"한 권으로 끝내는"

시원스쿨 기본토익 700+

시원스쿨어학연구소 지음

시원스쿨 LAB

시원스쿨
기본토익 700+

초판 1쇄 발행 2025년 10월 17일

지은이 시원스쿨어학연구소
펴낸곳 (주)에스제이더블유인터내셔널
펴낸이 양홍걸 이시원

홈페이지 www.siwonschool.com
주소 서울시 영등포구 영신로 166 시원스쿨
교재 구입 문의 02)2014-8151
고객센터 02)6409-0878

ISBN 979-11-7550-014-3 13740
Number 1-110404-18189900-06

이 책은 저작권법에 따라 보호받는 저작물이므로 무단복제와 무단전재를 금합니다. 이 책 내용의 전부 또는 일부를 이용하려면 반드시 저작권자와 ㈜에스제이더블유인터내셔널의 서면 동의를 받아야 합니다.

머리말

실전형 기본서: 700+ 문항으로 15일 만에 700+ 달성
시원스쿨 기본토익 700+

졸업, 취업, 승진, 이직, 공무원 시험의 첫 관문인 토익. 일단 700점 이상을 확보해 두어야 다음 단계의 준비를 마음 편히 할 수 있겠죠. 그런데 이 토익이라는 시험은 처음 방향을 잘못 잡거나 단기간에 집중해서 준비하지 않으면 6개월, 1년 까지도 늘어질 수 있고, 그러다 보면 다른 준비에 걸림돌이 되기 쉽습니다. 바로 그래서! 처음 시작을 어떻게 하는지가 매우 중요합니다.

입문 과정을 끝낸 학습자와 첫 토익에서 700+를 목표로 하는 수험자를 위해, 시원스쿨어학연구소는 「시원스쿨 기본토 익 700+」를 새롭게 선보입니다.

2025년 최신 개정판은 <LC + RC + VOCA> 통합 구성에 최신 기출 트렌드를 반영하고, 실전문제를 2배 이상 확대해 총 730문항을 담았습니다. 실전 모의고사 수준의 분량과 난이도로, 단 15일 만에 700점 달성을 목표로 하는 '실전형 기 본서'입니다.

시원스쿨 기본토익 700+는

❶ 실전형 기본서
기존 대비 2배 이상 늘어난 총 700문항 이상의 실전 문제를 수록했습니다. 최신 출제 포인트를 학습하고 즉시 문제 풀이에 적용하는 반복 훈련으로, 시험에 강한 실전 대비력을 갖출 수 있습니다.

❷ 최신 출제 경향 완벽 반영
2025년 기준 최신 출제 경향을 그대로 반영했습니다. 시험에 나오는 핵심 포인트만 학습하여, 빠르고 확실하게 700점 목표를 달성할 수 있습니다.

❸ 오답률 높은 파트 집중 공략
PART 3·4·5·6의 출제 유형과 풀이 방법, 문제 해결 순서, 오답 소거 전략까지 확실하게 익혀 정답률을 높입니다.

❹ 700+ 달성 필수 부가 자료 제공
RC 필수 특강(15강)으로 고난도 문제 해결 팁을 무료로 제공하며, 실전 모의고사 해설 또한 온라인으로 제공합니다.

이 책이 여러분의 토익 700+ 달성을 앞당기고, 더 높은 목표를 향해 나아가는 든든한 발판이 되길 바랍니다.

시원스쿨어학연구소 드림

목차

- 왜 「시원스쿨 기본토익 700+」인가?　　　　　　　　　　　　　　　　　　　6
- 이 책의 구성과 특징　　　　　　　　　　　　　　　　　　　　　　　　　8
- TOEIC이 궁금해　　　　　　　　　　　　　　　　　　　　　　　　　　12
- 초단기 완성 학습 플랜　　　　　　　　　　　　　　　　　　　　　　　14

LISTENING

Part 1
DAY 01　인물, 사물, 풍경 사진　　　　　　　　　　18
DAY 02　고난도 사진　　　　　　　　　　　　　　28
PART 1 FINAL TEST　　　　　　　　　　　　　　34

Part 2
DAY 03　의문사 의문문　　　　　　　　　　　　　38
DAY 04　일반 의문문　　　　　　　　　　　　　　48
DAY 05　제안·요청 의문문 / 선택 의문문　　　　　54
DAY 06　평서문 / 부가 의문문　　　　　　　　　　60
PART 2 FINAL TEST　　　　　　　　　　　　　　66

Part 3
DAY 07　주제 / 목적 / 문제점 문제　　　　　　　　70
DAY 08　장소 / 신분 / 직업 문제　　　　　　　　　78
DAY 09　세부사항 / say about 문제　　　　　　　86
DAY 10　제안·요청 사항 / do next 문제　　　　　94
DAY 11　의도 파악 문제 / 시각자료 연계 문제　　102
PART 3 FINAL TEST　　　　　　　　　　　　　112

Part 4
DAY 12　전화 메시지 / 라디오 방송　　　　　　　118
DAY 13　공지 및 안내　　　　　　　　　　　　　128
DAY 14　회의 발췌/소개　　　　　　　　　　　　136
DAY 15　광고/투어 가이드　　　　　　　　　　　144
PART 4 FINAL TEST　　　　　　　　　　　　　152

READING

Part 5

DAY 01	명사	158
DAY 02	대명사	164
DAY 03	동사의 종류 및 시제	170
DAY 04	동사의 특성	178
DAY 05	동명사 / to부정사	186
PART 5 FINAL TEST 1		194
DAY 06	분사	196
DAY 07	형용사 / 부사	202
DAY 08	접속사	212
DAY 09	전치사	220
DAY 10	관계사	228
PART 5 FINAL TEST 2		236

Part 6

DAY 11	접속부사	240
DAY 12	문맥파악 / 문장삽입	250
PART 6 FINAL TEST		264

Part 7

DAY 13	세부사항 / 주제·목적 / 사실확인	270
DAY 14	문맥파악	280
DAY 15	다중지문	290
PART 7 FINAL TEST		300

실전 모의고사 문제지   309

별책

- [해설서] 정답 및 해설
- [미니북] DAY 01-05 최빈출 정답 어휘_명사   2
  - DAY 06-08 최빈출 정답 어휘_동사   32
  - DAY 09-10 최빈출 정답 어휘_형용사   50
  - DAY 11-12 최빈출 정답 어휘_부사   62
  - DAY 13-15 최빈출 정답 어휘_숙어   74

시원스쿨랩 홈페이지
lab.siwonschool.com

- 본서 음원 (MP3)
- 미니북 어휘 시험지 (PDF)

왜 「시원스쿨 기본토익 700+」인가?

1 실전형 기본서: 기존 대비 2배 분량, 총 700문항 이상 수록!

- 최신 출제 포인트를 학습하고, 그 내용을 문제 풀이에 적용하는 반복 연습에 집중하여 실전 대비에 착실한 기본서입니다.
- 약 730문항에 달하는 실전 문제를 통해 점수 향상에도 탁월한 실전형 기본서입니다.

2 최신 출제 유형 완벽 반영으로 700+점 보장

- 2025년 기준 최신 출제 경향 그대로, 시험에 나오는 것을 중점으로 핵심 출제 포인트 이론만 학습하여 빠르고 확실하게 목표 점수에 도달할 수 있습니다.
- 연습 문제를 비롯한 모든 실전 문제는 기출 변형 문제이며 실제 토익의 출제 포인트와 동일합니다.

3 오답률 높은 파트 집중 공략

- PART 3·4·5·6의 출제 유형을 분석하고, 문제 풀이 방법과 순서, 오답 소거법까지 확실하게 학습하여 정답률을 높일 수 있습니다.

4 700+ 달성 필수 부가 자료 제공 (비매품 증정)

- 부가 자료 <RC 필수 특강>은 RC 문제 풀이에 필요한 고난도 실전 대비 팁을 담은 15강으로 구성되어 있으며, 무료강의와 함께 제공됩니다.

5 QR코드로 바로 듣는 편리한 음원

- 회원가입 없이도 교재 내 QR코드를 스캔하여 본서 음원을 모바일로 편리하게 들을 수 있습니다.
- 교재 음원은 시원스쿨랩 홈페이지(lab.siwonschool.com)에서 다운로드해 이용할 수도 있습니다.

6 15일 완성 학습 플랜

- LC, RC 섹션은 각각 15개 Day로 구성되어 있어 최대 30일 안에 [LC + RC + VOCA]로 이루어진 한 권을 거뜬히 끝낼 수 있습니다. 또한 누구나 따라하기 쉬운 명료한 학습플랜을 제시합니다.
- 동영상 강의(유료) 수강 시 더욱 쉽고 빠르게 700+ 기본기 완성이 가능합니다. 하루에 딱 2시간만 토익 공부에 시간을 할애할 수만 있다면, 단 15일 안에 본 교재 한 권을 끝낼 수 있습니다.

7 최신 기출 변형 실전 모의고사 1회분

- 최신 토익 시험과 난이도 및 유형 면에서 거의 유사한 기출 변형 실전 모의고사 1회분을 제공합니다.
- 모의고사의 음원, 스크립트, 상세한 해설도 모두 온라인으로 무료로 제공합니다.

이 책의 구성과 특징

LC

2026년 대비 최신 출제 경향 완벽 반영

시험에 실제로 출제되는 핵심 포인트만 선별하여 이론을 정리했습니다.

배운 즉시 적용하는 연습문제

배운 내용을 즉시 연습하는 PRACTICE(연습문제)를 통해 출제포인트를 완벽히 소화하고 넘어가도록 합니다.

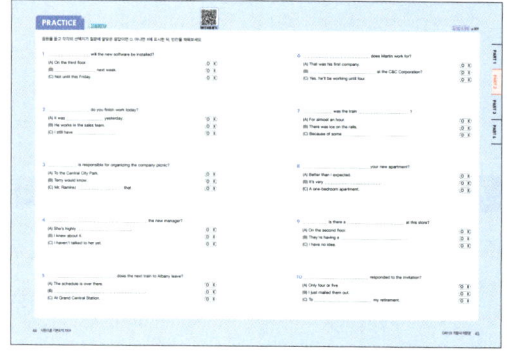

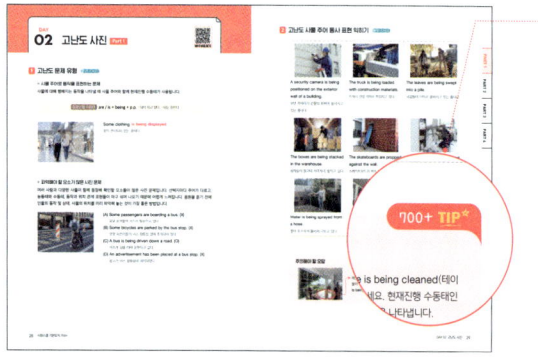

700+ TIP

주의해야 할 오답, 빈출은 아니지만 간헐적으로 출제되는 문제 유형 등과 같이 추가 학습 내용을 정리한 코너입니다.

RC

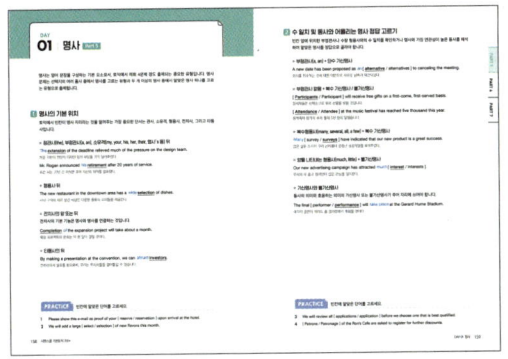

기출 유형 연습문제 수록

PART 5의 모든 예문은 기출 유형으로 제작되었으며, 2지 선다형의 예문도 포함되어 있어 효과적으로 출제 포인트를 체득할 수 있습니다.

예시 지문 및 풀이 전략 수록

PART 6, 7은 예시 지문과 함께 키워드, 정답의 단서를 파악하여 정답을 찾아가는 풀이 과정을 이해하기 쉽게 설명하여 어려움 없이 학습할 수 있습니다.

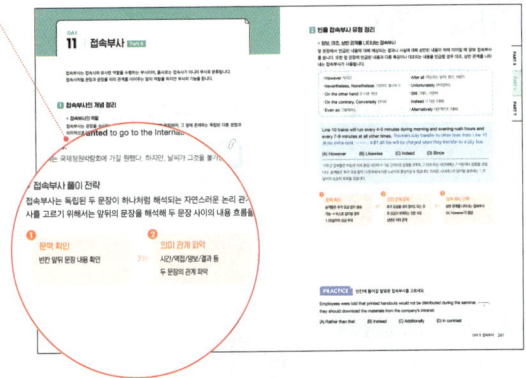

700제가 넘는 실전문제 수록

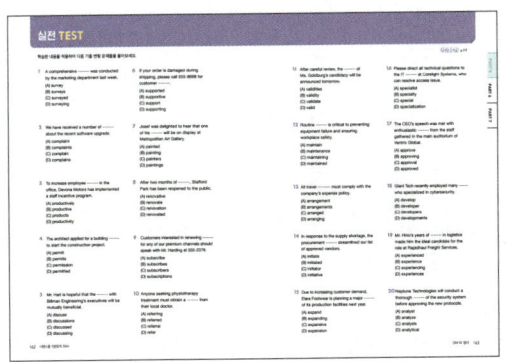

실전 분량의 실전 TEST

LC, RC 각각 15개의 챕터(DAY)가 끝나면 실전 TEST를 풀이하여 해당 챕터의 학습 내용을 실전 문제에 적용하여 풀이할 수 있도록 하였습니다.

이 책의 구성과 특징

700제가 넘는 실전문제 수록

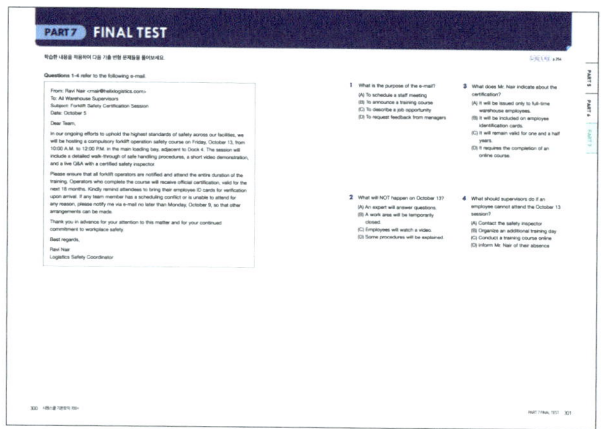

PART별 마무리 문제 풀이
FINAL TEST

각 PART에서 배운 출제 포인트에 대한 마무리 학습으로 모의고사형 실전 문제를 풀이하도록 하였습니다. 실전 TEST와 FINAL TEST는 모두 약 730제가 넘는 문항이며, 기출 유형으로 제작된 실전 문제입니다.

VOCA

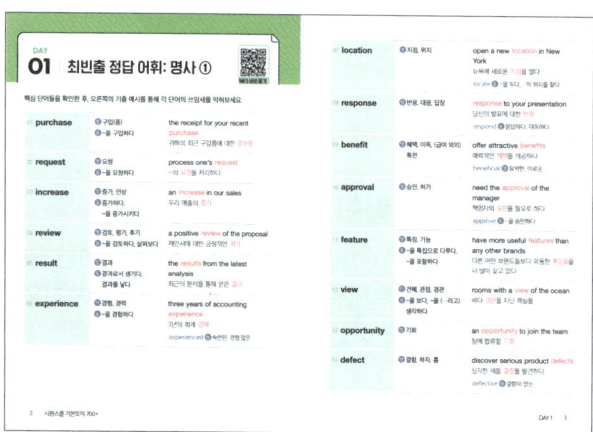

[미니북] 최빈출 정답 어휘

LC/RC에서 정답으로 나온 보기에서 자주 쓰인 필수 어휘들을 모아 휴대가 간편한 미니북으로 제작하였습니다.

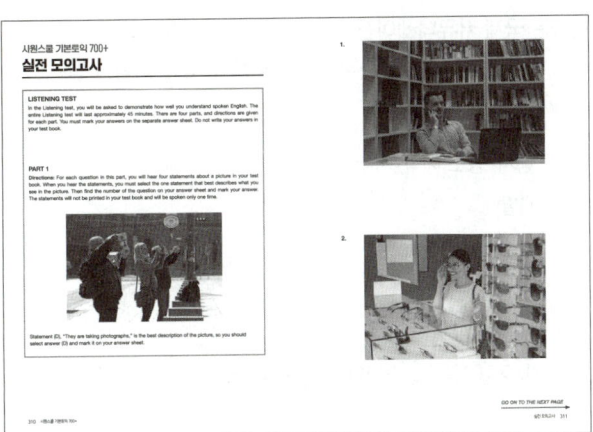

최신 기출 변형 실전 모의고사 1회분

최신 토익 시험과 난이도 및 유형면에서 거의 유사한 기출 변형 실전 모의고사 1회분을 제공합니다.
(해설: 온라인 제공)

[별책] 정답 및 해설

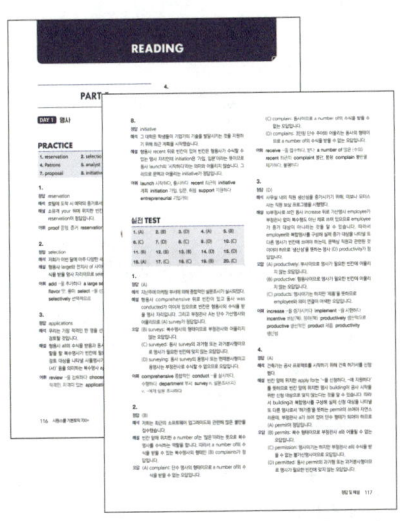

오답까지 해설하는 꼼꼼한 해설

정답이 되는 이유 뿐만 아니라, 각 선택지가 왜 오답인지까지 설명해 줌으로써 출제자가 의도한 함정에 빠지지 않는 센스를 길러줍니다.

TOEIC이 궁금해

토익은 어떤 시험이에요?

TOEIC은 ETS(Educational Testing Service)가 출제하는 국제 커뮤니케이션 영어 능력 평가 시험(Test Of English for International Communication)입니다. 즉, 토익은 영어로 업무적인 소통을 할 수 있는 능력을 평가하는 시험으로서, 다음과 같은 주제를 다룹니다.

기업 일반	계약, 협상, 홍보, 영업, 비즈니스 계획, 회의, 행사, 장소 예약, 사무용 기기
제조 및 개발	공장 관리, 조립 라인, 품질 관리, 연구, 제품 개발
금융과 예산	은행, 투자, 세금, 회계, 청구
인사	입사 지원, 채용, 승진, 급여, 퇴직
부동산	건축, 설계서, 부동산 매매 및 임대, 전기/가스/수도 설비
여가	교통 수단, 티켓팅, 여행 일정, 역/공항, 자동차/호텔 예약 및 연기와 취소, 영화, 공연, 전시

토익은 총 몇 문제인가요?

구성	파트	내용		문항 수 및 문항 번호		시간	배점
Listening Test	Part 1	사진 묘사		6	1-6	45분	495점
	Part 2	질의 응답		25	7-31		
	Part 3	짧은 대화		39 (13지문)	32-70		
	Part 4	짧은 담화		30 (10지문)	71-100		
Reading Test	Part 5	단문 빈칸 채우기 (문법, 어휘)		30	101-130	75분	495점
	Part 6	장문 빈칸 채우기 (문법, 문맥에 맞는 어휘/문장)		16 (4지문)	131-146		
	Part 7	독해	단일 지문	29 (10지문)	147-175		
			이중 지문	10 (2지문)	176-185		
			삼중 지문	15 (3지문)	186-200		
합계				200 문제		120분	990점

토익 시험을 보려고 해요. 어떻게 접수하나요?

- 한국 TOEIC 위원회 인터넷 사이트(www.toeic.co.kr)에서 접수 일정을 확인하고 접수합니다.
- 접수 시 최근 6개월 이내에 촬영한 jpg 형식의 사진이 필요하므로 미리 준비합니다.
- 토익 응시료는 (2025년 기준) 정기 접수 시 52,500원입니다.

시험 당일엔 뭘 챙겨야 하나요?

- 아침을 적당히 챙겨 먹습니다. 빈속은 집중력 저하의 주범이고 과식은 졸음을 유발합니다.
- 시험 준비물을 챙깁니다.
    - 신분증 (주민등록증, 운전면허증, 기간 만료 전 여권, 공무원증만 인정. 학생증 안됨. 단, 중고등학생은 국내 학생증 인정)
    - 연필과 깨끗하게 잘 지워지는 지우개 (볼펜이나 사인펜은 안됨. 연필은 뭉툭하게 깎아서 여러 자루 준비)
    - 아날로그 시계 (전자시계는 안됨)
    - 수험표 (필수 준비물은 아님. 수험 번호는 시험장에서 감독관이 답안지에 부착해주는 라벨을 보고 적으면 됨)
- 고사장을 반드시 확인합니다.

시험은 몇 시에 끝나나요?

오전 시험	오후 시험	내용
9:30 - 9:45	2:30 - 2:45	답안지 작성 오리엔테이션
9:45 - 9:50	2:45 - 2:50	수험자 휴식 시간
9:50 - 10:10	2:50 - 3:10	신분증 확인, 문제지 배부
10:10 - 10:55	3:10 - 3:55	리스닝 시험
10:55 - 12:10	3:55 - 5:10	리딩 시험

- 최소 30분 전에 입실을 마치고(오전 시험은 오전 9:20까지, 오후 시험은 오후 2:20까지) 지시에 따라 답안지에 기본 정보를 기입합니다.
- 안내 방송이 끝나고 시험 시작 전 5분의 휴식 시간이 주어지는데, 이때 화장실에 꼭 다녀옵니다.

시험 보고 나면 성적은 바로 나오나요?

- 시험일로부터 9일 후 낮 12시에 한국 TOEIC 위원회 사이트(www.toeic.co.kr)에서 성적이 발표됩니다.

초단기 완성 학습 플랜

- 다음의 학습 진도를 참조하여 **매일** 학습합니다.
- 해당일의 학습을 하지 못했더라도 **이전으로 돌아가지 말고 오늘에 해당하는 학습**을 하세요. 그래야 끝까지 완주할 수 있답니다.
- 교재의 학습을 모두 마치면 도서 맨 뒤에 수록된 토익 최신 경향이 반영된 **실전 모의고사**를 꼭 풀어보세요.
- 교재를 끝까지 한 번 보고 나면 **2회 학습**에 도전합니다. 두 번째 볼 때는 훨씬 빠르게 끝낼 수 있어요. 토익은 천천히 1회 보는 것보다 빠르게 2회, 3회 보는 것이 훨씬 효과가 좋습니다.

15일 완성 학습 플랜

1일	2일	3일	4일	5일
LC DAY 01	LC DAY 02	LC DAY 03	LC DAY 04	LC DAY 05
RC DAY 01	RC DAY 02	RC DAY 03	RC DAY 04	RC DAY 05
VOCA DAY 01	VOCA DAY 02	VOCA DAY 03	VOCA DAY 04	VOCA DAY 05

6일	7일	8일	9일	10일
LC DAY 06	LC DAY 07	LC DAY 08	LC DAY 09	LC DAY 10
RC DAY 06	RC DAY 07	RC DAY 08	RC DAY 09	RC DAY 10
VOCA DAY 06	VOCA DAY 07	VOCA DAY 08	VOCA DAY 09	VOCA DAY 10

11일	12일	13일	14일	15일
LC DAY 11	LC DAY 12	LC DAY 13	LC DAY 14	LC DAY 15
RC DAY 11	RC DAY 12	RC DAY 13	RC DAY 14	RC DAY 15
VOCA DAY 11	VOCA DAY 12	VOCA DAY 13	VOCA DAY 14	VOCA DAY 15

30일 완성 학습 플랜

1일	2일	3일	4일	5일
LC DAY 01 VOCA DAY 01	RC DAY 01 VOCA DAY 02	LC DAY 02 VOCA DAY 03	RC DAY 02 VOCA DAY 04	LC DAY 03 VOCA DAY 05
6일	**7일**	**8일**	**9일**	**10일**
RC DAY 03 VOCA DAY 06	LC DAY 04 VOCA DAY 07	RC DAY 04 VOCA DAY 08	LC DAY 05 VOCA DAY 09	RC DAY 05 VOCA DAY 10
11일	**12일**	**13일**	**14일**	**15일**
LC DAY 06 VOCA DAY 11	RC DAY 06 VOCA DAY 12	LC DAY 07 VOCA DAY 13	RC DAY 07 VOCA DAY 14	LC DAY 08 VOCA DAY 15
16일	**17일**	**18일**	**19일**	**20일**
RC DAY 08 VOCA DAY 01	LC DAY 09 VOCA DAY 02	RC DAY 09 VOCA DAY 03	LC DAY 10 VOCA DAY 04	RC DAY 10 VOCA DAY 05
21일	**22일**	**23일**	**24일**	**25일**
LC DAY 11 VOCA DAY 06	RC DAY 11 VOCA DAY 07	LC DAY 12 VOCA DAY 08	RC DAY 12 VOCA DAY 09	LC DAY 13 VOCA DAY 10
26일	**27일**	**28일**	**29일**	**30일**
RC DAY 13 VOCA DAY 11	LC DAY 14 VOCA DAY 12	RC DAY 14 VOCA DAY 13	LC DAY 15 VOCA DAY 14	RC DAY 15 VOCA DAY 15

기본토익 700+

PART 1

DAY 01 인물, 사물, 풍경 사진
DAY 02 고난도 사진
PART 1 FINAL TEST

PART 1 사진 묘사 문제 미리보기

- 문항수: 6문항 (1번~6번)
- 사진을 보고, 들려주는 네 개의 선택지 중에서 사진의 상황을 가장 잘 묘사한 것을 고르는 문제입니다.
- 소거법을 이용해 오답을 철저하게 가려내야 합니다.

문제지

1.

····· 문제지에는 사진만 제시됩니다.

음원

Number 1. Look at the picture marked number 1 in your test book.

(A) The man is looking at a monitor.
(B) The man is talking on the phone. ✓
(C) The man is crossing his legs.
(D) The man is holding a pen.

DAY 01 | 인물, 사물, 풍경 사진 Part 1

1 인물 사진 핵심 사항 🔊 01-1.mp3

■ 인물의 동작/상태 파악하기

주로 사람을 주어로 하는 문장이 나오며, 사진 속 사람의 동작이나 상태는 대부분 현재진행 동사로 제시됩니다.

현재진행형 am / are / is + 동사ing ~하고 있다, ~하는 중이다

▶ He **is wearing** eyeglasses.
남자가 안경을 쓴 상태이다.

▶ A man **is typing** on a keyboard.
남자가 키보드로 타이핑을 하고 있다.

■ 여러 사람이 등장하는 경우 주어에 주의해 듣기

등장인물 전부: They / People
전체 중 일부 사람들: Some people
남자들 중 한 명: One of the men / A man
여자들 중 한 명: One of the women / A woman

■ 여러 사람이 등장하는 경우 동작 / 상태 파악하기

여러 사람이 등장하는 사진에서는 인물들의 공통적인 동작이나 상태뿐만 아니라 개별적인 동작과 상태도 함께 재빠르게 파악해야 합니다.

▶ A woman **is wearing** eyeglasses.
한 여자가 안경을 쓴 상태이다.

▶ The men **are shaking** hands.
남자들이 악수를 하고 있다.

▶ They **are sitting** around the table.
사람들이 테이블 주위에 앉아 있다.

2 인물 사진 동사 표현 익히기 🔊 01-2.mp3

■ 보다, 읽다

reading a book 책을 읽고 있다	**examining** some clothing 옷을 살펴보고 있다
looking at a map 지도를 보고 있다	**browsing** through the shelves 선반을 살펴보고 있다
looking in a drawer 서랍 안을 들여다 보고 있다	**studying** a sign 표지판을 보고 있다

■ 걷다, 이동하다

walking along the beach 해변을 따라 걷고 있다	**walking up** the stairs 계단을 오르고 있다
crossing a street 길을 건너고 있다	**walking down** the stairs 계단을 내려가고 있다

■ 앉다, 서다, 기대다

sitting at a desk 책상에 앉아 있다	**waiting** in line 줄 서서 기다리고 있다
standing behind a man 남자 뒤에 서 있다	**leaning against** a wall 벽에 기대어 있다

■ 들다, 잡다, 이동시키다 / 손을 뻗다 / 담다

holding a piece of paper 종이 한 장을 잡고 있다	**removing** a piece of paper 종이 한 장을 빼고 있다
carrying a briefcase 서류 가방을 들고 있다	**reaching** for an item 물건을 향해 손을 뻗고 있다
pushing a cart 카트를 밀고 있다	**putting / loading** an item into a cart 카트 안으로 물건을 담고 있다

■ 착용하다 / 벗다

trying on headphones 헤드폰을 써보고 있다	**wearing** a necklace 목걸이를 착용한 상태이다 [상태]
putting on a hat 모자를 착용하는 중이다 [동작]	**taking off** a jacket 재킷을 벗는 중이다
removing eyeglasses 안경을 벗는 중이다	**tying** a shoe 신발 끈을 묶는 중이다

■ 일하다, 작업하다

sweeping the floor 바닥을 쓸고 있다	**preparing** some food 음식을 준비하고 있다
loading some boxes into a vehicle 상자를 차량에 싣고 있다	**working** at a construction site 공사장에서 작업하고 있다
typing on a keyboard 키보드로 타자를 치고 있다	**repairing** a car 자동차를 수리하고 있다
adjusting some equipment 장비를 조정하고 있다	**cleaning** a room 방을 청소하고 있다

■ 타다, 내리다

boarding a train 기차에 탑승하고 있다	**riding** a bicycle 자전거를 타고 있다
getting on a bus 버스에 탑승하고 있다	**getting off** a train 기차에서 내리고 있다

기타 빈출 표현

700+ TIP

pointing at a screen
화면을 가리키고 있다

shaking hands
악수하고 있다

facing each other
서로 마주 보고 있다

3 사물/풍경 사진 핵심 사항 🔊 01-3.mp3

■ 사물의 상태를 나타내는 수동태 동사 파악하기

주로 사물을 주어로 하는 문장이 나오며, 사진 속 사물의 상태는 대부분 현재시제 수동태나 현재완료시제 수동태로 제시됩니다.

> **현재 수동태** are / is + 과거분사[p.p.] ~되어 있다
> **현재완료 수동태** have/has been + 과거분사[p.p.] ~된 채로 있다

Boxes **are stacked**.
= Boxes **have been stacked**.
상자들이 쌓여 있다.

■ 사물의 상태를 나타내는 현재시제 동사 파악하기

> **단순 현재시제** 현재시제 동사 + 전치사구
> **There is / are 구문** There is/are + 주어 + 전치사구

A lamp **is on the desk**.
　　　　　　전치사구
= **There is** a lamp **on the desk**.
램프가 책상 위에 위치해 있다.

The staircase **leads to the beach**.
계단이 해변으로 이어져 있다.

4 사물/풍경 사진 동사 표현 익히기 🎧 01-4.mp3

■ 사무 장소

A laptop computer **is** on a desk. 노트북 컴퓨터가 책상 위에 있다.

Monitors **are positioned** side by side. 모니터들이 나란히 위치해 있다.

A potted plant **has been placed** in the corner. 화분에 담긴 식물이 구석에 놓여 있다.

Some luggage **has been left** in front of the door. 문 앞에 수화물이 놓여 있다.

Some documents **have been stacked** on top of the cabinet. 몇몇 서류들이 서랍 위에 쌓여 있다.

■ 상점

Bags **are displayed** on the shelves. 가방들이 선반에 진열되어 있다.

Some bags **are** on display. 몇몇 가방들이 진열되어 있다.

The shelves **have been filled with** items. 선반이 제품들로 가득 채워져 있다.

The shelves **have been stocked with** products. 선반이 제품들로 채워져 있다.

Clothing **is hanging** on racks. 옷이 옷걸이에 걸려 있다.

■ 주택

Cushions **are arranged** on chairs. 쿠션들이 의자에 정렬되어 있다.

Some artwork **has been mounted** on the wall. 몇몇 미술품이 벽에 걸려 있다.

Light fixtures **are hanging** from the ceiling. 조명 장치가 천장에 걸려 있다.

Light fixtures **are hanging** above the table. 조명 장치가 테이블 위에 걸려 있다.

There is a potted plant on a piece of furniture. 가구 한 점 위에 화분에 담긴 식물이 있다.

A table **is positioned** between two windows. 테이블이 두 창문 사이에 놓여져 있다.

A television **has been set** on a desk. 텔레비전이 책상 위에 설치되어 있다.

■ 교통수단

Train tracks **run** **alongside the coast**. 기찻길이 해변을 따라 뻗어 있다.

Cars **are parked** **in a row**. 차들이 한 줄로 주차되어 있다.

Some boats **are docked** **at a pier**. 몇몇 보트들이 부두에 정박되어 있다.
Some boats **are tied** **to a dock**.

Some vehicles **have stopped** **at a traffic signal**. 몇몇 차량들이 교통 신호에 멈췄다.

A car **is facing** **a wall**. 차 한대가 벽을 바라보고 있다.

■ 풍경

There's a fountain **in front of a building**. 분수대가 건물 앞에 있다.

Some buildings **are located** **near a hill**. 몇몇 건물들이 언덕 근처에 위치해 있다.

Trees **have been planted** **around the house**. 나무들이 집 주변에 심어져 있다.

There are some skyscrapers **overlooking** a lake. 호수를 내려보는 몇몇 고층 건물들이 있다.

A dock **has been built** **in a harbor**. 항구에 부두가 지어져 있다.

A bridge **crosses** **over a river**. 다리가 강 위를 가로지른다.

700+ TIP

사물/풍경 사진에서 필수인 위치 전치사구

1. [표면에 붙어] ~위에, ~에
   on the table, on the wall

2. [표면에서 떨어져서] ~위에
   above the desk / over a river

3. ~앞에 / 뒤에
   in front of a door / behind a door

4. ~가까이에
   near a building

5. 한 줄로 / 여러 줄로
   in a row / in rows

6. ~ 주변에 / 둥글게
   around the house / in a circle

7. 나란히
   side by side

8. ~를 따라
   along the street, alongside the coast

PRACTICE 🎧 01-5.mp3

음원을 듣고 주어진 사진을 바르게 묘사한 문장이면 O, 아니면 X에 표시하고, 빈칸을 채워보세요.

1

(A) She is _____ her jacket. (O X)
(B) She is _____ on a keyboard. (O X)
(C) She is _____ from a cup. (O X)
(D) She is _____ a drawer. (O X)

2

(A) The man is _____ a safety vest. (O X)
(B) The man is _____ some materials. (O X)
(C) The man is _____ the floor. (O X)
(D) The man is _____ boxes onto a cart. (O X)

3

(A) One of the men is _____ a building. (O X)
(B) They are _____ down some stairs. (O X)
(C) One of the men is _____ a cup. (O X)
(D) They are _____ a street. (O X)

4

(A) A light fixture is _____ from the ceiling. (O X)
(B) The chairs have been _____ in the corner. (O X)
(C) A table _____ for a meal. (O X)
(D) The curtains _____ _____. (O X)

5

(A) A door has been _____ _____. (O X)
(B) A staircase _____ a building. (O X)
(C) A light fixture has been _____ on the wall. (O X)
(D) There are benches _____ a building. (O X)

6

(A) The shelves have been _____ with items. (O X)
(B) Boxes have been _____ on top of each other. (O X)
(C) Some fruit _____ for sale. (O X)
(D) Some groceries have been _____ in a shopping cart. (O X)

실전 TEST

학습한 내용을 적용하여 다음 기출 변형 문제들을 풀어보세요.

1

2

3

4

5

6

7

8

9

10

11

12

DAY 02 | 고난도 사진 Part 1

1 고난도 문제 유형 🎧 02-1.mp3

■ **사물 주어로 동작을 표현하는 문제**

사물에 대해 행해지는 동작을 나타낼 때 사물 주어와 함께 현재진행 수동태가 사용됩니다.

현재진행 수동태 are / is + being + p.p. ~되어 지고 있다, ~되는 중이다

Some clothing **is being displayed**.
옷이 전시되어 있는 중이다.

■ **파악해야 할 요소가 많은 사진 문제**

여러 사람과 다양한 사물이 함께 등장해 확인할 요소들이 많은 사진 문제입니다. 선택지마다 주어가 다르고, 능동태와 수동태, 동작과 위치 관계 표현들이 마구 섞여 나오기 때문에 어렵게 느껴집니다. 음원을 듣기 전에 인물의 동작 및 상태, 사물의 위치를 미리 파악해 놓는 것이 가장 좋은 방법입니다.

(A) Some passengers are boarding a bus. (X)
　　몇몇 승객들이 버스에 탑승하고 있다.
(B) Some bicycles are parked by the bus stop. (X)
　　몇몇 자전거들이 버스 정류장 옆에 주차되어 있다.
(C) A bus is being driven down a road. (O)
　　버스가 길을 따라 운행되고 있다.
(D) An advertisement has been placed at a bus stop. (X)
　　광고가 버스 정류장에 위치되었다.

2 고난도 사물 주어 동사 표현 익히기 🎧 02-2.mp3

A security camera is being positioned on the exterior wall of a building.
보안 카메라가 건물의 외벽에 놓여지고 있는 중이다.

The truck is being loaded with construction materials.
트럭이 건설 자재로 채워지고 있다.

The leaves are being swept into a pile.
낙엽들이 더미로 쓸려지고 있는 중이다.

The boxes are being stacked in the warehouse.
상자들이 창고에 차곡차곡 쌓이고 있다.

The skateboards are propped against the wall.
스케이트보드가 벽에 기대어져 있다.

Repairs are being carried out on the broken water pipe.
고장 난 수도관의 수리가 진행되고 있다.

Water is being sprayed from a hose.
물이 호스에서 뿜어져 나오고 있다.

The damaged device is being examined.
손상된 기기가 점검되고 있다.

A light fixture is being repaired.
조명 장치가 수리되는 중이다.

700+ TIP

주의해야 할 오답

➤ 깨끗하게 닦여 있는 테이블의 상태만 보고 A table is being cleaned(테이블이 닦이고 있다)를 정답으로 고르지 않도록 주의하세요. 현재진행 수동태인 is being cleaned는 현재 사람에 의해 진행 중인 동작을 나타냅니다.

3 생소한 명사 어휘 익히기 🔊 02-3.mp3

평소에 자주 접하지 못한 생소한 어휘들이 등장해서 당황하게 만드는 경우가 종종 있습니다. 따라서 Part 1에 종종 나오는 생소한 어휘들을 미리 알아두는 것이 좋습니다.

curb 연석

ramp 경사로

railing 난간

wheelbarrow 외바퀴 손수레

patio 야외 테라스

lawnmower 잔디 깎는 기계

archway 아치형 길[입구]

ladder 사다리

scaffolding 비계
(공사장에서 높은 곳의 공사를 위해 임시로 설치한 가설물)

bushes 덤불, 관목

pedestrian 행인, 보행자

vendor 행상인, 판매자

PRACTICE 02-4.mp3

음원을 듣고 주어진 사진을 바르게 묘사한 문장이면 O, 아니면 X에 표시하고, 빈칸을 채워보세요.

1
(A) Some people are walking under an _____. ○ X
(B) A road is being _____ with bricks. ○ X
(C) A sign is being _____ on a wall. ○ X
(D) There are lampposts _____ _____. ○ X

2
(A) Some plants are being _____ along a walkway. ○ X
(B) Some windows are _____ by curtains. ○ X
(C) A bike is _____ against the building. ○ X
(D) There are _____ in a garden. ○ X

3
(A) A stage is being _____ indoors. ○ X
(B) People are _____ at an entrance. ○ X
(C) People _____ for a concert. ○ X
(D) A concert hall is _____. ○ X

정답 및 해설 p.006

실전 TEST 🎧 02-5.mp3

학습한 내용을 적용하여 다음 기출 변형 문제들을 풀어보세요.

1.

2.

3.

4.

5.

6.

7

8

9

10

11

12

PART 1 FINAL TEST

학습한 내용을 적용하여 다음 기출 변형 문제들을 풀어보세요.

1

2

3

4

5

6

7

8

9

10

11

12

기본토익 700+

PART 2

DAY 03	의문사 의문문
DAY 04	일반 의문문
DAY 05	제안·요청 의문문 / 선택 의문문
DAY 06	평서문 / 부가 의문문

PART 2 FINAL TEST

PART 2 질의 응답 문제 미리보기

- 문항수: 25문항 (7번~31번)
- 한 개의 질문을 들려주고, 이에 대한 (a), (b), (c) 세 개의 응답 중 가장 적절한 응답을 고르는 문제입니다.
- 소거법을 이용해 오답을 가려내는 방식으로 풀어야 합니다.

문제지

7. Mark your answer on your answer sheet.
8. Mark your answer on your answer sheet.
   ⋮
31. Mark your answer on your answer sheet.

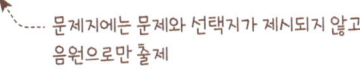
문제지에는 문제와 선택지가 제시되지 않고
음원으로만 출제

음원

Number 7. When did you leave the office?

(A) After you called me. ✓
(B) It's on the fifth floor.
(C) No, I haven't left anything.

DAY 03 | 의문사 의문문 Part 2

1 When 의문문 🔊 03-1.mp3

When은 '언제'를 의미하는 의문사이며, 시점(날짜, 요일, 시간 등)으로 대답하는 것이 기본입니다. 그래서 선택지 중 시점 표현이 나오는 것을 정답으로 고를 수 있도록 반드시 음원이 시작하자마자 언급되는 의문사 When을 들어야 합니다.

■ 가까운 미래 시점 응답

Q	When can I see the final version of the pamphlet?	제가 언제 팸플릿의 최종 버전을 볼 수 있을까요?
A1	Monday at the latest.	늦어도 월요일에요.
A2	Sometime in March.	3월 중이에요.
A3	Not until next week.	다음 주는 되어야 해요.

■ 과거 시점 응답

Q	When did you come back from your trip?	언제 여행에서 돌아오셨나요?
A1	Several days ago.	며칠 전이에요.
A2	Last week.	지난 주에요.

2 Where 의문문 🔊 03-2.mp3

Where 의문문은 '어디'를 묻는 질문이므로 특정 장소나 위치를 나타내는 「전치사 + 명사」 형태가 정답으로 제시되는 것이 일반적입니다. 영국 또는 호주 성우가 Where를 발음할 때 [r] 발음이 들리지 않기 때문에 순간적으로 의문사 When과 착각할 수 있습니다. 따라서 이러한 특성을 미리 염두에 두는 것이 좋습니다.

■ 장소/위치 응답

| Q | Where did you leave the invoice? | 거래 내역서를 어디에 두었나요? |
| A | It's on my desk. | 제 책상 위에 있어요. |

| Q | Where's the closest gas station? | 가장 가까운 주유소가 어디에 있나요? |
| A | **There's one** on Main Street. | 메인 스트리트에 하나 있어요. |

> 『There's one + 장소/위치』는 '~에 하나 있다'는 뜻으로, Where 의문문에 There's one ~으로 대답하면 90% 이상 정답.

3 Who 의문문 🎧 03-3.mp3

Who 의문문은 사람에 대해 묻는 질문으로, 이에 대한 응답으로 특정한 사람의 이름이나 구체적인 직책, 직업 등이 정답으로 나옵니다. 이때 사람 이름이 아닌 부서나 회사명으로 대답하는 것도 가능합니다.

■ 이름/직책/부서명 응답

Q	Who's leading the training workshop?	누가 교육 워크숍을 진행하나요?
A1	That's Mandy's job.	그건 맨디 씨의 일이에요.
A2	I asked Daniel to do it.	제가 대니얼 씨에게 해달라고 부탁했어요.
Q	Who authorized that purchase?	누가 그 구매를 승인했나요?
A1	The department manager.	부장님이요.
A2	Someone in the Accounting Department.	회계부의 누군가요.

4 간접 응답 / 의외의 응답 🎧 03-4.mp3

질문에 대한 직접적인 응답 대신 의외의 응답이 정답인 경우가 종종 등장합니다. 평소 [질문-응답]의 다양한 조합을 많이 듣고 익혀 두어야 PART 2에서 고득점을 할 수 있습니다.

■ ~에게 물어보세요 / 알아보겠습니다 / 모르겠어요

Q	When was the last safety inspection?	마지막 안전 검사가 언제였죠?
A1	You can find it online.	그건 온라인으로 찾아볼 수 있어요.
A2	Let me ask the manager.	매니저님에게 물어볼게요.
A3	I have no idea. / I'm not sure.	모르겠어요.

■ 아직 결정되지 않았어요

Q	Who is scheduled to give the keynote speech?	누가 기조연설을 하기로 했나요?
A	It hasn't been decided yet.	아직 결정되지 않았습니다.

■ 기타 의외의 응답

Q	When will Dr. Martin be available?	마틴 박사님이 언제 시간이 나실까요?
A1	He's busy all day.	그는 하루 종일 바쁘세요.
A2	Did you check the e-mail from him?	그에게서 온 이메일을 확인했나요?

5 What 의문문 🔊 03-5.mp3

What은 '무엇'을 뜻하며, 사람/사물의 이름, 사물의 상태, 목적, 금액, 수치, 상대방 의견 등을 묻는 다양한 질문에 사용됩니다. When, Where, Who 의문문과 달리 정형화된 응답 패턴이 없어 질문 내용을 정확히 이해해야만 풀 수 있습니다. 특히, What 뒤에 이어지는 명사나 동사에 유의해 질문의 의도를 파악하여 그에 맞는 응답을 골라야 합니다.

■ 구체적 사실을 묻는 질문

Q	**What's the problem with** the machine?	기계에 무슨 문제가 있나요?
A1	Some parts didn't arrive.	일부 부품들이 도착하지 않았어요.
A2	It's not working properly.	제대로 작동하지 않아요.

Q	**What happened** at the monthly meeting yesterday?	어제 월례 회의에서 무슨 일이 있었나요?
A1	I missed it, too.	저도 못 갔어요.
A2	We discussed the product design.	상품 디자인을 얘기했어요.

■ 의견을 묻는 질문

➤ What do you think of ~? 라는 의문문도 사용됩니다.

Q	**What do you think about** this coffee shop?	이 커피숍 어때요?
A1	It has a good dessert menu.	좋은 디저트 메뉴가 있어요.
A2	It's my favorite place.	제가 가장 좋아하는 곳이에요.

■ 액수 등 숫자 정보를 묻는 질문

Q	**What's the price** for this item on display?	전시되어 있는 이 상품은 얼마인가요?
A1	It's thirty-two dollars.	32달러입니다.
A2	Doesn't it have a price tag?	가격표가 있지 않나요?
A3	You can ask at the front desk.	프런트 데스크에 물어보세요.

■ 기타 질문

「What + 명사 ~?」 형태의 질문이 자주 나옵니다. What 바로 다음에 나오는 명사까지 주의해서 들어야 합니다.

Q **What time** do you usually get to work?
A1 Around 9 o'clock.
A2 It depends on the traffic.

보통 몇 시에 회사에 도착하세요?
9시 쯤에요.
교통 상황에 따라 달라요.

Q **What floor** is Ace Media on?
A1 It's on the third floor.
A2 Here's the building directory.

에이스 미디어 사가 몇 층에 있습니까?
3층에 있습니다.
여기 건물 안내도가 있어요.

Q **What kind of bicycle** do you have?
A1 I have a folding bike.
A2 Are you thinking of buying one?

어떤 종류의 자전거를 가지고 계세요?
접이식 자전거를 갖고 있어요.
한 대 구입할 생각이세요?

6 Which 의문문 🔊 03-6.mp3

Which는 '어느, 어느 것'을 뜻하며, What과 마찬가지로 상대방의 의견, 방법, 정보, 일/사건, 금액, 시간, 날짜, 수치 등을 묻는 다양한 질문에 사용됩니다. 「Which 명사 ~?」 혹은 「Which of 명사 ~?」 구조로 출제됩니다.

■ Which 명사 ~? (어느 ~?)

> Which 의문문에 대한 답변에 대명사 one이 등장하면 99% 정답입니다.

Q **Which restaurant** did you choose?
A1 The **one** on Brooks Street.
A2 I'm still considering a few.

어느 식당을 선택했나요?
브룩스 스트리트에 있는 것이요.
여전히 몇 군데를 고려하는 중이에요.

Q **Which envelopes** do we use to mail out invitations?
A1 The yellow **ones** in the second cabinet.
A2 I think we're out of them.

초대장을 우편으로 발송할 때 어느 봉투를 사용하나요?
두 번째 캐비닛에 있는 노란색의 것들이요.
그것들이 다 떨어진 것 같아요.

■ Which of 명사 ~? (~ 중에 어느 것?)

Q **Which of these seminars** should I attend?
A1 The one on photo editing.
A2 It's posted on the bulletin board.

이 세미나들 중 어느 것에 참석해야 하나요?
사진 편집에 관한 것이요.
알림판에 게시되어 있어요.

Q **Which of our company's books** has been the most successful this month?
A1 It hasn't been announced yet.
A2 *The Kingdom* by James Gold.

우리 회사 책들 중 어느 것이 이번 달에 가장 성공적이었나요?
아직 발표되지 않았어요.
제임스 골드의 『킹덤』이요.

7 How 의문문 🔊 03-7.mp3

How 의문문이 '어떻게'라는 뜻으로 쓰일 때는 방법이나 수단 등을 묻습니다. 이때 How 의문문의 동사 부분에 특히 집중해서 들어야 합니다.

■ 방법, 수단

Q	**How** do I **get to** the Tower Hotel?	타워 호텔에 어떻게 가나요?
A1	Take bus number 24 over there.	저기서 24번 버스를 타세요.
A2	Actually, it's my first time here.	사실, 전 여기 처음이에요.

Q	**How** can I **become a member** of the association?	어떻게 협회의 회원이 될 수 있죠?
A1	Fill out this form.	이 서식을 작성하세요.
A2	I applied on their Web site.	전 그곳의 웹사이트에서 지원했어요.

▶ 회사나 단체 등을 지칭할 때 그곳의 사람들을 가리키는 의미로 3인칭 복수 대명사 they/their/them을 사용합니다.

■ 상태, 의견

Q	**How was** the **movie festival** yesterday?	어제 영화제 어땠어요?
A1	It was very successful.	매우 성공적이었어요.
A2	There were too many people.	사람이 너무 많았어요.

■ How + 형용사/부사 (얼마나~?)

How 의문문이 '얼마나'라는 뜻으로 쓰일 때는 의문사 How가 형용사나 부사와 결합하여 기간, 빈도, 거리, 금액, 수량 등을 묻습니다. 따라서 How 다음에 이어지는 형용사 또는 부사를 반드시 들어야 합니다.

• How much[many] ~?	얼마나 많이/많은 ~인가요?
• How long ~?	얼마나 오래 ~인가요?
• How often ~?	얼마나 자주 ~인가요?
• How soon ~?	얼마나 곧 ~인가요?

Q	**How long** will it take to drive to the airport?	공항에 운전해서 가는데 얼마나 오래 걸릴까요?
A1	About an hour.	약 한 시간이요.
A2	I wouldn't recommend driving.	운전하는 건 추천하고 싶지 않아요.

Q	**How many** chairs will you need for the training?	교육에 얼마나 많은 의자가 필요할까요?
A1	At least 30, I guess.	적어도 30개일 것 같아요.
A2	Let me check with the Personnel Department.	제가 인사팀에 확인해 볼게요.

8 Why 의문문 🔊 03-8.mp3

Why 의문문은 '왜 ~?'라는 뜻으로, 특정 상황이나 사건이 발생한 원인 또는 이유를 묻습니다. 주로 「because + 주어 + 동사」 또는 「because of + 명사」 또는 「to + 동사원형」 형태의 to부정사구가 정답입니다.

■ 원인, 이유에 대한 응답

Q **Why** is there so much traffic this afternoon? 오늘 오후에 왜 이렇게 교통량이 많죠?
A1 **Because of** the festival in town. 시내에서 열리는 축제 때문에요.
A2 There was a car accident on Main Street. 메인 스트리트에 자동차 사고가 있었어요..

Q **Why didn't** the **shipment** of shoes **arrive** today? 신발 배송이 왜 오늘 도착하지 않았죠?
A1 **Because** the truck broke down. 트럭이 고장 났거든요.
A2 I'll call the warehouse right away. 지금 바로 창고에 전화해 볼게요.

■ 목적을 나타내는 to부정사구 응답

Q **Why** is the **supermarket closed** this week? 이번 주에 슈퍼마켓이 왜 문을 닫나요?
A To do some repairs. 수리 작업을 하기 위해서요.

Q **Why** did you **leave early** yesterday? 어제 왜 일찍 가셨어요?
A To pick up my daughter. 딸을 데리러 가기 위해서요.

700+ TIP

Why don't you[we] ~? (~하시겠어요?)

Why don't you[we] ~?는 이유를 묻는 부정 의문문이 아니라 주로 '~하시겠어요?'라고 제안하는 의문문으로 쓰입니다. 따라서 이 유형의 질문에 내용에 대한 이해없이 Because나 Because of로 대답한 것을 고르지 않도록 주의해야 합니다.

EX Why don't you join us for lunch? 우리랑 같이 점심 먹을래요?
(A) Because I was not hungry. (X) 배가 고프지 않았기 때문이에요.
(B) I'd love to. (O) 꼭 그러고 싶어요.

PRACTICE

음원을 듣고 각각의 선택지가 질문에 알맞은 응답이면 O, 아니면 X에 표시한 뒤, 빈칸을 채워보세요.

1 _____ will the new software be installed?
   (A) On the third floor. (O X)
   (B) _____ next week. (O X)
   (C) Not until this Friday. (O X)

2 _____ do you finish work today?
   (A) It was _____ yesterday. (O X)
   (B) He works in the sales team. (O X)
   (C) I still have _____. (O X)

3 _____ is responsible for organizing the company picnic?
   (A) To the Central City Park. (O X)
   (B) Terry would know. (O X)
   (C) Mr. Ramirez _____ that. (O X)

4 _____ the new manager?
   (A) She's highly _____. (O X)
   (B) I knew about it. (O X)
   (C) I haven't talked to her yet. (O X)

5 _____ does the next train to Albany leave?
   (A) The schedule is over there. (O X)
   (B) _____. (O X)
   (C) At Grand Central Station. (O X)

44 시원스쿨 기본토익 700+

6 _____ does Martin work for?

   (A) That was his first company.   O X
   (B) _____ at the C&C Corporation?   O X
   (C) Yes, he'll be working until four.   O X

7 _____ was the train _____?

   (A) For almost an hour.   O X
   (B) There was ice on the rails.   O X
   (C) Because of some _____.   O X

8 _____ your new apartment?

   (A) Better than I expected.   O X
   (B) It's very _____.   O X
   (C) A one-bedroom apartment.   O X

9 _____ is there a _____ at this store?

   (A) On the second floor.   O X
   (B) They're having a _____.   O X
   (C) I have no idea.   O X

10 _____ responded to the invitation?

   (A) Only four or five.   O X
   (B) I just mailed them out.   O X
   (C) To _____ my retirement.   O X

실전 TEST 🔊 03-10.mp3

학습한 내용을 적용하여 다음 기출 변형 문제들을 풀어보세요.

> **PART 2 실전 문제 풀이 지침**
> 1. 순식간에 지나가기 때문에 0.1초만 딴 생각을 해도 놓치게 됩니다. 최대한 집중력을 유지하세요.
> 2. 의문사 의문문이 나오면 문제지에 의문사를 적어야 해요. 안 적으면 선택지를 듣는 도중에 헷갈립니다.
> 3. 각 선택지를 들으면서 확실한 오답은 X, 확실한 정답은 O, 모호한 것은 △ 표시해 두세요. 듣는 도중 정답이라고 생각되는 것이 있더라도 끝까지 듣고 확인한 후 정답을 마킹하세요.

1   Mark your answer.   (A)   (B)   (C)

2   Mark your answer.   (A)   (B)   (C)

3   Mark your answer.   (A)   (B)   (C)

4   Mark your answer.   (A)   (B)   (C)

5   Mark your answer.   (A)   (B)   (C)

6   Mark your answer.   (A)   (B)   (C)

7   Mark your answer.   (A)   (B)   (C)

8   Mark your answer.   (A)   (B)   (C)

9   Mark your answer.   (A)   (B)   (C)

10 Mark your answer.   (A)   (B)   (C)

11 Mark your answer.   (A)   (B)   (C)

12 Mark your answer.   (A)   (B)   (C)

13 Mark your answer.   (A)   (B)   (C)

14 Mark your answer.   (A)   (B)   (C)

15 Mark your answer.   (A)   (B)   (C)

16 Mark your answer.   (A)   (B)   (C)

17 Mark your answer.   (A)   (B)   (C)

18 Mark your answer.   (A)   (B)   (C)

19 Mark your answer.   (A)   (B)   (C)

20 Mark your answer.   (A)   (B)   (C)

21 Mark your answer.   (A)   (B)   (C)

22 Mark your answer.   (A)   (B)   (C)

23 Mark your answer.   (A)   (B)   (C)

24 Mark your answer.   (A)   (B)   (C)

25 Mark your answer.   (A)   (B)   (C)

DAY 04 | 일반 의문문 Part 2

1 Do/Have 조동사 의문문, Be동사 의문문 🎧 04-1.mp3

Yes/No로 대답하는 것이 가능한 의문문이지만, 그렇지 않은 선택지가 정답인 경우가 상당히 많으므로 Yes/No만을 기다리기 보다는 질문과 선택지 사이의 연관성을 찾아내야 합니다.

■ Do 조동사 의문문

Q Do you **want me to send the document** by mail?
A Yes, that would be helpful.

제가 그 서류를 우편으로 보내기를 원하세요?
네, 그건 도움이 될 것입니다.

Q Does **this bus stop** at the National Museum?
A No, take the bus from the stop across the street.

이 버스는 국립 박물관에 정차하나요?
아니요, 길 건너 버스 정류장에서 타세요.

Q Did you **register for the seminar** next week?
A Thanks for reminding me. ·····▶ No 생략

다음주에 있을 세미나에 등록하셨나요?
상기시켜줘서 고마워요.

■ 간접 의문문

「Do you know + 의문사 ~?」와 같은 구조로 된 의문문을 간접 의문문이라고 합니다. 이때 Do you know는 가볍게 들어도 되지만 그 뒤에 나오는 의문사절은 집중해서 들어야 합니다. 간접 의문문은 일반 의문문의 형태(Do you know ~)이므로 Yes/No 응답도 가능하지만 주로 Yes/No를 생략하고 해당 의문사에 어울리는 답변을 하는 정답이 제시됩니다.

Q Do you know **who** will be **giving a keynote speech** at the conference today?
A Dr. Miller is. ·····▶ Yes 생략

오늘 컨퍼런스에서 기조 연설을 누가 할 것인지 알고 있나요?
밀러 박사님입니다.

Q Do you know **where** Ms. Garcia **is**?
A All the marketing staff are in a meeting.

가르시아 씨가 어디에 있는지 아시나요?
모든 마케팅 직원들은 회의에 가 있습니다.

■ Have 조동사 의문문

Q Have you **prepared** for **the tax audit**? 세무 조사에 대비했어요?
A It won't happen for a few more months. 몇 달 동안은 없을 거예요.

Q Have you **booked a venue** for Mr. Choi's retirement party? 최 씨의 퇴직 파티 장소를 예약하셨나요?
A Do you know how many people will come? 몇 명이 올지 아세요?

■ Be동사 의문문

Q Are we **buying a new copy machine** at the office? 사무실에 새로운 복사기를 사는 건가요?
A Yes, Cathleen just confirmed the purchase. 네, 캐틀린이 방금 구매를 확인했어요.

Q Is **this bed cover the right size** for your bed? 이 침대 커버가 당신의 침대에 맞는 크기인가요?
A I checked it last night. ----▶ Yes 생략 어젯밤에 확인했어요.

Q Was **the monthly meeting** scheduled for 1 P.M. **canceled**? 오후 1시에 예정되어 있던 월간 회의는 취소되었나요?
A That's what I heard. ----▶ Yes 생략 저는 그렇게 들었어요.

700+ TIP

be동사 숙어 표현

Part 2에 자주 나오는 be동사 숙어 표현들을 미리 숙지하면 질문을 들을 때 빠르게 의미를 파악할 수 있습니다.

be able to do ~할 수 있다	**Were** you **able to** register for the workshop? 워크숍에 등록할 수 있었나요?
be likely to do ~할 것 같다	**Is** Ms. Jones **likely to** attend the conference? 존스 씨가 컨퍼런스에 참석할 것 같나요?
be supposed to do ~하기로 되어 있다	**Aren't** we **supposed to** be meeting clients today? 우리가 오늘 고객들을 만나기로 되어 있지 않나요?
be familiar with ~을 잘 알다	**Are** you **familiar with** the company's policies? 회사 방침을 잘 알고 있나요?
be ready to do ~할 준비가 되다	**Are** you **ready to** go to lunch? 점심 먹으러 갈 준비 됐나요?

2 부정 의문문 🔊 04-2.mp3

부정 의문문은 일반 의문문의 조동사나 Be동사에 not을 붙인 형태로, 어떤 사실을 다시 한 번 확인하기 위한 질문입니다. 부정 의문문이 나오면 문장의 not은 신경 쓰지 말고 긍정 의문문으로 해석해야 헷갈리지 않습니다. 그런 다음 질문 내용에 대해 긍정이면 Yes, 부정이면 No라고 응답하는 것을 찾으면 됩니다. 단, 일반 의문문과 마찬가지로 Yes/No를 생략한 응답이나 의외의 응답이 정답이 되는 경우도 많습니다.

Q	Don't you **have to submit your expense report** by the end of today? = Do you **have to submit your expense report** by the end of today?	오늘 내에 당신의 지출 보고서를 제출해야 하지 않나요?
A1	No, my manager moved the deadline to tomorrow.	아니요. 부장님이 기한을 내일로 옮겼습니다.
A2	Actually, I already sent it this morning.	사실은 오늘 아침에 이미 제출했어요.

Q	Isn't **Dr. Greene's clinic open** on Saturdays? = Is **Dr. Greene's clinic open** on Saturdays?	토요일에 그린 선생님의 진료소는 열지 않나요?
A1	Yes, but it's by appointment only.	네, 하지만 예약 진료만 합니다.
A2	I'll give them a call now.	제가 지금 전화를 해볼게요.

Q	Haven't you **had your bicycle fixed** yet? = Have you **had your bicycle fixed** yet?	아직 당신의 자전거를 고치지 않았나요?
A1	I'm taking it to a repair shop tomorrow.	내일 수리점에 가지고 갈 거예요.
A2	The shop said they'll finish it by Friday.	수리점에서 금요일까지 완료할 것이라고 했어요.

700+ TIP ★

주의해야 할 부정 의문문의 연음

뒤에 이어지는 주어와 함께 빠르게 발음되어 연음이 될 경우, 당황해서 소리는 물론 의미까지 놓치기 쉬우므로 평소에 그 소리에 익숙해져 있어야 합니다.

Haven't you already got tickets for the show? — 이미 그 쇼의 입장권을 구하지 않으셨나요?
해븐츄

Shouldn't we update our company logo? — 우리 회사 로고를 업데이트해야 하지 않나요?
슈른위

Won't you be at the panel discussion tomorrow? — 내일 공개 토론회에 가시지 않나요?
워운츄

PRACTICE 🎧 04-3.mp3

음원을 듣고 각각의 선택지가 질문에 알맞은 응답이면 O, 아니면 X에 표시한 뒤, 빈칸을 채워보세요.

1 _____ lend out laptops?
- (A) You can return the books on the second floor. (O X)
- (B) Yes, _____. (O X)
- (C) Thanks, please put them on top of the pile. (O X)

2 Has _____ arrived yet?
- (A) Yes, I took the bus. (O X)
- (B) It _____ well now. (O X)
- (C) _____ by the server rack. (O X)

3 _____ to operate the video-conferencing system?
- (A) Sure, _____. (O X)
- (B) _____ will be at 11. (O X)
- (C) A few system files only. (O X)

4 _____ the in-person training sessions next week?
- (A) From Human Resources. (O X)
- (B) No, there were a few trainers. (O X)
- (C) They're going to _____ instead. (O X)

5 _____ be stored in the AV closet?
- (A) After I finish the project first. (O X)
- (B) _____. (O X)
- (C) Yes, we need to clean the room. (O X)

정답 및 해설 p.017

실전 TEST 🎧 04-4.mp3

학습한 내용을 적용하여 다음 기출 변형 문제들을 풀어보세요.

> **PART 2 실전 문제 풀이 지침**
> 1. 순식간에 지나가기 때문에 0.1초만 딴 생각을 해도 놓치게 됩니다. 최대한 집중력을 유지하세요.
> 2. 의문사 의문문이 나오면 문제지에 의문사를 적어야 해요. 안 적으면 선택지를 듣는 도중에 헷갈립니다.
> 3. 각 선택지를 들으면서 확실한 오답은 X, 확실한 정답은 O, 모호한 것은 △ 표시해 두세요. 듣는 도중 정답이라고 생각되는 것이 있더라도 끝까지 듣고 확인한 후 정답을 마킹하세요.

1 Mark your answer.   (A) (B) (C)

2 Mark your answer.   (A) (B) (C)

3 Mark your answer.   (A) (B) (C)

4 Mark your answer.   (A) (B) (C)

5 Mark your answer.   (A) (B) (C)

6 Mark your answer.   (A) (B) (C)

7 Mark your answer.   (A) (B) (C)

8 Mark your answer.   (A) (B) (C)

9 Mark your answer.   (A) (B) (C)

10 Mark your answer.   (A) (B) (C)

11 Mark your answer.   (A) (B) (C)

12 Mark your answer.   (A) (B) (C)

13 Mark your answer.   (A) (B) (C)

14 Mark your answer.   (A) (B) (C)

15 Mark your answer.   (A) (B) (C)

16 Mark your answer.   (A) (B) (C)

17 Mark your answer.   (A) (B) (C)

18 Mark your answer.   (A) (B) (C)

19 Mark your answer.   (A) (B) (C)

20 Mark your answer.   (A) (B) (C)

21 Mark your answer.   (A) (B) (C)

22 Mark your answer.   (A) (B) (C)

23 Mark your answer.   (A) (B) (C)

24 Mark your answer.   (A) (B) (C)

25 Mark your answer.   (A) (B) (C)

DAY 05 | 제안·요청 의문문/선택 의문문 Part 2

1 제안·요청 의문문 🔊 05-1.mp3

제안이나 요청, 부탁을 나타내는 의문문은 질문 내용에 대해 수락 또는 거절하는 응답이 상당히 많은 정답 비중을 차지합니다. 따라서 수락 및 거절을 나타내는 다양한 표현들을 충분히 익혀 두는 것이 좋습니다.

■ 수락/긍정의 응답

Q **Why don't we** start organizing the event schedule now?
행사 일정을 짜는 것을 지금 시작할까요?
A Yes, we have a lot to do.
네, 우리는 할 것이 많아요.

Q **Can you** review the budget proposal later?
예산 제안서를 나중에 검토해줄 수 있나요?
A I can do it after the meeting.
회의 후에 할 수 있어요.

Q **Would you mind** forwarding that e-mail to Jessica?
제시카 씨에게 그 이메일을 전달해주시겠습니까?
A1 Sure, I can do that.
물론이죠. 할 수 있어요.
A2 Not at all. / No, I don't mind.
그럼요, 좋습니다.

➡ Do you mind -ing? / Would you mind -ing?는 상대방에게 부탁할 때 쓰는 표현입니다. 동사 mind는 '꺼리다, 싫어하다'라는 뜻이므로 이 표현을 직역하면 '~하면 싫으세요?'라는 의미이기 때문에 No, I don't mind / No, not at all은 '아뇨, 싫지 않아요'라는 뜻으로 수락을 나타냅니다.

■ 거절/부정의 응답

Q **Would you like to** subscribe to our streaming service?
저희의 스트리밍 서비스를 구독하시겠어요?
A No, thanks. I'm already using one.
아니요, 감사합니다만 저는 이미 하나를 이용하고 있어요.

Q **Could you** call IT support now to fix the network issue?
IT 지원팀에 네트워크 문제를 해결해달라고 지금 전화해줄 수 있나요?
A I just need to finish backing up my files.
저는 제 파일들을 백업하는 걸 끝내야 해요.

700+ TIP

꼭 알아야 할 최빈출 제안·요청 의문문 표현

- Why don't you[we] ~? ~하는 게 어때요?
- Would[Could] you ~? ~해 주시겠어요?
- Do[Don't] you want to ~? ~하시겠어요?
- Would you mind –ing? / Do you mind if I ~? ~해 주시겠습니까? / ~해도 되겠습니까?
- How about ~? ~하는 게 어때요?
- Would you like[prefer] to ~? ~하시겠습니까?

■ 기타 응답

Q **Would you mind** if I opened the window for some fresh air?
상쾌한 공기를 위해 창문을 열어도 괜찮을까요?

A Isn't the traffic outside too loud?
밖에 교통 소음이 너무 크지 않나요?

Q **Can I** see the completed schedule for next month's conference?
다음 달 컨퍼런스의 최종 일정을 볼 수 있을까요?

A Registration for speakers is still open.
아직 연사 등록이 진행 중입니다.

Q **Would you** be interested in managing the summer internship program?
여름 인턴십 프로그램을 관리하는 것에 관심이 있을까요?

A How many interns will I supervise?
제가 얼마나 많은 인턴을 감독해야 하나요?

Q **Could you** check if the Wi-Fi router is powered on?
와이파이 라우터가 전원이 켜져 있는지 확인해 줄 수 있나요?

A Should I check all the network devices?
제가 모든 네트워크 장비들을 확인해야 하나요?

Q **Would you like me to** give you the samples today?
오늘 견본을 드릴까요?

A I'll only be in the office until 3.
저는 3시까지만 사무실에 있을 거예요.

700+ TIP ★

토익에 잘 나오는 수락 또는 거절 응답

수락
- That'll be great. / That would be good.
  그럼 좋겠어요.
- That's a good idea. 좋은 생각이에요.
- That sounds good. 좋아요.
- Sure, I'll do it right now.
  물론이죠, 지금 바로 할게요.
- I'd be happy to. 기꺼이 할게요.
- I'll be there in a minute. 잠시 후에 갈게요.
- Of course. 물론이죠.
  (= Absolutely, Certainly, Definitely)
- I'd appreciate that. 그럼 감사하죠.

거절
- I'm afraid I can't.
  유감스럽지만 못해드릴 것 같아요.
- I have other plans. 다른 계획이 있어요.
- I did already. 저는 이미 했어요.
- Sorry, I'm busy that day.
  죄송해요, 저 그날 바빠요.
- I wasn't planning to. 그럴 계획이 아니었어요.
- Thanks, but ~ 감사합니다만, ~
- I'd like to, but ~ 그러고 싶지만, ~

2 선택 의문문 🔊 05-2.mp3

선택 의문문은 'A or B'의 구조로 두 가지 선택 사항을 제시하는 의문문으로, 둘 중 한 가지 선택 사항을 택하는 내용이 정답인 경우가 가장 많습니다. 둘 다 아닌 제 3의 것을 언급하거나 '아직 결정나지 않았다', '잘 모르겠다'와 같은 유형의 응답도 정답이 될 수 있으니 이러한 응답에 대비하면서 듣도록 합니다.

■ A, B 중 하나를 선택

Q Do I have to **deliver the signed contract in person** (A) or **send you a scanned copy** (B)?
서명된 계약서를 제가 직접 전달해야 하나요, 아니면 당신에게 스캔본을 보내야 하나요?

A I prefer the scanned copy.
저는 스캔본을 선호합니다.

➤ 가장 흔한 정답 유형으로, A, B 둘 중 하나를 선택할 때 질문에 나온 단어나 표현을 그대로 씁니다.

Q Should we **order lunch now** (A) or **wait until 1 P.M.** (B)?
우리가 지금 점심을 주문해야 할까요, 아니면 1시까지 기다려야 할까요?

A I'm in no hurry.
저는 급하지 않아요.

➤ 고난도 문제의 경우 이와 같이 A, B 둘 중 하나를 선택해 다른 말로 바꿔 말합니다.

■ 둘 중 아무거나, 둘 다 아님

Q Would you rather **get tickets for Saturday** (A) or **Sunday** (B)?
토요일 티켓을 원하세요, 아니면 일요일 티켓을 원하세요?

A1 **Either** day is fine with me.
둘 중 어느 것
전 둘 중 아무 날이나 괜찮아요.

A2 **Neither**. I prefer Friday.
둘 중 아무 것도 아닌
둘 다 아니에요. 전 금요일이 좋아요.

■ 제 3의 선택, 의외의 응답

Q Are you booking **a window seat** (A) or **an aisle seat** (B)?
창가쪽 좌석을 예약할 건가요, 아니면 통로쪽 좌석을 예약할 건가요?

A I have to check the prices.
저는 가격을 확인해야 해요.

➤ A, B 이외의 제 3의 응답

Q Will we **schedule the team-building retreat in June** (A) or **July** (B)?
팀 단합회를 6월로 정할까요, 아니면 7월로 정할까요?

A1 The schedule hasn't been finalized.
그 일정은 아직 최종 결정되지 않았어요.

A2 I'm not sure.
잘 모르겠어요.

➤ 의외의 응답

PRACTICE 🔊 05-3.mp3

음원을 듣고 각각의 선택지가 질문에 알맞은 응답이면 O, 아니면 X에 표시한 뒤, 빈칸을 채워보세요.

1 Would you like to _____ to expedited shipping?

(A) How often do you use it?   O X
(B) I would like to add more toppings.   O X
(C) No, _____ is enough.   O X

2 Could you _____ the updated expense-reporting software?

(A) I've submitted mine already.   O X
(B) I _____ myself.   O X
(C) _____ is scheduled in July.   O X

3 _____ extra uniforms for the new employees?

(A) In the supply room.   O X
(B) I already did.   O X
(C) Oh, _____.   O X

4 Would you like to _____ in June or July?

(A) I'm OK _____.   O X
(B) It's two weeks ago.   O X
(C) _____ by next Monday?   O X

5 _____ go to that jazz concert on Tuesday or Wednesday night?

(A) I work _____.   O X
(B) My parents enjoyed it so much.   O X
(C) _____. I prefer Saturday.   O X

정답 및 해설 p.024

실전 TEST 🎧 05-4.mp3

학습한 내용을 적용하여 다음 기출 변형 문제들을 풀어보세요.

> **PART 2 실전 문제 풀이 지침**
> 1. 순식간에 지나가기 때문에 0.1초만 딴 생각을 해도 놓치게 됩니다. 최대한 집중력을 유지하세요.
> 2. 의문사 의문문이 나오면 문제지에 의문사를 적어야 해요. 안 적으면 선택지를 듣는 도중에 헷갈립니다.
> 3. 각 선택지를 들으면서 확실한 오답은 X, 확실한 정답은 O, 모호한 것은 △ 표시해 두세요. 듣는 도중 정답이라고 생각되는 것이 있더라도 끝까지 듣고 확인한 후 정답을 마킹하세요.

1 Mark your answer.　　(A)　(B)　(C)

2 Mark your answer.　　(A)　(B)　(C)

3 Mark your answer.　　(A)　(B)　(C)

4 Mark your answer.　　(A)　(B)　(C)

5 Mark your answer.　　(A)　(B)　(C)

6 Mark your answer.　　(A)　(B)　(C)

7 Mark your answer.　　(A)　(B)　(C)

8 Mark your answer.　　(A)　(B)　(C)

9 Mark your answer.　　(A)　(B)　(C)

10 Mark your answer.　　(A)　(B)　(C)

11 Mark your answer.　　(A)　(B)　(C)

12 Mark your answer.　　(A)　(B)　(C)

13 Mark your answer.   (A) (B) (C)

14 Mark your answer.   (A) (B) (C)

15 Mark your answer.   (A) (B) (C)

16 Mark your answer.   (A) (B) (C)

17 Mark your answer.   (A) (B) (C)

18 Mark your answer.   (A) (B) (C)

19 Mark your answer.   (A) (B) (C)

20 Mark your answer.   (A) (B) (C)

21 Mark your answer.   (A) (B) (C)

22 Mark your answer.   (A) (B) (C)

23 Mark your answer.   (A) (B) (C)

24 Mark your answer.   (A) (B) (C)

25 Mark your answer.   (A) (B) (C)

DAY 06 | 평서문 / 부가 의문문 Part 2

1 평서문 🎧 06-1.mp3

마침표로 끝나는 평서문이 제시되고, 그 말에 대한 적절한 반응을 고르는 유형으로 매회 2~4 문항이 출제됩니다. 상대방에게 궁금한 것을 묻는 질문이 아니기 때문에 정답으로 적절한 반응을 예측하기가 쉽지 않아 난이도가 높습니다. 강하게 발음되는 동사나 명사 위주로 듣고, 말하는 이의 의도를 재빨리 파악하여 각 선택지와의 의미 관계를 명확히 판단하는 것이 핵심입니다.

■ 정보/사실 전달

정보나 사실을 전달하는 평서문에 대해 되묻는 응답이나 제공된 정보에 대한 의견, 그리고 추가 정보를 제공하는 답변이 정답으로 등장합니다.

Q Our **online courses are free** for registered users.
저희의 온라인 강좌들은 등록된 사용자들에게 무료입니다.
A Can I download the materials too?
제가 자료도 다운로드 받을 수 있나요?

Q Mr. Reeds **approved** the marketing **budget**.
리즈 씨가 마케팅 예산을 승인했어요.
A I already saw the memo.
전 이미 회람을 봤어요.

Q We **plan to relocate** the main office next quarter.
저희는 다음 분기에 본사를 이전할 계획입니다.
A I heard it'll be somewhere near the central station.
중앙역 근처 어디일 것이라고 들었어요.

■ 문제 상황 알림

Q I **can't find the invoice** from the supplier.
공급업체로부터 받은 송장을 못 찾겠어요.
A I put it in your inbox tray.
제가 당신의 받은 편지함에 넣었어요.

Q I **didn't bring an umbrella,** and it's starting to rain.
우산을 가지고 오지 않았는데 비가 오기 시작하네요.
A I've got a spare one in my bag.
제 가방에 남는 게 하나 있어요.

Q Our team**'s looking for a graphic designer** for the new campaign.
저희 팀은 새로운 캠페인을 위한 그래픽 디자이너를 찾고 있어요.
A I know someone who recently graduated in design.
저는 최근에 디자인 전공으로 졸업한 사람을 알아요.

■ 감정/의견 표현

자신의 감정이나 의견을 밝히는 평서문에는 상대방의 말에 대한 의견을 제시하는 응답이 자주 정답으로 나옵니다.

Q The office **cafeteria will start serving breakfast** next week.
A I've always wanted to grab something warm before work.

회사 카페테리아가 다음 주에 아침식사를 제공하기 시작할 것입니다.
저는 항상 업무 전에 따뜻한 걸 먹고 싶었어요.

Q It's **fine if we postpone** the team lunch.
A Good, I wasn't sure I could make it today.

팀 점심회식을 연기해도 괜찮습니다.
잘됐네요. 저는 오늘 참석할 수 있을지 확실하지 않았거든요.

Q We **have to assign someone** to lead the next project.
A I think Jason would be a great fit.

우리는 다음 프로젝트를 이끌 누군가를 배정해야해요.
제 생각에 제이슨이 아주 적합한 사람일 것 같습니다.

■ 제안/요청

의문문이 아닌 평서문으로도 제안이나 요청을 할 수 있습니다. 이 유형의 다양한 표현들(Let's ~, I'd like you to ~, Please ~, We should ~)과 함께 제안이나 요청에 어울리는 응답도 알아두세요.

Q **Let's review the training schedule** for new hires.
A Are you available at the moment?

신입 직원들을 위한 교육 일정을 검토해봅시다.
지금 시간 되세요?

▶ I'd like you to do: 당신이 ~해주면 좋겠어요.
　 I'd like to do: 저는 ~하고 싶습니다.

Q **I'd like you to submit the expense report** by the end of the day.
A That shouldn't be a problem.

당신이 오늘까지 지출 보고서를 제출하면 좋겠어요.
문제 없습니다.

Q **Please confirm the reservation** for next Thursday.
A I'll handle it right now.

다음주 목요일의 예약을 확인해주세요.
지금 바로 처리하겠습니다.

2 부가 의문문 🔊 06-2.mp3

- 부가 의문문은 『평서문 + 꼬리말』의 구조로, 상대방으로부터 동의를 이끌어 내거나 사실을 확인하는 용도로 사용하는 의문문입니다.
- 평서문이 긍정문이면 꼬리말에 not이 붙고, 부정문으로 제시되면 꼬리말에 not이 붙지 않습니다.

> **EX** You're going to the party, aren't you?
> Mr. Chen didn't attend the meeting, did he?

- 대부분 Yes/No로 답한 후 관련 정보를 추가로 언급하는 방식으로 정답이 제시됩니다. 하지만 오답 선택지에도 Yes/No를 배치해 혼동을 유발하는 경우가 많으므로 각 선택지를 유심히 들으면서 질문 내용과의 연관성을 확인해야 합니다.

■ 긍정문 + 부정 꼬리말

문제를 풀 때 꼬리말의 형태는 전혀 신경 쓰지 않아도 됩니다. 앞에 제시되는 평서문을 잘 듣고 문장의 내용이 맞으면 Yes, 아니면 No로 대답하는 것을 고르면 됩니다. Yes/No를 생략하고 대답하는 경우나 의외의 응답을 하는 경우에 주의합니다.

Q **That hotel has a rooftop pool**, doesn't it? 그 호텔에는 루프탑 수영장이 있죠, 그렇지 않나요?
(= 그 호텔에 루프탑 수영장이 있죠?)
A1 Yes, they just renovated it last month. 맞아요, 지난 달에 막 개조공사를 했어요.
A2 I've never stayed there. 저는 거기 묵은 적이 없어요.

■ 부정문 + 긍정 꼬리말

부정문이 나오더라도 무조건 긍정으로 해석해서 문장의 내용이 맞으면 Yes, 아니면 No로 대답하는 것을 고르면 됩니다. 마찬가지로 Yes/No를 생략하고 대답하는 경우나 의외의 응답을 하는 경우에 주의해야 합니다.

Q **We don't need to bring our own headphones**, do we? 우리는 헤드폰을 가지고 갈 필요가 없죠, 그렇죠?
(= 우리는 헤드폰을 가져가야 하죠?)
= We need to bring our own headphones.
A1 No, they provide them at the entrance. 아니요, 입구에서 헤드폰을 제공해줘요.
A2 I'm not sure. Let me check. 모르겠어요. 확인해 볼게요.

■ 긍정문 + 꼬리말 right

Q **This ticket includes a free drink**, right? 이 티켓에는 무료 음료가 포함되어 있죠, 그렇죠?
A1 You'll need to present your voucher at the counter. 카운터에서 당신의 쿠폰을 보여줘야 할 겁니다.
A2 Sorry, that promotion expired last week. 죄송합니다. 그 프로모션은 지난 주에 끝났어요.

PRACTICE 🔊 06-3.mp3

음원을 듣고 각각의 선택지가 질문에 알맞은 응답이면 O, 아니면 X에 표시한 뒤, 빈칸을 채워보세요.

1 I just heard that the concert has been _____.
(A) No, I haven't heard from him. O X
(B) _____? O X
(C) That's very _____! O X

2 Please make sure to _____ by the deadline.
(A) _____ in the shared folder. O X
(B) Sure, I'm _____. O X
(C) Let me know if you need help. O X

3 Ms. Bowen _____ today, didn't she?
(A) Sure, I'll design it again. O X
(B) That's _____. O X
(C) Yes, this morning. O X

4 This month's budget report _____ yet, has it?
(A) I'll help with your proposal. O X
(B) It _____ discussed more. O X
(C) The manager just received it. O X

5 I'd like you to _____ before closing.
(A) Who should I send _____ to once it's done? O X
(B) Sure, I'll make sure it's done. O X
(C) Yes, it's scheduled tomorrow. O X

정답 및 해설 p.032

실전 TEST 🎧 06-4.mp3

학습한 내용을 적용하여 다음 기출 변형 문제들을 풀어보세요.

> **PART 2 실전 문제 풀이 지침**
> 1. 순식간에 지나가기 때문에 0.1초만 딴 생각을 해도 놓치게 됩니다. 최대한 집중력을 유지하세요.
> 2. 의문사 의문문이 나오면 문제지에 의문사를 적어야 해요. 안 적으면 선택지를 듣는 도중에 헷갈립니다.
> 3. 각 선택지를 들으면서 확실한 오답은 X, 확실한 정답은 O, 모호한 것은 △ 표시해 두세요. 듣는 도중 정답이라고 생각되는 것이 있더라도 끝까지 듣고 확인한 후 정답을 마킹하세요.

1. Mark your answer. (A) (B) (C)
2. Mark your answer. (A) (B) (C)
3. Mark your answer. (A) (B) (C)
4. Mark your answer. (A) (B) (C)
5. Mark your answer. (A) (B) (C)
6. Mark your answer. (A) (B) (C)
7. Mark your answer. (A) (B) (C)
8. Mark your answer. (A) (B) (C)
9. Mark your answer. (A) (B) (C)
10. Mark your answer. (A) (B) (C)
11. Mark your answer. (A) (B) (C)
12. Mark your answer. (A) (B) (C)

13 Mark your answer.   (A) (B) (C)

14 Mark your answer.   (A) (B) (C)

15 Mark your answer.   (A) (B) (C)

16 Mark your answer.   (A) (B) (C)

17 Mark your answer.   (A) (B) (C)

18 Mark your answer.   (A) (B) (C)

19 Mark your answer.   (A) (B) (C)

20 Mark your answer.   (A) (B) (C)

21 Mark your answer.   (A) (B) (C)

22 Mark your answer.   (A) (B) (C)

23 Mark your answer.   (A) (B) (C)

24 Mark your answer.   (A) (B) (C)

25 Mark your answer.   (A) (B) (C)

PART 2 FINAL TEST 🎧 FT-2.mp3

학습한 내용을 적용하여 다음 기출 변형 문제들을 풀어보세요.

> **PART 2 실전 문제 풀이 지침**
> 1. 순식간에 지나가기 때문에 0.1초만 딴 생각을 해도 놓치게 됩니다. 최대한 집중력을 유지하세요.
> 2. 의문사 의문문이 나오면 문제지에 의문사를 적어야 해요. 안 적으면 선택지를 듣는 도중에 헷갈립니다.
> 3. 각 선택지를 들으면서 확실한 오답은 X, 확실한 정답은 O, 모호한 것은 △ 표시해 두세요. 듣는 도중 정답이라고 생각되는 것이 있더라도 끝까지 듣고 확인한 후 정답을 마킹하세요.

1   Mark your answer.   (A)   (B)   (C)
2   Mark your answer.   (A)   (B)   (C)
3   Mark your answer.   (A)   (B)   (C)
4   Mark your answer.   (A)   (B)   (C)
5   Mark your answer.   (A)   (B)   (C)
6   Mark your answer.   (A)   (B)   (C)
7   Mark your answer.   (A)   (B)   (C)
8   Mark your answer.   (A)   (B)   (C)
9   Mark your answer.   (A)   (B)   (C)
10 Mark your answer.   (A)   (B)   (C)
11 Mark your answer.   (A)   (B)   (C)
12 Mark your answer.   (A)   (B)   (C)

13 Mark your answer.   (A) (B) (C)

14 Mark your answer.   (A) (B) (C)

15 Mark your answer.   (A) (B) (C)

16 Mark your answer.   (A) (B) (C)

17 Mark your answer.   (A) (B) (C)

18 Mark your answer.   (A) (B) (C)

19 Mark your answer.   (A) (B) (C)

20 Mark your answer.   (A) (B) (C)

21 Mark your answer.   (A) (B) (C)

22 Mark your answer.   (A) (B) (C)

23 Mark your answer.   (A) (B) (C)

24 Mark your answer.   (A) (B) (C)

25 Mark your answer.   (A) (B) (C)

기본토익 700+

PART 3

DAY 07 주제 / 목적 / 문제점 문제
DAY 08 장소 / 신분 / 직업 문제
DAY 09 세부 사항 / say about 문제
DAY 10 제안·요청 사항 / do next 문제
DAY 11 의도 파악 문제 / 시각자료 연계 문제
PART 3 FINAL TEST

PART 3 ★ 짧은 대화 문제 미리보기

- 문항수: 39문항 (32번~70번)
- 두 명, 혹은 세 명이 나누는 대화를 듣고 관련 질문에 대한 정답을 고르는 유형입니다.
- 총 13개 대화가 나오고, 대화 한 개당 세 문제씩 제시됩니다.
- 대화를 듣기 전에 문제지에 제시된 문제들을 미리 읽어 두어야 합니다.

📄 문제지

32. Where are the speakers?

    (A) In a gym
    (B) In an office
    (C) In a clinic
    (D) In a store ✓

33. What does the man inquire about?

    (A) Size options ✓
    (B) Special discounts
    (C) Available colors
    (D) Product prices

34. What does the woman suggest?

    (A) Coming back tomorrow
    (B) Looking for an item together ✓
    (C) Trying out a different product
    (D) Purchasing an item online

🎧 음원

Questions 32-34 refer to the following conversation.

M Hello, I'm looking for some running shoes. They're the Ultra Boost 301s. Do you carry them?

W Actually, we do. In fact, that style is currently available at 40 percent off.

M Great! And I was wondering if they're available in large sizes such as size 295 or 300.

W I'm not sure. Let's go to the display stands and take a look at what we have available.

Number 32. Where are the speakers?
Number 33. What does the man inquire about?
Number 34. What does the woman suggest?

----- 문제지에 문제와 선택지 (A)~(D)가 제시됨

DAY 07 | 주제/목적/문제점 문제 Part 3

1 주제 / 목적을 묻는 문제 🔊 07-1.mp3

Part 3에서는 대화 하나당 세 문제씩 출제되는데, 그 중 첫 번째 문제로 자주 출제되는 문제 유형입니다. 질문을 먼저 읽고 주제/목적 문제임을 파악한 후, 대화가 시작되면 첫 번째 화자의 말에 집중해 듣고 그 화자의 말이 다른 말로 약간 바뀌어 나온(Paraphrase) 선택지를 고르면 됩니다.

Q **What** are the speakers mainly **discussing**? ▶ 화자들이 주로 이야기하고 있는 것은?

(A) **A training session** ○----┐ 교육 시간
(B) A product launch   제품 출시
(C) A hiring decision   고용 결정
(D) A building renovation   건물 개조

M: Are you ready for **the staff orientation** this afternoon? → 오늘 오후 직원 오리엔테이션 준비됐어요?

W: Almost. I just need to print the **training handouts**. → 거의 다 됐어요. 교육 자료만 출력하면 됩니다.

M: I left some extra pens in the conference room for you. → 회의실에 여분의 펜을 두고 왔어요.

W: Perfect. **I'll set everything up** before the break. → 완벽해요. 쉬는 시간 전에 다 준비할게요.

■ 대화에서 주제나 목적이 드러나는 문장 유형

첫 번째 화자의 질문	**What do you think about** the new software program? 새 소프트웨어 프로그램에 대해 어떻게 생각해요? ❶ 예상 대화 주제 새로운 소프트웨어 프로그램
전화 용건을 말하는 문장	**I'm calling to inquire about** shipping items to some European countries. 몇몇 유럽 국가들로 제품을 발송하는 것에 대해 문의하기 위해 전화 드립니다. ❶ 예상 전화 목적 해외 발송 서비스에 대해 문의하는 것
요청 사항을 말하는 문장	**I'd like to make a reservation. I'm organizing a dinner** for 10 people. 예약을 하고 싶습니다. 저는 10명에 대한 저녁 식사 자리를 마련하는 중입니다. ❶ 예상 대화 주제 저녁 식사 예약

2 문제점을 묻는 문제 🎧 07-2.mp3

질문에 problem이 보이면 문제점에 대해 묻는 것이므로 대화에 부정적인 내용(ex. 작동이 안 된다, 너무 비싸다, 재고가 없다, 늦었다 등)이 나올 것을 예상하고 들어야 합니다. 문제점을 묻는 문제가 있으면 첫 번째 화자가 문제점 발생 상황을 언급하는 것으로 대화가 시작되기 때문에 첫 번째 화자의 말을 놓치지 않고 잘 들어야 합니다.

Q What **problem** does the **woman mention**? ▶ 여자가 말하는 문제점은?

(A) A passport is missing.
(B) A hotel reservation did not go through.
(C) **A flight was booked incorrectly.**
(D) The airport changed some departure times.

여권을 분실했다.
호텔 예약에 실패했다.
항공편이 잘못 예약되었다.
공항이 출발시간을 변경하였다.

W: Hi, Josh. I reviewed the team's travel bookings.
M: Thanks! Everything looked fine on my end.
W: **Except one thing—Elaine's flight was scheduled for the wrong day.**
M: I'll call the travel agency to have that fixed right away.

여 안녕하세요 조쉬. 전 팀원들의 여행 예약을 검토했어요.
남 고마워요! 제가 보기엔 전부 문제없어 보였어요.
여 한 가지만 제외하고요. 일레인의 항공편이 잘못된 날짜로 예약되어 있었어요.
남 바로 여행사에 전화해서 수정할게요.

■ 대화에서 문제점이 언급되는 문장 유형

문제점이 있다	We're currently **having some problems** with our Web site. 현재 우리 웹사이트에 몇몇 문제점들이 있어요.
~할 수 없다	**I can't** connect to the Internet, so **I can't** check my e-mail. 제가 인터넷에 접속할 수가 없어서, 제 이메일을 확인할 수 없어요.
부정적인 내용을 알리는 신호	**Unfortunately**, the cars you liked are not within your budget. 안타깝게도, 당신이 마음에 들어한 차들은 당신의 예산 내에 있지 않아요. ❶ 부정적인 표현 Unfortunately, I'm sorry, I'm afraid, but, actually, however

3 질문 유형 🔊 07-3.mp3

다양한 질문 형태를 미리 충분히 익혀 두세요. 그렇게 하면 실전에서 질문을 파악하는 데 0.5초밖에 걸리지 않으므로 어느 부분에 초점을 맞춰 들어야 하는지 미리 대비하고 대화를 들을 수 있어 유리합니다.

대화의 주제를 묻는 질문 유형

What is the conversation **(mainly) about**?
대화는 주로 무엇에 관한 것인가?

What are the speakers mainly **discussing**?
화자들은 주로 무엇을 얘기하고 있는가?

What is the **main topic** of the conversation?
대화의 주제는 무엇인가?

What are the **speakers planning**?
화자들은 무엇을 계획하고 있는가?

주제 문제의 단서는 대화의 첫 대사에 나오는 경우가 많으므로 대화가 시작되는 시점에 최대한 집중해 첫 대사를 놓치지 말고 들어야 합니다. 주제를 묻는 일반적인 질문 외에도 '화자들은 무엇을 계획하고 있는가?'와 같은 질문도 종종 출제됩니다.

전화의 목적을 묻는 질문 유형

Why is the man **calling**?
남자는 왜 전화하는가?

Why did[does] the man **call** the woman?
남자는 왜 여자에게 전화했는가[하는가]?

What is the **purpose** of the **call**?
전화의 목적은 무엇인가?

전화 대화에서 전화를 건 목적이나 이유를 묻는 문제가 잘 나옵니다. 대화가 시작될 때 전화를 건 사람의 첫 대사에 반드시 용건이 언급되므로 그 내용을 놓치지 말아야 합니다.

문제점을 묻는 질문 유형

What is the **problem**?
무엇이 문제인가?

What problem does the man/woman **mention[have]**?
남자/여자는 무슨 문제점을 언급하는가[가지고 있는가]?

What is the **man/woman concerned [worried] about**?
남자/여자는 무엇에 대해 우려[걱정]하는가?

특정 문제점이나 걱정거리가 무엇인지 묻는 유형으로, 부정적인 내용을 말하는 문장에 정답 단서가 있습니다. 따라서 이러한 유형의 질문이 보이면 대화에 부정적인 내용이 제시된다는 것을 미리 생각하고 듣는 것이 좋습니다.

PRACTICE 🎧 07-4.mp3

음원을 듣고 질문에 맞는 선택지를 고른 뒤, 빈칸을 채워보세요.

1 **Why** is the **man calling**?
(A) To collect feedback about a service 서비스에 대한 피드백을 얻기 위해
(B) To propose a new rental package 새로운 렌탈 패키지를 제안하기 위해
(C) To apologize for a cancellation 취소에 대해 사과하기 위해
(D) To update some contract terms 일부 계약 조항을 업데이트하기 위해

> M: Good afternoon, this is Aaron from Classic Rentals. I'm calling regarding _____ _____ for your event last weekend.
> W: Hi, Aaron. Everything went smoothly, though one microphone stopped working in the middle of the speech.
> M: I'm sorry to hear that. I'll make a note and follow up with the tech team.

2 **What problem** does **the woman mention**?
(A) An award ceremony has been postponed. 시상식이 연기되었다.
(B) A chart is missing. 차트가 분실되었다.
(C) Some names are incorrect. 일부 이름들이 잘못되어 있다.
(D) A device is malfunctioning. 기기가 제대로 작동하지 않고 있다.

> W: Hi, Daniel. Have you finalized the seating chart for the awards ceremony?
> M: Yes, everything's been arranged and sent to the printer.
> W: I'm afraid _____.
> M: Oh no. We'll need to fix that before the programs go out.

정답 및 해설 p.040

DAY 07 주제/목적/문제점 문제 73

실전 TEST 🔊 07-5.mp3

학습한 내용을 적용하여 다음 기출 변형 문제들을 풀어보세요.

> **PART 3 실전 문제 풀이 지침**
> 1. 대화가 나오기 전에 세 개의 문제를 빠르게 읽고 핵심을 파악합니다. 이때 키워드에 동그라미를 쳐 둡니다.
> 2. 미리 읽은 문제와 관련된 내용을 노려 듣습니다.
> 3. 정답을 찾으면 문제지에 바로 체크하고 다음 문제를 읽습니다. 답안지 마킹은 나중에 한꺼번에 해도 됩니다.

1 What are the speakers mainly discussing?

(A) A sales report
(B) A product launch
(C) A store opening
(D) A training session

2 What problem does the man mention?

(A) Some staff members are late.
(B) A meeting was postponed.
(C) Some information was not sent.
(D) A product has sold poorly.

3 What does the man agree to do by Tuesday?

(A) Arrange a meeting
(B) Speak with his manager
(C) E-mail a document
(D) Visit a client

4 What are the speakers discussing?

(A) Organizing a trip
(B) Purchasing a property
(C) Renovating a building
(D) Planning an event

5 Who most likely is Mr. Goldberg?

(A) An architect
(B) An interior designer
(C) A real estate agent
(D) A financial advisor

6 What does the woman recommend that the man do?

(A) Call an office
(B) Provide an e-mail address
(C) Visit a Web site
(D) Fill out a survey

7 Why is the man calling?

(A) To organize a meal
(B) To increase an order
(C) To request information
(D) To complain about some items

8 Where does the woman probably work?

(A) At a coffee shop
(B) At a supermarket
(C) At a factory
(D) At a hotel

9 What does the woman say she will do?

(A) Speak to her supervisor
(B) Provide a bulk discount
(C) Prepare some food items
(D) Change a delivery time

10 What is the problem?

(A) A blueprint has been misplaced.
(B) A computer is malfunctioning.
(C) A client has not arrived.
(D) Some information is wrong.

11 Why is the woman concerned?

(A) She has to finish some work.
(B) She is late for a meeting.
(C) She forgot to save a document.
(D) She lost some contact details.

12 What does the woman say she will do next?

(A) Cancel a meeting
(B) Back up her work
(C) Contact a client
(D) Install some software

실전 TEST 07-5.mp3

학습한 내용을 적용하여 다음 기출 변형 문제들을 풀어보세요.

13 What are the speakers trying to do?

(A) Organize a fundraiser
(B) Make a reservation
(C) Select an event venue
(D) Recruit some participants

14 What problem does the man mention?

(A) Some equipment is too large.
(B) Some paperwork was not submitted.
(C) A shipment has been delayed.
(D) A parking area is small.

15 What does the man say he will do?

(A) Create a survey
(B) Talk to a manager
(C) Apply for a permit
(D) Send some cost projections

16 What is the conversation about?

(A) A budget limit
(B) A supply shortage
(C) A design error
(D) Broken machinery

17 What does the man offer?

(A) A rental voucher
(B) An extended warranty
(C) An alternative product
(D) Free delivery

18 Why does the woman ask to visit the business?

(A) To view a new design
(B) To receive a discount coupon
(C) To drop off some materials
(D) To take some photos

19 What is the conversation mainly about?

(A) Purchasing a business
(B) Repairing a vehicle
(C) Renovating a work area
(D) Updating some software

20 How does the man say he could approach a project?

(A) By hiring more employees
(B) By doing research online
(C) By referring to a catalog
(D) By attending a conference

21 What is the woman worried about?

(A) Maintenance costs
(B) Construction noise
(C) An upcoming deadline
(D) A change in regulations

22 What product do the speakers make?

(A) Hamburgers
(B) Office supplies
(C) Sandwiches
(D) Lunch boxes

23 What problem does the woman mention?

(A) There are not enough staff members.
(B) The demand for a product is not high.
(C) The store cannot take online orders.
(D) A kitchen space is too small.

24 Who will the man contact?

(A) A packaging company
(B) A mobile app developer
(C) A delivery service provider
(D) A marketing specialist

DAY 08 | 장소/신분/직업 문제 Part 3

1 대화 장소를 묻는 문제 🎧 08-1.mp3

대화가 진행되는 장소를 묻는 문제는 대화 중에 드러나는 관련 단어들을 통해 장소를 유추해야 합니다. 이때 반드시 2개 이상의 키워드를 종합해 정답을 고르도록 하세요. 처음에 들리는 키워드 한 개만 듣고 섣불리 유추하면 오답 함정에 빠질 수 있습니다.

Q Where most likely are the **speakers**? ----▶ 화자들이 있는 곳은?

(A) At a library — 도서관
(B) At a design agency — 디자인 에이전시
(C) **At a museum** — 박물관
(D) At a theater — 극장

W: Hi, Javier. Have you finished **organizing the paintings for the new exhibit**?
M: Almost. I just need to double-check the lighting in **Gallery B**.

여 안녕하세요, 하비에르. 새로운 전시회를 위한 그림 정리는 끝났어요?
남 거의 다 됐어요. B 전시실 조명을 한 번 더 확인해야 해요.

■ 대화 장소 및 관련 직업 키워드

장소	관련 직업	키워드
store 매장	store clerk 매장 점원 sales representative 판매원 customer service representative 고객 서비스 담당 직원	in stock 재고가 있는 out of stock 재고가 없는 receipt 영수증 discount 할인 refund 환불, 환불해주다 exchange 교환, 교환하다 special offer 특가 accept credit card 신용 카드를 받다
hotel 호텔	front desk clerk 안내 데스크 직원	check in 입실 수속을 하다 check out 퇴실 수속을 하다 reservation 예약 room service 룸서비스 suite room 스위트 룸 banquet hall 연회장
auto repair shop 자동차 수리소	mechanic 정비사	auto parts 자동차 부품 inspection 점검, 검사 flat tire 펑크 난 타이어 garage 차량 정비소 have the tires replaced 타이어를 교체 받다
catering company 출장 요리 제공 업체	caterer 출장 요리 제공업자	catering service 출장 요리 서비스 food service 음식 서비스 cater an event 행사에 출장 음식을 제공하다 corporate party 회사 파티 food order 음식 주문

2 신분/직업/직책을 묻는 문제 🔊 08-2.mp3

화자들 중 한 사람의 신분을 묻는 문제는 정답 단서가 그 사람의 말이 아닌 상대방의 말에 언급되는 경우도 많으므로 두 사람 모두의 말에 집중해야 합니다.

Q **Who** most likely is the **man**? ······▶ 남자의 신분은?

(A) A sales representative — 영업 사원
(B) A cleaning service manager — 청소 서비스 관리자
(C) A landlord — 임대주
(D) **A repair technician** — 수리 기사

M: This is Jeff from Summit **Repairs.** I'm checking in about **the refrigerator service you requested**.
W: Thanks for calling. It's still making a loud humming sound. I wasn't sure it was fixed after the last visit.

🔵 서밋 리페어의 제프입니다. 요청하신 냉장고 수리 건으로 확인 차 연락드렸습니다.
🟠 전화해주셔서 감사합니다. 여전히 웅웅거리는 소리가 크게 나요. 지난번 수리 이후에 제대로 고쳐졌는지 확신이 안 들었어요.

■ 대화 장소 및 관련 직업 키워드

장소	관련 직업	키워드
real estate agency 부동산 중개업체	real estate agent 부동산 중개인 property manager 건물 관리자	resident 주민 tenant 세입자 lease 임대차 계약(서) rent 임대하다, 임대(료) office space 사무 공간 property 부동산, 건물
medical clinic, doctor's office 병원, 진료소	doctor 의사 nurse 간호사 receptionist 접수 직원 dentist 치과 의사	patient 환자 medical records 진료 기록 appointment 진료 예약 regular check-up 정기 검진 test results 검사 결과 medication 약물 (치료) dental appointment 치과 예약 cavity 충치
factory 공장 manufacturing facility 제조 시설	factory worker 공장 직원	give a tour 견학을 시켜주다 assembly line 조립 라인 conveyor belt 컨베이어 벨트 machine 기계, 장비 safety inspection 안전 점검 protective gear 보호 장비
magazine company 잡지사 newspaper company 신문사	journalist 언론인 reporter 기자 staff-writer 전속 기자 editor 편집자	article 기사 next issue 다음 호 subscribe to ~을 구독하다 sign up for ~을 신청하다 renew one's subscription 구독을 갱신하다 digital subscription 디지털 구독
library 도서관	librarian 사서	check out a book 책을 대출하다 overdue fee 연체료 return a book 책을 반납하다 borrow a book 책을 빌리다 owe a fine 벌금을 내야 하다 due + 시점: ~가 반납 기한인

DAY 08 장소/신분/직업 문제 79

3 장소/신분/직업 질문 유형 🔊 08-3.mp3

다양한 질문 형태를 미리 충분히 익혀 두세요. 그렇게 하면 실전에서 질문을 파악하는 데 0.5초밖에 걸리지 않으므로 어느 부분에 초점을 맞춰 들어야 하는지 미리 대비하고 대화를 들을 수 있어 유리합니다.

대화 장소 또는 근무 장소를 묻는 질문 유형

Where (most likely) are **the speakers**?
화자들은 어디에 있는 것 같은가?

Where is the conversation (most likely) **taking place**?
대화가 어디에서 이뤄지고 있는 것 같은가?

Where do the speakers (most likely) **work**?
화자들은 어디에서 근무하는 것 같은가?

Where does the man (most likely) **work**?
남자는 어디에서 근무하는 것 같은가?

What type of company does the **man** (most likely) **work** for?
남자는 어떤 종류의 회사에서 근무하는 것 같은가?

most likely는 '가장 가능성이 높은'이라는 뜻으로, 신경 쓰지 않아도 돼요. most likely에 괄호를 쳐보세요. 그럼 질문의 핵심이 더 잘 보일 것입니다.

화자(들)의 신분을 묻는 질문 유형

Who (most likely) are the (speakers)?
화자들은 누구일 것 같은가?

Who (most likely) is the (woman)?
여자는 누구일 것 같은가?

Who (most likely) is the (woman talking to)?
여자는 누구에게 말을 하고 있는 것 같은가?
(= 남자는 누구인가?)

질문을 읽을 때 누구에 대해 묻는지 해당 부분에 동그라미를 치면 헷갈리지 않습니다.

마지막 질문과 같이 대화 상대를 묻는 질문에 유의하세요. 질문의 주어가 여자인데 동사가 talking to로 나오면 남자가 누구인지 묻는 것이므로 여자에 대해 묻는 것으로 생각하지 말아야 합니다.

제3자의 신분을 묻는 질문 유형

Who is (Thomas Ventura)?
토마스 벤츄라는 누구인가?

질문에 특정한 사람 이름이 언급되면 재빨리 동그라미를 치고 대화에 그 이름이 언급되는 부분에서 단서를 찾아야 합니다. 이때 이름의 철자와 발음이 생소하면 당황할 수도 있으므로 유의하세요.

PRACTICE 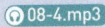 08-4.mp3

음원을 듣고 질문에 맞는 선택지를 고른 뒤, 빈칸을 채워보세요.

1 **Who** most likely is the **man**?
(A) A bank teller 은행 직원
(B) A librarian 도서관 사서
(C) A cashier 계산원
(D) A sales clerk 판매원

W: Hello, I received a notice in the mail _____.
My name is Jennifer Kim.
M: Hm, yes. It says in our system that you _____ books.
Would you like to pay that now?
W: Do you take credit cards?
M: We usually accept either cash or credit, but our card reader is malfunctioning. Let me see if it's working again.

2 **Who** is **Erica Sanders**?
(A) A sponsor 후원자
(B) A fund manager 펀드 매니저
(C) A lawyer 변호사
(D) A financial advisor 재무 상담가

M: Hi. I'm calling because _____ in drafting partnership agreements. Now that we've secured initial funding, I want to ensure our contracts are rock-solid.
W: Thank you for contacting our law firm. Could you tell me more about your business and legal needs?
M: Sure. My company develops renewable energy solutions, and we want to write up clear and strategic terms with our partners.
W: In that case, I recommend you speak with Erica Sanders. She has _____ _____, especially for startups like yours.

정답 및 해설 p.048

실전 TEST 08-5.mp3

학습한 내용을 적용하여 다음 기출 변형 문제들을 풀어보세요.

> **PART 3 실전 문제 풀이 지침**
> 1. 대화가 나오기 전에 세 개의 문제를 빠르게 읽고 핵심을 파악합니다. 이때 키워드에 동그라미를 쳐 둡니다.
> 2. 미리 읽은 문제와 관련된 내용을 노려 듣습니다.
> 3. 정답을 찾으면 문제지에 바로 체크하고 다음 문제를 읽습니다. 답안지 마킹은 나중에 한꺼번에 해도 됩니다.

1 Where most likely are the speakers?
(A) In a hotel
(B) On a ship
(C) At a travel agency
(D) In a train station

2 What does the woman ask about?
(A) Admission fees
(B) Room rates
(C) City tours
(D) Water sports

3 What will the man probably do next?
(A) Change a travel itinerary
(B) Call a hotel manager
(C) Print a ticket for the woman
(D) Give the woman a brochure

4 Who most likely is the man?
(A) A factory manager
(B) A repair technician
(C) A recruitment agent
(D) A safety inspector

5 What was the woman concerned about?
(A) The location of a building
(B) The condition of some machines
(C) The quality of some work
(D) The deadline for a project

6 What does the man say he will do?
(A) Speak to a colleague
(B) Order spare parts
(C) Send a document
(D) Reschedule a meeting

7 Who most likely is the man?

(A) A tour guide
(B) An art critic
(C) A store clerk
(D) A painter

8 Where did the woman get the man's contact information?

(A) From an article
(B) From a brochure
(C) From a Web site
(D) From a friend

9 According to the man, what is the problem with the largest artwork?

(A) It has been damaged.
(B) It is too heavy to hang.
(C) It is no longer available.
(D) Its price has increased.

10 Where does the woman most likely work?

(A) At a supermarket
(B) At a bakery
(C) At a restaurant
(D) At a clothing shop

11 Why is the woman calling the man?

(A) To request a payment
(B) To inform him that an item is ready
(C) To recommend some new products
(D) To confirm the date of an event

12 What service does the woman mention?

(A) Store membership
(B) Gift wrapping
(C) Bulk discounts
(D) Home delivery

실전 TEST 08-5.mp3

학습한 내용을 적용하여 다음 기출 변형 문제들을 풀어보세요.

13 What most likely is the man's job?

(A) Construction worker
(B) Event planner
(C) Highway engineer
(D) News reporter

14 Why is the woman concerned?

(A) A weather forecast is bad.
(B) A crew member is not feeling well.
(C) A schedule has been changed.
(D) Some equipment is malfunctioning.

15 What does the man say he will check for?

(A) Parking availability
(B) Customer complaints
(C) Surplus items
(D) Traffic congestion

16 Where does the man most likely work?

(A) At a hotel
(B) At an airport
(C) At a train station
(D) At a travel agency

17 What does the woman say she will do today?

(A) Go on a city tour
(B) Meet with a client
(C) Give a presentation
(D) Visit a government office

18 According to the man, how can the woman make a payment?

(A) By using a certain mobile app
(B) By scheduling a bank transfer
(C) By tapping a credit card
(D) By inserting cash

19 Who most likely is the woman?

(A) A professional athlete
(B) A dance instructor
(C) A personal trainer
(D) A medical doctor

20 What is the man looking forward to?

(A) Having a healthy lifestyle
(B) Becoming a certified teacher
(C) Working with an industry expert
(D) Completing a renovation project

21 What does the woman ask the man to do?

(A) Practice a task
(B) Review a contract
(C) Complete a form
(D) Provide his phone number

22 Where is the conversation most likely taking place?

(A) At a national park
(B) At a garden center
(C) At a health food store
(D) At an art gallery

23 What does the man ask about?

(A) The types of packaging offered
(B) The available colors for a flower
(C) The size options for a container
(D) The specifications of an electronic device

24 What will most likely happen next?

(A) The woman will arrange a delivery service.
(B) The woman will provide some bags.
(C) The man will choose a different item.
(D) The man will receive a discount.

DAY 09 | 세부 사항/say about 문제 Part 3

1 세부 사항을 묻는 문제 🔊 09-1.mp3

세부 사항 문제들 중에서 특정 과거 시점의 일을 묻는 문제와 특정 대상에 대해 묻는 문제가 가장 많이 출제됩니다. 반드시 문제를 미리 읽고 키워드를 확인한 후 대화에서 키워드가 언급될 때 함께 제시되는 관련 정보를 놓치지 말고 들어야 합니다. 키워드와 단서가 대화에서 잠깐 언급되고 지나가기 때문에 대화를 다 듣고 나서는 풀기가 어렵습니다.

Q What did the man do **this morning**? ▶ 남자가 오늘 아침에 한 일은?

(A) He held a project meeting. — 프로젝트 회의를 주최했다.
(B) He drafted a budget proposal. — 예산안을 작성했다.
(C) He wrote a project report. — 프로젝트 보고서를 작성했다.
(D) **He updated an online timeline.** — 온라인 일정표를 업데이트 했다.

M: Good morning, Theo. **I updated the project timeline on our web portal this morning**.
W: Perfect. Now everyone can see the new deadlines and milestones.

남 좋은 아침입니다. 테오. 전 오늘 아침 우리 웹 포털에 프로젝트 일정을 업데이트했어요.
여 좋아요. 이제 모두가 새로운 마감일과 주요 단계를 볼 수 있겠네요.

■ 세부 사항 문제에 대비하는 요령

질문	요령
What did the man do this morning? 남자는 오늘 아침에 무엇을 했는가?	대화 중에 this morning이 언급되는 부분에서 정보를 파악합니다.
How can the woman receive a free service? 여자는 어떻게 무료 서비스를 받을 수 있는가?	free(무료의)와 같은 의미인 complimentary, for free, at no cost 등이 언급되는 부분에 정답 단서가 제시된다는 점을 기억하고 듣습니다.
What does the man say is available on the Web site? 남자는 웹사이트에서 무엇이 이용 가능하다고 말하는가?	Web site를 다르게 표현한 homepage, online 등이 언급되는 부분에 정답 단서가 제시된다는 것을 예상하며 들어야 합니다.
What will happen on September 2? 9월 2일에 무슨 일이 있을 것인가?	요일이나 날짜 등의 키워드는 다른 말로 바꿔 제시하기 어려우므로 September 2가 그대로 언급되는 부분에 함께 제시되는 정보를 찾습니다.

2 say about 문제 🎧 09-2.mp3

- 한 화자가 특정 대상에 대해 말한 내용을 듣고 정확히 이해했는지 확인하는 문제로서, 질문에서 say about 다음에 나온 대상에 동그라미를 치고 대화에서 이 대상이 언급되는 곳을 잘 들어야 합니다.
- Part 3에서 가장 어려운 유형에 해당됩니다. 선택지가 문장으로 제시되기 때문에 대화에서 나온 말이 다른 말로 바뀌어 나온(Paraphrase) 정답 문장을 순간적으로 가려낼 수 있는 속독 능력이 요구됩니다.

Q What does the **woman** say about **the library**? ▶ 도서관에 대해 여자가 한 말은?

(A) It has extended hours. 운영 시간이 연장되었다.
(B) **It was recently renovated.** 최근에 개조되었다.
(C) It charges a new membership fee. 신규 회원비를 청구한다.
(D) It is always crowded on weekends. 주말에 항상 붐빈다.

M: Excuse me, I'm looking for **Redwood Public Library**. I have the address, but I can't seem to find it.
W: It's just down Main Street, across from City Hall. **It's just undergone major improvements**. You might want to check out the new café inside after you borrow some books.

🗣 실례합니다. 레드우드 공공 도서관을 찾고 있는 데요. 주소는 가지고 있지만 잘 못 찾겠어요.

🗣 메인 스트리트를 따라 가시면 시청 맞은편에 있어요. 막 주요 개선 작업을 마쳤답니다. 책 대여 후에 내부에 새로 생긴 카페도 들러 보세요.

■ say about 문제 빈출 유형 및 정답

say about 인물	He is very talented/creative/qualified. 재능이 있다/창의적이다/자격을 갖추고 있다. He is familiar with company policies. 회사 정책을 잘 알고 있다. She has recently joined the company. 최근에 입사했다.
say about 업체	It has a good reputation. 평판이 좋다. It is out of some items. 몇몇 물품이 떨어졌다. It opened/was renovated recently. 최근에 열었다/개조되었다.
say about 제품	It needs to be fixed. 수리되어야 한다. It received an award. 상을 받았다. It is out of stock. 재고가 없다. It is on sale now. 현재 할인 중이다. It is currently unavailable. 현재 이용할 수 없다.
say about 행사	It is closing soon. 곧 종료될 것이다. It will be rescheduled/postponed. 일정이 재조정될 것이다/연기될 것이다. It was crowded. 사람들로 붐볐다.

3 세부 사항 / say about 질문 유형 🎧 09-3.mp3

다양한 질문 형태를 미리 충분히 익혀 두세요. 그렇게 하면 실전에서 질문을 파악하는 데 0.5초 밖에 걸리지 않으므로 어느 부분에 초점을 맞춰 들어야 하는지 미리 대비하고 대화를 들을 수 있어 유리합니다.

세부 사항을 묻는 질문 유형

대상

What **information** does the **woman** ask for?
여자는 무슨 정보를 요청하는가?

특정 시점

(According to the **woman**,) what will **happen** next Monday?
(여자의 말에 따르면) 다음 주 월요일에 무슨 일이 있을 것인가?

What did the **man do** yesterday?
남자는 어제 무엇을 했는가?

이유

Why did the **man** take a new job?
남자는 왜 새 직장을 구했는가?

방법

(According to the **man**,) **how** can the **woman find** additional information?
(남자의 말에 따르면) 여자는 어떻게 추가 정보를 찾을 수 있는가?

다양한 질문이 제시되지만 중요한 점은 키워드를 빠르게 파악하고 키워드에 동그라미 표시를 해서 어떤 정보에 주의해 들어야 하는지 미리 대비하는 것입니다. 특히 'According to ~'라는 말이 질문에 포함되어 있으면, 남자와 여자 중 어느 화자의 말에 귀 기울여야 하는지 명확히 알 수 있습니다.

say about 질문 유형

What does the **man** say about Inez Bowman?
남자는 이네즈 보우먼 씨에 대해 뭐라고 말하는가?

What does the **woman** say about her office?
여자는 자신의 사무실에 대해 뭐라고 말하는가?

질문 형태가 단순해서 키워드를 파악하기 쉽습니다. 남자와 여자 중 누가 하는 말에 대해 묻는 것인지 확인하고, about 바로 뒤의 단어에 동그라미 표시해 둡니다.

PRACTICE

🎧 09-4.mp3

음원을 듣고 질문에 맞는 선택지를 고른 뒤, 빈칸을 채워보세요.

1 What did the **man do over the weekend**?
   (A) He bought a new digital camera. 새 디지털 카메라를 샀다.
   (B) He printed holiday photos. 휴일에 찍은 사진을 인화했다.
   (C) He organized his digital photos. 디지털 사진을 정리했다.
   (D) He deleted old files. 오래된 파일을 삭제했다.

> **W**: Hi, David! How was your weekend?
> **M**: Hi, Sarah. Over the weekend, I _____
>   by year and event.
> **W**: That system looks very organized. Which program did you use?
> **M**: PhotoSort Pro was a lifesaver—tagging batch after batch. I'll send you the download link.

2 What does the **woman** say about **Blue Mountain Hotel**?
   (A) It is far from public transit. 대중교통 이용과 거리가 멀다.
   (B) It is too expensive. 너무 비싸다.
   (C) It is too small for some guests. 몇몇 손님들에게는 크기가 너무 작다.
   (D) It does not have an audio system. 오디오 시스템이 없다.

> **M**: Hi, our product launch was supposed to be at Riverside Conference Center, but it's double-booked.
> **W**: We met at Blue Mountain Hotel's meeting room last quarter.
> **M**: That room was the perfect size.
> **W**: However, their service charge is _____ for this event.
> **M**: Understood. I'll check with the events team for alternatives.

정답 및 해설 p.055

실전 TEST 09-5.mp3

학습한 내용을 적용하여 다음 기출 변형 문제들을 풀어보세요.

> **PART 3 실전 문제 풀이 지침**
> 1. 대화가 나오기 전에 세 개의 문제를 빠르게 읽고 핵심을 파악합니다. 이때 키워드에 동그라미를 쳐 둡니다.
> 2. 미리 읽은 문제와 관련된 내용을 노려 듣습니다.
> 3. 정답을 찾으면 문제지에 바로 체크하고 다음 문제를 읽습니다. 답안지 마킹은 나중에 한꺼번에 해도 됩니다.

1 What does the man want to do?

(A) Hire new staff
(B) Organize a trip
(C) Hold some seminars
(D) Survey some customers

2 What will happen in April?

(A) An employee will be promoted.
(B) A company office will be moved.
(C) A store will be opened.
(D) A new product will be launched.

3 What is the woman concerned about?

(A) A busy work schedule
(B) A delivery delay
(C) The cost of an item
(D) The attendance at an event

4 Where are the speakers?

(A) In an art gallery
(B) In a library
(C) In a fitness center
(D) In a department store

5 What does the woman suggest that the man do?

(A) Watch a video
(B) Download an app
(C) Apply for a membership
(D) Use a coupon

6 What does the woman give to the man?

(A) A password
(B) A flyer
(C) A beverage
(D) A schedule

7 What does the woman want to reserve?

(A) A live performer
(B) A company vehicle
(C) A conference venue
(D) A dining room

8 What does the man offer to send to the woman?

(A) Discount vouchers
(B) Menu options
(C) Photographs
(D) A brochure

9 What does the man say about the rooms on the third floor?

(A) They are more expensive.
(B) They seat fewer people.
(C) They do not have windows.
(D) They are currently unavailable.

10 What does one of the men say they are accustomed to?

(A) Long drives
(B) Messy workspaces
(C) Short notices
(D) Late responses

11 Why are the men visiting the factory?

(A) To deliver a machine
(B) To install some software
(C) To repair some equipment
(D) To inspect the building

12 What does one of the men warn the woman about?

(A) work delay
(B) A high cost
(C) A poor service
(D) A contract term

실전 TEST

학습한 내용을 적용하여 다음 기출 변형 문제들을 풀어보세요.

13 What was the topic of the morning workshop?
(A) Sustainability
(B) Technology
(C) Product testing
(D) Public speaking

14 According to the woman, what problem did she encounter?
(A) Some attendees did not sign in.
(B) Some videos were slow to load.
(C) Several slides were missing information.
(D) An activity took longer than expected.

15 What does the man want to do?
(A) Write a report
(B) Distribute a survey
(C) Listen to a recording
(D) Calculate a budget

16 What is the woman planning?
(A) A company dinner
(B) A movie festival
(C) A panel discussion
(D) An employee retreat

17 What does the man say about evening showtimes?
(A) They usually cost more.
(B) They tend to sell out quickly.
(C) They must be reserved in person.
(D) They are not eligible for a discount.

18 What does the man ask the woman about?
(A) How she heard about a service
(B) How she will pay for a reservation
(C) Whether she needs a receipt
(D) When she will pick up a product

19 Why did the woman hire the man's company?

(A) To move her furniture
(B) To redesign a room layout
(C) To remodel her bathroom
(D) To install an air-conditioning unit

20 What will happen tomorrow afternoon?

(A) The crew will paint the walls.
(B) The woman will receive a delivery.
(C) An electrician will visit.
(D) A mechanic will fix a fan.

21 What does the man suggest doing?

(A) Using a larger machine
(B) Building windows
(C) Checking the weather forecast
(D) Expanding a space

22 Why are the speakers meeting?

(A) To tour a rental space
(B) To organize a company event
(C) To enjoy some coffee together
(D) To gather content for a magazine

23 What does the man say he will do later this year?

(A) Change a menu
(B) Sell a business
(C) Relocate overseas
(D) Hire new workers

24 What does Amanda say about a property?

(A) It is spacious.
(B) It is popular online.
(C) It has a nice view.
(D) It is a historical landmark.

DAY 10 | 제안·요청 사항/do next 문제 Part 3

1 제안·요청 사항을 묻는 문제 🔊 10-1.mp3

- 화자 한 명이 상대방에게 무엇을 하도록 제안 또는 요청하는지를 묻는 문제가 나옵니다. 그 단서가 제안·요청하는 표현과 함께 제시되므로 여러 가지 제안·요청 표현들을 미리 알고 있으면 쉽게 풀 수 있습니다.
- 문제를 읽을 때 누가 제안·요청하는지, 그리고 누가 제안·요청을 받는지를 정확히 파악해야 합니다.
- 선택지가 비교적 짧은 동사구나 동명사구로 나오므로 선택지까지 먼저 읽고 대화를 들으면 유리합니다.

Q What does the **woman suggest doing**? ┈┈▶ 여자가 제안하는 것은?

(A) Painting the walls 　　　　　　　　벽에 페인트칠 하기
(B) Buying new furniture 　　　　　　　새 가구 구입하기
(C) Hiring an interior designer 　　　　인테리어 디자이너 고용하기
(D) **Conducting an online survey of employees** 직원 온라인 설문조사 실시하기

M: Emma, the marketing team needs fresh ideas for our office redesign.
W: Why don't we **survey staff with an online poll** to gather their design preferences?

남: 엠마, 마케팅 팀이 사무실 인테리어 리모델링에 대한 새로운 아이디어를 필요로 해요.
여: 직원들의 디자인 선호도를 알아보기 위해 온라인 설문조사를 해보는 게 어때요?

■ 제안·요청 사항이 드러나는 문장 유형과 정답

단서 문장	정답
Would you be interested in attending our annual sales conference? 저희 연례 영업 컨퍼런스에 참석하는 것에 관심이 있으실까요?	Participate in a conference 컨퍼런스에 참석하기
Why don't you talk to one of our technicians? 저희 기술자들 중 한 명과 얘기해 보시는 건 어떠세요?	Speak to a technician 기술자와 얘기하기
I suggest you come back in an hour to pick it up. 한 시간 후에 다시 오셔서 가져가시는 것을 제안 드립니다.	Come back later 나중에 다시 오기
You will need to **fill out an application form**. 신청서를 작성하셔야 할 겁니다.	Complete a form 양식 작성하기
I was wondering if you could work late tonight. 오늘 밤 늦게까지 일하실 수 있는지 궁금했어요.	Work extra hours 초과 근무하기
I'd appreciate it if you could send me the cost estimate via e-mail. 저에게 이메일로 비용 견적서를 보내 주실 수 있다면 감사하겠습니다.	Send an e-mail 이메일 보내기

2 do next 문제 🔊 10-2.mp3

두 명의 화자 또는 한 명의 화자가 대화가 끝난 후에 이어서 할 일을 묻는 문제로, 질문이 '~ do next?'와 같이 제시됩니다. 대화의 마지막 부분에서 계획이나 일정 등과 관련해 미래시제로 말하거나 화자의 의지 등을 말하는 부분이 주로 단서가 됩니다.

Q What will the **woman do next**? ▶ 여자가 곧 이어 할 일은?

(A) **Pay a workshop fee**   워크숍 참가비 지불하기
(B) Buy baking ingredients   제빵 재료 구입하기
(C) Submit a recipe idea   조리법 아이디어 제출하기
(D) Confirm a schedule   일정 확인하기

W: I'd like to enroll in your weekend baking workshop.
M: Wonderful. We'll reserve your spot as soon as **we receive 100 dollars as a workshop fee**.
W: Got it. **I'll take care of that right away**.

여: 저는 주말 베이킹 워크숍에 등록하고 싶습니다.
남: 좋습니다. 참가비 100달러를 받는 즉시 자리를 확보해 드리겠습니다.
여: 네, 바로 처리하겠습니다.

■ do next 문제의 단서가 드러나는 문장 유형과 정답

단서 문장	정답
I'll go **put in an order** right now. 제가 가서 지금 바로 주문할게요.	Place an order 주문하기
I'll **take a look at the budget** and let you know. 제가 예산을 한번 확인해 보고 알려 드릴게요.	Review a budget 예산 검토하기
I just realized I forgot to **call my client**. Will you excuse me for a minute? 제 고객에게 전화하는 일을 잊었다는 걸 막 알았어요. 잠시 실례해도 될까요?	Make a phone call 전화하기
I'd be happy to **talk about the assignment** with you. 함께 할당 업무에 관해 기꺼이 얘기해 보고 싶습니다.	Discuss an assignment 할당 업무 이야기하기
Could you **offer our listeners some advice** on buying a car? 자동차 구입에 관해 저희 청취자들에게 조언 좀 해 주시겠습니까?	Give some advice 조언 제공하기
Just **go to our Web site**. It will have all the information you need. 그냥 저희 웹사이트로 가보세요. 필요하신 모든 정보가 있을 겁니다.	Visit a Web site 웹사이트 방문하기
I need your **signature on this registration form**. 이 등록 양식에 당신의 서명이 필요합니다.	Sign a form 양식에 서명하기

3 제안·요청 사항 / do next 질문 유형 🔊 10-3.mp3

다양한 질문 형태를 미리 충분히 익혀 두세요. 그렇게 하면 실전에서 질문을 파악하는 데 0.5초 밖에 걸리지 않으므로 어느 부분에 초점을 맞춰 들어야 하는지 미리 대비하고 대화를 들을 수 있어 유리합니다.

제안·요청 사항을 묻는 질문 유형

What does the **man ask** the woman to do? -----▶ 남자가 하는 말에 집중
　　　　　　남자가 요청하다
남자는 여자에게 무엇을 하도록 요청하는가?

What is the man asked to do? -----▶ 상대방인 여자가 하는 말에 집중
　　남자가 요청 받다
남자는 무엇을 하도록 요청 받는가?

What does the **man suggest** the woman do?
　　　　　　남자가 제안하다
남자는 여자에게 무엇을 하도록 제안하는가?

What does the **man recommend** doing?
　　　　　　남자가 추천하다
남자는 무엇을 하도록 추천하는가?

What does the **woman offer to do**? -----▶ 여자가 하는 말에 집중
　　　　　여자가 자신이 하겠다고 제안하다
여자는 무엇을 하겠다고 제안하는가?

> 가장 중요한 것은 누가 누구에게 제안하는지를 잘 파악하는 것입니다. 특히 남자 또는 여자가 요청하는 것을 묻는지(능동태로 표현), 요청 받는 것을 묻는지(수동태로 표현) 구분할 수 있어야 합니다.

do next 질문 유형

What will the **speakers** (most likely) **do next**?
화자들은 이어서 무엇을 할 것 같은가?

What will the **woman** (probably) **do next**?
여자는 아마도 이어서 무엇을 할 것인가?

What (does the man say) **he will do**?
남자는 무엇을 하겠다고 말하는가?

> most likely, probably, does the man say와 같은 형식적인 표현에 괄호를 치면 질문의 핵심이 더 잘 보입니다.

PRACTICE 🔊 10-4.mp3

음원을 듣고 질문에 맞는 선택지를 고른 뒤, 빈칸을 채워보세요.

1 What does the **man suggest**?
(A) Ordering extra ink cartridges 여분의 잉크 카트리지 주문하기
(B) Buying a heavy-duty printer 견고한 프린터 구매하기
(C) Hiring a printing service 인쇄 대행 서비스 이용하기
(D) Reducing a page count 페이지 수 줄이기

> W: Our office printer can't handle all these monthly reports. It keeps running out of ink and jamming.
> M: I suggest _____
> _____.
> W: That would save us from a lot of headaches.
> M: I'll research some models this afternoon.

2 **What** will the **man** most likely **do next**?
(A) Wait for desk staff to return 직원이 돌아오기를 기다린다
(B) Purchase a yoga mat 요가 매트를 구매한다
(C) Swap to a different time slot 다른 시간대로 교체한다
(D) Complete a sign-up through an app 앱을 통해 등록을 완료한다

> M: I want to sign up for today's yoga session, but the front desk isn't taking registrations.
> W: The reception area is closed for a staff meeting, so you can't register in person right now.
> M: Now I'm not on the roster, and the class starts soon.
> W: I think you will need to _____
> _____ on the wall.

📖 정답 및 해설 p.063

실전 TEST 🎧 10-5.mp3

학습한 내용을 적용하여 다음 기출 변형 문제들을 풀어보세요.

PART 3 실전 문제 풀이 지침

1. 대화가 나오기 전에 세 개의 문제를 빠르게 읽고 핵심을 파악합니다. 이때 키워드에 동그라미를 쳐 둡니다.
2. 미리 읽은 문제와 관련된 내용을 노려 듣습니다.
3. 정답을 찾으면 문제지에 바로 체크하고 다음 문제를 읽습니다. 답안지 마킹은 나중에 한꺼번에 해도 됩니다.

1 What does the man show to the woman?
(A) A work schedule
(B) A company ID card
(C) An employment contract
(D) An application form

2 What does the woman say about the man's job?
(A) He will be helping a supervisor.
(B) He will be responsible for finances.
(C) He will work on the weekends.
(D) He will be required to serve customers.

3 What does the woman ask the man to do?
(A) Join a group
(B) Fill out a form
(C) Give a presentation
(D) Read a handbook

4 Where does the man work?
(A) At a restaurant
(B) At a radio station
(C) At a dry cleaner
(D) At a grocery store

5 What is the woman concerned about?
(A) A service cost
(B) A delivery time
(C) A membership fee
(D) A seating capacity

6 What will the man most likely do next?
(A) Transfer the call
(B) Speak with a manager
(C) Refund a purchase
(D) Check an inventory

7 Where does the man most likely work?

(A) At a holiday resort
(B) At a sports stadium
(C) At a convention center
(D) At a government building

8 What does the woman inquire about?

(A) Changing a venue
(B) Transporting equipment
(C) Selling merchandise
(D) Purchasing tickets

9 What does the man suggest the woman do?

(A) Fill out a form
(B) Reschedule a presentation
(C) Visit an event site
(D) Speak to his manager

10 Where most likely are the speakers?

(A) At a dental clinic
(B) At a job center
(C) At a grocery store
(D) At an auto shop

11 What is the reason for the delay?

(A) A reservation error was made.
(B) Some equipment is faulty.
(C) There is heavy traffic.
(D) A staff member is sick.

12 What does the man offer to do?

(A) Provide a voucher
(B) Offer a refund
(C) Contact a supervisor
(D) Arrange a free service

실전 TEST

학습한 내용을 적용하여 다음 기출 변형 문제들을 풀어보세요.

13 What is the woman shopping for?

(A) A handbag
(B) A pair of jeans
(C) Hiking boots
(D) Camping gear

14 What is the woman concerned about?

(A) An event has been postponed.
(B) A price might be cheaper online.
(C) A specific color is not available for sale.
(D) An item may require a lot of maintenance.

15 What will the woman most likely do next?

(A) Try on an item
(B) Make a purchase
(C) Register for a class
(D) View a product catalog

16 Where most likely are the speakers?

(A) At a stationery shop
(B) At a medical facility
(C) At an electronics store
(D) At an engineering firm

17 What does the man say he has been reading about?

(A) Market trends
(B) A special technology
(C) Product testing feedback
(D) A company's history

18 What does the woman suggest that the man do?

(A) Check a product label
(B) Place an order online
(C) Sign up for a waitlist
(D) Go to a different location

19 Why are the speakers planning a lunch?

(A) To meet with a client
(B) To reward a team effort
(C) To support a local initiative
(D) To introduce a new executive

20 What does the woman say she likes about the Marigold Kitchen?

(A) Its reasonable prices
(B) Its extended store hours
(C) Its quiet environment
(D) Its delicious food

21 What does the man offer to do?

(A) Send out some instructions
(B) Arrange a reservation
(C) Ask for confirmation
(D) Change an event schedule

22 What is the purpose of the woman's visit?

(A) To change the engine of her car
(B) To buy a new set of wheels
(C) To identify an issue with some tires
(D) To receive regular maintenance

23 What does the man indicate about a task?

(A) He is very familiar with it.
(B) He will request additional assistance.
(C) It is easier to complete at night.
(D) It will take a couple of hours to finish.

24 What will the woman most likely do next?

(A) Visit a supermarket
(B) Wait in a designated area
(C) Call her car insurance provider
(D) Organize some paperwork

DAY 11 | 의도 파악 문제 / 시각자료 연계 문제 Part 3

1 화자가 한 말의 의미/속뜻은 무엇인가? 🔊 11-1.mp3

- 대화 중에 한 명의 화자가 하게 될 말을 문제에서 미리 보여주고, 대화 흐름상 그 말이 어떤 의미/속뜻을 갖는지 묻는 문제가 나옵니다. 세 개의 문제 중에 인용 문장이 포함된 질문이 보이면 먼저 밑줄을 긋고 재빨리 해석해 두세요.
- 의도 파악 문제는 인용 문장의 바로 앞부분에 결정적인 힌트가 나오는 경우가 많습니다. 따라서 대화의 흐름을 명확히 파악하는 것이 매우 중요합니다.

Q What does the **man imply** when he says, "I didn't expect that!"?
▶ "그건 예상하지 못했어요!"라는 말의 속뜻은?

(A) He needs to check some information.   일부 정보를 확인해야 한다.
(B) **He is pleased by some news.**   어떤 소식을 듣고 기뻐하고 있다.
(C) He wants to change the decision.   결정을 바꾸고 싶어 한다.
(D) He has a scheduling conflict.   일정이 겹친다.

W: Did you hear the news? **We're going on a cruise for our company trip. It will be amazing!**
M: I just heard! **I didn't expect that!** And we'll be stopping at several beautiful beaches.

여 소식 들으셨어요? 우리가 회사 야유회로 유람선 여행을 간대요. 놀라운 여행이 될 거예요!
남 저도 방금 들었어요! 그건 예상하지 못했어요! 여러 아름다운 해변에 들르게 되겠네요.

▶ 여자가 회사에서 유람선 여행을 간다는 소식을 전하면서 놀라운 여행이 될 것이라고 말하자 남자가 "그건 예상하지 못했어요!"라고 반응하였습니다. 이 말은 여자가 전한 유람선 여행 소식에 매우 기쁘다는 표현으로 볼 수 있습니다.

■ 의미 파악과 속뜻을 묻는 문제 질문 유형

의미를 묻는 질문 유형

What does the **woman mean** when she says, "That's the third time this year"?
여자가 "올해 세 번째예요"라고 말할 때 그 말의 의미는 무엇인가?

속뜻을 묻는 질문 유형

What does the **man imply** when he says, "Gina is leaving the company next month"?
남자가 "지나는 다음 달에 회사를 떠날 거예요."라고 말할 때 그 말의 속뜻은 무엇인가?

2 화자가 왜 "~"라고 말하는가? 🔊 11-2.mp3

한 명의 화자가 특정한 말을 하는 이유를 묻는 문제로, 이 유형의 문제에서 선택지는 To부정사구(~하기 위해) 형태로 제시되는 경우가 많습니다.

Q Why does the **woman say**, "the community center hosts a monthly potluck dinner for volunteers"? ----▶ "커뮤니티 센터에서 매달 자원봉사자를 위한 포틀럭 디너를 연다"라고 말하는 이유는?

(A) To ask for cooking   요리를 부탁하기 위해
(B) To note training constraints   교육 일정의 제약을 언급하기 위해
(C) **To suggest a social event** •······· 사교 행사를 제안하기 위해
(D) To describe the center's schedule   센터의 일정을 설명하기 위해

W: I'm glad you're joining our volunteer program. Its orientation is on May 5th. Do you have any questions?
M: Yes. **I'd love to meet other volunteers. What kinds of social activities will be held?**
W: Weekdays are packed with training, so most volunteers don't stick around. But the community center hosts a monthly potluck dinner for volunteers.

여 귀하께서 자원봉사 프로그램에 참여하셔서 기쁩 니다. 오리엔테이션은 5월 5일이에요. 질문 있으 세요?
남 네. 다른 자원봉사자들과 만나고 싶은데, 어떤 사 교 활동들이 열리나요?
여 평일은 교육으로 가득차서 대부분의 자원봉사자 는 남아 있지 않아요. 하지만 커뮤니티 센터에서 매달 자원봉사자를 위한 포틀럭 디너를 열어요.

----▶ 남자가 "다른 자원봉사자들과 친목 활동을 하고 싶다"고 말하고 어떤 활동들 이 있는지 물었고 여자가 친목 활동의 일환으로 커뮤니티 센터에 매달 열리는 포 틀럭 디너에 대해 언급하였습니다. 따라서 여자는 남자의 친목 활동에 대한 질 문에 답변하고, 친목 활동을 제안하는 것이라는 것을 알 수 있습니다.

■ **말하는 이유를 묻는 질문 유형**

의도 파악 문제는 단순히 주어진 문장 자체의 의미를 묻는 것이 아니라 그 말을 한 의도나 이유를 묻는 문제입 니다. 따라서 주어진 문장의 의미를 정확히 해석한 다음, 이 문장이 대화에서 어떤 의도로 사용되는지를 확인 해야 합니다. 단순히 인용 문장을 다른 말로 바꾼 선택지는 함정이라는 것을 명심하세요.

> **말하는 이유를 묻는 유형**
>
> **Why** does the **woman say**, "The café is just down the street"?
> 여자가 "카페는 길을 따라 조금만 내려가면 있어요"라고 말하는 이유는 무엇인가?

3 표/리스트형 시각자료 🔊 11-3.mp3

시각자료 연계 문제 중에서 가장 많이 출제되는 유형입니다. 이 유형 중에서도 가격 목록이 가장 자주 나오고, 그 다음으로 일정표, 건물의 층별 안내, 명부(사무실 및 내선 번호, 업무 담당자 정보) 등이 골고루 출제되고 있습니다. 대화를 잘 듣고 시각자료의 항목 중 어디에 해당하는지 찾아 내용을 확인하면 됩니다.

Ticket Prices (per person)	
Children (under 12)	$6
Senior (65+)	$8
Group Discount (at least 6 in a group)	**$10**
Adult	$12

Q Look at the graphic. **What ticket price** will the speakers probably **pay**? ┈┈▶ 화자들이 1인당 지불할 티켓 가격은?

(A) $6
(B) $8
(C) **$10**
(D) $12

W: Henry, a few of us are going to a baseball game after work on Friday. Would you like to come?
M: Yeah, that sounds great. How much are tickets?
W: There are different prices, but since **there will be six of us, we'll qualify for a special price**.
M: Good! I'm looking forward to it.

예 헨리 씨, 저희 중에 몇 명이 금요일 퇴근 후에 야구 경기를 보러 갈 거예요. 함께 가시겠어요?
답 네, 아주 좋을 것 같아요. 입장권이 얼마인가요?
예 서로 다른 가격들이 있기는 하지만, 저희가 6명이 될 것이기 때문에, 특가 이용 자격이 있을 거예요.
답 좋아요! 정말 기대가 되네요.

┈┈▶ 여자가 '우리는 6명이라서 특가 서비스에 대한 자격이 있을 것이다'라고 말하고 있습니다. 이제 시각자료에서 '6인 할인'에 해당하는 항목을 찾아보면, 세 번째 칸의 '최소 6명으로 된 단체에 대한 할인(Group Discount / at least 6 in a group)'에 해당된다는 것을 알 수 있습니다.

4 지도형 시각자료 🔊 11-4.mp3

특정 위치를 찾는 유형이므로 지도나 평면도가 시각자료로 제시되면 대화 중에 결정적인 단서가 되는 위치나 이동 방향과 관련된 표현에 반드시 집중해야 합니다.

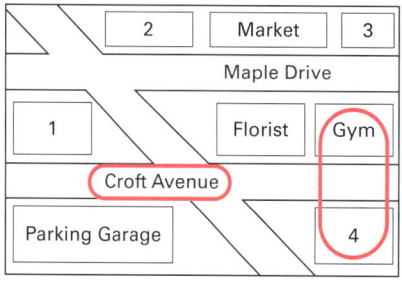

Q Look at the graphic. **Which building** will the speakers **go to tomorrow**?
┈┈▶ 화자들이 내일 갈 건물은?

(A) Building 1
(B) Building 2
(C) Building 3
(D) **Building 4**

M: Is it true that our clients at Sitwell aren't happy with the Web site we designed for them?
W: Yes, sadly. They want to meet tomorrow to discuss their issues with it. Why don't we have lunch with them at Mango Bistro? It's **across from the gym on Croft Avenue**.
M: That will work for me.

남 시트웰 사의 고객들이 우리가 디자인해 드린 웹사이트를 마음에 들어 하지 않는다는 게 사실인가요?
여 안타깝게도, 그렇습니다. 그분들이 그것과 관련된 사안들을 논의하기 위해 내일 만나고 싶어하십니다. 망고 비스트로에서 그분들과 함께 점심 식사하면 어떨까요? 크로프트 애비뉴에 있는 체육관 맞은편입니다.
남 저는 좋을 것 같아요.

▶ 여자가 망고 비스트로에서 고객들을 만날 것을 제안하면서 그곳의 위치를 '크로프트 애비뉴에 있는 체육관 맞은편'이라고 설명합니다. 시각자료에서 크로프트 애비뉴에 위치한 체육관 맞은편에 있는 건물이 '4'로 표기되어 있는 것을 확인할 수 있습니다.

5 그래프형 시각자료 🎧 11-5.mp3

원 그래프, 막대 그래프, 선 그래프 등이 제시되며, 파악하기 어렵고 복잡한 것은 나오지 않습니다. 대화에 '가장 많은(the most)', '가장 높은(the highest)', '두 번째로 많은(the second most)', '가장 저조한(the poorest)' 등의 최상급 표현이 결정적인 정답 단서로 제시되는 경우가 많습니다. 숫자 및 순위 표현에 주목하세요.

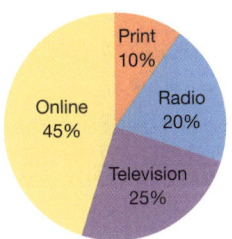

Q Look at the graphic. **Which advertising method** will the man probably **discuss next?**

▶ 다음 순서로 논의할 광고 방법은?

(A) Print
(B) Radio
(C) Television
(D) **Online**

M: Kathy, we need to discuss different advertising methods.
W: Right, I just saw the survey results. Our print ads only bring in 10% of our customers, and radio accounts for 20%.
M: I don't think they're our main concern. I'd rather **focus on the advertising method that attracts the most customers**.

남 캐시 씨, 우리는 다른 광고 방법들을 논의해야 합니다.
여 맞아요, 제가 방금 설문 조사 결과를 봤어요. 우리 인쇄물 광고는 우리 고객의 겨우 10퍼센트만 끌어들이고 있고, 라디오는 20퍼센트를 차지하고 있어요.
남 저는 그것들이 우리의 주된 우려 사항이라고 생각하지 않습니다. 저는 차라리 가장 많은 고객을 끌어들이는 광고 방법에 초점을 맞추고 싶어요.

▶ 남자가 가장 많은 고객들을 끌어들이는 광고 방법에 초점을 맞추고 싶다고 말하고 있는데, 그래프에 45퍼센트로 표기된 '온라인'이 가장 많은 비율을 차지하고 있는 것을 확인할 수 있습니다.

PRACTICE 🔊 11-6.mp3

음원을 듣고 질문에 맞는 선택지를 고른 뒤, 빈칸을 채워보세요.

1. **What** does the **woman mean** when she says, "this is a really popular location"?
   (A) The monthly rate includes utilities. 월 임대료에 공과금이 포함된다.
   (B) The furniture is ergonomically designed. 가구가 인체공학적으로 설계되었다.
   (C) The building has excellent security. 건물 보안이 훌륭하다.
   (D) They're being booked very quickly. 예약이 빠르게 진행되고 있다.

   M: I appreciate the tour of your co-working space. _____
   _____ for our start-up.
   W: Glad to hear that. Just so you know, this is a really popular location.
   M: I'll check with my team before we sign anything.
   W: No problem—let me know when you're ready to reserve.

2. **Why** does the **woman** say, "There's a power outage in my building, so I can't access the file"?
   (A) To ask doing the task on behalf of her 그 일을 대신해 달라고 요청하기 위해서
   (B) To request additional resources 추가 자원을 요청하기 위해
   (C) To suggest postponing a discussion 논의를 미루자고 제안하기 위해
   (D) To discuss new video elements 새로운 영상 요소에 대해 이야기하기 위해

   M: Hi, Alex. I want to review the revised training-video script.
   W: I added a clearer intro outlining our objectives.
   M: Perfect, that will tighten the message.
   W: I also rewrote the closing to include a stronger call to action.
   M: Can you run through those new lines now?
   W: I'm sorry. There's a power outage in my building, so I can't access the file.
   M: All right. _____.

Store Layout (Ground Floor)

[Entrance]

Aisle 1	Aisle 2	Aisle 3	Aisle 4
Produce (Fruits, Veg)	Paper Goods (Napkins, Towels)	Cleaning Products (Bleach, Soaps)	Pet Food (Dog & Cat)

3 Look at the graphic. **Which aisle** does the **woman direct** the man to?
(A) Aisle 1
(B) Aisle 2
(C) Aisle 3
(D) Aisle 4

M: I need supplies for my store's stockroom. Can you tell me where I can find bleach?

W: Sure, in the aisle with detergents.

M: Which aisle number is that?

W: The one _____.

M: Thanks.

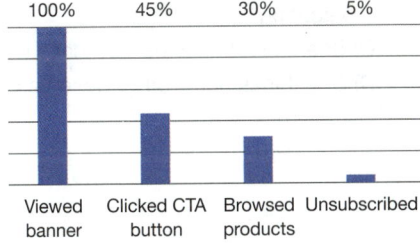

4 Look at the graphic. **Which percentage surprised the man**?
(A) 100%
(B) 45%
(C) 30%
(D) 5%

M: Did you review our homepage banner performance? I was amazed at _____ _____ the CTA button.

W: That's excellent! It should lead to more product views and, hopefully, sales.

M: Splitting the banner into two different color schemes was a smart move—those segments really stood out.

실전 TEST 🎧 11-7.mp3

학습한 내용을 적용하여 다음 기출 변형 문제들을 풀어보세요.

PART 3 실전 문제 풀이 지침

1. 대화가 나오기 전에 세 개의 문제를 빠르게 읽고 핵심을 파악합니다. 이때 키워드에 동그라미를 쳐 둡니다.
2. 미리 읽은 문제와 관련된 내용을 노려 듣습니다.
3. 정답을 찾으면 문제지에 바로 체크하고 다음 문제를 읽습니다. 답안지 마킹은 나중에 한꺼번에 해도 됩니다.

---

1 What position is the man inquiring about?

(A) Office manager
(B) Sales associate
(C) Graphic designer
(D) Maintenance worker

2 What does the man mean when he says, "that isn't an issue"?

(A) He is aware of a problem.
(B) He is familiar with a program.
(C) He already completed a task.
(D) He meets a requirement.

3 What does the woman ask the man to do?

(A) Attend an interview
(B) Provide contact information
(C) Submit a résumé
(D) Complete a form

4 According to the man, why are many people traveling to Miami?

(A) To attend a seminar
(B) To enjoy the weather
(C) To attend a music festival
(D) To participate in a sports event

5 What does the woman imply when she says, "He has been working so hard"?

(A) She has been helping her brother.
(B) She wants her brother to take a vacation.
(C) She cannot miss her brother's event.
(D) She thinks her brother deserves a reward.

6 What does the man suggest?

(A) Taking another bus
(B) Going to the train station
(C) Renting a vehicle
(D) Changing a schedule

7 Which field does the man most likely work in?

(A) Entertainment
(B) Catering
(C) Real estate
(D) Landscaping

8 What does the woman inquire about?

(A) A performance stage
(B) Some furniture
(C) A room size
(D) Some audio equipment

9 What does the woman mean when she says, "You know where the storage room is, right?"?

(A) She wants to reorganize an event area.
(B) She wants the man to give her directions.
(C) She wants the man to complete a task.
(D) She wants to look for a missing item.

10 What are the speakers mainly discussing?

(A) Planning an event
(B) Improving productivity
(C) Changing a business location
(D) Opening a new branch

11 Where does the woman plan to make an announcement?

(A) At a shareholder meeting
(B) At a work seminar
(C) At a staff dinner
(D) At a press conference

12 Why does the man say, "Kyle Firth has been with us for over five years"?

(A) To congratulate an employee
(B) To make a recommendation
(C) To express surprise
(D) To correct the woman's error

실전 TEST (11-7.mp3)

학습한 내용을 적용하여 다음 기출 변형 문제들을 풀어보세요.

Food	Price	Drink Size
French fries	$4.00	Small
Fried chicken	$5.00	Medium
Hamburger	$6.00	Large
Pizza	$8.00	Jumbo

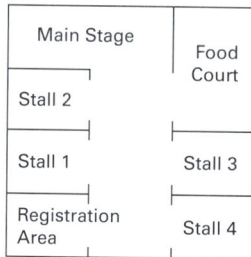

13 Where are the speakers?
 (A) At a sports stadium
 (B) At a movie theater
 (C) At a music festival
 (D) At an amusement park

14 Look at the graphic. What size of drink will the woman receive?
 (A) Small
 (B) Medium
 (C) Large
 (D) Jumbo

15 How will the woman pay?
 (A) With cash
 (B) With a coupon
 (C) With an app
 (D) With a credit card

16 Why is the woman familiar with the expo?
 (A) She was a volunteer.
 (B) She watched a video.
 (C) She is a journalist.
 (D) She knows the event organizer.

17 Look at the graphic. Which stall does the man recommend?
 (A) Stall 1
 (B) Stall 2
 (C) Stall 3
 (D) Stall 4

18 What will the man explain later?
 (A) A computer program
 (B) A schedule
 (C) A product
 (D) A customer policy

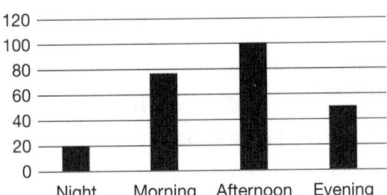

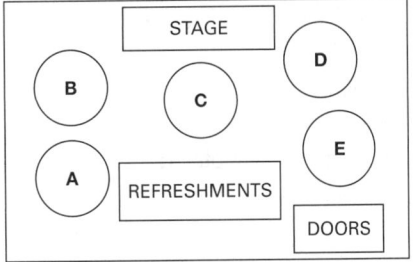

19 Look at the graphic. Which shift are the speakers discussing?
(A) Night
(B) Morning
(C) Afternoon
(D) Evening

20 According to the woman, what has been a problem?
(A) Low sales
(B) Customer complaints
(C) Shipping delays
(D) Employee shortages

21 What does the man say will happen next month?
(A) A new product will be launched.
(B) A restaurant will close.
(C) A business will be renovated.
(D) A price will increase.

22 Why are the speakers planning a banquet?
(A) To celebrate a milestone
(B) To recognize an employee
(C) To advertise a product launch
(D) To raise money for charity

23 What does the man say should be mentioned in a speech?
(A) A personal story
(B) A notable accomplishment
(C) Some sales figures
(D) Some research findings

24 Look at the graphic. Where will the woman be seated?
(A) In section A
(B) In section C
(C) In section D
(D) In section E

PART 3　FINAL TEST ⓟ FT-3.mp3

학습한 내용을 적용하여 다음 기출 변형 문제들을 풀어보세요.

1　What does the woman ask the man to do for her?

(A) Check a calendar
(B) Purchase an item
(C) Find some clothing
(D) Make some copies

2　What does the man say about a shipment?

(A) It includes a tracking number.
(B) It was ordered last week.
(C) It has been delayed before.
(D) It is missing items.

3　Where is the man?

(A) At a café
(B) At a print shop
(C) At a market
(D) At a post office

4　What has the man been contracted to do?

(A) Act in a commercial
(B) Design a model
(C) Photograph an event
(D) Advertise a product

5　What will happen next week?

(A) An industry conference
(B) An award ceremony
(C) A film festival
(D) A movie premiere

6　What does the woman remind the man to do?

(A) Sample some food
(B) Upload several pictures
(C) Write a review
(D) Look through a catalog

7 What most likely started last week?

(A) Business operations
(B) A recruitment period
(C) A training program
(D) A research project

8 Where are the speakers working?

(A) At a museum
(B) At a laboratory
(C) At a factory
(D) At a farm

9 What will the speakers do next?

(A) Weigh some items
(B) Collect a sample
(C) Set up a table
(D) Analyze some results

10 What news does the man share?

(A) The city mayor will be visiting.
(B) The public library will be relocated.
(C) A director changed departments.
(D) A new utility company has opened.

11 What improvement do the speakers hope to see?

(A) Diverse landscaping plants
(B) Energy-efficient machines
(C) An expanded parkland
(D) Additional water stations

12 What is scheduled for tomorrow morning?

(A) A board meeting
(B) A welcome party
(C) A brainstorming session
(D) A team-building workshop

PART 3 FINAL TEST

학습한 내용을 적용하여 다음 기출 변형 문제들을 풀어보세요.

13 What recently happened at the business?

(A) It has recruited new sales representatives.
(B) It has been receiving more complaints.
(C) It has sold out of a certain product.
(D) It has merged with another company.

14 According to the man, what will help the business?

(A) Rewarding employees
(B) Renting equipment
(C) Implementing a safety policy
(D) Changing a manufacturing technique

15 Who does Grace say she will call today?

(A) A mechanical parts supplier
(B) A fashion accessories supplier
(C) A fabric supplier
(D) A paper supplier

16 Who most likely is the man?

(A) A travel agent
(B) A physical trainer
(C) A hotel worker
(D) A gym employee

17 Why is Ms. Lee calling?

(A) She needs an expedited delivery.
(B) She misplaced one of her belongings.
(C) She did not receive a complimentary item.
(D) She was incorrectly charged a fee.

18 What will Ms. Lee most likely do next?

(A) Go to a storage room
(B) Put the speaker on hold
(C) Provide her phone number
(D) Schedule a pick-up time

19 What are the speakers meeting to discuss?

(A) A financial status
(B) A production process
(C) A retail advertisement
(D) A product evaluation

20 What does the man mean when he says, "it does cost more time and effort to make new designs"?

(A) He is volunteering to make changes.
(B) He is disappointed with some results.
(C) He is attempting to provide reasoning.
(D) He is excited to oversee product development.

21 Who most likely is David?

(A) A printmaker
(B) A marketer
(C) A retail worker
(D) A graphic designer

22 What problem does the woman mention?

(A) A transaction cannot be processed.
(B) A train has been delayed.
(C) An event has been postponed.
(D) Some fares have increased significantly.

23 What does the man suggest?

(A) Contacting a service provider
(B) Reading a manual
(C) Calling headquarters
(D) Verifying an address

24 What does the man imply when he says, "I made a purchase in-store"?

(A) He is requesting a proof of purchase.
(B) He is explaining why he was not in the office.
(C) He is offering an alternative solution.
(D) He is unsure how to help the woman.

기본토익 700+

PART 4

DAY 12 전화 메시지 / 라디오 방송
DAY 13 공지 및 안내
DAY 14 회의 발췌/소개
DAY 15 광고/투어 가이드

PART 4 FINAL TEST

PART 4 * 짧은 담화 문제 미리보기

- 문항수: 30문항 (71번~100번)
- 전화메시지, 방송, 광고 등 한 사람이 말하는 담화를 듣고 관련 질문에 대한 정답을 고르는 유형입니다.
- 총 10개 담화가 나오고, 담화 한 개당 세 문제씩 제시됩니다.
- 대화를 듣기 전에 문제지에 제시된 문제들을 미리 읽어 두어야 합니다.

📋 문제지

71. What is the purpose of the talk?

(A) To announce a job opening
(B) To introduce a speaker
(C) To welcome new employees
(D) To describe an event ✓

72. Where should the listeners go when they arrive?

(A) To the basement
(B) To the box office ✓
(C) To the banquet hall
(D) To the conference room

73. What will be given to all participants?

(A) A free meal
(B) A software package
(C) A reference letter
(D) A personal evaluation ✓

↖ 문제지에 문제와 선택지 (A)~(D)가 제시됨

🎧 음원

Questions 71-73 refer to the following announcement.

Good afternoon. I'd like to invite you to Career Showcase, which is scheduled to be held in the Atlantica Center. This career fair will connect you with employers who can offer you several job opportunities. When you turn up at the center, just go to the box office to get a visitor's pass. At the end of the job fair, you will be given a personal report evaluating your strengths as a job candidate.

Number 71. What is the purpose of the talk?
Number 72. Where should the listeners go when they arrive?
Number 73. What will be given to all participants?

DAY 12 | 전화 메시지/라디오 방송 Part 4

1 전화 메시지 🔊 12-1.mp3

전화 메시지는 Part 4에서 출제 빈도가 높은 유형이며, 예약이나 주문, 약속 등의 변경이나 확인, 취소, 상대방의 요청 사항에 대한 답변, 일정 조정 등이 주된 내용입니다. 메시지마다 내용 전개 방식이 거의 유사하고, 일정한 패턴을 지닌 문장들이 반복적으로 쓰이기 때문에 전화 메시지의 흐름과 빈출 표현들을 미리 익혀 두면 어렵지 않게 정답을 고를 수 있습니다.

■ 전화 메시지 지문 예시와 구성

Hello. **This is Sandra Park calling from Jenta's Online Market.**
-----▶ 저는 젠타스 온라인 마켓의 산드라 박입니다.

① 인사 및 자기 소개
화자가 자신의 이름과 소속을 밝힙니다.

I'm just looking at the order you placed last night on our Web site. I'm afraid that **the product you requested is currently sold out, so I'll give you a full refund.** -----▶ 요청하신 제품이 현재 품절이라 전액 환불해 드리겠습니다.

② 전화 용건
전화를 건 용건을 밝히거나 문제 상황을 알립니다.

However, in the e-mail I've just sent you, I've recommended some items that might suit your preferences. **If you want to purchase one of them today, please let me know as soon as possible.**
-----▶ 오늘 구매하길 원하시면 가능한 한 빨리 알려주세요.

③ 당부 또는 요청 사항
청자에게 당부의 말이나 요청 사항을 전달합니다.

Thank you for shopping at Jenta's Online Market.

④ 마무리 인사

안녕하세요. 저는 젠타스 온라인 마켓에서 전화 드리는 산드라 박입니다.

귀하께서 저희 웹사이트에서 어젯밤에 주문하신 사항을 보고 있습니다. 귀하께서 요청하신 제품이 현재 품절이어서, 전액 환불해 드리고자 합니다.

하지만, 제가 방금 보내 드린 이메일에, 귀하의 선호도에 어울릴 만한 몇몇 제품들을 추천해 드렸습니다. 만약 오늘 그 중 하나를 구매하고 싶으시면, 저에게 가능한 한 빨리 알려주시기 바랍니다.

젠타스 온라인 마켓을 이용해 주셔서 감사합니다.

2 전화 메시지 필수 표현 🎧 12-2.mp3

■ 인사 및 자기 소개

☐ I'm calling from ABC Company.	ABC Company에서 전화 드립니다.
☐ It's[This is] John Bailey (calling) from Accounting.	저는 회계부의 존 베일리입니다.
☐ You've reached ABC Company.	귀하는 ABC Company에 전화하셨습니다.
☐ Thanks for calling ABC Company.	ABC Company에 전화 주셔서 감사합니다.

■ 전화 용건 설명

☐ I'm calling about ~	~에 관해 전화 드립니다.
☐ I'm calling to let you know ~	~을 알려 드리기 위해 전화 드립니다.
☐ I'm calling to confirm ~	~을 확인하기 위해 전화 드립니다.
☐ I'm calling to respond to your inquiry about ~	~에 관한 귀하의 문의에 답변 드리기 위해 전화 드립니다.

■ 당부 또는 요청 사항

☐ I'd appreciate it if you could ~	~해 주실 수 있다면 감사하겠습니다.
☐ I suggest that you ~	~하시도록 권해 드립니다.
☐ Could[Can] you please ~?	~해 주시겠습니까?
☐ Please call me back at 375-4859.	375-4859번으로 저에게 다시 전화 주시기 바랍니다.
☐ Let me know what you think.	어떻게 생각하시는지 알려주세요.
☐ I'd like to do ~	~하고자 합니다.
☐ I'd like you to do ~	귀하께서 ~해 주셨으면 합니다.

> I'd like to do는 '내가 ~하고 싶다'는 뜻이고, I'd like you to do는 '당신이 ~하면 좋겠다'는 말이에요. Part 4에서 What does the speaker want to do?(화자가 무엇을 하고 싶어 하는가?)와 What does the speaker ask the listener to do?(화자가 청자에게 무엇을 하도록 요청하는가?) 질문의 정답 단서가 되는 표현이니 반드시 구분해 두세요.

■ 마무리 인사

☐ Please feel free to contact us.	언제든지 저희에게 연락 주십시오.
☐ Don't hesitate to contact me.	주저하지 말고 저에게 연락 주십시오.
☐ I'm looking forward to hearing from you soon.	곧 연락 주시기를 기대하고 있겠습니다.
☐ You can reach me at 375-4859.	375-4859번으로 저에게 연락하실 수 있습니다.
☐ If you have any questions, please call[contact] ~	문의 사항이 있으시면 ~로 전화[연락] 주세요.

3 라디오 방송 🔊 12-3.mp3

■ 일반 뉴스 보도

일반 뉴스 보도에는 지역 소식, 비즈니스, 경제, 선거, 개발 및 건설 등을 다루는 내용이 주로 나옵니다. 내용이 다소 딱딱하고 어려운 단어들이 꽤 등장하는 편이기 때문에 관련 어휘를 꼼꼼히 암기해 두어야 수월하게 들을 수 있습니다. 뉴스 보도는 주제를 명확하게 제시하는 것으로 시작해 관련 세부 정보를 전달하는 흐름으로 진행되는 경우가 많으므로 처음부터 집중해서 들어야 합니다.

This is Roger Smith **with WBN local news**.
　　　　　　　　-----▶ WBN 지역 뉴스를 전해드리는

| ① 인사 및 뉴스 소개 |

본인 소개와 함께 뉴스 시작을 알립니다.

The Richmond Theater, which was the oldest building in town, **was demolished yesterday**. -----▶ 리치몬드 극장이 어제 철거되었습니다

| ② 뉴스 내용 요약 |

보도할 주제를 간략히 언급합니다.

Having held many theatrical performances, the Richmond Theater was once a symbol of the city, but it has been removed to build the city's first skyscraper. **The government will use the site for its new International Business Center.**
　　　　　　　-----▶ 정부는 그 부지를 새로운 국제 비즈니스 센터로 사용할 것입니다

| ③ 상세 정보 제공 |

앞서 간략히 언급한 뉴스와 관련해 상세하게 이야기합니다.

For more details about the new building, check our radio station's Web site.

| ④ 마무리 |

해당 뉴스에 대한 추가 정보를 얻을 수 있는 방법을 안내합니다.

WBN 지역 뉴스를 전해 드리는 로저 스미스입니다.

우리 도시에서 가장 오래된 건물이었던 리치몬드 극장이 어제 철거되었습니다.

많은 연극 공연을 개최했던, 리치몬드 극장은 한때 우리 도시의 상징이었지만, 우리 도시의 첫 고층 건물을 짓기 위해 철거되었습니다. 정부는 그 부지를 새로운 국제 비즈니스 센터로 활용할 것입니다.

새 건물에 대해 더 많은 자세한 정보를 원하시면, 저희 라디오 방송국의 웹사이트를 확인하시기 바랍니다.

4 라디오 방송 필수 표현 🎧 12-4.mp3

■ 일반 뉴스

☐ And now for the local news.	이제 지역 뉴스를 전해드리겠습니다.
☐ Thanks for tuning in to *Business at Five*.	<5시의 비즈니스>를 청취해 주셔서 감사합니다.
☐ This is Andrew Jones with *World News Radio*.	<월드 뉴스 라디오>의 앤드류 존스입니다.
☐ Starting next week, the project will begin.	다음 주부터, 그 프로젝트가 시작될 것입니다.
☐ The city council has approved a proposal to ~	시의회가 ~하자는 제안을 승인했습니다.
☐ The CEO announced a merger yesterday.	대표이사가 어제 합병을 발표했습니다.
☐ On today's show, we're happy to have ~	오늘 프로그램에서, ~를 모시게 되어 기쁩니다.
☐ Ms. Whitman will be discussing ~	휘트먼 씨께서 ~에 관해 이야기해 주실 것입니다.

■ 교통 정보

☐ traffic congestion / heavy traffic	교통 체증, 교통 정체
☐ Traffic is backed up on the highways.	고속도로에 차량들이 밀려 있습니다.
☐ Traffic is moving slowly due to ~	~ 때문에 차량들이 느리게 이동하고 있습니다.
☐ Highway 80 will be closed until next month.	80번 고속도로가 다음 달까지 폐쇄될 것입니다.
☐ You may want to use Kings Avenue instead.	킹스 애비뉴를 대신 이용하시는 것이 좋겠습니다.
☐ I would suggest taking an alternate route.	대체 경로를 이용하시도록 권해 드립니다.

■ 일기 예보

☐ Today's forecast calls for[shows] ~	오늘의 일기 예보는 ~으로 예상됩니다.
☐ There is a high chance of rain showers on Friday.	금요일에 소나기가 내릴 가능성이 높습니다.
☐ We can expect a bit of snow on Monday.	월요일에 약간의 눈이 예상됩니다.
☐ Temperatures are expected to rise tomorrow.	내일 기온이 오를 것으로 예상됩니다.
☐ The roads will be slippery, so please drive slowly.	도로가 미끄러울 것이므로, 천천히 운전하세요.

■ 마무리 인사

☐ I'll be back with another traffic update.	또 다른 교통 소식과 함께 돌아오겠습니다.
☐ Stay tuned and keep listening.	채널을 고정하시고 계속 들어주세요.
☐ I'll be right back after a short commercial break.	짧은 광고 후에 바로 돌아오겠습니다.

PRACTICE 🎧 12-5.mp3

음원을 듣고 각 질문에 맞는 답을 고른 뒤, 스크립트를 보면서 빈칸을 채워보세요.

1 Where does the speaker work?
(A) At an architecture firm 건축 사무소
(B) At a gallery 미술관
(C) At a train operator 철도 회사
(D) At a construction materials supplier 건설 자재 공급업체

2 Why is the speaker calling?
(A) To review some design plans 설계 도면을 검토하기 위해
(B) To check a train schedule 기차 일정을 확인하기 위해
(C) To arrange some catering 음식 공급을 준비하기 위해
(D) To order some building materials 건축 자재를 주문하기 위해

3 What does the speaker mean when he says, "we won't be stopping by for the exhibit"?
(A) The gallery is closed. 미술관이 문을 닫았다.
(B) Tickets are sold out. 입장권이 매진되었다.
(C) Time will be limited. 시간이 제한적일 것이다.
(D) He does not like art. 그는 미술을 좋아하지 않는다.

Hey, Marcus. _____to EcoBuild Solutions this Thursday to showcase our sustainable materials to their architects. This collaboration is vital _____. So, our train arrives at 10:30 A.M. We'll head to their office for the demonstration and discussion, then tour their sample construction site. And we'll catch the 6 P.M. train home. I know you hoped we'd have time to drop into that modern art gallery downtown. It might not fit, so let's just say we won't be stopping by for the exhibit.

4 What is the broadcast mainly about?
   (A) Some event highlights 몇몇 행사의 하이라이트
   (B) A bus detour and delays 버스 우회 운행 및 지연
   (C) Library hours 도서관 운영 시간
   (D) Lecture cancellations 강의 취소

5 What are listeners encouraged to do?
   (A) Register for another term 다음 학기 등록하기
   (B) Check a Web site 웹사이트 확인하기
   (C) Call a transit office 교통국에 전화하기
   (D) Purchase a bus pass 버스 승차권 구매하기

6 What is taking place in the campus quad?
   (A) A music concert 음악회
   (B) A sports tournament 스포츠 대회
   (C) A science fair 과학 박람회
   (D) A food festival 음식 축제

> Now interrupting *Classics on Campus* for a transportation update from University Transit. Students taking Route 5 should be aware that _____ _____ on Elm Street. As a result, service during peak hours is running every twenty minutes, which is longer than usual. For a detour map and the revised timetable, _____. Also, _____ _____ in the campus quad, so foot traffic is heavy. And now, back to your scheduled programming.

실전 TEST 🔊 12-6.mp3

학습한 내용을 적용하여 다음 기출 변형 문제들을 풀어보세요.

> **PART 4 실전 문제 풀이 지침**
> 1. 담화가 나오기 전에 세 개의 문제를 빠르게 읽고 핵심을 파악합니다. 이때 키워드에 동그라미를 쳐 둡니다.
> 2. 미리 읽은 문제와 관련된 내용을 노려 듣습니다.
> 3. 정답을 찾으면 문제지에 바로 체크하고 다음 문제를 읽습니다. 답안지 마킹은 나중에 한꺼번에 해도 됩니다.

1 What department does the speaker work in?

(A) Customer Service
(B) Human Resources
(C) Marketing
(D) Technical Support

2 What problem does the speaker mention?

(A) A document is missing.
(B) A shipment has not arrived.
(C) A part needs to be replaced.
(D) A deadline is too soon.

3 What does the speaker offer to do?

(A) Talk to a supervisor
(B) Cancel an order
(C) Request a file
(D) Call a coworker

4 Who most likely is the message intended for?

(A) Local residents
(B) Travel agents
(C) Potential tourists
(D) Business owners

5 What does the speaker say about the downtown area?

(A) It is hosting a festival.
(B) It has limited parking.
(C) It has several landmarks.
(D) It is under construction.

6 What should listeners do to find out more information?

(A) Leave a message
(B) Make an appointment
(C) Visit a Web site
(D) Dial a number

7 What is the speaker calling about?

(A) A business expansion
(B) A job vacancy
(C) A staff orientation
(D) A holiday schedule

Expense Report	
Gasoline	$60
Accommodations	$250
Food	$120
Company pamphlets	$90
	Total: $520

8 What does the speaker mean when he says, "there have already been over 300 views"?

(A) A deadline should be changed.
(B) A recruiting method has been successful.
(C) A Web site is becoming more popular.
(D) A larger room might be required.

10 What did the listener do last week?

(A) Went on vacation
(B) Organized a staff trip
(C) Attended a job fair
(D) Spoke at a convention

9 What does the speaker advise the listener to do?

(A) Review some documents
(B) Submit a proposal
(C) Attend an interview
(D) Postpone a trip

11 Look at the graphic. Which amount needs to be checked?

(A) $60
(B) $250
(C) $120
(D) $90

12 What does the speaker ask the listener to do?

(A) Make a payment
(B) Send an e-mail
(C) Explain a procedure
(D) Purchase equipment

실전 TEST

학습한 내용을 적용하여 다음 기출 변형 문제들을 풀어보세요.

13 What does the speaker say will happen in August?
(A) A new airport terminal will be opened.
(B) An airline will launch a new route.
(C) A Web site will be improved.
(D) New employees will be recruited.

14 What benefit to customers does the speaker mention?
(A) Easier booking procedures
(B) Fewer delays
(C) Lower prices
(D) Reduced travel times

15 According to the speaker, who is pleased about the news?
(A) Government officials
(B) Board members
(C) Tourists
(D) Local business owners

16 What is the radio broadcast mainly about?
(A) Building maintenance
(B) Landscaping work
(C) Local weather
(D) Traffic conditions

17 What is causing a delay near Highway 150?
(A) A repair project
(B) A sporting event
(C) A store opening
(D) An outdoor concert

18 What will the listeners hear next?
(A) A weather update
(B) Some advertisements
(C) An interview
(D) Some business news

19 What is the main topic of the broadcast?

(A) A magazine article
(B) A library service
(C) An educational program
(D) A recycling project

Thursday	Friday	Saturday	Sunday
☁️🌧	⛅	☀️	☁️

20 What will users of the application be able to do?

(A) Upgrade a membership
(B) Consult a professional
(C) Sign up for an event
(D) Receive notifications

21 What does the speaker imply when he says, "And that's not all"?

(A) He thinks the app has some drawbacks.
(B) He will describe another feature of the app.
(C) He believes the app will be popular.
(D) He will recommend some different apps.

22 What type of event is the speaker describing?

(A) A store's grand opening
(B) An arts and crafts fair
(C) A music festival
(D) A sports competition

23 According to the speaker, what can the listeners find on a Web site?

(A) An event schedule
(B) A registration form
(C) A list of food vendors
(D) A parking map

24 Look at the graphic. On which day is the event being held?

(A) Thursday
(B) Friday
(C) Saturday
(D) Sunday

DAY 13 | 공지 및 안내 Part 4

1 사내 공지 🔊 13-1.mp3

사내 공지는 회사 내부에서 들을 수 있는 공지를 말합니다. 회사 내에서 새로 실시되는 규정, 예정된 공사나 시설 보수 작업 안내, 회사 위치 이전 일정, 사내 행사 안내 등과 관련된 내용이 자주 출제됩니다.

■ 사내 공지 지문 예시와 구성

Before we end the day, **I need to share a marketing department update**. ▶ 마케팅 부서의 업데이트된 소식을 전달합니다.

▶ 소셜미디어 전략가가 우리 팀 회의에 참석할 것입니다.
On Tuesday, **a social media strategist from Digital Pulse will join our team meeting to outline the new campaign strategy**. Our goal is to boost engagement across all channels. We'll review the content calendar and analyze last quarter's metrics. Also, I think we should refresh our hashtag-usage guidelines. So, I printed the campaign brief and hashtag best-practices list. **Please study them before the meeting.** I'll circulate copies around the table now. ▶ 미팅 전에 꼭 숙지해 주시기 바랍니다.

If you have any questions, **feel free to call me or send me an e-mail**.

① 공지 주제 안내
공지에서 다룰 주제를 간략히 언급합니다.

② 세부 사항 설명
공지 주제와 관련해, 변동 사항이나 일정, 유의 사항 등을 구체적으로 설명합니다. 날짜나 장소 등의 세부 사항에 유의해야 합니다.

③ 마무리 인사
문의 방법이나 추가 정보 확인 방법 등을 알려 줍니다.

오늘 일과 마무리 전에 마케팅 부서 업데이트를 전합니다.

화요일에 디지털 펄스의 소셜미디어 전략가가 우리 팀 미팅에 참석해 새 캠페인 전략을 설명할 예정입니다. 우리 목표는 모든 채널에서 고객 참여를 극대화하는 것입니다. 미팅에서 콘텐츠 캘린더를 검토하고 지난 분기 실적 지표를 분석할 것입니다. 또 해시태그 사용 지침도 새롭게 정비할 필요가 있다고 생각합니다. 그래서 캠페인 간략 설명서와 해시태그 모범 활용 가이드 목록을 출력해 두었습니다. 미팅 전까지 꼭 숙지해 주시기 바랍니다. 지금 테이블을 돌아가며 자료를 배포하겠습니다.

어떤 질문이든 있으실 경우, 언제든지 저에게 전화하시거나 이메일을 보내 주시기 바랍니다.

2 공공장소 공지 🔊 13-2.mp3

공공장소 공지는 공항이나 기차역, 지하철역, 버스 터미널에서 승객들에게 알리는 유형과 상점이나 쇼핑몰에서 고객들에게 알리는 유형이 자주 나옵니다. 특히, 교통편과 관련된 공지의 경우, 문제 상황 및 원인, 그리고 청자들에게 요청하는 일과 관련된 문제가 자주 나오므로 그 정보에 특히 주의를 기울여 들어야 합니다.

■ 공공장소 공지 지문 예시와 구성

Attention, all passengers on Viva City Bus.
----▶ 비바 시티 버스 승객 여러분께 알립니다.

① 공지 대상 언급
공지 대상을 짧게 언급합니다.

I apologize for **the delayed departure of our city sightseeing bus** today. The driver is stuck in roadwork and will arrive shortly.
----▶ 시티투어 버스 출발이 지연되었습니다

② 변경 사항 설명
출발 지연 및 항공편 취소 등 공지 대상이 알아야 할 공지 내용을 언급합니다.

While you wait, please help yourselves to chilled water and snacks at the bus stop. And **I'd like to remind you to have your tour wristbands visible before you board the bus. Once we're underway, the first landmark you'll pass is the Old Town Clock Tower.** As we roll by, your guide will share its role in the city's founding.
----▶ 버스 탑승 시 손목밴드 보여주세요. / 먼저 보실 명소는 올드 타운 시계탑입니다.

③ 추가 정보 및 요청사항
공지 내용에 따른 대처 사항이나 승객들에게 요청하는 일, 투어에 관한 안내 등을 전달합니다.

We apologize for this inconvenience. Thank you for your understanding and cooperation.

④ 마무리 인사

비바 시티 버스를 이용하시는 모든 승객 여러분께 알립니다.

오늘 시내 관광버스 출발이 늦어진 점 사과드립니다. 운전기사가 도로 공사 구간에 막혀 있었고, 곧 도착할 예정입니다.

기다리는 동안 버스 정류장에 마련된 시원한 물과 간식을 자유롭게 드시기 바랍니다. 탑승 전에는 투어 팔찌가 잘 보이도록 착용해 주시기를 다시 말씀드립니다. 버스가 출발하면 가장 먼저 보실 명소는 올드타운 시계탑입니다. 지나가면서 가이드가 이 시계탑이 도시 설립에 어떤 역할을 했는지 설명해 드립니다.

이러한 불편함에 대해 사과 드립니다. 여러분의 양해와 협조에 감사 드립니다.

3 필수 표현 🔊 13-3.mp3

■ 공지 시작 알림

☐ This is a reminder to all employees.	모든 직원들에게 다시 한 번 알립니다.
☐ Attention, employees.	직원 여러분께 알립니다.
☐ Attention, passengers[shoppers].	승객 여러분[쇼핑객 여러분]께 알립니다.
☐ Welcome aboard.	탑승을 환영합니다.
☐ May I have your attention, please?	주목해 주시겠습니까?(= 안내 말씀 드립니다.)

■ 공지 세부 정보

☐ We'll be upgrading the software program.	소프트웨어 프로그램을 업그레이드할 예정입니다.
☐ As you know, our office will move to the Gracia Building.	아시다시피, 우리 사무실이 그라시아 빌딩으로 이전할 것입니다.
☐ I'd like to tell you about a new vacation policy.	새 휴가 정책에 관해 말씀 드리고자 합니다.
☐ Safety inspectors will be visiting us this Friday.	안전 조사관들이 이번주 금요일에 방문할 예정입니다.

■ 지시 및 요청 사항

☐ All employees are required to ~	모든 직원들은 ~해야 합니다.
☐ Please be informed that ~ / Please note that ~	~임을 알아 두시기 바랍니다.
☐ Please be advised that ~	~라는 점에 유의하세요.
☐ I'd like you all to submit a report by the end of the day.	일과 종료 시점까지 모두 보고서를 제출해 주세요.
☐ Please remember to save all your work.	모든 작업물을 저장해야 한다는 점을 기억하세요.
☐ Make sure to stop by the Personnel Department.	반드시 인사부에 들르십시오.

■ 마무리 인사

☐ We are sorry for the inconvenience.	불편함에 대해 사과 드립니다.
☐ Thank you for your understanding.	여러분의 양해에 감사 드립니다.
☐ Please wait for further notice.	추가 공지를 기다려 주시기 바랍니다.
☐ We apologize for the delay.	지연에 대해 사과 드립니다.

PRACTICE 🔊 13-4.mp3

음원을 듣고 각 질문에 맞는 답을 고른 뒤, 스크립트를 보면서 빈칸을 채워보세요.

1 Where most likely is this announcement being made?
 (A) At a theater 극장
 (B) At a museum 박물관
 (C) At a concert hall 콘서트장
 (D) At a bookstore 서점

2 What does the speaker say has changed?
 (A) The admission price 입장료
 (B) The parking rules 주차 규정
 (C) The opening hours 개장 시간
 (D) A demonstration location 시연 장소

3 What does the speaker say is available at the front desk?
 (A) A lost item 분실물
 (B) A ticket stub 티켓 반쪽
 (C) A brochure 안내 책자
 (D) A membership card 회원 카드

Good morning, and welcome to the Spring Exhibition _____.
Please note that the live painting demonstration _____
_____ to make room for the sculpture unveiling. Gallery 7 is on the second floor, next to the Impressionist Wing. Also, will the guest who _____
_____ at the front desk please claim them? They have small buckles at the wrists.

📖 정답 및 해설 p.090

실전 TEST 🔊 13-5.mp3

학습한 내용을 적용하여 다음 기출 변형 문제들을 풀어보세요.

> **PART 4 실전 문제 풀이 지침**
> 1. 담화가 나오기 전에 세 개의 문제를 빠르게 읽고 핵심을 파악합니다. 이때 키워드에 동그라미를 쳐 둡니다.
> 2. 미리 읽은 문제와 관련된 내용을 노려 듣습니다.
> 3. 정답을 찾으면 문제지에 바로 체크하고 다음 문제를 읽습니다. 답안지 마킹은 나중에 한꺼번에 해도 됩니다.

1 What is the announcement about?
 (A) Moving to a new office space
 (B) Improving productivity at work
 (C) Installing new software
 (D) Purchasing office supplies

2 What does the speaker say about the North Riverside Building?
 (A) It is located next to a bus stop.
 (B) It has spacious offices.
 (C) It has fast Internet service.
 (D) It includes a cafeteria.

3 What are employees asked to do?
 (A) Move some furniture
 (B) Bring their personal items
 (C) Put documents into boxes
 (D) Turn off their computers

4 What will the business give to the listeners?
 (A) Company vehicles
 (B) Personal offices
 (C) New laptop computers
 (D) Extra vacation days

5 What benefit does the speaker mention?
 (A) Increased annual revenue
 (B) Improved customer service
 (C) Faster production rates
 (D) Higher employee satisfaction

6 According to the speaker, why should listeners send an e-mail to Mr. Harris?
 (A) To schedule a meeting
 (B) To volunteer for a role
 (C) To make a request
 (D) To confirm attendance

7 Why is the announcement being made?

(A) To describe the supermarket's amenities
(B) To announce a closing time
(C) To explain why a service is unavailable
(D) To advertise a new branch

Train Number	Departure Time	Destination
P12	09:00	Providence
B59	09:45	Boston
A46	10:30	Albany
S23	11:15	Springfield

8 Why does the woman say, "Make sure you check them out"?

(A) She is reminding the listeners to use store coupons.
(B) She wants the listeners to visit a different business.
(C) She hopes the listeners will take advantage of a deal.
(D) She is advising the listeners to check their receipts.

10 What is the main purpose of the announcement?

(A) To describe the station facilities
(B) To explain a new policy
(C) To apologize for upcoming construction
(D) To remind passengers about a platform change

9 According to the speaker, what will happen at the business next week?

(A) New products will be sold.
(B) A free delivery service will begin.
(C) Business hours will be extended.
(D) A special sale will begin.

11 According to the speaker, what can the listeners do in the station?

(A) Visit a gift shop
(B) Sample free food
(C) Charge their phones
(D) Obtain some pamphlets

12 Look at the graphic. Which train does the speaker say will be delayed?

(A) P12
(B) B59
(C) A46
(D) S23

실전 TEST

학습한 내용을 적용하여 다음 기출 변형 문제들을 풀어보세요.

13 Where most likely is the announcement being made?

(A) At a job fair
(B) At an auto show
(C) At a museum exhibit
(D) At a manufacturing plant

14 What does the speaker say has changed?

(A) Refreshment offerings
(B) A panel schedule
(C) A seating plan
(D) A speaker

15 What does the speaker say is available at the welcome desk?

(A) A parking pass
(B) A free gift
(C) A ticket
(D) Brochures

16 Why has a movie screening been delayed?

(A) A projector is being repaired.
(B) There was a scheduling error.
(C) Some guests have not arrived.
(D) An employee was late for the shift.

17 What are the listeners reminded to do?

(A) Silence their devices
(B) Hold onto their tickets
(C) Read a synopsis
(D) Pick up complimentary refreshments

18 What will be shown to guests first?

(A) The emergency exit routes
(B) A special presentation
(C) Movie trailers
(D) Product advertisements

19 Where does the announcement take place?

(A) At a community garden
(B) At a science museum
(C) At a hardware store
(D) At a national park

20 What does the speaker instruct the listeners to do?

(A) Work together in groups
(B) Help direct visitor traffic
(C) Paint some parking lines
(D) Investigate a hiking trail

21 What does the speaker say will be updated?

(A) A Web site
(B) A handbook
(C) A shuttle service
(D) A dress code policy

22 What is the speaker mainly discussing?

(A) A hiring process
(B) A mentorship program
(C) Internal transfer options
(D) Opportunities for promotion

23 What does the speaker say will not change?

(A) A required training timeline
(B) An online reservation system
(C) The hours of business operation
(D) Customer support procedures

24 What does the speaker mean when she says, "I'm meeting with Mr. Navarro later this week"?

(A) She will try to get approval for extra funds.
(B) She wants to organize a team-building event.
(C) She will be having a meal with Mr. Navarro.
(D) She plans to give Mr. Navarro a survey.

DAY 14 | 회의 발췌/소개 Part 4

1 회의 발췌 🔊 14-1.mp3

회의 발췌 담화는 Part 4에서 가장 많이 출제되는 유형 중의 하나로, 다른 담화 유형보다 난이도가 높은 편에 속합니다. 경쟁 업체의 성장, 판매 실적 부진, 변경된 회사 정책, 성과에 대한 칭찬, 외부 인사 방문에 대한 대비 등 주로 업무 진행이나 회사의 방향성과 관련된 내용이 등장합니다.

■ 회의 발췌 지문 예시와 구성

I'm glad you could make time in your busy schedules to come to this meeting. **I'd like to talk about our recent customer survey**.
─────▶ 최근의 고객 설문 조사에 관해 이야기하고자 합니다

① 인사 및 회의 소집 이유
간단한 인사와 함께 회의를 소집한 이유를 말합니다.

I reviewed some feedback from our mobile application users, and there's a common complaint. Most of them said that **it's too complicated to use**. So, **I've decided to hire a professional application developer** who can improve our application.
─────▶ 우리의 모바일 앱이 사용하기에 너무 복잡하다고 해서 전문 개발자를 고용하기로 결정했습니다

② 배경 설명 및 관련 정보 제공
회의를 통해 해결해야 하는 문제 상황 및 해결책, 의견 등을 제시합니다.

I'll post the job opening on Thursday. **If you have someone to recommend for this position, please contact the personnel manager**.

③ 요청 사항 및 전달 사항 언급
의견 제공, 설문지 작성, 자료 전달 등 업무상 요청 사항을 말합니다.

바쁜 일정에도 이번 회의에 오실 시간을 내주셔서 기쁩니다. 저는 최근의 고객 설문 조사에 관해 이야기하고자 합니다.

제가 우리 모바일 애플리케이션 사용자들로부터 받은 일부 의견을 검토했는데, 한 가지 공통적인 불만 사항이 있습니다. 그들 중 대부분이 그것이 사용하기에 너무 복잡하다고 말했습니다. 그래서 우리 애플리케이션을 향상시킬 수 있는 애플리케이션 전문 개발자를 고용하기로 결정했습니다.

목요일에 구인 공고를 게시할 것입니다. 이 직책에 추천할 만한 사람이 있으면, 인사부장님께 연락하시기 바랍니다.

2 소개 🔊 14-2.mp3

소개 담화는 크게 인물 소개와 행사 소개로 나뉘는데, 인물 소개 유형이 좀 더 자주 출제됩니다. 인물 소개에는 강연자나 특정 수상자, 해당 행사에 의미 있는 인물, 새로 입사하거나 은퇴하는 직원과 관련된 내용이 많습니다. 한 인물의 이력/경력에 관해 묻는 문제가 자주 나오므로 소개하는 인물의 특징에 해당되는 정보를 주의 깊게 들어야 합니다.

■ 소개 지문 예시와 구성

Welcome everyone to **Science Weekly's Annual Research Awards Ceremony**. ·····▶ 『사이언스 위클리』의 연례 연구 시상식

① 소개 대상 언급
간단한 인사와 함께 행사명을 소개합니다. 행사명이 담화 장소 문제의 단서가 될 수 있습니다.

As the editor of the region's leading publication on scientific breakthroughs, I'm honored **to introduce our guest of honor this evening, Dr. Alex Kim**. ·····▶ 오늘 밤 영예의 주인공 알렉스 킴 박사님을 소개합니다

② 행사의 목적 및 인물 소개
행사를 개최하는 목적과 소개하려는 인물을 언급합니다.

Dr. Kim has published groundbreaking research in our journal for over ten years. **What's truly special about his work is the paradigm-shifting experiments he pioneered in nanotechnology.** His studies have influenced dozens of laboratories worldwide.
·····▶ 그의 연구에서 진정으로 특별한 점은 나노기술 분야에서 개척하신 패러다임 전환 실험입니다

③ 특정 인물에 관한 상세 설명
소개하는 인물의 직책과 경력, 업적 등을 상세히 설명합니다.

·····▶ 이제 연단으로 올라와 수상하시기 바랍니다
Now, Dr. Kim, **please join me at the podium to accept this award** recognizing your contributions to scientific innovation.

④ 마무리 인사
소개하는 인물을 무대로 불러내는 것으로 마무리합니다.

여러분, 『사이언스 위클리』의 연례 연구 시상식에 오신 것을 환영합니다.

과학 분야 획기적 성과를 다루는 지역 최고의 간행물 편집장으로서 오늘 밤 영예의 주인공인 알렉스 킴 박사님을 소개하게 되어 영광입니다.

킴 박사님은 지난 10년 동안 본 저널에 획기적인 연구를 발표해 오셨습니다. 그의 연구에서 진정으로 특별한 점은 나노기술 분야에서 개척하신 패러다임 전환 실험입니다. 그 연구는 전 세계 수십 곳의 연구실에 영향을 미쳤습니다.

이제 킴 박사님은 이 자리에 올라 과학 혁신에 대한 공로를 인정하는 상을 받아 주시기 바랍니다.

3 필수 표현 🔊 14-3.mp3

■ 회의 시작 알림

☐ The first thing I want to discuss ~	제가 논의하고 싶은 첫 번째 안건은 ~입니다.
☐ As you've read in the notice, ~	공지 사항에서 읽어 보셨듯이, ~
☐ I'd like to start the meeting by ~	~하는 것으로 회의를 시작하려 합니다.
☐ I called this meeting to talk about ~	~에 관해 이야기하기 위해 이 회의를 소집했습니다.

■ 행사 소개

☐ Thank you for coming to our ~ event.	저희 ~ 행사에 와 주셔서 감사 드립니다.
☐ Welcome to Jane Lee's retirement party.	제인 리 씨의 은퇴 파티에 오신 것을 환영합니다.
☐ I'm pleased to welcome everyone to the Company of the Year award ceremony.	올해의 기업 시상식에 오신 여러분을 환영하게 되어 기쁩니다.
☐ I'm pleased to announce the winner of this award.	이 상의 수상자를 발표하게 되어 기쁩니다.
☐ This year's event will support ~	올해의 행사는 ~을 후원할 것입니다.

■ 인물 소개

☐ I'd like to introduce Risa to you ~	여러분들께 리사 씨를 소개해 드리겠습니다.
☐ Mr. Kim is best known for ~	킴 씨는 ~로 가장 잘 알려져 있습니다.
☐ Under her leadership, our business expansion has been really successful.	그녀의 리더십 하에, 우리의 사업 확장은 정말로 성공적이었습니다.
☐ Mr. Chang has served as the president of a design company.	창 씨는 디자인 회사의 사장으로 근무해 오셨습니다.
☐ She has been recognized as a marketing expert.	그녀는 마케팅 전문가로 인정 받아 왔습니다.

■ 마무리 인사

☐ Please welcome Collin Richardson.	콜린 리차드슨 씨를 환영해 주시기 바랍니다.
☐ Please give her a warm round of applause.	그녀에게 따뜻한 박수 갈채를 보내주시기 바랍니다.
☐ Before we invite Kate up to the stage,	케이트 씨를 무대 위로 모시기 전에,
☐ Please join me at the podium ~	여기 연단으로 와주시기 바랍니다.

PRACTICE 🔊 14-4.mp3

음원을 듣고 각 질문에 맞는 답을 고른 뒤, 스크립트를 보면서 빈칸을 채워보세요.

1. Who are the listeners?
   (A) Shareholders 주주
   (B) Warehouse staff 창고 직원
   (C) Conference attendees 회의 참석자
   (D) Members of the company's board 회사 이사회 구성원

2. What does the speaker imply when she says, "Ms. Patel is at the investor conference"?
   (A) An analysis is confidential. 분석 자료는 기밀이다.
   (B) Some final figures are wrong. 일부 최종 수치가 잘못되었다.
   (C) Some comments will be made later. 일부 의견이 나중에 전달될 것이다.
   (D) A conference was postponed. 회의가 연기되었다.

3. What will the listeners do next?
   (A) Draft a press release 보도 자료를 작성한다
   (B) Tour the Western hub 서부의 허브를 견학한다
   (C) Review a report on projected savings 예상 절감액 보고서를 검토한다
   (D) Contact some conference organizers 회의 주최측에 연락한다

We've called this morning's board meeting to discuss the proposed shutdown of our Eastern Distribution Center. _____, we all have a duty to protect shareholder interests and streamline operations. The purpose of the shutdown would be to consolidate logistics into the newer Western hub and cut costs. Before we vote on this proposal, _____, including Ms. Olivia Patel, our CFO. But as you know, Ms. Patel is at the investor conference, so instead, _____ _____ this morning. Please review page 22 in your board book.

정답 및 해설 p.098

DAY 14 회의 발췌/소개   139

실전 TEST

학습한 내용을 적용하여 다음 기출 변형 문제들을 풀어보세요.

> **PART 4 실전 문제 풀이 지침**
> 1. 담화가 나오기 전에 세 개의 문제를 빠르게 읽고 핵심을 파악합니다. 이때 키워드에 동그라미를 쳐 둡니다.
> 2. 미리 읽은 문제와 관련된 내용을 노려 듣습니다.
> 3. 정답을 찾으면 문제지에 바로 체크하고 다음 문제를 읽습니다. 답안지 마킹은 나중에 한꺼번에 해도 됩니다.

1 What is the speaker mainly discussing?
(A) A training workshop
(B) A staff reward system
(C) A store's annual sale
(D) A company merger

2 What will the listeners be selling?
(A) Mobile phones
(B) Home appliances
(C) Computer accessories
(D) Television services

3 What will happen in January?
(A) A business will be relocated.
(B) New employees will begin work.
(C) New products will be launched.
(D) Bonuses will be awarded to employees.

4 Where most likely is the event being held?
(A) At a convention center
(B) In a restaurant
(C) At a company headquarters
(D) In a government building

5 Who is being honored at the event?
(A) A company founder
(B) A CEO
(C) A public official
(D) A personnel director

6 What will the listeners most likely do next?
(A) Provide some feedback
(B) View a video
(C) Listen to a talk
(D) Watch a performance

7 What is the purpose of the meeting?

(A) To adjust a monthly work schedule
(B) To watch a demonstration
(C) To prepare for an inspection
(D) To announce a new safety policy

SUGGESTIONS FOR NUTRINA CHOCOLATE BAR

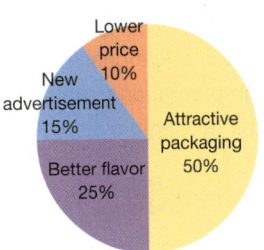

Lower price 10%
New advertisement 15%
Attractive packaging 50%
Better flavor 25%

8 What does the speaker imply when he says, "Failure is not an option"?

(A) He thinks some equipment needs to be fixed.
(B) He needs the listeners to take a task seriously.
(C) He believes a deadline should be extended.
(D) He wants the listeners to re-take a test.

10 Who most likely are the listeners?

(A) Product developers
(B) Market researchers
(C) Kitchen assistants
(D) Food critics

9 What will the listeners do next?

(A) Put on safety equipment
(B) Organize an event
(C) Discuss project goals
(D) Submit a survey

11 Look at the graphic. Which category is the speaker worried about?

(A) Attractive packaging
(B) Better flavor
(C) New advertisement
(D) Lower price

12 What has the company decided to do?

(A) Collaborate with a celebrity
(B) Open another store
(C) Hire more employees
(D) Launch an advertising campaign

실전 TEST 14-5.mp3

학습한 내용을 적용하여 다음 기출 변형 문제들을 풀어보세요.

13 What does the speaker most likely do at the museum?

(A) Manage the parking lot
(B) Organize educational events
(C) Design promotional materials
(D) Recruit new employees

14 According to the speaker, who is Natalia Peller?

(A) A movie producer
(B) A vegetable farmer
(C) A local historian
(D) A research scientist

15 What does the speaker mean when he says, "We have another speaker coming at 4 o'clock"?

(A) Guests must leave by a certain time.
(B) Sign-ups for another event will close soon.
(C) A schedule has been changed last minute.
(D) A follow-up activity is free of charge.

16 What industry do the listeners most likely work in?

(A) Agriculture
(B) Fishing
(C) Pharmaceutical
(D) Environmental science

17 According to the speaker, what will the project require?

(A) A specific sampling method
(B) A manual reporting system
(C) Data analysis
(D) Flexible scheduling

18 What are the listeners asked to find in a packet?

(A) A regional map
(B) An ID number
(C) Quality reports
(D) Location assignments

19 What does the speaker say is new about the event?

(A) It is happening in an outdoor stadium.
(B) It is free to attend.
(C) It will take place over two days.
(D) It has drawn a very large audience.

20 Why is Ms. Lindholm being recognized?

(A) She is an accomplished actress.
(B) She founded a famous theater company.
(C) She has created groundbreaking set designs.
(D) She directed a successful musical play.

21 According to the speaker, what will happen before Ms. Lindholm receives her award?

(A) Her colleague will give a speech.
(B) A video will be shown.
(C) A rehearsal will take place.
(D) Some reporters will ask questions.

22 What agenda topic is the speaker discussing?

(A) Streamlining company finances
(B) Boosting brand recognition
(C) Researching competitors' products
(D) Launching a recycling initiative

23 According to the speaker, who is Martin Delgado going to talk about?

(A) A fellow employee
(B) Social media influencers
(C) Real estate agents
(D) Internet users

24 What does the speaker imply when he says, "I don't want it to be a distraction"?

(A) An activity is expected to be difficult.
(B) The presentation will be postponed.
(C) A worksheet will be distributed later.
(D) A handout contains incorrect information.

DAY 15 | 광고/투어 가이드 Part 4

1 광고 🎧 15-1.mp3

광고에서는 전자제품, 사무용품, 가구, 여행 상품, 할인 행사 등 다양한 제품 또는 서비스를 다룬 내용이 제시됩니다. 광고되는 제품이나 서비스를 먼저 언급하는 것으로 담화가 시작되며, 담화 전반에 걸쳐 그 특징을 소개하는 흐름으로 진행되므로 난이도가 비교적 쉬운 편입니다.

■ 광고 지문 예시와 구성

-----▶ 새로운 언어를 완벽하게 배울 준비 되셨나요?
Are you ready to master a new language? At Fluent Edge Academy, we offer immersive, instructor-led courses that emphasize real-world conversation skills.

전부 온라인이고 상호 작용이 가능합니다 ◀-----
Unlike other language programs, **our classes are fully online and interactive,** so students can practice with native speakers from anywhere. **Our virtual classrooms are accessible 24/7** and across all time zones. -----▶ 가상 강의실은 24시간 매일 이용 가능합니다

Visit our Website today to sign up **for a free trial lesson**.
-----▶ 무료 체험 수업을 받으시려면

① 광고 제품 또는 서비스 소개
광고 제품이나 서비스를 소개합니다.

② 상세 정보 제공
광고하는 제품이나 서비스의 특징점이나 할인 혜택 등과 관련된 상세 정보를 제공합니다.

③ 구매 요령 및 당부의 말
제품 구매나 서비스 이용 시에 필요한 추가 정보를 전달합니다. 주로 영업 시간과 전화번호를 안내하고 웹사이트 이용 등을 권장합니다.

새로운 언어를 마스터할 준비가 되셨나요? 플루언트 엣지 아카데미에서는 실제 회화 능력에 중점을 둔 몰입형 강사 주도 강의를 제공합니다.

다른 언어 프로그램과 달리, 저희 수업은 전부 온라인이면서 상호작용이 가능해 언제 어디서나 원어민과 연습할 수 있습니다. 가상 강의실은 24시간 연중무휴, 전 세계 모든 시간대에서 이용 가능합니다.

지금 웹사이트를 방문해 무료 체험 수업에 등록해 보세요.

2 투어 가이드 🔊 15-2.mp3

투어 가이드는 여행객들을 대상으로 하는 가이드와 신입 직원 또는 외부 방문객에게 회사 시설 등을 소개하는 견학 가이드가 주된 내용입니다. 대부분 투어 장소 소개와 함께 진행 순서를 언급하는 흐름으로 담화가 이어지므로 비교적 어렵지 않은 유형에 속합니다.

■ 투어 가이드 지문 예시와 구성

Welcome, everyone. **My name is Marcus, and I'll be your guide on this city bike tour today.** ·····▶ 저는 마커스이고 오늘 투어 가이드입니다

Originally, I had planned to include the Westside Loop, but it's closed for a charity marathon. So **we'll be riding along the East Waterfront** instead, which covers a similar distance. One nice thing about that route is that it has a dedicated bike path with riverfront views.
·····▶ 우리는 자전거를 타고 이스트 워터프론트를 가겠습니다

·····▶ 출발 전에 헬멧을 확보하세요
As a reminder, you'll want to secure your helmets before we depart. Helmets are available at the rental kiosk if you need one.

So, let's get started. Please follow me.

① 환영 인사 및 본인 소개
환영 인사와 함께 투어를 진행할 사람을 소개합니다.

② 투어 일정 및 세부 정보
투어의 종류 또는 일정, 투어 진행 순서를 언급하면서 이동 장소에 관한 특징적인 정보를 언급합니다.

③ 당부 사항
방문객 준수 사항 등을 안내합니다.

④ 투어 시작 알림
투어가 시작된다는 말과 함께 담화를 마무리합니다.

여러분, 환영합니다. 제 이름은 마커스이며, 오늘 시내 자전거 투어의 가이드입니다.

원래 웨스트사이드 루프 코스를 포함하려 했지만, 그곳은 자선 마라톤 때문에 폐쇄되었습니다. 그래서 대신 비슷한 거리를 달릴 수 있는 이스트 워터프론트를 따라 탈 예정입니다. 그 경로의 장점 중 하나는 전용 자전거 도로가 있어 강변 전망을 즐길 수 있다는 것입니다.

다시 말씀드리면, 출발 전에 헬멧을 확보해 주시기 바랍니다. 필요하신 분은 대여소에서 헬멧을 받으실 수 있습니다.

그럼, 시작해 보겠습니다. 저를 따라오세요.

3 필수 표현 🔊 15-3.mp3

■ 제품/서비스 소개 및 혜택 안내

☐ If you are looking for ~ / Looking to ~	~을 찾고 계신다면 / ~하는 것을 찾고 계신다면
☐ (Are you) tired of ~? / Are you ready to ~?	~에 싫증 나셨나요? / ~할 준비 되셨나요?
☐ Now is the time to ~	이제 ~하실 때입니다.
☐ New Way Car Rental is here for you.	뉴웨이 렌터카가 여기 있습니다.
☐ You can get a 30% discount on your purchase.	구매품에 대해 30% 할인 받으실 수 있습니다.
☐ You will receive 50% off the regular price.	정가에서 50% 할인 받으시게 될 것입니다.
☐ The sale ends on December 15.	세일은 12월 15일에 종료됩니다.
☐ We'll be offering a voucher and a free gift.	상품권과 무료 선물을 제공해드릴 것입니다.
☐ Starting next week	다음 주부터
☐ For a limited time only	한정된 기간에 한해

■ 구매 방법

☐ For more information, visit our Web site.	더 많은 정보를 원하시면, 저희 웹사이트를 방문하세요.
☐ See our Web site at www.siwonschool.com.	저희 웹사이트 www.siwonschool.com을 확인해 보십시오.
☐ To order, just call our store.	주문하시려면, 저희 매장으로 전화 주십시오.

■ 투어 가이드

☐ We will be arriving shortly at ~	저희는 곧 ~에 도착할 것입니다.
☐ I'm Chris, and I'll be your tour guide.	저는 크리스이며, 여러분의 투어 가이드입니다.
☐ I'll be leading you on today's tour.	제가 오늘 투어에서 여러분을 안내할 것입니다.
☐ I'll show you around this facility.	제가 오늘 이 시설을 견학시켜 드릴 것입니다.
☐ Our tour will last approximately two hours.	저희 투어는 약 2시간 동안 지속될 것입니다.
☐ After lunch, we'll spend the afternoon exploring the History Museum.	점심 식사 후에, 역사 박물관을 답사하며 오후 시간을 보낼 것입니다.
☐ We'll head back to the entrance.	우리는 입구로 돌아갈 것입니다.
☐ This is the last stop on the tour.	이곳이 견학 중의 마지막 방문 장소입니다.
☐ Visitors are not allowed to take pictures of the artwork.	방문객들은 미술품 사진 촬영이 허용되지 않습니다.
☐ There's a brochure next to the information desk.	안내 데스크 옆에 안내 책자가 있습니다.

PRACTICE

음원을 듣고 각 질문에 맞는 답을 고른 뒤, 스크립트를 보면서 빈칸을 채워보세요.

1 What is being advertised?
(A) A highway rest stop 고속도로 휴게소
(B) A vehicle charge station 차량 충전소
(C) An auto-repair shop 자동차 정비소
(D) A new electric-car dealership 새로운 전기 자동차 대리점

2 According to the speaker, what will listeners appreciate most about Horizon Motors?
(A) The speed of charging process 충전 속도
(B) The size of a showroom 전시장의 크기
(C) The free home-charger setup 무료 가정용 충전기 설치
(D) The wide selection of electric-car models 다양한 전기차 모델

3 What does the speaker suggest listeners do online?
(A) Schedule a test drive 시승 예약하기
(B) Browse the virtual showroom 가상 전시장 둘러보기
(C) Sign up for a charging plan 충전 요금제 가입하기
(D) Compare financing option 금융 옵션 비교하기

> Looking to upgrade your daily commute this year? Horizon Motors is _____ _____ in the region, located on Greenway Drive just off the Highway 101. Our vehicles are more than just eco-friendly — they also come with access to fast-charging stations nearby. Not only that, but we believe you'll love _____ _____. Visit our Web site today to browse our virtual showroom. Make your drive greener by choosing Horizon Motors.

정답 및 해설 p.107

실전 TEST

학습한 내용을 적용하여 다음 기출 변형 문제들을 풀어보세요.

> **PART 4 실전 문제 풀이 지침**
> 1. 담화가 나오기 전에 세 개의 문제를 빠르게 읽고 핵심을 파악합니다. 이때 키워드에 동그라미를 쳐 둡니다.
> 2. 미리 읽은 문제와 관련된 내용을 노려 듣습니다.
> 3. 정답을 찾으면 문제지에 바로 체크하고 다음 문제를 읽습니다. 답안지 마킹은 나중에 한꺼번에 해도 됩니다.

1 What is being advertised?

(A) A data storage service
(B) An anti-virus program
(C) A home security device
(D) A computer repair shop

2 What has the business received an award for?

(A) Its exchange policies
(B) Its creative designs
(C) Its customer service
(D) Its competitive prices

3 What offer does the speaker mention?

(A) A product catalog
(B) A free trial opportunity
(C) A membership upgrade
(D) A monthly newsletter

4 Where is the tour most likely taking place?

(A) At a museum
(B) At a grocery store
(C) At a shopping mall
(D) At a production plant

5 What does the speaker say has changed about the tour?

(A) The cost
(B) The tour guide
(C) The duration
(D) The location

6 What does the speaker offer the listeners?

(A) A gift voucher
(B) A free shipping code
(C) A special discount
(D) A product sample

7 Who most likely are the listeners?

(A) Historical researchers
(B) Town officials
(C) Market vendors
(D) Tour group members

Sunshine Tours	
Tour Package	Duration
Traveler	5 days
Voyager	1 week
Explorer	2 weeks
Pioneer	1 month

8 What does the speaker imply when she says, "That's why I'm here"?

(A) She is asking the listeners to stay in a group.
(B) She is happy to answer the listeners' questions.
(C) She is encouraging the listeners to follow her.
(D) She hopes the listeners will stop by again in the future.

10 What is the main purpose of the advertisement?

(A) To seek volunteers
(B) To describe a resort facility
(C) To promote a travel company
(D) To describe overseas attractions

9 According to the speaker, why is there a delay?

(A) The weather is bad.
(B) A restaurant is overbooked.
(C) A street is closed to visitors.
(D) Some people haven't arrived yet.

11 What does the speaker mention about children?

(A) They must be old enough to participate.
(B) They will get a special coupon.
(C) They require adult supervision.
(D) They can enjoy several activities.

12 Look at the graphic. Which tour package is on sale?

(A) Traveler
(B) Voyager
(C) Explorer
(D) Pioneer

실전 TEST

학습한 내용을 적용하여 다음 기출 변형 문제들을 풀어보세요.

13 Where is the tour taking place?

(A) At a zoo
(B) At a farm
(C) In an aquarium
(D) On a hiking trail

14 What does the speaker say was recently completed?

(A) A building renovation
(B) A fencing installation
(C) An equipment upgrade
(D) A program implementation

15 What does the speaker encourage the listeners to do?

(A) Take pictures
(B) Remain silent
(C) Put on a hat
(D) Observe a space

16 According to the speaker, how is a product environmentally friendly?

(A) It does not use any packaging.
(B) It is made from recycled materials.
(C) It reduces energy consumption levels.
(D) It uses less water to manufacture.

17 How does an extra layer of security help clothing?

(A) By preventing damage
(B) By reducing discoloration
(C) By improving fragrance
(D) By saving space

18 What does the speaker say can be claimed on a Web site?

(A) A gift card
(B) A discount code
(C) A sample product
(D) A free membership

19 What is the class mainly about?

(A) Sewing clothes
(B) Making collages
(C) Watercolor painting
(D) Paper dyeing

Travis Park
Spartan Library
Cumberland District
Heritage District
Lakewood District
Ponderosa District
Remington Pond
Baylands Park

20 What is different about today's class?

(A) It will feature a guest speaker.
(B) It will include a written assignment.
(C) It will take place outside at a park.
(D) It will require partner work for some.

22 What type of service is being advertised?

(A) Catering
(B) Food delivery
(C) Car rental
(D) Package shipping

21 What will the speaker do next?

(A) Set up a presentation
(B) Distribute some supplies
(C) Show some artwork examples
(D) Choose an object for students

23 According to the speaker, how can the listeners use a new service?

(A) By submitting an online form
(B) By sending a text message
(C) By installing a mobile app
(D) By visiting a city Web site

24 Look at the graphic. In which of the following locations can the listeners receive a discount?

(A) Travis Park
(B) Spartan Library
(C) Remington Pond
(D) Baylands Park

PART 4 FINAL TEST

학습한 내용을 적용하여 다음 기출 변형 문제들을 풀어보세요.

1. Where most likely is the speaker?
   (A) At a manufacturing plant
   (B) At a construction site
   (C) On a cargo ship
   (D) At a delivery center

2. Why does the speaker recognize a team?
   (A) The team established a beneficial partnership.
   (B) The team reduced operating expenditure.
   (C) The city granted a permit.
   (D) The manager has been promoted.

3. What are the listeners required to do?
   (A) Read an e-mail
   (B) Look over some designs
   (C) Vote on a name
   (D) Sign-in to a Web site

4. What are the listeners invited to do?
   (A) Meet an artist
   (B) Visit a studio
   (C) Ask a question
   (D) Make a submission

5. What guideline does the speaker emphasize?
   (A) Providing specific details
   (B) Talking slowly
   (C) Including a phone number
   (D) Registering online

6. According to the speaker, what may happen during a broadcast?
   (A) A sponsored product will be advertised.
   (B) An audio recording will be used.
   (C) A special guest will be interviewed.
   (D) A new song will be played.

7 What kind of event is taking place?

(A) An arts-and-crafts fair
(B) A community contest
(C) A musical performance
(D) A local festival

8 Why did a company make a change?

(A) To meet some city regulations
(B) To promote its services
(C) To support community members
(D) To upgrade its brand image

9 Why should the listeners speak to an associate?

(A) To sign a form
(B) To receive a suggestion
(C) To find a seat
(D) To borrow an item

10 What does the speaker say he does for a living?

(A) He coordinates events.
(B) He oversees a business.
(C) He performs live music.
(D) He interviews job candidates.

11 What does the speaker imply when he says, "we had to improvise"?

(A) An audience was very disappointed.
(B) He tried to call an expert for help.
(C) There was a communication error.
(D) He forgot to reiterate a company policy.

12 What will the listeners most likely hear next?

(A) An expert analysis
(B) A news report
(C) A review
(D) A commercial

PART 4 — FINAL TEST

학습한 내용을 적용하여 다음 기출 변형 문제들을 풀어보세요.

13 Why has a tour been delayed?
(A) A trail is being cleared.
(B) There was a scheduling error.
(C) Some visitors forgot their equipment.
(D) A previous tour is ending late.

14 What are the listeners reminded to do?
(A) Fill their water bottles
(B) Wear sun protection
(C) Buy some food
(D) Explore a visitor center

15 What will a guide talk about first?
(A) The hike's duration
(B) Native plant life
(C) Stories about a tower
(D) A popular scenic viewpoint

16 What does the speaker's company sell?
(A) Blankets
(B) Flowers
(C) Carpets
(D) Curtains

17 What does the speaker praise about the listener's team?
(A) Their emphasis on practicality
(B) Their attention to detail
(C) Their unique approach
(D) Their sense of responsibility

18 Why does the speaker say, "many customers don't tend to prefer them"?
(A) The quality of a product is lacking.
(B) Consumer trends have been changing.
(C) A design will likely not be used.
(D) A survey has revealed surprising results.

19 Who is Vanessa Kim?

(A) A mechanic
(B) An artist
(C) A journalist
(D) A designer

20 What is the focus of today's podcast episode?

(A) Book publishing
(B) Home improvement
(C) Printing machines
(D) Virtual assistants

21 What does the speaker alert the listeners to?

(A) New visual content
(B) Exclusive merchandise
(C) A subscription program
(D) A job opportunity

```
┌─────────────┬──────────┬──────────┐
│             │ Sculptures│          │
│             ├──────────┤   Side   │
│  Oil paintings         │  Entrance│
│             ├──────────┼──────────┤
│             │          │ Portraits│
│  Ceramics   │          │          │
│             │          │          │
└─────────────┴──────────┴──────────┘
              Front Entrance
```

22 Why is the meeting taking place?

(A) To discuss an event venue
(B) To improve visitor numbers
(C) To honor some artists
(D) To update a shift schedule

23 Look at the graphic. Which art pieces will be moved on Sunday?

(A) Oil paintings
(B) Ceramics
(C) Sculptures
(D) Portraits

24 What does the speaker say he will do?

(A) Contact a restaurant
(B) Provide extra compensation
(C) Send out an invitation
(D) Cover meal expenses

기본토익 700+

PART 5

DAY 01 명사	**DAY 06** 분사
DAY 02 대명사	**DAY 07** 형용사 / 부사
DAY 03 동사의 종류 및 시제	**DAY 08** 접속사
DAY 04 동사의 특성	**DAY 09** 전치사
DAY 05 동명사 / to부정사	**DAY 10** 관계사
PART 5 FINAL TEST (1)	**PART 5 FINAL TEST (2)**

PART 5 단문 빈칸 채우기 문제 미리보기

- 문항수: 30문항 (101번~130번)
- 한 문장의 빈칸에 알맞은 단어나 표현을 고르는 유형입니다.
- 문법 문제와 어휘 문제가 섞여 나오는데, 출제 비중은 대략 문법 60%, 어휘 40% 정도입니다.
- 문제 당 권장 풀이 시간이 20초 정도로 매우 짧기 때문에 일일이 해석해서 풀 수 없으므로, 해석이 필요없는 문법 문제들은 단서만 가지고 최대한 빠르게 처리하도록 합니다.

📄 문법 문제

101. Ms. Brown requests that weekly reports ------- submitted to her no later than 4 P.M. each Friday.

(A) having been
(B) be ✓
(C) being
(D) were

📄 어휘 문제

102. To attract more people to join Glow Fitness Center, memberships are ------- by 50 percent this month.

(A) selected
(B) expected
(C) discounted ✓
(D) taken

DAY 01 | 명사 Part 5

명사는 영어 문장을 구성하는 기본 요소로서, 토익에서 매회 4문제 정도 출제되는 중요한 유형입니다. 명사 문제는 선택지의 여러 품사 중에서 명사를 고르는 유형과 두 개 이상의 명사 중에서 알맞은 명사 하나를 고르는 유형으로 출제됩니다.

1 명사의 기본 위치

토익에서 빈칸이 명사 자리라는 것을 알려주는 가장 중요한 단서는 관사, 소유격, 형용사, 전치사, 그리고 타동사입니다.

■ 정관사(the), 부정관사(a, an), 소유격(my, your, his, her, their, 명사's 등) 뒤

The **extension** of the deadline relieved much of the pressure on the design team.
마감 기한의 연장이 디자인 팀의 부담을 크게 덜어주었다.

Mr. Rogan announced his **retirement** after 20 years of service.
로건 씨는 20년 간 재직한 후에 자신의 퇴직을 발표했다.

■ 형용사 뒤

The new restaurant in the downtown area has a wide **selection** of dishes.
시내 구역에 새로 생긴 식당은 다양한 종류의 요리들을 제공한다.

■ 전치사의 앞 또는 뒤

전치사의 기본 기능은 명사와 명사를 연결하는 것입니다.

Completion of the expansion project will take about a month.
확장 프로젝트의 완료는 약 한 달이 걸릴 것이다.

■ 타동사의 뒤

By making a presentation at the convention, we can attract **investors**.
컨벤션에서 발표를 함으로써, 우리는 투자자들을 끌어들일 수 있습니다.

PRACTICE 빈칸에 알맞은 단어를 고르세요.

1. Please show this e-mail as proof of your [reserve / reservation] upon arrival at the hotel.
2. We will add a large [select / selection] of new flavors this month.

2 수 일치 및 동사와 어울리는 명사 정답 고르기

빈칸 앞에 위치한 부정관사나 수량 형용사와의 수 일치를 확인하거나 명사와 가장 연관성이 높은 동사를 해석하여 알맞은 명사를 정답으로 골라야 합니다.

■ 부정관사(a, an) + 단수 가산명사

A new date has been proposed as an [**alternative** / alternatives] to canceling the meeting.
회의를 취소하는 것에 대한 대안으로 새로운 날짜가 제안되었다.

■ 부정관사 없음 + 복수 가산명사 / 불가산명사

[**Participants** / Participant] will receive free gifts on a first-come, first-served basis.
참석자들은 선착순으로 무료 선물을 받을 것입니다.

[**Attendance** / Attendee] at the music festival has reached five thousand this year.
음악축제 참가자 수가 올해 5천 명에 달했습니다.

■ 복수형용사(many, several, all, a few) + 복수 가산명사

Many [survey / **surveys**] have indicated that our new product is a great success.
많은 설문 조사가 우리 신제품이 엄청난 성공작임을 보여주었다.

■ 양을 나타내는 형용사(much, little) + 불가산명사

Our new advertising campaign has attracted much [**interest** / interests].
우리의 새 광고 캠페인이 많은 관심을 일으켰다.

■ 가산명사와 불가산명사

동사의 의미와 호응하는 의미의 가산명사 또는 불가산명사가 주어 자리에 쓰여야 합니다.

The final [performer / **performance**] will take place at the Gerard Hume Stadium.
마지막 공연이 제라드 흄 경기장에서 개최될 것이다.

PRACTICE 빈칸에 알맞은 단어를 고르세요.

3 We will review all [applications / application] before we choose one that is best qualified.
4 [Patrons / Patronage] of the Ron's Cafe are asked to register for further discounts.

3 복합명사

일반적으로 형용사가 명사 앞에 위치해 명사를 수식하지만, 이 형용사 자리에 명사가 사용될 수도 있습니다. 즉, 「명사 + 명사」 구조에서 앞에 위치하는 명사가 형용사와 같은 역할을 합니다.

■ 하나의 명사를 선택하는 경우

주로 뒤의 명사를 선택하는 유형으로 출제됩니다. 빈칸 앞에 명사가 존재하는 구조이지만, 이 명사가 주변의 형용사나 동사 등과 의미 연결이 되지 않으므로 빈칸에 또 다른 명사가 추가로 필요합니다.

- travel arrangements 여행 준비
- sales representative 영업 사원
- product distribution 상품 유통
- employee safety 직원 안전
- photo identification 사진 신분증
- customer/client satisfaction 고객 만족
- customer suggestions 고객 제안
- design presentation 디자인 발표
- pay increase 급여 인상
- retail sales 소매 판매
- retirement celebrations 은퇴 기념식
- budget flight 저가 항공편

> 행위를 할 수 없는 명사이므로
> 동사 received의 주어가 될 수 없음

All sales representatives received a 10 % bonus for outstanding performance.
모든 영업사원들이 뛰어난 성과에 대해 10퍼센트의 보너스를 받았다.

> 단수 가산명사이지만 부정관사 없이 쓰여 있으므로
> customer가 take의 목적어가 될 수 없음

Randy's Organic Foods always take customer satisfaction seriously.
랜디즈 오가닉 푸드는 항상 고객 만족을 중요하게 생각합니다.

■ 두 개의 명사들 중 택일하는 경우

선택지에 두 개의 명사가 있다면 수 일치 또는 동사와의 의미 연결을 통해 정답을 선택합니다.

수 일치 확인	오답	동사와 의미 연결 확인	오답
all client concerns 모든 고객 우려들 a ticketing system 발권 시스템 retail sales 소매 판매 toy manufacturers 장난감 제조사들	concern systems sale manufacturer	contract negotiations 계약 협상 state regulations 주 규정 sales representative 영업사원 installation instructions 설치 안내	negotiator regulator representation instructors

Mr. Hobbs handles the product [distributor / **distribution**] in the company.
홉스 씨는 회사에서 제품 유통을 담당합니다.

> 동사 handle이 사물이나 일을 다룬다는 의미이므로
> 행위명사인 distribution이 정답

PRACTICE 빈칸에 알맞은 단어를 고르세요.

5 Our senior market [analysis / analyst] will visit your office tomorrow afternoon.

6 Effective contract [negotiators / negotiations] require strong communication skills and a deep understanding of legal terms.

4 헷갈리는 명사 형태

다음 명사들은 다른 품사로 착각하기 쉬운 형태들입니다. 빠르게 정답을 선택해야 하는 압박감에 순간적으로 착각하기 쉬우므로 매우 주의해야 합니다.

■ 분사로 착각하기 쉬운 -ing 명사

> 학위(degree)와 어울리는 분야를 나타내는 명사가 필요

All applicants for this position should hold a degree in [**accounting** / accountant].
이 직책에 대한 모든 지원자들은 회계학 학위를 소지하고 있어야 합니다.

토익 빈출 -ing 명사
- accounting 회계
- advertising 광고
- cleaning 청소
- opening 공석

■ 형용사로 착각하기 쉬운 -al 명사

> 타동사 receive 뒤에는 목적어가 필요

Employees should receive **approval** from their supervisor to stay late in the office.
직원들은 늦게 사무실에 남아 있으려면 소속 부서장의 승인을 받아야 합니다.

토익 빈출 -al 명사
- approval 승인
- potential 잠재력
- referral 추천, 소개
- renewal 갱신, 개선
- arrival 도착
- proposal 제안(서)
- removal 제거
- rental 대여

■ 형용사로 착각하기 쉬운 -tive 명사

> 부정관사 뒤에는 단수명사가 필요

A new proposal was submitted as an [**alternative** / alternatives] to the previous one.
이전의 것에 대한 대안으로 새로운 제안서가 제출되었다.

토익 빈출 -tive 명사
- alternative 대안
- objective 목표
- perspective 관점
- initiative 계획
- representative 직원

PRACTICE 빈칸에 알맞은 단어를 고르세요.

7. Before submitting a business [proposal / proposing], it's essential to conduct thorough market research.

8. The university launched a recent [initiation / initiative] to support students in developing entrepreneurial skills.

실전 TEST

학습한 내용을 적용하여 다음 기출 변형 문제들을 풀어보세요.

1. A comprehensive ------- was conducted by the marketing department last week.
   (A) survey
   (B) surveys
   (C) surveyed
   (D) surveying

2. We have received a number of ------- about the recent software upgrade.
   (A) complaint
   (B) complaints
   (C) complain
   (D) complains

3. To increase employee ------- in the office, Devona Motors has implemented a staff incentive program.
   (A) productively
   (B) productive
   (C) products
   (D) productivity

4. The architect applied for a building ------- to start the construction project.
   (A) permit
   (B) permits
   (C) permission
   (D) permitted

5. Mr. Hart is hopeful that the ------- with Billman Engineering's executives will be mutually beneficial.
   (A) discuss
   (B) discussions
   (C) discussed
   (D) discussing

6. If your order is damaged during shipping, please call 555-8698 for customer -------.
   (A) supported
   (B) supportive
   (C) support
   (D) supporting

7. Josef was delighted to hear that one of his ------- will be on display at Metropolitan Art Gallery.
   (A) painted
   (B) painting
   (C) painters
   (D) paintings

8. After two months of -------, Stafford Park has been reopened to the public.
   (A) renovative
   (B) renovate
   (C) renovation
   (D) renovated

9. Customers interested in renewing ------- for any of our premium channels should speak with Mr. Harding at 555-2376.
   (A) subscribe
   (B) subscribes
   (C) subscribers
   (D) subscriptions

10. Anyone seeking physiotherapy treatment must obtain a ------- from their local doctor.
    (A) referring
    (B) referred
    (C) referral
    (D) refer

11 After careful review, the ------- of Ms. Goldburg's candidacy will be announced tomorrow.

(A) validities
(B) validity
(C) validate
(D) valid

12 Routine ------- is critical to preventing equipment failure and ensuring workplace safety.

(A) maintain
(B) maintenance
(C) maintaining
(D) maintained

13 All travel -------- must comply with the company's expense policy.

(A) arrangement
(B) arrangements
(C) arranged
(D) arranging

14 In response to the supply shortage, the procurement ------- streamlined our list of approved vendors.

(A) initiate
(B) initiated
(C) initiator
(D) initiative

15 Due to increasing customer demand, Elara Footwear is planning a major ------- of its production facilities next year.

(A) expand
(B) expanding
(C) expansive
(D) expansion

16 Please direct all technical questions to the IT ------- at Corelight Systems, who can resolve access issue.

(A) specialist
(B) specialty
(C) special
(D) specialization

17 The CEO's speech was met with enthusiastic ------- from the staff gathered in the main auditorium of Ventrix Global.

(A) approve
(B) approving
(C) approval
(D) approved

18 Giant Tech recently employed many ------ who specialized in cybersecurity.

(A) develop
(B) developer
(C) developers
(D) developments

19 Mr. Hino's years of ------- in logistics made him the ideal candidate for the role at Rapidhaul Freight Services.

(A) experienced
(B) experience
(C) experiencing
(D) experiences

20 Neptune Technologies will conduct a thorough ------- of the security system before approving the new protocols.

(A) analyst
(B) analyze
(C) analysis
(D) analytical

DAY 02 | 대명사 Part 5

대명사는 앞서 언급된 명사의 반복을 피하기 위해 사용하는 품사이며 토익에서 매월 2-3문제 정도 꾸준히 출제되고 있습니다. 대명사가 가리키는 대상의 수일치(단수/복수), 그리고 문장 내 빈칸에 알맞은 대명사의 '격'을 묻는 문제가 주로 출제됩니다.

1 인칭대명사

사람 또는 사물을 대신해서 사용하는 대명사입니다. 역할에 따라 주격, 소유격, 목적격으로 나뉘고, 「~의 것」을 의미하는 소유대명사와 자기 자신을 가리키는 재귀대명사가 있습니다.

	인칭	주격	소유격	목적격	소유대명사	재귀대명사
단수	1	I	my	me	mine	myself
	2	you	your	you	yours	yourself
	3	she	her	her	hers	herself
		he	his	him	his	himself
		it	its	it	-	itself
복수	1	we	our	us	ours	ourselves
	2	you	your	you	yours	yourselves
	3	they	their	them	theirs	themselves

■ **주격: 주어 자리**

주격은 주어 자리에서 동사의 행위자를 나타내므로, 인칭대명사를 고르는 문제에서 동사 앞에 빈칸이 있다면 주격이 정답입니다.

Before making a reservation, **you** should check the schedule first.
예약하기 전에, 일정을 먼저 확인하셔야 합니다.

■ **소유격: 명사 앞 /「own + 명사」 앞**

소유격은 명사 앞에서 소유자를 나타내므로, 인칭대명사를 고르는 문제에서 명사 또는 「own + 명사」 앞에 빈칸이 있다면 소유격이 정답입니다.

After years of research, Dr. Han finally published **his** findings in a renowned journal.
수년간의 연구 끝에, 한 박사는 마침내 자신의 연구 결과를 저명한 학술지에 발표했다.

「on + 소유격 + own」으로 '혼자, 스스로'라는 의미를 나타내는 부사로 출제되기도 합니다.

Mr. Franklin had to handle all the customer complaints **on his own**.
프랭클린 씨는 모든 고객 불만 사항을 스스로 처리해야 했다.

■ 목적격: 타동사 또는 전치사의 목적어 자리

→ 타동사 introduce의 목적어 자리

If you meet the new intern today, don't forget to introduce **him** to the team.
만약 오늘 새로운 인턴을 만난다면, 그를 팀에 소개하는 것을 잊지 마세요.

→ 전치사 to의 목적어 자리

The company offered a promotion to **him** after years of dedicated service.
그 회사는 수년간의 헌신적인 근무 후에 그에게 승진을 제안했다.

■ 소유대명사: 명사 자리

소유대명사는 「소유격 + 앞에 언급된 명사」를 나타내며, 같은 단어의 반복을 피하기 위해 명사를 생략한 형태입니다.

→ = your business

We specialize in supporting businesses like **yours** and help them attract qualified candidates.
저희는 귀사와 같은 기업을 전문적으로 지원하며, 자격을 갖춘 인재를 유치할 수 있도록 돕습니다.

■ 목적어 역할을 하는 재귀대명사

주어와 목적어가 동일할 경우, 목적어 자리에는 재귀대명사(-self 또는 -selves)를 사용합니다.

She taught **herself** how to play the piano by watching online tutorials.
그녀는 온라인 강의를 보고 혼자서 피아노를 연주하는 법을 배웠다.

■ 부사 역할을 하는 재귀대명사

부사로 쓰이는 재귀대명사는 「직접, 스스로」라고 해석하며, 주로 주어 바로 뒤 또는 문장 맨 끝에 위치합니다. 인칭대명사를 고르는 문제에서 빈칸을 제외하고 문장의 구성 요소가 모두 갖춰진 완전한 문장일 때 재귀대명사를 고르면 됩니다.

→ 주어, 동사, 목적어로 구성된 완전한 문장이므로 그 뒤는 재귀대명사 자리

She booked the entire trip **herself** without using a travel agency.
그녀는 여행사를 이용하지 않고 직접 여행 전체를 예약했다.

■ 전치사의 목적어 역할을 하는 재귀대명사

재귀대명사는 명사 또는 목적격 대명사처럼 전치사의 목적어로 사용될 수 있으며, 토익에서는 주로 전치사 by, for 또는 among과 함께 출제됩니다.

The students organized the event by **themselves** without any help from the faculty.
학생들은 교수진의 도움 없이 스스로 행사를 준비했다.

PRACTICE 빈칸에 알맞은 단어를 고르세요.

1   Professor Langley is known for [her / hers] groundbreaking research in neuroscience.
2   Despite the risk, Daniel repaired the electrical wiring [him / himself] late at night.

2 지시대명사

지시대명사는 가리키는 대상의 수와 거리에 따라 다르게 사용되는 대명사입니다. 가까이 있는 사람이나 사물 하나를 가리킬 때는 this, 가까이 있는 여럿을 가리킬 때는 these를 사용합니다. 멀리 있는 사람이나 사물 하나를 가리킬 때는 that, 멀리 있는 여럿을 가리킬 때는 those를 사용합니다.

■ 지시대명사

토익에서 지시대명사는 주로 복수형인 these와 those가 출제되며, 단수형은 거의 출제되지 않습니다. 토익에서 this는 주로 지시형용사 또는 강조부사(이렇게, 이만큼)로 출제되며, that은 명사절 접속사와 관계대명사 관련 문제로 출제되기 때문입니다.

▶ 복수명사인 mobile devices를 대신함

We will focus on mobile devices as **these** are very popular on the market today.
저희는 모바일 기기에 집중할 것인데, 이것들이 요즘 시장에서 매우 인기가 있기 때문입니다.

토익에서 지시대명사 those는 사람들(= people)을 가리키는 부정대명사로 많이 출제됩니다. 주로 those 뒤에 who절, 형용사구, 분사구, 전치사구 등의 수식어구가 동반됩니다.

▶ ~하는 사람들

Those who arrive early will receive a complimentary welcome drink at the venue.
일찍 도착하는 분들은 행사장에서 환영 음료를 무료로 받게 됩니다.

▶ ~을 가진 사람들

Only **those** with valid security clearance may enter the restricted area.
유효한 보안 인증을 가진 사람들만 제한 구역에 들어갈 수 있습니다.

▶ ~인 사람들

Those interested in the marketing class should contact Mr. Madison for more information.
마케팅 수업에 관심 있으신 분들은 더 많은 정보를 얻으시려면 매디슨 씨에게 연락하셔야 합니다.

■ 지시형용사

지시대명사들은 같은 의미를 가지면서 명사를 수식하는 역할을 하는 형용사로도 사용될 수 있는데, 이것을 지시형용사라고 합니다. 토익에서는 지시형용사 출제 빈도가 지시대명사보다 높은 편입니다.

Please review **these** documents carefully before signing the agreement.
이 계약서에 서명하기 전에 이 문서들을 꼼꼼히 검토해 주세요.

PRACTICE 빈칸에 알맞은 단어를 고르세요.

3 The company offers remote work options for [that / those] who prefer flexible schedules.

4 The employee lounge on the 4th floor will be temporarily inaccessible [this / that] week.

3 부정대명사

     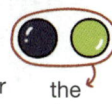

We have two types of security alarms, one for home use and **the other** for office use.
저희는 두 가지 유형의 보안 알람을 보유하고 있는데, 하나는 가정용이고 나머지 하나는 사무실용입니다.

Some like Mr. Amaron's enthusiastic personality, while **others** find him too loud.
어떤 사람들은 아마론 씨의 열정적인 성격을 좋아하는 반면, 다른 사람들은 그가 너무 시끄럽다고 생각한다.

4 수량대명사 및 기타 대명사

■ 복수대명사(Some, Most, All, Several, Many, None) + of the 복수명사 + 복수동사

During the hike, **some** of the tourists decided to take an alternate trail.
하이킹 중에 관광객들 중 일부는 다른 경로를 선택했다.

■ 불가산대명사(Little, Most, All) + (of the 불가산명사) + 단수동사

Most of the time was spent introducing Dext Technology's new device.
대부분의 시간이 덱스트 테크놀로지의 새로운 기기를 소개하는 데 쓰였다.

■ one another: 서로

The members of the orchestra listened to **one another** carefully to stay in harmony.
오케스트라 단원들은 조화를 이루기 위해 서로의 연주를 주의 깊게 들었다.

■ each other: 서로, 협력하여

The dancers relied on **each other** to maintain perfect timing during the performance.
공연 중에 무용수들은 완벽한 타이밍을 유지하기 위해 서로에게 의지했다.

PRACTICE 빈칸에 알맞은 단어를 고르세요.

5 Some employees prefer to work independently, while [another / others] thrive in collaborative environments.

6 [Some / Little] of the applicants forgot to submit their portfolios before the deadline.

실전 TEST

학습한 내용을 적용하여 다음 기출 변형 문제들을 풀어보세요.

1. In addition to ------- ability to communicate with others, Mr. Moore's skill at planning is also remarkable.
   (A) his
   (B) him
   (C) he
   (D) himself

2. If you are looking for Ms. Kite, you can find ------- in the accounting office.
   (A) she
   (B) hers
   (C) her
   (D) herself

3. Unlike other department supervisors, Ms. Trasker would prefer to complete the monthly work schedule -------.
   (A) hers
   (B) her
   (C) herself
   (D) her own

4. All new class members receive an information package in order to familiarize ------- with the course curriculum.
   (A) itself
   (B) yourself
   (C) ourselves
   (D) themselves

5. ------- who are interested in attending the seminar should contact their managers before 6 P.M.
   (A) There
   (B) They
   (C) Which
   (D) Those

6. Ascot Bank's Main Street and Harp Road locations will remain open on Christmas Eve, as ------- branches have customer service departments.
   (A) whose   (B) theirs
   (C) these   (D) ours

7. ------- of the employees who attended the industrial engineering conference felt that it was helpful.
   (A) None
   (B) Whoever
   (C) Anyone
   (D) Nobody

8. The company will reserve one business class flight ticket for Ms. Dobson and ------- for Mr. Salman.
   (A) those
   (B) others
   (C) another
   (D) the others

9. Because all of her assistants were on vacation, Ms. Clarkson had to revise the budget report by -------.
   (A) she
   (B) herself
   (C) hers
   (D) her

10. Job applicants should take the job proficiency test on ------- within the time allocated.
    (A) they
    (B) their own
    (C) them
    (D) themselves

11 Mr. Rawlins offered to handle the negotiations ------- rather than assign the task to a less experienced colleague.

(A) him
(B) himself
(C) he
(D) his

12 In the language exchange program, participants helped ------- improve their speaking skills.

(A) one another
(B) each
(C) its own
(D) other

13 The customer support staff should resolve minor issues ------- without escalating them to the management team.

(A) them
(B) themselves
(C) theirs
(D) they

14 We asked five consultants to review the design, but ------- of them offered useful feedback.

(A) any
(B) none
(C) both
(D) someone

15 Please ensure that ------- of the online training courses are uploaded to the company portal before Friday.

(A) every
(B) much
(C) all
(D) each

16 Ms. Ortega instructed the interns to submit the completed designs directly to ------- before the end of the day.

(A) she
(B) her
(C) hers
(D) herself

17 Although the prototype design still contains several flaws, ------- impressed everyone who attended the demonstration session.

(A) it
(B) they
(C) that
(D) those

18. Mr. Clarke's new regional office in Calgary is much smaller than ------- here in Edmonton.

(A) us
(B) ours
(C) our
(D) we

19. Mr. Lew is aware that the final draft is due today, as we already sent ------- a message about it this morning.

(A) he
(B) him
(C) his
(D) himself

20 Employees at Moo Dairy Inc. were asked to evaluate their performance as well as that of ------- colleagues.

(A) their
(B) theirs
(C) them
(D) they

DAY 03 | 동사의 종류 및 시제 Part 5

토익에서 동사는 목적어를 가지지 않는 자동사와 목적어를 반드시 가져야 하는 타동사를 구분하는 문제, 그리고 시점 표현을 보고 빈칸에 들어갈 동사의 시제를 고르는 문제가 출제됩니다.

1 동사의 종류

■ 2형식 자동사

아래와 같은 2형식 자동사 뒤에는 보어(주격보어)가 위치합니다. 보어는 주어에 대한 설명으로서 형용사 또는 명사가 쓰일 수 있지만, 토익에서는 주격보어 자리에 주로 형용사가 출제됩니다. 명사가 주격보어로 사용될 경우, 이 명사는 주어와 동격 관계가 되어야 하므로 주격보어를 고를 때 이 관계를 꼭 확인해야 합니다.

> **토익 빈출 2형식 자동사**
> - be ~이다
> - become ~이 되다
> - remain 계속 ~한 상태이다
> - seem ~처럼 보이다
> - appear ~처럼 보이다
> - sound ~처럼 들리다
> - prove ~한 것으로 판명되다

▶ 주어 The Dawson Bridge의 상태를 설명하는 형용사 보어

The Dawson Bridge will **remain** closed until Saturday for urgent repairs.
도슨 다리는 긴급 수리를 위해 토요일까지 폐쇄된 상태로 있을 것이다.

▶ 주어 this intern = 보어 a valuable asset

With enough training, this intern could **become** a valuable asset to the company.
충분한 훈련으로, 이 인턴은 회사에 귀중한 인재가 될 수도 있습니다.

■ 3형식 타동사와 목적어

• **자동사와 타동사의 구분**

3형식 타동사는 뒤에 반드시 하나의 목적어를 가져야 합니다. 그래서 주로 목적어를 가질 수 없는 자동사와 구분하는 유형으로 출제되므로 둘을 구분하는 연습을 미리 해 두는 것이 좋습니다.

▶ 자동사 arrive는 목적어를 가질 수 없으므로 오답

All participants must [**reach** / arrive] the training center no later than 8:45 A.M.
모든 참가자는 오전 8시 45분까지 교육 센터에 도착해야 한다.

> **타동사로 혼동하기 쉬운 토익 빈출 1형식 자동사**
>
> - **expire** 만료되다
> - **proceed** 진행하다
> - **differ from** ~와 다르다
> - **participate in** ~에 참여하다
> - **result in** ~의 결과를 낳다
> - **belong to** ~에 속하다
> - **respond to** ~에 응답하다, ~에 대응하다
> - **reply to** ~에게 답장하다
> - **communicate with** ~와 의사소통하다
> - **comply with** ~을 준수하다
>
> * 자동사는 목적어를 가질 수 없으므로 대부분 in, from, to, with 등과 같은 전치사와 함께 쓰고, 그 뒤에 목적어가 위치하는 형태로 쓰입니다.

• 3형식 타동사의 목적어 자리

3형식 타동사의 목적어 자리에는 명사, 대명사, 동명사, to부정사, 명사절이 올 수 있는데, 이 중에서 가장 많이 출제되는 것은 that 명사절을 목적어로 취하는 동사를 선택하는 유형입니다.

▶ 자동사 comply는 명사 목적어가 바로 올 수 없으므로 오답

To ensure safety, please [comply / **follow**] all posted guidelines while using the laboratory equipment.
안전을 위해 실험 장비 사용 시 게시된 모든 지침을 준수해 주세요.

▶ 타동사 suggest는 동명사를 목적어로 가지므로 오답

We suggested [host / **hosting**] a charity event during the holiday season.
우리는 휴가철에 자선 행사를 개최하는 것을 제안했다.

▶ 타동사 plan은 to부정사를 목적어로 가지므로 오답

The IT department plans [upgrade / **to upgrade**] the security system over the weekend.
IT 부서는 이번 주말 동안 보안 시스템을 업그레이드할 계획이다.

▶ 동사 encourage는 that절을 목적어로 취하지 않으므로 오답

The marketing team [**announced** / encouraged] that the new campaign would launch in early May.
마케팅팀은 새 캠페인이 5월 초에 시작될 예정이라고 발표했다.

The quarterly report from Orion Motors [**indicates** / represents] that production costs have decreased due to automation.
오리온 모터스의 분기 보고서는 자동화로 인해 생산 비용이 감소했음을 나타냅니다.

PRACTICE 빈칸에 알맞은 단어를 고르세요.

1. All staff members must [comply / observe] with the updated workplace safety regulations.
2. The technician proceeded [caution / cautiously] after detecting a possible malfunction in the system.

■ 4형식 타동사와 2개의 목적어

4형식 타동사는 간접목적어와 직접목적어, 즉 2개의 목적어를 가집니다. 간접목적어는 받는 사람을 나타내는 목적어로 '~에게'라고 해석하고, 직접목적어는 사람에게 주어지는 사물을 나타내는 목적어로 '~을/를'이라고 해석합니다. 이러한 동사들은 사람에게 사물을 준다는 의미를 가지고 있기 때문에 수여동사라고 부릅니다.

▶ 수여동사 뒤 간접목적어, 직접목적어 순서로 쓰임

Ms. Patterson **sent** **the client an updated version of the contract** yesterday.
　　　　　　　　간접목적어(~에게)　　　　직접목적어(~을)

패터슨 씨는 어제 고객에게 계약서 최신 버전을 보냈습니다.

토익 빈출 4형식 타동사
- give 주다
- offer 제공하다
- grant 주다
- teach 가르쳐주다
- show 보여주다
- award 수여하다
- send 보내주다
- assign 할당하다
- bring 가져다주다
- lend 빌려주다
- charge 부과하다

수여동사 중에는 직접목적어 자리에 that 명사절이 전달 내용으로 쓰여야 하는 remind(상기시키다), notify(알리다), inform(알리다), assure(확신시키다)과 같은 동사도 있습니다. that 명사절 대신에 「of + 명사(전달내용)」가 쓰이기도 합니다.

▶ 타동사 announce는 사람 목적어를 가지지 않음

We regret to [**inform** / announce] **you that the product you ordered is currently out of stock**.
　　　　　　　　　　　　사람 목적어　　　　　　that + 전달 내용

귀하가 주문하신 제품은 현재 품절 상태임을 알려드리게 되어 유감입니다.

■ 5형식 타동사와 목적보어

5형식 타동사는 동사 뒤에 「목적어 + 목적보어」 구조를 사용합니다. 여기서 목적보어는 목적어를 설명하는 것으로서 명사, 형용사, to부정사, 분사 등이 목적보어로 쓰일 수 있습니다. 목적보어 자리에 명사가 올 경우, 목적어와 명사는 동격 관계를 이뤄야 합니다. 「목적어 + 목적보어」는 「~을 …라고」 또는 「~을 …로」 등과 같이 해석합니다.

The CEO **named** **Ms. Park** **the new director of marketing**.
　　　　　　　　목적어　　　　목적보어(명사)

CEO는 박 씨를 마케팅 부서의 새 책임자로 임명했습니다.

The team **found** **the revised schedule** **more convenient** for everyone.
　　　　　　　목적어　　　　　　목적보어(형용사)

팀은 수정된 일정이 모두에게 더 편리하다고 판단했다.

토익 빈출 5형식 타동사
- make 만들다
- appoint 임명하다
- keep 유지하다
- deem 간주하다
- consider 여기다
- leave ~한 상태로 두다
- find 생각하다
- name 지명하다, 임명하다

■ to부정사를 목적보어로 가지는 5형식 타동사

5형식 타동사의 목적보어 자리에 to부정사가 사용되어 「동사 + 목적어 + to부정사」의 구조로 쓰이는 동사가 있습니다. 「~에게 …하도록 하다」라고 해석하며, 빈칸 뒤에 위치한 「목적어 + to부정사」의 구조를 확인해 이 구조와 어울리는 5형식 타동사를 정답으로 선택하는 문제가 출제됩니다.

「allow + 목적어 + to부정사」: (목적어)가 ~할 수 있도록 허용하다

This software **allows** managers to monitor project progress in real time.
이 소프트웨어는 관리자가 프로젝트 진행 상황을 실시간으로 모니터링할 수 있도록 허용합니다.

「목적어 + to부정사」 구조와 어울리는 토익 빈출 5형식 타동사

- ask 요청하다
- require 요구하다
- recommend 권하다
- advise 조언하다
- allow 허용하다
- enable 할 수 있게 하다
- encourage 권고하다

■ 사역동사

사역동사는 「~에게 …하게 하다」라는 의미로 누군가에게 어떤 행동을 하도록 만드는 동사를 의미합니다. 사역동사로 have, let, make가 자주 출제되며, 「사역동사 + 목적어 + 동사원형」의 구조로 쓰입니다. 또한 help는 준사역동사로, 목적보어 자리에 동사원형과 to부정사 둘 다 쓰일 수 있습니다.

The supervisor **let** the staff **leave** early after the meeting.
회의 후 감독자는 직원들이 일찍 퇴근하는 것을 허락했다.

have의 경우, 「have + 목적어 + 과거분사(p.p.)」의 구조로도 자주 사용됩니다. 위에 설명한 것처럼 목적어 뒤에 동사원형이 쓰일 경우에는 목적어가 동사의 행위 주체이지만, 목적어 뒤에 과거분사가 쓰이면 목적어가 행위를 당하는 대상이 됩니다.

회비(their dues)가 출금되는 대상이므로 수동을 의미하는 과거분사 사용

All members must **have** their dues **withdrawn** by the 5th to maintain active status.
모든 회원은 5일까지 회비가 출금되어야 활동 상태가 유지됩니다.

PRACTICE 빈칸에 알맞은 단어를 고르세요.

3 The company considers flexible work arrangements [benefit / beneficial] to productivity.

4 The company made all employees [attend / to attend] the safety training.

2 동사의 시제: 단순 시제

■ 현재: ~하다, ~한다

현재시제는 과학적인 원리, 변하지 않는 현상, 반복적 행위나 습관 등을 나타낼 때 사용하며, 토익에서는 주로 기업의 활동 또는 사람의 직무, 그리고 단체 규정 등에 현재시제를 사용합니다.

> 반복성을 나타내는 표현

The sales department **usually** **holds** team meetings **every Monday morning**.
영업부는 보통 매주 월요일 오전에 팀 회의를 진행한다.

현재시제와 어울리는 시간 표현
- **frequently** 자주
- **normally** 보통
- **regularly** 정기적으로
- **commonly** 일반적으로, 흔히
- **every** + 시간명사: ~마다
- **typically** 일반적으로
- **generally** 일반적으로
- **occasionally** 가끔
- **routinely** 정기적으로
- **often** 종종, 자주
- **usually** 보통

■ 과거: ~했다

과거시제는 **과거의 특정 시점에 발생한 일 또는 상태**를 나타낼 때 사용합니다. 주로 동사원형 뒤에 「-(e)d」를 붙여 만들고, 불규칙 형태로 과거를 나타내는 동사도 있습니다.

> 과거시간 표현

Green Food Inc. **implemented** new procedures regarding returning goods **last year**.
그린푸드 사는 상품을 반품하는 것에 대한 새로운 절차를 작년에 시행했다.

과거시제와 어울리는 시간 표현
- **last** + 시간명사: 지난 ~에
- **ago** ~ 전에
- **yesterday** 어제
- **recently** 최근에

■ 미래: ~할 것이다

미래시제는 **미래의 특정 시점에 일어날 일을 예측**할 때 사용합니다. 주로 「will + 동사원형」 형태 또는 「will be -ing」 형태의 미래진행시제도 정답으로 출제됩니다. 미래 시점을 나타내는 시간 표현이 단서로 제시됩니다.

> 미래시간 표현

Customer support representatives **will respond** to all inquiries **shortly**.
고객지원 담당자는 곧 모든 문의에 응답할 예정입니다.

미래시제와 어울리는 시간 표현
- **tomorrow** 내일
- **shortly** 곧
- **until[by] the end of this +** 시간명사: 이번 ~까지
- **soon** 곧
- **next** + 시간명사: 다음 ~에

3 동사의 시제: 복합 시제

■ 현재진행: ~하는 중이다, ~하고 있다

화자가 말을 하고 있는 현재 일시적으로 어떤 행위가 진행 중임을 강조하는 현재진행시제는 「am/is/are + -ing」 형태를 지닙니다. 현재 시점을 나타내는 시간 표현이 단서로 제시됩니다.

GreenLine Energy **is launching** a new eco-friendly product line these days.
그린라인 에너지 사는 요즘 친환경 신제품군을 출시하고 있다.

> these days는 현재시점을 기준으로 일시적인 기간에 진행 중임을 의미

현재진행시제와 어울리는 시간 표현
- currently 현재
- (right) now (바로) 지금
- at the moment 지금
- these days 요즘

■ 현재완료: ~했다

「have/has + p.p.」의 형태를 지니는 현재완료시제는 **과거에 시작된 행위가 현재까지 영향을 미치는 경우**를 나타낼 때 사용합니다.

The sales of men's footwear **have increased** continuously over the past five years.
남성 신발 판매량이 지난 5년간 꾸준히 증가했다. [5년 전에 오르기 시작해 계속 증가함]

> 현재완료의 단서인 기간 표현 (5년의 기간)

현재완료시제와 어울리는 시간 표현
- lately 최근에
- just 이제 막
- since 그 이래로
- since + 과거시점: ~ 이래로
- over[for, in, during] the last[past] + 기간: 지난 ~의 동안
- for + 기간: ~ 동안에
- recently 최근에

■ 과거완료: ~했었다

과거완료는 **과거의 한 시점을 기준으로 그보다 더 이전에 발생한 일을 강조**하기 위해 사용하며, 「had + p.p.」로 나타냅니다.

The technician **had inspected** all equipment before the factory reopened.
기술자는 공장이 재개되기 전에 모든 장비를 점검했습니다.

과거완료시제와 어울리는 시간 표현
- Before/By the time + 주어 + 과거시제, 주어 + had p.p.: ~하기 전에/했을 때쯤에, …했었다

PRACTICE 빈칸에 알맞은 단어를 고르세요.

5 The board of directors [holds / will hold] a strategic planning workshop early next quarter.

6 Mr. Swen [is warning / had warned] about potential system failures before the outage occurred.

실전 TEST

학습한 내용을 적용하여 다음 기출 변형 문제들을 풀어보세요.

1. Although Mr. Walsh has been interested in the house on Denham Street, he ------- hesitant to buy it.
   (A) seems
   (B) meets
   (C) applies
   (D) goes

2. All membership cards for Millglen Public Library will ------- valid for two years from the issuing date.
   (A) send
   (B) remain
   (C) achieve
   (D) provide

3. After months of negotiations, Zenistar Inc. has ------- an agreement with Roper & Co.
   (A) reached
   (B) talked
   (C) experienced
   (D) decided

4. NCH Group will ------- several new luxury hotels that are conveniently located near major train stations.
   (A) notice
   (B) invite
   (C) open
   (D) enter

5. The restaurant manager ------- Ms. Ritchie a free meal voucher to apologize for the poor service.
   (A) traveled
   (B) offered
   (C) told
   (D) asked

6. All temporary employees must ------- the head of the personnel department a weekly work report.
   (A) send
   (B) attend
   (C) review
   (D) arrive

7. The marketing team ------- us that the deadline for completing the market survey would be extended by one week.
   (A) required
   (B) announced
   (C) informed
   (D) released

8. The mayor of Riverside ------- all local residents to attend a public hearing at City Hall.
   (A) agreed
   (B) purchased
   (C) discussed
   (D) encouraged

9. Jarrod Inc. develops services to help business owners ------- the changing needs of potential customers.
   (A) apply
   (B) wait
   (C) seem
   (D) meet

10. Please ------- our tour guides know whether you would like more information about certain buildings and landmarks.
    (A) join
    (B) visit
    (C) let
    (D) allow

11. Now that the grounds of the restaurant have been landscaped, most of our diners typically ------- to sit outside on the terrace.
    (A) choose
    (B) chose
    (C) will have chosen
    (D) chooses

12. At yesterday's meeting, the CEO of Bentley Corporation ------- a contract with Dunlevy Catering.
    (A) sign
    (B) will sign
    (C) have signed
    (D) signed

13. The office intranet and access to data files ------- unavailable until tomorrow due to the maintenance work.
    (A) are being
    (B) were
    (C) had been
    (D) will be

14. For those who are allergic to pork, many restaurants ------- more vegetarian menu options in the last ten years.
    (A) will introduce
    (B) have introduced
    (C) will have introduced
    (D) to introduce

15. The salespeople at our branch in Camden reached their monthly target six days earlier than we -------.
    (A) expect
    (B) are expecting
    (C) were expected
    (D) had expected

16. By the time Ms. Rushden began her new management role at headquarters, the personnel team ------- a new office for her.
    (A) prepared
    (B) preparing
    (C) had prepared
    (D) will have prepared

17. We at Global Fitness appreciate that you ------- our weekly yoga classes for the past 18 months.
    (A) enjoyed
    (B) enjoying
    (C) have enjoyed
    (D) had enjoyed

18. Omni Telecom's head office ------- experienced employees to assist new recruits in handling customer complaints for 10 years.
    (A) assigns
    (B) is assigning
    (C) has been assigned
    (D) has assigned

19. Oil prices ------- over the past six months, but they are expected to stabilize towards the end of this year.
    (A) increase
    (B) increasing
    (C) have increased
    (D) will increase

20. Recently, a government committee ------- to make dramatic modifications to the current tax system.
    (A) is created
    (B) will create
    (C) has been created
    (D) is creating

DAY 04 | 동사의 특성 Part 5

영어의 동사는 능동태/수동태의 태와 단수/복수의 수를 일치시켜야 하는데, 토익에서는 태와 수 또는 시제를 복합적으로 확인하는 방식으로 출제됩니다. 예를 들어, 먼저 주어와 수가 일치하는 선택지를 2개 고른 뒤, 그 중에서 태 또는 시제 변화에 맞는 최종 정답을 선택하게 되는데, 이 과정을 한 번에 끝낼 수 있도록 연습해야 합니다.

1 태

문장 속에서 주어와 행위 대상의 관계를 나타내는 동사의 태는 능동태와 수동태로 나뉩니다. 능동태는 주어가 동사의 행위를 직접 하는 경우에 쓰이며, 「타동사 + 목적어」 구조입니다. 수동태는 주어가 동사의 행위를 당하는 대상일 경우에 쓰이며, 타동사의 목적어가 주어로 사용됩니다.

■ 수동태 문장

동사의 행위 대상, 즉 목적어를 주어로 사용하는 문장입니다. 「주어 + be p.p. + (by 행위자)」의 구조를 지니며 「~이 …되다」라고 해석합니다. **타동사 뒤에 목적어가 없다면 수동태**라는 것을 명심하세요.

▶ 타동사 뒤에 목적어가 없으므로 오답

The employee attendance records [reviewed / **are reviewed**] weekly by the HR department.
직원 출근 기록은 인사부서에서 매주 검토된다.

수동태 문장은 능동태 동사의 목적어가 주어 자리로 이동한 구조이기 때문에 목적어를 가질 수 없는 자동사는 수동태 자리에 올 수 없습니다.

◀ respond는 1형식 자동사이므로 수동태가 될 수 없음

All packages arriving after working hours should be [responded / **delivered**] to Ms. Davis.
업무 종료 후에 도착하는 모든 소포는 데이비스 씨에게 전달되어야 합니다.

수동태 자리에 오답으로 자주 출제되는 자동사

- work 일하다
- travel 출장 가다
- stay 머무르다
- arrive 도착하다
- respond 응답하다
- rise 상승하다
- agree 동의하다
- last 지속되다
- reply 답장하다

■ **수동태 시제**

수동태의 형태 「be + p.p.」에서 시제를 나타내는 것은 be동사입니다. 따라서 p.p.는 그대로 두고 be동사만 해당 시제에 맞게 변화시켜 시제를 나타냅니다.

> 현재시제 **is/are** + p.p. ~되다
> 과거시제 **was/were** + p.p. ~되었다
> 미래시제 **will be** + p.p. ~될 것이다
> 현재진행시제 **is/are being** + p.p. ~되고 있다 / ~되는 중이다
> 과거진행시제 **was/were being** + p.p. ~되고 있었다 / ~되는 중이었다
> 미래진행시제 **will be being** + p.p. ~되고 있을 것이다 / ~되는 중일 것이다
> 현재완료시제 **has/have been** + p.p. ~되었다
> 과거완료시제 **had been** + p.p. ~되었다
> 미래완료시제 **will have been** + p.p. ~될 것이다

The meeting schedule **was revised** to accommodate the clients' availability last Friday.
고객들의 일정에 맞추기 위해 지난 금요일에 회의 일정이 수정되었다.

The company's IT infrastructure **is being adjusted** to improve data security and performance.
회사의 IT 인프라는 데이터 보안 및 성능 향상을 위해 조정되고 있다.

■ **능동태와 수동태를 구분하는 방법**

타동사 자리인 빈칸 뒤에 명사 목적어가 있다면 능동태, 목적어가 없고 전치사구나 부사가 있다면 수동태가 정답입니다.

▶ 명사 앞은 타동사 능동태 자리
Rockwell Cable Network [is announced / **announced**] their plan to increase subscription fees.
락웰 케이블 네트워크는 시청료를 인상한다는 계획을 발표했다. [능동태]

▶ 전치사구 앞은 타동사 수동태 자리
The final report [prepared / **was prepared**] by the accounting team on time.
최종 보고서는 회계팀에 의해 제시간에 작성되었다.

PRACTICE 빈칸에 알맞은 단어를 고르세요.

1 The new marketing strategy was [worked / implemented] across all regions.
2 The elevator in Tower B is [inspecting / being inspected] to ensure it meets updated safety standards.

■ 빈출 수동태 구문

다음 수동태 구문들은 토익에서 자주 출제되는 구문들입니다. 「수동태 + 전치사」 구문의 경우 빈칸 앞에 있는 수동태 동사를 보고 함께 쓰이는 전치사를 고르는 방식으로 출제되고, 「수동태 + to부정사」 구문의 경우 빈칸 뒤의 to부정사를 보고 함께 쓰이는 수동태 동사를 고르거나 그 반대의 경우로 자주 출제됩니다.

> **토익 빈출 「수동태 + 전치사」 구문**
>
> - be associated with ~와 연관되다
> - be satisfied with ~에 만족하다
> - be equipped with ~을 갖추고 있다
> - be interested in ~에 관심이 있다
> - be committed[dedicated, devoted] to ~에 전념하다
> - be concerned[worried] about ~에 대해 걱정하다
>
> - be intended for ~을 위해 의도되다
> - be faced with ~에 직면하다
> - be pleased with ~에 기뻐하다
> - be involved in ~에 관여되다
> - be related to ~에 관련되다
> - be surprised at ~에 놀라다
> - be based on ~을 기반으로 하다
> - be regarded as ~로 여겨지다

▶ to부정사의 to가 아니라 전치사 to이므로 동명사 목적어가 필요

Our sales representatives **are committed to offering** the lowest rates in the industry.
저희 영업사원들은 업계 최저 가격을 제공하는 데 전념하고 있습니다.

Executives **are concerned about** meeting the quarterly revenue targets.
임원진은 분기 수익 목표 달성에 대해 걱정하고 있다.

> **토익 빈출 「수동태 + to부정사」 구문**
>
> - be asked to do ~하도록 요청받다
> - be allowed to do ~하도록 허용되다
> - be required to do ~해야 하다
> - be encouraged to do ~하도록 권장되다
> - be pleased to do ~해서 기쁘다
>
> - be advised to do ~하도록 권고되다
> - be expected to do ~할 것으로 예상되다
> - be scheduled to do ~할 예정이다
> - be invited to do ~하도록 요청받다
> - be prepared to do ~하도록 준비되다

▶ to부정사 앞의 빈칸은 require의 수동태 자리

Guests [require / **are required**] to show valid identification when entering the facility.
방문객들은 시설에 들어갈 때 유효한 신분증을 제시해야 합니다.

Team leaders [expect / **are expected**] to submit progress reports every Friday afternoon.
팀장들은 매주 금요일 오후마다 진행 보고서를 제출할 것으로 예상됩니다.

■ 4형식 타동사(수여동사)의 수동태

목적어를 2개 가지는 4형식 타동사 즉, 수여동사의 수동태는 간접목적어와 직접목적어 모두 주어 자리에 위치할 수 있기 때문에 두 가지 수동태 문장을 만들 수 있습니다.

Mr. Littleton **assigned** **the assistant** **the task of ordering the office supplies**.
　　　　　　　　　간접목적어(=사람)　　　　　직접목적어(= 사물, 일)

리틀턴 씨는 비서에게 사무용품을 주문하는 업무를 배정했다. [능동태]

- **4형식 수동태 (1): 간접목적어가 주어 자리로 이동**

> 능동태 문장의 과거시제 assigned에 맞추어 과거시제 was assigned 사용

The assistant **was assigned** the task of ordering the office supplies by Mr. Littleton.

비서는 리틀턴 씨에 의해 사무용품을 주문하는 업무를 배정받았다.

- **4형식 수동태 (2): 직접목적어가 주어 자리로 이동**

> 직접목적어가 주어 자리로 이동하면 동사 뒤의 간접목적어 앞에 전치사 필요

The task of ordering the office supplies **was assigned** to the assistant by Mr. Littleton.

사무용품을 주문하는 업무가 리틀턴 씨에 의해 비서에게 배정되었다.

■ 5형식 타동사의 수동태

The marketing team **made** **the presentation** **more engaging** for potential clients.
　　　　　　　　능동태(과거시제)　　목적어　　　목적보어(형용사)

마케팅팀은 그 발표를 잠재 고객들에게 더 매력적으로 만들었다. [능동태]

The presentation **was made** **more engaging** for potential clients by the marketing team.
　　　　　　　　수동태(과거시제)　목적보어(형용사)

그 발표는 마케팅팀에 의해 잠재 고객들에게 더 매력적으로 만들어졌다.

PRACTICE 빈칸에 알맞은 단어를 고르세요.

3 All passengers [advise / are advised] to arrive at the airport at least two hours before departure.

4 The new employee [considered / was considered] highly motivated and well-prepared.

2 수일치

동사의 현재시제와 현재완료시제, 그리고 수동태는 항상 주어와 수가 일치해야 하는데, 주어가 단수 가산명사이거나 불가산명사일 때, 그리고 단수 취급하는 회사명 등 고유명사일 때, 동사 자리에 단수 형태가 와야 합니다.

■ 주의해야 하는 주어-동사 수일치

⤳ 회사명 및 고유 명사는 항상 단수 취급

Kingston Foods **offers** a wide range of organic frozen meals to health-conscious consumers.
킹스턴 푸드 사는 건강을 중시하는 소비자에게 다양한 유기농 냉동 식품을 제공합니다.

to부정사, 동명사, 명사절 등도 주어 자리에 위치하면 모두 단수명사 취급됩니다.

To maintain consistent service quality **is** one of the company's top priorities.
일관된 서비스 품질을 유지하는 것이 회사의 최우선 과제 중 하나입니다.

Attending international trade shows **helps** companies expand their global network.
국제 무역 박람회에 참석하는 것은 기업이 글로벌 네트워크를 확장하는 데 도움이 됩니다.

Whether the sales team can meet the quarterly targets or not **depends** on the success of the product launch.
영업팀이 분기 목표를 달성할 수 있을지 없을지는 제품 출시의 성공 여부에 달려 있습니다.

■ 주어-동사 수일치의 예외

동사 앞에 조동사가 사용되는 경우에는 주어와 동사의 수일치가 발생하지 않습니다.

⤳ 조동사 뒤는 동사원형 자리

Anyone available for overtime this season should **contact** the scheduling coordinator.
이번 시즌에 초과 근무가 가능한 사람은 일정 조정 담당자에게 연락해야 합니다.

3 동사 자리 출제 유형 정리

문장의 동사 자리에 알맞은 동사 형태를 고르는 문제에서는 선택지에 명사 또는 to부정사나 동명사 같은 명백한 오답들이 자주 포함됩니다. 빈칸이 동사 자리임을 확인한 후, 동사의 형태인 선택지들 중에서 (1) 수일치 (2) 태 (3) 시제를 따져 정답을 찾습니다.

■ 주어-동사의 수일치 문제

동사의 수일치 여부를 확인하기 위해서는 문장의 주어를 제일 먼저 찾는 것이 중요합니다. 이후, 수일치 여부와 상관없는 조동사나 과거시제의 유무를 확인합니다.

> 회사명은 항상 단수 취급

Horizon Electronics ------- compact audio systems for home and office use.
(A) design   (B) designs   (C) designing   (D) to design

■ 동사의 태 문제

동사 자리인 빈칸 뒤에 목적어가 있으면 능동태, 목적어 없이 전치사구 또는 부사 등이 있다면 수동태 동사를 고릅니다.

> 동사 자리 뒤에 전치사구가 있다면 수동태 자리

The marketing campaign ------- by industry critics for its creative approach.
(A) praise   (B) praised   (C) to praise   (D) was praised

■ 동사의 시제 문제

동사의 시제를 확인하기 위해서는 단서가 되는 시간 표현을 찾습니다.

> 과거 시간 표현

All office computers ------- by the IT team before the system crashed yesterday.
(A) were checked   (B) are checking   (C) check   (D) have checked

---

PRACTICE 빈칸에 알맞은 단어를 고르세요.

5 Anyone entering the restricted area must [is escorted / be escorted] by security personnel.

6 Promotional events for The King cakes at Pampano's Bakery [holds / are held] every three months.

실전 TEST

학습한 내용을 적용하여 다음 기출 변형 문제들을 풀어보세요.

1. Professor Adison Chopra is highly ------- by leading scientists in the field of genetic engineering.
   (A) regard
   (B) regarding
   (C) regarded
   (D) regards

2. Employees should find alternative places to have lunch while the workers ------- the cafeteria renovations.
   (A) complete
   (B) completing
   (C) to complete
   (D) are completed

3. Agate Electronics will ------- its new cell phone model at the upcoming technology convention in Portland.
   (A) demonstrate
   (B) demonstrates
   (C) demonstrating
   (D) be demonstrated

4. Multico Enterprises ------- steady growth into markets overseas over the next few years.
   (A) anticipates
   (B) anticipating
   (C) to anticipate
   (D) is anticipated

5. The sales manager is surprised ------- the recent surge in sales after the new marketing campaign.
   (A) into
   (B) over
   (C) at
   (D) from

6. All rooms listed in Raffles Golf Resort's brochure are fully equipped ------- kitchen utensils.
   (A) at
   (B) to
   (C) in
   (D) with

7. The discounts for subscriptions of 6 months or more are ------- only to those on our newsletter mailing list.
   (A) to offer
   (B) offering
   (C) offer
   (D) offered

8. Paid vacations and cash bonuses will be ------- to the employees with the best attendance record in October.
   (A) assumed
   (B) awarded
   (C) agreed
   (D) accepted

9. Arko Petroleum Inc.'s new company policy for the staff dress code ------- only to its full-time employees.
   (A) apply
   (B) applies
   (C) applying
   (D) are applied

10. Head Chef Leah McKellan ------- kitchen staff to clean the food preparation stations before health inspections.
    (A) ask
    (B) has been asked
    (C) has asked
    (D) are asking

11 Several proposals for the new marketing initiative ------- by the end of the week.
(A) was submitted
(B) is submitting
(C) has submitted
(D) were submitted

12 The financial statements -------- thoroughly reviewed before the investor meeting next month.
(A) will be
(B) were being
(C) is
(D) have

13 All incoming shipments ------- upon arrival by the inventory team at Felsen Imports.
(A) inspects
(B) is inspected
(C) are inspected
(D) was inspecting

14 A detailed summary of the training modules ------- to all new employees next Monday.
(A) distribute
(B) was distributed
(C) are distributing
(D) will be distributed

15 Neither of the pending contracts ------- finalized due to budget restrictions.
(A) have been
(B) is being
(C) has been
(D) are being

16 All of the invoices from Keller & Rowe ------- as paid in the accounting system.
(A) is marked
(B) are marking
(C) was marked
(D) have been marked

17 The final decision regarding the product launch date ------- by the board of directors.
(A) were made
(B) is being made
(C) have made
(D) makes

18 The quarterly sales reports for three regions ------- electronically yesterday.
(A) was submitted
(B) were submitted
(C) has been submitted
(D) submitted

19 The renovation plans for the Darnell Café branch ------- currently being revised by the design team.
(A) are
(B) is
(C) has
(D) be

20 A collection of client testimonials ------- on the new section of our Web site.
(A) were posted
(B) are posted
(C) has been posted
(D) have posted

DAY 05 | 동명사 / to부정사 **Part 5**

동명사와 to부정사는 모두 동사에서 변화된 형태이며, 동사의 특성을 유지한 채로 문장에서 동사가 아닌 다른 품사의 역할을 합니다. 동명사는 이름에서 알 수 있듯이 주어, 목적어, 보어 등 명사의 주요 기능이 모두 가능하며, to부정사는 명사, 형용사, 부사의 기능을 할 수 있습니다.

1 동명사의 명사적 특성

동명사는 주어, 목적어, 보어 등 명사가 하는 역할을 할 수 있습니다.

■ 주어 역할

→ 이미 문장의 동사 can lead가 있으므로 또 다른 동사는 오답

[**Gathering** / Gather] customer feedback can lead to significant improvements in service quality.
고객의 피드백을 수집하는 것은 서비스 품질의 상당한 개선으로 이어질 수 있습니다.

■ 타동사 또는 전치사의 목적어 역할

→ the contract라는 목적어가 연결되려면 전치사가 필요하므로 오답

The legal counsel recommended [revision / **revising**] the contract before final approval.
법률 고문은 최종 승인 전에 계약서를 수정할 것을 권장했다.

> **동명사를 목적어로 취하는 토익 빈출 타동사**
> - recommend 추천하다
> - consider 고려하다
> - avoid 피하다
> - enjoy 즐기다
> - finish 끝마치다
> - suggest 제안하다
> - mind 꺼리다
> - admit 인정하다, 시인하다

→ brand awareness라는 목적어가 연결되려면 전치사가 필요하므로 오답

The marketing team is focused on [improvement / **improving**] brand awareness across digital platforms.
마케팅팀은 디지털 플랫폼 전반에서 브랜드 인지도를 향상시키는 데 집중하고 있다.

■ 보어 역할

launching은 현재분사가 아니라 동명사 ◄   → be동사 is 뒤에는 동사원형이 쓰일 수 없으므로 오답

The company's primary goal for this year is [**launching** / launch] a variety of new items.
회사의 올해 주요 목표는 다양한 신제품을 출시하는 것이다.

2 동명사의 동사적 특성

동명사는 동사가 변형된 것이므로 목적어/보어 유무, 부사의 수식, 시제 변화 등 동사적 특성을 그대로 유지하며, 이 특성이 동명사의 주요 출제 포인트에 해당됩니다.

■ 목적어를 가질 수 있음

→ 명사가 또 다른 명사와 결합하려면 전치사가 필요하므로 오답

[**Maintaining** / Maintenance] accurate financial records is essential for annual audits.
정확한 재무 기록을 유지하는 것이 연례 감사에 필수적입니다.

■ 보어를 가질 수 있음

→ 동명사 keeping의 목적어 sensitive files를 설명하는 목적보어

Keeping sensitive files accessible to all employees could result in a data breach.
민감한 파일을 모든 직원이 접근 가능하게 유지하는 것은 데이터 유출로 이어질 수 있다.

■ 부사의 수식을 받음

← 부사의 수식을 받음과 동시에 전치사의 목적어 역할을 할 수 있는 동명사

The manager emphasized the importance of thoroughly [**reviewing** / review] the contract before signing it.
부장님은 계약서에 서명하기 전에 철저하게 검토하는 것의 중요성을 강조했다.

■ 동명사 VS 명사

동명사는 관사나 형용사의 수식을 받지 못하고, 명사는 부사의 수식을 받지 못합니다. 또한 명사는 목적어를 가지지 못한다는 것이 동명사와의 차이점입니다.

← 동명사는 관사의 수식을 받을 수 없으므로 오답

The advertising campaign was designed for the [**improvement** / improving] of our annual profits.
그 광고 캠페인은 우리의 연간 수익 개선을 위해 기획되었습니다.

← 동명사는 형용사의 수식을 받지 못하므로 오답

We can improve our productivity by carrying out a thorough [inspecting / **inspection**].
우리는 철저한 점검을 실시함으로써 생산성을 향상시킬 수 있습니다.

PRACTICE 빈칸에 알맞은 단어를 고르세요.

1. Mr. Lee suggested [postpone / postponing] the meeting due to scheduling conflicts.
2. The team succeeded by efficiently [coordination / coordinating] their efforts across departments.

3 명사로 굳어진 동명사

토익에서는 동명사 또는 분사처럼 ing로 끝나는 형태를 가진 단어들이 명사 자리 문제에 자주 출제됩니다. 이 단어들의 품사가 동명사 또는 분사가 아니라 명사라는 것을 명확히 알고 있지 않으면 문장 구조 파악에 혼동을 일으켜 정답을 놓칠 수 있으므로 잘 숙지하도록 합니다.

■ ing형 명사

We are pleased to invite you to the [open / **opening**] of our Beijing office on August 10.
귀하를 8월 10일에 저희 베이징 지사의 개장 행사에 초대하게 되어 기쁩니다.

토익 빈출 ing형 명사

- building 건물, 건축
- seating 좌석 (설비)
- shipping 배송
- housing 주택 (제공)
- opening 개회, 개장, 공석
- planning 기획
- spending 지출, 소비
- handling 취급
- manufacturing 제조
- advertising 광고 (활동)
- boarding 탑승
- writing 글자, 저술
- training 교육
- accounting 회계
- understanding 이해
- working 작동, 작업

■ ing형 명사가 포함된 빈출 복합명사

All orders placed before 3 P.M. will be shipped the same day, provided that the [**shipping** / shipment] charge has been paid.
오후 3시 이전에 접수된 모든 주문은 배송 요금이 결제된 경우에 한해 당일 배송될 것입니다.

토익 빈출 ing형 복합명사

- building permit 건축 허가
- manufacturing process 제조 과정
- planning meeting 기획 회의
- shipping charge 배송 요금
- opening ceremony 개회식, 개장식
- training session 교육 시간
- accounting department 회계부
- spending pattern 소비 패턴
- job opening 공석, 빈자리
- seating capacity 좌석 수용력
- advertising campaign 광고 캠페인
- boarding pass 탑승권

PRACTICE 빈칸에 알맞은 단어를 고르세요.

3 We need to revise our travel policy to reduce [spends / spending].

4 All leased vehicles must be returned in clean and proper working [conditional / condition].

4 to부정사의 명사 역할

명사 역할을 하는 to부정사는 문장 내에서 주어, 목적어, 보어의 자리에 사용됩니다. 토익에서는 주로 목적어와 보어의 역할에 대해 출제됩니다.

■ **특정 동사와 결합하는 to부정사**

특정 동사들은 to부정사와 결합하는데, 이 동사들 뒤에 위치할 to부정사를 선택하는 문제가 자주 출제됩니다.

----▶ 동사 hope는 to부정사를 목적어로 취함

The management hopes [**to open** / opening] the new branch office in Seoul by early autumn.
경영진은 초가을까지 서울에 새로운 지사를 개설하기를 희망한다.

to부정사와 결합하는 토익 빈출 동사

- hope 희망하다
- hesitate 망설이다
- decide, choose 결정하다
- attempt 시도하다
- plan 계획하다
- offer 제안하다
- aim 목표로 하다
- tend (~ 하는) 경향이 있다
- would like 하고 싶다
- intend 계획하다
- strive 노력하다
- promise 약속하다
- expect 예상하다
- wish 바라다
- fail 실패하다
- seem, appear (~처럼) 보이다

■ **보어로 쓰이는 to부정사**

----▶ be동사의 주격보어로 사용된 to부정사

Our goal for next year is [expand / **to expand**] our business into the Asian market.
우리의 내년 목표는 사업을 아시아 시장으로 확대하는 것이다.

to부정사 보어와 어울리는 토익 빈출 명사

- goal 목표
- aim 목표, 목적
- plan 계획
- job 일, 직무
- mission 임무, 사명
- intension 의도
- objective 목표

■ **목적보어로 쓰이는 to부정사**

5형식 동사의 목적보어로 사용되는 to부정사는 5형식 타동사를 정답으로 고르는 데 결정적 단서가 됩니다.

----▶ make는 「make + 목적어 + 동사원형」와 같이 목적보어로 동사원형이 사용됨

The new system will [make / **allow**] our employees to maximize their work efficiency.
새로운 시스템은 저희 직원들에게 작업 효율을 극대화할 수 있게 해줄 것입니다.

목적보어로 to부정사를 취하는 토익 빈출 5형식 동사

- allow 허용하다
- enable 가능하게 하다
- instruct 지시하다, 안내하다
- expect 기대하다
- remind 상기시키다
- invite 요청하다
- permit 허용하다
- ask 요청하다
- force 강요하다
- advise 조언하다
- encourage 권하다, 장려하다
- require, request 요청하다

5 to부정사의 형용사 역할

to부정사는 명사를 뒤에서 수식하여 「~하게 될, ~할, ~하는」이라는 미래의 의미를 가지는 형용사처럼 사용될 수 있습니다. 특히, 특정 명사를 뒤에서 수식하는 to부정사 형태를 묻는 문제가 자주 출제됩니다.

→ 명사 a plan을 뒤에서 수식하는 to부정사

The HR department proposed **a plan to provide** leadership training for new managers.
인사부는 신임 관리자들을 위한 리더십 교육을 제공할 계획을 제안했다.

→ 명사 a great way를 뒤에서 수식하는 to부정사

Establishing clear objectives is **a great way** [improving / **to improve**] team performance.
명확한 목표를 설정하는 것은 팀 성과를 향상시키는 좋은 방법이다.

> **to부정사의 수식을 받는 토익 빈출 명사**
> - right 권리
> - ability 능력
> - intention 의도
> - time 때
> - decision 결정
> - way 방법
> - opportunity 기회
> - request 요청
> - effort 노력
> - plan 계획
> - moment 시간

6 to부정사의 부사 역할

주로 사람의 감정을 나타내는 형용사 뒤에 오거나, 5형식 동사의 수동태 뒤에 위치하는 문제, 그리고 목적을 나타내는 「in order to do」 구조로 출제됩니다.

■ 형용사를 뒤에서 수식

We are **pleased to help** you with the problem you are experiencing with our service.
저희는 귀하께서 저희 서비스에 대해 겪고 계신 문제에 대해 도움을 드리게 되어 기쁩니다.

> **토익에서 주로 to부정사의 수식을 받는 감정 형용사**
> - pleased 만족한, 기쁜
> - delighted 즐거운
> - happy 기쁜
> - excited 신이 난, 들뜬
> - proud 자랑스러운
> - surprised 놀란
> - honored 영광인
> - sorry 안타까운, 유감인
>
> **토익에서 주로 to부정사의 수식을 받는 일반 형용사**
> - willing 의향이 있는
> - eligible 자격이 있는
> - reluctant 꺼리는
> - likely 가능성 있는
> - set 예정된
> - eager 간절히 원하는
> - ready 준비된
> - able[unable] 할 수 있는[없는]
> - hesitant 주저하는
> - available 가능한
> - fortunate 다행인
> - sure 확신하는

■ **수동태 뒤에 위치하는 to부정사**

「주어 + be p.p. + to부정사」의 구조로 수동태 뒤에 빈칸이 위치하는 문제가 자주 출제됩니다. 이 때 대부분 5형식 동사의 수동태가 쓰입니다.

Employees are strongly advised [**to change** / changing] their passwords every 90 days.
직원들은 90일마다 비밀번호를 변경할 것을 강력히 권고 받습니다.

to부정사와 결합하는 토익 빈출 수동태

- be allowed to do
  ~하도록 허용되다
- be expected to do
  ~할 것으로 예상되다
- be advised to do
  ~하도록 권고되다
- be asked to do
  ~하도록 요청받다
- be encouraged to do
  ~하도록 권장되다
- be invited to do
  ~하도록 요청받다
- be forced to do
  어쩔 수 없이 ~하다
- be required to do
  ~해야 하다
- be scheduled to do
  ~하도록 예정되다
- be permitted to do
  ~하도록 허락받다
- be prepared to do
  ~하도록 준비되다
- be designed to do
  ~하도록 기획되다
- be authorized to do
  ~하도록 허가받다
- be reminded to do
  ~하도록 상기되다

■ **목적을 나타내는 to부정사 숙어**

to부정사가 완전한 문장 맨 뒤에 위치하여 '~하기 위해서'라는 의미를 나타냅니다. 이렇게 행위의 목적을 나타낼 경우 「in order to부정사」 구조로도 출제됩니다. 이때 오답 선택지들이 전치사 또는 접속사 등으로 출제되기 때문에 빈칸 뒤의 동사원형만 보고 쉽게 정답을 고를 수 있습니다.

You should complete an online form [**in order to** / for] apply for the advertised position.
광고된 직책에 지원하시려면 온라인 양식을 작성하셔야 합니다.

7 to부정사의 의미상 주어

대부분 to부정사의 행위자는 문장의 주어이거나 목적어인데, 그렇지 않을 경우 to부정사의 행위자를 따로 문장에 밝힐 필요가 있습니다. 이를 to부정사의 의미상 주어라고 하며, to부정사 앞에 「전치사 for + 목적격」의 형태로 씁니다.

→ 동사 hire의 행위자는 '우리'(us)

It is important **for us** [hiring / **to hire**] more experts in the field of finance.
우리가 금융 분야의 더 많은 전문가들을 고용하는 것이 중요하다.

PRACTICE 빈칸에 알맞은 단어를 고르세요.

5 Zenith Pharmaceuticals aims [to increase / increasing] its market penetration by partnering with local distributors.

6 Applicants should be prepared [to submit / submitting] additional documentation upon request.

실전 TEST

학습한 내용을 적용하여 다음 기출 변형 문제들을 풀어보세요.

1. ------- to Eagle Mountain can be difficult due to the poorly maintained roads in the area.
   (A) Driving
   (B) Drives
   (C) Drive
   (D) Driven

2. Gaston Grill and Bistro hopes to attract many new customers by ------- healthy side dishes to its menu.
   (A) add
   (B) adding
   (C) addition
   (D) added

3. The Wishing Well Foundation established by researchers at Hampshire University is committed to ------- rare animal species.
   (A) protect
   (B) protected
   (C) protection
   (D) protecting

4. We would like ------- that your office furniture design has been selected as a finalist in our national design competition.
   (A) announce
   (B) announcing
   (C) announced
   (D) to announce

5. The value of our stock continually decreases in spite of ------- to improve the image of our headphones brand.
   (A) issues
   (B) efforts
   (C) opinions
   (D) responses

6. Freshways Supermarket has decided ------- its overtime rate for employees who work on night shifts.
   (A) increases
   (B) to increase
   (C) increasing
   (D) increased

7. Our warehouse employees treat merchandise with the utmost care to avoid ------- any items.
   (A) damage
   (B) damaging
   (C) to damage
   (D) damages

8. To ------- his résumé, Mr. O'Donnell completed courses in business management and financial planning.
   (A) enhance
   (B) enhancement
   (C) enhanced
   (D) enhancing

9. We would ------- arriving at our office no later than 3 P.M. so that you can finish any remaining paperwork.
   (A) ask
   (B) decide
   (C) suggest
   (D) continue

10. The marketing director ------- to attract more customers with the release of the new social media-based advertising campaign.
    (A) continues
    (B) finishes
    (C) expects
    (D) considers

11 The door-to-door sales team's ability ------- well in adverse circumstances has really impressed the regional manager.

(A) performs
(B) performing
(C) to perform
(D) performance

12 At the Verdant Hotel, we are willing ------- our guests to make their stay more enjoyable.

(A) assist
(B) to assist
(C) assisting
(D) assisted

13 Mr. Ramirez, the head consultant, is responsible for ------- the communication skills workshop and networking events.

(A) organize
(B) organization
(C) organizing
(D) to organize

14 No intern may be offered a full-time position with Sylar Engineering without fully ------- the internship program.

(A) complete
(B) completing
(C) completes
(D) be completed

15 ------- compensate Ms. Wincott for the damage caused to her dress, the dry cleaner offered her a $100 gift certificate.

(A) So that
(B) In order to
(C) When
(D) Even if

16 The national ------- of our newsletters and promotional flyers will be carried out by the public relations manager, Jessica Lowe.

(A) to distribute
(B) distributing
(C) distributor
(D) distribution

17 Mitchum's Department Store has a managerial employment ------- for qualified individuals in the local area.

(A) opens
(B) opened
(C) open
(D) opening

18 Only musicians aged between 8 and 15 are ------- to enter the music competition at the town fair.

(A) accessible
(B) variable
(C) capable
(D) eligible

19 Mr. Harrison will move to an office on the third floor ------- closer to the marketing team.

(A) being
(B) to be
(C) is
(D) will be

20 All chemicals in the laboratory should be stored in containers that are labeled with the ------- clearly visible.

(A) writing
(B) written
(C) write
(D) writer

PART 5　FINAL TEST 1

학습한 내용을 적용하여 다음 기출 변형 문제들을 풀어보세요.

1. The museum's recent ------- has attracted tens of thousands of art lovers from across the country.
   (A) exhibit
   (B) exhibiting
   (C) exhibited
   (D) exhibits

2. The quarterly sales figures ------- sent to the board members by e-mail at the end of each month.
   (A) is
   (B) are
   (C) was
   (D) has

3. It is essential ------- the office supply order form before the deadline to avoid processing delays.
   (A) to submit
   (B) submitted
   (C) submit
   (D) submitting

4. A team of twenty people designed the mobile app, but only two of ------- will conduct the presentation to potential investors.
   (A) them
   (B) they
   (C) their
   (D) theirs

5. Several significant ------- were made to the first draft of the building blueprint after the architect received the client's feedback.
   (A) alter
   (B) altered
   (C) altering
   (D) alterations

6. ------- the customer service department directly can greatly reduce the time required to exchange a defective item.
   (A) Contact
   (B) Contacting
   (C) Contacts
   (D) Contacted

7. All faulty items ------- from the assembly lines immediately by the quality assurance team.
   (A) remove
   (B) removed
   (C) are removed
   (D) removes

8. Please remind factory ------- to put on safety gear before operating any of the assembly line machines.
   (A) employees
   (B) employ
   (C) employment
   (D) employing

9. The finance director intends ------- a full report on next quarter's revenue projections.
   (A) prepares
   (B) preparing
   (C) to prepare
   (D) prepared

10. Please inform Ms. Rivera that her flight itinerary was sent to ------- this morning.
    (A) her
    (B) she
    (C) hers
    (D) herself

11 The ------- of the urban development project will require coordination among three departments.

(A) complete
(B) completion
(C) completely
(D) completing

12 Mr. Lyle offered to lead the orientation session ------- due to several members of the HR department being absent.

(A) him
(B) his
(C) he
(D) himself

13 Many of our guests enjoy ------- the woodland areas and nature trails that surround the hotel.

(A) explore
(B) exploring
(C) to explore
(D) explored

14 Due to a decline in customer -------, the restaurant launched a promotional campaign on several social media platforms.

(A) satisfy
(B) satisfied
(C) satisfaction
(D) satisfying

15 GlobalFin Solutions will ------- new clients to access financial records through the upgraded dashboard.

(A) offer   (B) send
(C) find   (D) allow

16 According to the customer survey, ------- of the respondents said they would recommend Shining Tech's newest wearable device to others.

(A) that   (B) most
(C) every   (D) both

17 The facilities team installed air purifiers throughout the building ------- airborne particles during peak production hour.

(A) reduce
(B) reduction
(C) reduced
(D) to reduce

18 Ms. Carter's proposal ------- by the board members during the meeting this morning.

(A) discusses
(B) discussing
(C) discussed
(D) was discussed

19 New orders for Veritas Medical Solutions' equipment ------- to increase following the trade show.

(A) was expected
(B) is expecting
(C) are expected
(D) to expect

20 In addition to ------- webinars, DLS Consulting will launch a series of in-person workshops in October.

(A) host   (B) hosts
(C) hosting   (D) hosted

DAY 06 | 분사 Part 5

동사가 변형되어 형용사로 기능하는 분사는 ing형 현재분사와 ed형 과거분사로 나뉩니다. 현재분사가 be동사와 결합하여 진행시제를 구성하고, 과거분사가 be동사와 결합하여 수동태, 그리고 have와 결합하여 완료시제를 구성하는 내용은 이미 앞에서 공부했으므로 이번 「분사」편에서는 분사의 형용사 기능에 대해 학습합니다.

1 명사를 수식하는 분사의 위치

분사는 명사를 앞 또는 뒤에서 수식하는 형용사의 기능을 할 수 있고, 형용사처럼 부사의 수식을 받을 수 있습니다. 따라서, 빈칸이 형용사 자리인데 선택지에 형용사가 없다면 분사를 고르면 됩니다.

■ **명사를 앞에서 수식하는 분사**

The [rise / **rising**] energy costs have affected our production budget.
상승하는 에너지 비용은 우리의 생산 예산에 영향을 미쳤다.

The company expects its product to satisfy even [**demanding** / demanded] customers.
회사는 자사 제품이 까다로운 고객들까지 만족시키기를 기대한다.

The [approve / **approved**] budget for next year was announced at the board meeting.
내년에 대해 승인된 예산이 이사회에서 발표되었다.

▶ 분사를 수식하는 부사는 분사 앞에 위치함

All of the newly [**hired** / hire] employees should attend the orientation.
새로 채용된 직원들 모두가 오리엔테이션에 참석해야 합니다.

■ **명사를 뒤에서 수식하는 분사**

분사가 명사를 뒤에서 수식할 때 함께 쓰이는 목적어, 부사 또는 전치사구 때문에 문장 구조가 어려워 보일 수 있습니다.

▶ 문장에 이미 동사 should attend가 있으므로 오답

Employees [work / **working**] remotely should attend the virtual team briefing every Monday.
원격 근무 중인 직원들은 매주 월요일에 가상 팀 브리핑에 참여해야 합니다.

▶ 문장에 이미 동사 will be repaired가 있으므로 오답

The machines [damage / **damaged**] during transit will be repaired at no additional cost.
운송 중 손상된 기계는 추가 비용 없이 수리될 것입니다.

2 일반동사의 분사

분사의 수식을 받는 명사가 분사의 행위를 당하는 대상이면 과거분사, 명사가 행위를 하는 주체면 현재분사를 선택합니다.

▶ 배송은 사람에 의해 지연되는 것이므로 능동을 의미하는 현재분사는 오답

The [delaying / **delayed**] shipments have caused inventory shortages across the region.
지연된 배송으로 인해 해당 지역 전역에서 재고 부족 현상이 발생했습니다.

또한, 타동사의 분사가 명사를 뒤에서 수식하는 자리가 빈칸일 때, 빈칸 뒤에 목적어 없이 전치사구나 부사가 있으면 과거분사 자리입니다.

▶ 타동사의 현재분사는 바로 뒤에 목적어가 필요하므로 오답

Please review the proposals [submitting / **submitted**] by the marketing team before the meeting.
회의 전에 마케팅팀이 제출한 제안서를 검토해 주세요.

■ 능동을 의미하는 현재분사: ~하는

분사가 명사를 앞에서 수식할 때, 명사가 행위를 하는 주체이면 능동을 의미하는 현재분사가 정답입니다. 이 경우, 자동사의 현재분사를 고르는 유형으로 출제될 가능성이 높습니다.

▶ 수동태가 될 수 없는 자동사는 과거분사 형태로 명사를 수식할 수 없음

[**Remaining** / Remained] seats on the international flight are available on a first-come, first-served basis.
국제선의 남은 좌석은 선착순으로 이용 가능합니다.

타동사의 분사가 명사를 뒤에서 수식하는 구조일 때, 빈칸 뒤에 목적어가 있으면 현재분사 자리입니다.

▶ 서류가 보여주는 것이므로 수동을 의미하는 과거분사는 오답

I have attached documents [**detailing** / detailed] my experience in the IT industry.
정보통신 분야의 제 경력을 상세히 설명하는 서류들을 첨부했습니다.

▶ 과거분사는 뒤에 목적어를 가질 수 없음

Candidates [**meeting** / met] the qualifications will be invited to the interview next week.
자격 요건을 충족하는 지원자는 다음 주에 인터뷰에 초대될 것입니다.

PRACTICE 빈칸에 알맞은 단어를 고르세요.

1 The documents [containing / contained] sensitive information must be stored securely.
2 The customer support center will operate during [extending / extended] weekend hours.

3 감정동사의 분사 형태

「~을 즐겁게 하다, ~을 만족시키다」처럼 사람명사를 목적어로 취해 감정을 일으키는 동사를 감정동사라고 합니다. 이 감정동사가 분사로 쓰일 때는 감정을 유발하는 원인에 대해서는 현재분사를, 그리고 감정을 느끼는 사람에 대해서는 과거분사를 사용해 수식합니다. 이 분사들은 대부분 형용사로 굳어져 사용되고 있으므로 하나의 형용사로 기억해두면 문제 풀이가 더 쉬워집니다.

■ 감정을 유발하는 원인에 대해 사용하는 현재분사

We received several [**confusing** / confused] messages regarding the system upgrade.
저희는 시스템 업그레이드에 관한 헷갈리는 메시지를 여러 개 받았습니다.

→ 감정 유발 원인

감정의 원인을 나타내는 토익 빈출 현재분사

- exciting 신나는
- pleasing 기쁘게 하는
- surprising 놀라게 하는
- boring 지루하게 하는
- annoying 짜증나게 하는
- satisfying 만족시키는
- interesting 흥미롭게 하는
- worrying 걱정시키는
- frustrating 좌절감을 주는
- relaxing 편안하게 하는
- disappointing 실망시키는
- confusing 혼동시키는
- fascinating 매력적인
- embarrassing 당황스럽게 하는
- shocking 충격적인

■ 감정을 느끼는 사람에 대해 사용하는 과거분사

사람명사를 수식하는 감정동사의 분사는 수동을 나타내는 과거분사 형태입니다. 또한 토익에서 사람명사를 수식하는 감정동사의 분사는 대부분 명사의 뒤에서 수식하는 구조로 출제됩니다.

→ 감정을 느끼는 사람

This survey shows that most customers have been [pleasing / **pleased**] with our services.
이 설문조사는 대부분의 고객들이 우리 서비스에 즐거워 해왔다는 것을 보여준다.

사람의 감정을 나타내는 토익 빈출 과거분사

- excited 신난
- pleased 기쁜, 즐거운
- surprised 놀란
- frustrated 좌절한
- relaxed 편안한
- satisfied 만족한
- interested 흥미를 느낀
- delighted 기쁜
- embarrassed 당황한
- shocked 충격 받은
- disappointed 실망한
- impressed 감동받은
- bored 지루한
- annoyed 짜증난

4 형용사로 굳어진 분사

특정 현재분사나 과거분사는 수식하는 명사와의 의미 관계에 상관없이 특정 의미를 나타내는 형용사로 사용됩니다. 이렇게 형용사로 굳어진 분사들을 암기해 두면 빠르게 정답을 찾을 수 있습니다.

■ 형용사로 굳어진 현재분사

토익에서 특정 분사들은 자동사이든 타동사이든 상관없이 주로 현재분사의 형태로 명사를 수식하도록 출제되므로 잘 암기해 두어야 합니다.

▶ 자동사 lead의 현재분사로서 「선도적인」이라는 의미의 능동형 형용사

Maxwell Systems is recognized as a **leading** manufacturer of industrial equipment in Southeast Asia.
맥스웰 시스템즈는 동남아시아 산업 장비 분야의 선도적인 제조업체로 인정받고 있습니다.

토익 빈출 현재분사형 형용사

- promising 장래성 있는
- leading 선도적인
- lasting 지속적인
- existing 기존의
- missing 사라진, 빠진
- rewarding 보람 있는
- remaining 남아있는
- participating 참가하는
- surrounding 주변의
- following 다음의
- demanding 힘든
- coming 다가오는
- rising 증가하는, 상승하는
- growing 성장하는, 늘어나는
- challenging 해볼 만한

■ 형용사로 굳어진 과거분사

토익에서 특정 분사들은 자동사이든 타동사이든 상관없이 주로 과거분사의 형태로 명사를 수식하도록 출제되므로 잘 암기해 두어야 합니다.

▶ 동사 qualify의 과거분사로서 「자격을 갖춘」이라는 뜻의 수동형 형용사

We are looking to hire a [qualifying / **qualified**] technician with experience in electrical maintenance.
저희는 전기 유지보수 경험이 있는 자격을 갖춘 기술자를 채용하려고 합니다.

토익 빈출 과거분사형 형용사

- increased 증가된
- respected 존경받는
- experienced 경험 많은, 능숙한
- dedicated 헌신적인
- complicated 복잡한
- attached 첨부된
- damaged 손상된
- established 자리를 잡은, 인정된
- skilled 능숙한, 숙련된
- qualified 자격을 갖춘
- limited 한정된
- detailed 상세한

PRACTICE 빈칸에 알맞은 단어를 고르세요.

3. Our clients found the service experience surprisingly [satisfying / satisfied].
4. The [attaching / attached] invoice includes additional charges for expedited shipping.

실전 TEST

학습한 내용을 적용하여 다음 기출 변형 문제들을 풀어보세요.

1. A dinner party will be arranged at Waldorf Hotel to welcome the newly ------- branch managers.
   (A) appoint
   (B) appointing
   (C) appointed
   (D) appoints

2. A hiring strategy ------- by Mr. Patel is being reviewed by the personnel department at Portable Phones Inc.
   (A) propose
   (B) proposal
   (C) proposed
   (D) proposing

3. Holiday Travel Ltd. is an internationally ------- travel agency, and its head office is located in New York City.
   (A) recognized
   (B) recognize
   (C) recognizing
   (D) recognizes

4. Mr. Komiya describes Goldway Cosmetics as a new store ------- a variety of items, such as moisturizer, shampoo, and bodycare cream.
   (A) sell
   (B) sells
   (C) sold
   (D) selling

5. All employees at Crowder Corporation say they are ------- with the team-based office environment.
   (A) satisfy
   (B) satisfied
   (C) satisfying
   (D) satisfaction

6. The CEO of Bellco Electronics is expected to make a ------- announcement about the collaboration with Indigo Software.
   (A) surprises
   (B) surprised
   (C) surprising
   (D) surprisingly

7. The screen of our new Proteus 3 cell phone is much larger than that of any ------- foldable cell phone on the market.
   (A) exist
   (B) exists
   (C) existed
   (D) existing

8. ------- research on consumer spending trends was carried out by the Markham Marketing Group.
   (A) Detail
   (B) Details
   (C) Detailing
   (D) Detailed

9. Patients' medical notes ------- by the physician include confidential information that should not be disclosed to anyone.
   (A) record
   (B) recorded
   (C) recording
   (D) records

10. Sayid Ibrahim is a ------- economist who works in close collaboration with several US financial institutions.
    (A) lead
    (B) leader
    (C) led
    (D) leading

11 The ------- schedule for the BlueRise Technologies Convention resulted in poor attendance for several events.
(A) confusing
(B) confused
(C) confusion
(D) confuse

12 The employees ------- by the CEO's announcement regarding early retirement incentives expressed concern during the meeting.
(A) frustrating
(B) frustrated
(C) frustrate
(D) frustrates

13 All clients must submit the ------- form before entering the secure area.
(A) signing
(B) sign
(C) signed
(D) signature

14 Mr. Emoto submitted a list of ------- vendors for next quarter's supply contract.
(A) consider
(B) considered
(C) considering
(D) consideration

15 The company released a statement ------- the delay in product shipping.
(A) explaining
(B) explained
(C) explanation
(D) explains

16 We were impressed by the ------- presentation given by the entrepreneurs seeking investment.
(A) convincing
(B) convinced
(C) conviction
(D) convinces

17 The ------- data suggest that our newest product line is exceeding expectations.
(A) analyze
(B) analyzing
(C) analyzed
(D) analyses

18 The ------- form should be submitted to the accounting department by Friday.
(A) complete
(B) completing
(C) completion
(D) completed

19 The -------- noise from the construction site has made it difficult for our employees to concentrate.
(A) annoying
(B) annoyed
(C) annoy
(D) annoyance

20 The HR manager spoke to the ------- employees about the change in overtime policy.
(A) concerning
(B) concern
(C) concerned
(D) concerns

DAY 07 | 형용사 / 부사 Part 5

토익에서 형용사는 명사 앞 또는 뒤에 위치한 빈칸에 쓰일 형용사를 고르는 유형으로, 부사는 동사 또는 형용사를 수식하는 자리를 묻는 유형으로, 각각 90% 정도 출제됩니다. 그러므로 형용사와 부사의 다양한 위치를 파악하는 것이 가장 중요합니다.

1 형용사의 역할과 위치

형용사는 명사를 앞 또는 뒤에서 수식하거나 2형식 자동사의 보어로서 주어를 보충 설명해주는 역할을 하며, 5형식 타동사의 목적보어로서 목적어를 보충 설명하는 역할을 합니다.

■ 관사(the, a, an)와 명사 사이

The report highlights a **critical** issue that must be addressed immediately.
그 보고서는 즉시 해결되어야 할 중대한 문제를 강조하고 있습니다.

■ 타동사와 목적어 사이

The supervisor praised **creative** solutions proposed by the engineering team.
관리자는 엔지니어링 팀이 제시한 창의적인 해결책을 칭찬했습니다.

■ 2형식 자동사 다음

▶ 형용사의 의미를 강조하기 위해 앞에 부사가 추가되기 함

Our new products have become very **popular** since the successful marketing campaign.
우리의 신제품들은 성공적인 마케팅 캠페인 이후 매우 큰 인기를 얻었다.

■ 5형식 타동사의 목적어 다음

The committee **considers** **the new policy** **beneficial** for improving productivity.
　　　　　　　동사　　　　목적어　　　목적보어

위원회는 새로운 정책이 생산성 향상에 유익하다고 보고 있습니다.

2 수량형용사

명사를 수식하는 명사의 수에 적합한 수량형용사가 빈칸으로 출제되기도 합니다. 특히, 가산명사의 단수형과 복수형, 그리고 불가산명사를 각각 수식하는 수량형용사들을 잘 알아 두어야 합니다.

■ 단수명사 수식

└─→ 단수 가산명사인 applicant를 수식할 수 있는 Every가 정답

[**Every** / All] applicant must submit a résumé by the end of the month.
모든 지원자는 반드시 이번 달 말일까지 이력서를 제출해야 한다.

단수 가산명사를 수식하는 토익 빈출 수량형용사

- every 모든
- each 각각의
- another 또 하나의
- one 하나의

■ 복수명사 수식

└─→ 복수 가산명사

The technician conducted [**several** / every] tests to ensure the equipment was working properly.
기술자는 장비가 제대로 작동하는지 확인하기 위해 여러 테스트를 실시했다.

복수 가산명사를 수식하는 토익 빈출 수량형용사

- several 여럿의
- many 많은
- a few 몇몇의
- some 몇몇의
- a lot of 많은
- all 모든
- most 대부분의
- few 거의 없는
- numerous 수많은

■ 불가산명사 수식

└─→ 불가산명사

There was [few / **little**] progress in completing the renovations before the deadline.
마감 전에 공사를 완료하는 것에 있어 진전이 거의 없었다.

불가산명사를 수식하는 토익 빈출 수량형용사

- much 많은
- a little 약간의
- little 거의 없는
- some 일부의, 조금의
- all 모든
- most 대부분의
- a lot of 많은

PRACTICE 빈칸에 알맞은 단어를 고르세요.

1 The final report became more [thorough / thoroughly] after additional data was included.
2 Please verify [all / each] item on the checklist before submitting your report.

3 부정형용사

무엇인지 **구체적으로 밝혀지지 않은 대상을 가리킬 때 사용하는 형용사**를 부정형용사라고 하며, **수식하는 명사와 수를 일치시키는 것**이 출제의 핵심입니다.

■ another + 단수명사: (앞에 제시된 것 외에) 또 하나의 ~

> ▶ 복수 가산명사 앞에 쓰이므로 오답

The client requested [**another** / other] sample to compare with existing products.
그 고객은 기존 제품과 비교하기 위해 샘플을 하나 더 요청했습니다.

■ other + 복수명사: (앞에 제시된 것 외에) 다른 ~

> ▶ 단수 가산명사 앞에 쓰이므로 오답

If you have any questions, feel free to reach out to [another / **other**] staff members in your department.
질문이 있으시면 부서 내의 다른 직원들에게 언제든지 연락하세요.

■ the other + 단수/복수명사: (앞에 제시된 것 외에) 나머지의 ~

> 특정 범위 내의 일부를 제외한 나머지 모두를 가리킬 때 사용 ◀

Mr. Hamilton's office is more spacious than [other / **the other**] ones on the 3rd floor.
해밀턴 씨의 사무실이 3층에 있는 나머지 것들보다 더 널찍하다.

■ some + 복수명사/불가산명사: 일부의 ~, 어떤 ~

> ▶ 단수명사 앞에 쓰이므로 오답

The company has partnered with [**some** / another] vendors to improve supply chain efficiency.
그 회사는 공급망 효율성을 높이기 위해 몇몇 업체들과 협력했습니다.

■ any + 단수/복수명사/불가산명사: 어떤 ~이든

The warranty does not cover **any** damage caused by improper use.
보증은 부적절한 사용으로 발생한 어떤 손상도 보장하지 않습니다.

4 특이한 형태의 형용사

부사처럼 보이는 형용사 또는 부사와 동일한 형태의 형용사들이 있으므로 순간적으로 헷갈리지 않도록 미리 확인해 둡시다.

■ ly로 끝나는 형용사

> ▶ 명사 + ly = 형용사

Employing an advertisement agency has proven to be [**costly** / cost].
광고 대행사를 고용하는 것이 비용이 많이 드는 것으로 드러났다.

> ▶ 명사 + ly = 형용사

The manager ensured that the evacuation proceeded in an [order / **orderly**] manner.
관리자는 대피가 질서 있게 진행되도록 보장했습니다.

부사로 착각하기 쉬운 토익 빈출 형용사

- **timely** 시기적절한
- **costly** 비용이 많이 드는
- **weekly** 매주의
- **orderly** 정돈된, 질서 있는
- **monthly** 매달의
- **friendly** 친근한
- **leisurely** 여유로운

■ 부사와 동일한 형태의 형용사

→ 「관사 + 형용사 + 명사」 구조

The **early** stages of product development require careful planning.
제품 개발의 초기 단계는 신중한 계획을 필요로 한다.

→ 「주어 + 자동사 + 부사」 구조

The store opened **early** on the day of the sale.
그 매장은 세일 당일에 일찍 문을 열었다.

→ 「소유격 + 형용사 + 명사」 구조

Because of his **hard** attitude, cooperation was difficult.
그의 완고한 태도 때문에 협력이 어려웠다.

→ 「주어 + 자동사 + 부사」 구조

The printer is running **hard** due to high-volume orders.
다량의 주문으로 인해 프린터가 세게 작동하고 있다.

5 특정 전치사가 뒤따르는 형용사

어떤 형용사들은 대상을 나타낼 때 특정 전치사와 결합합니다. 이때 형용사와 전치사를 하나의 숙어처럼 외워 두면 빈칸 뒤에 위치한 전치사만 보고도 쉽게 정답을 선택할 수 있습니다.

■ 빈칸 뒤의 전치사가 형용사 선택의 중요 단서인 경우

→ 뒤의 전치사가 by가 아니므로 수동태가 될 수 없음

The XV 500 vacuum cleaner is [**representative** / represented] **of** all our home appliances.
XV 500 진공청소기는 저희 가전제품을 대표합니다.

토익 빈출 「형용사 + 전치사」 숙어

- be appreciative of
  ~에 감사하다
- be considerate of
  ~을 배려하다
- be accustomed to
  ~에 익숙하다
- be representative of
  ~을 대표하다
- be skilled at
  ~에 능숙하다
- be relevant to
  ~와 관련되다
- be associated with
  ~와 관련되다
- be similar to
  ~와 유사하다
- be distinct from
  ~와 다르다

PRACTICE 빈칸에 알맞은 단어를 고르세요.

3 Employees must obtain approval before making [some / any] purchase on behalf of the company.

4 Most overseas staff are already [associated / accustomed] to working in multicultural environments.

6 부사의 역할과 위치

동사와 형용사를 수식하는 부사의 위치를 묻는 기본적인 문제가 80% 정도 출제되지만, 또 다른 부사, 분사, 명사구, 동명사구 또는 문장 전체 등 다양한 대상을 수식하는 부사의 기능을 묻는 문제들도 종종 출제됩니다.

■ 동사 수식

▶ 주어와 동사 사이는 동사를 수식하는 부사 자리

The marketing team [careful / **carefully**] reviewed the presentation before the product launch.
마케팅 팀은 제품 출시 전에 발표 자료를 신중히 검토했습니다.

▶ 자동사 뒤는 부사 자리

The factory now operates [efficient / **efficiently**] than it did last year.
그 공장은 현재 작년보다 더 효율적으로 운영되고 있습니다.

▶ 3형식 동사 / ▶ 3형식 타동사의 목적어 뒤는 부사 자리

Please read **the instructions** [thorough / **thoroughly**] before installing the software.
　　　　　　목적어
소프트웨어를 설치하기 전에 설명서를 꼼꼼히 읽어주시기 바랍니다.

▶ 수동태 be 동사와 과거분사(p.p) 사이는 부사 자리

After a long period of development, our new line of products was [final / **finally**] released.
오랜 개발 기간 끝에, 우리의 새로운 제품군이 마침내 출시되었다.

■ 형용사 수식

▶ 형용사를 앞에서 수식하는 것은 부사

Nanosoft's newest software is [wide / **widely**] compatible with most operating systems.
나노소프트의 최신 소프트웨어는 대부분의 운영 체제와 폭넓게 호환됩니다.

▶ 형용사를 앞에서 수식하는 것은 부사

Customer feedback has been [consistent / **consistently**] positive since the update was released.
업데이트가 출시된 이후 고객 피드백은 지속적으로 긍정적이었다.

■ 분사 수식

▶ 형용사는 분사를 수식할 수 없음

All shipments must be handled [gentle / **gently**] to avoid damage.
모든 배송물은 손상을 방지하기 위해 부드럽게 다뤄져야 합니다.

[Serious / **Seriously**] considering the deadline, the team decided to skip the additional revisions.
마감 기한을 진지하게 고려하면서, 그 팀은 추가 수정을 생략하기로 결정하였다.

■ 명사구 수식

→ 형용사는 관사 앞에 올 수 없음

The newly-opened shopping mall was [former / **formerly**] a manufacturing plant.
새롭게 개장된 쇼핑몰은 이전에 제조 공장이었다.

■ 동명사 수식

→ 형용사는 동명사를 수식할 수 없음

The company improved productivity by [regular / **regularly**] monitoring employee performance.
그 회사는 직원 성과를 정기적으로 관찰함으로써 생산성을 향상시켰습니다.

Mr. Choi emphasized [strict / **strictly**] following the updated safety procedures.
최 씨는 업데이트 된 안전 절차를 엄격하게 따르는 것을 강조했습니다.

■ 전치사구 수식

→ 접속사 뒤에는 「주어 + 동사」가 필요

Please make sure the inspection checklist is completed [when / **promptly**] at the beginning of the shift.
근무 시작과 동시에 점검표 작성을 반드시 완료해 주세요.

특정 전치사와 자주 쓰이는 토익 빈출 부사

- **directly to[from]** 장소: ~로[~로부터] 곧장
- **precisely at** 시간: 정확히 ~시에
- **directly[immediately, shortly] after** ~ 직후에
- **promptly at** 시간: ~시 정각에
- **directly[immediately, shortly] before** ~ 직전에

■ 문장 수식

→ 형용사는 문장을 수식할 수 없음

[Apparent / **Apparently**], the revised proposal meets all of the client's expectations.
분명히, 수정된 제안서가 고객의 모든 기대를 충족하는 것 같습니다.

→ 형용사는 문장을 수식할 수 없음

[Late / **Lately**], clients have shown interest in our team's business proposals.
최근에, 고객들이 우리 팀의 사업 제안들에 관심을 보였다.

PRACTICE 빈칸에 알맞은 단어를 고르세요.

5 The customer service representatives responded [prompt / promptly] to the complaint.

6 The convention center is [convenient / conveniently] located close to the airport.

7 특수한 부사

■ 강조부사

▶ 형용사를 강조하는 부사

The new marketing strategy is **quite** effective in increasing customer engagement.
새로운 마케팅 전략은 고객 참여를 늘리는 데 꽤 효과적이다.

▶ 동사를 수식하는 부사

The committee **highly** regarded the applicant's leadership experience.
위원회는 그 지원자의 리더십 경험을 높이 평가했다.

'더 ~한'이라는 의미를 가진 「형용사 + er」 또는 「more + 형용사」와 같은 비교급 형용사를 강조하는 even, much, still, far, a lot, considerably, significantly가 있습니다.

▶ 형용사 great의 비교급

The updated model is faster than the previous one and offers **much** greater reliability.
업데이트된 모델은 이전 모델보다 더 빠르며, 훨씬 더 높은 신뢰성을 제공합니다.

토익 빈출 강조부사

- **only** 오직
- **fairly** 아주, 꽤
- **extremely** 매우, 극히
- **even** 심지어, 훨씬[비교급 수식]
- **highly** 매우, 대단히
- **well** 훨씬
- **significantly** 상당히
- **still** 훨씬[비교급 수식]
- **fully** 완전히, 전적으로
- **heavily** 심하게
- **considerably** 상당히
- **far** 훨씬[비교급 수식]
- **quite** 상당히, 꽤
- **greatly** 대단히, 크게
- **much** 훨씬[비교급 수식]
- **a lot** 훨씬[비교급 수식]

■ 혼동하기 쉬운 부사

▶ 높이를 강조하는 부사

Star Express's new tracking system has been proved to be [high / **highly**] effective.
스타 익스프레스의 새 배송 추적 시스템은 매우 효율적인 것으로 입증되었다.

▶ 부정의 의미를 나타내는 부사

Hamond Footwear's newest products are [**hardly** / hard] visible on the street.
해몬드 풋웨어의 신제품들은 좀처럼 거리에서 보이지 않는다.

토익 빈출 혼동부사

- **high** 높이 / **highly** 매우
- **late** 늦게 / **lately** 최근에
- **short** 짧게 / **shortly** 곧, 즉시
- **hard** 열심히 / **hardly** 거의 ~않다
- **close** 가까이, 엄밀히 / **closely** 면밀하게, 긴밀하게

■ 숫자 표현과 어울리는 부사

> 형용사/분사를 강조하는 부사

The shipment weighs [**approximately** / extremely] 200 kilograms and must be handled with care.
그 화물은 약 200kg의 무게이며 주의 깊게 다뤄야 합니다.

> 동사 행위를 수식하는 부사

Each participant can receive a reimbursement of [**up to** / gradually] $250 for travel expenses.
각 참가자는 여행 경비로 최대 $250까지 환급받을 수 있습니다.

숫자 표현 앞에 쓰이는 토익 빈출 부사

- approximately, about 약, 대략
- at least 최소한, 적어도
- nearly, almost 거의
- up to 최대 ~까지
- over ~가 넘는
- only, just 단지, 그저
- more than ~을 넘는

■ Still, Yet, Already

	의미	주요 시제 결합 빈도	구문 (각 부사 위치에 주의)
still	여전히 (상태 지속)	현재=현재완료>미래>과거	still + 현재시제: 여전히 ~하다 still + have not p.p.: 여전히 ~하지 않았다 will + still + 동사원형: 여전히 ~할 것이다
yet	아직 (부정적 의미)	현재완료	have + yet + to부정사: 아직도 ~해야 하다 have not + yet + p.p: 아직 ~하지 않았다
already	이미, 벌써 (완료)	현재완료=현재=과거완료= 과거	have + already + p.p.: 이미 ~했다 be + already + p.p.: 이미 ~되어 있다 may + already + be: 벌써 ~일 수도 있다

> to부정사 또는 부정어 not과 어울리는 부사

The software update was released a month ago, but some users [**still** / yet] use the old version.
소프트웨어 업데이트는 한 달 전에 배포되었지만 일부 사용자는 여전히 이전 버전을 사용하고 있습니다.

> have to부정사 사이에 yet 위치

Our engineers have **yet** to identify the cause of the system malfunction.
저희의 기술진은 아직 시스템 오작동의 원인을 밝혀내지 못했습니다.

PRACTICE 빈칸에 알맞은 단어를 고르세요.

7 Mr. Turner's concert was [quite / well] attended despite the lack of promotion last week.
8 The product is [still / yet] under warranty even though it was purchased a year ago.

실전 TEST

학습한 내용을 적용하여 다음 기출 변형 문제들을 풀어보세요.

1. Make sure that you give yourself a ------- amount of time to arrive at the airport during rush hour.
   (A) consideration
   (B) consider
   (C) considerable
   (D) considerably

2. Most customers find it ------- to browse our latest product brochure online before visiting our store.
   (A) benefit
   (B) beneficial
   (C) beneficially
   (D) benefits

3. The event planning team considered ------- locations for the company's annual banquet.
   (A) every
   (B) each
   (C) several
   (D) much

4. While some people visit Splash Canyon to experience the exciting rides, ------- visitors simply want to walk around and enjoy the scenery.
   (A) another
   (B) any
   (C) everyone
   (D) other

5. The relocation of headquarters to Melbourne proved to be more ------ than initially anticipated.
   (A) cost
   (B) costs
   (C) costly
   (D) costing

6. Blue Fabric Company produces ------- priced textiles such as cotton, silk, leather, and wool.
   (A) reason
   (B) reasoned
   (C) reasonable
   (D) reasonably

7. The film festival was announced two months ago, but the list of featured films ------- has not been released publicly.
   (A) still
   (B) yet
   (C) already
   (D) only

8. Last year's recycling initiative was a great success, as ------- 80 percent of the company's annual waste was recycled.
   (A) approximate
   (B) approximating
   (C) approximately
   (D) approximation

9. Marty McInnes was ------- an intern, but he was promoted to manager of the public relations team last month.
   (A) origin
   (B) original
   (C) originality
   (D) originally

10. Ms. Carp worked as a journalist for 22 years at *The Chicago Post*, where she wrote numerous ------- regarded articles.
    (A) high
    (B) highly
    (C) higher
    (D) highest

11 We made the instructions ------- so that all users can understand them.

(A) clear
(B) clearing
(C) clearly
(D) clarity

12 Please distribute the ------- brochures to all participants before the seminar begins.

(A) informing
(B) inform
(C) information
(D) informative

13 We completed some of the performance evaluations yesterday, and ------- reports will be finished by tomorrow.

(A) another
(B) the other
(C) a little
(D) each other

14 You may contact the support center regarding ------- concern you have about your subscription.

(A) any
(B) few
(C) all
(D) other

15 The risks ------- with investing in foreign markets should be carefully considered.

(A) associated
(B) association
(C) associate
(D) associates

16 Several departments worked ------- to launch the product ahead of schedule.

(A) collaborate
(B) collaborative
(C) collaboratively
(D) collaborated

17 -------, the accounting department failed to notice the duplication error.

(A) Regret
(B) Regrettable
(C) Regretted
(D) Regrettably

18 Bravetech Inc.'s new color printers are ------- more affordable than similar models that were released in September.

(A) very
(B) much
(C) too
(D) such

19 Inspectors are required to ------- check safety protocols at each construction site.

(A) close
(B) closeness
(C) closely
(D) closer

20 The supplier has ------- to confirm the shipping date despite multiple requests.

(A) still
(B) yet
(C) already
(D) hardly

DAY 08 | 접속사 Part 5

접속사는 토익에서 매월 3~5개 문제가 출제되는 중요한 영역입니다. 주로 빈칸 앞뒤의 구조 또는 의미에 따라 정답이 결정되지만, 상관접속사처럼 단서만 찾으면 바로 해결되는 유형도 종종 출제됩니다.

1 등위접속사

등위접속사는 주어와 동사를 각각 포함하는 두 개의 절을 동등하게 연결합니다. 이때 두 개의 절에서 중복되는 요소를 생략하고 대비되는 요소만 남겨서 두 개의 구나 단어를 연결하기도 합니다. 보통 선택지에 접속사, 전치사, 부사 등이 섞여 제시되며, 이 경우 빈칸 앞뒤 구조만 확인해 어울리는 품사만 고르면 됩니다. 종종 선택지에 접속사가 2개 이상 제시되기도 하는데, 이 경우에는 해석을 통해 자연스럽게 연결되는 접속사를 골라야 합니다.

> **등위접속사의 종류**
> - **and** 그리고, ~와 (순차 연결)
> - **or** 또는 (선택)
> - **but** 그러나 (상반, 역접)
> - **so** 그래서 (결과)
> - **nor** ~도 아니다 (부정문에 사용)

■ 절과 절을 연결

→ 서로 상반된 내용을 연결
Mr. Chow approved the marketing budget, [and / **but**] he expressed concern about the advertising timeline.
초우 씨는 마케팅 예산을 승인했지만, 광고 일정에 대해서는 우려를 표했습니다.

■ 구와 구를 연결

also는 연결 기능을 하지 못하는 부사이므로 오답 ◄   ► 로그인 후에 순차적으로 발생한 행위
Ms. Swindle logged into the system [also / **and**] submitted the expense report right away.
스윈들 씨는 시스템에 로그인했고 곧바로 지출 보고서를 제출했습니다.

■ 단어와 단어를 연결

앞뒤의 명사들이 모두 컨퍼런스의 특징이 되는 것을 나타내므로 순차 연결을 나타내는 접속사가 필요 ◄   ► 부정을 나타내는 nor는 긍정문에 사용하지 않음
The conference will feature keynote speeches [**and** / nor] panel discussions throughout the day.
컨퍼런스는 하루 종일 기조연설과 패널 토론을 특징으로 할 것입니다.

2 상관접속사

상관접속사는 등위접속사 구조 앞에 특정한 의미를 나타내는 부사를 추가한 연결 구조입니다. 한쪽 단어를 단서로 나머지 단어를 선택하도록 출제되므로 서로 짝을 이루는 조합만 외워 두면 상관접속사 문제를 아주 쉽게 풀 수 있습니다.

■ both A and B: A와 B 둘 모두

→ and와 짝을 이뤄 상관접속사를 구성하는 것은 both이므로 either는 오답

[Either / **Both**] full-time and part-time employees have to attend the annual event.
정규직과 시간제 직원들 모두 연례 행사에 참석해야 합니다.

■ either A or B: A 또는 B 둘 중 하나

→ either는 선택을 나타내는 부사이므로 선택 접속사가 필요

Candidates must submit either a printed résumé [**or** / and] a digital portfolio before the interview.
지원자는 인터뷰 전에 인쇄된 이력서 또는 디지털 포트폴리오 중 하나를 제출해야 합니다.

■ neither A or B: A와 B 둘 다 아닌

→ 전체 부정을 나타내는 접속사 nor과 짝을 이루는 부사

The shipment was [both / **neither**] delivered on time nor properly labeled.
배송은 제시간에 이루어지지도 않았고, 라벨이 제대로 붙여지지도 않았습니다.

■ not only A but (also) B: A뿐만 아니라 B도

→ not only와 짝을 이뤄 상관접속사를 구성하는 but이 정답. also는 종종 생략됨

The new policy will impact not only full-time employees [and / **but**] also contract workers.
새로운 정책은 정규직 직원뿐만 아니라 계약직 근로자에게도 영향을 줄 것입니다.

■ A as well as B: B뿐만 아니라 A도

→ both는 부사이므로 접속사 자리에 사용할 수 없음

The brochure highlights the resort's dining options [both / **as well as**] its recreational facilities.
그 안내 책자는 다양한 오락 시설뿐만 아니라 리조트의 식사 옵션도 강조하고 있습니다.

PRACTICE 빈칸에 알맞은 단어를 고르세요.

1. Mr. Han did not attend the meeting, [and / but] he submitted a detailed report in advance.
2. The training session covered [both / either] company policies and emergency procedures.

3 부사절 접속사

주어와 동사가 포함된 완전한 절을 이끌어 부사의 역할을 하도록 해주는 접속사입니다. 선택지가 접속사로만 구성된 경우 두 문장을 해석하여 연결 관계를 파악하면 되지만, 오답으로 전치사나 부사가 포함되는 경우 품사와 빈칸 뒤의 구조를 꼭 확인해야 합니다.

시간	when ~할 때 after ~한 후에 before ~하기 전에 since ~한 이후로 once ~하는 대로 until ~할 때까지 while ~하는 동안 as soon as ~하자마자 as ~할 때 by the time + 절: ~무렵에
조건	if ~한다면 unless ~가 아니라면 as long as ~하는 한 even if 설사 ~라 하더라도 as if 마치 ~처럼 assuming (that) ~라면 provided (that) ~라면 in the event that ~하는 경우에
양보	although, though, even though 비록 ~이지만, ~함에도 불구하고 however 아무리 ~하더라도 no matter + wh 의문사: ~하더라도
이유	because ~하기 때문에 since ~하므로 as ~하므로 now that (이제) ~이므로 in that ~라는 점에서
목적	so that ~할 수 있도록 in order that ~하기 위해
대조	while ~하는 반면, ~이지만 whereas ~하는 반면
결과	so ~ that …: 너무 ~해서 …하다

[**Since** / Although] the building is located downtown, it may take more time to get there.
그 건물은 도심에 위치해 있기 때문에, 거기까지 가는 데 더 많은 시간이 걸릴 수 있다.

so that 뒤에 이어지는 절에는 조동사 can이 쓰여서 '~할 수 있도록'이라는 의미를 나타냄

Ms. Liu adjusted the schedule [**so that** / whereas] the team **can** finish testing before the product launch.
제품 출시 전에 팀이 테스트를 끝낼 수 있도록 리우 씨가 일정을 조정했습니다.

You can begin entering data [while / **once**] the login credentials have been verified.
로그인 정보가 인증되면 데이터를 입력하기 시작할 수 있습니다.

전치사는 절을 이끌지 못하므로 오답

Please avoid making loud noises [**while** / during] the video conference is in progress.
화상 회의가 진행 중일 때는 큰 소음을 일으키는 걸 피해주세요.

Employees at Horizon Tech are required to complete a security training [**before** / if] they can access the main laboratory.
호라이즌 테크의 직원들은 본 실험실에 출입하기 전에 보안 교육을 완료해야 합니다.

The warranty remains valid [because / **as long as**] the product is not modified by third-party technicians.
제품이 제 3의 기술자에 의해 수정되지 않는 한 보증은 유효합니다.

■ 분사구문

부사절 접속사가 이끄는 절에서 주어를 생략하고 동사를 분사로 만들어 사용하는 구조이며, 주로 분사가 능동인지, 수동인지를 구분하는 유형으로 출제되므로 빈칸 뒤의 구조에 특히 주의해야 합니다.

▶ 뒤에 목적어가 있으므로 타동사 handle의 현재분사가 정답

Protective gear is mandatory when [**handling** / handled] hazardous material.
위험 물질을 다룰 때는 보호 장비가 의무적입니다.

▶ 타동사 complete 뒤에 목적어가 없으므로 과거분사가 정답

Once [completing / **completed**], the center will be the largest building in the city.
일단 완공되고 나면, 그 센터는 시에서 가장 큰 건물이 될 것이다.

가끔 접속사까지 생략되고 분사만 남는 경우가 출제되기도 하는데, 빈칸 앞의 절이 분사의 주어 역할을 합니다. 이 경우 대부분 선택지에 다양한 품사 형태가 제시되므로 그 중에서 분사를 정답으로 고르면 됩니다.

▶ 주어 없이 동사가 쓰여야 하므로 주어가 생략된 형태인 분사가 정답

BGL Enterprise had to delay hiring new staff, [**considering** / consider] current financial constraints.
현재 재정 상황을 고려하여 BGL 엔터프라이즈 사는 신규 직원 채용을 연기해야 했다.

■ 분사구문과 to부정사의 구분

가끔 분사구문은 접속사가 생략되어 출제되기도 합니다. 이때 선택지에 to부정사가 함께 제시되면, 문장 구조상으로 분사구문과 부정사를 구분하기가 어렵기 때문에 분사와 to부정사를 각각 빈칸에 대입하여 해석을 해야 합니다. 그런데, 분사구문은 여러 의미로 해석될 수 있으므로, 먼저 목적을 나타내는 to부정사를 대입하여 해석합니다. '~하기 위해서'라는 목적의 의미가 맞다면 to부정사를, 아니라면 분사를 정답으로 고르는 식으로 시간을 줄일 수 있습니다.

▶ 업무를 끝마치는 것이 커피를 사러 밖에 나가는 행위의 직접적인 목적이 될 수 없으므로 to부정사는 오답

[**Having** / To have] finished the assigned task, Ms. Lee went out to buy a cup of coffee.
배정된 업무를 끝마치고 나서, 리 씨는 커피를 한 잔 사러 나갔다.

▶ 일정이 지연되는 것은 초과 근무를 하기 위한 목적이 아니라 이유이므로 분사구문이 정답

[**Running** / To run] behind schedule, the construction team decided to work overtime over the weekend.
일정이 지연되고 있어서, 건설 팀은 주말에 초과 근무를 하기로 결정했다.

▶ 최근의 보안 문제를 해결하는 것은 새로운 방화벽 프로토콜을 도입한 목적이므로 to부정사가 정답

[Addressing / **To address**] the recent security issues, BH Systems implemented a new firewall protocol.
최근 보안 문제를 해결하기 위해, BH 시스템즈는 새로운 방화벽 규정을 시행했다.

PRACTICE 빈칸에 알맞은 단어를 고르세요.

3 Visitors can take photographs [since / while] strolling through the historic district.
4 The meeting will start at 10 A.M., [depends / depending] on when the executives arrive.

4 명사절 접속사

주어와 동사가 포함된 하나의 절을 이끌어 명사와 같은 역할을 하도록 해주는 접속사입니다.

■ 명사절 접속사의 기본 위치

명사절을 이끄는 접속사로는 that, whether, 그리고 WH 의문사(what, who/whose/whom, where, when, why, which, how)의 순으로 많이 출제됩니다. 명사절은 절이 명사의 역할을 하는 것이므로 문장 내에서 주어, 동사 및 전치사의 목적어, 그리고 보어로 쓰일 수 있습니다.

▶ 타동사 estimate의 목적어인 명사절을 이끄는 접속사

Several market analysts estimate **that** demand for electric vehicles will continue to climb.
여러 시장 분석가들은 전기차 수요가 계속해서 증가할 것이라고 예측한다.

▶ 전치사 of의 목적어인 명사절을 이끄는 접속사

The HR team is still finalizing plans and will soon inform us of **who** will serve as the new team leader.
인사팀은 아직 계획을 마무리하고 있는 중이며 누가 새 팀장으로 임명될지 곧 알려줄 예정입니다.

▶ 문장 전체의 주어 역할을 하는 명사절을 이끄는 접속사

Whether the new software update will resolve all reported bugs remains to be confirmed.
새 소프트웨어 업데이트가 모든 보고된 버그를 해결할지는 아직 확인되지 않았습니다.

▶ be동사 뒤에서 보어 역할을 하는 명사절을 이끄는 접속사

The CEO's question was **when** the redesigned Web site would be launched.
CEO의 질문은 재설계된 웹사이트가 언제 개시될 것인지였다.

---

that 명사절을 목적어로 취하는 토익 빈출 동사[확정된 내용]

- believe that ~라고 생각하다
- note that ~라는 것에 주목하다
- request that ~하도록 요청하다
- state that ~라고 진술하다
- hear that ~라고 듣다
- ask that ~하도록 요청하다
- find that ~라는 것을 알게 되다
- announce that ~라고 발표하다
- suggest that ~하도록 제안하다, ~임을 암시하다
- indicate[show] that ~라는 것을 보여주다

---

whether 명사절을 목적어로 취하는 토익 빈출 동사[불확실한 내용]

- determine whether ~인지를 결정하다
- let A know whether ~인지를 A에게 알려주다
- decide whether ~인지를 결정하다
- choose whether ~인지를 결정하다
- ask whether ~인지를 묻다

■ 완전한 절을 이끄는 명사절 접속사

> where 뒤에 「주어 + 동사 + 목적어」로 구성된 완전한 절이 이어진 구조

The board agreed on **where** we should hold the annual shareholders meeting.
이사회는 연례 주주총회를 어디에서 개최해야 하는지에 대해 합의했습니다.

> that 뒤에 「주어 + 1형식 자동사 + 전치사구」로 구성된 완전한 절이 이어진 구조

The company's annual report reveals **that** profits have risen by 20 percent over year.
회사의 연례 보고서는 이익이 전년 대비 20퍼센트 증가했다고 밝힙니다.

> 완전한 절을 이끄는 토익 빈출 명사절 접속사
> - that (확정된 내용)
> - where (장소)
> - why (이유)
> - whether (미결정 내용)
> - when (시간)
> - how (방법)

■ 불완전한 절을 이끄는 명사절 접속사

> 동사 know의 목적어가 빠진 불완전한 절

The seminar will focus on **what** young professionals need to know about effective networking.
세미나는 젊은 전문가들이 효과적인 네트워킹에 관해 알아야 할 내용을 중점적으로 다룰 것입니다.

> 불완전한 절을 이끄는 토익 빈출 명사절 접속사
> - who (주어 없음)
> - whose (소유격 없음)
> - which (주어, 목적어, 또는 보어 없음)
> - whom (목적어 없음)
> - what (주어, 목적어, 또는 보어 없음)
> - how (보어 또는 부사 없음)

■ to부정사를 이끄는 명사절 접속사

Mr. Simpson inquired about **how to apply** for the advertised position.
심슨 씨는 광고된 직책에 어떻게 지원하는지에 대해 문의했다.

> to부정사를 이끄는 토익 빈출 명사절 접속사
> - whether to do ~할지의 여부
> - what to do 무엇을 할지
> - when to meet 언제 만날지
> - how to register 어떻게 등록할지
> - where to go 어디에 가야할지
> - which to use 어느 것을 사용할지
> - whom to select 누구를 선택할지

PRACTICE   빈칸에 알맞은 단어를 고르세요.

5   The government report suggests [that / whether] stricter regulations would reduce emissions.

6   The committee has not decided [which / that] proposal requires immediate revision.

실전 TEST

학습한 내용을 적용하여 다음 기출 변형 문제들을 풀어보세요.

1. Without a valid receipt, we cannot provide customers with a refund, ------- we can offer to exchange a returned product.
   (A) or
   (B) and
   (C) as
   (D) but

2. ------- she has worked at WJE Engineering for over 20 years, the company has never offered Ms. Graves a leading role.
   (A) Once
   (B) Before
   (C) Since
   (D) Although

3. ------- Eddard Manufacturing's output has declined this year, its monthly net profits have increased significantly.
   (A) Because
   (B) While
   (C) Until
   (D) As long as

4. A complimentary mat and towel will be included ------- you sign up for one of our yoga courses.
   (A) if
   (B) with
   (C) but
   (D) either

5. ------- written several best-selling novels, Timothy Cook never won an award for his work.
   (A) To have
   (B) Have
   (C) Having
   (D) Had

6. Medical researchers at NorthPharm will determine ------- the new pain medication causes any negative side effects.
   (A) about
   (B) that
   (C) unless
   (D) whether

7. MJD Foods International announced this morning ------- it will expand its popular range of frozen pizzas.
   (A) what
   (B) that
   (C) because
   (D) while

8. The board members should decide ------- will lead the product presentation at the seminar in Hong Kong.
   (A) who
   (B) that
   (C) where
   (D) why

9. ------- Mr. Hartigan or Ms. Rhodes will assume the role of CFO at Manning Enterprises.
   (A) Both
   (B) Each
   (C) Either
   (D) Neither

10. By implementing an employee incentive program, we can not only improve the atmosphere of the office ------- boost our productivity.
    (A) so that
    (B) both
    (C) much
    (D) but

11 You may take a longer lunch break today ------- you finish the morning reports on time.

(A) while
(B) since
(C) if
(D) unless

12 Ms. Palomares was promoted to regional director ------- she had only been with Fritzen Labs for one year.

(A) during
(B) so that
(C) because
(D) even though

13 Neither the sales director ------- the marketing manager was available for the budget meeting.

(A) or
(B) and
(C) nor
(D) but

14 The shipment from Rymax Co. will be delayed ------- the roads are closed due to the storm.

(A) although
(B) because
(C) whereas
(D) despite

15 Both the legal department ------- the compliance team must review the new contract.

(A) either
(B) or
(C) and
(D) nor

16 The budget proposal was approved ------- several board members raised objections.

(A) because
(B) though
(C) whether
(D) so that

17 Ms. Wu submitted the revised draft, ------- she forgot to include the updated pricing table.

(A) but
(B) once
(C) hence
(D) because

18 The IT department rescheduled the maintenance to avoid disruptions ------- several employees were working overtime.

(A) since
(B) unless
(C) although
(D) whereas

19 Management has stated ------- all employees must complete the compliance training by June 30th.

(A) since
(B) that
(C) whether
(D) unless

20 The sales team will choose ------- to launch the new product this fall or early next year.

(A) whether
(B) until
(C) before
(D) when

DAY 09 | 전치사 Part 5

전치사는 토익에서 매월 4~5문항 정도 출제되는 빈출 품사 중 하나이며, 주로 전치사끼리 의미를 비교하거나 또는 의미가 비슷한 접속사와 구분하는 유형으로 출제됩니다. 전치사의 기본 의미를 구분하는 문제로 출제되기도 하지만, 다른 단어와 결합된 숙어 형태로 출제되는 경우가 더 많기 때문에, 어휘 학습처럼 암기로 접근해야 합니다.

1 시간 전치사

■ 기간

────▶ 유효기간 앞에 사용

The package must be returned **within** seven days of receipt to qualify for a full refund.
전액 환불을 받을 자격을 얻기 위해서 상품은 수령 후 7일 이내에 반품되어야 합니다.

숫자 없는 기간 명사를 목적어로 취함 ◀────   ────▶ 숫자가 포함된 기간 명사를 목적어로 취하므로 오답

Customers can contact technical support [**during** / for] regular business hours.
고객은 정규 영업시간 동안 기술 지원팀에 연락할 수 있습니다.

> **기간 명사를 목적어로 취하는 전치사**
> - 숫자 있는 기간 명사: **during** ~동안 **within** ~ 이내에 **for** ~ 동안 **over** ~ 동안에 걸쳐 **after** ~ 후에 **in** ~ 후에
> - 숫자 없는 기간 명사: **during** ~ 중에, ~ 동안 **throughout** ~ 내내

■ 시점

────▶ 날짜, 요일 앞에는 전치사 on

The annual safety inspection is scheduled to take place **on** September 14.
연례 안전 점검은 9월 14일에 진행될 예정입니다.

until은 특정 시점까지 행위가 지속되는 것을 나타내므로 오답 ◀────   ────▶ by는 특정 시점까지 행위가 완료되는 마감 시한을 의미

Please make sure the final report is reviewed [until / **by**] the end of the business day.
영업일 종료 시점까지 최종 보고서가 검토되었는지 반드시 확인해주세요.

> **시점 명사를 목적어로 취하는 전치사**
> - **at** (시간 등) ~에
> - **by** (기한) ~까지
> - **past** ~을 지나서
> - **on** (날짜, 요일 등) ~에
> - **until** (지속) ~까지
> - **from A to B**: A부터 B까지
> - **in** (월, 연도 등) ~에
> - **before** ~ 전에
> - **toward(s)** ~쯤, ~경에
> - **since** ~ 이후로
> - **after** ~ 후에
> - **between A and B**: A와 B 사이에

2 장소/위치 이동 전치사

■ 장소/위치/이동

강이나 도로처럼 길게 뻗어있는 장소에 대해 사용 ◀----   ----▶ 전체 범위에 걸친 장소에 대해 사용하므로 오답

Several luxury resorts are located [**along** / throughout] the coastline of the island.
여러 고급 리조트가 섬의 해안선을 따라 위치해 있다.

장소/위치/이동을 나타내는 전치사

- in (도시, 국가 등) ~에
- at (장소) ~에
- near ~ 근처에
- along (길 등) ~을 따라
- for ~을 향해
- within ~ 내에
- around ~ 주위에
- throughout ~ 전역에
- on (도로, 표면 등) ~에
- over ~ 너머에
- above ~ 위에
- next to ~ 옆에
- beside ~ 옆에
- below[under] ~ 밑에
- across 건너서, 전체에
- across from ~ 맞은편에
- onto ~ 위로
- into ~ 안으로
- out of ~ 밖으로
- behind ~ 뒤에
- in front of ~ 앞에
- to, toward(s) ~ 쪽으로
- from A to B: A에서 B까지
- between A and B: A와 B 사이에

3 이유/목적 전치사

■ 이유   ----▶ 이익, 혜택을 받은 것에 대한 이유를 나타냄

[**Owing to** / Thanks to] unexpected maintenance issues, the plant remained closed for two additional days.
예기치 못한 정비 문제 때문에 공장이 이틀 더 폐쇄되었습니다.

이유를 나타내는 전치사

- because of ~ 때문에
- due to ~로 인해, ~ 때문에
- thanks to ~ 때문에, ~ 덕분에
- owing to ~ 때문에
- on account of ~ 때문에
- for ~ 때문에, ~해서

■ 목적

After a business trip, employees should submit their receipts [within / **for**] reimbursement.
출장 후에, 직원들은 비용 환급을 위해 영수증을 제출해야 합니다.

PRACTICE   빈칸에 알맞은 단어를 고르세요.

1 The number of online orders steadily increased [over / for] the holiday period.
2 The agreement outlines shared responsibilities [from / between] our firm and its overseas partner.

4 주제/소속/범위/수단/자격 전치사

■ 주제

> '복리후생 제도의 변화'가 인사부에 연락할 내용의 주제에 해당함

Please contact the HR department [**regarding** / over] any changes to your benefits package.
복리후생 제도 변경에 관해서는 인사부에 연락해주세요.

주제를 나타내는 전치사
- about ~에 관해, ~와 관련해
- as to ~에 관해, ~와 관련해
- concerning ~에 관해, ~와 관련해
- over ~에 관해
- in regard to ~와 관련해
- with regard to ~와 관련해
- on ~에 관해(논문, 신문, 뉴스 등 전문적인 내용)
- regarding ~에 관해, ~와 관련해

■ 소속/범위

> 연령별 그룹이 차이를 보이는 대상 범위에 해당
> between은 범위의 대상이 둘 일 때 사용

The survey found significant differences [**among** / between] age groups in their spending habits.
그 설문조사에서 연령별 그룹들 사이에서 소비 습관에 상당한 차이가 있는 것으로 나타났습니다.

소속/범위를 나타내는 전치사
- at ~에 근무하는
- among ~ 사이에서
- of ~의
- from A to B: A에서 B까지
- from ~ 소속의
- in ~의 분야에서, ~하는 데
- within ~의 범위 내에

■ 수단/자격

> 맞춤형 후속 전화를 한 것이 분기 목표를 초과 달성한 방법이므로 by가 정답

The sales team exceeded quarterly targets [**by** / in] making personalized follow-up calls to prospective clients.
영업팀은 잠재 고객에게 맞춤형 후속 전화를 실시함으로써 분기 목표를 초과 달성했습니다.

수단/자격을 나타내는 전치사
- with ~로, ~을 갖고
- as ~로서
- through ~을 통해
- via ~을 통해
- on behalf of ~을 대신해
- by ~로, ~함으로써, ~을 타고

5 순서/양보/대체/동반/제외 전치사

■ 순서

두 가지 일의 전후 관계를 나타냄

Certificates will be awarded [**following** / concerning] successful completion of the training program.
연수 과정의 성공적인 수료 후에 수료증이 수여될 것입니다.

순서를 나타내는 전치사
- after ~ 후에
- following ~ 후에
- before ~ 전에
- prior to ~ 전에, ~에 앞서
- ahead of ~보다 빨리, 앞서
- behind ~보다 늦게
- upon ~하자마자

■ 양보/대체

주어진 조건 또는 벌어진 상황에서 예상되는 결과나 반응에 대한 상반된 결과를 나타내는 내용을 양보라고 합니다.

'~에도 불구하고 침착하고 전문적으로 대응했다'와 같은 양보의 의미가 구성되어야 알맞으므로 despite이 정답

The support staff responded calmly and professionally [because of / **despite**] the unexpected system outage.
예상치 못한 시스템 장애에도 불구하고 지원팀은 침착하고 전문적으로 대응했습니다.

양보/대체를 나타내는 전치사
- despite ~에도 불구하고
- in spite of ~에도 불구하고
- rather than ~ 대신에, ~가 아니라
- regardless of ~에 상관없이
- instead of ~ 대신에, ~하지 않고
- notwithstanding ~에도 불구하고

■ 동반/제외

The hotel's amenities are extensive, [**including** / aside from] a rooftop pool, fitness center, and 24-hour concierge service.
호텔의 편의 시설은 옥상 수영장, 피트니스 센터, 24시간 컨시어지 서비스를 포함하여 광범위합니다.

동반/제외를 나타내는 전치사
- with ~와 함께, ~을 가지고
- excluding ~을 제외하고
- apart from ~ 외에
- including ~을 포함하여
- along with ~와 함께, ~와 더불어
- aside from ~은 별도로 하고
- without ~없이, ~가 없다면
- except (for) ~을 제외하고

PRACTICE 빈칸에 알맞은 단어를 고르세요.

3 The board appointed Ms. Harrison [as / about] the company's new chief operating officer.

4 The marketing team decided to focus on digital channels [in spite of / rather than] print advertising this quarter.

6 다양한 의미로 사용되는 전치사

■ for의 다양한 의미

단일 전치사로 가장 많이 출제되는 전치사 for는 이동 방향(~로, ~을 향해), 행위의 대상(~에게, ~을 대상으로), 목적 또는 용도(~을 위해, ~용으로), 이유(~ 때문에, ~로 인해), 기간(~ 동안), 특정 시점(~에), 자격(~을 받을, ~에 대해) 등 아주 다양한 의미로 사용된다는 것을 꼭 기억해 두어야 합니다.

▶ 강의를 들어야 할 대상을 나타내므로 for가 정답

According to the Web site, the course is intended [to / **for**] amateur photographers.
웹사이트에 따르면, 그 강좌는 아마추어 사진가들을 대상으로 하고 있다.

▶ 회사의 퇴직연금 제도에 대한 자격을 나타내므로 for가 정답

New hires will be eligible [with / **for**] the company's retirement plan after one year of service.
신입 사원은 1년 근속 후 회사 퇴직연금 제도에 가입할 자격이 주어질 것입니다.

■ by의 다양한 의미

전치사 by도 for와 마찬가지로 매우 다양한 의미로 사용됩니다. 방법(~함으로써, ~을 통해), 수치 변화 또는 차이(~만큼), 교통 수단(~을 타고, ~을 이용해), 위치(~ 옆에), 마감 기한(~까지), 행위 주체(~에 의해) 등의 의미로 자주 출제된다는 것을 알아 두시기 바랍니다.

▶ by는 증가 또는 감소를 나타내는 동사 뒤에서 숫자 표현과 함께 수치 변화를 나타냄

The membership of our fitness center has increased [**by** / prior to] 20 percent this quarter.
우리 헬스클럽의 회원 수가 이번 분기에 20퍼센트 증가했습니다.

▶ by + -ing: ~함으로써 (방법)

GreenNova reduced packaging waste **by** switching to biodegradable materials.
그린노바 사는 생분해성 소재로 전환함으로써 포장 폐기물을 줄였습니다.

■ from의 다양한 의미

전치사 from도 사용되는 의미의 수가 많으며, 출제 빈도 또한 높습니다. 자주 출제되는 의미로는 시작 지점(~부터, ~로부터), 출처(~에서 나온), 소속(~ 소속의, ~ 출신의), 분리 또는 격리(~로부터, ~에서), 재료(~로 만들어진), 구별(~로부터, ~와), 금지 또는 방지(~하지 않도록), 변화(~에서)가 있습니다.

▶ 동사 prevent, stop 등과 함께 쓰이는 from은 방지 또는 중단의 의미를 가짐

Management is striving to prevent similar accidents [instead of / **from**] occurring again.
경영진은 유사 사고들이 다시 발생하는 것을 막기 위해 노력하고 있습니다.

▶ 변화되기 전의 상태나 형태를 나타낼 때 '~에서'라는 의미

Production costs have decreased by 10 percent [than / **from**] what they were five years ago.
생산 비용이 5년 전 그랬던 것에서 10% 감소했다.

7 특수 전치사

■ 현재분사에서 변형된 전치사

기자회견의 주제가 '회사의 최근 인수'이므로 concerning이 정답

The director held a press conference [following / **concerning**] the company's recent acquisition.
이사는 회사의 최근 인수에 관하여 기자 회견을 열었다.

현재분사형 전치사

- beginning (with/on/in) ~부터 (시작해)
- considering ~을 고려해, 감안해
- excluding ~을 제외하고
- owing to ~ 때문에
- regarding ~와 관련해
- starting (with/on/in) ~부터 (시작해)
- following ~ 후에
- notwithstanding ~에도 불구하고
- concerning ~와 관련해
- including ~을 포함해
- according to ~에 따르면
- surrounding ~주위에, ~을 둘러싼

■ 명사 결합형 전치사구

연장 보증도 프리미엄 요금제에 포함되므로 '추가'의 의미를 나타내는 in addition to가 정답

Our premium plan offers priority support [**in addition to** / in response to] extended warranty coverage.
저희의 프리미엄 요금제는 연장 보증 뿐만 아니라 우선 지원을 제공합니다.

악천후가 일정이 연기될 수 있는 한 가지 요인에 해당되므로 In case of가 정답

[In recognition of / **In case of**] inclement weather, the final match will be delayed.
악천후가 발생할 경우에, 결승전은 연기될 것입니다.

명사 결합형 전치사구

- in addition to ~에 더해, ~뿐만 아니라
- on behalf of ~을 대표해, 대신해
- in the event of ~의 경우에
- in recognition of ~을 인정해
- in accordance with ~에 따라, ~을 준수해
- as a result of ~에 따른 결과로
- in case of ~의 경우에
- in observance of ~을 준수해
- under the direction of ~의 감독[지휘] 하에
- beyond description 이루 말할 수 없는
- in response to ~에 대응해, 응답하여

PRACTICE 빈칸에 알맞은 단어를 고르세요.

5 The new application is ideal [by / for] those who don't have enough time for shopping.

6 [As a result of / According to] the records in our database, your order was delivered last Friday.

실전 TEST

학습한 내용을 적용하여 다음 기출 변형 문제들을 풀어보세요.

1. The new security protocols go into effect ------- April 3 and will remain in place indefinitely.
   (A) by
   (B) since
   (C) on
   (D) for

2. All customer inquiries should be directed ------- the support team rather than the product manager.
   (A) onto
   (B) to
   (C) from
   (D) by

3. The legal department reviewed the agreement carefully ------- sending it to the client.
   (A) before
   (B) during
   (C) among
   (D) through

4. Our finance office is located ------- the second floor, next to the elevator.
   (A) over
   (B) under
   (C) on
   (D) across

5. The technician found a fault ------- the wiring that caused the outage.
   (A) in
   (B) at
   (C) to
   (D) of

6. Employees are asked to refrain ------- using personal devices during training sessions.
   (A) with
   (B) of
   (C) by
   (D) from

7. Plyus Appliances received confirmation of the delivery ------- e-mail late yesterday afternoon.
   (A) in
   (B) by
   (C) over
   (D) with

8. Ms. Harrigan placed the revised forms ------- the shared drive so the entire team could access them.
   (A) at
   (B) from
   (C) on
   (D) to

9. The monthly sales meeting will be held ------- Room B unless staff are otherwise notified.
   (A) in
   (B) on
   (C) at
   (D) to

10. Ms. Takada has worked at Insen Transport ------- nearly a decade and is now head of operations.
    (A) for
    (B) during
    (C) since
    (D) by

11 Numerous classical musicians from all over the world will perform ------- the Fifth Annual Vancouver Music Festival.
(A) among
(B) between
(C) during
(D) while

12 Payments for all Pacific Telecom services are normally due ------- the 20th of each month.
(A) in
(B) on
(C) at
(D) with

13 Mr. Treadstone and the real estate agent will meet ------- 452 Jones Street to view the vacant building.
(A) along
(B) on
(C) under
(D) at

14 Dr. Miranda Silva was awarded the Sherwood Prize ------- her research on the importance of good body posture.
(A) of
(B) for
(C) to
(D) about

15 Starting next month, only those ------- a permit will be allowed to use the North Bay parking lot.
(A) toward
(B) for
(C) of
(D) with

16 According to the data, traffic congestion on Fifth Avenue is at its worst ------- 7 A.M. and 9 A.M.
(A) among
(B) under
(C) between
(D) both

17 Frank Lyles, a business professor from Hampton University, will be delivering a lecture ------- time management skills.
(A) by
(B) to
(C) with
(D) on

18 Please contact Ms. Scott in the personnel office if you did not receive the memorandum ------- the new corporate security policies.
(A) without
(B) regarding
(C) following
(D) throughout

19 ------- its affordable housing and large number of schools, the Repford neighborhood is very popular with young families.
(A) Owing to
(B) Assuming
(C) Rather
(D) Because

20 Greenberg Marketing Group has decided to conduct an extensive customer survey on behalf ------- the Denham Department Store.
(A) for
(B) of
(C) with
(D) to

DAY 10 | 관계사 (Part 5)

관계사는 동일한 것을 지칭하는 요소를 가진 두 문장을 하나로 연결하는 방법으로, 하나의 절을 다른 절의 명사(=선행사)에 연결합니다. 이때 선행사가 관계사절에서 명사의 기능을 하면 관계대명사, 선행사가 관계사절에서 부사의 역할을 하면 관계부사라고 합니다. 관계사가 포함된 문장은 구조가 복잡해 어려워 보이지만, 토익에서 출제되는 관계사 문제는 50% 이상이 사람/사물 선행사를 구분하는 유형과 관계대명사의 주격/소유격/목적격을 구분하는 유형 등 기초 원리를 묻는 유형으로 출제됩니다.

1 관계대명사

관계대명사가 이끄는 절은 하나의 명사를 뒤에서 수식하는 역할을 합니다. 수식 대상인 명사(선행사)가 사람인지 사물인지 구분하고, 동사의 수를 일치시키고, 관계대명사의 격을 맞추면 됩니다. 관계대명사는 선행사가 관계대명사절에서 하는 역할에 따라 주격, 소유격, 그리고 목적격으로 구분되며 주격, 소유격, 목적격 순으로 자주 출제됩니다.

■ 관계대명사의 격

	주격	목적격	소유격
사람	who / that	whom / that	whose
사물	which / that	which / that	whose / of which

▶ 사람 선행사 Customers를 수식하는 주격 관계대명사

Customers **who enroll** in the loyalty program gain access to exclusive discounts.
로열티 프로그램에 등록하는 고객은 특별 할인 혜택을 받을 수 있습니다.

▶ 사물 선행사 proposal을 수식하는 주격 관계대명사

We approved the proposal **which outlines** the new employee benefits program.
우리는 새로운 복리후생 제도를 설명하는 제안서를 승인했습니다.

▶ 사람명사 candidate와 사물명사 résumé 사이의 소유 관계를 나타내면서 candidate를 수식하는 소유격 관계대명사

Mr. Kane interviewed the candidate **whose résumé** included international experience.
케인 씨는 국제 경력이 포함된 이력서를 가진 지원자를 면접했습니다.

▶ 사물 선행사 presentation을 수식하는 목적격 관계대명사. 목적격은 생략 가능

Ms. Jung completed the presentation **(that) the client requested** urgently.
정 씨는 고객이 긴급히 요청한 발표 자료를 완성했다.

■ 전치사 + 관계대명사

관계대명사는 대명사의 성격을 지니고 있어서 전치사의 목적어로 사용될 수 있습니다. 전치사의 목적어로는 whom과 which만 사용되며, that은 전치사의 목적어로 사용되지 않습니다.

▶ 전치사 in과 관계대명사 which가 결합되어 사물명사 report를 수식

We analyzed the report **in which** quarterly sales figures were compared across regions.
저희는 분기별 판매 수치가 지역별로 비교된 보고서를 분석했습니다.

▶ 「수량 부정대명사 + of + 목적격 관계대명사」

The seminar attracted over 300 participants, **some of whom** traveled from overseas.
그 세미나는 300명 이상의 참석자를 끌어 모았으며, 그 중 일부는 해외에서 왔습니다.

목적격 whom/which와 결합하는 토익 빈출 수량 표현

- most of ~의 대부분
- many of ~의 다수
- some of ~의 일부
- a few of ~의 몇몇
- all of ~의 모두
- both of ~의 둘 다
- several of ~의 몇몇
- any of ~하는 누구든/무엇이든
- each of ~의 각각
- none of ~중 아무도 (않다)

■ 관계대명사의 수일치

주격 관계대명사가 이끄는 절의 동사는 수식받는 명사(선행사)에 맞춰 수를 일치시키고, 소유격 관계대명사가 이끄는 절의 동사는 소유격 관계대명사 뒤에 쓰이는 명사에 수를 일치시킵니다.

▶ 선행사인 단수명사 supervisor에 맞춰 3인칭 단수 형태로 수일치

The supervisor who [monitor / **monitors**] production quality will attend tomorrow's meeting.
생산 품질을 관리하는 관리자가 내일 회의에 참석할 것입니다.

▶ 소유격 뒤의 복수명사 responsibilities에 맞춰 복수 형태로 수일치

The supervisor whose responsibilities [**include** / includes] performance reviews meets with staff every quarter.
성과 평가가 책무에 포함되어 있는 관리자는 매 분기마다 직원들과 면담합니다.

PRACTICE 빈칸에 알맞은 단어를 고르세요.

1 I forwarded the e-mail [which / whose] explains the travel reimbursement policy.

2 The consultant who [advise / advises] on market expansion strategies joined the project yesterday.

2 관계부사

관계부사는 시간, 장소, 이유 또는 방법을 나타내는 명사를 수식하며, 관계대명사와 달리 격에 따라 구분하지 않습니다.

■ 장소 관계부사 where

'그 곳에서' (= at the conference hall / at the place)

The conference hall **where** the keynote speech takes place can accommodate over 500 guests.
기조 연설이 진행되는 컨퍼런스 홀은 500명 이상의 관객을 수용할 수 있다.

■ 시간 관계부사 when

'그 때에' (= on the day / at the time)

The day **when** all invoices must be approved is this Thursday.
모든 청구서가 승인되어야 하는 날은 이번 주 목요일입니다.

▶ 토익에서는 선행사 the time이 생략된 구조로 출제

The second quarter of each year is **when** our profits reach record highs.
매년 2분기는 우리 수익이 최대치를 기록하는 시기이다.

■ 이유 관계부사 why

'그 이유 때문에' (= for that reason)

The committee reviewed the reasons **why** the marketing campaign underperformed.
위원회는 마케팅 캠페인이 예상보다 실적을 내지 못했던 이유들을 검토했습니다.

▶ 토익에서는 선행사 the reason이 생략된 구조로 출제

That's **why** we have kept a close relationship with our local communities.
그것이 우리가 지역 사회들과 긴밀한 관계를 유지해 온 이유입니다.

■ 방법 관계부사 how

▶ 방법을 나타낼 때 관계부사 how 또는 선행사 the way 중 하나만 사용

The IT team documented the procedure on **how** employees can reset their passwords.
IT 팀은 직원들이 비밀번호를 재설정할 수 있는 방법에 대한 절차를 문서화했습니다.

3 복합관계사

복합관계대명사와 복합관계부사로 나뉘는 복합관계사는 관계대명사와 관계부사 끝에 ever가 붙은 형태이며, 「~하는 …이든」이라는 의미를 나타냅니다. 복합관계대명사가 이끄는 절은 명사절 또는 부사절의 역할을 하며, 복합 관계부사가 이끄는 절은 부사절의 역할을 합니다. 명사를 수식하는 역할이 아니므로 선행사가 없다는 것이 특징입니다.

■ 복합관계대명사

> whoever/whomever ~하는 누구든, 누구를 ~하든 (= anyone who(m), no matter who(m))
> whatever ~하는 무엇이든, 무엇을 ~하든 (= anything that, no matter what)
> whichever ~하는 어느 것이든, 어느 것을 ~하든 (= anything which, no matter which)

= anyone who: ~하는 누구라도

The bonus will go to **whoever exceeds** their quarterly targets by more than 10 percent.
분기 목표를 10% 이상 초과 달성하는 누구라도 그 사람에게 보너스가 지급될 것입니다.

= No matter what: ~하는 것은 무엇이든지

The company will provide **whatever** is necessary for remote work.
그 회사는 원격 근무에 필요한 것은 무엇이든지 제공할 것이다.

■ 복합관계부사

> wherever ~하는 어디든, ~하는 곳마다 (= at any place where, no matter where)
> whenever ~하는 언제든, ~할 때마다 (= at any time when, no matter when)
> however 아무리 ~해도, 얼마나 ~하든 (= no matter how)

= at any time when: ~할 때 언제든
= no matter when

Employees can use company vehicles **whenever** they have off-site meetings.
직원들은 외부 회의가 있을 때 언제든 회사 차량을 이용할 수 있습니다.

= No matter how: 얼마나 ~하든

However complex the new software is, our IT department will provide useful hands-on training.
새로운 소프트웨어가 아무리 복잡하더라도 저희 IT 부서는 유용한 실습형 교육을 제공할 것입니다.

PRACTICE 빈칸에 알맞은 단어를 고르세요.

3 Mr. Song reserved a meeting room [when / where] both teams can collaborate without interruptions.

4 The emergency lighting activates [whenever / however] normal power fails.

4 다양한 관계사의 구분

각 관계사는 특정 구조로 된 절을 이끄는데, 그 특징과 관련된 부분이 토익의 주요 출제 포인트입니다. 따라서, 관계사별로 어떤 구조적인 특징이 있는지 명확히 알아 두어야 합니다.

■ 불완전한 절을 이끄는 관계대명사 who, whom, that, which

관계대명사 who, whom, that, which는 관계대명사절에서 주어, 목적어, 보어의 역할을 하므로 그 역할에 해당하는 주어, 목적어 또는 보어가 빠진 불완전한 절이 이어집니다. 그러므로 빈칸 뒤의 절이 불완전한 구조라면, 빈칸은 관계대명사의 자리입니다.

▶ who가 purchases의 주어이므로 주어가 빠진 불완전한 절

A discount coupon will be provided to anyone **who purchases** items on our Web site.
저희 웹사이트에서 제품을 구입하시는 모든 분께 할인 쿠폰이 제공될 것입니다.

▶ that이 visited의 목적어이므로 목적어가 빠진 불완전한 절

The restaurant **that we visited** yesterday will close next week for renovation.
우리가 어제 방문했던 식당은 개조 공사를 위해 다음 주에 문을 닫을 것이다.

■ 완전한 절을 이끄는 관계부사 where, when, why, how

관계부사 where, when, why, how는 관계부사절에서 부사(장소, 시간, 이유, 방법)의 역할을 하므로 그 뒤에는 주어, 동사, 목적어, 보어 등 문장 구성 요소가 모두 갖춰진 완전한 절이 이어집니다. 그러므로 빈칸 뒤의 절이 완전한 구조라면, 빈칸은 관계부사의 자리입니다.

▶ 「주어 + 수동태 동사(be p.p.)」로 구성된 완전한 절

The inspectors will examine the warehouse **where surplus inventory is stored**.
검사관들이 잉여 재고가 보관되어 있는 창고를 조사할 것이다.

▶ 「주어 + 자동사」로 구성된 완전한 절

The quarter **when most product launches occur** usually shows higher revenue.
대부분의 제품 출시가 이루어지는 분기에는 일반적으로 더 높은 수익이 발생한다.

▶ 선행사 the reason이 생략됨

The research team identified **why the prototype failed the stress test**.
그 연구팀은 프로토타입이 스트레스 테스트에 실패한 이유를 확인하였다.

How의 수식을 받는 형용사 + 주어 + 동사 ◀

All employees are asked to take short breaks, no matter **how busy they are**.
아무리 바쁘더라도, 모든 직원은 잠깐씩 휴식을 취하는 것이 요청됩니다.

■ **불완전한 절을 이끄는 복합관계대명사 who(m)ever, whatever, whichever**

복합관계사 문제는 네 개의 선택지가 모두 복합관계사들로만 구성됩니다. 따라서 먼저 빈칸 뒤의 절이 완전한 구조인지를 확인해 복합관계대명사 자리인지 또는 복합관계부사 자리인지를 구분한 뒤, 의미를 통해 정답을 고릅니다.

전치사의 목적어 자리지만 토익에서는 whomever 대신 whoever를 사용 ◀------ ┆ ┆ ------▶ 동사 has의 주어가 빠진 불완전한 절

The company will offer an incentive trip to **whoever has** the highest sales record this year.
회사는 올해 가장 높은 판매 실적을 올린 사람에게 인센티브 여행을 제공할 것이다.

------▶ 타동사 decide의 목적어가 빠진 불완전한 절

Whatever management **decides** on this matter, we will support it.
경영진이 이 문제에 대해 무엇을 결정하든, 우리는 그것을 지지할 것입니다.

■ **완전한 절을 이끄는 복합관계부사 wherever, whenever, however**

「주어 + be동사 + 보어」로 구성된 완전한 절 ◀------

Automatic updates are installed [**whenever** / wherever] **the computer is** not in use.
컴퓨터가 사용되지 않을 때마다 자동 업데이트가 설치됩니다.

------▶ 「주어 + 동사 + 목적어」로 구성된 완전한 절

Managers must review financial records **wherever they detect unusual transactions**.
이상 거래가 발견되는 곳이라면 어디든 관리자는 재무 기록을 검토해야 합니다.

■ **명사(=선행사)를 가지지 않는 what**

선행사를 포함한 관계대명사인지, 아니면 명사절 접속사인지 what의 역할에 대한 논란이 있지만, 토익에서 그 구분은 중요하지 않습니다. 다만 두 가지의 역할 모두 what이 명사 뒤에 쓰이지 않으므로, what이 선택지에 포함되어 있는 경우에 문제에서 빈칸 앞에 명사가 위치한다면 what을 오답으로 소거하고 관계대명사를 정답으로 골라야 합니다.

------▶ what은 앞에 위치한 선행사를 수식하지 않으므로 오답

The software update [what / **that**] was released last week improved system security.
지난주에 출시된 소프트웨어 업데이트는 시스템 보안을 향상시켰습니다.

PRACTICE 빈칸에 알맞은 단어를 고르세요.

5 Please submit your application form to Ms. Reynor via e-mail or fax, depending on [however / whichever] is easier for you.

6 New hires toured the distribution facility [which / where] orders are processed and shipped.

실전 TEST

학습한 내용을 적용하여 다음 기출 변형 문제들을 풀어보세요.

1. The marketing director, ------- ideas have transformed the company's image, will be retiring next month.
   (A) who
   (B) whose
   (C) whom
   (D) which

2. The device ------- was returned by the customer had a manufacturing defect.
   (A) who
   (B) whom
   (C) that
   (D) whose

3. We hired an external consultant ------- specializes in energy efficiency to design our new solar-powered battery.
   (A) whose
   (B) who
   (C) which
   (D) what

4. The office ------- we held the client meeting is being renovated this week.
   (A) that
   (B) what
   (C) which
   (D) where

5. Ms. Ortega, ------- you met at the conference, is leading the training session today.
   (A) who
   (B) which
   (C) whose
   (D) when

6. The company released a report ------- outlines its strategy for the next fiscal year.
   (A) whose
   (B) who
   (C) that
   (D) where

7. This is the application ------- needs to be completed by all new employees.
   (A) what
   (B) who
   (C) that
   (D) where

8. The technician ------- fixed the server did an excellent job and charged a reasonable fee.
   (A) who
   (B) which
   (C) whom
   (D) whose

9. The seminar, ------- was organized by the human resources department, covered workplace health and safety.
   (A) who
   (B) what
   (C) how
   (D) which

10. Employees ------- performance exceeds expectations will be considered for promotion every three months.
    (A) which
    (B) whose
    (C) in which
    (D) who

11 Guests ------- are interested in the guided tour of the Empire State Building should meet in the lobby at 10 A.M.
(A) who
(B) which
(C) whose
(D) whom

12 All staff were informed by the company president about the merger with Vortex Entertainment, ------- is based in Los Angeles.
(A) who
(B) whose
(C) how
(D) which

13 The festival organizer announced a shuttle bus service that ------- the event venue with several bus and subway lines.
(A) connect
(B) connection
(C) connecting
(D) connects

14 Full-time employees with over five years of service who ------- to take paid vacation in August must submit a request form no later than April 30.
(A) wish
(B) wishes
(C) wishing
(D) wishful

15 Many businesses in Aspen hire additional workers during the winter ------- the number of tourists is at its highest.
(A) where
(B) why
(C) when
(D) how

16 Ms. Grey accidentally left her purse in the conference room ------- her interview took place.
(A) what
(B) which
(C) that
(D) where

17 Customers who misplace their instruction manual can visit our Web site to see ------- our furniture should be assembled.
(A) which
(B) what
(C) how
(D) whom

18 Mr. Bentley will provide two weeks of training and support to ------- replaces him as payroll manager next month.
(A) whichever
(B) whoever
(C) whenever
(D) wherever

19 Our market research survey shows ------- our products are most popular with consumers aged between 17 and 25.
(A) why
(B) which
(C) what
(D) those

20 Ms. Johnson visited the factory yesterday to inspect the manufacturing machines ------- were installed last year.
(A) what
(B) that
(C) who
(D) there

PART 5 FINAL TEST 2

학습한 내용을 적용하여 다음 기출 변형 문제들을 풀어보세요.

1. The ------- documents were distributed to everyone who attended the product demonstration.
   (A) print
   (B) printing
   (C) printed
   (D) prints

2. The keynote speaker greeted all guests ------- before starting his talk on genetic engineering.
   (A) warmly
   (B) warm
   (C) warmest
   (D) warmth

3. Please place all job application forms ------- the tray on Ms. Cooper's desk.
   (A) at
   (B) in
   (C) to
   (D) over

4. Argo Sportswear's main distribution warehouse is located ------- the industrial park, just off Highway 9.
   (A) among
   (B) across
   (C) through
   (D) within

5. The merchandise ------ is included in our summer sale promotion should be labeled with a yellow sticker.
   (A) what
   (B) that
   (C) it
   (D) this

6. Every department needs to develop a ------- plan before the reorganization of the business begins.
   (A) clear
   (B) clearly
   (C) clarity
   (D) clearing

7. The safety inspector gave the restaurant a high score, ------- he identified several things that can be improved.
   (A) unless
   (B) because
   (C) so that
   (D) although

8. Discount vouchers may be redeemed only at ------- branches of Sunrise Bubble Tea.
   (A) participant
   (B) participate
   (C) participating
   (D) participated

9. The new technical support Web chat feature is ------- effective, reducing response times by 30 percent.
   (A) high
   (B) highly
   (C) higher
   (D) highest

10. The payment to the client was delayed ------- the accounting system experienced technical issues.
    (A) however
    (B) but
    (C) so
    (D) because

11 The new air conditioning units will be installed ------- the weekend to minimize disruption to our workflow.

(A) despite
(B) until
(C) while
(D) during

12 The consultant ------- we hired last month specializes in renewable energy projects.

(A) who
(B) which
(C) them
(D) where

13 Lazarus Engineering submitted a ------- bid, making the firm a strong contender for the monorail development project.

(A) compete
(B) competitor
(C) competitive
(D) competitively

14 According to the user manual, a red ------- light indicates that the machine is overheating.

(A) blink
(B) blinking
(C) blinks
(D) blinked

15 The organizers of the tennis tournament will need to adjust the schedule ------- unforeseen delays.

(A) for
(B) of
(C) about
(D) between

16 Our contract with the accounting firm remains valid ------- the end of the fiscal year.

(A) until
(B) since
(C) toward
(D) across

17 The function rooms ------- companies will hold their year-end banquets have been thoroughly cleaned by the housekeeping staff.

(A) what
(B) when
(C) which
(D) where

18 Due to high demand, ------- all seats for the Elmwood Conference were reserved within two hours.

(A) next to
(B) nearly
(C) somewhat
(D) approximately

19 Because Mr. Ramirez completed the project ahead of schedule ------- multiple setbacks, he received a performance bonus.

(A) against
(B) except for
(C) regardless of
(D) nevertheless

20 The final round of the Startup Pitch Contest was so ------- that several audience members gave standing ovations.

(A) thrill
(B) thrills
(C) thrilled
(D) thrilling

기본토익 700+

PART 6

DAY 11 접속부사
DAY 12 문맥파악 / 문장삽입
PART 6 FINAL TEST

PART 6 ★ 지문 빈칸 채우기 문제 미리보기

- 문항수: 16문항 (131번~146번)
- 한 개의 지문에 네 개의 빈칸이 들어 있고, 그 빈칸에 들어갈 문법적으로, 또는 의미적으로 알맞은 어휘/문장을 고르는 유형으로서, 총 네 개의 지문이 출제됩니다.

Questions 131-134 refer to the following instructions.

Thank you for purchasing plants from our store. Stick to these easy-to-follow guidelines to ------- **131.** your plants and help them to flourish.

↳ 알맞은 어휘 고르기

First, your plants require water, light, and warmth in order to survive. Place your plants in suitable pots or troughs filled with nutrient-rich soil. Then, ------- **132.** position them

↳ 단어의 알맞은 형태 고르기

somewhere where they can receive ample sunlight. Make sure that you water your plants on a regular basis. -------, **133.** they will begin to wither and will eventually die. -------. **134.**

↳ 알맞은 접속부사 고르기   ↳ 문맥상 알맞은 문장 고르기

131. (A) preserve
(B) select ✓
(C) order
(D) review

132. (A) simplify
(B) simply ✓
(C) simple
(D) simplistically

133. (A) Meanwhile
(B) However
(C) Thus
(D) Otherwise ✓

134. (A) By following these instructions, you can keep your plants healthy. ✓
(B) These can be purchased at affordable prices from Palmerstone Plants.
(C) We wish to apologize for any inconvenience this may have caused you.
(D) Please note that the devices should be cleaned on a regular basis.

DAY 11 | 접속부사 Part 6

접속부사는 접속사와 유사한 역할을 수행하는 부사이며, 품사로는 접속사가 아니라 부사로 분류됩니다. 접속사처럼 문장과 문장을 의미 관계를 이어주는 말의 역할을 하지만 부사의 기능을 합니다.

1 접속부사의 개념 정리

■ **접속부사의 역할**

접속부사는 문장을 수식하는 부사로서 문장의 시작 부분에 위치하며, 그 앞에 존재하는 독립된 다른 문장과 의미적으로 어떤 관계인지를 나타냅니다.

> 주어 + 동사 + (목적어/보어/수식어구). 접속부사, 주어 + 동사.

Mr. Pederson wanted to go to the International Garden Expo. However, **the weather made** it impossible.
페더슨 씨는 국제정원박람회에 가길 원했다. 하지만, 날씨가 그것을 불가능하게 하였다.

■ **접속부사 풀이 전략**

접속부사는 독립된 두 문장이 하나처럼 해석되는 자연스러운 논리 관계를 나타냅니다. 따라서 알맞은 접속부사를 고르기 위해서는 앞뒤의 문장을 해석해 두 문장 사이의 내용 흐름을 파악해야 합니다.

문맥 확인
빈칸 앞뒤 문장 내용 확인

의미 관계 파악
시간/역접/양보/결과 등
두 문장의 관계 파악

접속 부사 선택
해당 관계에 적합한 접속부사 선택

2 빈출 접속부사 유형 정리

■ 양보, 대조, 상반 관계를 나타내는 접속부사

앞 문장에서 언급된 내용에 대해 예상되는 결과나 사실에 대해 상반된 내용이 뒤에 이어질 때 양보 접속부사를 씁니다. 또한 앞 문장에 언급된 내용과 다른 특징이나 대조되는 내용을 언급할 경우 대조, 상반 관계를 나타내는 접속부사가 사용됩니다.

- However 하지만
- Nevertheless, Nonetheless 그럼에도 불구하고
- On the other hand 또 다른 한편
- On the contrary, Conversely 반대로
- Even so 그럴지라도
- After all (예상과는 달리) 결국, 어쨌든
- Unfortunately 안타깝게도
- Still 그래도, 여전히
- Instead 그 대신 (대체)
- Alternatively 대안적으로 (대체)

Line 10 trains will run every 4-5 minutes during morning and evening rush hours and every 7-9 minutes at all other times. Travelers may transfer to other lines from Line 10 at no extra cost. -------, a $1.35 fee will be charged when they transfer to a city bus.

(A) However (B) Likewise (C) Indeed (D) Since

10호선 열차들은 아침과 저녁 혼잡 시간에 4~5분 간격으로 운행될 것이며, 그 외의 모든 시간대에는 7~9분마다 운행될 것입니다. 승객들은 추가 요금 없이 10호선에서 다른 노선으로 환승하실 수 있습니다. 하지만, 시내버스로 갈아탈 경우에는 1.35달러의 요금이 부과될 것입니다.

1 문맥 확인
승객들은 추가 요금 없이 환승 가능 → 버스로 갈아탈 경우 1.35달러의 요금 부과

2 의미 관계 파악
추가 요금을 내지 않아도 되는 것과 요금이 부과되는 것은 서로 상반된 의미 관계

3 접속 부사 선택
상반 관계를 나타내는 접속부사
(A) However가 정답

PRACTICE 빈칸에 들어갈 알맞은 접속부사를 고르세요.

Employees were told that printed handouts would not be distributed during the seminar. -------, they should download the materials from the company's Intranet.

(A) Rather than that (B) Instead (C) Additionally (D) In contrast

■ 추가 관계를 나타내는 접속부사

앞 문장에 언급된 것과 같은 성격의 내용이 추가되는 흐름을 나타낼 때 사용합니다.

- In addition, Additionally 덧붙이면
- Similarly 유사하게
- Besides, Plus 그 밖에
- Also 또한, 역시
- Likewise 마찬가지로
- In fact 사실은, 실제로 (자세한 내용 추가)
- Moreover, Furthermore 게다가, 또한, 더 나아가

This e-mail is to confirm the terms we drafted during our meeting yesterday. As we discussed, your firm will provide state-of-the-art security equipment, and the start date of installation will be August 15. We would prefer if you could have the work finished within 2 or 3 days. -------, the full cost of the installation will be no more than $5,000, as we agreed yesterday.

(A) For example   (B) Therefore   (C) In contrast   (D) In addition

이 이메일은 어제 회의 중에 저희가 초안을 작성한 계약 조건을 확인해 드리기 위한 것입니다. 저희가 논의했던 대로, 귀사가 첨단 보안 장비를 제공할 것이며, 설치 작업 시작일은 8월 15일이 될 것입니다. 저희는 2~3일 내에 작업이 마무리될 수 있도록 해주시면 좋겠습니다. 덧붙여, 모든 설치 비용은 어제 합의한 대로 5,000달러를 넘지 않을 것입니다.

문맥 확인
2~3일 이내 작업 완료하면 좋겠다 → 모든 설치 비용은 합의대로 5000달러 미만

의미 관계 파악
장비 설치 작업 기한 언급 후 설치 비용 언급이므로 장비 설치에 관한 정보 추가 관계

접속 부사 선택
추가 내용을 언급할 때 사용하는 접속부사 (D) In addition이 정답

PRACTICE   빈칸에 들어갈 알맞은 접속부사를 고르세요.

The office installed energy-efficient LED lighting throughout the building, reducing overall power consumption. Monthly electricity expenses have dropped by nearly 20 percent. -------, maintenance costs for lighting fixtures have been cut in half. The facilities team continues to monitor performance.

(A) In contrast   (B) For example   (C) In fact   (D) Nevertheless

■ 인과 관계를 나타내는 접속부사

두 개의 문장이 「원인 + 결과」 또는 「근거 + 결론」의 흐름일 때 결과 또는 결론을 나타내는 두 번째 문장의 시작 부분에 인과 접속부사를 사용합니다.

- Therefore 그러므로, 따라서
- As a result 그 결과
- Accordingly 그에 따라서
- Thus 그리하여
- Consequently, Ultimately 결국
- Eventually 결국, 마침내

Simon ENG is planning to have a year-end banquet to celebrate what has been a very successful year for us so far. Approximately 150 members of our staff will attend. The Beverly Hotel has been recommended to me by a number of my colleagues. -------, I would like to check if it will be able to meet our requirements.

(A) However   (B) Therefore   (C) Furthermore   (D) Similarly

사이먼 ENG는 지금까지 매우 성공적이었던 한 해를 기념하기 위해 연말 연회를 열 계획입니다. 약 150명의 직원들이 참석할 것입니다. 많은 동료들이 저에게 비벌리 호텔을 추천해 주었습니다. 그러므로, 귀 호텔이 저희의 요구 사항을 충족할 수 있을지 확인하고 싶습니다.

① 문맥 확인
비벌리 호텔을 추천받았다 → 그 호텔이 요구사항을 충족할 수 있을지 확인하고 싶다

② 의미 관계 파악
행사 장소로 많은 추천을 받았기 때문에 그 호텔에 대해 확인하는 것은 인과 관계

③ 접속 부사 선택
「원인 + 결과」의 인과 관계를 나타내는 (B) Therefore가 정답

PRACTICE 빈칸에 들어갈 알맞은 접속부사를 고르세요.

The warehouse operations team adopted an automated inventory tracking system last quarter. This system reduced human error in stock management. -------, product discrepancy reports reached an all-time low. The team is now exploring similar tools for packaging and logistics.

(A) As a result   (B) Instead   (C) In contrast   (D) Furthermore

■ 시점 관계를 나타내는 접속부사

- Afterward(s) 나중에
- Then 그 다음에
- Since then 그 이래로
- Currently, At present 현재
- After this/that 그 이후에
- First 우선
- At the same time 동시에
- As usual 늘 그렇듯이
- In the meantime 그동안, 한편
- Previously 이전에
- Finally, Eventually 마침내

Ace Graphics Suite incorporates many cutting-edge applications such as PhotoAce 6, DesignAce 7, and IllustrationAce 6, which means that experienced experts can use it to create virtually anything. -------, Ace Graphics Suite is easily accessible to nonprofessional users.

(A) Subsequently   (B) For instance   (C) At the same time   (D) In this case

에이스 그래픽스 스위트는 포토에이스 6, 디자인에이스 7, 그리고 일러스트레이션에이스 6와 같은 여러 첨단 애플리케이션들을 포함하며, 이는 숙련된 전문가들이 이것을 사용하여 거의 모든 것을 창작해낼 수 있다는 것을 뜻합니다. 동시에, 에이스 그래픽스 스위트는 비전문가 사용자들도 손쉽게 사용할 수 있습니다.

❶ 문맥 확인
전문가들이 이것을 사용하여 거의 모든 것을 창작할 수 있다
→ 비전문가 사용자들도 손쉽게 이 제품을 사용할 수 있다

❷ 의미 관계 파악
제품에 관해 숙련된 전문가와 비전문가 측면에 관한 두 가지 내용의 장점을 동시에 언급

❸ 접속 부사 선택
동시 발생을 나타내는 시간 접속부사인 (C) At the same time이 정답

PRACTICE   빈칸에 들어갈 알맞은 접속부사를 고르세요.

The annual security audit is scheduled to run through Friday afternoon. Access to the internal network will be restricted until the audit is complete. -------, employees may use the guest Wi-Fi for non-confidential tasks. Thank you for your cooperation.

(A) For instance   (B) On the other hand   (C) In the meantime   (D) Moreover

■ 조건, 예시 관계를 나타내는 접속부사

- Otherwise 그렇지 않다면(가정)
- In this case 이 경우에(가정)
- If possible 가능하다면(가정)
- If so 그렇다면(가정)
- For example 예를 들면(예시)
- For instance 예를 들면(예시)

Your subscription to *Do It Yourself Monthly* is due to expire at the end of this month. There are several reasons for you to renew it now. First, if you do so before August 15, we can offer you a special price of only $20 for twelve more issues. -------, you will be required to pay the standard 12-month price of $35.

(A) However   (B) Besides   (C) Additionally   (D) Otherwise

귀하의 <월간 Do It Yourself> 구독이 이달 말에 만료될 예정입니다. 지금 구독을 갱신하셔야 할 몇 가지 이유들이 있습니다. 우선, 만약 8월 15일 전에 그렇게 하신다면, 12권 추가에 대해 단 20달러라는 특별 가격을 제공해 드릴 수 있습니다. 그렇지 않다면, 귀하는 35달러라는 12개월 정상 가격을 지불하셔야 할 것입니다.

❶ 문맥 확인
8/15 전에 갱신하면 12권 추가에 대해 특별 가격 20달러로 제공 가능 → 35달러라는 12개월 정상 가격을 지불해야 한다

❷ 의미 관계 파악
뒷문장에서 20달러가 아닌 35달러가 언급된 것은 8월 15일 전에 갱신하지 않는 조건에 따른 부정적인 결과

❸ 접속 부사 선택
부정적인 결과에 대해 나타내는 가정 접속부사 (D) Otherwise가 정답

PRACTICE 빈칸에 들어갈 알맞은 접속부사를 고르세요.

Wilson Tech has implemented a series of cost-saving measures this quarter. These include reducing energy consumption and modifying equipment usage. -------, machines are turned off during non-peak hours to lower electricity bills. Such efforts are expected to improve operational efficiency.

(A) For example   (B) However   (C) In conclusion   (D) As a result

실전 TEST

학습한 내용을 적용하여 다음 기출 변형 문제들을 풀어보세요.

Questions 1-4 refer to the following e-mail.

Dear Mr. Pratt,

You have made an excellent decision in hiring our company ------- nutritious meals for the workers at your headquarters. I am writing this message to finalize some of the terms we discussed during our meeting last Friday.

As we agreed, you will contact us at approximately 9:30 A.M. each day, Monday through Friday, to ------- us how many meals you require on that particular day. We will then prepare the lunches for your employees and deliver them to your offices no later than noon. If any of your staff members have dietary requirements, we will be happy to accommodate them. -------, we are also able to fully customize our set menus for you, as long as you notify us at least one week in advance.

Once you have confirmed that you are satisfied with the arrangement outlined above, I will have a formal contract drawn up and sent to you. -------.

Best wishes,
Cheryl Boone, Greenfields Catering

1. (A) providing
   (B) will provide
   (C) provides
   (D) to provide

2. (A) remember
   (B) inform
   (C) describe
   (D) clarify

3. (A) Consequently
   (B) Recently
   (C) Instead
   (D) Furthermore

4. (A) I am confident that we will establish a strong business relationship.
   (B) I look forward to welcoming you on your first day at Greenfields.
   (C) Please let me know when you are free to discuss the event menu.
   (D) We truly appreciate your feedback on our products and services.

Questions 5-8 refer to the following e-mail.

Hello,

I am planning to take my employees on a trip to thank them for their hard work over the past year. A colleague of mine recommended Pine Valley Park as an ideal destination for a staff outing and team-building session, so I am considering making a booking with you. -------, I have some concerns about the suitability of your facilities.
　　5.

First of all, there will be approximately 50 managers and employees in total, and I'm not sure whether you have enough cabins to ------- our group. Also, I'd like to make sure
　　　　　　　　　　　　　　　　　　　　　　　6.
that you have a large meeting room that ------- a public address system and a screen for
　　　　　　　　　　　　　　　　　　7.
presentations and group activities.

I would be very grateful if you could provide more details about the cabins and meeting space, and also a full list of the available outdoor activities at Pine Valley Park. -------.
　　　　　　　　　　　　　　　　　　　　　　　　　　　　　　　　　　　　　　8.
Assuming that you can meet all of our needs, I will be happy to make a reservation immediately.

Kindest regards,
Colin Connell, JKX Publishing Group

5　(A) However
　　(B) Therefore
　　(C) Furthermore
　　(D) Similarly

6　(A) compromise
　　(B) mediate
　　(C) accommodate
　　(D) gather

7　(A) include
　　(B) includes
　　(C) to include
　　(D) included

8　(A) Several employees have inquired about hiking opportunities.
　　(B) Our workers particularly enjoyed your tours of the local area.
　　(C) As such, I would like to reserve at least twenty of your cabins.
　　(D) Thank you for applying the group discount to our booking.

실전 TEST

Questions 9-12 refer to the following memo.

Dear Team,

As you know, our headquarters will undergo interior renovations starting next month. ------- (9.), we have decided to temporarily relocate all warehouse storage to the Hillbrook facility, as space at headquarters will be limited during this period.

The Hillbrook site is not only spacious but also conveniently located near the freeway, which is why we have chosen to move items there. ------- (10.) this, the facilities team is working to ensure that climate controls and security measures are properly installed before the move. A checklist is being compiled to track which departments are storing materials, and how much space each one requires.

Please make sure to respond with your department's storage needs in a ------- (11.) manner by June 17. Late submissions may not be accommodated due to space constraints. Additionally, only essential inventory should be transferred.

------- (12.). As such, be sure to label your containers clearly with the department name and contents to prevent confusion. If you have questions, reach out to logistics@brolinlogix.com. Thank you for your cooperation.

Harold Collins, Facilities Manager
Portland Daily News

9
(A) Instead
(B) Despite
(C) On the other hand
(D) Accordingly

10
(A) Prior to
(B) Adjacent to
(C) As opposed to
(D) In favor of

11
(A) time
(B) timely
(C) timing
(D) timed

12
(A) The storage facility is not in use.
(B) This relocation phase has already been completed.
(C) Accuracy is essential to this process.
(D) No departments are currently using extra space.

Questions 13-16 refer to the following article.

Using Micro-Influencers to Build Authentic Brand Loyalty

In today's digital landscape, consumers are increasingly drawn to brands that feel personal and authentic. -------, large-scale influencer campaigns may not always foster
             13.
the same level of trust that smaller, more relatable creators can inspire.

Micro-influencers—those with between 1,000 and 50,000 followers—are gaining popularity due to their strong engagement rates and niche audiences. Their content tends to be more targeted, and followers often feel a stronger sense of connection. For companies with modest advertising budgets, working with micro-influencers can be both cost-effective and -------.
                    14.

Success ------- on careful brand alignment. Businesses should collaborate with
         15.
influencers who genuinely support their values and missions. However, some companies make the mistake of focusing only on follower count without considering audience demographics or content style. This can lead to a campaign that falls flat or feels inauthentic.

-------. The most successful campaigns emphasize shared values, authentic messaging,
16.
and audience compatibility rather than scale alone.

To maximize long-term results, companies should also monitor campaign performance and maintain ongoing relationships with key creators.

---

13 (A) Although
    (B) Consequently
    (C) For example
    (D) Previously

14 (A) impactful
    (B) limited
    (C) seasonal
    (D) reversible

15 (A) depending
    (B) dependent
    (C) depended
    (D) depends

16 (A) This strategy has proven costly in the past.
    (B) Therefore, brands should prioritize relevance when selecting influencers.
    (C) Some influencers provide free merchandise to viewers.
    (D) Online marketing budgets have been increasing.

DAY 12 | 문맥파악 / 문장삽입 Part 6

1 동사의 시제 고르기

Part 6에서 출제되는 동사의 시제 문제는 Part 5와는 달리 정답의 단서가 같은 문장이 아니라 지문의 다른 문장에 들어 있습니다. 가장 일반적인 풀이 방법은 지문 상단의 날짜, 시간부사, 주변 문장의 동사에 쓰인 시제에서 정답 단서를 찾는 것이며, 문맥의 흐름을 전체적으로 파악해야 하는 고난도 문제 유형도 가끔 출제됩니다. 특히, 단서를 찾기 위해서는 지문의 첫 문장을 읽는 것이 매우 중요합니다.

■ 첫 문장 또는 첫 단락에서 단서 찾기

첫 문장 또는 첫 단락에서 시제 문제의 단서를 찾을 수 있습니다. 시제를 직접적으로 나타내는 시점이나 날짜를 나타내는 표현을 찾거나 빈칸 앞뒤 문장의 동사를 보고 빈칸에 쓰일 동사의 시제를 유추합니다.

The Deputy Mayor of Ferrytown, Ron Jenkins, has announced plans for the Ferrytown Street Parade. The event ------- every summer on the last Saturday in July. The first ever parade is scheduled for July 29 this year, and a route has already been tentatively mapped out.

(A) took place (B) taking place (C) had taken place (D) will take place

---

론 젠킨스 페리타운 부시장이 페리타운 거리 축제 계획을 발표했습니다. 이 행사는 매해 여름 7월의 마지막 토요일에 개최될 것입니다. 최초의 거리 축제는 올해 7월 29일로 예정되어 있고, 경로도 이미 잠정적으로 설정되었습니다.

❶ 문맥 확인
부시장이 페리타운 거리 축제 계획을 발표했다
→ 최초의 거리 축제는 올해 7월 29일로 예정되어 있고, 경로도 이미 설정되었다

❷ 시제 단서 파악
다음 문장의 주어 The first ever parade가 결정적 단서이며, 행사 계획이 발표되었는데, 최초의 행사가 예정되어 있다고 언급

❸ 정답 시제 선택
예정된 행사에 대한 내용은 미래에 일어날 일을 뜻하므로 미래시제인 (D) will take place가 정답

■ 날짜 비교해서 단서 찾기

편지, 이메일, 회람 등의 상단에 적힌 날짜와 지문 내에 제시되는 특정 날짜를 비교하여 알맞은 시제를 고르는 유형입니다.

Date: April 28

Last week, I placed an order for two books, *Innovation Mindset* and *Digital Growth Strategies* through your online store. According to the shipping confirmation, the package ------- at 3:15 P.M. on April 26. I appreciate your prompt delivery and look forward to reading them over the weekend.

(A) is arriving   (B) has arrived   (C) arrived   (D) will arrive

작성일: 4월 28일
저는 지난주에 온라인 매장을 통해 『혁신적 사고방식』과 『디지털 성장 전략』 이렇게 두 권을 주문했습니다. 배송 확인서에 따르면 소포는 **4월 26일 오후 3시 15분에 도착했습니다**. 빠른 배송에 감사드리며, 주말에 책을 읽는 것이 기대됩니다.

 작성 날짜 확인
지문 상단에 나타난 작성 날짜가 4월 28일(April 28)인 것을 확인

 날짜 비교하기
빈칸이 포함된 문장에 언급된 날짜는 4월 26일(April 26)이므로 작성 날짜보다 과거시점에 대한 내용인 것을 확인

③ 정답 시제 선택
선택지 중에서 과거시제를 나타내는 (C) arrived가 정답

오답 풀이   현재완료 시제 has arrived는 과거-현재 사이의 기간에 일어나는 일을 나타내는 시제이므로 4월 26일 오후 3시 15분과 같이 정확한 과거 시점이 언급된 문장에는 쓸 수 없습니다.

PRACTICE   빈칸에 들어갈 알맞은 동사의 시제를 고르세요.

The Riverside Annual Charity Run has grown into one of the city's largest community events. The race ------- every spring on the second Sunday of April. Participants can register online or on race day starting at 7 A.M.
1

(A) took place   (B) takes place   (C) had taken place   (D) will take place

2 대명사 고르기

Part 5에서 출제되는 대명사 문제는 대명사의 알맞은 격을 찾는 문제로 출제되는 반면, Part 6에서 출제되는 대명사 문제는 빈칸이 포함된 문장의 앞 문장을 확인해 가리키는 대상을 찾아야 합니다. Part 6 대명사 문제는 주로 인칭대명사와 부정대명사를 고르는 문제가 출제됩니다.

■ 인칭대명사 고르기

인칭대명사는 앞서 언급된 명사를 대신하는 대명사입니다. 따라서 선택지에 she, he, it, they 등의 인칭대명사가 제시되면 앞 문장에서 그 지칭 대상을 찾아야 하며, 단/복수의 수일치도 확인해야 합니다.

The Department of Environmental Affairs recently published its annual findings on urban pollution and waste management across major cities. The statistics show a notable rise in air pollutant levels, particularly in densely populated industrial zones. Several recommendations for addressing these issues were presented in the report. ------- focus on expanding green spaces, regulating factory emissions, and promoting eco-friendly public transportation.

(A) They (B) Them (C) It (D) You

환경부는 최근 주요 도시의 도시 오염 및 폐기물 관리에 대한 연례 조사 결과를 발표했다. 통계에 따르면 대기 오염 수치가 특히 인구 밀도가 높은 산업 지구에서 눈에 띄게 증가한 것으로 나타났다. 이 문제들을 해결하기 위한 여러 가지 권고 사항이 보고서에 제시되었다. **이 권고 사항들은** 녹지 공간 확대, 공장 배출물 규제, 친환경 대중교통 장려 등을 중심으로 구성되어 있다.

① 문맥 확인
이 문제들을 해결하기 위한 여러 가지 권고 사항이 보고서에 제시됨 → 녹지 공간 확대, 공장 배출물 규제, 친환경 대중교통 장려 등에 초점을 맞춘다

② 인칭대명사 단서 파악
빈칸은 주어 자리이며, 뒤에 위치한 동사 focus는 현재시제 복수동사이므로 앞문장에 언급된 복수명사 중 하나를 지칭

③ 정답 선택
녹지 공간 확대, 공장 배출물 규제, 친환경 대중교통 장려는 앞 문장의 Several recommendations의 예시이므로 주격 복수대명사 (A) They가 정답

PRACTICE 빈칸에 들어갈 알맞은 대명사를 고르세요.

The Metropolitan Environmental Council has opened nominations for the Clean Sky Award. Prospective nominees are required to complete the official application form before submitting their entries. ------- can be downloaded from the Council's Web site at www.mec.org/cleansky/application.

2

(A) They (B) Them (C) It (D) You

■ 부정대명사 고르기

Part 6에서 출제되는 부정대명사는 앞 문장에 언급된 명사의 수와 관련되는 경우가 많습니다. 따라서 선택지에 부정대명사가 제시되는 경우, 앞 문장에서 해당 명사를 찾은 다음 이 명사와 수가 일치하는 부정대명사를 선택지에서 찾습니다. 토익 빈출 부정대명사에는 one, each, either, both, some, most, all 등이 있습니다.

> The finalists for the National Graphic Design Competition have been announced following three rounds of evaluation. The selected candidates will present their portfolios to a panel of industry professionals next Thursday. ------- of the submissions vary in style, content, and format, showcasing a wide range of creative approaches. Each has been reviewed individually to ensure fair judgment based on originality and clarity.
>
> (A) Either   (B) Every   (C) All   (D) Both
>
> 전국 그래픽 디자인 경연 대회의 최종 후보자들이 세 차례의 심사를 거쳐 발표되었다. 선정된 후보자들은 다음주 목요일에 업계 전문가들로 구성된 심사위원단 앞에서 자신의 포트폴리오를 발표할 예정이다. **제출된** 모든 **작품은** 스타일, 내용, 형식 면에서 다양하며, 창의적인 접근 방식이 폭넓게 드러난다. 각 작품은 독창성과 명료성을 기준으로 공정하게 심사되도록 개별적으로 검토되었다.

❶ 문맥 확인
선정된 후보자들은 다음주 목요일에 자신의 포트폴리오를 발표할 예정 → 제출물들은 스타일, 내용, 형식 면에서 다양함

❷ 대명사 단서 파악
선정된 후보자들이 발표할 포트폴리오(their portfolios)를 지칭하는 단어로 다음 문장에 the submissions가 언급됨

❸ 정답 선택
전치사 of와 함께 복수명사 the submissions를 지칭할 수 있는 (C) All이 정답

오답 풀이   Either와 Both는 「either of 복수명사」「both of 복수명사」로 쓸 수 있으나 모두 두 개의 대상을 가리키는 복수명사에만 사용할 수 있으므로 다수의 대상을 지칭하는 자리에 쓰일 수 없습니다. Every는 항상 명사를 수식하는 수량 형용사로, 부정대명사로 사용되지 않습니다.

PRACTICE   빈칸에 들어갈 알맞은 대명사를 고르세요.

Greenfield Community Theater has launched seasonal acting workshops open to performers of all skill levels. The workshops take place on weekday evenings and weekend afternoons. Some sessions focus on improvisation, while others explore classical scene study. ------- of the sessions are led by professional Broadway actors. Participants can register online or in person at the theater box office.

(A) Every   (B) Some   (C) Either   (D) Both

3 어휘 고르기

Part 6 어휘 문제는 주어진 문장에서 단서를 찾아 빈칸에 알맞은 단어를 고르는 Part 5 어휘 문제와 달리, 지문의 다른 부분에 단서가 주어지기 때문에 문맥을 파악해야 하는 유형입니다. 따라서, 어휘력뿐만 아니라 지문의 내용 흐름을 이해하는 능력도 필요합니다.

■ 지시어 또는 형용사를 활용한 어휘 찾기

지시어/대명사/소유격/정관사/형용사 등이 빈칸이 포함된 문장에 있는 경우, 앞 문장과 연계해 정답을 찾아야 합니다.

Millerton Publishing recently announced plans to release a series of nonfiction books focusing on global economic trends. The initial titles will cover topics such as emerging markets, supply chain disruptions, and shifts in consumer behavior. The books are scheduled for release next quarter and will be promoted through an international campaign. A complete list of all the ------- is available on the company's Web site for early order placement.

(A) events   (B) volumes   (C) documents   (D) products

밀러튼 퍼블리싱은 최근 세계 경제 흐름을 주제로 한 논픽션 서적 시리즈를 출시할 계획을 발표했다. 초기의 도서들은 신흥 시장, 공급망 혼란, 소비자 행동의 변화와 같은 주제를 다룰 예정이다. 그 도서들은 다음 분기에 출간될 예정이며, 국제적인 캠페인을 통해 홍보가 이루어질 것이다. 모든 권들에 대한 전체 목록은 조기 주문을 위해 회사 웹사이트에서 확인할 수 있다.

---

❶ 문맥 확인
그 책들은 다음 분기에 출간될 예정이고 국제적인 캠페인으로 홍보 예정 → 각 ~의 전체 목록은 조기 주문을 위해 웹사이트에서 확인 가능

❷ 단서 파악
빈칸은 '모든'이라는 의미의 형용사 all의 수식을 받고 있으며, 빈칸 앞에 있는 A complete list와 관련된 앞 문장의 주어 The books를 주요 단서로 확인

❸ 정답 선택
The books를 가리키는 명사가 필요하므로 도서 시리즈의 '권'을 뜻하는 (B) volumes가 정답

PRACTICE 빈칸에 들어갈 알맞은 단어를 고르세요.

Applications for the summer internship program are now open. Prospective interns should review the latest ------- before submitting their materials.
4

(A) essays   (B) contracts   (C) guidelines   (D) publications

■ 첫 문장을 활용한 어휘 찾기

Part 6 지문에서 첫 문장은 항상 꼼꼼하게 확인해야 합니다. 글의 주제와 성격을 알 수 있을 뿐만 아니라 지문 중반이나 끝부분에 출제되는 어휘 문제의 단서가 첫 문장에 제시되는 경우도 많기 때문입니다.

Starting next Monday, the IT department will shut down the internal messaging system for two days to perform major software updates. Employees are encouraged to use e-mail or phone until the work is completed. The system outage is expected to begin early Monday morning. Should you experience any difficulties during the ------- disruption, please contact the help desk at extension 235.

(A) frequent (B) sudden (C) possible (D) temporary

다음주 월요일부터 IT 부서는 주요 소프트웨어 업데이트를 진행하기 위해 내부 메시징 시스템을 이틀 동안 종료할 예정입니다. 작업이 완료될 때까지 직원들은 이메일이나 전화 통신을 사용하도록 권장됩니다. 시스템 중단은 월요일 오전 일찍 시작될 것으로 예상됩니다. 일시적인 장애가 있는 동안 어려움을 겪으신다면 내선 235번으로 헬프데스크에 연락해 주세요.

❶ 단서 위치 파악
빈칸에 들어갈 형용사는 빈칸 뒤에 위치한 명사 disruption을 수식해야 하므로 disruption과 관련된 단어를 첫 문장에서 확인

❷ 첫 문장 내용 확인
첫 문장에서 언급된 shut down the internal messaging system이 disruption(장애)을 나타내는 것을 확인

❸ 정답 선택
첫 문장에서 언급된 shut down의 동작이 '이틀 동안'(for two days) 발생할 것이라고 하였으므로 이 기간을 표현하는 형용사로 '일시적인'이라는 의미의 (D) temporary를 정답으로 선택

PRACTICE 빈칸에 들어갈 알맞은 단어를 고르세요.

Beginning March 1, the Finance Department introduced revised expense-reporting guidelines for all employees. Should you have questions about the ------- policy update, direct them to finance@company.com.

(A) detailed (B) mandatory (C) previous (D) recent

4 문장 삽입 유형 풀이 전략

토익 Part 6에서 가장 고난도에 속하는 문장 삽입 유형은 내용 흐름상 빈칸에 가장 알맞은 문장을 선택하는 유형입니다. 빈칸 앞뒤에 위치한 문장을 비롯해 지문의 전체 흐름을 파악하여 정답을 찾아야 합니다. 하지만 아래 내용을 미리 익혀두면 문제를 푸는 데 필요한 단서들을 빠르게 찾고, 경우에 따라 지문 전체에 대한 해석 없이 정답을 고를 수도 있습니다.

■ 빈칸 위치에 따른 삽입 문장 내용 및 유형 파악
① 지문의 첫 문장 → 주제 또는 목적 전달: 인사말, 소개, 사과, 알림 등
② 지문 중간 위치 → 앞뒤 문장과의 논리 흐름 연결 중요
③ 지문의 마지막 문장 → 전체 내용 요약 또는 마무리 인사, 기대, 요청 등

■ 앞뒤 문장과의 논리 관계 확인
① 빈칸 전후 문장을 연결하는 논리 관계: 역접(그러나), 추가 설명(또한), 인과(그래서)
② 흐름을 알 수 있는 표현과 단어에 주목 → 정답의 단서로 활용

■ 논리 연결 단서 확인하기
① 빈칸 전후 문장에 나타나는 단서: 지시어(this, that), 대명사(they, it), 접속부사(however, therefore), 특정 명사(the + 명사)
② 선택지 문장 검토: 문장 사이의 논리 관계 파악 후 내용 흐름상 적절한 문장 선택
  - 시제 일치: 앞뒤 문장의 시제와 어울리는지 확인
  - 어휘 적합성: 빈칸 앞뒤 문맥에서 요구하는 정보(수정, 요약, 예시 등)를 담고 있는지 확인

■ 빈칸 뒤에 단서가 주어지는 경우 [고난도]
빈칸 앞에 지시어, 대명사, 접속부사 등에 해당하는 단서가 없는 경우 빈칸 뒤에서 부연 설명 하는 내용과 관련된 특정 주제를 언급한 문장을 정답으로 선택

> 앞문장과 각 선택지가 서로 연결되는 단서(지시어, 대명사, 접속부사)가 없음

Next Monday, the IT department will be setting up the new computerized inventory system on all computers. Also, **a workshop** will be held at 11:45 A.M. in order to **familiarize employees** with the new software. -------------- It is most important that all of **our employees can understand and use it easily**.

모든 직원들이 새로운 소프트웨어를 이해하고 쉽게 사용할 수 있는 것이 가장 중요하다. → 워크숍이 매우 중요하므로 참석은 의무적이다

(A) We appreciate your interest in additional staff training opportunities.
(B) Unfortunately, there are no spaces left.
(C) The new computers should arrive on Monday.
(D) Please note that the participation is mandatory.

다음 주 월요일에, IT 부서가 모든 컴퓨터에 새 전산 재고 시스템을 설치할 예정입니다. 또한, 직원들이 새 소프트웨어에 익숙해질 수 있도록 오전 11시 45분에 워크숍이 열릴 예정입니다. <u>참석은 의무적이라는 점을 알아 두시기 바랍니다</u>. 모든 직원들이 해당 시스템을 쉽게 이해하고 사용할 수 있는 것이 가장 중요합니다.

(A) 추가 직원교육 기회에 관심을 가져 주셔서 감사합니다.
(B) 안타깝게도, 남아 있는 공간이 없습니다.
(C) 새로운 컴퓨터가 월요일에 도착할 것입니다.
(D) 참석은 의무적이라는 점을 알아 두시기 바랍니다.

5 지시어를 활용한 삽입 문장 찾기

We will adopt a new document-management system next month to improve file accessibility and security. Users will receive training and step-by-step guides before the transition. If you have any questions about this migration, please contact your IT coordinator. -------.

(A) We apologize for any inconvenience the switch may cause.
(B) The existing documents are scheduled to be shredded next week.
(C) File access may be temporarily restricted due to scheduled maintenance.
(D) Your feedback on the workshop is welcome.

우리는 파일 접근성과 보안을 개선하기 위해 다음 달에 새로운 문서 관리 시스템을 도입할 예정입니다. 사용자들은 이전 전에 교육과 단계별 안내서를 받을 것입니다. 이번 이전에 관해 문의사항이 있으면 IT 코디네이터에게 연락해 주십시오. **이전으로 인해 불편을 끼쳐 드려 죄송합니다.**

(A) 이전으로 인해 불편을 끼쳐 드려 죄송합니다.
(B) 기존의 문서들은 다음주에 파쇄될 예정입니다.
(C) 정기 점검으로 인해 파일 접근이 일시적으로 제한될 수 있습니다.
(D) 워크숍에 대한 여러분의 의견을 환영합니다.

지시어 확인
빈칸 앞 문장에 this migration이 포함되어 있는 것을 확인

지시어 대상 파악
this migration이 the transition, a new document-management system을 지칭하는 것을 확인

정답 선택
this migration을 the switch로 언급하고, 지문의 마지막에 위치한 문장이므로 the switch로 인한 불편에 대한 사과의 내용이 적절하므로 (A)가 정답

PRACTICE 빈칸에 들어갈 알맞은 문장을 고르세요.

The cafeteria will introduce a new vegan menu next week in response to growing demand. If you have any feedback on the revised menu, please send your comments to foodservices@campus.edu. -------.
6

(A) These dishes are prepared fresh daily.
(B) We look forward to hearing your thoughts.
(C) Lunch service runs until 2 P.M.
(D) The new menu features seasonal produce.

6 접속부사를 활용한 삽입 문장 찾기

문장 삽입 유형에서 선택지 문장에 접속부사가 있는 경우 해당 문장을 먼저 해석하여 의미 관계를 파악합니다.

Thank you for your interest in our online learning platform. The OL100 series you inquired about has been upgraded to the OL200 Pro, which includes interactive quizzes and real-time analytics. -------. We have attached a brief tutorial video for your review. Thank you again for considering our solutions.

(A) However, enrollment slots are limited and fill up quickly.
(B) Therefore, we suggest you register early to secure your spot.
(C) For instance, learners have praised its user-friendly interface.
(D) Furthermore, the platform allows course materials to be downloaded in advance for offline study.

저희의 온라인 학습 플랫폼에 관심 가져 주셔서 감사합니다. 문의하신 OL100 시리즈는 OL200 Pro로 업그레이드되었으며, 그것은 인터랙티브 퀴즈와 실시간 분석 기능을 포함합니다. **게다가, 해당 플랫폼은 이동 중 학습을 위해 오프라인 다운로드를 지원합니다.** 검토를 위해 간단한 튜토리얼 영상을 첨부해 드렸습니다. 다시 한 번 저희 솔루션을 고려해 주셔서 감사합니다.

(A) 하지만, 등록 인원이 한정되어 있어 빠르게 마감됩니다.
(B) 따라서, 조기 등록을 통해 자리를 확보하실 것을 권장합니다.
(C) 예를 들어, 학습자들은 사용자 친화적인 인터페이스를 칭찬했습니다.
(D) 게다가, 해당 플랫폼은 이동 중 학습을 위해 오프라인 다운로드를 지원합니다.

① 접속부사 확인
(A)~(D)에 포함된 각각의 접속부사의 의미와 앞문장과의 관계를 확인

② 앞뒤 문맥 확인
업그레이드된 제품의 기능(인터랙티브 퀴즈, 실시간 분석) 소개 → 간단한 튜토리얼 영상 첨부

③ 정답 선택
사용자의 편리성을 위해 추가적인 기능에 대한 설명으로 이어지는 것이 자연스러운 흐름이므로 오프라인 학습을 위해 미리 다운로드를 받을 수 있는 기능을 알리는 (D)가 정답

PRACTICE 빈칸에 들어갈 알맞은 문장을 고르세요.

Thank you for your question about our Oceanview Suite. The accommodation has been refurbished with modern décor and now includes complimentary breakfast service. -------. Please see the enclosed brochure for booking rates.

(A) I hope you enjoy your stay.
(B) Additionally, guests receive a welcome drink upon arrival.
(C) Both rates apply to all room types.
(D) For example, the lunch menu changes daily.

7 패러프레이징을 활용한 삽입 문장 찾기

Greenwood Public Library recently introduced its new digital catalog system, featuring an intuitive interface and advanced search filters. It delivers personalized recommendations based on each patron's reading history, making it easier to uncover relevant titles. -------. Patrons can access the catalog on in-library terminals or through the Greenwood Library mobile app.

(A) Users can refine search results by genre, publication date, or author name.
(B) This feature analyzes reading patterns to suggest titles aligned with individual preferences.
(C) Library staff will collect feedback and share reports quarterly.
(D) As a result, membership renewals increased by 30 percent.

그린우드 공공 도서관에서는 최근 직관적인 인터페이스와 고급 검색 필터를 갖춘 새로운 디지털 카탈로그 시스템을 도입했습니다. 이 시스템은 각 이용자의 독서 이력에 기반한 개인화된 추천을 제공하여 관련 자료를 더 쉽게 찾을 수 있도록 돕습니다. **이 기능은 이용자의 독서 패턴을 분석하여 개인 취향에 맞춘 도서를 추천합니다.** 이용자들은 도서관 내 공용 단말기나 그린우드 도서관 모바일 앱을 통해 카탈로그에 접속할 수 있습니다.

(A) 이용자는 장르, 출간일, 저자명으로 검색 결과를 세분화할 수 있습니다.
(B) 이 기능은 이용자의 독서 패턴을 분석하여 개인 취향에 맞춘 도서를 추천합니다.
(C) 도서관 직원은 분기별로 피드백을 수집하여 보고서를 공유할 예정입니다.
(D) 그 결과, 회원 갱신률이 30% 증가했습니다.

---

❶ 문맥 파악
디지털 카탈로그의 주요 기능(직관적 인터페이스·고급 검색 필터) 소개 → 개인화 추천으로 자료 탐색이 용이해지는 효과 강조

❷ 패러프레이징 확인
앞문장에 언급된 "각 이용자의 독서 이력에 기반한 개인화된 추천 제공"과 관련된 내용의 선택지 찾기

❸ 정답 선택
personalized recommendations → individual preferences, reading history → reading patterns로 패러프레이징한 (B)가 정답

PRACTICE 빈칸에 들어갈 알맞은 문장을 고르세요.

On Friday, the Safety Office will conduct a fire evacuation drill in the main building. This drill aims to familiarize all occupants with emergency procedures. Participation is required for everyone. -------.

8

(A) The online training session was held yesterday afternoon.
(B) The Safety Office recently updated its emergency guidelines.
(C) It is crucial that you evacuate immediately.
(D) We hope this activity will improve overall safety awareness.

실전 TEST

학습한 내용을 적용하여 다음 기출 변형 문제들을 풀어보세요.

Questions 1-4 refer to the following advertisement.

Here at Cajun Fried Chicken, we want to celebrate our 50th year in business with our customers. So, for this weekend only, a free ice cream sundae and large soft drink ------- with any purchase of a chicken sandwich, burger, or bucket from our main menu.
                                                                                                          1.

You can take advantage of this ------- at any of our 33 branches throughout California until closing time on Sunday, November 16.
                                            2.

Additionally, we are giving our customers a chance to enter a contest to win exciting prizes throughout November. Simply check the unique code found on ------- receipt and enter it at www.cfc.com/prizedraw. -------.
                                                                                              3.
                                                               4.

1. (A) including
   (B) to include
   (C) are being included
   (D) had been included

2. (A) item
   (B) offer
   (C) vacancy
   (D) range

3. (A) his
   (B) her
   (C) your
   (D) their

4. (A) Congratulations on winning one of our amazing prizes.
   (B) We hope you enjoy the new additions to our menus.
   (C) This is our way of thanking our customers for their patronage.
   (D) Once again, we apologize for closing some of our branches.

Questions 5-8 refer to the following e-mail.

Dear Ms. Henderson,

------- 5. You ------- 6. a basic salary of $63,000 per year, which can increase annually based on the outcome of your performance review. Your first day of employment here at BioKing Inc. has been tentatively set for Monday, October 23. However, this may be rearranged if you have any schedule conflicts ------- 7. you from starting on that date.

Later this week, Peter Faraday, whom you met during the interview, will send you an information pack which contains detailed information regarding ------- 8. role and responsibilities here at BioKing. Please review this prior to your first day, and contact me at 555-0139 if you have any queries.

Sincerely,

Barbara Staples, HR Director
BioKing Inc.

5. (A) We would be grateful if you would come in for an interview.
   (B) Unfortunately, we are not currently hiring new staff.
   (C) Congratulations on your recent promotion to management.
   (D) We are pleased to offer you a place at our firm.

6. (A) receiving
   (B) received
   (C) to receive
   (D) will receive

7. (A) opposing
   (B) recommending
   (C) preventing
   (D) finalizing

8. (A) you
   (B) your
   (C) his
   (D) their

실전 TEST

Questions 9-12 refer to the following article.

Portland Daily News

PORTLAND (June 5) - According to a recent survey, the city council's plan to pedestrianize Harp Street in downtown Portland has been met with an overwhelmingly ------- response from local residents.
  9.

Approximately eighty-five percent of survey respondents criticized the idea, noting that it was an important route for commuters who use personal vehicles. The road ------- to all
  10.
vehicles in August in an effort to boost the attractiveness of the road as a shopping and dining area.

-------, Harp Street serves as an important commuter route for those who need to cross
  11.
the city from east to west, or vice versa, and it also plays a significant role in the city's bus route network. -------.
  12.

9. (A) contented
   (B) negative
   (C) favorable
   (D) faulty

10. (A) will be closed
    (B) had been closed
    (C) was closed
    (D) is closed

11. (A) Gradually
    (B) Currently
    (C) Eventually
    (D) Fortunately

12. (A) Portland residents are proud of the city's affordable public transportation.
    (B) The city council aims to widen the road to reduce traffic congestion.
    (C) For example, the route will be useful to those who work in other cities.
    (D) As such, many people will need to make alternative travel arrangements.

Questions 13-16 refer to the following instructions.

Cosmic Dimensions - Rare Comic Book Seller

Buying Rare Comic Books

At Cosmic Dimensions, we keep all of our stock in perfect condition by ensuring it is stored and handled properly. Some of our older and rarer comic books are rather fragile and, as such, are susceptible to damage. -------, it is up to you to take care of any comic books you purchase by following some simple guidelines. All of our comic books come in a sealed plastic pouch, and they should ------- inside this at all times when not in use. Also, be gentle when reading the comic to avoid accidental tears or wrinkles. ------- may occur when pages are turned too quickly or gripped too firmly. -------. However, should you require information about repairs or restoration, please speak with one of our employees at 555-2828.

13. (A) Otherwise
    (B) For instance
    (C) Similarly
    (D) Therefore

14. (A) remain
    (B) place
    (C) look
    (D) hold

15. (A) Theirs
    (B) Either
    (C) These
    (D) Every

16. (A) This advice will help you preserve the condition of your comics.
    (B) We apologize that the items were not to your satisfaction.
    (C) All products are shipped in special packaging within 2 business days.
    (D) The comic book you inquired about is currently out of stock.

PART 6 FINAL TEST

학습한 내용을 적용하여 다음 기출 변형 문제들을 풀어보세요.

Questions 1-4 refer to the following memo.

Date: March 3
Subject: Quarterly Report Submissions

Dear staff,

This is a reminder that all quarterly financial reports must be submitted by Friday, March 10. Reports should be checked thoroughly for ------- before submission. Any errors must
1.
be corrected and approved by a department manager. ------- your department require
2.
additional time, please notify me no later than Tuesday. Any late reports ------- our
3.
compliance with internal audit procedures. We appreciate your cooperation in this matter. -------.
4.

Regards,

Marisol Grant
Finance Director

---

1 (A) accuracy
(B) efficiency
(C) diligence
(D) potential

2 (A) If
(B) Because
(C) Should
(D) Provided

3 (A) have affected
(B) were affecting
(C) is affected
(D) will affect

4 (A) Several key details were missing from your report.
(B) The new procedures are outlined on the company Web site.
(C) It is important to seek a prompt resolution to this problem.
(D) Documents should be sent directly to me by e-mail.

Questions 5-8 refer to the following notice.

Springfield Museum: Extended Opening Hours

The Springfield Museum is pleased to announce that starting April 1, our new opening hours will be from 9 A.M. to 8 P.M., Tuesday through Sunday. -------5.-------. This change should make it easier for more guests -------6.------- our exhibits, especially working professionals. As always, admission is free on the first Sunday of every month. On other days, we are currently offering a "pay-what-you-please" admission policy, -------7.------- our standard ticket price is $8.50. Anyone who cannot -------8.------- this due to financial difficulties is welcome to pay less or visit the museum for free. Group tours may be booked in advance through our Web site.

5. (A) We will remain closed on Mondays for maintenance.
   (B) We hope to see you at our grand opening event.
   (C) We apologize for this temporary inconvenience.
   (D) We expect the work to be finished by the end of April.

6. (A) are enjoying
   (B) enjoy
   (C) have enjoyed
   (D) to enjoy

7. (A) unless
   (B) before
   (C) although
   (D) since

8. (A) attend
   (B) invest
   (C) afford
   (D) exchange

PART 6 FINAL TEST

Questions 9-12 refer to the following memo.

Subject: Change in Prototype Submission Procedure
Date: February 14

R&D Department Staff,

Please be aware that starting next Monday, all prototype submissions must be processed through the revised digital tracking system. This will help ensure that every flashlight model ------- (9.) consistently and reviewed in a timely manner. All team members will receive login credentials and user guides by the end of this week. ------- (10.), make sure that you check your e-mail for these before leaving on Friday. The system is being launched ------- (11.) recent delays in getting new product versions officially approved, which were traced back to gaps in manual documentation. ------- (12.).

Kendra Matsuura
Product Development Lead

9 (A) documented
   (B) to document
   (C) documenting
   (D) is documented

10 (A) Therefore
   (B) However
   (C) Meanwhile
   (D) On the other hand

11 (A) regardless of
   (B) in response to
   (C) concerning
   (D) while

12 (A) Please submit the new flashlight model design in person.
   (B) We believe this change will improve both transparency and workflow efficiency.
   (C) All product development will be carried out using a manual documentation process.
   (D) This new system was implemented primarily to reduce production costs.

Questions 13-16 refer to the following Web page.

---

www.palmeradigitalcamera.com/question

Question   7/24 13:14

I just bought the digital camera C300 and the images look overly dark indoors. What can I do to fix this?

→ **Expert Answer (Chris Stein):** This is likely due to the default light sensitivity (ISO) setting being too low for indoor environments. We recommend increasing the ISO to 800 or higher ----13.---- shooting in low light conditions. ----14.----. Make sure to ----15.---- the shutter speed as well, since it affects exposure time. Also, using a tripod can improve photo quality in poorly lit spaces. If you continue ----16.---- the same problem, contact our support team for guided troubleshooting.

---

13 (A) then
(B) so
(C) when
(D) though

14 (A) This helps the camera capture more light without using flash.
(B) Additionally, we kindly ask that you conduct a shooting session outdoors.
(C) I'm afraid that Palmera C300 model is not available in your region at the moment.
(D) Please note that your item will be repaired and shipped within seven business days.

15 (A) run
(B) purchase
(C) compare
(D) adjust

16 (A) experience
(B) experiencing
(C) experienced
(D) were experienced

기본토익 700+

PART 7

- **DAY 13** 세부사항 / 주제·목적 / 사실확인
- **DAY 14** 문맥파악
- **DAY 15** 다중지문

PART 7 FINAL TEST

PART 7 독해 문제 미리 보기

- 문항수: 54문항 (147번~200번)
- 주어진 글을 읽고 질문에 답하는 유형입니다. 한 개의 지문을 읽고 푸는 유형, 두 개의 지문을 읽고 푸는 유형, 세 개의 지문을 읽고 푸는 유형이 있으며, 지문당 문제 개수는 지문에 따라 2~5개로 달라집니다.

Questions 151-152 refer to the following memo.

To: All Customer Service Staff
From: Human Resources
Date: May 8

In order to serve the needs of our clients, we will be opening an additional shift. The schedule for this shift will be Saturday through Thursday, 4 P.M. to 12:30 A.M. Current employees who **volunteer to move to this shift** will earn an extra 50% of their pay per hour. ····· 152번 문제 키워드

Interested employees should send a cover letter expressing their interest to Carrie Waters in Human Resources at cwaters@abccompany.com. There are 23 customer service slots open, and 2 management slots. Furthermore, successful external applicants that you refer can earn YOU $100 after their first 30 days of employment!

문제의 키워드를 지문에서 찾기

151. What is being announced in the memo?

(A) Strategies for better client support
(B) New time slots for workers ✓
(C) A chance for promotion
(D) A revised vacation policy

152. What incentive is offered to employees who **work the new time shift**?

(A) A $100 bonus
(B) Extra time off
(C) A higher pay rate ✓
(D) A decrease in work hours

DAY 13 | 세부정보/주제·목적/사실확인 Part 7

1 세부정보

단편적인 사항을 묻는 세부정보 찾기는 Part 7에서 비교적 쉬운 유형이므로 이 유형을 가장 먼저 푸는 것이 좋습니다. 질문에 주어진 키워드를 지문에서 찾아 질문의 의문사에 해당하는 정보를 선택지에서 고르면 됩니다. 이때 이름이나 날짜처럼 단서가 선택지에 그대로 제시되는 단순 정보도 있지만, 대부분 지문의 단서를 살짝 다른 말로 바꾸어서 제시하는 패러프레이징이 사용된다는 점에 유의해야 합니다.

■ 빈출 질문 유형

단순 정보: What [무엇인가?]
- **What** does Mr. Richardson offer to do? 리처드슨 씨는 무엇을 하겠다고 제안하는가?
- **What** did Ms. Jameson send with her letter? 제임슨 씨는 편지와 함께 무엇을 보냈는가?
- **What** is included in the rental fee? 임대료에 무엇이 포함되어 있는가?

요청사항: What [무엇을 ~하는가?]
- **What** information does Ms. Kelly **request**? 켈리 씨는 무슨 정보를 요청하는가?
- **What** are employees **asked to do**? 직원들은 무엇을 하도록 요청받는가?
- **What** is Ms. O'Brian **advised to do**? 오브라이언 씨는 무엇을 하도록 권고받는가?

인물/신분: Who [누구인가?]
- **Who** is Ms. Jones? 존스 씨는 누구인가?

방법/수량/기간/빈도: How [어떻게, 얼마나 많이, 얼마나 오래, 얼마나 자주 ~하는가?]
- **How did** Mr. Smith learn about the event? 스미스 씨는 어떻게 이 행사를 알게 되었나?
- **How much** did Ms. Rogan pay for her subscription? 로건 씨는 구독료로 얼마를 지불하였는가?

장소/지명: Where [어디에 ~인가?]
- **Where** is Mr. Taylor's office located? 타일러 씨의 사무실은 어디에 위치해 있는가?

시점: When [언제 ~인가?]
- **When** did Ms. Parker leave for a trip? 파커 씨는 언제 출장을 떠났는가?

■ 세부정보 유형 예제

질문에 제시된 키워드를 지문에서 찾은 다음, 앞 또는 뒤에 언급되는 관련 정보 중에서 정답 단서를 찾아봅니다.

To accommodate increasing consumer demand for our items, we have found it necessary to expand our current facilities. By expanding our showroom and storage area, we will be able to display and stock a larger variety of items.

The renovations will take place this winter over a two-month period. Although Salaman Furniture will be closed between December 21 and February 21, our online shop will still be operational.

Q. What does Salaman Furniture plan to do? 살라만 가구점은 무엇을 할 계획인가?
(A) It will open a second location. 두 번째 지점을 개장할 것이다.
(B) It will expand its customer services. 자사의 고객 서비스를 확대할 것이다.
(C) It will launch a new Web site. 새로운 웹사이트를 공개할 것이다.
(D) It will remodel its store. 자사의 매장을 개조할 것이다.

우리 제품에 대해 증가하는 고객 수요를 수용하기 위해, 우리는 현재의 시설을 확장하는 것이 필수임을 알게 되었습니다. 우리의 진열 공간과 보관 구역을 확장함으로써, 우리는 더 다양한 상품들을 진열하고 재고로 갖춰 놓을 수 있을 것입니다.

이 개조 공사는 올 겨울에 두 달의 기간에 걸쳐 진행될 것입니다. 살라만 가구점이 12월 21일부터 2월 21일까지 문을 닫기는 하지만, 우리 온라인 매장은 그대로 영업을 할 것입니다.

질문 키워드 확인
질문의 키워드 Salaman Furniture, plan to do에 관련된 내용을 지문에서 찾습니다.

지문 속 단서 찾기
계획에 관련된 정보: 이 개조 공사는 올 겨울에 두 달의 기간에 걸쳐 진행될 것입니다.

선택지 고르기
개조 공사가 진행된다는 말은 자사의 매장을 개조한다는 뜻이므로 (D)가 정답입니다.

PRACTICE

To all gym members:
The locker room showers will be undergoing maintenance this Friday. We apologize for the inconvenience and recommend using the facilities on the second floor. Signage will be posted to help direct members to the appropriate location.

1 What will be done to help members locate the temporary facilities?
(A) Staff will escort them personally.
(B) Directions will be sent out via e-mail.
(C) Floor maps will be distributed in the lobby.
(D) Signs will be put up in the gym.

2 주제·목적

토익 Part 7에서 비교적 쉬운 유형인 글의 주제 또는 글을 쓴 목적을 묻는 문제도 먼저 풀어야 하는 유형들 중 하나입니다. 대부분 지문 첫 문장 또는 첫 단락에 문의, 요청, 지시, 발표, 공유 등을 나타내는 표현과 함께 제시됩니다. 따라서 지문의 첫 부분에 주제·목적의 정답 단서를 알리는 표현과 함께 언급되는 정보에 주목해야 합니다.

■ 빈출 질문 유형

주제

- What is the main subject of the article? 이 기사의 주제는 무엇인가?
- What does the article primarily discuss? 이 기사는 주로 무엇을 논의하고 있는가?
- What is the e-mail about? 이 이메일은 무엇에 관한 것인가?

목적

- What is the purpose of the notice? 이 공지의 목적은 무엇인가?
- Why was the memo written? 이 회람이 쓰여진 이유는 무엇인가?
- Why was the information sent? 이 정보가 보내진 이유는 무엇인가?

■ 빈출 단서 유형

주제

- This letter[e-mail] is to confirm 이 편지는[이메일은] ~을 확인해 드리기 위한 것입니다.
- I am writing to apologize for ~에 대해 사과드리기 위해 씁니다.

목적

- The purpose of this letter[e-mail] is to do 이 편지[이메일]의 목적은 ~하는 것입니다.
- I am happy to inform you about ~에 대해 알려드리게 되어 기쁩니다.

■ 주제·목적 유형 예제

질문에 제시된 키워드와 본문 시작 부분의 내용에 유의해 정답 단서를 찾아봅니다.

Dear Mr. Simon,

This e-mail is to express regret for causing you inconvenience. Recently, I received your e-mail describing the damage to your customized Aurora lamp you ordered. We at Aurora Lamps and Lighting strive to ensure that this does not happen to our products, and we take care to pack all items very carefully. We will be more than willing to send you a replacement item.

Q. Why was the e-mail **sent** to Mr. Simon? 이 이메일은 왜 사이먼 씨에게 보내졌는가?
(A) To acknowledge a problem with an order 주문품의 문제를 시인하기 위해
(B) To express thanks to him for his patronage 그의 성원에 대해 감사를 표하기 위해
(C) To complain about a faulty product 결함 제품에 대해 불만을 제기하기 위해
(D) To request some customer feedback 고객 의견을 요청하기 위해

사이먼 씨께,

본 이메일은 귀하에게 불편을 끼쳐드린 것에 대해 사과드리기 위함입니다. 최근, 귀하께서 주문하신 맞춤형 오로라 램프에 대한 손상을 설명하는 귀하의 이메일을 받았습니다. 저희 오로라 램프조명 사는 저희 제품에 이런 일이 발생하지 않도록 보장하기 위해 애쓰고 있으며, 모든 상품을 매우 조심스럽게 포장하도록 주의를 기울이고 있습니다. 귀하께 기꺼이 교체품을 보내 드릴 것입니다.

❶ 질문 키워드 확인
질문의 키워드 Why ~ sent?는 편지를 보낸 목적을 나타냅니다.

❷ 지문 속 단서 찾기
단락에서 「This e-mail is to do ~」와 같은 표현과 함께 제시되며, to부정사 부분이 목적을 나타냅니다.

❸ 선택지 고르기
사이먼 씨가 「불편」을, 「주문품에 발생한 손상」이라고 표현했으므로 이 표현을 「주문품에 발생한 문제」라고 표현한 (A)가 정답입니다.

PRACTICE

Dear Mr. Lee,

Thank you for agreeing to lead our weekly marketing strategy session. This is to confirm the meeting will take place on July 12 at 2 P.M. in Conference Room A. Please let me know if you need any AV equipment or additional handouts. We look forward to your presentation.

2. Why was the e-mail sent to Mr. Lee?
   (A) To confirm the date and location of a meeting
   (B) To request a change in a meeting time
   (C) To apologize for double-booking a session
   (D) To cancel an upcoming workshop

3 사실확인

사실확인 유형은 특정 대상에 대해 옳게 말한 것을 고르는 일치 유형과 옳지 않게 설명한 것을 고르는 불일치 유형의 두 가지로 출제되는데, 일치 유형이 70% 정도로 출제 비중이 훨씬 높습니다.

일치와 불일치 유형 모두 풀이 방법은 질문의 키워드를 지문에서 찾아 단서를 선택지와 비교하는 세부정보 유형 풀이법과 비슷하지만, 단서가 지문 곳곳에 흩어져 있어서 지문의 많은 부분을 읽어야 합니다. 또한 일치하는 것 하나를 찾는 순간 풀이가 끝나는 일치 유형과 달리, 불일치 유형은 일치하는 것 세 개를 모두 찾아야 불일치하는 하나를 정답으로 고를 수 있으므로 시간이 더 많이 필요합니다.

■ 빈출 질문 유형

일치하는 것 찾기

- What is indicated about Mr. Banks? 뱅크스 씨에 대해 알려진 것은 무엇인가?
- What is mentioned about Mr. Austin's proposal? 오스틴 씨의 제안에 대해 언급된 것은 무엇인가?
- What is stated about Milton Corporation? 밀턴 사에 대해 서술된 것은 무엇인가?
- What is included in the rental price? 대여료에 포함된 것은 무엇인가?
- What is true about the promotional event? 홍보 행사에 관해 사실인 것은 무엇인가?

일치하지 않는 것 찾기

- What is NOT mentioned about Mr. Simpson? 심슨 씨에 대해 언급되지 않은 것은 무엇인가?
- What is NOT indicated in the letter? 편지에서 밝혀지지 않은 것은 무엇인가?
- What is NOT stated about Ms. Hamilton? 해밀턴 씨에 대해 서술되지 않은 것은 무엇인가?
- What is NOT included in Mr. Black's e-mail? 블랙 씨의 이메일에 포함되지 않은 것은 무엇인가?

■ 사실확인 유형 예제

질문에 제시된 키워드를 지문에서 찾은 다음, 앞 또는 뒤에 언급되는 관련 정보 중에서 정답 단서를 찾아봅니다.

Dear Desmond,

I wanted to thank you for taking the time to show me the facility on Southern Avenue yesterday. It looks like it may be a good fit for our company's new location. The size is perfect, **and the location is very convenient for highway access**. However, I do have a couple of quick questions about the property.

Q. **What is true** about **the facility**? 이 시설에 대해 사실인 것은 무엇인가?
(A) It can be remodeled. 개조될 수 있다.
(B) It has underground parking. 지하 주차장이 있다.
(C) It is not far from the highway. 고속도로와 멀리 떨어져 있지 않다.
(D) Its parking may be insufficient. 주차 공간이 충분하지 않을 수도 있다.

데즈몬드 씨,

어제 시간을 내셔서 저를 서던 애비뉴에 있는 시설로 안내해 주신 것에 대해 감사드리고 싶었습니다. 그곳은 우리 회사의 새로운 사옥으로 꼭 맞는 것처럼 보입니다. 크기가 완벽했고, 위치는 고속도로 이용에 매우 편리합니다. 하지만, 그 건물에 관해 두어 가지 간단한 질문이 있습니다.

질문 키워드 확인
질문의 키워드 the facility에 관해 지문에 언급된 것을 정답으로 고릅니다.

지문 속 단서 찾기
the facility에 관련해서 언급된 '고속도로 이용에 매우 편리한 위치'라는 내용을 확인합니다.

선택지 고르기
고속도로 이용에 편리하다는 것은 고속도로와 멀지 않다는 의미와 문맥이 통하므로 (C)가 정답입니다.

PRACTICE

Notice from: Building Management

Starting April 1, our underground parking garage will reserve four spaces exclusively for electric vehicles with Level 2 chargers. General parking spaces remain available on a first-come, first-served basis. Monthly parking permits must be renewed by the third business day of each month. Please display your permit clearly at all times.

3 What is true about the parking garage after April 1?
(A) All parking spaces will incur an hourly fee.
(B) Some spots will be set aside for electric vehicles.
(C) Monthly permits will no longer be necessary.
(D) General spaces will be removed.

실전 TEST

학습한 내용을 적용하여 다음 기출 변형 문제들을 풀어보세요.

Questions 1-2 refer to the following advertisement.

Check Out Perseus Direct!

Do you have a busy schedule these days? Are you finding it difficult to find time to shop for groceries or other goods? If so, then you should install the Perseus Direct application on your mobile devices. Perseus Direct has partnered with more than 3,000 businesses in Carver City and the surrounding area, and we are ready and waiting to pick up a wide variety of items for you and bring them to your door. From fresh produce and baked goods to exercise equipment and vitamin supplements, we can get these to you quickly and conveniently. We already employed a team of around 30 drivers, and are in the process of adding another 20. So, you will always find one who is available to meet your needs. Download Perseus Direct from your preferred app store or find out more by visiting www.perseusdirectonline.ca.

1 What kind of business is Perseus Direct?

(A) A grocery store
(B) A software developer
(C) A delivery service
(D) A fitness center

2 What is indicated about Perseus Direct?

(A) It is expanding overseas.
(B) It has won several awards.
(C) It requires a registration fee.
(D) It is hiring more employees.

Questions 3-5 refer to the following letter.

Dear Hiring Manager,

Please find my résumé attached for your review in regard to the sales executive position posted on Global Transit's Web site. I have extensive experience in direct consumer sales, and I am currently looking for a new career opportunity. I am particularly interested in your company as I have recently moved to an area where Global Transit conducts a great deal of business.

In my previous sales role, I increased sales revenues by expanding existing markets and making contacts in new markets. I received the Top Salesperson Award for four consecutive years, and also the Innovator Award for creating a highly successful sales manual.

Attached you will find my detailed job history with several letters of reference with contact information. Please consider me for the advertised position.

Sincerely,

Michael Wilson

3 What is the purpose of the letter?
(A) To announce a job opening
(B) To request more information
(C) To express interest in a job
(D) To honor an employee

4 What is true about Mr. Wilson?
(A) He works for Global Transit.
(B) He is an award recipient.
(C) He has advertising experience.
(D) He started a new company.

5 What is enclosed with the letter?
(A) Recommendation letters
(B) A college transcript
(C) A list of clients
(D) A business card

Questions 6-8 refer to the following memo.

To: All Regional Sales Associates
From: Camille Foster, Operations Manager
Subject: Regarding Our Weekly Sales Meeting
Date: April 3

Due to renovation work on the 4th floor conference room, this week's sales meeting will be held in the Willow Training Room on the 2nd floor. The meeting time remains unchanged—Thursday at 10:30 A.M.—and remote access will still be available via OfficeNet. Please arrive ten minutes early to allow time for setup, especially if you are presenting.

6 What is the main purpose of the memo?
 (A) To seek additional presenters for an upcoming sales meeting
 (B) To notify employees about a change in meeting location
 (C) To announce a delay in the start time of a regular meeting
 (D) To inform staff of a new policy regarding conference room use.

7 Why are employees asked to arrive early?
 (A) The meeting will begin earlier than usual.
 (B) Attendees will receive printed handouts at the door.
 (C) Some equipment needs to be set up in advance.
 (D) Security checks will be conducted before the meeting.

8 Which of the following is NOT mentioned in the memo?
 (A) The meeting is moved because of renovation work.
 (B) Participants can join remotely via OfficeNet.
 (C) Attendees should arrive early if they are presenting.
 (D) Everyone must bring printed handouts to the meeting.

Questions 9-11 refer to the following review.

Customer Review: Mesa Audio M60 Bluetooth Speaker
☆☆☆☆☆

Reviewer: Edward Berg
Date: August 7

I bought the M60 speaker two weeks ago and have been blown away by the sound quality—it's surprisingly powerful for its size. I also like the minimalist design and the battery life, which lasts about 10 hours on a full charge. The only downside is that it takes a while to pair with my phone, especially the first time. Still, overall, it's a great value for the price and perfect for casual listening. I wouldn't hesitate to let my friends know about the M60's blend of portability and power.

---

9 What is Mr. Berg's opinion of the speaker's sound quality?

(A) It is disappointing.
(B) It is better than expected.
(C) Its volume is too high.
(D) It is average for the price.

10 What feature did Mr. Berg's device have a problem with?

(A) Battery life
(B) Volume controls
(C) Wireless connectivity
(D) Product weight

11 What is indicated about Mr. Berg?

(A) He uses the speaker mostly for professional purposes.
(B) He plans to return the speaker soon.
(C) He would recommend the speaker to others.
(D) He has owned several Mesa Audio products.

DAY 14 | 문맥파악 Part 7

1 동의어 찾기

지문 속의 특정 위치에 나타나 있는 단어를 문제에서 제시한 후, 그 단어와 유사한 의미를 지닌 단어를 고르는 유형입니다. 동의어 찾기 유형 문제에서 가장 중요한 점은 단순히 특정 단어가 지니는 사전적 의미가 아니라 주어진 문장에서 어떤 의미를 나타내는지를 파악하는 것입니다.

■ 빈출 질문 유형

- The word "concerning" in paragraph 1, line 2, is closest in meaning to
  첫 번째 단락, 두 번째 줄의 단어 "concerning"과 의미가 가장 가까운 것은 무엇인가?

- In the first e-mail, the word "perform" in paragraph 3, line 1, is closest in meaning to
  첫 번째 이메일에서, 세 번째 단락, 첫 번째 줄의 단어 "perform"과 의미가 가장 가까운 것은 무엇인가?

■ 동의어 찾기 문제 풀이 순서

① 문제를 먼저 읽고 제시된 단어의 위치를 지문에서 찾습니다.
② 제시된 단어가 포함된 문장을 읽고 의미를 파악합니다.
③ 이때, 해당 문장뿐만 아니라 앞뒤에 위치한 문장들도 함께 읽어 흐름을 파악합니다.
④ 해당 문장 및 앞뒤 문장들을 통해 파악한 문맥 속에서 제시된 단어가 어떤 의미를 나타내는지 생각합니다.
⑤ 그 의미와 가장 유사한 의미를 지닌 단어를 선택지에서 고릅니다.

■ 동의어 찾기 문제 주의사항

- 다양한 의미를 지니는 단어가 출제되므로 자신이 알고 있는 의미만 생각하고 성급하게 답을 고르지 말아야 합니다.
- 제시된 단어의 의미 또는 지문의 전체적인 내용을 정확히 알지 못하더라도 앞뒤 문장을 읽고 흐름을 파악해 풀 수 있으므로 반드시 문맥을 파악하는 데 집중합니다.

■ 동의어 찾기 유형 예제

질문에 제시된 단어를 지문에서 찾아 해당 문장 및 앞뒤 문장을 읽고 문맥을 파악합니다.

Summer Breeze Hotel is now offering early bird specials for guests who book their stay before June 30. Guests can reserve a room up to a year in advance, locking in the lowest available rates. Complimentary breakfast is included with every booking, and pool access is free to hotel guests. Visit our Web site today to take advantage of these limited-time offers.

Q. The word "rates" in paragraph 1, line 3, is closest in meaning to
첫 번째 단락, 세 번째 줄의 단어 "rates"와 의미가 가장 가까운 것은 무엇인가?
(A) discounts 할인
(B) fees 요금
(C) rankings 순위
(D) benefits 혜택

썸머 브리즈 호텔에서는 6월 30일 이전에 숙박을 예약하시는 고객님께 얼리버드 특가를 제공하고 있습니다. 고객님께서는 최대 1년 전까지 객실을 사전 예약하여 가장 저렴한 요금을 확정하실 수 있습니다. 모든 예약에는 무료 조식이 포함되며, 호텔 투숙객은 수영장을 무료로 이용하실 수 있습니다. 오늘 바로 웹사이트를 방문하셔서 이 한정 기간의 특별 혜택을 누리세요.

❶ 문장 해석하기
질문에 제시된 단어가 포함된 문장 해석: "고객님께서는 최대 1년 전까지 객실을 사전 예약하여 가장 저렴한 rates로 확정하실 수 있습니다."

❷ 지문 속 단서 찾기
1. 얼리버드 특가 제공(offering early bird specials)
2. 1년 전까지 사전 예약(reserve a room up to a year in advance)

❸ 정답 찾기
사전 예약 시 특가로 예약할 수 있다는 내용이므로 the lowest의 수식을 받는 명사 rates는 '요금', '가격'을 의미합니다. 따라서 정답은 (B) fees(요금)입니다.

PRACTICE

Join us at the Seoul Tech Expo! The expo will feature over 50 tech startups showcasing innovations in AI, robotics, and VR. Attendees can participate in hands-on demos, keynote speeches, and networking events. Food trucks and live music will complete the festival atmosphere. Plan your visit at www.seoultechexpo.com.

1 The word "feature" in paragraph 1, line 1, is closest in meaning to
   (A) present   (B) attribute   (C) function   (D) represent

2 표현의도 파악하기

문자 메시지 지문 또는 채팅 지문에서 한 메시지 작성자가 쓴 특정 문장을 문제에서 제시한 후, 그 문장이 어떤 의도로 쓰였는지 알아내는 유형입니다. 동의어 찾기 문제와 마찬가지로, 단순히 해당 문장이 지니는 의미를 찾는 것이 아니라 지문의 내용 흐름 속에서 어떤 의도로 쓰였는지를 파악하는 것이 가장 중요합니다.

■ 빈출 질문 유형

- At 10:24 A.M., what does Ms. Laine most likely mean when she writes, "Well, I hope you still write everything in your planner"?
  오전 10시 24분에, 레인 씨가 "당신이 여전히 일정표에 모든 것을 기록하고 있기를 바랍니다"라고 쓴 의도는 무엇인가?

- At 5:17 P.M., what does Mr. Kang most likely mean when he writes, "I'll contact Mr. Stewart before dinner"?
  오후 5시 17분에, 강 씨가 "저녁 식사 전에 제가 스튜어트 씨에게 연락할게요"라고 쓴 의도는 무엇인가?

■ 표현의도 파악하기 문제 풀이 순서

① 문제에 제시된 특정 문장을 먼저 확인합니다.
② 해당 문장의 내용을 파악합니다.
③ 해당 문장을 지문 속에서 찾습니다.
④ 해당 문장의 앞뒤에 위치한 문장을 읽고 대화의 흐름을 파악합니다.
⑤ 대화의 흐름과 관련하여 제시된 문장이 표면적인 의미 외에 어떤 의도로 쓰였는지 생각합니다.
⑥ 그 의도를 가장 잘 나타내는 문장을 선택지에서 고릅니다.

■ 표현의도 파악하기 문제 주의 사항

- 문제를 읽으면서 제시된 문장을 확인한 후, 해당 문장이 지니는 기본적인 의미를 그대로 말한 선택지를 고르지 않도록 주의합니다.
- 제시된 문장 앞뒤에 위치한 문장을 통해 제시된 문장의 숨은 의도를 알아내는 것이 핵심이므로 반드시 문맥을 파악하는 데 집중합니다.
- 제시된 문장과 멀리 떨어진 문장을 읽고 의도를 파악해야 하는 문제도 종종 있으므로, 제시된 문장 바로 앞 또는 뒤에 위치한 문장으로 의도를 파악하기 어렵다면, 그보다 더 앞에 위치한 문장을 읽어보아야 합니다.

■ 표현의도 파악하기 유형 예제

질문에 제시된 문장을 지문에서 찾아 해당 문장 및 앞뒤 문장을 읽고 내용 흐름을 파악합니다.

Leo [2:10 P.M.] Did the vendor confirm delivery for our event supplies?
Mina [2:12 P.M.] Yes, but the timing isn't ideal—they'll drop everything off at 8 A.M. the day of the event.
Leo [2:14 P.M.] That's cutting it close. We need more time to set up.
Mina [2:17 P.M.] I know. I'll ask if they can move it up to the afternoon before.
Leo [2:20 P.M.] Good idea. Let's not leave it to the last minute again.

Q. At 2:20 P.M., what does Leo most likely mean when he writes, "Let's not leave it to the last minute again"?
오후 2시 20분에, 레오 씨가 "또다시 마지막 순간까지 미루지 않도록 해요"라고 쓴 의도는 무엇인가?
(A) He regrets placing a supply order too late. 공급 주문을 너무 늦게 했던 것을 후회한다.
(B) He suggests delaying an event to allow more setup time.
준비 시간을 더 허용하기 위해 행사를 연기하는 것을 제안한다.
(C) He wants to avoid tight delivery timing in the future. 향후 촉박한 배송 일정을 피하기를 원한다.
(D) He is worried a vendor will cancel without notice. 판매자가 예고 없이 취소할 것이라고 걱정한다.

레오 [오후 2:10] 판매사가 행사 용품 배달 일정을 확정했나요?
미나 [오후 2:12] 네. 그런데 시간이 좀 안 좋아요—행사 당일 오전 8시에 물품을 전달한다고 하네요.
레오 [오후 2:14] 그건 너무 촉박한데요. 준비 시간이 더 필요해요.
미나 [오후 2:17] 그러게요. 전날 오후로 일정을 앞당길 수 있는지 물어볼게요.
레오 [오후 2:20] 좋아요. 또다시 마지막 순간까지 미루지 않도록 해요.

❶ **해당 문장 해석하기**
질문에 제시된 문장 해석:
"또다시 마지막 순간까지 미루지 않도록 해요."

❷ **지문 속 단서 찾기**
1. 행사 당일 오전 8시에 물품 전달 예정이라 시간이 좀 안 좋다(timing isn't ideal)고 언급
2. 시간이 너무 촉박하다(That's cutting it close)는 우려 표현

❸ **정답 찾기**
"또다시 마지막 순간까지 미루지 않도록 해요" → 이전에도 비슷한 일이 있었고, 앞으로는 준비를 더 여유 있게 하고 싶다는 의미이므로 (C)가 정답입니다.

PRACTICE

[12:48 P.M.] Daniel Hunt: Hello, thank you for contacting Jabes Apparel. I'm Daniel Hunt from Customer Support. What can I help you with today?
[12:49 P.M.] Rachel Rohan: Hi, I requested a refund last week but haven't seen it processed yet.
[12:50 P.M.] Daniel Hunt: Let me check the status for you. Can you share your order number?
[12:51 P.M.] Rachel Rohan: Sure. Order #92317 — the backpack I returned.
[12:52 P.M.] Daniel Hunt: Ah, that explains it. The refund wasn't issued because the return item hasn't arrived at our warehouse yet.
[12:53 P.M.] Rachel Rohan: Oh I see. I'll wait a few more days then.

2 At 12:52 P.M., what does Daniel Hunt most likely mean when he writes, "Ah, that explains it"?
(A) He no longer needs the order number.
(B) He cannot help the customer any further.
(C) He wants the customer to file a complaint.
(D) He has figured out the reason for the delay.

3 문장삽입 위치 파악하기

하나의 문장이 주어지고 지문의 내용 흐름상 그 문장의 위치로 가장 적절한 곳을 찾는 유형의 문제입니다. Part 6에서 정해진 위치에 알맞은 문장을 찾아 넣는 유형과 비슷한 원리로 출제됩니다. 지문 속에서 단락별 내용 전개와 관계 확인 등을 통한 전체적인 내용 흐름을 파악해야 하는 어려운 문제이지만, 그 속에 연계성을 찾는 데 필요한 단서가 반드시 제시되므로 그 단서를 빠르게 찾고 정확한 내용 흐름을 파악하는 것이 중요합니다.

■ 빈출 질문 유형

- In which of the positions marked [1], [2], [3], and [4] does the following sentence best belong?
  [1], [2], [3], 그리고 [4] 중에서 다음 문장이 가장 잘 어울리는 위치는 어느 것인가?

■ 문장삽입 위치 파악하기 문제 풀이 순서

① 문제에 제시된 문장을 먼저 해석하면서 문장 내에 존재하는 지시어, 대명사, 특정 명사, 접속부사 등을 단서로 확인합니다.
② 지문에서 [1]~[4]로 표시된 부분을 찾아 각 위치에 문장을 넣어 의미 연결이 자연스러운지 확인합니다.
③ 이때, 이미 확인해 둔 단서(지시어, 대명사, 특정 명사, 접속부사 등)를 활용해 앞뒤 문장과의 관계를 보고 파악합니다.

■ 빈출 단서 유형

- 지시어/대명사: this, that, these, those, they, them, such, it, he, she, both 등
- 접속부사: however, therefore, accordingly, for example, instead, furthermore, also 등
- 시간 및 순서 표현: before, after, prior to, then, first, finally 등
- 정관사(the) + 명사

■ 문장삽입 위치 파악하기 문제 주의 사항

- 문맥을 파악해야 하는 유형이므로 해당 지문에 있는 다른 문제를 먼저 푸는 것이 좋습니다. 세부정보 유형 문제나 주제/목적 문제를 먼저 풀면서 지문의 내용을 파악할 수 있으므로 그 이후에 문장삽입 위치 파악하기 문제를 푸는 것이 효율적입니다.
- 각 숫자로 표기된 위치에 넣어 앞뒤 문장과 자연스럽게 연결되는지 확인해야 합니다.

■ 문장삽입 위치 파악하기 유형 예제

질문에 제시된 문장에서 단서를 확인해 내용 흐름상 알맞게 연결되는 위치를 찾습니다.

— [1] —. A front desk attendant at the Trinity Hotel will be responsible for helping our guests. — [2] —. The front desk attendant will oversee check-ins and check-outs and respond to any of the guests' requests or inquiries. — [3] —. Applicants who hold a university degree are preferred, but it is not required. — [4] —.

Q. In which of the positions marked [1], [2], [3] and [4] does the following sentence best belong?

[1], [2], [3] 그리고 [4] 중에서 다음 문장이 가장 잘 어울리는 위치는 어느 것인가?

"They should also have at least one year of experience in the hotel industry."
"그들은 또한 호텔 업계에서 최소 1년 동안의 경력을 지니고 있어야 합니다."

(A) [1]   (B) [2]   (C) [3]   (D) [4]

-[1]-. 트리니티 호텔의 프런트 데스크 직원은 고객을 돕는 일을 담당하게 됩니다. -[2]-. 프런트 데스크 직원은 체크인과 체크아웃을 관리하고 고객의 요청이나 문의에 응답합니다. -[3]-. 대학 학위 소지자가 우대되지만, 필수 조건은 아닙니다. -[4]-.

❶ 해당 문장 해석하기
질문에 제시된 문장 해석: "그들은 또한 호텔 업계에서 최소 1년 동안의 경력을 지니고 있어야 합니다"

❷ 해당 문장 속 단서 찾기
1. 최소 1년의 호텔 업계 경력 언급
2. 인칭대명사 They
3. 첨가의 부사 also

❸ 정답 찾기
부사 also가 있으므로 해당 문장의 내용과 유사한 의미가 앞서 언급되어야 하므로 [4]가 정답입니다.

- Applicants = They
- hold a university degree → also have ~ experience

PRACTICE

The City Library will introduce a new policy for study-room reservations starting July 1. — [1] —. Students and faculty can book rooms up to two weeks in advance. — [2] —. Reservations must be canceled at least 24 hours before the start time to avoid penalties. — [3] —. Nominal fees will apply for late cancellations. — [4] —.

3 In which position does the following sentence best belong?

"Non-library members, however, must register for a guest pass before making a reservation."

(A) [1]   (B) [2]   (C) [3]   (D) [4]

실전 TEST

학습한 내용을 적용하여 다음 기출 변형 문제들을 풀어보세요.

Questions 1-3 refer to the following online chat discussion.

Grant [10:35 A.M.] Hey, Olivia… The top floor of our headquarters will be closed all of next week while the remodeling work is underway. That means we'll need to find a new workspace for the marketing department staff.

Olivia [10:37 A.M.] Yes, I know. At least half of the marketing team will be in London next week for a skills development workshop, so we only need to find a new temporary space for the remaining staff.

Grant [10:39 A.M.] Oh, that's right. So, there'll only be about ten department members here next week?

Olivia [10:40 A.M.] Exactly. So, I was thinking we could fit them in with the graphic design team on the third floor. The last time I checked, there were several empty desks there.

Grant [10:42 A.M.] Things have changed. They have recently recruited a lot of new workers.

Olivia [10:45 A.M.] Hmm... in that case, I'll see if we can set up some temporary workstations in Meeting Room 3. It isn't being used that much these days.

---

1 What is indicated about the business?

(A) It has moved to a new headquarters.
(B) It has scheduled some renovations.
(C) It recently hired more marketing staff.
(D) It will be closed for one week.

2 What did Olivia mention about some marketing department workers?

(A) They often collaborate with graphic designers.
(B) They requested new work equipment.
(C) They are based at a London branch.
(D) They will attend a training event.

3 At 10:42 A.M., what does Grant mean when he writes, "Things have changed"?

(A) He recommends that some work be postponed.
(B) He doubts there are enough workspaces available.
(C) He thinks the marketing team should remain on the top floor.
(D) He believes some new desks have been ordered.

Questions 4-6 refer to the following letter.

Dear Mr. Hannigan,

On behalf of Royale Bank, I am pleased to inform you that your bank loan application has been accepted and processed. Therefore, we will grant you the $10,000 sum in accordance with the terms and conditions laid out in the enclosed agreement. — [1] —.

We have already received copies of your pay slips covering the past six months, your two pieces of state-issued photo ID, and your social security number. — [2] —. Once the funds have been deposited into your business bank account, you will be notified by SMS and receive written confirmation by mail that you may keep for your reference. — [3] —.

As detailed in the agreement, the full sum plus interest must be paid back within 10 years. We can offer you an interest rate of 9 percent, which is a fairly competitive rate among Oregon banks. We expect a repayment of $126 on the 1st of each month, and failure to adhere to these terms may result in additional administration charges or fees.
— [4] —.

Please feel free to contact me directly at 555-1103 should you have any questions or concerns.

Sincerely,
Rajesh Suleman, Corporate Loans Manager
Royale Bank

---

4 Why was the letter sent to Mr. Hannigan?

(A) To confirm the opening of an account
(B) To provide advice on starting a business
(C) To approve a request for financing
(D) To request additional information

5 What is Mr. Hannigan asked to do on a monthly basis?

(A) Make a payment
(B) Visit the bank
(C) Submit a document
(D) Call Mr. Suleman

6 In which of the positions marked [1], [2], [3], and [4] does the following sentence best belong?

"As such, we have all the necessary information and do not need to trouble you for anything else."

(A) [1]
(B) [2]
(C) [3]
(D) [4]

Questions 7-9 refer to the following notice.

Shipping Policy – Autumn & Lake Home Décor

We aim to dispatch all orders within two business days of purchase. — [1] —. Orders shipped within the continental U.S. typically arrive within five to seven business days. Please note that processing times may be longer during peak holiday seasons. — [2] —. International shipping is available, but delivery times vary by region and may be affected by customs procedures. — [3] —. Express shipping options are offered at checkout for customers who need faster service. — [4] —.

7 What is the main purpose of notice?

(A) To promote discounted shipping rates
(B) To update store hours for the holidays
(C) To describe a return process for defect items
(D) To inform customers of fulfillment timelines

8 The word "dispatch" in paragraph 1, line 1, is closest in meaning to

(A) ship
(B) replace
(C) remove
(D) track

9 In which of the positions marked [1], [2], [3], and [4] does the following sentence best belong?

"Delays are particularly likely in the weeks prior to Christmas."

(A) [1]
(B) [2]
(C) [3]
(D) [4]

Questions 10-12 refer to the following online chat discussion.

[10:12 A.M.] Arun Davies: Hi team, any update on the draft layout for the EcoSave campaign? We were hoping to review it before tomorrow.

[10:14 A.M.] Leena Jensen: We're still waiting on the product dimensions from the client. They said they'd confirm yesterday, but we've heard nothing yet.

[10:16 A.M.] Jason Kim: I tried to follow up with them again this morning by e-mail. If we don't hear back by noon, I'll mock up a placeholder layout.

[10:18 A.M.] Leena Jensen: Good idea. Also, the tagline needs to be finalized—should we just go with the last version from Marketing?

[10:20 A.M.] Arun Davies: Let's hold off. They sent us a revised one late last night, but it hasn't been approved.

[10:23 A.M.] Jason Kim: OK. I'll try the client's contact number since they aren't responding to e-mails.

[10:25 A.M.] Arun Davies: Thanks, Jason. Let me know if you hear anything.

---

10 What problem are the writers mainly discussing?

(A) A delay in client communication
(B) A defect in a product design
(C) A fault with some design software
(D) An unsuccessful marketing campaign

11 At 10:20 A.M., what does Mr. Davies mean when he says, "Let's hold off"?

(A) He would like to push back a work deadline.
(B) He believes that a meeting is unnecessary.
(C) He would prefer to wait for approval.
(D) He wants to meet a client in person.

12 What will Mr. Kim most likely do next?

(A) Revise a tagline
(B) Send an e-mail
(C) Make a phone call
(D) Meet with Mr. Davies

DAY 15 | 다중지문 Part 7

1 다중지문 풀이 전략

2개의 지문이 1세트로 구성되는 이중지문, 그리고 3개의 지문이 1세트로 구성되는 삼중지문이 토익 Part 7의 마지막에 등장합니다. 이중지문과 삼중지문 모두 1세트당 5문제씩 다양한 유형의 문제가 출제되지만, 이중지문과 삼중지문의 가장 큰 특징은 1개의 지문이 아닌 2개의 지문에 나뉘어 제시되는 단서를 종합해 푸는 연계 문제가 세트마다 반드시 1문제 이상 출제된다는 점입니다.

■ 다중지문 간단히 파악하기

	이중지문	삼중지문
문제 번호	176~180번, 181~185번 (총 2세트, 10문제)	186~190번, 191~195번, 196~200번 (총 3세트, 15문제)
지문별 문제 배치 순서	· 첫째 지문: 1~2번 문제 · 둘째 지문: 4~5번 문제 · 대체로 3번 문제가 연계 문제	· 첫째 지문: 1~2번 문제(연계 문제 포함) · 둘째 지문: 3~4번 문제(연계 문제 포함) · 셋째 지문: 5번 문제
문제 유형	주제/목적 문제, 세부정보 문제, 사실확인 문제, 동의어 문제, 연계 문제 (표현의도 파악 및 문장삽입 유형은 제외)	

■ 다중지문 구성 예시

	지문 구성
이중지문	웹페이지 공지 - 고객의 이용후기(칭찬/불만) 특정 주제에 관한 문의 - 문의에 대한 답변 예정된 행사/공사/회의 공지 - 구체적 일정 및 유의 사항 설문조사/행사 참여 권유 - 참가 신청서 불만 및 문제점 제기 - 해결책 제시 제품 및 서비스 광고 - 고객 혜택 특정 주제에 관한 공지 - 관련 기사
삼중지문	제품 관련 할인/하자/정책 변경 안내 공지 - 고객의 영수증 - 고객의 이메일 특정 주제에 관한 기사 - 해당 주제에 관한 문의 - 담당자 답변 웹페이지 광고 - 제품/서비스 등의 주문/신청 - 관련 양식 특정 행사 공지 - 행사 일정표 - 행사 결과/반응 지면 광고 - 제품/서비스 등의 주문/신청 - 영수증 웹페이지 광고 - 소비자 이용 후기 - 업체 측 답변

■ 다중지문 문제 풀이 순서

이중지문과 삼중지문은 지문 순서와 문제 순서가 대체로 일치하므로 출제되는 문제 유형에 따라 우선 순위를 정해서 푸는 것이 좋습니다. 또한 세트당 대략 5분 내에 지문 내용을 파악하고 문제 풀이하는 것이 효율적입니다.

| 개별 지문에 대한 주제/목적, 동의어 문제 | ≫ | 개별 지문에 대한 세부정보, 사실확인 문제 | ≫ | 두 개의 지문에 대한 연계 문제 |

① 주제/목적 문제와 동의어 문제부터 풀이

- 각 세트에 출제되는 다섯 문제들 중에서 개별 지문의 초반부에서 비교적 쉽게 단서를 찾을 수 있는 주제/목적 문제부터 풀이합니다.
- 동의어 문제는 제시된 단어가 포함된 문장 또는 그 앞뒤 문장들의 내용 흐름만 파악해도 풀 수 있으므로 주제/목적 문제와 함께 먼저 풀이합니다.

② 세부정보 및 사실확인 문제는 나중에 풀이

- 세부정보, 사실확인 문제는 찾아야 할 정보도 많고 각 선택지와 대조하는 과정을 거쳐야 해서 많은 시간이 소모되므로 나중에 풀이합니다.
- 지문의 단서를 다른 말로 바꿔 표현하는 패러프레이징에 주의해야 하며, 단서와 선택지를 대조하는 과정에서 확인되는 오답은 소거합니다.

③ 연계 문제는 나중에 풀이

- 한 지문에서 찾은 단서를 바탕으로 관련 정보가 언급된 다른 지문에서 추가 단서를 찾은 다음, 두 가지 정보를 종합해 유추 가능한 것을 정답으로 골라야 합니다.
- 삼중지문 연계 문제의 경우, 기본적인 문제 풀이 과정은 이중지문과 같으며, 세 개의 지문 중 두 개 지문에 제시되는 단서를 바탕으로 풀이합니다. 한 문제에 대한 단서가 세 개의 지문에 모두 제시되는 경우는 없습니다.

■ 다중지문 문제 풀이 주의사항

- 지문을 읽을 때 짝지어 나오는 지문들이 서로 어떤 관계인지 먼저 파악해야 합니다. 문제 풀이에 핵심적인 역할을 하는 특정 날짜나 장소, 서비스 종류, 비용, 방법 등과 같이 중요한 정보에 유의하여 읽어야 합니다.
- 한 지문을 읽고 나머지 지문을 읽을 때 앞서 확인한 중요 정보 중 중복되는 요소가 언급되는 부분을 놓치지 않는 것이 중요합니다.
- 단, 삼중지문 연계 문제에서는 단서가 1번 지문과 3번 지문에 숨어 있거나 2번 지문과 3번 지문에 제시되는 등 일관적이지 않으므로 지문을 읽는 동안 연계성을 파악하는 것이 중요합니다.

2 이중지문 연습

가장 중요한 것은 2개의 지문이 1세트를 구성하므로 두 지문 사이의 관계를 빠르게 파악하는 것입니다. 쉬운 유형의 문제를 먼저 풀이하면서 각 지문의 내용 및 두 지문 사이의 관계를 대략적으로 파악한 다음, 세부적인 정보 확인 및 대조 과정이 필요한 어려운 유형의 문제로 넘어가는 방식으로 풀이합니다.

■ 이중지문 풀이 단계

① 두 지문의 종류를 먼저 파악하고 각 문제의 유형을 확인해 풀이할 순서를 정합니다. 각 세트에 있는 다섯 문제를 반드시 순차적으로 풀지 않아도 됩니다.
② 주제/목적 문제와 동의어 문제 등 쉬운 유형의 문제를 먼저 풀면서 각 지문의 내용과 두 지문 사이의 관계를 간략하게 파악합니다.
③ 세부정보 및 사실확인 문제를 풀이합니다. According to나 In the e-mail 등과 같이 특정 지문을 가리키는 말이 질문에 쓰인 경우 해당 지문 하나만 보고 풀 수 있으므로 이것을 먼저 풀이합니다. 이 유형의 문제를 풀이하기 위해 세부적인 정보를 파악하는 동안 두 지문 사이의 연계성을 염두에 두고 읽는 것이 좋습니다.
④ 두 지문 사이에 연계된 정보를 파악해 연계 문제를 마지막으로 풀이합니다.

■ 이중지문 연습 예제

Outdoor Acoustic Festival Being Planned by University

May 5 (Columbus) – Ripley University is organizing an outdoor music festival to be held in June, but the final date and location have not yet been decided. According to Dan Nutter, the event organizer, the festival will either be held at Roger Park on June 15 or on June 22 at Dow Lake Park. Nutter says that the decision should be finalized by the weekend.

Ripley Outdoor Acoustic Festival

Gold Pass Ticket: June 22
Headliner: Tracy Reynolds, 8 P.M.
Supporting act: The Blue Hill Pickers, 7 P.M.

Q. Where did the Ripley Outdoor Acoustic Festival most likely take place?
리플리 야외 어쿠스틱 축제는 어디에서 열렸을 것 같은가?
(A) Roger Park 로저공원
(B) Dow Lake Park 도우레이크 공원
(C) Ripley University 리플리 대학교
(D) Columbus Community Center 콜럼버스 지역문화센터

대학에 의해 계획된 야외 어쿠스틱 음악 축제

5월 5일 (콜럼버스) – 리플리 대학이 야외 음악 축제를 6월에 개최하려고 준비 중이지만, 최종 날짜 및 장소는 아직 결정되지 않았다. 행사 주최 책임자인 댄 너터 씨에 따르면, 이 축제는 6월 15일에 로저 공원 또는 6월 22일에 도우레이크 공원 중 한 곳에서 개최될 것이다. 너터 씨는 이 결정이 이번 주말까지 최종 확정될 것이라고 밝혔다.

리플리 야외 어쿠스틱 음악 축제
골드 입장권: 6월 22일
메인 공연자: 트레이시 레이놀즈, 오후 8시
찬조 공연자: 더 블루 힐 피커즈, 오후 7시

첫 지문에서 질문의 키워드 찾기
질문의 키워드는 Ripley Outdoor Acoustic Festival이며, 질문의 의문사는 Where이므로 지문에서 행사 장소에 대해 언급된 부분을 확인

첫 지문 속 단서 찾기
해당 축제가 일자별로 개최장소가 다른 것을 확인
1. 6월 15일 로저 공원
2. 6월 22일 도우레이크 공원

두 번째 지문 속 단서 찾고 정답 고르기
두 번째 지문인 입장권에 기재된 축제 일자가 6월 22일(June 22)인 것을 확인 → 도우레이크 공원이 축제 장소이므로 (B)가 정답

PRACTICE

Sole Comfort Shoe Store

To ensure customer satisfaction, Sole Comfort Shoe Store offers the following refund policy. Returns made within seven days of purchase, with the original shoes and receipt, will receive a 100% refund. Returns made between eight and thirty days of purchase, with the original shoes and receipt, will receive a 50% refund. No refunds will be issued for returns made more than thirty days after purchase. Shoes must be in unworn condition and accompanied by the original receipt.

Date: August 20

To whom it may concern,
I purchased a pair of "Metro Walk" loafers on August 10 for $120. Unfortunately, they didn't fit as expected. The shoes are unworn and I still have the original receipt. Please let me know how much I will be refunded and the next steps. Thank you.

Rita Harrison

1 How much refund will Ms. Harrison receive?
(A) $0   (B) $60   (C) $120   (D) $90

3 삼중지문 연습

삼중지문은 이중지문보다 읽어야 할 지문이 하나 더 있다는 것 외에는 이중지문과 큰 차이가 없습니다. 따라서 이중지문의 문제를 풀이할 때와 동일한 순서 및 방식을 적용해 풀이합니다. 단, 연계 문제의 단서가 세 지문 중 어디에 위치하는지를 파악할 때 주의해야 합니다.

■ 삼중지문 풀이 단계

① 세 지문의 종류를 먼저 파악하고 각 문제의 유형을 확인해 풀이할 순서를 정합니다. 각 세트에 있는 다섯 문제를 반드시 순차적으로 풀지 않아도 됩니다.
② 쉬운 유형의 문제를 먼저 풀면서 각 지문의 내용과 세 지문 사이의 관계를 간략하게 파악합니다.
③ 세부사항 및 사실확인 문제를 풀이합니다. 이 유형의 문제를 풀이하기 위해 세부적인 정보를 파악하는 동안 세 지문 사이의 연계성을 염두에 두고 읽는 것이 좋습니다. 삼중지문 연계 문제의 단서는 세 지문 중 첫째-둘째, 둘째-셋째, 또는 첫째-셋째 등 두 개의 지문에서만 찾을 수 있습니다.
④ 세 지문 중 두 지문 사이에 연계된 정보를 파악해 연계 문제를 마지막으로 풀이합니다.

■ 삼중지문 연습 예제

Miguel,

I just made your reservation for the upcoming Tech Entrepreneur Seminar being held at the Estates Hotel. Your pass costs $40, but the company will cover it with our employee development budget. Keep in mind that parking around the hotel is expensive, and you'll likely have to pay $25 for a spot.

Rosa,

Thanks for making the arrangements. I think I'll learn a lot at the seminar. It should be a good networking opportunity, too. I'll keep any other travel receipts I receive and turn them in to you on Monday when I return to the office.

Tech Entrepreneur Seminar

Estates Hotel, 9786 North Avenue, Salt Lake City
One-Day Pass - $25
Two-Day Pass - $40

Q. What type of pass was most likely booked for Miguel?
어떤 종류의 입장권이 미구엘 씨를 위해 예약되었을 것 같은가?

(A) One-Day Pass 1일 입장권
(B) Two-Day Pass 2일 입장권
(C) Guest Speaker Pass 초청 연설자 입장권
(D) Priority Registration Pass 사전 등록자 입장권

미구엘 씨,
에스테이츠 호텔에서 곧 개최되는 기술 사업가 세미나에 귀하를 막 예약해 드렸습니다. 귀하의 입장권은 비용이 40달러이지만, 회사에서 직원 능력 개발 예산으로 비용을 충당해 드릴 것입니다. 이 호텔 주변의 주차는 비싸며 한 자리를 이용하는데 25달러를 지불하셔야 할 가능성이 있다는 점을 유념하시기 바랍니다.

로사 씨,
준비해 주셔서 감사드립니다. 세미나에서 많이 배울 것이라고 생각합니다. 좋은 인적 교류 기회도 될 것입니다. 제가 받을 어떤 출장 영수증이든 보관하고 있다가 사무실로 복귀하는 월요일에 그것들을 제출하겠습니다.

기술 사업가 세미나

에스테이츠 호텔, 노스 애비뉴 9786번지, 솔트 레이크 시티
1일 입장권 – 25달러
2일 입장권 - 40달러

---

1 첫 지문에서 질문의 키워드 찾기
질문의 키워드는 What type of pass, for Miguel이므로 지문에서 Miguel에게 보내는 이메일인 첫 지문에서 관련된 pass에 관한 부분을 확인

2 첫 지문 속 단서 찾기
미구엘의 입장권(pass)이 40달러라고 언급된 것을 확인

3 세 번째 지문 속 단서 찾고 정답 고르기
첫 지문에서 파악한 단서 40달러에 해당하는 입장권이 2일권(Two-Day Pass)인 것을 확인하고 (B)를 정답으로 선택

실전 TEST

학습한 내용을 적용하여 다음 기출 변형 문제들을 풀어보세요.

Questions 1-5 refer to the following e-mails.

Subject: Mariposa Bistro
Date: November 4

Dear Sir/Madam,

I dined at your restaurant with some friends two days ago, and we really enjoyed your extensive seafood menu and the table we reserved out on the patio. Nevertheless, I am writing to you because I wish to bring an incident regarding a member of your staff to your attention. The employee, whose name tag identified him as Steven, carelessly dropped a bowl of ice cream while bringing out the dessert course. Unfortunately, this landed on my cell phone, which was on the table, cracking the screen and damaging the leather phone case.

I am still very unhappy about this situation, as he was carrying too many dishes at the time and an accident was bound to happen. As a result, I had no choice but to visit a phone store yesterday and pay $120 for screen repairs. The phone case is worth an additional $50, but luckily, I have managed to clean that and it's almost back to its original appearance. So, I do not expect to be compensated for the full $170, but I hope to at least have the cost of repairs covered.

I hope to hear back from you soon regarding this matter.

Sincerely,
Lisa Mulvaney

Date: November 5
Subject: Mariposa Bistro

Dear Ms. Mulvaney,

I am terribly sorry to hear about the incident that spoiled your otherwise enjoyable experience at my restaurant. I have spoken to the employee you mentioned and arranged for all staff to undergo retraining this week. As a token of goodwill, I insist on covering the cost of both the repairs and the case, which you mentioned is still not in perfect condition. I would be happy to send you a direct bank transfer, if that suits you. Please let me know your banking information at your earliest possible convenience, and I will take care of this immediately. Once again, please accept my apologies, and I look forward to seeing you again at Mariposa Bistro.

Best regards,

Alan Crandall
Proprietor, Mariposa Bistro

1. What is the main purpose of the first e-mail?

   (A) To reserve a table
   (B) To make a complaint
   (C) To inquire about a menu
   (D) To praise an employee

2. When did Ms. Mulvaney visit Mariposa Bistro?

   (A) On November 2
   (B) On November 3
   (C) On November 4
   (D) On November 5

3. How much money will Mr. Crandall send to Ms. Mulvaney?

   (A) $50
   (B) $120
   (C) $170
   (D) $220

4. In the second e-mail, the word "suits" in paragraph 1, line 5, is closest in meaning to

   (A) adapts
   (B) satisfies
   (C) confirms
   (D) outfits

5. Who is Mr. Crandall?

   (A) A business owner
   (B) A cleaner
   (C) A chef
   (D) A server

Questions 6-10 refer to the following Web page, press release, and instant message.

	www.moscowballetgroup.com/about		
ABOUT	DANCERS	PERFORMANCES	CONTACT

THE MOSCOW BALLET GROUP

The Moscow Ballet Group was founded by Dimitri Popov in 2002 and has toured extensively all over the world on an annual basis since it was first established. Several of Russia's top ballet dancers are currently active group members, including Nikolai Nureyev, who is frequently cited as the world's leading contemporary ballet dancer. Our upcoming North American tour kicks off in Los Angeles on March 20 and ends in New York City on April 23. The performances will include completely original dance routines devised by our brilliant choreographer, Olga Vaganova, and feature stunning hand-painted backdrops produced by the famous artist Ivan Somova. We would like to thank our performance director, Natalia Geltzer, for bringing all of these wonderful elements together to create our most amazing show yet.

Ballet fans should note that the Moscow Ballet Group will be taking the rest of the year off to focus on practice and training to prepare ourselves for a full world tour next year, so this will be your last chance to see one of our performances for a while. Tickets can be purchased by clicking the 'PERFORMANCES' tab above.

OFFICIAL PRESS RELEASE
MOSCOW BALLET GROUP
Contact: inquiries@mbg.com

(April 5) – It has recently come to our attention that we did not include enough dates in Canada on our current North American tour. Our Canadian fans are very important to us, so we have decided to extend the tour by adding some additional performances in the provinces of Ontario and Quebec. Details of the additional performances are as follows:

Palisade Music Center (Quebec City) - April 27
Frederic Building (Montreal) - April 29
GQ Convention Center (Ottawa) - May 1
Lovett Concert Hall (Toronto) - May 3

Tickets for the above dates are on sale now, and may be purchased directly from the venues or by visiting our Web site at www.moscowballetgroup.com/performances.

Angela Lowden [3:25 P.M.]

Hi Selma. Mary and I would really like to go and see the Moscow Ballet Group at the GQ Convention Center, and we figured you would be interested in joining us. As you probably know, the venue is just a short drive from my house, so I'd be happy to have you and Mary over for dinner first before we go and see the performance. I watched an interview on Channel 4 with the person who choreographs all the dancers' moves, and I was amazed. Let me know if you're interested!

6 What is indicated about Nikolai Nureyev?

(A) He established the Moscow Ballet Group.
(B) He has won awards for his dancing.
(C) He is unable to join an upcoming tour.
(D) He is often praised for his expertise.

7 According to the Web page, what is true about the Moscow Ballet Group's North American tour?

(A) It runs for three months.
(B) It begins in New York City.
(C) It includes an original music score.
(D) It is the group's final tour this year.

8 In the message, the word "figured" in paragraph 1, line 2, is closest in meaning to

(A) counted
(B) guessed
(C) solved
(D) outlined

9 In which city does Ms. Lowden most likely live?

(A) Quebec City
(B) Montreal
(C) Ottawa
(D) Toronto

10 Who did Ms. Lowden see being interviewed on television?

(A) Ivan Somova
(B) Natalia Geltzer
(C) Dimitri Popov
(D) Olga Vaganova

PART 7 FINAL TEST

학습한 내용을 적용하여 다음 기출 변형 문제들을 풀어보세요.

Questions 1-4 refer to the following e-mail.

From: Ravi Nair <rnair@helixlogistics.com>
To: All Warehouse Supervisors
Subject: Forklift Safety Certification Session
Date: October 5

Dear Team,

In our ongoing efforts to uphold the highest standards of safety across our facilities, we will be hosting a compulsory forklift operation safety course on Friday, October 13, from 10:00 A.M. to 12:00 P.M. in the main loading bay, adjacent to Dock 4. The session will include a detailed walk-through of safe handling procedures, a short video demonstration, and a live Q&A with a certified safety inspector.

Please ensure that all forklift operators are notified and attend the entire duration of the training. Operators who complete the course will receive official certification, valid for the next 18 months. Kindly remind attendees to bring their employee ID cards for verification upon arrival. If any team member has a scheduling conflict or is unable to attend for any reason, please notify me via e-mail no later than Monday, October 9, so that other arrangements can be made.

Thank you in advance for your attention to this matter and for your continued commitment to workplace safety.

Best regards,

Ravi Nair
Logistics Safety Coordinator

1. What is the purpose of the e-mail?

   (A) To schedule a staff meeting
   (B) To announce a training course
   (C) To describe a job opportunity
   (D) To request feedback from managers

2. What will NOT happen on October 13?

   (A) An expert will answer questions.
   (B) A work area will be temporarily closed.
   (C) Employees will watch a video.
   (D) Some procedures will be explained.

3. What does Mr. Nair indicate about the certification?

   (A) It will be issued only to full-time warehouse employees.
   (B) It will be included on employee identification cards.
   (C) It will remain valid for one and a half years.
   (D) It requires the completion of an online course.

4. What should supervisors do if an employee cannot attend the October 13 session?

   (A) Contact the safety inspector
   (B) Organize an additional training day
   (C) Conduct a training course online
   (D) Inform Mr. Nair of their absence

Questions 5-9 refer to the following article and review.

Healthy Office Digest
March Edition

Small Wellness Habits for Busy Professionals

Staying healthy while working full time can be difficult, especially for employees with long hours or desk-based roles. However, developing a few simple wellness habits can make a meaningful difference over time.

- Make time for movement. Try to stand or walk for a few minutes every hour, even if it's just a lap around the office. Over time, this can help reduce stiffness and improve energy levels.
- Keep nutritious snacks nearby. Instead of reaching for chips or candy, prepare sliced fruit or mixed nuts in advance and store them in individual containers.
- Drink more water. Many people confuse thirst for hunger, which leads to unnecessary snacking. Staying hydrated also improves concentration.

Have your own workplace wellness tips? Write to us and we might feature them in an upcoming issue!

Reader Submission

Thanks for the great suggestions in your recent article. I used to work at Moira Communications, and I would always encourage my colleagues to keep healthy habits throughout the day. One strategy that worked for me was switching from coffee to fruit smoothies in the morning. It helped me stay alert without the caffeine crash.

Also, because I kept spilling drinks on my commute, I designed a reusable bottle that's perfect for smoothies. My brand-new company, Rivermix, just released the FreshGo Flask. It's insulated, leakproof, and fits easily into car cup holders and work bags. We designed it to help busy professionals start their day in a healthier way.

—Kiera Nolan

5 What is NOT recommended in the article?

(A) Taking brief walks during the day
(B) Eating healthy snacks
(C) Getting extra sleep during work hours
(D) Consuming more fluids

6 What does the article indicate about staying properly hydrated?

(A) It can help reduce the desire to eat.
(B) It can decrease the likelihood of illness.
(C) It may lead to more frequent breaks.
(D) It improves athletic performance.

7 What is indicated about *Healthy Office Digest*?

(A) It is published daily by Moira Communications.
(B) It accepts health-related ideas from readers.
(C) It is focused on product reviews.
(D) It is intended only for medical professionals.

8 What is true about the FreshGo Flask?

(A) It was reviewed in a health magazine.
(B) It was inspired by a design competition.
(C) It is available in many different colors.
(D) It was launched onto the market recently.

9 What can be inferred about Ms. Nolan?

(A) She was the founder of Moira Communications.
(B) She writes articles for several publications.
(C) She read the March issue of *Healthy Office Digest*.
(D) She no longer drinks fruit smoothies.

PART 7 FINAL TEST

Questions 10-14 refer to the following e-mails and a price list.

To: info@blossomandbelleweddings.com
From: clara.finchley@hawthornmedia.co.uk
Subject: Wedding Reception Plans
Date: April 4

Hello,

I'm writing regarding my upcoming wedding reception on May 18, which your company is helping to coordinate. As you know, I've already arranged catering and floral decorations through your firm, and you have been very communicative and helpful throughout the planning process. However, due to the unpredictable weather lately, I'm now considering setting up a large-scale tent as a precaution for the garden area. Could you please send me the available options and pricing for outdoor tents that could accommodate approximately 60 guests? My budget is already stretched thin, so I would have to keep the price below $1,400.

Thank you,
Clara Finchley

To: clara.finchley@hawthornmedia.co.uk
From: info@blossomandbelleweddings.com
Subject: RE: Wedding Reception Plans
Date: April 5

Dear Ms. Finchley,

Thank you for your message. We would be happy to arrange a tent for your event. Please refer to the attached price list, which outlines several tent options depending on size, style, and included furnishings. I understand that you wish to keep costs down, but I encourage you to consider our brand-new style, which includes wood panel flooring and sophisticated lighting.

For your estimated guest count, both the Garden View and Heritage Style options would be suitable. Please let us know your preference by April 12 so that we have time to secure your booking and confirm setup. If you'd like to discuss this further by phone, feel free to reach me directly at 555-4921.

Sincerely,

Amanda Yeung
Lead Coordinator
Blossom & Belle Weddings

Outdoor Tent Rental Options – Spring Wedding Season

Tent Type	Capacity	Features	Price (Flat Rate)
Basic Pavilion	Up to 40	Open-sided, no furnishings	$800
Garden View	50–80	Includes string lighting, side panels	$1,200
Heritage Style	40–90	Includes chandeliers, wooden flooring	$1,550
Grand Pavilion	Up to 150	Includes full lighting, stage, carpeting	$2,100

Notes:
Bookings must be confirmed at least 10 days before event date.
All tents include setup and dismantling.
In the event of high winds, side panels may be removed for safety.

10 What does Ms. Finchley say she has already done?

(A) Booked food and flowers
(B) Increased the number of guests
(C) Changed an event date
(D) Paid for her event in full

11 What is suggested about the original reception plan?

(A) It was intended to be outdoors.
(B) It included a backup location.
(C) It required a Basic Pavilion.
(D) It did not involve a tent.

12 Which rental option would be most appropriate for Ms. Finchley's needs?

(A) Basic Pavilion
(B) Garden View
(C) Heritage Style
(D) Grand Pavilion

13 What is the rental price for the company's newest type of tent?

(A) $800
(B) $1,200
(C) $1,550
(D) $2,100

14 What is indicated about all tent options?

(A) They must be booked in advance.
(B) They include furniture and lighting.
(C) They must be set up by the client.
(D) They are the same price all year-round.

시원스쿨 **한 권 토익** 시리즈

시원스쿨
기본토익
700⁺

LC/RC 인강

속전속결 토익 졸업
하승연 선생님

실전형
기본 완성 강의

700+ 목표달성을 위해
엄선된 출제포인트 및
실전문제 양치기 학습으로
15일 커리큘럼 목표점수 달성

안정적인
점수 확보 솔루션

700점 이상 달성에 필수적인
PART 3, 4 & PART 6, 7에서
전략적인 점수 확보
솔루션 제시

만점 강사
스킬 전수

시험영어 전문가,
토익 만점 하승연 쌤의
친절하고 상세한 맞춤 설명으로
만점 풀이 전략 완벽 전수

시원스쿨랩 사이트에서(lab.siwonschool.com) 유료로 수강 가능합니다.

기본토익 700+

실전 모의고사

실전 모의고사 음원

실전 모의고사 해설

시원스쿨 기본토익 700+
실전 모의고사

LISTENING TEST

In the Listening test, you will be asked to demonstrate how well you understand spoken English. The entire Listening test will last approximately 45 minutes. There are four parts, and directions are given for each part. You must mark your answers on the separate answer sheet. Do not write your answers in your test book.

PART 1

Directions: For each question in this part, you will hear four statements about a picture in your test book. When you hear the statements, you must select the one statement that best describes what you see in the picture. Then find the number of the question on your answer sheet and mark your answer. The statements will not be printed in your test book and will be spoken only one time.

Statement (D), "They are taking photographs," is the best description of the picture, so you should select answer (D) and mark it on your answer sheet.

1.

2.

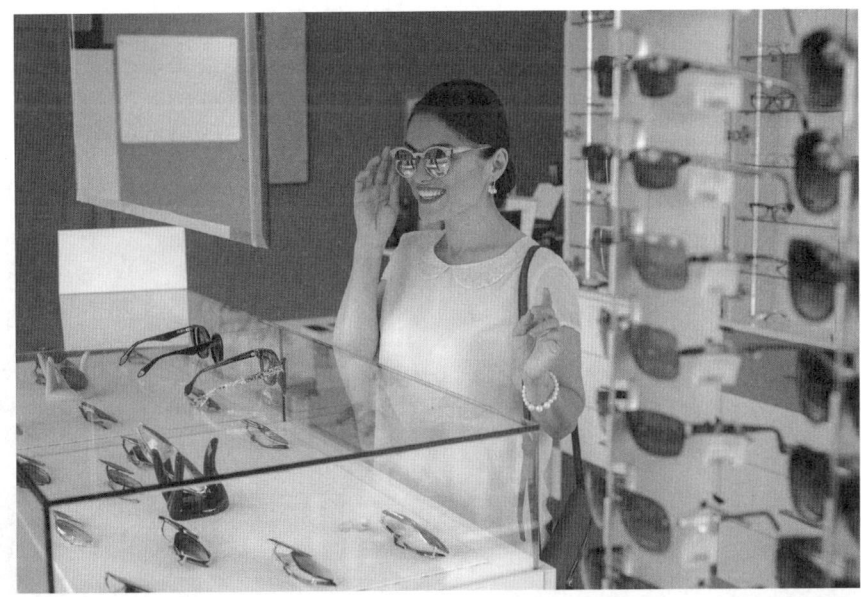

3.

4.

5.

6.

PART 2

Directions: You will hear a question or statement and three responses spoken in English. They will not be printed in your test book and will be spoken only one time. Select the best response to the question or statement and mark the letter (A), (B), or (C) on your answer sheet.

7. Mark your answer on your answer sheet.
8. Mark your answer on your answer sheet.
9. Mark your answer on your answer sheet.
10. Mark your answer on your answer sheet.
11. Mark your answer on your answer sheet.
12. Mark your answer on your answer sheet.
13. Mark your answer on your answer sheet.
14. Mark your answer on your answer sheet.
15. Mark your answer on your answer sheet.
16. Mark your answer on your answer sheet.
17. Mark your answer on your answer sheet.
18. Mark your answer on your answer sheet.
19. Mark your answer on your answer sheet.
20. Mark your answer on your answer sheet.
21. Mark your answer on your answer sheet.
22. Mark your answer on your answer sheet.
23. Mark your answer on your answer sheet.
24. Mark your answer on your answer sheet.
25. Mark your answer on your answer sheet.
26. Mark your answer on your answer sheet.
27. Mark your answer on your answer sheet.
28. Mark your answer on your answer sheet.
29. Mark your answer on your answer sheet.
30. Mark your answer on your answer sheet.
31. Mark your answer on your answer sheet.

PART 3

Directions: You will hear some conversations between two or more people. You will be asked to answer three questions about what the speakers say in each conversation. Select the best response to each question and mark the letter (A), (B), (C) or (D) on your answer sheet. The conversations will not be printed in your test book and will be spoken only one time.

32. What did the woman do last weekend?

    (A) Meet with investors
    (B) Test some products
    (C) Attend a convention
    (D) Talk at a fundraiser

33. What field do the speakers most likely work in?

    (A) Computer accessories
    (B) Home appliances
    (C) Cooking utensils
    (D) Building supplies

34. What does the man say will happen in September?

    (A) A marketing campaign will begin.
    (B) A retail outlet will be opened.
    (C) New products will be sold.
    (D) Customers will be surveyed.

35. What does the man ask the woman to do?

    (A) Send out invitations
    (B) Reserve an event venue
    (C) Create a seating plan
    (D) Organize transportation

36. What kind of event will take place?

    (A) A retirement dinner
    (B) An awards ceremony
    (C) A staff orientation
    (D) A charity banquet

37. What will the man probably do next?

    (A) Visit a venue
    (B) Purchase equipment
    (C) Review a document
    (D) Have lunch with the woman

38. Where most likely are the speakers?

    (A) In a university
    (B) In a museum
    (C) In a hospital
    (D) In a library

39. According to the woman, what will happen at 3 P.M.?

    (A) A seminar will be held.
    (B) A staff meeting will start.
    (C) A building will be closed.
    (D) An announcement will be made.

40. What does the woman suggest doing?

    (A) Cleaning a room
    (B) Handing out maps
    (C) Putting up signs
    (D) Changing a schedule

41. What type of service are the speakers discussing?

    (A) Vehicle rental
    (B) Event planning
    (C) Food delivery
    (D) IT maintenance

42. What is the man concerned about?

    (A) Preparing orders
    (B) Purchasing vehicles
    (C) Obtaining licenses
    (D) Training employees

43. What does the woman say she will do?

    (A) Place an advertisement
    (B) Conduct more interviews
    (C) Lead an orientation
    (D) Check job requirements

GO ON TO THE NEXT PAGE

44. Where most likely do the speakers work?
    (A) In a factory
    (B) In a laboratory
    (C) In a warehouse
    (D) In an office

45. Why did the woman leave her previous job?
    (A) She was dissatisfied with her salary.
    (B) She moved to a different city.
    (C) She did not enjoy the work.
    (D) She decided to resume her education.

46. What will the woman most likely do next?
    (A) Fill out some forms
    (B) Meet her colleagues
    (C) Watch a presentation
    (D) Join a training class

47. What is the problem with the changing room?
    (A) It is closed for renovations.
    (B) Its showers are broken.
    (C) Its door cannot be opened.
    (D) It has been flooded.

48. What does Tony suggest?
    (A) Performing warm-up exercises
    (B) Purchasing a beverage
    (C) Signing up for a gym class
    (D) Borrowing some clothes

49. What does the woman plan to do in April?
    (A) Join a sports team
    (B) Go on vacation
    (C) Attend a family event
    (D) Extend a membership

50. Who most likely is the man?
    (A) A repairman
    (B) A cleaner
    (C) A server
    (D) A cook

51. What does the woman ask the man to do?
    (A) Tidy a stock room
    (B) Assist a customer
    (C) Fix some appliances
    (D) Clean some surfaces

52. What does the man recommend?
    (A) Postponing an inspection
    (B) Keeping an area clear
    (C) Holding a meeting
    (D) Opening the business early

53. What problem does the man mention about his room?
    (A) It is locked.
    (B) It has not been cleaned.
    (C) It is too hot.
    (D) It is missing some items.

54. What does the woman mean when she says, "All of our standard rooms are booked"?
    (A) She is pleased with the hotel's popularity.
    (B) She recommends upgrading a room.
    (C) She will provide the man with a refund.
    (D) She cannot fulfill the man's request.

55. What does the man say he will do in the morning?
    (A) Move to a different room
    (B) Speak with a manager
    (C) Interview for a job
    (D) Attend a conference

56. What does the woman suggest doing?

    (A) Relocating a head office
    (B) Organizing training classes
    (C) Replacing some furniture
    (D) Installing new software

57. What does the man mean when he says, "But there are more than 300 workspaces in our headquarters"?

    (A) A building may not be large enough.
    (B) An idea might not be affordable.
    (C) Some positions must be filled quickly.
    (D) Some workers will be transferred.

58. What will the man probably do next?

    (A) Make a payment
    (B) Speak with a colleague
    (C) Test some merchandise
    (D) Visit a supplier

59. What does the woman want to purchase at the bakery?

    (A) A loaf of bread
    (B) A selection of muffins
    (C) A box of donuts
    (D) A birthday cake

60. What does Simon say about the items sold in the bakery?

    (A) They can be gift wrapped.
    (B) They are freshly made.
    (C) They are currently discounted.
    (D) They can be personalized.

61. What does Jeremy suggest that the woman do?

    (A) Enter a contest
    (B) Obtain a membership
    (C) Order a beverage
    (D) Look at some images

Event Duties (Wesley)	
Time	Duty
9:00 A.M.–11:00 A.M.	Taking tickets
11:00 A.M.–1:00 P.M.	Distributing flyers
1:00 P.M.–5:00 P.M.	Moving equipment
5:00 P.M.–7:00 P.M.	Tidying up the site

62. What is the woman organizing?

    (A) A film festival
    (B) A trade show
    (C) A concert
    (D) A parade

63. What does the woman ask the man to do?

    (A) Operate a food stall
    (B) Sell event merchandise
    (C) Supervise a parking area
    (D) Construct a stage

64. Look at the graphic. Which duty will the man ask Peter to do?

    (A) Taking tickets
    (B) Distributing flyers
    (C) Moving equipment
    (D) Tidying up the site

GO ON TO THE NEXT PAGE

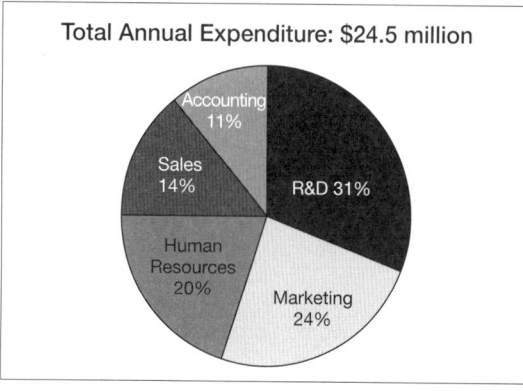

Shipping Options (Domestic)	Shipping Time
Standard	Within 7 days
Standard Plus	3-5 days
Express	1-2 days
Express Plus	Within 24 hours

65. What type of business do the speakers most likely work for?

    (A) An electronics manufacturer
    (B) A publishing company
    (C) A pharmaceutical firm
    (D) A software developer

66. According to the woman, what will take place next month?

    (A) A recruitment fair
    (B) A business seminar
    (C) A department merger
    (D) A shareholder meeting

67. Look at the graphic. What department does the man work in?

    (A) R&D
    (B) Marketing
    (C) Human Resources
    (D) Sales

68. What industry do the speakers work in?

    (A) Fitness equipment
    (B) Online auctions
    (C) Home improvement
    (D) Health foods

69. Look at the graphic. Which shipping option did the man choose?

    (A) Standard
    (B) Standard Plus
    (C) Express
    (D) Express Plus

70. What does the woman suggest the man do?

    (A) Call a customer
    (B) Provide a partial refund
    (C) Cancel an order
    (D) Send a discount voucher

PART 4

Directions: You will hear some talks given by a single speaker. You will be asked to answer three questions about what the speaker says in each talk. Select the best response to each question and mark the letter (A), (B), (C), or (D) on your answer sheet. The talks will not be printed in your test book and will be spoken only one time.

71. Who most likely is the listener?

(A) A security guard
(B) A real estate agent
(C) An office supervisor
(D) A maintenance worker

72. What information does the speaker need?

(A) A business address
(B) An opening time
(C) A building pass code
(D) A telephone number

73. What does the speaker ask the listener to do?

(A) Join her for coffee
(B) Provide her with directions
(C) Send her a message
(D) Call her back

74. What is the speaker mainly discussing?

(A) Job vacancies
(B) Sales figures
(C) Marketing strategies
(D) Staff evaluations

75. What does the speaker want the listeners to do?

(A) Review work policies
(B) Train new employees
(C) Work overtime
(D) Submit a report

76. According to the speaker, what will outstanding workers receive?

(A) A voucher
(B) A promotion
(C) A bonus
(D) An award

77. Who most likely are the listeners?

(A) Authors
(B) Book critics
(C) Customers
(D) Store workers

78. What does the speaker mention about Prism Publishing?

(A) It is seeking new writers.
(B) It has delayed a book release.
(C) It is hosting a special event.
(D) It has gone out of business.

79. What does the speaker mean when she says, "I'd like to know what you think"?

(A) She wants help in making an advertising decision.
(B) She is looking for ways to improve work conditions.
(C) She wants to hear opinions about a book.
(D) She will conduct a survey about reading habits.

80. Where most likely does the speaker work?

(A) At a travel agency
(B) At an airport
(C) At a train station
(D) At a bus terminal

81. What does the speaker imply when she says, "It's the least we can do"?

(A) She is announcing a ticket discount.
(B) She feels sorry about a situation.
(C) Some passengers will receive a refund.
(D) Some workers are available to offer assistance.

82. What does the speaker say she will do?

(A) Assist with some repairs
(B) Change a departure schedule
(C) Keep passengers informed
(D) Issue new tickets to passengers

GO ON TO THE NEXT PAGE

83. What field do the listeners most likely work in?
  (A) Human resources
  (B) Finance
  (C) Web design
  (D) Product development

84. What does the speaker suggest doing?
  (A) Increasing an advertising budget
  (B) Researching rival companies
  (C) Expanding a range of products
  (D) Recruiting new employees

85. What will happen next month?
  (A) A new retail outlet will open.
  (B) A sales report will be released.
  (C) A marketing campaign will end.
  (D) A product will be launched.

86. According to the speaker, what will Happy Valley do this summer?
  (A) Launch new products
  (B) Move its headquarters
  (C) Open a new branch
  (D) Lower its prices

87. What does Happy Valley most likely sell?
  (A) Clothing
  (B) Fast food
  (C) Children's toys
  (D) Kitchen appliances

88. Why are the listeners encouraged to visit a Web site?
  (A) To submit suggestions
  (B) To receive a free gift
  (C) To enter a contest
  (D) To apply for a job

89. Who most likely are the listeners?
  (A) Theater directors
  (B) Screenwriters
  (C) Film critics
  (D) Aspiring actors

90. Why does the speaker say, "He is now in demand for both movies and plays"?
  (A) To emphasize how stressful a career is
  (B) To announce some job opportunities
  (C) To show the importance of hard work
  (D) To suggest that the listeners change their careers

91. What will the listeners receive later today?
  (A) A certificate
  (B) A job offer
  (C) A copy of a book
  (D) A ticket for a play

92. According to the speaker, what will happen in January?
  (A) A workplace will be renovated.
  (B) A survey will be conducted.
  (C) A convention will be held.
  (D) A product will be launched.

93. What recommendation does the speaker make?
  (A) Increasing an order
  (B) Changing a design
  (C) Postponing an event
  (D) Offering accessories

94. What does the speaker ask the listeners to do by the end of tomorrow?
  (A) Fill out a form
  (B) Contact customers
  (C) Submit suggestions
  (D) Install some applications

Thursday	Friday	Saturday	Sunday
☀️⛅	☁️☁️	🌧️	💨

95. What type of work is the speaker calling about?

(A) Road maintenance
(B) Equipment installation
(C) Park landscaping
(D) Building repairs

96. Look at the graphic. When will the work be done?

(A) Thursday
(B) Friday
(C) Saturday
(D) Sunday

97. What does the speaker ask the listener to do?

(A) Meet with a client
(B) Contact a supplier
(C) Submit a report
(D) Return to head office

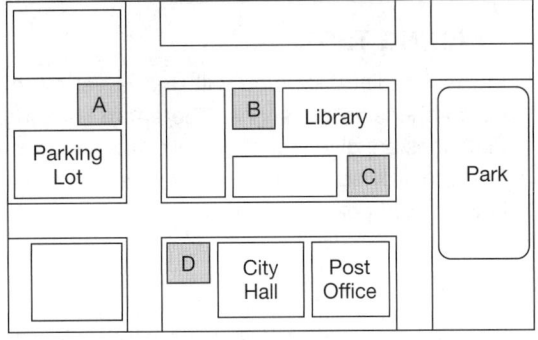

98. What is the speaker mainly discussing?

(A) A park
(B) A fountain
(C) A building
(D) A statue

99. Look at the graphic. Which site does the speaker prefer?

(A) Site A
(B) Site B
(C) Site C
(D) Site D

100. What will the listeners do next?

(A) Look at photographs
(B) Check a blueprint
(C) Visit a location
(D) Watch a video

This is the end of the Listening test. Turn to Part 5 in your test book.

GO ON TO THE NEXT PAGE

READING TEST

In the Reading test, you will read a variety of texts and answer several different types of reading comprehension questions. The entire Reading test will last 75 minutes. There are three parts, and directions are given for each part. You are encouraged to answer as many questions as possible within the time allowed. You must mark your answers on the separate answer sheet. Do not write your answers in your test book.

PART 5

Directions: A word or phrase is missing in each of the sentences below. Four answer choices are given below each sentence. Select the best answer to complete the sentence. Then mark the letter (A), (B), (C), or (D) on your answer sheet.

101. Atlus Logistics will ------- with a rival shipping and moving business in early summer.
(A) merger
(B) merge
(C) merging
(D) merged

102. Mr. Colman enjoyed working ------- the interior designer on the layout for the new office.
(A) on
(B) for
(C) around
(D) with

103. All construction permit ------- should be handled by the council's City Planning Department.
(A) inquire
(B) inquiringly
(C) inquiries
(D) inquirer

104. All gallery workers are reminded that artworks must be hung ------- for display.
(A) carefully
(B) careful
(C) care
(D) caring

105. Shoppers on a tight budget might prefer the Praxis L5 cell phone over the best-selling Praxis XLg, but this model ------- exclude several features.
(A) has
(B) does
(C) makes
(D) causes

106. Buzzsaw Events marketing team leaders recruit local students to assist with ------- concert promotions.
(A) them
(B) theirs
(C) themselves
(D) their

107. The proposed site for the music festival must pass a safety inspection, ------- the event cannot be held there.
(A) how
(B) however
(C) or
(D) moreover

108. Successful applicants for the sales representative positions will be notified ------- one week of their interview.
(A) within
(B) until
(C) among
(D) along

109. While leading the marketing team at Aitken Enterprises, Ms. Barker displayed many ------- qualities.
    (A) admirable
    (B) admiration
    (C) admire
    (D) admiring

110. Last year, the Birch Valley region recorded its ------- annual tourism figures ever.
    (A) high
    (B) higher
    (C) highly
    (D) highest

111. The Mandolin Restaurant ------- monthly expenses by making slight changes to its recipes and portion sizes.
    (A) to reduce
    (B) reducing
    (C) is reduced
    (D) reduced

112. The city council is grateful ------- the valuable assistance of the volunteers who joined the river clean-up program.
    (A) but
    (B) for
    (C) truly
    (D) to

113. Now that its new call center is nearing -------, Westside Energy is hiring individuals to fill fifty telephone operator positions.
    (A) complete
    (B) completely
    (C) completion
    (D) completes

114. The drops in average monthly attendance ------- a decline in popularity for musical stage performances.
    (A) represent
    (B) represents
    (C) representing
    (D) representative

115. Kai Kojima has ------- negotiated a contract to construct a 175-floor skyscraper in Dubai.
    (A) success
    (B) successful
    (C) successes
    (D) successfully

116. ------- in the Scottish Heritage Association is open to anyone who makes a financial donation to the organization.
    (A) Analysis
    (B) Purpose
    (C) Membership
    (D) Awareness

117. The fees ------- on the invoice are non-negotiable, and must be paid in full no later than May 31.
    (A) show
    (B) shown
    (C) had shown
    (D) are showing

118. Because the tour group did not visit the mountain early -------, the members were unable to enjoy the spectacular sunrise.
    (A) around
    (B) before
    (C) rather
    (D) enough

119. The opening times and admission fees listed in the Globetrotter series of travel guides are ------- very up-to-date.
    (A) quickly
    (B) wisely
    (C) generally
    (D) expertly

120. The company offered Mr. Henderson a ------- salary, but he was still not satisfied with the terms of the employment contract.
    (A) competed
    (B) competitive
    (C) competitively
    (D) competition

GO ON TO THE NEXT PAGE

121. Due to concerns over his health, Mr. Lipman ------- the promotion offered to him by the managing director.
    (A) inquired
    (B) rejected
    (C) pretended
    (D) misled

122. Despite only having five years of experience in the field, Lily Kwon made the best case for selecting her ------- our public relations expert.
    (A) in
    (B) so
    (C) by
    (D) as

123. Our message forum members cannot post ------- online while our server is undergoing urgent maintenance.
    (A) none
    (B) whichever
    (C) neither
    (D) anything

124. Erasmus Solutions creates ------- marketing campaigns that appeal to a wide demographic of consumers.
    (A) compelling
    (B) attentive
    (C) concerned
    (D) opposite

125. We are pleased to see that the waste disposal regulations imposed last year are having the ------- impact on the local ecosystem.
    (A) surviving
    (B) desired
    (C) organized
    (D) eventful

126. The flood relief workers have used sandbags to create a temporary ------- around the public library.
    (A) source
    (B) inventory
    (C) building
    (D) boundary

127. Concertgoers are encouraged to take their seats at least 15 minutes prior to the band's ------- performance time.
    (A) anticipated
    (B) selective
    (C) responsible
    (D) capable

128. Please take note of the error message and code ------- the printer malfunctions.
    (A) likewise
    (B) whenever
    (C) altogether
    (D) including

129. ------- you do not currently have a valid passport, please present a different form of photo ID such as a driver's license.
    (A) Regarding
    (B) Therefore
    (C) As a result of
    (D) In the event that

130. Some customer records became mixed up ------- being transferred to the new database system.
    (A) in the process of
    (B) in exchange for
    (C) for the reason that
    (D) in contrast to

PART 6

Directions: Read the texts that follow. A word, phrase, or sentence is missing in parts of each text. Four answer choices for each question are given below the text. Select the best answer to complete the text. Then mark the letter (A), (B), (C) or (D) on your answer sheet.

Questions 131-134 refer to the following e-mail.

Dear Ms. Webber,

I am contacting you to give you advance notice of an unavoidable ------- to our catering service
131.
between May 5 and May 7. We will be closing down our kitchens for necessary renovations, including the installation of new machines and appliances. -------. The work will require three full days, -------
132. **133.**
which time we cannot prepare orders for our clients. ------- any disappointment, please consider
134.
using our sister company, Heavenly Sandwiches, while we are temporarily closed.

Regards,

Walter King
Customer Support Manager
Taste of Heaven Catering

---

131. (A) increase
(B) complaint
(C) process
(D) disruption

132. (A) This will improve our ability to make delicious food.
(B) We would like to receive an estimate for the proposed work.
(C) The catering field is becoming increasingly competitive.
(D) Your orders will be delivered at the pre-arranged time.

133. (A) rather than
(B) due to
(C) during
(D) above

134. (A) To avoid
(B) Having avoided
(C) Avoids
(D) Avoided

GO ON TO THE NEXT PAGE

Questions 135-138 refer to the following e-mail.

From: Desmond Feeney
To: All staff members
Subject: Workshop series
Date: Wednesday, February 7

Dear employees,

The next installment of our Building Better Relationships workshops is taking place on March 2. This ------- workshop features a guest appearance from Jonah Montero, a renowned motivational speaker and business expert. Mr. Montero ------- the importance of socializing with coworkers outside of the workplace. Mr. Montero's workshop is the only one in the series that will be held here at head office. -------.

We would like all staff to attend the workshop, but we are aware that some teams will be working on that day, even though it is a Saturday. As such, make sure you receive ------- your department supervisor before coming to the event.

Best wishes,

Desmond Feeney, Personnel Manager
Whizz Electronics

135. (A) recent
(B) vacant
(C) possible
(D) upcoming

136. (A) discussed
(B) will discuss
(C) has discussed
(D) will have discussed

137. (A) We apologize for the late-minute change of speaker.
(B) The workshop series will resume early next year.
(C) Mr. Montero hopes each of you found his talk highly informative.
(D) The others will take place in our training center and retail stores.

138. (A) approving
(B) being approved
(C) the approval of
(D) who approves

Questions 139-142 refer to the following article.

DPRA Town Forum
November 8
By Arnie Lovett

The Dunhaven Parks & Recreation Association (DPRA) will hold a town forum at the public library on Tuesday, November 14 at 6:30 P.M. to review a plan to create new parking facilities at the main entrance of Seafield Park in downtown Dunhaven.

-------. Several local residents who live near the park entrance have already objected to the proposal as they believe it will result in traffic congestion on the surrounding streets. -------, the DPRA is considering working with the Urban Planning Committee to widen certain streets from two lanes to four lanes. During the forum, Craig Teller, the head of Urban Planning at Dunhaven Council, will describe how much traffic congestion residents can ------- to experience with widened roads. A ------- by Richard Ashford, the DPRA's president, will take place immediately afterwards.

139. (A) The DPRA announced that the project was completed under budget.
(B) The parking lot will accommodate around 200 vehicles.
(C) The public library has been in need of repairs for several years.
(D) The DPRA proposed several potential sites for the park.

140. (A) In addition
(B) In time
(C) In response
(D) In conclusion

141. (A) prefer
(B) accept
(C) limit
(D) expect

142. (A) present
(B) presenting
(C) presenter
(D) presentation

GO ON TO THE NEXT PAGE

Questions 143–146 refer to the following e-mail.

From: eswinton@grillking.com
To: opankow@valleyfoods.com
Subject: Valley Meatless Patties

Dear Mr. Pankow,

I am responsible for sourcing and purchasing supplies for the Grill King fast food chain, which is now in the process of ------- its menu to include plant-based burgers that are suitable for our
143.
vegan and vegetarian customers. We would like to try out some of your Valley Meatless Patties on a trial basis in select stores. I noted that this ------- consistently scores highly in online
144.
reviews, and is a top seller in many major supermarkets throughout the country. At first, I thought this might be a retail-only product, but after browsing your Web site, it seems that you do -------
145.
supply products to restaurant chains. As I mentioned, we would prefer to start out by testing the patties in a few specific stores. -------. Would you be prepared to offer a price reduction for large
146.
monthly deliveries?

I hope to hear from you soon.

Regards,

Edith Swinton
Grill King Inc.

143. (A) expanding
(B) expanded
(C) expands
(D) expand

144. (A) method
(B) activity
(C) location
(D) variety

145. (A) indeed
(B) along
(C) quite
(D) ever

146. (A) Our fast food chain prides itself on its commitment to good nutrition.
(B) Unfortunately, many of our customers disliked the plant-based burgers.
(C) However, we plan to make a purchase for all stores later.
(D) If this interests you, please view our menu on our Web site.

PART 7

Directions: In this part you will read a selection of texts, such as magazine and newspaper articles, e-mails, and instant messages. Each text or set of texts is followed by several questions. Select the best answer for each question and mark the letter (A), (B), (C), or (D) on your answer sheet.

Questions 147-148 refer to the following invitation.

You are invited to attend a special seminar here at Ferrell University.

Special Guest Speaker:
Professor Andrew Morton
Renowned Psychologist and Celebrated Author of
Promoting Inclusivity and Diversity in our Academic Institutions

Topic: Student Welfare
Date: November 25, 1:30 P.M. - 3:30 P.M.
Venue: Hanover Lecture Hall

This seminar is open only to Ferrell University faculty who teach undergraduate and postgraduate students. Only 100 spots are available.
Call Ms. Polly Kidman at Extension 223 to secure a place.

---

147. For whom is the invitation most likely intended?

(A) Undergraduate students
(B) University administration staff
(C) Lecturers and instructors
(D) Recent college graduates

148. What are interested individuals advised to do?

(A) Register for a course
(B) Buy Professor Morton's book
(C) Take lecture notes
(D) Contact Ms. Kidman

Questions 149-150 refer to the following instructions.

Welcome to Silver Hills Hotel in Chicago! To use your staff discount for reservations at any Silver Hills hotel or resort, please follow the guidelines below:

1. Make your reservation through our newly-designed Web site at www.silverhillshotels.com.
2. On the payment screen, click on the tab that says Silver Hills Partners.
3. Enter your unique employee identification number. As it will be your first time using this feature, your initial password will be Silverhills123, which we recommend that you change immediately.
4. You will be prompted to create your own password, which must be at least 8 characters long and contain at least one number. If you encounter any problems, consult with the Human Resources Manager at your specific workplace.
5. Click on "Confirm" to finalize the reservation. You should see your 20 percent staff discount on the printable receipt provided.

SILVER HILLS HOTEL CHICAGO

149. For whom are the instructions most likely intended?

(A) New employees
(B) Hotel guests
(C) Web site designers
(D) Human resources managers

150. What is the reader asked to do?

(A) Provide contact details
(B) Create a social media profile
(C) Attend an information session
(D) Change an online password

Questions 151-152 refer to the following text message chain.

Craig Corman [12:44 P.M.]
Wendy, are you on your way back to the office?

Wendy Statler [12:45 P.M.]
Yes, I just finished lunch. What's up?

Craig Corman [12:46 P.M.]
Our office supplies shipment is delayed, and I really need a pack of A4 paper and some printer toner to create my presentation handouts. I can't believe we've run out already.

Wendy Statler [12:47 P.M.]
Do you know where I can get those items around here?

Craig Corman [12:48 P.M.]
Yes, the store on Fourth Avenue.

Wendy Statler [12:49 P.M.]
There are lots of stores on Fourth Avenue.

Craig Corman [12:51 P.M.]
Oh, right! It's right beside the post office, not far from the Willis Street intersection. You can't miss it.

Wendy Statler [12:53 P.M.]
I think I know the place. Does it normally have products displayed out front?

Craig Corman [12:54 P.M.]
That's the one! Thanks, Wendy. I'll settle up with you once you're back.

151. What's Mr. Corman's problem?

(A) He cannot turn on a printer.
(B) He has misplaced some handouts.
(C) He is out of some supplies.
(D) He is unable to access an office.

152. At 12:49 P.M., what does Ms. Statler imply when she writes, "There are lots of stores on Fourth Avenue"?

(A) She recommends a business on Fourth Avenue.
(B) She needs more detailed directions.
(C) Mr. Corman should visit a store himself.
(D) Mr. Corman should compare some prices.

Questions 153-154 refer to the following e-mail.

From:	Lily Platt
To:	Ravi Mahood
Date:	February 17
Subject:	Re: Requests

Dear Mr. Mahood,

I received your recent e-mail containing specific requests related to your upcoming appearance at the Glendale Comedy Festival. I'm happy to tell you that we are able to accommodate all of the requests you made. A dressing room will be provided for your convenience, and it will have 4 liters of mineral water and assorted snacks. You will go on stage at 7 P.M. sharp, and the event organizers will ensure that your props and additional drinking water are placed on stage beforehand, as per your request. You have been allocated one hour for your comedy set, but you may stay on stage for an additional 15 minutes if necessary.

Please keep in mind that I am still waiting to receive a rough transcript of the material you intend to use during your performance. It is important for us to evaluate this to make sure that the jokes are suitable for our all-ages audience. I would appreciate it if you could include this as an attachment when you reply to this message.

Regards,

Lily Platt
Event Coordinator
Glendale Comedy Festival

153. What is a purpose of the e-mail?

(A) To confirm the details of a performance
(B) To promote an upcoming comedy festival
(C) To suggest changes to a comedy routine
(D) To apologize for an event schedule change

154. What is Mr. Mahood asked to do?

(A) Select his preferred time
(B) Set up some stage props
(C) Attend an audition
(D) E-mail a transcript

Questions 155-157 refer to the following form.

Service Contract

Destiny IT Solutions
E-mail: admin@destinyit.com
Phone: 555-2881
Web site: http://www.destinyitsolutions.com

Client's Name: Edwin Johnson
Service Location: Room 411, 4th Floor, Ace Lux Building, Arnett Boulevard, Dallas
Type of Service: IT Maintenance for Businesses
Service Date/Time: June 17, 1:00 P.M. - 5:00 P.M.
Cost Breakdown of Services Carried Out:

1) Quarterly server maintenance (2nd Quarter) $450.00
2) Anti-virus Software Upgrade $250.00
3) Voice-Activated Software Integration $350.50

Full Balance Due: $1,050.00
Advance Payment (Received on June 10): $500.00
Remaining Amount to be Paid Upon Completion of Work: $550.00

155. What is indicated about the work?

(A) It covers the repair of laptops.
(B) It was fully paid in advance.
(C) It will be performed in the morning.
(D) It includes a regular task.

156. Where most likely will the work take place?

(A) In a building lobby
(B) At a computer store
(C) At Mr. Johnson's workplace
(D) At Mr. Johnson's home

157. What payment amount will Destiny IT Solutions receive on June 17?

(A) $450
(B) $500
(C) $550
(D) $1,050

Questions 158-160 refer to the following press release.

FOR IMMEDIATE RELEASE
Contact: Annabelle Carver, acarver@autosure.co.uk

London (January 21) - Autosure is delighted to announce the addition of several electric cars to its fleet of vehicles at its main rental facility in Croydon, South London. —[1]—. The fleet will initially include 20 electric cars, with a view to doubling this number over the next two years.

Each car features a top-of-the-range satellite navigation system, a spacious boot that can accommodate two large suitcases, and an automatic parking system. The interiors include leather upholstery, drinks holders, and two television screens in the back of the headrests. —[2]—. Every car also boasts a cutting-edge collision avoidance detection system, which alerts the driver when an accident is imminent.

The electric cars are environmentally-friendly and come with full motor insurance coverage. —[3]—. Additionally, drivers can enjoy the reduced costs of charging the car compared with the price of filling a traditional car up with petrol.

We welcome you to stop by our Croydon location and check out all of the vehicles we have in our large fleet. —[4]—. If you wish to test drive one of the electric cars prior to renting it, you may do so by sending an e-mail to agillies@autosure.co.uk.

158. What most likely is Autosure?
(A) A car manufacturer
(B) A rental company
(C) An insurance provider
(D) A vehicle repair firm

159. What is indicated about the electric vehicles?
(A) They cost more to run than traditional cars.
(B) They are available for a limited time.
(C) They include an advanced safety feature.
(D) They have been advertised on television.

160. In which of the positions marked [1], [2], [3], and [4] does the following sentence best belong?

"One of our qualified team members will be happy to assist you."

(A) [1]
(B) [2]
(C) [3]
(D) [4]

Questions 161-163 refer to the following notice.

Valleyside Golf Course & Clubhouse

PARKING LOT GUIDELINES
- PERMIT RULES

Use of the main clubhouse parking lot is restricted to Valleyside Golf Club members and employees. Permits are required for long-term parking and must always be displayed on the inside of each vehicle's windscreen. Short-term parking (up to 30 minutes) at the east side of the clubhouse is allowed for delivery drivers and taxi pick-ups.

- Long-term parking permits are issued to each club member on the first day of their membership period and can be renewed whenever their club membership is renewed. Please remember to check the appropriate box to request/renew a permit when filling out a membership application or renewal form.
- Short-term parking permits may be obtained from the security office at the main entrance on Wilshire Avenue and must be returned within 30 minutes.
- Any vehicle found in the parking lot without a permit will be noted and the owner will be required to pay a $100 fine.

161. What is the purpose of the notice?

(A) To describe changes to a membership application procedure
(B) To announce a plan to construct a new parking lot
(C) To encourage employees to take advantage of a service
(D) To specify who is permitted to use a parking area

162. What is indicated about long-term parking permits?

(A) They must be visible at all times.
(B) They cost 100 dollars to replace.
(C) They can be used by non-members of the club.
(D) They require the payment of a monthly fee.

163. How can delivery drivers acquire a permit?

(A) By filling out an application form
(B) By parking at the east side of a building
(C) By visiting the golf clubhouse
(D) By stopping at a security office

GO ON TO THE NEXT PAGE

Questions 164-167 refer to the online chat discussion.

Grace Chan	Hello, fellow parents. I'm looking for some suggestions. I'm considering Little Explorer Summer Camps for my son, but there are so many to choose from: Twin Valley, Beaver Creek, High Falls... [2:44 P.M.]
Jim Thornton	My daughters went to the High Falls Little Explorer camp last year. They said it was a lot of fun. [2:52 P.M.]
Grace Chan	That's what all the online reviews say, too. The Little Explorer's Web page says that they operate a bus to the campsite, but I was thinking about driving myself. What do you think? [2:55 P.M.]
Peter Bosman	I put my son on the bus a couple of years back and it was pretty convenient. They have pick-up points all over the city. [3:04 P.M.]
Grace Chan	Is the bus relatively affordable, Peter? [3:06 P.M.]
Jim Thornton	Driving yourself means that you can make sure he gets there safely. Personally, I'd be worried about my daughters going on the bus. [3:09 P.M.]
Peter Bosman	It was quite cheap, actually. Around $45 extra for a return trip. [3:14 P.M.]
Michael Witkowski	Grace, the campsite at High Falls isn't really far from the city. An hour's drive at the most. [3:18 P.M.]
Grace Chan	That's pretty reasonable, Peter. And Jim, that's an excellent point! I'll take him myself. [3:27 P.M.]
Michael Witkowski	Just make sure you take Highway 401 instead of 405. I drove along 405 last night and traffic was terrible due to ongoing construction work. [3:33 P.M.]
Grace Chan	Thanks, everyone! I really appreciate it. [3:40 P.M.]

164. With whom was Ms. Chan most likely chatting?

(A) People who work at summer camps
(B) People who posted online reviews
(C) People who have children
(D) People who use a bus regularly

165. Why has Ms. Chan decided to drive herself?

(A) Because a campsite is located far away
(B) Because a bus pick-up point is inconvenient
(C) Because it is cheaper than taking a bus
(D) Because she can ensure her son's safety

166. At 3:27 P.M., what does Ms. Chan most likely mean when she writes, "That's pretty reasonable"?

(A) She is pleased with a camp schedule.
(B) She thinks a ticket price is fair.
(C) She is impressed with Peter's directions.
(D) She agrees that a destination is close.

167. What does Mr. Witkowski indicate about Highway 401?

(A) It is undergoing construction work.
(B) It is known for heavy traffic.
(C) It is the fastest way to the camp.
(D) It is part of a bus route.

Questions 168-171 refer to the following article.

Riverfront Development Scheduled to Start

(March 13) - A significant riverfront development project is set to begin in Newmarket. The project will start with the demolition of several abandoned structures, such as warehouses and factories, situated along the edge of Fern River. Several hotels and smaller lodgings will then be constructed in the area in order to accommodate the influx of people anticipated to arrive for next summer's International Athletics Competition.

The riverfront area, however, has suffered extensive flooding over the past few years, so there is some concern over the suitability of the land for construction. If the ground is too soft, or susceptible to further flooding, it would pose a serious safety risk to anyone using the proposed buildings.

To address the problem, officials handling the Newmarket Riverside Development project are collaborating with a team of experts from Triton Surveying to evaluate whether the land is safe to build on. The surveying team will conduct a comprehensive analysis of the soil and riverbanks in the last week of March, and if their results prove satisfactory, the demolition stage will take place in early April.

Flooding has become an increasing problem in and around Newmarket. Frequent downpours between March and June often cause river levels to rise drastically, and the overspill of water has become a significant problem, particularly for farmers growing crops in the area.

168. Why is the city's riverfront area undergoing development?
 (A) To provide accommodation for event attendees
 (B) To improve the condition of several warehouses
 (C) To create more recreational facilities for tourists
 (D) To construct a new sports stadium

169. What has Triton Surveying been hired to do?
 (A) Check the potential risks of construction
 (B) Identify an alternative construction site
 (C) Demolish buildings along the riverside
 (D) Analyze water samples taken from a river

170. In paragraph 3, line 1, the word "handling" is closest in meaning to
 (A) carrying
 (B) overseeing
 (C) transitioning
 (D) securing

171. What is suggested about Newmarket?
 (A) It is known for its local produce.
 (B) It regularly hosts international events.
 (C) Its crop yields are at an all-time high.
 (D) It receives heavy rainfall.

GO ON TO THE NEXT PAGE

Questions 172-175 refer to the following letter.

October 7

Dear Ms. Santiago,

I am delighted that you have agreed to be our keynote speaker at this year's Genetically Modified Foods & Organisms (GMFO) Conference. —[1]—. Your speech on advances in GM technology and research will take place at approximately 9 A.M. on December 20th, the first day of our three-day event. As I mentioned previously, we moved the event to a more spacious venue this year: the Humberside Convention Center. This is mainly because we anticipate a larger crowd than ever before. In fact, we expect around 20,000 people to be in attendance for your speech. —[2]—.

On the day of your speaking appearance, you will be assisted by Simon Cartwright, one of my most trusted and experienced event coordinators. Mr. Cartwright will meet you at the East Entrance of the convention center and show you to our speakers lounge, where you can relax and refresh yourself. He will also be happy to help you practice your speech, print additional documents, or modify presentation slides, if necessary. —[3]—.

Please find enclosed a VIP parking permit that you should use when you arrive at the convention center. This should be activated immediately to ensure that you are assigned a space as close to the entrance as possible. To do so, visit our event Web site, click on the "Event Speakers" tab, and then the "My Details" tab. Then, type in the unique code printed on your enclosed permit. —[4]—.

Best regards,

Joseph Ellison
Senior Event Coordinator
GMFO Conference

Enclosure

172. What aspect of Ms. Santiago's conference appearance is NOT mentioned?

(A) The topic she will discuss
(B) The duration of her speech
(C) The location of the event
(D) The size of an audience

173. What does the letter indicate about Mr. Cartwright?

(A) He will give a speech at an upcoming conference.
(B) He created Ms. Santiago's presentation slides.
(C) He will distribute handouts at an event.
(D) He is one of Mr. Ellison's employees.

174. What will Ms. Santiago most likely do next?

(A) Respond to Mr. Ellison
(B) Enter an activation code
(C) Set up an online account
(D) Print out a parking permit

175. In which of the positions marked [1], [2], [3], and [4] does the following sentence best belong?

"This doesn't even account for those who choose to livestream the event at home."

(A) [1]
(B) [2]
(C) [3]
(D) [4]

GO ON TO THE NEXT PAGE

Questions 176-180 refer to the following instructions and e-mail.

Millburn Classics Collection

With the steady addition of almost 100 more titles over the past two years, the Millburn Classics Collection now consists of more than 300 classic works of literature, reproduced as beautifully illustrated and annotated paperback and hardback books by Millburn Publishing House. Future additions will include *To Kill a Mockingbird* by Harper Lee and *Anna Karenina* by Leo Tolstoy.

How to care for your books:

There are various ways in which you can preserve the condition and prolong the lifespan of your Millburn Classics. First, make sure you store your books in a moderate, comfortable environment. Too much heat or moisture can accelerate deterioration and encourage mold growth. This is commonly seen in books stored in hot attics or moist basements. Similarly, keep your books away from direct sunlight, which will cause fading and discoloration of the paper and covers.

When shelving your books, make sure that you stand them upright and support them with bookends so that they will not slump or fall down. When removing books from a shelf, do not pull on the top of the book's spine. This can cause the spine of the book to be detached from the pages over time. Instead, grip the middle of the spine on both sides and pull. Lastly, never attempt to repair damaged books yourself, as this can cause more serious long-lasting damage.

We provide a free professional book rebinding service for damaged paperbacks and hardbacks, which is subject to a small fee for return shipping. When sending your books in for repair, package them carefully in a sturdy box and send it to the following address: Millburn Publishing House (Workshop), 461 Stratford Road, Nottingham, UK NG1 1AP. Please include a check or cash. Each book costs £25 to repair, and we charge a flat fee of £10 for shipping. All books will be sent back to the owner within two weeks of receipt.

For any correspondence not related to book repairs, please write to us at Millburn Publishing House (Head Office), 45 Beach Street, Nottingham, UK NG2 1AT.

We hope that you take good care of your Millburn Classics books so that they last for several generations!

To:	Millburn Publishing House <helpdesk@millburnpub.co.uk>
From:	Harry Mapother <hmapother@duomail.co.uk>
Date:	September 29
Re:	Update request

Dear sir/madam,

Almost one month ago, I sent two of my Millburn Classics Collection paperbacks in for rebinding. I honestly expected them to have been returned by now. I'd appreciate it if you could let me know when they will be sent back to me. When I sent the books to your Beach Street address, I included a check for £60 (£50 for the books plus the shipping fee) and my name and home address were clearly marked on the package label.

Best wishes,

Harry Mapother

176. What is suggested about the Millburn Classics Collection?

(A) It is consistently growing in size.
(B) It primarily consists of hardback books.
(C) It includes nearly 100 works of literature.
(D) It was compiled by renowned authors.

177. What is NOT mentioned in the instructions as a potential cause of damage to books?

(A) Mold
(B) Moisture
(C) Sunlight
(D) Dust

178. What recommendation is made in the instructions?

(A) Storing books in a basement
(B) Stacking books in piles
(C) Handling books properly
(D) Repairing books at home

179. Why did Mr. Mapother send the e-mail?

(A) To confirm that a payment has been made
(B) To complain about the condition of books
(C) To inquire about new additions to a book series
(D) To find out how long a delay will be

180. What mistake did Mr. Mapother make?

(A) He included the wrong amount of money.
(B) He sent books to the wrong location.
(C) He forgot to include a return address.
(D) He sent the wrong type of books.

GO ON TO THE NEXT PAGE

Questions 181-185 refer to the following e-mails.

To: customerservices@britannia.com
From: bzelenski@solarmail.net
Date: February 4
Subject: Statement help

Dear Customer Service Team,

I am unable to view my monthly electronic statement, which is supposed to be a feature of my new Britannia Bank account. I clicked on all the tabs and links on my online banking page, including the E-statements and Transaction History tabs, but I could not find an actual statement for January. The bank clerk who served me in the High Street branch was unable to figure out what the problem is, and told me that I should e-mail you with my account details to troubleshoot my online banking problems. My name is Bruno Zelenski and my account number is 34776254. I hope you can solve this issue for me.

Regards,

Bruno Zelenski

To: Bruno Zelenski <bzelenski@solarmail.net>
From: Customer Services <customerservices@britannia.com>
Date: February 5
Subject: Re: Statement help
Attachment: printable_1

Dear Mr. Zelenski,

Thank you for contacting Britannia Bank Customer Services. Based on your e-mail address and the information you have provided, I have confirmed that you have a Premium Saver online account with us. This type of account should indeed include monthly electronic statements. I have taken the necessary steps to activate this feature in your online banking account. After logging in, please click on the E-statements tab in order to view any previous statements.

If you require assistance with any other online banking matters in the future, you might find our Live Chat feature to be even more convenient and efficient than using e-mail. You can find the link to this feature in the top-right corner of our main page at www.britanniabank.com. To use the chat, you will be required to enter your customer name, account number, and online banking password. However, if you are more comfortable corresponding by e-mail, this is also perfectly fine with us.

Please accept our apologies for the inconvenience regarding your E-statement. As a token of apology, please take advantage of the printable coupons that I have attached on behalf of Britannia Bank. These can be redeemed in several local retail outlets in return for some savings.

Regards,

Olivia Allen
Customer Service Representative
Britannia Bank

181. What did Mr. Zelenski do before writing his e-mail on February 4?

(A) He changed his online banking password.
(B) He visited a local bank branch.
(C) He referred to a troubleshooting guide.
(D) He installed some new software.

182. How did Ms. Allen check what type of account Mr. Zelenski has?

(A) By asking him a security question
(B) By contacting the High Street branch
(C) By reading a monthly bank statement
(D) By matching his name and account number

183. According to Ms. Allen, where can Mr. Zelenski find the Live Chat link?

(A) In a Britannia Bank e-mail
(B) On his Online Banking profile page
(C) On his monthly E-statement
(D) On the bank's main Web page

184. In the second e-mail, the word "regarding" in paragraph 3, line 1, is closest in meaning to

(A) watching
(B) considering
(C) concerning
(D) reviewing

185. What did Ms. Allen attach to her e-mail?

(A) A bank statement
(B) A feedback form
(C) Discount vouchers
(D) Information pamphlets

GO ON TO THE NEXT PAGE

Questions 186-190 refer to the following article, e-mail, and online review.

The Ballywick Times

September 20 - A new stone monument is being constructed at a workshop on the outskirts of Ballywick, and once finished, it will be erected in the downtown area, in the middle of Plaza Square. Work on the Sherman Monument began almost one year ago. Benjamin Turner, a senior partner at Pinnacle Architecture, drafted the original design and is leading the construction phase of the project, assisted by members of the Ballywick Heritage Association.

Pinnacle Architecture is no stranger to the design and construction of urban monuments, having previously worked on the Victory Arch and the Beaumont Column, in New Haven and Garretville, respectively. Understanding the sheer scale of the Sherman Monument project, which will take approximately two years in total to complete, Pinnacle founder and chairman Leonard Kratz has promised to make a sizable donation to the Ballywick Heritage Association if the monument is erected in time for the Ballywick 250th Anniversary Founding Celebration next August. Mr. Turner and his team have promised to have the project finished ahead of schedule and under budget.

The monument honors the contribution of Civil War General Tobias Sherman, who is seen as a hero among local residents of Ballywick and the surrounding area, and is expected to boost tourism. Mr. Turner's original design drew inspiration from several portraits of General Sherman that are part of the permanent art exhibit at Ballywick History Museum.

E-Mail Message

To: Benjamin Turner <bturner@pinnacle.com>
From: Terry Carlson <tcarlson@pinnacle.com>
Date: August 11
Subject: You did it!

Hi, Benjamin,

I just wanted to congratulate you on completing the Sherman Monument in time for the city's founding celebration. This achievement has really raised the profile of our company on a nationwide scale, and we are already seeing a rise in the number of new clients we are taking on. Mr. Kratz is over the moon and looks forward to seeing you at the official unveiling ceremony next week. Also, he has stayed true to his word and fulfilled the promise he made last September.

Best wishes,

Terry Carlson
Pinnacle Architecture

http://www.thehartleyhotel.com/reviews

| OUR HOTEL | ROOMS | RATES | REVIEWS |

The Hartley Hotel
September 5, by Maria Lanegan

Some of my college friends in Boston grew up in Ballywick, and they invited me to their hometown for the city's 250th Anniversary Founding Celebration last month. I had a really great time. The Hartley Hotel overlooks Plaza Square in downtown Ballywick, so we had a fantastic view of several local sights and all of the festivities. I stayed at The Hartley Hotel for the entirety of my week-long vacation, and I would highly recommend it. Aside from being close to all of the city's best sightseeing spots, its rooms are very comfortable and I really enjoyed relaxing by the swimming pool. The restaurant didn't meet my expectations, as did the room service I ordered, but there are plenty of good places to eat at nearby.

186. What is the purpose of the article?

(A) To describe a rise in tourism in Ballywick
(B) To discuss an ongoing construction project
(C) To provide details about an upcoming celebration
(D) To profile a successful local architect

187. In the article, the word "drew" in paragraph 3, line 3, is closest in meaning to

(A) gathered
(B) sketched
(C) outlined
(D) prompted

188. What is suggested in the e-mail?

(A) Mr. Kratz helped to design a monument.
(B) Mr. Turner won an award for his architectural design.
(C) Mr. Carlson assisted Mr. Turner with a recent project.
(D) Mr. Kratz has made a donation to an association.

189. What is most likely true about Ms. Lanegan?

(A) She is an employee at Pinnacle Architecture.
(B) She met Mr. Turner during her vacation.
(C) She saw the Sherman Monument.
(D) She attended a college in Ballywick.

190. What aspect of the hotel was Ms. Lanegan disappointed with?

(A) The guest rooms
(B) The location
(C) The food
(D) The swimming pool

GO ON TO THE NEXT PAGE

Questions 191-195 refer to the following e-mails and invitation.

From:	Edwina Merton <emerton@cifa.com>
To:	Lars Elberg <leberg@cifa.com>
Date:	December 2
Subject:	Invitation draft
Attachment:	CIFA invitation

Hello, Lars,

Please find attached the draft for the event invitations we need to have printed. The event venue accommodates 600 guests and we assume that all invitees will attend. I would suggest printing 700 invitations, just so we have some extra ones in case we need them. I'd like you to make the award winners names bold, and please increase the font size of our president's name. Also, I'm afraid I just heard that we will be using a different catering company than originally planned, and I didn't have time to take the chef's name off. I'd appreciate it if you could take care of that for me.

Just to make sure we don't need to make any further changes, you should let Mr. Silver review the draft invitation before you submit it to be printed.

Thanks for your help, Lars.

Edwina Merton
CIFA Events Coordinator

The Canadian Independent Film Association (CIFA)

You are cordially invited to attend
The 6th Annual CIFA Awards Ceremony

@The Ivy Hotel, 346 Seventh Avenue, Toronto
Friday, December 29

6:30 P.M. ~ 7:00 P.M. - Welcome Address (CIFA President, Bob Silver)
7:00 P.M. ~ 8:00 P.M. - 5-Course Banquet (Prepared by Chef Miguel Cortez)
8:00 P.M. ~ 9:30 P.M. - Presentation of Awards (Hosted by Paul Wagner)
9:30 P.M. ~ 11:00 P.M. - Live Performance (Meredith Corr & Band)

Main Award Winners:
Best Picture - Future Imperfect (AFK Motion Pictures)
Best Director - William Oakley (Days of Winter)
Best Acting Performance (Male) - Ian Ritchie (Future Imperfect)
Best Acting Performance (Female) - Amy Costner (Wild Horses)

From:	Bob Silver
To:	Edwina Merton
Date:	December 3
Subject:	CIFA Invitation

Edwina,

Thank you for your work on the invitations for this year's CIFA Awards Ceremony. Lars just sent me the final draft in order to get my feedback. I'm very impressed with the layout and the presentation, and I told Lars to go ahead with the printing.

As this will be the third consecutive year that the Best Director award has gone to the same individual, we plan to honor him by showing a short film clip compilation of his work prior to presenting him with the award. I'd like you to get together with Adrian Belmont to work on that tomorrow afternoon. Also, we plan to have the male and female winners in the Best Acting Performance category present the awards for Best Original Screenplay and Best Cinematography at the start of the awards ceremony. Lastly, I'd like to allocate more time for the acceptance speech of the winners of Best Picture. Please keep this in mind while you are working on the scheduling and general running of the event.

I look forward to seeing you at the rehearsal show on the 22nd. If you have any questions, feel free to contact me at any time.

Regards,

Bob Silver
President, CIFA

191. What is one reason that Ms. Merton sent the e-mail?

(A) To invite Mr. Elberg to an event
(B) To suggest changing an event schedule
(C) To provide some instructions
(D) To inquire about a seating capacity

192. Which name will most likely be removed from the invitation?

(A) Bob Silver
(B) Miguel Cortez
(C) Paul Wagner
(D) Meredith Corr

193. In the first e-mail, the word "assume" in paragraph 1, line 2, is closest in meaning to

(A) adopt
(B) undertake
(C) pretend
(D) believe

194. What is indicated about Mr. Oakley?

(A) He has won several awards during his career.
(B) He will give the longest acceptance speech at the event.
(C) He will present an award during the ceremony.
(D) He will be recognized for his acting performance.

195. What will Ms. Merton probably do on December 4?

(A) Attend a rehearsal show
(B) Work on some film clips
(C) Print event invitations
(D) Meet with Mr. Silver

GO ON TO THE NEXT PAGE

Questions 196-200 refer to the following online feedback form, e-mail, and Web site.

http://www.condimentking.com/feedback

CONDIMENT KING
Your best choice for the widest range of sauces, dressings, and seasonings!

We value your feedback!

If you have any comments or suggestions for how Condiment King can improve its service or products, please let us know by completing the e-form below.

Name: Colin Paxman
Address: 477 Wayside Avenue, Seattle (Pear Tree Diner)
Email: cpaxman@peartree.com

Feedback:

As the head chef at Pear Tree Diner, I have been using numerous Condiment King products for several years now, and I am typically very happy with the way they taste. In particular, I exclusively use Condiment King dressings when preparing salads at the diner. Customers often comment on how delicious they are. However, the last batch of dressings I purchased a month ago seem markedly different. Many customers brought to my attention that the Caesar and Thousand Island dressings were blander than before, and upon trying them myself, I had to agree!

To: cpaxman@peartree.com
From: egainsbourg@condimentking.com
Date: April 18
Subject: Your feedback

Dear Mr. Paxman,

Please accept my apologies for the issue you mentioned in the feedback section of our Web site. We recently made some changes to the ingredients and preparation process for several items, and based on the feedback we have received, it may have been a poor decision. As such, we plan to revert to the traditional, popular formula immediately.

To make amends, we have issued a refund to you for the products you were dissatisfied with. We also would like to send you a complimentary 200ml bottle of one of our new hot sauces. I have selected the least hot among our four signature hot sauces, so I hope you will find it agreeable and delicious! Please consider ordering more bottles for use in your restaurant. For this month only, we are offering a discount of 25 percent on all bulk hot sauce orders consisting of 20 bottles or more.

We always value your loyal patronage.

Kindest regards,

Elizabeth Gainsbourg
Condiment King Inc.
Customer Service Supervisor

http://www.condimentking.com/hotsauces

Condiment King: Hot Sauce Range

Our brand new range of signature hot sauces can help you to spice up a wide variety of dishes, from chicken wings to pizza to burgers! We offer the following range of hot sauces, so you are sure to find one to suit your preferred heat level!

Product Name	Heat Level	Price (200ml)
Heatwave	***	$12.00
Red Sizzle	****	$13.50
Volcano	****	$15.00
Inferno	*****	$16.50

196. What does Mr. Paxman mention in his feedback form?

(A) His latest Condiment King order was late.
(B) A range of dressings should be expanded.
(C) The quality of some products has changed.
(D) Some food items were damaged during shipping.

197. What is the main purpose of the e-mail?

(A) To respond to a complaint
(B) To thank Mr. Paxman for his assistance
(C) To explain a problem with a Web site
(D) To apologize for a price increase

198. What is indicated about Condiment King's Thousand Island dressing?

(A) Its production will be discontinued.
(B) It is being manufactured by a different company.
(C) It is the company's most popular dressing.
(D) It is being made using a new recipe.

199. What does Ms. Gainsbourg encourage Mr. Paxman to do?

(A) Make a change to an existing order
(B) Take advantage of a limited-time offer
(C) Provide a refund to his customers
(D) Remove some items from his menu

200. What type of hot sauce does Ms. Gainsbourg offer Mr. Paxman?

(A) Heatwave
(B) Red Sizzle
(C) Volcano
(D) Inferno

Stop! This is the end of the test. If you finish before time is called, you may go back to Parts 5, 6, and 7 and check your work.

시원스쿨 LAB

"한 권으로 끝내는"
시원스쿨 기본토익 700+
정답 및 해설

시원스쿨 LAB

LISTENING

PART 1

DAY 1 인물, 사물, 풍경 사진

PRACTICE

1. (A) X (B) O (C) X (D) X
2. (A) O (B) O (C) X (D) X
3. (A) X (B) O (C) O (D) X
4. (A) O (B) X (C) O (D) X
5. (A) X (B) O (C) O (D) O
6. (A) X (B) X (C) O (D) X

1.
(A) She is taking off her jacket.
(B) She is typing on a keyboard.
(C) She is drinking from a cup.
(D) She is looking in a drawer.

(A) 여자가 자신의 재킷을 벗는 중이다. [X]
(B) 여자가 키보드로 타자를 치고 있다. [O]
(C) 여자가 컵에 든 것을 마시고 있다. [X]
(D) 여자가 서랍 안을 들여다보고 있다. [X]

어휘 take off ~을 벗다 type on a keyboard 키보드로 타자를 치다 drink from a cup 컵에 든 것을 마시다 look in ~ 안을 들여다 보다 drawer 서랍

2.
(A) The man is wearing a safety vest.
(B) The man is moving some materials.
(C) The man is sweeping the floor.
(D) The man is loading boxes onto a cart.

(A) 남자가 안전 조끼를 착용한 상태이다. [O]
(B) 남자가 일부 자재를 옮기고 있다. [O]
(C) 남자가 바닥을 빗자루로 쓸고 있다. [X]
(D) 남자가 상자들을 카트에 싣고 있다. [X]

어휘 vest 조끼 material 물품, 재료, 자재 sweep ~을 빗자루로 쓸다 load A onto B: A를 B 위에 싣다

3.
(A) One of the men is entering a building.
(B) They are walking down some stairs.
(C) One of the men is holding a cup.
(D) They are crossing a street.

(A) 남자들 중 한 명이 건물에 들어가고 있다. [X]
(B) 사람들이 계단을 걸어 내려가고 있다. [O]
(C) 남자들 중 한 명이 컵을 들고 있다. [O]
(D) 사람들이 거리를 건너고 있다. [X]

어휘 enter ~에 들어가다 walk down ~을 걸어 내려가다 hold ~을 들다, 붙잡다, 쥐다 cross ~을 건너다, 가로지르다

4.
(A) A light fixture is hanging from the ceiling.
(B) The chairs have been placed in the corner.
(C) A table has been set for a meal.
(D) The curtains have been closed.

(A) 조명 기구가 천장에 매달려 있다. [O]
(B) 의자들이 구석에 놓여 있다. [X]
(C) 테이블이 식사를 위해 차려져 있다. [O]
(D) 커튼이 닫혀 있다. [X]

어휘 light fixture 조명 기구 hang 걸려 있다, 매달리다 ceiling 천장 place v. ~을 놓다, 두다 in the corner 구석에 meal 식사

5.
(A) A door has been left open.
(B) A staircase leads to a building.
(C) A light fixture has been mounted on the wall.
(D) There are benches in front of a building.

(A) 문 하나가 열린 채로 있다. [X]
(B) 계단이 건물로 이어져 있다. [O]
(C) 조명 기구가 벽에 설치되어 있다. [O]
(D) 건물 앞에 벤치들이 있다. [O]

어휘 be left + 형용사: ~한 채로 있다 staircase 계단 lead to ~로 이어지다, 연결되다 light fixture 조명 기구 mount ~을 설치하다, 고정시키다 in front of ~ 앞에

6.
(A) The shelves have been filled with items.
(B) Boxes have been stacked on top of each other.
(C) Some fruit is displayed for sale.
(D) Some groceries have been put in a shopping cart.

(A) 선반이 물품으로 가득 차 있다. [X]
(B) 상자들이 차곡차곡 쌓여 있다. [X]
(C) 일부 과일이 판매용으로 진열되어 있다. [O]
(D) 일부 식료품들이 쇼핑 카트에 놓여 있다. [X]

어휘 shelf 선반 be filled with ~로 가득 차 있다 item 물품, 제품 stack ~을 쌓다 on top of each other 차곡차곡 display ~을 진열하다, 전시하다 for sale 판매용의, 판매 중인 grocery 식료품 put ~을 놓다, 두다

실전 TEST

1. (A)	2. (C)	3. (D)	4. (B)	5. (B)
6. (B)	7. (C)	8. (A)	9. (B)	10. (A)
11. (C)	12. (C)			

1.
(A) A man is wearing a pair of gloves.
(B) A man is watering a bush.
(C) A man is leaning over a fence.
(D) A man is cutting some wooden panels.

(A) 남자는 장갑을 착용하고 있다.
(B) 남자는 관목에 물을 주고 있다.
(C) 남자는 울타리에 기대고 있다.
(D) 남자는 나무판을 자르고 있다.

정답 (A)
해설 인물 사진이므로 인물의 행동, 자세, 복장 등에 초점을 맞춰 들어야 합니다.
(A) 남자는 장갑을 착용하고 있으므로 정답.
(B) 남자가 들고 있는 것이 전정가위이므로 오답.
(C) 사진에 울타리가 없으므로 오답.
(D) 사진에 나무판이 없으므로 오답.

어휘 a pair of 한 쌍의 water 물을 주다 bush 관목, 덤불 lean over ~에 기대다 fence 울타리 panel 판

2.
(A) She's organizing some pens and paper.
(B) She's dusting off a counter.
(C) She's facing a monitor on a table.
(D) She's taking notes in a library.

(A) 그녀는 펜과 종이를 정리하고 있다.
(B) 그녀는 조리대를 털고 있다.
(C) 그녀는 탁자 위의 모니터를 바라보고 있다.
(D) 그녀는 도서관에서 필기를 하고 있다.

정답 (C)
해설 인물 및 사물 사진이므로 인물의 자세와 행동, 사물의 명칭과 위치 관계에 초점을 맞춰 들어야 합니다.
(A) 여자의 손에 펜과 종이가 없으므로 오답.
(B) 여자는 책상에 앉아 있으므로 오답.
(C) 여자가 모니터를 보고 있으므로 정답.
(D) 여자는 필기를 하고 있지 않으므로 오답.

어휘 organize 정리하다 dust off 먼지를 털다 counter 조리대 face 마주보다 take notes 필기하다

3.
(A) She is strolling along a beach.
(B) She is swimming in the ocean.
(C) She is fishing from a pier.
(D) She is resting outdoors.

(A) 여자가 해변을 따라 거닐고 있다.
(B) 여자가 바다에서 수영하고 있다.
(C) 여자가 부두에서 낚시하고 있다.
(D) 여자가 야외에서 휴식하고 있다.

정답 (D)
해설 1인 사진이므로 등장 인물의 동작이나 자세, 관련 사물에 초점을 맞춰 들어야 합니다.
(A) 여자가 해변에서 걷는 동작을 하는 것이 아니므로 오답.
(B) 여자가 수영하는 동작을 하고 있지 않으므로 오답.
(C) 여자가 낚시하는 동작을 하고 있지 않으므로 오답.
(D) 여자가 야외에서 휴식을 취하는 상황이므로 정답.

어휘 stroll 거닐다, 산책하다 along (길 등) ~을 따라 pier 부두 rest 휴식하다, 쉬다 outdoors 야외에서, 옥외에서

4.
(A) A woman is pushing a shopping cart.
(B) A woman is paying for her purchase.
(C) A man is opening a cash register.
(D) A man is wrapping some merchandise.

(A) 한 여자가 쇼핑 카트를 밀고 있다.
(B) 한 여자가 구입품 비용을 지불하고 있다.
(C) 한 남자가 금전 등록기를 열고 있다.
(D) 한 남자가 몇몇 상품을 포장하고 있다.

정답 (B)
해설 2인 사진이므로 사람들의 공통된 동작이나 자세, 주변 사물에 함께 초점을 맞춰 들어야 합니다.
(A) 여자가 쇼핑 카트를 미는 동작을 하고 있지 않으므로 오답.
(B) 여자가 카운터 앞에 서서 비용을 지불하는 동작을 하고 있으므로 정답.
(C) 남자가 금전 등록기를 여는 동작을 하고 있지 않으므로 오답.

(D) 남자가 상품을 포장하는 동작을 하고 있지 않으므로 오답.

어휘 push a cart 카트를 밀다 pay for ~에 대한 비용을 지불하다 purchase 구입(품) cash register (상점의) 금전 등록기 wrap ~을 포장하다 merchandise 상품, 제품

5.

(A) They're shaking hands.
(B) They're seated next to each other.
(C) They're setting the table.
(D) They're facing each other.

(A) 사람들이 악수를 하고 있다.
(B) 사람들이 서로 나란히 앉아 있다.
(C) 사람들이 상을 차리고 있다.
(D) 사람들이 서로 마주 보고 있다.

정답 (B)

해설 2인 사진이므로 사람들의 공통된 동작이나 자세, 주변 사물에 함께 초점을 맞춰 들어야 합니다.
(A) 악수하고 있는 모습이 아니므로 오답.
(B) 두 사람이 나란히 앉아 있는 상태이므로 정답.
(C) 상을 차리고 있는 사람들을 찾아볼 수 없으므로 오답.
(D) 두 사람이 서로 마주 보는 자세를 취하고 있지 않으므로 오답.

어휘 shake hands 악수를 하다 be seated 앉아 있다, 착석하다 next to ~ 옆에 each other 서로 set the table 상을 차리다 face each other 서로 마주 보다

6.

(A) A man is trimming some bushes.
(B) One of the women is watering a plant.
(C) The women are bending over the flowers.
(D) They are kneeling under a tree.

(A) 한 남자가 일부 덤불을 다듬고 있다.
(B) 여자들 중 한 명이 식물에 물을 주고 있다.
(C) 여자들이 꽃 위로 몸을 숙이고 있다.
(D) 사람들이 나무 밑에서 무릎을 꿇고 있다.

정답 (B)

해설 다인 사진이므로 등장 인물들의 공통된 동작이나 개별 자세, 주변 사물에 함께 초점을 맞춰 들어야 합니다.
(A) 남자가 덤불을 다듬는 동작을 하고 있지 않으므로 오답.
(B) 두 여자 중 한 명이 물을 주는 동작을 하고 있으므로 정답.
(C) 두 여자가 서로 마주 보는 자세를 하고 있지 않으므로 오답.
(D) 나무 밑에서 무릎 꿇고 있는 사람들이 없으므로 오답.

어휘 trim ~을 다듬다 bush 덤불, 관목 water v. ~에 물을 주다 plant 식물 bend over ~위로 몸을 숙이다 kneel 무릎을 꿇다

7.

(A) A yard is surrounded by trees.
(B) A wooden fence has been built outside.
(C) The walls of a house are made of bricks.
(D) Some tools have been left on the ground.

(A) 마당이 나무로 둘러싸여 있다.
(B) 바깥쪽에 나무 울타리가 설치되어 있다.
(C) 집의 벽은 벽돌로 지어져 있다.
(D) 몇몇 도구들이 땅에 놓여 있다.

정답 (B)

해설 풍경 사진이므로 풍경 속 사물의 명칭과 위치 관계에 초점을 맞춰 들어야 합니다.
(A) 마당이 보이지 않으므로 오답.
(B) 야외로 보이는 곳에 나무 울타리가 보이므로 정답.
(C) 울타리는 나무로 만들어져 있으므로 오답.
(D) 도구가 보이지 않으므로 오답.

어휘 be surrounded by ~로 둘러싸여 있다 wooden 나무의 fence 울타리 be made of ~로 만들어 지다 brick 벽돌 tool 도구 ground 땅, 바닥

8.

(A) A potted plant is positioned next to a desk.
(B) Some boxes have been placed on a shelf.
(C) There are some pillows on a bed.
(D) A light fixture is mounted on the wall.

(A) 화분 하나가 책상 옆에 놓여 있다.
(B) 몇몇 상자가 선반 위에 놓여 있다.
(C) 침대 위에 베개가 몇 개 있다.
(D) 벽에 조명 기구가 설치되어 있다.

정답 (A)

해설 사물 사진이므로 각 사물의 명칭과 위치 관계에 초점을 맞춰 들어야 합니다.
(A) 책상 옆에 화분이 놓여져 있으므로 정답.
(B) 선반에는 박스가 없으므로 오답.
(C) 침대와 베개가 보이지 않으므로 오답.
(D) 벽에는 시계와 선반이 있으므로 오답.

어휘 potted plant 화분 be positioned 위치해 있다 next to ~옆에 be placed 놓여 있다 shelf 선반 pillow 베개 light fixture 조명 기구, 조명 장치 be mounted 걸려 있다, 설치되어 있다

9.

(A) A swimming pool has been filled.
(B) A boat is tied to a dock.
(C) A bridge crosses over a waterway.
(D) A ship is approaching a pier.

(A) 수영장이 꽉 차 있다.
(B) 보트 한 대가 부두에 정박되어 있다.
(C) 다리가 수로 위를 가로지르고 있다.
(D) 배 한 척이 부두에 다가가고 있다.

정답 (B)

해설 풍경 사진이므로 풍경 속 사물의 명칭과 위치 관계에 초점을 맞춰 들어야 합니다.
(A) 수영장을 찾아볼 수 없으므로 오답.
(B) 보트 한 대가 부두에 정박된 상태이므로 정답.
(C) 다리는 보이지 않으므로 오답.
(D) 배 한 척이 어딘가로 이동하는 것이 아니라 정박된 상태이므로 오답.

어휘 filled 꽉 찬, 가득 찬 be tied to ~에 정박되다, 묶여 있다 dock 부두 bridge 다리 cross ~을 가로지르다 over ~위로 waterway (강, 운하 등의) 수로 approach ~에 다가가다, 다가오다 pier 부두

10.
(A) A fence is surrounding the house.
(B) A building is under construction.
(C) A field of grass is being mowed.
(D) Potted plants have been placed outside.

(A) 담장이 집을 둘러싸고 있다.
(B) 건물이 공사 중이다.
(C) 잔디밭이 깎이는 중이다.
(D) 화분에 담긴 식물이 밖에 놓여 있다.

정답 (A)

해설 풍경 사진이므로 풍경 속 사물의 명칭과 위치 관계에 초점을 맞춰 들어야 합니다.
(A) 담장이 지어져 집 외부를 둘러싼 상태이므로 정답.
(B) 건물에 공사가 진행되는 상황이 아니므로 오답.
(C) 잔디밭을 깎는 동작을 하는 사람을 찾아볼 수 없으므로 오답.
(D) 화분에 담긴 식물을 찾아볼 수 없으므로 오답.

어휘 fence 담장 outside prep. ~ 외부에, ~ 바깥에 ad. 외부에, 밖에 under construction 공사 중인 field of grass 잔디밭, 풀밭 mow (잔디, 풀 등) ~을 깎다, 베다 potted plant 화분에 담긴 식물 place v. ~을 놓다, 두다

11.
(A) A library is being cleaned.
(B) A librarian is putting materials on a cart.
(C) Shelves are stocked with books.
(D) Some books are spread out on a counter.

(A) 도서관이 청소되고 있다.
(B) 사서가 카트에 자료를 담고 있다.
(C) 선반에 책들이 채워져 있다.
(D) 몇몇 책들이 카운터에 흩어져 있다.

정답 (C)

해설 사물 사진이므로 각 사물의 명칭과 위치 관계에 초점을 맞춰 들어야 합니다.
(A) 도서관을 청소하는 동작을 하는 사람을 찾아볼 수 없으므로 오답.
(B) 사람(사서)을 찾아볼 수 없으므로 오답.
(C) 선반이 책으로 가득 차 있는 상태이므로 정답.
(D) 카운터 뿐만 아니라 흩어져 있는 책들을 찾아볼 수 없으므로 오답.

어휘 librarian 사서 put A on B: A를 B에 놓다, 두다 material 물품, 재료, 자료 shelf 선반 be stocked with ~가 갖춰져 있다 spread out ~을 펼쳐 놓다, 늘어 놓다

12.
(A) A sidewalk is being repaired.
(B) Some people are walking through an archway.
(C) There are lampposts along the walkway.
(D) Some trees have been cut down.

(A) 보도가 수리되고 있다.
(B) 몇몇 사람들이 아치형 길을 통과해 걷고 있다.
(C) 보도를 따라 가로등이 서 있다.
(D) 몇몇 나무들이 잘려 넘어져 있다.

정답 (C)

해설 풍경 사진이므로 풍경 속 사물의 명칭과 위치 관계에 초점을 맞춰 들어야 합니다.
(A) 보도에 수리 작업을 하고 있는 사람이 없으므로 오답.
(B) 길을 걷는 사람들을 찾아볼 수 없으므로 오답.
(C) 보도를 따라 가로등들이 서 있는 상태이므로 정답.
(D) 잘려 넘어진 나무들을 찾아볼 수 없으므로 오답.

어휘 sidewalk 보도 repair ~을 수리하다 archway 아치형 길, 아치형 입구 lamppost 가로등 along (길 등) ~을 따라 walkway 보도, 통행로 cut down (나무 등) ~을 잘라 넘어뜨리다

DAY 2 고난도 사진

PRACTICE

1. (A) O (B) X (C) X (D) O
2. (A) X (B) X (C) O (D) X
3. (A) X (B) X (C) O (D) X

1.
(A) Some people are walking under an archway.
(B) A road is being paved with bricks.
(C) A sign is being posted on a wall.
(D) There are lampposts along the walkway.

(A) 몇몇 사람들이 아치형 길 밑으로 걸어가고 있다. [O]
(B) 길이 벽돌로 포장되고 있다. [X]
(C) 표지판이 벽에 게시되고 있다. [X]
(D) 보도를 따라 가로등이 서 있다. [O]

어휘 archway 아치형 길, 아치형 입구 road 도로, 길 pave (도로 등) ~을 포장하다 brick 벽돌 sign 간판, 표지판 post ~을 게시하다 lamppost 가로등 along (길 등) ~을 따라 walkway 보도

2.
(A) Some plants are being planted along a walkway.
(B) Some windows are covered by curtains.
(C) A bike is propped up against the building.
(D) There are potted plants in a garden.

(A) 몇몇 식물들이 통로를 따라 심어지고 있다. [X]
(B) 몇몇 창문이 커튼으로 가려져 있다. [X]
(C) 자전거 한 대가 건물에 받쳐져 있다. [O]
(D) 화분에 담긴 식물들이 정원에 있다. [X]

어휘 be lined up 줄지어져 있다 walkway 통로, 보도 be covered 덮여져 있다, 가려져 있다 be propped up 받쳐져 있다, 기대어져 있다 potted plant 화분에 담긴 식물

3.
(A) A stage is being set up indoors.
(B) People are waiting in line at an entrance.
(C) People have gathered for a concert.
(D) A concert hall is unoccupied.

(A) 무대가 실내에 설치되고 있다. [X]
(B) 사람들이 입구에 줄 서서 대기하고 있다. [X]
(C) 사람들이 콘서트를 보기 위해 모여 있다. [O]
(D) 콘서트 홀이 비어 있다. [X]

어휘 stage 무대 set up ~을 설치하다 indoors 실내에 wait in line 줄 서서 기다리다 entrance 입구 gather 모이다 unoccupied (자리 등이) 비어 있는, 사람이 없는

실전 TEST

1. (A) 2. (D) 3. (C) 4. (C) 5. (D)
6. (A) 7. (C) 8. (A) 9. (D) 10. (A)
11. (D) 12. (B)

1.
(A) A pedestrian is crossing the street.
(B) There are cars parked along the street.
(C) Some trees are growing alongside a building.
(D) Columns line a walkway.

(A) 보행자 한 명이 길을 건너고 있다.
(B) 길을 따라 주차된 자동차들이 있다.
(C) 몇몇 나무들이 건물 옆에 나란히 자라고 있다.
(D) 기둥들이 보도를 따라 늘어서 있다.

정답 (A)

해설 1인 사진이므로 등장 인물의 동작이나 자세, 관련 사물에 초점을 맞춰 들어야 합니다.
(A) 보행자 한 명이 길을 건너는 동작을 하고 있으므로 정답.
(B) 차량들이 주차된 것이 아니라 횡단보도 앞에 잠시 정차한 상황이므로 오답.
(C) 건물 옆에 나란히 자라는 나무를 찾아볼 수 없으므로 오답.
(D) 보도를 따라 늘어선 기둥들을 찾아볼 수 없으므로 오답.

어휘 pedestrian 보행자 cross the street 길을 건너다 There is A p.p.: ~된 A가 있다 park v. ~을 주차하다 along (길 등) ~을 따라 grow 자라다 alongside ~ 옆에 나란히 column 기둥 line v. ~을 따라 늘어서다 walkway 보도, 통로

2.
(A) Some people are unloading luggage.
(B) Airplanes are parked side by side.
(C) Some people are opening suitcases.
(D) Steps are positioned next to an aircraft.

(A) 몇몇 사람들이 수하물을 내리고 있다.
(B) 비행기들이 나란히 세워져 있다.
(C) 몇몇 사람들이 여행 가방을 열고 있다.
(D) 계단이 비행기 옆에 위치해 있다.

정답 (D)

해설 다인 사진이므로 등장 인물들의 공통된 동작이나 개별 자세, 주변 사물에 함께 초점을 맞춰 들어야 합니다.
(A) 수하물을 내리는 동작을 하는 사람을 찾아볼 수 없으므로 오답.

(B) 옆에 나란히 서 있는 다른 비행기를 찾아볼 수 없으므로 오답.
(C) 여행 가방을 여는 동작을 하는 사람을 찾아볼 수 없으므로 오답.
(D) 비행기 옆에 비행기로 오르는 계단이 위치해 있으므로 정답.

어휘 unload (짐 등) ~을 내리다 luggage 수하물, 짐 park v. ~을 세워 놓다, 주차하다 side by side 나란히 suitcase 여행 가방 steps 계단 be positioned 위치해 있다 next to ~의 옆에 aircraft 비행기

3.

(A) A man is carrying a bucket.
(B) A man is planting some flowers.
(C) Water is being sprayed from a hose.
(D) A fence is being built around a yard.

(A) 한 남자가 양동이를 옮기고 있다.
(B) 한 남자가 꽃을 심고 있다.
(C) 물이 호스에서 뿌려지고 있다.
(D) 담장이 마당 주변에 지어지고 있다.

정답 (C)
해설 1인 사진이므로 등장 인물의 동작이나 자세, 관련 사물에 초점을 맞춰 들어야 합니다.
　　(A) 남자가 양동이를 옮기는 동작을 하는 것이 아니므로 오답.
　　(B) 남자가 꽃을 심는 동작을 하는 것이 아니므로 오답.
　　(C) 물이 호스를 통해 뿌려지고 있으므로 정답.
　　(D) 담장을 짓는 동작을 하는 사람을 찾아볼 수 없으므로 오답.

어휘 carry ~을 옮기다, 나르다 bucket 양동이 plant ~을 심다 spray ~을 뿌리다 around ~ 주변에, ~을 둘러 yard 마당

4.

(A) Some fruit has been put in a shopping cart.
(B) Food is on display in a cafeteria.
(C) An outdoor area is crowded with people.
(D) Picnic tables are being cleaned.

(A) 몇몇 과일이 쇼핑 카트에 놓여 있다.
(B) 음식이 구내 식당에 진열되어 있다.
(C) 한 야외 장소가 사람들로 붐비고 있다.
(D) 피크닉용 탁자들이 말끔히 치워지고 있다.

정답 (C)
해설 다인 사진이므로 등장 인물들의 공통된 동작이나 개별 자세, 주변 사물에 함께 초점을 맞춰 들어야 합니다.
　　(A) 쇼핑 카트를 찾아볼 수 없으므로 오답.
　　(B) 사진 속 장소가 구내 식당이 아니므로 오답.
　　(C) 야외에 마련된 장소가 사람들로 가득하므로 정답.
　　(D) 피크닉 테이블을 치우고 있는 모습은 보이지 않으므로 오답.

어휘 put A in B: A를 B에 놓다, 두다 on display 진열된, 전시된 cafeteria 구내 식당 be crowded with ~로 붐비다 clean ~을 말끔히 치우다

5.

(A) Carts are being loaded with bricks.
(B) A sign is being posted.
(C) Some wheels are being replaced.
(D) Wheelbarrows are propped against a wall.

(A) 카트들에 벽돌이 실리고 있다.
(B) 표지판이 게시되고 있다.
(C) 몇몇 바퀴가 교체되고 있다.
(D) 외바퀴 손수레들이 벽에 기대어져 있다.

정답 (D)
해설 사물 사진이므로 각 사물의 명칭 및 위치 관계를 함께 파악하며 들어야 합니다.
　　(A) 카트에 벽돌을 싣는 동작은 보이지 않으므로 오답.
　　(B) 표지판은 이미 게시되어 있으며, 게시되는 중이 아니므로 오답.
　　(C) 바퀴를 교체하는 동작은 보이지 않으므로 오답.
　　(D) 외바퀴 손수레들이 벽에 기대어져 있는 모습을 묘사한 정답.

어휘 load ~을 싣다 brick 벽돌 sign 표지판 post ~을 게시하다 wheel 바퀴 replace ~을 교체하다 wheelbarrow 외바퀴 손수레 be propped against ~에 기대어져 있다

6.

(A) Some plants are hanging from the ceiling.
(B) Some artwork is being framed.
(C) Some chairs have been stacked in the corner.
(D) A seating area has been set up outside.

(A) 몇몇 식물들이 천장에 매달려 있다.
(B) 일부 예술품이 액자에 넣어지고 있다.
(C) 몇몇 의자들이 구석에 쌓여 있다.
(D) 좌석 공간이 외부에 설치되어 있다.

정답 (A)
해설 사물 사진이므로 각 사물의 명칭 및 위치 관계를 함께 파악하며 들어야 합니다.
　　(A) 천장에 식물들이 매달려 있는 상태이므로 정답.
　　(B) 예술품을 액자에 넣는 동작을 하는 사람이 없으므로 오답.
　　(C) 쌓여 있는 의자를 찾아볼 수 없으므로 오답.
　　(D) 사진 속 공간은 실내이므로 오답.

어휘 hang 매달리다, 걸려 있다 ceiling 천장 artwork 예술품 frame v. ~을 액자에 넣다 in the corner 구석에 seating area 좌석 공간 set up ~을 설치하다 outside 외부에, 바깥에

7.

(A) Some bushes are being trimmed.
(B) Some people are hiking through a forest.
(C) There are some people cycling outdoors.
(D) Some bicycles have been parked along a railing.

(A) 몇몇 덤불이 다듬어지고 있다.
(B) 몇몇 사람들이 숲 속을 지나 하이킹을 하고 있다.
(C) 야외에서 자전거를 타는 몇몇 사람들이 있다.
(D) 몇몇 자전거들이 난간을 따라 세워져 있다.

정답 (C)
해설 풍경 사진이므로 풍경 속 사물의 명칭과 위치 관계에 초점을 맞춰 들어야 합니다.
　　(A) 덤불을 다듬는 동작을 하는 사람이 없으므로 오답.
　　(B) 하이킹하는 사람들을 찾아볼 수 없으므로 오답.
　　(C) 몇몇 사람들이 자전거를 타고 있는 상황이므로 정답.
　　(D) 난간을 따라 세워진 자전거를 찾아볼 수 없으므로 오답.
어휘 bush 덤불, 관목 trim ~을 다듬다 hike 하이킹하다, 도보 여행하다 through ~을 지나, 통과해 There is A -ing: ~하는 A가 있다 cycle 자전거를 타다 outdoors 야외에서, 옥외에서 park v. ~을 세워 놓다, 주차하다 along (길 등) ~을 따라 railing 난간

8.

(A) Boxes are stacked on a warehouse floor.
(B) A ladder is leaning against a shelving unit.
(C) Some packages are being inspected.
(D) Items are being placed into boxes.

(A) 창고 바닥에 상자들이 쌓여 있다.
(B) 사다리가 선반에 기대어져 있다.
(C) 몇몇 포장 상자들이 검사되고 있다.
(D) 물건들이 박스에 넣어지고 있다.

정답 (A)
해설 사물 사진이므로 각 사물의 명칭 및 위치 관계를 함께 파악하며 들어야 합니다.
　　(A) 창고로 보이는 곳 바닥에 상자들이 쌓여 있으므로 정답.
　　(B) 사다리는 보이지 않으므로 오답.
　　(C) 포장 상자를 검사하는 모습이 보이지 않으므로 오답.
　　(D) 상자에 물건을 담는 모습이 보이지 않으므로 오답.
어휘 stack ~을 쌓다 warehouse 창고 floor 바닥 ladder 사다리 lean against ~에 기대다 shelving unit 선반 package 포장 상자, 소포 inspect ~을 검사하다 place A into B: A를 B에 넣다

9.

(A) Some curtains are being installed.
(B) Vegetables are being washed in a sink.
(C) Potted plants have been placed in front of the window.
(D) The containers have been filled with food.

(A) 커튼이 설치되고 있다.
(B) 야채가 싱크대에서 씻겨지고 있다.
(C) 화분에 담긴 식물이 창문 앞에 놓여져 있다.
(D) 용기들에 음식이 가득 차 있다.

정답 (D)
해설 사물 사진이므로 각 사물의 명칭 및 위치 관계를 함께 파악하며 들어야 합니다.
　　(A) 커튼은 이미 설치되어 있고, 설치되는 모습이 아니므로 오답.
　　(B) 야채를 씻는 모습이 보이지 않으므로 오답.
　　(C) 창문 앞에 화분이 놓여있지 않으므로 오답.
　　(D) 많은 용기들에 음식이 가득 차 있는 모습이므로 정답.
어휘 install ~을 설치하다 vegetable 야채, 채소 wash ~을 씻다 sink 싱크대 potted plant 화분에 담긴 식물 place ~을 놓다, 두다 in front of ~의 앞에 container 그릇, 용기 be filled with ~로 가득 차다

10.

(A) Some cars are parked along a street.
(B) Some branches are piled beside a truck.
(C) Some vehicles have stopped at an intersection.
(D) A pathway leads to a parking area.

(A) 몇몇 자동차들이 길을 따라 주차되어 있다.
(B) 몇몇 나뭇가지들이 트럭 옆에 쌓여 있다.
(C) 몇몇 차량들이 교차로에서 멈췄다.
(D) 길이 주차장으로 이어진다.

정답 (A)
해설 풍경 사진이므로 풍경 속 사물의 명칭과 위치 관계에 초점을 맞춰 들어야 합니다.
　　(A) 사진 속 보이는 여러 대의 자동차가 모두 길가에 주차되어 있으므로 정답.
　　(B) 나뭇가지 더미와 트럭을 찾아볼 수 없으므로 오답.
　　(C) 사진 속 장소는 교차로가 아니므로 오답.
　　(D) 주차장을 찾아볼 수 없으므로 오답.
어휘 park 주차하다 along ~을 따라서 branch 나뭇가지 pile 쌓다 beside ~ 옆에 vehicle 차량 intersection 교차로 pathway 길 lead to ~로 이어지다 parking area 주차장

11.

(A) Some shelves are being restocked.
(B) Some bins have been stacked in rows.
(C) A sign has been set up next to a door.
(D) Some items are displayed in refrigerators.

(A) 몇몇 선반들에 상품들이 다시 채워지고 있다.
(B) 몇몇 쓰레기통이 줄지어 쌓여 있다.
(C) 표지판이 문 옆에 설치되어 있다.
(D) 몇몇 물건들이 냉장고 안에 진열되어 있다.

정답 (D)

해설 사물 사진이므로 각 사물의 명칭 및 위치 관계를 함께 파악하며 들어야 합니다.
  (A) 냉장고 안의 선반 위에는 이미 상품들이 채워져 있는 상태이므로 오답.
  (B) 쓰레기통이 보이지 않으므로 오답.
  (C) 표지판은 보이지 않으므로 오답.
  (D) 냉장고 안에 상품들이 진열되어 있으므로 정답.

어휘 shelf 선반 restock 다시 채우다 bin 쓰레기통 stack 쌓다 in rows 줄지어 sign 표지판 set up 설치하다 next to ~옆에 display 진열하다, 전시하다 refrigerator 냉장고

12.

(A) The man is holding onto a railing.
(B) The man is descending some stairs.
(C) There's a door beneath the staircase.
(D) A stone structure is being constructed.

(A) 남자가 난간을 붙잡고 있다.
(B) 남자가 계단을 내려가고 있다.
(C) 계단 밑에 문이 하나 있다.
(D) 석조 구조물이 지어지고 있다.

정답 (B)

해설 1인 사진이므로 등장 인물의 동작이나 자세, 관련 사물에 초점을 맞춰 들어야 합니다.
  (A) 남자가 난간을 붙잡은 자세를 취하고 있지 않으므로 오답.
  (B) 남자가 계단을 내려가는 동작을 하고 있으므로 정답.
  (C) 계단 밑에 문이 위치해 있지 않으므로 오답.
  (D) 석조 구조물이 지어지는 것이 아니라 이미 지어진 상태이므로 오답.

어휘 hold onto ~을 붙잡다 railing 난간 descend ~을 내려가다, 내려오다 beneath ~ 밑에, 아래에 staircase 계단 structure 구조물 construct ~을 짓다, 건설하다

PART 2

DAY 3 의문사 의문문

PRACTICE

1. (A) X   (B) O   (C) O
2. (A) X   (B) X   (C) O
3. (A) X   (B) O   (C) O
4. (A) O   (B) X   (C) O
5. (A) X   (B) O   (C) X
6. (A) X   (B) O   (C) X
7. (A) X   (B) O   (C) O
8. (A) O   (B) O   (C) X
9. (A) X   (B) O   (C) O
10. (A) O   (B) O   (C) X

1. When will the new software be installed?
   (A) On the third floor.
   (B) Sometime next week.
   (C) Not until this Friday.

   언제 새 소프트웨어가 설치될 건가요?
   (A) 3층에서요. [X]
   (B) 다음 주 중으로요. [O]
   (C) 이번 주 금요일이나 되어야 합니다. [O]

해설 새 소프트웨어가 언제 설치되는지 묻는 When 의문문입니다.
  (A) 위치 표현으로서 Where 의문문에 어울리는 답변이므로 오답.
  (B) When에 어울리는 대략적인 미래 시점으로 답변하고 있으므로 정답.
  (C) When에 어울리는 특정 미래 시점으로 답변하고 있으므로 정답.

어휘 install ~을 설치하다 Not until + 시점: ~나 되어야 한다

2. When do you finish work today?
   (A) It was due yesterday.
   (B) He works in the sales team.
   (C) I still have a lot to do.

   오늘 언제 일을 끝마치시나요?
   (A) 그건 어제가 기한이었어요. [X]
   (B) 그는 영업팀에서 근무합니다. [X]
   (C) 아직 할 게 많아요. [O]

해설 오늘 언제 일을 끝마치는지 묻는 When 의문문입니다.

(A) 답변자 자신의 업무 종료 시점이 아닌 과거 시점의 마감 기한을 말하고 있으므로 오답.
(B) 대상을 알 수 없는 He에 관해 말하는 답변이므로 오답.
(C) 할 일이 많다는 말로 언제 업무를 종료할지 알 수 없음을 나타내는 정답.

어휘 due ~가 기한인 still 아직

3. Who is responsible for organizing the company picnic?
   (A) To the Central City Park.
   (B) Terry would know.
   (C) Mr. Ramirez handles that.
   누가 회사 야유회 준비를 책임지고 있나요?
   (A) 센트럴 시티 공원으로요. [X]
   (B) 테리 씨가 알 거예요. [O]
   (C) 라미레즈 씨가 그 일을 처리합니다. [O]

해설 회사 야유회 준비를 누가 책임지고 있는지 묻는 Who 의문문입니다.
   (A) Where에 어울리는 장소 전치사구로 답변하고 있으므로 오답.
   (B) Who에 해당되는 답변 대신 그 정보를 알 수 있는 사람을 언급하는 정답.
   (C) Who에 어울리는 사람 이름과 함께 야유회를 준비하는 일을 that으로 지칭해 담당자를 알려주는 정답.

어휘 be responsible for ~을 책임지고 있다 organize ~을 준비하다, 마련하다 handle ~을 처리하다, 다루다

4. What do you think about the new manager?
   (A) She's highly qualified.
   (B) I knew about it.
   (C) I haven't talked to her yet.
   신임 부장님에 대해서 어떻게 생각하세요?
   (A) 매우 뛰어난 자격을 갖추신 분이에요. [O]
   (B) 그것에 대해 알고 있었어요. [X]
   (C) 아직 그분과 얘기해 보지 못했어요. [O]

해설 신임 부서장에 대해 어떻게 생각하는지 의견을 묻는 What 의문문입니다.
   (A) 신임 부서장의 자격과 관련된 답변자 자신의 의견을 밝히는 답변이므로 정답.
   (B) 사람이 아닌 특정 대상(it)에 대해 알고 있었다는 사실을 말하는 답변이므로 오답.
   (C) 아직 얘기해 보지 않아 어떻게 생각하는지 의견을 말할 수 없다는 뜻을 밝히는 답변이므로 정답.

어휘 What do you think about ~? ~에 대해 어떻게 생각하세요? highly 매우, 대단히 qualified 자격을 갖춘, 적격인

5. What time does the next train to Albany leave?
   (A) The schedule is over there.
   (B) It leaves in half an hour.
   (C) At Grand Central Station.
   알바니로 가는 다음 기차가 몇 시에 출발하나요?
   (A) 일정표가 저기 저쪽에 있어요. [O]
   (B) 그건 30분 후에 떠나요. [O]
   (C) 그랜드 센트럴 역에서요. [X]

해설 알바니로 가는 다음 기차가 몇 시에 출발하는지 묻는 What 의 문문입니다.
   (A) 특정 시간을 직접 말하는 대신 그 정보를 확인할 방법을 알려주는 답변이므로 정답.
   (B) What time에 어울리는 미래 시점으로 답변하고 있으므로 정답.
   (C) Where에 어울리는 장소 전치사구로 답변하고 있으므로 오답.

어휘 leave 출발하다, 떠나다 over there 저기 저쪽에 in + 시간/기간: ~ 후에

6. Which firm does Martin work for?
   (A) That was his first company.
   (B) Doesn't he work at the C&C Corporation?
   (C) Yes, he'll be working until four.
   마틴 씨가 어느 회사에서 근무하나요?
   (A) 그게 그분의 첫 번째 회사였어요. [X]
   (B) 그분은 C&C 주식회사에서 근무하시지 않나요? [O]
   (C) 네, 그분은 4시까지 근무할 겁니다. [X]

해설 마틴 씨가 어느 회사에서 근무하는지 묻는 Which 의문문입니다.
   (A) That은 앞서 언급된 특정 대상을 가리키는데, 그 대상을 알 수 없어 질문에 맞지 않는 답변이므로 오답.
   (B) Which firm에 어울리는 특정 회사를 언급해 마틴 씨의 근무 여부를 확인하기 위해 되묻는 말이므로 정답.
   (C) 의문사 의문문에 어울리지 않는 Yes로 답변하는 오답. 의문사 의문문에 대해 Yes나 No로 시작되는 답변은 바로 오답 소거해야 합니다.

어휘 firm 회사 work for ~에서 근무하다

7. Why was the train delayed?
   (A) For almost an hour.
   (B) There was ice on the rails.
   (C) Because of some mechanical problems.
   기차가 왜 지연되었나요?
   (A) 약 1시간 동안이요. [X]
   (B) 철로에 얼음이 있었어요. [O]
   (C) 몇몇 기계적인 문제들 때문에요. [O]

해설 기차가 지연된 이유를 묻는 Why 의문문입니다.
(A) How long에 어울리는 지속 시간을 말하는 답변이므로 오답.
(B) 철로에 얼음이 있었다는 말로 기차가 지연된 이유를 언급하는 답변이므로 정답.
(C) Why와 어울리는 Because of와 함께 기계적인 문제를 언급하는 것으로 지연 이유를 밝히고 있으므로 정답.

어휘 delay ~을 지연시키다, 미루다 rail 철로, 선로 mechanical 기계적인

8. How do you like your new apartment?
(A) Better than I expected.
(B) It's very spacious.
(C) A one-bedroom apartment.

당신의 새 아파트가 마음에 드시나요?
(A) 제가 예상했던 것보다 더 좋아요. [O]
(B) 아주 널찍해요. [O]
(C) 침실 1개짜리 아파트입니다. [X]

해설 상대방에게 새 아파트가 마음에 드는지 묻는 How 의문문입니다.
(A) 예상보다 더 좋다는 말로 아파트에 대한 의견을 밝히는 답변이므로 정답.
(B) 아주 널찍하다는 말로 아파트가 마음에 든다는 이유를 말하는 답변이므로 정답.
(C) 단순히 침실 1개짜리 아파트라는 특성을 나타내는 말로서, 마음에 드는지 아닌지를 말하는 특성으로 볼 수 없으므로 오답.

어휘 How do you like ~? ~은 마음에 드시나요?, ~은 어떠세요? expect 예상하다, 기대하다 spacious 넓은, 널찍한

9. Why is there a large crowd at this store?
(A) On the second floor.
(B) They're having a clearance sale.
(C) I have no idea.

왜 이 매장에 사람들이 많은 건가요?
(A) 2층에요. [X]
(B) 정리 세일 행사 중입니다. [O]
(C) 잘 모르겠어요. [O]

해설 매장에 사람들이 많은 이유를 묻는 Why 의문문입니다.
(A) Where에 어울리는 위치 전치사구로 답변하고 있으므로 오답.
(B) 정리 세일 행사 중이라는 말로 사람들이 모여든 이유를 언급하는 답변이므로 정답.
(C) 잘 모르겠다는 말로 사람들이 많은 이유와 관련해 불확실성을 나타내는 답변이므로 정답.

어휘 crowd 사람들, 군중 clearance sale 정리 세일 행사

10. How many people responded to the invitation?
(A) Only four or five.
(B) I just mailed them out.
(C) To celebrate my retirement.

얼마나 많은 사람들이 초대에 응했나요?
(A) 겨우 4~5명이요. [O]
(B) 제가 그것들을 막 우편으로 보냈습니다. [O]
(C) 제 퇴직을 기념하기 위해서요. [X]

해설 얼마나 많은 사람들이 초대에 응했는지 묻는 How 의문문입니다.
(A) How many people에 어울리는 인원수로 답변하고 있으므로 정답.
(B) 초대장들을 뜻하는 them과 함께 막 우편으로 보냈기 때문에 아직 정확한 인원수를 알 수 없다는 뜻을 나타내는 답변이므로 정답.
(C) 행사 참석 인원수가 아닌 행사 개최 목적을 나타내는 말이므로 오답.

어휘 respond to ~에 응하다, 답변하다 invitation 초대(장) mail A out: A를 우편으로 발송하다 celebrate ~을 축하하다, 기념하다 retirement 은퇴, 퇴직

실전 TEST

1. (C)	2. (A)	3. (A)	4. (A)	5. (C)
6. (C)	7. (B)	8. (C)	9. (A)	10. (C)
11. (B)	12. (A)	13. (C)	14. (B)	15. (A)
16. (A)	17. (A)	18. (A)	19. (B)	20. (C)
21. (C)	22. (B)	23. (C)	24. (B)	25. (B)

1. When will the new accounting software be installed?
(A) I already knew.
(B) It's still there.
(C) In about three weeks.

언제 새 회계 소프트웨어가 설치될 건가요?
(A) 저는 이미 알고 있었어요.
(B) 그건 아직 거기 있어요.
(C) 약 3주 후에요.

정답 (C)

해설 새 회계 소프트웨어가 언제 설치되는지 묻는 When 의문문입니다.
(A) 특정 사실에 대해 아는지 확인하는 의문문에 어울리는 답변이므로 오답.
(B) Where에 어울리는 위치 표현으로 답변하고 있으므로 오답.
(C) When에 어울리는 대략적인 미래 시점으로 답변하고 있으므로 정답.

어휘 accounting 회계 install ~을 설치하다 in + 시간/기간: ~후에 about 약, 대략

2. Where is the investment seminar being held?
   (A) In the conference room.
   (B) The handouts are ready.
   (C) Some budget information.

어디에서 투자 세미나가 개최되나요?
   (A) 대회의실에서요.
   (B) 유인물이 준비되어 있습니다.
   (C) 일부 예산 관련 정보요.

정답 (A)
해설 투자 세미나가 어디에서 개최되는지 묻는 Where 의문문입니다.
   (A) Where에 어울리는 장소 전치사구로 답변하고 있으므로 정답.
   (B) 세미나 개최 장소가 아닌 자료 준비 상태를 말하고 있으므로 오답.
   (C) 세미나 개최 장소가 아닌 특정 정보의 종류를 말하고 있으므로 오답.

어휘 investment 투자(금) hold ~을 개최하다, 열다 handout 유인물 budget 예산

3. Who is in charge of sending invitations?
   (A) It hasn't been decided yet.
   (B) For the fundraising event.
   (C) No, I wasn't invited.

누가 초대장을 보내는 일을 책임지고 있나요?
   (A) 아직 결정되지 않았어요.
   (B) 기금 마련 행사를 위해서요.
   (C) 아뇨, 저는 초대받지 못했어요.

정답 (A)
해설 초대장을 보내는 일을 누가 책임지고 있는지 묻는 Who 의문문입니다.
   (A) 아직 결정되지 않았다는 말로 알 수 없음을 나타내는 정답.
   (B) 초대장을 보내는 일을 책임지고 있는 사람이 아닌 초대장 발송 목적을 말하고 있으므로 오답.
   (C) 의문사 의문문에 어울리지 않는 No로 답변하는 오답. 의문사 의문문에 대해 Yes나 No로 시작되는 답변은 바로 오답 소거해야 합니다.

어휘 in charge of ~을 책임지는, 맡고 있는 invitation 초대(장) decide ~을 결정하다 fundraising 기금 마련, 모금 invite ~을 초대하다

4. When can I get the copy of the rental contract?
   (A) On Monday morning, I guess.
   (B) Of course, you can.
   (C) Put it on my desk, please.

언제 제가 임대 계약서 사본을 받을 수 있나요?
   (A) 월요일 아침일 것 같아요.
   (B) 물론, 하실 수 있습니다.
   (C) 그걸 제 책상에 놓아 주세요.

정답 (A)
해설 임대 계약서 사본을 언제 받을 수 있는지 묻는 When 의문문입니다.
   (A) When에 어울리는 특정 시점으로 답변하고 있으므로 정답.
   (B) 상대방의 말에 대해 확인을 해주거나 허락을 할 때 사용하는 말이므로 오답.
   (C) 물건을 놓아둘 위치를 알리는 말로서 Where 의문문에 어울리는 답변이므로 오답.

어휘 copy 사본, 한 장, 한 부 rental 임대, 대여 contract 계약(서) put A on B: A를 B에 놓다, 두다

5. Who is going to pick up Mark from the airport?
   (A) At Pearson Airport.
   (B) Not yet.
   (C) I can do that.

누가 공항에서 마크 씨를 데려올 건가요?
   (A) 피어슨 공항에서요.
   (B) 아직 아니에요.
   (C) 제가 할 수 있어요.

정답 (C)
해설 공항에서 마크 씨를 누가 데려올 건지 묻는 Who 의문문입니다.
   (A) Where에 어울리는 장소 전치사구로 답변하고 있으므로 오답.
   (B) 어떤 일의 시작 또는 완료 여부와 관련된 부정 답변이므로 오답.
   (C) 공항에서 데려오는 일을 that으로 지칭해 답변자 자신이 할 수 있다는 가능성을 말하는 답변이므로 정답.

어휘 pick up (차로) ~를 데려오다, 데리러 가다 not yet 아직 아니다

6. When will you decide on the date for the banquet?
   (A) The annual staff party.
   (B) A little more color.
   (C) I picked one already.

언제 연회 날짜를 결정하실 건가요?
   (A) 연례 직원 회식입니다.
   (B) 색을 좀 더 많이요.
   (C) 이미 날짜를 선택했어요.

정답 (C)
해설 연회 날짜를 언제 결정할 것인지 묻는 When 의문문입니다.
   (A) 연회 날짜 결정 시점이 아닌 연회 목적을 말하는 답변이므로 오답.

(B) 연회 날짜 결정 시점이 아닌 색 추가를 요청하는 말이므로 오답.
(C) 질문에 포함된 date를 대신하는 one과 함께 이미 어떤 날을 선택했다는 의미이므로 정답.

어휘 decide on ~을 결정하다 annual 연례적인, 해마다의 pick ~을 선택하다, 정하다

7. Who will be the keynote speaker at the conference?
(A) We'll arrive at 9.
(B) I heard it's Mr. Choi.
(C) At the headquarters.

누가 컨퍼런스에서 기조 연설자가 되는 건가요?
(A) 우리는 9시에 도착할 겁니다.
(B) 최 씨라고 들었어요.
(C) 본사에서요.

정답 (B)
해설 컨퍼런스에서 누가 기조 연설자가 될 것인지 묻는 Who 의문문입니다.
(A) When에 어울리는 도착 시점을 알리는 답변이므로 오답.
(B) 특정 인물의 이름과 함께 자신이 들은 정보를 밝히는 답변이므로 정답.
(C) Where에 어울리는 장소 전치사구로 답변하고 있으므로 오답.

어휘 keynote speaker 기조 연설자 arrive 도착하다 headquarters 본사, 본부

8. When did you send that order?
(A) To the branch in Texas.
(B) Well, that should be enough time.
(C) Several days ago.

언제 그 주문 사항을 보내셨나요?
(A) 텍사스에 있는 지점으로요.
(B) 저, 그거면 충분한 시간일 거예요.
(C) 며칠 전에요.

정답 (C)
해설 주문 사항을 언제 보냈는지 묻는 When 의문문입니다.
(A) Where에 어울리는 위치 전치사구로 답변하고 있으므로 오답.
(B) 질문에서 말하는 과거 시점이 아닌 지속 시간과 관련된 답변이므로 오답.
(C) When에 어울리는 대략적인 과거 시점으로 답변하고 있으므로 정답.

어휘 order 주문 (사항), 주문품 branch 지점, 지사 several 몇몇의, 여럿의

9. What do you think of our new office?
(A) It looks great.
(B) The desk is over there.
(C) On the 4th floor.

우리 새 사무실에 대해 어떻게 생각하세요?
(A) 아주 좋아 보여요.
(B) 그 책상은 저기 저쪽에 있어요.
(C) 4층에요.

정답 (A)
해설 사무실에 대해 어떻게 생각하는지 의견을 묻는 What 의문문입니다.
(A) new office를 It으로 지칭해 아주 좋아 보인다는 의견을 밝히고 있으므로 정답.
(B) 새 사무실에 대한 의견이 아닌 책상이 놓인 위치를 말하는 답변이므로 오답.
(C) Where에 어울리는 위치 전치사구로 답변하고 있으므로 오답.

어휘 What do you think of ~? ~에 대해서 어떻게 생각하세요? look + 형용사: ~하게 보이다, ~한 것 같다 over there 저기 저쪽에

10. What's the extension for Customer Service?
(A) At the service desk.
(B) 100 dollars.
(C) It's 8160.

고객 서비스부의 내선 번호가 무엇인가요?
(A) 서비스 데스크에서요.
(B) 100달러입니다.
(C) 8160입니다.

정답 (C)
해설 고객 서비스부의 내선 번호를 묻는 What 의문문입니다.
(A) Where에 어울리는 위치 전치사구로 답변하고 있으므로 오답.
(B) 질문에 포함된 Service와 연관성 있게 들리는 비용 수준을 말하는 것으로 혼동을 유발하는 오답.
(C) extension에 해당되는 특정 번호를 말하는 답변이므로 정답.

어휘 extension 내선 (번호)

11. Which hotel is hosting this year's conference?
(A) Over 3,000 attendees.
(B) The same one as last year.
(C) You can register online.

어느 호텔에서 올해의 컨퍼런스를 주최하나요?
(A) 3,000명이 넘는 참석자들이요.
(B) 작년과 같은 곳이요.
(C) 온라인으로 등록하실 수 있어요.

정답 (B)
해설 올해의 컨퍼런스를 주최하는 호텔을 묻는 Which 의문문입니다.
(A) How many에 어울리는 행사 참석자 규모를 말하는 답변이므로 오답.
(B) 질문에 포함된 hotel을 대신하는 대명사 one과 함께 작년과 같은 곳이라는 말로 행사 주최 호텔을 알려주는 답변이므로 정답.
(C) 방법을 묻는 How에 어울리는 등록 방법을 말하는 답변이므로 오답.
어휘 host ~을 주최하다 over ~가 넘는 attendee 참석자 register 등록하다

12. What did the client say about our budget proposal?
(A) **She was very impressed.**
(B) The sales figures.
(C) Without his approval.

그 고객이 저희의 예산 제안서에 대해 뭐라고 하시던가요?
(A) 그분께서는 매우 깊은 인상을 받으셨어요.
(B) 매출 수치요.
(C) 그분의 승인 없이요.

정답 (A)
해설 고객이 예산 제안서에 대해 무슨 말을 했는지 묻는 What 의문문입니다.
(A) 질문에 포함된 the client를 She로 지칭해 그 사람이 느낀 점을 전달하는 답변에 해당되므로 정답.
(B) 고객의 의견이 아닌 어떤 정보의 종류를 말하는 답변이므로 오답.
(C) 제안서에 대한 고객의 의견이 아닌 누군가의 승인 여부와 관련된 말이므로 오답.
어휘 budget 예산 proposal 제안(서) impressed 깊은 인상을 받은 sales 매출, 영업, 판매(량) figure 수치, 숫자 approval 승인

13. Which department am I training in today?
(A) The train departs every 30 minutes.
(B) Everyone is pleased with your work.
(C) **Didn't you check the bulletin board?**

저는 오늘 어느 부서에서 교육 받을 건가요?
(A) 기차가 30분마다 출발합니다.
(B) 모든 사람이 당신의 작업물에 만족하고 있어요.
(C) 게시판을 확인해 보시지 않았나요?

정답 (C)
해설 어느 부서에서 교육 받는지 묻는 Which 의문문입니다.
(A) 질문의 training과 발음이 비슷한 train으로 혼동을 노린 오답.

(B) 교육 받는 부서가 아닌 상대방의 작업물에 대한 사람들의 의견을 말하는 답변이므로 오답.
(C) 게시판을 확인해 봤는지 되묻는 것으로 질문자가 원하는 정보를 찾을 수 있는 방법을 언급하는 답변이므로 정답.
어휘 department 부서 train v. 교육 받다 depart 출발하다 every 30 minutes 30분마다 be pleased with ~에 만족하다, 기뻐하다 work 작업(물) bulletin board 게시판

14. What's tomorrow's meeting about?
(A) At 10 A.M.
(B) **A new vacation policy.**
(C) I met them on Tuesday.

내일 있을 회의는 무엇에 관한 것인가요?
(A) 오전 10시에요.
(B) 새로운 휴가 정책이요.
(C) 저는 그분들을 화요일에 만났어요.

정답 (B)
해설 내일 있을 회의가 무엇에 관한 것인지 묻는 What 의문문입니다.
(A) When에 어울리는 시간 표현으로 답변하고 있으므로 오답.
(B) 새 휴가 정책이라는 회의 주제를 말하는 답변이므로 정답.
(C) 질문에 포함된 meeting과 연관성 있게 들리는 met을 활용해 혼동을 유발하는 답변으로, 회의 주제가 아닌 누군가를 만난 시점을 밝히는 답변이므로 오답.
어휘 vacation 휴가 policy 정책, 방침

15. What time does the bus arrive?
(A) **It should be here in 10 minutes.**
(B) Four bus tickets, please.
(C) No, I'm not too busy.

그 버스가 몇 시에 도착하나요?
(A) 10분 후에 여기로 올 겁니다.
(B) 버스표 4장 주세요.
(C) 아뇨, 저는 그렇게 바쁘지 않아요.

정답 (A)
해설 버스가 몇 시에 도착하는지 묻는 What 의문문입니다.
(A) What time에 어울리는 특정 미래 시점으로 답변하고 있으므로 정답.
(B) 버스 도착 시간이 아닌 버스 티켓 구매 수량을 말하는 답변이므로 오답.
(C) 의문사 의문문에 어울리지 않는 No로 답변하는 오답. 의문사 의문문에 대해 Yes나 No로 시작되는 답변은 바로 오답 소거해야 합니다.
어휘 arrive 도착하다 in + 시간/기간: ~ 후에

16. Which of these paintings would look best in the dining room?
   (A) I like the yellow one.
   (B) No, it's in the living room.
   (C) I didn't get a chance to see him.

이 그림들 중에 어느 것이 식사 공간에 가장 잘 어울릴까요?
   (A) 저는 노란색으로 된 것이 좋아요.
   (B) 아뇨, 그건 거실에 있어요.
   (C) 저는 그분을 볼 기회가 없었어요.

정답 (A)
해설 식사 공간에 가장 잘 어울릴 수 있는 그림을 묻는 Which 의문문입니다.
   (A) 질문에 포함된 painting을 대신하는 대명사 one과 함께 특정 색상으로 된 것이 좋다는 의견을 제시하는 답변이므로 정답.
   (B) 의문사 의문문에 어울리지 않는 No로 답변하는 오답. 의문사 의문문에 대해 Yes나 No로 시작되는 답변은 바로 오답 소거해야 합니다.
   (C) 그림이 아닌 특정 인물(him)과 관련된 말이므로 오답.

어휘 painting 그림 look + 형용사: ~하게 보이다, ~한 것 같다 get a chance to do ~할 기회가 있다

17. Why was the music festival canceled?
   (A) Due to the bad weather.
   (B) Yes, I heard about it.
   (C) I like that song.

왜 그 음악 축제가 취소된 거죠?
   (A) 악천후 때문이에요.
   (B) 네, 그것에 관해 들었어요.
   (C) 저는 그 노래가 마음에 들어요.

정답 (A)
해설 음악 축제가 취소된 이유를 묻는 Why 의문문입니다.
   (A) Why와 어울리는 이유 전치사 Due to와 함께 악천후 때문이라는 말로 축제 취소 이유를 밝히는 답변이므로 정답.
   (B) 의문사 의문문에 어울리지 않는 Yes로 답변하는 오답. 의문사 의문문에 대해 Yes나 No로 시작되는 답변은 바로 오답 소거해야 합니다.
   (C) 질문에 포함된 music과 연관성 있게 들리는 song을 활용해 혼동을 유발하는 답변으로, 축제 취소 이유가 아닌 특정 노래에 대한 의견을 밝히는 말이므로 오답.

어휘 cancel ~을 취소하다 due to ~ 때문에, ~로 인해 bad weather 악천후

18. Why was the file cabinet moved from the corner?
   (A) To make more space for a new printer.
   (B) Right around the corner.
   (C) It's on my desk.

왜 그 파일 캐비닛이 구석에서 옮겨진 거죠?
   (A) 새 프린터를 놓을 공간을 더 확보하기 위해서요.
   (B) 바로 모퉁이를 돈 곳에요.
   (C) 그건 제 책상 위에 있습니다.

정답 (A)
해설 파일 캐비닛이 구석에서 옮겨진 이유를 묻는 Why 의문문입니다.
   (A) Why와 어울리는 목적을 나타내는 to부정사구와 함께 공간 확보를 위해 캐비닛이 옮겨졌다는 목적을 밝히는 답변이므로 정답.
   (B) 질문에 포함된 corner를 반복 사용해 혼동을 유발하는 답변으로, Where에 어울리는 위치 전치사구로서 캐비닛이 옮겨진 이유와 관련 없는 오답.
   (C) Where에 어울리는 위치를 알려주는 답변이므로 캐비닛이 옮겨진 이유와 관련 없는 오답.

어휘 move A from B: A를 B에서 옮기다 make more space 공간을 더 확보하다 right around the corner 바로 모퉁이를 돈 곳에

19. How often is the software upgraded?
   (A) Let me show you how.
   (B) Once a month.
   (C) About a couple of days ago.

얼마나 자주 그 소프트웨어가 업그레이드되나요?
   (A) 제가 어떻게 하는지 보여 드리겠습니다.
   (B) 한 달에 한 번이요.
   (C) 약 이틀 전에요.

정답 (B)
해설 얼마나 자주 소프트웨어가 업그레이드되는지 묻는 How 의문문입니다.
   (A) 특정 방법을 알려주겠다는 말이므로 소프트웨어 업그레이드 빈도와 관련 없는 오답.
   (B) How often에 어울리는 빈도를 말하는 답변이므로 정답.
   (C) When에 어울리는 대략적인 과거 시점을 말하는 답변이므로 오답.

어휘 Let me do 제가 ~해 드리겠습니다 show A how: A에게 어떻게 하는지 보여주다 about 약, 대략

20. How many computers will we need for the training session?
   (A) I enjoyed the speech.
   (B) It's raining now.
   (C) At least 20, I guess.

얼마나 많은 컴퓨터가 교육 시간에 필요할까요?
   (A) 저는 그 연설이 즐거웠습니다.
   (B) 지금 비가 내리고 있어요.
   (C) 최소 20대일 것 같아요.

정답 (C)
해설 얼마나 많은 컴퓨터가 교육 시간에 필요한지 묻는 How 의문문입니다.
(A) 컴퓨터 수량이 아닌 과거 시점에 참석한 연설에 대한 의견을 밝히는 답변이므로 오답.
(B) 질문에 포함된 training과 일부 발음이 같은 raining을 활용해 혼동을 유발하는 답변으로, 컴퓨터 수량과 관련 없는 오답.
(C) How many에 어울리는 대략적인 수량으로 답변하고 있으므로 정답.

어휘 training 교육 session (특정 활동을 위한) 시간 at least 최소한, 적어도

21. Why is there so much traffic in the city today?
(A) My car is stuck in traffic.
(B) That's okay.
(C) Because of the construction.

오늘 시내에 왜 그렇게 많은 차량이 있는 건가요?
(A) 제 차가 교통 혼잡에 갇혀 있어요.
(B) 괜찮습니다.
(C) 공사 때문이에요.

정답 (C)
해설 오늘 시내에 차량이 많은 이유를 묻는 Why 의문문입니다.
(A) 질문에 포함된 traffic을 반복 사용해 혼동을 유발하는 답변으로, 차량이 많은 이유가 아닌 자신의 차량이 혼잡한 상황에 갇혀 있다는 사실을 언급하는 말이므로 오답.
(B) 상대방의 사과 등에 괜찮다는 뜻으로 사용하는 말이므로 오답.
(C) Why에 어울리는 이유 전치사 Because of와 함께 공사 때문이라는 말로 차량이 많은 이유를 밝히는 답변이므로 정답.

어휘 traffic 차량, 교통 be stuck in ~에 갇혀 있다 construction 공사, 건설

22. How long will it take to drive to the hotel?
(A) In room 804.
(B) About 30 minutes.
(C) For three nights.

그 호텔까지 차를 운전해서 가는 데 얼마나 걸릴까요?
(A) 804호실에요.
(B) 약 30분이요.
(C) 3박이요.

정답 (B)
해설 호텔까지 차를 운전해서 가는 데 얼마나 걸리는지 묻는 How 의문문입니다.
(A) 질문에 포함된 hotel과 연관성 있게 들리는 객실 번호를 말하는 답변으로, 이동 시간과 관련 없는 오답.
(B) How long에 어울리는 대략적인 이동 소요 시간을 말하는 답변이므로 정답.
(C) 질문에 포함된 hotel과 연관성 있게 들리는 숙박 기간을 말하는 답변이므로 오답.

어휘 take ~의 시간이 걸리다 drive to ~로 차를 운전해서 가다 about 약, 대략

23. Why did we purchase the office supplies from a different store?
(A) Every Monday.
(B) On their Web site.
(C) The other one closed.

왜 우리가 다른 매장에서 사무용품을 구입한 거죠?
(A) 매주 월요일이요.
(B) 그곳의 웹사이트에서요.
(C) 다른 쪽 매장이 문을 닫았어요.

정답 (C)
해설 다른 매장에서 사무용품을 구입한 이유를 묻는 Why 의문문입니다.
(A) How often에 어울리는 반복 주기 또는 When에 어울리는 시점에 해당되는 답변이므로 오답.
(B) Where에 어울리는 제품 구입 장소에 해당되는 답변이므로 오답.
(C) 두 가지 특정 대상 중 하나를 제외한 나머지 하나를 지칭할 때 사용하는 The other와 함께 그곳이 문을 닫았다는 말로 다른 곳에서 구입한 이유를 말하는 정답.

어휘 purchase ~을 구입하다 supplies 용품, 물품 the other (둘 중 하나를 제외한) 나머지 하나

24. How much are the tickets for the concert?
(A) At the box office.
(B) They cost 30 euros each.
(C) It was very exciting.

그 콘서트 입장권은 얼마인가요?
(A) 매표소에서요.
(B) 각각 30유로의 비용이 듭니다.
(C) 아주 흥미로웠어요.

정답 (B)
해설 콘서트 입장권이 얼마인지 묻는 How 의문문입니다.
(A) Where에 어울리는 위치 전치사구로 답변하고 있으므로 오답.
(B) How much에 어울리는 특정 가격으로 답변하고 있으므로 정답.
(C) 질문에 포함된 concert와 연관성 있게 들리는 exciting을 활용해 혼동을 유발하는 답변으로, 입장권 가격이 아닌 콘서트에 대한 의견을 밝히는 말이므로 오답.

어휘 cost ~의 비용이 들다 exciting 흥미로운

25. How was your trip to Vietnam?
  (A) Only for seven days.
  (B) I had a great time.
  (C) I would like to take the train.

베트남으로 떠났던 여행은 어떠셨나요?
  (A) 겨우 7일 동안이요.
  (B) 아주 즐거운 시간을 보냈습니다.
  (C) 저는 그 기차를 타고 싶습니다.

정답 (B)

해설 베트남으로 떠났던 여행이 어땠는지 묻는 How 의문문입니다.
  (A) How long에 어울리는 지속 기간으로 답변하고 있으므로 오답.
  (B) 즐거운 시간을 보냈다는 말로 베트남 여행에 대한 의견을 밝히고 있으므로 정답.
  (C) 질문에 포함된 trip과 연관성 있게 들리는 교통 수단으로 답변하고 있으므로 오답.

어휘 would like to do ~하고 싶다, ~하고자 하다
take (교통편) ~을 타다, 이용하다

DAY 4 일반 의문문

PRACTICE

1. (A) X	(B) O	(C) X
2. (A) X	(B) X	(C) O
3. (A) O	(B) X	(C) X
4. (A) X	(B) X	(C) O
5. (A) X	(B) O	(C) X

1. Does your library lend out laptops?
  (A) You can return the books on the second floor.
  (B) Yes, except on weekends.
  (C) Thanks, please put them on top of the pile.

당신의 도서관은 노트북 컴퓨터를 대여해주나요?
  (A) 그 책들은 2층에 반납하실 수 있습니다. [X]
  (B) 네, 주말 제외하고요. [O]
  (C) 고맙습니다. 더미 위에 놓아주세요. [X]

해설 도서관이 노트북 컴퓨터를 대여하는지 묻는 일반 의문문입니다.
  (A) 노트북 컴퓨터가 아닌 도서 반납에 대한 답변이므로 오답.
  (B) Yes/No 중에 대답해야 하는 일반 의문문에 어울리는 답변이며, '주말 제외'라는 내용 또한 질문에 대한 답변이 될 수 있으므로 정답.
  (C) 고맙다는 답변에 어울리지 않는 질문이며, 노트북 컴퓨터를 어디에 놓는지에 대한 질문도 아니므로 오답.

어휘 lend out 대여해주다 laptop 노트북 컴퓨터 return 반납하다 except ~을 제외하고 on top of ~의 위에 pile 더미, 쌓아둔 것

2. Has the technician arrived yet?
  (A) Yes, I took the bus.
  (B) It is working well now.
  (C) His toolbox is by the server rack.

기사님은 아직 도착하지 않으셨나요?
  (A) 네, 저는 버스를 탔습니다. [X]
  (B) 그건 지금은 잘 작동하고 있습니다. [X]
  (C) 그의 도구함은 서버 랙 옆에 있습니다. [O]

해설 기사가 도착했는지 묻는 일반 의문문입니다.
  (A) 기사에 대해 물었으므로 I에 대해 답변하는 것은 오답.
  (B) it이 가리키는 것이 무엇인지 알 수 없으므로 오답.
  (C) 그의 도구함이 서버 랙 옆에 있다는 말은 그가 도착했다는 의미를 나타낼 수 있으므로 정답.

어휘 technician 기사, 기술자 work well 잘 작동하다
toolbox 도구함, 장비함 server rack 서버 랙(서버를 올려두는 선반)

3. Do you know how to operate the video-conferencing system?
  (A) Sure, I can show you.
  (B) The conference will be at 11.
  (C) A few system files only.

화상 회의 시스템을 작동시키는 법을 아시나요?
  (A) 물론이죠, 보여드릴 수 있습니다. [O]
  (B) 컨퍼런스는 11시에 있을 예정입니다. [X]
  (C) 몇몇의 시스템 파일만요. [X]

해설 화상 회의 시스템을 작동시키는 방법을 아는지 묻는 간접 의문문입니다.
  (A) Yes에 해당하는 Sure로 답변하였으며, 화상 회의 시스템을 작동시키는 법을 보여준다는 내용이므로 정답.
  (B) 컨퍼런스의 시간에 대한 답변이므로 오답.
  (C) 질문은 시스템 파일에 관한 내용이 아니므로 오답.

어휘 operate 작동시키다, 운영하다 video-conferencing 화상 회의

4. Aren't you starting the in-person training sessions next week?
  (A) From Human Resources.
  (B) No, there were a few trainers.
  (C) They're going to be conducted online instead.

당신이 대면 교육 훈련 시간을 다음 주부터 시작하는 것 아닌가요?
(A) 인사부에서요. [X]
(B) 아니요. 몇몇의 트레이너들만 있습니다. [X]
(C) 그것들은 온라인으로 대신 실시될 것입니다. [O]

해설 대면 교육 훈련 시간이 다음주에 시작하는지 묻는 부정 의문문입니다.
(A) 교육 훈련이 누구로부터 실시되는지에 대한 답변이므로 오답.
(B) 몇몇의 트레이너들만 있다는 답변이므로 오답.
(C) 대면 교육이 아니라 온라인으로 실시될 것이라는 내용이므로 정답.

어휘 in-person 대면의, 직접적인 trainer 트레이너, 교관, 훈련사 conduct 실시하다, 시행하다 instead 대신에

5. Isn't the projector supposed to be stored in the AV closet?
(A) After I finish the project first.
(B) The Sales department is using it today.
(C) Yes, we need to clean the room.

프로젝터가 영상 장비함에 저장되어야 하는 것 아닌가요?
(A) 제가 그 프로젝트를 먼저 완료한 후에요. [X]
(B) 영업부에서 오늘 그것을 사용할 것입니다. [O]
(C) 네, 저희는 그 방을 청소해야 합니다. [X]

해설 프로젝트가 영상 장비함에 저장되어야 하는 것이 아닌지 묻는 부정 의문문입니다.
(A) 프로젝터가 아닌 프로젝트에 대한 답변이므로 오답.
(B) 프로젝터를 영업부에서 오늘 사용할 것이라는 내용을 나타내는 것이므로 정답.
(C) 영상 장비함과 프로젝터에 관한 내용이 아닌 방을 청소해야 한다는 답변이므로 오답.

어휘 be supposed to do ~해야 하다, ~하기로 예정되어 있다 store 저장하다 AV closet 영상 장비함 sales department 영업부 need to do ~해야 하다

실전 TEST

1. (C)	2. (A)	3. (A)	4. (B)	5. (B)
6. (B)	7. (B)	8. (B)	9. (C)	10. (C)
11. (B)	12. (A)	13. (B)	14. (C)	15. (B)
16. (C)	17. (B)	18. (A)	19. (B)	20. (C)
21. (A)	22. (A)	23. (C)	24. (B)	25. (C)

1. Do you have time to help me fill out this form?
(A) It seems informative.
(B) Fill it to the top.
(C) Of course. What can I do?

제가 이 양식을 작성하는 것을 도와줄 시간이 있으신가요?
(A) 그건 유익한 것 같아요.
(B) 맨 위까지 가득 채워 주세요.
(C) 물론입니다. 무엇을 하면 될까요?

정답 (C)

해설 자신이 양식을 작성하는 것을 도와줄 시간이 있는지 확인하는 일반 의문문입니다.
(A) 시간이 나는지에 대한 여부가 아닌 특정 대상(It)의 성격을 나타내는 말이므로 오답.
(B) 질문에 포함된 동사 fill의 다른 의미(채우다)를 활용해 혼동을 유발하는 답변으로, 무언가를 가득 채워 달라고 요청하는 말이므로 질문과 관련 없는 오답.
(C) 시간이 있다는 긍정의 뜻을 나타내는 Of course와 함께 무엇을 하는 것으로 도울 수 있는지 되묻는 말을 덧붙인 답변이므로 정답.

어휘 help A do: A가 ~하는 것을 돕다 fill out ~을 작성하다 form 양식, 서식 seem + 형용사: ~한 것 같다, ~한 것처럼 보이다 informative 유익한 fill ~을 채우다, 메우다 to the top 맨 위까지

2. Don't you have an appointment with the public relations manager?
(A) Yes, I'm leaving for it now.
(B) She made a very good point.
(C) Go to the second floor.

홍보부장님과 약속이 있지 않나요?
(A) 네, 지금 그것을 위해 출발하는 중입니다.
(B) 그녀가 아주 좋은 지적을 해주었어요.
(C) 2층으로 가세요.

정답 (A)

해설 홍보부장과 약속을 하지 않았는지 확인하는 부정 의문문입니다.
(A) 긍정을 나타내는 Yes와 함께 지금 출발한다는 말로 약속이 있음을 확인해주는 답변이므로 정답.

(B) 질문의 appointment와 일부 발음이 비슷한 point를 이용하여 혼동을 유발하는 오답.
(C) 상대방이 약속이 있는지 확인하는 질문의 내용과 관련 없는 오답.

어휘 appointment 약속, 예약 public relations 홍보 leave 출발하다, 떠나다 make a good point 좋은 지적을 하다

3. Do you think I should reserve a table at the restaurant?
   (A) It's not supposed to be busy.
   (B) I had a wonderful time.
   (C) The grilled fish, please.

제가 그 레스토랑에 테이블을 하나 예약해야 한다고 생각하세요?
(A) 그곳은 붐비지 않을 겁니다.
(B) 저는 아주 즐거운 시간을 보냈습니다.
(C) 구운 생선으로 부탁합니다.

정답 (A)
해설 레스토랑에 테이블을 하나 예약해야 한다고 생각하는지 확인하기 위해 묻는 일반 의문문입니다.
(A) 레스토랑이 붐비지 않을 것이라고 말하는 것은 예약할 필요가 없다는 뜻이므로 정답.
(B) 즐거운 시간을 보냈다는 말로 과거 시점의 일에 대한 의견을 밝히는 답변이므로 예약 여부와 관련 없는 오답.
(C) 질문에 포함된 restaurant과 연관성 있게 들리는 grilled fish를 활용해 혼동을 유발하는 답변으로, 음식 주문 시에 할 수 있는 말이므로 질문과 관련 없는 오답.

어휘 reserve ~을 예약하다 be supposed to do ~할 예정이다, ~하기로 되어 있다 grilled 구운

4. Aren't you wearing a suit for your interview?
   (A) A position in marketing.
   (B) I'm considering it.
   (C) Let's check the schedule.

면접을 위해 정장을 입을 것이 아닌가요?
(A) 마케팅 부서의 직책이요.
(B) 그것을 고려 중입니다.
(C) 일정표를 확인해 봅시다.

정답 (B)
해설 면접 자리에 정장을 입고 가지 않는지 확인하기 위한 부정 의문문입니다.
(A) 정장 착용 여부가 아닌 특정 부서의 직책을 언급하는 말이므로 질문과 관련 없는 오답.
(B) 질문에서 언급하는 '정장을 입는 일'을 it으로 지칭해 그렇게 하는 것을 고려 중이라는 말로 아직 확정하지 않은 상황임을 말하고 있으므로 정답.
(C) 일정표를 확인해 보자고 권하는 답변으로, 정장 착용 여부와 관련해 제안할 수 있는 일이 아니므로 오답.

어휘 suit 정장 position 직책, 일자리 consider ~을 고려하다

5. Have you checked your e-mail account yet?
   (A) So does she.
   (B) I've been too busy.
   (C) Near the post office.

혹시 당신 이메일 계정을 확인해 보셨나요?
(A) 그녀도 그렇습니다.
(B) 제가 계속 너무 바빴어요.
(C) 우체국 근처에요.

정답 (B)
해설 이메일 계정을 확인해 보았는지를 묻는 일반 의문문입니다.
(A) 앞서 언급된 일에 대해 동의하거나 동일한 상황에 처해 있음을 나타낼 때 사용하는 말이므로 오답.
(B) 계속 너무 바빴다는 말로 아직 확인해 보지 못했다는 뜻을 나타내는 답변이므로 정답.
(C) 질문에 포함된 e-mail의 mail과 연관성 있게 들리는 post office를 활용해 혼동을 유발하는 답변으로, 이메일 계정 확인 여부와 관련 없는 답변이므로 오답.

어휘 account 계정, 계좌 near ~ 근처에

6. Do you know who's coming to the dinner party tonight?
   (A) I don't know where to go.
   (B) All of the staff members.
   (C) It was very delicious.

오늘 저녁 만찬에 누가 오는지 아시나요?
(A) 저는 어디로 가는지 몰라요.
(B) 전 직원이요.
(C) 아주 맛있었습니다.

정답 (B)
해설 저녁 만찬에 누가 오는지 확인하기 위해 묻는 일반 의문문입니다.
(A) 참석 대상자가 아닌 행사 개최 장소와 관련된 답변이므로 오답.
(B) 질문에 포함된 의문사 who에 어울리는 참석 대상자를 밝히는 답변이므로 정답.
(C) 질문에 포함된 dinner와 연관성 있게 들리는 delicious를 활용해 혼동을 유발하는 답변으로, 참석 대상자가 아닌 특정 음식에 대한 의견을 밝히는 말이므로 오답.

어휘 where to go 어디로 가는지, 가는 곳 staff member 직원

7. Has anyone checked the sales figures yet?
   (A) That sounds pretty accurate.
   (B) Mr. Camby might have.
   (C) They are having a sale.

혹시 누가 매출 수치를 확인해 보셨나요?
(A) 아주 정확한 것 같네요.
(B) 캠비 씨가 했을 수도 있습니다.
(C) 그곳은 할인 판매 중입니다.

정답 (B)
해설 매출 수치를 확인해 본 사람이 있는지 확인하기 위해 묻는 일반 의문문입니다.
(A) 매출 수치를 확인해 본 사람이 아닌 자료의 정확성과 관련된 답변이므로 오답.
(B) 특정 인물을 언급해 그 사람이 매출 수치를 확인했을 가능성을 말하는 답변이므로 정답.
(C) 질문에 포함된 sale의 다른 의미(할인 판매)를 활용해 혼동을 유발하는 답변으로, 매출 수치 확인 여부와 관련 없는 오답.

어휘 sales 매출, 영업, 판매(량), 할인 판매 figure 수치, 숫자 pretty 아주, 꽤 accurate 정확한 might have p.p. ~했을 수도 있다

8. Are you supposed to take our guests out to lunch?
(A) Where did you go?
(B) No, they're leaving before noon.
(C) Help yourself.

우리 손님들을 모시고 점심 식사하러 나갈 예정인가요?
(A) 어디로 가셨어요?
(B) 아뇨, 그분들께서는 정오 전에 떠나실 거예요.
(C) 마음껏 드세요.

정답 (B)
해설 손님들을 모시고 점심 식사하러 나갈 예정인지 확인하기 위해 묻는 일반 의문문입니다.
(A) 과거 시점(did)의 일에 대해 되묻고 있으므로 질문과 관련 없는 오답.
(B) 부정을 나타내는 No 및 guests를 대신하는 they와 함께 정오 전에 그들이 떠난다는 말로 점심 식사하러 가지 않을 것이라는 뜻을 나타내는 답변이므로 정답.
(C) 식사 자리에서 상대방에게 마음껏 먹도록 권할 때 사용하는 말이므로 오답.

어휘 be supposed to do ~할 예정이다, ~하기로 되어 있다 take A out to B: A를 데리고 B하러 나가다 leave 출발하다, 떠나다 noon 정오 Help yourself 마음껏 드세요

9. Is there a computer that I can use to print?
(A) The library opened at 9 A.M.
(B) Thanks for printing it.
(C) It's out of order right now.

제가 인쇄하는 데 사용할 수 있는 컴퓨터가 있나요?
(A) 도서관이 오전 9시에 열었습니다.
(B) 그것을 인쇄해 주셔서 감사합니다.
(C) 그게 지금은 고장 나 있습니다.

정답 (C)
해설 인쇄하는 데 사용할 수 있는 컴퓨터가 있는지 확인하기 위해 묻는 일반 의문문입니다.
(A) 이용 가능한 컴퓨터의 존재 여부가 아닌 도서관 개장 시간을 말하고 있어 질문과 관련 없는 오답.
(B) 질문에 포함된 print를 반복 사용해 혼동을 유발하는 답변으로, 이용 가능한 컴퓨터의 존재 여부와 관련 없는 감사 인사이므로 오답.
(C) 이용 가능한 컴퓨터를 It으로 지칭해 그것이 고장 나 있다는 말로 사용할 수 없음을 나타내는 답변이므로 정답.

어휘 out of order 고장 난

10. Is this year's job fair going to be in Germany?
(A) It is fairly big.
(B) No, it's next month.
(C) Why don't you ask Emma?

올해 취업 박람회가 독일에서 있을 건가요?
(A) 그건 꽤 큽니다.
(B) 아뇨, 다음 달에요.
(C) 엠마 씨에게 물어보시는 게 어때요?

정답 (C)
해설 취업 박람회가 독일에서 있을 건지 확인하기 위해 묻는 일반 의문문입니다.
(A) 질문에 포함된 fair와 일부 발음이 같은 fairly를 활용해 혼동을 유발하는 답변으로, 행사 개최 장소가 아닌 행사 규모를 말하고 있어 질문과 관련 없는 오답.
(B) 부정을 나타내는 No 뒤에 이어지는 말이 시점 표현이므로 질문과 관련 없는 오답.
(C) 질문 내용에 대해 확인해 주는 대신 그 정보를 확인할 수 있는 방법을 제안하는 답변이므로 정답.

어휘 job fair 취업 박람회 fairly 꽤, 상당히 Why don't you ~? ~하는 게 어때요?

11. Didn't Mr. Shin tell you to cancel the award ceremony?
(A) No, I didn't win it.
(B) Yes, but he changed his mind.
(C) We'll try again next year.

신 씨가 시상식을 취소하라고 말씀하시지 않았나요?
(A) 아뇨, 저는 그 상을 받지 않았어요.
(B) 네, 하지만 마음을 바꾸셨어요.
(C) 우리는 내년에 다시 시도할 겁니다.

정답 (B)

해설 신 씨가 시상식을 취소하라고 얘기하지 않았는지 확인하기 위해 묻는 부정 의문문입니다.
(A) 질문에 포함된 award와 연관성 있게 들리는 win을 활용해 혼동을 유발하는 답변으로, 부정을 나타내는 No 뒤에 이어지는 말이 행사 취소 여부와 관련 없는 내용이므로 오답.
(B) 긍정을 나타내는 Yes 및 Mr. Shin을 지칭하는 he와 함께 취소 요청이 있었지만 다시 마음을 바꿨다는 말로 취소하지 않는다는 뜻을 나타내는 답변이므로 정답.
(C) 내년에 다시 해보겠다는 뜻이므로 행사 취소 여부와 관련 없는 오답.

어휘 tell A to do: A에게 ~하라고 말하다 cancel ~을 취소하다 award ceremony 시상식 win (상 등) ~을 받다, 타다 try 시도하다, 노력하다

12. Have the product samples come yet?
 (A) They're on your desk.
 (B) Ten pieces, please.
 (C) Every day next week.

혹시 제품 샘플이 왔나요?
 (A) 당신 책상 위에 있습니다.
 (B) 10개 부탁합니다.
 (C) 다음 주에 매일이요.

정답 (A)
해설 제품 샘플이 왔는지 확인하기 위해 묻는 일반 의문문입니다.
(A) 질문에 포함된 samples를 They로 지칭해 상대방 책상 위에 있다는 말로 샘플이 도착했음을 알리는 답변이므로 정답.
(B) 질문에 포함된 product와 연관성 있게 들리는 제품 수량을 말해 혼동을 유발하는 답변으로, 제품 주문 시에 할 수 있는 말이므로 샘플 도착 여부와 관련 없는 오답.
(C) 반복 주기를 나타내는 말이므로 샘플 도착 여부와 관련 없는 오답.

어휘 piece 한 개, 한 조각

13. Will the library be open this Saturday?
 (A) Can you close the door for me?
 (B) No, it's a public holiday.
 (C) I loved that book series.

도서관이 이번 주 토요일에 문을 열까요?
 (A) 저를 위해 문을 닫아 주시겠어요?
 (B) 아뇨, 그날은 공휴일입니다.
 (C) 그 도서 시리즈가 아주 마음에 들었어요.

정답 (B)
해설 도서관이 이번 주 토요일에 문을 여는지 확인하기 위해 묻는 일반 의문문입니다.
(A) open에서 연상 가능한 close를 이용해 혼동을 유발하는 오답이며, 문을 닫아 달라고 부탁하는 말이므로 질문의 의도에 맞지 않는 오답.
(B) 부정을 뜻하는 No와 함께 공휴일이라는 말로 도서관이 운영되지 않는 이유를 언급하고 있으므로 정답.
(C) library에서 연상 가능한 book series를 이용해 혼동을 유발하는 오답이며, 특정 도서 시리즈에 대한 의견을 밝히는 답변이므로 질문의 의도에 맞지 않는 오답.

어휘 public holiday 공휴일

14. Are you buying tickets to the basketball game next week?
 (A) Oh, I don't play video games.
 (B) He was asked to take some photos.
 (C) I heard it's already sold out.

다음 주에 있을 농구 경기 입장권을 구입하시나요?
 (A) 아, 저는 비디오 게임을 하지 않아요.
 (B) 그가 몇몇 사진을 촬영하도록 요청 받았어요.
 (C) 그게 이미 매진되었다고 들었어요.

정답 (C)
해설 다음 주에 있을 농구 경기 입장권을 구입하는지 확인하기 위해 묻는 일반 의문문입니다.
(A) game을 반복해 혼동을 유발하는 오답이며, 비디오 게임을 하지 않는다는 사실을 밝히는 답변이므로 질문의 의도에 맞지 않는 오답.
(B) 대상을 알 수 없는 He가 사진을 촬영하도록 요청 받은 사실을 언급하는 답변이므로 질문의 의도에 맞지 않는 오답.
(C) 이미 매진된 사실을 언급해 경기 입장권을 구입할 수 없는 상태임을 나타내고 있으므로 정답.

어휘 be asked to do ~하도록 요청 받다 sold out 매진된, 품절된

15. Is Mr. Miyazaki planning to retire soon?
 (A) The party was very fun.
 (B) No, I don't think so.
 (C) Almost 30 years.

미야자키 씨가 곧 은퇴하실 계획을 세우고 계시는 건가요?
 (A) 그 파티는 아주 재미있었어요.
 (B) 아뇨, 저는 그렇게 생각하지 않아요.
 (C) 거의 30년이요.

정답 (B)
해설 미야자키 씨가 곧 은퇴할 계획인지 확인하기 위해 묻는 일반 의문문입니다.
(A) 파티에 대한 자신의 의견을 알리는 답변이므로 질문의 의도에 맞지 않는 오답.
(B) 부정을 뜻하는 No와 함께 그렇게 생각하지 않는 말로 미야자키 씨가 곧 은퇴할 것 같지 않다는 의견을 나타내고 있으므로 정답.

(C) 시간을 언급하는 답변이므로 질문의 의도에 맞지 않는 오답.

어휘 plan to do ~할 계획이다 retire 은퇴하다, 퇴직하다 think so (앞선 말에 대해) 그런 것 같다, 그렇게 생각하다

16. Do we have enough coffee beans for the rest of the day?
(A) How about this afternoon?
(B) I'm sorry, we don't carry that brand.
(C) Yes, I double-checked to be safe.

우리가 오늘 나머지 하루 동안 쓸 커피 콩이 충분히 있나요?
(A) 오늘 오후는 어떠세요?
(B) 죄송하지만, 저희가 그 브랜드는 취급하지 않습니다.
(C) 네, 안전하게 하기 위해 제가 재확인했습니다.

정답 (C)
해설 나머지 하루 동안 쓸 커피 콩이 충분히 있는지 확인하기 위해 묻는 일반 의문문입니다.
(A) the day와 연관성 있게 들리는 this afternoon을 이용해 혼동을 유발하는 오답이며, 뭔가를 하기 위한 시점을 제안하는 말이므로 질문의 의도에 맞지 않는 오답.
(B) coffee와 연관성 있게 들리는 brand를 이용해 혼동을 유발하는 오답이며, 매장에서 직원이 고객에게 하는 말이므로 질문의 의도에 맞지 않는 오답.
(C) 긍정을 뜻하는 Yes와 함께 안전을 위해 재확인했다는 말로 커피 콩이 충분히 있음을 강조하고 있으므로 정답.

어휘 the rest of ~의 나머지 How about ~? ~는 어때요? carry (제품 등) ~을 취급하다 double-check ~을 재확인하다, ~을 이중으로 확인하다

17. Are you having any difficulties with the copier?
(A) She's very hardworking.
(B) No, everything's fine.
(C) I have a few extra copies if you'd like.

복사기에 대해 어떤 어려움이라도 있으신가요?
(A) 그녀는 아주 근면합니다.
(B) 아뇨, 모든 게 잘됩니다.
(C) 원하시다면 저한테 추가 복사본이 몇 장 있습니다.

정답 (B)
해설 복사기를 이용하는 데 어떤 어려움이라도 있는지 확인하기 위해 묻는 일반 의문문입니다.
(A) 대상을 알 수 없는 She가 근면하다는 사실을 언급하는 답변이므로 질문의 의도에 맞지 않는 오답.
(B) 부정을 뜻하는 No와 함께 모든 게 잘된다는 말로 전혀 어려움이 없다는 뜻을 나타내고 있으므로 정답.
(C) copier와 일부 발음이 유사한 copies를 이용해 혼동을 유발하는 답변이며, 복사기 이용상의 어려움과 관련된 답변이 아니므로 질문의 의도에 맞지 않는 오답.

어휘 copier 복사기 hardworking 근면한 a few 몇몇의 extra 추가의, 별도의, 여분의 if you'd like 원하시다면

18. Isn't there a pharmacy somewhere in this building?
(A) Yes, it's on the second floor.
(B) In the waiting lounge.
(C) I visited their farm recently.

이 건물 어딘가에 약국이 하나 있지 않나요?
(A) 네, 2층에 있습니다.
(B) 대기실에요.
(C) 제가 그분들의 농장을 최근에 방문했습니다.

정답 (A)
해설 현재 있는 건물 어딘가에 약국이 하나 있지 않은지 확인하기 위해 묻는 부정 의문문입니다.
(A) 긍정을 뜻하는 Yes와 함께 2층에 있다는 말로 약국의 위치를 알려 주고 있으므로 정답.
(B) 대기실에 있다는 말은 약국의 위치로 맞지 않으므로 오답.
(C) pharmacy와 일부 발음이 유사한 farm을 이용해 혼동을 유발하는 답변이며, 약국의 존재 여부와 관련 없는 말이므로 질문의 의도에 맞지 않는 오답.

어휘 pharmacy 약국 waiting lounge 대기실 farm 농장 recently 최근에

19. Did you apply for a monthly parking permit?
(A) No, there's a surplus.
(B) Yes, I should be getting it today.
(C) Make sure to check with our manager.

월간 주차 허가증을 신청하셨나요?
(A) 아뇨, 여분이 있습니다.
(B) 네, 오늘 받게 될 겁니다.
(C) 반드시 우리 부장님께 확인해 보세요.

정답 (B)
해설 월간 주차 허가증을 신청했는지 확인하기 위해 묻는 일반 의문문입니다.
(A) 부정을 뜻하는 No 뒤에 이어지는 말이 주차 허가증 신청 여부와 관련 없는 말이므로 질문의 의도에 맞지 않는 오답.
(B) 긍정을 뜻하는 Yes와 함께 a monthly parking permit을 it으로 지칭해 오늘 받을 것이라는 말로 신청 사실을 확인해 주고 있으므로 정답.
(C) 책임자에게 꼭 확인해 보라고 당부하는 말이므로 질문의 의도에 맞지 않는 오답.

어휘 apply for ~을 신청하다, ~에 지원하다 monthly 월간의, 달마다의 parking 주차(장) permit n. 허가증 v. ~을 허가하다 surplus n. 여분, 잉여 make sure to do 반드시 ~하도록 하다 check with ~에게 확인해 보다

20. Will you be visiting the manufacturing plant today?
(A) It should be watered daily.
(B) Sure, I know a good mechanic.
(C) No, I have to work on a presentation.

오늘 그 제조 공장을 방문하실 예정이신가요?
(A) 매일 물이 뿌려져야 합니다.
(B) 물론이죠, 제가 좋은 정비사를 한 분 알고 있어요.
(C) 아뇨, 저는 발표에 대한 작업을 해야 합니다.

정답 (C)
해설 오늘 제조 공장을 방문할 예정인지 확인하기 위해 묻는 일반 의문문입니다.
(A) plant의 다른 의미(식물)에서 연상 가능한 watered를 이용해 혼동을 유발하는 답변이며, 공장 방문 일정과 관련 없는 말이므로 질문의 의도에 맞지 않는 오답.
(B) 긍정을 뜻하는 Sure 뒤에 아는 정비사가 있음을 밝히는 말이 이어지고 있으므로 질문의 의도에 맞지 않는 오답.
(C) 부정을 뜻하는 No와 함께 발표 관련 작업을 해야 한다는 말로 오늘 방문할 수 없는 이유를 밝히고 있으므로 정답.

어휘 manufacturing 제조 plant n. 공장, 식물 v. ~을 심다 water v. ~에게 물을 주다 mechanic 정비사 work on ~에 대한 작업을 하다 presentation 발표(회)

21. Am I required to submit a copy of my passport?
(A) No, that won't be necessary.
(B) Please pass me that form.
(C) We offer both part- and full-time roles.

제 여권 사본을 한 부 제출해야 하나요?
(A) 아뇨, 그러실 필요 없을 겁니다.
(B) 그 양식을 제게 건네 주세요.
(C) 저희는 시간제와 정규직 역할을 모두 제공합니다.

정답 (A)
해설 여권 사본을 한 부 제출해야 하는지 확인하기 위해 묻는 일반 의문문입니다.
(A) 부정을 뜻하는 No와 함께 그럴 필요가 없을 것이라는 말로 제출하지 않아도 된다는 뜻을 나타내고 있으므로 정답.
(B) passport와 일부 발음이 유사한 pass를 이용해 혼동을 유발하는 답변이며, 여권 사본 제출 여부와 관련된 답변이 아니므로 질문의 의도에 맞지 않는 오답.
(C) 제공 가능한 일자리의 종류를 밝히는 답변이므로 질문의 의도에 맞지 않는 오답.

어휘 be required to do ~해야 하다, ~할 필요가 있다 submit ~을 제출하다 necessary 필요한, 필수의 pass A B: A에게 B를 건네 주다 form 양식, 서식 both A and B: A와 B 둘 모두

22. Do we have any empty tables outside on the patio?
(A) Yes, but only two.
(B) I didn't bring a jacket with me.
(C) Are you renovating your garden?

우리가 밖에 있는 테라스 구역에 어떤 빈 테이블이든 있나요?
(A) 네, 하지만 겨우 두 개뿐입니다.
(B) 저는 재킷을 챙겨 오지 않았어요.
(C) 정원을 보수하고 계시는 건가요?

정답 (A)
해설 테라스 구역에 빈 테이블이 있는지 확인하기 위해 묻는 일반 의문문입니다.
(A) 긍정을 나타내는 Yes와 함께 빈 테이블이 겨우 두 개뿐이라는 사실을 덧붙이고 있으므로 정답.
(B) 재킷을 챙겨 오지 않은 사실을 언급하는 답변으로 질문의 의도에 맞지 않는 오답.
(C) 정원을 보수하고 있는지 되묻고 있으므로 빈 테이블의 존재 여부와 관련 없는 오답.

어휘 patio 테라스 renovate ~을 보수하다, ~을 개조하다

23. Isn't a new water dispenser being installed this afternoon?
(A) Let's reorganize the window display.
(B) Sure, I'll have some tea.
(C) The technician is already here.

새 급수 장치가 오늘 오후에 설치될 것이지 않나요?
(A) 진열창을 다시 정리합시다.
(B) 물론이죠, 저는 차를 좀 마실 거예요.
(C) 그 기술자가 이미 이곳에 와 있어요.

정답 (C)
해설 새 급수 장치가 오늘 오후에 설치되지 않는지 확인하기 위해 묻는 부정 의문문입니다.
(A) dispenser와 일부 발음이 유사한 display를 이용해 혼동을 유발하는 답변이며, 새 급수 장치의 설치 여부와 관련 없는 오답.
(B) 긍정을 뜻하는 Sure 뒤에 차를 마실 것이라는 말이 이어지고 있으므로 새 급수 장치의 설치 여부와 관련 없는 오답.
(C) 기술자가 이미 와 있다는 말로 설치 작업이 진행 중이라는 뜻을 나타내고 있으므로 정답.

어휘 water dispenser 급수 장치 install ~을 설치하다 reorganize ~을 다시 정리하다, ~을 재구성하다 display n. 진열(품), 전시(품) v. ~을 진열하다, ~을 전시하다

24. Aren't we going to find another voice actor for the recording?
(A) Yes, that movie was a huge hit.

(B) We're already behind schedule.
(C) I know how to edit videos.

우리는 그 녹음 작업을 위해 또 다른 성우를 찾지 않을 건가요?
(A) 네, 그 영화는 엄청나게 흥행했어요.
(B) 우리는 이미 일정보다 뒤처진 상태입니다.
(C) 제가 동영상을 편집하는 방법을 알고 있습니다.

정답 (B)

해설 녹음 작업을 위해 또 다른 성우를 찾지 않는지 확인하기 위해 묻는 부정 의문문입니다.
   (A) actor를 통해 연상 가능한 단어 movie를 이용해서 혼동을 유발하는 답변이며, 성우를 찾는 일과 관련 없는 오답.
   (B) 이미 일정보다 뒤처진 상태라는 말로 다른 성우를 찾을 여유가 없다는 뜻을 나타내고 있으므로 정답.
   (C) recording에서 연상 가능한 videos를 이용해 혼동을 유발하는 답변이며, 성우를 찾는 일과 관련 없는 말이므로 질문의 의도에 맞지 않는 오답.

어휘 voice actor 성우 recording 녹음, 녹화 huge 엄청난 behind schedule 일정보다 뒤처진 how to do ~하는 방법 edit ~을 편집하다

25. Are there any cardboard boxes that need to be recycled?
(A) Here's my business card.
(B) For storing office supplies.
(C) There's some in the break room.

재활용되어야 하는 어떤 판지 상자든 있나요?
(A) 여기 제 명함입니다.
(B) 사무용품을 보관하기 위해서요.
(C) 휴게실에 좀 있습니다.

정답 (C)

해설 재활용되어야 하는 판지 상자가 있는지 확인하기 위해 묻는 일반 의문문입니다.
   (A) cardboard와 일부 발음이 유사한 business card를 이용해 혼동을 유발하는 답변이며, 판지 상자의 존재 여부와 관련된 답변이 아니므로 질문의 의도에 맞지 않는 오답.
   (B) boxes에서 연상 가능한 storing office supplies를 이용해 혼동을 유발하는 답변이며, 목적을 알리는 말이므로 판지 상자의 존재 여부와 관련 없는 오답.
   (C) 휴게실에 좀 있다는 말로 재활용되어야 하는 판지 상자가 있는 곳을 밝히는 말이므로 정답.

어휘 cardboard 판지 recycle ~을 재활용하다 business card 명함 store v. ~을 보관하다, ~을 저장하다 supplies 용품, 물품 break room 휴게실

DAY 5 제안·요청 의문문 / 선택 의문문

PRACTICE

1. (A) X (B) X (C) O
2. (A) X (B) O (C) X
3. (A) X (B) O (C) O
4. (A) O (B) X (C) O
5. (A) O (B) X (C) O

1. Would you like to upgrade to expedited shipping?
(A) How often do you use it?
(B) I would like to add more toppings.
(C) No, the standard option is enough.

빠른 배송으로 업그레이드하시겠습니까?
(A) 얼마나 자주 사용하시나요? [X]
(B) 토핑을 더 추가하고 싶습니다. [X]
(C) 아니요, 일반 배송 옵션이면 충분합니다. [O]

해설 빠른 배송으로 업그레이드 하는 것을 원하는지 묻는 제안 의문문입니다.
   (A) 얼마나 자주 사용하는지 묻는 의문사 의문문으로, 빠른 배송 업그레이드와 무관하므로 오답.
   (B) 빠른 배송 업그레이드와 무관한 토핑에 관한 답변이므로 오답.
   (C) 빠른 배송의 반대 개념인 일반 배송 옵션이 언급하였으며, 이는 제안에 대한 거절 답변이므로 정답.

어휘 expedited shipping 빠른 배송, 신속배송 often 자주 topping 토핑, (음식 위에 얹는) 고명 standard 일반적인, 보통의

2. Could you help me set up the updated expense reporting software?
(A) I've submitted mine already.
(B) I haven't received any instructions myself.
(C) The next update is scheduled in July.

새로운 지출 보고 소프트웨어를 설정하는 데 도와주실 수 있나요?
(A) 저는 이미 제 것을 제출했습니다. [X]
(B) 저는 아직 안내서를 받지 못했습니다. [O]
(C) 다음 업데이트는 7월로 예정되어 있습니다. [X]

해설 소프트웨어 설정하는 것을 도와줄 수 있는지 묻는 요청 의문문입니다.
   (A) 자신의 것이 무엇인지, 왜 제출하는지에 대해 알 수 없으므로 오답.
   (B) 안내서를 받지 못했다는 것은 지출 보고 소프트웨어를 설정하는 것을 도와줄 수 없다는 의미로, 요청에 대한 거절

의 표현으로 볼 수 있으므로 정답.
(C) 업데이트 시기에 대한 내용은 질문과 무관하므로 오답.

어휘 set up 설정하다, 설치하다 updated 업데이트 된 expense 지출, 경비 submit 제출하다 instruction 참안내서, 지시, 설명 be scheduled 예정되어 있다

3. How about ordering extra uniforms for the new employees?
   (A) In the supply room.
   (B) I already did.
   (C) Oh, that's a good idea.

신입 직원들을 위해 추가 유니폼을 주문하는 것이 어떠세요?
(A) 비품실에요. [X]
(B) 제가 이미 했어요. [O]
(C) 아, 좋은 생각입니다. [O]

해설 신입 직원들을 위해 추가 유니폼을 주문해야 하지 않는지 묻는 제안 의문문입니다.
(A) 장소 전치사구이므로 추가 유니폼 주문 여부와 관련 없는 오답.
(B) 자신이 이미 추가 유니폼을 주문했다고 말하는 정답.
(C) 상대방의 말에 동의를 나타내는 답변으로서, 추가 유니폼을 주문해야 한다는 의미이므로 정답.

어휘 order ~을 주문하다 extra 추가의, 여분의

4. Would you like to launch the marketing campaign in June or July?
   (A) I'm OK with either.
   (B) It was two weeks ago.
   (C) Can I let you know by next Monday?

마케팅 캠페인을 6월에 시작하시겠어요, 아니면 7월에 시작하시겠어요?
(A) 저는 어느 쪽이든 괜찮습니다. [O]
(B) 그건 2주 전 일이에요. [X]
(C) 다음 주 월요일까지 알려드려도 될까요? [O]

해설 마케팅 캠페인을 6월에 시작할지, 7월에 시작할지를 묻는 선택 의문문입니다.
(A) 6월과 7월 어느 것이든 괜찮다는 의미이므로 정답.
(B) 2주 전이라는 과거시점은 질문과 무관하므로 오답.
(C) 6월과 7월 중에 지금 선택하지 않고 다음주 월요일에 알려줘도 되는지 묻는 말이므로 정답.

어휘 launch 출시하다, 시작하다 campaign 캠페인, 조직적 활동 let A know A에게 알리다

5. Should we go to that jazz concert on Tuesday or Wednesday night?
   (A) I work both nights.
   (B) My parents enjoyed it so much.
   (C) Neither. I prefer Saturday.

화요일이나 수요일 밤에 그 재즈 콘서트에 갈까요?
(A) 저는 두 날 저녁에 다 근무해요. [O]
(B) 제 부모님은 그 공연을 정말 즐기셨어요. [X]
(C) 둘 다 안돼요. 저는 토요일이 더 좋아요. [O]

해설 재즈 콘서트에 화요일에 갈지, 수요일에 갈지를 묻는 선택 의문문입니다.
(A) 화요일과 수요일 저녁 모두 일을 한다는 의미로 거절의 답변이므로 정답.
(B) 부모님이 재즈 콘서트를 즐겼다는 의미로 질문과 무관하므로 오답.
(C) 화요일과 수요일 모두 거절하고 토요일이 더 좋다는 의미로 질문에 대한 제 3의 답변을 나타내므로 정답.

어휘 both 둘 다 neither 둘 다 아닌 prefer 선호하다

실전 TEST

1. (B)	2. (B)	3. (C)	4. (C)	5. (A)
6. (A)	7. (A)	8. (C)	9. (A)	10. (A)
11. (B)	12. (B)	13. (B)	14. (C)	15. (A)
16. (C)	17. (C)	18. (A)	19. (A)	20. (A)
21. (B)	22. (C)	23. (B)	24. (C)	25. (B)

1. Could you make me a copy of this sales report?
   (A) It hasn't been reported yet.
   (B) I'm afraid the copy machine is out of order.
   (C) OK, you can contact him by e-mail.

이 매출 보고서의 사본을 만들어 주시겠어요?
(A) 그건 아직 보고되지 않았습니다.
(B) 복사기가 고장 난 것 같습니다.
(C) 좋아요, 그에게 이메일로 연락하시면 됩니다.

정답 (B)

해설 매출 보고서의 사본을 만들어 줄 수 있는지 묻는 요청 의문문입니다.
(A) 질문에 포함된 report의 다른 의미(보고하다)를 활용해 혼동을 유발하는 답변으로, 상대방의 요청에 대한 반응으로 어울리지 않는 오답.
(B) 복사기가 고장 났다는 말로 상대방의 요청을 들어줄 수 없다는 뜻을 나타내는 답변이므로 정답.
(C) 수락을 나타내는 OK로 답변이 시작되고 있지만 정작 OK 뒤에 상대방의 요청과 관련 없는 말이 이어지고 있으므로 오답.

어휘 make A B: A에게 B를 만들어 주다 copy 사본, 한 부, 한 장 sales 매출, 영업, 판매(량) I'm afraid (that) (부정적인 일에 대해) ~한 것 같아요 out of order 고장 난 contact ~에게 연락하다

2. Would you like to come to the cooking demonstration?
(A) In the shopping mall.
(B) Who else is attending?
(C) Every Monday.

요리 시연회에 오시겠어요?
(A) 쇼핑몰에서요.
(B) 그 밖에 누가 또 참석하나요?
(C) 매주 월요일이요.

정답 (B)
해설 요리 시연회에 올 의향이 있는지 묻는 제안 의문문입니다.
(A) 장소 전치사구이므로 상대방의 제안에 대한 반응으로 어울리지 않는 오답.
(B) 시연회 행사 참석 여부를 결정하기 위한 일종의 조건으로서 누가 참석하는지 먼저 확인하기 위해 되묻는 질문이므로 정답.
(C) 반복 주기를 나타내는 말이므로 상대방의 제안에 대한 반응으로 어울리지 않는 오답.

어휘 Would you like to do? ~하시겠어요? demonstration 시연(회) Who else ~? 그 밖에 누가 ~? attend 참석하다

3. Would you rather book a room downtown or near the beach?
(A) How about at noon?
(B) Yes, I have one.
(C) Either is fine.

시내에 있는 방을 예약하시겠어요, 아니면 해변 근처에 있는 것으로 하시겠어요?
(A) 정오는 어떠세요?
(B) 네, 하나 있습니다.
(C) 둘 중 어느 것이든 좋습니다.

정답 (C)
해설 예약할 방의 위치와 관련해 시내 또는 해변 근처 중에 어느 곳이 나은지 묻는 선택 의문문입니다.
(A) 방의 위치가 아닌 시점과 관련해 되묻는 답변이므로 질문에 어울리지 않는 오답.
(B) 선택 의문문에 어울리지 않는 Yes로 답변하는 오답. 선택 의문문에 Yes나 no로 답변하는 선택지는 일부 소수의 경우를 제외하고 거의 오답입니다.
(C) 둘 중 아무 방이라도 좋다는 뜻을 나타내는 말이므로 정답. 선택 의문문에서 either를 이용해 '둘 중 어느 것이든 좋다'라는 의미를 나타내는 답변은 정답일 확률이 높습니다.

어휘 Would you rather ~? ~하시겠어요? book v. ~을 예약하다 downtown ad. 시내에 near ~ 근처에 How about ~? ~는 어때요? noon 정오 either 둘 중 어느 것이든

4. Do we have enough printing paper, or should we order more?
(A) I prefer the colored copy.
(B) That's a good deal.
(C) I'll check the storage room.

우리가 인쇄 용지를 충분히 갖고 있나요, 아니면 더 주문해야 하나요?
(A) 저는 컬러 복사를 선호합니다.
(B) 좋은 거래네요.
(C) 보관실을 확인해 볼게요.

정답 (C)
해설 인쇄 용지가 충분한지, 아니면 더 주문해야 하는지 묻는 선택 의문문입니다.
(A) 복사와 관련해 답변자 자신의 선호 사항을 말하는 답변이므로 용지 보유량과 관련 없는 오답.
(B) 좋은 거래라고 말하는 That이 지칭하는 대상을 알 수 없고, 용지 보유량과도 관련 없는 오답.
(C) 둘 중 하나를 선택하기 위한 조건으로서 용지 보유량을 확인할 수 있는 방법을 언급하는 답변이므로 정답.

어휘 order ~을 주문하다 prefer ~을 선호하다 deal 거래(조건), 거래 상품 storage 보관, 저장

5. Would you mind if I closed the window?
(A) No, I don't mind.
(B) It's a nice closet.
(C) The bakery opens at 9.

창문을 좀 닫아도 괜찮을까요?
(A) 그럼요, 괜찮습니다.
(B) 좋은 벽장이네요.
(C) 그 제과점은 9시에 문을 엽니다.

정답 (A)
해설 창문을 닫아도 괜찮은지 묻는 제안 의문문입니다.
(A) mind가 포함된 질문에 대해 긍정의 의미로 쓰이는 No와 함께 '괜찮다'는 말을 덧붙인 답변이므로 정답.
(B) 질문에 포함된 closed와 연관성 있게 들리는 closet을 활용해 혼동을 유발하는 답변으로, 상대방의 제안에 대한 반응으로 어울리지 않는 오답.
(C) 질문에 포함된 closed와 연관성 있게 들리는 opens를 활용해 혼동을 유발하는 답변으로, 상대방의 제안에 대한 반응으로 어울리지 않는 오답.

어휘 Would you mind if I ~? 제가 ~해도 괜찮을까요? I don't mind (mind로 묻는 질문에 대해) 괜찮습니다, 상관없습니다 closet 벽장

6. Are you going anywhere over the weekend or are you staying home?
(A) I'm going camping.

(B) We'll stay a little longer.
(C) Isn't it too boring?

주말 동안 어디라도 가시나요, 아니면 댁에 계시나요?
(A) 캠핑하러 갑니다.
(B) 우리는 조금 더 머무를 거예요.
(C) 너무 지루하지 않나요?

정답 (A)
해설 주말에 어디 가는지, 아니면 집에 있는지 묻는 선택 의문문입니다.
(A) 캠핑하러 간다는 말로 어딘가로 간다는 뜻을 나타내는 답변이므로 정답.
(B) 질문에 포함된 stay를 반복 사용해 혼동을 유발하는 답변으로, 주말 일정에 대한 선택과 관련 없는 추가 숙박 기간에 해당되는 말이므로 오답.
(C) 주말 일정에 대한 답변자 자신의 선택과 관련 없는 오답.

어휘 anywhere 어디든지 over ~ 동안에 걸쳐 a little 조금, 약간 boring 지루하게 만드는

7. Would you like a paper or a plastic bag for your purchases?
(A) Neither, actually.
(B) Extra bread, please.
(C) I wrote it on the paper.

구입 제품에 대해 종이 봉지가 좋으세요, 아니면 비닐 봉지가 좋으세요?
(A) 사실, 둘 다 원하지 않습니다.
(B) 빵 좀 추가해 주세요.
(C) 제가 그걸 종이에 써놨어요.

정답 (A)
해설 종이 봉지와 비닐 봉지 중에 어느 것이 더 좋은지 묻는 선택 의문문입니다.
(A) 두 가지 선택 대상을 모두 부정하는 Neither와 함께 둘 다 원하지 않는 뜻을 나타내는 답변이므로 정답.
(B) 봉지 선택과 관련 없는 빵 추가를 요청하는 말이므로 오답.
(C) 질문에 포함된 paper를 반복 사용해 혼동을 유발하는 답변으로, 봉지 선택과 관련 없는 말이므로 오답.

어휘 Would you like A or B? A가 좋으세요, 아니면 B가 좋으세요? purchase 구매(품) neither 둘 다 아니다 actually 실은, 사실은 extra 추가의, 여분의

8. Could you help me set up these tables on the first floor?
(A) Perhaps we can hold it indoors.
(B) At the back of the building.
(C) Sure, just give me a moment.

이 탁자들을 1층에 설치할 수 있게 도와 주실 수 있나요?
(A) 아마 우리는 실내에서 그걸 개최할 수 있을 겁니다.
(B) 건물 뒤편에서요.
(C) 그럼요, 잠깐만 시간을 주세요.

정답 (C)
해설 탁자 설치를 도와줄 수 있는지 묻는 요청 의문문입니다.
(A) 개최 가능성이 있는 장소를 말하는 답변으로, 상대방의 요청에 대한 반응으로 어울리지 않는 오답.
(B) 위치 전치사구이므로 상대방의 요청에 대한 반응으로 어울리지 않는 오답.
(C) 수락을 나타내는 Sure와 함께 잠깐 시간을 달라는 말로 잠시 후에 도울 수 있다고 알리는 답변이므로 정답.

어휘 help A do: A가 ~하는 것을 돕다 set up ~을 설치하다 perhaps 아마 hold ~을 개최하다, 열다 indoors 실내에서 at the back of ~ 뒤편에 give A a moment: A에게 잠깐 시간을 주다

9. Would you prefer a room with a balcony or one without?
(A) I have no preference.
(B) To see the river view.
(C) I appreciate it.

발코니가 있는 방이 좋으세요, 아니면 없는 것이 좋으세요?
(A) 따로 선호하는 건 없습니다.
(B) 강 풍경을 보기 위해서요.
(C) 그것에 대해 감사 드립니다.

정답 (A)
해설 발코니가 있는 방과 없는 방 중에 어느 것이 더 좋은지 묻는 선택 의문문입니다.
(A) 따로 선호하는 것이 없다는 말은 둘 중 어느 것이 선택되어도 상관없다는 의미를 나타내는 답변이므로 정답.
(B) 특정한 방을 선택한 경우에 그에 대한 이유로 언급할 수 있는 말이므로 질문과 관련 없는 오답.
(C) 감사 인사이므로 객실 선택과 관련 없는 오답.

어휘 Would you prefer ~? ~가 좋으세요?, ~로 하시겠어요? without ~ 없이, ~ 없는 preference 선호하는 것 view 풍경, 경관 appreciate ~에 대해 감사하다

10. Do you want to pick up the books or would you rather have them delivered?
(A) I'll stop by your store after 6 P.M.
(B) I just need four copies.
(C) Yes, she arrived last night.

책들을 직접 가져가시겠어요, 아니면 배송 받고 싶으신가요?
(A) 오후 6시 이후에 당신의 매장에 들를게요.
(B) 저는 4권만 필요합니다.
(C) 네, 그녀는 어젯밤에 도착했어요.

정답 (A)
해설 책들을 직접 가져갈지, 아니면 배송 받을 것인지 묻는 선택 의문문입니다.
(A) 매장에 들르겠다는 말로 직접 가져가겠다는 뜻을 나타내는 답변이므로 정답.
(B) 책 수령 방식이 아닌 필요 수량을 말하는 답변이므로 질문과 관련 없는 오답.
(C) 질문에 포함된 deliver와 연관성 있게 들리는 도착 시점을 말하는 답변으로, 책 수령 방식과 관련 없는 말이므로 오답.

어휘 pick up ~을 가져가다 would you rather ~? ~하시겠어요? have A p.p.: A가 ~되게 하다 stop by ~에 들르다 copy 한 권, 한 부, 한 장 arrive 도착하다

11. Would you like to join us for a coffee after work?
(A) No, I didn't receive a memo.
(B) Sure, that would be lovely.
(C) It starts in August.

퇴근 후에 저희와 함께 커피 한잔 하시겠어요?
(A) 아뇨, 저는 회람을 받지 못했어요.
(B) 그럼요, 아주 좋을 것 같아요.
(C) 그건 8월에 시작됩니다.

정답 (B)
해설 퇴근 후에 함께 커피를 마실 의향이 있는지 묻는 제안 의문문입니다.
(A) 거절을 나타내는 No 뒤에 이어지는 회람에 대한 말은 함께 커피를 마시는 일과 관련 없으므로 오답.
(B) 수락을 나타내는 Sure와 함께 상대방과 커피를 마시는 일을 that으로 지칭해 좋을 것 같다고 덧붙이는 답변이므로 정답.
(C) 질문에 포함된 work와 연관성 있게 들리는 작업 시작 시점을 말하는 답변으로, 상대방의 제안에 대한 반응으로 어울리지 않는 말이므로 오답.

어휘 Would you like to do? ~하시겠어요? join ~와 함께 하다, 합류하다 receive ~을 받다 lovely 아주 좋은, 아주 기쁜

12. Would you prefer to meet at lunch time, or another time?
(A) I'd prefer chicken.
(B) Whatever is convenient for you.
(C) It was delicious, thank you.

점심 시간에 만나는 게 좋으세요, 아니면 다른 시간이 좋으세요?
(A) 저는 닭고기로 할게요.
(B) 무엇이든 당신에게 편리한 것으로요.
(C) 맛있었어요, 고맙습니다.

정답 (B)
해설 만나는 시점과 관련해 점심 시간과 다른 시간 중에 어느 것이 더 좋은지 묻는 선택 의문문입니다.
(A) 질문에 포함된 lunch와 연관성 있게 들리는 chicken을 활용해 혼동을 유발하는 답변으로, 만나는 시점과 관련 없는 오답.
(B) '무엇이든 상대방에게 편리한 것'이라는 말은 상대방에게 선택권을 주겠다는 뜻이며, 어느 것이 선택되어도 상관없다는 의미이므로 정답.
(C) 질문에 포함된 lunch와 연관성 있게 들리는 delicious를 활용해 혼동을 유발하는 답변으로, 만나는 시점과 관련 없는 오답.

어휘 Would you prefer to do? ~하시겠어요? I'd prefer ~로 할게요, ~가 좋을 것 같아요 whatever 무엇이든 ~하는 것 convenient 편리한

13. Would you like me to make a summary of the test results?
(A) Alan Crawford is our research director.
(B) We still need to run more tests.
(C) It took about an hour.

제가 테스트 결과를 요약해 드릴까요?
(A) 앨런 크로포드 씨가 저희 연구소장님이십니다.
(B) 저희는 여전히 더 많은 테스트를 진행해야 합니다.
(C) 약 1시간 걸렸습니다.

정답 (B)
해설 테스트 결과를 요약해 줄지 묻는 제안 의문문입니다.
(A) test에서 연상 가능한 research를 이용해 혼동을 유발하는 답변이며, 연구소장의 이름을 밝히는 답변이므로 질문의 의도에 맞지 않는 오답.
(B) 여전히 더 많은 테스트를 진행해야 한다는 말로 지금 결과를 요약할 필요가 없다는 뜻을 나타내고 있으므로 정답.
(C) test에서 연상 가능한 소요 시간을 언급해 혼동을 유발하는 답변이며, 테스트 결과를 요약할지 제안하는 질문에 대한 답변으로 어울리지 않으므로 오답.

어휘 Would you like me to do? 제가 ~해 드릴까요? make a summary of ~을 요약하다, ~의 요약본을 만들다 result 결과(물)

14. Can you please help me set up the projector in the meeting room?
(A) At the back of the room.
(B) Who is the project lead?
(C) It's already ready to go.

회의실에 프로젝터를 설치하도록 저 좀 도와 주시겠어요?
(A) 그 방 뒤쪽에요.
(B) 누가 그 프로젝트 책임자인가요?
(C) 그건 이미 이용하실 준비가 되어 있습니다.

정답 (C)
해설 회의실에 프로젝터를 설치하도록 도와 달라고 묻는 요청 의문문입니다.
(A) Where 의문문에 어울리는 위치 표현이므로 오답이다.
(B) projector와 일부 발음이 유사한 project를 이용해 혼동을 유발하는 답변이며, 도움을 요청하는 질문에 대한 답변으로 어울리지 않으므로 오답.
(C) 이미 준비되어 있는 상태라는 말로 설치할 필요가 없다는 뜻을 나타내고 있으므로 정답

어휘 help A do: ~하도록 A를 돕다 set up ~을 설치하다, ~을 설정하다, ~을 준비하다 lead n. 책임자, 이끄는 사람 be ready to do ~할 준비가 되다

15. Could you remind Kevin to complete the online training?

(A) Oh, but he's off today.
(B) Yes, I agree completely.
(C) The train is almost here.

케빈 씨에게 온라인 교육을 완료하라고 상기시켜 주시겠어요?
(A) 아, 하지만 그분이 오늘 휴무입니다.
(B) 네, 전적으로 동의합니다.
(C) 기차가 거의 이곳에 도착했어요.

정답 (A)
해설 케빈 씨에게 온라인 교육을 완료하도록 상기시켜 달라고 요청하는 의문문입니다.
(A) Kevin을 he로 지칭해 오늘 휴무라는 말로 요청대로 상기시켜 줄 수 없다는 뜻을 나타내고 있으므로 정답.
(B) 요청에 대한 수락을 뜻하는 Yes 뒤에 동의를 나타내는 말이 이어지고 있으므로 질문의 의도에 맞지 않는 오답.
(C) training과 일부 발음이 유사한 train을 이용해 혼동을 유발하는 답변이며, 기차의 도착 상황과 관련된 말이므로 질문의 의도에 맞지 않는 오답.

어휘 remind A to do: A에게 ~하도록 상기시키다 complete ~을 완료하다 training 교육, 훈련 off 휴무인, 일을 쉬는 agree 동의하다, 합의하다 completely 전적으로, 완전히

16. Why don't we organize a team outing this summer?

(A) A local organization.
(B) No, I've never been hiking before.
(C) I'll start thinking of activities.

우리가 이번 여름에 팀 야유회를 마련하면 어떨까요?
(A) 한 지역 단체요.
(B) 아뇨, 저는 전에 하이킹하러 가 본 적이 전혀 없어요.
(C) 제가 활동들을 생각해 보기 시작할게요.

정답 (C)
해설 여름에 팀 야유회를 마련하면 어떨지 묻는 제안 의문문입니다.
(A) organize와 일부 발음이 유사한 organization을 이용해 혼동을 유발하는 답변이며, 야유회를 마련하자고 제안하는 질문에 대한 반응으로 어울리지 않는 오답.
(B) 제안에 대한 거절을 뜻하는 No 뒤에 답변자 자신의 경험을 언급하는 말이 이어지고 있으므로 질문의 의도에 맞지 않는 오답.
(C) 야유회에서 할 활동들을 생각해 보기 시작하겠다는 말로 야유회를 마련하는 것에 대해 동의를 나타내고 있으므로 정답.

어휘 Why don't we ~? ~하면 어떨까요?, ~할까요? outing 야유회 local 지역의, 현지의 organization 단체, 조직(체), 마련, 준비, 주최 activity 활동

17. Why don't we check out the construction site tomorrow?

(A) Which Web site did you use?
(B) Yes, they own the entire building.
(C) We'll need to get approval first.

내일 공사 현장을 확인해 보면 어떨까요?
(A) 어느 웹사이트를 이용하셨나요?
(B) 네, 그 사람들이 그 건물 전체를 소유하고 있어요.
(C) 우리는 먼저 승인을 받아야 할 겁니다.

정답 (C)
해설 내일 공사 현장을 확인해 보면 어떨지 묻는 제안 의문문입니다.
(A) site의 다른 의미(현장-웹 사이트)를 이용해 혼동을 유발하는 답변이며, 내일 공사 현장을 확인해 보자고 제안하는 질문에 대한 반응으로 어울리지 않는 오답.
(B) 제안에 대한 수락을 뜻하는 Yes 뒤에 대상을 알 수 없는 they의 건물 소유 상태를 알리는 말이 이어지고 있으므로 질문의 의도에 맞지 않는 오답.
(C) 먼저 승인을 받아야 할 것이라는 말로 공사 현장을 확인하러 가기 위한 조건을 언급하고 있으므로 정답.

어휘 Why don't we ~? ~하면 어떨까요?, ~할까요? site 현장, 부지, 장소, 웹 사이트 own ~을 소유하다 entire 전체의 will need to do ~해야 할 것이다 approval 승인

18. Would you like to go watch the movie premiere with us this Sunday?

(A) Didn't that pass already?
(B) A premium membership.
(C) I went to AGC Theaters.

이번 주 일요일에 저희랑 함께 그 영화 시사회를 보러 가시겠어요?
(A) 그 행사는 이미 지나가지 않았나요?
(B) 프리미엄 회원 자격이요.
(C) 저는 AGC 씨어터스에 갔어요.

정답 (A)
해설 일요일에 함께 영화 시사회를 보러 가자고 묻는 제안 의문문입니다.
(A) the movie premiere를 that으로 지칭해 이미 지나가지 않았는지 되묻는 것으로 갈 수 없는 행사가 아닌지 확인하고 있으므로 정답.
(B) premiere와 일부 발음이 유사한 premium을 이용해 혼동을 유발하는 답변이며, 회원 등급과 관련된 말이므로 질문의 의도에 맞지 않는 오답.
(C) movie에서 연상 가능한 Theaters를 언급해 혼동을 유발하는 답변이며, 답변자 자신이 과거에 간 영화관 이름을 언급하고 있으므로 질문의 의도에 맞지 않는 오답.

어휘 Would you like to do? ~하시겠어요?, ~하고 싶으세요? premiere 시사회, 초연, 첫 방송 pass 지나가다 premium 고급의, 상급의, 고가의

19. Would you please turn on the air conditioning?
   (A) Sure, no problem.
   (B) Next to the entryway.
   (C) The airline just called me back.

에어컨 좀 틀어 주시겠어요?
(A) 물론이죠, 문제 없습니다.
(B) 입구 옆에요.
(C) 그 항공사에서 방금 제게 다시 전화했어요.

정답 (A)
해설 에어컨 틀어 달라고 묻는 요청 의문문입니다.
(A) 요청에 대한 수락을 뜻하는 Sure 뒤에 문제 없다는 말을 덧붙여 에어컨을 틀어 주겠다는 뜻을 나타내고 있으므로 정답.
(B) Where 의문문에 어울리는 위치 표현이므로 요청 질문에 대한 반응으로 어울리지 않는 오답.
(C) air와 일부 발음이 유사한 airline을 이용해 혼동을 유발하는 답변이며, 항공사의 연락을 받은 사실을 알리는 말이므로 질문의 의도에 맞지 않는 오답.

어휘 turn on ~을 틀다, ~을 켜다 air conditioning 에어컨 next to ~ 옆에 entryway 입구 call A back: A에게 다시 전화하다

20. Can I help you find anything in our store?
   (A) No, thanks. I'm just browsing.
   (B) Yes, I found it very useful.
   (C) A coupon for 50 percent off.

저희 매장에서 무엇이든 찾으시는 걸 도와 드릴까요?
(A) 아뇨, 괜찮습니다. 그냥 둘러 보는 중이에요.
(B) 네, 저는 그게 아주 유용하다고 생각했어요.
(C) 50퍼센트 할인되는 쿠폰이요.

정답 (A)

해설 매장에서 무엇이든 찾는 것을 도와 줄지 묻는 제안 의문문입니다.
(A) 제안에 대한 거절을 뜻하는 No, thanks와 함께 그냥 둘러 보는 중이라는 말로 도움이 필요 없는 이유를 밝히고 있으므로 정답.
(B) find의 다른 의미(생각하다)를 이용해 혼동을 유발하는 답변이며, 특정 대상에 대한 자신의 의견을 밝히는 말이므로 질문의 의도에 맞지 않는 오답.
(C) store에서 연상 가능한 coupon과 50 percent off를 언급해 혼동을 유발하는 답변이며, 쿠폰의 할인 비율을 언급하고 있으므로 질문의 의도에 맞지 않는 오답.

어휘 help A do: ~하도록 A를 돕다 browse 둘러 보다 find A 형용사: A를 ~하다고 생각하다 off 할인하여

21. Would you like to grab lunch with the interns?
   (A) The usual catering company.
   (B) The expense report is due by the end of today.
   (C) Everyone had a great time.

인턴 직원들과 함께 점심 식사하시겠어요?
(A) 평소와 같은 출장 요리 제공 회사요.
(B) 지출 보고서가 오늘 일과 종료 시점까지 기한입니다.
(C) 모든 사람이 아주 즐거운 시간을 보냈어요

정답 (B)
해설 인턴 직원들과 함께 점심 식사하고 싶은지 묻는 제안 의문문입니다.
(A) lunch에서 연상 가능한 catering을 언급해 혼동을 유발하는 답변이며, 특정 출장 요리 업체를 언급하는 답변이므로 질문의 의도에 맞지 않는 오답.
(B) 지출 보고서가 오늘 일과 종료 시점까지 기한이라는 말로 해당 업무로 인해 인턴 직원들과 점심 식사할 시간이 없다는 뜻을 나타내고 있으므로 정답.
(C) 모든 사람이 과거에 아주 즐거운 시간을 보냈다는 사실을 밝히는 말이므로 제안에 대한 반응으로 어울리지 않는 오답.

어휘 grab lunch 점심 식사하다 usual 평소와 같은, 일반적인, 보통의 catering 출장 요리 제공(업) expense 지출(비용), 경비 due ~가 기한인 by (기한) ~까지

22. Should we go to the Thai restaurant or the Italian one?
   (A) An extra side of rice, please.
   (B) For a party of six.
   (C) They both sound delicious.

우리가 태국 레스토랑으로 가야 하나요, 아니면 이탈리아 레스토랑으로 가야 하나요?
(A) 추가로 쌀밥을 곁들여 주세요.
(B) 여섯 명의 일행을 위해서요.
(C) 둘 모두 맛있을 것 같아요.

정답 (C)
해설 태국 레스토랑과 이탈리아 레스토랑 중 어디로 가야 하는지 묻는 선택 의문문입니다.
(A) restaurant에서 연상 가능한 rice를 언급해 혼동을 유발하는 답변이며, 레스토랑이 아닌 음식 메뉴를 언급하고 있으므로 질문의 의도에 맞지 않는 오답.
(B) 인원수를 알리는 답변이므로 질문의 의도에 맞지 않는 오답.
(C) 둘 모두 맛있을 것 같다는 말로 질문에 제시된 두 레스토랑 중 어느 쪽이든 좋다는 의미를 나타내고 있으므로 정답.

어휘 extra 추가의, 별도의 side 곁들임 요리 party 일행, 사람들, 당사자 both 둘 모두 sound + 형용사: ~한 것 같다, ~하게 들리다

23. Would you like to give your speech in the morning or after lunchtime?
(A) I couldn't reach her.
(B) In the afternoon sounds good.
(C) Mike is a fantastic presenter.

오전에 연설하시고 싶으세요, 아니면 점심 시간 후에 하시고 싶으세요?
(A) 저는 그녀와 연락이 되지 않았어요.
(B) 오후에 하는 게 좋은 것 같아요.
(C) 마이크 씨는 환상적인 발표자입니다.

정답 (B)
해설 오전에 연설하고 싶은지, 아니면 점심 시간 후에 하고 싶은지 묻는 선택 의문문입니다.
(A) 대상을 알 수 없는 her와 연락이 되지 않은 사실을 밝히고 있으므로 질문의 의도에 맞지 않는 오답.
(B) 오후에 하는 게 좋은 것 같다는 말로 질문에 제시된 선택 사항 중 하나를 언급하고 있으므로 정답.
(C) 마이크 씨에 대한 의견을 말하는 답변이므로 질문의 의도에 맞지 않는 오답.

어휘 Would you like do? ~하고 싶으세요?, ~하시겠어요? reach ~에게 연락하다 sound + 형용사: ~한 것 같다, ~하게 들리다 presenter 발표자

24. Does Ms. Choi oversee the Kirkland branch or the Huntington branch?
(A) On weekday evenings.
(B) Sure, I can go with you.
(C) You should ask our boss.

최 씨가 커크랜드 지점을 총괄하고 있나요, 아니면 헌팅턴 지점을 총괄하고 있나요?
(A) 주중 저녁 시간마다요.
(B) 물론이죠, 당신과 함께 갈 수 있어요.
(C) 우리 사장님께 여쭤 보세요.

정답 (C)
해설 최 씨가 커크랜드 지점과 헌팅턴 지점 중 어느 곳을 총괄하고 있는지 묻는 선택 의문문입니다.
(A) When 의문과 어울리는 시점 표현이므로 오답.
(B) 함께 갈 수 있다는 뜻을 알리는 답변이므로 질문의 의도에 맞지 않는 오답.
(C) 사장님께 여쭤 보라는 말로 질문과 관련된 정보를 확인할 방법을 제시하고 있으므로 정답.

어휘 oversee ~을 총괄하다, ~을 감독하다 branch 지점, 지사

25. Are you interviewing the author on Thursday or Friday?
(A) Yes, they gave us a great review.
(B) I'm taking those days off.
(C) It was an attractive offer.

그 작가를 목요일에 인터뷰하시나요, 아니면 금요일에 하시나요?
(A) 네, 그분들께서 우리에게 훌륭한 평가를 제공해 주셨어요.
(B) 그 날들은 제가 휴무입니다.
(C) 매력적인 제안이었어요.

정답 (B)
해설 특정 작가를 목요일에 인터뷰하는지, 아니면 금요일에 하는지 묻는 선택 의문문입니다.
(A) 대상을 알 수 없는 they를 언급해 그 사람들이 훌륭한 평가를 제공한 사실을 언급하는 말이므로 질문의 의도에 맞지 않는 오답.
(B) 질문에 제시된 Thursday or Friday를 those days로 지칭해 두 요일에 휴무라는 말로 다른 날에 인터뷰한다는 뜻을 나타내고 있으므로 정답.
(C) 매력적인 제안이었다는 의견을 밝히는 답변이므로 질문의 의도에 맞지 않는 오답.

어휘 author 작가, 저자 review 평가, 후기, 검토 take A off: A만큼 휴무하다, A만큼 일을 쉬다 attractive 매력적인 offer n. 제안, 제공(되는 것), 특가 서비스 v. ~을 제안하다, ~을 제공하다

DAY 6 평서문 / 부가 의문문

PRACTICE

1. (A) X (B) O (C) O
2. (A) O (B) O (C) X
3. (A) X (B) O (C) O
4. (A) X (B) O (C) O
5. (A) O (B) O (C) X

1. I just heard that the concert has been postponed.
   (A) No, I haven't heard from him.
   (B) Until what day?
   (C) That's very disappointing!

   콘서트가 연기되었다는 얘기를 막 들었어요.
   (A) 아뇨, 그에게서 아무 말도 듣지 못했어요. [X]
   (B) 언제까지요? [O]
   (C) 아주 실망스럽네요! [O]

   해설 콘서트가 연기되었다는 사실을 말하는 평서문입니다.
   (A) heard를 반복 사용해 혼동을 유발하는 답변으로, 대상을 알 수 없는 him을 언급한 오답.
   (B) 언제까지인지 되묻는 것으로 연기된 콘서트의 재개 시점을 확인하려는 말이므로 정답.
   (C) 아주 실망스럽다는 말로 콘서트 연기 사실에 대한 감정을 드러낸 답변이므로 정답.

   어휘 postpone ~을 연기하다, 미루다 hear from ~에게 얘기를 듣다, 소식을 듣다 until (지속) ~까지 disappointing 실망시키는

2. Please make sure to upload the revised designs by the deadline.
   (A) The files are already in the shared folder.
   (B) Sure. I'm almost done.
   (C) Let me know if you need help.

   기한 내에 수정된 디자인 파일을 꼭 업로드해 주세요.
   (A) 파일은 이미 공유 폴더에 있습니다 [O].
   (B) 네, 거의 다 끝났어요. [O]
   (C) 도움이 필요하시면 말씀해 주세요. [X]

   해설 수정된 디자인 파일을 기한 내에 업로드하라는 평서문입니다.
   (A) 이미 공유 폴더에 있다는 내용으로 업로드를 완료했다는 답변이므로 정답.
   (B) 긍정의 대답과 함께 거의 다 완료했다는 답변이므로 정답.
   (C) 도움이 필요하면 알려달라는 내용은 질문과 무관하므로 오답.

   어휘 make sure to do 반드시 ~하다, 꼭 ~하다 revised 수정된 deadline 마감 기한 let A know: A에게 알리다

3. Ms. Bowen resigned today, didn't she?
   (A) Sure, I'll design it again.
   (B) That's what I heard.
   (C) Yes, this morning.

   보웬 씨가 오늘 사임하셨죠, 그렇지 않나요?
   (A) 그럼요, 그것을 다시 디자인할게요. [X]
   (B) 그렇다고 들었어요. [O]
   (C) 네, 오늘 아침에요. [O]

   해설 보웬 씨가 오늘 사임한 것인지 확인하기 위해 묻는 부가 의문문입니다.
   (A) 질문에 포함된 resigned와 발음이 일부 같은 design을 활용해 혼동을 유발하는 답변으로, 보웬 씨의 사임 여부와 관련 없는 오답.
   (B) 보웬 씨의 사임 사실을 That으로 지칭해 그것이 자신이 들은 정보임을 확인해 주는 답변이므로 정답.
   (C) 긍정을 나타내는 Yes와 함께 '오늘 아침'이라는 구체적인 시점을 덧붙이는 답변이므로 정답.

   어휘 resign 사임하다

4. This month's budget report hasn't been approved yet, has it?
   (A) I'll help with your proposal.
   (B) It needs to be discussed more.
   (C) The manager just received it.

   이번 달 예산 보고서가 아직 승인되지 않았죠, 그렇죠?
   (A) 제가 당신 제안서 작업을 도와 드릴게요. [X]
   (B) 그건 더 논의되어야 합니다. [O]
   (C) 부장님께서 막 그걸 받으셨어요. [O]

   해설 이번 달 예산 보고서가 아직 승인되지 않은 것이 맞는지 확인하기 위해 묻는 부가 의문문입니다.
   (A) 제안서 작업에 대해 도움을 주겠다고 제안하는 말이므로 예산 보고서 승인 여부와 관련 없는 오답.
   (B) budget report를 It으로 지칭해 그것이 더 논의되어야 한다는 말로 아직 승인되지 않았음을 나타내는 답변이므로 정답.
   (C) budget report를 It으로 지칭해 부서장이 그것을 막 받았다는 말로 아직 검토 전이어서 승인 여부를 알 수 없다는 뜻을 나타내는 답변이므로 정답.

   어휘 budget 예산 approve ~을 승인하다 help with ~하는 것을 돕다 proposal 제안(서) discuss ~을 논의하다, 이야기하다 receive ~을 받다

5. I'd like you to update the inventory list before closing.
   (A) Who should I send the updated list to once it's done?
   (B) Sure, I'll make sure it's done.
   (C) Yes, it's scheduled tomorrow.

저는 당신이 마감 전에 재고 목록을 업데이트해 주길 바랍니다.
(A) 완료되면 누구에게 업데이트된 목록을 보내면 될까요? [O]
(B) 알겠습니다. 꼭 해두겠습니다. [O]
(C) 네, 그건 내일로 예정되어 있어요. [X]

해설 마감 전에 재고 목록을 업데이트 해주길 바란다는 평서문입니다.
(A) 업데이트를 끝낸다면 업데이트된 목록을 누구에게 보낼지 묻는 의미로, 재고 목록 업데이트 작업을 완료한 상황에 대해 묻는 답변이므로 정답.
(B) 긍정의 답변 Sure과 꼭 완료하겠다는 답변이므로 정답.
(C) 긍정의 답변 Yes와 내일 예정되어 있다는 내용은 마감 전에 재고 목록을 업데이트 하라는 말과 무관하므로 오답.

어휘 I'd like you to do 당신이 ~하길 바랍니다 inventory list 재고 목록 once 일단 ~하면 make sure 반드시 ~하다 be scheduled 예정되어 있다

실전 TEST

1. (A)	2. (B)	3. (A)	4. (A)	5. (C)
6. (B)	7. (B)	8. (A)	9. (C)	10. (B)
11. (B)	12. (B)	13. (A)	14. (C)	15. (C)
16. (A)	17. (B)	18. (B)	19. (A)	20. (B)
21. (A)	22. (C)	23. (C)	24. (A)	25. (B)

1. Today is the perfect day for a golf tournament, isn't it?
   (A) Right, the weather is beautiful.
   (B) It will start soon.
   (C) Usually every weekend.

   오늘은 골프 경기를 개최하기에 완벽한 날이죠, 그렇지 않요?
   (A) 맞아요, 날씨가 정말 좋아요.
   (B) 곧 시작할 겁니다.
   (C) 보통 매주 주말이에요.

정답 (A)
해설 오늘이 골프 경기를 개최하기에 완벽한 날이라는 점에 대해 확인하기 위해 묻는 부가 의문문입니다.
(A) 동의를 나타내는 Right과 함께 골프 경기를 개최하기에 완벽한 날이라고 생각하는 이유를 덧붙이는 답변이므로 정답.
(B) 경기가 시작되는 대략적인 미래 시점을 말하는 답변이므로 골프 경기를 개최하기에 완벽한 날이라는 점에 대해 확인하기 위해 묻는 말과 관련 없는 오답.
(C) 반복 주기와 관련된 답변이므로 골프 경기를 개최하기에 완벽한 날이라는 점에 대해 확인하기 위해 묻는 말과 관련 없는 오답.

어휘 usually 보통, 일반적으로

2. You've met Mr. Hawkins before, haven't you?
   (A) Sometime next week.
   (B) No, I don't think so.
   (C) He's the most qualified.

   전에 호킨스 씨를 만나신 적이 있죠, 그렇지 않나요?
   (A) 다음 주 중으로요.
   (B) 아뇨, 그런 것 같지 않아요.
   (C) 그분이 가장 적격입니다.

정답 (B)
해설 전에 호킨스 씨를 만난 적이 있지 않은지 확인하기 위해 묻는 부가 의문문입니다.
(A) 과거의 경험을 묻는 것에 어울리지 않는 대략적인 미래 시점을 말하는 답변이므로 오답.
(B) 부정을 나타내는 No와 함께 그렇지 않은 것 같다는 말로 만난 적이 없음을 알리는 답변이므로 정답.
(C) Mr. Hawkins를 He로 지칭하고 있지만 만난 경험이 아닌 자격 여부를 말하고 있으므로 관련 없는 오답.

어휘 think so (앞서 언급된 것에 대해) 그렇게 생각하다 qualified 적격인, 자격을 갖춘

3. I'd like to make a reservation for a rental car.
   (A) Your name, please?
   (B) I thought I returned it.
   (C) Thanks, I'd love to.

   렌터카 예약을 하고 싶습니다.
   (A) 성함이 어떻게 되시죠?
   (B) 제가 그걸 반납한 것 같은데요.
   (C) 고마워요, 꼭 그러고 싶어요.

정답 (A)
해설 렌터카 예약을 하고 싶다는 요청 사항을 말하는 평서문입니다.
(A) 상대방의 이름을 묻는 것으로 렌터카 예약에 필요한 조건을 묻는 답변이므로 정답.
(B) 고객이 할 수 있는 말이므로 렌터카 예약 요청을 받는 사람, 즉 직원의 반응으로 어울리지 않는 오답.
(C) 감사의 인사와 함께 앞서 언급된 일에 대한 수락을 나타내는 말인데, 이는 렌터카 예약 요청을 받는 직원이 보일 수 있는 반응으로 어울리지 않으므로 오답.

어휘 make a reservation 예약하다 rental car 렌터카 return ~을 반납하다, 반품하다 I'd love to (제안에 대한 수락) 꼭 그러고 싶어요, 좋아요

4. I heard the project manager is going on a business trip to South Africa.
   (A) How long will it be?
   (B) A factory in Taiwan.
   (C) Yes, he came back from his trip.

프로젝트 매니저께서 남아프리카로 출장을 가신다고 들었어요.
(A) 그게 얼마나 오래 걸릴까요?
(B) 타이완에 있는 공장이요.
(C) 네, 그는 여행에서 돌아왔어요.

정답 (A)
해설 프로젝트 매니저가 남아프리카로 출장을 간다는 소식을 들은 사실을 말하는 평서문입니다.
   (A) 출장 가는 일을 it으로 지칭해 그 기간을 묻는 말이므로 정답.
   (B) project 및 business와 연관성 있게 들리는 factory를 활용해 혼동을 유발하는 답변으로, 매니저의 남아프리카 출장 소식과 관련 없는 타 지역 공장을 언급하는 말이므로 오답.
   (C) 제시 문장에 나온 trip을 그대로 이용한 함정으로 오답.
어휘 go on a business trip 출장을 가다

5. You're going to the music festival, aren't you?
   (A) There were many musicians.
   (B) Could you turn the volume down?
   (C) Only if I can get a day off.

음악 축제에 가시죠, 그렇지 않나요?
(A) 많은 음악가들이 있었습니다.
(B) 소리 좀 줄여 주시겠어요?
(C) 제가 하루 쉴 수 있는 경우에만요.

정답 (C)
해설 상대방이 음악 축제에 가지 않는지 확인하기 위해 묻는 부가 의문문입니다.
   (A) 답변자 자신의 음악 축제 참석 여부가 아닌 축제 공연자 규모와 관련된 답변이므로 오답.
   (B) music과 연관성 있게 들리는 turn the volume down을 활용해 혼동을 유발하는 답변으로, 답변자 자신의 음악 축제 참석 여부를 말하는 것이 아니므로 오답.
   (C) 음악 축제에 참석하는 데 필요한 조건을 언급하는 답변이므로 정답.
어휘 turn A down: A를 줄이다, 낮추다 get A off: A만큼 쉬다, 휴무이다

6. Sales of our new menu items have been lower than we expected.
   (A) At tomorrow's meeting.
   (B) I know. It's disappointing.
   (C) It's on sale now.

우리의 새 메뉴 품목 매출이 우리가 예상했던 것보다 낮았습니다.
(A) 내일 회의에서요.
(B) 알아요. 실망스럽네요.
(C) 그건 지금 세일 중입니다.

정답 (B)
해설 새 메뉴 품목의 매출이 예상했던 것보다 낮았다는 문제점을 말하는 평서문입니다.
   (A) 매출 저조와 관련 있을 법한 회의를 언급하지만 제시 문장의 내용에 어울리지 않는 반응이므로 오답.
   (B) 상대방이 말하는 매출 관련 정보를 알고 있다는 말과 함께 매출이 낮은 것에 대한 실망감을 나타내는 답변이므로 정답.
   (C) Sale의 다른 의미(할인 판매)를 활용해 혼동을 유발하는 답변으로, 제품이 할인 판매 중임을 말하고 있으므로 저조한 매출과 관련 없는 오답.
어휘 sales 매출, 판매(량), 영업, 할인 판매 item 품목, 제품 expect ~을 예상하다, 기대하다 disappointing 실망시키는 on sale 할인 판매 중인

7. That was the last session of the workshop, right?
   (A) Last semester.
   (B) No, there were a couple more.
   (C) Yes, I registered in advance.

그게 워크숍의 마지막 시간이었죠, 그렇죠?
(A) 마지막 학기요.
(B) 아뇨, 두 가지 더 있어요.
(C) 네, 저는 미리 등록했습니다.

정답 (B)
해설 워크숍의 특정 시간을 That으로 지칭해 그것이 워크숍의 마지막 시간이었는지 확인하기 위해 묻는 부가 의문문입니다.
   (A) last를 반복 사용해 혼동을 유발하는 답변으로, 워크숍 마지막 시간이었는지에 대해 확인하는 질문과 관련 없는 오답.
   (B) 부정을 나타내는 No와 함께 워크숍의 남아 있는 시간을 알려주는 말을 덧붙이고 있으므로 정답.
   (C) 긍정을 나타내는 Yes로 답변이 시작되고 있지만, 정작 Yes 뒤에 이어지는 말은 워크숍의 마지막 시간이었는지에 대한 확인과 관련 없는 오답.
어휘 session (특정 활동을 위한) 시간 semester 학기 register 등록하다 in advance 미리, 사전에

8. Rhonda has offered to organize the design workshop.
   (A) That will be a great help.
   (B) Place the sign by the front door.

(C) It's open to all team members.

론다 씨가 디자인 워크숍을 준비하겠다고 제안하셨어요.
(A) 그건 아주 큰 도움이 될 거예요.
(B) 표지판을 정문 옆에 놓아두세요.
(C) 모든 팀원에게 열려 있습니다.

정답 (A)

해설 론다 씨가 디자인 워크숍을 준비하겠다고 제안한 사실을 말하는 평서문입니다.
(A) 론다 씨가 디자인 워크숍을 준비하는 일을 That으로 지칭해 그렇게 하면 큰 도움이 될 것이라는 의견을 밝히는 답변이므로 정답.
(B) design과 일부 발음이 유사한 sign을 활용해 혼동을 유발하는 답변으로, 표지판을 놓아둘 위치를 알리는 말이므로 론다 씨의 디자인 워크숍 준비 제안과 관련 없는 오답.
(C) 행사 참가 대상자와 관련된 말이므로 론다 씨의 디자인 워크숍 준비 제안과 관련 없는 오답.

어휘 offer to do ~하겠다고 제안하다 organize ~을 준비하다, 조직하다 place v. ~을 놓다, 두다 sign 표지(판) by ~ 옆에 open to ~에게 열려 있는, 공개된

9. We should send travel receipts to the Personnel Department, shouldn't we?
(A) Thanks, we had an amazing trip.
(B) I'll give you a ride.
(C) No, to Cathy in Accounting.

우리가 인사부에 출장 영수증들을 보내야 하죠, 그렇지 않나요?
(A) 고맙습니다, 저희는 놀라운 여행을 했어요.
(B) 제가 차로 태워 드릴게요.
(C) 아뇨, 회계부의 캐시 씨에게요.

정답 (C)

해설 인사부에 출장 영수증들을 보내야 하지 않는지 확인하기 위해 묻는 부가 의문문입니다.
(A) travel과 연관성 있게 들리는 trip을 활용해 혼동을 유발하는 답변으로, 과거의 여행에 대한 의견을 말하고 있으므로 출장 영수증 제출 부서와 관련 없는 오답.
(B) travel과 연관성 있게 들리는 ride를 활용해 혼동을 유발하는 답변으로, 상대방에게 차로 태워 주겠다고 제안하고 있으므로 출장 영수증 제출 부서와 관련 없는 오답.
(C) 부정을 나타내는 No와 함께 영수증을 수령하는 실제 부서를 알려주는 것으로 상대방의 정보가 잘못되었음을 말하는 답변이므로 정답.

어휘 receipt 영수증 Personnel Department 인사부 amazing 놀라운 give A a ride: A를 차로 태워 주다 Accounting 회계부

10. We should check for any errors in these blueprints.
(A) Building designs, I think.
(B) Alex already reviewed them.
(C) Yes, for a new shopping mall.

우리는 이 설계도에 어떤 오류라도 있는지 확인해야 합니다.
(A) 건물 디자인인 것 같아요.
(B) 알렉스 씨가 이미 검토했습니다.
(C) 네, 새 쇼핑몰을 위한 것입니다.

정답 (B)

해설 설계도에 어떤 오류라도 있는지 확인해야 한다고 제안하는 평서문입니다.
(A) 어떤 대상에 대해 건물 디자인인 것 같다는 의견을 말하는 답변이므로, 설계도의 오류 확인 제안에 대한 반응으로 어울리지 않는 오답.
(B) 알렉스 씨가 이미 검토했다는 말로 오류가 있는지 확인할 필요가 없다는 뜻을 나타내는 답변이므로 정답.
(C) 동의를 나타내는 Yes로 답변이 시작되고 있지만, 정작 Yes 뒤에 이어지는 말은 설계도의 용도를 알리고 있으므로 설계도의 오류 확인 제안에 대한 반응으로 어울리지 않는 오답.

어휘 check for (문제 등) ~가 있는지 확인하다 blueprint 설계도, 청사진 review ~을 검토하다

11. I think Luis will be the top salesman this month, don't you?
(A) Well, it was on sale.
(B) Yeah, he's done very well.
(C) No, in Human Resources.

루이스 씨가 이번 달 최고의 영업 사원이 되실 것 같아요, 그렇게 생각하지 않으세요?
(A) 저, 그건 할인 판매 중이었습니다.
(B) 네, 그분이 아주 잘해 주셨어요.
(C) 아뇨, 인사부에서요.

정답 (B)

해설 루이스 씨가 이번 달 최고의 영업 사원이 될 것 같다는 의견을 말하고 동의를 구하는 부가 의문문입니다.
(A) salesman과 일부 발음이 같은 sale을 활용해 혼동을 유발하는 답변으로, 최고의 영업 사원이 될 것 같다는 의견과 관련 없는 할인 판매를 말하고 있으므로 오답.
(B) 긍정을 나타내는 Yeah와 함께 Luis를 he로 지칭해 최고의 영업 사원이 될 수 있는 이유를 덧붙인 답변이므로 정답.
(C) 질문의 내용과 관련 없는 부서명을 언급하는 오답.

어휘 salesman 영업 사원 on sale 할인 판매 중인 human resources 인사팀, 인사부

12. I don't know where my ID card is.
   (A) We'll find out tomorrow.
   (B) I saw it in the break room.
   (C) Let's get a rental car.

   제 신분증이 어디 있는지 모르겠어요.
   (A) 우리는 내일 알게 될 겁니다.
   (B) 그걸 휴게실에서 봤어요.
   (C) 렌터카를 한 대 빌립시다.

   정답 (B)
   해설 자신의 신분증이 어디 있는지 모르겠다는 문제점을 말하는 평서문입니다.
   (A) 상대방이 분실한 신분증과 관련해 답변자가 속한 여러 사람들(We)이 그것이 어디 있는지 알게 될 것이라는 말은 앞뒤가 맞지 않으므로 오답. 또한 find out은 '정보 등을 알아내다, 알게 되다'라는 의미로 사용되기 때문에 사물인 신분증이 어디 있는지 모르겠다는 문제점과 관련 없는 답변이므로 오답.
   (B) ID card를 it으로 지칭해 그것을 본 장소를 알려주는 답변이므로 정답.
   (C) card와 발음이 유사한 car를 활용해 혼동을 유발하는 답변으로, 렌터카를 빌리자고 제안하는 말이므로 신분증 분실과 관련 없는 오답.

   어휘 find out 알아내다, 알게 되다 break room 휴게실 rental car 렌터카

13. Mr. Ericsson called in sick just now.
   (A) Alright, I'll let our staff know.
   (B) At the pick-up counter.
   (C) I can call for a quote after this meeting.

   에릭슨 씨가 지금 막 전화로 병가를 냈습니다.
   (A) 알겠습니다, 제가 우리 직원들에게 알릴게요.
   (B) 물품 수령 카운터에서요.
   (C) 제가 이 회의 후에 비용 견적서를 요청할 수 있습니다.

   정답 (A)
   해설 에릭슨 씨가 지금 막 전화로 병가를 냈다는 문제를 알리는 평서문입니다.
   (A) 직원들에게 알리겠다는 말로 에릭슨 씨가 병가를 낸 것에 따라 필요한 조치를 언급하고 있으므로 정답.
   (B) Where 의문문에 어울리는 장소 표현이며, 에릭슨 씨가 병가를 낸 것에 따른 영향 등과 전혀 관련 없는 말이므로 오답.
   (C) call을 반복해 혼동을 유발하는 답변이며, 비용 견적서 요청 시점을 언급하는 말이므로 에릭슨 씨의 병가 사실을 알리는 평서문과 어울리지 않는 오답.

   어휘 call in sick 전화로 병가를 내다 let A know: A에게 알리다 pick-up (물품 등을) 가져가기, 가져오기, (사람을) 차에 태우러 가기 call for ~을 요청하다 quote 견적(서)

14. I'm planning to fill out the employee survey today.
   (A) By clicking the link in the e-mail.
   (B) We finished filling the order on time.
   (C) I already submitted mine.

   저는 오늘 직원 설문 조사지를 작성할 계획입니다.
   (A) 이메일에 있는 링크를 클릭해서요.
   (B) 우리는 제때 그 주문을 이행하는 것을 끝마쳤습니다.
   (C) 저는 이미 제 것을 제출했어요.

   정답 (C)
   해설 오늘 직원 설문 조사지를 작성할 계획임을 밝히는 평서문입니다.
   (A) How 의문문에 어울리는 접속 방법을 언급하는 답변이므로 직원 설문 조사지 작성 계획을 밝히는 평서문과 어울리지 않는 오답.
   (B) fill의 다른 의미(이행하다)를 이용해 혼동을 유발하는 답변이며, 제때 주문을 이행한 사실을 언급하고 있으므로 직원 설문 조사지 작성 계획을 밝히는 평서문과 어울리지 않는 오답.
   (C) 자신의 설문지를 mine(= my survey)으로 지칭해 이미 제출했다는 말로 직원 설문 조사를 위해 필요한 일을 완료한 상태임을 밝히고 있으므로 정답.

   어휘 plan to do ~할 계획이다 fill out ~을 작성하다 survey n. 설문 조사(지) v. ~에게 설문 조사하다 by (방법) ~해서, ~함으로써 fill ~을 이행하다, ~을 충족하다, ~을 채우다 on time 제때 submit ~을 제출하다

15. There's a twenty five-dollar charge for cancellations.
   (A) No, they didn't.
   (B) My hotel reservation.
   (C) Can I pay that through bank transfer?

   취소에 대해 25달러의 청구 요금이 있습니다.
   (A) 아뇨, 그들은 그러지 않았어요.
   (B) 제 호텔 예약이요.
   (C) 은행 계좌 이체를 통해 지불할 수 있나요?

   정답 (C)
   해설 취소에 대해 25달러의 청구 요금이 있다는 사실을 알리는 평서문입니다.
   (A) 어떤 사실을 확인하기 위해 묻는 일반 의문문에 어울리는 답변이므로 오답.
   (B) 답변자 자신의 호텔 예약을 언급하고 있으므로 취소 수수료 금액을 밝히는 평서문과 어울리지 않는 오답.
   (C) 25달러의 취소 수수료를 지불할 방법과 관련해 은행 계좌 이체가 가능한지 묻고 있으므로 정답.

   어휘 charge 청구 요금, 부과 요금 cancellation 취소 reservation 예약 bank transfer 은행 계좌 이체

16. I'd like to purchase a memory foam mattress.
   (A) No, in the furniture section.
   (B) What's your price range?
   (C) Here's some images of the Memorial Hall.

   메모리 폼 매트리스를 구입하고 싶습니다.
   (A) 아뇨, 가구 판매 구역에서요.
   (B) 원하시는 가격대가 어떻게 되시나요?
   (C) 여기 기념관을 담은 몇몇 이미지가 있습니다.

정답 (B)
해설 메모리 폼 매트리스 구입 의사를 밝히는 평서문입니다.
   (A) mattress에서 연상 가능한 furniture를 언급해 혼동을 유발하는 답변이며, 어떤 장소와 관련해 잘못 알고 있는 정보를 바로잡아 주는 말에 해당하므로 제품 구매 의사를 밝히는 평서문과 어울리지 않는 오답.
   (B) 원하는 가격대가 어떻게 되는지 묻는 것으로 제품 구입을 위한 조건을 확인하고 있으므로 정답.
   (C) memory와 일부 발음이 유사한 Memorial을 언급해 혼동을 유발하는 답변이며, 기념관 이미지를 언급하고 있으므로 제품 구매 의사를 밝히는 평서문과 어울리지 않는 오답.

어휘 would like to do ~하고 싶다 purchase v. ~을 구입하다 n. 구입(품) price range 가격대

17. Our director would like to see the latest drafts of the design.
   (A) Yes, the decision is final.
   (B) With or without our entire team?
   (C) It was delivered a few days late.

   저희 이사님께서 최신 디자인 안을 확인해 보고 싶어 하십니다.
   (A) 네, 그 결정은 최종입니다.
   (B) 우리 팀 전체와 함께요, 아니면 우리 팀 없이요?
   (C) 그건 며칠 늦게 전달되었습니다.

정답 (B)
해설 이사가 최신 디자인 안을 확인해 보고 싶어 한다는 사실을 알리는 평서문입니다.
   (A) 최종 결정이 내려졌음을 밝히는 말이므로 이사가 최신 디자인 안을 확인해 보고 싶어 한다고 알리는 평서문과 어울리지 않는 오답.
   (B) 팀 전체가 함께 하는 것인지, 아니면 그렇지 않은지 묻는 것으로 디자인 안을 확인해 보는 방식과 관련해 묻고 있으므로 정답.
   (C) 과거에 전달된 시점과 관련된 답변이므로 이사가 최신 디자인 안을 확인해 보고 싶어 한다고 알리는 평서문과 어울리지 않는 오답.

어휘 would like to do ~하고 싶다 latest 최신의, 최근의 draft 초안 decision 결정 entire 전체의

18. The customer didn't schedule a consultation, did she?
   (A) Yes, a big consulting firm.
   (B) No, unfortunately not.
   (C) The new desk calendars are useful.

   그 고객께서 상담 일정을 잡지 않으셨네요, 그렇죠?
   (A) 네, 대형 컨설팅 업체요.
   (B) 잡지 않으셨어요, 아쉽게도요.
   (C) 새 책상용 달력이 유용해요.

정답 (B)
해설 특정 고객이 상담 일정을 잡지 않았는지 확인하기 위해 묻는 부가 의문문입니다.
   (A) consultation과 일부 발음이 유사한 consulting을 이용해 혼동을 유발하는 답변이며, 컨설팅 업체를 한 곳 언급하고 있으므로 질문의 의도에 맞지 않는 오답.
   (B) 부정을 뜻하는 No와 함께 상담 일정을 잡지 않은 것에 대한 아쉬움을 나타내는 말이므로 정답.
   (C) schedule에서 연상 가능한 calendars를 이용해 혼동을 유발하는 답변이며, 책상용 달력의 유용함을 언급하고 있으므로 질문의 의도에 맞지 않는 오답.

어휘 schedule ~의 일정을 잡다 consultation 상담, 상의 firm 업체, 회사 unfortunately 아쉽게도, 안타깝게도 useful 유용한

19. All of the tax forms have been prepared, right?
   (A) Yes, they're on your desk.
   (B) The fax machine in the back.
   (C) OK, that should work for me.

   모든 세금 신고 양식이 준비되어 있는 거죠, 맞죠?
   (A) 네, 당신 책상에 있습니다.
   (B) 뒤쪽에 있는 팩스 기계요.
   (C) 좋습니다, 그럼 저는 괜찮을 겁니다.

정답 (A)
해설 모든 세금 신고 양식이 준비되어 있는지 확인하기 위해 묻는 부가 의문문입니다.
   (A) 긍정을 뜻하는 Yes와 함께 tax forms를 they로 지칭해 상대방 책상에 놓여 있다고 알리는 답변이므로 정답.
   (B) tax와 거의 발음이 유사한 fax를 이용해 혼동을 유발하는 답변이며, 특정 팩스 기계를 언급하고 있으므로 질문의 의도에 맞지 않는 오답.
   (C) 긍정을 뜻하는 OK 뒤에 어떤 조건 등이 괜찮다는 뜻을 나타내는 말이 이어지고 있으므로 질문의 의도에 맞지 않는 오답.

어휘 form 양식, 서식 prepare ~을 준비하다 in the back 뒤쪽에 work for (조건, 일정 등이) ~에게 괜찮다, ~에게 좋다

20. We should clear those chairs before the meeting, shouldn't we?

(A) Several seats are unavailable.
(B) I'd rather leave them just in case.
(C) Yes, our weekly meetings are on Fridays.

우리가 회의 시간 전에 저 의자들을 치워야 하죠, 그렇지 않아요?
(A) 몇 개의 좌석이 이용 불가능합니다.
(B) 만일에 대비해서 놔뒀으면 합니다.
(C) 네, 우리 주간 회의는 금요일마다 있어요.

정답 (B)
해설 회의 시간 전에 의자들을 치워야 하는지 확인하기 위해 묻는 부가 의문문입니다.
(A) chairs에서 연상 가능한 seats를 이용해 혼동을 유발하는 답변이며, 좌석 이용 가능성과 관련된 정보를 언급하고 있으므로 질문의 의도에 맞지 않는 오답.
(B) those chairs를 them으로 지칭해 만일에 대비해서 그냥 두기를 원한다는 말로 의자를 치우지 말자고 제안하는 의미를 나타내고 있으므로 정답.
(C) 긍정을 뜻하는 Yes 뒤에 주간 회의 일정을 알리는 말이 이어지고 있으므로 질문의 의도에 맞지 않는 오답.

어휘 clear ~을 치우다, ~을 청소하다 unavailable (사물) 이용할 수 없는, (사람) 시간이 없는 would rather do ~하고 싶다 leave ~을 놓아 두다, ~을 남겨 놓다 just in case 만일에 대비해서, 혹시 모르니까

21. The pieces at the art exhibition were nice, weren't they?

(A) I've been to better galleries.
(B) Sure, I'll take another piece.
(C) There must've been an error.

그 미술 전시회의 작품들이 훌륭했어요, 그렇지 않았나요?
(A) 저는 더 좋은 미술관에 가 본 적이 있어요.
(B) 물론이죠, 한 조각 더 가져갈게요.
(C) 오류가 있었던 게 틀림없어요.

정답 (A)
해설 특정 미술 전시회의 작품들이 훌륭했는지 확인하기 위해 묻는 부가 의문문입니다.
(A) 더 나은 미술관에 가 본 적이 있다는 말로 상대방이 언급하는 미술관의 작품들에 관한 의견에 동의하지 않는다는 뜻을 나타내고 있으므로 정답.
(B) piece의 다른 의미(조각)를 이용해 혼동을 유발하는 답변이며, 피자나 케이크 등을 한 조각 더 먹어야 할 때 사용하는 표현이므로 질문의 의도에 맞지 않는 오답.
(C) 오류가 존재했던 것으로 강하게 추측하는 말에 해당하므로 질문의 의도에 맞지 않는 오답.

어휘 piece (글, 그림, 음악 등) 작품 exhibition 전시(회) have been to ~에 가 본 적이 있다 must have p.p. ~했던 것이 틀림없다

22. Mr. Nguyen has a dentist appointment tomorrow morning, doesn't he?

(A) No, I don't have a reservation.
(B) This dental center opened just last month.
(C) Yes, I think you're right.

은구옌 씨가 내일 오전에 치과 예약이 있으시죠, 그렇지 않아요?
(A) 아뇨, 저는 예약하지 않았어요.
(B) 이 치과는 지난 달에 막 개원했어요.
(C) 네, 당신 말이 맞는 것 같아요.

정답 (C)
해설 은구옌 씨가 내일 오전에 치과 예약이 있는지 확인하기 위해 묻는 부가 의문문입니다.
(A) 은구옌 씨의 예약 여부가 아닌 답변자 자신의 예약과 관련해 언급하고 있으므로 오답.
(B) dentist과 일부 발음이 유사한 dental을 이용해 혼동을 유발하는 답변이며, 은구옌 씨의 예약 여부가 아닌 한 치과의 개원 시점을 언급하고 있으므로 질문의 의도에 맞지 않는 오답.
(C) 긍정을 뜻하는 Yes 뒤에 상대방의 말이 맞는 것 같다고 덧붙이는 것으로 은구옌 씨가 내일 오전에 치과 예약이 있음을 확인해 주고 있으므로 정답.

어휘 dentist 치과 의사 appointment 예약, 약속 reservation 예약 dental 치과의, 치아의

23. We didn't receive your cover letter with your application.

(A) The secretary position.
(B) I've been working here since March.
(C) I can send it again.

저희는 귀하의 자기 소개서를 지원서와 함께 받지 못했습니다.
(A) 비서 직책이요.
(B) 저는 3월부터 계속 이곳에 근무해 오고 있습니다.
(C) 다시 보내 드릴 수 있습니다.

정답 (C)
해설 상대방의 자기 소개서를 지원서와 함께 받지 못했다는 문제를 알리는 평서문입니다.
(A) application에서 연상 가능한 position을 언급해 혼동을 유발하는 답변이며, 특정 직책을 언급하는 말이므로 자기 소개서를 받지 못했다는 문제를 알리는 평서문과 어울리지 않는 오답.
(B) 답변자 자신의 근무 시작 시점을 밝히는 말이므로 자기 소개서를 받지 못했다는 문제를 알리는 평서문과 어울리지 않는 오답.

(C) cover letter를 it으로 지칭해 다시 보낼 수 있다는 말로 해결 방법을 언급하고 있으므로 정답.

어휘 receive ~을 받다 cover letter 자기 소개서 application 지원(서), 신청(서) secretary 비서 position 직책, 일자리 since + 과거 시점: ~부터, ~ 이후로

24. I can give you a paper copy of your bank statement.

(A) Oh, that would be great.
(B) During the first quarter.
(C) Why don't you pass them out later?

귀하의 은행 계좌 거래 내역서 사본을 제공해 드릴 수 있습니다.
(A) 아, 그러면 아주 좋을 겁니다.
(B) 1분기 동안에요.
(C) 나중에 그것들을 나눠 주시면 어떨까요?

정답 (A)

해설 상대방의 은행 계좌 거래 내역서 사본을 제공해 줄 수 있다고 제안하는 평서문입니다.
(A) 은행 계좌 거래 내역서 사본을 제공하는 일을 that으로 지칭해 그 조치에 대한 긍정적인 반응을 표현하는 답변이므로 정답.
(B) 특정 기간을 언급하는 말이므로 은행 계좌 거래 내역서 사본을 제공해 줄 수 있다는 사실을 알리는 평서문과 어울리지 않는 오답.
(C) give에서 연상 가능한 pass out을 이용해 혼동을 유발하는 답변이며, 은행 계좌 거래 내역서 사본을 제공해 줄 수 있다는 사실을 알리는 평서문과 어울리지 않는 오답.

어휘 bank statement 은행 계좌 거래 내역서 quarter 분기, 4분의 1 Why don't you ~? ~하면 어떨까요? pass A out: A를 나눠 주다

25. Ms. Franklin requested that we work on the Hamilton account.

(A) The construction work is still going on.
(B) Is there an urgent deadline?
(C) A licensed accountant.

프랭클린 씨께서 우리가 해밀턴 고객사에 대한 작업을 해야 한다고 요청하셨습니다.
(A) 그 공사 작업이 여전히 계속 진행되고 있습니다.
(B) 긴급한 마감 기한이 있나요?
(C) 자격증이 있는 회계사요.

정답 (B)

해설 프랭클린 씨의 요청 사항으로서 자신들이 해밀턴 고객사에 대한 작업을 하는 것을 언급하는 평서문입니다.
(A) work을 반복해 혼동을 유발하는 답변이며, 특정 공사의 진행 상황을 알리고 있으므로 해밀턴 고객사 작업에 대한 프랭클린 씨의 요청 사항을 언급하는 평서문과 어울리지 않는 오답.
(B) 긴급한 마감 기한이 있는지 묻는 것으로 해밀턴 고객사 작업에 대한 조건을 확인하는 말이므로 정답.
(C) account와 일부 발음이 유사한 accountant를 이용해 혼동을 유발하는 답변이며, 자격증이 있는 회계사를 언급하는 말이므로 해밀턴 고객사 작업에 대한 프랭클린 씨의 요청 사항을 언급하는 평서문과 어울리지 않는 오답.

어휘 request that ~라고 요청하다 work on ~에 대한 작업을 하다 account 고객사, 거래처, 계정, 계좌 go on 계속 진행되다 urgent 긴급한 deadline 마감 기한 licensed 자격증이 있는, 면허가 있는 accountant 회계사

PART 3

DAY 7 주제 / 목적 / 문제점 문제

PRACTICE

1. (A)   **2.** (C)

Question 1 refers to the following conversation.

> **M:** Good afternoon, this is Aaron from Classic Rentals. **I'm calling regarding the sound system we provided** for your event last weekend.
> **W:** Hi, Aaron. Everything went smoothly, though one microphone stopped working in the middle of the speech.
> **M:** I'm sorry to hear that. I'll make a note and follow up with the tech team.

남: 안녕하세요, 클래식 렌탈스의 아론입니다. 지난 주말 귀하의 행사에 제공해드린 음향 시스템과 관련해 전화 드립니다.
여: 안녕하세요, 아론. 모든 것이 잘 진행되었어요, 다만 연설 도중 마이크 하나가 작동을 멈추었어요.
남: 유감이네요. 메모를 해서 기술팀과 확인하도록 하겠습니다.

어휘 regarding ~에 관하여 provide 제공하다 go smoothly 순조롭게 진행되다, 잘 진행되다 stop working 작동을 멈추다 in the middle of ~ 중간에 speech 연설 make a note 메모하다 follow up 확인하다, 더 알아보다

1. 남자는 왜 전화하는가?
(A) 서비스에 대한 피드백을 얻기 위해
(B) 새로운 렌탈 패키지를 제안하기 위해
(C) 취소에 대해 사과하기 위해
(D) 일부 계약 조항을 업데이트하기 위해

정답 (A)
해설 남자는 지난 주말에 행사를 위해 제공한 음향 시스템에 관련하여 전화를 한다고(I'm calling regarding the sound system we provided for your event last weekend)라고 말하며 지난 행사에 제공된 서비스에 대해 언급하였습니다. 여자는 서비스가 대체로 잘 이루어졌다고 하며, 마이크 문제를 언급해 피드백을 제공하고 있으므로 정답은 (A)입니다.

어휘 collect 얻다, 모으다 propose 제안하다 apologize for ~에 대해 사과하다 cancellation 취소 contract term 계약 조항

Question 2 refers to the following conversation.

> **W:** Hi, Daniel. Have you finalized the seating chart for the awards ceremony?
> **M:** Yes, everything's been arranged and sent to the printer.
> **W:** **I'm afraid two guest names are misspelled.**
> **M:** Oh no. We'll need to fix that before the programs go out.

여: 안녕하세요, 다니엘. 시상식 좌석 배치는 마무리했나요?
남: 네, 모두 정리돼서 인쇄소로 보냈습니다.
여: 그런데 손님 이름 두 개가 잘못 표기된 것 같아요.
남: 안돼, 프로그램이 나오기 전에 고쳐야겠어요.

어휘 finalize 마무리하다 seating chart 좌석 배치도 awards ceremony 시상식 arrange 정리하다, 마련하다 misspell 철자를 잘못 쓰다, 철자가 틀리다 fix 고치다 program 프로그램, 진행 순서

2. 여자는 어떤 문제를 언급하는가?
(A) 시상식이 연기되었다.
(B) 차트가 분실되었다.
(C) 일부 이름들이 잘못되어 있다.
(D) 기기가 제대로 작동하지 않고 있다.

정답 (C)
해설 여자가 두 명의 손님 이름이 잘못 쓰였다(two guest names are misspelled)고 언급하였으므로 (C)가 정답입니다.

어휘 postpone 연기하다 missing 분실된 incorrect 정확하지 않은, 틀린 device 기기 malfunction 제대로 작동하지 않다

실전 TEST

1. (A)	**2.** (C)	**3.** (C)	**4.** (B)	**5.** (C)
6. (C)	**7.** (B)	**8.** (A)	**9.** (C)	**10.** (B)
11. (A)	**12.** (C)	**13.** (C)	**14.** (D)	**15.** (B)
16. (B)	**17.** (C)	**18.** (A)	**19.** (B)	**20.** (C)
21. (A)	**22.** (C)	**23.** (A)	**24.** (C)	

Questions 1-3 refer to the following conversation.

> W: Good afternoon, Terry. **1** I'm calling about the report you are writing. You've been adding up the sales of all our products, right?
> M: Yes, that's right. But, **2** some figures from our Chicago branch haven't been sent yet. As a result, I think the report might be delayed by a couple of days.
> W: That's not a problem. But **3** I'd appreciate it if you could e-mail the document to me as soon as it's finished. I'll need it for next week's management meeting.
> M: Sure. **3** I'll get it to you by Tuesday at the latest.

여: 안녕하세요, 테리 씨. 당신이 작성 중인 보고서와 관련해서 전화드립니다. 모든 우리 제품의 매출액을 더해 오고 계셨죠, 그렇죠?
남: 네, 맞습니다. 하지만, 우리 시카고 지사로부터 아직 몇몇 수치를 받지 못했어요. 결과적으로, 보고서가 며칠 지연될 수도 있을 것 같아요.
여: 그건 괜찮습니다. 하지만 완료되는 대로 저에게 이메일로 그 문서를 보내주실 수 있다면 감사하겠습니다. 다음 주에 있을 경영진 회의에 필요합니다.
남: 물론입니다. 늦어도 화요일까지는 보내 드리겠습니다.

어휘 add up ~을 더하다, 추가하다 sales 매출(액), 판매(량), 매출 figure 수치, 숫자 as a result 결과적으로 delay ~을 지연시키다, 지체하다 by (차이) ~만큼, (기한) ~까지 I'd appreciate it if you could ~: ~해 주실 수 있다면 감사하겠습니다 as soon as ~하는 대로, ~하자마자 get A to B: A를 B에게 주다 at the latest 늦어도

1. 화자들은 주로 무엇을 이야기하고 있는가?
   (A) 매출 보고서
   (B) 제품 출시
   (C) 매장 개장
   (D) 교육 시간

정답 (A)
해설 여자가 대화 초반부에 상대방이 작성 중인 보고서를 언급하면서 매출액을 더하는 일을 해오고 있었던 게 맞는지(I'm calling about the report you are writing. You've been adding up the sales of all our products ~) 물은 뒤로 그 보고서 작성과 관련된 내용으로 대화가 진행되고 있습니다. 따라서 매출 보고서가 대화 주제임을 알 수 있으므로 (A)가 정답입니다.

어휘 launch 출시, 공개 training 교육 session (특정 활동을 위한) 시간

2. 남자는 무슨 문제점을 언급하는가?
   (A) 일부 직원들이 지각을 한다.
   (B) 회의가 연기되었다.
   (C) 일부 정보가 보내지지 않았다.
   (D) 제품이 저조하게 판매되었다.

정답 (C)
해설 남자가 언급하는 문제점을 묻고 있으므로 남자의 말에서 부정적인 내용을 찾아야 합니다. 대화 중반부에 남자가 시카고 지사로부터 아직 수치를 받지 못한 사실을(some figures from our Chicago branch haven't been sent yet) 알리고 있는데, 이는 정보가 보내지지 않은 것에 해당되므로 (C)가 정답입니다.

어휘 postpone ~을 연기하다 poorly 저조하게, 형편 없이
Paraphrase some figures ⇒ Some information

3. 남자는 화요일까지 무엇을 하는 데 동의하는가?
   (A) 회의 마련하기
   (B) 소속 부서장과 이야기하기
   (C) 이메일로 문서 보내기
   (D) 고객 방문하기

정답 (C)
해설 대화 후반부에 여자가 문서를 이메일로 보내 달라고 요청하는 것에 대해(I'd appreciate it if you could e-mail the document to me ~) 남자가 화요일까지 보내겠다고(I'll get it to you by Tuesday ~) 답변하고 있으므로 (C)가 정답입니다.

어휘 agree to do ~하는 데 동의하다 arrange ~을 마련하다, 조치하다

Questions 4-6 refer to the following conversation.

> M: Hi, Joanna. **4** I'm considering buying a new house, and I heard you mention that you bought yours through Goldberg Realty. Were they helpful?
> W: Definitely. You should go to their offices and have a chat with **5** Jeff Goldberg. He has so much experience in finding the perfect homes for his clients, especially young families.
> M: That sounds perfect. Where is his agency?
> W: It's on the corner of Mitchum and Twelfth. But, **6** I would strongly recommend visiting the company's Web site first. There's a lot of useful information on it that will help you prepare for your meeting.

남: 안녕하세요, 조애나 씨. 제가 새 주택 구입을 고려 중인데, 당신이 골드버그 리얼티를 통해서 주택을 구입하셨다고 말씀하신 것을 들었어요. 도움이 되셨나요?
여: 당연하죠. 그곳 사무실에 가셔서 제프 골드버그 씨와 얘기해 보셔야 해요. 그분은 고객들을 위해 완벽한 주택을 찾으시는데 경험이 아주 많으신 분이에요. 특히 젊은 부부들을 위해서요.
남: 아주 좋은 것 같네요. 그분 업체가 어디에 있나요?
여: 미첨 가와 12번 가가 만나는 모퉁이에 있어요. 하지만, 먼저 그 회사 웹사이트를 방문해 보실 것을 적극 권해 드리고 싶어요. 그 사이트에 만남을 준비하는 데 도움이 될 유용한 정보가 많이 있어요.

어휘 consider -ing ~하는 것을 고려하다 hear A do: A가 ~하는 것을 듣다 mention that ~라고 말하다 through ~을 통해 helpful 도움이 되는, 유익한 Definitely (강한 긍정) 당연하죠, 틀림 없어요 experience in -ing ~하는 데 있어서의 경험 especially 특히 agency 업체, 대행사 on the corner of A and B: A와 B가 만나는 모퉁이에 strongly recommend -ing ~하는 것을 적극 권하다 useful 유용한 help A do: A가 ~하는 데 도움을 주다 prepare for ~을 준비하다, ~에 대비하다

4. 화자들은 무엇을 이야기하고 있는가?
 (A) 여행을 준비하는 것
 (B) 부동산을 구입하는 것
 (C) 건물을 개조하는 것
 (D) 행사를 계획하는 것

정답 (B)
해설 대화를 시작하면서 남자가 새 주택 구입을 고려하고 있다고(I'm considering buying a new house ~) 언급한 뒤로 그와 관련된 방법에 관해 이야기하는 것으로 대화가 진행되고 있으므로 (B)가 정답입니다.

어휘 organize ~을 준비하다, 조직하다 purchase ~을 구입하다 property 부동산, 건물 renovate ~을 개조하다, 보수하다

Paraphrase buying a new house
⇒ Purchasing a property

5. 골드버그 씨는 누구일 것 같은가?
 (A) 건축가
 (B) 인테리어 디자이너
 (C) 부동산 중개업자
 (D) 금융 상담 전문가

정답 (C)
해설 골드버그 씨의 이름이 언급되는 대화 중반부에, 여자가 골드버그 씨가 고객들을 위해 완벽한 주택을 찾아주는 일에 경험이 많다고(~ Jeff Goldberg. He has so much experience in finding the perfect homes for his clients ~) 말하고 있습니다. 이는 부동산 중개업자가 하는 일에 해당되므로 (C)가 정답입니다.

어휘 postpone ~을 연기하다 poorly 저조하게, 형편 없이

6. 여자는 남자에게 무엇을 하도록 권하는가?
 (A) 사무실에 전화하기
 (B) 이메일 주소 제공하기
 (C) 웹사이트 방문하기
 (D) 설문조사지 작성하기

정답 (C)
해설 여자가 권하는 일을 묻고 있으므로 여자의 대사 중 권고나 제안과 관련된 표현이 언급되는 부분에서 단서를 찾아야 합니다. 대화 마지막에 여자가 회사 웹사이트를 방문하는 것을 적극 권한다고(I would strongly recommend visiting the company's Web site first) 말하는 내용이 있으므로 이를 언급한 (C)가 정답입니다.

어휘 provide ~을 제공하다 fill out ~을 작성하다 survey 설문조사(지)

Questions 7-9 refer to the following conversation.

M: Hi, this is Jim Thorpe from the Bridges Corporation. I called you earlier this morning to place an order for 25 beverages for our lunchtime meeting. **7 I'd like to increase the order to 50 beverages.** Can you still bring those up to our offices by 1 P.M. today?
W: I'm sorry, sir, but **8 our coffee shop** is understaffed today, and lunchtime is our busiest period. If you require 50 beverages, we might not manage to deliver them until around 2.
M: Really? Well, maybe we can just take the 25 drinks, but **9 could you include 25 muffins as well?**
W: Yes, that will be possible. **9 I can warm those up quite quickly and bring them along with your drinks at 1 P.M.**

남: 안녕하세요, 저는 브릿지스 사의 짐 소프입니다. 아까 아침에 저희 점심 모임에 필요한 음료 25개를 주문하려고 전화했었습니다. 그 주문을 음료 50개로 늘리려고 합니다. 여전히 오늘 오후 1시까지 저희 사무실로 그것들을 가져다 주실 수 있으세요?
여: 고객님, 죄송하지만, 오늘 저희 커피 매장에 직원이 부족한데, 점심 시간이 가장 바쁜 시간대입니다. 50개의 음료가 필요하시다면, 2시쯤이나 되어야 간신히 배달해 드릴 수 있을 겁니다.
남: 정말요? 저, 아마 그냥 음료 25개로 해도 될 것 같은데, 그럼 머핀 25개도 포함해 주실 수 있으세요?

여: 네, 그렇게는 가능할 겁니다. 그 머핀들을 아주 빨리 데운 다음, 오후 1시에 음료와 함께 가져다 드릴 수 있습니다.

어휘 place an order for ~을 주문하다 beverage 음료 would like to do ~하고 싶다, ~하고자 하다 increase ~을 늘리다, 증가시키다 bring A up to B: A를 B로 가져오다, 가져가다 understaffed 직원이 부족한, 일손이 모자라는 require ~을 필요로 하다 not A until B: B나 되어야 A하다 manage to do 간신히 ~해내다 around ~쯤, 약, 대략 include ~을 포함하다 as well ~도, 또한 warm A up: A를 데우다 quite 꽤, 아주 along with ~와 함께

7. 남자는 왜 전화를 거는가?
(A) 식사 자리를 준비하기 위해
(B) 주문량을 늘리기 위해
(C) 정보를 요청하기 위해
(D) 일부 제품에 대해 불평하기 위해

정답 (B)
해설 대화 초반부에 화자가 자신을 소개한 뒤로 주문량을 음료 50개로 늘리고 싶다고(I'd like to increase the order to 50 beverages) 말하고 있습니다. 따라서 이를 언급한 (B)가 정답입니다.

어휘 organize ~을 준비하다, 조직하다 request ~을 요청하다 complain about ~에 대해 불평하다

8. 여자는 어디에서 일하고 있을 것 같은가?
(A) 커피숍에서
(B) 슈퍼마켓에서
(C) 공장에서
(D) 호텔에서

정답 (A)
해설 남자의 요청 사항을 들은 여자가 대화 중반부에 'our coffee shop'이라는 말로 자신이 근무하는 곳을 밝히고 있으므로 (A)가 정답입니다.

9. 여자는 자신이 무엇을 할 것이라고 말하는가?
(A) 자신의 상사와 이야기하기
(B) 대량 할인 제공하기
(C) 일부 음식품 준비하기
(D) 배달 시간 변경하기

정답 (C)
해설 대화 후반부에 남자가 머핀 25개를 포함해 달라고(could you include 25 muffins as well?) 요청하는 것에 대해 여자가 그것들을 데워서 음료와 함께 갖다 주겠다고(I can warm those up quite quickly and bring them ~) 대답하고 있습니다. 이는 음식을 준비하겠다는 뜻을 나타내는 것이므로 (C)가 정답입니다.

어휘 supervisor 상사, 책임자, 부서장 bulk 대량의 prepare ~을 준비하다

Paraphrase
· muffins ⇒ food items
· warm those up ⇒ Prepare

Questions 10-12 refer to the following conversation.

M: Good morning, Ms. Lang. I am here to fix the laptop that you called about. What exactly is the matter with it?
W: **10 The laptop keeps shutting down by itself every 10 minutes or so. 11 I need to finish working on a blueprint that I should send to a client within the hour.** Will you be able to fix the problem quickly?
M: I think I'll need to download and install some software and reboot the system. It'll probably take at least 30 minutes.
W: Oh, then I'm not going to have much time left for my work. **12 I'd better call my client and let him know about the delay.**

남: 안녕하세요, 랭 씨. 전화로 말씀하신 노트북 컴퓨터를 고치러 왔습니다. 정확히 무엇이 문제인가요?
여: 그 노트북 컴퓨터가 10분 정도마다 계속 저절로 멈춰요. 저는 1시간 내로 고객에게 보내 드려야 하는 설계도 작업을 마쳐야 합니다. 빨리 그 문제를 바로잡아 주실 수 있으세요?
남: 제 생각엔 몇몇 소프트웨어를 다운로드해 설치한 다음, 시스템을 재부팅해야 할 것 같습니다. 아마 최소 30분은 걸릴 겁니다.
여: 아, 그럼 제가 일할 시간이 많이 남지 않게 되는 거네요. 제가 고객에게 전화해서 이 지연 문제에 관해 말씀 드리는 게 낫겠어요.

어휘 fix ~을 고치다, 바로잡다 exactly 정확히 keep -ing 계속 ~하다 shut down (장치 등이) 멈추다, 정지하다 by itself (사물) 저절로 or so (숫자 표현 뒤에서) ~ 정도 work on ~에 대한 작업을 하다 within ~ 이내에 be able to do ~할 수 있다 install ~을 설치하다 reboot ~을 재부팅하다 take ~의 시간이 걸리다 at least 최소한, 적어도 have A p.p.: ~된 A가 있다, A를 ~되게 하다 had better + 동사원형: ~하는 게 낫다 let A know about B: A에게 B에 관해 알리다 delay 지연, 지체

10. 무엇이 문제점인가?
(A) 설계도가 분실되었다.
(B) 컴퓨터가 오작동하고 있다.

(C) 고객이 도착하지 않았다.
(D) 일부 정보가 잘못되었다.

정답 (B)

해설 문제점이 무엇인지 묻는 문제이므로 부정적인 정보를 찾아야 합니다. 대화 초반부에 여자가 노트북 컴퓨터가 10분 정도마다 계속 저절로 멈춘다는(The laptop keeps shutting down by itself every 10 minutes or so) 말로 문제점을 밝히고 있는데, 이는 노트북 컴퓨터가 오작동하는 상황을 말하는 것이므로 (B)가 정답입니다.

어휘 misplace ~을 분실하다, ~을 둔 곳을 잊다 malfunction 오작동하다 arrive 도착하다 wrong 잘못된, 엉뚱한

11. 여자는 왜 우려하는가?
(A) 일부 업무를 끝마쳐야 한다.
(B) 회의에 늦은 상태이다.
(C) 문서를 저장하는 것을 잊었다.
(D) 몇몇 연락처를 잃어버렸다.

정답 (A)

해설 대화 중반부에 여자가 1시간 내로 고객에게 보낼 설계도 작업을 마쳐야 한다는(I need to finish working on a blueprint that I should send to a client within the hour) 말로 우려 사항을 언급하고 있습니다. 이는 업무를 끝내는 것을 의미하므로 (A)가 정답입니다.

Paraphrase finish working on a blueprint
⇒ finish some work

12. 여자는 자신이 곧이어 무엇을 할 것이라고 말하는가?
(A) 회의 취소하기
(B) 자신의 작업물 백업하기
(C) 고객에게 연락하기
(D) 일부 소프트웨어 설치하기

정답 (C)

해설 대화 마지막 부분에 여자가 고객에게 전화를 걸어 지연 문제를 알리겠다고(I'd better call my client and let him know about the delay) 언급하고 있습니다. 이는 고객에게 연락하는 일을 말하는 것이므로 (C)가 정답입니다.

어휘 cancel ~을 취소하다 contact ~에게 연락하다

Paraphrase call ⇒ Contact

Questions 13-15 refer to the following conversation.

M: Jennifer, **13** how about we hold our annual spring music festival at this park?
W: Oh! I've been there before. It's very nice.
M: Really? But there may be one problem. **14** It has a small parking lot, so it can't really accommodate large crowds.
W: That's true. Maybe we should keep looking for other venues.
M: **15** I'll ask our project manager for her opinion first. She might have some good ideas.

남: 제니퍼 씨, 이 공원에서 우리 연례 봄철 음악 축제를 개최하면 어떨까요?
여: 아! 전에 그곳에 가 본 적 있어요. 아주 멋진 곳이에요.
남: 그래요? 하지만 한 가지 문제가 있을 수도 있어요. 주차장이 작기 때문에, 실제로 대규모 인파를 수용할 수 없어요.
여: 맞아요. 아마 우리가 계속 다른 개최 장소를 찾아 봐야 할 거예요.
남: 제가 우리 프로젝트 매니저께 의견을 먼저 여쭤 볼게요. 몇몇 좋은 아이디어를 갖고 계실지도 몰라요.

어휘 how about + 주어 + 동사?: ~하면 어떨까요? hold ~을 개최하다 annual 연례적인, 해마다의 parking lot 주차장 accommodate ~을 수용하다 crowd 인파, 군중 keep -ing 계속 ~하다 look for ~을 찾다 venue 개최 장소, 행사장 ask A for B: A에게 B를 요청하다

13. 화자들은 무엇을 하려 하고 있는가?
(A) 모금 행사를 마련하는 일
(B) 예약하는 일
(C) 행사 개최 장소를 선택하는 일
(D) 몇몇 참가자를 모집하는 일

정답 (C)

해설 남자가 대화를 시작하면서 특정 공원에서 연례 봄철 음악 축제를 개최하면 어떨지(how about we hold our annual spring music festival at this park?) 물은 뒤로 그 장소의 장단점에 관해 이야기하고 있으므로 (C)가 정답입니다.

어휘 organize ~을 마련하다, ~을 조직하다 fundraiser 모금 행사, 기금 마련 행사 make a reservation 예약하다 select ~을 선택하다 recruit ~을 모집하다 participant 참가자

Paraphrase annual spring music festival / this park
⇒ an event venue

14. 남자는 어떤 문제를 언급하는가?
(A) 일부 장비가 너무 크다.
(B) 일부 서류가 제출되지 않았다.
(C) 배송이 지연되었다.
(D) 주차 공간이 좁다.

정답 (D)

해설 남자가 대화 중반부에 주차장이 작기 때문에 대규모 인파를 수용할 수 없다는(It has a small parking lot, so it can't really accommodate large crowds) 문제를 언급하고 있

으므로 (D)가 정답입니다.

어휘 equipment 장비 paperwork 서류 (작업) submit ~을 제출하다 shipment 배송(품) delay ~을 지연시키다

Paraphrase a small parking lot
⇒ A parking area is small

15. 남자는 무엇을 할 것이라고 말하는가?
(A) 설문 조사지를 만드는 일
(B) 매니저와 이야기하는 일
(C) 허가증을 신청하는 일
(D) 몇몇 예상 비용 정보를 보내는 일

정답 (B)

해설 대화 후반부에 남자가 프로젝트 매니저에게 의견을 먼저 물어보겠다고(I'll ask our project manager for her opinion first) 말하고 있으므로 (B)가 정답입니다.

어휘 create ~을 만들어 내다 survey 설문 조사(지) apply for ~을 신청하다, ~에 지원하다 permit n. 허가증 v. ~을 허가하다 projection 예상, 예측

Paraphrase ask our project manager for her opinion first ⇒ Talk to a manager

Questions 16-18 refer to the following conversation.

> M: Hello, I'm Kamal calling from Printing Palace. I have an update regarding 17 **your order for 100 custom tote bags**. Unfortunately, 16 **our inventory of bags is running low due to a supply issue**.
> W: Oh, that's not good. Our grand opening is next week.
> M: 17 **We offer customizable backpacks as well**, but they are more expensive. To make up for the inconvenience, I can provide you with a $50 discount off your total.
> W: OK. 18 **I'd like to see a sample of the new design in person though.** May I drop by tomorrow morning to confirm it before it goes into production?

남: 안녕하세요, 저는 프린팅 팰리스에서 전화 드리는 카말입니다. 귀하의 맞춤 제작 토트백 100개에 대한 주문과 관련된 최신 소식이 있습니다. 유감스럽게도, 저희 가방 재고가 공급 문제로 인해 부족해지고 있습니다.
여: 아, 그럼 안되는데요. 저희 개장식이 다음 주에 있거든요.
남: 저희가 맞춤 제작 가능한 배낭도 제공하고 있는데, 이 제품들은 더 비쌉니다. 불편함에 대해 보상해 드리기 위해, 귀하의 총액에서 50달러 할인 서비스를 제공해 드릴 수 있습니다.

여: 알겠습니다. 하지만 새 디자인의 샘플을 직접 확인해 보고 싶습니다. 생산에 돌입하기 전에 확정할 수 있도록 내일 오전에 잠깐 들러도 될까요?

어휘 regarding ~와 관련된, ~에 관한 order 주문(품) custom 맞춤 제작하는, 주문 제작하는 unfortunately 유감스럽게도, 안타깝게도 inventory 재고 (목록), 재고 조사 run low 부족해지다, 다 떨어져가다 due to ~로 인해, ~때문에 supply 공급(품) issue 문제, 사안 customizable 맞춤 제작 가능한 as well ~도, 또한 make up for ~에 대해 보상하다, ~을 만회하다 inconvenience 불편함 provide A with B: A에게 B를 제공하다 total 총액, 총합 would like to do ~하고 싶다 in person 직접 (가서) though (문장 끝이나 중간에서) 하지만 drop by 잠깐 들르다 confirm ~을 확정하다, ~을 확인해 주다 go into ~에 돌입하다 production 생산, 제작

16. 대화는 무엇에 관한 것인가?
(A) 예산 제한
(B) 공급 부족
(C) 디자인 오류
(D) 고장 난 기계

정답 (B)

해설 남자가 대화 초반부에 자사의 가방 재고가 공급 문제로 인해 부족해지고 있다는(our inventory of bags is running low due to a supply issue) 문제를 언급한 뒤로 그 해결 방법에 관해 이야기하고 있으므로 (B)가 정답입니다.

어휘 budget 예산 limit n. 제한, 한정 v. ~을 제한하다 shortage 부족 broken 고장 난, 망가진, 깨진 machinery 기계(류)

Paraphrase running low due to a supply issue
⇒ A supply shortage

17. 남자는 무엇을 제안하는가?
(A) 대여 쿠폰
(B) 품질 보증 연장
(C) 대체 제품
(D) 무료 배송

정답 (C)

해설 남자가 여자의 주문품인 토트백과(your order for 100 custom tote bags) 관련된 문제를 언급한 다음, 대화 중반부에 맞춤 제작 가능한 배낭도 제공한다는(We offer customizable backpacks as well) 말로 대안을 제시하고 있습니다. 이는 다른 제품으로 대체하도록 제안하는 것이므로 (C)가 정답입니다.

어휘 rental 대여, 임대 voucher 쿠폰, 상품권 extend

~을 연장하다, ~을 확장하다 warranty 품질 보증(서) alternative a. 대체의, 대안의 n. 대안 free 무료의

Paraphrase custom tote bags / offer customizable backpacks as well
⇒ An alternative product

18. 여자는 왜 업체를 방문하기를 요청하는가?
(A) 새로운 디자인을 보기 위해
(B) 할인 쿠폰을 받기 위해
(C) 몇몇 재료를 갖다 주기 위해
(D) 몇몇 사진을 촬영하기 위해

정답 (A)
해설 여자가 대화 후반부에 새 디자인의 샘플을 직접 확인해 보고 싶다고(I'd like to see a sample of the new design in person though) 밝히면서 내일 오전에 잠깐 들러도 되는지 묻고 있으므로 (A)가 정답입니다.

어휘 ask to do ~하기를 요청하다 view ~을 보다 receive ~을 받다 drop off (사물) ~을 갖다 놓다, ~을 내려 놓다, (사람) ~을 차에서 내려 주다 material 재료, 자재, 물품

Paraphrase
· drop by ⇒ visit
· see a sample of the new design ⇒ view a new design

Questions 19-21 refer to the following conversation.

W: **19** **My car here is a classic model from the 1970s.** It still runs, but the engine is very loud, and some parts are outdated. **19** **I'm not sure if I should replace the engine or try to fix it.**
M: I actually specialize in restoring vintage cars to their original condition. Plus, **20** **I own a catalog of other vehicles from that time period, which I can use as a reference to fix yours accordingly.**
W: Really? I'm just worried about whether the original engine is fuel efficient. **21** **I wonder if maintaining it will end up costing a lot.**

여: 여기 제 자동차는 1970년대에 나온 클래식 모델입니다. 여전히 운행되긴 하지만, 엔진이 소리가 아주 크고, 몇몇 부품들은 낡은 상태입니다. 엔진을 교체하거나 고치려 해 봐야 하는 건지 잘 모르겠습니다.
남: 저는 사실 구형 자동차들을 원래의 상태로 복원하는 일을 전문으로 하고 있습니다. 게다가, 그 시대에 나온 다른 자동차들의 카탈로그도 소유하고 있어서, 그것을 참고 자료로 이용해 그에 따라 고쳐 드릴 수 있습니다.

여: 정말인가요? 저는 그저 원래의 엔진이 연비가 좋은 건지에 대해 걱정됩니다. 그걸 유지 관리하는 게 결국 많은 비용이 들게 될지 궁금해요.

어휘 run 운행되다, 작동되다 part 부품 outdated 낡은, 구식의 replace ~을 교체하다, ~을 대체하다 try to do ~하려 하다 fix ~을 고치다 specialize in ~을 전문으로 하다 restore ~을 복원하다, ~을 회복시키다 vintage 구형의, 골동품의 original 애초의, 원래의, 원본의 own ~을 소유하다 vehicle 차량 reference 참고 자료, 추천서, 추천인 accordingly 그에 따라 whether ~인지 (아닌지) fuel efficient 연비가 좋은 wonder if ~인지 궁금하다 maintain ~을 유지 관리하다 end up -ing 결국 ~하게 되다 cost ~의 비용이 들다

19. 대화가 주로 무엇에 관한 것인가?
(A) 업체를 매입하는 일
(B) 차량을 수리하는 일
(C) 작업 구역을 개조하는 일
(D) 일부 소프트웨어를 업데이트하는 일

정답 (B)
해설 여자가 대화를 시작하면서 자신의 자동차 모델을 소개하고(My car here is a classic model from the 1970s), 그 엔진을 교체하거나 고치는 문제에 대해 확신하지 못하고 있음을(I'm not sure if I should replace the engine or try to fix it) 밝힌 뒤로, 그 차량 수리 문제에 관해 이야기하고 있으므로 (B)가 정답입니다.

어휘 purchase ~을 매입하다, ~을 구입하다 repair ~을 수리하다 renovate ~을 개조하다, ~을 보수하다

Paraphrase My car / fix it ⇒ Repairing a vehicle

20. 남자는 어떻게 프로젝트에 접근할 수 있을 거라고 말하는가?
(A) 추가 직원을 고용해서
(B) 온라인으로 조사해서
(C) 카탈로그를 참고해서
(D) 컨퍼런스에 참석해서

정답 (C)
해설 대화 중반부에 남자가 당시에 나온 다른 자동차들의 카탈로그도 소유하고 있어서 그것을 참고 자료로 이용해 고칠 수 있다고(I own a catalog of other vehicles from that time period, which I can use as a reference to fix yours accordingly) 밝히고 있으므로 (C)가 정답입니다.

어휘 approach ~에 접근하다 hire ~을 고용하다 refer to ~을 참고하다 attend ~에 참석하다

Paraphrase a catalog / use as a reference
⇒ referring to a catalog

21. 여자는 무엇에 대해 걱정하는가?
(A) 유지 관리 비용
(B) 공사 소음
(C) 다가오는 마감 기한
(D) 규정상의 변화

정답 (A)

해설 여자가 대화 후반부에 유지 관리하는 게 결국 많은 비용이 들게 될지 궁금하다는(I wonder if maintaining it will end up costing a lot) 말로 우려를 표하고 있으므로 (A)가 정답입니다.

어휘 maintenance 유지 관리, 정비 upcoming 다가오는, 곧 있을 deadline 마감 기한 regulation 규정, 규제

Paraphrase maintaining it / costing a lot
⇒ Maintenance costs

Questions 22-24 refer to the following conversation.

M: I've noticed a lot of nearby office workers ordering **22 our sandwiches** for lunch. Maybe we should start offering a delivery option.
W: We'd need to prepare big batches quickly and have drivers to send out the deliveries. **23 The problem is, we're already short of staff during lunch hours.**
M: True. But if we want to expand our business, we have to make some changes. **24 I'll talk to a delivery company** and see what they would charge.

남: 근처의 많은 사무 직원들이 점심 식사로 우리 샌드위치를 주문하고 있다는 걸 알게 되었어요. 아마 우리가 배달 선택권을 제공하기 시작해야 할 거예요.
여: 우리는 많은 제공량을 신속히 준비해야 하고 배달 제품을 보내기 위해 기사들이 있어야 할 겁니다. 문제는, 우리가 이미 점심 시간 중에 직원이 부족하다는 겁니다.
남: 맞아요. 하지만 우리가 사업을 확장하기를 원한다면, 몇 가지 변화를 줘야 합니다. 제가 배달 회사 한 곳과 이야기해서 비용을 얼마나 청구할지 확인해 볼게요.

어휘 notice A -ing: A가 ~하는 것을 알게 되다 nearby 근처의 order v. ~을 주문하다 n. 주문(품) offer ~을 제공하다 prepare ~을 준비하다 batch (한 번의) 제공량, 한 회분 send out ~을 보내다, ~을 발송하다 be short of ~이 부족하다 expand ~을 확장하다, ~을 확대하다 make a change 변화를 주다, 변경하다 charge ~을 청구하다

22. 화자들은 어떤 제품을 만드는가?
(A) 햄버거
(B) 사무용품
(C) 샌드위치
(D) 점심 도시락

정답 (C)

해설 남자가 대화 초반부에 소속 업체의 제품을 our sandwiches로 지칭하고 있으므로 (C)가 정답입니다.

어휘 supplies 용품, 물품

23. 여자는 어떤 문제를 언급하는가?
(A) 직원들이 충분히 있지 않다.
(B) 한 제품에 대한 수요가 높지 않다.
(C) 매장이 온라인 주문을 받을 수 없다.
(D) 주방 공간이 너무 좁다.

정답 (A)

해설 대화 중반부에 여자가 문제가 있음을 언급하면서 이미 점심 시간 중에 직원이 부족하다는(The problem is, we're already short of staff during lunch hours) 사실을 밝히고 있으므로 (A)가 정답입니다.

어휘 demand n. 수요, 요구 v. ~을 요구하다 take an order 주문을 받다

Paraphrase we're already short of staff
⇒ There are not enough staff members

24. 남자는 누구에게 연락할 것인가?
(A) 포장 회사
(B) 모바일 앱 개발업체
(C) 배달 서비스 제공업체
(D) 마케팅 전문가

정답 (C)

해설 남자가 대화 후반부에 배달 회사 한 곳과 이야기해서(I'll talk to a delivery company) 비용 관련 정보를 알아보겠다고 밝히고 있으므로 (C)가 정답입니다.

어휘 packaging 포장(재) developer 개발업체, 개발업자 specialist 전문가

Paraphrase a delivery company
⇒ A delivery service provider

DAY 8 장소 / 신분 / 직업 문제

PRACTICE

1. (B)　　　　**2.** (C)

Question 1 refers to the following conversation.

> W: Hello, I received a notice in the mail about an overdue fee for my book loan. My name is Jennifer Kim.
> M: Hm, yes. It says in our system that you owe $5 for overdue books. Would you like to pay that now?
> W: Do you take credit cards?
> M: We usually accept either cash or credit, but our card reader is malfunctioning. Let me see if it's working again.

> 여: 안녕하세요. 도서 대출 연체료에 대한 우편 통지를 받았어요. 제 이름은 제니퍼 킴입니다.
> 남: 음, 네. 저희 시스템에 따르면 연체된 도서에 대해 5달러를 내셔야 해요. 지금 결제하시겠어요?
> 여: 신용카드도 받으시나요?
> 남: 보통은 현금이나 신용카드 모두 받지만, 지금 카드 단말기가 제대로 작동하지 않네요. 다시 작동하는지 확인해볼게요.

어휘 notice 공지, 통지　overdue 기한이 지난, 연체의　fee 요금　loan 대출, 대여　owe 지불해야 하다, 빚지다　pay 지불하다　accept 받아들이다, 수락하다　cash 현금　malfunction 제대로 작동하지 않다

1. 남자는 누구일 것 같은가?
　(A) 은행 직원
　(B) 도서관 사서
　(C) 계산원
　(D) 판매원

정답 (B)

해설 남자는 여자에게 연체된 책에 대해 5달러를 내야 한다고(you owe $5 for overdue books) 언급하였으므로 책을 대여해 주는 곳은 도서관이며, 연체료를 받는 사람은 도서관 사서임을 알 수 있습니다. 따라서 정답은 (B)입니다.

Question 2 refers to the following conversation.

> M: Hi. I'm calling because my startup needs legal assistance in drafting partnership agreements. Now that we've secured initial funding, I want to ensure our contracts are rock-solid.
> W: Thank you for contacting our law firm. Could you tell me more about your business and its legal needs?
> M: Sure. My company develops renewable energy solutions, and we want to write up clear and strategic terms with our partners.
> W: In that case, I recommend you speak with Erica Sanders. She has extensive experience in corporate law, especially for startups like yours.

> 남: 안녕하세요. 제 스타트업이 파트너십 계약서를 작성하는 데 법률 지원이 필요해서 전화드렸습니다. 이제 저희는 초기 자금을 확보해서, 저는 계약을 철저히 준비하고 싶습니다.
> 여: 저희 로펌에 연락주셔서 감사합니다. 귀사의 사업과 법률적 필요에 대해 좀 더 자세히 말씀해주시겠어요?
> 남: 네. 저희 회사는 재생에너지 솔루션을 개발하고 있으며, 저희는 파트너들과 명확하고 전략적인 계약 조항을 작성하고 싶습니다.
> 여: 그렇다면 에리카 샌더스 씨와 상담하시는 것을 권합니다. 그녀는 기업법 분야에서 폭넓은 경험을 갖고 있으며, 특히 귀하의 회사같은 스타트업 전문입니다.

어휘 startup 스타트업, 신규 업체　legal 법률의, 합법의　assistance 지원, 도움, 진행 순서　draft (문서 등을) 작성하다, 쓰다　partnership 동업 관계, 파트너십　agreement 계약, 합의　now that ~이니까, ~해서　secure 확보하다　initial 초기의　funding 자금　ensure 보장하다, 확실히 하다　contract 계약　rock-solid 확실한, 절대로 깨지지 않는　contact 연락하다　renewable 재생가능한　clear 명확한, 분명한　strategic 전략적인　extensive 광범위한, 폭넓은　corporate 기업의, 법인의

2. 에리카 샌더스는 누구인가?
　(A) 후원자
　(B) 펀드 매니저
　(C) 변호사
　(D) 재무 상담가

정답 (C)

해설 여자가 법률 회사에 전화해준 것에 감사하다고 말한 것으로 여자가 일하는 곳이 법률 회사임을 알 수 있습니다. 그리고 에리카 샌더스에 대해서 기업법 분야에 폭넓은 경험을 가지고 있다고(She has extensive experience in corporate law) 언급한 것으로 보아 에리카 샌더스가 변호사임을 알 수 있습

니다. 따라서 정답은 (C)입니다.

실전 TEST

1. (C)	2. (C)	3. (D)	4. (D)	5. (B)
6. (C)	7. (D)	8. (C)	9. (C)	10. (B)
11. (B)	12. (D)	13. (D)	14. (A)	15. (D)
16. (C)	17. (B)	18. (A)	19. (C)	20. (A)
21. (C)	22. (B)	23. (C)	24. (B)	

Questions 1-3 refer to the following conversation.

M: What do you think about this 8-day cruise in the Mediterranean Sea? **1** **The package includes a first-class cabin. It's great for people who want to relax and enjoy some beautiful views of the sea.**

W: It seems nice, but I would prefer to travel by train, and **2** **I'd like to join some guided tours in European cities. Do you have any packages that include these?**

M: Sure, we have several packages that include that kind of thing. **3** **Just let me grab some brochures for you.**

남: 지중해에서 8일을 보내는 이 여객선 여행은 어떠세요? 이 패키지 여행에는 1등급 객실이 포함되어 있습니다. 휴식을 취하고 아름다운 바다 경치를 즐기고 싶어하는 분들에게 아주 좋습니다.

여: 아주 좋은 것 같기는 하지만, 저는 기차로 여행하고 싶고, 여러 유럽 도시에서 가이드를 동반한 투어에 함께 하고 싶어요. 이런 서비스를 포함한 패키지 여행이 있나요?

남: 물론이죠, 그런 종류의 것을 포함한 여러 패키지 여행이 있습니다. 제가 몇몇 안내 책자를 가져다 드리겠습니다.

어휘 cruise 여객선 package 패키지 여행 include ~을 포함하다 cabin 객실, 선실 relax 휴식하다 view 경치, 풍경 would prefer to do ~하고 싶다 guided 가이드가 동반된 several 여럿의, 몇몇의 grab ~을 가져오다 brochure 안내 책자

1. 화자들은 어디에 있을 것 같은가?
   (A) 호텔
   (B) 선박
   (C) 여행사
   (D) 기차역

정답 (C)

해설 대화의 시작 부분에서 남자가 특정 패키지 여행을 제안하면서 그 여행의 특징을 간단히 언급하고 있는데(The package includes a first-class cabin. It's great for people who want to relax and enjoy some beautiful views of the sea), 이는 여행사 직원이 고객에게 할 수 있는 말에 해당하므로 (C)가 정답입니다.

2. 여자는 무엇에 관해 묻는가?
   (A) 입장료
   (B) 객실 요금
   (C) 도시 투어
   (D) 수상 스포츠

정답 (C)

해설 대화 중반부에서 여자가 유럽 도시에서 가이드를 동반한 투어를 하고 싶다고 알리면서 그런 투어가 있는지(I'd like to join some guided tours in European cities. Do you have any packages that include these?) 묻고 있습니다. 따라서 (C)가 정답입니다.

어휘 admission 입장 (허가) fee 요금, 수수료 rate (이용) 요금

3. 남자는 곧이어 무엇을 할 것 같은가?
   (A) 여행 일정 변경하기
   (B) 호텔 지배인에게 전화하기
   (C) 여자를 위해 표 출력하기
   (D) 여자에게 안내 책자 제공하기

정답 (D)

해설 대화 맨 마지막에 남자가 안내 책자를 갖다 주겠다고(Just let me grab some brochures for you) 말하고 있으므로 이를 언급한 (D)가 정답입니다.

어휘 itinerary 일정(표)

Paraphrase let me grab some brochures
⇒ Give the woman a brochure

Questions 4-6 refer to the following conversation.

M: Ms. Barton, **4** **I've just completed the inspection of your factory.** You'll be pleased to hear that the factory meets all of the safety regulations.

W: That's great news. **5** **I was worried that some of the older manufacturing machines might be in poor condition.** And, I can't really afford to replace those right now.

M: Don't worry. All of the manufacturing and packaging machines were closely inspected, and they are still functioning perfectly. **6 I'll be preparing my report tomorrow, and I'll e-mail a copy of it to you before the end of the week.**

남: 바튼 씨, 제가 막 당신의 공장에 대한 점검 작업을 완료했습니다. 이 공장이 모든 안전 규정을 충족한다는 말을 들으시면 기쁘실 겁니다.
여: 아주 좋은 소식이네요. 저는 몇몇 오래된 제조 기계들이 좋지 않은 상태일 수 있어서 걱정했어요. 그리고, 지금 바로 그것들을 교체할 여유가 많이 있지 않거든요.
남: 걱정하지 마세요. 모든 제조 기계와 포장 기계가 면밀히 점검되었으며, 여전히 완벽히 작동하고 있습니다. 제가 내일 보고서를 준비할 예정인데, 이번 주말 전까지 그 사본을 이메일로 보내 드리겠습니다.

어휘 complete ~을 완료하다 inspection 점검, 검사 be pleased to do ~해서 기쁘다 meet (조건 등) ~을 충족하다 regulation 규정, 규제 be worried that ~해서 걱정하다 manufacturing 제조 poor 좋지 못한, 형편없는 can't afford to do ~할 여유가 없다 replace ~을 교체하다, 대체하다 packaging 포장(재) closely 면밀히 inspect ~을 점검하다, 검사하다 function v. 작동하다, 기능하다 prepare ~을 준비하다

4. 남자는 누구일 것 같은가?
   (A) 공장 관리 책임자
   (B) 수리 기사
   (C) 채용 담당자
   (D) 안전 점검관

정답 (D)

해설 남자가 대화 시작 부분에 상대방 공장에 대한 점검을 완료했다고(I've just completed the inspection of your factory) 말하고 있습니다. 이는 안전 점검을 실시하는 사람이 할 수 있는 말이므로 (D)가 정답입니다.

어휘 repair 수리 recruitment 채용, 모집 agent 직원, 대리인 inspector 점검관

5. 여자는 무엇에 대해 우려했는가?
   (A) 건물 위치
   (B) 일부 기계의 상태
   (C) 일부 작업물의 수준
   (D) 프로젝트 마감 기한

정답 (B)

해설 여자의 우려 사항을 묻는 문제이므로 여자의 말에서 부정적인 정보를 찾아야 합니다. 대화 중반부에 여자가 몇몇 오래된 제조 기계들이 좋지 않은 상태일 수 있어서 걱정했다고(I was worried that some of the older manufacturing machines might be in poor condition) 말하고 있으므로 (B)가 정답입니다.

어휘 be concerned about ~에 대해 우려하다 location 위치, 지점 quality 수준, 질 deadline 마감 기한

6. 남자는 자신이 무엇을 할 것이라고 말하는가?
   (A) 동료 직원에게 이야기하기
   (B) 여분의 부품 주문하기
   (C) 문서 보내기
   (D) 회의 일정 재조정하기

정답 (C)

해설 대화 마지막 부분에 남자가 보고서를 준비해 이번 주말 전까지 이메일로 보내 주겠다고(I'll be preparing my report tomorrow, and I'll e-mail a copy of it to you before the end of the week) 말하고 있으므로 (C)가 정답입니다.

어휘 colleague 동료 직원 part 부품 reschedule ~의 일정을 재조정하다

Paraphrase report / e-mail a copy of it
⇒ Send a document

Questions 7-9 refer to the following conversation.

W: Hi, **7 I just saw some pictures of your paintings online, and I'm very impressed with your talent.** In fact, I'd like to buy one for my new apartment. **8 I found your mobile number on your Web site,** so I thought I'd call you directly.
M: Yes, thanks for calling. Which artwork are you interested in?
W: The largest one, which shows a beautiful view of the ocean. It would look fantastic on the wall in my new dining room.
M: Oh, **9 I'm afraid the largest artwork has already been sold.** I do have some smaller ones that are quite similar in style. If you'd like to drop by my art studio, I can let you have a look at them.

여: 안녕하세요, 제가 온라인으로 귀하의 그림을 찍은 몇몇 사진들을 막 봤는데, 그 재능에 매우 깊은 인상을 받았습니다. 실은, 새로운 제 아파트에 놓을 것을 하나 구입하고 싶습니다. 귀하의 웹사이트에서 귀하의 휴대전화 번호를 발견해서, 직접 전화하는 게 좋겠다고 생각했습니다.
남: 네, 전화 주셔서 감사합니다. 어느 미술품에 관심이 있으신가요?
여: 아름다운 바다 경치를 보여주는 가장 큰 것이요. 새로운 제 식사 공간의 벽에 걸면 환상적일 것 같아요.

남: 아, 유감이지만 가장 큰 미술품은 이미 판매되었습니다. 스타일이 꽤 비슷하면서 더 작은 것들도 분명 있습니다. 제 화실에 들러 보고 싶으시면, 그것들을 한번 보여 드릴 수 있습니다.

어휘 be impressed with ~에 깊은 감명을 받다, ~에 깊은 인상을 받다 talent 재능 would like to do ~하고 싶다 directly 직접 artwork 미술품, 예술 작품 be interested in ~에 관심이 있다 dining room 식사 공간 quite 꽤, 아주 drop by ~에 들르다

7. 남자는 누구일 것 같은가?
  (A) 투어 가이드
  (B) 미술 평론가
  (C) 매장 점원
  (D) 화가

정답 (D)

해설 대화 시작 부분에 여자가 상대방의 그림을 찍은 사진을 본 사실과 함께 그 재능에 깊은 인상을 받았다고(I just saw some pictures of your paintings online, and I'm very impressed with your talent) 말하고 있습니다. 따라서 남자는 그림을 그리는 사람임을 알 수 있으므로 (D)가 정답입니다.

어휘 critic 평론가 clerk 점원

8. 여자는 어디서 남자의 연락처를 구했는가?
  (A) 기사에서
  (B) 안내 책자에서
  (C) 웹사이트에서
  (D) 친구에게서

정답 (C)

해설 대화 초반부에 여자가 상대방의 웹사이트에서 휴대전화 번호를 발견했다고(I found your mobile number on your Web site ~) 말하고 있으므로 (C)가 정답입니다.

어휘 contact information 연락처 brochure 안내 책자

9. 남자의 말에 따르면, 가장 큰 미술품에 무슨 문제가 있는가?
  (A) 손상되었다.
  (B) 걸어 놓기에 너무 무겁다.
  (C) 더 이상 구매할 수 없다.
  (D) 가격이 올랐다.

정답 (C)

해설 가장 큰 그림과 관련된 정보가 제시되는 대화 후반부에, 남자가 가장 큰 그림이 이미 판매되었다고(I'm afraid the largest artwork has already been sold) 알리고 있습니다. 이는 구매할 수 없다는 뜻이므로 (C)가 정답입니다.

어휘 damaged 손상된, 피해를 입은 too A to do: ~하기에는 너무 A하다 no longer 더 이상 ~ 않다 available 구매

가능한, 이용 가능한 increase 오르다, 증가하다

Paraphrase has already been sold
⇒ no longer available

Questions 10-12 refer to the following conversation.

W: Hi, Mr. Miller. 🔟 **This is Jessie from Harvest Baked Goods.** 1️⃣1️⃣ **I'm just calling to let you know that the personalized birthday cake you ordered is now finished and available for pick-up.**

M: Oh, that was fast! I'm kind of busy during lunchtime, though. I might not be able to make it to your store until late afternoon. What time do you close?

W: We shut at 5:30 P.M. today. 1️⃣2️⃣ **We'd be happy to deliver the cake directly to your house**, if you'd like. The service only costs an additional five dollars. If you're interested, what time works best for you?

M: That would be convenient. Let's say 4 o'clock. Thanks.

여: 안녕하세요, 밀러 씨. 저는 하비스트 베이크드 굿즈의 제시입니다. 주문하신 맞춤 제작 생일 케이크가 지금 완성되어서 가져가실 수 있다는 사실을 알려 드리기 위해 전화 드립니다.
남: 아, 빠르시네요! 하지만, 제가 점심 시간에는 좀 바쁩니다. 오후 늦은 시간에나 매장으로 갈 수 있을 것 같아요. 몇 시에 문 닫으시죠?
여: 저희가 오늘은 오후 5시 30분에 닫습니다. 원하신다면, 저희가 기꺼이 댁으로 직접 케이크를 배달해 드리겠습니다. 이 서비스는 추가로 5달러밖에 들지 않습니다. 관심 있으시면, 몇 시가 가장 좋으신가요?
남: 그럼 편리할 것 같네요. 4시로 해요. 감사합니다.

어휘 let A know that: A에게 ~임을 알리다 personalize ~을 개인의 필요에 맞추다 order ~을 주문하다 available for ~가 가능한 pick-up 가져가기, 가져오기 though (문장 끝이나 중간에서) 하지만 not A until B: B나 되어야 A하다 be able to do ~할 수 있다 make it to ~로 가다, ~에 도착하다 be happy to do 기꺼이 ~하다 directly 곧장, 직접 cost ~의 비용이 들다 additional 추가의 interested 관심 있는 work best for (시간 등이) ~에게 가장 좋다 convenient 편리한 Let's say A: A로 합시다, A면 될 겁니다

10. 여자는 어디에서 근무하고 있을 것 같은가?
  (A) 슈퍼마켓에서
  (B) 제과점에서
  (C) 레스토랑에서

(D) 의류 매장에서

정답 (B)

해설 대화를 시작하면서 여자가 자신이 속한 업체를 Harvest Baked Goods라고 하고, 뒤이어 상대방이 주문한 케이크와 관련해 전화했다고(I'm just calling to let you know that the personalized birthday cake you ordered ~) 언급하고 있습니다. 따라서 여자는 제과점에서 근무하는 사람임을 알 수 있으므로 (B)가 정답입니다.

11. 여자는 왜 남자에게 전화하는가?
(A) 비용 지불을 요청하기 위해
(B) 제품이 준비된 상태임을 알리기 위해
(C) 몇몇 신제품을 추천하기 위해
(D) 행사 날짜를 확인해 주기 위해

정답 (B)

해설 대화 초반부에 여자가 상대방이 주문한 케이크가 완료되어 가져갈 수 있다고(I'm just calling to let you know that the personalized birthday cake you ordered is now finished and available for pick-up) 알리고 있습니다. 이는 제품이 준비되어 있다는 뜻이므로 (B)가 정답입니다.

어휘 request ~을 요청하다 payment 지불(액) inform A that: A 에게 ~임을 알리다 recommend ~을 추천하다 confirm ~을 확인해주다

Paraphrase the personalized birthday cake you ordered ⇒ an item

12. 여자는 무슨 서비스를 언급하는가?
(A) 매장 회원제
(B) 선물 포장
(C) 대량 할인
(D) 자택 배달

정답 (D)

해설 여자가 언급하는 서비스를 묻는 문제이므로 여자의 말에서 특정 서비스와 관련된 정보를 찾아야 합니다. 대화 후반부에 여자가 상대방 집으로 케이크를 배달해 주겠다고(We'd be happy to deliver the cake directly to your house ~) 말하고 있으므로 (D)가 정답입니다.

어휘 wrapping 포장 bulk 대량의

Questions 13-15 refer to the following conversation.

W: Good morning, Jacob! I saw **13** **you've been assigned to report on the grand opening of Lombard Bridge today**. What time are you leaving?
M: Oh, I was going to leave around 3 o'clock since my coverage is for our evening news segment. Did the broadcast schedule change?
W: No, but **14** **I'm concerned about the weather later. It's going to be raining in the afternoon**, so make sure you and your crew all bring a rain jacket.
M: Thanks for the advice. **15** **I'll also check the traffic conditions before we head out to see if there are any slowdowns**.

여: 안녕하세요, 제이콥 씨. 오늘 롬바드 다리 개통식을 보도하도록 배정되셨다는 걸 알았어요. 몇 시에 출발하시나요?
남: 아, 제 취재 내용이 우리 저녁 뉴스 코너를 위한 것이기 때문에 3시쯤 출발하려고 했습니다. 그 방송 일정이 변경되었나요?
여: 아뇨, 하지만 이따가 날씨가 우려되어서요. 오후에 비가 내릴 거라서, 반드시 당신과 당신 팀원들 모두 우비를 챙겨 가시도록 하세요.
남: 조언 감사합니다. 어떤 정체 문제라도 있는지 알아보기 위해 출발하기 전에 교통 상황도 확인해 볼 겁니다.

어휘 be assigned to do ~하도록 배정되다 leave 출발하다, 떠나다 around ~쯤, 약, 대략 since ~하기 때문에, ~한 이후로 coverage 취재, 보도 news segment 뉴스 코너 broadcast n. 방송 v. ~을 방송하다 be concerned about ~을 우려하다 make sure (that) 반드시 ~하도록 하다 crew (함께 작업하는) 팀, 조 traffic 교통(량), 차량들 condition 상황, 상태, 조건, 환경 head out 출발하다 see if ~인지 알아보다 slowdown 정체, 지연, 둔화

13. 남자의 직업은 무엇일 것 같은가?
(A) 공사장 인부
(B) 행사 기획자
(C) 고속도로 엔지니어
(D) 뉴스 기자

정답 (D)

해설 대화를 시작하면서 여자가 남자에게 오늘 롬바드 다리 개통식을 보도하도록 배정된(you've been assigned to report on the grand opening of Lombard Bridge today) 사실을 언급하고 있으므로 (D)가 정답입니다.

14. 여자가 걱정하는 이유는 무엇인가?
(A) 일기 예보가 좋지 않다.
(B) 팀원 한 명이 몸이 좋지 않다.
(C) 일정이 변경되었다.
(D) 일부 장비가 오작동하고 있다.

정답 (A)

해설 여자가 대화 중반부에 이따가 날씨가 우려된다고 말하면서 오후에 비가 내릴 거라고(I'm concerned about the weather later. It's going to be raining in the afternoon) 알리고 있으므로 (A)가 정답입니다.

어휘 feel well 건강이 좋다, 기분이 좋다 equipment 장비 malfunction 오작동하다

Paraphrase the weather later / raining in the afternoon
⇒ A weather forecast is bad

15. 남자는 무엇에 대해 확인해 볼 것이라고 말하는가?
(A) 주차 공간 이용 가능성
(B) 고객 불만 사항
(C) 여분의 제품
(D) 교통 혼잡

정답 (D)

해설 대화 마지막 부분에 남자가 어떤 정체 문제라도 있는지 알아보기 위해 교통 상황도 확인해 볼 것이라고(I'll also check the traffic conditions ~ to see if there are any slowdowns) 알리고 있습니다. 이는 교통 혼잡 문제가 있는지 미리 알아보려는 것이므로 (D)가 정답입니다.

어휘 parking 주차(장) availability 이용 가능성 complaint 불만, 불평 surplus 여분의, 잉여의 congestion 혼잡

Paraphrase traffic conditions / any slowdowns
⇒ Traffic congestion

Questions 16-18 refer to the following conversation.

> W: Excuse me, **16** I'm going to catch a train here later this evening, but I was wondering if there's anywhere I can store my suitcase.
> M: Yes, there are storage lockers by exits 1 and 3. You can pay using your transportation card.
> W: Oh, **17** I'm only in this city for today because I have a client meeting, so I didn't buy a transportation card. Is there any other way to pay?
> M: **18** There's a Rockford Transit mobile app that you can use, too. But you'll have to input your credit card information to reserve the locker.
> 여: 실례지만, 제가 이따가 오늘 저녁에 여기서 기차를 탈 건데, 제 여행 가방을 보관할 곳이 있는지 궁금했습니다.
> 남: 네, 1번과 3번 출구 옆에 보관용 사물함이 있습니다. 교통 카드를 이용해서 결제하실 수 있습니다.
> 여: 아, 제가 고객 회의가 있기 때문에 오늘만 이 도시에 와 있는 거라서, 교통 카드를 구입하지 않았습니다. 결제할 수 있는 다른 어떤 방법이라도 있을까요?
> 남: 이용하실 수 있는 록포드 교통 모바일 앱도 있습니다. 하지만, 사물함을 예약하시려면 신용카드 정보를 입력하셔야 할 겁니다.

어휘 catch (교통편) ~을 타다 wonder if ~인지 궁금하다 store v. ~을 보관하다, ~을 저장하다 suitcase 여행 가방 storage 보관, 저장 by ~ 옆에 transportation 교통(편) way to do ~할 수 있는 방법 will have to do ~해야 할 것이다 input ~을 입력하다 reserve ~을 예약하다

16. 남자는 어디에 근무하고 있을 것 같은가?
(A) 호텔
(B) 공항
(C) 기차역
(D) 여행사

정답 (C)

해설 여자가 대화를 시작하면서 남자에게 이따가 오늘 저녁에 현재 있는 곳에서 기차를 탄다는 사실과 함께 여행 가방을 보관할 수 있는 어떤 곳이든 있는지 궁금했다고(I'm going to catch a train here later this evening, but I was wondering if there's anywhere I can store my suitcase) 알리고 있습니다. 따라서, 기차역에서 고객이 직원에게 문의하는 상황임을 알 수 있으므로 (C)가 정답입니다.

17. 여자는 오늘 무엇을 할 것이라고 말하는가?
(A) 시내 여행을 가는 일
(B) 고객과 만나는 일
(C) 발표하는 일
(D) 관공서 한 곳을 방문하는 일

정답 (B)

해설 대화 중반부에 여자가 고객 회의가 있기 때문에 오늘만 와 있는 거라고(I'm only in this city for today because I have a client meeting) 밝히고 있으므로 (B)가 정답입니다.

어휘 give a presentation 발표하다 government office 관공서, 관청

Paraphrase a client meeting ⇒ Meet with a client

18. 남자의 말에 따르면, 여자는 어떻게 결제할 수 있는가?
(A) 특정 모바일 앱을 이용해서
(B) 은행 계좌 이체 일정을 잡아서
(C) 신용카드를 갖다 대서
(D) 현금을 넣어서

정답 (A)

해설 남자가 대화 후반부에 여자의 비용 결제 문제와 관련해 록포드 교통 모바일 앱을 이용해도 된다고(There's a Rockford Transit mobile app that you can use, too) 알리고 있으므로 (A)가 정답입니다.

어휘 make a payment 결제하다, 지불하다 certain 특정한, 일정한 bank transfer 은행 계좌 이체 tap ~을 살짝 갖다 대다, ~을 톡 두드리다 insert ~을 넣다, ~을 삽입하다

Paraphrase a Rockford Transit mobile app that you can use ⇒ using a certain mobile app

Questions 19-21 refer to the following conversation.

W: Hi, **19** thanks for coming to this orientation session for your fitness program.
M: No problem. **20** I'm excited to get fit and start living healthier, especially through workout routines that are personalized for me.
W: Well, I'm excited to help you achieve your goals. Today, we're just going to go over your fitness profile and discuss what exactly you want to focus on. First, **21** can you fill out this quick health questionnaire for me?
M: Of course.

여: 안녕하세요, 이용하실 피트니스 프로그램에 필요한 오리엔테이션 시간에 와 주셔서 감사합니다.
남: 별 말씀을요. 몸매를 가꾸고 더 건강한 생활을 시작하게 되어 기대됩니다. 특히 제게 맞춤 제공되는 운동 루틴을 통해 그렇게 하게 되어서요.
여: 음, 목표를 달성하시도록 도와 드리게 되어 기쁩니다. 오늘, 고객님의 피트니스 프로필을 살펴 보고 정확히 무엇에 초점을 맞추고 싶으신지 이야기해 볼 겁니다. 우선, 저를 위해 이 간단한 건강 설문 조사지를 작성해 주시겠습니까?
남: 물론이죠.

어휘 session (특정 활동을 위한) 시간 get fit 몸매를 가꾸다, 건강을 유지하다 especially 특히, 특별히 workout 운동 routine 반복하는 특정 동작의 순서와 방법 personalized 개인에게 맞춰 제공되는 help A do: ~하도록 A를 돕다 achieve ~을 달성하다, ~을 이루다 go over ~을 살펴 보다, ~을 검토하다 fitness profile 피트니스 프로필(신체 건강 수준에 대한 평가) discuss ~을 이야기하다, ~을 논의하다 exactly 정확히 focus on ~에 초점을 맞추다 fill out ~을 작성하다 questionnaire 설문 조사지

19. 여자는 누구일 것 같은가?
(A) 프로 운동 선수
(B) 댄스 강사
(C) 개인 트레이너
(D) 의학 박사

정답 (C)

해설 여자가 대화를 시작하면서 남자의 피트니스 프로그램에 필요한 오리엔테이션 시간에 온 것에 대해 감사하다는(thanks for coming to this orientation session for your fitness program) 인사를 전하고 있습니다. 이를 통해 개인 몸매 및 건강 관리를 담당하는 트레이너임을 알 수 있으므로 (C)가 정답입니다.

20. 남자는 무엇을 하기를 고대하고 있는가?
(A) 건강한 생활 방식을 가지는 것
(B) 자격증이 있는 교사가 되는 것
(C) 업계 전문가와 협업하는 것
(D) 개조 공사 프로젝트를 완료하는 것

정답 (A)

해설 대화 초반부에 남자가 몸매를 가꾸고 더 건강한 생활을 시작하는 것에 대한 기대감을(I'm excited to get fit and start living healthier) 나타내고 있으므로 (A)가 정답입니다.

어휘 look forward to -ing ~하기를 고대하다 certified 자격증이 있는, 공인된 industry 업계 expert 전문가 complete ~을 완료하다 renovation 개조, 보수

Paraphrase
· excited ⇒ looking forward to
· get fit and start living healthier
  ⇒ Having a healthy lifestyle

21. 여자는 남자에게 무엇을 하도록 요청하는가?
(A) 한 가지 일을 실행할 것
(B) 계약서를 살펴 볼 것
(C) 양식을 작성 완료할 것
(D) 전화번호를 제공할 것

정답 (C)

해설 대화 후반부에 여자가 간단한 건강 설문 조사지를 작성해 달라고(can you fill out this quick health questionnaire for me?) 요청하고 있습니다. 이는 일종의 양식을 작성 완료하는 것을 의미하므로 (C)가 정답입니다.

어휘 practice ~을 실행하다 task 일, 업무 review ~을 살펴 보다, ~을 검토하다 contract 계약(서) complete ~을 완료하다 form 양식, 서식

Paraphrase fill out this quick health questionnaire
  ⇒ Complete a form

Questions 22-24 refer to the following conversation.

W: Hi, there. Do you need help looking for anything?
M: Hi, yes. **22 I want to buy some rose plants.**
W: All of our roses are over here. Follow me.
M: Oh, I like this red one. **23 Do you have any in a smaller-sized pot?**
W: Unfortunately, those are the smallest pot sizes we have. **24 We can give you plastic bags with handles for easier transport, though.**
M: Great! In that case, **24 I'll take three, please.**

여: 안녕하세요. 무엇이든 찾으시는 데 도움이 필요하신가요?
남: 안녕하세요, 네. 저는 장미를 좀 구입하려고 합니다.
여: 저희 장미는 모두 여기 이쪽에 있습니다. 따라오세요.
남: 아, 저는 이 붉은색 장미가 마음에 들어요. 더 작은 크기의 화분에 담긴 게 있나요?
여: 유감스럽게도, 그것들이 저희가 보유하고 있는 가장 작은 화분 크기입니다. 하지만, 더 수월한 이동을 위해 손잡이가 있는 비닐 봉지를 제공해 드릴 수 있습니다.
남: 잘됐네요! 그럼, 세 개 가져가겠습니다.

어휘 look for ~을 찾다 plant 식물 over here 여기 이쪽에 follow ~을 따라가다 smaller-sized 더 작은 크기의 pot 화분, 항아리, 단지 unfortunately 유감스럽게도, 아쉽게도 transport n. 이동, 운송 v. ~을 운송하다 though (문장 끝이나 중간에서) 하지만 in that case (앞선 말에 대해) 그럼, 그런 경우라면

22. 대화는 어디에서 진행되고 있을 것 같은가?
(A) 국립 공원
(B) 원예 용품점
(C) 건강 식품 매장
(D) 미술관

정답 (B)
해설 대화 초반부에 남자가 도움이 필요한지 묻는 여자에게 장미를 구입하려 한다고(I want to buy some rose plants) 알리고 있으므로 식물을 구입할 수 있는 장소인 (B)가 정답입니다.

어휘 take place 진행되다, 개최되다, 발생하다

23. 남자는 무엇에 관해 묻는가?
(A) 제공되는 포장재 유형
(B) 구입 가능한 꽃 색상
(C) 용기의 크기 선택
(D) 전자 기기의 사양

정답 (C)
해설 남자가 대화 중반부에 더 작은 크기의 화분에 담긴 게 있는지(Do you have any in a smaller-sized pot?) 묻고 있는데,

이는 식물을 담을 보관 용기의 크기와 관련해 묻는 것이므로 (C)가 정답입니다.

어휘 packaging 포장(재) offer ~을 제공하다 available (사물) 구입 가능한, 이용 가능한, (사람) 시간이 있는 container 용기, 그릇 specifications (제품의) 사양, 설명서 device 기기, 장치

Paraphrase have any in a smaller-sized pot ⇒ The size options for a container

24. 곧이어 무슨 일이 있을 것 같은가?
(A) 여자가 배송 서비스를 조치해 줄 것이다.
(B) 여자가 몇몇 봉지를 제공할 것이다.
(C) 남자가 다른 제품을 선택할 것이다.
(D) 남자가 할인을 받을 것이다.

정답 (B)
해설 여자가 대화 후반부에 손잡이가 있는 비닐 봉지를 제공해 줄 수 있다고(We can give you plastic bags with handles for easier transport, though) 제안하는 것에 대해, 남자가 그럴 경우에 세 개 가져가겠다고(I'll take three, please) 대답하고 있습니다. 따라서, 여자가 비닐 봉지를 제공할 것으로 볼 수 있으므로 (B)가 정답입니다.

어휘 arrange ~을 조치하다, ~을 처리하다, ~을 마련하다 choose ~을 선택하다 receive ~을 받다

Paraphrase give you plastic bags ⇒ provide some bags

DAY 9 세부사항 / say about 문제

PRACTICE

1. (C) **2.** (B)

Question 1 refers to the following conversation.

W: Hi, David! How was your weekend?
M: Hi, Sarah. **Over the weekend, I reorganized my entire digital photo library by year and event.**
W: That system looks very organized. Which program did you use?
M: PhotoSort Pro was a lifesaver—tagging batch after batch. I'll send you the download link.

여: 안녕하세요, 데이빗! 주말은 어땠어요?
남: 안녕하세요, 사라. 주말 동안 저는 디지털 사진 라이브러리 전체를 연도별, 행사별로 다시 정리했어요.
여: 그 방식 정말 체계적으로 보이네요. 어떤 프로그램을 사용했나요?
남: '포토소트 프로'가 정말 도움이 되었어요—사진을 묶음으로 태그하는 것이 그랬어요. 제가 다운로드 링크를 보내줄게요.

어휘 reorganize 다시 정리하다 entire 전체의 organized 정리된, 체계적인 lifesaver 큰 도움이 되는 것, 목숨을 구해 주는 것 batch 묶음

1. 남자는 주말에 무엇을 했는가?
   (A) 새 디지털 카메라를 샀다.
   (B) 휴일에 찍은 사진을 인화했다.
   (C) 디지털 사진을 정리했다.
   (D) 오래된 파일을 삭제했다.

정답 (C)

해설 남자는 주말 동안 디지털 사진 라이브러리 전체를 연도별, 행사별로 다시 정리했다고(Over the weekend, I reorganized my entire digital photo library by year and event) 언급하였으므로 정답은 (C)입니다.

어휘 print 인쇄하다, 인화하다

Question 2 refers to the following conversation.

M: Hi, our product launch was supposed to be at Riverside Conference Center, but it's double-booked.
W: We met at Blue Mountain Hotel's meeting room last quarter.
M: That room was the perfect size.
W: However, **their service charge is way over our budget** for this event.
M: Understood. I'll check with the events team for alternatives.

남: 안녕하세요, 원래 저희 제품 출시 행사는 리버사이드 컨퍼런스 센터에서 열릴 예정이었는데, 일정이 중복 예약되었어요.
여: 지난 분기에는 블루 마운틴 호텔 회의실에서 만났었죠.
남: 그 방은 크기가 딱 좋았어요.
여: 하지만 이번 행사를 하기에 그곳의 서비스 요금이 예산을 너무 초과해요.
남: 알겠습니다. 대안이 있는지 이벤트팀에 확인해볼게요.

어휘 launch 출시 be supposed to do ~하기로 예정되어 있다 double-booked 중복 예약된 quarter 분기 charge 요금 budget 예산 alternative 대안, 대체

2. 블루 마운틴 호텔에 대해 여자는 뭐라고 말하는가?
   (A) 대중교통 이용과 거리가 멀다.
   (B) 너무 비싸다.
   (C) 몇몇 손님들에게는 크기가 너무 작다.
   (D) 오디오 시스템이 없다.

정답 (B)

해설 여자가 블루 마운틴 호텔의 회의실에 대해 언급하고, 그 후에 그곳의 서비스 요금이 예산을 훨씬 초과한다고(their service charge is way over our budget) 말했으므로 정답은 (B)입니다.

어휘 public transit 대중교통 be far from ~에서 거리가 먼

실전 TEST

1. (C)	2. (C)	3. (A)	4. (C)	5. (A)
6. (C)	7. (D)	8. (C)	9. (B)	10. (A)
11. (C)	12. (B)	13. (D)	14. (B)	15. (B)
16. (D)	17. (A)	18. (B)	19. (C)	20. (B)
21. (A)	22. (D)	23. (B)	24. (B)	

Questions 1-3 refer to the following conversation.

M: Nina, I wanted to ask you about **1** the customer service seminars for our employees. Is it okay to hold them during the first week of April?
W: Well, we have several crucial work deadlines at the beginning of **2 3** April. We'll also be busy opening the newest branch of our supermarket chain that month. It might not be the best time. Could you hold the seminars in May instead?
M: Sure, that'll work, too. I totally forgot that April will be such a busy time for us.

남: 니나 씨, 우리 직원들을 위한 고객 서비스 세미나에 관해 여쭤보고 싶었어요. 4월 첫째 주에 개최하는 것이 괜찮은가요?
여: 저, 저희가 4월 초에 몇 가지 중대한 작업 마감 기한이 있어요. 또한 그 달에 우리 슈퍼마켓 체인의 최신 지점도 개장하느라 바쁠 거예요. 그때가 가장 좋은 시기가 아닐 수도 있어요. 대신 5월에 그 세미나를 개최해 주시겠어요?
남: 물론이죠, 그렇게 해도 될 겁니다. 4월이 우리에게 그렇게 바쁜 시기일 거라는 사실을 완전히 잊고 있었어요.

어휘 hold ~을 개최하다, 열다 several 몇몇의, 여럿의 crucial 중대한 deadline 마감 기한 be busy -ing ~하느라

바쁘다 branch 지점, 지사 instead 대신 totally 완전히, 전적으로 forget that ~임을 잊다

1. 남자는 무엇을 하고 싶어하는가?
(A) 신입 사원 고용하기
(B) 여행 준비하기
(C) 몇몇 세미나 개최하기
(D) 몇몇 고객들에게 설문조사하기

정답 (C)

해설 대화 초반부에 남자가 고객 서비스 세미나를 언급하면서 4월 첫째 주에 개최하는 것이 괜찮은지(the customer service seminars for our employees. Is it okay to hold them during the first week of April?) 묻고 있으므로 (C)가 정답입니다.

어휘 hire ~을 고용하다 organize ~을 준비하다, 조직하다 survey v. ~에게 설문조사하다

2. 4월에 무슨 일이 있을 것인가?
(A) 직원이 승진될 것이다.
(B) 회사 사무실이 이전될 것이다.
(C) 매장이 개장될 것이다.
(D) 신제품이 출시될 것이다.

정답 (C)

해설 4월이라는 시점이 언급되는 대화 중반부에, 여자가 4월에 있을 일을 말하면서 신규 지점을 개장할 거라고(~ April. We'll also be busy opening the newest branch of our supermarket chain that month) 알리고 있으므로 (C)가 정답입니다.

어휘 promote ~을 승진시키다 launch ~을 출시하다, 공개하다

Paraphrase opening the newest branch
⇒ store will be opened

3. 여자는 무엇에 대해 우려하는가?
(A) 바쁜 업무 일정
(B) 배송 지연
(C) 제품의 가격
(D) 행사의 참석자 수

정답 (A)

해설 여자가 대화 중반부에 4월에 있을 마감 기한 및 신규 지점 개장으로 바쁜 상황일 것임을 알리는 것으로 볼 때(~ April. We'll also be busy opening the newest branch of our supermarket chain that month), 바쁜 업무 일정으로 인해 우려하고 있다는 것을 알 수 있으므로 (A)가 정답입니다.

어휘 be concerned about ~에 대해 우려하다 delay 지연, 지체 attendance 참석(자의 수)

Questions 4-6 refer to the following conversation.

M: Excuse me. 4 **This is my first time coming to Mayer's Gym.** Are there any classes I could join?
W: Well, there aren't any scheduled for today, but 5 **you can watch our introductory video**. Just play it here on this tablet. It will teach you the basics of 4 **using our fitness equipment**.
M: Oh, that sounds good. And, I saw a flyer that says 6 **I can get a sports drink**.
W: Right, 6 **here you go. You can get one for free each day** as part of our special promotion.

남: 실례합니다. 오늘 메이어스 체육관에 처음 오는데요. 어떤 수업이든 제가 함께 할 수 있는 게 있을까요?
여: 저, 오늘 예정되어 있는 것은 아무것도 없지만, 저희 소개 동영상을 보실 수 있습니다. 이 태블릿에서 재생하시기만 하면 됩니다. 저희 피트니스 장비 이용에 대한 기본 사항들을 가르쳐 드릴 겁니다.
남: 아, 좋은 것 같아요. 그리고, 제가 스포츠 음료를 받을 수 있다고 쓰여 있는 전단을 봤어요.
여: 맞습니다, 여기 있습니다. 저희 특별 홍보 행사의 일환으로 매일 무료로 1개 받으실 수 있습니다.

어휘 join ~에 함께 하다, 참가하다 scheduled for + 시점: ~로 예정된 introductory 소개용의, 입문의 basics 기본, 기초 equipment 장비 flyer 전단 say (문서 등에) ~라고 쓰여 있다 for free 무료로 as part of ~의 일환으로 promotion 홍보, 판촉 (행사)

4. 화자들은 어디에 있는가?
(A) 미술관
(B) 도서관
(C) 피트니스 센터
(D) 백화점

정답 (C)

해설 대화 초반부에 남자가 Mayer's Gym에 처음 온다고 말하는 부분(This is my first time coming to Mayer's Gym)과 중반부에 여자가 피트니스 장비를 이용하는 일(using our fitness equipment)을 언급하는 것으로 볼 때 피트니스 센터에 있다는 것을 알 수 있으므로 (C)가 정답입니다.

5. 여자는 남자에게 무엇을 하도록 제안하는가?
(A) 동영상 시청하기
(B) 앱 다운로드하기
(C) 회원 자격 신청하기
(D) 쿠폰 사용하기

정답 (A)

해설 여자가 제안하는 일을 묻고 있으므로 여자의 말에서 권고나 제안 관련 표현과 함께 제시되는 정보를 찾아야 합니다. 대화 초반부에 여자가 소개 동영상을 시청하도록(you can watch our introductory video) 권하는 부분이 있으므로 이를 언급한 (A)가 정답입니다.

어휘 apply for ~을 신청하다, ~에 지원하다

6. 여자는 남자에게 무엇을 주는가?
   (A) 비밀번호
   (B) 전단
   (C) 음료
   (D) 일정표

정답 (C)

해설 대화 후반부에 남자가 스포츠 음료를 받는 일을(I can get a sports drink) 언급하는 것에 대해 여자가 여기 있다고(here you go) 하면서 매일 무료로 1개를 받을 수 있다고(You can get one for free each day ~) 말해주고 있으므로 (C)가 정답입니다.

Questions 7-9 refer to the following conversation.

W: Hi, **7** **I'm interested in reserving one of your private dining rooms.** A colleague of mine held a celebration at your restaurant last month and he highly recommends your food and service.

M: That's nice to hear. **8** **Would you like me to e-mail you some photos and additional details for each of our private rooms?**

W: That would be great. My address is sarasmith@gomail.com. By the way, I'd prefer a room that has a good view, if possible.

M: Well, **9** **our rooms on the third floor provide a nice view of the sea. However, they have a slightly lower seating capacity than our other rooms.**

여: 안녕하세요, 저는 개별 식사 공간들 중의 하나를 예약하는 데 관심이 있습니다. 제 동료 직원 한 명이 지난 달에 귀 레스토랑에서 기념 행사를 열었는데, 음식과 서비스를 적극 추천해 줬어요.
남: 그 말씀을 듣게 되어 기쁩니다. 저희 개별 식사 공간 각각에 대한 몇몇 사진과 추가 세부 사항을 이메일로 보내 드릴까요?
여: 그럼 아주 좋을 것 같아요. 제 주소는 sarasmith@gomail.com입니다. 그건 그렇고, 가능하다면 전망이 좋은 방이면 좋겠습니다.
남: 저, 3층에 있는 방들은 훌륭한 바다 전망을 제공합니다. 하지만, 다른 방들보다 좌석 수용 규모가 약간 작습니다.

어휘 be interested in ~하는 데 관심 있다 reserve ~을 예약하다 private 개별의, 개인의, 사적인 colleague 동료 (직원) hold ~을 개최하다, 열다 celebration 기념 행사, 축하 행사 highly recommend ~을 적극 추천하다 would like A to do: A가 ~하기를 원하다 additional 추가적인 details 세부 사항, 상세 정보 by the way (화제 전환 시) 그건 그렇고 would prefer ~을 원하다, ~하고 싶다 if possible 가능하다면 provide ~을 제공하다 slightly 약간, 조금 seating capacity 좌석 수용 규모, 수용 가능한 좌석 인원

7. 여자는 무엇을 예약하고 싶어하는가?
   (A) 라이브 연주자
   (B) 회사 차량
   (C) 컨퍼런스 개최 장소
   (D) 식사 공간

정답 (D)

해설 여자가 예약하고 싶어하는 것을 묻는 문제이므로 여자의 말에서 예약 대상으로 언급되는 정보를 찾아야 합니다. 대화를 시작하면서 여자가 식사 공간을 예약하는 데 관심이 있다고(I'm interested in reserving one of your private dining rooms) 말하고 있으므로 (D)가 정답입니다.

어휘 vehicle 차량 venue 개최 장소

8. 남자는 여자에게 무엇을 보내겠다고 제안하는가?
   (A) 할인 쿠폰
   (B) 메뉴 선택권
   (C) 사진
   (D) 안내 책자

정답 (C)

해설 남자가 제안하는 일을 묻는 문제이므로 남자의 말에서 제안 표현과 함께 제시되는 정보를 찾아야 합니다. 대화 중반부에 남자가 개별 식사 공간의 사진과 세부 사항을 이메일로 보내 주겠다고(Would you like me to e-mail you some photos and additional details for each of our private rooms?) 제안하고 있으므로 이 둘 중 사진을 언급한 (C)가 정답입니다.

어휘 voucher 쿠폰, 상품권 brochure 안내 책자, 소책자

9. 남자는 3층에 있는 방에 관해 무슨 말을 하는가?
   (A) 더 비싸다.
   (B) 더 적은 인원을 앉힐 수 있다.
   (C) 창문이 없다.
   (D) 현재 이용할 수 없다.

정답 (B)

해설 3층에 있는 방은 대화 후반부에 언급되는데, 남자가 그곳의 방이 지니는 특징으로 바다 전망이 제공된다는 점과 다른 방들보다 좌석 수용 규모가 약간 작다는 점을(our rooms on the third floor provide a nice view of the sea. However, they have a slightly lower seating capacity ~) 알리고 있습니다. 따라서 좌석 수용 규모가 더 작다는 점에 해당되는 의미를 지닌 (B)가 정답입니다.

어휘 seat ~을 앉히다 currently 현재 unavailable 이용할 수 없는

Paraphrase have a slightly lower seating capacity
⇒ seat fewer people

Questions 10-12 refer to the following conversation with three speakers.

> W: Thanks for coming to our factory. I know we're far away from the city.
> M1: It's no problem. **10 We always drive all over the place doing repairs.**
> M2: Right, it's just part of our job. So, you mentioned on the phone that your packaging machine hasn't been working properly. Does it operate?
> W: It runs, but the cutter isn't functioning well.
> M1: OK. We'll take a look at it. **11 Hopefully it's an easy fix**, but you did mention that it's an old model. If we can't fix it, you might have to buy a new unit. And, as you know, **12 these machines can be costly**.

여: 저희 공장에 와 주셔서 감사합니다. 저희가 시내에서 멀리 있다는 걸 알고 있어요.
남1: 문제 없습니다. 저희는 늘 모든 곳을 다니며 수리를 하니까요.
남2: 맞아요, 그건 저희 일의 일부이죠. 자, 전화로 말씀하시기를 포장 기계가 제대로 작동하지 않고 있다고 하셨죠. 작동은 됩니까?
여: 기계가 돌아가긴 해요, 하지만 절단기가 제대로 작동하지 않아요.
남1: 알겠습니다. 저희가 한번 살펴 볼게요. 쉽게 수리되면 좋겠지만, 그게 오래된 모델이라고 하셨죠. 만일 저희가 고치지 못하면, 새 기계를 구입하셔야 할 겁니다. 그리고, 아시다시피, 이 기계들은 비쌀 수 있어요.

어휘 factory 공장 far away from ~로부터 먼 all over the place (넓은 지역에 걸쳐) 모든 곳에, 사방에 do repairs 수리하다 mention that ~라고 언급하다 packaging 포장 work (기계 장치 등이) 작동되다(= operate, run, function) cutter 절단기 take a look at ~을 한번 살펴보다 hopefully 바라건대 fix n. 수리, 해결책 v. ~을 수리하다 unit 기계, 장치 as you know 아시다시피 costly 많은 돈이 드는

10. 남자들 중 한 명이 자신들은 무엇에 익숙하다고 말하는가?
(A) 장거리 운전
(B) 지저분한 작업 공간
(C) 촉박한 공지
(D) 늦은 응답

정답 (A)

해설 여자가 먼 길을 온 것에 대해 고맙다고 인사하자 남자1이 괜찮다고 말하며 자신들은 늘 수리하러 모든 곳을 다닌다고(We always drive all over the place doing repairs) 덧붙이고 있습니다. all over the place는 '넓은 지역에 걸쳐 있는 모든 곳'을 뜻하므로, 이들이 익숙하다고 말하는 것은 먼 거리를 다니는 장거리 운전입니다. 따라서 정답은 (A)입니다.

어휘 messy 지저분한, 엉망인 workspace 작업 공간 short notice 촉박한 공지 response 반응

11. 남자들은 왜 공장을 방문하고 있는가?
(A) 기계를 배송하기 위해
(B) 몇몇 소프트웨어를 설치하기 위해
(C) 몇몇 장비를 수리하기 위해
(D) 건물을 검사하기 위해

정답 (C)

해설 여자가 일하는 공장의 포장 기계가 작동이 되지 않아서 남자들이 이를 수리하기 위해 방문한 상황입니다. 대화 후반부에 남자 1이 쉽게 고쳐지길 바란다고(Hopefully it's an easy fix) 말한 것을 통해 이들의 방문 목적을 알 수 있습니다. 따라서 정답은 (C)입니다.

어휘 deliver ~을 배송하다 install ~을 설치하다 equipment 장비 inspect ~을 검사하다

12. 남자들 중 한 명이 여자에게 무엇에 대해 경고하는가?
(A) 작업 지연
(B) 높은 비용
(C) 형편없는 서비스
(D) 계약 조항

정답 (B)

해설 대화 마지막에 남자가 만일 수리가 안되면 새 기계를 사야 하는데, 기계가 비싸다고(these machines can be costly) 경고해 주고 있으므로 (B)가 정답입니다.

어휘 delay 지연 cost 비용 poor 형편없는, 잘 못하는 contract 계약 term 조항

Questions 13-15 refer to the following conversation.

M: Hannah, how was the workshop this morning?
W: Attendance was great. **13** **I think people really enjoyed learning how to present clearly and confidently in front of an audience.**
M: I'm glad to hear that!
W: But **14** **some of the video clips in the presentation loaded very slowly**. Next time, I think I should download them instead of relying on the Wi-Fi connection.
M: Yeah, that sounds like a good solution. Actually, I came to ask if I could have the participants' contact information. **15** **I want to send out a follow-up survey to everyone**.

남: 한나 씨, 오늘 아침에 있었던 워크숍은 어떠셨나요?
여: 참석자 수가 아주 많았어요. 사람들은 청중 앞에서 명확하고 자신감 있게 발표하는 방법을 배우는 것을 정말로 즐거워했던 것 같아요.
남: 그 말씀을 들으니 기쁘네요!
여: 하지만 발표 중에 동영상들 중 일부가 아주 느리게 로딩되었어요. 다음 번에는, 와이파이 연결에 의존하는 대신 다운로드해야 할 것 같아요.
남: 네, 그게 좋은 해결책인 것 같아요. 실은, 참가자들의 연락처를 받을 수 있을지 여쭤 보러 왔어요. 제가 모든 분께 후속 설문 조사지를 발송하고 싶어서요.

어휘 how was A?: A는 어땠나요? attendance 참석, 참석자 수 how to do ~하는 방법 present 발표하다 clearly 명확히, 분명히 confidently 자신감 있게 in front of ~ 앞에 audience 청중, 관객, 시청자들 video clip 동영상 presentation 발표(회) load (프로그램, 데이터 등이) 로딩되다 instead of ~ 대신 rely on ~에 의존하다 connection 연결 (상태) sound like ~인 것 같다, ~인 것처럼 들리다 solution 해결책 ask if ~인지 묻다 participant 참가자 contact information 연락처 send out ~을 발송하다 follow-up 후속적인, 후속 조치의 survey 설문 조사(지)

13. 오전 워크숍의 주제는 무엇이었는가?
(A) 지속 가능성
(B) 기술
(C) 제품 테스트
(D) 대중 연설

정답 (D)
해설 대화 초반부에 남자가 여자에게 오전 워크숍이 어땠는지 묻자, 여자가 사람들이 청중 앞에서 명확하고 자신감 있게 발표하는 방법을 배우는 것을 즐거워했다고(I think people really enjoyed learning how to present clearly and confidently in front of an audience) 밝히고 있습니다. 이를 통해 대중 앞에서 연설하는 방법을 배우는 워크숍이었음을 알 수 있으므로 (D)가 정답입니다.

Paraphrase present clearly and confidently in front of an audience ⇒ Public speaking

14. 여자의 말에 따르면, 그녀는 어떤 문제에 직면했는가?
(A) 일부 참석자들이 입장 서명을 하지 않았다.
(B) 일부 동영상이 느리게 로딩되었다.
(C) 여러 슬라이드에 정보가 빠져 있었다.
(D) 한 활동이 예상보다 더 오래 걸렸다.

정답 (B)
해설 여자가 대화 중반부에 발표 중에 동영상들 중 일부가 아주 느리게 로딩되었다는(some of the video clips in the presentation loaded very slowly) 문제를 언급하고 있으므로 (B)가 정답입니다.

어휘 encounter ~에 직면하다, ~을 접하다 attendee 참석자 sign in (행사 등에) 서명하고 입장하다, 출입 확인을 받다 miss ~을 빠트리다, ~을 놓치다, ~을 지나치다 take long 오래 걸리다 than expected 예상보다

15. 남자는 무엇을 하고 싶어 하는가?
(A) 보고서를 작성하는 일
(B) 설문 조사지를 나눠 주는 일
(C) 녹음 내용을 들어 보는 일
(D) 예산을 계산하는 일

정답 (B)
해설 남자가 대화 맨 마지막 부분에 모든 사람에게 후속 설문 조사지를 발송하고 싶다는(I want to send out a follow-up survey to everyone) 바람을 알리고 있습니다. 이는 설문 조사지를 나눠 주고 싶다는 뜻이므로 (B)가 정답입니다.

어휘 distribute ~을 나눠 주다, ~을 배부하다 calculate ~을 계산하다 budget 예산

Paraphrase send out a follow-up survey ⇒ Distribute a survey

Questions 16-18 refer to the following conversation.

M: Callaway Cinema, how can I help you?
W: Hello, I'd like to make a group ticket order for one of your movie showings. **16 I'm planning a one-day retreat for my team at work.**
M: Sure, which film and showtime are you interested in? We do provide group booking discounts, but **17 please note that evening showtimes tend to be more expensive.**
W: That won't be a problem. I'd like to reserve fifteen seats for *Infinite Skies* this Saturday at 8 P.M.
M: Alright, and **18 would you like to pay online or on site?**

남: 캘러웨이 시네마입니다, 무엇을 도와 드릴까요?
여: 안녕하세요, 그곳 영화 상영회들 중 한 회차에 대해 단체 관람권을 주문하고자 합니다. 저는 회사에 있는 저희 팀을 위해 일일 단합 대회를 계획하고 있습니다.
남: 네, 어느 영화와 어느 상영 시간에 관심이 있으신가요? 저희가 분명 단체 예약 할인을 제공해 드리고 있기는 하지만, 저녁 상영회는 더 비싼 경향이 있다는 점에 유의하시기 바랍니다.
여: 그건 문제가 되지 않을 겁니다. 이번 주 토요일, 오후 8시에 <인피니트 스카이> 좌석 15개를 예매하고 싶습니다.
남: 알겠습니다, 그리고 온라인에서 결제하시겠습니까, 아니면 현장에서 하시겠습니까?

어휘 would like to do ~하고 싶다 make an order 주문하다 showing 상영회, 상연회 retreat n. 단합 대회, 야유회 be interested in ~에 관심이 있다 booking 예약 note that ~라는 점에 유의하다, ~임에 주목하다 tend to do ~하는 경향이 있다 reserve ~을 예약하다 on site 현장에서

16. 여자는 무엇을 계획하고 있는가?
(A) 회사 저녁 회식
(B) 영화제
(C) 패널 토론회
(D) 직원 단합 대회

정답 (D)
해설 여자가 대화 초반부에 단체 관람권에 관해 문의하면서 회사의 팀을 위해 일일 단합 대회를 계획하고 있다는(I'm planning a one-day retreat for my team at work) 사실을 밝히고 있으므로 (D)가 정답입니다.

Paraphrase a one-day retreat for my team at work
⇒ An employee retreat

17. 남자는 저녁 상영 시간과 관련해 무슨 말을 하는가?
(A) 일반적으로 더 많은 비용이 든다.
(B) 빠르게 매진되는 경향이 있다.
(C) 반드시 직접 가서 예매해야 한다.
(D) 할인 대상이 되지 않는다.

정답 (A)
해설 대화 중반부에 남자가 저녁 상영회는 더 비싼 경향이 있다는 점에 유의하라고(please note that evening showtimes tend to be more expensive) 당부하는 말을 전하고 있습니다. 이는 더 많은 비용이 든다는 뜻이므로 (A)가 정답입니다.

어휘 usually 일반적으로, 보통 sell out 매진되다, 품절되다 in person 직접 (가서) be eligible for ~의 대상이 되다, ~에 대한 자격이 있다

Paraphrase tend to be more expensive
⇒ usually cost more

18. 남자는 여자에게 무엇에 관해 묻는가?
(A) 서비스에 관해 어떻게 들었는지
(B) 예약에 대해 어떻게 결제할 것인지
(C) 영수증이 필요한지
(D) 언제 제품을 가져갈 것인지

정답 (B)
해설 남자가 대화 맨 마지막 부분에 온라인에서 결제할 것인지, 아니면 현장에서 할 것인지(would you like to pay online or on site?) 묻고 있으므로 (B)가 정답입니다.

어휘 reservation 예약 whether ~인지 (아닌지) receipt 영수(증), 수령, 수취 pick up ~을 가져가다, ~을 가져오다

Paraphrase pay online or on site ⇒ How she will pay

Questions 19-21 refer to the following conversation.

M: Ms. Choi, **19 my crew just finished installing your new bathroom sink and bathtub. We're going to start laying down the floor tiles soon.** We're right on schedule.
W: That's great! **20 I just called Lena's Furniture Store regarding the mirror. They're going to deliver it tomorrow afternoon**, which means you can probably start painting the walls whenever you're ready. And for the lights, I plan to call an electrician after you're all done.
M: OK. Also, **21 I think you should consider installing a larger ventilation fan.** I noticed this part of your home gets a lot of direct sunlight, so it gets pretty hot in here.
W: Oh, thanks for that suggestion. I'll consider it.

정답 및 해설 61

남: 최 씨, 저희 작업팀이 방금 새 욕실 세면대와 욕조를 설치하는 일을 끝마쳤습니다. 저희가 곧 바닥 타일을 까는 작업을 시작할 겁니다. 일정에 맞게 잘 진행되고 있습니다.

여: 아주 좋습니다! 제가 거울과 관련해서 방금 레나스 가구점에 전화했습니다. 내일 오후에 배송해 줄 예정인데, 이는 언제든 준비가 되실 때 아마 벽면에 페인트칠을 시작하실 수 있을 거라는 의미입니다. 그리고 조명에 대해서는, 작업을 모두 완료하신 후에 제가 전기 기사님께 전화 드릴 계획입니다.

남: 좋습니다. 그리고, 더 큰 환풍기를 설치하시는 걸 고려해 보셔야 할 것 같습니다. 주택 내에서 이쪽 부분이 직사광선을 많이 받고 있기 때문에, 이곳이 꽤 더워진다는 사실을 알게 되었습니다.

여: 아, 제안에 대해 감사 드립니다. 고려해 볼게요.

어휘 crew (함께 작업하는) 팀, 조 install ~을 설치하다 lay down (타일, 벽돌 등) ~을 깔다 on schedule 일정대로인, 예정대로 regarding ~와 관련해, ~에 관한 whenever 언제든 ~할 때 plan to do ~할 계획이다 electrician 전기 기사 done 완료된 consider -ing ~하는 것을 고려하다 ventilation fan 환풍기 notice (that) ~임을 알게 되다, ~임에 주목하다 direct sunlight 직사광선 pretty 꽤, 아주, 상당히 suggestion 제안, 의견

19. 여자는 왜 남자의 회사를 고용했는가?
(A) 가구를 옮기기 위해
(B) 방 배치를 다시 디자인하기 위해
(C) 욕실을 개조하기 위해
(D) 에어컨 기기를 설치하기 위해

정답 (C)
해설 남자가 대화를 시작하면서 자신의 작업팀이 새 욕실 세면대와 욕조를 설치하는 일을 끝마친 사실과 함께 곧 바닥 타일을 까는 작업을 시작할 것이라고(my crew just finished installing your new bathroom sink and bathtub. We're going to start laying down the floor tiles soon) 알리고 있습니다. 이를 통해 욕실 개조 공사를 진행하고 있다는 것을 알 수 있으므로 (C)가 정답입니다.

어휘 hire ~을 고용하다 layout 배치(도), 구획 remodel ~을 개조하다 air-conditioning 에어컨 unit 기기 한 대, 상품 한 개, 구성 단위

Paraphrase installing your new bathroom sink and bathtub ⇒ remodel her bathroom

20. 내일 오후에 무슨 일이 있을 것인가?
(A) 작업팀이 벽면을 페인트칠할 것이다.
(B) 여자가 배송품을 받을 것이다.
(C) 전기 기사가 방문할 것이다.
(D) 정비 기사가 환풍기를 고칠 것이다

정답 (B)
해설 내일 오후라는 시점이 언급되는 중반부에, 여자가 거울과 관련해서 방금 레나스 가구점에 전화했다고 언급하면서 내일 오후에 배송해 줄 것이라고(I just called Lena's Furniture Store regarding the mirror. They're going to deliver it tomorrow afternoon) 알리고 있으므로 (B)가 정답입니다.

어휘 receive ~을 받다 delivery 배송(품) mechanic 정비 기사 fix ~을 고치다, ~을 바로잡다

Paraphrase are going to deliver it ⇒ will receive a delivery

21. 남자는 무엇을 하는 것을 제안하는가?
(A) 더 큰 기계를 이용할 것
(B) 창문을 만들 것
(C) 일기 예보를 확인할 것
(D) 한 공간을 확장할 것

정답 (A)
해설 남자가 대화 후반부에 더 큰 환풍기를 설치하시는 걸 고려해 봐야 할 것 같다고(I think you should consider installing a larger ventilation fan) 제안하고 있으므로 (A)가 정답입니다.

어휘 suggest -ing ~하는 것을 제안하다 forecast n. 예보 v. ~을 예보하다 expand ~을 확장하다, ~을 확대하다

Paraphrase installing a larger ventilation fan ⇒ Using a larger machine

Questions 22-24 refer to the following conversation with three speakers.

W1: **22 Thank you for allowing us to take pictures of your café, Benji.** This is my coworker, Amanda. As I mentioned, **22 we're both staff writers for an interior design magazine**.
W2: Hello. Nice to meet you. I love the architecture here.
M: Thank you. I've been running this shop for almost two decades now, but **23 I plan to sell it later this year**. I want to pursue a different business venture.
W1: Oh, that's exciting! But I really hope the new owner keeps the property as a café.
W2: I agree. Now that I'm seeing it in person, **24 I get why so many people post about this place on social media!**

여1: 귀하의 카페를 촬영하도록 허용해 주셔서 감사 드립니다, 벤지 씨. 이쪽은 제 동료인 아만다 씨입니다. 제가 언급해 드린 대로, 저희 둘 모두 실내 디자인 잡지를 위해 일하는 전속 기자입니다.

여2: 안녕하세요. 만나 뵙게 되어서 기쁩니다. 이곳 건축 양식이 너무 마음에 듭니다.

남: 감사합니다. 제가 지금 거의 20년 동안 이 매장을 계속 운영해 오고 있지만, 올해 후반기에 매각할 계획입니다. 제가 다른 벤처 사업을 추구하기를 원하고 있거든요.

여1: 아, 흥미롭네요! 하지만 저는 새로운 소유주께서 이 건물을 카페로 유지하시기를 정말로 바라고 있어요.

여2: 동감이에요. 직접 확인해 보고 있으니까, 왜 그렇게 많은 사람들이 소셜 미디어에 이곳과 관련된 게시글을 올리는지 알겠어요.

어휘 allow A to do: A에게 ~하도록 허용하다, A에게 ~할 수 있게 해 주다 coworker 동료 (직원) mention 언급하다 staff writer 전속 기자 architecture 건축 양식, 건축학 run ~을 운영하다 decade 10년 plan to do ~할 계획이다 pursue ~을 추구하다, ~을 계속 하다 business venture (모험적인) 벤처 사업 owner 소유주, 주인 property 건물, 부동산, 자산 agree 동의하다, 합의하다 now that (이제) ~이므로 in person 직접 (가서) post 게시글을 올리다

22. 화자들은 왜 만나고 있는가?
   (A) 임대 공간을 둘러보기 위해
   (B) 회사 행사를 준비하기 위해
   (C) 함께 커피를 즐기기 위해
   (D) 잡지에 필요한 콘텐츠를 수집하기 위해

정답 (D)

해설 여자 한 명이 대화를 시작하면서 남자에게 카페를 촬영하도록 허용해 준 것에 대해 감사하다는(Thank you for allowing us to take pictures of your café, Benji) 말과 함께 자신들이 실내 디자인 잡지의 전속 기자라고(we're both staff writers for an interior design magazine) 언급하고 있습니다. 따라서, 두 여자가 잡지에 필요한 콘텐츠 제작과 관련해 해당 카페를 방문한 상황임을 알 수 있으므로 (D)가 정답입니다.

어휘 tour v. ~을 둘러보다, ~을 견학하다 rental 임대, 대여 organize ~을 준비하다, ~을 조직하다 gather ~을 수집하다, ~을 모으다

23. 남자는 올해 후반기에 무엇을 할 것이라고 말하는가?
   (A) 메뉴를 변경하는 일
   (B) 업체를 매각하는 일
   (C) 해외로 이전하는 일
   (D) 신입 직원을 고용하는 일

정답 (B)

해설 대화 중반부에 남자가 자신의 카페를 it으로 지칭해 올해 후반기에 매각할 계획이라고(I plan to sell it later this year) 알리고 있으므로 (B)가 정답입니다.

어휘 relocate 이전하다, 재배치되다 overseas ad. 해외로, 해외에 a. 해외의 hire ~을 고용하다

24. 아만다 씨는 건물과 관련해 무슨 말을 하는가?
   (A) 널찍하다.
   (B) 온라인에서 인기 있다.
   (C) 멋진 경관을 지니고 있다.
   (D) 역사적인 명소이다

정답 (B)

해설 첫 번째 여자가 대화 초반부에 동료 직원이라고 소개한 두 번째 여자가 아만다이며, 아만다는 대화 후반부에 왜 그렇게 많은 사람들이 소셜 미디어에 해당 건물과 관련된 게시글을 올리는지 알겠다고(I get why so many people post about this place on social media) 말하고 있습니다. 이는 사람들이 아주 많은 게시글을 올릴 정도로 인기 있다는 뜻이므로 (B)가 정답입니다.

어휘 spacious 널찍한 historical 역사적인, 역사상의 landmark 명소, 인기 장소

Paraphrase so many people post about this place on social media ⇒ popular online

---

DAY 10 제안·요청 사항 / do next 문제

PRACTICE

1. (B)   2. (D)

Question 1 refers to the following conversation.

> W: Our office printer can't handle all these monthly reports. It keeps running out of ink and jamming.
> M: **I suggest we invest in a high-capacity laser printer that handles large volumes.**
> W: That would save us from a lot of headaches.
> M: I'll research some models this afternoon.

여: 저희 사무실의 프린터는 이 모든 월간 보고서들을 처리할 수가 없어요. 잉크도 자꾸 떨어지고 종이 걸림도 계속됩니다.

남: 저는 대용량 인쇄에 적합한 고성능 레이저 프린터에 투자하는 것을 제안합니다.
여: 그게 있으면 진짜 골치 아픈 일이 많이 줄겠어요.
남: 제가 오늘 오후에 몇 가지 모델을 알아 볼게요.

어휘 handle 처리하다, 다루다 monthly 월간의, 월례의 keep -ing 계속 ~하다 run out of ~가 다 떨어지다 jam 막힘, 걸림 suggest 제안하다 invest 투자하다 volume 용량 high-capacity 고성능의 save A from B: A를 B에서 구하다 headache 두통, 골칫거리 research 조사하다

1. 남자는 무엇을 제안하는가?
(A) 여분의 잉크 카트리지 주문하기
(B) 견고한 프린터 구매하기
(C) 인쇄 대행 서비스 이용하기
(D) 페이지 수 줄이기

정답 (B)
해설 남자는 "I suggest ~"로 시작하는 문장에서 대용량 인쇄에 적합한 고성능 레이저 프린터에 투자하는 것을(we invest in a high-capacity laser printer that handles large volumes) 제안하였습니다. 따라서 정답은 (B)입니다.

어휘 extra 여분의 heavy-duty 튼튼한, 견고한 hire 고용하다, 이용하다 reduce 줄이다

Question 2 refers to the following conversation.

M: I want to sign up for today's yoga session, but the front desk isn't taking registrations.
W: The reception area is closed for a staff meeting, so you can't register in person right now.
M: Now I'm not on the roster, and the class starts soon.
W: **I think you will need to register via our mobile app by scanning that QR code on the wall.**

남: 저는 오늘 요가 수업에 등록하고 싶은데, 프런트 데스크에서 접수를 안 받아요.
여: 지금 리셉션 구역이 직원 회의로 인해 닫혀 있어서, 직접 등록은 불가능해요.
남: 그럼 지금 명단에 제 이름도 없고, 수업도 곧 시작하잖아요.
여: 벽에 붙은 QR 코드를 스캔해서 저희 모바일 앱으로 등록하셔야 할 것 같아요.

어휘 sign up for ~에 등록하다 registration 등록 reception 접수, 응대 staff meeting 직원 회의 register 등록 in person 직접 roster 등록 명단 via ~을 통해 by -ing ~함으로써

2. 남자는 이어서 무엇을 할 것 같은가?
(A) 직원이 돌아오기를 기다린다
(B) 요가 매트를 구매한다
(C) 다른 시간대로 교체한다
(D) 앱을 통해 등록을 완료한다

정답 (D)
해설 남자가 요가 수업에 등록을 하지 못한다고 하자 대화 마지막 부분에서 여자가 남자에게 벽에 붙은 QR 코드를 스캔해서 저희 모바일 앱으로 등록하셔야 할 것 같다고(I think you will need to register via our mobile app by scanning that QR code on the wall) 말하는 것을 듣고 남자가 앱을 통해 등록을 완료할 것이라는 것을 알 수 있습니다. 따라서 정답은 (D)입니다.

어휘 wait for ~을 기다리다 swap to ~으로 교체하다, 바꾸다 complete 완료하다 sign-up 등록 through ~을 통해

실전 TEST

1. (C)	2. (A)	3. (D)	4. (D)	5. (B)
6. (D)	7. (C)	8. (C)	9. (A)	10. (A)
11. (D)	12. (D)	13. (C)	14. (D)	15. (A)
16. (C)	17. (B)	18. (C)	19. (D)	20. (C)
21. (C)	22. (C)	23. (A)	24. (B)	

Questions 1-3 refer to the following conversation.

W: Good morning, and welcome to Muller Corporation's orientation session for new interns. Have you been assigned to a department?
M: Yes, **1 I just received my employment contract from the personnel manager. Here it is.** It says I've been placed in the general affairs department.
W: I see. It actually says **2 you'll be assisting the manager of the department**, so that's a very important role. Now, while we are waiting for the others to arrive, **3 please have a quick read through the employee handbook** that you can find on your chair.

여: 안녕하세요, 그리고 뮬러 사의 신입 인턴 오리엔테이션 시간에 오신 것을 환영합니다. 부서를 배정 받으셨나요?
남: 네, 방금 인사부장님으로부터 제 고용 계약서를 받았습니다. 여기 있습니다. 제가 총무부에 배치되었다고 쓰여 있습니다.

여: 알겠습니다. 실제로는 그 부서의 부장님을 도와드릴 예정이라고 쓰여 있어요. 그래서 그것은 매우 중요한 역할입니다. 자, 다른 분들이 도착하기를 기다리는 동안, 당신의 의자 위에서 찾아보실 수 있는 직무 안내서를 한번 빠르게 훑어보시기 바랍니다.

어휘 session (특정 활동을 위한) 시간 assign ~을 배정하다, 할당하다 department 부서 receive ~을 받다 employment contract 고용 계약(서) personnel manager 인사부장 say (문서 등에) ~라고 쓰여 있다 place ~을 배치하다, 두다 general affairs department 총무부 actually 실제로, 사실 assist ~을 돕다 role 역할 while ~하는 동안 wait for A to do: A가 ~하기를 기다리다 arrive 도착하다 have a read through ~을 죽 읽어보다 employee handbook 직무 안내서

1. 남자는 여자에게 무엇을 보여주는가?
(A) 업무 일정표
(B) 사원증
(C) 고용 계약서
(D) 지원서

정답 (C)

해설 남자가 여자에게 보여주는 것을 묻는 문제이므로 전달 또는 제공 등을 나타내는 표현과 함께 언급되는 것을 찾아야 합니다. 대화 중반부에 남자가 인사부장으로부터 고용 계약서를 받은 사실과 함께 그것을 전달하는 말을 하고 있으므로 (I just received my employment contract from the personnel manager. Here it is) (C)가 정답입니다.

어휘 application 지원, 신청 form 양식, 서식

2. 여자는 남자의 일과 관련해 무슨 말을 하는가?
(A) 부서장을 도울 것이다.
(B) 재무를 책임질 것이다.
(C) 주말마다 근무할 것이다.
(D) 고객들에게 서비스를 제공해야 할 것이다.

정답 (A)

해설 여자가 남자의 일과 관련하여 하는 말을 묻는 문제이므로 여자의 말에서 단서를 찾아야 합니다. 대화 후반부에 여자가 남자를 you로 지칭해 부서장을 돕는 일을 할 것이라고 (~ you'll be assisting the manager of the department) 말하고 있으므로 (A)가 정답입니다.

어휘 supervisor 부서장, 책임자, 상사 be responsible for ~을 책임지다 finance 재무, 재정, 금융 be required to do ~해야 하다 serve ~에게 서비스를 제공하다

Paraphrase assisting the manager of the department
⇒ helping a supervisor

3. 여자는 남자에게 무엇을 하도록 요청하는가?
(A) 그룹에 합류하기
(B) 양식 작성하기
(C) 발표하기
(D) 안내서 읽어보기

정답 (D)

해설 여자가 요청하는 일을 묻고 있으므로 여자의 말에서 요청 관련 표현과 함께 제시되는 정보를 찾아야 합니다. 대화 후반부에 여자가 직무 안내서를 한번 빠르게 훑어보도록(please have a quick read through the employee handbook ~) 요청하는 말이 있으므로 이를 언급한 (D)가 정답입니다.

어휘 ask A to do: A에게 ~하도록 요청하다 join ~에 합류하다, ~와 함께 하다 fill out ~을 작성하다 give a presentation 발표하다

Questions 4-6 refer to the following conversation.

M: This is Kohlman's Supermarket. How can I help you today?
W: Hello. I just heard on the radio that **4** you now deliver grocery orders. I'd like some more information about it.
M: Sure, what would you like to know?
W: 5 Won't the order take a few days to arrive?
M: Actually, it's same-day delivery, guaranteed.
W: Oh, fantastic. I'll try it this week. Umm… and since I have you on the line, **6** could you check if you have any Roma pasta sauce in stock?
M: 6 Of course. Let me do a quick search for you.

남: 콜만스 슈퍼마켓입니다. 오늘 무엇을 도와드릴까요?
여: 안녕하세요. 이제 식료품 주문 사항을 배송해 주신다는 말을 라디오에서 막 들었어요. 좀 더 많은 정보를 알려 주셨으면 합니다.
남: 물론입니다, 무엇을 알고 싶으신가요?
여: 주문품이 도착하는 데 며칠씩 걸리지 않을까요?
남: 실은, 당일 배송을 보장해 드리고 있습니다.
여: 아, 정말 좋은데요. 이번 주에 한 번 해보겠습니다. 음… 그리고 통화하는 김에, 로마 파스타 소스 재고가 있는지 확인 좀 해주시겠어요?
남: 물론입니다. 빠르게 찾아보겠습니다.

어휘 grocery 식료품 order 주문(품) I'd like ~을 원하다, ~하고 싶다 take ~의 시간이 걸리다 arrive 도착하다 same-day 당일의 delivery 배송 guaranteed 보장되는 try ~을 한 번 해보다 on the line 통화 중인 have A in stock: A를 재고로 갖추고 있다 do a search 찾다

4. 남자는 어디에서 근무하는가?
(A) 레스토랑에서
(B) 라디오 방송국에서
(C) 세탁소에서
(D) 식료품 매장에서

정답 (D)

해설 대화 초반부에 여자가 남자가 소속된 업체를 you로 지칭해 식료품 주문 사항을 배송해 준다는(you now deliver grocery orders) 소식을 들은 사실을 언급하고 있으므로 (D)가 정답입니다.

5. 여자는 무엇에 대해 우려하는가?
(A) 서비스 비용
(B) 배송 기간
(C) 회비
(D) 좌석 수용 규모

정답 (B)

해설 여자가 우려하는 것을 묻는 문제이므로 여자의 말에서 언급되는 부정적인 정보를 찾아야 합니다. 대화 중반부에 여자가 주문품이 도착하는 데 며칠씩 걸리지 않을지(Won't the order take a few days to arrive?) 질문하는 부분이 있는데, 이는 배송 기간을 우려하는 말에 해당되므로 (B)가 정답입니다.

어휘 be concerned about ~에 대해 우려하다

6. 남자는 곧이어 무엇을 할 것 같은가?
(A) 전화 돌려주기
(B) 부서장과 이야기하기
(C) 구입품 환불해주기
(D) 재고 확인하기

정답 (D)

해설 대화 후반부에 여자가 특정 파스타 소스 재고를 확인해 달라고 요청하는 것에 대해(could you check if you have any Roma pasta sauce in stock?) 남자가 Of course라는 말로 수락하고 있으므로 (D)가 정답입니다.

어휘 transfer a call (다른 곳으로) 전화를 돌리다 refund ~을 환불 해주다 purchase 구입(품) inventory 재고 (목록)

Paraphrase check if you have any Roma pasta sauce in stock ⇒ Check an inventory

---

Questions 7-9 refer to the following conversation.

M: Hi, **7** this is Richard Davis calling from Metro Convention Center. I'd just like to confirm your reservation for next month's software convention. You requested to use Public Hall 2 on September 14, didn't you?

W: Yes, that's right. And, **8** I was wondering if we will be allowed to sell any of our branded merchandise during our presentation. Just some hats and T-shirts.

M: No problem. But **9** you'll need to complete a form in order to have permission for that. I'll send you one by e-mail now. Please send the completed one back to me as quickly as possible.

남: 안녕하세요, 저는 메트로 컨벤션 센터의 리차드 데이비스입니다. 다음 달에 있을 소프트웨어 컨벤션 행사의 예약 사항을 확인해 드리고자 합니다. 9월 14일에 2번 공개홀을 이용하겠다고 요청하셨죠, 그렇지 않나요?

여: 네, 맞습니다. 그리고, 저희 발표 시간 중에 저희 브랜드가 들어간 어떤 상품이든 판매하도록 허용될 수 있는지 궁금합니다. 그저 몇몇 모자와 티셔츠뿐입니다.

남: 문제 없습니다. 하지만 그 부분에 대해 승인 받으시려면 양식을 작성하셔야 할 겁니다. 제가 지금 이메일로 한 부 보내 드리겠습니다. 작성 완료하신 것을 가능한 한 빨리 저에게 다시 보내 주시기 바랍니다.

어휘 confirm ~을 확인해 주다 reservation 예약 request to do ~하도록 요청하다 wonder if ~인지 궁금하다 be allowed to do ~하도록 허용되다 branded 브랜드가 들어간 merchandise 상품 during ~ 중에, ~ 동안 presentation 발표 complete ~을 작성 완료하다 form 양식, 서식 in order to do ~하기 위해 permission 승인, 허가 as quickly as possible 가능한 한 빨리

7. 남자는 어디에서 근무하고 있을 것 같은가?
(A) 휴양 리조트에서
(B) 스포츠 경기장에서
(C) 컨벤션 센터에서
(D) 정부 건물에서

정답 (C)

해설 대화 시작 부분에 남자가 'this is Richard Davis calling from Metro Convention Center'라는 말로 자신의 이름과 소속 단체를 밝히고 있으므로 (C)가 정답입니다.

8. 여자는 무엇에 관해 문의하는가?
(A) 행사 장소를 변경하는 것
(B) 장비를 운송하는 것
(C) 상품을 판매하는 것
(D) 표를 구입하는 것

정답 (C)

해설 여자가 문의하는 것을 묻는 문제이므로 여자의 말에서 단서를 찾아야 합니다. 대화 중반부에 여자가 발표 중에 상품을 판매하도록 허용되는지 궁금하다고(I was wondering if we will be allowed to sell any of our branded merchandise during our presentation) 말하고 있으므로 (C)가 정답입니다.

어휘 inquire about ~에 관해 문의하다 venue (행사 등의) 장소 transport ~을 운송하다 equipment 장비

9. 남자는 여자에게 무엇을 하도록 권하는가?
(A) 양식 작성하기
(B) 발표 일정 재조정하기
(C) 행사 장소 방문하기
(D) 자신의 부서장과 이야기하기

정답 (A)

해설 남자가 권하는 일을 묻고 있으므로 남자의 말에서 권고 또는 제안 관련 표현과 함께 언급되는 정보를 찾아야 합니다. 대화 후반부에 남자가 승인을 받으려면 양식을 작성해야 한다고(you'll need to complete a form in order to have permission ~) 말하는 부분이 있으므로 이를 언급한 (A)가 정답입니다.

어휘 fill out ~을 작성하다 reschedule ~의 일정을 재조정하다 site 장소, 부지, 현장

Paraphrase complete a form ⇒ Fill out a form

Questions 10-12 refer to the following conversation.

> W: Excuse me, 10 it's been almost an hour since I arrived for my dental appointment. Do you know why it is taking so long? I have to be at a job interview at noon.
> M: Oh, I'm sorry. 11 One of our dentists had to go home ill this morning, so the other one, Dr. Martinez, is seeing all patients today. Hopefully, he'll be able to see you soon. As an apology for the delay, 12 I can offer you a free teeth cleaning service.
> W: That would be appreciated. But, I doubt I'll have time to take advantage of it today. I don't want to be late for my interview.

여: 실례합니다, 제가 치과 예약 때문에 도착한지 거의 한 시간이 다 되었습니다. 왜 이렇게 오래 걸리는지 아시나요? 제가 정오에는 구직 면접 자리에 가봐야 합니다.
남: 아, 죄송합니다. 저희 치과 의사 선생님들 중 한 분께서 오늘 아침에 편찮으셔서 댁으로 돌아 가셔야 했기 때문에, 다른 의사 선생님이신 마르티네즈 선생님께서 오늘 모든 환자분들을 보고 계십니다. 바라건대, 곧 진료해 드릴 수 있을 겁니다. 지연 문제에 대한 사과로, 무료 치석 제거 서비스를 제공해 드릴 수 있습니다.
여: 그렇게 해주시면 감사하겠습니다. 하지만, 오늘 그것을 이용할 시간이 있을 것 같지 않네요. 제 면접 시간에 늦고 싶지 않아서요.

어휘 since ~한 이후로 arrive 도착하다 dental 치아의, 치과의 appointment 예약, 약속 take ~의 시간이 걸리다 noon 정오 dentist 치과 의사 go home ill 아파서 집에 가다 the other (둘 중 하나를 제외한) 나머지 다른 하나의 patient 환자 hopefully 바라건대 be able to do ~할 수 있다 apology for ~에 대한 사과 delay 지연, 지체 offer A B: A에게 B를 제공하다 free 무료의 teeth cleaning 치석 제거 appreciate ~에 대해 감사하다 doubt (that) ~할 것 같지 않다, ~인지 의심 스럽다 take advantage of ~을 이용하다

10. 화자들은 어디에 있을 것 같은가?
(A) 치과 진료소에
(B) 취업 안내 센터에
(C) 식료품 매장에
(D) 자동차 수리소에

정답 (A)

해설 대화를 시작하면서 여자가 치과 예약 때문에 도착한지 거의 한 시간이 다 되었다고(it's been almost an hour since I arrived for my dental appointment) 말하고 있으므로 치과 진료소를 뜻하는 (A)가 정답입니다.

11. 지연 문제의 원인은 무엇인가?
(A) 예약상의 실수가 발생했다.
(B) 일부 장비에 결함이 있다.
(C) 교통량이 극심하다.
(D) 의료진의 일원이 아프다.

정답 (D)

해설 대화 중반부에 남자가 치과 의사 선생님들 중 한 명이 오늘 아침에 편찮으셔서 댁으로 돌아 가셔야 했기 때문에 다른 의사 선생님이 오늘 모든 환자를 보고 있다고(One of our dentists had to go home ill this morning, so the other one, Dr. Martinez, is seeing all patients today) 알리는 것으로 지연 문제의 원인을 말해주고 있습니다. 따라서 이와 같은 사실을 언급한 (D)가 정답입니다.

어휘 reservation 예약 make an error 실수하다 equipment 장비 faulty 결함이 있는 heavy traffic 극심한 교통량

12. 남자는 무엇을 하겠다고 제안하는가?
(A) 쿠폰 제공하기
(B) 환불 해주기
(C) 상사에게 연락하기
(D) 무료 서비스 마련하기

정답 (D)

해설 남자가 제안하는 일을 묻고 있으므로 남자의 말에서 제안 관련 표현과 함께 제시되는 정보를 찾아야 합니다. 대화 후반부에 남자가 사과의 뜻으로 무료 치석 제거 서비스를 제공해 줄 수 있다고(I can offer you a free teeth cleaning service) 제안하고 있으므로 (D)가 정답입니다.

어휘 offer to do ~하겠다고 제안하다 provide ~을 제공하다(= offer) voucher 쿠폰, 상품권 refund 환불(액) contact ~에게 연락하다 supervisor 상사, 책임자, 부서장 arrange ~을 마련하다, 조치하다 free 무료의

Questions 13-15 refer to the following conversation.

> W: Hi, **13** **can you recommend me a good pair of boots?** I'm going hiking next week and want to get a sturdy pair.
> M: Sure. Do you have any color or style preferences?
> W: Not really, but **14** **I'm worried about keeping the shoes clean. I'd like some that are easy to manage.**
> M: Well, most of our outdoor boots are waterproof and made of leather or durable nylon. So even if they get dirty, they'll be easy to clean. If you want an affordable option, I'd suggest these Agoda Trekkers.
> W: Great. **15** **Can I try them on right now?**
>
> 여: 안녕하세요, 좋은 등산화 한 켤레 추천해 주시겠어요? 제가 다음 주에 하이킹하러 가기 때문에 튼튼한 것으로 한 켤레 구입하고 싶습니다.
> 남: 물론입니다. 선호하시는 어떤 색상이나 스타일이 있으신가요?
> 여: 꼭 그렇진 않은데, 신발을 깨끗하게 유지하는 것이 걱정입니다. 관리하기 쉬운 것이면 좋겠습니다.
> 남: 음, 대부분의 저희 야외 등산화들이 방수인데다, 가죽 또는 내구성이 뛰어난 나일론으로 만들어집니다. 그래서 더러워진다 하더라도, 닦아내기 쉬울 겁니다. 가격이 저렴한 선택 대상을 원하시면, 이 아고다 트레커스를 권해 드리고 싶습니다.
> 여: 아주 좋습니다. 지금 바로 착용해 볼 수 있나요?

어휘 sturdy 튼튼한, 견고한 preference 선호(하는 것) Not really (앞선 말에 대해) 꼭 그렇지는 않다 be worried about ~을 걱정하다 keep A 형용사: A를 ~하게 유지하다 would like A: A를 원하다, A로 하고 싶다 waterproof 방수의 be made of ~로 만들어지다 leather 가죽 durable 내구성이 좋은 even if ~한다 하더라도 get + 형용사: ~해지다, ~한 상태가 되다 affordable 가격이 저렴한, 감당할 수 있는 try A on: A를 착용해 보다

13. 여자는 무엇을 쇼핑하고 있는가?
(A) 핸드백
(B) 청바지
(C) 등산화
(D) 캠핑 장비

정답 (C)

해설 여자가 대화를 시작하면서 좋은 등산화 한 켤레 추천해 달라고(can you recommend me a good pair of boots?) 요청하고 있으므로 (C)가 정답입니다.

14. 여자가 걱정하는 이유는 무엇인가?
(A) 행사가 연기되었다.
(B) 가격이 온라인에서 더 저렴할지도 모른다.
(C) 특정 색상이 판매 가능하지 않다.
(D) 제품이 많은 유지 관리를 필요로 할 수 있다.

정답 (D)

해설 대화 중반부에 여자가 신발을 깨끗하게 유지하는 것이 걱정이라고 언급하면서 관리하기 쉬운 것이면 좋겠다고(I'm worried about keeping the shoes clean. I'd like some that are easy to manage) 알리고 있습니다. 이는 제품의 유지 관리가 어렵지 않을지, 즉 많은 유지 관리가 필요하지 않을지 걱정하는 것이므로 (D)가 정답입니다.

어휘 be concerned about ~을 걱정[우려]하다 postpone ~을 연기하다, ~을 미루다 specific 특정한, 구체적인 available (사물) 이용 가능한, 구입 가능한, (사람) 시간이 있는 for sale 판매용의, 판매용으로 내놓은 require ~을 필요로 하다 maintenance 유지 관리, 정비

Paraphrase keeping the shoes clean / would like some that are easy to manage ⇒ An item may require a lot of maintenance

15. 여자는 곧이어 무엇을 할 것 같은가?
(A) 제품을 착용해 보는 일
(B) 제품을 구입하는 일
(C) 한 강좌에 등록하는 일
(D) 제품 카탈로그를 확인해 보는 일

정답 (A)

해설 여자가 대화 맨 마지막 부분에 남자가 추천하는 신발 한 켤레에 대해 지금 바로 착용해 볼 수 있는지(Can I try them on right now?) 묻고 있으므로 (A)가 정답입니다.

어휘 make a purchase 구입하다 register for ~에 등록하다
view ~을 보다

Questions 16-18 refer to the following conversation.

> W: Hi, there. **16** **I noticed you've been eyeing our display of Infinitize Robot Vacuums, especially the VL9 series.**
> M: Yes, **17** **I've been reading about the special technology behind this new brand.** Many reviews are saying its products are amazing, so I wanted to buy one today. But I don't see the model I'm looking for.
> W: Oh yes, these vacuums are our hottest items right now. **18** **Why don't you register for our waitlist?** All I need is your name and phone number, and you'll be able to claim any item within the next batch we get.

여 안녕하세요, 고객님. 저희 인피니타이즈 로봇 진공 청소기, 특히 VL9 시리즈의 진열품을 계속 눈여겨 보고 계신다는 걸 알게 되었습니다.
남 네, 이 새로운 브랜드의 이면에 존재하는 특수 기술에 관한 글을 계속 읽어 오고 있었거든요. 많은 후기에서 이 브랜드의 제품들이 놀랍다고 말하고 있어서, 오늘 하나 구입하고 싶었습니다. 하지만 제가 찾고 있는 모델은 보이지 않네요.
여 아, 네, 이 브랜드의 진공 청소기들이 지금 가장 인기 있는 제품입니다. 저희 대기 명단에 등록해 보시면 어떨까요? 성함과 전화번호만 있으면 되는데, 저희가 받는 다음 번 물량 내에 있는 어떤 제품이든 요청하실 수 있으실 겁니다.

어휘 notice (that) ~임을 알게 되다, ~임에 주의하다 eye v. ~을 눈여겨 보다 display n. 진열(품), 전시(품) v. ~을 진열하다, ~을 전시하다 vacuum n. 진공 청소기 v. ~을 진공 청소기로 청소하다 especially 특히, 특별히 behind ~의 이면에 존재하는 review n. 후기, 평가, 검토 v. ~의 후기를 작성하다, ~을 평가하다, ~을 검토하다 look for ~을 찾다 Why don't you ~? ~하시면 어떨까요? register for ~에 등록하다 waitlist 대기 명단 All I need is A: A만 있으면 됩니다 be able to do ~할 수 있다 claim ~을 요청하다, ~을 주장하다 batch 한 회분의 물량

16. 화자들은 어디에 있을 것 같은가?
(A) 문구점
(B) 의료 시설
(C) 전자제품 매장
(D) 엔지니어링 회사

정답 (C)

해설 여자가 대화를 시작하면서 남자에게 인피니타이즈 로봇 진공 청소기, 특히 VL9 시리즈의 진열품을 계속 눈여겨 보고 있다는 것을 알게 되었다고(I noticed you've been eyeing our display of Infinitize Robot Vacuums, especially the VL9 series) 말하고 있습니다. 따라서, 진공 청소기를 구입할 수 있는 매장인 (C)가 정답입니다.

어휘 stationery 문구(류) facility 시설(물) electronics 전자제품 firm 회사, 업체

Paraphrase Robot Vacuums ⇒ electronics

17. 남자는 무엇에 관해 계속 읽어 오고 있다고 말하는가?
(A) 시장 동향
(B) 특수 기술
(C) 제품 테스트 의견
(D) 한 회사의 역사

정답 (B)

해설 대화 중반부에 남자가 한 새로운 브랜드의 이면에 존재하는 특수 기술에 관한 글을 계속 읽어 오고 있었다고(I've been reading about the special technology behind this new brand) 밝히고 있으므로 (B)가 정답입니다.

어휘 trend 동향, 추세, 유행 feedback 의견

18. 여자는 남자에게 무엇을 하도록 제안하는가?
(A) 제품 라벨을 확인할 것
(B) 온라인으로 주문할 것
(C) 대기 명단에 등록할 것
(D) 다른 지점으로 가 볼 것

정답 (C)

해설 여자가 대화 후반부에 제품의 인기와 관련해 언급하면서 대기 명단에 등록해 보면 어떨지(Why don't you register for our waitlist?) 제안하고 있으므로 (C)가 정답입니다.

어휘 place an order 주문하다 sign up for ~에 등록하다, ~을 신청하다 location 지점, 위치

Paraphrase register for our waitlist
⇒ Sign up for a waitlist

Questions 19-21 refer to the following conversation.

W: Hi, Derek. You know how 19 **Sunita Peterson is going to be our new executive director? She told me that she wants to have a meal with our team to get to know everyone.**
M: Alright then, let's arrange a lunch for this Friday. Any ideas where to go?
W: 20 **How about the Marigold Kitchen on Bryan Avenue? It usually isn't too crowded or loud,** which means we can have a good conversation altogether in there.
M: Good idea. 21 **I'll contact Ms. Peterson right now to ask whether Friday lunchtime is okay. After she confirms, we can send out a notice to everyone.**

여: 안녕하세요, 데릭 씨. 수니타 피터슨 씨께서 우리 신임 전무 이사님이 되실 예정이라는 것을 알고 계시죠? 그분께서 저에게 모든 사람을 알게 될 수 있도록 우리 팀과 식사를 하고 싶으시다고 말씀하셨어요.
남: 알겠습니다. 그럼, 이번 주 금요일로 점심 식사 자리를 마련해 보죠. 어디로 갈지 좋은 생각 있으세요?
여: 브라이언 애비뉴에 있는 매리골드 키친은 어떠세요? 이곳이 평소에 그렇게 붐비거나 시끄럽지 않은데, 이는 우리가 그곳에서 모두 좋은 대화를 나눌 수 있다는 뜻입니다.
남: 좋은 생각입니다. 제가 지금 바로 피터슨 씨께 연락해서 금요일 점심 시간이 괜찮으신지 여쭤 보겠습니다. 이분께서 확인해 주신 후에, 모두에게 공지를 발송할 수 있습니다.

어휘 executive director 전무 이사, 상무 이사 get to do ~하게 되다 arrange ~을 마련하다, ~을 조치하다, ~을 처리하다 where to do 어디서 ~할지, ~하는 곳 How about ~? ~는 어때요? usually 평소에, 일반적으로 crowded (사람들로) 붐비는 altogether 전체적으로, 모두 contact ~에게 연락하다 whether ~인지 (아닌지) confirm 확인해 주다 send out ~을 발송하다 notice 공지, 알림, 안내(문)

19. 화자들은 왜 점심 식사를 계획하고 있는가?
(A) 고객과 만나기 위해
(B) 팀의 노력에 대해 보상하기 위해
(C) 지역 내의 한 계획을 지지하기 위해
(D) 신임 이사를 소개하기 위해

정답 (D)
해설 여자가 대화를 시작하면서 수니타 피터슨 씨가 신임 전무 이사가 된다는 사실과 함께 그 사람이 모두를 알 수 있도록 함께 식사하고 싶어한다는(Sunita Peterson is going to be our new executive director? She told me that she wants to have a meal with our team to get to know everyone) 사실을 알리고 있습니다. 따라서, 신임 전무 이사를 소개하는 자리가 될 것임을 알 수 있으므로 (D)가 정답입니다.

어휘 reward ~에 대해 보상하다 support ~을 지지하다, ~을 지원하다 local 지역의, 현지의 initiative 계획, 주도(권), 솔선 수범, 진취성 introduce ~을 소개하다, ~을 도입하다

20. 여자는 매리골드 키친과 관련해 무엇이 마음에 든다고 말하는가?
(A) 합리적인 가격
(B) 연장된 매장 운영 시간
(C) 조용한 환경
(D) 맛있는 음식

정답 (C)
해설 대화 중반부에 여자가 매리골드 키친을 권하면서 평소에 그렇게 붐비거나 시끄럽지 않다는(How about the Marigold Kitchen on Bryan Avenue? It usually isn't too crowded or loud) 점을 언급하고 있습니다. 이는 그 식당이 조용한 환경을 지니고 있다는 뜻이므로 (C)가 정답입니다.

어휘 reasonable 합리적인, 가격이 알맞은 extend ~을 연장하다, ~을 확장하다

Paraphrase isn't too crowded or loud
⇒ quiet environment

21. 남자는 무엇을 하겠다고 제안하는가?
(A) 몇몇 안내 사항을 발송하는 일
(B) 예약 일정을 잡는 일
(C) 확인을 요청하는 일
(D) 행사 일정을 변경하는 일

정답 (C)
해설 남자가 대화 마지막 부분에 피터슨 씨에게 연락해서 금요일 점심 시간이 괜찮은지 물어 보겠다고 말하면서 확인을 받은 후에 공지를 발송하겠다고(I'll contact Ms. Peterson right now to ask whether Friday lunchtime is okay. After she confirms, we can send out a notice to everyone) 알리고 있으므로 (C)가 정답입니다.

어휘 reservation 예약 ask for ~을 요청하다 confirmation 확인(서)

Questions 22-24 refer to the following conversation.

M: OK, **22** **I finished looking at all four wheels on your car.**
W: **22** **Were you able to figure out the problem?**
M: Yes. One of the rear tires has a hole in it, so the loss of pressure is making your vehicle unstable when driving. The tire needs to be replaced completely.
W: Will that take a long time?
M: Luckily, **23** **this is such a common issue that I have lots of experience with it.** I can get it done within the next hour.
W: Wow, that's a relief. **24** **I'll just sit in your waiting area in the meantime.**

남: 좋습니다, 고객님 자동차의 바퀴 네 개를 모두 살펴 보는 일을 끝마쳤습니다.
여: 문제를 파악하실 수 있으셨나요?
남: 네. 뒤쪽 타이어들 중 하나에 구멍이 생겼기 때문에, 압력 손실이 운전하실 때 차량을 불안정하게 만들고 있습니다. 이 타이어는 완전히 교체되어야 합니다.
여: 그게 시간이 오래 걸릴까요?
남: 다행히, 이는 너무 흔한 문제라서 제가 이에 대해 많은 경험을 지니고 있습니다. 앞으로 1시간 내에 완료해 드릴 수 있습니다.
여: 와우, 그럼 안심입니다. 저는 그 동안 그냥 대기실에 앉아 있을게요.

어휘 wheel (차량 등의) 바퀴 be able to do ~할 수 있다 figure out ~을 파악하다, ~을 알아내다 rear 뒤쪽의 loss 손실, 분실, 상실 pressure 압력, 압박(감) make A + 형용사: A를 ~하게 만들다 vehicle 차량 unstable 불안정한 replace ~을 교체하다 completely 완전히, 전적으로 take ~의 시간이 걸리다 such a 명사(구) that: 너무 ~해서 하다 common 흔한, 보통의, 공동의 issue 문제, 사안 get A p.p.: A를 ~되게 하다 relief 안심, 안도(감) in the meantime 그 사이에, 그러는 동안

22. 여자의 방문 목적은 무엇인가?
(A) 자동차 엔진을 교체하는 것
(B) 새로운 바퀴 세트를 구입하는 것
(C) 몇몇 타이어에 생긴 문제를 확인하는 것
(D) 정기 유지 관리 작업을 받는 것

정답 (C)
해설 남자가 대화를 시작하면서 여자의 자동차 바퀴 네 개를 모두 살펴 보는 일을 끝마쳤다고(I finished looking at all four wheels on your car) 알리자, 여자가 문제를 파악할 수 있었는지(Were you able to figure out the problem?) 묻고 있으므로 (C)가 정답입니다.

어휘 identify ~을 확인하다, ~을 알아보다 regular 정기적인, 규칙적인 maintenance 유지 관리, 정비

Paraphrase wheels on your car / figure out the problem
⇒ identify an issue with some tires

23. 남자가 한 가지 일과 관련해 언급하는 것은 무엇인가?
(A) 그것에 아주 익숙하다.
(B) 추가 도움을 요청할 것이다.
(C) 야간에 완료하기 더 쉽다.
(D) 끝마치는 데 두어 시간이 걸릴 것이다.

정답 (A)
해설 남자가 대화 후반부에 해당 타이어 교체 작업과 관련해 너무 흔한 문제라서 그에 대해 많은 경험을 지니고 있다고(this is such a common issue that I have lots of experience with it) 밝히고 있습니다. 이는 아주 익숙한 작업임을 의미하는 말이므로 (A)가 정답입니다.

어휘 task 일, 업무 be familiar with ~에 익숙하다, ~을 잘 알다 request ~을 요청하다 additional 추가적인 assistance 도움, 지원 complete ~을 완료하다

Paraphrase have lots of experience with it
⇒ is very familiar with it

24. 여자는 곧이어 무엇을 할 것 같은가?
(A) 슈퍼마켓을 방문하는 일
(B) 지정된 구역에서 대기하는 일
(C) 자신의 자동차 보험 회사에 전화하는 일
(D) 몇몇 서류를 정리하는 일

정답 (B)
해설 여자가 대화 맨 마지막 부분에 남자가 작업하는 사이에 대기실에 앉아 있겠다고(I'll just sit in your waiting area in the meantime) 말하고 있으므로 (B)가 정답입니다.

어휘 designated 지정된 insurance 보험 provider 제공업체 organize ~을 정리하다, ~을 준비하다 paperwork 서류 (작업)

Paraphrase sit in your waiting area
⇒ Wait in a designated area

DAY 11 의도 파악 문제/시각자료 연계 문제

PRACTICE

1. (D) 2. (C) 3. (C) 4. (B)

Question 1 refers to the following conversation.

> M: **I appreciate the tour of your co-working space.** The layout and natural light are perfect for our start-up.
> W: **Glad to hear that. Just so you know, this is a really popular location.**
> M: I'll check with my team before we sign anything.
> W: No problem—let me know when you're ready to reserve.

남: 공동 업무 공간을 둘러보게 해주셔서 감사합니다. 공간 구성과 자연광이 우리 스타트업에 딱 맞네요.
여: 그렇게 말씀해주시니 기쁘네요. 참고로 여기는 정말 인기가 많은 위치예요.
남: 계약하기 전에 팀원들과 먼저 상의해볼게요.
여: 좋습니다—예약하실 준비가 되시면 말씀해주세요.

어휘 appreciate 감사하다 tour 둘러보기, 순회 co-working space 공동 업무 공간 lay out 공간 구성, 배치 natural light 자연광 start-up 스타트업, 신규 기업 popular 인기가 많은 sign 서명하다 reserve 예약하다

1. 여자가 "여기는 정말 인기가 많은 위치예요."라고 말할 때 그 말의 의미는 무엇인가?
(A) 월 임대료에 공과금이 포함된다.
(B) 가구가 인체공학적으로 설계되었다.
(C) 건물 보안이 훌륭하다.
(D) 예약이 빠르게 진행되고 있다.

정답 (D)

해설 남자에게 공동 업무 공간을 둘러보게 해주는 여자는 부동산 중개인 또는 임대인으로 보이며, "인기가 많은 위치이다"라는 말은 이 공동 업무 공간을 예약하려는 사람이 많다는 것을 의미합니다. 따라서 예약이 빠르게 진행되고 있다는 것을 알 수 있으므로 정답은 (D)입니다.

어휘 monthly rate 월 임대료 utilities (수도, 전기, 가스 등) 공과금 furniture 가구 ergonomically 인체 공학적으로 security 보안 book 예약하다

Question 2 refers to the following conversation.

> M: Hi, Alex. I want to review the revised training-video script.
> W: I added a clearer intro outlining our objectives.
> M: Perfect, that will tighten the message.
> W: I also rewrote the closing to include a stronger call to action.
> M: **Can you run through those new lines now?**
> W: I'm sorry. There's a power outage in my building, so I can't access the file.
> M: All right. **Let's resume once your power is back.**

남: 안녕하세요, 알렉스. 저는 수정된 교육 영상 대본을 검토하고 싶어요.
여: 제가 도입부에 목표를 명확하게 설명하는 메시지를 추가했어요.
남: 완벽해요, 그게 메시지를 훨씬 강화되게 할거예요.
여: 행동으로 옮기기 위한 더 강력한 요구를 포함시켜서 마무리 부분도 다시 썼어요.
남: 지금 그 새 대사들을 한번 읽어줄 수 있어요?
여: 미안해요. 지금 우리 건물에 정전이 나서 파일에 접근할 수가 없어요.
남: 알겠어요. 전기가 복구되면 다시 이어서 해요.

어휘 review 검토하다 revised 수정된 script 대본 clearer 더 명확한 intro 도입부 outline (대략적으로) 설명하다, 개요를 서술하다 objective 목표 tighten 강화되게 하다, 단단하게 하다 closing 마무리, 끝부분 stronger 더 강력한 call to action 행동 개시 요구 run through 읽다, 연습하다 line 대사 power outage 정전 access 접근하다 resume 재개하다, 다시 이어지다 once 일단 ~하면 power 전기

2. 여자가 "우리 건물에 정전이 나서 파일에 접근할 수 없어요."라고 말하는 이유는 무엇인가?
(A) 그 일을 대신해 달라고 요청하기 위해
(B) 추가 자원을 요청하기 위해
(C) 논의를 미루자고 제안하기 위해
(D) 새로운 영상 요소에 대해 이야기하기 위해

정답 (C)

해설 남자가 여자에게 "그 새로운 대사들을 지금 읽어 줄 수 있어요?"라고 요청한 것에 대한 답변으로 건물의 정전에 대해 언급하였으므로 지금 새로운 대사를 읽어줄 수 없다는 것을 나타낸다는 것을 알 수 있습니다. 따라서 정답은 (C)입니다.

어휘 task 업무, 일 on behalf of ~을 대신해서 request 요청하다 additional 추가적인 resource 자원 postpone 연기하다, 미루다 discussion 논의 discuss 논의하다, 이야기 하다 element 요소

Question 3 refers to the following conversation and floor plan.

> M: I need supplies for my store's stockroom. Can you tell me where I can find bleach?
> W: Sure, in the aisle with detergents.
> M: **Which aisle number is that?**
> W: **The one between paper goods and pet food.**
> M: Thanks.

> 남: 제 가게 창고에 물품이 좀 필요합니다. 표백제를 어디서 찾을 수 있을까요?
> 여: 네, 세제 진열대 쪽에 있습니다.
> 남: 그 진열대는 몇 번 통로인가요?
> 여: 종이 제품과 애완동물 사료 사이에 있는 통로입니다.
> 남: 감사합니다.

```
         매장 배치도 (1층)

              [입구]

  통로 1    통로 2    통로 3    통로 4
  농작물   종이류    청소용품   애완동물
  (과일,   제품      (표백제,   사료
  채소)   (냅킨,    비누)      (개, 고양이)
          타올)
```

어휘 supply 물품, 공급품 store 매장 stockroom 창고 bleach 표백제 aisle 통로 detergent 세제 paper goods 종이 제품

3. 시각자료를 보시오. 여자가 남자에게 알려주는 통로는 어느 통로인가?
   (A) 1번 통로
   (B) 2번 통로
   (C) 3번 통로
   (D) 4번 통로

정답 (C)

해설 남자가 표백제가 있는 통로가 몇 번 통로인지 묻자 여자는 종이 제품과 애완동물 사료 사이에 있는 통로라고(The one between paper goods and pet food)라고 언급했습니다. 안내도에 따르면 종이 제품과 애완동물 사료 사이에 있는 통로는 3번 통로이므로 정답은 (C)입니다.

Question 4 refers to the following conversation and chart.

> M: Did you review our homepage banner performance? **I was amazed at how many visitors clicked the CTA button.**
> W: That's excellent! It should lead to more product views and, hopefully, sales.
> M: Splitting the banner into two different color schemes was a smart move—those segments really stood out.

> 남: 저희 홈페이지 배너 성과를 검토하셨어요? 저는 얼마나 많은 방문자들이 행동 개시 요구 버튼을 눌렀는지를 보고 놀랐어요.
> 여: 그거 훌륭하네요! 그게 사람들의 더 많은 상품 조회와, 바라건대, 판매로도 이어져야 해요.
> 남: 배너를 2가지 색으로 나누는 계획은 현명한 조치였어요—그 부분들이 정말 눈에 띄네요.

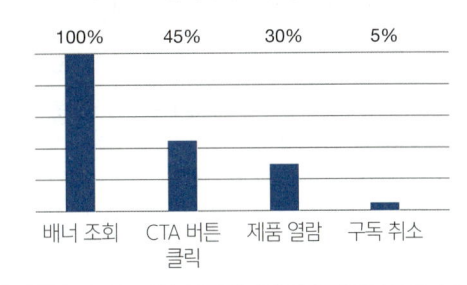

어휘 review 검토하다 performance 성과 be amazed at ~에 놀라다 CTA 행동 개시 요구(call-to-action) lead to ~로 이어지다 view 조회 hopefully 바라건대 sales 판매 split 나누다, 쪼개다 scheme 계획 smart 현명한, 영리한 move 행동, 조치 segment 부분, 조각 stand out 눈에 띄다

4. 시각자료를 보시오. 어떤 퍼센트 수치가 남자를 놀라게 하였는가?
   (A) 100%
   (B) 45%
   (C) 30%
   (D) 5%

정답 (B)

해설 남자는 대화 첫 부분에서 자신이 얼마나 많은 방문자들이 행동 개시 요구 버튼을 클릭했는지를 보고 놀랐다고(I was amazed at how many visitors clicked the call-to-action button) 언급하였습니다. 막대 그래프에서 CTA 버튼을 클릭한 것의 퍼센트 수치는 45%이므로 정답은 (B)입니다.

어휘 surprise 놀라게 하다

실전 TEST

1. (C)	2. (D)	3. (A)	4. (C)	5. (C)
6. (A)	7. (B)	8. (B)	9. (C)	10. (D)
11. (C)	12. (B)	13. (D)	14. (C)	15. (D)
16. (A)	17. (C)	18. (B)	19. (D)	20. (D)
21. (B)	22. (D)	23. (B)	24. (D)	

Questions 1-3 refer to the following conversation.

M: Hi, **1** I saw the job posting for your design agency. Have you hired anyone yet?
W: No, we haven't. **2** We need someone who has been working in graphic design for a while.
M: Well, that isn't an issue. I have over ten years of experience, and I brought my portfolio. It showcases some of my best work.
W: Let's see… **3** do you have time for an interview now? The personnel manager just got back from lunch.

남: 안녕하세요, 저는 귀하의 디자인 회사 구인 공고를 봤습니다. 혹시 누군가를 고용하셨나요?
여: 아뇨, 하지 않았습니다. 저희는 한동안 그래픽 디자인 분야에서 근무해 오신 분이 필요합니다.
남: 저, 그건 문제가 아닙니다. 저는 10년이 넘는 경력을 지니고 있으며, 제 포트폴리오도 챙겨 왔습니다. 포트폴리오는 저의 가장 뛰어난 몇몇 작업들을 보여줍니다.
여: 어디 보자… 지금 면접 보실 시간이 있으신가요? 인사부장님께서 막 점심 식사를 마치고 돌아오셨거든요.

어휘 job posting 구인 공고 hire ~을 고용하다 for a while 한동안 issue 문제, 사안 over ~가 넘는 experience 경력, 경험 portfolio (구직 시 제출하는) 포트폴리오, 작품집 showcase ~을 보여주다, 선보이다 work 작품, 작업(물) personnel manager 인사부장 get back from ~에서 돌아오다, 돌아가다

1. 남자는 무슨 직책에 관해 문의하고 있는가?
(A) 사무실 관리 책임자
(B) 영업 사원
(C) 그래픽 디자이너
(D) 시설 관리 직원

정답 (C)
해설 대화 시작 부분에 남자가 상대방 회사를 your design agency 라고 지칭하면서 그 디자인 회사의 구인 공고를 본 사실을 언급하고 누군가가 고용되었는지(I saw the job posting for your design agency. Have you hired anyone yet?) 확인하고 있습니다. 따라서 그래픽 디자이너 직책에 관해 문의하는 것으로 볼 수 있으므로 (C)가 정답입니다.

어휘 inquire about ~에 관해 문의하다 maintenance 시설 관리, 유지 보수

2. 남자가 "그건 문제가 아닙니다"라고 말할 때 그 말의 의미는 무엇인가?
(A) 문제점을 알고 있다.
(B) 프로그램에 익숙하다.
(C) 이미 한 가지 일을 완료했다.
(D) 필수 요건을 충족한다.

정답 (D)
해설 대화 중반부에 여자가 그래픽 디자인 분야에서 근무해 온 사람이 필요하다고(We need someone who has been working in graphic design for a while) 말하자 남자가 '그건 문제가 아니다'라고 말하면서 자신의 경력 기간을 언급하는 내용입니다. 이는 회사측 채용 요건을 충족한다는 의미이므로 (D)가 정답입니다.

어휘 be aware of ~을 알고 있다, 인식하고 있다 be familiar with ~에 익숙하다, ~을 잘 알고 있다 complete ~을 완료하다 task 일, 업무 meet (조건 등) ~을 충족하다 requirement 필수 요건, 필요한 것

3. 여자는 남자에게 무엇을 하도록 요청하는가?
(A) 면접 자리에 참석하기
(B) 연락처 제공하기
(C) 이력서 제출하기
(D) 서식 작성하기

정답 (A)
해설 여자가 요청하는 일을 묻고 있으므로 여자의 말에서 요청 관련 표현과 함께 언급되는 정보를 찾아야 합니다. 대화 마지막에 여자는 남자에게 지금 면접을 볼 시간이 있는지(~ do you have time for an interview now?) 묻는 것으로 면접 참석을 요청하고 있습니다. 따라서 이를 언급한 (A)가 정답입니다.

어휘 attend ~에 참석하다 provide ~을 제공하다 contact information 연락처 submit ~을 제출하다, 내다 résumé 이력서 complete ~을 작성하다, 완료하다 form 서식

Questions 4-6 refer to the following conversation.

W: Hello, I would like a round trip ticket for the bus to Miami that leaves at 9:00 A.M.
M: I'm sorry, but those tickets are sold out. **4 A lot of people are traveling to Miami this weekend to attend the Summertime Music Festival** on South Beach.
W: Oh, no! But **5 I have to get to Miami by 5 P.M. for my brother's graduation. He has been working so hard.**
M: Well, **6 there are a couple of seats left on a bus that leaves at 9:30**, but it makes several stops along the way. But, that should still get you to Miami by 4:30. Hopefully that works for you.

여: 안녕하세요, 오전 9시에 출발하는 마이애미행 버스 왕복 티켓 주세요.
남: 죄송하지만, 그 티켓은 매진되었습니다. 많은 사람들이 사우스 비치에서 열리는 서머타임 음악 축제에 참석하기 위해 이번 주말에 마이애미로 가고 있습니다.
여: 아, 이런! 하지만 제 남동생 졸업식 때문에 오후 5시까지 마이애미에 도착해야 해요. 남동생이 아주 열심히 해 왔거든요.
남: 저, 9시 30분에 출발하는 버스에 좌석이 두 개 남아 있기는 하지만, 가는 길에 여러 번 정차합니다. 하지만, 그래도 그 버스는 당신을 오후 4시 30분까지 마이애미에 도착할 수 있게 할 겁니다. 그렇게 하시는 게 괜찮길 바랍니다.

어휘 would like ~을 원하다, ~하고 싶다 leave 출발하다, 떠나다, ~을 남기다 sold out 매진된 travel to ~로 가다, 이동하다 attend ~에 참석하다 get to ~에 도착하다 by (기한) ~까지 graduation 졸업(식) there is A p.p.: ~된 A가 있다 make a stop 정차하다, 서다 several 여럿의, 몇몇의 hopefully 희망하여, 바라건대, (일, 상황 등이) 잘 되면 work for (일정, 시간 등이) ~에게 좋다

4. 남자의 말에 따르면, 왜 많은 사람이 마이애미로 가고 있는가?
(A) 세미나에 참석하기 위해
(B) 날씨를 즐기기 위해
(C) 음악 축제에 참석하기 위해
(D) 스포츠 행사에 참가하기 위해

정답 (C)
해설 대화 초반부에 남자가 많은 사람들이 서머타임 뮤직 페스티벌에 참석하기 위해 이번 주말에 마이애미로 가고 있다고(A lot of people are traveling to Miami this weekend to attend the Summertime Music Festival ~) 말하고 있으므로 (C)가 정답입니다.

어휘 attend ~에 참석하다 participate in ~에 참가하다

5. 여자가 "남동생이 아주 열심히 해 왔거든요"라고 말할 때 그 말의 속뜻은 무엇인가?
(A) 남동생을 계속 도와주었다.
(B) 남동생이 휴가를 떠나기를 원하고 있다.
(C) 남동생의 행사를 놓칠 수 없다.
(D) 남동생이 보상 받을 자격이 있다고 생각한다.

정답 (C)
해설 대화 중반부에 여자가 남동생 졸업식에 가야 한다고(~ I have to get to Miami by 5 P.M. for my brother's graduation) 알리면서 '남동생이 아주 열심히 해 왔다'라고 말하는 흐름입니다. 이는 반드시 그 졸업식에 참석해야 한다는 뜻을 강조하기 위해 한 말이므로 (C)가 정답입니다.

어휘 want A to do: A가 ~하기를 원하다 miss ~을 놓치다, 지나치다 deserve ~을 받을 자격이 있다, ~을 받을 만하다

6. 남자는 무엇을 제안하는가?
(A) 다른 버스 타기
(B) 기차역으로 가기
(C) 차량 대여하기
(D) 일정 변경하기

정답 (A)
해설 남자가 제안하는 일을 묻고 있으므로 남자의 말에서 제안 관련 표현과 함께 제시되는 정보를 찾아야 합니다. 대화 후반부에 남자가 9시 30분에 출발하는 버스에 자리가 있음을(~ there are a couple of seats left on a bus that leaves at 9:30 ~) 알리면서 그 버스가 시간에 맞게 도착하게 해준다는 사실을 말해주고 있습니다. 이는 다른 버스를 타도록 제안하는 것이므로 (A)가 정답입니다.

어휘 rent ~을 대여하다, 임대하다 vehicle 차량

Questions 7-9 refer to the following conversation.

M: Hello, Ms. Wexler. **7 My team has just finished setting up the buffet.** Once the roasted chicken is finished, all the food should be ready for your luncheon.
W: We're right on schedule, then. Thank you, Matt. I'm very pleased with your services. Oh, and **8 have the chairs arrived yet for the seating area?**
M: **8 Yes**, they were unloaded from the truck, but **9 haven't been set up.**
W: **9 OK. I think we'll need some extra.** You know where the storage room is, right?

남: 안녕하세요, 웩슬러 씨. 저희 팀이 뷔페를 마련하는 일을 방금 마쳤습니다. 구운 닭 요리가 완료되기만 하면, 귀하의 오찬 행사에 필요한 모든 음식이 준비될 겁니다.
여: 그럼 예정대로 잘 되어가고 있는 거네요. 고마워요, 매트 씨. 제공해 주시는 서비스에 매우 만족합니다. 아, 그리고 혹시 좌석 공간에 놓을 의자들이 도착했나요?
남: 네, 트럭에서 내리기는 했지만, 설치되지는 않았습니다
여: 알겠어요. 여분이 좀 필요할 것 같습니다. 물품 보관실이 있는 곳이 어딘지 알고 계시죠, 그렇죠?

어휘 set up ~을 마련하다, 설치하다 once ~하기만 하면, 일단 ~하는 대로 be ready for ~에 대한 준비가 되다 luncheon 오찬 be right on schedule 예정대로 잘 되어가다 then 그럼, 그렇다면 be pleased with ~에 만족하다, ~에 기쁘다 arrive 도착하다 seating area 좌석 공간 unload (짐 등) ~을 내리다 extra 여분(의 것) storage 보관, 저장

7. 남자는 어느 분야에 근무하고 있을 것 같은가?
 (A) 접대
 (B) 출장 요리 제공
 (C) 부동산
 (D) 조경

정답 (B)
해설 대화 초반부에 남자가 자신의 팀을 My team으로 지칭해 뷔페를 마련하는 일을 방금 마쳤다고(My team has just finished setting up the buffet) 알리고 있습니다. 이는 요리를 제공하는 팀에 속한 사람이 할 수 있는 말에 해당되므로 (B)가 정답입니다.

어휘 field 분야 catering 출장 요리 제공(업)

8. 여자는 무엇에 대해 문의하는가?
 (A) 공연 무대
 (B) 가구
 (C) 방 크기
 (D) 음향 장비

정답 (B)
해설 여자가 대화 중반부에 의자들이 도착했는지(~ have the chairs arrived yet for the seating area?) 묻는 것에 대해 남자가 'Yes'라는 말로 확인해 주고 있으므로 의자 제품이 속하는 범주에 해당되는 단어인 (B)가 정답입니다.

어휘 equipment 장비

Paraphrase chairs ⇒ furniture

9. 여자가 "물품 보관실이 있는 곳이 어딘지 알고 계시죠, 그렇죠?"라고 말할 때 그 말의 의미는 무엇인가?
 (A) 행사 공간을 재배치하고 싶어한다.

(B) 남자가 자신에게 길을 알려주기를 원하고 있다.
(C) 남자가 어떤 일을 완료하기를 원하고 있다.
(D) 빠진 물품을 찾아보고 싶어한다.

정답 (C)
해설 남자가 대화 후반부에 의자가 설치되지 않은 사실을(~ haven't been set up) 언급하자 여자가 알겠다고 하면서 여분의 의자가 필요하다고(OK. I think we'll need some extra) 알리면서 '물품 보관실이 있는 곳이 어딘지 알고 계시죠?'라고 묻는 상황입니다. 이는 여분의 의자를 꺼내 설치 작업을 완료하도록 요청하는 것, 즉 남자가 일을 완료하도록 원하는 것이므로 (C)가 정답입니다.

어휘 reorganize ~을 재배치하다, 재편하다 want A to do: A가 ~하기를 원하다 give A directions: A에게 길을 알려주다 complete ~을 완료하다 look for ~을 찾다 missing 빠진, 없는

Questions 10-12 refer to the following conversation.

M: Hi, Samantha. Since our pizza shop is becoming so popular, 10 **I think it's time to open a second location in Circleville.**
W: I was thinking the same thing. Maybe 11 **we can tell our employees next week at our staff appreciation dinner.**
M: That would be perfect. Plus, I think it would be best to make one of our current workers the manager of the new shop.
W: I agree. 12 **We need someone who is responsible.**
M: Right, but loyalty is important, too. You know, Kyle Firth has been with us for over five years.
W: Hmm… he has been a great employee.

남: 안녕하세요, 사만다 씨. 저희 피자 매장이 아주 많은 인기를 얻고 있기 때문에, 서클빌에 두 번째 지점을 개장할 때인 것 같아요.
여: 저도 같은 생각을 하고 있었어요. 아마 다음 주에 있을 직원 감사 회식 시간에 직원들에게 말할 수 있을 거예요.
남: 그렇게 하시면 완벽할 거예요. 그리고, 현재 근무 중인 우리 직원들 중 한 명을 새 매장 관리 책임자로 만드는 게 가장 좋을 것 같습니다.
여: 동의합니다. 책임감 있는 사람이 필요해요.
남: 맞아요, 하지만 충성도도 중요합니다. 있잖아요, 카일 퍼스 씨가 5년 넘게 우리와 함께 해 왔어요.
여: 음… 그분은 언제나 훌륭한 직원이셨죠.

어휘 become + 형용사: ~한 상태가 되다 popular 인기 있는 location 지점, 위치 appreciation 감사(의 뜻) plus 그리고, 게다가 make A B: A를 B로 만들다 current

현재의 agree 동의하다 responsible 책임감 있는, 책임을 맡은 loyalty 충성(심) over ~ 넘게

10. 화자들은 주로 무엇을 이야기하고 있는가?
(A) 행사를 계획하는 것
(B) 생산성을 향상시키는 것
(C) 업체 위치를 변경하는 것
(D) 신규 지점을 개장하는 것

정답 (D)

해설 대화 시작 부분에 남자가 서클빌에 두 번째 지점을 개장할 때라고(I think it's time to open a second location in Circleville) 알린 뒤로 그 지점 개장과 관련된 내용으로 대화가 이어지고 있으므로 (D)가 정답입니다.

어휘 improve ~을 향상시키다 productivity 생산성 branch 지점, 지사

Paraphrase open a second location
⇒ Opening a new branch

11. 여자는 어디에서 공지할 계획인가?
(A) 주주 총회에서
(B) 업무 세미나에서
(C) 직원 회식에서
(D) 기자 회견에서

정답 (C)

해설 여자가 어디에서 공지할 계획인지를 묻고 있으므로 여자의 말에서 공지 장소와 관련된 정보를 찾아야 합니다. 대화 중반부에 여자가 다음 주에 있을 직원 감사 회식 자리에서 직원들에게 말할 수 있을 거라고(we can tell our employees next week at our staff appreciation dinner) 언급하고 있으므로 (C)가 정답입니다.

어휘 plan to do ~할 계획이다 make an announcement 공지하다, 발표하다 shareholder 주주

12. 남자가 "카일 퍼스 씨가 5년 넘게 우리와 함께 해 왔어요"라고 말하는 이유는 무엇인가?
(A) 직원을 축하하기 위해
(B) 추천하기 위해
(C) 놀라움을 표하기 위해
(D) 여자의 오류를 정정해주기 위해

정답 (B)

해설 대화 중반부에 여자가 신규 지점과 관련해 책임감 있는 사람이 필요하다고(We need someone who is responsible) 알린 뒤로 "카일 퍼스 씨가 5년 넘게 우리와 함께 해 왔어요"라고 말하는 흐름입니다. 이는 카일 퍼스 씨를 관리 책임자로 추천한다는 뜻을 나타내는 말이므로 (B)가 정답입니다.

어휘 congratulate ~을 축하하다 make a recommendation 추천하다 express (감정 등) ~을 표현하다 surprise 놀라움 correct v. ~을 수정하다, 정정하다 error 실수, 오류

Questions 13-15 refer to the following conversation and sign.

W: **13** There's a long line for the roller coaster, so I want something to eat while I wait. And, when I bought my admission ticket, I heard that the park has a special offer right now.
M: Yes, just check this sign. Different snacks come with a free drink, but the size depends on what you order. So, a pizza comes with a jumbo sized soft drink.
W: Oh, I get it. **14** I want a hamburger then.
M: OK, that's $6.00.
W: **15** I only have a credit card. Is that OK?
M: **15** Of course. We accept all different types of cards here.

여: 롤러 코스터 줄이 길어서, 기다리는 동안 먹을 것 좀 사고 싶어요. 그리고, 제가 입장권을 구입했을 때, 공원에 지금 특가 서비스가 있다고 들었어요.
남: 네, 이 안내표를 확인해 보세요. 서로 다른 간식에 무료 음료가 딸려 있기는 하지만, 무엇을 주문하시는지에 따라 크기가 다릅니다. 그래서, 피자에는 점보 사이즈 탄산 음료가 딸려 있습니다.
여: 아, 알겠어요. 그럼 전 햄버거로 하겠습니다.
남: 알겠습니다, 6달러입니다.
여: 제가 신용 카드밖에 없어요. 그래도 괜찮나요?
남: 물론입니다. 이곳에서 저희는 서로 다른 모든 종류의 카드를 받습니다.

음식	가격	음료 크기
감자 튀김	4달러	소
프라이드 치킨	5달러	중
햄버거	6달러	대
피자	8달러	점보

어휘 while ~하는 동안 admission 입장 (허가) special offer 특가 서비스 come with (제품 등에) ~가 딸려 있다, ~을 포함하다 free 무료의 depend on ~에 따라 다르다, ~에 달려 있다 then 그럼, 그렇다면 accept ~을 받아들이다, 수용하다

13. 화자들은 어디에 있는가?
(A) 스포츠 경기장에
(B) 영화관에

정답 및 해설 **77**

(C) 음악 축제에
(D) 놀이 공원에

정답 (D)

해설 여자가 대화를 시작하면서 '롤러 코스터 줄이 길다(There's a long line for the roller coaster ~)'라고 언급하고 있는데, 이는 놀이 공원에 있는 사람이 할 수 있는 말에 해당되므로 (D)가 정답입니다.

어휘 stadium 경기장 festival 축제 amusement park 놀이 공원

14. 시각자료를 보시오. 여자는 어떤 크기의 음료를 받을 것인가?
(A) 소
(B) 중
(C) 대
(D) 점보

정답 (C)

해설 시각자료에 음료 크기를 확인하기 위한 기준이 되는 항목으로 음식 종류와 가격이 쓰여 있으므로 이 두 가지와 관련된 정보를 찾아야 합니다. 대화 중반부에 여자가 햄버거로 하겠다고(I want a hamburger then) 말하고 있는데, 시각자료에 햄버거 선택 시의 음료 크기가 'Large'로 표기되어 있으므로 (C)가 정답입니다.

어휘 receive ~을 받다

15. 여자는 어떻게 비용을 지불할 것인가?
(A) 현금으로
(B) 쿠폰으로
(C) 앱으로
(D) 신용 카드로

정답 (D)

해설 대화 후반부에 여자가 신용 카드밖에 없다는 말과 함께 괜찮은지 묻자(I only have a credit card. Is that OK?) 남자가 Of course라는 말로 수락하고 있으므로 (D)가 정답입니다.

Questions 16-18 refer to the following conversation and floor plan.

M: Hi Susan, welcome to the Tennyson Tech Expo. I'm Steve, the event director. **16 You mentioned you volunteered last year, so you're already familiar with the event**. So, all you need to do is select which stall you want.
W: Thanks. I'd like to be in a visible area, if that's possible. Any suggestions?
M: Well, Stall 1 is already taken, but it's by the registration area, so a lot of people will ignore it. **17 How about the spot over there, next to the food court?**
W: Great. And, when can I do my product demonstration on the main stage?
M: Oh, **18 I'll explain that later. We made some changes to the event schedule, so there's a lot to cover.**

남: 안녕하세요, 수잔 씨, 테니슨 기술 박람회에 오신 것을 환영합니다. 저는 행사 진행 책임자인 스티브입니다. 작년에 자원 봉사를 하셨다고 말씀해 주셨기 때문에, 이미 행사에 익숙하시겠죠. 따라서, 어느 판매대를 원하시는지를 선택해 주시기만 하면 됩니다.
여: 감사합니다. 저는 가능하면 눈에 잘 보이는 곳에 있고 싶습니다. 추천해 주실 만한 곳이라도 있나요?
남: 저, 판매대 1은 이미 선택되었는데, 등록 구역 옆에 있기 때문에 많은 사람들이 그냥 지나칠 겁니다. 저기 저쪽에 푸드 코트 옆 자리는 어떠신가요?
여: 아주 좋습니다. 그리고, 언제 중앙 무대에서 제품 시연회를 할 수 있죠?
남: 아, 그건 나중에 설명해 드리겠습니다. 저희가 행사 일정을 좀 변경했기 때문에, 다룰 내용이 많습니다.

어휘 mention (that) ~라고 말하다, 언급하다 volunteer 자원 봉사하다 be familiar with ~에 익숙하다, ~을 잘 알다 all you need to do is + 동사원형: ~하기만 하면 됩니다 select ~을 선택하다 stall 판매대 visible 눈에 잘 보이는 suggestion 추천, 제안, 의견 registration 등록 ignore ~을 무시하다 How about ~? ~는 어떠세요? spot 자리, 장소 next to ~ 옆에 demonstration 시연(회) explain ~을 설명하다 make a change to ~을 변경하다 cover (주제, 내용 등) ~을 다루다

16. 여자는 왜 박람회에 익숙한가?
(A) 자원봉사자였다.
(B) 동영상을 시청했다.
(C) 기자이다.
(D) 행사 주최자를 알고 있다.

정답 (A)

해설 대화 시작 부분에 남자가 여자에게 작년에 자원 봉사를 한 사실과 함께 그로 인해 행사에 이미 익숙한 상태라고(You mentioned you volunteered last year, so you're already familiar with the event) 말하고 있으므로 (A)가 정답입니다.

어휘 volunteer 자원 봉사자 journalist 기자 organizer 주최자, 조직자

17. 시각자료를 보시오. 남자는 어느 판매대를 추천하는가?
(A) 판매대 1
(B) 판매대 2
(C) 판매대 3
(D) 판매대 4

정답 (C)

해설 평면도가 시각자료로 제시되어 있으므로 각 구역 사이의 위치 관계에 유의해 들어야 합니다. 대화 중반부에서 남자가 푸드 코트 옆 공간은 어떻게 생각하는지 묻는 것으로(How about the spot over there, next to the food court?) 이 자리를 추천하고 있는데, 평면도를 확인해 보면 푸드 코트 옆 자리가 Stall 3로 표기되어 있으므로 (C)가 정답입니다.

18. 남자가 나중에 무엇을 설명할 것인가?
(A) 컴퓨터 프로그램
(B) 일정
(C) 제품
(D) 고객 정책

정답 (B)

해설 대화 마지막 부분에 남자가 나중에 설명하겠다는 말과 함께 일정에 변동 사항이 있어 할 얘기가 많다고(I'll explain that later. We made some changes to the event schedule, so there's a lot to cover) 말하고 있습니다. 따라서 일정과 관련해 나중에 설명해주는 것으로 볼 수 있으므로 (B)가 정답입니다.

어휘 policy 정책, 방침

Questions 19-21 refer to the following conversation and graph.

W: Stan, have you checked the latest report yet? We need to do something to improve this one shift. I think we might need to hire a new manager.
M: What's the problem? 19 **That shift only gets an average of 50 orders.**
W: 20 **Some workers have recently quit, so there aren't enough employees to work that shift.**
M: Oh, I see. 21 **With our main competitor Burger Zone closing next month**, we'll probably become a lot busier. We need to make sure each shift is ready.

여: 스탠 씨, 혹시 최신 보고서를 확인해 보셨나요? 이 교대 근무 하나를 개선하기 위해 뭔가 해야 합니다. 제 생각엔 우리가 신임 관리 책임자를 고용해야 할 것 같아요.
남: 뭐가 문제인가요? 그 교대 근무는 겨우 평균 50개의 주문만 받고 있어요.
여: 일부 직원들이 최근에 그만두었기 때문에, 그 근무조로 일할 직원이 충분하지 않습니다.
남: 아, 알겠습니다. 우리 주요 경쟁업체인 버거 존이 다음 달에 문을 닫는 상황이라, 우리는 아마 훨씬 더 바빠질 것입니다. 각 교대 근무조가 반드시 준비되도록 해야 합니다.

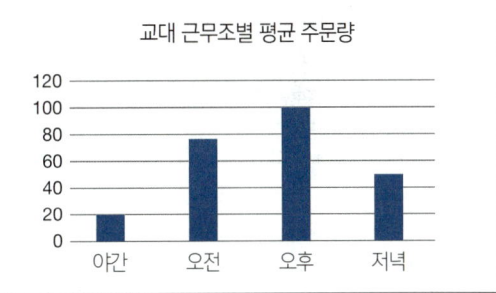

어휘 improve ~을 개선하다, 향상시키다 shift 교대 근무(조) hire ~을 고용하다 average n. 평균 a. 평균의 recently 최근에 quit 그만두다 with A -ing: A가 ~하면서 competitor 경쟁 업체, 경쟁자 a lot (비교급 수식) 훨씬 make sure (that) 반드시 ~하도록 하다

19. 시각자료를 보시오. 화자들은 어느 근무조를 이야기하고 있는가?
(A) 야간
(B) 오전
(C) 오후
(D) 저녁

정답 (D)

해설 시각자료가 그래프일 경우, 각 항목의 명칭과 수치 정보를 확인하고 순위의 우열과 관련된 내용에 주의해 들어야 합니다. 대화 중반부에 남자가 평균 50개의 주문만 받는 특정 근무조를(That shift only gets an average of 50 orders) 언급한 뒤로 그 근무조와 관련해 이야기하고 있는데, 그래프에서 주문량 50개에 해당되는 근무조가 Evening이므로 (D)가 정답입니다.

20. 여자의 말에 따르면, 무엇이 문제였는가?
(A) 저조한 매출
(B) 고객 불만
(C) 배송 지연
(D) 직원 부족

정답 (D)

해설 여자가 말하는 문제점을 묻는 문제이므로 여자의 말에서 부

정적인 정보를 찾아야 합니다. 대화 중반부에 여자가 일부 직원들이 그만두면서 직원이 충분하지 못한 상황(Some workers have recently quit, so there aren't enough employees to work that shift) 알리고 있으므로 '직원 부족'을 뜻하는 (D)가 정답입니다.

어휘 sales 매출, 판매(량), 영업 complaint 불만 shipping 배송 delay 지연, 지체 shortage 부족

Paraphrase there aren't enough employees
⇒ Employee shortages

21. 남자는 다음 달에 무슨 일이 있을 것이라고 말하는가?
(A) 신제품이 출시될 것이다.
(B) 레스토랑이 문을 닫을 것이다.
(C) 업체가 개조될 것이다.
(D) 가격이 오를 것이다.

정답 (B)

해설 다음 달(next month)이 언급되는 대화 후반부에, 주요 경쟁 업체인 버거 존이 다음 달에 문을 닫는다고(With our main competitor Burger Zone closing next month ~) 언급되고 있으므로 (B)가 정답입니다.

어휘 launch ~을 출시하다 renovate ~을 개조하다, 보수하다 increase 오르다, 증가되다

Paraphrase main competitor Burger Zone
⇒ a restaurant

Questions 22-24 refer to the following conversation and room layout.

> M: I can't believe **22** it's already time to plan this year's charity banquet again. Alison, did we finalize which foundation we're raising funds to support this year?
> W: Yes, it's called Thread of Hope. They recycle old and used clothes. I heard they collected over 200 tons of clothes last year, **23** which is a huge accomplishment!
> M: That's amazing! **23** We definitely shouldn't forget to mention that in the opening remarks.
> W: I agree. Oh yeah, and since I'll be in charge of attendance tracking, **24** I'd like to be seated near the conference room doors, if that's alright.
> M: OK. I'll make sure to keep that in mind.

남: 저는 벌써 올해의 자선 연회를 또 계획할 때가 되었다는 게 믿기지 않아요. 앨리슨 씨, 우리가 올해 어느 재단을 지원하기 위해 모금하는지 최종 확정하셨나요?

여: 네, '쓰레드 오브 호프'라고 불리는 곳입니다. 이곳은 오래된 중고 의류를 재활용하고 있어요. 이곳이 작년에 200톤이 넘는 의류를 수집했다고 들었는데, 이는 엄청난 성과입니다!

남: 놀랍네요! 우리는 반드시 개회사 중에 그 부분을 언급하는 것을 잊지 말아야 합니다.

여: 동의해요. 아, 맞아요, 그리고 제가 참석자 수 파악을 책임질 것이기 때문에, 괜찮으시다면, 대회의실 출입문 근처에 앉았으면 합니다.

남: 좋습니다. 제가 반드시 그 부분을 명심하도록 하겠습니다.

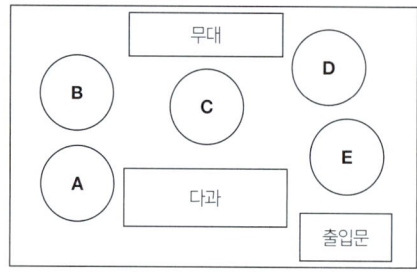

어휘 charity 자선 (활동), 자선 단체 banquet 연회 finalize ~을 최종 확정하다 foundation 재단 raise funds 모금하다, 기금을 마련하다 support ~을 지원하다, ~을 후원하다 recycle ~을 재활용하다 used 중고의 clothes 의류 collect ~을 수집하다, ~을 모으다 huge 엄청난 accomplishment 성과, 업적, 성취 definitely 분명히, 확실히 forget to do ~하는 것을 잊다 mention ~을 언급하다 opening remarks 개회사 agree 동의하다, 합의하다 since ~하기 때문에, ~한 이후로 in charge of ~을 책임지고 있는, ~을 맡고 있는 attendance 참석, 참석자 수 tracking 파악, 추적 would like to do ~하고 싶다 be seated 앉다, 착석하다 make sure to do 반드시 ~하도록 하다 keep A in mind: A를 명심하다 refreshments 다과, 간식

22. 화자들은 왜 연회를 계획하고 있는가?
(A) 획기적인 일을 기념하기 위해
(B) 한 직원을 표창하기 위해
(C) 제품 출시 행사를 광고하기 위해
(D) 자선 활동에 필요한 기금을 마련하기 위해

정답 (D)

해설 남자가 대화를 시작하면서 올해의 자선 연회를 계획할 때가 되었다고 언급하면서 여자에게 어느 재단을 지원하기 위해 모금하는지를 최종 확정했는지(it's already time to plan this year's charity banquet again. Alison, did we finalize which foundation we're raising funds to support this year?) 묻고 있으므로 (D)가 정답입니다.

어휘 celebrate ~을 기념하다, ~을 축하하다 milestone 획기적인 일, 중대 시점 recognize ~을 표창하다, ~을

인정하다 **advertise** ~을 광고하다 **launch** n. 출시 (행사), 시작 v. ~을 출시하다, ~을 시작하다

Paraphrase raising funds ⇒ raise money

23. 남자는 무엇이 연설 중에 언급되어야 한다고 말하는가?
(A) 개인적인 이야기
(B) 주목할 만한 업적
(C) 몇몇 판매 수치
(D) 몇몇 연구 결과물

정답 (B)

해설 여자가 대화 중반부에 한 가지 일에 대해 엄청난 성과라고 (which is a huge accomplishment!) 놀라워하는 것에 대해, 남자가 분명히 개회사 중에 그 부분을 언급하는 것을 잊지 말아야 한다고(We definitely shouldn't forget to mention that in the opening remarks) 말하고 있으므로 (B)가 정답입니다.

어휘 **notable** 주목할 만한, 중요한, 현저한 **sales** 판매(량), 영업, 매출 **figure** 수치, 숫자 **findings** 결과(물)

Paraphrase a huge accomplishment
⇒ A notable accomplishment

24. 시각자료를 보시오. 여자는 어디에 앉을 것인가?
(A) A 구역
(B) C 구역
(C) D 구역
(D) E 구역

정답 (D)

해설 대화 후반부에 여자가 대회의실 출입문 근처에 앉고 싶다고(I'd like to be seated near the conference room doors) 말하자, 남자가 명심하겠다고 대답하였습니다. 시각자료에서 하단에 DOORS가 표기된 곳과 가장 가까운 구역이 E이므로 (D)가 정답입니다.

PART 4

DAY 12 전화 메시지/라디오 방송

PRACTICE

1. (A) **2.** (B) **3.** (C) **4.** (B) **5.** (B) **6.** (C)

Questions 1-3 refer to the following telephone message.

Hey, Marcus. Everything's scheduled for our trip to EcoBuild Solutions this Thursday to showcase our sustainable materials to their architects. **1** This collaboration is vital for our architecture firm. So, **2** our train arrives at 10:30 A.M. We'll head to their office for the demonstration and discussion, then tour their sample construction site. And **2** we'll catch the 6 P.M. train home. I know you hoped we'd have time to drop into that modern art gallery downtown. **3** It might not fit, so let's just say we won't be stopping by for the exhibit.

마커스 씨, 안녕하세요. 이번 주 목요일 에코빌드 솔루션스 방문 일정이 모두 확정되었습니다. 저희 지속 가능한 자재를 그들의 건축가 분들께 선보일 예정입니다. 이번 협업은 저희 건축사무소에 있어 매우 중요합니다. 그래서, 기차는 오전 10시 30분에 도착하고, 바로 그들의 사무실로 이동해 시연 및 논의를 진행할 예정입니다. 그 후에는 샘플 시공 현장을 둘러볼 계획입니다. 그리고 돌아오는 기차는 오후 6시입니다. 당신이 현대 미술관에도 들르고 싶다는 것을 알고 있습니다. 시간이 안 될 것 같아서, 저희는 전시관에 들리지 않는 것으로 합시다.

어휘 **be scheduled** 일정이 정해지다 **showcase** 선보이다, 소개하다 **sustainable** 지속 가능한 **materials** 자재, 재료 **architect** 건축가 **collaboration** 협업, 공동 작업 **vital** 중대한, 중요한 **head to** ~로 향하다, ~에 가다 **demonstration** 시연, 설명 **construction site** 공사 현장 **drop into** ~에 들르다 **fit** (시간이) 맞다 **let's say** 그러니까, ~합시다 **stop by** 들르다 **exhibit** 전시관, 전시

1. 화자는 어디에서 일하는가?
(A) 건축 사무소
(B) 미술관
(C) 철도 회사

정답 및 해설 **81**

(D) 건설 자재 공급업체

정답 (A)

해설 화자가 에코빌드 솔루션스 방문 일정에 대해 언급한 뒤에 이 협업이 그들의 건축사무소에 있어 매우 중요하다고(This collaboration is vital for our architecture firm) 언급한 것을 듣고 화자가 일하는 곳이 건축 회사임을 알 수 있습니다. 따라서 정답은 (A)입니다.

어휘 architecture 건축 operator 운영자, 운영 회사 construction 건설, 건축 supplier 공급업체

2. 화자가 전화를 하는 이유는 무엇인가?
(A) 설계 도면을 검토하기 위해
(B) 기차 일정을 확인하기 위해
(C) 음식 공급을 준비하기 위해
(D) 건축 자재를 주문하기 위해

정답 (B)

해설 화자는 담화 중반부에 오전 10시 30분에 도착하는 기차를 타고 에코빌드 솔루션스를 방문할 것이라고 언급하고, 그 뒤에 투어가 끝나고 오후 6시 기차를 타고 집으로 돌아올 것이라고 언급하고 있습니다. 이를 통해 전화를 한 목적이 기차 일정을 알려주기 위한 것임을 알 수 있으므로 정답은 (B)입니다.

어휘 review 검토하다 plan 도면 arrange 준비하다, 마련하다 catering 음식 공급, 출장 조리 서비스 building material 건축 자재

3. 화자가 "저희는 전시관에 들리지 않는 것으로 합시다"라고 말할 때 그 말의 의미는 무엇인가?
(A) 미술관이 문을 닫았다.
(B) 입장권이 매진되었다.
(C) 시간이 제한적일 것이다.
(D) 그는 미술을 좋아하지 않는다.

정답 (C)

해설 화자가 "저희는 전시관에 들리지 않을 것입니다"라고 말하기 전에 시간이 맞지 않을지도 모른다고(It might not fit) 언급하였으므로, 전시관에 들를 시간이 부족할 것이라는 것을 알 수 있습니다. 따라서 정답은 (C)입니다.

어휘 gallery 미술관 sold out 매진된, 다 팔린 limited 제한된

Questions 4-6 refer to the following broadcast.

Now interrupting *Classics on Campus* for a transportation update from University Transit. **4** Students taking Route 5 should be aware that the bus is being detoured due to construction on Elm Street. As a result, service during peak hours is running every twenty minutes, which is longer than usual. **5** For a detour map and the revised timetable, check the University Transit Web site.

Also, **6** the annual science fair is underway in the campus quad, so foot traffic is heavy. And now, back to your scheduled programming.

지금부터는 <캠퍼스 클래식> 방송을 잠시 중단하고, 대학 교통국에서 제공하는 교통 안내를 전해드립니다. 5번 버스를 타는 학생들은 엘름 스트리트에서 진행 중인 공사로 인해 버스 노선이 우회 운행되고 있다는 점을 알아 두시기 바랍니다. 그 결과로, 최대 혼잡 시간대에는 평소보다 간격이 긴, 20분 간격으로 운행되고 있습니다. 우회 경로 지도와 변경된 시간표는 대학 교통국 웹사이트에서 확인하실 수 있습니다. 또한 캠퍼스 광장에서는 연례 과학 박람회가 열리고 있어 보행자 통행이 많습니다. 그럼 다시 예정된 방송으로 돌아가겠습니다.

어휘 interrupt 중단시키다, 방해하다 transportation 수송, 이동 transit 교통 체계 be aware that ~에 대해 알다 route 경로, 노선 detour 우회하다 due to ~로 인해 as a result 그 결과 peak hours 최고 절정의 시간, 최대 혼잡 시간 than usual 평소보다 revised 수정된 annual 연례의, 매년의 fair 박람회 underway 진행 중인 quad 광장, 사각형 안뜰 foot traffic 보행자 통행량

4. 방송은 주로 무엇에 관한 내용인가?
(A) 몇몇 행사의 하이라이트
(B) 버스 우회 운행 및 지연
(C) 도서관 운영 시간
(D) 강의 취소

정답 (B)

해설 대학 교통국에서 업데이트 소식을 알려준다고 언급한 뒤로 엘름 스트리트의 공사로 인해 5번 버스가 우회 운행되고 있다는 점을 알아두라는(Students taking Route 5 should be aware that the bus is being detoured due to construction on Elm Street) 내용과 그 뒤에 버스 배차 간격이 20분으로 늘어날 것이라는 내용이 언급되므로 정답은 (B)입니다.

어휘 delay 지연, 연기 lecture 강의 cancellation 취소

5. 청자들은 무엇을 하도록 권장되는가?
(A) 다음 학기 등록하기
(B) 웹사이트 확인하기
(C) 교통국에 전화하기
(D) 버스 승차권 구매하기

정답 (B)

해설 우회 경로 지도와 변경된 시간표를 보기 위해서 대학 교통국 웹사이트를 확인하라는(For a detour map and the revised timetable, check the University Transit Web site) 내용이 언급되었으므로 청자들에게 웹사이트 확인을 요

청하는 것임을 알 수 있습니다. 따라서 정답은 (B)입니다.

어휘 register for ~에 등록하다 bus pass 승차권

6. 캠퍼스 광장에서 무슨 일이 일어나고 있는가?
   (A) 음악회
   (B) 스포츠 대회
   (C) 과학 박람회
   (D) 음식 축제

정답 (C)

해설 화자가 담화 마지막 부분에서 캠퍼스 광장에서 연례 과학 박람회가 열리고 있다고(the annual science fair is underway in the campus quad) 언급하였으므로 정답은 (C)입니다.

어휘 tournament 토너먼트, 대회

실전 TEST

1. (D)	2. (C)	3. (A)	4. (C)	5. (D)
6. (D)	7. (B)	8. (B)	9. (A)	10. (C)
11. (D)	12. (B)	13. (B)	14. (C)	15. (A)
16. (D)	17. (A)	18. (B)	19. (B)	20. (D)
21. (B)	22. (C)	23. (A)	24. (C)	

Questions 1-3 refer to the following telephone message.

Hello, Joanne. **1** **This is Logan calling from Technical Support.** You left a message about the problems you are having with the printer in your office. I had a look at it, and I found out what the problem is. **2** **One of the parts is broken, so I called the technician. The repairman should be arriving in an hour to replace it.** I heard that this is the fourth time that this has happened. If the machine has the same problem again, **3** **I'll speak to your department manager and suggest buying a new one.** If you have any questions, don't hesitate to call me back. Thanks.

안녕하세요, 조앤 씨. 저는 기술 지원부에서 전화 드리는 로건입니다. 귀하의 사무실에 있는 프린터에서 발생되고 있는 문제점과 관련해서 메시지를 남겨 주셨습니다. 제가 살펴봤는데, 무엇이 문제점인지 알아냈습니다. 부품들 중의 하나가 고장나 있어서, 저는 기술자를 불렀습니다. 수리 기사가 그것을 교체하기 위해 1시간 후에 도착할 겁니다. 이 문제가 발생한 게 이번이 네 번째라고 들었습니다. 만일 그 기계에 다시 동일한 문제점이 생기면, 제가 귀하의 부장님과 얘기해서 새 것을 구입하도록 제안할 것입니다. 어떤 질문이든 있으시면, 주저하지 마시고 저에게 다시 전화 주세요. 감사합니다.

어휘 leave a message 메시지를 남기다 have a problem with ~에 문제가 있다 have a look at ~을 한 번 보다 find out ~을 알아내다 part 부품 broken 고장 난 repairman 수리 기사 arrive 도착하다 in + 시간: ~ 후에 replace ~을 교체하다 suggest -ing ~하도록 제안하다, 권하다 hesitate to do ~하는 것을 주저하다, 꺼리다

1. 화자는 무슨 부서에서 근무하는가?
   (A) 고객 서비스부
   (B) 인사부
   (C) 마케팅부
   (D) 기술 지원부

정답 (D)

해설 담화를 시작하면서 화자가 자신의 신분과 관련해 기술 지원부에서 전화하는 로건이라고(This is Logan calling from Technical Support) 알리고 있으므로 (D)가 정답입니다.

2. 화자는 무슨 문제점을 언급하는가?
   (A) 문서 하나가 빠져 있다.
   (B) 배송 물품이 도착하지 않았다.
   (C) 부품 하나가 교체되어야 한다.
   (D) 마감 기한이 너무 이르다.

정답 (C)

해설 문제점이 언급되는 담화 중반부에, 부품 하나가 고장나 있고 수리 기사가 그것을 교체하러 올 것이라고(One of the parts is broken, ~ The repairman should be arriving in an hour to replace it) 알리고 있으므로 이를 말한 (C)가 정답입니다.

어휘 missing 빠져 있는, 없는 shipment 배송(품) arrive 도착하다 deadline 마감 기한

3. 화자는 무엇을 하겠다고 제안하는가?
   (A) 부서장과 얘기하기
   (B) 주문 취소하기
   (C) 파일 요청하기
   (D) 동료 직원에게 전화하기

정답 (A)

해설 화자가 제안하는 일이 언급되는 후반부에, 동일한 문제점이 다시 발생하면 상대방의 부서장과 얘기해 새 제품 구입을 제안하겠다고(I'll speak to your department manager and suggest buying a new one) 말하고 있습니다. 따라서 부서장과 얘기하는 일을 말한 (A)가 정답입니다.

어휘 supervisor 부서장, 책임자, 상사 cancel ~을 취소하다

order 주문(품) request ~을 요청하다 coworker 동료 직원

Questions 4-6 refer to the following recorded message.

> **4 Thank you for calling the Auckland Tourism office line.** We are pleased to help you with any inquiries you might have regarding Auckland and the various activities we have here in the city. Please be aware that, **5 due to extensive renovation work, some downtown areas may currently have restricted access or services.** The project is expected to be completed by the end of the year. **6 Please press 1 if you wish to speak with one of our customer service operators for more information** about our tourist attractions and landmarks.

오클랜드 관광 사무소 회선으로 전화 주셔서 감사합니다. 오클랜드에 관해, 그리고 저희가 이 도시 내에서 운영하고 있는 다양한 활동에 관해 귀하께서 가지고 계실 수 있는 어떤 문의 사항에 대해서도 기꺼이 도움을 드리겠습니다. 대규모 개조 공사로 인해, 현재 일부 시내 지역들에 출입 또는 서비스 제공이 제한될 수 있다는 점에 유의하시기 바랍니다. 이 프로젝트는 올 연말까지 완료될 것으로 예상됩니다. 저희 관광 명소 및 주요 지형지물에 관한 추가 정보를 얻기 위해 저희 고객 서비스 전화 안내원들 중 한 명과 통화하기를 원하시면 1번을 눌러 주십시오.

어휘 line 전화(선) be pleased to do 기꺼이 ~하다, ~해서 기쁘다 help A with B: B에 대해 A를 돕다 inquiry 문의 regarding ~와 관련해 various 다양한 activity 활동 be aware that ~ 임에 유의하다 due to ~로 인해 extensive 대규모의, 광범위한 renovation 개조, 보수 currently 현재 restricted 제한된 access 출입, 이용 be expected to do ~할 것으로 예상되다 complete ~을 완료하다 by (기한) ~까지 operator 전화 안내원 attraction 명소, 인기 장소 landmark (건물 등의) 주요 지형지물

4. 이 메시지는 누구를 대상으로 할 것 같은가?
  (A) 지역 주민들
  (B) 여행사 직원들
  (C) 잠재적인 관광객들
  (D) 사업주들

정답 (C)

해설 화자가 담화를 시작하면서 오클랜드 관광 사무소 회선으로 전화한 것에 대해 감사하다는(Thank you for calling the Auckland Tourism Office) 인사를 하고 있습니다. 이는 잠재적인 관광객들을 대상으로 하는 안내 메시지임을 나타내는 것이므로 (C)가 정답입니다.

어휘 be intended for ~을 대상으로 하다 local 지역의, 현지의 resident 주민 potential 잠재적인 owner 소유주, 주인

5. 화자는 시내 지역에 관해 무슨 말을 하는가?
  (A) 축제를 주최하고 있다.
  (B) 주차 공간이 제한되어 있다.
  (C) 여러 주요 지형지물이 있다.
  (D) 공사 중이다.

정답 (D)

해설 시내 지역이 언급되는 중반부에 개조 공사로 인해 일부 시내 지역에 발생될 수 있는 문제점을(due to extensive renovation work, some downtown areas may ~) 말하는 부분이 있으므로 공사 중이라는 사실을 말한 (D)가 정답입니다.

어휘 host ~을 주최하다 limited 제한된 parking 주차 (공간) several 여럿의, 몇몇의 under construction 공사 중인

Paraphrase renovation work ⇒ construction

6. 청자들이 더 많은 정보를 알아내려면 무엇을 해야 하는가?
  (A) 메시지 남기기
  (B) 예약하기
  (C) 웹사이트 방문하기
  (D) 번호 누르기

정답 (D)

해설 담화 마지막 부분에 추가 정보를 얻기 위한 방법으로 1번을 눌러 고객 서비스 전화 안내원과 얘기하도록(Please press 1 if you wish to speak with one of our customer service operators for more information ~) 권하고 있으므로 (D)가 정답입니다.

어휘 find out ~을 알아내다 leave ~을 남기다 make an appointment 예약하다 dial ~ 번으로 전화하다, 다이얼을 돌리다

Questions 7-9 refer to the following telephone message.

> Hi, Sally. This is Josh. I hope you hear this before you leave the office for the holiday. I have an update on **7 the job opening we posted for the assistant position in the accounting department. 8 You were concerned that people would not see it on the job recruiting site and felt that we should have advertised it in the newspaper.** Well, I just logged in and there have already been over 300 views. By Wednesday, **9 we'll have received a lot of applications, so I think you should start going**

through them for the upcoming interviews. Have a nice holiday.

안녕하세요, 샐리 씨. 조쉬입니다. 휴가를 위해 사무실을 떠나시기 전에 이 메시지를 들으시길 바랍니다. 우리가 회계부의 보조 직원 직책에 대해 게시한 직무 공석과 관련된 새로운 소식이 있습니다. 당신은 사람들이 이것을 구인 사이트에서 보지 않을 거라고 우려하시면서 우리가 이것을 신문에 광고했어야 했다고 생각하셨습니다. 저, 제가 막 로그인해 봤는데, 이미 300회가 넘는 조회수가 있었습니다. 수요일쯤에, 우리는 많은 지원서를 받게 될 것이기 때문에, 제 생각에 당신이 곧 있을 면접에 대비해 그 지원서들을 검토하기 시작하셔야 할 겁니다. 휴가 잘 다녀오세요.

어휘 leave ~에서 떠나다, 나가다 job opening 직무 공석 post ~을 게시하다 assistant 보조의, 조수의 accounting 회계 department 부서 be concerned that ~라는 점을 우려하다 job recruiting site 구인 사이트 should have p.p. ~했어야 했다 over ~가 넘는 view 조회수 by ~쯤에 receive ~을 받다 application 지원(서), 신청(서) go through ~을 검토하다 upcoming 곧 있을, 다가오는

7. 화자는 무엇에 관해 전화했는가?
   (A) 사업 확장
   (B) 직무 공석
   (C) 직원 오리엔테이션
   (D) 휴가 일정

정답 (B)
해설 담화 초반부에 화자가 자신과 상대방이 회계부의 보조 직원 직책에 대해 게시한 직무 공석(the job opening we posted for the assistant position in the accounting department)을 언급하고 있으며, 이 이후에도 이것과 관련된 내용을 말하고 있습니다. 이를 통해, 화자가 직무 공석에 관련된 이야기를 하기 위해 상대방에게 전화했다는 것을 알 수 있으므로 (B)가 정답입니다.

어휘 expansion 확장 job vacancy 직무 공석

Paraphrase job opening ⇒ job vacancy

8. 화자가 "이미 300회가 넘는 조회수가 있었습니다"라고 말할 때 그 말의 의미는 무엇인가?
   (A) 마감 기한이 변경되어야 한다.
   (B) 구인 방법이 성공적이었다.
   (C) 웹사이트가 더욱 유명해지고 있다.
   (D) 더 큰 방이 요구될 것이다.

정답 (B)
해설 화자가 담화 중반부에 사람들이 구인 사이트에서 보지 않을 거라고 우려한 사실과 함께 신문에 광고했어야 했다고 (You were concerned that people would not see it on the job recruiting site ~) 하는 상대방의 의견을 언급한 후에 "이미 300회가 넘는 조회수가 있었습니다"라고 말하고 있습니다. 이는 구인 사이트로 구인 활동을 한 것이 성공적이었음을 나타내는 것으로 볼 수 있으므로 (B)가 정답입니다.

어휘 deadline 마감 기한 recruiting 구인, 모집 method 방법 successful 성공적인 popular 유명한 be required 요구되다

9. 화자는 청자에게 무엇을 하도록 권하는가?
   (A) 몇몇 문서들 검토하기
   (B) 제안서 제출하기
   (C) 인터뷰 참여하기
   (D) 여행 미루기

정답 (A)
해설 담화 후반부에 메시지 수신자인 샐리를 you로 지칭해 곧 있을 면접에 대비해 그 지원서들을 검토하기 시작해야 한다고(we'll have received a lot of applications, so I think you should start going through them for the upcoming interviews) 요청하고 있습니다. 이는 문서를 검토하는 일을 말하는 것이므로 (A)가 정답입니다.

어휘 advise A to do: A에게 ~하도록 권하다 review ~을 검토하다 document 문서 submit ~을 제출하다 proposal 제안(서) attend 참석하다 postpone ~을 미루다

Paraphrase going through ⇒ Review

Questions 10-12 refer to the following telephone message and expense report.

Hello, Christopher. This is Amy from Accounting. The reason that I am calling is that I have a question about the expense report from 10 **your business trip to the career fair last week**. I've looked over your document and the receipts you submitted, but there's a problem. 11 **You reported purchasing pamphlets, and I've added up all the receipts. I think you may have written down a higher amount than what you actually spent.** Could you check it out for me and 12 **let me know by e-mail** at your earliest convenience? Thank you.

안녕하세요, 크리스토퍼 씨. 저는 회계부의 에이미입니다. 제가 전화 드리는 이유는 지난 주에 취업 박람회로 떠나셨던 출장에서 생긴 비용 보고서와 관련해 질문이 있어서입니다. 제출해 주신 문서와 영수증들을 검토해 봤는데, 문제가 하나 있습니다. 팸플릿을 구입하신 것으로 보고해 주셨고, 제가 모든 영수증들을 합산해 봤습니다. 제 생각에는 실제로 귀하께서 소비하신 것보다 더 높은 액수를 기재해 주셨던 것 같습니다. 가급적 빨리 이것을 확인해 보시고 저에게 이메일로 알려 주시겠습니까? 감사합니다.

비용 보고서	
휘발유	60달러
숙박 시설	250달러
식사	120달러
회사 팸플릿	90달러
	총액: 520달러

어휘 expense report 비용 보고서 career fair 취업 박람회 look over ~을 검토하다 receipt 영수증 submit ~을 제출하다 purchase ~을 구입하다 pamphlet 팸플릿, 안내 책자 add up ~을 합산하다 amount 액수, 금액 actually 실제로, 사실 let A know: A에게 알리다 at your earliest convenience 가급적 빨리 accommodation 숙박 시설

10. 청자는 지난 주에 무엇을 했는가?
 (A) 휴가를 갔다.
 (B) 직원 여행을 준비했다.
 (C) 취업 박람회에 참여했다.
 (D) 협의회에서 연설을 했다.

정답 (C)

해설 지난 주라는 시점이 제시되는 초반부에, 상대방을 your로 지칭해 상대방이 지난 주에 취업 박람회로 떠났던 출장(your business trip to the career fair last week)을 언급하고 있습니다. 이를 통해 청자가 지난 주에 취업 박람회에 참여한 것을 알 수 있으므로 (C)가 정답입니다.

어휘 organize ~을 준비하다, 조직하다

Paraphrase career ⇒ job

11. 시각자료를 보시오. 어느 액수가 확인되어야 하는가?
 (A) 60달러
 (B) 250달러
 (C) 120달러
 (D) 90달러

정답 (D)

해설 담화 중반부에 상대방이 팸플릿을 구입한 사실과 함께 그 부분이 실제 소비 액수보다 더 높게 기재된 것 같다고(You reported purchasing pamphlets, ~ you may have written down a higher amount than what you actually spent) 말하고 있습니다. 시각자료를 보면, 팸플릿 항목의 액수가 90달러로 표기되어 있으므로 (D)가 정답입니다.

12. 화자는 청자에게 무엇을 하도록 요청하는가?
 (A) 지불하기
 (B) 이메일 보내기
 (C) 절차 설명하기
 (D) 장비 구입하기

정답 (B)

해설 화자가 담화 마지막 부분에서 상대방에게 자신이 말하는 문제점을 확인해서 이메일로 알려 달라고(let me know by e-mail ~) 요청하고 있으므로 (B)가 정답입니다.

어휘 make a payment 지불하다 explain ~을 설명하다 procedure 절차 equipment 장비

Paraphrase let me know by e-mail ⇒ Send an e-mail

Questions 13-15 refer to the following news report.

I'm Lucy Moore with your travel news update. Yesterday, **13** Star Airlines announced that it will be opening a direct flight between Seoul and Vancouver. The airline will begin offering this route in August. A press release from Star Airlines also indicated that **14** the company is starting a "budget flight" service, meaning that its potential passengers should expect to pay a lower price for their Pan-Pacific flight. **15** City officials from both Seoul and Vancouver are excited about the many benefits that will come with the increased tourism.

저는 최신 여행 뉴스를 전해 드리는 루시 무어입니다. 어제, 스타 항공사가 서울과 밴쿠버를 오가는 직항편을 운항할 예정이라고 발표했습니다. 이 항공사는 8월에 이 노선에 대한 서비스를 제공하기 시작할 것입니다. 또한, 스타 항공사의 보도 자료에 따르면 이 회사는 "저가 항공편" 서비스를 시작한다고 나타나 있으며, 이는 잠재 승객들이 범태평양의 항공편에 대해 더 낮은 가격을 지불할 것으로 예상하게 된다는 뜻입니다. 서울과 밴쿠버 양쪽 도시의 공무원들은 관광 산업 증대와 함께 생길 많은 이점들에 대해 들떠 있습니다.

어휘 direct flight 직항편 between A and B: A와 B 사이에 offer ~을 제공하다 route 경로, 노선 press release 보도 자료 indicate that ~임을 나타내다 budget a. 저가의 potential 잠재적인 expect to do ~할 것으로 예상하다 official 공무원, 관계자 benefit 이점, 혜택 increased 증대된, 늘어난 tourism 관광

13. 화자는 8월에 무슨 일이 있을 것이라고 말하는가?
 (A) 새 공항 터미널이 열릴 것이다.
 (B) 항공사가 새 노선 운항을 시작할 것이다.
 (C) 웹사이트가 개선될 것이다.
 (D) 새로운 직원들이 모집될 것이다.

정답 (B)

해설 8월이라는 시점이 제시되는 초반부에, 스타 항공사가 서울과 밴쿠버를 오가는 직항편을 운항할 예정이라고 발표한 사실과 함께 8월에 서비스를 제공하기 시작할 것이라고(Star Airlines announced that it will be opening a direct flight ~ The airline will begin offering this route in August) 알리고 있습니다. 따라서 새 노선의 운항을 시작하는 일을 언급한 (B)가 정답입니다.

어휘 launch ~을 시작하다, ~에 착수하다 improve ~을 개선하다 recruit ~을 모집하다

Paraphrase will be opening a direct flight
⇒ will launch a new route

14. 화자는 고객들이 누릴 어떤 이점을 언급하는가?
(A) 더 쉬운 예약 절차
(B) 더 적은 지연
(C) 더 낮은 가격
(D) 줄어든 여행 시간

정답 (C)

해설 화자는 담화 중반부에 고객들이 누리게 될 혜택으로 저가 항공편 서비스를 언급하면서 더 낮은 가격을 지불하는 이점(the company is starting a "budget flight" service, meaning that its potential passengers should expect to pay a lower price ~)을 말하고 있습니다. 따라서 (C)가 정답입니다.

어휘 booking 예약 procedure 절차 delay 지연 reduced 줄어든, 감소된

15. 화자의 말에 따르면, 누가 해당 소식에 대해 기뻐하는가?
(A) 정부 공무원들
(B) 이사회 임원들
(C) 관광객들
(D) 지역 사업체 소유주들

정답 (A)

해설 누군가가 기뻐하는 일은 담화 후반부에 언급되고 있는데, 서울과 밴쿠버 양쪽 도시의 공무원들이 관광 산업 증대와 함께 생길 많은 이점에 대해 들떠 있다고(City officials from both Seoul and Vancouver are excited about the many benefits ~) 알리고 있습니다. 따라서 (A)가 정답입니다.

어휘 government 행정, 정부 board 이사회 local 지역의 owner 소유주

Paraphrase City officials ⇒ Government officials

Questions 16-18 refer to the following radio broadcast.

Good morning, listeners, and 16 **welcome to the Saturday morning traffic report**. The roads are clear this morning, and traffic in the northern parts of the city is minimal. However, 17 **there is a delay near Highway 150 due to repair work**. Workers have closed down the highway and it'll take approximately six weeks to finish the construction project. So, I recommend taking Route 18 instead. Also, if you are planning to visit shops along Dermott Road on Sunday, remember that it will be inaccessible by car due to the annual marathon. 18 **I'll be back with some local news after this commercial break.**

안녕하세요, 청취자 여러분, 그리고 토요일 아침 교통 소식 시간에 오신 것을 환영합니다. 오늘 아침에는 도로들이 한산하며, 도시 북부의 교통량이 아주 적습니다. 하지만, 보수 공사 작업으로 인해 150번 고속도로 근처에 지연 문제가 있습니다. 작업자들은 이 고속도로를 폐쇄했으며, 해당 공사 프로젝트를 완료하는 데 약 6주의 시간이 걸릴 것입니다. 따라서, 대신 18번 도로를 이용하시도록 권해 드립니다. 또한, 일요일에 더멋 로드를 따라 위치한 매장들을 방문하실 계획이라면, 연례 마라톤 대회로 인해 차량으로 접근할 수 없을 것이라는 점을 기억하시기 바랍니다. 저는 광고 방송 후에 몇 가지 지역 소식과 함께 돌아오겠습니다.

어휘 traffic 교통(량), 차량들 clear (길 등이) 한산한 minimal 아주 적은 delay 지연, 지체 due to ~로 인해 repair 수리 close down ~을 폐쇄하다 take ~의 시간이 걸리다 approximately 약, 대략 recommend -ing ~하도록 권하다, 추천하다 instead 대신 plan to do ~할 계획이다 along (길 등) ~을 따라 inaccessible 접근할 수 없는, 이용할 수 없는 annual 연례적인, 해마다의 commercial break 광고 방송 시간

16. 라디오 방송은 주로 무엇에 관한 것인가?
(A) 건물 시설 관리
(B) 조경 작업
(C) 지역 날씨
(D) 교통 상황

정답 (D)

해설 화자가 담화를 시작하면서 인사말로 토요일 아침 교통 소식 시간에 온 것을 환영한다고(welcome to the Saturday morning traffic report) 알리고 있습니다. 따라서 교통 상황에 관한 라디오 방송임을 알 수 있으므로 (D)가 정답입니다.

어휘 maintenance 시설 관리, 유지 관리 landscaping 조경 local 지역의, 현지의

정답 및 해설 **87**

17. 무엇이 150번 고속 도로 근처의 교통을 지연시키는가?
  (A) 보수 공사 프로젝트
  (B) 스포츠 행사
  (C) 매장 개장
  (D) 야외 콘서트

정답 (A)

해설 문제에 제시된 키워드 near Highway 150(150번 고속 도로 근처)가 언급되는 곳을 들어보면 이곳에 정체가 발생했는데 이것이 보수 공사 작업 때문이라고(there is a delay near Highway 150 due to repair work) 언급합니다. 따라서 정답은 (A)입니다.

어휘 opening 개장, 개점 outdoor 야외의

18. 청자들은 곧이어 무엇을 들을 것인가?
  (A) 날씨 최신 정보
  (B) 몇몇 광고
  (C) 인터뷰
  (D) 몇몇 비즈니스 뉴스

정답 (B)

해설 담화 맨 마지막에 광고 방송 후에 다시 돌아오겠다고(I'll be back with some local news after this commercial break) 알리고 있으므로 (B)가 정답입니다.

어휘 advertisement 광고

Paraphrase commercial break ⇒ advertisements

Questions 19-21 refer to the following broadcast.

Good afternoon, I'm Andrew Huffman. Today, **19 we have a report about a new service developed by the city library that should help local residents**. Community readers are always concerned about forgetting the return dates of their books, magazines and videos. But now, **20 21 an application has been provided by the library that will automatically send a notification to users to remind them of an approaching due date**. And that's not all. **21 The application will also recommend materials to read based on the user's reading preference**. Download the application for free and check it out.

안녕하세요, 저는 앤드류 허프만입니다. 오늘, 저희는 시립 도서관에 의해 개발되어 지역 주민들께 도움이 될 새로운 서비스에 관한 소식을 가지고 있습니다. 독서를 좋아하시는 지역 주민들께서는 항상 도서, 잡지, 그리고 비디오 반납 날짜를 잊는 것에 대해 우려합니다. 하지만 이제, 이용자들에게 다가오는 반납 기일을 상기시켜 주는 알림을 자동으로 보내줄 애플리케이션이 이 도서관에 의해 제공되었습니다. 그리고 그게 다가 아닙니다. 이 애플리케이션은 또한 이용자의 독서 선호도를 바탕으로 읽을거리를 추천해 줄 것입니다. 무료로 이 애플리케이션을 다운로드하셔서 확인해 보십시오.

어휘 develop ~을 개발하다 local 지역의 resident 주민 community 지역 사회 be concerned about ~에 대해 우려하다 forget ~을 잊다 provide ~을 제공하다 automatically 자동으로 notification 알림 remind A of B: A에게 B를 상기 시키다 approaching 다가오는 due date 반납 기일, 마감일 recommend ~을 추천하다 material 자료, 재료, 물품 based on ~을 바탕으로 preference 선호(하는 것) for free 무료로

19. 방송의 주제는 무엇인가?
  (A) 잡지 기사
  (B) 도서관 서비스
  (C) 교육용 프로그램
  (D) 재활용 프로젝트

정답 (B)

해설 담화를 시작하면서 화자가 오늘 보도 내용으로 시립 도서관에 의해 개발된 새로운 서비스에 관한 소식을 가지고 있다고(we have a report about a new service developed by the city library that should help local residents) 알리고 있으므로 (B)가 정답입니다.

어휘 article (잡지 등의) 기사 educational 교육적인 recycling 재활용

20. 애플리케이션의 사용자들은 무엇을 할 수 있을 것인가?
  (A) 회원 자격 업그레이드하기
  (B) 전문가와 상담하기
  (C) 한 행사에 등록하기
  (D) 알림 받기

정답 (D)

해설 담화 중반부에 주민들을 대상으로 제공되는 서비스로 이용자들에게 반납 기일을 상기시켜주는 알림을 보내줄 애플리케이션이 제공된다고(an application has been provided by the library that will automatically send a notification to users to remind them of an approaching due date) 알리고 있습니다. 따라서 알림을 받는 일을 뜻하는 (D)가 정답입니다.

어휘 be able to do ~할 수 있다 consult ~와 상담하다 professional n. 전문가 sign up for ~에 등록하다, ~을 신청하다 receive ~을 받다

Paraphrase send a notification to users ⇒ Receive notifications

21. 화자가 "그리고 그게 다가 아닙니다"라고 말할 때 그 말의 속뜻은 무엇인가?

(A) 앱이 몇몇 결점을 가지고 있다고 생각한다.
(B) 앱의 또 다른 특징을 설명할 것이다.
(C) 앱이 유명해질 것이라고 믿는다.
(D) 몇몇 다른 앱들을 추천할 것이다.

정답 (B)

해설 담화 중반부에 주민들을 대상으로 제공되는 서비스인 애플리케이션의 특징으로, 이용자들에게 반납 기일을 상기시켜주는 알림을 보내줄 것이라고(an application has been provided by the library that will automatically send a notification to users to remind them of an approaching due date) 말한 후에 '그게 다가 아닙니다'라고 말하고 있습니다. 또한, 주어진 문장 뒤에서 앱의 또 다른 특징으로, 이용자의 독서 선호도를 바탕으로 읽을거리도 추천해 줄 것(The application will also recommend materials to read based on the user's reading preference)이라고 언급하고 있습니다. 이를 통해, 주어진 문장이 앱의 또 다른 특징을 다음에 설명할 것이라고 알려주는 문장이라는 것을 알 수 있으므로 (B)가 정답입니다.

어휘 drawback 결점 describe ~을 설명하다 feature 특징 popular 유명한 recommend ~을 추천하다

Questions 22-24 refer to the following news report and weather forecast.

Good morning, listeners. I'm Mary Wells, and I'm here with your local news update. As many of you know, **22 the annual Canterbury Jazz Festival is taking place soon in Remuera Park**, and everyone can enjoy it at no cost. It's a great way to enjoy some popular jazz music. This year's headlining artist is jazz singer Lucas Mason, and everyone is looking forward to his performance. If you're interested, **23 you can visit the official Web site at www.canterburyfestival.com to see a full performance schedule**. As for the weather, **24 we're expecting a sunny day without any clouds on the big day**, so make sure to bring your sunglasses.

안녕하세요, 청취자 여러분. 저는 메리 웰스이고, 여러분의 지역 뉴스 최신 정보를 전해드리기 위해 여기에 왔습니다. 여러분들 중 많은 분들이 아시다시피, 연례 캔터베리 재즈 축제가 곧 레무에라 공원에서 열릴 예정이며 모든 분들이 이것을 무료로 즐기실 수 있습니다. 이것은 몇몇 인기 있는 재즈 음악을 즐길 수 있는 아주 좋은 방법입니다. 올해의 주요 공연자는 재즈 가수인 루카스 메이슨 씨이며, 모든 분들께서 이분의 공연을 고대하고 계십니다. 관심 있으실 경우, 전체 공연 일정표를 확인해 보시기 위해 공식

웹사이트인 www.canterburyfestival.com을 방문하시기 바랍니다. 날씨와 관련해서는, 이 중요한 날에 구름 한 점 없이 화창한 날이 예상되고 있으므로 반드시 선글라스를 챙겨 가시기 바랍니다.

목요일	금요일	토요일	일요일

어휘 local 지역 annual 연례적인, 해마다의 take place (행사 등이) 열리다 enjoy ~을 즐기다 at no cost 무료로 way to do ~하는 방법 headlining artist 주요 공연자 look forward to ~을 고대하다 interested 관심 있는 official 공식의, 공식적인 as for ~와 관련해서는, ~에 관해 말하자면 expect ~을 예상하다 big day 중요한 날 make sure to do 반드시 ~하도록 하다

22. 화자는 무슨 종류의 행사를 설명하고 있는가?

(A) 매장의 개장식
(B) 미술 및 공예 박람회
(C) 음악 축제
(D) 운동 대회

정답 (C)

해설 화자가 담화 초반부에서 연례 캔터베리 재즈 축제가 곧 열릴 것이라고(the annual Canterbury Jazz Festival is taking place soon in Remuera Park) 알리면서 이 축제와 관련된 전반적인 정보를 제공하는 것으로 담화를 이어가고 있습니다. 따라서 (C)가 정답입니다.

어휘 describe ~을 설명하다 grand opening 개장식 craft 공예 fair 박람회 competition (경연) 대회

23. 화자의 말에 따르면, 청자들은 웹사이트에서 무엇을 찾을 수 있는가?

(A) 행사 일정표
(B) 등록 양식
(C) 식품 판매 업체 목록
(D) 주차 안내도

정답 (A)

해설 웹사이트가 언급되는 후반부에, 전체 공연 일정표를 확인해 보기 위해 공식 웹사이트를 방문하라고(you can visit the official Web site at www.canterburyfestival.com to see a full performance schedule) 언급하고 있습니다. 이를 통해, 웹사이트에서 행사 일정표를 찾을 수 있다는 것을 알 수 있으므로 (A)가 정답입니다.

어휘 registration 등록 form 양식, 서식 vendor 판매 업체, 판매 업자

Paraphrase full performance schedule
⇒ event schedule

24. 시각자료를 보시오. 행사는 어느 날에 개최될 것인가?
(A) 목요일
(B) 금요일
(C) 토요일
(D) 일요일

정답 (C)
해설 날씨 정보가 제공되는 맨 마지막 부분에, 구름 한 점 없이 화창한 날이 예상된다고(we're expecting a sunny day without any clouds on the big day) 알리고 있습니다. 시각자료에서 화창한 날에 해당되는 요일이 토요일이므로 (C)가 정답입니다.

DAY 13 공지 및 안내

PRACTICE

1. (B)   2. (D)   3. (A)

Questions 1-3 refer to the following announcement.

Good morning, and **1** welcome to the Spring Exhibition at the National Art Museum. Please **2** note that the live painting demonstration has been moved to Gallery 7 to make room for the sculpture unveiling. Gallery 7 is on the second floor, next to the Impressionist Wing. Also, **3** will the guest who left a pair of grey leather gloves at the front desk please claim them? They have small buckles at the wrists.

안녕하십니까, 국립미술박물관의 춘계 전시에 오신 것을 환영합니다. 실시간 작화 시연이 조각 작품 공개를 위한 공간 확보로 인해 제 7전시실로 장소가 변경되었음을 안내드립니다. 제 7전시실은 2층 인상파 전시실 옆에 있습니다. 또한, 안내 데스크에 회색 가죽 장갑 한 켤레를 두고 가신 관람객께서는 수령해 주시겠습니까? 손목 부분에 작은 버클이 달려 있습니다.

어휘 exhibition 전시(회) national 국립의 note that ~라는 점을 알아두세요 live 실시간의 painting 작화, 그림 그리기 demonstration 시연 room 공간 sculpture 조각 unveiling 공개 Impressionist 인상주의자 wing (건물의) 동, 부속 건물 a pair of 한 쌍의 leather 가죽 claim (분실물 등을) 찾아가다, (자신의 것을) 요구하다, 요청하다 wrist 손목

1. 이 안내는 어디서 이뤄지고 있는 것 같은가?
(A) 극장
(B) 박물관
(C) 콘서트장
(D) 서점

정답 (B)
해설 화자가 국립미술박물관의 춘계 전시에 오신 것을 환영한다고 (welcome to the Spring Exhibition at the National Art Museum) 언급한 것을 듣고 장소가 박물관임을 알 수 있습니다. 따라서 정답은 (B)입니다.

2. 화자는 무엇이 변경되었다고 말하는가?
(A) 입장료
(B) 주차 규정
(C) 개장 시간
(D) 시연 장소

정답 (D)
해설 화자는 실시간 작화 시연이 조각 작품 공개를 위한 공간 확보로 인해 제 7전시실로 장소가 변경되었음을 안내드린다고(live painting demonstration has been moved to Gallery 7 to make room for the sculpture unveiling) 언급하고 있으므로, 시연의 장소가 변경되었다는 것을 알 수 있습니다. 따라서 정답은 (D)입니다.

어휘 admission 입장료 location 위치, 장소

3. 화자는 프런트 데스크에서 무엇을 얻을 수 있다고 말하는가?
(A) 분실물
(B) 티켓 반쪽
(C) 안내 책자
(D) 회원 카드

정답 (A)
해설 화자가 안내 데스크에 회색 가죽 장갑 한 켤레를 두고 가신 관람객에게 그것을 찾아갈 것을(will the guest who left a pair of grey leather gloves at the front desk please claim them?) 언급하는 내용에서 회색 가죽 장갑이 분실물임을 알 수 있습니다. 따라서 정답은 (A)입니다.

어휘 lost 분실된 ticket stub 입장 후 찢어서 받는 입장권의 반쪽

실전 TEST

1. (A)	2. (C)	3. (C)	4. (B)	5. (B)
6. (C)	7. (B)	8. (C)	9. (A)	10. (A)
11. (C)	12. (C)	13. (B)	14. (B)	15. (C)
16. (A)	17. (A)	18. (C)	19. (D)	20. (B)
21. (B)	22. (B)	23. (A)	24. (A)	

Questions 1-3 refer to the following announcement.

As you all know, **① we are scheduled to relocate our offices to the North Riverside Building** in the City Center next week. I'm sure that you are all excited about moving to such a state-of-the art building. Personally, **② I can't wait to take advantage of the high-speed WiFi Internet** that is available for free throughout the entire building. The IT department will back up all your work files and pack up your computers, and the maintenance team will handle the office furniture. So, **③ all you need to do is empty out any file cabinets you may use and put the files into labeled boxes.** Please do this before we start moving everything on Friday.

여러분들 모두 아시다시피, 우리는 다음 주에 도심에 위치한 노스 리버사이드 빌딩으로 사무실을 이전할 예정입니다. 분명 여러분 모두가 그러한 최신 건물로 옮기는 것에 대해 들떠 있으실 겁니다. 개인적으로, 저는 건물 전체에 걸쳐 무료로 이용 가능한 초고속 와이파이 인터넷을 빨리 이용해 보고 싶습니다. IT 부서에서 여러분의 업무 파일 전부를 백업하고 여러분의 컴퓨터를 포장할 것이며, 시설 관리팀에서 사무용 가구를 처리할 것입니다. 따라서, 여러분은 이용하실 수도 있는 어떤 파일 캐비닛이든지 깨끗이 비운 다음, 파일들을 라벨이 표기된 상자에 담기만 하면 됩니다. 금요일에 우리가 모든 것을 옮기는 일을 시작하기 전에 이 일을 해 주시기 바랍니다.

어휘 be scheduled to do ~할 예정이다 relocate ~을 이전하다 be sure that 분명 ~할 것이다, ~임을 확신하다 state-of-the-art 최신의 can't wait to do 빨리 ~하고 싶다 take advantage of ~을 이용하다 available 이용 가능한 for free 무료로 throughout ~ 전체에 걸쳐 entire 전체의 pack up ~을 포장하다, 꾸리다 maintenance 시설 관리, 유지 관리 handle ~을 처리하다, 다루다 all you need to do is + 동사원형: 여러분은 ~하기만 하면 됩니다 empty out ~을 깨끗이 비우다 put A into B: A를 B에 담다, 넣다 labeled 라벨이 표기된

1. 공지는 무엇에 관한 내용인가?
 (A) 새로운 사무 공간으로 이사하는 것
 (B) 직장에서 생산성을 향상시키는 것
 (C) 새 소프트웨어를 설치하는 것
 (D) 사무 용품을 구매하는 것

정답 (A)
해설 공지의 주제는 담화의 첫 부분에 나타나므로 담화 초반부를 제대로 들어야 합니다. 첫 문장에서 사무실 이전에 대해 언급한(we are scheduled to relocate our offices to North Riverside Building ~) 다음, 직원들이 해야 할 일들을 안내하고 있으므로, 새 사무 공간으로의 이전을 뜻하는 (A)가 정답입니다.

어휘 improve ~을 향상시키다 productivity 생산성 at work 직장에서 install ~을 설치하다 purchase ~을 구매하다 office supplies 사무 용품

2. 화자는 노스 리버사이드 빌딩에 대해 뭐라고 말하는가?
 (A) 버스 정류장 옆에 위치해 있다.
 (B) 널찍한 사무실을 가지고 있다.
 (C) 빠른 인터넷 서비스를 가지고 있다.
 (D) 구내 식당을 포함하고 있다.

정답 (C)
해설 담화 중반부에 화자가 새 건물 내의 특징과 관련해 초고속 와이파이 인터넷을 빨리 이용해 보고 싶다고(I can't wait to take advantage of the high-speed WiFi Internet ~) 말하고 있으므로 (C)가 정답입니다.

어휘 be located next to ~ 옆에 위치해 있다 spacious 널찍한 include ~을 포함하다 cafeteria 구내 식당

3. 직원들은 무엇을 하도록 요청 받는가?
 (A) 일부 가구 옮기기
 (B) 각자의 개인 물품 챙겨 가기
 (C) 문서를 상자에 담기
 (D) 각자의 컴퓨터 끄기

정답 (C)
해설 직원들이 요청 받는 일을 묻고 있으므로 요청 관련 표현이 제시되는 부분에서 단서를 찾아야 합니다. 담화 후반부에 화자가 'all you need to do is ~'라는 말로 요청 사항을 알리고 있는데, 파일 캐비닛들을 깨끗이 비우고 그 파일들을 라벨이 표기된 상자에 담으라고(empty out any file cabinets you may use and put the files into labeled boxes) 요청하고 있습니다. 따라서 이 중 한 가지에 해당되는 (C)가 정답입니다.

어휘 be asked to do ~하도록 요청 받다 supplies 물품, 용품 item 물품, 제품 turn off ~을 끄다

Questions 4-6 refer to the following announcement.

Before we start today's management meeting, I have an announcement to make. You may remember that **4 I suggested that each of you be provided with your own personal office. Well, the CEO of our firm has reviewed my proposal and finally approved it. 5 This change will allow us to better serve our valuable customers.** The offices will be assigned according to your individual needs and preferences, so to select which one you want, **6 download a request form online and submit it to Mr. Harris in Personnel by e-mail by the end of the day.**

우리가 금일 운영 회의를 시작하기에 앞서, 공지 사항이 하나 있습니다. 제가 여러분 각자에게 여러분의 개인 사무실이 제공되도록 제안한 사실을 기억하실 겁니다. 저, 우리 회사의 대표이사님께서 제 제안을 검토하신 다음, 최종적으로 그것을 승인하셨습니다. 이러한 변화는 우리가 우리의 소중한 고객들에게 더 나은 서비스를 제공할 수 있게 해줄 것입니다. 사무실은 여러분의 개인 필요성 및 선호도에 따라 배정될 것이므로, 원하시는 것을 선택하시려면, 온라인에서 요청 양식을 다운로드하신 다음, 이것을 오늘 일과 종료 시점까지 이메일로 인사부에 있는 해리스 씨에게 제출하십시오.

어휘 management 운영, 경영, 관리 announcement 공지, 발표 suggest that ~하도록 제안하다 provide A with B: A에게 B를 제공하다 review ~을 검토하다 proposal 제안(서) approve ~을 승인하다 allow A to do: A가 ~할 수 있게 해주다 serve ~에게 서비스를 제공하다 valuable 소중한 assign ~을 배정하다, 할당하다 according to ~에 따라 individual 개인의, 개별적인 preference 선호(하는 것) select ~을 선택하다 request 요청 form 양식, 서식 submit ~을 제출하다 by (기한) ~까지

4. 회사는 청자들에게 무엇을 제공할 것인가?
(A) 회사 차량
(B) 개인 사무실
(C) 새 노트북 컴퓨터
(D) 추가 휴무 일수

정답 (B)
해설 담화 시작 부분에 화자 자신이 직원 각자에게 그들의 사무실이 제공되도록 제안한 사실과 그것이 승인된 사실을(I suggested that each of you be provided with your own personal office. Well, the CEO of our firm has reviewed my proposal and finally approved it) 함께 알리고 있습니다. 따라서 (B)가 정답입니다.

어휘 extra 추가의 vacation 휴무, 휴가

5. 화자는 무슨 이점을 언급하는가?
(A) 늘어난 연간 수익
(B) 향상된 고객 서비스
(C) 더 빠른 생산 속도
(D) 더 높은 직원 만족도

정답 (B)
해설 담화 중반부에 변화가 자신들이 소중한 고객들에게 더 나은 서비스를 제공할 수 있게 해줄 것이라고(This change will allow us to better serve our valuable customers) 언급하고 있습니다. 이를 통해, 향상된 고객 서비스가 이점이라는 것을 알 수 있으므로 (B)가 정답입니다.

어휘 benefit 이점, 혜택 increased 늘어난, 증가된 annual 연간의, 해마다의 revenue 수익 improved 향상된 production rate 생산 속도, 생산율 employee satisfaction 직원 만족도

6. 화자의 말에 따르면, 청자들은 왜 해리스 씨에게 이메일을 보내야 하는가?
(A) 회의 일정을 잡기 위해
(B) 역할에 대한 일을 자진해서 맡기 위해
(C) 요청하기 위해
(D) 참석을 확인하기 위해

정답 (C)
해설 이메일을 보내는 일이 언급되는 담화 후반부에, 화자는 온라인에서 요청 양식을 다운로드해 이것을 해리스 씨에게 이메일로 제출하도록(~ download a request form online and submit it to Mr. Harris in Personnel by e-mail by the end of the day) 요청하고 있습니다. 즉 요청 사항을 제출하기 위해 이메일을 보내야 하므로 (C)가 정답입니다.

어휘 schedule ~의 일정을 잡다 role 역할 make a request 요청하다 confirm ~을 확인하다 attendance 참석, 출석

Paraphrase download a request form online and submit it ⇒ make a request

Questions 7-9 refer to the following announcement.

Attention, shoppers. Please start making your way to the checkouts to pay for your items. **7 Our supermarket will be closing in 30 minutes.** Remember that we have various special items on display at the checkouts. **8 We have a special buy-one-get-one-free offer on Creme Deluxe chocolate bars this week.** Make sure you check them out! Also, we are currently handing out free samples of Naturolife beauty products on the second floor. **9 Starting from next week, our store will be carrying a new range of Naturolife skin moisturizers and cleansers.** Thank you for shopping with us today.

쇼핑객 여러분께 알립니다. 구입 제품에 대한 비용을 지불하기 위해 계산대로 이동하기 시작해 주십시오. 저희 슈퍼마켓은 30분 후에 문을 닫을 예정입니다. 저희가 계산대 옆에 다양한 특별 제품을 진열해 두고 있다는 점을 기억해 주시기 바랍니다. 저희는 이번 주에 크렘 딜럭스 초콜릿 바에 대해 1+1 특가 서비스를 제공합니다. 반드시 이것들을 확인해 보시기 바랍니다! 또한, 저희는 현재 2층에서 네이쳐오라이프 미용 제품의 무료 샘플을 나눠 드리고 있습니다. 다음 주부터, 저희 매장은 새로운 종류의 네이쳐오라이프 스킨 보습제와 세안제 제품을 취급할 것입니다. 오늘 저희 매장에서 쇼핑해 주셔서 감사드립니다.

어휘 make one's way to ~로 이동하다, 가다 checkout 계산대 pay for ~에 대한 비용을 지불하다 item 제품, 물품 have A on display: A를 진열해 두다, 전시해 두다 various 다양한 buy-one-get-one-free 1+1으로 제공하는 offer 제공 (서비스) make sure (that) 반드시 ~하도록 하다 check A out: A를 확인해 보다 currently 현재 hand out ~을 나눠 주다 free 무료의 carry (매장에서) ~을 취급하다, 갖춰 놓다 range (제품) 종류, 제품군

7. 왜 공지가 이뤄지고 있는가?
   (A) 슈퍼마켓의 편의 시설을 설명하기 위해
   (B) 마감 시간을 알리기 위해
   (C) 한 서비스가 왜 이용 불가능한지 설명하기 위해
   (D) 새로운 지점을 광고하기 위해

정답 (B)

해설 담화 시작 부분에서 쇼핑객들에게 계산대로 이동하도록 요청하면서 매장이 30분 후에 문을 닫을 예정이라고(Our supermarket will be closing in 30 minutes) 알리고 있습니다. 따라서 마감 시간을 알리는 것이 공지의 목적임을 알 수 있으므로 (B)가 정답입니다.

어휘 describe ~을 설명하다 amenities 편의 시설 announce ~을 알리다, 발표하다 explain ~을 설명하다 unavailable 이용할 수 없는 advertise ~을 광고하다 branch 지점, 지사

8. 여자가 "반드시 이것들을 확인해 보시기 바랍니다"라고 말하는 이유는 무엇인가?
   (A) 청자들에게 매장 쿠폰을 사용할 것을 상기시키고 있다.
   (B) 청자들이 다른 업체를 방문하기를 원한다.
   (C) 청자들이 거래 서비스를 이용하기를 바란다.
   (D) 청자들에게 영수증을 확인하는 것을 권하고 있다.

정답 (C)

해설 담화 중반부에 화자가 이번 주에 크렘 딜럭스 초콜릿 바에 대해 1+1 특가 서비스를 제공한다고(We have a special buy one-get-one-free offer on Creme Deluxe chocolate bars this week) 알린 뒤로 "반드시 이것들을 확인해 보시기 바랍니다"라는 말이 이어지고 있습니다. 이는 그 특가 서비스를 이용하도록 권하는 말에 해당되므로 (C)가 정답입니다.

어휘 remind A to do: A에게 ~하는 것을 상기시키다 want A to do: A가 ~하기를 바라다 take advantage of ~을 이용하다 deal 거래 서비스, 거래 제품 advise A to do: A에게 ~하는 것을 권하다 receipt 영수증

9. 화자의 말에 따르면, 다음 주에 업체에서 무슨 일이 있을 것인가?
   (A) 신제품이 판매될 것이다.
   (B) 무료 배송 서비스가 시작될 것이다.
   (C) 영업 시간이 연장될 것이다.
   (D) 특가 할인 판매가 시작될 것이다.

정답 (A)

해설 '다음 주'라는 시점은 담화 후반부에 언급되고 있으며, 여기서 다음 주부터 새로운 보습제와 세안제 제품을 취급할 것이라고(Starting from next week, our store will be carrying a new range of Naturolife skin moisturizers and cleansers) 알리고 있습니다. 이는 신제품이 판매될 것이라는 뜻이므로 (A)가 정답입니다.

어휘 happen 일어나다, 발생하다 free 무료의 delivery 배송, 배달 extend ~을 연장하다, 확대하다

Paraphrase will be carrying a new range of Naturolife skin moisturizers and cleansers
⇒ New products will be sold

Questions 10-12 refer to the following announcement and schedule.

Good morning, everyone. **10 On behalf of Karma Train Station, I'd like to tell you about the new facilities in our station.** Our three-month long refurbishment project was completed last month, and the station now includes a wide variety of excellent restaurants and cafes. Also, **11 you can use free WiFi and phone charging centers throughout the station.** And don't forget… reserving tickets is easier than ever thanks to the new ticket kiosks. **12 As a side note for those waiting for the 10:30 train to Albany, I'm sorry to say that it has been delayed by one hour.** We are sorry for the inconvenience.

안녕하세요, 여러분. 카르마 기차역을 대표해, 저희 역의 새로운 시설물에 관해 말씀드리고자 합니다. 저희의 3개월 동안의 재단장 프로젝트가 지난 달에 완료되었으며, 저희 역은 현재 아주 다양하면서도 훌륭한 레스토랑과 카페를 포함합니다. 또한, 역 전체에 걸쳐 무료 와이파이와 휴대 전화 충전소를 이용하실 수 있습니다. 그리고 잊지 마셔야 하는 점은… 티켓 예매가 새로운 티켓 판매기로 인해 그 어느 때보다 더 쉽습니다. 올바니 행 10시 30분 기차를 기다리시는 분들을 위한 별도의 공지로서, 이 기차가 1시간 지연되었다는 사실을 알려 드리게 되어 유감스럽게 생각합니다. 불편을 드려 죄송합니다.

열차 번호	출발 시간	도착지
P12	09:00	프로비던스
B59	09:45	보스턴
A46	10:30	올바니
S23	11:15	스프링필드

어휘 on behalf of ~을 대표해, 대신해 facility 시설(물) refurbishment 재단장 complete ~을 완료하다 include ~을 포함하다 a wide variety of 아주 다양한 free 무료의 charging center 충전소 throughout ~ 전역에 걸쳐 reserve ~을 예약하다 than ever 그 어느 때보다 thanks to ~로 인해, ~ 덕분에 ticket kiosk 티켓 판매기 side note 별도의 공지 those -ing ~하는 사람들 delayed 지연된, 지체된 by (차이 등) ~만큼 inconvenience 불편

10. 공지의 주 목적은 무엇인가?
 (A) 역내 시설물을 설명하는 것
 (B) 새로운 정책을 설명하는 것
 (C) 곧 있을 공사에 대해 사과하는 것
 (D) 승객들에게 승강장 변경에 관해 상기시키는 것

정답 (A)
해설 담화를 시작하면서 화자가 카르마 역을 대표해 역의 새로운 시설물에 관해 얘기하고자 한다고(On behalf of Karma Train Station, I'd like to tell you about the new facilities in our station) 알리고 있으므로 (A)가 정답입니다.

어휘 describe ~을 설명하다 explain ~을 설명하다 policy 정책 apologize for ~에 대해 사과하다 upcoming 곧 있을, 다가오는 remind A about B: A에게 B에 관해 상기시키다

Paraphrase tell you about the new facilities in our station ⇒ describe the station facilities

11. 화자의 말에 따르면, 청자들은 역에서 무엇을 할 수 있는가?
 (A) 선물 매장 방문하기
 (B) 무료 음식 시식하기
 (C) 자신들의 휴대폰 충전하기
 (D) 몇몇 팸플릿 얻기

정답 (C)
해설 이용 가능한 서비스가 언급되는 담화 중반부에, 역 전체에 걸쳐 무료 와이파이와 휴대 전화 충전소를 이용할 수 있다고(you can use free WiFi and phone charging centers throughout the station) 알리고 있습니다. 따라서 이 서비스들 중의 하나에 해당되는 (C)가 정답입니다.

어휘 sample ~을 시식하다 free 무료의 charge ~을 충전하다 obtain ~을 얻다, 획득하다

12. 시각자료를 보시오. 화자는 어느 기차가 지연될 것이라고 말하는가?
 (A) P12
 (B) B59
 (C) A46
 (D) S23

정답 (C)
해설 열차 지연 문제가 언급되는 담화 후반부에, 10시 30분에 올바니로 가는 기차가 1시간 지연되었다고(As a side note for those waiting for the 10:30 train to Albany, I'm sorry to say that it has been delayed by one hour) 알리고 있습니다. 시각자료에서 10시 30분에 올바니로 출발하는 기차의 번호가 A46이므로 (C)가 정답입니다.

Questions 13-15 refer to the following announcement.

Good afternoon, and 13 we hope that you are enjoying the fifth annual Metro City Auto Show. Please note that due to popular demand, 14 the expert panel on autonomous cars will now run until 3:30 instead of 3 o'clock to allow extra time for the question-and-answer session. Also, 15 if you have yet to pick up your raffle ticket for the prize giveaway, please come to the welcome desk. Each attendee can be entered once, so don't forget to test your luck!

안녕하세요, 그리고 저희는 여러분께서 제5회 연례 메트로 시티 자동차 전시회에서 즐거운 시간 보내고 계시기를 바랍니다. 많은 분들의 요구로 인해, 자율 주행 자동차에 관한 전문가 패널이 이제 질의 응답 시간에 추가 시간을 할당해 드리기 위해 3시 대신 3시 30분까지 운영될 것이라는 점에 유의하시기 바랍니다. 또한, 경품 증정을 위한 추첨 행사 티켓을 아직 가져가시지 않은 경우, 환영 데스크로 오시기 바랍니다. 각 참석자께서 한 차례 응모하실 수 있으므로, 잊지 마시고 여러분의 행운을 테스트해 보십시오.

어휘 annual 연례적인, 해마다의 note that ~라는 점에 유의하다, ~임에 주목하다 due to ~로 인해, ~ 때문에 popular 많은 사람들의, 대중의, 인기 있는 demand n. 요구, 수요 v. ~을 요구하다 expert 전문가 autonomous 자율적인 run 운영되다, 진행되다 instead of ~ 대신 allow ~을 할당하다, ~을 허용하다 extra 추가의, 별도의 question-and-answer session 질의 응답 시간 have yet to do 아직 ~하지 않았다 pick up ~을 가져가다, ~을 가져오다 raffle 추첨 행사 prize 경품, 상품 giveaway 증정(품) attendee 참석자 enter ~에 응모하다, ~에 참가하다 forget to do ~하는 것을 잊다

13. 공지는 어디에서 이뤄지고 있는 것 같은가?
(A) 취업 박람회에서
(B) 자동차 전시회에서
(C) 박물관 전시회에서
(D) 제조 공장에서

정답 (B)

해설 화자가 담화를 시작하면서 제5회 연례 메트로 시티 자동차 전시회에서 즐거운 시간 보내고 있기를 바란다는(we hope that you are enjoying the fifth annual Metro City Auto Show) 인사를 전하고 있으므로 (B)가 정답입니다.

어휘 fair 박람회, 축제 마당 exhibit 전시회, 전시물 manufacturing 제조(업) plant 공장

14. 화자는 무엇이 변경되었다고 말하는가?
(A) 다과 제공
(B) 패널 일정
(C) 좌석 배치도
(D) 연설자

정답 (B)

해설 화자가 담화 중반부에 자율 주행 자동차에 관한 전문가 패널이 3시 대신 3시 30분까지 운영된다고(the expert panel on autonomous cars will now run until 3:30 instead of 3 o'clock) 알리는 것으로 패널 일정이 변경되었음을 밝히고 있으므로 (B)가 정답입니다.

어휘 refreshment 다과, 간식 offering 제공(되는 것)

15. 화자는 환영 데스크에서 무엇이 이용 가능하다고 말하는가?
(A) 주차권
(B) 무료 선물
(C) 티켓
(D) 안내 책자

정답 (C)

해설 담화 후반부에 화자가 경품 증정을 위한 추첨 행사 티켓을 아직 가져가지 않은 사람은 환영 데스크로 오라고(if you have yet to pick up your raffle ticket for the prize giveaway, please come to the welcome desk) 알리고 있으므로 (C)가 정답입니다.

어휘 available (사물) 이용 가능한, 구입 가능한, (사람) 시간이 있는 pass 입장권, 출입증, 탑승권 free 무료의

Questions 16-18 refer to the following announcement.

Good evening, everyone. Thank you for your patience – 16 tonight's outdoor movie screening is starting a bit late because the projector is having some last-minute repairs done. Once it's all set, we'll begin immediately. While you wait, feel free to purchase some popcorn and drinks near the front entrance. And 17 as a friendly reminder, please silence all electronic devices at this time. Alright… Now, we're all set! 18 We're kicking off with a few movie previews before our main program, *The Star Grove Adventure*. Sit back, relax, and enjoy the show.

안녕하세요, 여러분. 여러분의 인내에 감사 드리며, 오늘밤 야외 영화 상영회는 프로젝터에 마지막 순간의 수리 작업이 진행되고 있어서 조금 늦게 시작됩니다. 모든 것이 준비되는 대로, 즉시 시작할 것입니다. 기다리시는 동안, 부담 갖지 마시고 정면 입구 근처에서 팝콘과 음료를 구입하셔도 됩니다. 그리고 혹시나 해서 상기시켜 드리는 것으로서, 이제 모든 전자 기기는 무음으로 해 주시기 바랍니다. 좋습니다… 자, 저희는 모두 준비되었습니다! 본

프로그램인 <스타 그로브 어드벤처>에 앞서 몇몇 영화 예고편으로 시작하겠습니다. 편안히 기대어 앉아, 긴장을 푸시고, 상영을 즐기시기 바랍니다!

어휘 patience 인내(심), 참을성 screening 상영(회) have A p.p.: A를 ~되게 하다 last-minute 마지막 순간의 repair n. 수리 v. ~을 수리하다 immediately 즉시 feel free to do 부담 갖지 말고 ~하세요, 마음껏 ~하세요 as a friendly reminder 혹시나 해서 상기시켜 드리는 것으로서 silence v. ~을 무음으로 하다 device 기기, 장치 set 준비된, 예정된, 설치된 kick off 시작하다 preview 예고편 relax 긴장을 풀다, 느긋하게 시간을 보내다

16. 영화 상영회는 왜 지연되었는가?
(A) 프로젝터가 수리되고 있다.
(B) 일정 관리상의 실수가 있었다.
(C) 일부 손님들이 도착하지 않았다.
(D) 한 직원이 교대 근무에 늦었다.

정답 (A)

해설 화자가 담화를 시작하면서 야외 영화 상영회가 프로젝터에 마지막 순간의 수리 작업이 진행되고 있어서 조금 늦게 시작된다고(tonight's outdoor movie screening is starting a bit late because the projector is having some last-minute repairs done) 밝히고 있으므로 (A)가 정답입니다.

어휘 scheduling 일정 관리 shift 교대 근무(조)

17. 청자들은 무엇을 하도록 상기되는가?
(A) 각자의 기기를 무음으로 할 것
(B) 티켓을 소지하고 있을 것
(C) 줄거리를 읽어 볼 것
(D) 무료 간식을 가져올 것

정답 (A)

해설 담화 중반부에 화자가 혹시나 해서 상기시키는 메시지임을 알리면서 모든 전자 기기를 무음으로 해 달라고(as a friendly reminder, please silence all electronic devices at this time) 당부하고 있으므로 (A)가 정답입니다.

어휘 be reminded to do ~하도록 상기되다 hold onto ~을 소지하다, ~을 붙잡다 synopsis 줄거리, 개요 pick up ~을 가져오다, ~을 가져가다 complimentary 무료의 refreshments 간식, 다과

18. 무엇이 손님들에게 먼저 보여질 것인가?
(A) 비상구 경로
(B) 특별 발표
(C) 영화 예고편
(D) 제품 광고

정답 (C)

해설 화자가 담화 후반부에 본 프로그램에 앞서 몇몇 영화 예고편으로 시작하겠다는 말로(We're kicking off with a few movie previews before our main program) 행사 진행 순서를 전달하고 있으므로 (C)가 정답입니다.

어휘 emergency exit 비상구 route 경로, 노선 presentation 발표(회) trailer (영화 등의) 예고편 advertisement 광고

Paraphrase movie previews ⇒ Movie trailers

Questions 19-21 refer to the following announcement.

> **19** Hello, Lassen Volcanic National Park staff. As we enter the peak summer season, we must be prepared to assist with parking overflow, especially near the Loomis Museum and Summit Lake areas. **20** **When the main lots fill up, please direct guests to the designated overflow sections and remind them to park only in marked areas.** We're also expecting heavy foot traffic on all trails, so please encourage visitors to follow trail etiquette. **21** **We're still updating some of the safety protocols in our employee handbook,** but the revised version will be sent out soon!
>
> 안녕하세요, 라센 화산 국립 공원 직원 여러분. 우리가 여름 성수기에 돌입함에 따라, 반드시 주차 과잉 문제에 대해 지원할 준비가 되어 있어야 하며, 특히 루미스 박물관과 서밋 호수 구역 근처가 그렇습니다. 주요 주차 구역들이 가득 차는 경우, 손님들을 지정된 초과 주차 구역으로 안내해 주시고 오직 표시된 구역 내에만 주차하도록 상기시켜 드리기 바랍니다. 모든 등산로에서도 많은 유동 인구가 예상되고 있으므로, 방문객들께 등산로 이용 에티켓을 따르도록 권장해 주십시오. 우리가 여전히 직원용 직무 안내서의 일부 안전 규정을 업데이트하고 있기는 하지만, 개정된 버전이 곧 발송될 것입니다.

어휘 peak season 성수기 be prepared to do ~할 준비가 되다 assist with ~에 대해 지원하다, ~을 돕다 parking 주차(장) overflow 과잉, 초과, 넘쳐 흐름 especially 특히, 특별히 lot 주차장 fill up 가득 차다 direct A to B: A를 B로 안내하다[보내다] designated 지정된 remind A to do: A에게 ~하도록 상기시키다 park 주차하다 marked 표시된 expect ~을 예상하다, ~을 기대하다 heavy (정도, 수량 등이) 많은, 심한 foot traffic 유동 인구 trail 등산로, 산길 encourage A to do: A에게 ~하도록 권장하다 follow ~을 따르다 etiquette 에티켓, 예의 protocol 규정, 규약 employee handbook 직원용 직무 안내서 revise ~을 개정하다, ~을 수정하다 send out ~을 발송하다

19. 공지는 어디에서 이뤄지고 있는 것 같은가?
   (A) 지역 공동체 정원
   (B) 과학 박물관
   (C) 철물점
   (D) 국립 공원

정답 (D)

해설 화자가 담화를 시작하면서 라센 화산 국립 공원 직원들을 부르면서(Hello, Lassen Volcanic National Park staff) 인사하는 부분을 통해 장소를 파악할 수 있으므로 (D)가 정답입니다.

어휘 **take place** 진행되다, 개최되다, 발생하다 **community** 지역 공동체, 지역 사회

20. 화자는 청자들에게 무엇을 하도록 지시하는가?
   (A) 무리를 지어 함께 일할 것
   (B) 방문객 통행을 안내하는 데 도움을 줄 것
   (C) 일부 주차선을 페인트칠할 것
   (D) 등산로 한 곳을 조사할 것

정답 (B)

해설 담화 중반부에 화자가 주요 주차 구역들이 가득 차는 경우에 손님들을 지정된 초과 주차 구역으로 안내하고 표시된 구역 내에만 주차하도록 상기시켜 주라고(When the main lots fill up, please direct guests to the designated overflow sections and remind them to park only in marked areas) 지시하고 있습니다. 이는 주차를 위해 손님들의 통행을 안내하는 일을 의미하므로 (B)가 정답입니다.

어휘 **instruct A to do:** A에게 ~하도록 지시하다[설명하다] **help do** ~하는 데 도움을 주다 **traffic** 통행(량), 교통(량) **investigate** ~을 조사하다

Paraphrase direct guests to the designated overflow sections ⇒ direct visitor traffic

21. 화자는 무엇이 업데이트될 것이라고 말하는가?
   (A) 웹사이트
   (B) 안내서
   (C) 셔틀 서비스
   (D) 복장 규정 정책

정답 (B)

해설 화자가 담화 후반부에 직원용 직무 안내서의 일부 안전 규정을 업데이트하고 있다는(We're still updating some of the safety protocols in our employee handbook) 사실을 밝히고 있으므로 (B)가 정답입니다.

어휘 **dress code** 복장 규정 **policy** 정책, 방침

Questions 22-24 refer to the following announcement.

Starting next month, we're updating how we welcome new hires to make their first few weeks on the job more productive. **22** We will be assigning a mentor to each new employee. **23** The duration of the mandatory training period will remain the same – this change just adds a more personal support element to help new hires settle in smoothly. I know **24** some of you have asked about allocating more funds for team lunches with new members as well. While I can't promise anything yet, I'm meeting with Mr. Navarro later this week. I'll give more updates later.

다음 달부터, 우리는 신입 사원들의 첫 근무 몇 주 동안 그들을 더욱 생산적으로 만들기 위해 환영하는 방식을 업데이트합니다. 우리는 각 신입 사원에게 멘토를 배정할 예정입니다. 의무 교육 시간의 지속 기간은 계속 동일하게 유지될 것이며, 이 변동 사항은 단지 신입 사원들이 순조롭게 적응하도록 돕기 위해 더욱 개인적인 지원 요소를 더하는 것뿐입니다. 여러분 중 일부가 새로운 구성원들과 함께 하는 팀 점심 식사를 위해 추가 자금을 할당하는 것에 관해서도 문의하셨다는 사실을 알고 있습니다. 제가 아직 어떤 것도 약속할 수는 없지만, 제가 이번 주 후반에 나바로 씨와 만납니다. 제가 나중에 더 많은 소식을 전해 드리겠습니다.

어휘 **new hire** 신입 사원 **make A 형용사:** A를 ~하게 만들다 **productive** 생산적인 **assign** ~을 배정하다 **mentor** 멘토(조언 등을 해 주는 유경험자나 선배) **duration** 지속 기간 **mandatory** 의무적인 **training** 교육, 훈련 **remain** 계속 ~한 상태로 유지되다 **add** ~을 더하다, ~을 추가하다 **support** 지원, 지지, 후원 **element** 요소 **help A do:** ~하도록 A를 돕다 **settle in** 적응하다, 정착하다 **smoothly** 순조롭게 **allocate** ~을 할당하다 **fund** 자금, 기금 **as well** ~도, 또한 **promise** ~을 약속하다

22. 화자는 주로 무엇을 이야기하고 있는가?
   (A) 고용 과정
   (B) 멘토십 프로그램
   (C) 내부 부서 이동 선택권
   (D) 승진 기회

정답 (B)

해설 화자가 담화 초반부에 신입 사원 환영 방식의 변화를 언급하면서 각 신입 사원에게 멘토를 배정할 것이라고(We will be assigning a mentor to each new employee) 알린 다음, 그에 관해 설명하고 있으므로 (B)가 정답입니다.

어휘 **hiring** 고용, 채용 **process** 과정 **internal** 내부의 **transfer** (자리 등의) 이동, 전근 **opportunity** 기회

promotion 승진, 촉진, 홍보, 판촉 (행사)

Paraphrase assigning a mentor to each new employee
⇒ A mentorship program

23. 화자는 무엇이 변경되지 않을 것이라고 말하는가?
(A) 필수 교육 진행 일정
(B) 온라인 예약 시스템
(C) 업체 운영 시간
(D) 고객 지원 절차

정답 (A)

해설 담화 중반부에 화자가 의무 교육 시간의 지속 기간은 계속 동일한 상태로 유지된다고(The duration of the mandatory training period will remain the same) 알리는 것으로 변동되지 않는 부분을 언급하고 있으므로 (A)가 정답입니다.

어휘 required 필수의, 필요한 reservation 예약 operation 운영, 영업, 가동, 작동 procedure 절차

Paraphrase
· will remain the same ⇒ will not change
· The duration of the mandatory training period ⇒ A required training timeline

24. 화자가 "제가 이번 주 후반에 나바로 씨와 만납니다"라고 말할 때 무엇을 의미하는가?
(A) 추가 자금에 대한 승인을 받기 위해 노력할 것이다.
(B) 팀 단합 행사를 마련하고 싶어 한다.
(C) 나바로 씨와 식사하고 있을 것이다.
(D) 나바로 씨에게 설문 조사지를 줄 계획이다.

정답 (A)

해설 화자가 담화 후반부에 청자들 중 일부가 새로운 구성원들과 함께 하는 팀 점심 식사를 위해 추가 자금을 할당하는 것에 관해 문의한 사실을(some of you have asked about allocating more funds for team lunches with new members as well) 언급하면서 '제가 이번 주 후반에 나바로 씨와 만납니다'라고 말하는 흐름입니다. 따라서, 해당 자금을 할당받기 위해 나바로 씨와 만나 이야기하려 한다는 것을 알 수 있으므로 (A)가 정답입니다.

어휘 approval 승인 extra 추가의, 별도의 organize ~을 마련하다, ~을 조직하다 plan to do ~할 계획이다 survey 설문 조사(지)

DAY 14 회의 발췌 / 소개

PRACTICE

1. (D) **2.** (C) **3.** (C)

Questions 1-3 refer to the following excerpt from a meeting.

We've called this morning's board meeting to discuss the proposed shutdown of our Eastern Distribution Center. **1** As directors of this company, we all have a duty to protect shareholder interests and streamline operations. The purpose of the shutdown would be to consolidate logistics into the newer Western hub and cut costs. Before we vote on this proposal, **2** we need comments from the Financial Committee, including Ms. Olivia Patel, our CFO. But as you know, Ms. Patel is at the investor conference, so instead, **3** we'll go over the latest cost-savings analysis this morning. Please review page 22 in your board book.

금일 오전 이사회는 동부 유통 센터 폐쇄 제안에 대해 논의하고자 소집되었습니다. 이 회사의 이사로서, 저희는 주주의 이익을 보호하고 운영을 능률화할 책임이 있습니다. 이번 폐쇄 제안의 목적은 물류를 최신식 서부 허브로 통합하고 비용을 절감하는 것입니다. 이 제안에 대한 투표 전에, 저희는 최고재무책임자(CFO)인 올리비아 파텔 씨를 포함한 재무위원회의 의견이 필요합니다. 하지만, 아시다시피, 파텔 씨는 현재 투자자 회의에 참석 중이므로, 대신에 금일 오전 회의에서는 최신 비용 절감 분석을 검토하겠습니다. 이사회 자료집 22페이지를 검토해주시기 바랍니다.

어휘 board meeting 이사회 회의 discuss 논의하다 shutdown 폐쇄 distribution 유통 corporate director (기업의) 이사, 임원 duty 의무 protect 보호하다 shareholder 주주 interest 이익 streamline 능률화하다, 간소화하다 operation 운영 purpose 목적 consolidate A into B: A를 B에 통합하다 logistics 물류 hub 허브, 중심지 cut cost 비용을 절감하다 vote on ~에 대해 투표하다 proposal 제안 comment 의견 investor 투자자 instead 대신에 go over 검토하다 latest 최신의 cost-saving 비용 절감의 analysis 분석 review 검토하다

1. 청자는 누구인가?
(A) 주주

98 시원스쿨 기본토익 700+

(B) 창고 직원
(C) 회의 참가자
(D) 회사 이사회 구성원

정답 (D)

해설 화자가 '이 회사의 이사로서, 우리는 ~ 의무를 가지고 있다'라고(As directors of this company, we all have a duty ~) 언급하는 것을 통해 화자를 포함한 청자가 모두 기업의 이사임을 알 수 있습니다. 따라서 정답은 (D)입니다. 화자가 말하는 상황은 회의(conference)가 아닌 이사회 회의(board meeting)이므로 (C)는 오답입니다.

2. 화자가 "파텔 씨는 현재 투자자 회의에 참석 중이다"라고 말할 때, 그 말의 속뜻은 무엇인가?
(A) 분석 자료는 기밀이다.
(B) 일부 최종 수치가 잘못되었다.
(C) 일부 의견이 나중에 전달될 것이다.
(D) 회의가 연기되었다.

정답 (C)

해설 화자는 파텔 씨의 의견이 필요하다고 말한 다음, 파텔 씨가 현재 투자자 회의에 참석 중이므로, 대신에 금일 오전 회의에서는 최신 비용 절감 분석을 검토하겠다고(Ms. Patel is at the investor conference, so instead, we'll go over the latest cost-savings analysis this morning) 언급하는 것을 통해 지금 파텔 씨의 의견이 필요하지만 당장 의견을 듣기 어려우므로 다음에 진행할 것이라는 것을 알 수 있습니다. 따라서 정답은 (C)입니다.

어휘 analysis 분석 confidential 기밀의 final 최종의, 마지막의 figure 수치 postpone 미루다, 연기하다

3. 청자는 다음에 무엇을 할 것인가?
(A) 보도 자료를 작성한다
(B) 서부의 허브를 견학한다
(C) 예상 절감액 보고서를 검토한다
(D) 회의 주최측에 연락한다

정답 (C)

해설 화자는 담화의 마지막 부분에서 금일 오전 회의에서는 최신 비용 절감 분석을 검토하겠다고(we'll go over the latest cost-savings analysis this morning) 언급하였으므로 청자들이 할 일은 예상 절감액 보고서를 검토하는 것임을 알 수 있습니다. 따라서 정답은 (C)입니다.

어휘 draft (문서, 서류 등을) 작성하다 press release 보도 자료 tour 견학하다, 둘러보다 projected savings 예상 절감액 organizer 주최자, 기획자

실전 TEST

1. (B)	2. (A)	3. (D)	4. (A)	5. (B)
6. (C)	7. (C)	8. (B)	9. (A)	10. (A)
11. (B)	12. (C)	13. (B)	14. (C)	15. (A)
16. (D)	17. (A)	18. (D)	19. (D)	20. (C)
21. (B)	22. (B)	23. (B)	24. (C)	

Questions 1-3 refer to the following excerpt from a meeting.

Good morning, and thanks for coming. The personnel manager asked me to gather you all **1** **to explain the new employee incentives program** which will be implemented from the second week of July. This program aims to encourage you all to achieve higher sales records. The most outstanding sales representatives will receive cash bonuses in recognition of their hard work. From October 1 to December 31, **2** **I will be closely monitoring your sales of our state-of-the-art mobile phone to new customers**, and **3** **bonuses will be given to the top three salespeople at our company banquet in January**. Good luck, everyone!

안녕하세요, 그리고 와주셔서 감사합니다. 인사부장님께서 7월 둘째 주부터 시행될 새로운 직원 보상책 프로그램을 설명하기 위해 여러분 모두를 한 자리에 모으도록 저에게 요청하셨습니다. 이 프로그램은 여러분 모두에게 더 높은 판매 기록을 달성하도록 장려하는 것을 목적으로 합니다. 가장 우수한 영업 사원들은 그 노고를 인정해 현금 보너스를 받게 될 것입니다. 10월 1일부터 12월 31일까지, 제가 신규 고객들을 대상으로 하는 우리 최신 휴대 전화기에 대한 여러분의 판매량을 면밀히 관찰할 것이며, 보너스는 1월에 있을 우리 회사 연회에서 최고의 영업 사원 세 명에게 제공될 것입니다. 행운을 빕니다, 여러분!

어휘 personnel manager 인사부장 ask A to do: A에게 ~하도록 요청하다 gather ~을 모으다 explain ~을 설명하다 incentive 보상책 implement ~을 시행하다 aim to do ~하는 것을 목적으로 하다 encourage A to do: A에게 ~하도록 장려하다, 권장하다 achieve ~을 달성하다 sales 판매(량), 영업, 매출 outstanding 우수한 representative n. 직원 receive ~을 받다 in recognition of ~을 인정해 monitor ~을 관찰하다 state-of-the-art 최신의 banquet 연회

1. 화자는 주로 무엇을 논의하고 있는가?
(A) 교육 연수
(B) 직원 보상 시스템
(C) 매장의 연례 할인 판매
(D) 회사 합병

정답 (B)

해설 담화 초반부에서 화자가 새 직원 보상책 프로그램을 설명하기 위해(~ to explain the new employee incentives program ~) 청자들을 한 자리에 모았다고 말하고 있습니다. 이후에 이와 관련된 설명을 계속 이어 나가고 있으므로 (B)가 정답입니다.

어휘 reward 보상 annual 연례적인, 해마다의 merger 합병

Paraphrase new employee incentives program
⇒ staff reward system

2. 청자들은 무엇을 판매할 예정인가?
(A) 휴대 전화기
(B) 가정용 가전 기기
(C) 컴퓨터 부대용품
(D) 텔레비전 서비스

정답 (A)

해설 청자들의 업무 특징과 관련된 정보는 담화 중반부에 제시되는데, 화자가 직접 신규 고객들을 대상으로 하는 최신 휴대 전화기에 대한 청자들의 판매량을 면밀히 관찰할 것이라고(I will be closely monitoring your sales of our state-of-the-art mobile phone to new customers ~) 알리고 있습니다. 따라서 청자들이 휴대 전화기를 판매할 것이라는 것을 알 수 있으므로 (A)가 정답입니다.

어휘 appliance (가전) 기기 accessories 부대용품

3. 1월에 무슨 일이 있을 것인가?
(A) 업체가 이전할 것이다.
(B) 신입 직원들이 일을 시작할 것이다.
(C) 새로운 제품들이 출시될 것이다.
(D) 직원들에게 보너스가 지급될 것이다.

정답 (D)

해설 January는 담화 후반부에 언급되고 있습니다. 1월에 최고의 영업 사원 3명에게 보너스가 제공될 것이라고(bonuses will be given to the top three salespeople at our company banquet in January) 알리고 있으므로 (D)가 정답입니다.

어휘 business 업체 relocate ~을 이전하다 launch ~을 출시하다 award ~을 주다, 수여하다

Questions 4-6 refer to the following introduction.

> **4 Welcome, everyone, to the Victoria Convention Hall.** I'm delighted to have you all here tonight **5 to celebrate the retirement of our company's CEO, Ms. Olivia Jasper**. And, I appreciate all the work that the Personnel Department has done to organize the party. When you look around, it's obvious that they put a lot of effort into making tonight a memorable event. I hope you all have also had a chance to try the delicious food. And now **6 I'd like to introduce the founder of our great company, who will give a short speech about the company's history** and tell us about Ms. Jasper's many achievements over the past 20 years.
>
> 빅토리아 컨벤션홀에 오신 것을 환영합니다, 여러분. 저는 우리 회사의 올리비아 재스퍼 대표이사님의 은퇴를 기념하기 위해 오늘 밤 여러분 모두를 여기에 모시게 되어 기쁩니다. 그리고, 저는 이 파티를 준비하기 위해 인사부에서 해오신 모든 노력에 대해 감사드립니다. 주변을 돌아보시면, 그들이 오늘 밤을 기억에 남을 만한 행사로 만드는 데 많은 노력을 기울여 주셨다는 것이 분명하게 보입니다. 저는 또한 여러분 모두가 맛있는 음식을 드셔 보실 기회도 가지셨기를 바랍니다. 그리고 이제 훌륭한 우리 회사의 창업주를 소개해 드리고자 합니다. 창업주께서는 회사의 연혁에 관해 간단히 연설하시고 지난 20년 동안에 걸친 재스퍼 대표이사님의 많은 업적에 관해 우리에게 말씀해 주실 것입니다.

어휘 celebrate ~을 기념하다, 축하하다 retirement 은퇴, 퇴직 appreciate ~에 대해 감사하다 organize ~을 준비하다, 조직하다 look around 주변을 둘러보다 obvious 분명한, 명백한 put a lot of effort into ~에 많은 노력을 기울이다 make A B: A를 B로 만들다 memorable 기억에 남을 만한 have a chance to do ~할 기회를 갖다 try ~을 한 번 먹어 보다 introduce ~을 소개하다 founder 설립자 give a speech 연설하다 achievement 업적, 성취 over ~ 동안에 걸쳐

4. 어디에서 행사가 개최되고 있는가?
(A) 컨벤션 센터에서
(B) 레스토랑에서
(C) 회사 본사에서
(D) 정부 건물에서

정답 (A)

해설 담화를 시작하면서 화자가 빅토리아 컨벤션홀에 온 것을 환영한다고(Welcome, everyone, to the Victoria Convention Hall) 알리는 것으로 인사하고 있습니다. 따라서 (A)가 정답입니다.

어휘 hold ~을 개최하다 headquarters 본사, 본부

5. 행사에서 누구를 기리고 있는가?
(A) 회사 설립자
(B) 대표이사
(C) 공무원
(D) 인사부장

정답 (B)

해설 담화 초반부에 대표이사인 올리비아 재스퍼 씨의 은퇴를 기념하기 위한 행사라고(~ to celebrate the retirement of our company's CEO, Ms. Olivia Jasper) 알리고 있으므로 (B)가 정답입니다.

어휘 honor ~을 기리다, ~에게 영예를 주다 public official 공무원 personnel director 인사부장

6. 청자들은 곧이어 무엇을 할 것 같은가?
(A) 몇몇 의견 제공하기
(B) 동영상 시청하기
(C) 연설 듣기
(D) 공연 관람하기

정답 (C)

해설 담화 후반부에서 화자가 회사의 연혁에 관해 간단히 연설하고 재스퍼 씨의 업적에 관해 얘기해 줄 창업주를 소개한다고(I'd like to introduce the founder of our great company, who will give a short speech about the company's history ~) 말하고 있습니다. 따라서 청자들은 곧이어 회사의 연혁에 관한 연설을 듣게 된다는 것을 알 수 있으므로 (C)가 정답입니다.

어휘 provide ~을 제공하다 feedback 의견 performance 공연

Questions 7-9 refer to the following excerpt from a meeting.

Good morning, everyone. First, I'd like to thank you for attending this meeting at such short notice. **7** I want to remind you all that our factory will receive an inspection tomorrow. As production line manager, **8** I must stress the importance of achieving a high score on this factory inspection, so we need to be ready before the safety inspector arrives. Failure is not an option. I want you all to check our manufacturing machines and clean around the working areas. Also, **9** I see that many of you are not wearing your safety hats and goggles. I want you to put these on before you start any cleaning work inside the factory.

안녕하세요, 여러분. 우선, 급한 공지에도 불구하고 이번 회의에 참석해 주신 것에 대해 감사드리고자 합니다. 저는 여러분 모두에게 우리 공장이 내일 점검을 받는다는 사실을 상기시켜 드리고자 합니다. 생산 라인 책임자로서, 저는 이번 공장 점검에 대해 높은 점수를 달성하는 것의 중요성을 강조해야겠습니다. 그래서 우리는 안전 검사관이 도착하기 전에 준비가 되어 있어야 합니다. 실패는 선택사항이 아닙니다. 저는 여러분 모두가 우리 제조 기계들을 확인하고 작업장 주변을 청소해 주셨으면 합니다. 또한, 여러분 중 많은 분들이 안전모와 보호 안경을 착용하지 않고 있는 것이 보입니다. 공장 내에서 어떤 청소 작업이든 시작하시기 전에 이것들을 착용해 주시기 바랍니다.

어휘 attend ~에 참석하다 at such short notice 급한 공지에도 remind A that: A에게 ~라는 점을 상기시키다 receive ~을 받다 inspection 점검 stress ~을 강조하다 importance 중요(성) achieve ~을 달성하다, 이루다 safety 안전 inspector 검사관 arrive 도착하다 failure 실패, 하지 못함 want A to do: A가 ~하기를 원하다 manufacturing 제조 put A on: A를 착용하다 cleaning 청소 inside ~ 내에서

7. 회의의 목적은 무엇인가?
(A) 월간 업무 일정을 조정하기 위해
(B) 시연회를 보기 위해
(C) 점검에 대비하기 위해
(D) 새 안전 정책을 발표하기 위해

정답 (C)

해설 담화 시작 부분에 화자가 내일 공장이 점검을 받는다는 사실을 알리면서(I want to remind you all that our factory will receive an inspection tomorrow) 그 일과 관련해서 해야 하는 일들을 간략히 설명하는 것으로 담화가 진행되고 있습니다. 이는 점검에 대비하고자 하는 것이므로 (C)가 정답입니다.

어휘 adjust ~을 조정하다 monthly 월간의, 달마다의 demonstration 시연(회) prepare for ~에 대비하다 announce ~을 발표하다, 알리다 policy 정책, 방침

8. 화자가 "실패는 선택 사항이 아닙니다"라고 말할 때 그 말의 속뜻은 무엇인가?
(A) 일부 장비가 수리되어야 한다고 생각한다.
(B) 청자들이 작업을 진지하게 받아들일 필요가 있다고 생각한다.
(C) 마감 기한이 연장되어야 한다고 생각한다.
(D) 청자들이 재시험을 치기를 바란다.

정답 (B)

해설 담화 중반부에 화자는 점검에서 높은 점수를 받는 것의 중요성을 반드시 강조해야 한다고(I must stress the importance

101

of achieving a high score on this factory inspection) 말한 뒤로 "실패는 선택 사항이 아닙니다"라는 말을 하고 있습니다. 이는 실패를 해서는 안된다는 의미로, 점검에서 반드시 높은 점수를 받기 위해 언급된 작업을 진지하게 받아들이고 점검에 대비하라고 하는 말이므로 (B)가 정답입니다.

어휘 equipment 장비 fix ~을 수리하다, 고치다 take A seriously: A를 진지하게 받아들이다 task 작업, 일, 업무 deadline 마감 기한 extend ~을 연장하다, 확대하다 retake a test 재시험을 치다

9. 청자들은 곧이어 무엇을 할 것인가?
(A) 안전 장비 착용하기
(B) 행사 준비하기
(C) 프로젝트 목표 논의하기
(D) 설문조사지 제출하기

정답 (A)

해설 담화 마지막 부분에 공장 내에서 어떤 청소 작업이든 시작하기 전에 안전모와 보호 안경을 착용하도록(I want you to put these on before you start any cleaning work inside the factory) 요청하고 있으므로 안전 장비 착용을 의미하는 (A)가 정답입니다.

어휘 organize ~을 준비하다, 조직하다 discuss ~을 논의하다, 이야기하다 submit ~을 제출하다 survey 설문조사(지)

Questions 10-12 refer to the following excerpt from a meeting and chart.

So now let's move on to the last agenda item. **10** We will look at the results of our recent customer survey to help us develop and improve our popular Nutrina chocolate bar. As you can see, half of the respondents suggested that we improve the packaging. This did not come as a surprise, and I know that the marketing team is already changing the wrapper design. **11** The thing that concerns me is the suggestion made by 25 percent of survey takers. This is an issue that we need to seriously address. Therefore, to meet this demand, **12** we've decided to hire more professional staff members to deal with it. We'll hold a meeting to discuss it this week.

자, 이제 마지막 의제 항목으로 넘어가 보겠습니다. 우리의 인기 있는 뉴트리나 초콜릿 바를 진전시키고 개선시키는데 도움이 되도록, 우리는 최근 고객 설문조사의 결과를 살펴볼 것입니다. 여러분이 보시다시피, 응답자의 절반이 우리가 포장재를 개선해야 한다고 제안했습니다. 이것은 놀라운 일이 아니었고, 저는 마케팅 팀이 이미 포장지 디자인을 바꾸고 있다는 것을 알고 있습니다.

저를 걱정시키는 것은 설문조사 참여자들의 25퍼센트에 의해 만들어진 제안입니다. 이것은 우리가 진지하게 처리해야 할 문제입니다. 따라서, 이 요구를 충족하기 위해, 우리는 이 문제를 처리할 전문 직원들을 더 고용하기로 결정했습니다. 우리는 이것을 논의하기 위해 이번 주에 회의를 개최할 것입니다.

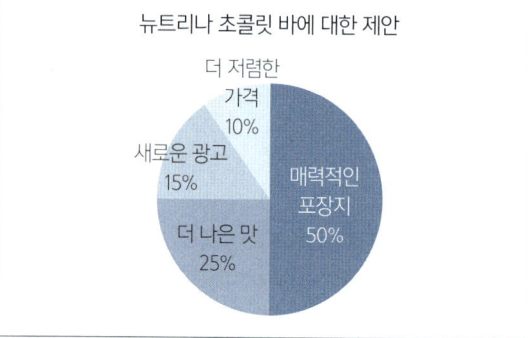

어휘 move onto ~로 넘어가다, 옮겨가다 agenda item 의제 항목 result 결과(물) recent 최근의 survey 설문조사 develop ~을 진전시키다, 개발하다 improve ~을 개선하다 respondent 응답자 suggest that ~라고 제안하다 packaging 포장(지) come as a surprise 놀라운 일이다 wrapper 포장지 concern ~을 걱정스럽게 만들다, 걱정하다 make a suggestion 제안하다 seriously 진지하게, 심각하게 address ~을 처리하다, 다루다 meet ~을 충족하다 demand 요구, 수요 decide to do ~하기로 결정하다 hire ~을 고용하다 deal with ~을 처리하다, 다루다 discuss ~을 논의하다 attractive 매력적인 packaging 포장 flavor 맛, 풍미

10. 청자들은 누구일 것 같은가?
(A) 제품 개발자들
(B) 시장 조사자들
(C) 주방 보조들
(D) 음식 평론가들

정답 (A)

해설 화자는 청자들에게 자신들의 인기 있는 뉴트리나 초콜릿 바를 진전시키고 개선시키는데 도움이 되도록, 자신들의 최근 고객 설문조사의 결과를 살펴볼 거라고(We will look at the results of our recent customer survey to help us develop and improve our popular Nutrina chocolate bar) 언급하고 있습니다. 이는 제품을 개발하는 입장에 있는 사람이 하는 일로 볼 수 있으므로 (A)가 정답입니다.

어휘 developer 개발자 researcher 조사자, 연구자 assistant 보조, 조수 critic 평론가, 비평가

11. 시각자료를 보시오. 화자는 어느 항목에 대해 걱정하고 있는가?
(A) 매력적인 포장지
(B) 더 나은 맛
(C) 새로운 광고
(D) 더 저렴한 가격

정답 (B)

해설 화자의 우려 사항, 즉 부정적인 정보가 제시되는 담화 중반부에, 화자가 자신을 걱정시키는 것은 설문조사 참여자들의 25퍼센트에 의해 만들어진 제안이라고(The thing that concerns me is the suggestion made by 25 percent of survey takers) 언급하고 있습니다. 시각자료에서 25퍼센트의 비율을 차지하는 것이 Better flavor로 쓰여 있으므로 (B)가 정답입니다.

어휘 be worried about ~에 대해 걱정하다

12. 회사는 무엇을 하기로 결정했는가?
(A) 유명 인사와 협업하기
(B) 또 다른 매장 개장하기
(C) 직원을 더 고용하기
(D) 광고 캠페인 시작하기

정답 (C)

해설 결정 사항이 언급되는 담화 후반부에, 이 문제를 처리할 전문 직원들을 더 고용하기로 결정했다고(we've decided to hire more professional staff members to deal with it) 언급하고 있으므로 (C)가 정답입니다.

어휘 collaborate with ~와 협업하다 celebrity 유명 인사 launch ~을 시작하다, ~에 착수하다 advertising 광고(활동)

Questions 13-15 refer to the following introduction.

Hello, I'm Mr. Monroe, and I'm delighted to welcome you to the Rosewood History Museum. Today, **13** **14 I've invited Natalia Peller, who's an expert on the history of agricultural and industrial development in this region, to give a talk.** Natalia is a familiar face here at our museum, and visitors are always deeply impressed by her knowledge about and enthusiasm for our town's history. **15 You'll be able to ask her questions at the end of the session,** but please keep in mind – we have another speaker coming at 4 o'clock.

안녕하세요, 저는 먼로이며, 로즈우드 역사 박물관에 오신 여러분을 맞이하게 되어 기쁩니다. 오늘은, 제가 이 지역의 농업 및 산업 발전 역사에 관한 전문가이신, 나탈리아 펠러 씨께 강연을 하시도록 요청 드렸습니다. 나탈리아 씨는 이곳 저희 박물관에서 익숙하신 분이시며, 방문객들께서 우리 도시의 역사에 관한 이분의 지식과 그에 대한 열정에 항상 깊은 인상을 받고 계십니다. 여러분께서는 이번 시간이 종료될 때 질문을 하실 수 있겠지만, 명심하셔야 하는 부분은, 4시에 또 다른 강연자께서 오신다는 점입니다.

어휘 be delighted to do ~해서 기쁘다 invite A to do: A에게 ~하도록 요청하다 expert 전문가 agricultural 농업의 industrial 산업의 development 발전, 발달, 개발 region 지역 familiar 익숙한, 잘 아는 be deeply impressed by ~에 깊은 인상을 받다 knowledge 지식 enthusiasm 열정 be able to do ~할 수 있다 session (특정 활동을 위한) 시간 keep in mind (that) ~임을 명심하다 have A -ing: ~하는 A가 있다

13. 화자는 박물관에서 무슨 일을 하고 있을 것 같은가?
(A) 주차장을 관리하는 일
(B) 교육 행사를 마련하는 일
(C) 홍보 자료를 디자인하는 일
(D) 신입 직원을 모집하는 일

정답 (B)

해설 화자가 담화 초반부에 전문가인 나탈리아 펠러 씨에게 강연하도록 요청한(I've invited Natalia Peller ~ to give a talk) 사실을 언급하고 있습니다. 따라서, 강연 등의 교육 행사를 마련하는 일을 담당하는 사람임을 알 수 있으므로 (B)가 정답입니다.

어휘 parking lot 주차장 organize ~을 마련하다, ~을 조직하다 promotional 홍보의, 판촉의 material 자료, 재료, 물품 recruit ~을 모집하다, ~을 채용하다

Paraphrase have invited ~ to give a talk
⇒ Organize educational events

14. 화자의 말에 따르면, 나탈리아 펠러 씨는 누구인가?
(A) 영화 제작자
(B) 채소 농부
(C) 지역 역사가
(D) 연구가

정답 (C)

해설 담화 초반부에 화자가 나탈리아 펠러 씨를 소개하면서 그 지역의 농업 및 산업 발전 역사에 관한 전문가라고(Natalia Peller, who's an expert on the history of agricultural and industrial development in this region) 소개하고 있으므로 (C)가 정답입니다.

어휘 local 지역의, 현지의

Paraphrase an expert on the history of agricultural and industrial development in this region
⇒ A local historian

15. 화자가 "4시에 또 다른 강연자께서 오신다는 점입니다"라고 말할 때 무엇을 의미하는가?

(A) 손님들은 반드시 특정 시간까지 떠나야 한다.
(B) 또 다른 행사에 대한 등록이 곧 마감될 것이다.
(C) 일정이 마지막 순간에 변경되었다.
(D) 후속 활동이 무료이다.

정답 (A)

해설 담화 후반부에 화자가 해당 강연 시간이 종료될 때 질문을 할 수 있을 것이라고(You'll be able to ask her questions at the end of the session) 알리면서, 명심해야 하는 부분으로 '4시에 또 다른 강연자께서 오신다는 점입니다'라고 언급하는 흐름입니다. 이는 4시가 되기 전에 질문 시간을 끝으로 해당 강연 일정이 마무리되어야 한다는 뜻으로서, 다음 강연을 위해 손님인 청자들이 반드시 떠나야 한다는 의미이므로 (A)가 정답입니다.

어휘 leave 떠나다, 나가다, 출발하다 by (기한) ~까지 certain 특정한, 일정한 sign-up 등록, 신청 last minute 마지막 순간에 follow-up 후속적인 activity 활동 free of charge 무료인

Questions 16-18 refer to the following excerpt from a meeting.

This morning, **16 we'll be going over logistics for the environmental survey project in the Clearwater region**. As you know, we'll be collecting water quality data over the next several weeks. **17 There are strict sampling procedures we're required to follow.** I'll go over those in detail soon, as well as how to report the samples. But first, **18 please check the first page in your information packet. It lists the specific area you'll each be working in.** Please make sure you're familiar with it before we move on.

오늘 오전에, 우리는 클리어워터 지역 내에서의 환경 조사 프로젝트를 위한 실행 계획을 살펴 볼 예정입니다. 아시다시피, 우리는 앞으로 몇 주 동안에 걸쳐 수질 데이터를 수집할 예정입니다. 우리가 준수해야 하는 엄격한 샘플 추출 절차가 존재합니다. 저는 곧 그것들뿐만 아니라, 샘플을 보고하는 방법도 상세히 짚어 드릴 것입니다. 하지만 먼저, 갖고 계신 정보 안내 자료집의 첫 페이지를 확인해 주시기 바랍니다. 여기에 여러분 각자가 작업할 예정인 특정 구역이 기재되어 있습니다. 우리가 다음 내용으로 넘어가기 전에 반드시 여러분은 그 구역에 익숙해 지시기를 바랍니다.

어휘 go over ~을 살펴 보다, ~을 짚어 주다 logistics 실행 계획 survey (설문) 조사 region 지역 collect ~을 수집하다, ~을 모으다 quality 질, 품질 strict 엄격한 sampling 샘플 추출 procedure 절차 be required to do ~해야 하다, ~할 필요가 있다 follow ~을 준수하다, ~을 따르다 in detail 상세히 as well as ~뿐만 아니라 … 도 how to do ~하는 방법 information packet 정보 안내 자료집 list ~이 기재되어 있다, ~을 목록에 올리다 specific 특정한, 구체적인 make sure (that) 반드시 ~하도록 하다 be familiar with ~에 익숙하다, ~을 잘 알다 move on (순서 등) 넘어가다, 진행하다

16. 청자들은 어떤 업계에 종사하고 있을 것 같은가?

(A) 농업
(B) 어업
(C) 제약
(D) 환경 과학

정답 (D)

해설 화자가 담화를 시작하면서 클리어워터 지역 내에서의 환경 조사 프로젝트를 위한 실행 계획을 살펴 볼 것이라고(we'll be going over logistics for the environmental survey project in the Clearwater region) 밝히고 있습니다. 따라서, 환경 조사를 실시할 수 있는 업계인 (D)가 정답입니다.

어휘 scheduling 일정 관리 shift 교대 근무(조)

17. 화자의 말에 따르면, 해당 프로젝트는 무엇을 필요로 할 것인가?

(A) 특정 샘플 추출 방식
(B) 수기 보고 시스템
(C) 데이터 분석
(D) 탄력적인 일정 관리

정답 (A)

해설 담화 중반부에 화자가 자신들이 준수해야 하는 엄격한 샘플 추출 절차가 있다고(There are strict sampling procedures we're required to follow) 언급하고 있습니다. 이는 특정 방식에 따라 샘플을 수집해야 한다는 뜻이므로 (A)가 정답입니다.

어휘 method 방식, 방법 manual 수기의, 수동의, 수작업의 analysis 분석 (결과) flexible 탄력적인, 유연한

Paraphrase strict sampling procedures we're required to follow ⇒ A specific sampling method

18. 청자들은 자료집에서 무엇을 찾도록 요청 받는가?

(A) 지역 지도
(B) 사원 번호
(C) 품질 보고서
(D) 배정된 장소

정답 (D)

해설 화자가 담화 후반부에 자료집을 언급하면서 청자들 각자가 작업할 예정인 특정 구역이 기재되어 있다고(please check the first page in your information packet. It lists the specific area you'll each be working in) 알리고 있습니다. 청자들 각자에게 배정된 작업 장소가 있다는 뜻이므로 (D)가 정답입니다.

어휘 be asked to do ~하도록 요청 받다 regional 지역의, 지방의 location 장소, 위치, 지점 assignment 배정(된 것), 할당(된 것)

Paraphrase the specific area you'll each be working in ⇒ Location assignments

Questions 19-21 refer to the following introduction.

Welcome to the annual Pinnacle Theater Awards. **19** For the first time ever, we're proud to have gathered an audience of over 3,000 guests here at the Altemus Amphitheater. **20** Tonight's special honoree, Jasmine Lindholm, has spent the past decade designing innovative sets that use virtual reality to bring stories to life. Her work has completely revolutionized the world of theater, and so, in recognition of her achievements, **21** we've created a short video featuring scenes from her most iconic productions. Before she comes up to accept her award, please take a moment to enjoy the clip.

연례 피너클 연극 시상식에 오신 것을 환영합니다. 사상 최초로, 저희가 이곳 알테무스 원형 극장에 3,000명이 넘는 손님들로 구성된 청중을 모시게 되어 자랑스럽습니다. 오늘밤 특별 수상자이신, 재스민 린드홀름 씨께서는 이야기에 생명력을 불어넣기 위해 가상 현실을 이용하는 혁신적인 무대 세트를 디자인하시면서 지난 10년을 보내셨습니다. 이분의 작업물은 연극계를 완전히 혁신시켜 왔으며, 그에 따라, 이분의 업적을 기리기 위해, 저희가 이분의 가장 상징적인 창작품의 장면들을 특징으로 하는 짧은 동영상을 만들었습니다. 이분께서 상을 받으시기 위해 올라오시기 전에, 잠시 시간을 갖고 동영상을 즐겨 보시기 바랍니다.

어휘 annual 연례적인 for the first time 처음으로 be proud to do ~해서 자랑스럽다 gather ~을 모으다 audience 청중, 관객, 시청자들 honoree 수상자, 수상작 spend A -ing: ~하면서 A의 시간을 보내다 decade 10년 innovative 혁신적인 virtual reality 가상 현실 bring A to life: A에 생명력을 불어넣다 completely 완전히, 전적으로 revolutionize ~을 혁신시키다 in recognition of ~을 기리기 위해, ~을 인정해 achievement 업적, 달성, 성취 create ~을 만들어 내다 feature v. ~을 특징으로 하다 n. 특징 iconic 상징적인 production 창작품 accept one's award 상을 받다 take a moment to do 잠시 시간을 갖고 ~하다 clip 동영상

19. 화자는 행사와 관련해 무엇이 새로운 것이라고 말하는가?
(A) 야외 경기장에서 개최되고 있다.
(B) 참석하는 데 무료이다.
(C) 이틀 동안에 걸쳐 진행될 것이다.
(D) 아주 많은 청중을 끌어들였다.

정답 (D)

해설 담화 시작 부분에 화자가 사상 최초로 3,000명이 넘는 손님들로 구성된 청중이 모인 사실을(we're proud to have gathered an audience of over 3,000 guests here at the Altemus Amphitheater) 언급하고 있으므로 (D)가 정답입니다.

어휘 free 무료의 attend 참석하다 take place 진행되다, 개최되다, 발생하다 draw ~을 끌어들이다

Paraphrase · For the first time ever ⇒ new
· have gathered an audience of over 3,000 guests ⇒ has drawn a very large audience

20. 린드홀름 씨는 왜 공로를 인정 받는가?
(A) 능력이 뛰어난 배우이다.
(B) 유명한 극단을 설립했다.
(C) 획기적인 무대 세트 디자인을 만들어 냈다.
(D) 성공적인 뮤지컬을 연출했다.

정답 (C)

해설 화자가 담화 중반부에 수상자 재스민 린드홀름 씨를 소개하면서 가상 현실을 이용하는 혁신적인 무대 세트를 디자인한 사실을(Tonight's special honoree, Jasmine Lindholm, has spent the past decade designing innovative sets that use virtual reality) 알리고 있으므로 이러한 공로에 해당하는 (C)가 정답입니다.

어휘 recognize ~을 인정하다, ~에게 표창하다 accomplished 능력이 뛰어난, 재주가 많은 found ~을 설립하다 groundbreaking 획기적인 direct ~을 연출하다, ~을 감독하다 musical play 뮤지컬

Paraphrase has spent the past decade designing innovative sets ⇒ has created groundbreaking set designs

21. 화자의 말에 따르면, 린드홀름 씨가 상을 받기 전에 무슨 일이 있을 것인가?
(A) 동료가 연설할 것이다.
(B) 동영상이 보여질 것이다.
(C) 예행 연습이 진행될 것이다.
(D) 몇몇 기자들이 질문할 것이다.

정답 (B)

해설 화자가 담화 마지막 부분에 린드홀름 씨의 작품에 담긴 장면들을 특징으로 하는 동영상을 만든 사실과 함께 수상 전

정답 및 해설 105

에 잠시 시간을 갖고 이 동영상을 즐기도록(we've created a short video featuring scenes from her most iconic productions. Before she comes up to accept her award, please take a moment to enjoy the clip) 요청하고 있으므로 (B)가 정답입니다.

어휘 receive ~을 받다 colleague 동료 (직원) give a speech 연설하다 rehearsal 예행 연습

Questions 22-24 refer to the following excerpt from a meeting.

> **22** **Let's begin with our first agenda item: how to increase our brand recognition.** Martin Delgado from the marketing department is here to introduce a new initiative that'll require participation from all employees. **23** **He's going to talk about searching for and identifying suitable social media influencers to work with.** Collaborating with influencers can help us reach more diverse customer groups. **24** **I was going to hand out a worksheet before the presentation**, but I don't want it to be a distraction.

첫 번째 안건 항목인, 우리의 브랜드 인지도를 높이는 방법으로 시작해 보겠습니다. 마케팅부의 마틴 델가도 씨가 전 직원의 참여를 필요로 하게 될 새로운 계획을 소개해 주시기 위해 이 자리에 오셨습니다. 그는 협업하기 적합한 소셜 미디어 인플루언서들을 찾고 확인하는 일에 관해 말씀해 주실 것입니다. 인플루언서들과 협업하는 것은 더욱 다양한 고객 그룹에 다가가도록 우리에게 도움을 줄 수 있습니다. 제가 발표 전에 작업 진행표를 나눠 드리려고 했지만, 그것이 방해가 되기를 원치 않습니다.

어휘 agenda 안건, 의제 how to do ~하는 방법 increase ~을 높이다, ~을 증가시키다 recognition 인지(도), 인식 introduce ~을 소개하다, ~을 도입하다 initiative n. 계획, 솔선 수범, 진취(성) require ~을 필요로 하다 participation 참여, 참가 search for ~을 찾다, ~을 검색하다 identify ~을 확인하다, ~을 발견하다 suitable 적합한, 알맞은 collaborate with ~와 협업하다, ~와 공동 작업하다 help A do: ~하도록 A에게 도움을 주다 reach ~에게 다가가다, ~에 이르다 diverse 다양한 hand out ~을 나눠 주다 worksheet 작업 진행표 presentation 발표(회) want A to do: A가 ~하기를 원하다 distraction 방해(하는 것), 지장(을 주는 것)

22. 화자는 어떤 안건 주제를 이야기하고 있는가?
(A) 회사 재무를 능률화하는 일
(B) 브랜드 인지도를 증진하는 일
(C) 경쟁사들의 제품을 연구하는 일
(D) 재활용 계획을 시작하는 일

정답 (B)

해설 화자가 담화를 시작하면서 첫 번째 안건 항목인 브랜드 인지도를 높이는 방법으로 시작하겠다고(Let's begin with our first agenda item: how to increase our brand recognition) 밝히고 있으므로 (B)가 정답입니다.

어휘 streamline ~을 능률화하다, ~을 간소화하다 finance 재무, 재정, 금융 boost ~을 증진하다, ~을 촉진하다 competitor 경쟁사, 경쟁자 launch v. ~을 시작하다, ~을 출시하다 n. 시작, 출시 recycling 재활용

Paraphrase increase our brand recognition
⇒ Boosting brand recognition

23. 화자의 말에 따르면, 마틴 델가도 씨는 누구에 관해 이야기할 것인가?
(A) 동료 직원
(B) 소셜 미디어 인플루언서들
(C) 부동산 중개업자들
(D) 인터넷 이용자들

정답 (B)

해설 담화 중반부에 화자가 델가도 씨를 He로 지칭해 협업하기 적합한 소셜 미디어 인플루언서들을 찾고 확인하는 일에 관해 이야기할 것이라고(He's going to talk about searching for and identifying suitable social media influencers to work with) 밝히고 있으므로 (B)가 정답입니다.

어휘 fellow a. 동료의, 같은 처지에 있는 n. 동료, 또래 real estate 부동산

24. 화자가 "그것이 방해가 되기를 원치 않습니다"라고 말할 때 무엇을 암시하는가?
(A) 한 가지 활동이 어려울 것으로 예상된다.
(B) 발표가 연기될 것이다.
(C) 작업 진행표가 나중에 배부될 것이다.
(D) 유인물이 부정확한 정보를 포함하고 있다.

정답 (C)

해설 화자가 담화 맨 마지막 부분에 발표 전에 작업 진행표를 나눠 줄 생각이었다고(I was going to hand out a worksheet before the presentation) 알리면서 '그것이 방해가 되기를 원치 않습니다'라고 말하는 흐름입니다. 이는 방해가 되지 않기 위해 애초의 계획과 달리 나중에 나눠 주겠다는 뜻이므로 (C)가 정답입니다.

어휘 activity 활동 be expected to do ~할 것으로 예상되다 postpone ~을 연기하다, ~을 미루다 distribute ~을 배부하다, ~을 나눠 주다, ~을 유통시키다 handout 유인물 contain ~을 포함하다, ~을 담고 있다 incorrect 부정확한

DAY 15 광고 / 투어 가이드

PRACTICE

1. (D) 2. (C) 3. (B)

Questions 1-3 refer to the following advertisement.

Looking to upgrade your daily commute this year? **1** **Horizon Motors is the newest and most state-of-the-art electric-vehicle showroom in the region**, located on Greenway Drive just off Highway 101. Our vehicles are more than just eco-friendly — they also come with access to fast-charging stations nearby. Not only that, but **2 we believe you'll love our complimentary home-charger installation service. 3 Visit our Web site today to browse our virtual showroom.** Make your drive greener by choosing Horizon Motors.

올해 귀하의 출퇴근을 업그레이드할 생각이신가요? 호라이즌 모터스는 이 지역에서 가장 최신식 전기차 전시장으로, 101번 고속도로 인근 그린웨이 드라이브에 위치해 있습니다. 당사 차량은 단순한 친환경 차량 그 이상으로, 인근의 고속 충전소 이용 혜택을 함께 제공합니다. 또한, 가정용 충전기 무료 설치 서비스를 가장 마음에 들어 하실 것이라 믿습니다. 당사 웹사이트를 방문하셔서 가상 전시장을 둘러보시기 바랍니다. 호라이즌 모터스를 선택하시고 보다 친환경적인 운전을 실현해보세요.

어휘 look to do ~하기를 생각하다 newest 최신의 state-of-the-art 최첨단의 electric-vehicle 전기 자동차 showroom 전시실 region 지역 located 위치한 fast-charging 고속 충전의 nearby 근처에 not only A but (also) B: A뿐만 아니라 B도 complimentary 무료의 installation 설치 browse 둘러보다 virtual 가상의 greener 더 친환경적인

1. 무엇이 광고되고 있는가?
(A) 고속도로 휴게소
(B) 차량 충전소
(C) 자동차 정비소
(D) 새로운 전기 자동차 대리점

정답 (D)

해설 화자가 호라이즌 모터스에 대해 소개하면서 '이 지역에서 가장 최신식 전기차 전시장'(Horizon Motors is the newest and most state-of-the-art electric-vehicle showroom in the region)이라고 언급하는 것을 통해 최신의 전기 자동차 대리점을 광고하고 있음을 알 수 있습니다. 따라서 정답은 (D)입니다.

2. 화자에 따르면, 호라이즌 모터스에 대해 청자가 가장 높이 평가할 것은 무엇인가?
(A) 충전 속도
(B) 전시장의 크기
(C) 무료 가정용 충전기 설치
(D) 다양한 전기 자동차 모델

정답 (C)

해설 화자는 청자들에게 가정용 충전기 무료 설치 서비스를 가장 마음에 들어 할 것이라고 믿는다고(we believe you'll love our complimentary home-charger installation service) 언급하는 것을 통해 청자들이 가장 높이 평가할 것은 가정용 충전기 설치임을 알 수 있습니다. 따라서 정답은 (C)입니다.

어휘 charging process 충전 과정 setup 설치 wide selection of 다양한

3. 화자는 청자가 온라인에서 무엇을 하도록 제안하는가?
(A) 시승 예약하기
(B) 가상 전시장 둘러보기
(C) 충전 요금제 가입하기
(D) 금융 옵션 비교하기

정답 (B)

해설 광고 마지막에 화자는 웹사이트에 방문해서 가상전시실을 둘러보라고(Visit our Web site today to browse our virtual showroom) 언급하므로 정답은 (B)입니다.

어휘 schedule 일정을 정하다 test drive 시승, 시운전 sign up for ~에 등록하다, 가입하다 charging plan 충전 요금제 compare 비교하다 financing option 금융 옵션

실전 TEST

1. (A)	2. (C)	3. (B)	4. (D)	5. (B)
6. (C)	7. (D)	8. (B)	9. (D)	10. (C)
11. (D)	12. (B)	13. (A)	14. (B)	15. (D)
16. (B)	17. (A)	18. (C)	19. (C)	20. (D)
21. (B)	22. (B)	23. (D)	24. (C)	

Questions 1-3 refer to the following advertisement.

Have you ever lost an important electronic file? And do you want to make sure that it never happens again? Then ■1 **Mega Cloud by SNT Technologies will keep your data safe and accessible whether you're at the office, at home, or even on vacation**. You can upload any file to your Mega Cloud storage account and then access it from any of your mobile devices. And if you have any problems, you can contact ■2 **our customer service department, which recently won the National Best Service Award**. Would you like to try out Mega Cloud before paying full price? ■3 **We are offering a one-week trial on our Web site for a limited time only**.

중요한 전자 파일을 분실하신 적이 있으신가요? 그리고 그런 일이 반드시 절대로 다시 발생되지 않도록 하고 싶으신가요? 그러시다면 저희 SNT 테크놀로지 사의 메가 클라우드가 여러분의 데이터를 안전하게 그리고 사무실과 자택에 있든, 또는 심지어 휴가 중이든 상관없이 이용 가능하도록 유지해 드릴 것입니다. 여러분은 어떤 파일이든 여러분의 메가 클라우드 저장 계정에 업로드하실 수 있으며, 그 후에 어떤 모바일 기기에서도 이것을 이용하실 수 있습니다. 그리고 어떤 문제든지 발생할 경우, 최근 전국 최고의 서비스 상을 수상한 저희 고객 서비스부에 연락하실 수 있습니다. 비용 전액을 지불하시기 전에 메가 클라우드를 시험 삼아 이용해 보고 싶으신가요? 저희는 저희 웹사이트에서 한정된 기간에 한해 1주일 동안의 체험 서비스를 제공해 드리고 있습니다.

어휘 make sure that 반드시 ~하도록 하다 then 그럼, 그렇다면, 그 후에 keep A 형용사: A를 ~하게 유지하다, 보관하다 accessible 이용 가능한, 접근 가능한 whether A, B, or C: A 나 B, 또는 C이든 (상관없이) even 심지어 on vacation 휴가 중인 storage 저장, 보관 account 계정 access ~을 이용하다, ~에 접근하다 contact ~에게 연락하다 recently 최근에 win an award 상을 받다 try out ~을 시험 삼아 이용해 보다 offer ~을 제공하다 trial 체험 서비스 for a limited time only 한정된 기간에 한해

1. 무엇이 광고되고 있는가?
   (A) 데이터 저장 서비스
   (B) 바이러스 퇴치용 프로그램
   (C) 주택 보안 장치
   (D) 컴퓨터 수리점

정답 (A)

해설 특정 서비스 및 그 특징이 언급되는 담화 시작 부분에, SNT 테크놀로지 사의 메가 클라우드가 데이터를 안전하게 그리고 어디에서도 이용 가능하도록 유지해 줄 것이라고(Mega Cloud by SNT Technologies will keep your data safe and accessible whether you're at the office, at home, or even on vacation) 알리고 있습니다. 이는 데이터 저장 서비스를 말하는 것이므로 (A)가 정답입니다.

어휘 anti-virus 바이러스 퇴치용의 security 보안 device 장치, 기기 repair 수리

2. 업체는 무엇에 대해 상을 받았는가?
   (A) 제품 교환 정책
   (B) 창의적인 디자인
   (C) 고객 서비스
   (D) 경쟁력 있는 가격

정답 (C)

해설 상을 받은 일이 언급되는 담화 후반부에, 최근에 상을 받은 고객 서비스부를(our customer service department, which recently won the National Best Service Award) 언급하는 부분이 있습니다. 이를 통해, 업체가 고객 서비스상을 받았음을 알 수 있으므로 (C)가 정답입니다.

어휘 receive ~을 받다 exchange 교환 policy 정책, 방침 creative 창의적인 competitive 경쟁력 있는, 경쟁하는

3. 화자는 무슨 제공 서비스를 언급하는가?
   (A) 제품 카탈로그
   (B) 무료 체험 기회
   (C) 회원 자격 업그레이드
   (D) 월간 소식지

정답 (B)

해설 업체 측에서 제공하는 서비스는 담화 맨 마지막에 제시되고 있는데, 웹사이트에서 한정된 기간에 한해 1주일 동안의 체험 서비스를 제공하고 있다는(We are offering a one-week trial on our Web site for a limited time only) 말이 있습니다. 이는 무료 체험 기회를 뜻하는 것이므로 (B)가 정답입니다.

어휘 offer 제공(되는 것) free 무료의 opportunity 기회 monthly 월간의, 달마다의

Paraphrase a one-week trial ⇒ free trial opportunity

Questions 4-6 refer to the following tour information.

> **4** Welcome to the Cannington Glass factory tour. Cannington has been a world-famous producer of high-quality glassware for over 150 years, and during the tour, you'll get to see how we make some of our most popular pieces. **5** Usually, I would guide the tour, but only for today, the senior glassblower Charlie Stonesman will lead you through the whole process himself and show you a demonstration of his exceptional skills. Of course, at the end of the tour, we are going to visit the gift shop, and **6** all of you participating in this tour can get 30 percent off all items in the shop. Just present the tour ticket to the cashier when you make a payment.

캐닝턴 유리 공장 견학에 오신 것을 환영합니다. 캐닝턴 사는 150년이 넘는 기간 동안 세계적으로 유명한 고품질 유리 제품 생산 업체였으며, 견학 시간 중에, 저희가 가장 인기 있는 제품 몇몇을 어떻게 만드는지 보시게 될 것입니다. 일반적으로, 제가 견학을 안내하지만, 오늘 하루에 한해, 수석급의 유리를 불어 만드는 직공이신 찰리 스톤스먼 씨께서 직접 여러분을 모시고 모든 과정을 진행하실 것이며, 자신의 뛰어난 기술을 시연하는 것을 보여드릴 것입니다. 물론, 견학 마지막에 선물 매장을 방문할 것이며, 이번 견학에 참가하시는 여러분 모두가 이 매장 내의 모든 제품에 대해 30퍼센트 할인을 받으실 수 있습니다. 비용을 지불하실 때 계산 담당 직원에게 견학 티켓을 제시하시기만 하면 됩니다.

어휘 producer 생산 업체 high-quality 고품질의 glassware 유리 제품 over ~ 넘게 get to do ~하게 되다 popular 인기 있는 piece 제품, 작품 usually 일반적으로, 보통 glassblower 유리를 불어 만드는 직공 lead ~을 이끌다 through ~(동안) 내내, ~을 거쳐, ~을 통해 whole 전체의 oneself (부사처럼 쓰여) 직접 demonstration 시연(회) exceptional 뛰어난, 우수한 participate in ~에 참가하다 get A off: A만큼 할인 받다 present ~을 제시하다 make a payment 비용을 지불하다

4. 어디에서 견학이 진행되고 있는 것 같은가?
   (A) 박물관에서
   (B) 식료품 매장에서
   (C) 쇼핑몰에서
   (D) 생산 공장에서

정답 (D)
해설 화자가 담화를 시작하면서 담화 장소와 관련해 캐닝턴 유리 공장 견학에 온 것을 환영한다고(Welcome to the Cannington Glass factory tour) 말하고 있습니다. 그 뒤에 이 장소에 대한 설명으로, 캐닝턴 사가 세계적으로 유명한 고품질 유리 제품 생산 업체(Cannington has been a world famous producer of high-quality glassware~)라고 언급하고 있으므로 (D)가 정답입니다.

어휘 take place (일, 행사 등이) 진행되다, 개최되다 plant 공장

5. 화자는 견학과 관련해 무엇이 변경되었다고 말하는가?
   (A) 비용
   (B) 견학 가이드
   (C) 지속 시간
   (D) 위치

정답 (B)
해설 담화 중반부에 일반적으로 화자 자신이 견학을 안내하지만 오늘에 한해 수석급의 유리를 불어 만드는 직공인 찰리 스톤스먼 씨가 직접 청자들을 이끌 것이라고(Usually, I would guide the tour, but only for today, the senior glassblower Charlie Stonesman will lead you through the whole process himself ~) 알리고 있습니다. 이는 견학 가이드가 변경되었다는 뜻이므로 (B)가 정답입니다.

어휘 duration 지속 시간 location 위치, 지점

6. 화자는 청자들에게 무엇을 제공하는가?
   (A) 상품권
   (B) 무료 쇼핑 코드
   (C) 특별 할인
   (D) 제품 샘플

정답 (C)
해설 청자들이 제공받는 것은 담화 후반부에 제시되고 있는데, 견학에 참가하는 모든 사람이(~ all of you participating in this tour can get 30 percent off all items in the shop) 매장에서 30퍼센트 할인을 받을 수 있다고 알리고 있습니다. 따라서 (C)가 정답입니다.

어휘 gift voucher 상품권 free 무료의

Questions 7-9 refer to the following talk.

7 **Thank you for joining our tour of Vonokusa City's Old Town.** I'll be your guide for today's tour. We'll be visiting the city's historic market and port districts, which have been the heart and soul of this city's thriving trade industry for more than 200 years. **8** **There are so many things to see and do in this area, and you may have many questions to ask.** That's why I'm here. We'll kick off the tour by visiting the historic docks, and then we'll go to the open-air market that covers a few blocks. **9** **We're running a little behind schedule because we're still waiting for several participants to arrive.** They should be here any minute, though, so we should be able to start shortly.

저희 보노쿠사 시의 구시가지 견학에 함께 해 주셔서 감사드립니다. 제가 오늘 견학의 가이드가 될 것입니다. 우리는 200년 넘게 이 도시에서 번성했던 무역 업계의 심장이자 혼이 담긴 곳인 도시의 역사적인 시장과 항구 구역을 방문할 예정입니다. 이 구역에서 보고, 할 수 있는 것들이 아주 많으므로, 질문이 많으실 수도 있습니다. 그것이 바로 제가 여기 있는 이유입니다. 우리는 역사적인 부두를 방문하는 것으로 견학을 시작할 것이며, 그 후 몇 블록에 걸쳐 있는 노천 시장으로 갈 것입니다. 우리가 일정에 조금 뒤처져 있는데, 이것은 우리가 여전히 몇몇 참가자들이 도착하기를 기다리고 있기 때문입니다. 하지만 금방 그들이 이곳으로 오실 것이므로, 곧 출발할 수 있을 것입니다.

어휘 join ~에 함께 하다, 합류하다 historic 역사적인 port 항구 district 구역, 지구 thriving 번성하는 trade 무역 industry 업계 kick off ~을 시작하다, 출발하다 by (방법) ~하는 것으로, ~함으로써 dock 부두 then 그 후에, 그런 다음 open-air market 노천 시장, 야외 시장 cover (장소 등) ~을 잇다, 이어지다 behind schedule 일정에 뒤처진 several 몇몇의, 여럿의 participant 참가자 arrive 도착하다 any minute 금방 though (문장 중간이나 끝에서) 하지만 be able to do ~할 수 있다 shortly 곧, 머지않아

7. 청자들은 누구일 것 같은가?
   (A) 역사 연구가들
   (B) 시 관계자들
   (C) 시장 노점 상인
   (D) 단체 견학 구성원들

정답 (D)
해설 화자가 담화를 시작하면서 Thank you for joining our tour of Vonokusa City's Old Town이라는 말로 견학에 함께 하는 것에 대해 청자들에게 감사의 인사를 전하고 있으므로 (D) 가 정답입니다.

어휘 historical 역사의, 역사와 관련된 researcher 연구자 official 관계자, 당국자 vendor 노점 상인

8. 화자가 "그것이 바로 제가 여기 있는 이유입니다"라고 말할 때 그 말의 속뜻은 무엇인가?
   (A) 청자들에게 그룹 내에 모여 있도록 요청하고 있다.
   (B) 기꺼이 청자들의 질문에 답변해 줄 것이다.
   (C) 청자들에게 자신을 따라오도록 장려하고 있다.
   (D) 청자들이 향후에 다시 들러 주기를 바란다.

정답 (B)
해설 담화 중반부에 청자들이 해당 구역에서 보고, 할 수 있는 것이 많아 질문이 많을 수도 있다고(There are so many things to see and do in this area, and you may have many questions to ask) 말한 후에 "그것이 바로 제가 여기 있는 이유입니다"라고 말하고 있습니다. 이는 청자들이 질문한 내용에 대해 답변해 주겠다는 뜻이므로 (B)가 정답입니다.

어휘 ask A to do: A에게 ~하도록 요청하다 stay in ~ 내에 머물러 있다 be happy to do 기꺼이 ~하다 encourage A to do: A에게 ~하도록 장려하다, 권장하다 follow ~을 따라오다 stop by ~에 들르다

9. 화자에 따르면, 지연이 있는 이유는 무엇인가?
   (A) 날씨가 좋지 못하다.
   (B) 레스토랑이 초과 예약되어 있다.
   (C) 거리가 방문객들에게 폐쇄되어 있다.
   (D) 몇몇 사람들이 아직 도착하지 않았다.

정답 (D)
해설 지연 문제가 언급되는 후반부에 일정이 뒤처진 사실과 함께 그 이유로 여전히 몇몇 참가자들이 도착하기를 기다리고 있기 때문이라고(We're running a little behind schedule because we're still waiting for several participants to arrive) 말하고 있으므로 (D)가 정답입니다.

어휘 overbooked 초과 예약된 closed to ~에게 폐쇄된

Paraphrase
 · behind schedule ⇒ delay
 · still waiting for several participants to arrive ⇒ Some people haven't arrived yet

Questions 10-12 refer to the following advertisement and list.

> **10** Are you looking for a memorable holiday package for your family? Then, Sunshine Tours is here for you. We've been in business for over 20 years, offering the best one-stop tour services available. We will arrange your flight, your accommodation, and even your entertainment options. **11** For customers with young children, we also provide excellent child-care options with a variety of activities that will keep your child safe and entertained. For this month only, **12** we are offering 20 percent discounts on our one-week trips. You can spend the whole week on a cruise ship while visiting the world's most exotic locations. For more information, check out our Web site at www.sunshinetours.com.
>
> 여러분의 가족을 위해 기억에 남을 만한 휴가 여행 패키지를 찾고 계신가요? 그러시다면, 여기 저희 선샤인 투어즈가 있습니다. 저희는 이용 가능한 최고의 원스톱 여행 서비스를 제공하면서 20년 넘게 업계에서 영업 중입니다. 저희는 여러분의 항공편, 숙박 시설, 그리고 심지어 여러분의 오락 선택권까지 마련해 드릴 것입니다. 유아동 동반 고객들께는, 아이를 계속해서 안전하고 즐겁게 해 줄 다양한 활동들과 함께 훌륭한 아이 돌봄 선택권도 제공해 드립니다. 이번 달에 한해, 저희는 일주일 기간의 여행에 대해 20 퍼센트의 할인을 제공해 드리고 있습니다. 여러분께서는 세계에서 가장 이국적인 곳들을 방문하시는 동안 여객선에서 일주일 전체를 보내실 수 있습니다. 추가 정보가 필요하실 경우, 저희 웹사이트 www.sunshinetours.com을 확인해 보시기 바랍니다.

선샤인 여행	
여행 패키지 상품	기간
트래블러	5일
12 보야저	**12** 1주
익스플로러	2주
파이오니어	1달

어휘 look for ~을 찾다 memorable 기억에 남을 만한 then 그럼, 그렇다면 be in business 영업 중인, 운영 중인 over ~ 넘게 offer ~을 제공하다 one-stop 원스톱의(한 장소에서 많은 종류의 제품과 서비스를 제공하는) available 이용 가능한 arrange ~을 마련하다, 조치하다 accommodation 숙박 시설 even 심지어 (~도) entertainment 오락, 여흥 provide ~을 제공하다 child-care 아이 돌봄, 아이 관리 a variety of 다양한 activity 활동 keep A 형용사: A를 ~하게 유지하다 safe 안전한 entertained 즐거워진 whole 전체의, 모든 cruise ship 여객선 while ~하면서, ~하는 동안 exotic 이국적인 location 장소, 위치 check out ~을 확인해 보다 duration 기간, 지속 시간

10. 광고의 주 목적은 무엇인가?
(A) 자원 봉사자를 찾기 위해
(B) 리조트 시설물을 설명하기 위해
(C) 여행사를 홍보하기 위해
(D) 해외 명소를 설명하기 위해

정답 (C)
해설 화자는 담화를 시작하면서 청자에게 기억에 남을 만한 휴가 여행 패키지를 찾고 있는지 물으면서 소속 여행사 이름을 언급하고 있습니다(Are you looking for a memorable holiday package for your family? Then, Sunshine Tours is here for you). 이를 통해, 여행사 홍보가 광고의 주 목적임을 알 수 있으므로 (C)가 정답입니다.

어휘 seek ~을 찾다 volunteer 자원 봉사자 describe ~을 설명하다 facility 시설(물) promote ~을 홍보하다 overseas 해외의 attraction 명소

11. 화자는 아이들에 관해 무엇을 언급하는가?
(A) 반드시 참가하기에 충분한 나이여야 한다.
(B) 특별 쿠폰을 받을 것이다.
(C) 성인의 통제가 필요하다.
(D) 여러 활동을 즐길 수 있다.

정답 (D)
해설 아이들과 관련된 정보가 제시되는 담화 중반부에, 아이를 계속해서 안전하고 즐겁게 해줄 다양한 활동들과 함께 훌륭한 아이 돌봄 선택권도 제공한다고(For customers with young children, we also provide excellent child-care options with a variety of activities ~) 말하고 있습니다. 따라서 이 서비스들 중에서 다양한 활동에 관해 언급한 (D)가 정답입니다.

어휘 participate 참가하다 require ~을 필요로 하다 supervision 통제, 관리

12. 시각자료를 보시오. 어느 여행 패키지가 할인 중인가?
(A) 트래블러
(B) 보야저
(C) 익스플로러
(D) 파이오니어

정답 (B)
해설 할인 정보가 제시되는 담화 후반부에, 일주일 기간의 여행에 대해 20퍼센트 할인을 제공해 주고 있다고(we are offering 20 percent discounts on our one-week trips) 언급하고 있습니다. 시각자료를 보면, 일주일 기간에 해당하는 여행 패키지 상품으로 Voyager가 표기되어 있으므로 (B)가 정답입니다.

니다.

어휘 on sale 할인 중인

Questions 13-15 refer to the following tour information.

> Alright everyone, may I have your attention? **13 Our zoo bus tour has brought us to this new Grassland Habitat zone.** This area houses several grass-feeding species and is one of the largest enclosures on site. **14 The fencing around the perimeter was just completed after a summer-long upgrade,** so this is one of the first public viewings. A lot of visitors find the animal interactions here especially fun to watch. We'll stop for about 15 minutes, so **15 I encourage you to observe their behavior and habitat during this short stop.**
>
> 좋습니다, 여러분, 잠시 주목해 주시겠습니까? 우리 동물원 버스 투어를 통해 이 새로운 목초 서식지 구역에 도착했습니다. 이 구역에 풀을 뜯어 먹는 여러 종이 살고 있으며, 부지 내에서 가장 규모가 큰 울타리 보호 구역들 중 하나입니다. 경계를 둘러싼 울타리는 여름 내 이어진 업그레이드 작업 끝에 막 완성되었기 때문에, 이번이 첫 일반인 관람 시간들 중 하나입니다. 많은 방문객들께서 이곳의 동물 교류 모습이 특히 재미있는 볼거리라고 생각하고 계십니다. 우리가 약 15분 동안 정차할 것이므로, 이 짧은 정차시간 동안 동물들의 행동과 서식지를 관찰해 보시기를 권해 드립니다.

어휘 attention 주목, 관심, 주의(력) grassland 목초지 habitat 서식지 house v. ~에게 살 곳을 제공하다 grass-feeding 풀을 뜯어 먹는 species (동식물의) 종 enclosure 울타리를 친 곳 on site 부지 내에, 현장에, 현지에 fencing 울타리 perimeter 경계(선), 주위 complete ~을 완성하다, ~을 완료하다 viewing 관람, 보기 find A 형용사: A를 ~하다고 생각하다 interaction 교류, 상호 작용 especially 특히, 특별히 about 약, 대략 encourage A to do: A에게 ~하도록 권하다 observe ~을 관찰하다, ~을 준수하다 scenery 풍경, 경치

13. 투어는 어디에서 진행되고 있는가?
(A) 동물원
(B) 농장
(C) 수족관
(D) 등산로

정답 (A)

해설 화자가 담화 초반부에 동물원 버스 투어를 통해 새로운 목초 서식지 구역에 도착했음을(Our zoo bus tour has brought us to this new Grassland Habitat zone) 알리고 있으므로

(A)가 정답입니다.

어휘 take place 진행되다, 개최되다, 발생하다

14. 화자는 무엇이 최근에 완료되었다고 말하는가?
(A) 건물 개조 공사
(B) 울타리 설치 작업
(C) 장비 업그레이드
(D) 프로그램 시행

정답 (B)

해설 담화 중반부에 화자가 경계를 둘러싼 울타리가 여름 내내 이어진 업그레이드 작업 끝에 막 완성되었다고(The fencing around the perimeter was just completed after a summer-long upgrade) 밝히고 있으므로 (B)가 정답입니다.

어휘 recently 최근에 renovation 개조, 보수 installation 설치 equipment 장비 implementation 시행

Paraphrase just ⇒ recently

15. 화자는 청자들에게 무엇을 하도록 권하는가?
(A) 사진을 촬영하는 일
(B) 정숙을 유지하는 일
(C) 모자를 착용하는 일
(D) 한 공간을 관찰하는 일

정답 (D)

해설 화자가 담화 맨 마지막 부분에 15분 동안 정차한다는 사실과 함께 동물들의 행동과 서식지를 관찰해 보도록(I encourage you to observe their behavior and habitat during this short stop) 권하고 있으므로 (D)가 정답입니다.

어휘 remain + 형용사: ~한 상태를 계속 유지하다, 여전히 ~한 상태이다 put on ~을 착용하다

Questions 16-18 refer to the following advertisement.

Are you noticing that your clothes wear out faster than they should? Try Riley's Mesh Laundry Bags for all your laundry needs! **16 Our mesh bags are environmentally friendly since they're produced using 100 percent recycled fabrics.** Even in the most powerful of washes, our durable zippers keep items secure. **17 This extra layer of security helps protect your favorite clothes from tangling, stretching, and getting damaged. 18 Visit our Web site to claim a free sample of Riley's Mesh Laundry Bags with your first order**, available only for a limited time.

여러분의 의류가 원래 그래야 하는 것보다 더 빨리 해진다 사실을 알아차리고 계신가요? 세탁과 관련해 필요로 하시는 모든 부분에 대해 저희 라일리스 메쉬 런드리 백을 한번 사용해 보십시오! 저희 세탁망은 100퍼센트 재활용된 직물을 이용해 생산되고 있으므로 환경 친화적입니다. 심지어 가장 강력한 세탁 설정에도, 내구성이 뛰어난 저희 지퍼가 세탁물을 안전하게 유지해 드립니다. 한층 더 추가된 이 보호 수단이 여러분께서 가장 좋아하시는 의류가 엉키고, 늘어나고, 손상되는 것으로부터 보호하는 데 도움을 드립니다. 저희 웹사이트를 방문하셔서 첫 주문과 함께 라일리스 메쉬 런드리 백 무료 샘플을 요청해 보시기 바라며, 이는 오직 한시적으로만 이용 가능합니다.

어휘 notice that ~임을 알아차리다, ~임에 주목하다 clothes 의류 wear out 해지다, 낡아서 떨어지다 environmentally friendly 환경 친화적인 since ~하기 때문에, ~한 이후로 produce ~을 생산하다 recycled 재활용된 fabric 직물, 천 wash n. 세탁, 씻기 durable 내구성이 좋은 keep A 형용사: A를 ~하게 유지하다 secure a. 안전한, 안정된 v. ~을 확보하다, ~을 얻다 extra 추가의, 별도의 layer 층, 막, 겹 security 보호, 보안 help do ~하는 데 도움을 주다 protect A from -ing: A가 ~하는 것으로부터 보호하다 tangle 엉키다, 헝클어지다 stretch 늘어나다 damaged 손상된, 피해를 입은 claim ~을 요청하다, ~을 주장하다 free 무료의 order 주문(품) available (사물) 이용 가능한, 구입 가능한, (사람) 시간이 있는 limited 한정된, 제한된

16. 화자의 말에 따르면, 제품은 어떻게 환경 친화적인가?
(A) 어떤 포장재도 이용하지 않는다.
(B) 재활용된 소재로 만들어진다.
(C) 에너지 소비 수준을 감소시켜 준다.
(D) 제조하는 데 물을 덜 이용한다.

정답 (B)
해설 화자가 담화 중반부에 제품의 특징을 언급하면서 100퍼센트 재활용된 직물을 이용해 생산되기 때문에 환경 친화적이라고(Our mesh bags are environmentally friendly since they're produced using 100 percent recycled fabrics) 소개하고 있으므로 (B)가 정답입니다.

어휘 packaging 포장(재) be made from ~로 만들어지다 material 소재, 재료, 물품 reduce ~을 감소시키다, ~을 줄이다 consumption 소비 manufacture ~을 제조하다

Paraphrase are produced using 100 percent recycled fabrics ⇒ is made from recycled materials

17. 한층 더 추가된 보호 수단은 어떻게 의류에 도움이 되는가?
(A) 손상을 방지함으로써
(B) 변색을 줄여 줌으로써
(C) 향을 개선함으로써
(D) 공간을 절약함으로써

정답 (A)
해설 화자가 담화 중반부에 한층 더 추가된 보호 수단이 가장 좋아하는 옷이 엉키고, 늘어나고, 손상되는 것으로부터 보호하는 데 도움을 준다고(This extra layer of security helps protect your favorite clothes from tangling, stretching, and getting damaged) 설명하고 있습니다. 이는 결국 의류 손상을 방지하는 데 도움을 준다는 뜻이므로 (A)가 정답입니다.

어휘 prevent ~을 방지하다, ~을 예방하다 discoloration 변색, 퇴색 improve ~을 개선하다, ~을 향상시키다 fragrance 향, 향기

Paraphrase protect your favorite clothes from tangling, stretching, and getting damaged ⇒ preventing damage

18. 화자는 웹사이트에서 무엇이 요청될 수 있다고 말하는가?
(A) 선물 카드
(B) 할인 코드
(C) 샘플 제품
(D) 무료 회원 자격

정답 (C)
해설 담화 후반부에 화자가 자사의 웹사이트를 방문해서 첫 주문과 함께 라일리스 메쉬 런드리 백 무료 샘플을 요청해 보라고(Visit our Web site to claim a free sample of Riley's Mesh Laundry Bags with your first order) 권하고 있으므로 (C)가 정답입니다.

어휘 be asked to do ~하도록 요청 받다 regional 지역의, 지방의 location 장소, 위치, 지점 assignment 배정(된 것), 할당(된 것)

Paraphrase a free sample of Riley's Mesh Laundry Bags ⇒ A sample product

Questions 19-21 refer to the following talk.

Welcome to this beginner art class hosted by the Lakeside Community Center. I'm Carla Mendes, and **19 I'll be showing you some techniques for washing, blending, and layering watercolors.** Usually, we have enough supply kits for every single person, but **20 due to a headcount miscalculation some of you will have to work in pairs.** So, while I pass out the materials, please look around the room and pick one object or view you might want to paint today. **21 We'll talk about what makes a good subject for watercolor once everyone has their supplies.**

저희 레이크사이드 지역 문화 센터에서 주최하는 초보자 미술 강좌에 오신 것을 환영합니다. 저는 칼라 멘데스이며, 제가 수채 물감을 엷게 칠하고, 혼합하며, 층을 이루는 데 필요한 몇 가지 기법들을 가르쳐 드릴 예정입니다. 보통, 저희가 개인별 물품 세트가 충분히 있지만, 인원수 착오로 인해, 여러분 중 일부는 짝을 지어 작업하셔야 할 것입니다. 자, 제가 재료를 나눠 드리는 동안, 실내 곳곳을 둘러 보시면서 오늘 그리고 싶어하실 수 있는 물체나 장면을 골라 보시기 바랍니다. 모든 분께서 물품을 받으시는 대로 무엇이 수채화에 있어 좋은 대상이 되는지에 관해 이야기해 보겠습니다.

어휘 host ~을 주최하다 wash (색깔) ~을 엷게 칠하다 blend ~을 혼합하다 layer ~의 층을 이루다 watercolor 그림 물감, 수채화 usually 보통, 일반적으로 supply 물품, 공급(품) kit 세트 due to ~로 인해, ~ 때문에 headcount 인원수 miscalculation 착오, 오산 will have to do ~해야 할 것이다 pass out ~을 나눠 주다 material 재료, 소재, 물품 pick ~을 고르다 object 물체 view 장면, 경관, 관점 subject 대상, 주제 once (일단) ~하는 대로, ~하자마자

19. 강좌는 주로 무엇에 관한 것인가?
  (A) 바느질로 옷 만들기
  (B) 콜라주 만들기
  (C) 수채화 그리기
  (D) 종이 염색하기

정답 (C)

해설 화자가 담화 초반부에 자신을 소개하면서 수채 물감을 엷게 칠하고, 혼합하며, 층을 이루는 데 필요한 몇 가지 기법을 가르쳐 줄 것이라고(I'll be showing you some techniques for washing, blending, and layering watercolors) 알리고 있으므로 (C)가 정답입니다.

어휘 sew 바느질로 ~을 만들다, ~을 바느질하다 collage 콜라주(색종이 등의 조각들로 하나의 그림을 만드는 기법) dyeing 염색(업)

Paraphrase washing, blending, and layering watercolors ⇒ Watercolor painting

20. 오늘 강좌와 관련해 무엇이 다른가?
  (A) 초청 연사를 특징으로 할 것이다.
  (B) 서면 과제를 포함할 것이다.
  (C) 야외에 있는 공원에서 진행될 것이다.
  (D) 일부 사람들에게 짝과 함께 하는 작업이 필요할 것이다.

정답 (D)

해설 담화 중반부에 화자가 평소와 달리 인원수 착오로 인해 청자들 중 일부는 짝을 지어 작업해야 한다고(due to a headcount miscalculation some of you will have to work in pairs) 알리고 있으므로 (D)가 정답입니다.

어휘 feature v. ~을 특징으로 하다 n. 특징 include ~을 포함하다 assignment 과제, 배정(된 일) take place 진행되다, 개최되다, 발생하다 require ~을 필요로 하다

Paraphrase some of you will have to work in pairs ⇒ will require partner work for some

21. 화자는 곧이어 무엇을 할 것인가?
  (A) 발표 시간을 마련하는 일
  (B) 몇몇 물품을 나눠 주는 일
  (C) 몇몇 예시 미술품을 보여 주는 일
  (D) 수강생들을 위해 물체를 선택하는 일

정답 (B)

해설 화자가 담화 맨 마지막 부분에 모든 사람이 물품을 받는 대로 무엇이 수채화에 있어 좋은 대상이 되는지에 관해 이야기하겠다고(We'll talk about what makes a good subject for watercolor once everyone has their supplies) 밝히고 있습니다. 따라서, 물품을 나눠 주는 일이 우선임을 알 수 있으므로 (B)가 정답입니다.

어휘 set up ~을 마련하다, ~을 설치하다, ~을 설정하다 presentation 발표(회) distribute ~을 나눠 주다, ~을 배부하다, ~을 유통시키다 choose ~을 선택하다

Questions 22-24 refer to the following advertisement and map.

> 22 Want an easy way to get your favorite meals delivered? 23 The city of Sunnyvale now offers on-demand deliveries for a wide range of local foods. Simply visit www.SunnyvaleEats.com to place your order. Our web platform aims to encourage residents to support our local eateries and restaurants. We'll help bring delicious meals straight to you – whether you're at home, at work, or even at the park. And for a limited time only, 24 if you're ordering from within the Ponderosa district, we're offering a 10 percent discount! Don't miss out!

여러분께서 가장 좋아하시는 식사를 배달시킬 수 있는 쉬운 방법을 원하시나요? 써니베일 시에서는 현재 아주 다양한 지역 음식에 대해 주문형 배달 서비스를 제공해 드리고 있습니다. www.SunnyvaleEats.com을 방문하셔서 주문하시기만 하면 됩니다. 저희 웹 플랫폼은 주민들께 지역 음식점과 레스토랑을 지원하시도록 권장해 드리는 것을 목표로 합니다. 여러분께서 댁에 계시든, 아니면, 직장이나 심지어 공원에 계시든 상관없이, 맛있는 식사를 여러분께 곧장 가져다 드리는 데 도움이 되어 드리겠습니다. 그리고 오직 한시적으로, 폰데로사 구역 내에서 주문하시는 경우, 저희가 10퍼센트 할인을 제공해 드립니다! 좋은 기회를 놓치지 마시기 바랍니다.

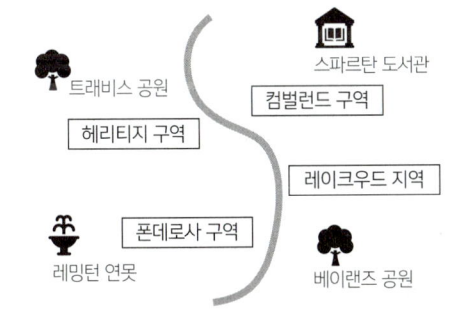

어휘 way to do ~하는 방법 get A p.p.: A를 ~되게 하다 favorite a. 가장 좋아하는 n. 가장 좋아하는 것 offer ~을 제공하다 on-demand 주문형의, 요구가 있을 시에 a wide range of 아주 다양한 local 지역의, 현지의 place one's order 주문하다 aim to do ~하는 것을 목표로 하다 encourage A to do: A에게 ~하도록 권장하다 resident 주민 support ~을 지원하다, ~을 지지하다, ~을 후원하다 eatery 음식점 help do ~하는 데 도움이 되다 straight 곧장 whether A, B, or C: A이든, B이든, 아니면 C이든 상관없이 limited 한정된, 제한된 district 구역, 지역, 지구 miss out 좋은 기회를 놓치다

22. 어떤 종류의 서비스가 광고되고 있는가?
(A) 출장 요리 제공
(B) 음식 배달
(C) 자동차 대여
(D) 포장물 배송

정답 (B)

해설 화자가 담화를 시작하면서 가장 좋아하는 식사를 배달시킬 수 있는 쉬운 방법을 원하는지(Want an easy way to get your favorite meals delivered?) 질문한 뒤로, 그 배달 서비스와 관련해 설명하고 있으므로 (B)가 정답입니다.

어휘 catering 출장 요리 제공(업) rental 대여, 임대 package 포장물, 소포, 배송품 shipping 배송,선적 launch v. ~을 시작하다, ~을 출시하다 n. 시작, 출시 recycling 재활용

Paraphrase way to get your favorite meals delivered
⇒ Food delivery

23. 화자의 말에 따르면, 청자들이 어떻게 새로운 서비스를 이용할 수 있는가?
(A) 온라인 양식을 제출해서
(B) 문자 메시지를 보내서
(C) 모바일 앱을 설치해서
(D) 시의 웹사이트를 방문해서

정답 (D)

해설 담화 초반부에 화자가 써니베일 시에서 제공하는 주문형 배달 서비스임을 언급한 다음, www.SunnyvaleEats.com이라는 웹사이트 주소와 함께 그곳에 방문해서 주문하기만 하면 된다고(The city of Sunnyvale now offers on-demand deliveries for a wide range of local foods. Simply visit www.SunnyvaleEats.com to place your order) 알리고 있으므로 (D)가 정답입니다.

어휘 submit ~을 제출하다 form 양식, 서식 text message 문자 메시지 installing ~을 설치하다

24. 시각자료를 보시오. 다음 장소들 중 어느 곳에서 청자들이 할인을 받을 수 있는가?
(A) 트래비스 공원
(B) 스파르탄 도서관
(C) 레밍턴 연못
(D) 베이랜즈 공원

정답 (C)

해설 화자가 담화 후반부에 폰데로사 구역 내에서 주문하면 10퍼센트 할인을 제공한다고(if you're ordering from within the Ponderosa district, we're offering a 10 percent discount!) 알리고 있습니다. 시각자료에서 왼쪽 하단에 Ponderosa district로 쓰여 있는 곳에 표기된 장소명이 Remington Pond이므로 (C)가 정답입니다.

어휘 following 다음의, 아래의 location 장소, 위치, 지점 receive ~을 받다

READING

PART 5

DAY 1 명사

PRACTICE

1. reservation
2. selection
3. applications
4. Patrons
5. analyst
6. negotiators
7. proposal
8. initiative

1.
정답 reservation
해석 호텔에 도착 시 예약의 증거로서 이 이메일을 보여주세요.
해설 소유격 your 뒤에 위치한 빈칸에는 명사가 올 수 있으므로 reservation이 정답입니다.
어휘 proof 증명, 증거 reservation 예약 arrival 도착

2.
정답 selection
해석 저희가 이번 달에 아주 다양한 새로운 맛들을 추가할 것입니다.
해설 형용사 large와 전치사 of 사이에 위치한 빈칸은 형용사의 수식을 받을 명사 자리이므로 selection이 정답입니다.
어휘 add ~을 추가하다 a large selection of 아주 다양한 flavor 맛, 풍미 select ~을 선택하다 selective 선택적인 selectively 선택적으로

3.
정답 applications
해석 우리는 가장 적격인 한 명을 선택하기에 앞서 모든 지원서를 검토할 것입니다.
해설 형용사 all의 수식을 받음과 동시에 동사 review의 목적어 역할을 할 복수명사가 빈칸에 필요한데, review의 목적어로서 검토 대상을 나타낼 사물명사가 필요하므로 '지원(서), 신청(서)' 등을 의미하는 복수명사 applications가 정답입니다.
어휘 review ~을 검토하다 choose ~을 선택하다 qualified 적격인, 자격이 있는 application 지원(서), 신청(서)

4.
정답 Patrons
해석 론스 카페의 고객은 추가 할인을 위해 등록해 주세요.
해설 동사가 복수형 are이므로 주어 역시 복수명사여야 합니다. Patronage은 불가산 명사로 단수 취급되기 때문에 복수명사인 Patrons가 정답입니다.
어휘 patron 후원자, 단골손님 Patronage 후원 register 등록하다, 기재하다 further 그 이상의, 여분의

5.
정답 analyst
해석 저희 선임 시장 분석가가 내일 오후에 귀하의 사무실을 방문하실 것입니다.
해설 형용사 senior의 수식을 받음과 동시에 명사 market과 복합명사를 구성할 또 다른 명사가 빈칸에 필요한데, 동사 visit의 행위 주체가 되어야 하므로 사람명사인 analyst가 정답입니다.
어휘 analysis 분석 analyze ~을 분석하다 analytic 분석적인 analyst 분석 전문가

6.
정답 negotiators
해석 효과적인 계약 협상자는 강력한 의사소통 기술과 법률 용어에 대한 깊은 이해가 필요합니다.
해설 형용사 effective의 수식을 받음과 동시에 명사 contract와 복합명사를 구성할 또 다른 명사가 필요한데, 동사 require의 행위 주체가 되어야 하므로 사람명사인 negotiators가 정답입니다.
어휘 effective 효과적인 contract 계약 negotiator 협상자 negotiation 협상 deep 깊은, 난해한 legal terms 법률 용어

7.
정답 proposal
해석 사업 제안서를 제출하기 전에 철저한 시장 조사를 수행하는 것이 필수적입니다.
해설 빈칸 뒤에 business는 명사입니다. 문맥상 제출을 할 수 있는 것은 제안서이므로 복합명사를 구성할 수 있는 명사인 proposal이 정답입니다.
어휘 submit 제출하다 business proposal 사업 제안서 essential 필수적인 conduct 수행하다, 실시하다 thorough 철저한, 면밀한

8.

정답 initiative

해석 그 대학은 학생들이 기업가의 기술을 발달시키는 것을 지원하기 위해 최근 계획을 시작했습니다.

해설 형용사 recent 뒤로 빈칸이 있어 빈칸은 형용사가 수식할 수 있는 명사 자리인데 initiation은 '가입, 입문'이라는 뜻이므로 동사 launch의 '시작하다'라는 의미와 어울리지 않습니다. 그러므로 문맥과 어울리는 initiative가 정답입니다.

어휘 launch 시작하다, 출시하다 recent 최근의 initiative 계획 initiation 가입, 입문, 취임 support 지원하다 entrepreneurial 기업가의

실전 TEST

1. (A)	2. (B)	3. (D)	4. (A)	5. (B)
6. (C)	7. (D)	8. (C)	9. (D)	10. (C)
11. (B)	12. (B)	13. (B)	14. (D)	15. (D)
16. (A)	17. (C)	18. (C)	19. (B)	20. (C)

1.

정답 (A)

해석 지난주에 마케팅 부서에 의해 종합적인 설문조사가 실시되었다.

해설 형용사 comprehensive 뒤로 빈칸이 있고 동사 was conducted가 이어져 있으므로 빈칸은 형용사의 수식을 받을 명사 자리입니다. 그리고 부정관사 A는 단수 가산명사와 어울리므로 (A) survey가 정답입니다.

오답 (B) surveys: 복수명사의 형태이므로 부정관사와 어울리지 않는 오답입니다.
(C) surveyed: 동사 survey의 과거형 또는 과거분사형이므로 명사가 필요한 빈칸에 맞지 않는 오답입니다.
(D) surveying: 동사 survey의 동명사 또는 현재분사형이고 동명사는 부정관사로 수식할 수 없으므로 오답입니다.

어휘 comprehensive 종합적인 conduct ~을 실시하다, 수행하다 department 부서 survey n. 설문조사(지) v. ~에게 설문 조사하다

2.

정답 (B)

해석 저희는 최근의 소프트웨어 업그레이드와 관련해 많은 불만을 접수했습니다.

해설 빈칸 앞에 위치한 a number of는 '많은'이라는 뜻으로 복수명사를 수식하는 역할을 합니다. 따라서 a number of의 수식을 받을 수 있는 복수명사의 형태인 (B) complaints가 정답입니다.

오답 (A) complaint: 단수 명사의 형태이므로 a number of의 수식을 받을 수 없는 오답입니다.
(C) complain: 동사이므로 a number of의 수식을 받을 수 없는 오답입니다.
(D) complains: 3인칭 단수 주어와 어울리는 동사의 형태이므로 a number of의 수식을 받을 수 없는 오답입니다.

어휘 receive ~을 접수하다, 받다 a number of 많은 (수의) recent 최근의 complaint 불만, 불평 complain 불만을 제기하다, 불평하다

3.

정답 (D)

해석 사무실 내의 직원 생산성을 증가시키기 위해, 데보나 모터스 사는 직원 보상 프로그램을 시행했다.

해설 to부정사로 쓰인 동사 increase 뒤로 가산명사 employee가 부정관사 없이 복수형도 아닌 채로 쓰여 있으므로 employee가 증가 대상이 아니라는 것을 알 수 있습니다. 따라서 employee와 복합명사를 구성해 실제 증가 대상을 나타낼 또 다른 명사가 빈칸에 쓰여야 하는데, 문맥상 직원과 관련된 것이어야 하므로 '생산성'을 뜻하는 명사 (D) productivity가 정답입니다.

오답 (A) productively: 부사이므로 명사가 필요한 빈칸에 어울리지 않는 오답입니다.
(B) productive: 형용사이므로 명사가 필요한 빈칸에 어울리지 않는 오답입니다.
(C) products: 명사이기는 하지만 '제품'을 뜻하므로 employee와 의미 연결이 어색한 오답입니다.

어휘 increase ~을 증가시키다 implement ~을 시행하다 incentive 보상(책), 장려(책) productively 생산적으로 productive 생산적인 product 제품 productivity 생산성

4.

정답 (A)

해석 건축가는 공사 프로젝트를 시작하기 위해 건축 허가서를 신청했다.

해설 빈칸 앞에 위치한 apply for는 '~을 신청하다, ~에 지원하다'를 뜻하므로 빈칸 앞에 위치한 명사 building이 공사 시작을 위한 신청 대상으로 맞지 않는다는 것을 알 수 있습니다. 따라서 building과 복합명사를 구성해 실제 신청 대상을 나타낼 또 다른 명사로서 '허가증'을 뜻하는 permit이 쓰여야 자연스러운데, 부정관사 a가 쓰여 있어 단수 형태가 되어야 하므로 (A) permit이 정답입니다.

오답 (B) permits: 복수 형태이므로 부정관사 a와 어울릴 수 없는 오답입니다.
(C) permission: 명사이기는 하지만 부정관사 a의 수식을 받을 수 없는 불가산명사이므로 오답입니다.
(D) permitted: 동사 permit의 과거형 또는 과거분사형이므로 명사가 필요한 빈칸에 맞지 않는 오답입니다.

어휘 architect 건축가 apply for ~을 신청하다, ~에 지원하다
permit n. 허가서 v. ~을 허용하다, 가능하게 하다
permission 허가, 승인

5.
정답 (B)
해석 하트 씨는 빌먼 엔지니어링 사의 임원들과 함께 하는 논의가 상호 이득이 되는 것이기를 바라고 있다.
해설 정관사 the와 전치사 with 사이에 위치한 빈칸은 the의 수식을 받을 명사 자리이므로 선택지에서 유일한 명사인 (B) discussions가 정답입니다.
오답 (A) discuss: 동사이므로 정관사 the의 수식을 받을 수 없는 오답입니다.
(C) discussed: 동사 discuss의 과거형 또는 과거분사형이므로 정관사 the의 수식을 받을 수 없는 오답입니다.
(D) discussing: 동사 discuss의 동명사 또는 현재분사형이므로 정관사 the의 수식을 받을 수 없는 오답입니다.
어휘 be hopeful that ~이기를 바라다 executive 임원 mutually 상호, 서로 간에 beneficial 이득이 되는, 유익한 discuss ~을 논의하다, 이야기하다 discussion 논의

6.
정답 (C)
해석 귀하의 주문품이 배송 중에 손상된 경우, 고객 지원 서비스를 위해 555-8698번으로 전화 주십시오.
해설 빈칸 앞에 위치한 customer는 가산명사로서 부정관사 a를 동반하거나 복수형으로 쓰여야 합니다. 둘 중 어디에도 해당하지 않는 상태인데, 이는 customer와 복합명사를 구성할 또 다른 명사가 빈칸에 필요하다는 뜻입니다. 따라서 선택지에서 유일한 명사인 (C) support가 정답입니다.
오답 (A) supported: 동사 support의 과거형 또는 과거분사형이므로 customer와 복합명사를 구성할 수 없는 오답입니다.
(B) supportive: 형용사이므로 customer와 복합명사를 구성할 수 없는 오답입니다.
(D) supporting: 동사 support의 동명사 또는 현재분사형이므로 customer와 복합명사를 구성할 수 없는 오답입니다.
어휘 order 주문(품) damaged 손상된, 피해를 입은 during ~ 중에 shipping 배송 support v. ~을 지원하다, 지지하다 n. 지원, 지지 supportive 지원하는

7.
정답 (D)
해석 조세프 씨는 자신의 작품 중 하나가 메트로폴리탄 미술관에 전시될 것이라는 말을 듣고 기뻐했다.
해설 빈칸 앞에 위치한 his는 소유격이므로 빈칸에 명사가 와야 합니다. 또한 이 문장에서는 will be의 주어로서 전시되는(on display) 것을 나타내는 명사여야 하므로 '작품'을 뜻하는 사물명사가 필요합니다. 따라서 「one of + 복수명사」 구조와 어울리는 (D) paintings가 정답입니다.
오답 (A) painted: 동사 paint의 과거형 또는 과거분사형이므로 소유격 대명사 his의 수식을 받을 수 없는 오답입니다.
(B) painting: 단수명사이므로 one of의 목적어로 쓸 수 없는 오답입니다.
(C) painters: 복수명사이기는 하지만, 전시 대상이 될 수 없는 사람명사이므로 오답입니다.
어휘 be delighted to do ~해서 기쁘다 on display 전시된, 진열

8.
정답 (C)
해석 두 달 동안의 개조 공사 후에, 스태포드 공원은 일반 대중에게 다시 개방되었다.
해설 전치사 of 뒤에 위치한 빈칸은 of의 목적어 역할을 할 명사 자리이므로 선택지에서 유일한 명사인 (C) renovation이 정답입니다.
오답 (A) renovative: 형용사이므로 전치사의 목적어 역할을 할 수 없는 오답입니다.
(B) renovate: 동사이므로 전치사의 목적어 역할을 할 수 없는 오답입니다.
(D) renovated: 동사 renovate의 과거형 또는 과거분사형이므로 전치사의 목적어 역할을 할 수 없는 오답입니다.
어휘 reopen ~을 다시 개방하다, 재개장하다 the public 일반 대중 renovative 혁신하는 renovate ~을 개조하다, 보수하다 renovation 개조 (공사), 보수 (공사)

9.
정답 (D)
해석 저희의 프리미엄 채널에 대한 서비스 이용을 갱신하시는 것에 관심이 있으신 고객들께서는 555-2376번의 하딩 씨와 이야기하시기 바랍니다.
해설 타동사 renew의 동명사 renewing 뒤에 위치한 빈칸에 목적어 역할을 할 명사가 필요한데, 갱신 대상이 되는 것은 사물이어야 하므로 사물명사인 (D) subscriptions가 정답입니다.
오답 (A) subscribe: 동사이므로 renew의 목적어 역할을 할 수 없는 오답입니다.
(B) subscribes: 3인칭 단수 주어와 어울리는 동사 형태이므로 renew의 목적어 역할을 할 수 없는 오답입니다.
(C) subscribers: 사람명사이므로 갱신 대상이 될 수 없는 오답입니다.
어휘 renew ~을 갱신하다, 재개하다 subscribe 서비스에 가입하다, 구독 신청하다 subscriber 서비스 가입자, 구독자 subscription 서비스 가입, 구독 신청

10.
정답 (C)

해석 물리 치료를 받고자 하는 사람은 누구든 반드시 지역 의사의 추천서를 받아야 합니다.

해설 부정관사 a와 전치사 from 사이에 위치한 빈칸은 a의 수식을 받을 명사 자리이므로 선택지에서 유일하게 명사인 (C) referral이 정답입니다. -al로 끝나지만 명사임을 기억해 두는 것이 좋습니다.

오답 (A) referring: 동사 refer의 동명사 또는 현재분사형이므로 부정관사의 수식을 받을 수 없는 오답입니다.
(B) referred: 동사 refer의 과거형 또는 과거분사형이므로 부정관사의 수식을 받을 수 없는 오답입니다.
(D) refer: 동사이므로 부정관사의 수식을 받을 수 없는 오답입니다.

어휘 seek ~을 찾다, 구하다 physiotherapy treatment 물리 치료법 obtain ~을 얻다, 획득하다 local 지역의, 현지의 refer 참조하다, 조회하다 referral 추천(서), 위탁

11.
정답 (B)

해석 신중한 검토 후에, 골드버그 씨의 후보 자격에 대한 타당성이 내일 발표될 것입니다.

해설 빈칸은 정관사 the와 전치사 of 사이에 위치하므로 빈칸은 명사 자리임을 알 수 있습니다. 따라서 보기 중에서 '유효성, 타당성'을 의미하는 (B) validity가 정답입니다.

오답 (A) validities: 셀 수 없는 추상 명사이므로 복수형으로 잘 쓰이지 않으며 문맥상 부적절한 오답입니다.
(C) validate: 동사이므로 명사 자리에는 올 수 없습니다.
(D) valid: 형용사이므로 명사 자리에는 올 수 없는 오답입니다.

어휘 candidacy 입후보, 후보 자격 announce 발표하다 validity 유효성, 타당성 validate 유효하게 하다, 입증하다 valid 유효한, 타당한

12.
정답 (B)

해석 정기 점검은 장비 고장을 예방하고 작업장의 안전을 보장하는 데 중요하다.

해설 빈칸은 형용사 routine과 동사 is 사이에 위치하므로, 명사 자리임을 알 수 있습니다. 따라서 보기 중에서 '정기적인 점검' 또는 '유지관리'를 의미하는 (B) maintenance가 정답입니다. "routine maintenance"는 토익에서 자주 등장하는 표현이며, 고유한 명사 덩어리처럼 쓰이는 숙어로 기억해 두면 좋습니다.

오답 (A) maintain: 동사원형으로 명사 자리에는 올 수 없는 오답입니다.
(C) maintaining: 동명사는 routine처럼 형용사의 수식을 받지 않습니다.
(D) maintained: 과거분사로 형용사 역할은 가능하나 이 문장에서는 명사 역할이 필요한 자리이므로 오답입니다.

어휘 routine 정기적인, 일상적인 maintenance 유지관리, 정비 prevent 예방하다, 막다 equipment failure 장비 고장 workplace safety 작업장 안전

13.
정답 (B)

해석 모든 출장 준비 사항은 회사의 경비 처리 정책을 준수해야 합니다.

해설 빈칸은 형용사 travel과 동사 must comply 사이에 위치하며, 전체적으로 「All + 명사」 구조를 이루므로 빈칸은 명사 자리임을 알 수 있습니다. 따라서 보기 중에서 '여행 준비, 계획'이라는 뜻의 복수 명사인 (B) arrangements가 정답입니다. travel arrangements는 토익에서 자주 등장하는 고유 표현으로 기억해 두는 것이 좋습니다.

오답 (A) arrangement: 수량 형용사 all 뒤에는 복수명사가 위치하므로 단수명사인 arrangement는 오답입니다.
(C) arranged: 과거분사형으로 형용사 역할은 가능하나, 이 문장에서는 명사 역할이 필요하므로 오답입니다.
(D) arranging: 동명사 또는 현재분사로, 명사 자리에는 어울리지 않으며 어색한 표현입니다.

어휘 travel arrangements 여행 준비, 여행 계획 comply with ~을 준수하다 expense policy 비용 정책, 경비 처리 규정

14.
정답 (D)

해석 공급 부족에 대응하여, 그 조달 계획은 승인된 공급업체 목록을 간소화했습니다.

해설 빈칸은 정관사 the와 동사 streamlined 사이에 위치하므로 빈칸은 명사 자리임을 알 수 있습니다. 따라서 보기 중에서 '조치, 계획'이라는 의미의 명사인 (D) initiative가 정답입니다.

오답 (A) initiate: 동사 원형이므로 명사 자리에는 올 수 없습니다.
(B) initiated: 과거형 또는 과거분사형이며, 이 문장에서는 명사 역할이 필요하므로 오답입니다.
(C) initiator: 명사이긴 하나 '행동을 시작한 사람'이라는 의미로, 여기서는 조직 또는 부서의 행동을 지칭하는 단어로 어울리지 않습니다.

어휘 procurement 구매 부서, 조달 담당 streamline 간소화하다, 능률화하다 approved vendors 승인된 공급업체 supply shortage 공급 부족 initiative 계획, 조치, (상황에 대한) 주도적 대응 initiate 개시되게 하다, 착수시키다 initiator 개시인

15.
정답 (D)

해석 증가하는 고객 수요로 인해, 엘라라 풋웨어 사는 내년에 자사 생산 시설들의 대대적인 확장을 계획하고 있다.

해설 형용사 major와 전치사 of 사이에 위치한 빈칸은 형용사의 수식을 받을 명사 자리이므로 (D) expansion이 정답입니다.

오답 (A) expand: 동사이므로 명사가 필요한 빈칸에 쓰일 수 없습니다.
(B) expanding: 동명사 또는 현재분사이므로 명사가 필요한 빈칸에 쓰일 수 없습니다.
(C) expansive: 형용사이므로 명사가 필요한 빈칸에 쓰일 수 없습니다.

어휘 due to ~로 인해, ~ 때문에 increasing 증가하는, 늘어나는 demand 수요, 요구 major 대대적인, 주요한 facility 시설(물) expand ~을 확장하다, ~을 확대하다 expansive 광범위한, 포괄적인 expansion 확장, 확대

16.
정답 (A)

해석 모든 기술적인 질문은 저희 코어라이트 시스템 사의 IT 전문가에게 전달해 주시기 바라며, 이분께서 접속 관련 문제들을 해결해 드릴 수 있습니다.

해설 빈칸에는 IT와 복합명사를 구성해 기술적인 질문을 전달 받고 문제를 해결해 줄 수 있는 사람을 나타낼 명사가 필요하므로 '전문가'를 뜻하는 (A) specialist가 정답입니다.

오답 (B) specialty: '전문 분야'라는 의미의 추상 명사로, 사람을 지칭하지 않으므로 문맥상 맞지 않습니다.
(C) special: 형용사이므로 명사 자리에 올 수 없어 오답입니다.
(D) specialization: '전문화, 전문 분야'라는 뜻의 명사지만, 사람을 나타내지 않기 때문에 오답입니다.

어휘 direct A to B A를 B에게 전달하다 technical question 기술적인 질문 resolve 해결하다 access issue 접근 문제 specialist 전문가 specialty 전문, 특제품, 특색 special 특별한, 특수한 specialization 특수화, 전문 분야

17.
정답 (C)

해석 대표이사의 연설은 벤트릭스 글로벌 사의 대강당에 모인 직원들의 열광적인 인정을 받았다.

해설 형용사 enthusiastic과 전치사 from 사이에 위치한 빈칸은 형용사의 수식을 받을 명사가 필요한 자리이므로 (C) approval이 정답입니다.

오답 (A) approve: 동사이므로 명사가 필요한 빈칸에 쓰일 수 없습니다.
(B) approving: 동명사 또는 현재분사이므로 명사가 필요한 빈칸에 쓰일 수 없습니다.
(D) approved: 동사의 과거형 또는 과거분사형이므로 명사가 필요한 빈칸에 쓰일 수 없습니다.

어휘 be met with ~을 받다, ~에 부딪치다 enthusiastic 열광적인, 열렬한 gather ~을 모으다, 모이다 approve ~을 인정하다, ~을 승인하다 approval 인정, 승인

18.
정답 (C)

해석 자이언트 테크 사는 최근 사이버 보안 분야를 전문으로 하는 많은 개발자들을 채용했습니다.

해설 many는 복수 수량 형용사이므로, 빈칸은 반드시 복수 명사가 쓰여야 하는 자리임을 알 수 있습니다. 따라서 보기 중에서 복수형이며, 사람을 의미하는 명사인 (C) developers가 정답입니다.

오답 (A) develop: 동사원형으로 명사 자리에는 올 수 없는 오답입니다.
(B) developer: 단수명사로 many와 수 일치하지 않기 때문에 오답입니다.
(D) developments: 복수명사이긴 하지만 '발전, 개발'이라는 추상 개념이므로 사람을 의미하는 문맥에는 적합하지 않습니다.

어휘 employ 고용하다 developer 개발자 specialize in ~ ~을 전문으로 하다 cybersecurity 사이버 보안 develop 개발하다 developer 개발자 development 개발, 발달

19.
정답 (B)

해석 히노 씨가 물류업 분야에서 지니고 있는 수년 동안의 경력은 그를 래피드홀 화물 서비스 사의 그 직책에 대한 이상적인 후보자로 만들어 주었다.

해설 전치사 of와 in 사이에 위치한 빈칸은 of의 목적어 역할을 할 명사 자리입니다. 또한, 일반적인 '경력, 경험'을 의미할 때 experience는 셀 수 없는 명사이므로 단수명사의 형태인 (B) experience가 정답입니다.

오답 (A) experienced: 형용사 또는 동사의 과거형/과거분사형이므로 명사 자리인 빈칸에 쓰일 수 없습니다.
(C) experiencing: 동명사 또는 현재분사이므로 명사 자리인 빈칸에 쓰일 수 없습니다.
(D) experiences: 복수명사이므로 단수명사가 필요한 빈칸에 쓰일 수 없습니다.

어휘 logistics 물류(업) make A B A를 B로 만들다 ideal 이상적인 candidate 후보자, 지원자 experienced 경험 많은 experience n. 경력, 경험 v. ~을 경험하다

20.
정답 (C)

해석 넵튠 테크놀로지 사는 새로운 규정을 승인하기 전에 보안 시

스템에 대해 철저한 분석을 실시할 것이다.
해설 형용사 thorough와 전치사 of 사이에 위치한 빈칸은 형용사의 수식을 받는 명사가 필요한 자리입니다. 선택지에서 명사는 (A) analyst와 (C) analysis인데, 동사 conduct의 목적어로서 실시 대상이 되는 일을 나타내야 하므로 '분석'을 뜻하는 (C) analysis가 정답입니다.
오답 (A) analyst: conduct의 목적어로서 실시 대상이 될 수 없는 사람명사이므로 오답입니다.
(B) analyze: 동사이므로 명사 자리인 빈칸에 쓰일 수 없는 오답입니다.
(D) analytical: 형용사이므로 명사 자리인 빈칸에 쓰일 수 없는 오답입니다.
어휘 conduct ~을 실시하다, ~을 수행하다 thorough 철저한, 꼼꼼한 approve ~을 승인하다 protocol 규정, 규약 analyst 분석가 analyze ~을 분석하다 analysis 분석 (결과) analytical 분석적인

DAY 2 대명사

PRACTICE

1. her 2. himself 3. those
4. this 5. others 6. Some

1.
정답 her
해석 랭리 교수는 신경과학 분야에서 그녀의 획기적인 연구로 잘 알려져 있습니다.
해설 빈칸 뒤에 명사인 research가 있으므로 명사 앞에서 소유를 나타낼 수 있는 소유격인 her이 정답입니다.
어휘 groundbreaking 획기적인, 혁신적인 neuroscience 신경과학 be known for ~으로 잘 알려져 있다

2.
정답 himself
해석 위험에도 불구하고, 대니얼은 밤늦게 직접 전기 배선을 수리했습니다.
해설 빈칸 앞에 문장의 구조를 살펴보면 주어, 동사, 목적어로 구성된 완전한 문장입니다. 따라서 완벽한 문장 뒤에서 '직접'이라는 의미로 쓰이는 부사 역할을 할 수 있는 재귀대명사 himself가 정답입니다.
어휘 despite ~에도 불구하고 risk 위험 repair 수리하다 electrical wiring 전기 배선

3.
정답 those
해석 그 회사는 유연한 근무 일정을 선호하는 사람들에게 재택근무를 제공합니다.
해설 관계대명사 who는 사람을 나타내는 명사를 수식하므로, 빈칸에 들어갈 대명사가 사람을 지칭하는 대명사이어야 합니다. 따라서 '사람들'이라는 의미를 나타내는 대명사 those가 정답입니다.
어휘 offer 제공하다 remote work 재택근무 prefer 선호하다 flexible schedules 유연한 일정

4.
정답 this
해석 4층에 있는 직원 라운지가 이번 주에 일시적으로 이용 불가능할 것입니다.
해설 빈칸 뒤에 오는 단어 week는 단수 명사이기 때문에 이를 수식할 수 있는 품사는 형용사여야 합니다. 따라서 단수 명사를 꾸밀 수 있는 지시형용사 this가 정답입니다.
어휘 temporarily 일시적으로, 임시로 inaccessible 이용 불가능한, 접근할 수 없는

5.
정답 others
해석 어떤 직원들은 독립적으로 일하는 것을 선호하는 반면, 다른 직원들은 협력적인 환경에서 잘 성장합니다.
해설 문맥상 문장 앞의 주어 Some employees는 복수형이므로, 이들과 구별되는 또 다른 복수 집단을 나타내는 표현이 필요합니다. 빈칸 뒤의 동사 thrive와도 수일치가 되는 '다른 직원들'이라는 의미를 나타내는 부정대명사 others가 정답입니다.
어휘 prefer 선호하다 thrive 잘 자라다, 번성하다

6.
정답 Some
해석 지원자 중 일부는 마감일 전에 포트폴리오를 제출하는 것을 잊었습니다.
해설 빈칸 뒤에는 「of the 복수명사 + 복수동사」로 되어 있으므로 셀 수 있는 명사인 applicants와 함께 쓸 수 있는 복수대명사 Some이 정답입니다.
어휘 applicant 지원자 submit 제출하다 deadline 마감일

실전 TEST

1. (A) 2. (C) 3. (C) 4. (D) 5. (D)
6. (C) 7. (A) 8. (C) 9. (B) 10. (B)
11. (B) 12. (A) 13. (B) 14. (B) 15. (C)
16. (B) 17. (A) 18. (B) 19. (B) 20. (A)

1.
정답 (A)

해석 다른 사람들과 의사소통하는 능력 외에도, 무어 씨의 계획 수립 능력은 매우 뛰어납니다.

해설 빈칸은 ability to communicate with others라는 명사구 앞에 위치하며, 소유격이 필요한 자리입니다. 이 명사구는 Mr. Moore의 능력을 수식하는 구조이므로, 빈칸은 소유격이 되어야 합니다. 따라서 보기 중에서 (A) his가 정답입니다.

오답 (B) him: 목적격으로 소유를 나타낼 수 없으므로 오답입니다.
(C) he: 주격으로 명사 앞에서 수식하는 용법이 아니므로 부적절한 오답입니다.
(D) himself: 재귀대명사는 소유를 나타내지 못하므로 오답입니다.

어휘 in addition to ~ 외에도, ~에 더하여 communicate with others 다른 사람들과 소통하다 skill at planning 계획 수립 능력 remarkable 주목할 만한, 훌륭한

2.
정답 (C)

해석 카이트 씨를 찾고 계신다면, 회계부 사무실에서 찾으실 수 있습니다.

해설 목적어를 필요로 하는 타동사 find와 전치사 in 사이에 위치한 빈칸은 find의 목적어 역할을 할 단어가 필요한 자리입니다. 그리고 찾는 대상으로서 앞서 언급된 Ms. Kite를 가리킬 목적격 대명사가 쓰여야 하므로 (C) her가 정답입니다.

오답 (A) she: 주격 대명사는 동사의 목적어 역할을 하지 못하므로 오답입니다.
(B) hers: 소유대명사가 동사의 목적어 역할을 할 수는 있지만, hers가 지칭하는 명사가 없으므로 오답입니다.
(D) herself: 재귀대명사도 동사의 목적어 역할을 할 수는 있지만, 행위 주체(주어)와 대상(목적어)이 동일할 때 사용하므로 오답입니다.

어휘 look for ~을 찾다 find ~을 찾아내다, 발견하다 accounting 회계

3.
정답 (C)

해석 다른 부서장들과 달리, 트래스커 씨는 직접 월간 업무 일정표를 완성하고 싶어합니다.

해설 빈칸 앞부분을 보면, Unlike 전치사구 뒤로 주어 Ms. Trasker와 동사, to부정사구로 이어지는 완전한 문장입니다. 따라서 맨 뒤에 위치한 빈칸은 부사처럼 부가적인 요소에 해당되는 단어가 쓰여야 하는데, 이 역할이 가능한 것이 재귀대명사이므로 (C) herself가 정답입니다.

오답 (A) hers: 소유대명사는 부사처럼 부가적인 역할을 하지 못하므로 오답입니다.
(B) her: 소유격 또는 목적격 대명사인데, 부사처럼 부가적인 역할을 하지 못하므로 오답입니다.
(D) her own: 명사를 수식하는 역할을 하므로 오답입니다.

어휘 unlike ~와 달리 department 부서 supervisor 부서장, 책임자, 상사 would prefer to do ~하고 싶어하다 complete ~을 완성하다, 완료하다 monthly 월간의, 달마다의 oneself (부사처럼 쓰여) 직접, 스스로 one's own 자신만의

4.
정답 (D)

해석 모든 신규 수강생들은 강의 교과 과정에 익숙해질 수 있도록 안내 책자 패키지를 받습니다.

해설 선택지가 모두 재귀대명사이므로 가리키는 대상이 무엇인지 파악해야 합니다. 빈칸은 타동사 familiarize의 목적어 자리이며, 그 앞에 주어로 쓰인 All new class members가 스스로를 익숙하게 만든다는 의미가 되어야 알맞습니다. 따라서 3인칭 복수 재귀대명사인 (D) themselves가 정답입니다.

오답 (A) itself: 3인칭 단수 재귀대명사이므로 오답입니다.
(B) yourself: 2인칭 단수 재귀대명사이므로 오답입니다.
(C) ourselves: 1인칭 복수 재귀대명사이므로 오답입니다.

어휘 receive ~을 받다 information package 안내 책자 묶음 in order to do ~할 수 있도록 familiarize oneself with ~에 익숙해지다, ~을 숙지하다 curriculum 교육 과정

5.
정답 (D)

해석 세미나에 참석하는 데 관심이 있는 분들께서는 오후 6시 전에 소속 부서장님께 연락하셔야 합니다.

해설 빈칸 뒤에 관계대명사 who가 이끄는 절이 있으므로 who절의 수식을 받을 수 있는 대명사 (D) Those가 정답입니다.

오답 (A) There: who절의 수식을 받지 못하므로 오답입니다.
(B) They: who절의 수식을 받지 못하므로 오답입니다.
(C) Which: who절의 수식을 받지 못하므로 오답입니다.

어휘 those who ~하는 사람들 be interested in ~에 관심이 있다 attend ~에 참석하다 contact ~에게 연락하다

6.
정답 (C)

해석 애스콧 은행의 메인 스트리트 지점과 하프 로드 지점은 크리스마스 이브에 문을 여는데, 이 지점들이 고객 서비스부를 포

함하고 있기 때문입니다.
해설 접속사 as와 명사 주어 branches 사이에 위치한 빈칸은 주어인 branches를 수식할 단어가 필요한 자리이므로 이 역할이 가능한 지시형용사 (C) these가 정답입니다.
오답 (A) whose: 접속사의 역할을 하는 소유격 관계대명사로서 다른 접속사 as 바로 뒤에 나란히 쓰일 수 없으므로 오답입니다.
(B) theirs: 소유대명사는 명사를 수식하지 못하므로 오답입니다.
(D) ours: 소유대명사는 명사를 수식하지 못하므로 오답입니다.
어휘 location 지점, 위치 remain + 형용사: ~한 상태로 있다, 유지되다 branch 지점, 지사 department 부서

7.
정답 (A)
해석 산업 공학 컨퍼런스에 참석했던 직원들 누구도 그것이 유익했다고 느끼지 않았다.
해설 빈칸 뒤에 위치한 「of the 복수명사」의 수식을 받을 수 있는 대명사인 (A) None이 정답입니다.
오답 (B) Whoever: 「of the 복수명사」의 수식을 받을 수 없는 복합관계대명사이므로 오답입니다.
(C) Anyone: 「of the 복수명사」의 수식을 받을 수 없는 대명사이므로 오답입니다.
(D) Nobody: 「of the 복수명사」의 수식을 받을 수 없는 대명사이므로 오답입니다.
어휘 attend ~에 참석하다 industrial engineering 산업 공학 helpful 유익한, 도움이 되는 none 아무도 ~ 않다 whoever ~하는 사람은 누구든

8.
정답 (C)
해석 회사는 돕슨 씨를 위해 비즈니스 클래스 항공권 한 장을, 샐먼 씨를 위해 또 한 장을 예약할 것이다.
해설 돕슨 씨에게 제공되는 비즈니스 클래스 항공권 한 장(one business class flight ticket)과 같은 종류의 것으로 샐먼 씨에게도 제공되는 것을 나타낼 대명사가 필요합니다. 따라서 one과 짝을 이뤄 같은 종류의 또 다른 하나를 가리킬 때 사용하는 부정대명사 (C) another가 정답입니다.
오답 (A) those: 복수인 특정 대상을 지칭할 때 사용하므로 문장의 의미에 맞지 않는 오답입니다.
(B) others: 복수대명사이므로 문장의 의미에 맞지 않는 오답입니다.
(D) the others: 특정 범위 내의 일부를 제외한 나머지를 가리키는 복수대명사이므로 2인만 등장하는 상황에 맞지 않는 오답입니다.

어휘 reserve ~을 예약하다 those (수식어구와 함께) ~하는 사람들 another 또 다른 하나

9.
정답 (B)
해석 자신의 업무 보조 직원들이 모두 휴가 중이었기 때문에, 클락슨 씨는 스스로 예산 보고서를 수정해야 했다.
해설 전치사 by 뒤에 빈칸이 있으므로 목적어 역할이 가능한 대명사를 찾아야 하는데, 여기서 by의 목적어는 주절의 주어 Ms. Clarkson을 가리킵니다. 따라서 주어와 동일 대상을 가리킬 때 사용하는 재귀대명사 (B) herself가 정답입니다.
오답 (A) she: 주격 대명사는 전치사의 목적어로 쓰일 수 없으므로 오답입니다.
(C) hers: 소유대명사이며, 소유대명사가 전치사의 목적어로 쓰일 수는 있지만 주어와 동일한 대상이 아니므로 오답입니다.
(D) her: 전치사의 목적어 역할이 가능한 목적격 대명사이지만, 주절의 주어 Ms. Clarkson과 다른 사람을 가리키는 의미가 되므로 오답입니다.
어휘 assistant 보조, 조수 on vacation 휴가 중인 revise ~을 수정하다 budget 예산 by oneself 스스로, 혼자

10.
정답 (B)
해석 구직 지원자들은 배정된 시간 내에 스스로 직무 능력 시험을 쳐야 합니다.
해설 빈칸 앞에 위치한 on과 결합할 수 있는 대명사 특수 구조를 골라야 하므로 (B) their own이 정답입니다.
오답 (A) they: 주어 자리에 올 수 있는 주격 대명사이므로 오답입니다.
(C) them: 전치사의 목적어 자리에 올 수 있는 목적격 대명사이지만 시험 대상으로 맞지 않으므로 오답입니다.
(D) themselves: 주어와 목적어가 동일할 때 목적어 자리에 오거나 부사 역할을 하는 재귀대명사이므로 오답입니다.
어휘 applicant 지원자, 신청자 take a test 시험을 치다 proficiency 능숙, 숙달 on one's own 혼자, 스스로 within ~ 이내에 allocated 배정된, 할당된

11.
정답 (B)
해석 롤린스 씨는 경험이 더 적은 동료 직원에게 그 협상 업무를 할당하는 대신, 그가 직접 그 업무를 처리하겠다고 제안했다.
해설 빈칸이 속한 주절에 주어와 동사(offered), 그리고 to부정사구가 이어져 있어 이미 구성이 완전한 상태입니다(rather than 이하 부분은 부가적인 요소). 따라서 '직접'이라는 의미로 부사처럼 부가적인 역할을 할 수 있는 재귀대명사 (B) himself가 정답입니다.

오답 (A) him: 목적격대명사로서 부사와 같은 역할을 할 수 없으므로 오답입니다.
(C) he: 주격대명사로서 부사와 같은 역할을 할 수 없으므로 오답입니다.
(D) his: 소유격대명사 또는 소유대명사(그의 것)로서 부사와 같은 역할을 할 수 없으므로 오답입니다.

어휘 offer to do ~하겠다고 제안하다 handle ~을 처리하다, ~을 다루다 negotiation 협상, 협의 rather than ~ 대신, ~가 아니라 assign ~을 할당하다, ~을 배정하다 task 일, 업무 less experienced 경험이 더 적은 colleague 동료(직원)

12.

정답 (A)
해석 언어 교환 프로그램에서 참가자들은 서로의 말하기 능력 향상을 도왔습니다.
해설 빈칸은 동사 helped 다음에 오는 목적어 역할을 하며, 이 문장은 참가자들끼리 서로 도움을 주는 관계를 표현하고 있으므로 상호 관계를 나타내는 대명사가 필요합니다. 보기 중에서 유일하게 서로를 뜻하는 상호대명사인 (A) one another가 정답입니다.
오답 (B) each: 형용사나 대명사로 '각각'을 뜻하지만, 상호 관계보다는 개별적인 의미를 나타내므로 문맥상 어색합니다.
(C) its own: 단수 주어를 받을 때 사용하는 표현이며, 복수 주어 participants와 수가 일치하지 않으므로 오답입니다.
(D) other: 보통 형용사로 쓰이며, 명사처럼 쓰일 때에도 상호 관계를 명확히 나타내지 못하므로 이 문장에는 적절하지 않습니다.
어휘 language exchange program 언어 교환 프로그램 participant 참가자 help ~ improve ~가 향상되도록 돕다 speaking skills 말하기 능력

13.

정답 (B)
해석 고객 지원 담당 직원들은 사소한 문제들을 경영진까지 확대시키지 않고 직접 해결해야 합니다.
해설 부가적인 요소인 without 전치사구를 제외하고, 빈칸 앞까지 주어와 동사(should resolve), 그리고 명사구 목적어 minor issues가 이어져 있어 문장의 구성이 완전한 상태입니다. 따라서 '직접'이라는 의미로 부사처럼 부가적인 역할을 할 수 있는 재귀대명사 (B) themselves가 정답입니다.
오답 (A) them: 목적격대명사로서 부사와 같은 역할을 할 수 없으므로 오답입니다.
(C) theirs: 소유대명사(그들의 것)로서 부사와 같은 역할을 할 수 없으므로 오답입니다.
(D) they: 주격대명사로서 부사와 같은 역할을 할 수 없으므로 오답입니다.

어휘 support 지원, 지지, 후원 resolve ~을 해결하다 minor 사소한, 중요하지 않은 issue 문제, 사안 without -ing ~하지 않고, ~하지 않은 채 escalate A to B: A를 B로 확대시키다 management 경영(진), 관리(진)

14.

정답 (B)
해석 우리는 다섯 명의 컨설턴트들에게 그 디자인을 살펴 보도록 요청했지만, 그들 중 누구도 유용한 의견을 제공하지 않았습니다.
해설 빈칸 뒤에 위치한 of 전치사구의 수식을 받을 수 있는 대명사가 필요하며, but과 어울려 주절과 대조되는 부정적인 의미를 나타내어 '그들 중 누구도 유용한 의견을 제공하지 않았다'를 뜻해야 자연스러우므로 '누구도 ~ 않다'를 의미하는 대명사 (B) none이 정답입니다.
오답 (A) any: of 전치사구의 수식을 받을 수는 있지만, 부정적인 의미를 나타내는 대명사가 아니므로 오답입니다.
(C) both: of 전치사구의 수식을 받을 수는 있지만, 부정적인 의미를 나타내는 대명사가 아니므로 오답입니다.
(D) someone: of 전치사구의 수식을 받을 수도 없고, 부정적인 의미를 나타내는 대명사도 아니므로 오답입니다.
어휘 ask A to do: A에게 ~하도록 요청하다 consultant 컨설턴트, 상담 전문가, 자문 review ~을 살펴 보다, ~을 검토하다 offer ~을 제공하다, ~을 제안하다 useful 유용한 feedback 의견 both (A and B): (A와 B) 둘 모두

15.

정답 (C)
해석 반드시 모든 온라인 교육 강좌들이 회사 포털에 금요일 전까지 업로드되도록 해 주시기 바랍니다.
해설 빈칸 뒤에 위치한 of the online training courses처럼 「of + 복수명사」의 수식을 받을 수 있는 대명사는 (C) all과 (D) each인데, 복수동사 are와 수 일치되어야 하므로 복수대명사 (C) all이 정답입니다.
오답 (A) every: of 전치사구의 수식을 받을 수 없는 형용사이므로 오답입니다.
(B) much: 「of + 셀 수 없는 명사」의 수식을 받는 대명사이므로 오답입니다.
(D) each: 「of + 복수명사」의 수식을 받을 수는 있지만, 복수동사 are와 수 일치되지 않는 단수대명사이므로 오답입니다.
어휘 ensure that 반드시 ~하도록 하다, ~임을 보장하다 training 교육, 강좌

16.

정답 (B)
해석 오르테가 씨는 오늘 일과 시간 종료 전까지 자신에게 직접 완료된 디자인을 제출하도록 인턴 직원들에게 지시했습니다.

해설 전치사 to의 목적어 역할을 할 대명사가 필요하며, 인턴들이 오르테가 씨에게 제출하는 것이므로 행위 주체와 대상자가 다를 때 사용하는 목적격대명사 (B) her가 정답입니다.

오답 (A) she: 전치사의 목적어 역할을 할 수 없는 주격대명사이므로 오답입니다.
(C) hers: 전치사의 목적어 역할은 할 수 있지만, '그녀의 것'을 의미하므로 제출물을 받는 사람을 나타내야 하는 빈칸에 어울리지 않는 오답입니다.
(D) herself: 전치사의 목적어 역할은 할 수 있지만, 행위 주체와 대상자가 동일인일 때 사용하는 재귀대명사이므로 오답입니다.

어휘 **instruct A to do:** A에게 ~하도록 지시하다[안내하다/설명하다] **submit** ~을 제출하다 **complete** ~을 완료하다 **directly** 직접, 곧장

17.
정답 (A)

해석 비록 그 시제품 디자인이 여전히 여러 결함을 포함하고 있기는 하지만, 그것이 시연 시간에 참석한 모든 사람에게 깊은 인상을 남겼다.

해설 사람들에게 깊은 인상을 남긴 것이 주절에 언급된 the prototype design이므로 앞서 언급된 단수 사물명사 자체를 가리킬 때 사용하는 대명사 (A) it이 정답입니다.

오답 (B) they: 복수대명사이므로 오답입니다.
(C) that: 단수대명사이기는 하지만, 앞서 언급된 상황이나 멀리 떨어져 있는 사물을 가리킬 때 사용하므로 오답입니다.
(D) those: 복수대명사이므로 오답입니다.

어휘 **prototype** 시제품, 원형 **contain** ~을 포함하다, ~을 담고 있다 **several** 여럿의, 몇몇의 **flaw** 결함, 흠 **impress** ~에게 깊은 인상을 남기다 **attend** ~에 참석하다 **demonstration** 시연(회) **session** (특정 활동을 위한) 시간

18.
정답 (B)

해석 캘거리에 있는 클락 씨의 새 지역 사무소는 이곳 에드먼튼에 있는 우리 것보다 훨씬 더 작다.

해설 클락 씨의 새 지역 사무소와 대비되는 '우리들의 사무소'가 than 뒤에 비교 대상으로 쓰여야 하며, '우리들의 사무소'는 동일 단어의 반복을 피해 '우리들의 것'을 뜻하는 소유대명사로 대신할 수 있으므로 (B) ours가 정답입니다.

오답 (A) us: 비교 대상이 되는 '우리들의 사무소'를 대신할 수 없는 목적격대명사이므로 오답입니다.
(C) our: 비교 대상이 되는 '우리들의 사무소'를 대신할 수 없는 소유격이므로 오답입니다.
(D) we: 비교 대상이 되는 '우리들의 사무소'를 대신할 수 없는 주격대명사이므로 오답입니다.

어휘 **regional** 지역의, 지방의 **much** (비교급 강조) 훨씬

19.
정답 (B)

해설 루 씨는 그 최종안이 오늘 마감 기한이라는 것을 알고 있는데, 저희가 오늘 아침에 그에게 그에 관한 메시지를 이미 보내 드렸기 때문입니다.

해설 「send + 사람 + 사물」의 4형식 구조에서 간접목적어 자리에 쓰여 받는 사람을 나타낼 대명사가 필요하며, 우리가 '그에게' 보낸 것이므로 목적격대명사 (B) him이 정답입니다.

오답 (A) he: 간접목적어 자리에 쓰일 수 없는 주격대명사이므로 오답입니다.
(C) his: 간접목적어 자리에 쓰일 수 없는 소유격 또는 소유대명사(그의 것)이므로 오답입니다.
(D) himself: 행위 주체와 대상자가 동일일 때 사용하는 재귀대명사이므로 오답입니다.

어휘 **be aware that** ~라는 것을 알고 있다 **draft** 초안, 원고 **due** ~가 기한인

20.
정답 (A)

해석 무 유제품 주식회사의 직원들은 자신들의 성과뿐만 아니라 그들의 동료 직원들의 그것도 평가하도록 요청 받았다.

해설 전치사 of의 목적어인 명사 colleagues 앞에 명사를 수식할 단어가 쓰여야 하므로 이 역할이 가능한 소유격 (A) their가 정답입니다.

오답 (B) theirs: 명사를 수식할 수 없는 소유대명사(그들의 것)이므로 오답입니다.
(C) them: 명사를 수식할 수 없는 목적격대명사(그들을/에게)이므로 오답입니다.
(D) they: 명사를 수식할 수 없는 주격대명사(그들은/이)이므로 오답입니다.

어휘 **be asked to do** ~하도록 요청 받다 **evaluate** ~을 평가하다 **performance** 성과, 실적, 수행 (능력), 공연, 연주(회) **as well as** ~뿐만 아니라 도 **colleague** 동료 (직원)

DAY 3 동사의 종류 및 시제

PRACTICE

1. comply   2. cautiously   3. beneficial
4. attend   5. will hold   6. had warned

1.
정답 comply
해석 모든 직원은 개정된 직장 내 안전 규정을 준수해야 합니다.
해설 빈칸 앞에 조동사가 위치해 있으므로, 해당 빈칸은 동사 자리에 해당합니다. comply는 1형식 자동사이기 때문에 뒤에 명사나 목적어가 바로 올 수 없으며, 전치사 with와 함께 '~을 따르다, 준수하다'라는 의미를 나타냅니다. 따라서 정답은 comply입니다.
어휘 comply (with) ~을 따르다, 준수하다 observe 관찰하다, 준수하다 workplace safety 직장 내 안전 regulation 규정

2.
정답 cautiously
해석 기술자는 시스템에서 잠재적인 고장을 감지한 후 조심스럽게 작업을 진행했습니다.
해설 proceed는 목적어 없이도 쓰일 수 있는 자동사이므로, 그 뒤에는 명사가 아닌 부사가 위치해야 합니다. 따라서 부사 cautiously가 정답입니다.
어휘 proceed 진행하다 cautiously 조심스럽게 malfunction 고장 detect 감지하다, 발견하다

3.
정답 beneficial
해석 그 회사는 유연한 근무 형태가 생산성에 도움이 된다고 생각합니다.
해설 빈칸 앞 동사 considers가 있으므로 동사 benefit은 답이 될 수 없습니다. consider은 5형식 타동사이며 「consider + 목적어 + 형용사」 구조로 쓰이므로 형용사 beneficial이 정답입니다.
어휘 consider ~라고 여기다, 간주하다 beneficial 유익한, 도움이 되는

4.
정답 attend
해석 그 회사는 모든 직원들이 안전 교육에 참석하게 했다.
해설 사역동사 make는 「사역동사 + 목적어 + 동사원형」의 구조로 쓰이므로 동사원형인 attend가 정답입니다.
어휘 make ~하게 만들다 employee 직원 safety training 안전 교육

5.
정답 will hold
해석 이사회는 전략기획 워크숍을 다음 분기 초에 열 것이다.
해설 문장 맨 뒤에 위치한 early next quarter라는 미래 시간을 나타내는 부사구가 있으므로 동사 또한 미래시제로 쓰여야 합니다. 따라서 정답은 will hold입니다.
어휘 board of directors 이사회 hold 열다, 가지다, 개최하다 strategic 전략적인 planning 계획, 기획 quarter 분기

6.
정답 had warned
해석 스웬 씨는 정전이 발생하기 전에 잠재적인 시스템 고장에 대해 경고했습니다.
해설 문장 맨 뒤에 위치한 부사절 before the outage occurred에 시제가 과거시제이고, 문맥상 그 과거시제보다 더 이전에 스웬 씨가 했던 동작을 나타내는 시제가 쓰여야 하므로 과거완료시제 동사가 필요합니다. 따라서 정답은 had warned입니다.
어휘 warn about ~에 대해 경고하다 potential 잠재적인 failure 고장, 기능 부전 outage 정전, 기능 중단 occur 발생하다

실전 TEST

1. (A)	2. (B)	3. (A)	4. (C)	5. (B)
6. (A)	7. (C)	8. (D)	9. (D)	10. (C)
11. (A)	12. (D)	13. (D)	14. (B)	15. (D)
16. (C)	17. (C)	18. (D)	19. (C)	20. (C)

1.
정답 (A)
해석 월시 씨가 데넘 스트리트에 있는 주택에 관심을 계속 갖고 있기는 하지만, 그것을 구매하기를 주저하는 것 같다.
해설 빈칸 바로 뒤에 형용사 hesitant가 있으므로 형용사를 보어로 취하는 2형식 동사가 필요합니다. 따라서 선택지 중에 '~한 것 같다'를 뜻하는 (A) seems가 정답입니다.
오답 (B) meets: 형용사 보어를 취하는 2형식 동사가 아니므로 오답입니다.
    (C) applies: 형용사 보어를 취하는 2형식 동사가 아니므로 오답입니다.
    (D) goes: 토익에서는 주로 형용사 보어를 취하지 않는 1형식 자동사로 쓰이므로 오답입니다.
어휘 although 비록 ~이기는 하지만 be interested in ~에 관심이 있다 hesitant to do ~하기를 주저하는, 망설이는 seem + 형용사: ~한 것 같다 apply 신청하다, 지원하다

2.
정답 (B)

해석 밀글렌 공공 도서관의 모든 회원카드는 발급일로부터 2년간 유효합니다.

해설 빈칸 바로 뒤에 형용사 valid가 있으므로 형용사를 보어로 취하는 2형식 동사인 (B) remain이 정답입니다.

오답 (A) send: 목적어를 취하는 3형식 또는 4형식 동사이므로 오답입니다.
(C) achieve: 목적어를 취하는 3형식 동사이므로 오답입니다.
(D) provide: 목적어를 취하는 3형식 동사이므로 오답입니다.

어휘 valid 유효한 issuing date 발급일 remain + 형용사: 계속 ~한 상태이다, ~한 상태로 유지되다 achieve ~을 달성하다, 이루다 provide ~을 제공하다

3.
정답 (A)

해석 수개월 동안의 협의 끝에, 제니스타 사는 로퍼 앤 코 사와 합의에 이르렀다.

해설 빈칸 뒤에 목적어 an agreement가 쓰여 있으므로 목적어를 취하는 타동사가 필요하며, an agreement와 어울려 '합의에 이르다'라는 의미를 나타내는 타동사 reach의 과거분사인 (A) reached가 정답입니다.

오답 (B) talked: 목적어를 취할 수 없는 자동사 talk의 과거분사이므로 오답입니다.
(C) experienced: 목적어를 취할 수 있는 타동사이지만 agreement와 의미가 맞지 않으므로 오답입니다.
(D) decided: 목적어를 취할 수 있는 타동사이지만 agreement와 의미가 맞지 않으므로 오답입니다.

어휘 negotiation 협의, 협상 agreement 합의, 동의 reach ~에 이르다, 다다르다 experience v. ~을 경험하다, 겪다 decide ~을 결정하다

4.
정답 (C)

해석 NCH 그룹은 주요 기차역과 가까운 곳에 편리하게 위치하는 여러 새 고급 호텔을 개장할 것이다.

해설 빈칸 뒤에 목적어 several new luxury hotels가 있으므로 목적어를 취할 수 있는 타동사 중에서 의미가 적절한 것을 찾아야 합니다. 목적어 several new luxury hotels에 대해 취해질 행위로는 '새 호텔들을 개장하다'라는 의미가 자연스러우므로 '~을 개장하다, 열다'를 뜻하는 타동사 (C) open이 정답입니다.

오답 (A) notice: 타동사이지만 의미가 맞지 않으므로 오답입니다.
(B) invite: 타동사이지만 의미가 맞지 않으므로 오답입니다.
(D) enter: 자동사 및 타동사이며 의미가 맞지 않으므로 오답입니다.

어휘 several 여럿의, 몇몇의 conveniently 편리하게 be located 위치해 있다 notice v. ~을 알아차리다 invite ~을 초대하다, ~에게 요청하다 enter ~에 들어가다, 참가하다

5.
정답 (B)

해석 레스토랑 매니저는 좋지 못한 서비스에 대해 사과하기 위해 리치 씨에게 무료 식사 쿠폰을 제공했다.

해설 빈칸 뒤에 두 개의 목적어 Ms. Ritchie와 a free meal voucher가 나란히 위치해 있습니다. 따라서 목적어를 두 개 취할 수 있는 4형식 수여동사가 필요하므로 '~에게 …을 제공하다'를 의미하는 (B) offered가 정답입니다.

오답 (A) traveled: 목적어를 취할 수 없는 자동사이므로 오답입니다.
(C) told: 목적어를 두 개 취할 수 있는 동사이기는 하지만 meal voucher와 의미가 맞지 않으므로 오답입니다.
(D) asked: 목적어를 두 개 취할 수 있는 동사이기는 하지만 meal voucher와 의미가 맞지 않으므로 오답입니다.

어휘 free 무료의 voucher 쿠폰, 상품권 apologize for ~에 대해 사과하다 poor 좋지 못한, 형편 없는 travel 여행하다, 이동하다 offer A B: A에게 B를 제공하다

6.
정답 (A)

해석 모든 임시직 직원들은 반드시 인사부장에게 주간 업무 보고서를 보내야 합니다.

해설 빈칸 뒤에 두 개의 목적어 the head of the personnel department와 a weekly work report가 나란히 위치해 있습니다. 따라서 목적어를 두 개 취할 수 있는 4형식 수여동사인 (A) send가 정답입니다.

오답 (B) attend: 두 개의 목적어를 취하지 않는 타동사이므로 오답입니다.
(C) review: 두 개의 목적어를 취하지 않는 타동사이므로 오답입니다.
(D) arrive: 목적어를 취할 수 없는 자동사이므로 오답입니다.

어휘 temporary 임시의, 일시적인 head 장, 책임자 personnel department 인사부 weekly 주간의, 매주의 send A B: A에게 B를 보내다 attend ~에 참석하다 review ~을 검토하다, 살펴보다 arrive 도착하다

7.
정답 (C)

해석 마케팅팀에서 우리에게 시장 설문조사 완료 마감기한이 일주일 정도 연장될 것이라고 알려주었다.

정답 및 해설 **127**

해설 빈칸 뒤에 「목적어 + that + 전달 내용」 구조가 이어져 있으므로 이 구조와 어울려 쓰이는 타동사 (C) informed가 정답입니다.
오답 (A) required: that절이 목적어로서 동사 바로 뒤에 이어지는 구조로 쓰이므로 오답입니다.
(B) announced: that절이 목적어로서 동사 바로 뒤에 이어지는 구조로 쓰이므로 오답입니다.
(D) released: 목적어를 하나만 가지므로 오답입니다.
어휘 **inform A that**: A에게 ~라고 알리다 **deadline** 마감기한 **complete** ~을 완료하다 **survey** 설문조사(지) **extend** ~을 연장하다 **by** (차이) ~정도, 만큼 **require** ~을 요구하다 **announce** ~을 알리다 **release** ~을 출시하다, 발표하다

8.
정답 (D)
해석 리버사이드 시장은 모든 지역 주민들에게 시청에서 열리는 공청회에 참석하도록 권고했다.
해설 빈칸 뒤에 「목적어 + to부정사」 구조가 이어져 있으므로 이 구조와 어울리는 타동사 (D) encouraged가 정답입니다.
오답 (A) agreed: 「agree to do」 구조로 쓰이는 동사이므로 오답입니다.
(B) purchased: 「목적어 + to부정사」 구조와 함께 사용하지 않는 타동사이므로 오답입니다.
(C) discussed: 「목적어 + to부정사」 구조와 함께 사용하지 않는 자동사 및 타동사이므로 오답입니다.
어휘 **mayor** 시장 **encourage A to do**: A에게 ~하도록 권하다, 장려하다 **local** 지역의, 현지의 **resident** 주민 **attend** ~에 참석하다 **public hearing** 공청회 **agree** 동의하다 **purchase** ~을 구입하다 **discuss** ~을 논의하다, 이야기하다

9.
정답 (D)
해석 재러드 사는 기업체 소유주들이 잠재 고객들의 변화하는 필요를 충족시키도록 돕는 서비스를 개발합니다.
해설 빈칸 뒤에 목적어 the changing needs가 있으므로 목적어 needs와 어울리는 동사를 찾아야 합니다. 여기서 the changing needs는 변화하는 잠재 고객들의 필요를 의미하므로 그 필요를 충족시킨다는 뜻이 되어야 자연스럽습니다. 따라서 '~을 충족하다'를 의미하는 (D) meet가 정답입니다.
오답 (A) apply: 타동사와 자동사로 모두 쓰이는데, 타동사일 때 needs와 의미가 맞지 않으므로 오답입니다.
(B) wait: 목적어를 취하지 않는 자동사이므로 오답입니다.
(C) seem: 주격 보어를 취하는 2형식 자동사이므로 오답입니다.
어휘 **develop** ~을 개발하다 **help A do**: A가 ~하도록 돕다 **owner** 소유주 **potential** 잠재적인 **apply** 지원하다, 신청하다, ~을 적용하다 **seem** ~한 것 같다 **meet** (조건 등) ~을 충족하다

10.
정답 (C)
해석 여러분께서 특정 건물과 명소에 관해 더 많은 정보를 원하시는지를 저희 투어 가이드들에게 알려 주시기 바랍니다.
해설 빈칸 뒤에 「목적어 + 동사원형」 구조가 이어져 있으므로 이 구조와 어울리는 사역동사 (C) let이 정답입니다.
오답 (A) join: 「목적어 + 동사원형」 구조와 어울려 쓰이지 않는 타동사이므로 오답입니다.
(B) visit: 「목적어 + 동사원형」 구조와 어울려 쓰이지 않는 타동사이므로 오답입니다.
(D) allow: 「목적어 + to부정사」 구조와 어울려 쓰이는 타동사이므로 오답입니다.
어휘 **let A know B**: A에게 B를 알리다 **whether** ~인지 (아닌지) **would like** ~을 원하다 **certain** 특정한, 일정한 **landmark** 명소, 인기 장소 **join** ~에 합류하다, 가입하다, 함께하다 **allow** ~을 허용하다, ~하게 해주다

11.
정답 (A)
해석 레스토랑 구내에 조경 작업이 이뤄져 있어서, 대부분의 우리 손님들이 일반적으로 바깥의 테라스 구역에 앉는 것을 택합니다.
해설 선택지가 모두 능동태 동사이고 시제만 다르므로 시제 단서를 찾아야 합니다. 빈칸 앞에 위치한 부사 typically는 '일반적으로, 보통'이라는 의미로 현재시제 동사와 어울리는 부사입니다. 또한 빈칸 앞에 위치한 주절의 주어 most of our diners는 복수 명사구이므로 이 명사구와 수 일치되는 현재시제 복수 동사 형태인 (A) choose가 정답입니다.
오답 (B) chose: 과거시제 동사이므로 typically와 어울리지 않는 오답입니다.
(C) will have chosen: 미래완료시제 동사이므로 typically와 어울리지 않는 오답입니다.
(D) chooses: 현재시제 동사이지만 3인칭 단수 주어와 수 일치되는 형태이므로 오답입니다.
어휘 **now that** (이제) ~이므로 **grounds** 부지, 구내 **landscape** ~에 조경 작업을 하다 **diner** 식사 손님 **typically** 일반적으로, 보통 **choose to do** ~하기로 결정하다, 선택하다 **terrace** 테라스

12.
정답 (D)
해석 어제 있었던 회의에서, 벤틀리 사의 대표이사가 던레비 케이터링 사와의 계약서에 서명했다.

해설 선택지가 모두 능동태 동사이고 시제만 다르므로 시제 단서를 찾아야 합니다. 문장 시작 부분에 At yesterday's meeting 이라는 과거 시간 표현이 쓰여 있으므로 과거시제인 (D) signed가 정답입니다.

오답 (A) sign: 현재시제 동사이므로 과거 시간 표현과 맞지 않는 오답입니다.
(B) will sign: 미래시제 동사이므로 과거 시간 표현과 맞지 않는 오답입니다.
(C) have signed: 현재완료시제 동사이므로 특정 과거 시간 표현과 맞지 않는 오답입니다.

어휘 sign a contract 계약(서)에 서명하다

13.
정답 (D)

해설 회사 인트라넷 및 데이터 파일이 유지 관리 작업으로 인해 내일까지 이용할 수 없을 것이다.

해설 선택지가 모두 능동태 동사이고 시제만 다르므로 시제 단서를 찾아야 합니다. 빈칸 뒤에 until tomorrow라는 미래 시간 표현이 있으므로 미래시제 (D) will be가 정답입니다.

오답 (A) are being: 현재진행시제 동사이므로 오답입니다.
(B) were: 과거시제 동사이므로 미래 시간 표현과 맞지 않는 오답입니다.
(C) had been: 과거완료시제 동사이므로 미래 시간 표현과 맞지 않는 오답입니다.

어휘 access to ~의 이용, ~에 대한 접근 unavailable 이용할 수 없는 until (지속) ~까지 due to ~로 인해 maintenance 유지 관리, 시설 보수

14.
정답 (B)

해설 돼지고기에 알레르기가 있는 사람들을 위해, 많은 레스토랑들이 지난 10년 동안 더 많은 채식 음식들을 소개해 왔다.

해설 빈칸 앞에 For 전치사구와 주어가 있고 빈칸 뒤로 명사 구와 in 전치사구가 있으므로 빈칸은 문장의 동사 자리입니다. 또한 in the last ten years라는 과거에서 현재에 이르는 기간 표현과 어울리려면 현재완료시제 동사가 쓰여야 하므로 (B) have introduced가 정답입니다.

오답 (A) will introduce: 미래시제 동사이므로 과거에서 현재에 이르는 기간 표현과 어울리지 않는 오답입니다.
(C) will have introduced: 미래완료시제 동사이므로 과거에서 현재에 이르는 기간 표현과 어울리지 않는 오답입니다.
(D) to introduce: 동사의 형태가 아니므로 동사가 필요한 빈칸에 맞지 않는 오답입니다.

어휘 those who ~하는 사람들 be allergic to ~에 알레르기가 있다 introduce ~을 소개하다, 도입하다

15.
정답 (D)

해설 우리의 캠든 지점 영업사원들이 우리가 예상했던 것보다 6일 더 빨리 월간 목표에 도달했다.

해설 비교 대상을 나타낼 때 사용하는 than 뒤로 주어 we와 빈칸만 위치한 구조입니다. we가 예상하는 행위의 주체이므로 능동태 동사가 필요하며, 예상하는 일을 한 시점은 주절에 과거시제로 쓰여 있는 reached보다 더 이전 시점의 일이어야 합니다. 따라서 과거시제보다 더 이전의 과거를 나타낼 때 사용하는 과거완료시제 (D) had expected가 정답입니다.

오답 (A) expect: 현재시제 동사이므로 시점이 맞지 않는 오답입니다.
(B) are expecting: 현재진행시제 동사이므로 시점이 맞지 않는 오답입니다.
(C) were expected: 수동태 동사이므로 행위 주체인 we와 어울리지 않는 오답입니다.

어휘 salespeople 영업사원들 branch 지점, 지사 reach ~에 도달하다, 이르다 monthly 월간의, 달마다의 expect ~을 예상하다, 기대하다

16.
정답 (C)

해설 러시든 씨가 본사에서 새로운 관리자 직책을 시작할 때쯤에 인사팀이 그녀를 위한 새 사무실을 준비했었다.

해설 빈칸이 속한 주절에서 빈칸 앞뒤로 주어와 목적어, 그리고 for 전치사구만 있으므로 빈칸은 주절의 동사 자리입니다. 또한 By the time이 이끄는 절의 동사가 시제(began)일 때, 주절의 동사는 과거완료시제를 사용하므로 (C) had prepared가 정답입니다.

오답 (A) prepared: 과거시제 동사이며, By the time이 이끄는 절의 동사가 과거시제일 때 사용하는 주절의 동사 시제로 맞지 않는 오답입니다.
(B) preparing: 동사의 형태가 아니므로 주절의 동사 자리인 빈칸에 맞지 않는 오답입니다.
(D) will have prepared: By the time이 이끄는 절의 동사가 현재시제일 때 주절에 사용하는 미래완료시제이므로 오답입니다.

어휘 by the time ~할 때쯤 management role 관리자 직책 headquarters 본사 personnel team 인사팀 prepare A for B: B를 위해 A를 준비하다

17.
정답 (C)

해설 저희 글로벌 피트니스는 귀하께서 지난 18개월 동안 저희 주중 요가 강좌를 즐기오신 것에 대해 감사 드립니다.

해설 for가 이끄는 기간 전치사구는 완료시제와 어울리므로 현재 완료진행시제인 (C) have enjoyed와 과거완료시제인

(D) had enjoyed 중에서 하나를 골라야 합니다. 그런데 주절에서 현재시제 동사 appreciate가 사용되므로 과거에서 현재까지의 기간을 나타낼 수 있는 현재완료시제 (C) have enjoyed가 정답입니다.

오답 (A) enjoyed: 과거시제 동사이므로 현재가 포함된 기간을 나타내지 못하는 오답입니다.
(B) enjoying: 동사의 형태가 아니므로 동사 자리인 빈칸에 맞지 않는 오답입니다.
(D) had enjoyed: 과거와 그보다 더 이전 사이의 기간을 나타내는 과거완료시제이므로 오답입니다.

어휘 appreciate that ~한 것에 대해 감사하다 past 지난, 과거의

18.
정답 (D)
해석 옴니 텔레콤 사의 본사는 10년 동안 신입사원들이 고객 불만을 처리하는 것을 돕도록 경험 많은 직원들을 배정해 오고 있다.
해설 선택지가 모두 동사의 형태이고 시제가 다르므로 시제 단서부터 찾아야 합니다. 문장 마지막에 위치한 기간을 나타내는 for 전치사구는 현재완료시제와 어울리며, 빈칸 뒤에 위치한 experienced employees를 목적어로 취할 수 있는 능동태인 (D) has assigned가 정답입니다.

오답 (A) assigns: 현재시제 동사이므로 기간을 나타내는 for 전치사구와 어울리지 않는 오답입니다.
(B) is assigning: 현재진행시제 동사이므로 기간을 나타내는 for 전치사구와 어울리지 않는 오답입니다.
(C) has been assigned: 현재완료시제 동사이지만 빈칸 뒤에 위치한 목적어(명사구)를 취할 수 없는 수동태이므로 오답입니다.

어휘 head office 본사 experienced 경험 많은 assist A in -ing: A가 ~하는 데 도움을 주다 new recruits 신입 사원 handle ~을 처리하다, 다루다 complaint 불만, 불평 assign ~을 배정하다, 할당하다

19.
정답 (C)
해석 유가가 지난 6개월에 걸쳐 상승해 왔지만, 올 연말쯤에 가까워질수록 안정될 것으로 예상된다.
해설 우선, 빈칸이 속한 주절에서 주어와 빈칸 뒤로 over 전치사구만 있으므로 빈칸은 주절의 동사 자리입니다. 또한 과거에서 현재까지의 기간을 나타내는 over 전치사구는 현재완료시제와 어울리므로 (C) have increased가 정답입니다.

오답 (A) increase: 현재시제 동사이므로 문장의 over 전치사구와 어울리지 않는 오답입니다.
(B) increasing: 동사의 형태가 아니므로 주절의 동사 자리인 빈칸에 맞지 않는 오답입니다.
(D) will increase: 미래시제 동사이므로 문장의 over 전치사구와 어울리지 않는 오답입니다.

어휘 over ~ 동안에 걸쳐 past 지난, 과거의 be expected to do ~할 것으로 예상되다 stabilize 안정화되다 towards + 시점: ~쯤에 가까워질수록 increase 인상되다, 증가되다

20.
정답 (C)
해석 최근, 현재의 조세 제도에 급격한 변화를 주기 위해 정부 위원회가 구성되었다.
해설 문장 시작 부분에 쓰여 있는 Recently라는 부사는 과거 또는 현재완료시제와 어울립니다. 또한 '위원회'를 뜻하는 주어 a government committee는 사람에 의해 만들어지는 대상이므로 create가 수동태로 쓰여야 합니다. 따라서 수동태 현재완료시제 동사인 (C) has been created가 정답입니다.

오답 (A) is created: Recently와 어울리지 않는 현재시제 수동태이므로 오답입니다.
(B) will create: Recently와 어울리지 않는 미래시제 동사이며 능동태이므로 오답입니다.
(D) is creating: Recently와 어울리지 않는 현재진행시제 동사이며 능동태이므로 오답입니다.

어휘 recently 최근에 committee 위원회 make a modification 변경하다, 수정하다 dramatic 급격한 current 현재의 tax system 조세 제도 create ~을 만들다

DAY 4 동사의 특성

PRACTICE

1. implemented   2. being inspected   3. are advised
4. was considered   5. be escorted   6. are held

1.
정답 implemented
해석 새로운 마케팅 전략이 모든 지역에 걸쳐 시행되었다.
해설 빈칸 앞 be 동사가 있고 빈칸 뒤에는 목적어가 없고 전치사구가 있으므로 빈칸은 수동태 자리입니다. 자동사 worked는 수동태로 쓰일 수 없으므로 implemented가 정답입니다.
어휘 strategy 전략 implement 시행되다 region 지역

2.
정답 being inspected
해석 B동의 엘리베이터는 최신 안전 기준을 충족하는지 확인하기 위해 점검 받고 있다.

해설 inspecting은 능동 형태로, 주어가 직접 점검하는 상황을 나타냅니다. 그러나 엘리베이터는 스스로 점검할 수 없기 때문에, 외부에 의해 점검받는다는 수동의 의미를 가진 being inspected가 정답입니다.

어휘 inspect 점검하다 ensure 보장하다, 확인하다 meet (기준 등을) 충족하다

3.

정답 are advised

해석 모든 승객은 출발 최소 두 시간 전에 공항에 도착하도록 권고된다.

해설 advise는 타동사이므로 목적어가 필요합니다. 이 문장에서는 승객들이 권고를 받는 대상이므로 수동태인 are advised가 정답입니다.

어휘 advise 권고하다, 조언하다 at least 최소한 departure 출발

4.

정답 was considered

해석 그 신입 직원은 매우 의욕적이고 준비가 잘 되어 있다고 여겨졌다.

해설 타동사 consider 뒤에 목적어가 위치하지 않고, 문맥상 주어인 The new employee는 consider의 대상이므로 수동태인 was considered가 정답입니다.

어휘 highly 매우 well-prepared 준비가 잘 된

5.

정답 be escorted

해석 제한 구역에 들어가는 사람은 모두 보안 요원에게 동행 되어야 합니다.

해설 빈칸 앞 조동사 must 뒤에는 동사원형이 와야 합니다. 또한 해석상 사람들이 요원에게 동행 되어야 한다는 의미로 수동태 형태인 be escorted가 정답입니다.

어휘 restricted 제한된 security personnel 보안 요원

6.

정답 are held

해석 팜파노 베이커리의 킹 케이크 판촉 행사는 3개월마다 개최된다.

해설 타동사 hold 뒤에 목적어가 위치하지 않고, 문맥상 주어인 Promotional events는 타동사 hold(개최하다)의 대상에 해당하므로 동사는 수동태가 되어야 합니다. 따라서 정답은 are held입니다.

어휘 promotional event 판촉 행사 hold 개최하다, (행사 등을) 열다

실전 TEST

1. (C)	2. (A)	3. (A)	4. (A)	5. (C)
6. (D)	7. (D)	8. (B)	9. (B)	10. (C)
11. (D)	12. (A)	13. (C)	14. (D)	15. (C)
16. (D)	17. (B)	18. (B)	19. (A)	20. (C)

1.

정답 (C)

해석 애디슨 초프라 교수는 유전 공학 분야의 선도적인 과학자들에 의해 매우 존경받고 있다.

해설 be동사 뒤에서 부사(highly)의 수식을 받을 수 있는 것은 현재분사 또는 과거분사입니다. 그런데 빈칸 뒤에 목적어 없이 by 전치사구만 쓰여 있어 수동태 동사를 구성하는 과거분사가 필요하다는 것을 알 수 있으므로 (C) regarded가 정답입니다. highly regarded를 하나의 숙어로 기억해두면 좋습니다.

오답 (A) regard: 명사 또는 동사원형인데, 명사일 경우에 부사의 수식을 받을 수 없고, 동사일 경우에 be동사 is 뒤에 위치할 수 없어 오답입니다.

(B) regarding: is 뒤에 위치하면 능동태 현재진행시제를 구성하게 되는데, regard가 타동사여서 목적어를 필요로 하므로 빈칸 뒤에 목적어가 쓰여 있지 않는 이 문장에 맞지 않는 오답입니다. 참고로, regarding은 전치사의 형태이기도 합니다.

(D) regards: 복수 명사 또는 3인칭 단수 주어와 어울리는 동사의 형태인데, 명사일 경우 부사의 수식을 받을 수 없고, 동사일 경우에 be동사 is 뒤에 위치할 수 없어 오답입니다.

어휘 highly regarded 매우 존경받는, 높이 평가 받는 leading 선도적인, 앞서 가는 field 분야 genetic engineering 유전 공학 regard n. 관련, 고려, 존중, 주목 v. ~을 존경하다, (높이) 평가하다 regarding ~와 관련해

2.

정답 (A)

해석 작업자들이 구내식당 개조 공사를 완료하는 동안 직원들은 점심 식사를 할 대체 장소를 찾아야 합니다.

해설 접속사 while 뒤로 주어 the workers와 빈칸, 그리고 명사구만 쓰여 있으므로 빈칸에 while절의 동사가 쓰여야 하며, 빈칸 뒤에 위치한 명사구를 목적어로 취해야 하므로 능동태 동사인 (A) complete가 정답입니다.

오답 (B) completing: 동명사 또는 현재분사형이므로 while절의 동사 자리인 빈칸에 쓰일 수 없는 오답입니다.

(C) to complete: 동사의 형태가 아니므로 while절의 동사 자리인 빈칸에 쓰일 수 없는 오답입니다.

(D) are completed: 수동태 동사이므로 빈칸 뒤에 위치한

정답 및 해설 131

명사구를 목적어로 취할 수 없는 오답입니다.

어휘 alternative 대체의, 대안의 while ~하는 동안, ~인 반면 cafeteria 구내식당 renovation 개조 (공사), 보수 (공사) complete ~을 완료하다

3.
정답 (A)

해석 애거트 일렉트로닉스 사가 포틀랜드에서 곧 열리는 기술 컨벤션에서 자사의 새 휴대전화 제품 사용법을 시연할 것이다.

해설 조동사 다음은 동사원형이 필요한 자리입니다. 그런데 빈칸 뒤에 명사구(its new cell phone model)가 있으므로 이 명사구를 목적어로 취할 수 있는 능동태 동사원형인 (A) demonstrate이 정답입니다.

오답 (B) demonstrates: 3인칭 단수 주어와 수 일치되는 동사 형태이므로 오답입니다.
(C) demonstrating: 동사의 형태가 아니므로 오답입니다.
(D) be demonstrated: 빈칸 뒤에 위치한 명사구를 목적어로 취할 수 없는 수동태이므로 오답입니다.

어휘 upcoming 곧 있을, 다가오는 demonstrate ~의 사용법을 시연하다, 시범 보이다

4.
정답 (A)

해석 멀티코 엔터프라이즈 사는 향후 몇 년에 걸쳐 해외 시장으로의 지속적인 확장을 예상하고 있다.

해설 주어와 빈칸 뒤로 명사구와 전치사구들만 있으므로 빈칸은 문장의 동사 자리이며, 빈칸 바로 뒤에 위치한 명사구를 목적어로 취해야 하므로 능동태 동사인 (A) anticipates가 정답입니다.

오답 (B) anticipating: 동사의 형태가 아니므로 문장의 동사 자리인 빈칸에 쓰일 수 없는 오답입니다.
(C) to anticipate: 동사의 형태가 아니므로 문장의 동사 자리인 빈칸에 쓰일 수 없는 오답입니다.
(D) is anticipated: 수동태 동사이므로 빈칸 뒤에 위치한 명사구를 목적어로 취할 수 없는 오답입니다.

어휘 steady 지속적인, 꾸준한 growth 성장 into (이동 방향) ~ 안으로, 속으로 (변화 등) ~로, ~의 상태로 overseas ad. 해외에 a. 해외의 over ~ 동안에 걸쳐 anticipate ~을 예상하다, 기대하다

5.
정답 (C)

해석 그 영업부장은 새 마케팅 캠페인 이후로 최근의 매출 급등에 대해 놀라워하고 있다.

해설 빈칸 앞에 위치한 is surprised는 전치사 at과 결합해 놀라움의 대상을 나타내므로 (C) at이 정답입니다.

오답 (A) into: is surprised와 결합하는 전치사가 아니므로 오답입니다.

(B) over: is surprised와 결합하는 전치사가 아니므로 오답입니다.
(D) from: is surprised와 결합하는 전치사가 아니므로 오답입니다.

어휘 sales 영업, 매출, 판매(량) be surprised at ~에 대해 놀라워하다 recent 최근의 surge in ~의 급등

6.
정답 (D)

해석 래플스 골프 리조트의 안내 책자에 실린 모든 객실에는 주방용품이 완전히 갖춰져 있다.

해설 빈칸 앞에 위치한 are equipped는 전치사 with와 결합해 갖춰진 물품을 나타내므로 (D) with가 정답입니다.

오답 (A) at: are equipped와 결합하는 전치사가 아니므로 오답입니다.
(B) to: are equipped와 결합하는 전치사가 아니므로 오답입니다.
(C) in: are equipped와 결합하는 전치사가 아니므로 오답입니다.

어휘 listed in ~에 수록된, 나열된 brochure 안내 책자, 소책자 be equipped with A: A가 갖춰져 있다, A가 구비되어 있다 fully 완전히, 전부, 최대로 kitchen utensils 주방용품

7.
정답 (D)

해석 6개월 이상의 구독 신청에 대한 할인은 오직 저희 소식지 우편 발송 대상자 명단에 포함된 분들에게만 제공됩니다.

해설 be동사 are와 전치사 to 사이에 빈칸이 있으므로 목적어를 필요로 하는 타동사 offer의 과거분사가 빈칸에 들어가 수동태 동사를 구성해야 알맞은 구조가 됩니다. 따라서 (D) offered가 정답입니다.

오답 (A) to offer: 능동태 to부정사여서 여전히 목적어를 필요로 하므로 오답입니다.
(B) offering: 현재분사로서 are와 함께 능동태 현재진행시제를 구성하게 되는데, 빈칸 뒤에 목적어가 나타나 있지 않으므로 빈칸에 맞지 않는 오답입니다.
(C) offer: 동사원형이므로 be동사 are 뒤에 나란히 위치할 수 없는 오답입니다.

어휘 subscription 구독 신청, 서비스 가입 or more (숫자 표현 뒤에서) ~ 이상 those (수식어구와 함께) ~하는 사람들 mailing list 우편물 발송 대상자 명단 offer A to B: A를 B에게 제공하다

8.
정답 (B)

해석 유급 휴가 및 현금 보너스가 10월에 가장 뛰어난 출근 기록을

보유한 직원들에게 주어질 것이다.

해설 빈칸 앞에는 사물 주어(Paid vacations and cash bonuses)가, 빈칸 뒤에는 대상자를 나타내는 to 전치사구가 쓰여 있습니다. 이는 수여동사가 수동태로 쓰일 때 어울리는 구조이므로 수여동사의 과거분사인 (B) awarded가 정답입니다.

오답 (A) assumed: 빈칸 앞뒤 구조에 어울리는 수여동사의 과거분사가 아니므로 오답입니다.
(C) agreed: 빈칸 앞뒤 구조에 어울리는 수여동사의 과거분사가 아니므로 오답입니다.
(D) accepted: 빈칸 앞뒤 구조에 어울리는 수여동사의 과거분사가 아니므로 오답입니다.

어휘 paid vacation 유급 휴가 attendance 출근, 참석(자 수) assume ~라고 생각하다, (책임 등) ~을 맡다 award A to B: A를 B에게 주다, 수여하다 agree 동의하다 accept ~을 받아들이다, 수용하다

9.

정답 (B)

해석 직원 복장 규정에 대한 아르코 정유회사의 새로운 사내 정책은 오직 정규직 직원들에게만 적용된다.

해설 빈칸 앞에는 주어와 for 전치사구가 있고, 빈칸 뒤에는 부사 only와 to 전치사구만 있으므로 빈칸이 문장의 동사 자리임을 알 수 있습니다. 또한 주어 Arko Petroleum Inc.'s new company policy는 3인칭 단수이므로 3인칭 단수 주어와 수일치되는 형태인 (B) applies가 정답입니다.

오답 (A) apply: 3인칭 단수 주어와 수일치되는 형태가 아니므로 오답입니다.
(C) applying: 동사의 형태가 아니므로 문장의 동사 자리인 빈칸에 쓰일 수 없는 오답입니다.
(D) are applied: 3인칭 단수 주어와 수일치되는 형태가 아니므로 오답입니다.

어휘 policy 정책, 방침 dress code 복장 규정 apply (to) (~에) 적용되다

10.

정답 (C)

해석 레아 맥켈란 주방장이 위생 검열 전에 음식 조리대를 청소하도록 주방 직원들에게 요청했다.

해설 선택지가 모두 동사의 형태이므로 수일치와 능/수동, 시제 단서를 통해 알맞은 것을 찾아야 합니다. 빈칸 앞에 위치한 Head Chef Leah McKellan이 3인칭 단수 주어이므로 단수 동사의 형태를 찾아야 하며, 빈칸 뒤에 위치한 명사구를 목적어로 취해야 하므로 능동태여야 합니다. 따라서 이 조건들을 만족하는 (C) has asked가 정답입니다.

오답 (A) ask: 3인칭 단수 주어와 수일치되는 형태가 아니므로 오답입니다.
(B) has been asked: 3인칭 단수 주어와 수일치되는 형태이기는 하지만 수동태이므로 오답입니다.
(D) are asking: 3인칭 단수 주어와 수일치되는 형태가 아니므로 오답입니다.

어휘 ask A to do A에게 ~하도록 요청하다 preparation station 조리대 inspection 점검, 검열

11.

정답 (D)

해석 새로운 마케팅 계획에 대한 여러 제안서가 주말까지 제출되었다.

해설 제안서는 사람에 의해 제출되는 대상이므로 '~을 제출하다'를 뜻하는 타동사 submit이 수동태로 쓰여야 알맞습니다. 그리고 복수명사구인 주어 Several proposals와 수 일치되는 복수동사가 쓰여야 하므로 (D) were submitted가 정답입니다.

오답 (A) was submitted: 수동태이기는 하지만, 단수동사이므로 오답입니다.
(B) is submitting: 능동태이며 단수동사이므로 오답입니다.
(C) has submitted: 능동태이며 단수동사이므로 오답입니다.

어휘 several 여럿의, 몇몇의 proposal 제안(서) initiative n. 계획, 솔선 수범, 진취(성), 주도(권) by (기한) ~까지 submit ~을 제출하다

12.

정답 (A)

해석 재무 제표가 다음 달에 있을 투자자 회의에 앞서 철저히 검토될 것입니다.

해설 재무 제표는 사람에 의해 검토되는 대상이므로 이러한 수동의 의미를 나타낼 수 있도록 과거분사 reviewed와 함께 수동태 동사를 구성할be동사가 필요합니다. 그리고 미래 시점 표현 next month와 어울리는 미래시제여야 하므로 (A) will be가 정답입니다.

오답 (B) were being: 수동태 과거진행시제를 구성하므로 오답입니다.
(C) is: 수동태 현재시제를 구성하므로 오답입니다.
(D) have: 능동태 현재완료시제를 구성하므로 오답입니다.

어휘 financial statements 재무 제표 thoroughly 철저히, 꼼꼼히 review ~을 검토하다, ~을 살펴 보다 investor 투자자

13.

정답 (C)

해석 입고되는 모든 배송품은 펠센 임포츠 사의 재고 관리팀에 의해 도착 즉시 점검된다.

해설 입고되는 배송품은 사람에 의해 점검되는 대상이므로 '~을 점검하다'를 뜻하는 타동사 inspect가 수동태로 쓰여야 알맞습니다. 그리고 복수명사구인 주어 All incoming shipments와 수 일치되는 복수동사가 쓰여야 하므로 (C) are inspected가

정답입니다.
오답 (A) inspects: 능동태이며 단수동사이므로 오답입니다.
(B) is inspected: 수동태이기는 하지만, 단수동사이므로 오답입니다.
(D) was inspecting: 능동태이며 단수동사이므로 오답입니다.
어휘 incoming 입고되는, 들어오는 shipment 배송(품), 선적(품) upon ~ 즉시, ~하자마자 arrival 도착 inventory 재고(품), 재고 조사, 재고 목록 inspect ~을 점검하다, ~을 검사하다

14.
정답 (D)
해석 교육 이수 단위들에 대한 상세 요약본이 다음주 월요일에 모든 신입 사원들에게 배부될 것입니다.
해설 요약본은 사람에 의해 배부되는 대상이므로 '~을 배부하다'를 뜻하는 타동사 distribute이 수동태로 쓰여야 알맞습니다. 그리고 미래 시점 표현 next Monday와 어울리는 미래시제여야 하므로 (D) will be distributed가 정답입니다.
오답 (A) distribute: 능동태 현재시제이므로 오답입니다.
(B) was distributed: 수동태 과거시제이므로 오답입니다.
(C) are distributing: 능동태 현재진행시제이므로 오답입니다.
어휘 detailed 상세한 summary 요약(본) training 교육, 훈련 module (과목 등의) 이수 단위, 기본 단위 distribute ~을 배부하다, ~을 나눠 주다, ~을 유통시키다

15.
정답 (C)
해석 미결 중인 두 계약 모두 예산 제한으로 인해 최종 확정되지 않았다.
해설 계약은 사람에 의해 최종 확정되는 대상이므로 이러한 수동의 의미를 나타낼 수 있도록 과거분사 finalized와 함께 수동태 동사를 구성할 be동사가 필요합니다. 그리고 예산 제한으로 인해 확정되지 못한 상태임을 나타내는 현재완료시제가 알맞으며, 단수대명사 주어 Neither와 어울리는 수동태 단수동사를 구성하는 (C) has been이 정답입니다.
오답 (A) have been: finalized와 함께 수동태 복수동사를 구성하므로 오답입니다.
(B) is being: 수동태 현재진행시제를 구성하므로 확정되지 못한 상태를 나타낼 동사로 어울리지 않는 오답입니다.
(D) are being: finalized와 함께 수동태 복수동사를 구성하므로 오답입니다.
어휘 neither (A nor B): (A도 B도) 둘 다 ~ 않다 pending 미결 중인, 임박한 contract 계약(서) finalize ~을 최종 확정하다 due to ~로 인해, ~ 때문에 budget 예산 restriction 제한, 제약

16.
정답 (D)
해석 켈러 & 로우 사에서 발급한 모든 거래 내역서가 회계 시스템에 지급 처리된 것으로 표시되었다.
해설 주어가 「All of the + 복수명사」일 때 복수로 취급됩니다. 그리고 문맥상 주어인 All of the invoice는 동사 mark의 주체가 아닌 객체이므로는 수동태 복수동사를 구성하는 (D) have been marked가 정답입니다. 참고로, 「All of the + 셀 수 없는 명사」는 단수 취급합니다.
오답 (A) is marked: 수동태 단수동사를 구성하므로 오답입니다.
(B) are marking: 현재진행시제 능동태 복수동사를 구성하므로 오답입니다.
(C) was marked: 수동태 단수동사를 구성하므로 오답입니다.
어휘 invoice 거래 내역서 mark A as B: A를 B라고 표시하다 accounting 회계

17.
정답 (B)
해석 제품 출시 날짜와 관련된 최종 결정이 이사회에 의해 이뤄지고 있다.
해설 단수명사구 The final decision이 문장의 주어이므로 수 일치되는 수동태 단수동사를 구성하는 (B) is being made가 정답입니다.
오답 (A) were made: 수동태 복수동사를 구성하므로 오답입니다.
(C) have made: 능동태 현재완료시제 복수동사를 구성하므로 오답입니다.
(D) makes: 능동태 현재시제 단수동사를 구성하므로 오답입니다.
어휘 decision 결정 regarding ~와 관련된 launch 출시(행사), 공개, 시작 board of directors 이사회

18.
정답 (B)
해석 세 곳의 지역에 대한 분기 영업 보고서들이 어제 온라인상에서 제출되었다.
해설 복수명사구 The quarterly sales reports가 문장의 주어이므로 수 일치되는 수동태 복수동사를 구성하는 (B) were submitted가 정답입니다.
오답 (A) was submitted: 수동태 단수동사를 구성하므로 오답입니다.
(C) has been submitted: 수동태 단수동사를 구성하므로 오답입니다.
(D) submitted: 능동태 과거시제를 구성하므로 오답입니다.
어휘 quarterly 분기의 sales 영업, 판매(량), 매출 region 지역, 지방 submit ~을 제출하다 electronically 온라인으로, 전자식으로

19.

정답 (A)

해석 다넬 카페 지점에 대한 개조 공사 도면이 현재 디자인팀에 의해 수정되고 있습니다.

해설 복수명사구 The renovation plans가 문장의 주어이므로 수 일치되는 수동태 복수동사를 구성하는 (A) are가 정답입니다.

오답 (B) is: being revised와 함께 수동태 단수동사를 구성하므로 오답입니다.
(C) has: being revised와 어울려 적절한 동사의 형태를 구성하는 요소가 아니므로 오답입니다.
(D) be: 조동사 뒤에 위치하거나 「Please + 동사원형」으로 시작하는 명령문을 구성할 때 사용하는 동사원형이므로 오답입니다.

어휘 renovation 개조, 보수 plan 도면, 설계도 branch 지점, 지사 currently 현재 revise ~을 수정하다, ~을 변경하다

20.

정답 (C)

해석 고객 추천 후기 모음이 저희의 웹사이트의 새로운 영역에 게시되었습니다.

해설 단수명사구 A collection이 문장의 주어이므로 수 일치되는 수동태 단수동사를 구성하는 (C) has been posted가 정답입니다.

오답 (A) were posted: 수동태 복수동사를 구성하므로 오답입니다.
(B) are posted: 수동태 복수동사를 구성하므로 오답입니다.
(D) have posted: 능동태 현재완료시제 복수동사를 구성하므로 오답입니다.

어휘 collection 모음, 선정 testimonial 추천서, 추천의 글 section 영역 post 게시하다

DAY 5 동명사 / to부정사

PRACTICE

1. postponing 2. coordinating 3. spending
4. condition   5. to increase   6. to submit

1.

정답 postponing

해석 이 씨는 일정 충돌로 인해 회의를 연기할 것을 제안했다.

해설 suggest는 동명사를 목적어로 취하는 타동사입니다. 그러므로 동명사 postponing이 정답입니다.

어휘 suggest 제안 due to ~때문에 conflict 충돌 postpone 연기하다, 미루다

2.

정답 coordinating

해석 그 팀은 부서 간의 노력을 효율적으로 조율함으로써 성공했다.

해설 전치사 by 뒤에는 동명사가 와야 하므로 coordinating이 정답입니다.

어휘 succeed 성공하다 efficiently 효율적으로 effort 노력

3.

정답 spending

해석 우리는 여행 정책을 수정하여 지출을 줄일 필요가 있다.

해설 reduce는 타동사이므로 뒤에 목적어로 명사가 필요합니다. 따라서 '지출'이라는 의미를 지닌 명사 spending이 정답입니다.

어휘 revise 수정하다, 개정하다 spending 지출, 소비

4.

정답 condition

해석 모든 임대 차량은 깨끗하고 정상 작동하는 상태로 반납되어야 합니다.

해설 conditional은 '조건부의'라는 뜻의 형용사로, 형용사가 명사를 수식할 수는 있지만, 이 문맥에서는 working condition이라는 복합 명사가 되어야 자연스럽습니다. 따라서 명사인 condition이 정답입니다.

어휘 vehicle 차량 proper 적절한, 알맞은

5.

정답 to increase

해석 제니스 제약은 지역 유통업체들과의 협력을 통해 자사의 시장 점유율을 확대하는 것을 목표로 하고 있습니다.

해설 동사 aim은 to부정사를 목적어로 취하는 타동사입니다. 그러

므로 to increase가 정답입니다.

어휘 aim (to) ~을 목표로 하다 market penetration 시장 침투율 local distributor 지역 유통업체

6.
정답 to submit

해석 지원자들은 요청 시 추가 서류를 제출할 준비가 되어 있어야 합니다.

해설 수동태 be prepared 뒤에는 to부정사가 위치하여 '~할 준비가 되다'라는 의미를 나타냅니다. 따라서 정답은 to submit입니다.

어휘 additional 추가의 documentation 서류

실전 TEST

1. (A)	2. (B)	3. (D)	4. (D)	5. (B)
6. (B)	7. (B)	8. (A)	9. (C)	10. (C)
11. (C)	12. (B)	13. (C)	14. (B)	15. (B)
16. (D)	17. (D)	18. (D)	19. (B)	20. (A)

1.
정답 (A)

해석 이글 산으로 차를 운전해 가는 일은 그 지역의 형편없이 관리된 도로들로 인해 어려울 수 있다.

해설 동사 can be 앞은 문장의 주어 자리입니다. 따라서 빈칸 뒤의 to 전치사구와 결합해 문장의 주어 역할을 할 수 있는 동명사 (A) Driving이 정답입니다.

오답 (B) Drives: 3인칭 단수 주어와 어울리는 동사의 형태이므로 주어 역할을 할 수 없는 오답입니다.
(C) Drive: 동사원형이므로 주어 역할을 할 수 없는 오답입니다.
(D) Driven: Drive의 과거분사형이므로 주어 역할을 할 수 없는 오답입니다.

어휘 due to ~로 인해, ~ 때문에 poorly 형편없이, 좋지 못하게 maintain 유지하다, 관리하다

2.
정답 (B)

해석 개스턴 그릴 앤 비스트로는 건강에 좋은 곁들임 요리들을 메뉴에 추가함으로써 많은 신규 고객들을 끌어들이기를 바라고 있다.

해설 빈칸 뒤에 위치한 명사구(healthy side dishes)를 목적어로 취함과 동시에 전치사 by의 목적어 역할을 할 동명사가 빈칸에 필요하므로 (B) adding이 정답입니다.

오답 (A) add: 동사원형이므로 전치사의 목적어 역할을 할 수 없는 오답입니다.
(C) addition: 명사가 다른 명사(구)와 결합하려면 전치사가 필요하므로 오답입니다.
(D) added: add의 과거형 또는 과거분사형이므로 전치사의 목적어 역할을 할 수 없는 오답입니다.

어휘 hope to do ~하기를 바라다 attract ~을 끌어들이다 by (방법) ~함으로써, ~해서 add ~을 추가하다 addition 추가(되는 것)

3.
정답 (D)

해석 햄프셔 대학의 연구가들에 의해 설립된 위싱 웰 재단은 희귀동물 종을 보호하는 데 전념하고 있다.

해설 빈칸 뒤에 위치한 명사구(rare animal species)를 목적어로 취함과 동시에 전치사 to의 목적어 역할을 할 동명사가 빈칸에 필요하므로 (D) protecting이 정답입니다.

오답 (A) protect: 동사원형이므로 전치사의 목적어 역할을 할 수 없는 오답입니다.
(B) protected: protect의 과거형 또는 과거분사형이므로 전치사의 목적어 역할을 할 수 없는 오답입니다.
(C) protection: 명사가 다른 명사(구)와 결합하려면 전치사가 필요하므로 오답입니다.

어휘 establish ~을 설립하다, 확립하다 be committed to -ing ~ 하는 데 전념하다, 헌신하다 rare 희귀한 species (동식물의) 종 protect ~을 보호하다 protection 보호

4.
정답 (D)

해석 귀하의 사무 가구 디자인이 저희 전국 디자인 경연대회의 결선 진출작으로 선정되었음을 알려 드리고자 합니다.

해설 빈칸 앞에 위치한 would like는 to부정사를 목적어로 취하므로 (D) to announce가 정답입니다.

오답 (A) announce: 동사원형이므로 would like 바로 뒤에 나란히 위치할 수 없는 오답입니다.
(B) announcing: would like는 동명사를 목적어로 취하지 않으므로 오답입니다.
(C) announced: announce의 과거형 또는 과거분사형이므로 would like 바로 뒤에 나란히 위치할 수 없는 오답입니다.

어휘 would like to do ~하고자 하다, ~하고 싶다 be selected as ~로 선정되다 finalist 결선 진출작, 결선 진출자 competition 경연대회 announce (that) (~라고) 알리다, 발표하다

5.
정답 (B)

해석 우리의 주가가 우리 헤드폰 브랜드의 이미지를 개선하기 위한 노력에도 불구하고 지속적으로 하락하고 있다.

해설 선택지가 모두 명사인데, 빈칸 뒤에 to부정사가 위치해 있으므로 to부정사의 수식을 받을 수 있는 명사인 (B) efforts가 정답입니다.

오답 (A) issues: to부정사의 수식을 받지 않는 명사이므로 오답입니다.
(C) opinions: to부정사의 수식을 받지 않는 명사이므로 오답입니다.
(D) responses: 전치사 to와 어울려 쓰이는 명사이므로 오답입니다.

어휘 value 가치, 값어치 stock 주식 continually 지속적으로 decrease 하락하다, 감소하다 in spite of ~에도 불구하고 improve ~을 개선하다, 향상시키다 issue 문제, 사안 opinion 의견 effort (to do) (~하려는) 노력 response (to) (~에 대한) 대응, 반응, 답변

6.
정답 (B)

해석 프레시웨이즈 슈퍼마켓은 야간 교대 근무조로 일하는 직원들을 대상으로 초과 근무 수당을 인상하기로 결정했다.

해설 빈칸 앞에 현재완료 시제로 쓰인 동사 decide는 to부정사를 목적어로 취하므로 (B) to increase가 정답입니다.

오답 (A) increases: 3인칭 단수 주어와 어울리는 동사의 형태이므로 동사 has decided 뒤에 나란히 위치할 수 없는 오답입니다.
(C) increasing: decide는 동명사를 목적어로 취하지 않으므로 오답입니다.
(D) increased: increase의 과거형 또는 과거분사형이므로 오답입니다.

어휘 decide to do ~하기로 결정하다 overtime rate 초과 근무 수당 shift 교대 근무(조) increase ~을 인상하다, 증가시키다

7.
정답 (B)

해석 저희 창고 직원들은 어떤 상품이든 손상시키는 것을 피하기 위해 정말로 세심하게 상품을 다룹니다.

해설 빈칸 뒤에 위치한 명사구(any items)를 목적어로 취함과 동시에 to부정사로 쓰인 동사 avoid의 목적어 역할을 할 동명사가 빈칸에 필요하므로 (B) damaging이 정답입니다.

오답 (A) damage: 동사 또는 명사의 형태인데, 동사일 경우에 avoid의 목적어 역할을 하지 못하며, 명사일 경우에 뒤에 이어지는 명사구와 연결시켜주는 전치사가 필요하므로 오답입니다.
(C) damaged: 동사의 과거형 또는 과거분사형인데, 과거분사로 명사를 수식하는 경우에 any 다음에 위치해야 알맞은 어순이 되므로 오답입니다.
(D) damages: 동사 또는 명사의 형태인데, 동사일 경우에 avoid의 목적어 역할을 하지 못하며, 명사일 경우에 뒤에 이어지는 명사구와 연결시켜주는 전치사가 필요하므로 오답입니다.

어휘 warehouse 창고 treat ~을 다루다, 처리하다 merchandise 상품 with the utmost care 정말로 세심하게, 극도로 주의해서 avoid -ing ~하는 것을 피하다 damage v. ~을 손상시키다 n. 손상, 피해

8.
정답 (A)

해석 이력서를 강화하기 위해, 오도넬 씨는 비즈니스 경영과 재무 기획 강좌들을 이수했다.

해설 빈칸 뒤에 위치한 명사구(his résumé)를 목적어로 취하면서 To와 결합해 목적을 나타내는 to부정사구를 이룰 수 있는 동사원형인 (A) enhance가 정답입니다.

오답 (B) enhancement: 명사로서, 명사구를 목적어로 가질 수 없으므로 오답입니다.
(C) enhanced: enhance의 과거형 또는 과거분사형이므로 to부정사를 구성할 동사원형이 필요한 빈칸에 맞지 않는 오답입니다.
(D) enhancing: enhance의 동명사 또는 현재분사형이므로 to부정사를 구성할 동사원형이 필요한 빈칸에 맞지 않는 오답입니다.

어휘 résumé 이력서 complete ~을 완수하다, 완료하다 management 경영, 운영, 관리 financial 재무의, 금융의 planning 기획 enhance ~을 향상시키다, 강화하다 enhancement 향상, 강화

9.
정답 (C)

해석 저희는 여러분께서 남은 어떤 문서 작업이든 끝마치실 수 있도록 늦어도 오후 3시까지는 저희 사무실에 도착하시기를 권해 드립니다.

해설 빈칸 뒤에 위치한 동명사 arriving을 목적어로 취해야 하므로 동명사를 목적어로 취하는 동사인 (C) suggest가 정답입니다.

오답 (A) ask: 동명사를 목적어로 취하지 않으므로 오답입니다.
(B) decide: 동명사를 목적어로 취하지 않으므로 오답입니다.
(D) continue: 동명사를 목적어로 취하기는 하지만 문장의 의미에 맞지 않는 오답입니다.

어휘 suggest -ing ~하도록 권하다, 제안하다 arrive 도착하다 no later than + 시간: 늦어도 ~까지는 so that (목적) ~할 수 있도록 remaining 남아 있는 paperwork 문서 (작업) ask (A to do): (A에게 ~하도록) 요청하다 decide (to do) (~하기로) 결정하다 continue (to do) (~하기를) 계속하다, 지속하다

10.
정답 (C)

해석 마케팅 이사는 새로운 소셜 미디어 기반의 광고 캠페인 시행과 더불어 더 많은 고객들을 끌어들이기를 기대하고 있다.

해설 선택지가 모두 동사이며, 빈칸 뒤에 to부정사가 위치한 구조이므로 to부정사를 목적어로 취하는 (A) continues와 (C) expects 중에서 의미가 알맞은 것을 골라야 하는데, '광고 캠페인의 목적이 고객을 늘리는 것이므로 '기대하고 있다'와 같은 의미가 되어야 알맞으므로 '~하기를 기대하다'를 뜻하는 (C) expects가 정답입니다.

오답 (A) continues: to부정사를 목적어로 취하기는 하지만 문장의 의미에 맞지 않는 오답입니다.
(B) finishes: 동명사를 목적어로 취하는 동사이므로 오답입니다.
(D) considers: 동명사를 목적어로 취하는 동사이므로 오답입니다.

어휘 expect to do ~하기를 기대하다, 예상하다 attract ~을 끌어 들이다 release 공개, 출시, 발표 A-based: A를 기반으로 하는, 바탕으로 하는 advertising 광고 (활동) continue (to do) (~하는 것을) 계속하다 finish (-ing) (~하는 것을) 끝마치다 consider (-ing) (~하는 것을) 고려하다

11.
정답 (C)

해석 어려운 여건 속에서 업무를 잘 수행하는 방문영업팀의 능력이 지사장에게 정말로 깊은 인상을 남겼다.

해설 빈칸 앞에 위치한 명사 ability는 to부정사의 수식을 받는 명사 이므로 (C) to perform이 정답입니다.

오답 (A) performs: 3인칭 단수 주어와 어울리는 동사의 형태인데, 문장에 이미 동사 has impressed가 있으므로 오답입니다.
(B) performing: 동사 perform의 동명사 또는 현재분사형인데, 둘 모두 명사 ability를 수식하지 않으므로 오답입니다.
(D) performance: 명사 ability와 복합명사를 구성하지 않는 명사이므로 오답입니다.

어휘 door-to-door sales 방문 영업 ability to do ~할 수 있는 능력 adverse 어려운, 불리한 circumstance 여건, 사정, 상황 impress ~에게 깊은 인상을 남기다 perform 수행하다, 실시하다 performance 수행 능력, 성과, 실적, 공연

12.
정답 (B)

해석 저희 버던트 호텔은 숙박을 더욱 즐겁게 만들어 드리기 위해 저희 손님들께 기꺼이 도움을 드립니다.

해설 빈칸 앞에 위치한 willing은 to부정사와 어울려 쓰이는 형용사이므로 (B) to assist가 정답입니다.

오답 (A) assist: 동사원형이므로 형용사 willing 바로 뒤에 나란히 위치할 수 없는 오답입니다.
(C) assisting: assist의 동명사 또는 현재분사의 형태로서 형용사 willing 바로 뒤에 나란히 위치할 수 없는 오답입니다.
(D) assisted: assist의 과거형 또는 과거분사형이므로 형용사 willing 바로 뒤에 나란히 위치할 수 없는 오답입니다.

어휘 be willing to do 기꺼이 ~하다 make A 형용사: A를 ~하게 만들다 enjoyable 즐거운 assist ~을 돕다

13.
정답 (C)

해석 수석 컨설턴트인 라미레즈 씨가 의사소통 능력 워크숍 및 인적 교류 행사들을 준비하는 일을 책임지고 있습니다.

해설 빈칸 뒤에 위치한 명사구(the communication skills workshop and networking events)를 목적어로 취함과 동시에 전치사 for의 목적어 역할을 할 동명사가 빈칸에 필요하므로 (C) organizing이 정답입니다.

오답 (A) organize: 동사원형이므로 전치사의 목적어 역할을 할 수 없는 오답입니다.
(B) organization: 명사가 다른 명사(구)와 결합하려면 전치사가 필요하므로 오답입니다.
(D) to organize: organize의 to부정사형이므로 전치사의 목적어 역할을 할 수 없는 오답입니다.

어휘 be responsible for ~에 대한 책임을 지다 skill 능력, 기술 networking 인적 교류 organize ~을 준비하다, 조직하다 organization 단체, 조직

14.
정답 (B)

해석 인턴십 프로그램을 완전히 끝내지 않는다면, 어떤 인턴도 사일러 엔지니어링 사에서 정규직 일자리를 제안받을 수 없을 것입니다.

해설 빈칸 뒤에 위치한 명사구(the internship program)를 목적어로 취함과 동시에 부사 fully의 수식을 받으면서 전치사 without의 목적어 역할을 할 동명사가 빈칸에 필요하므로 (B) completing이 정답입니다.

오답 (A) complete: 동사원형이므로 전치사의 목적어 역할을 할 수 없는 오답입니다.
(C) completes: 3인칭 단수 주어와 어울리는 동사의 형태이므로 전치사의 목적어 역할을 할 수 없는 오답입니다.
(D) be completed: 수동태 동사의 형태이므로 전치사의 목적어 역할을 할 수 없는 오답입니다.

어휘 offer A B: A에게 B를 제안하다, 제공하다 position 일자리, 직책 without ~하지 않는다면, ~없이 fully 완전히,

모두, 전적으로 complete ~을 완료하다

15.
정답 (B)

해석 드레스에 생긴 손상에 대해 윈콧 씨에게 보상하기 위해, 세탁소에서 100달러의 상품권을 제공했다.

해설 빈칸 바로 뒤에 동사원형 compensate이 쓰여 있으므로 동사원형과 결합해 '~하기 위해'라는 의미를 나타낼 때 사용하는 (B) In order to가 정답입니다.

오답 (A) So that: 주어와 동사를 포함한 절을 이끌어야 하는 접속사이므로 오답입니다.
(C) When: 주어와 동사를 포함한 절을 이끌어야 하는 접속사이며, 주어가 없을 경우에 「When -ing」의 구조로 된 분사구문을 이끌어야 하므로 오답입니다.
(D) Even if: 주어와 동사를 포함한 절을 이끌어야 하는 접속사이므로 오답입니다.

어휘 compensate A for B: B에 대해 A에게 보상하다 damage 손상, 피해 cause ~을 발생시키다, 야기하다 offer A B: A에게 B를 제공하다 gift certificate 상품권 so that (목적) ~할 수 있도록 in order to do ~하기 위해 even if 설사 ~라 하더라도

16.
정답 (D)

해석 우리 소식지 및 홍보용 전단의 국내 배포 작업이 제시카 로우 홍보부장에 의해 실시될 것이다.

해설 정관사 The 및 형용사 national과 전치사 of 사이는 정관사와 형용사의 수식을 받는 명사 자리인데, 실시되는(be carried out) 일을 나타낼 명사가 필요하므로 '배포, 유통'을 뜻하는 (D) distribution이 정답입니다.

오답 (A) to distribute: to부정사이므로 정관사와 형용사의 수식을 받을 수 없는 오답입니다.
(B) distributing: 동명사는 정관사와 형용사의 수식을 받지 못하므로 오답입니다.
(C) distributor: 명사이지만 사람을 나타내므로 의미가 맞지 않아 오답입니다.

어휘 national 국내의, 국가의 promotional 홍보의 flyer 전단 carry out ~을 실시하다, 수행하다 public relations manager 홍보부장 distribute ~을 배부하다, 나눠주다 distributor 유통회사 distribution 배포, 유통

17.
정답 (D)

해석 밋첨스 백화점에 지역 내 자격 있는 사람들을 대상으로 하는 관리직 공석이 있다.

해설 빈칸 앞에 위치한 명사 employment는 부정관사 a로 수식할 수 없는 불가산명사이므로 빈칸에 가산명사가 들어가 복합명사를 구성해야 알맞습니다. 따라서 가산명사인 (D) opening이 정답입니다.

오답 (A) opens: 3인칭 단수 주어와 어울리는 동사의 형태이므로 복합명사를 구성할 수 없는 오답입니다.
(B) opened: open의 과거형 또는 과거분사형이므로 복합명사를 구성할 수 없는 오답입니다.
(C) open: 동사 또는 형용사의 형태이므로 복합명사를 구성할 수 없는 오답입니다.

어휘 managerial 관리의, 운영의 employment 일자리, 고용, 직업 qualified 자격이 있는, 적격인 individual n. 사람, 개인 local 지역의, 현지의 opening 공석, 빈자리

18.
정답 (D)

해석 오직 8세에서 15세 사이의 음악인들만 도시 축제의 음악 경연 대회에 참가할 자격이 있습니다.

해설 빈칸 앞뒤에 각각 위치한 be동사 및 to부정사와 어울리는 형용사로서 '~할 자격이 있다'라는 의미를 나타낼 때 사용하는 (D) eligible이 정답입니다.

오답 (A) accessible: be동사 및 to부정사와 어울리는 형용사가 아니므로 오답입니다.
(B) variable: be동사 및 to부정사와 어울리는 형용사가 아니므로 오답입니다.
(C) capable: 전치사 of와 어울리는 형용사이므로 오답입니다.

어휘 aged 연령의, ~세의 between A and B: A와 B 사이에 enter 참가하다, 들어가다 competition 대회 fair 축제, 박람회 accessible 접근 가능한 variable 변동이 심한, 가변적인 capable 할 수 있는 eligible 자격이 있는, 가질 수 있는

19.
정답 (B)

해석 해리슨 씨는 마케팅팀과 더 가까이 있기 위해 3층에 있는 사무실로 옮길 것이다.

해설 문장에 이미 동사 will move가 있으므로 빈칸은 동사 자리가 아니며, 「주어 + 동사 + 전치사구」로 구성된 완전한 절 뒤에서 부가적인 요소로서 목적을 의미할 때 사용하는 수식어구인 to 부정사 (B) to be가 정답입니다.

오답 (A) being: 3층으로 사무실을 옮기는 목적을 나타내는 수식어구를 이끌지 못하므로 오답입니다.
(C) is: 동사의 형태이므로 동사 자리가 아닌 빈칸에 쓰일 수 없는 오답입니다.
(D) will be: 동사의 형태이므로 동사 자리가 아닌 빈칸에 쓰일 수 없는 오답입니다.

어휘 move to ~로 옮기다, 이동하다 close to ~와 가까운

20.
정답 (A)

해석 실험실의 모든 화학 물질은 글자가 선명히 보이는 상태로 라벨을 붙인 용기에 담아 보관되어야 합니다.

해설 전치사 with와 정관사 the 다음은 정관사의 수식을 받음과 동시에 전치사의 목적어 역할을 할 명사 자리입니다. 그런데 눈에 보이는 것으로서 라벨로 붙여질 수 있는 것을 나타내야 하므로 '글자, 글(쓰기)' 등을 뜻하는 (A) writing이 정답입니다. with 전치사구는 「with + 목적어(writing) + 목적보어(visible)」의 구조로 '~인 채로, ~상태로'라고 해석됩니다.

오답 (B) written: write의 과거분사형이므로 정관사의 수식을 받거나 전치사의 목적어 역할을 하지 못하는 오답입니다.
(C) write: 동사원형이므로 정관사의 수식을 받거나 전치사의 목적어 역할을 하지 못하는 오답입니다.
(D) writer: 명사이지만 사람명사로서 문장에 맞지 않는 의미를 지니고 있으므로 오답입니다.

어휘 chemical n. 화학 물질 laboratory 실험실, 연구실 store v. ~을 보관하다, 저장하다 container 용기, 그릇 label v. ~에 라벨을 붙이다 with A 형용사: A가 ~한 상태로, A가 ~한 채로 clearly 선명히, 분명히 visible 눈에 보이는 writing n. 글자, 글(쓰기)

DAY 6 분사

PRACTICE

1. containing 2. extended 3. satisfying 4. attached

1.
정답 containing

해석 민감한 정보가 담긴 문서들은 안전하게 보관되어야 합니다.

해설 목적어인 sensitive information이 뒤에 위치해 있으므로 능동의 의미를 나타내는 분사 containing이 정답입니다.

어휘 sensitive 민감한 securely 안전하게

2.
정답 extended

해석 고객 지원 센터는 연장된 주말 운영 시간 동안 운영될 것입니다.

해설 주말 운영 시간은 연장되는 대상이므로 수동의 의미를 나타내는 과거분사인 extended가 정답입니다.

어휘 customer support center 고객 지원 센터 during ~동안

3.
정답 satisfying

해석 저희 고객들은 그 서비스 경험이 놀랍도록 만족스러웠다고 느꼈습니다.

해설 서비스 경험이 만족을 주는 것이므로 만족감이라는 감정을 일으킨다는 의미의 현재분사 satisfying이 정답입니다.

어휘 found A + 형용사: A를 ~하다고 생각하다 surprisingly 놀랍게도

4.
정답 attached

해석 첨부된 송장에는 빠른 배송에 대한 추가 요금이 포함되어 있다.

해설 attached는 동사 attach의 과거분사로서 수동형 형용사로 굳어진 과거분사입니다. 송장에 첨부되었다는 수동의 뜻으로 쓰였으므로 attached가 정답입니다.

어휘 attach 붙이다, 달다, 바르다, 첨부하다 invoice 송장 charge 청구하다, 값을 매기다 expedited 촉진된

실전 TEST

1. (C)	2. (C)	3. (A)	4. (D)	5. (B)
6. (C)	7. (D)	8. (D)	9. (B)	10. (D)
11. (A)	12. (B)	13. (C)	14. (B)	15. (A)
16. (A)	17. (C)	18. (D)	19. (A)	20. (C)

1.
정답 (C)

해석 새롭게 선임된 지점장들을 환영하기 위해 저녁 만찬이 월도프 호텔에서 마련될 것이다.

해설 「관사 + 부사 + ----- + 명사」의 구조에서 빈칸은 부사의 수식을 받음과 동시에 명사를 수식할 분사 자리입니다. 그리고 '지점장'은 다른 사람들에 의해 선임되는 것이므로 수동의 의미를 나타낼 수 있는 과거분사 (C) appointed가 정답입니다.

오답 (A) appoint: 동사원형이므로 명사를 수식할 수 없는 오답입니다.
(B) appointing: 수동의 의미를 나타낼 수 없는 현재분사이므로 오답입니다.
(D) appoints: 3인칭 단수 주어와 어울리는 동사의 형태이므로 명사를 수식할 수 없는 오답입니다.

어휘 arrange ~을 마련하다, 조치하다 branch 지점, 지사 appoint ~을 선임하다, 임명하다

2.
정답 (C)

해석 파텔 씨에 의해 제안된 고용 전략이 포터블 폰즈 사의 인사부에 의해 검토되고 있다.

해설 문장에 이미 동사 is being reviewed가 있으므로 빈칸은 동사 자리가 아니며, by 전치사구와 결합해 명사구 A hiring strategy를 뒤에서 수식하는 구조가 되어야 합니다. 빈칸 뒤에 목적어 없이 by 전치사구만 있으므로 목적어를 필요로 하지 않는 과거분사 (C) proposed가 정답입니다.

오답 (A) propose: 동사원형이므로 동사 자리가 아닌 빈칸에 쓰일 수 없는 오답입니다.
(B) proposal: 명사가 앞뒤의 다른 명사(구)와 결합하려면 전치사가 필요하므로 오답입니다.
(D) proposing: 타동사 propose의 현재분사로서 목적어를 필요로 하므로 오답입니다.

어휘 hiring 고용 strategy 전략 review ~을 검토하다 personnel department 인사부 propose ~을 제안하다 proposal 제안 (서)

3.
정답 (A)
해설 홀리데이 트래블 사는 세계적으로 인정받는 여행사이며, 본사는 뉴욕 시에 위치해 있다.
해설 「관사 + 부사 + ----- + 명사」의 구조에서 빈칸은 부사의 수식을 받음과 동시에 명사를 수식할 분사 자리입니다. 그리고 여행사(travel agency)는 사람들에 의해 인정받는 것이므로 수동의 의미를 나타낼 수 있는 과거분사 (A) recognized가 정답입니다.

오답 (B) recognize: 동사원형이므로 명사를 수식할 수 없는 오답입니다.
(C) recognizing: 수동의 의미를 나타낼 수 없는 현재분사이므로 오답입니다.
(D) recognizes: 3인칭 단수 주어와 어울리는 동사의 형태이므로 명사를 수식할 수 없는 오답입니다.

어휘 travel agency 여행사 head office 본사 be located + 전치사: ~에 위치해 있다 recognize ~을 인정하다

4.
정답 (D)
해설 코미야 씨는 골드웨이 코즈메틱스 사를 보습제와 샴푸, 그리고 바디케어 크림 같은 다양한 제품을 판매하는 신개념 매장이라고 설명합니다.
해설 문장에 이미 동사 describes가 있으므로 또 다른 동사 sell은 분사의 형태로 쓰여 명사구 a new store를 뒤에서 수식하는 구조를 이뤄야 알맞습니다. 그리고 빈칸 뒤에 위치한 명사구(a variety of items)를 목적어로 취해야 하므로 현재분사인 (D) selling이 정답입니다.

오답 (A) sell: 동사원형이므로 명사를 뒤에서 수식할 수 없는 오답입니다.
(B) sells: 3인칭 단수 주어와 어울리는 동사의 형태이므로 명사를 뒤에서 수식할 수 없는 오답입니다.
(C) sold: 바로 뒤에 위치한 명사구를 목적어로 취할 수 없는 과거분사이므로 오답입니다.

어휘 describe A as B: A를 B라고 설명하다, 묘사하다 a variety of 다양한 such as ~와 같은

5.
정답 (B)
해설 크라우더 코퍼레이션 사의 모든 직원은 팀 기반의 사무실 환경에 만족하고 있다고 말합니다.
해설 be동사 뒤에 보어로 쓰일 분사가 필요한데, are 앞의 주어 they가 가리키는 사람명사 All employees의 감정을 나타낼 과거분사가 쓰여야 알맞으므로 (B) satisfied가 정답입니다.

오답 (A) satisfy: 동사원형이므로 be동사 are 바로 뒤에 나란히 위치할 수 없는 오답입니다.
(C) satisfying: 만족감을 유발하는 원인에 대해 사용되는 현재분사이므로 오답입니다.
(D) satisfaction: 빈칸 앞뒤에 위치한 be동사 및 전치사 with와 어울려 쓰이지 않으므로 오답입니다.

어휘 A-based: A를 기반으로 하는, 바탕으로 하는 environment 환경 satisfy ~을 만족시키다 satisfying 만족시키는 satisfied (with) (사람이 ~에) 만족한 satisfaction 만족(도)

6.
정답 (C)
해설 벨코 일렉트로닉스 사의 대표이사가 인디고 소프트웨어 사와의 협업에 관해 놀라운 발표를 할 것으로 예상된다.
해설 부정관사 a와 명사 announcement 사이는 명사를 수식할 단어가 필요한 자리이므로 이 역할이 가능한 과거분사 또는 현재분사 중에서 하나를 골라야 합니다. '발표' 등을 뜻하는 announcement는 사람을 놀라게 만드는 주체이므로 '놀라게 하는'이라는 의미로 감정을 유발하는 원인에 대해 사용하는 현재분사 (C) surprising이 정답입니다.

오답 (A) surprises: 동사 또는 명사의 형태인데, 동사일 경우에 명사를 수식할 수 없고, 명사일 경우에 뒤에 위치한 명사 announcement와 복합명사를 구성하지 않으므로 오답입니다.
(B) surprised: 감정을 느끼는 사람에 대해 사용하므로 오답입니다.
(D) surprisingly: 명사를 수식할 수 없는 부사이므로 오답입니다.

어휘 be expected to do ~할 것으로 예상되다 make an announcement 발표하다, 공지하다 collaboration 협업, 공동 작업 surprise v. ~을 놀라게 하다 n. 놀라움 surprising 놀라게 하는 surprised (사람이) 놀란 surprisingly 놀라울 정도로, 놀랍게도

7.
정답 (D)

해석 새로운 저희 프로테우스 3 휴대전화의 화면은 시중에 나와 있는 기존의 어떤 접이식 휴대전화기의 화면보다 훨씬 더 큽니다.

해설 전치사 of와 명사구 목적어 any foldable cell phone 사이에 위치한 빈칸은 명사구를 수식할 단어가 필요한 자리인데, 자동사 exist는 현재분사의 형태로만 명사구를 수식할 수 있으므로 (D) existing이 정답입니다.

오답 (A) exist: 동사원형이므로 명사구를 수식할 수 없는 오답입니다.
(B) exists: 3인칭 단수 주어와 어울리는 동사의 형태이므로 오답입니다.
(C) existed: exist의 과거형 또는 과거분사형인데, 자동사 exist는 과거분사의 형태로 명사구를 수식할 수 없으므로 오답입니다.

어휘 much (비교급 수식) 훨씬 foldable 접이식의, 접을 수 있는 on the market 시중에 나와 있는 exist 존재하다 existing 기존의

8.
정답 (D)

해석 소비자 소비 경향에 관한 상세한 조사가 마컴 마케팅 그룹에 의해 실시되었다.

해설 동사 was carried out 앞에 위치한 주어 research 앞에 빈칸이 있으므로 빈칸은 주어인 명사 research를 수식할 단어가 쓰여야 하는 자리입니다. 따라서 동사 detail의 분사들 중 하나를 골라야 하는데, '조사'는 사람에 의해 상세화 되는 대상이므로 수동의 의미를 나타내는 과거분사 (D) Detailed가 정답입니다.

오답 (A) Detail: 동사 또는 명사의 형태인데, 동사일 경우에 명사 research를 앞에서 수식할 수 없고, 명사일 경우에 전치사를 통해 또 다른 명사 research와 연결되어야 하므로 오답입니다.
(B) Details: 3인칭 단수 주어와 어울리는 동사 또는 복수형 명사의 형태인데, 동사일 경우에 명사를 앞에서 수식할 수 없고, 또 다른 명사 research와 연결되려면 전치사가 필요하므로 오답입니다.
(C) Detailing: 수동의 의미를 나타낼 수 없는 현재분사이므로 오답입니다.

어휘 research 조사, 연구 consumer 소비자 spending 소비, 지출 trend 경향, 추세 carry out ~을 실시하다, 수행하다 detail v. ~을 상세히 설명하다 n. 상세 정보, 세부 사항 detailed 상세한

9.
정답 (B)

해석 의사에 의해 기록된 환자 의료 기록은 누구에게도 공개되지 말아야 하는 기밀 정보를 포함하고 있다.

해설 record는 동사와 명사로 모두 쓰이는데, 문장에 이미 동사 include가 있으므로 빈칸은 동사 자리가 아니며, 명사로서 앞에 위치한 다른 명사와 어울리려면 전치사가 필요합니다. 따라서 분사의 형태로 쓰여 명사 notes를 뒤에서 수식해야 하는데, 빈칸 뒤에 목적어가 없으므로 과거분사인 (B) recorded가 정답입니다.

오답 (A) record: 동사 또는 명사의 형태인데, 빈칸이 동사 자리가 아니므로 동사로 쓰일 수 없고, 명사일 경우에 전치사를 통해 또 다른 명사 notes와 연결되어야 하므로 오답입니다
(C) recording: 타동사 record의 현재분사는 목적어를 필요로 하므로 빈칸에 맞지 않는 오답입니다.
(D) records: 3인칭 단수 주어와 어울리는 동사 또는 복수형 명사의 형태인데, 동사일 경우에 명사를 뒤에서 수식할 수 없고, 또 다른 명사 notes와 연결되려면 전치사가 필요하므로 오답입니다

어휘 patient n. 환자 medical note 의료 기록 physician (내과) 의사 include ~을 포함하다 confidential 기밀의 disclose ~을 공개하다, 드러내다

10.
정답 (D)

해석 사이드 이브라힘 씨는 미국의 여러 금융 기관과 긴밀한 협업 관계로 일하는 손꼽히는 경제 전문가이다.

해설 부정관사 a와 명사 economist 사이에 위치한 빈칸은 명사를 수식할 단어가 필요한 자리이므로 분사에서 형용사로 굳어진 (D) leading이 정답입니다.

오답 (A) lead: 동사원형이므로 명사를 수식할 수 없는 오답입니다.
(B) leader: 바로 뒤에 위치한 명사 economist와 복합명사를 구성하지 않는 명사이므로 오답입니다.
(C) led: lead의 과거형 또는 과거분사형인데, 과거분사일 때 사물명사를 수식하므로 오답입니다.

어휘 economist 경제 전문가 in close collaboration with ~와 긴밀한 협업 관계로 several 여럿의, 몇몇의 financial 금융의, 재무의 institution 기관, 단체, 협회 lead ~을 이끌다, 진행하다 leading 손꼽히는, 선도적인

11.
정답 (A)

해석 혼란스럽게 만드는 블루라이즈 테크놀로지 컨벤션 일정이 여러 행사에 대해 저조한 참석률을 초래했다.

해설 정관사 The와 명사 schedule 사이에 위치한 빈칸은 명사

를 수식할 형용사 또는 분사가 쓰일 자리입니다. 선택지에 형용사가 없어 현재분사 (A) confusing와 과거분사 (B) confused 중에서 하나를 골라야 하는데, 일정(schedule)이 사람을 혼란스럽게 만드는 원인이므로 '혼란스럽게 만드는'을 뜻하는 현재분사 (A) confusing이 정답입니다.

오답 (B) confused: '(사람이) 혼란스러워 하는'이라는 의미로 사람명사를 수식하는 과거분사이므로 오답입니다.

(C) confusion: 명사로서 복합명사를 구성하는 경우를 생각해 볼 수는 있지만, schedule과 복합명사를 구성하지 않으므로 오답입니다.

(D) confuse: 동사이므로 형용사 또는 분사가 필요한 빈칸에 쓰일 수 없는 오답입니다.

어휘 result in ~을 초래하다, ~라는 결과를 낳다 poor 저조한, 좋지 못한 attendance 참석(률), 참석자 수 several 여럿의, 몇몇의 confuse ~을 혼란스럽게 만들다, ~을 헷갈리게 하다 confusion 혼란, 혼동

12.

정답 (B)

해석 조기 퇴직 보상책에 관한 대표이사님의 발표에 좌절한 직원들은 회의 중에 우려를 표했다.

해설 주어인 The employees를 뒤에서 수식하면서 by 전치사구와 어울려 '~에 좌절한'이라는 의미를 나타내는 과거분사 (B) frustrated가 정답입니다.

오답 (A) frustrating: by 전치사구와 함께 쓰일 수 없는 현재분사이므로 오답입니다.

(C) frustrate: 문장의 동사는 expressed이므로 또다른 동사를 쓸 수 없으므로 동사원형은 오답입니다.

(D) frustrates: 문장의 동사는 expressed이므로 또다른 동사를 쓸 수 없으므로 「동사+(e)s」 형태 또한 오답입니다.

어휘 announcement 발표, 공지, 알림 regarding ~에 관한 retirement 퇴직, 은퇴 incentive n. 보상책, 장려책 express 표현하다 concern 우려, 걱정 frustrate 좌절감을 주다, 불만스럽게 만들다

13.

정답 (C)

해석 모든 고객들께서는 보안 구역에 들어가시기 전에 반드시 서명된 양식을 제출하셔야 합니다.

해설 정관사 the와 명사 form 사이에 위치한 빈칸은 명사를 수식할 형용사 또는 분사가 쓰일 자리입니다. 선택지에 형용사가 없어 현재분사 (A) signing과 과거분사 (C) signed 중에서 하나를 골라야 하는데, 양식(form)은 사람에 의해 서명되는 것이므로 이러한 수동의 의미(서명된)를 나타내는 과거분사 (C) signed가 정답입니다.

오답 (A) signing: 현재분사이며, 수동의 의미를 나타내지 못하므로 오답입니다.

(B) sign: 명사 또는 동사이며, 명사로 쓰일 때 form과 복합명사를 구성하지 않으므로 오답입니다.

(D) signature: 명사이며, form과 복합명사를 구성하지 않으므로 오답입니다

어휘 submit ~을 제출하다 form 양식, 서식 secure 안전한, 안심하는 signature 서명

14.

정답 (B)

해석 에모토 씨는 다음 분기 공급 계약에 대해 고려된 판매업체의 목록을 제출했다.

해설 전치사 of와 명사 목적어 vendors 사이에 위치한 빈칸은 명사를 수식할 형용사 또는 분사가 쓰일 자리입니다. 빈칸 앞뒤 부분의 내용으로 볼 때, '다음 분기 공급 계약에 대해 고려된 판매업체들의 목록'을 의미해야 자연스러우므로 '고려된'을 뜻하는 과거분사 (B) considered가 정답입니다.

오답 (A) consider: 명사를 수식할 수 없는 동사이므로 오답입니다.

(C) considering: 동명사, 현재분사, 또는 전치사(~을 고려하면)이며, 현재분사로 쓰일 때 고려 대상임을 뜻하는 수동의 의미를 나타내지 못하므로 오답입니다.

(D) consideration: 명사이기는 하지만 '고려'라는 의미로 빈칸 뒤에 위치한 또다른 명사 vendors와 복합명사를 구성하지 않으므로 오답입니다.

어휘 vendor 판매업체, 판매업자 quarter 분기 supply 공급(품) contract 계약(서) consider ~을 고려하다, ~을 라고 여기다 consideration 사려, 고려 사항

15.

정답 (A)

해석 그 회사는 제품 배송에 있어 지연 문제를 설명하는 입장문을 발표했다.

해설 빈칸 앞에 주어와 동사, 그리고 명사구 목적어로 구성된 완전한 절이 쓰여 있으므로 빈칸 이하 부분은 부가적인 수식어구의 역할을 해야 합니다. 또한, 빈칸 앞뒤 명사구들로 볼 때, 빈칸과 the delay가 분사구를 구성해 '지연 문제를 설명하는'이라는 의미로 a statement를 수식해야 알맞으므로 명사구 the delay를 목적어로 취할 수 있는 현재분사 (A) explaining이 정답입니다.

오답 (B) explained: 동사의 과거형 또는 과거분사형이며, 과거분사로 쓰일 때 바로 뒤에 위치한 명사구를 목적어로 취할 수 없으므로 오답입니다.

(C) explanation: 명사이며, 두 개의 명사구들 사이에 전치사 없이 또 다른 명사가 쓰일 수 없으므로 오답입니다.

(D) explains: 3인칭 단수 주어에 대한 동사이므로 분사가 필요한 빈칸에 쓰일 수 없는 오답입니다.

어휘 release ~을 발표하다, ~을 공개하다, ~을 출시하다 statement 입장문, 성명(서), 진술(서) delay 지연, 지체

shipping 배송, 선적 explain ~을 설명하다
explanation 설명, 해명

16.
정답 (A)
해석 저희는 투자금을 구하고 있는 기업가들에 의해 진행된 설득력 있는 발표에 깊은 인상을 받았습니다.
해설 정관사 the와 명사 presentation 사이에 위치한 빈칸은 명사를 수식할 형용사 또는 분사가 쓰일 자리입니다. 선택지에 형용사가 없어 현재분사 (A) convincing과 과거분사 (B) convinced 중에서 하나를 골라야 하는데, 발표 내용(presentation)이 사람들을 설득하는 원인이므로 '설득하는(설득력 있는)'을 뜻하는 현재분사 (A) convincing이 정답입니다.
오답 (B) convinced: 과거분사이며, '(사람이) 설득된'을 뜻하므로 의미가 맞지 않는 오답입니다.
(C) conviction: 명사이며, presentation과 복합명사를 구성하지 않으므로 오답입니다.
(D) convinces: 명사를 수식할 수 없는 동사이므로 오답입니다.
어휘 be impressed by ~에 깊은 인상을 받다 presentation 발표(회) entrepreneur 기업가 seek ~을 구하다, ~을 찾다 investment 투자(금) convince ~을 설득하다, ~을 납득시키다 conviction 납득시키기, 확신

17.
정답 (C)
해석 분석된 데이터는 우리 최신 제품 라인이 기대치를 초과하고 있음을 나타낸다.
해설 정관사 The와 명사 data 사이에 위치한 빈칸은 명사를 수식할 형용사 또는 분사가 쓰일 자리입니다. 선택지에 형용사가 없어 현재분사 (B) analyzing과 과거분사 (C) analyzed 중에서 하나를 골라야 하는데, 데이터는 사람에 의해 분석되는 것이므로 이러한 수동의 의미를 나타내는 과거분사 (C) analyzed가 정답입니다.
오답 (A) analyze: 명사를 수식할 수 없는 동사이므로 오답입니다.
(B) analyzing: 현재분사이며, 수동의 의미를 나타낼 수 없으므로 오답입니다.
(D) analyses: 명사 analysis의 복수형이며, 정관사 The와 명사 사이에 쓰일 수 없으므로 오답입니다.
어휘 suggest that ~임을 나타내다, ~하도록 제안하다 exceed ~을 초과하다, ~을 넘어서다 expectation 기대(치), 예상 analyze ~을 분석하다 analysis 분석 (결과)(analyses는 복수형)

18.
정답 (D)
해석 완성된 양식은 금요일까지 회계 부서에 제출되어야 합니다.
해설 빈칸은 관사 the와 명사 form 사이에 위치하므로, 빈칸은 명사를 수식하는 형용사 자리임을 알 수 있습니다. 양식(form)은 작성되는 대상이므로 수동의 의미가 포함된 형용사가 필요합니다. 따라서 '완성된', '완료된'이라는 의미의 과거분사 (D) completed가 정답입니다.
오답 (A) complete: 형용사로 '완전한'이라는 뜻이지만, "complete form"은 어색하며 일반적으로 쓰이지 않습니다.
(B) completing: 현재분사로 명사를 수식할 수 있으나, 제출되어야 한다는 수동적 의미와 맞지 않아 문맥상 부적절합니다.
(C) completion: 명사이므로 형용사 자리에는 올 수 없어 오답입니다.
어휘 accounting department 회계 부서

19.
정답 (A)
해석 짜증스러운 공사 현장 소음이 우리 직원들이 집중하는 것을 어렵게 만들었다.
해설 정관사 the와 명사 noise 사이에 위치한 빈칸은 명사를 수식할 형용사 또는 분사가 쓰일 자리입니다. 선택지에 형용사가 없어 현재분사 (A) annoying과 과거분사 (B) annoyed 중에서 하나를 골라야 하는데, 소음(noise)이 직원들을 짜증스럽게 만드는 것이므로 '짜증스러운'을 뜻하는 현재분사 (A) annoying이 정답입니다.
오답 (B) annoyed: 과거분사이며, '(사람이) 짜증난, 짜증을 느끼는'이라는 의미를 나타내므로 오답입니다.
(C) annoy: 동사이므로 정관사와 명사 사이에 쓰일 수 없는 오답입니다.
(D) annoyance: 명사이며, noise와 복합명사를 구성하지 않으므로 오답입니다.
어휘 site 현장, 부지, 장소 make it 형용사 for A to do: A가 ~하는 것을 …하게 만들다 concentrate 집중하다 annoy 짜증나게 하다 annoyance 짜증, 골칫거리

20.
정답 (C)
해석 인사부장은 초과 근무 정책상의 변동 사항과 관련해 우려하는 직원들에게 이야기하였다.
해설 정관사 The와 명사 employees 사이에 위치한 빈칸은 명사를 수식할 형용사 또는 분사가 쓰일 자리입니다. 선택지에 형용사가 없어 현재분사 (A) concerning과 과거분사 (C) concerned 중에서 하나를 골라야 하는데, 사람이 어떤 원인(정책 변화)에 의해 우려하게 되는 것이므로 이러한 수동의 의미를 나타내는 과거분사 (C) concerned가 정답입니다.

오답 (A) concerning: 현재분사이며, 수동의 의미를 나타낼 수 없으므로 오답입니다. 참고로, concerning은 '~와 관련된'을 뜻하는 전치사로도 쓰입니다.
(B) concern: 동사 또는 명사이며, 명사로 쓰일 때 employees와 복합명사를 구성하지 않으므로 오답입니다.
(D) concerns: 동사 또는 명사이며, 명사로 쓰일 때 employees와 복합명사를 구성하지 않으므로 오답입니다.

어휘 HR 인사(부), 인적 자원 overtime 초과 근무, 야근 policy 정책, 방침 concern v. ~을 우려하게 만들다, ~을 걱정시키다 n. 우려, 걱정 concerned (사람이) 우려하게 된, 우려하는

DAY 7 형용사 / 부사

PRACTICE

1. thorough   2. each   3. any
4. accustomed   5. promptly   6. conveniently
7. well   8. still

1.
정답 thorough
해석 추가 데이터가 포함된 후, 최종 보고서는 더 철저해졌다.
해설 자동사 뒤에 주격보어로서 형용사가 위치해야 하므로 형용사 thorough가 정답입니다.
어휘 thorough 철저한, 꼼꼼한 include 포함하다 report 보고서 additional 추가적인

2.
정답 each
해석 보고서를 제출하기 전에 체크리스트의 각 항목을 확인해 주세요.
해설 item은 단수 가산명사로 이를 수식하는 수량 형용사인 each가 정답입니다.
어휘 verify 확인하다, 검증하다 item 항목 checklist 점검표 submit 제출하다

3.
정답 any
해석 직원들은 회사를 대신하여 어떠한 구매든 하기 전에 승인을 받아야 합니다.
해설 「any+ 단수/복수명사/불가산명사」로 '어떤 ~이든지'라는 뜻을 가지고 있습니다. 따라서 단수명사인 purchase를 수식하는 any가 정답입니다.

어휘 obtain 얻다, 획득하다 approval 승인 purchase 구매 on behalf of ~을 대신하여

4.
정답 accustomed
해석 대부분의 해외 직원들은 다문화 환경에서 일하는 데 이미 익숙하다.
해설 be accustomed to는 '~에 익숙하다'라는 숙어입니다. 따라서 accustomed가 정답입니다.
어휘 accustomed to ~에 익숙한 associated with ~와 관련된 multicultural 다문화의 environment 환경

5.
정답 promptly
해석 고객 서비스 담당자들은 불만 제기에 신속하게 대응했다.
해설 respond는 주격보어가 필요없는 자동사이며, 부사의 수식을 받으므로 부사인 promptly가 정답입니다.
어휘 promptly 신속하게, 즉시 respond 응답하다, 대응하다 complaint 불만, 항의 representative 대표자, 직원

6.
정답 conveniently
해석 그 컨벤션 센터는 공항 근처에 편리하게 위치해 있다.
해설 빈칸 뒤에 위치한 과거분사 located는 부사의 수식을 받으므로 부사 conveniently가 정답입니다.
어휘 be located 위치해 있다 convention center 컨벤션 센터, 회의장 close to ~에 가까이 conveniently 편리하게

7.
정답 well
해석 지난주에 홍보 부족에도 불구하고 터너 씨의 콘서트는 많은 관객이 참석했다.
해설 well attended는 관용적인 표현으로, 행사가 많은 사람들의 참석을 받은 상태를 나타냅니다. 따라서 '많은 사람들이 참석했다'의 의미를 나타내는 well이 정답입니다.
어휘 attend 참석하다 promotion 홍보 despite ~에도 불구하고 well attended 많은 사람이 참석한

8.
정답 still
해석 그 제품은 구매한 지 1년이 지났음에도 불구하고 아직도 보증 기간이 남아 있다.
해설 yet은 보통 부정문이나 의문문에서 '아직 ~하지 않았다'는 의미로 사용됩니다. 부사 still은 어떤 상태가 지금까지도 지속되고 있음을 나타내는 부사로, 보증(warranty)이 현재도 유효함

정답 및 해설 145

을 뜻하는 문맥이므로 still이 정답입니다.

어휘 still 아직도 warranty 보증(기간) even though ~일지라도 purchase 구매하다

실전 TEST

1. (C)	2. (B)	3. (C)	4. (D)	5. (C)
6. (D)	7. (A)	8. (C)	9. (D)	10. (B)
11. (A)	12. (D)	13. (B)	14. (A)	15. (A)
16. (C)	17. (D)	18. (B)	19. (C)	20. (B)

1.
정답 (C)

해석 혼잡 시간대에는 공항에 도착하는 데 있어 충분한 시간 여유를 갖도록 하시기 바랍니다.

해설 부정관사 a와 명사 amount 사이에 위치한 빈칸은 명사를 수식할 단어가 필요한 자리이므로 이 역할이 가능한 형용사 (C) considerable이 정답입니다.

오답 (A) consideration: 바로 뒤에 위치한 amount와 복합명사를 구성하지 않으므로 오답입니다.
(B) consider: 동사원형이며, 부정관사와 명사 사이에 위치할 수 없는 오답입니다.
(D) considerably: 부사이며, 부정관사와 명사 사이에 위치할 수 없는 오답입니다.

어휘 make sure that 반드시 ~하도록 하다 give A B: A에게 B를 주다, 제공하다 a considerable amount of time 상당한 시간 arrive 도착하다 rush hour (교통) 혼잡 시간대 consideration 고려, 숙고, 배려 consider ~을 고려하다, ~을 …라고 여기다 considerably 많이, 상당히

2.
정답 (B)

해석 대부분의 고객들이 저희 매장을 방문하기에 앞서 온라인으로 저희의 최신 제품 안내 책자를 훑어보는 것이 유익하다고 생각합니다.

해설 동사 find와 목적어 it 뒤에 위치한 빈칸은 it을 설명하는 목적보어 자리인데, 가목적어 it이 가리키는 진목적어인 to부정사구에서 말하는 일의 성격을 나타낼 형용사가 쓰여야 알맞으므로 (B) beneficial이 정답입니다.

오답 (A) benefit: 명사 또는 동사이며, 진목적어인 to부정사구에 대한 목적보어로 쓰이지 않으므로 오답입니다.
(C) beneficially: 부사는 진목적어인 to부정사구에 대한 목적보어로 쓰이지 않으므로 오답입니다.
(D) benefits: 복수명사 또는 3인칭 단수 주어와 어울리는 동사이며, 동사는 진목적어인 to부정사구에 대한 목적보어로 쓰이지 않으므로 오답입니다.

어휘 find it 형용사 to do: ~하는 것을 …하다고 생각하다 browse ~을 훑어보다, 둘러보다 latest 최신의 brochure 안내 책자 online 온라인으로 benefit n. 혜택, 이득 v. 이득을 얻다, ~에게 이득이 되다 beneficially 유익하게 beneficial 유익한, 이득이 되는

3.
정답 (C)

해석 행사 기획팀이 회사의 연례 연회를 위해 여러 장소를 검토했다.

해설 빈칸 뒤에 동사 considered의 목적어로 복수 가산명사 locations가 쓰여 있으므로 복수 가산명사를 수식하는 (C) several이 정답입니다.

오답 (A) every: 단수 가산명사를 수식하므로 오답입니다.
(B) each: 단수 가산명사를 수식하므로 오답입니다.
(D) much: 불가산명사를 수식하므로 오답입니다.

어휘 planning 기획 consider ~을 고려하다 location 장소, 위치, 지점 annual 연례적인, 해마다의 banquet 연회 several 여럿의, 몇몇의

4.
정답 (D)

해석 어떤 사람들은 신나는 놀이기구를 경험하기 위해 스플래시 캐년을 방문하는 반면, 다른 방문객들은 그저 걸어서 돌아다니며 경치를 즐기고 싶어 합니다.

해설 접속사 While이 이끄는 절이 끝나는 콤마 뒤로 빈칸과 주절의 주어 visitors가 있으므로 빈칸은 visitors를 수식할 형용사가 필요한 자리입니다. 또한 복수 가산명사인 visitors를 수식하는 some과 대응되어 다른 일부를 나타내야 하므로 (D) other가 정답입니다.

오답 (A) another: 단수 가산명사를 수식하므로 오답입니다.
(B) any: 복수 가산명사를 수식할 수는 있지만 '어떠한 ~이든'이라는 의미로 일부 사람들 외의 다른 사람들을 가리키는 뜻으로 쓰일 수 없으므로 오답입니다.
(C) everyone: 대명사이므로 명사를 앞에서 수식할 수 없는 오답입니다.

어휘 while ~인 반면 experience v. ~을 경험하다, 겪다 ride n. 놀이기구 simply 그저, 단순히 walk around 걸어서 돌아다니다 scenery 경치, 경관

5.
정답 (C)

해석 본사를 멜버른으로 이전하는 것은 처음 예상보다 비용이 더 많이 드는 것으로 나타났습니다.

해설 빈칸 앞 비교급을 나타내는 부사 more이 있으므로 빈칸은 형용사 자리임을 알 수 있습니다. 따라서 선택지 중에서 형용사는 '비용이 드는', '값비싼'이라는 의미를 나타내는 (C) costly

가 정답입니다.
오답 (A) cost: 명사 또는 동사로 쓰이는 형태이며, 비교급 부사 more의 수식을 받을 수 없으므로 오답입니다.
(B) costs: 명사 또는 동사로 쓰이는 형태이며, 비교급 부사 more의 수식을 받을 수 없으므로 오답입니다.
(D) costing: 타동사 cost의 현재분사 형태이며, 단독으로 쓰이는 현재분사가 아니므로 오답입니다.
어휘 relocation 이전 headquarters 본사 prove to do ~하는 것으로 드러나다, 나타나다 initially 처음에 than anticipated 예상한 것보다 cost n. 값, 비용 v. 비용이 들다, 잃게 하다

6.
정답 (D)
해석 블루 패브릭 사는 면, 비단, 가죽, 그리고 양모 같이 저렴하게 가격이 책정된 직물을 생산합니다.
해설 「동사 + ----- + 과거분사 + 명사」의 구조에서 빈칸은 동사의 목적어로 쓰인 명사를 수식하는 과거분사를 앞에서 수식할 부사 자리이므로 (D) reasonably가 정답입니다.
오답 (A) reason: 명사 또는 동사이며, 빈칸 뒤에 위치한 과거분사를 수식할 수 없는 오답입니다.
(B) reasoned: 동사 reason의 과거형 또는 과거분사형으로 빈칸 뒤에 위치한 과거분사를 수식할 수 없는 오답입니다.
(C) reasonable: 형용사이며, 빈칸 뒤에 위치한 과거분사를 수식할 수 없는 오답입니다.
어휘 produce ~을 생산하다 priced 가격이 책정된 textile 직물, 섬유 such as ~와 같은 reason n. 이유 v. ~라고 판단하다 reasonable 저렴한, 합리적인 reasonably 저렴하게, 합리적으로

7.
정답 (A)
해석 그 영화제는 두 달 전에 발표되었지만, 주요 영화 목록은 여전히 공개적으로 발표되지 않았다.
해설 빈칸 뒤에 위치한 부정어 not과 어울릴 수 있는 부사 (A) still과 (B) yet 중에서, 현재완료시제를 구성하는 have 앞에 위치할 수 있는 (A) still이 정답입니다.
오답 (B) yet: 현재완료시제를 구성하는 have 앞에 위치할 수 없는 부사이므로 오답입니다.
(C) already: 현재완료시제를 구성하는 have 앞에 위치할 수 없는 부사이므로 오답입니다.
(D) only: 현재완료시제를 구성하는 have 앞에 위치할 수 없는 부사이므로 오답입니다.
어휘 announce ~을 발표하다 featured 주연의, 특별한, 주요한 release ~을 공개하다 publicly 공개적으로

8.
정답 (C)
해석 작년의 재활용 계획은 대단한 성공이었는데, 회사 내 연간 쓰레기의 약 80퍼센트가 재활용되었기 때문이다.
해설 접속사 as와 빈칸 뒤로 숫자 표현이 포함된 명사구가 as절의 주어로 쓰여 있습니다. 따라서 숫자 표현 앞에 위치하는 부사인 (C) approximately가 정답입니다.
오답 (A) approximate: 형용사 또는 동사이며, 숫자 표현 앞에 위치하지 않으므로 오답입니다.
(B) approximating: 동사 approximate의 동명사 또는 현재분사형이며, 숫자 표현 앞에 위치하지 않으므로 오답입니다.
(D) approximation: 명사이며, 숫자 표현 앞에 위치하지 않으므로 오답입니다.
어휘 recycling 재활용 initiative n. 계획 success 성공 annual 연간의, 해마다의 waste 쓰레기, 폐기물 recycle ~을 재활용하다 approximate a. 근사치의 v. (수량 등이) ~와 거의 비슷하다, ~에 근접하다 approximately 약, 대략 approximation 근사치, 비슷한 것

9.
정답 (D)
해석 마티 맥킨즈 씨는 원래 인턴이었지만, 지난달에 홍보팀 팀장으로 승진되었다.
해설 be동사 was와 보어로 쓰인 명사구 an intern 사이에 빈칸이 위치해 있으므로 명사(구) 앞에 쓰일 수 있는 부사 (D) originally가 정답입니다.
오답 (A) origin: 사람주어와 동격이 되지 않아 보어로 쓰일 수 없는 명사이며, 빈칸 뒤에 위치한 부정관사 an과 어순도 맞지 않으므로 오답입니다.
(B) original: 형용사이며, 부정관사 an 앞에 위치할 수 없으므로 오답입니다.
(C) originality: 사람주어와 동격이 되지 않아 be동사 뒤에서 보어로 쓰일 수 없는 명사이며, 빈칸 뒤에 위치한 부정관사 an과 어순도 맞지 않으므로 오답입니다.
어휘 promote ~를 승진시키다 public relations 홍보 origin 기원, 유래 originality 독창성 original 원래의, 원본의, 독창적인 originally 원래, 애초에

10.
정답 (B)
해석 카프 씨는 『더 시카고 포스트』에서 22년 동안 기자로 근무했는데, 그곳에서 높이 평가받은 수많은 기사를 썼다.
해설 명사 articles를 수식하는 과거분사 regarded를 앞에서 수식해 강조하는 역할을 하는 부사 (B) highly가 정답입니다.
오답 (A) high: 형용사 또는 부사이며, 과거분사를 앞에서 수식해 강조하는 역할을 하지 않으므로 오답입니다.

(C) higher: 비교급 형용사 또는 비교급 부사의 형태이며, 과거분사를 앞에서 수식해 강조하는 역할을 하지 않으므로 오답입니다.

(D) highest: 최상급 형용사의 형태이며, 과거분사를 앞에서 수식해 강조하는 역할을 하지 않으므로 오답입니다.

어휘 journalist 기자 numerous 수많은, 다수의
highly regarded 높이 평가받는

11.
정답 (A)

해석 저희는 모든 사용자가 이해할 수 있도록 지침을 명확하게 만들었습니다.

해설 빈칸은 목적어 the instructions 뒤에서 목적보어로 들어가는 자리이며, 「made + 목적어 + 형용사」라는 구조로 되어 있습니다. 이 구조는 '~을 …하게 만들다'라는 뜻을 나타내며, 빈칸에 형용사가 와야 자연스러운 문장이 됩니다. 따라서 형용사인 (A) clear가 정답입니다.

오답 (B) clearing: 현재분사로 형용사 역할을 할 수는 있지만, clearing의 목적어가 없으므로 오답입니다.

(C) clearly: 부사는 목적보어 자리에 위치할 수 없으므로 오답입니다.

(D) clarity: '명확성'이라는 의미를 나타내는 명사이며 목적보어 자리에 위치할 수 있지만 '지침을 명확성으로 만들었다'라는 의미가 문맥상 어울리지 않으므로 오답입니다.

어휘 instruction 지침 user 사용자 clear 명확한 clearly 명확하게 clarity 명확성

12.
정답 (D)

해석 세미나 시작 전에 모든 참가자에게 유익한 안내 책자를 배포해 주세요.

해설 빈칸은 the라는 정관사와 brochures라는 복수 명사 사이에 위치하므로, 형용사 자리임을 알 수 있습니다. 문맥상 브로셔는 정보를 전달하는 목적으로 사용되며, 참가자에게 도움이 되는 내용이 담겨 있을 것이므로 '유익한, 유용한'이라는 뜻의 형용사 (D) informative가 정답입니다.

오답 (A) informing: 현재분사이며, 빈칸 뒤에 위치한 brochure는 동사 inform의 목적어가 아니라 수식하는 대상이므로 오답입니다.

(B) inform: 동사원형이며, 정관사 the와 명사 사이에 위치할 수 없으므로 오답입니다.

(C) information: 명사이며, 빈칸 뒤에 위치한 brochure와 복합명사를 구성하지 않으므로 오답입니다.

어휘 distribute 배포하다, 나누어주다 brochure 안내 책자, 브로셔 participant 참가자 inform 알리다 information 정보 informative 유익한

13.
정답 (B)

해석 저희는 어제 일부 성과 평가를 완료했고, 나머지 보고서는 내일까지 완료될 예정입니다.

해설 빈칸은 some of the performance evaluations이 가리키는 것에 대한 나머지 보고서들을 지칭해야 하므로, 복수 명사를 수식할 수 있는 표현이 필요합니다. 보기 중에서 복수 명사 reports를 수식하면서 전체 중 나머지를 지칭하는 표현은 (B) the other입니다.

오답 (A) another: 단수 명사를 수식하는 부정형용사이며, 복수 명사 reports와 쓸 수 없으므로 오답입니다.

(C) a little: 셀 수 없는 명사를 수식하는 표현으로, 가산 복수 명사 reports와 쓸 수 없으므로 오답입니다.

(D) each other: 상호 관계를 나타내는 표현으로, 문맥상 나머지를 지칭하는 의미와 맞지 않으므로 오답입니다.

어휘 performance evaluations 성과 평가 report 보고서 complete 완료하다 the other 나머지의 by tomorrow 내일까지

14.
정답 (A)

해석 구독에 대해 당신이 가지고 있는 어떤 걱정이든 지원 센터로 문의하셔도 됩니다.

해설 빈칸은 전치사 regarding 바로 뒤에 위치하면서 명사 concern을 수식해야 하므로 형용사 자리임을 알 수 있습니다. 이 문장은 사용자가 가지고 있는 어떤 종류의 걱정도 지원 센터에 문의할 수 있다는 의미이므로, (A) any가 정답입니다.

오답 (B) few: 형용사이지만 복수명사를 수식하므로 오답입니다.

(C) all: 복수명사 또는 셀 수 없는 명사를 수식하므로 오답입니다.

(D) other: 보통 비교 대상이 있을 때 쓰이며, 앞 문장에서 언급된 concern이 없기 때문에 문맥상 부적절하므로 오답입니다.

어휘 contact 연락하다 regarding ~에 관하여 concern 걱정, 우려 subscription 구독, 가입

15.
정답 (A)

해석 해외 시장에 투자와 관련된 위험은 신중히 고려되어야 합니다.

해설 빈칸은 명사 risks를 수식하며, 전치사 with와 함께 쓰여 '~와 관련된'이라는 의미를 나타내는 형용사 (A) associated가 정답입니다.

오답 (B) association: '연관, 협회'라는 의미의 명사로서 형용사 자리에는 쓸 수 없으므로 오답입니다.

(C) associate: 문장에 동사가 should be considered이므로 또다른 동사는 오답입니다.

(D) associates: '동료' 또는 '제휴 회사' 등의 뜻을 가진 명사로, risks와 복합명사를 구성하지 않으므로 오답입니다.

어휘 risk 위험 associated with ~와 관련된 invest in ~에 투자하다 foreign market 해외 시장 carefully 신중하게

16.
정답 (C)
해석 여러 부서들이 그 제품을 예정보다 앞서 출시하기 위해 협력하여 일했습니다.
해설 자동사 work는 부사의 수식을 받으므로 (C) collaboratively가 정답입니다.
오답 (A) collaborate: 동사원형이며, 동사 work와 함께 쓸 수 없으므로 오답입니다.
(B) collaborative: work는 형용사 보어를 가지지 않는 자동사이므로 오답입니다.
(D) collaborated: 과거형 동사로서 동사 work와 함께 쓸 수 없으므로 오답입니다.

어휘 launch 출시하다 ahead of schedule 예정보다 앞서 collaborate 협력하다 collaborative 협력적인 collaboratively 협력적으로, 협업하여

17.
정답 (D)
해석 안타깝게도, 회계 부서는 중복 오류를 알아차리지 못했습니다.
해설 빈칸은 문장의 맨 앞에 위치하며, 뒤에 콤마(,)가 있고 완전한 문장이 이어지므로, 빈칸은 문장 전체를 수식하는 부사 자리임을 알 수 있습니다. 따라서 정답은 (D) Regrettably입니다.
오답 (A) Regret: 명사로 문장 전체를 수식할 수 없으므로 오답입니다.
(B) Regrettable: 형용사로 문장 전체를 수식할 수 없으므로 오답입니다.
(C) Regretted: 과거형 동사 또는 과거분사로, 이 문장에서 필요한 부사 역할을 할 수 없기 때문에 오답입니다.

어휘 accounting department 회계부서 fail to do ~하지 못하다 notice 알아차리다 duplication 중복 error 오류 regret 후회하다 regrettable 유감스러운 regrettably 유감스럽게도, 안타깝게도

18.
정답 (B)
해석 브레이브테크 사의 새로운 컬러 프린터는 9월에 출시된 유사 모델보다 훨씬 더 저렴합니다.
해설 빈칸은 비교급 표현 more affordable 앞에 위치하므로, 비교급을 수식할 수 있는 부사 자리임을 알 수 있습니다. 따라서 보기 중에서 비교급을 강조하는 부사인 (B) much가 정답입니다.
오답 (A) very: 일반적으로 원급 형용사나 최상급을 수식하므로 오

답입니다.
(C) too: '너무'라는 부정적 의미를 나타내는 부사이므로 오답입니다.
(D) such: 「such + 형용사 + 명사」 구조로 쓰이므로 오답입니다.

어휘 affordable 가격이 알맞은, 구입 가능한 release 출시하다

19.
정답 (C)
해석 검사관들은 각 건설 현장에서 안전 수칙을 면밀히 확인하도록 요구받습니다.
해설 빈칸은 동사 check 앞에 위치하며, 동작이 어떻게 수행되는지를 설명하는 부사 자리입니다. 이 문장은 검사관들이 정확하고 세밀하게 안전 수칙을 점검해야 한다는 의미를 전달하므로, 동사를 수식하는 부사 (C) closely가 정답입니다.
오답 (A) close: '가까이', '가깝게'라는 부사로도 쓰이지만 문맥상 어울리지 않으므로 오답입니다.
(B) closeness: '친밀함, 가까움'을 의미하는 명사이며, 동사 check를 수식할 수 없으므로 오답입니다.
(D) closer: 비교급 형용사 또는 부사로, 문장 흐름상 비교 대상이 없으므로 오답입니다.

어휘 inspector 검사관 be required to do ~하는 것을 요구받다, ~해야 하다 check 확인하다 safety protocol 안전 수칙 construction site 건설 현장

20.
정답 (B)
해석 여러 차례 요청에도 불구하고 공급업체는 아직 배송 날짜를 확인하지 않았습니다.
해설 빈칸은 has 다음에 오는 자리이며, to confirm이라는 부정사가 이어지는 「has yet to + 동사원형」 구조로 쓰였음을 알 수 있습니다. 문맥상 '아직 배송 날짜를 확인하지 않았다'는 내용을 전달해야 하므로 (B) yet이 정답입니다.
오답 (A) still: '여전히'라는 의미로, has/have to와 함께 쓰이지 않는 부사이므로 오답입니다.
(C) already: '이미'라는 뜻으로, has/have to와 함께 쓰이지 않는 부사이므로 오답입니다.
(D) hardly: '거의 ~않다'라는 뜻의 부사지만, has/have to와 함께 쓰이지 않는 부사이므로 오답입니다.

어휘 supplier 공급업체 shipping date 배송 날짜 confirm 확인하다 have yet to do 아직 ~하지 않다 despite ~에도 불구하고 multiple 여러 번의, 여러 개의 request 요청 hardly 거의 ~ 않다

DAY 8 접속사

PRACTICE

1. but
2. both
3. while
4. depending
5. that
6. which

1.
정답 but
해석 한 씨는 회의에 참석하지는 않았지만, 사전에 상세한 보고서를 제출했습니다.
해설 and는 단순히 동등한 내용을 이어주는 접속사이므로 문맥상 어색합니다. 앞뒤 문장이 대조적이므로 반대의 의미를 연결 수 있는 접속사 but이 정답입니다.
어휘 attend 참석하다 submit 제출하다 in advance 사전에 detailed 자세한, 상세한

2.
정답 both
해석 교육 세션에서는 회사 정책과 긴급 대응 절차를 둘 다 다뤘다.
해설 either은 선택을 나타내는 부사이지만 문장에서 회사 정책과 긴급 대응 절차가(company policies and emergency procedures) 두 항목이 and로 연결되어 있으므로 상관접속사 both가 정답입니다.
어휘 cover 다루다, 포함하다 policy 정책 emergency procedure 긴급 대처 절차

3.
정답 while
해석 방문객들은 역사적인 구역을 거니는 동안 사진을 찍을 수 있다.
해설 두 동작(take photographs + strolling)이 동시에 일어나는 상황이므로, while이 정답입니다. since는 보통 이유 또는 과거 시점 이후의 시간 경과를 나타낼 때 사용됩니다.
어휘 take photograph 사진을 찍다 stroll 거닐다, 산책하다 historic district 역사 지구

4.
정답 depending
해석 회의는 임원들이 언제 도착하는지에 따라 오전 10시에 시작될 예정이다.
해설 depends는 단수형 동사로 이 문장에서 직접 사용할 수 없고, 이미 주절에 will start라는 동사가 있으므로 그 뒤에는 조건을 설명해주는 분사구문이 이어지는 게 자연스럽습니다. 따라서 '~에 따라'라는 의미를 갖고 있는 depending이 정답입니다.
어휘 depend ~에 달려 있다, ~에 따라 다르다 executive 임원

5.
정답 that
해석 정부 보고서는 보다 엄격한 규제가 배출량을 줄일 것이라는 점을 시사하고 있다.
해설 빈칸 앞에 위치한 동사 suggest는 '~을 제안하다, 시사하다'는 뜻으로, that절을 목적어로 취할 수 있는 동사이므로 정답은 that입니다.
어휘 suggest 제안하다, 시사하다 regulation 규제 reduce 줄이다 emission 배출(량), 배출물

6.
정답 which
해석 위원회는 어느 제안서가 즉각적인 수정이 필요한지 아직 결정하지 못했다.
해설 which proposal은 '어떤 제안서'라는 「의문사 + 명사」 구조로 명사절을 이끄므로 which가 정답입니다.
어휘 committee 위원회 decide 결정하다 proposal 제안서 immediate revision 즉각적인 수정

실전 TEST

1. (D) 2. (D) 3. (B) 4. (A) 5. (C)
6. (D) 7. (B) 8. (A) 9. (C) 10. (D)
11. (C) 12. (D) 13. (C) 14. (B) 15. (C)
16. (B) 17. (A) 18. (A) 19. (B) 20. (A)

1.
정답 (D)
해석 유효한 영수증이 없다면, 저희는 고객들께 환불을 제공해 드릴 수 없지만, 반품된 제품을 교환해 드리겠다고 제안할 수 있습니다.
해설 빈칸 앞뒤로 주어와 동사가 각각 포함된 절이 하나씩 위치해 있으므로 이 절들을 연결할 접속사가 빈칸에 필요하며, '환불해 줄 수는 없지만, 교환해 줄 수는 있다'와 같은 상반 관계가 되어야 알맞으므로 '하지만, 그러나' 등을 뜻하는 등위접속사 (D) but이 정답입니다.
오답 (A) or: '또는'을 뜻하는 등위접속사이므로 의미가 맞지 않는 오답입니다.
(B) and: '그리고'를 뜻하는 등위접속사이므로 의미가 맞지 않는 오답입니다.
(C) as: 등위접속사가 아니므로 문장 구조상 맞지 않는 오답입니다.
어휘 without ~ 없이, ~가 없다면 valid 유효한 receipt 영수증 provide A with B: A에게 B를 제공하다 refund 환불 offer to do ~하겠다고 제안하다 exchange ~을 교환하다 returned 반품된, 반납된

2.
정답 (D)

해석 비록 WJE 엔지니어링 사에서 비록 20년 넘게 근무해 왔지만, 그 회사는 그레이브스 씨에게 한 번도 책임자 역할을 제안한 적이 없었다.

해설 선택지가 모두 부사절 접속사이므로 의미가 어울리는 것을 찾아야 합니다. '비록 20년 넘게 근무했지만, 한 번도 책임자 역할을 제안하지 않았다'와 같은 상반 관계가 되어야 알맞으므로 '비록 ~지만'을 뜻하는 (D) Although가 정답입니다.

오답 (A) Once: '일단 ~한다면, ~하자마자'를 뜻하는 접속사이므로 의미가 맞지 않는 오답입니다.
(B) Before: '~하기 전에'를 뜻하는 접속사이므로 의미가 맞지 않는 오답입니다.
(C) Since: '~하기 때문에, ~한 이후로'를 뜻하는 접속사이므로 의미가 맞지 않는 오답입니다.

어휘 over ~ 넘게 offer A B: A에게 B를 제안하다, 제공하다 leading 이끄는, 선도적인 role 역할 once 일단 ~하는 대로, ~하자마자 although 비록 ~지만 since ~하기 때문에, ~한 이후로

3.
정답 (B)

해석 에다드 제조사의 생산량이 올해 감소한 반면, 월간 순수익은 상당히 증가해 왔다.

해설 선택지가 모두 부사절 접속사이므로 의미가 어울리는 것을 찾아야 합니다. '생산량이 감소한 반면, 월간 순수익은 상당히 증가했다'와 같은 상반 관계가 되어야 알맞으므로 '~한 반면'을 뜻하는 접속사 (B) While이 정답입니다.

오답 (A) Because: '~하기 때문에'를 뜻하는 접속사이므로 의미가 맞지 않는 오답입니다.
(C) Until: '~할 때까지'를 뜻하는 접속사이므로 의미가 맞지 않는 오답입니다.
(D) As long as: '~하는 한, ~하기만 하면'을 뜻하는 접속사이므로 의미가 맞지 않는 오답입니다.

어휘 output 생산량 decline 감소하다, 하락하다 monthly 월간의, 달마다의 net profit 순수익, 순이익 increase 증가하다, 오르다 significantly 상당히 while ~한 반면 until (지속) ~할 때 까지 as long as ~하는 한, ~하기만 하면

4.
정답 (A)

해석 저희 요가 강좌들 중 하나에 등록하시면 무료 매트와 수건이 포함될 것입니다.

해설 빈칸 앞뒤로 주어와 동사가 각각 포함된 절이 하나씩 위치해 있습니다. 따라서 빈칸은 이 절들을 연결할 접속사가 필요한 자리인데 '등록하면, 무료 선물이 포함된다'와 같은 의미가 되어야 알맞으므로 조건 접속사인 (A) if가 정답입니다.

오답 (B) with: 전치사이므로 두 개의 절을 연결할 수 없는 오답입니다.
(C) but: 접속사이지만 의미가 맞지 않으므로 오답입니다.
(D) either: 「A or B」의 구조와 짝을 이뤄 상관접속사를 구성하므로 오답입니다.

어휘 complimentary 무료의 include ~을 포함하다 sign up for ~에 등록하다, ~을 신청하다 either (A or B): (A 또는 B) 둘 중 의 하나

5.
정답 (C)

해석 여러 베스트셀러 소설을 집필했지만, 티모시 쿡 씨는 자신의 작품에 대해 한 번도 상을 받지 못했다.

해설 접속사와 주어가 없는 채로 과거분사 written과 결합해야 하므로 목적을 나타내는 to부정사구를 구성할 수 있는 (A) To have와 분사구문을 구성할 수 있는 (C) Having 중에서 하나를 골라야 합니다. 구조적으로는 둘 다 어울리므로 해석을 통해 알맞은 것을 골라야 하는데, 목적을 나타내는 to부정사구가 되면 '베스트셀러 소설을 쓰기 위해, 상을 받은 적이 없다'라는 어색한 의미가 되므로 분사구문을 구성하는 (C) Having이 정답입니다.

오답 (A) To have: 목적을 말하는 to부정사구를 구성하게 되는데, 어색한 의미를 나타내므로 오답입니다.
(B) Have: 과거분사와 함께 현재완료시제 동사를 구성하는 요소인데, 접속사와 주어가 없는 상태에서 빈칸에 쓰일 수 없는 오답입니다.
(D) Had: 과거분사와 함께 과거완료시제 동사를 구성하는 요소인데, 접속사와 주어가 없는 상태에서 빈칸에 쓰일 수 없는 오답입니다.

어휘 several 여럿의, 몇몇의 novel 소설 win an award 상을 받다 work 작품, 작업(물)

6.
정답 (D)

해석 노스팜의 의료 연구가들이 새로운 진통제가 부정적인 부작용을 야기하는지 밝힐 것이다.

해설 목적어를 필요로 하는 타동사 determine 뒤로 빈칸이 있고 그 뒤로 주어와 동사가 포함된 절이 하나 이어져 있습니다. 따라서 이 절이 determine의 목적어 역할을 하는 명사절이 되어야 하는데, '부작용을 야기하는지를 밝힐 것이다'와 같은 불확실성을 포함한 의미가 되어야 알맞으므로 '~인지 (아닌지)'를 뜻하는 명사절 접속사 (D) whether가 정답입니다.

오답 (A) about: 전치사이므로 빈칸 뒤에 이어지는 절을 이끌 수 없는 오답입니다.
(B) that: 명사절 접속사이지만 '~라는 점, ~라는 사실' 등의 의미로 확실한 내용을 말할 때 사용하므로 문장의 의미에 어울리지 않는 오답입니다.

(C) unless: 부사절 접속사이므로 명사절 접속사가 필요한 빈칸에 쓰일 수 없는 오답입니다.

어휘 determine ~을 밝히다, 알아내다 pain medication 진통제 cause ~을 야기하다, 초래하다 negative 부정적인 side effect 부작용 whether ~인지 (아닌지) unless ~가 아니라면, ~하지 않는다면

7.
정답 (B)

해석 MJD 푸드 인터내셔널은 자사의 인기 있는 냉동 피자 제품군을 확장할 것이라고 오늘 아침에 발표했다.

해설 목적어를 필요로 하는 타동사 announced 뒤로 시점 부사 this morning과 빈칸이 있고, 그 뒤로 주어와 동사가 포함된 절이 하나 이어져 있습니다. 따라서 이 절이 announced의 목적어 역할을 하는 명사절이 되어야 하는데, 빈칸 뒤로 「주어 + 동사 + 목적어」로 구성된 완전한 절이 있으므로 완전한 명사절을 이끄는 접속사 (B) that이 정답입니다.

오답 (A) what: 불완전한 명사절을 이끄는 접속사이므로 오답입니다.
(C) because: 부사절 접속사이므로 명사절 접속사가 필요한 빈칸에 쓰일 수 없는 오답입니다.
(D) while: 부사절 접속사이므로 명사절 접속사가 필요한 빈칸에 쓰일 수 없는 오답입니다.

어휘 announce that ~라고 발표하다 expand ~을 확대하다, 확장하다 range 제품군, 종류, 범위 while ~인 반면, ~하는 동안

8.
정답 (A)

해석 이사진은 홍콩에서 열리는 세미나에서 누가 제품 발표를 진행할 것인지 결정해야 합니다.

해설 목적어를 필요로 하는 타동사 decide 뒤로 빈칸이 있고 그 뒤로 주어 없이 동사부터 시작되는 불완전한 절이 이어져 있습니다. 따라서 이 절이 decide의 목적어 역할을 하는 명사 절이 되어야 하므로 불완전한 절을 이끄는 명사절 접속사 (A) who가 정답입니다.

오답 (B) that: 명사절 접속사로 쓰일 때 완전한 절을 이끌어야 하므로 오답입니다.
(C) where: 완전한 절을 이끄는 명사절 접속사이므로 오답입니다.
(D) why: 완전한 절을 이끄는 명사절 접속사이므로 오답입니다.

어휘 board members 이사진, 이사회 decide ~을 결정하다 lead ~을 진행하다, 이끌다 presentation 발표(회)

9.
정답 (C)

해석 하티건 씨 또는 로즈 씨 둘 중 한 사람이 매닝 엔터프라이즈 사의 최고재무이사 자리를 맡을 것이다.

해설 빈칸 뒤로 문장의 주어가 「A or B」의 구조로 쓰여 있습니다. 따라서 이 구조와 함께 「A 또는 B 둘 중의 하나」라는 의미로 상관접속사를 구성하는 (C) Either가 정답입니다.

오답 (A) Both: 「A and B」의 구조와 함께 상관접속사를 구성하므로 오답입니다.
(B) Each: 형용사 또는 대명사로 쓰이므로 빈칸에 맞지 않는 오답입니다.
(D) Neither: 「A nor B」의 구조와 함께 상관접속사를 구성하므로 오답입니다.

어휘 either A or B: A 또는 B 둘 중의 하나 assume (역할, 책임 등) ~을 맡다 role 자리, 직책, 역할 both (A and B): (A와 B) 둘 모두 neither (A nor B): (A도 B도) 둘 다 아닌

10.
정답 (D)

해석 직원 보상 프로그램을 시행함으로써, 우리는 사무실 분위기를 개선할 수 있을 뿐만 아니라 생산성도 증대시킬 수 있다.

해설 빈칸 앞에 첫 번째 동사구와 함께 쓰인 not only와 짝을 이뤄 상관접속사를 구성하는 요소인 (D) but이 정답입니다.

오답 (A) so that: 부사절 접속사이므로 오답입니다.
(B) both: 「A and B」의 구조와 함께 상관접속사를 구성하므로 오답입니다.
(C) much: 대명사, 형용사 또는 부사로 쓰이므로 빈칸에 맞지 않는 오답입니다.

어휘 by (방법) ~함으로써, ~해서 implement ~을 시행하다 incentive 보상(책), 장려(책) not only A but (also) B: A뿐만 아니라 B도 improve ~을 개선하다, 향상시키다 atmosphere 분위기 boost ~을 증대시키다, 촉진하다 productivity 생산성 so that (목적) ~할 수 있도록 both (A and B): (A와 B) 둘 모두

11.
정답 (C)

해석 오전 보고서들을 제때 끝내신다면 오늘 점심 시간을 더 길게 가지셔도 됩니다.

해설 선택지가 모두 접속사이므로 의미가 알맞은 것을 찾아야 합니다. 빈칸 뒤에 위치한 절이 '오전 보고서들을 제때 끝내신다면'이라는 의미로 점심 시간을 더 길게 가질 수 있는 조건을 나타내야 알맞으므로 '~한다면'이라는 뜻으로 조건을 말할 때 사용하는 (C) if가 정답입니다.

오답 (A) while: '~하는 동안, ~하는 반면'을 뜻하는 접속사이므로 의미가 맞지 않는 오답입니다.
(B) since: '~하기 때문에, ~한 이후로'를 뜻하는 접속사이므

(D) unless: '~하지 않는다면, ~가 아니라면'을 뜻하는 접속사이므로 의미가 맞지 않는 오답입니다.

어휘 take a lunch break 점심 시간을 갖다 on time 제때, 제시간에

12.

정답 (D)

해석 팔로마레스 씨는 프릿즈 랩스에 불과 1년밖에 있지 않았지만, 지부장으로 승진되었다.

해설 빈칸 뒤에 주어와 동사를 포함한 절이 쓰여 있어 이 절을 이끌 접속사가 필요하며, '팔로마레스 씨가 프릿즈 랩스에 불과 1년밖에 있지 않았지만'이라는 의미로 승진 조건과 대조되는 사실을 나타내야 알맞으므로 '(비록) ~하기는 하지만'이라는 뜻으로 대조적인 내용을 말할 때 사용하는 접속사 (D) even though가 정답입니다.

오답 (A) during: 전치사(~ 중에, ~ 동안)이므로 접속사 자리인 빈칸에 쓰일 수 없는 오답입니다.
(B) so that: '(목적) ~하도록, (결과) 그래서, 그러므로'를 뜻하는 접속사이므로 의미가 맞지 않는 오답입니다.
(C) because: '~하기 때문에'를 뜻하는 접속사이므로 의미가 맞지 않는 오답입니다.

어휘 promote ~을 승진시키다, ~을 홍보하다, ~을 촉진하다 regional 지역의, 지방의

13.

정답 (C)

해석 영업부장님과 마케팅부장님 두 분 모두 예산 회의에 참석하실 시간을 내실 수 없었습니다.

해설 neither는 nor와 짝을 이뤄 'A도 B도 둘 다 ~ 않다'를 뜻하는 상관접속사 「neither A nor B」를 구성하므로 (C) nor가 정답입니다.

오답 (A) or: either와 짝을 이뤄 'A 또는 B 둘 중 하나'를 뜻하는 상관접속사 「either A or B」를 구성하므로 오답입니다.
(B) and: both와 짝을 이뤄 'A와 B 둘 모두'를 뜻하는 상관접속사 「both A and B」를 구성하므로 오답입니다.
(D) but: not only와 짝을 이뤄 'A뿐만 아니라 B도'를 뜻하는 상관접속사 「not only A but (also) B」를 구성하므로 오답입니다.

어휘 sales 영업, 판매(량), 매출 available (사람) 시간이 있는, (사물) 이용 가능한, 구입 가능한 budget 예산

14.

정답 (B)

해석 도로들이 폭풍으로 인해 폐쇄되어 있기 때문에 라이맥스 주식회사에서 보내는 배송품이 지연될 것입니다.

해설 빈칸 뒤에 주어와 동사를 포함한 절이 쓰여 있어 이 절을 이끌 접속사가 필요하며, '도로들이 폭풍으로 인해 폐쇄되어 있기 때문에'라는 의미로 배송이 지연되는 이유를 나타내야 알맞으므로 '~하기 때문에'라는 뜻으로 이유를 말할 때 사용하는 접속사 (B) because가 정답입니다.

오답 (A) although: '(비록) ~지만'을 뜻하는 접속사이므로 의미가 맞지 않는 오답입니다.
(C) whereas: '~하는 반면'을 뜻하는 접속사이므로 의미가 맞지 않는 오답입니다.
(D) despite: 전치사(~에도 불구하고)이므로 접속사 자리인 빈칸에 쓰일 수 없는 오답입니다.

어휘 shipment 배송(품), 선적(물) delay ~을 지연시키다 due to ~로 인해, ~ 때문에

15.

정답 (C)

해석 법무팀과 준법 관리팀 둘 모두 반드시 그 새로운 계약서를 검토해야 합니다.

해설 both는 'A와 B 둘 모두'를 뜻하는 상관접속사 「both A and B」를 구성하므로 (C) and가 정답입니다.

오답 (A) either: or와 짝을 이뤄 'A 또는 B 둘 중 하나'를 뜻하는 상관접속사 「either A or B」를 구성하므로 오답입니다.
(B) or: either와 짝을 이뤄 'A 또는 B 둘 중 하나'를 뜻하는 상관접속사 「either A or B」를 구성하므로 오답입니다.
(D) nor: neither와 짝을 이뤄 'A도 B도 둘 다 ~ 않다'를 뜻하는 상관접속사 「neither A nor B」를 구성하므로 오답입니다.

어휘 legal department 법무 부서 compliance team 준법감시 팀 both (A and B): (A와 B) 둘 모두 review 검토하다 contract 계약(서)

16.

정답 (B)

해석 여러 이사회 임원들의 반대 의견을 제기했음에도 불구하고 그 예산 제안서가 승인되었다.

해설 선택지가 모두 접속사이므로 의미가 알맞은 것을 찾아야 합니다. 빈칸 뒤에 위치한 절이 '여러 이사회 임원들의 반대 의견을 제기했지만'이라는 의미로 승인된 사실과 대조되는 부정적인 의견을 나타내야 알맞으므로 '(비록) ~지만'이라는 뜻으로 대조적인 내용을 말할 때 사용하는 접속사 (B) though가 정답입니다.

오답 (A) because: '~하기 때문에'를 뜻하는 접속사이므로 의미가 맞지 않는 오답입니다.
(C) whether: '~인지 (아닌지), ~와 상관없이'를 뜻하는 명사절 접속사이므로 의미가 맞지 않는 오답입니다.
(D) so that: '(목적) ~하도록, (결과) 그래서, 그러므로'를 뜻하는 접속사이므로 의미가 맞지 않는 오답입니다.

어휘 budget 예산 proposal 제안(서) approve ~을 승인하다

several 여럿의, 몇몇의 board 이사회 raise (문제 등)
~을 제기하다 objection 반대 (의견)

17.
정답 (A)

해석 우 씨는 수정안을 제출했지만, 업데이트된 가격표를 포함시키는 것을 잊었습니다.

해설 빈칸은 두 개의 완전한 절을 연결하는 접속사 자리입니다. 앞 절은 '제출했다', 뒤 절은 '잊었다'는 내용을 담고 있으며, 두 행동이 대조되는 의미를 가집니다. 따라서 대조나 예외를 나타낼 수 있는 접속사인 (A) but이 정답입니다.

오답 (B) once: '일단 ~하면'이라는 의미를 나타내는 부사절 접속사이며, 이 문장의 문맥과 어울리지 않으므로 오답입니다.
(C) hence: 인과 관계를 나타내며 '그러므로'라는 의미를 부사이므로 오답입니다.
(D) because: 원인을 나타내는 부사절 접속사이며, 문맥상 어울리지 않으므로 오답입니다.

어휘 submit 제출하다 revised 수정된 draft 초안, 작성물 forget to do ~할 일을 잊다 pricing table 가격표

18.
정답 (A)

해석 몇몇 직원들이 초과 근무를 하고 있었기 때문에 혼란을 피하기 위해 IT 부서는 유지 관리 작업 일정을 재조정했다.

해설 선택지가 모두 접속사이므로 의미가 알맞은 것을 찾아야 합니다. 빈칸 뒤에 위치한 절이 '직원들이 초과 근무를 하고 있었기 때문에'라는 지장을 피하기 위해 유지 관리 작업 일정을 재조정한 이유를 나타내야 알맞으므로 '~하기 때문에'라는 뜻으로 이유를 말할 때 사용하는 접속사 (A) since가 정답입니다.

오답 (B) unless: '~하지 않는다면, ~가 아니라면'을 뜻하는 접속사이므로 의미가 맞지 않는 오답입니다.
(C) although: '(비록) ~지만'을 뜻하는 접속사이므로 의미가 맞지 않는 오답입니다.
(D) whereas: '~하는 반면'을 뜻하는 접속사이므로 맞지 않는 오답입니다.

어휘 reschedule ~의 일정을 재조정하다 maintenance 유지 관리, 시설 관리 avoid ~을 피하다 disruption 방해, 중단, 혼란 work overtime 초과 근무하다

19.
정답 (B)

해석 경영진은 모든 직원이 6월 30일까지 준법 교육을 완료해야 한다고 명시했습니다.

해설 빈칸은 동사 has stated 뒤에 이어지는 명사절을 이끄는 접속사 자리입니다. 빈칸 뒤에는 완전한 절이 있고, 이 절이 동사 state의 목적어가 되어야 하므로 빈칸에는 명사절 접속사가 필요합니다. 따라서 '~라는 것'이라는 의미를 나타내는 명사절 접속사 (B) that이 정답입니다.

오답 (A) since: '~이래로' 또는 '~때문에'라는 의미의 부사절 접속사이므로 명사절 접속사 자리에 쓸 수 없습니다.
(C) whether: '~인지 아닌지'의 의미로 명사절 접속사로 쓰일 수 있으나 동사 state의 목적어로 쓸 수 없으므로 오답입니다.
(D) unless: '~하지 않는다면'이라는 의미를 나타내는 부사절 접속사이므로 명사절 접속사 자리에 쓸 수 없습니다.

어휘 management 경영진 state 명시하다, 진술하다 complete 완료하다 compliance training 준법 교육 by ~까지

20.
정답 (A)

해석 영업팀은 이번 가을에 신제품을 출시할지 내년 초에 신제품을 출시할지를 결정할 예정입니다.

해설 빈칸은 동사 choose 뒤에 위치하며, 의문 또는 선택의 내용을 담는 명사절을 이끌어야 합니다. 문맥상 영업팀이 신제품을 출시할지 말지를 결정할 것이라는 내용이므로, '~할지'의 의미를 나타내는 명사절 접속사 (A) whether가 정답입니다.

오답 (B) until: '~할 때까지'라는 의미를 나타내는 시간 부사절 접속사이므로 타동사의 목적어 자리에 쓸 수 없습니다.
(C) before: '~하기 전에'라는 의미를 나타내는 시간 부사절 접속사이므로 타동사의 목적어 자리에 쓸 수 없습니다.
(D) when: '~할 때'라는 의미를 나타내는 시간 부사절 접속사이므로 타동사의 목적어 자리에 쓸 수 없습니다.

어휘 sales team 영업팀 choose 결정하다, 선택하다 launch 출시하다 product 제품

DAY 9 전치사

PRACTICE

1. over   2. between   3. as
4. rather than 5. for   6. According to

1.
정답 over

해석 온라인 주문 수는 휴일 기간 동안 꾸준히 증가했다.

해설 over는 특정 기간 전체에 걸쳐 무언가가 지속적으로 발생했을 때 사용하는 표현으로, 'holiday period 동안 주문 수가 꾸준히 증가했다'는 의미와 어울리므로 over가 정답입니다.

어휘 steadily 꾸준히 increase 증가하다 over ~에 걸쳐, ~동안 holiday period 휴일 기간

2.
정답 between

해석 합의서는 우리 회사와 해외 파트너 간의 공동 책임을 설명하고 있다.

해설 문장에서 our firm and its overseas partner는 「A and B」의 구조이므로, 「between A and B」의 구조로 장소/위치/이동을 나타내는 전치사인 between이 정답입니다.

어휘 outline 개략적으로 설명하다 responsibility 책임 firm 회사

3.
정답 as

해석 이사회는 해리슨씨를 회사의 새로운 최고운영책임자로 임명했다.

해설 문장에서 해리슨이 맡게 된 직책을 소개하고 있으므로 as가 정답입니다. about은 주제나 관련성에 사용되는 전치사이므로 동사 appointed(임명했다)와는 어울리지 않습니다.

어휘 appoint A as B: A를 B로 임명하다 board 이사회

4.
정답 rather than

해석 마케팅팀은 이번 분기에 인쇄 광고보다는 디지털 채널에 집중하기로 결정했다.

해설 rather than은 '~보다는' 선택적 비교 표현으로, 이 문장에서 강조하고자 하는 digital channels와 잘 어울리므로 rather than이 정답입니다. In spite of는 ~에도 '불구하고'라는 의미를 가진 양보 표현으로, 이 문장에서는 문맥상 적절하지 않습니다.

어휘 focus on ~에 집중하다

5.
정답 for

해석 그 새로운 애플리케이션은 쇼핑할 시간이 부족한 사람들에게 이상적이다.

해설 애플리케이션이 쇼핑할 시간이 부족한 사람들(those)에게 적합하다는 대상의 의미를 전달하고 있으므로 for가 정답입니다. by는 행위의 주체를 나타내는 전치사이므로 오답입니다.

어휘 ideal 이상적인

6.
정답 According to

해석 저희 데이터베이스의 기록에 따르면, 귀하의 주문은 지난 금요일에 배송되었습니다.

해설 선택지에 접속사와 전치사가 섞여 있어 빈칸 뒤의 구조를 보고 정답을 찾아야 합니다. 빈칸 뒤에 '기록'을 의미하는 명사가 쓰여 있으므로 빈칸에는 전치사가 위치해야 합니다. 따라서 '~에 따르면'이라는 의미로 출처 또는 근거를 말할 때 사용하는 전치사 According to가 정답입니다.

어휘 package 물품, 소포 deliver ~을 배송하다, 배달하다 even though 비록 ~이지만 in case (that) ~인 경우에 provided that ~라면

실전 TEST

1. (C)	2. (B)	3. (A)	4. (C)	5. (A)
6. (D)	7. (B)	8. (C)	9. (A)	10. (A)
11. (C)	12. (B)	13. (D)	14. (B)	15. (D)
16. (C)	17. (D)	18. (B)	19. (A)	20. (B)

1.
정답 (C)

해석 새로운 보안 협약이 4월 3일에 시행되어 무기한으로 동일하게 유지될 것입니다.

해설 선택지가 모두 전치사이므로 빈칸 뒤에 위치한 명사(구)와 어울리는 것을 찾아야 합니다. April 3 같은 날짜 앞에 사용하는 전치사가 필요하며, 시행되는 시점을 나타내야 하므로 '~에'를 뜻하는 (C) on이 정답입니다.

오답 (A) by: 날짜 앞에 사용할 수는 있지만, 기한을 나타내어 '~까지'를 의미하므로 어울리지 않는 오답입니다.
(B) since: 날짜 앞에 사용할 수는 있지만, 과거의 시점을 나타내어 '~ 이후로'를 의미하므로 어울리지 않는 오답입니다.
(D) for: '~ 동안'이라는 의미로 숫자를 포함해 기간을 나타내는 명사구를 목적어로 취하므로 오답입니다.

어휘 protocol 협약, 규약, 규정 go into effect 시행되다 remain ~한 상태로 유지되다, 여전히 ~한 상태이다 in place 가동되어, 제자리에, 시행되어 indefinitely 무기한으로 by (기한) ~까지, (위치) ~ 옆에, (수단, 방법) ~로, (함으로써, (차이) ~만큼, (행위 주체) ~에 의해 since prep. ~ 이후로 conj. ~한 이후로, ~하기 때문에 ad. 그 이후로 for (기간) ~ 동안, (목적, 대상, 추구 등) ~에 대해, ~을 위해, ~을 향해, ~으로

2.
정답 (B)

해석 모든 고객 문의 사항은 제품 관리부장님이 아니라 지원팀에 전달되어야 합니다.

해설 선택지가 모두 전치사이므로 빈칸 뒤에 위치한 명사(구)와 어울리는 것을 찾아야 합니다. 빈칸 뒤에 위치한 명사구 the support team이 문의 사항을 처리하기 위해 그 내용을 전달 받는 팀이므로 '~에게, ~로' 등의 의미로 전달 대상자를 나타내는 전치사 (B) to가 정답입니다.

오답 (A) onto: 전달 대상자를 나타내는 전치사가 아니므로 오답입니다.
(C) from: 전달 대상자를 나타내는 전치사가 아니므로 오답입니다.
(D) by: 전달 대상자를 나타내는 전치사가 아니므로 오답입니다.

어휘 inquiry 문의, 질문 support 지원, 지지, 후원 rather than ~가 아니라, ~ 대신 onto (이동) ~ 위로

3.
정답 (A)
해석 법무팀에서 계약서를 고객에게 보내기 전에 신중히 그것을 검토했다.
해설 선택지가 모두 전치사이므로 빈칸 뒤에 위치한 동명사(구)와 어울리는 것을 찾아야 합니다. 빈칸 앞뒤에 각각 위치한 동사구와 동명사구가 '계약서를 고객에게 보내기 전에 신중히 그것을 검토했다'와 같은 의미로 일의 진행 순서를 나타내야 알맞으므로 '~ 전에'를 뜻하는 전치사 (A) before가 정답입니다.
오답 (B) during: 일의 진행 순서를 나타내는 전치사가 아니므로 오답입니다.
(C) among: 일의 진행 순서를 나타내는 전치사가 아니므로 오답입니다.
(D) through: 일의 진행 순서를 나타내는 전치사가 아니므로 오답입니다.

어휘 legal 법과 관련된, 합법적인 review ~을 검토하다, ~을 살펴 보다 agreement 계약(서), 합의(서) carefully 신중히, 주의 깊게 during ~ 중에, ~ 동안 among ~ 사이에서, ~ 중에서 through (이동) ~을 통과해, ~을 거쳐, (수단) ~을 통해, (기간) ~ 동안 내내, ~까지, (장소) ~을 전역에 걸쳐

4.
정답 (C)
해석 저희 재무팀 사무실은 2층에, 엘리베이터 옆에 위치해 있습니다.
해설 선택지가 모두 전치사이므로 빈칸 뒤에 위치한 명사(구)와 어울리는 것을 찾아야 합니다. the second floor 같은 명사구와 함께 건물 등의 층을 나타낼 때 사용하는 전치사 (C) on이 정답입니다.
오답 (A) over: 건물 등의 층을 나타내는 전치사가 아니므로 오답입니다.
(B) under: 건물 등의 층을 나타내는 전치사가 아니므로 오답입니다.
(D) across: 건물 등의 층을 나타내는 전치사가 아니므로 오답입니다.

어휘 finance 재무, 재정, 금융 be located 위치해 있다 next to ~ 옆에 over (위치, 이동 등) ~ 위로 가로질러, ~을 넘어, ~을 뒤집어, (수량 등) ~ 넘게, (기간) ~ 동안에 걸쳐, (장소) ~ 전역에, (종료 등) ~을 지난, ~을 넘긴 across (장소, 위치 등) ~을 가로질러, ~ 건너편에, ~ 전역에

5.
정답 (A)
해석 그 기술자는 정전을 초래한 배선 장치 내의 결함을 발견했다.
해설 선택지가 모두 전치사이므로 빈칸 뒤에 위치한 명사(구)와 어울리는 것을 찾아야 합니다. 빈칸 앞뒤에 위치한 명사구들로 볼 때, '배선 장치 내의 결함'을 의미해야 자연스러우므로 '~ 내의, ~ 안에 (있는)'을 뜻하는 전치사 (A) in이 정답입니다.
오답 (B) at: 배선 장치 내부를 나타낼 수 있는 전치사가 아니므로 오답입니다.
(C) to: 배선 장치 내부를 나타낼 수 있는 전치사가 아니므로 오답입니다.
(D) of: 배선 장치 내부를 나타낼 수 있는 전치사가 아니므로 오답입니다.

어휘 fault 결함, 흠 wiring 배선 (장치), 배선 공사 cause ~을 초래하다 outage 정전, 단수

6.
정답 (D)
해석 직원들은 교육 시간 중에 개인 기기를 이용하는 것을 삼가도록 요청 받았다.
해설 동사 refrain과 어울려 '~하는 것을 삼가다[자제하다]'를 뜻하는 「refrain from -ing」를 구성해야 하므로 (D) from이 정답입니다.
오답 (A) with: 동사 refrain과 어울려 쓰이는 전치사가 아니므로 오답입니다.
(B) of: 동사 refrain과 어울려 쓰이는 전치사가 아니므로 오답입니다.
(C) by: 동사 refrain과 어울려 쓰이는 전치사가 아니므로 오답입니다.

어휘 be asked to do ~하도록 요청 받다 device 기기, 장치 during ~ 중에, ~ 동안 training 교육, 훈련 session (특정 활동을 위한) 시간

7.
정답 (B)
해석 플라이어스 어플라이언스 사는 어제 오후 늦게 이메일로 배송 확인서를 받았다.
해설 선택지가 모두 전치사이므로 빈칸 뒤에 위치한 명사(구)와 어울리는 것을 찾아야 합니다. e-mail과 함께 '이메일로'라는 의미로 연락 수단을 나타낼 때 사용하는 전치사 (B) by가 정답입니다.
오답 (A) in: e-mail과 함께 연락 수단을 나타낼 때 사용하는 전치사가 아니므로 오답입니다.

(C) over: e-mail과 함께 연락 수단을 나타낼 때 사용하는 전치사가 아니므로 오답입니다.

(D) with: e-mail과 함께 연락 수단을 나타낼 때 사용하는 전치사가 아니므로 오답입니다.

어휘 receive ~을 받다 confirmation 확인(서)

8.
정답 (C)

해석 해리건 씨는 팀 전체가 이용할 수 있도록 수정된 양식들을 공유 드라이브에 올려 두었다.

해설 선택지가 모두 전치사이므로 빈칸 뒤에 위치한 명사(구)와 어울리는 것을 찾아야 합니다. the shared drive 같은 온라인상의 저장 공간에 대해 'A를 B에 올려 두다'를 뜻하는 「place A on B」를 구성해야 하므로 (C) on이 정답입니다.

오답 (A) at: 온라인상의 저장 공간에 대해 place와 어울려 쓰이는 전치사가 아니므로 오답입니다.

(B) from: 온라인상의 저장 공간에 대해 place와 어울려 쓰이는 전치사가 아니므로 오답입니다.

(D) to: 온라인상의 저장 공간에 대해 place와 어울려 쓰이는 전치사가 아니므로 오답입니다.

어휘 place v. ~을 두다, ~을 놓다 revise ~을 수정하다, ~을 변경하다 form 양식, 서식 shared 공유된 entire 전체의 access ~을 이용하다, ~에 접근하다, ~에 접속하다

9.
정답 (A)

해석 직원들이 별도로 통보 받지 않는다면 월간 영업 회의가 B 회의실에서 열릴 것입니다.

해설 선택지가 모두 전치사이므로 빈칸 뒤에 위치한 명사(구)와 어울리는 것을 찾아야 합니다. Room B 안에서 회의가 열리는 것이므로 공간의 내부나 넓은 공간에 대해 '~ 안에서, ~ 내부에서'를 의미할 때 사용하는 전치사 (A) in이 정답입니다.

오답 (B) on: 공간의 내부나 넓은 공간에 대해 사용하는 전치사가 아니므로 오답입니다.

(C) at: 공간의 내부나 넓은 공간에 대해 사용하는 전치사가 아니므로 오답입니다.

(D) to: 공간의 내부나 넓은 공간에 대해 사용하는 전치사가 아니므로 오답입니다.

어휘 monthly 월간의, 달마다의 sales 영업, 판매(량), 매출 hold (행사 등) ~을 열다, ~을 개최하다 unless ~하지 않는다면, ~가 아니라면 otherwise 별도로, 그 외에는, 그렇지 않으면 notify ~에게 통보하다, ~에게 알리다

10.
정답 (A)

해석 타카다 씨는 거의 10년 동안 잉센 트랜스포트에서 근무해 오셨으며, 현재 운영부장님이십니다.

해설 선택지가 모두 전치사이므로 빈칸 뒤에 위치한 명사(구)와 어울리는 것을 찾아야 합니다. 빈칸 뒤에 위치한 nearly a decade가 타카다 씨가 근무해 온 기간에 해당하므로 '~동안'이라는 의미로 어떤 일이나 상태가 지속되어 온 기간을 나타낼 때 사용하는 (A) for가 정답입니다.

오답 (B) during: 기간을 나타내는 전치사이기는 하지만, 어떤 일이 지속되는 동안 발생한 다른 일을 나타낼 때 사용하는 전치사이므로 오답입니다.

(C) since: 전치사(~ 이후로)일 때 과거의 시작 시점을 나타내는 명사(구)를 목적어로 취하므로 오답입니다.

(D) by: '~까지'라는 의미로 완료 기한을 나타낼 때 사용하는 전치사이므로 오답입니다.

어휘 nearly 거의 decade 10년 operation 운영, 영업, 가동, 작동

11.
정답 (C)

해석 전 세계에서 오는 수많은 클래식 음악가들이 제5회 연례 밴쿠버 음악 축제 중에 공연할 것이다.

해설 빈칸 뒤에 명사구가 위치해 있으므로 빈칸은 명사구를 목적어로 취하는 전치사 자리이며, the Fifth Annual Vancouver Music Festival은 기간의 의미를 포함하고 있는 명사구이므로 기간 명사 앞에 사용하는 전치사 (C) during이 정답입니다.

오답 (A) among: 복수명사를 목적어로 취하는 전치사이므로 오답입니다.

(B) between: 「A and B」 또는 복수명사로 된 목적어를 취하는 전치사이므로 오답입니다.

(D) while: 접속사이므로 전치사 자리인 빈칸에 맞지 않는 오답입니다.

어휘 numerous 수많은, 다수의 perform 공연하다, 연주하다 among ~ 사이에서 between (A and B): (A 또는 B) 사이에 during ~ 중에, ~ 동안 while ~하는 동안, ~인 반면

12.
정답 (B)

해석 퍼시픽 텔레콤 사의 모든 서비스에 대한 비용 지불은 보통 매달 20일이 기한이다.

해설 빈칸 뒤에 위치한 명사구는 날짜를 나타내므로 날짜 앞에 사용하는 전치사 (B) on이 정답입니다.

오답 (A) in: 월 또는 연도 앞에 사용하는 전치사이므로 오답입니다.

(C) at: 시각 앞에 사용하는 전치사이므로 오답입니다.

(D) with: 날짜 앞에 사용하는 전치사가 아니므로 오답입니다.

어휘 payment 지불(금)　normally 보통, 일반적으로　due + 날짜: ~가 기한인

13.
정답 (D)

해석 트레드스톤 씨와 부동산 중개업자는 그 빈 건물을 보기 위해 존스 스트리트 452번지에서 만날 것이다.

해설 빈칸 뒤에 위치한 명사구는 주소를 나타내므로 하나의 지점 앞에 사용하는 전치사 (D) at이 정답입니다.

오답 (A) along: 도로나 해변처럼 길게 이어져 있는 장소 앞에 사용하는 전치사이므로 오답입니다.
(B) on: 주소 앞에 사용할 수 있는 전치사가 아니므로 오답입니다.
(C) under: 주소 앞에 사용할 수 있는 전치사가 아니므로 오답입니다.

어휘 real estate agent 부동산 중개업자　view v. ~을 보다　vacant 비어 있는　along (길 등) ~을 따라

14.
정답 (B)

해석 미란다 실바 박사는 좋은 신체 자세의 중요성에 관한 연구로 셔우드 상을 받았다.

해설 빈칸 뒤에 위치한 명사구는 '연구'를 뜻하는데, 실바 박사가 상을 받은 이유에 해당되는 것으로 볼 수 있으므로 이유를 나타내는 전치사 (B) for가 정답입니다.

오답 (A) of: 이유를 나타내는 전치사가 아니므로 오답입니다.
(C) to: 이유를 나타내는 전치사가 아니므로 오답입니다.
(D) about: 이유를 나타내는 전치사가 아니므로 오답입니다.

어휘 award A B: A에게 B를 주다, 수여하다　research 연구, 조사　importance 중요성　posture 자세

15.
정답 (D)

해석 다음 달부터, 오직 허가증을 가진 사람들만 노스 베이 주차장을 이용하는 것이 허용될 것입니다.

해설 빈칸 앞에 위치한 those는 수식어구를 동반해 '~하는 사람들'이라는 의미를 나타내는 대명사이며, 빈칸 뒤에 위치한 명사구 a permit은 '허가증'을 나타냅니다. 따라서 '허가증을 가진 사람들'이라는 뜻이 되어야 알맞으므로 '~을 가진'의 의미를 나타내는 동반 전치사 (D) with가 정답입니다.

오답 (A) toward: 동반을 나타내는 전치사가 아니므로 오답입니다.
(B) for: 동반을 나타내는 전치사가 아니므로 오답입니다.
(C) of: 동반을 나타내는 전치사가 아니므로 오답입니다.

어휘 starting + 날짜: ~부터　those (수식어구와 함께) ~하는 사람들　permit 허가증　be allowed to do ~하는 것이 허용되다　parking lot 주차장　toward (방향 등) ~ 쪽으로, ~을 향해

16.
정답 (C)

해석 자료에 따르면, 5번가의 교통 혼잡은 오전 7시와 9시 사이에 최악의 수준에 이른다.

해설 빈칸 뒤에 기준이 되는 두 시점이 「A and B」의 구조로 쓰여 있습니다. 따라서 이와 같은 구조와 함께 'A와 B 사이에'라는 의미를 나타낼 때 사용하는 전치사 (C) between이 정답입니다.

오답 (A) among: 「A and B」의 구조와 어울리는 전치사가 아니므로 오답입니다.
(B) under: 「A and B」의 구조와 어울리는 전치사가 아니므로 오답입니다.
(D) both: 「A and B」의 구조와 어울리기는 하지만 전치사가 아니며, 의미도 맞지 않는 오답입니다.

어휘 according to ~에 따르면　traffic congestion 교통 혼잡　at one's worst 최악의 수준인　between A and B: A와 B 사이에　among ~ 사이에서　both (A and B): (A와 B) 둘 모두

17.
정답 (D)

해석 햄튼 대학교의 경영학 교수인 프랭크 라일즈 씨가 시간 관리 기술에 관해 강연하실 것입니다.

해설 빈칸 뒤에 '시간 관리 기술'을 뜻하는 명사구가 쓰여 있는데, 이는 빈칸 앞에 언급된 강연(lecture)의 주제인 것으로 판단할 수 있습니다. 따라서 주제를 나타내는 전치사 (D) on이 정답입니다.

오답 (A) by: 주제를 나타내는 전치사가 아니므로 오답입니다.
(B) to: 주제를 나타내는 전치사가 아니므로 오답입니다.
(C) with: 주제를 나타내는 전치사가 아니므로 오답입니다.

어휘 deliver a lecture 강연하다　management 관리, 운영, 경영　skill 기술, 능력

18.
정답 (B)

해석 새로운 사내 보안 정책과 관련된 회람을 받지 못하셨다면, 인사부의 스콧 씨에게 연락하십시오.

해설 빈칸 뒤에 '새로운 사내 보안 정책'을 뜻하는 명사구가 쓰여 있는데, 이는 빈칸 앞에 언급된 회람(memorandum)의 주제인 것으로 판단할 수 있습니다. 따라서 주제를 나타내는 전치사 (B) regarding이 정답입니다.

오답 (A) without: 주제를 나타내는 전치사가 아니므로 오답입니다.

(C) following: 주제를 나타내는 전치사가 아니므로 오답입니다.

(D) throughout: 주제를 나타내는 전치사가 아니므로 오답입니다.

어휘 contact ~에게 연락하다 personnel 인사(부) receive ~을 받다 memorandum 회람 corporate 기업의 security 보안 policy 정책, 방침 without ~없이, ~하지 않고 following ~ 후에 regarding ~와 관련해 throughout (기간) ~ 동안에 걸쳐, (장소) ~ 전역에 걸쳐

19.
정답 (A)

해석 가격이 적당한 주택 및 많은 수의 학교들 때문에, 렙포드 지역은 젊은 가정들에게 매우 인기가 있다.

해설 빈칸과 콤마 사이에 두 개의 명사구가 and로 연결되어 있습니다. 따라서 이 두 개의 명사구들을 목적어로 취할 전치사가 빈칸에 쓰여야 알맞으므로 선택지에서 유일한 전치사인 (A) Owing to가 정답입니다.

오답 (B) Assuming: 주어와 동사가 포함된 절을 이끌어야 하는 접속사이므로 오답입니다.

(C) Rather: 부사이므로 명사구를 목적어로 취할 수 없는 오답입니다.

(D) Because: 주어와 동사가 포함된 절을 이끌어야 하는 접속사이므로 오답입니다.

어휘 affordable 가격이 적당한 housing 주택 neighborhood 지역, 인근 popular with ~에게 인기 있는 owing to ~ 때문에 assuming (that) ~라고 가정하면 rather 다소, 오히려, 좀, 약간

20.
정답 (B)

해석 그린버그 마케팅 그룹은 데넘 백화점을 대신해 광범위한 고객 설문조사를 실시하기로 결정했다.

해설 빈칸 앞에 위치한 on behalf는 전치사 of와 결합해 '~을 대신해, 대표해'라는 의미를 나타내는 전치사구를 구성하므로 (B) of가 정답입니다.

오답 (A) for: on behalf와 어울려 전치사구를 구성하지 않으므로 오답입니다.

(C) with: on behalf와 어울려 전치사구를 구성하지 않으므로 오답입니다.

(D) to: on behalf와 어울려 전치사구를 구성하지 않으므로 오답입니다.

어휘 decide to do ~하기로 결정하다 conduct ~을 실시하다, 수행하다 extensive 광범위한, 폭넓은 survey 설문조사(지) on behalf of ~을 대신해, 대표해

DAY 10 관계사

PRACTICE

1. which 2. advises 3. where
4. whenever 5. whichever 6. where

1.
정답 which

해석 나는 여행 경비 환급 정책을 설명하는 이메일을 전달했다.

해설 선택지가 모두 관계대명사이므로 빈칸 앞의 명사 및 빈칸 뒤의 구조를 통해 알맞은 것을 찾아야 합니다. whose는 보통 '~의'라는 소유격으로, 빈칸 뒤에는 명사가 와야 합니다. 하지만 이 문장에서는 동사가 오기 때문에 whose는 답이 되지 못합니다. which는 선행사(e-mail)를 받아서 주격 관계대명사 역할을 하므로 정답은 which입니다.

어휘 forward 전달하다 reimbursement policy 환급 정책

2.
정답 advises

해석 시장 확장 전략에 대해 조언하는 그 컨설턴트가 어제 프로젝트에 합류했다.

해설 who는 빈칸 앞의 명사 consultant를 수식하는 주격 관계대명사이며, 선행사 consultant에 해당하는 단수 명사에 맞춰 단수 동사인 advises가 정답입니다.

어휘 advise 조언하다

3.
정답 where

해석 송 씨는 두 팀이 방해 없이 협업할 수 있는 회의실을 예약했다.

해설 When은 시간을 나타내는 관계부사로서, 시간 관련 상황에 쓰입니다. 하지만 문맥상 빈칸 뒤에 나오는 meeting room은 장소를 의미하기 때문에, 해당 장소에서 어떤 일이 이루어졌다는 점을 설명하려면 관계부사 where이 정답입니다.

어휘 collaborate 협업하다 interruption 방해

4.
정답 whenever

해석 정전이 발생할 때마다, 비상 조명이 작동합니다.

해설 whenever는 '~할 때마다'를 뜻하는 관계부사로서, '정전이 발생할 때마다 비상 조명이 작동한다'는 상황을 자연스럽게 전달하므로 whenever이 정답입니다. However는 '아무리 ~하더라도, 얼마나 ~하든지' 라는 의미의 복합관계부사로, 이 문장에서는 문맥상 어울리지 않습니다.

어휘 activate 작동하다 emergency lighting 비상 조명

5.
정답 whichever

해석 이메일이든 팩스든, 더 쉬운 방식에 따라 레이노어 씨에게 신청서를 제출해 주세요.

해설 빈칸 앞에 전치사 on이 있고, 빈칸 뒤에 be동사와 주격보어 easier가 있으므로 주어가 없는 절이 이어져 있으므로 주격관계대명사 또는 복합관계대명사가 위치할 수 있습니다. 따라서 선택지 중에 복합관계대명사인 whichever이 정답입니다. 복합관계부사 however는 전치사 뒤에 쓰일 수 없으며, 그 뒤에는 형용사나 부사가 위치하거나, 완전한 절이 이어져야 하므로 오답입니다.

어휘 submit 제출하다 application form 신청서, 지원서 via ~을 통해서 depending on ~에 따라

6.
정답 where

해석 신입 사원들은 주문이 처리되고 배송되는 유통 시설을 견학했다.

해설 빈칸 뒤에는 「주어 + 수동태 동사(be p.p.)」 구조의 완전한 절이 오며, 빈칸 앞에 distribution facility는 장소를 나타냅니다. 따라서 그 장소에서 발생하는 동작을 설명하기 위해서는 관계부사 where이 적절합니다. 관계대명사 which 뒤에는 주어 또는 목적어가 없는 불완전한 절이 이어지므로 오답입니다.

어휘 hire 고용하다, (사람의) 고용 distribution facility 유통시설

실전 TEST

1. (B)	2. (C)	3. (B)	4. (D)	5. (A)
6. (C)	7. (C)	8. (A)	9. (D)	10. (B)
11. (A)	12. (D)	13. (D)	14. (A)	15. (C)
16. (D)	17. (C)	18. (B)	19. (A)	20. (B)

1.
정답 (B)

해석 여러 아이디어들로 회사의 이미지를 변모시켜 오신, 마케팅 이사님께서 다음 달에 퇴직하실 예정입니다.

해설 선택지가 모두 관계대명사이므로 빈칸 뒤에 이어지는 절의 구조 및 선행사를 통해 알맞은 것을 찾아야 합니다. 선행사 The marketing director가 사람이며, 빈칸 뒤에 위치한 명사 ideas가 The marketing director's ideas(마케팅 이사의 아이디어들)에 해당하는 소유 관계이므로 소유격관계대명사 (B) whose가 정답입니다.

오답 (A) who: 주격관계대명사이며, 바로 뒤에 관계대명사절의 동사가 이어져야 하므로 오답입니다.
(C) whom: 목적격관계대명사이며, 바로 뒤에 동사나 전치사의 목적어가 빠진 불완전한 관계대명사절이 이어져야 하므로 오답입니다.
(D) which: 사람명사를 수식하는 관계대명사가 아니므로 오답입니다.

어휘 transform ~을 변모시키다, ~을 탈바꿈시키다 retire 퇴직하다, 은퇴하다

2.
정답 (C)

해석 고객에 의해 반품된 그 기기에는 제조상의 결함이 있었다.

해설 선택지가 모두 관계대명사이므로 빈칸 뒤에 이어지는 절의 구조 및 선행사를 통해 알맞은 것을 찾아야 합니다. 선행사 The device는 사물이므로 사물명사를 수식할 수 있는 관계대명사 (C) that이 정답입니다.

오답 (A) who: 사람명사를 수식할 때 사용하는 주격관계대명사이므로 오답입니다.
(B) whom: 사람명사를 수식할 때 사용하는 목적격관계대명사이므로 오답입니다.
(D) whose: 소유격관계대명사이므로 오답입니다.

어휘 device 기기, 장치 return ~을 반품하다, ~을 반납하다 manufacturing 제조(업) defect 결함

3.
정답 (B)

해석 우리는 새 태양열 충전식 배터리를 고안하기 위해 에너지 효율을 전문으로 하는 외부 자문을 고용했습니다.

해설 선택지가 모두 관계대명사이므로 빈칸 뒤에 이어지는 절의 구조 및 선행사를 통해 알맞은 것을 찾아야 합니다. 선행사 an external consultant는 사람명사이며, 빈칸 뒤에 동사 specializes가 있으므로 사람명사를 수식하는 주격관계대명사 (B) who가 정답입니다.

오답 (A) whose: 소유격관계대명사이며, 빈칸 뒤에 소유 관계에 해당하는 명사가 이어져야 하므로 오답입니다.
(C) which: 사람명사를 수식하는 관계대명사가 아니므로 오답입니다.
(D) what: 선행사를 수식하는 역할을 하지 않으므로 오답입니다.

어휘 hire ~을 고용하다 external 외부의 consultant 자문, 컨설턴트, 상담 전문가 specialize in ~을 전문으로 하다 efficiency 효율(성) solar-powered 태양열 충전식의, 태양열로 동력을 얻는

4.
정답 (D)

해석 우리가 고객 회의를 열었던 사무실이 이번 주에 개조되고 있습니다.

해설 선택지가 관계대명사 또는 관계부사이므로 빈칸 뒤에 이어지는 절의 구조 및 선행사를 통해 알맞은 것을 찾아야 합니다. 선

행사 The office가 장소사물명사이며, 이를 수식하는 절 we held the client meeting이 빠진 요소 없이 구성이 완전한 상태이므로 장소사물명사를 수식하면서 완전한 절을 이끄는 관계부사 (D) where가 정답입니다.

오답 (A) that: 장소사물명사를 수식할 수는 있지만, 주어나 목적어 등이 빠진 불완전한 절을 이끄는 관계대명사이므로 오답입니다.

(B) what: 선행사를 수식하는 역할을 하지 않으므로 오답입니다.

(C) which: 장소사물명사를 수식할 수는 있지만, 주어나 목적어 등이 빠진 불완전한 절을 이끄는 관계대명사이므로 오답입니다.

어휘 hold (행사 등) ~을 열다, ~을 개최하다 renovate ~을 개조하다, ~을 보수하다

5.
정답 (A)

해석 당신이 컨퍼런스에서 만났던 오르테가 씨가 오늘 교육을 진행합니다.

해설 선택지가 모두 관계대명사이므로 빈칸 뒤에 이어지는 절의 구조 및 선행사를 통해 알맞은 것을 찾아야 합니다. 선행사 Ms. Ortega는 사람이며, 빈칸 뒤에 타동사 met의 목적어가 빠진 불완전한 절이 있고, 콤마 뒤에 위치해야 하므로 사람명사를 수식하는 목적격관계대명사로서 콤마 뒤에 쓰일 수 있는 (A) who가 정답입니다.

오답 (B) which: 사람명사를 수식하는 관계대명사가 아니므로 오답입니다.

(C) whose: 사람명사를 수식하는 소유격관계대명사이며, 빈칸 뒤에 소유 관계에 해당하는 명사와 동사가 이어지는 구조에 쓰이므로 오답입니다.

(D) when: 시간을 나타내는 관계부사이므로 오답입니다.

어휘 lead ~을 진행하다, ~을 이끌다 training 교육, 훈련 session (특정 활동을 하는) 시간

6.
정답 (C)

해석 그 회사는 다음 회계 연도에 대한 자사의 전략을 개괄적으로 설명하는 보고서를 공개했다.

해설 선택지가 모두 관계대명사이므로 빈칸 뒤에 이어지는 절의 구조 및 선행사를 통해 알맞은 것을 찾아야 합니다. 선행사 a report가 사물이므로 사물명사를 수식할 수 있는 관계대명사 (C) that이 정답입니다.

오답 (A) whose: 소유격관계대명사이며, 빈칸 뒤에 소유 관계에 해당하는 명사가 이어져야 하므로 오답입니다.

(B) who: 사람명사를 수식할 때 사용하는 관계대명사이므로 오답입니다.

(D) where: 장소명사를 수식할 때 사용하는 관계부사이므로 오답입니다.

어휘 release ~을 공개하다, ~을 발표하다, ~을 출시하다 outline ~을 개괄적으로 설명하다 strategy 전략 fiscal year 회계 연도

7.
정답 (C)

해석 이것은 모든 신입 직원들에 의해 작성 완료되어야 하는 신청서입니다.

해설 선택지가 관계대명사 또는 관계부사이므로 빈칸 뒤에 이어지는 절의 구조 및 선행사를 통해 알맞은 것을 찾아야 합니다. 선행사 the application이 사물이므로 사물명사를 수식할 수 있는 관계대명사 (C) that이 정답입니다.

오답 (A) what: 선행사를 수식하는 역할을 하지 않으므로 오답입니다.

(B) who: 사람명사를 수식할 때 사용하는 관계대명사이므로 오답입니다.

(D) where: 장소를 나타내는 명사를 수식할 때 사용하는 관계부사이므로 오답입니다.

어휘 application 신청(서), 지원(서) complete ~을 완료하다

8.
정답 (A)

해석 서버를 고쳐 준 기술자가 작업을 훌륭하게 해 주었으며, 합리적인 요금을 청구했습니다.

해설 선택지가 모두 관계대명사이므로 빈칸 뒤에 이어지는 절의 구조 및 선행사를 통해 알맞은 것을 찾아야 합니다. 선행사 The technician이 사람이며, 빈칸 뒤에 동사 fixed가 있으므로 사람명사를 수식하는 주격관계대명사 (A) who가 정답입니다.

오답 (B) which: 사람명사를 수식하는 관계대명사가 아니므로 오답입니다.

(C) whom: 사람명사를 수식하는 목적격 관계대명사이며, 빈칸 뒤에 동사나 전치사의 목적어가 빠진 절이 위치한 구조에 쓰이므로 오답입니다.

(D) whose: 사람명사를 수식하는 소유격 관계대명사이며, 빈칸 뒤에 소유 관계에 해당하는 명사가 이어져야 하므로 오답입니다.

어휘 fix ~을 고치다, ~을 바로잡다 do a excellent job 일을 훌륭하게 하다 charge ~을 청구하다 reasonable 합리적인 fee 요금, 수수료

9.
정답 (D)

해석 그 세미나는, 인사부에 의해 마련된 것으로서, 직장 내 보건과 안전을 다뤘습니다.

해설 선택지가 모두 관계대명사이므로 빈칸 뒤에 이어지는 절의 구조 및 선행사를 통해 알맞은 것을 찾아야 합니다. 선행사 The seminar가 사물명사의 범위에 해당하며, 빈칸 뒤에 수동태

동사 was organized가 있고, 콤마 뒤에 위치해야 하므로 사물명사를 수식하는 주격관계대명사로서 콤마 뒤에 쓰일 수 있는 (D) which가 정답입니다.

오답 (A) who: 사람명사를 수식하는 주격관계대명사이므로 오답입니다.
(B) what: 선행사를 수식하는 역할을 하지 않으므로 오답입니다.
(C) how: 방법을 나타내는 관계부사이므로 오답입니다.

어휘 organize ~을 마련하다, ~을 조직하다 human resources 인사(부), 인적 자원 cover (주제 등) ~을 다루다, ~을 포함하다

10.
정답 (B)
해석 성과가 기대치를 초과하는 직원들은 3개월마다 승진 대상으로 고려될 것입니다.
해설 선택지가 모두 관계대명사이므로 빈칸 뒤에 이어지는 절의 구조 및 선행사를 통해 알맞은 것을 찾아야 합니다. 선행사 Employees가 사람이며, 빈칸 뒤에 위치한 명사 performance가 Employees' performance(직원들의 성과)에 해당하는 소유 관계이므로 소유격관계대명사 (B) whose가 정답입니다.

오답 (A) which: 사람명사를 수식하는 관계대명사가 아니므로 오답입니다.
(C) in which: 「전치사 + 관계대명사」 구조로, 장소명사 또는 시간명사를 수식하는 관계대명사이므로 오답입니다.
(D) who: 주격관계대명사이며, 바로 뒤에 관계대명사절의 동사가 이어져야 하므로 오답입니다.

어휘 performance 성과, 실적, 수행 (능력) exceed ~을 초과하다, ~을 넘어서다 expectation 기대(치), 예상 consider ~을 고려하다 promotion 승진, 판촉 (행사), 홍보

11.
정답 (A)
해석 엠파이어 스테이트 빌딩의 가이드 동반 투어에 관심 있으신 손님들께서는 오전 10시까지 로비에 모이셔야 합니다.
해설 선택지가 모두 관계대명사이므로 수식받는 명사(선행사) 및 빈칸 뒤의 구조에 어울리는 것을 찾아야 합니다. 빈칸 앞에 사람명사 Guests가 있고 빈칸 뒤로 주어 없이 동사 are가 쓰여 있습니다. 따라서 사람명사를 수식하는 주격 관계대명사인 (A) who가 정답입니다.

오답 (B) which: 사물명사를 수식하는 관계대명사이므로 오답입니다.
(C) whose: 바로 뒤에 명사가 딸려 있어야 하는 소유격 관계대명사이므로 오답입니다.
(D) whom: 사람명사를 수식하지만, 바로 뒤에 주어와 동사가 위치하는 구조에 어울리므로 오답입니다.

어휘 be interested in ~에 관심이 있다 guided 가이드를 동반한

12.
정답 (D)
해석 전 직원이 회사 대표를 통해 로스앤젤레스에 본사를 둔 보텍스 엔터테인먼트 사와의 합병에 관해 들었다.
해설 선택지가 관계대명사와 관계부사로 구성되어 있으므로 수식 받는 명사(선행사) 및 빈칸 뒤의 구조에 어울리는 것을 찾아야 합니다. 빈칸 앞에 업체명에 해당되는 사물명사 Vortex Entertainment가 있고 빈칸 뒤로 주어 없이 동사 is가 쓰여 있습니다. 따라서 사물명사를 수식하는 주격 관계대명사인 (D) which가 정답입니다.

오답 (A) who: 사람명사를 수식하는 관계대명사이므로 오답입니다.
(B) whose: 사람명사 또는 사물명사를 수식하지만, 바로 뒤에 명사가 딸려 있어야 하는 소유격 관계대명사이므로 오답입니다.
(C) how: 방법을 나타내는 관계부사이므로 오답입니다.

어휘 inform ~에게 알리다 merger with ~와의 합병 be based in ~에 본사를 두다, 기반을 두다

13.
정답 (D)
해석 축제 주최자가 행사 개최 장소와 여러 버스 및 지하철 노선을 연결하는 셔틀버스 서비스를 발표했다.
해설 명사구 a shuttle bus service 뒤로 관계대명사 that과 빈칸이 있고 그 뒤로 명사구와 전치사구만 쓰여 있습니다. 따라서 빈칸에 that절의 동사가 쓰여야 하는데, 이 that절이 수식하는 명사(선행사)인 a shuttle bus service가 단수이므로 단수 명사와 수일치되는 단수 동사 (D) connects가 정답입니다.

오답 (A) connect: 복수명사와 수일치되는 복수동사이므로 오답입니다.
(B) connection: 명사이므로 that절의 동사가 필요한 빈칸에 맞지 않는 오답입니다.
(C) connecting: 동명사 또는 현재분사형이므로 that절의 동사가 필요한 빈칸에 맞지 않는 오답입니다.

어휘 organizer 주최자, 조직자 announce ~을 발표하다, 공지하다 venue 개최 장소 several 여럿의, 몇몇의 connect (A with B): (A를 B와) 연결하다 connection 연결, 접속, 관련

14.
정답 (A)

해석 근속 기간이 5년이 넘으면서 8월에 유급 휴가를 떠나기를 희망하는 정규직 직원들은 늦어도 4월 30일까지 요청 양식을 제출해야 합니다.

해설 사람명사 Full-time employees를 수식하는 관계대명사 who 뒤로 빈칸과 to부정사가 이어져 있습니다. 따라서 빈칸에 who절의 동사가 쓰여야 하는데, 이 who절이 수식하는 명사(선행사) Full-time employees가 복수형이므로 복수 동사의 형태인 (A) wish가 정답입니다.

오답 (B) wishes: 단수 명사와 수일치되는 단수 동사의 형태이므로 오답입니다.
(C) wishing: 동명사 또는 현재분사형이므로 who절의 동사가 필요한 빈칸에 맞지 않는 오답입니다.
(D) wishful: 형용사이므로 who절의 동사가 필요한 빈칸에 맞지 않는 오답입니다.

어휘 paid vacation 유급 휴가 submit ~을 제출하다 request 요청 form 양식, 서식 no later than 늦어도 ~까지는 wishful 바라는, 갈망하는

15.
정답 (C)

해석 애스펜에 있는 많은 업체들이 관광객 숫자가 최고 수준에 이르는 겨울 중에 직원을 추가로 고용합니다.

해설 선택지가 모두 관계부사들이므로 빈칸 앞에 위치한 명사의 특성에 따라 알맞은 것을 골라야 합니다. 빈칸 앞에 시점을 나타내는 the winter가 쓰여 있으므로 시간 관계부사인 (C) when이 정답입니다.

오답 (A) where: 장소 관계부사이므로 빈칸에 맞지 않는 오답입니다.
(B) why: 이유 관계부사이므로 빈칸에 맞지 않는 오답입니다.
(D) how: 방법 관계부사이므로 빈칸에 맞지 않는 오답입니다.

어휘 business 업체, 회사 hire ~을 고용하다 additional 추가적인 during ~ 중에, ~ 동안 the number of ~의 수, 숫자 at one's highest 최고 수준인, 최고치인

16.
정답 (D)

해석 그레이 씨는 자신의 면접이 진행되었던 대회의실에 실수로 지갑을 놓고 왔다.

해설 선택지에 관계대명사와 관계부사가 섞여 있는데, 빈칸 뒤에 주어와 자동사로 구성된 완전한 절을 이끌 수 있는 것은 관계부사이므로 관계부사 (D) where가 정답입니다.

오답 (A) what: 불완전한 절을 이끌어야 하므로 오답입니다.
(B) which: 불완전한 절을 이끄는 관계대명사이므로 오답입니다.
(C) that: 불완전한 절을 이끄는 관계대명사이므로 오답입니다.

어휘 accidentally 실수로, 우연히 leave ~을 놓다, 두다 take place (일, 행사 등이) 발생되다, 개최되다

17.
정답 (C)

해석 사용 설명서를 분실하신 고객들께서 저희 가구가 어떻게 조립되는지 보시려면 저희 웹사이트를 방문하시면 됩니다.

해설 선택지가 관계대명사와 관계부사로 구성되어 있으므로 수식받는 명사(선행사) 및 빈칸 뒤의 구조에 어울리는 것을 찾아야 합니다. 그런데 빈칸 앞에 명사(선행사) 없이 to부정사로 쓰인 동사 see만 있으므로 선행사 the way만 사용하거나 the way 없이 사용하는 관계부사 (C) how가 정답입니다.

오답 (A) which: 수식해야 하는 명사(선행사)가 필요한 관계대명사이므로 오답입니다.
(B) what: 뒤에 불완전한 절을 이끌어야 하므로 오답입니다.
(D) whom: 수식해야 하는 명사(선행사)가 필요한 관계대명사이므로 오답입니다.

어휘 misplace ~을 분실하다, ~을 둔 곳을 잊다 instruction manual 사용 설명서 assemble ~을 조립하다

18.
정답 (B)

해석 벤틀리 씨는 다음 달에 급여 업무 책임자로 자신의 후임자가 되는 사람이 누구든지 2주간의 교육 및 지원을 제공할 것이다.

해설 선택지가 모두 복합 관계사들이므로 빈칸 이하 부분의 역할 및 구조를 확인해 알맞은 것을 찾아야 합니다. 전치사 to 다음에 빈칸이 있고 그 뒤로 주어 없이 동사 replaces부터 시작되는 불완전한 절이 위치해 있습니다. 따라서 불완전한 명사절을 이끌 수 있는 복합관계대명사가 필요한데, replaces의 주어로서 누군가의 후임이 되는 것은 사람이어야 하므로 사람을 의미하는 주격 복합관계대명사인 (B) whoever가 정답입니다.

오답 (A) whichever: 불완전한 명사절을 이끌 수 있는 복합관계대명사이지만, 사람을 의미하지 않으므로 오답입니다.
(C) whenever: 부사절의 역할을 하는 완전한 절을 이끄는 복합관계부사이므로 오답입니다.
(D) wherever: 부사절의 역할을 하는 완전한 절을 이끄는 복합관계부사이므로 오답입니다.

어휘 provide ~을 제공하다 training 교육 support 지원, 지지 replace ~의 후임이 되다, ~을 대체하다 payroll 급여 대상자 명단 whoever ~하는 누구든 whichever ~하는 어느 것이든, 어느 것을 ~하든 whenever ~하는 언제든, ~할 때마다 wherever ~하는 어디든

19.

정답 (A)

해석 우리의 시장 조사 설문 결과는 왜 우리 제품이 17세에서 25세 사이의 소비자들에게 가장 인기가 높은지를 보여준다.

해설 목적어를 필요로 하는 타동사 shows 뒤로 빈칸이 있고, 그 뒤로 주어와 동사를 포함한 완전한 절이 이어지는 구조입니다. 따라서 이 절이 shows의 목적어 역할을 하는 관계부사인 (A) why가 정답입니다. 참고로, why 앞에 이유의 명사 the reason이 생략되었습니다.

오답 (B) which: 불완전한 명사절을 이끄는 관계대명사이므로 오답입니다.

(C) what: 불완전한 명사절을 이끄는 접속사이므로 오답입니다.

(D) those: 대명사이므로 주어와 동사가 포함된 절을 이끌 수 없으므로 오답입니다.

어휘 research 조사, 연구 survey 설문조사(지) show 보여주다, 나타내다 consumer 소비자 aged + 연령: 나이가 ~인 between A and B: A와 B 사이에

20.

정답 (B)

해석 존슨 씨는 작년에 설치된 제조 기계들을 점검하기 위해 어제 공장을 방문했다.

해설 빈칸 뒤에 주어 없이 동사 were installed부터 시작되는 불완전한 절이 있습니다. 따라서 이 불완전한 절은 빈칸 바로 앞에 위치한 사물명사 manufacturing machines를 수식하는 역할을 해야 알맞으므로 불완전한 절을 이끌어 명사(선행사)를 수식하는 주격 관계대명사 (B) that이 정답입니다.

오답 (A) what: 불완전한 절을 이끌기는 하지만 명사(선행사)가 필요하지 않으므로 오답입니다.

(C) who: 불완전한 절을 이끄는 주격 관계대명사이지만 사람 명사를 수식해야 하므로 오답입니다.

(D) there: 부사 또는 명사로 쓰이므로 절을 이끌 수 없는 오답입니다.

어휘 inspect ~을 점검하다 manufacturing 제조 install ~을 설치하다

PART 6

DAY 11 접속부사

PRACTICE

1. (B) 2. (C) 3. (A) 4. (C) 5. (A)

1.

정답 (B)

직원들은 세미나 동안 인쇄된 유인물이 배포되지 않을 것이라고 들었다. 그 대신, 그들은 회사의 인트라넷에서 자료를 다운로드해야 한다.

(A) 그것보다는
(B) 그 대신
(C) 게다가, 추가로
(D) 반대로

해설 세미나 동안 인쇄된 유인물이 배포되지 않는다는 안내를 받은 직원들에게 대안으로 자료를 인트라넷에서 다운로드해야 한다는 내용입니다. 앞 문장의 내용에 대한 대안의 내용이 이어지고 있으므로 이러한 문맥에서 사용될 수 있는 적절한 연결어는 '그 대신'을 의미하는 (B) Instead가 정답입니다.

어휘 employee 직원 printed 인쇄된 handout 유인물, 배포 자료

2.

정답 (C)

사무실은 건물 전체에 에너지 효율적인 LED 조명을 설치하여 전체 전력 소비를 줄였다. 월간 전기 요금은 거의 20% 감소했다. 사실상, 조명 기구의 유지 보수 비용은 절반으로 줄었다. 시설 관리팀은 성능을 계속해서 모니터링하고 있다.

(A) 반대로
(B) 예를 들어
(C) 사실상, 실제로
(D) 그럼에도 불구하고

해설 빈칸 앞 문장에서 LED 조명 도입으로 전기 요금이 20% 감소했다는 사실을 언급했고, 이어지는 문장은 관리 비용도 절반으로 줄었다는 추가적인 사실을 강조합니다. 따라서 앞서 말한 내용을 뒷받침하거나 강화하는 추가 정보를 제시할 때 쓰이는 접속부사인 (C) in fact가 정답입니다.

어휘 install 설치하다 lighting 조명 consumption 소비 expense 비용 drop 감소하다 maintenance 유지보수

3.

정답 (A)

> 창고 운영팀은 지난 분기에 자동 재고 추적 시스템을 도입했다. 이 시스템은 재고 관리에서의 인적 오류를 줄였다. 그 결과, 제품 불일치 신고가 역대 최저치에 달했다. 그 팀은 현재 포장과 물류 분야에서도 유사한 도구들을 탐색하고 있다.

(A) 그 결과
(B) 대신에
(C) 대조적으로
(D) 더욱이

해설 문장 시작 부분에 콤마와 함께 빈칸이 위치하는 경우, 접속부사 문제이므로 앞뒤 문장의 의미를 확인해 그 관계를 파악합니다. 앞 문장에는 자동 재고 추적 시스템을 도입했다는 내용이 언급되었고, 그 뒤에 제출 불일치(오류)가 역대 최저라는 결과가 뒤에 나오므로 '그 결과'를 의미하는 접속부사 (A) As a result 가 정답입니다.

어휘 warehouse 창고 operations team 운영팀 automated 자동화된 inventory tracking system 재고 추적 시스템 quarter 분기 reduce 줄이다 stock management 재고 관리 as a result 그 결과 discrepancy 불일치, 차이, 오류 all-time 역대의 explore 탐색하다, 검토하다 logistics 물류

4.

정답 (C)

> 연례 보안 감사가 금요일 오후까지 진행될 예정입니다. 내부 네트워크에 대한 접근은 감사가 완료될 때까지 제한될 것입니다. 그동안, 직원들은 기밀이 아닌 업무에는 게스트 와이파이를 사용할 수 있습니다. 협조해 주셔서 감사합니다.

(A) 예를 들어
(B) 그러는 한편
(C) 그동안, 그 사이에
(D) 게다가

해설 문장 시작 부분에 콤마와 함께 빈칸이 위치하는 경우, 접속부사 문제이므로 앞뒤 문장의 의미를 확인해 그 관계를 파악합니다. 뒷 문장에는 감사가 끝날 때까지 사용할 수 있는 대체 수단을 소개하고 있으므로, '그동안에, 그 사이에'를 의미하는 (C) In the meantime이 정답입니다.

어휘 annual 매년의, 연례의 security audit 보안 감사 scheduled 예정된 run through ~까지 진행되다 restricted 제한된 complete 완료되다 in the meantime 그동안

5.

정답 (A)

> 윌슨 테크는 이번 분기에 일련의 비용 절감 조치를 시행했다. 여기에는 에너지 소비 감소와 장비 사용 조정이 포함된다. 예를 들어, 전기 요금을 낮추기 위해 비혼잡 시간대에는 기계의 전원이 꺼진다. 그러한 노력은 운영 효율성 향상에 도움이 될 것으로 기대된다.

(A) 예를 들어
(B) 그러나, 하지만
(C) 결론적으로
(D) 그 결과

해설 문장 시작 부분에 콤마와 함께 빈칸이 위치하는 경우, 접속부사 문제이므로 앞뒤 문장의 의미를 확인해 그 관계를 파악합니다. 앞 문장에는 에너지 소비 감소와 장비 사용의 조정에 대한 내용이 언급이 되고, 빈칸 뒤에 전기 요금을 낮추기 위해 비혼잡 시간대에 기계의 전원이 꺼진다는 내용이 언급되는데, 이는 에너지 소비 감소와 장비 사용 조정의 예시에 해당하므로, '예를 들어'라는 의미의 접속부사 (A) For example이 정답입니다.

어휘 implement 시행하다, 도입하다 cost-saving measure 비용 절감 조치 energy consumption 에너지 소비 modify 수정하다, 조정하다 equipment 장비 non-peak hours 비혼잡 시간대 electricity bill 전기 요금 efficiency 효율성

실전 TEST

1. (D)   2. (B)   3. (D)   4. (A)   5. (A)
6. (C)   7. (B)   8. (A)   9. (D)   10. (A)
11. (B) 12. (C) 13. (B) 14. (A) 15. (D)
16. (B)

1-4 다음 이메일을 참조하시오.

> 프랫 씨께,
>
> 귀사의 본사에 근무하는 직원들에게 영양가 있는 식사를 **1** 제공하기 위해 저희 회사를 고용하는 데 있어 훌륭한 결정을 내리셨습니다. 저는 지난주 금요일에 있었던 회의 중에 저희가 논의했던 몇몇 조건들을 최종 확정하고자 이 메시지를 씁니다.
>
> 합의한 바와 같이, 귀사에서 특정 요일에 얼마나 많은 식사를 필요로 하시는지 저희에게 **2** 알려 주시기 위해 월요일부터 금요일까지 매일 대략 오전 9시 30분에 저희에게 연락하시게 됩니다. 저희는 그 후에 귀사의 직원들을 위해 점심 식사를 준비해 늦어도

정오까지는 사무실로 배달해 드릴 것입니다. 귀사의 직원들 중 어느 분이든 식사와 관련된 요구 사항이 있으시면, 저희는 기꺼이 그것들을 수용할 것입니다. **3** 게다가, 귀사에서 최소 일주일 전에 미리 저희에게 알려주시기만 하면, 저희 세트 메뉴를 전적으로 맞춤 제공해 드릴 수도 있습니다.

위에 간략히 말씀드린 준비사항에 만족하신다고 확인해 주시는 대로, 정식 계약서를 작성해 보내 드리겠습니다. **4** 저는 저희가 함께 긴밀한 사업 관계를 형성할 것이라고 확신합니다.

안녕히 계십시오.
쉐릴 분, 그린필즈 케이터링

어휘 make a decision 결정을 내리다 hire ~을 고용하다 nutritious 영양가 있는 headquarters 본사 finalize ~을 최종 확정하다 terms (계약 등의) 조건, 조항 discuss ~을 논의하다, 이야기하다 agree 합의하다 contact ~에게 연락하다 approximately 약, 대략 require ~을 필요로 하다 particular 특정한 prepare ~을 준비하다 no later than 늦어도 ~까지는 dietary 식사의 requirement 요구, 요건 be happy to do 기꺼이 ~하다 accommodate ~을 수용하다 be able to do ~할 수 있다 fully 전적으로, 완전히 customize ~을 맞춤 제공하다 as long as ~하기만 하면, ~하는 한 notify ~에게 알리다 at least 최소한, 적어도 in advance 미리, 사전에 once 일단 ~하는 대로, ~하자마자 confirm that ~임을 확인해 주다 be satisfied with ~에 만족하다 arrangement 준비, 조치, 조정 outline v. ~을 간략히 말하다 above ad. 위에 have A p.p.: A가 ~되게 하다 formal 정식의, 공식적인 contract 계약(서) draw up ~을 작성하다

1.

정답 (D)

해설 선택지가 동사 provide의 여러 형태이므로 빈칸의 역할부터 파악합니다. 문장에 이미 동사 have made가 있으므로 provide는 동사의 형태로 쓰일 수 없으며, '직원들에게 영양가 있는 식사를 제공하기 위해'라는 목적을 나타내는 역할을 해야 알맞습니다. 따라서 목적을 나타낼 때 사용하는 to부정사의 형태인 (D) to provide가 정답입니다.

오답 (A) providing: 동명사 또는 현재분사형이므로 목적을 나타낼 수 없는 오답입니다.
(B) will provide: 조동사 will을 포함한 동사의 형태이므로 동사 자리가 아닌 빈칸에 쓰일 수 없는 오답입니다.
(C) provides: 3인칭 단수 주어와 어울리는 동사의 형태이므로 빈칸에 쓰일 수 없는 오답입니다.

어휘 provide ~을 제공하다

2.

정답 (B)

해설 빈칸 다음을 보면, 사람을 가리키는 목적어 us가 있고 의문사 how가 이끄는 명사절이 곧바로 이어지는 구조입니다. 따라서 「사람 목적어 + 의문사 명사절」의 구조와 함께 쓰일 수 있는 동사 (B) inform이 정답입니다.

오답 (A) remember: 「사람 목적어 + 의문사 명사절」의 구조와 함께 쓰이지 않는 동사이므로 오답입니다.
(C) describe: 「사람 목적어 + 의문사 명사절」의 구조와 함께 쓰이지 않는 동사이므로 오답입니다.
(D) clarify: 「사람 목적어 + 의문사 명사절」의 구조와 함께 쓰이지 않는 동사이므로 오답입니다.

어휘 inform A how: 얼마나 ~한지 A에게 알리다 describe ~을 설명하다, 묘사하다 clarify ~을 분명히 말하다, 명확하게 하다

3.

정답 (D)

해설 문장 시작 부분에 콤마와 함께 빈칸이 위치하는 경우, 접속부사 문제이므로 앞뒤 문장의 의미를 확인해 그 관계를 파악합니다. 앞 문장에는 식사 관련 요구 사항들을 수용하겠다는 말이 있고, 빈칸 뒤에는 세트 메뉴를 맞춤 제공해 주겠다는 말이 쓰여 있습니다. 따라서 업체 측에서 해줄 수 있는 서비스를 추가로 알리는 흐름임을 알 수 있으므로 추가 접속부사 (D) Furthermore가 정답입니다.

오답 (A) Consequently: 결과를 말할 때 사용하는 접속부사이므로 오답입니다.
(B) Recently: 접속부사로 쓰이지 않으며, 대략적인 과거 시점을 나타내므로 오답입니다.
(C) Instead: 대체되는 것을 말할 때 사용하는 접속부사이므로 오답입니다.

어휘 consequently 결과적으로 recently 최근에 instead 대신에 furthermore 게다가, 더욱이

4.

정답 (A)

해석 **(A) 저는 저희가 함께 긴밀한 사업 관계를 형성할 것이라고 확신합니다.**
(B) 그린필즈에서의 첫 근무일에 귀하를 맞이할 수 있기를 고대합니다.
(C) 행사 메뉴를 논의할 시간이 있으실 때 저에게 알려 주시기 바랍니다.
(D) 저희 제품 및 서비스에 관한 귀하의 의견에 진심으로 감사드립니다.

해설 지문 전체적으로 첫 거래를 위해 가진 회의 내용을 요약하고 있고, 빈칸 바로 앞에는 그 요약 내용에 만족할 경우에 정식 계약서를 보내겠다고 알리고 있습니다. 따라서 이제 막 계약이

성사되려는 시점이므로 상대 업체와 함께 좋은 관계를 형성하기를 원하는 바람을 담은 (A)가 정답입니다.

오답 (B) 지문 전체적으로 상대방의 첫 근무와 관련된 내용이 아니므로 흐름상 맞지 않는 오답입니다.
(C) 지문 전체적으로 행사 메뉴와 관련된 내용이 아니므로 흐름상 맞지 않는 오답입니다.
(D) 지문 전체적으로 제품 및 서비스에 관한 상대방의 의견과 관련된 내용이 아니므로 흐름상 맞지 않는 오답입니다.

어휘 be confident that ~임을 확신하다 establish ~을 형성하다, 확립하다 relationship 관계 look forward to -ing ~하기를 고대하다 let A know B: A에게 B를 알려주다 be free to do ~할 시간이 있다 appreciate ~에 대해 감사하다 feedback 의견

5-8 다음 이메일을 참조하시오.

안녕하세요,

저는 지난 한 해에 걸친 노고에 감사하기 위해 저희 직원들을 데리고 여행을 떠날 계획을 세우고 있습니다. 제 동료 중 한 명이 직원 야유회 및 팀 단합 시간에 이상적인 장소로 파인 밸리 파크를 추천해 주었기 때문에, 귀사에 예약하는 것을 고려하고 있습니다. **5** 하지만, 귀사 시설물의 적합성에 관해 몇 가지 우려 사항이 있습니다.

가장 먼저, 대략 총 50명의 관리자와 직원들이 있을 것이기 때문에, 저희 단체를 **6** 수용하기에 충분한 객실들이 있는지 잘 모르겠습니다. 또한, 발표 및 그룹 활동에 필요한 장내 방송 시스템과 스크린을 **7** 포함하는 대규모 모임 공간이 있는지도 확실히 해 두고 싶습니다.

객실과 모임 장소에 관한 추가 상세 정보를 비롯해 파인 밸리 파크에서 이용 가능한 야외 활동들을 담은 전체 목록도 제공해 주실 수 있다면 감사하겠습니다. **8** 여러 직원들이 하이킹 기회에 관해서 문의했습니다. 귀사에서 저희의 모든 필요 사항들을 충족해 주실 수 있다면, 기꺼이 즉시 예약하겠습니다.

안녕히 계십시오,
콜린 코넬, JKX 출판그룹

어휘 plan to do ~할 계획이다 take A on a trip: A를 데리고 여행을 떠나다 thank A for B: B에 대해 A에게 고마워하다 over ~ 동안에 걸친 colleague 동료 (직원) ideal 이상적인 destination 도착지, 목적지 outing 야유회 session (특정 활동을 위한) 시간 consider -ing ~하는 것을 고려하다 make a booking 예약하다 concern 우려, 걱정 suitability 적합성 facility 시설(물) approximately 약, 대략 in total 총, 전부 합쳐 whether ~인지 (아닌지) cabin 객실 make sure that ~인지 확실히 하다, 반드시 ~하도록 하다 public address system 장내 방송 시스템 presentation 발표 grateful 감사하는 provide ~을 제공하다 details 상세 정보, 세부 사항 available 이용 가능한 assuming that ~한다면, ~라고 가정하면 meet (조건 등) ~을 충족하다 be happy to do 기꺼이 ~하다 make a reservation 예약하다 immediately 즉시

5.
정답 (A)
해설 문장 시작 부분에 콤마와 함께 빈칸이 위치하는 경우, 접속부사 문제이므로 앞뒤 문장의 의미를 확인해 그 관계를 파악합니다. 앞 문장에는 예약하는 것을 고려하고 있다는 긍정적인 말이 있고, 빈칸 뒤에는 우려 사항이 있다는 부정적인 말이 쓰여 있습니다. 따라서 상반되는 내용을 말하는 흐름임을 알 수 있으므로 양보 접속부사 (A) However가 정답입니다.

오답 (B) Therefore: 결과를 말할 때 사용하는 접속부사이므로 오답입니다.
(C) Furthermore: 추가 사항을 말할 때 사용하는 접속부사이므로 오답입니다.
(D) Similarly: 유사성을 말할 때 사용하는 접속부사이므로 오답입니다.

어휘 however 하지만, 그러나 therefore 따라서, 그러므로 furthermore 게다가, 더욱이 similarly 마찬가지로

6.
정답 (C)
해설 선택지가 모두 타동사이므로 문장의 의미에 어울리는 동사를 찾아야 합니다. 빈칸 앞에 '충분한 객실이 있는지'라는 말이 쓰여 있고 빈칸 뒤에는 목적어로 '우리 단체'를 뜻하는 명사구가 쓰여 있습니다. 이 둘의 의미 관계로 볼 때 '우리 단체를 수용할 만큼 충분한 객실이 있는지'라는 뜻이 되어야 적절하므로 '~을 수용하다'를 뜻하는 (C) accommodate이 정답입니다.

오답 (A) compromise: '~을 타협하여 해결하다'를 뜻하므로 문장의 의미에 어울리지 않는 오답입니다.
(B) mediate: '~을 중재하다, 조정하다'를 뜻하므로 문장의 의미에 어울리지 않는 오답입니다.
(D) gather: '~을 모으다'를 뜻하므로 문장의 의미에 어울리지 않는 오답입니다.

어휘 compromise ~을 타협하여 해결하다 mediate ~을 중재하다, 조정하다 accommodate ~을 수용하다 gather ~을 모으다

7.
정답 (B)
해설 선택지가 동사 include의 여러 형태이므로 빈칸의 역할부터 파악합니다. 명사구 a large meeting room 뒤로 that

이 바로 이어져 있으므로 a large meeting room을 수식하는 that절임을 알 수 있고, 빈칸 뒤로 명사구와 전치사구만 있으므로 빈칸은 이 that절의 동사 자리입니다. 그리고 모임 공간이 지닌 일반적인 특성을 나타내야 하므로 include가 현재시제로 쓰여야 합니다. 또한 that이 수식하는 명사(선행사) a large meeting room이 3인칭 단수이므로 3인칭 단수 명사와 수일치되는 형태인 (B) includes가 정답입니다.

오답 (A) include: 현재시제이지만 3인칭 단수 명사와 수일치되는 형태가 아니므로 오답입니다.
(C) to include: 동사의 형태가 아니므로 that절의 동사 자리인 빈칸에 쓰일 수 없는 오답입니다.
(D) included: 과거시제이므로 모임 공간이 지닌 일반적인 특성을 나타내는 의미로 쓰일 수 없는 오답입니다.

어휘 include ~을 포함하다

8.

정답 (A)

해석 (A) 여러 직원들이 하이킹 기회에 관해서 문의했습니다.
(B) 저희 직원들이 귀사의 지역 투어를 특히 즐거워했습니다.
(C) 따라서, 귀사의 객실들 중 최소 20개를 예약하고자 합니다.
(D) 저희 예약에 단체 할인을 적용해 주셔서 감사드립니다.

해설 바로 앞 문장에 이용 가능한 야외 활동에 관한 세부 정보도 제공해 달라는 말이 있으므로 그렇게 요청하는 이유로서 여러 직원들이 하이킹 기회에 관해 문의했음을 언급하는 (A)가 정답입니다.

오답 (B) 빈칸 앞뒤 내용이 과거에 이미 즐겁게 경험한 일과 관련된 것이 아니므로 흐름상 맞지 않는 오답입니다.
(C) 빈칸 앞뒤 내용이 예약하기로 결정한 상황이 아니므로 흐름상 맞지 않는 오답입니다.
(D) 빈칸 앞뒤 내용이 할인 서비스와 관련된 것이 아니므로 흐름상 맞지 않는 오답입니다.

어휘 several 여럿의, 몇몇의 inquire about ~에 관해 문의하다 opportunity 기회 particularly 특히, 특별히 as such 따라서, 그러한 이유로 would like to do ~하고자 하다, ~하고 싶다 reserve ~을 예약하다 at least 최소한, 적어도 apply ~을 적용하다 booking 예약

9-12 다음 회람을 참조하시오.

팀원 여러분,

아시다시피, 우리 본사가 다음 달부터 실내 개조 공사를 거칠 것입니다. **9** 그에 따라, 우리는 일시적으로 모든 창고 보관 설비를 힐브룩 시설로 이전하기로 결정했습니다. 이 기간 중에 본사의 공간이 제한될 것이기 때문입니다.

힐브룩 부지는 널찍할 뿐만 아니라 고속도로 근처에 편리하게 위치해 있기도 합니다. 그것이 우리가 그곳으로 물품을 이동시키기로 정한 이유입니다. **10** 이에 앞서, 시설 관리팀에서 반드시 이전하기 전에 온도 조절 장치 및 보안 수단이 적절히 설치되어 있도록 작업할 것입니다. 어느 부서에서 물품을 보관하고, 얼마나 많은 공간을 각 부서에서 필요로 하는지 파악하기 위한 점검 사항 확인표가 만들어지는 중입니다.

반드시 6월 17일까지 **11** 때에 맞춰 여러분의 부서에서 보관과 관련해 필요로 하는 사항들과 함께 답변해 주시기 바랍니다. 늦은 제출은 공간 제약으로 인해 수용되지 않을 수 있습니다. 추가로, 오직 필수 재고품만 옮겨질 것입니다.

12 정확성이 이 과정에 필수적입니다. 따라서, 꼭 여러분의 보관 용기에 부서명과 내용물을 명확히 라벨로 표기해 혼란을 방지하시기 바랍니다. 질문이 있으실 경우, logistics@brolinlogix.com으로 연락 주십시오. 여러분의 협조에 감사 드립니다.

해럴드 콜린스, 시설 관리팀장
포틀랜드 데일리 뉴스

어휘 storage 보관 (설비), 저장 (공간) relocation (위치) 이전, 재배치 headquarters 본사 undergo ~을 거치다, ~을 겪다 renovation 개조, 보수 limited 제한된 available 이용 가능한 temporarily 일시적으로, 임시로 facility 시설(물) site 부지, 현장 not only A but also B: A뿐만 아니라 B도 spacious 널찍한 conveniently 편리하게 located 위치한 ensure that 반드시 ~하도록 하다, ~임을 보장하다 climate control 온도 조절 장치 measures 수단, 조치 properly 적절히, 제대로 install ~을 설치하다 compile (자료 등을 모아) ~을 만들다, ~을 정리하다 track ~을 파악하다, ~을 추적하다 store v. ~을 보관하다 material 물품, 재료 make sure to do 반드시 ~하도록 하다 respond 답변하다, 대응하다 submission 제출(물) accommodate ~을 수용하다 due to ~로 인해, ~ 때문에 constraint 제약, 제한 essential 필수적인 inventory 재고(품), 재고 조사 transfer ~을 옮기다 as such 따라서 be sure to do 꼭 ~하다 label v. ~을 라벨로 표기하다 container 용기, 그릇 content 내용(물) prevent ~을 방지하다 confusion 혼란, 혼동 reach out to ~에 연락하다 cooperation 협조, 협력

9.

정답 (D)

해설 빈칸 뒤에 콤마(,)가 있고, 그 뒤에 완전한 문장이 이어지므로 빈칸은 접속부사 자리임을 알 수 있습니다. 앞 문장에서 본사에서 실내 개조 공사가 진행될 것이라는 내용이 언급되어 있고, 그 뒤에 모든 창고 보관 설비를 이전할 것이라는 내용이 언

급되어 있습니다. 문맥상 원인과 결과의 관계를 나타내는 접속부사가 필요하므로 '그에 따라'라는 의미의 접속부사 (D) Accordingly가 정답입니다.

오답 (A) Instead: '대신에'라는 의미로 대안의 내용을 나타내는 접속부사이므로 오답입니다.
(B) Despite: 전치사며, 의미가 맞지 않으므로 오답입니다.
(C) On the other hand: '그러는 한편'이라는 의미로 대조적인 내용을 연결하는 접속부사이므로 오답입니다.

어휘 instead 대신에 despite ~에도 불구하고 on the other hand 그러는 한편 accordingly 그에 따라

10.
정답 (A)
해설 선택지가 모두 전치사이므로 의미가 알맞은 것을 찾아야 합니다. 빈칸 뒤에 위치한 this가 앞 단락에 언급된 힐브룩 부지로 이전하는 일을 가리키며, 그에 앞서 시설 관리팀에서 이전하기 전에 필요한 설치 작업을 한다는 의미를 나타내야 자연스러우므로 '~에 앞서, ~ 전에'를 뜻하는 (A) Prior to가 정답입니다.

오답 (B) Adjacent to: '~에 인접한'을 뜻하므로 의미가 어울리지 않는 오답입니다.
(C) As opposed to: '~와 반대로, ~와 대조적으로'를 뜻하므로 의미가 어울리지 않는 오답입니다.
(D) In favor of: '~을 위해, ~에 찬성해'를 뜻하므로 의미가 어울리지 않는 오답입니다.

어휘 adjacent to ~에 인접한 as opposed to ~와 반대로, ~와 대조적으로 in favor of ~을 위해, ~에 찬성해

11.
정답 (B)
해설 빈칸 앞뒤에 위치한 전치사 in과 부정관사 a, 그리고 명사 manner와 어울려 '때에 맞춰, 제때, 적시에'를 뜻하는 「in a timely manner」를 구성해야 알맞으므로 (B) timely가 정답입니다.

오답 (A) time: 전치사 in과 부정관사 a, 그리고 명사 manner와 어울리는 표현을 구성하지 않으므로 오답입니다.
(C) timing: 전치사 in과 부정관사 a, 그리고 명사 manner와 어울리는 표현을 구성하지 않으므로 오답입니다.
(D) timed: 전치사 in과 부정관사 a, 그리고 명사 manner와 어울리는 표현을 구성하지 않으므로 오답입니다.

어휘 timing 타이밍, 시기 (선택) timed 시간이 맞춰진

12.
정답 (C)
해석 (A) 그 보관 시설은 이용되지 않고 있습니다.
(B) 이 이전 단계는 이미 완료되었습니다.
(C) 정확성이 이 과정에 필수적입니다.
(D) 어느 부서도 현재 추가 공간을 이용하고 있지 않습니다.

해설 빈칸 뒤에 '따라서'라는 의미로 결과를 말할 때 사용하는 As such와 함께 부서명과 내용물을 명확히 라벨로 표기해 혼란을 방지하도록 당부하는 말이 쓰여 있습니다. 이는 물품 이전 작업을 정확히 진행하기 위한 방법에 해당하므로 그 정확성을 강조하는 (C)가 정답입니다.

오답 (A) 빈칸 다음 내용이 특정 보관 시설의 이용 여부와 관련된 내용이 아니므로 흐름상 맞지 않는 오답입니다.
(B) 빈칸 다음 내용이 이미 완료된 단계와 관련된 내용이 아니므로 흐름상 맞지 않는 오답입니다.
(D) 빈칸 다음 내용이 추가 공간 이용 여부와 관련된 내용이 아니므로 흐름상 맞지 않는 오답입니다.

어휘 in use 이용 중인 phase 단계 complete ~을 완료하다 accuracy 정확(성) essential 필수적인 process 과정 currently 현재 extra 추가의, 별도의

13-16 다음 기사를 참조하시오.

> **마이크로 인플루언서를 이용해 진정한 브랜드 충성도 구축하기**
>
> 오늘날의 디지털 분야에서, 소비자들은 개인적이면서 진짜라고 느끼는 브랜드에 점점 더 이끌리고 있습니다. **13** 결과적으로, 대형 인플루언서를 활용한 캠페인은 더 소규모이면서 더 많은 공감대를 형성하는 창작자들이 영감을 줄 수 있는 동일한 수준의 신뢰도를 항상 조성하지 못할 수 있습니다.
>
> 마이크로 인플루언서들, 즉 1천명에서 5만명 사이의 팔로워들을 지닌 이들이, 뛰어난 참여율과 틈새 구독자들로 인해 인기를 얻고 있습니다. 이들의 콘텐츠는 더욱 목표가 되어 있고, 팔로워들은 종종 더 강한 유대감을 느낍니다. 적당한 광고 예산을 가진 기업에게, 마이크로 인플루언서들과 협업하는 것은 비용 효율이 높고, **14** 영향력이 강력합니다.
>
> 성공은 신중한 브랜드 일관성에 **15** 달려 있습니다. 업체들은 진심으로 자사의 가치와 사명을 지지하는 인플루언서들과 협업해야 합니다. 그러나, 일부 기업들은 구독자층 또는 콘텐츠 스타일은 고려하지 않고 오직 팔로워 수에만 초점을 맞추는 실수를 저지릅니다. 이는 완전히 실패하거나 가식적으로 느껴지는 캠페인으로 이어질 수 있습니다.
>
> **16** 따라서, 브랜드는 인플루언서를 선택할 때 관련성을 최우선으로 고려해야 합니다. 가장 성공적인 캠페인은 규모보다는 공유된 가치, 진정성 있는 메시지, 그리고 청중과의 공존 가능성을 중시합니다.
>
> 장기적인 성과를 극대화하기 위해, 기업은 캠페인 성과를 지켜보고 핵심 크리에이터들과의 지속적인 관계를 유지해야 합니다.

어휘 authentic 진정한, 진짜의 landscape 분야, ~계 consumer 소비자 increasingly 점점 더 be drawn to ~에 이끌리다 large-scale 대형의, 대규모의 foster 조성하다, 발전시키다 the same level of 동일한 수준의 relatable 공감대를 형성하는 creator 창작자 inspire 영감을 주다, 격려하다 gain popularity 인기를 얻다 engagement rate (온라인 콘텐츠 등의) 참여율 niche (시장의) 틈새 audience 구독자들, 시청자들, 청중 targeted 목표가 된 connection 유대(감) modest 보통의, 적당한 advertising 광고 (활동) budget 예산 both A and B: A와 B 둘 모두 cost-effective 비용 효율적인 careful 신중한, 조심스러운 alignment 일관성, 방향성의 일치 genuinely 진심으로 mission 사명, 임무 make the mistake of ~하는 실수를 저지르다 focus on ~에 초점을 맞추다 without -ing ~하지 않고, ~하지 않은 채 consider ~을 고려하다 audience demographics 구독자층, 시청자층 lead to ~로 이어지다 fall flat 완전히 실패하다 inauthentic 가식적인, 진짜가 아닌 prioritize ~에 우선 순위를 두다 emphasize 강조하다, 중시하다 shared 공유된 value 가치(관) messaging 메시지 전달 compatibility 공존 가능성, 양립성 scale 규모, 범위, 등급 along (명사 뒤에서) ~ 하나만으로 maximize 극대화하다 long-term 장기적인 monitor 감시하다, 지켜보다 performance 성과 maintain 유지하다 ongoing 지속적인

13.
정답 (B)

해설 콤마와 함께 문장 시작 부분에 빈칸이 위치하는 경우, 앞뒤 문장들의 의미 흐름을 나타내는 접속부사가 쓰여야 합니다. 빈칸 뒤에 위치한 문장은 오늘날의 디지털 분야에서 소비자들이 보이는 경향에 따라 대형 인플루언서를 활용한 캠페인이 가져올 수 있는 부정적인 결과를 말하고 있습니다. 따라서 '그 결과, 결과적으로'라는 의미로 어떤 원인에 따른 결과를 말할 때 사용하는 (B) Consequently가 정답입니다.

오답 (A) Although: 주어와 동사를 각각 포함한 두 개의 절을 연결해 하나의 문장으로 만들어 주는 접속사이므로 오답입니다.
(C) For example: '예를 들어'를 뜻하므로 원인과 결과를 말하는 흐름에 어울리지 않는 오답입니다.
(D) Previously: '이전에'를 뜻하므로 원인과 결과를 말하는 흐름에 어울리지 않는 오답입니다.

어휘 although (비록) ~하기는 하지만, ~함에도 불구하고 consequently 그 결과, 결과적으로 for example 예를 들어 previously 이전에

14.
정답 (A)

해설 선택지가 모두 형용사이므로 의미가 알맞은 것을 찾아야 합니다. 빈칸에 쓰일 형용사는 앞에 and로 연결된 cost-effective와 함께 예산 수준이 보통인 회사들에게 앞서 언급된 접근 방식이 어떤 긍정적인 영향을 미칠 수 있는지를 나타내야 합니다. 따라서 금전적 측면의 장점을 나타낼 형용사가 쓰여야 자연스러우므로 '영향력이 강한'을 뜻하는 (A) impactful이 정답입니다.

오답 (B) limited: '제한적인'을 뜻하므로 문장의 의미에 어울리지 않는 오답입니다.
(C) seasonal: '계절적인'을 뜻하므로 문장의 의미에 어울리지 않는 오답입니다.
(D) reversible: '되돌릴 수 있는, 뒤집을 수 있는'을 뜻하므로 문장의 의미에 어울리지 않는 오답입니다.

어휘 impactful 영향력이 강한 limited 제한적인 seasonal 계절적인 reversible 되돌릴 수 있는, 뒤집을 수 있는

15.
정답 (D)

해설 주어와 빈칸 뒤로 on 전치사구만 쓰여 있으므로 빈칸이 문장의 동사 자리임을 알 수 있습니다. 또한, 성공의 조건을 말하는 내용으로서 일반적인 사실 또는 불변의 법칙 등을 나타낼 때 사용하는 현재시제 동사가 쓰여야 알맞으므로 (D) depends가 정답입니다.

오답 (A) depending: 동명사 또는 현재분사이므로 동사 자리에 쓰일 수 없는 오답입니다.
(B) dependent: 형용사이므로 동사 자리에 쓰일 수 없는 오답입니다.
(C) depended: 과거시제 동사이므로 문장의 의미에 어울리지 않는 오답입니다.

어휘 depend (on) (~에) 달려 있다, 좌우되다, 의존하다 dependent 의존하는, 의지하는

16.
정답 (B)

해석 (A) 이 전략은 과거에 비용이 많이 드는 것으로 입증된 바 있습니다.
(B) 따라서, 브랜드는 인플루언서를 선택할 때 관련성을 최우선으로 고려해야 합니다.
(C) 일부 인플루언서들은 시청자들에게 무료 상품을 제공합니다.
(D) 온라인 마케팅 예산이 계속 상승해 오고 있습니다.

해설 빈칸 뒤에 최고의 캠페인은 공유되는 가치 및 명확한 메시지 전달에 우선 순위를 둔다는 핵심적인 조언이 제시되어 있습니다. 따라서 앞서 지문 전체적으로 설명하는 인플루언서 활용 캠페인에 관한 조언에 해당하는 내용이 이어져야 자연스러우

므로 (B)가 정답입니다.

오답 (A) 빈칸 다음 내용이 비용과 관련된 내용이 아니므로 흐름상 맞지 않는 오답입니다.

(C) 빈칸 다음 내용이 일부 인플루언서들이 제공하는 특전과 관련된 내용이 아니므로 흐름상 맞지 않는 오답입니다.

(D) 빈칸 다음 내용이 온라인 마케팅 예산 규모의 변화와 관련된 내용이 아니므로 흐름상 맞지 않는 오답입니다.

어휘 strategy 전략 prove + 형용사: ~한 것으로 입증되다 costly 비용이 많이 드는 in the past 과거에 select ~을 선정하다 prioritize 최우선으로 고려하다 relevance 관련성 free 무료의 merchandise 상품 viewer 시청자, 보는 사람 increase 상승하다, 증가하다

DAY 12 문맥파악 / 문장삽입

PRACTICE

1. (B) 2. (C) 3. (B) 4. (C)
5. (D) 6. (B) 7. (B) 8. (D)

1.
정답 (B)

리버사이드 연례 자선 달리기 행사는 도시에서 가장 큰 지역 행사 중 하나로 성장해 왔다. 이 경주는 매년 봄, 4월 둘째 주 일요일에 개최된다. 참가자는 온라인 또는 행사 당일 오전 7시부터 등록할 수 있다.

(A) 개최되었다
(B) 개최된다
(C) 개최되었다
(D) 개최될 것이다

해설 동사 take place의 시제를 고르는 문제입니다. 빈칸 뒤에 위치한 every summer는 반복적인 발생을 나타내므로 현재시제 동사가 필요합니다. 따라서 정답은 (B) takes place입니다.

어휘 annual 매년의, 연례의 charity 자선단체 grown into ~로 성장했다 community event 지역 행사 take place 열리다, 개최되다

2.
정답 (C)

메트로폴리탄 환경 의회는 클린스카이 상에 대한 후보 추천을 시작했다. 후보자는 출품작을 제출하기 전에 정식 지원서를 작성해야 한다. 그것은 위원회의 웹사이트 www.mec.org/cleansky/application에서 다운로드할 수 있다.

(A) 그들은
(B) 그들을
(C) 그것은
(D) 당신은

해설 빈칸에 들어갈 알맞은 주격 대명사를 고르는 문제입니다. 빈칸이 포함된 문장의 내용에 따르면 다운로드 받을 수 있는 것이 주어가 되어야 하므로 앞문장에서 언급된 the official application form을 가리키는 대명사가 주어임을 알 수 있습니다. 따라서 단수 명사에 대한 주격 인칭대명사 (C) It이 정답입니다.

어휘 nomination 후보 추천 prospective 예상된, 기대되는 nominee 지명[임명, 추천]된 사람 submit 제출하다 entry 제출물, 출품작

3.
정답 (B)

그린필드 커뮤니티 극장은 모든 실력의 공연자들을 위한 계절별 연기 워크숍을 시작했다. 워크숍은 평일 저녁과 주말 오후에 진행된다. 일부 세션은 즉흥 연기에 중점을 두며, 다른 세션은 고전적인 장면 연구를 탐구한다. 일부 세션은 브로드웨이 전문 배우들이 진행한다. 참가자들은 온라인이나 극장 매표소에서 직접 등록할 수 있다.

(A) 모두(의)
(B) 일부의
(C) 둘 중 하나
(D) 양자의

해설 빈칸 뒤에 동사가 있으므로 주어 역할이 가능한 대명사를 골라야 합니다. 앞 문장에서는 워크숍의 다양성을 강조하고 모든 세션이 동일하지 않음을 반복적으로 강조합니다. 빈칸이 속한 문장에서는 브로드웨이 배우에 의해 진행되는 세션은 모든 세션 중에 일부에 해당하므로 '일부'를 의미하는 (B) Some이 정답입니다.

어휘 performer 공연자, 연기자 improvisation 즉흥 연기 explore 탐구하다 classical scene study 고전 연극 장면 분석 register 등록하다 in person 직접 box office 매표소

4.
정답 (C)

여름 인턴십 프로그램 지원이 현재 열려 있습니다. 예비 인턴들은 서류를 제출하기 전에 최신 안내물을 검토해야 합니다.

(A) 에세이

정답 및 해설 171

(B) 계약서
(C) 지침, 안내서
(D) 출판물

해설 빈칸에 들어갈 알맞은 명사를 고르는 문제입니다. 빈칸 앞 문장에서는 인턴십에 지원하기 위해 필요한 사전 검토 사항을 말하고 있으며, 예비 인턴들이 검토할 대상으로 '지침, 안내서'가 자연스러우므로 (C) guidelines이 정답입니다.

어휘 review 검토하다 submit 제출하다 essay 에세이 guideline 지침, 안내서 publication 출판물

5.

정답 (D)

> 3월 1일부터 재무 부서는 모든 직원들을 대상으로 수정된 비용 보고 지침을 도입했습니다. 이 최근 정책 업데이트에 대해 질문이 있을 경우, finance@company.com으로 문의해 주세요.

(A) 상세한
(B) 의무적인
(C) 앞의, 이전의
(D) 최근의

해설 문장에서 특정 시점(March 1)에 재무 부서에서 새로운 지침을 도입했다는 내용을 담고 있으므로 빈칸에는 '정책 업데이트'라는 명사를 수식하기에 적절한 '최근의'라는 의미의 형용사가 자연스럽습니다. 따라서 정답은 (D) recent입니다.

어휘 Finance Department 재무 부서 revised 수정된, 개정된 expense-reporting 경비 보고

6.

정답 (B)

> 카페테리아는 수요 증가에 대응하여 다음 주에 새로운 비건 메뉴를 도입할 예정입니다. 수정된 메뉴에 대한 의견이 있으시면, foodservices@campus.edu로 보내주시기 바랍니다. 귀하의 의견을 기대하고 있습니다.

(A) 이 요리들은 매일 신선하게 준비됩니다.
(B) 귀하의 의견을 기대하고 있습니다.
(C) 점심 서비스는 오후 2시까지 운영됩니다.
(D) 새로운 메뉴는 제철 농산물을 특징으로 합니다.

해설 빈칸 앞 문장은 수정된 비건 메뉴에 대한 피드백을 요청하는 내용이므로, 그에 관련된 문장이 이어져야 합니다. 따라서 그 의견을 기대한다는 점을 언급한 (B)가 정답입니다.

어휘 in response to ~에 대한 응답으로 demand 요구 dish 요리, 한 접시 daily 매일의, 나날의 look forward to 고대하다 feature 특징, 특색 seasonal 계절의 produce 생산물

7.

정답 (B)

> 오션뷰 스위트에 대한 문의에 감사드립니다. 해당 숙소는 현대적인 인테리어로 새롭게 단장되었으며, 무료 조식 서비스가 포함되어 있습니다. 게다가, 숙박객이 도착 시 환영 음료가 제공됩니다. 예약 요금은 동봉된 안내 브로셔를 참고해 주시기 바랍니다.

(A) 즐거운 숙박 되시길 바랍니다.
(B) 게다가, 숙박객이 도착 시 환영 음료가 제공됩니다.
(C) 두 요금 모두 모든 객실 유형에 적용됩니다.
(D) 예를 들어, 점심 식단은 매일 변경됩니다.

해설 빈칸 앞 문장은 숙소의 변경 사항(모던 인테리어, 무료 아침 식사 등)을 안내하고 있습니다. 이러한 혜택을 보강하며 추가 정보로 환영 음료를 제공한다는 내용인 (B)가 정답입니다.

어휘 accommodation 숙박 refurbish 재단장하다, 새로 꾸미다 complimentary 무료의 enclosed 동봉하다 additionally 게다가 rate 요금

8.

정답 (D)

> 금요일에 안전 관리 부서가 본관에서 화재 대피 훈련을 실시할 예정입니다. 이번 훈련은 모든 입주자가 비상 절차에 익숙해지도록 하는 데 목적이 있습니다. 모든 사람이 반드시 참여해야 합니다. 이러한 훈련이 전반적인 안전 의식을 향상시키길 바랍니다.

(A) 온라인 교육 세션은 어제 오후에 실시되었습니다.
(B) 안전 관리 부서는 최근 비상 지침을 업데이트했습니다.
(C) 즉시 대피하는 것이 매우 중요합니다.
(D) 이러한 훈련이 전반적인 안전 의식을 향상시키길 바랍니다.

해설 금요일에 시행될 화재 대피 훈련의 목적과 필수 참여 사항을 설명한 뒤 훈련의 기대 효과인 안전 의식 향상을 자연스럽게 강조하는 문장인 (D)가 정답입니다.

어휘 conduct 실시하다 evacuation 피난, 대피 drill 훈련, 연습 aim 목표하다 familiarize 익숙하게 하다 occupant 입주자 recently 최근에, 근래에 crucial 결정적인, 중대한 awareness 자각, 인식

실전 TEST

1. (C)	2. (B)	3. (C)	4. (C)	5. (D)
6. (D)	7. (C)	8. (B)	9. (B)	10. (A)
11. (B)	12. (D)	13. (D)	14. (A)	15. (C)
16. (A)				

1-4 다음 광고를 참조하시오.

저희 케이준 프라이드 치킨에서, 저희 고객들과 함께 개업 50주년을 기념하고자 합니다. 따라서, 이번 주말에 한해, 저희의 주 메뉴에서 치킨 샌드위치, 버거, 또는 버킷 중 어느 것을 주문하시든지 무료 선데 아이스크림과 라지 사이즈의 탄산 음료가 **1** 포함될 것입니다.

고객 여러분께서는 11월 16일 일요일 영업 종료 시간까지 캘리포니아 전역에 있는 저희 지점 33곳 어디에서든 이 **2** 특별 서비스를 이용하실 수 있습니다.

추가로, 저희는 11월 한 달 내내 흥미진진한 상품을 받으실 수 있는 콘테스트 참가 기회를 고객 여러분께 제공해 드릴 것입니다. 단지 **3** 여러분의 영수증에서 찾아보실 수 있는 고유 코드를 확인하신 다음, www.cfc.com/prizedraw에서 입력하시기만 하면 됩니다. **4** 이런 방법으로 저희는 고객 여러분의 성원에 감사드리고자 합니다.

어휘 celebrate ~을 기념하다, 축하하다 free 무료의 purchase 구매(품) take advantage of ~을 이용하다 branch 지점, 지사 throughout (장소) ~ 전역에 걸쳐, (기간) ~ 동안 내내 additionally 추가로, 게다가 give A B: A에게 B를 주다, 제공 하다 enter ~에 참가하다, ~을 입력하다 win (상 등) ~을 받다, 타다 prize 상품, 상 unique 고유한, 독특한 receipt 영수증

1.

정답 (C)

해설 빈칸 앞에는 for 전치사구와 주어에 해당되는 명사구가 있고, 빈칸 뒤에는 with 전치사구만 있으므로 빈칸에 문장의 동사가 쓰여야 합니다. 또한 for this weekend only라는 말로 서비스가 제공되는 특정 미래 시점을 나타내는 표현이 쓰여 있으므로 미래시제를 대신할 수 있는 현재진행시제인 (C) are being included가 정답입니다.

오답 (A) including: 동사의 형태가 아니므로 문장의 동사 자리인 빈칸에 맞지 않는 오답입니다.
(B) to include: 동사의 형태가 아니므로 문장의 동사 자리인 빈칸에 맞지 않는 오답입니다.
(D) had been included: 서비스가 제공되는 특정 미래 시점 표현 for this weekend only와 어울리지 않는 과거완료시제이므로 오답입니다.

어휘 include ~을 포함하다

2.

정답 (B)

해설 선택지가 모두 명사이므로 의미가 알맞은 것을 찾아야 합니다. 빈칸 앞에 앞서 언급된 것을 가리킬 때 사용하는 지시형용사 this가 쓰여 있고 그것을 이용할 수 있는 장소를 알리는 문장입니다. 앞 문장에 기념을 위해 이번 주말에 한해 이용할 수 있는 특별 서비스가 언급되어 있으므로 이를 한 단어로 가리킬 명사로 '제안'을 뜻하는 (B) offer가 정답입니다.

오답 (A) item: '제품, 품목, 항목' 등을 뜻하므로 앞서 언급된 주말 동안 이용할 수 있는 특별 서비스를 대신하기에 알맞지 않은 오답입니다.
(C) vacancy: '공석, 빈 자리' 등을 뜻하므로 앞서 언급된 주말 동안 이용할 수 있는 특별 서비스를 대신하기에 알맞지 않은 오답입니다.
(D) range: '제품군, 범위, 종류' 등을 뜻하므로 앞서 언급된 주말 동안 이용할 수 있는 특별 서비스를 대신하기에 알맞지 않은 오답입니다.

어휘 item 제품, 품목, 항목 offer 제안 vacancy 공석, 빈 자리 range 제품군, 범위, 종류

3.

정답 (C)

해설 빈칸 앞의 내용으로 보아 receipt는 고유 코드가 적힌 영수증을 의미한다는 것을 알 수 있습니다. 여기서 영수증은 이 광고에 담긴 정보를 보는 사람들, 즉 고객들(our customers)이 갖고 있는 영수증이어야 하므로 상대방을 지칭할 때 사용하는 대명사인 (C) your가 정답입니다.

오답 (A) his: 이 광고를 보는 고객들을 지칭하는 대명사로 맞지 않으므로 오답입니다.
(B) her: 이 광고를 보는 고객들을 지칭하는 대명사로 맞지 않으므로 오답입니다.
(D) their: 이 광고를 보는 고객들을 지칭하는 대명사로 맞지 않으므로 오답입니다.

4.

정답 (C)

해석 (A) 놀라운 저희 경품들 중 하나를 받게 되신 것에 대해 축하드립니다.
(B) 저희 메뉴의 새로운 추가 품목을 즐기시기를 바랍니다.
(C) 이런 방법으로 저희는 고객 여러분의 성원에 감사드리고자 합니다.
(D) 다시 한 번, 일부 저희 지점들을 닫는 것에 대해 사과드립니다.

해설 지문 전체적으로, 50주년을 기념하기 위해 제공하는 무료 서

비스 이용 방법과 콘테스트 참가 기회에 관해 설명하고 있습니다. 따라서 이와 같은 혜택을 하나로 가리키는 This와 함께 그러한 행사들을 진행하는 이유로서 고객에게 감사하는 방법임을 언급하는 내용을 담은 (C)가 정답입니다.

오답 (A) 경품 추첨이 완료되어 경품 당첨자에게 보내는 축하의 의미이므로 지문의 내용과 맞지 않습니다.
(B) 메뉴 추가에 관한 내용이 언급되지 않았으므로 오답입니다.
(D) 지점의 폐점과 관련된 내용은 언급되지 않았으므로 오답입니다.

어휘 Congratulations on ~에 대해 축하드립니다 amazing 놀라운 addition 추가(되는 것) one's way of -ing ~하는 방법 patronage 성원, 단골 이용 apologize for ~에 대해 사과하다

5-8 다음 이메일을 참조하시오.

헨더슨 씨께,

5 저희 회사의 일자리를 귀하께 제안해 드리게 되어 기쁩니다. 귀하께서는 매년 63,000달러를 기본 급여로 **6** 받으실 것이며, 이는 귀하의 업무 능력 평가 결과를 바탕으로 해마다 인상될 수 있습니다. 저희 바이오킹 주식회사에서의 귀하의 첫 근무일은 10월 23일 월요일로 잠정적으로 정해졌습니다. 하지만, 그날 근무를 시작하지 **7** 못하게 하는 어떠한 일정상의 충돌 문제라도 있으실 경우에 재조정될 수 있습니다.

이번 주 후반에, 면접 중에 만나셨던 피터 패러데이 씨께서 저희 바이오킹 내에서 **8** 귀하의 역할 및 직무와 관련된 상세 정보를 담은 안내 책자 묶음을 보내 드릴 것입니다. 첫 근무일 이전에 이것을 살펴보시기 바라며, 어떤 문의 사항이든 있으시면, 저에게 555-0139번으로 연락 주시기 바랍니다.

안녕히 계십시오.

바바라 스테이플스, 인사부장
바이오킹 주식회사

어휘 salary 급여, 봉급 increase 인상되다, 증가되다 annually 해마다 based on ~을 바탕으로, 기반으로 outcome 결과 performance 업무 수행 능력, 실적, 성과 review n. 평가, 검토 v. ~을 살펴보다, 검토하다 tentatively 잠정적으로 be set for + 날짜: ~로 정해지다 however 하지만, 그러나 rearrange ~을 재조정하다 schedule conflict 일정상의 충돌, 겹침 information pack 안내 책자 묶음 contain ~을 포함하다, 담고 있다 detailed 상세한 regarding ~와 관련된 role 역할 responsibility 책임, 직무 prior to ~에 앞서, ~ 전에 contact ~에게 연락하다 query 문의 (사항)

5.

정답 (D)

해석 (A) 면접을 위해 오신다면 감사할 것입니다.
(B) 안타깝게도, 저희가 현재 신입 직원을 고용하고 있지 않습니다.
(C) 관리직으로의 최근 승진에 대해 축하드립니다.
(D) 저희 회사의 일자리를 귀하께 제안해 드리게 되어 기쁩니다.

해설 빈칸 뒤에 이어지는 내용을 보면, 상대방이 받는 급여 및 첫 근무 시작 시점 등과 관련된 정보가 제공되고 있습니다. 이는 새로 입사하는 직원에게 할 수 있는 말이므로 입사가 확정된 직원에게 할 수 있는 인사말에 해당되는 (D)가 정답입니다.

오답 (A) 지문 전체적으로 면접과 관련된 내용이 아니므로 흐름상 어울리지 않는 오답입니다.
(B) 지문 전체적으로 고용 불가능성과 관련된 내용이 아니므로 흐름상 어울리지 않는 오답입니다.
(C) 지문 전체적으로 상대방의 승진과 관련된 내용이 아니므로 흐름상 어울리지 않는 오답입니다.

어휘 grateful 감사하는 come in for ~하러 오다 unfortunately 안타깝게도, 아쉽게도 currently 현재 hire ~을 고용하다 Congratulations on ~에 대해 축하 드립니다 recent 최근의 promotion 승진 management 관리(직), 경영(진) offer A B: A에게 B를 제안하다, 제공하다 firm 회사, 업체

6.

정답 (D)

해설 우선, 주어 You 뒤로 빈칸이 있고 그 뒤에 명사구 및 which절이 있으므로 빈칸은 주절의 동사 자리임을 알 수 있습니다. 또한 입사가 확정된 직원의 첫 근무가 아직 시작되지 않았으므로 빈칸 뒤에 쓰여 있는 급여를 받는 것도 미래의 일이어야 합니다. 따라서 미래시제 동사 (D) will receive가 정답입니다.

오답 (A) receiving: 동사의 형태가 아니므로 주절의 동사 자리인 빈칸에 맞지 않는 오답입니다.
(B) received: 동사이기는 하지만 과거시제이므로 뒤에 이어지는 문장과 흐름상 맞지 않는 오답입니다.
(C) to receive: 동사의 형태가 아니므로 주절의 동사 자리인 빈칸에 맞지 않는 오답입니다.

어휘 receive ~을 받다

7.

정답 (C)

해설 선택지가 모두 동사의 현재분사형 또는 동명사이므로 문장의 구조 또는 의미에 적절한 것을 찾아야 합니다. 빈칸 다음을 보면 「목적어 + from -ing」 구조가 이어져 있는데, 이는 동사 prevent와 함께 '~가 …하는 것을 막다, 방해하다' 등을 의미할 때 사용하므로 (C) preventing이 정답입니다.

174 시원스쿨 기본토익 700+

오답 (A) opposing: 「목적어 + from -ing」 구조와 어울리는 동사가 아니므로 오답입니다.
(B) recommending: 「목적어 + from -ing」 구조와 어울리는 동사가 아니므로 오답입니다.
(D) finalizing: 「목적어 + from -ing」 구조와 어울리는 동사가 아니므로 오답입니다.

어휘 oppose ~을 반대하다 recommend ~을 추천하다, 권하다 prevent (A from -ing): (A가 ~하는 것을) 막다, 방해하다 finalize ~을 최종 확정하다

8.
정답 (B)

해설 우선 전치사 regarding과 명사 목적어 사이에 위치한 빈칸은 명사를 수식할 수 있는 소유격 자리입니다. 또한 빈칸 앞뒤를 보면, 상대방(you)에게 상세 정보를 담은 책자 묶음을 보내 줄 거라는 말이 쓰여 있습니다. 따라서 빈칸 뒤에 위치한 role and responsibilities는 상대방의 '역할과 직무'를 의미하는 것이어야 자연스러우므로 (B) your가 정답입니다.

오답 (A) you: 주격 또는 목적격 대명사이므로 명사를 수식할 수 없는 오답입니다.
(C) his: 상대방을 가리킬 수 없는 3인칭 대명사이므로 오답입니다.
(D) their: 상대방을 가리킬 수 없는 3인칭 대명사이므로 오답입니다.

9-12 다음 기사를 참조하시오.

포틀랜드 데일리 뉴스

포틀랜드 (6월 5일) - 최근의 설문조사에 따르면, 포틀랜드 시내의 하프 스트리트를 보행자 전용 도로로 만들겠다는 시의회의 계획이 지역 주민들의 압도적으로 **9** **부정적인** 반응에 직면했습니다.

약 85퍼센트의 설문조사 응답자들은 그곳이 개인 차량을 이용하는 통근자들에게 중요한 경로라는 점을 특별히 언급하면서 그 아이디어를 비난했습니다. 이 도로는 쇼핑 및 외식 구역으로서의 매력을 증대하기 위한 노력의 일환으로 8월에 모든 차량을 대상으로 **10** 폐쇄될 것입니다.

11 현재, 하프 스트리트는 도시를 동쪽에서 서쪽 방향으로 또는 그 반대로 가로질러 이동해야 하는 사람들에게 중요한 통근 경로의 역할을 하고 있으며, 또한 시내버스 노선에 있어서도 중요한 역할을 하고 있습니다. **12** 따라서, 많은 사람들이 대체 이동 수단을 마련해야 할 것입니다.

어휘 according to ~에 따르면 recent 최근의 survey 설문조사(지) council 시의회 plan to do ~하려는 계획 pedestrianize ~을 보행자 전용 도로로 만들다 be met with ~에 직면하다, ~에 부딪히다 overwhelmingly 압도적으로 response 반응, 대응 local 지역의, 현지의 resident 주민 approximately 약, 대략 respondent 응답자 criticize ~을 비난하다 note that ~임을 특별히 언급하다, ~임에 주목하다 route 경로, 노선 commuter 통근자 vehicle 차량 in an effort to do ~하기 위한 노력의 일환으로 boost ~을 증대하다, 촉진하다 attractiveness 매력 serve as ~의 역할을 하다 those who ~하는 사람들 cross ~을 가로지르다 vice versa (앞서 언급된 것에 대해) 그 반대로 play a significant role in ~에 있어 중요한 역할을 하다

9.
정답 (B)

해설 선택지가 모두 형용사이므로 의미가 알맞은 것을 찾아야 합니다. 빈칸에 쓰일 형용사는 바로 뒤에 위치한 response를 수식해 지역 주민들이 보인 반응의 특성을 나타내야 합니다. 다음 문장을 보면 85퍼센트의 설문조사 응답자들이 비난했다는 말이 있으므로 좋지 못한 반응을 보였다는 것을 알 수 있습니다. 따라서 '부정적인'을 뜻하는 (B) negative가 정답입니다.

오답 (A) contented: '만족하는'을 뜻하므로 다음 문장과 흐름상 맞지 않는 의미를 나타내는 오답입니다.
(C) favorable: '호의적인' 등을 뜻하므로 다음 문장과 흐름상 맞지 않는 의미를 나타내는 오답입니다.
(D) faulty: '결함이 있는'을 뜻하므로 다음 문장과 흐름상 맞지 않는 의미를 나타내는 오답입니다.

어휘 contented 만족하는 negative 부정적인 favorable 호의적인 faulty 결함이 있는

10.
정답 (A)

해설 선택지가 모두 수동태 동사이고 시제만 다르므로 시점 관련 단서를 찾아야 합니다. 빈칸 뒤에 발생 시점으로 8월(in August)이 언급되어 있는데, 이는 지문 상단의 기사 작성 시점(June 5)보다 미래입니다. 따라서 미래시제 동사인 (A) will be closed가 정답입니다.

오답 (B) had been closed: 과거완료시제이므로 알맞은 시점 관계를 나타내지 못하는 오답입니다.
(C) was closed: 과거시제이므로 알맞은 시점 관계를 나타내지 못하는 오답입니다.
(D) is closed: 현재시제이므로 알맞은 시점 관계를 나타내지 못하는 오답입니다.

11.
정답 (B)

해설 빈칸 뒤에 쓰인 동사 serves가 현재시제이므로 하프 스트리트가 현재 어떤 역할을 하고 있는지 말하는 문장임을 알 수 있습니다. 따라서 현재시제 동사와 어울리는 부사 (B) Currently

가 정답입니다.

오답 (A) Gradually: '점차적으로'를 뜻하므로 현재 하프 스트리트의 역할을 나타내는 문장에 맞지 않는 오답입니다.
(C) Eventually: '결국, 마침내'를 뜻하므로 현재 하프 스트리트의 역할을 나타내는 문장에 맞지 않는 오답입니다.
(D) Fortunately: '다행히'를 뜻하므로 현재 하프 스트리트의 역할을 나타내는 문장에 맞지 않는 오답입니다.

어휘 gradually 점차적으로 currently 현재 eventually 결국, 마침내 fortunately 다행히

12.

정답 (D)

해석 (A) 포틀랜드 주민들은 요금이 적절한 시의 대중 교통을 자랑스러워하고 있습니다.
(B) 시의회가 교통 혼잡을 줄이기 위해 그 도로를 넓히는 것을 목표로 삼고 있습니다.
(C) 예를 들어, 그 경로는 다른 도시에서 근무하는 사람들에게 유용할 것입니다.
(D) 따라서, 많은 사람들이 대체 이동 수단을 마련해야 할 것입니다.

해설 바로 앞에 하프 스트리트가 통근과 시내버스 노선에 중요한 역할을 한다고 설명하므로 이 도로가 폐쇄될 때 사람들이 해야 하는 일, 즉 대체 이동 수단을 마련해야 한다는 점을 언급한 (D)가 정답입니다.

오답 (A) 빈칸 앞부분의 내용이 대중 교통의 요금과 관련되어 있지 않으므로 흐름상 맞지 않는 오답입니다.
(B) 빈칸 앞부분의 내용이 도로 확장과 관련되어 있지 않으므로 흐름상 맞지 않는 오답입니다.
(C) 이 도로가 현재 통근자들에게 중요하다는 빈칸 앞부분의 내용과 맞지 않는 오답입니다.

어휘 be proud of ~을 자랑스러워 하다 affordable 가격이 적정한 public transportation 대중 교통 aim to do ~하는 것을 목표로 삼다 widen ~을 넓히다, 확장하다 reduce ~을 줄이다, 감소시키다 traffic congestion 교통 혼잡 those who ~하는 사람들 as such 따라서, 그러한 이유로 make an arrangement 마련하다, 조치하다 alternative 대안의, 대체의 travel 이동

13-16 다음 안내를 참조하시오.

코즈믹 디멘션즈 – 희귀 만화책 판매 업체

희귀 만화책 구입하기

저희 코즈믹 디멘션즈에서는, 모든 재고를 반드시 적절하게 보관하고 취급함으로써 완벽한 상태로 유지합니다. 일부 더 오래되고 희귀한 만화책들은 다소 망가지기 쉬우며, 그로 인해 손상에 취약합니다. **13** 따라서, 구매하시는 어떤 만화책이든 몇몇 간단한 가이드라인을 따라 함으로써 관리하는 일은 여러분이 직접 하시기 바랍니다. 저희의 모든 만화책은 밀봉된 비닐 가방에 담긴 채로 나오며, 이용하지 않으실 때는 항상 이 가방 안에 **14** 보관되어야 합니다. 또한, 우발적인 찢김이나 구겨짐을 피하기 위해 만화책을 읽으실 때 조심스럽게 다루셔야 합니다. **15** 이런 일들은 페이지를 너무 빨리 넘기시거나 너무 꽉 붙잡으실 때 발생될 수 있습니다. **16** 이 조언이 여러분의 만화책 상태를 보존하는 데 도움이 될 것입니다. 하지만, 수선 또는 복원과 관련된 정보가 필요하실 경우, 555-2828번을 통해 저희 직원들 중 한 명과 이야기하시기 바랍니다.

어휘 rare 희귀한 keep A in perfect condition: A를 완벽한 상태로 유지하다, 보관하다 stock 재고(품) by (방법) ~함으로써 ensure (that) 반드시 ~하도록 하다, ~임을 보장하다 store ~을 보관하다 handle ~을 취급하다, 다루다 properly 적절히, 제대로 rather 다소, 좀, 오히려 fragile 망가지기 쉬운, 손상되기 쉬운 as such 그로 인해, 따라서 be susceptible to ~에 취약하다, ~되기 쉽다 damage 손상, 피해 up to ~에게 달려 있는 take care of ~을 관리하다, 돌보다, 처리하다 purchase ~을 구매하다 follow ~을 따르다, 준수하다 sealed 밀봉된 at all times 항상 when not in use 이용하지 않을 때 gentle 조심스러운, 부드러운, 온화한 avoid ~을 피하다 accidental 우연한, 우발적인 tear 찢김 wrinkle 구겨짐, 주름 occur 발생되다 turn a page 페이지를 넘기다 grip ~을 붙잡다 firmly 꽉, 단단히 require ~을 필요로 하다 repair 수선, 수리 restoration 복원, 복구

13.

정답 (D)

해설 선택지가 모두 접속부사이므로 앞뒤 문장을 확인해 의미의 흐름을 파악해야 합니다. 앞 문장에는 망가지기 쉽고 손상에 취약하다는 말이, 뒤에 위치한 문장에는 구매자(you)에게 잘 관리할 책임이 있음을 알리는 말이 쓰여 있습니다. 이는 '취약한 특성'이라는 원인에 따른 '관리 책임'이라는 결과를 말하는 것이므로 '따라서, 그러므로' 등의 의미로 결과를 나타내는 접속부사 (D) Therefore가 정답입니다.

오답 (A) Otherwise: 특정 조건에 따른 부정적인 결과를 말할 때 사용하므로 오답입니다.
(B) For instance: 예시를 나타낼 때 사용하므로 오답입니다.
(C) Similarly: 유사 정보를 언급할 때 사용하므로 오답입니다.

어휘 otherwise 그렇지 않으면 for instance 예를 들어 similarly 마찬가지로, 유사하게 therefore 따라서, 그러므로

14.

정답 (A)

해설 선택지가 모두 동사이므로 문장의 구조 및 의미를 확인해 알맞은 것을 골라야 합니다. 조동사(should)와 전치사구(inside this) 사이는 자동사 자리이며, they가 지칭하는 만화책들이 이용되지 않을 때 보관되는 곳을 나타내는 의미가 되어야 하므로 '유지되다, 남아 있다' 등을 뜻하는 (A) remain이 정답입니다.

오답 (B) place: 목적어를 필요로 하는 타동사이므로 문장 구조에 맞지 않는 오답입니다.
(C) look: 자동사이지만 의미가 어울리지 않는 오답입니다.
(D) hold: 목적어를 필요로 하는 타동사이므로 문장 구조에 맞지 않는 오답입니다.

어휘 remain (~한 상태로) 유지되다, 남아 있다 place v. ~을 놓다, 두다 look 보다 hold ~을 붙잡다, 보유하다, 개최하다

15.

정답 (C)

해설 바로 뒤에 조동사와 동사가 있으므로 주어 역할이 가능한 대명사를 골라야 합니다. 또한 동사 occur를 통해 발생 가능성을 말하는 것을 볼 때, 빈칸 바로 앞에 언급된 두 가지 부정적인 일(tears or wrinkles)을 지칭할 대명사가 필요하다는 것을 알 수 있으므로 이 역할이 가능한 복수 지시대명사 (C) These가 정답입니다.

오답 (A) Theirs: '그들의 것'을 뜻하는 소유대명사이므로 의미가 맞지 않는 오답입니다.
(B) Either: 앞서 언급된 것을 대신하는 대명사가 아니므로 오답입니다.
(D) Every: 형용사이므로 주어 자리인 빈칸에 쓰일 수 없는 오답입니다.

어휘 either (A or B): (A 또는 B) 둘 중의 하나

16.

정답 (A)

해석 (A) 이 조언이 여러분의 만화책 상태를 보존하는 데 도움이 될 것입니다.
(B) 저희는 그 제품들이 귀하께 만족스럽지 못했다는 점에 대해 사과드립니다.
(C) 모든 제품은 영업일로 2일 이내에 특별 포장되어 배송됩니다.
(D) 귀하께서 문의하신 만화책은 현재 재고가 없는 상태입니다.

해설 빈칸에 앞서 지문 전체적으로 만화책 관리 방법을 간략히 설명하고 있으므로 이를 '조언'(This advice)'이라는 말로 대신해 이 글을 읽는 구매자(you)에게 도움을 줄 것이라고 말하는 (A)가 정답입니다.

오답 (B) 지문 전체적으로 고객의 불만과 관련된 내용이 아니므로 흐름상 맞지 않는 오답입니다.
(C) 지문 전체적으로 제품 배송과 관련된 내용이 아니므로 흐름상 맞지 않는 오답입니다.
(D) 지문 전체적으로 특정 제품의 재고 보유 여부와 관련된 내용이 아니므로 흐름상 맞지 않는 오답입니다.

어휘 help A do: ~하는 데 A에게 도움이 되다 preserve ~을 보존하다 apologize that ~라는 점에 대해 사과하다 item 제품, 물품, 품목 to one's satisfaction ~에게 만족스러운 ship ~을 배송하다 packaging 포장(재) within ~ 이내에 inquire about ~에 관해 문의하다 currently 현재 out of stock 재고가 없는

PART 7

DAY 13 세부사항 / 주제·목적 / 사실확인

PRACTICE

1. (D)　　**2.** (A)　　**3.** (B)

헬스장 회원 여러분께:
락커룸 샤워실은 이번 금요일에 유지 보수 작업이 진행될 예정입니다. 이용에 불편을 드려 죄송하며, 2층 시설을 이용해주시길 권장 드립니다. 회원들이 적절한 장소로 이동하도록 돕기 위해 안내 표지판이 게시될 것입니다.

---

1. 회원들이 임시 시설을 찾을 수 있도록 어떤 조치가 취해질 예정인가?
(A) 직원이 직접 안내할 것이다.
(B) 이메일로 안내 지도가 발송될 것이다.
(C) 로비에서 층별 안내도가 배포될 것이다.
(D) 체육관에 안내 표지판이 게시될 것이다.

해설 (D)
해설 공지문에 따르면, 샤워실에 유지 보수 작업이 진행될 것이며 마지막 문장에 체육관 내에 안내 표지판이 설치될 예정이라는 문장이 나와 있으므로 정답은 (D)입니다.

어휘 undergo 겪다, 경험하다　maintenance 유지 관리, 보수　inconvenience 불편　facility 시설　signage 안내판　appropriate 적절한　temporary 임시의　sent out 발송하다　distribute 배포하다　put up (표지·광고 등을) 게시하다, 설치하다

Paraphrase　Signage will be posted ⇒ Signs will be put up

이 씨께,
주간 마케팅 전략 회의를 진행해주시기로 동의해 주셔서 감사합니다. 이것은 회의가 7월 12일 오후 2시, A 회의실에서 진행될 예정임을 확인해 드리기 위한 것입니다. AV 장비나 추가 자료가 필요하시면 알려주세요. 귀하의 발표를 기대하고 있겠습니다.

---

2. 이메일은 왜 이 씨에게 발송되었는가?
(A) 회의의 날짜와 장소를 확인하기 위해
(B) 회의 시간을 변경해 달라고 요청하기 위해
(C) 회의가 중복 예약된 것에 대해 사과하기 위해
(D) 다가오는 워크숍을 취소하기 위해

해설 (A)
해설 이메일 첫 번째 줄의 "This is to confirm the meeting will take place on July 12 at 2 P.M. in Conference Room A"라는 문장은 이 씨에게 이메일을 보낸 목적을 나타냅니다. 이 문장을 통해 회의의 일정과 장소를 확실히 안내하고 있으므로 정답은 (A)입니다.

어휘 agree 동의하다　lead 이끌다, 안내하다, 진행하다　confirm 확인하다　additional 부가적인　look forward to ~을 고대하다　apologize 사과하다

건물 관리팀 공지
4월 1일부터, 저희의 지하 주차장 내에 Level 2 충전기가 설치된 전기차 전용 공간 4개가 별도로 지정됩니다. 일반 차량용 주차 공간은 선착순으로 계속 이용 가능하며, 월별 주차 허가증은 매달 셋째 영업일 이전에 갱신되어야 합니다. 항상 주차 허가증이 잘 보이도록 해주세요.

---

3. 4월 1일 이후 주차장에 대해 사실인 것은 무엇인가?
(A) 모든 주차 공간은 시간당 요금이 부과될 것이다.
(B) 일부 공간이 전기차 전용으로 지정될 것이다.
(C) 월간 주차 허가는 더 이상 필요하지 않을 것이다.
(D) 일반 주차 공간이 폐지될 것이다.

해설 (B)
해설 첫 문장 our underground parking garage will reserve four spaces exclusively for electric vehicles with Level 2 chargers에서 Level 2 충전기가 설치된 전기차 전용 공간 4개가 별도로 지정됨을 공지하고 있으므로 정답은 (B)입니다.

어휘 notice 통지, 통보　reserve 예약해 두다, 지정하다　exclusively 전적으로, 오로지　vehicle 운송 수단　permit 허가증　renew 갱신[계속]하다　display 전시하다　incur 초래하다　no longer 더 이상 ~하지 않다　eliminate 제거하다

실전 TEST

1. (C)　**2.** (D)　**3.** (C)　**4.** (B)　**5.** (A)
6. (B)　**7.** (C)　**8.** (D)　**9.** (B)　**10.** (C)
11. (C)

1-2 다음 광고를 참조하시오.

> **페르세우스 다이렉트를 확인해 보십시오!**
>
> 요즘 일정이 바쁘신가요? 식료품이나 기타 상품을 쇼핑하실 시간을 찾기 어렵다고 생각하고 계신가요? 그러시다면, 모바일 기기에 '페르세우스 다이렉트' 애플리케이션을 설치하셔야 합니다. '페르세우스 다이렉트'는 카버 시티 및 인근 지역에 위치한 3,000개가 넘는 업체들과 제휴를 맺고 있으며, **1** 여러분을 위해 아주 다양한 제품을 받아 자택으로 가져다 드릴 준비가 되어 대기하고 있습니다. 신선한 농산품과 제과 제품에서부터 운동 장비와 비타민 보충제에 이르기까지, 신속하고 편리하게 전달해 드릴 수 있습니다. **2** 저희는 이미 약 30명의 기사들로 구성된 팀을 고용하고 있으며, 20명을 더 추가하는 과정에 있습니다. 따라서, 여러분의 필요를 충족시켜 드릴 수 있는 사람을 언제든지 찾아보실 수 있을 것입니다. 선호하시는 앱 스토어에서 '페르세우스 다이렉트'를 다운로드하시거나 www.perseusdirectonline.ca를 방문하셔서 더 많은 정보를 알아보시기 바랍니다.

어휘 check out ~을 확인해 보다 find A 형용사: A를 ~하다고 생각하다 groceries 식료품 goods 상품 if so 그렇다면 install ~을 설치하다 device 기기, 장치 partner with ~와 제휴하다 more than ~가 넘는 surrounding 인근의, 주변의 pick up ~을 가져오다, 가져가다 a wide variety of 아주 다양한 produce n. 농산품 equipment 장비 supplement 보충(제) get A to B: A를 B에게 갖다 주다 conveniently 편리하게 employ ~을 고용하다 around 약, 대략 in the process of -ing ~하는 과정에 있는 add ~을 추가하다 available 이용 가능한, 시간이 나는 meet (조건 등) ~을 충족하다 preferred 선호하는 find out 알아보다

1. 페르세우스 다이렉트는 무슨 종류의 업체인가?
(A) 식료품 매장
(B) 소프트웨어 개발업체
(C) 배달 서비스 회사
(D) 피트니스 센터

정답 (C)

해설 해당 업체의 업무 특성이 드러나는 중반부에, 아주 다양한 제품을 받아 자택으로 가져다줄 준비가 되어 대기하고 있다고(we are ready and waiting to pick up a wide variety of items for you and bring them to your door) 알리고 있습니다. 이는 배달 서비스를 말하는 것이므로 (C)가 정답입니다.

어휘 developer 개발업체, 개발자

2. 페르세우스 다이렉트에 관해 알려진 것은 무엇인가?
(A) 해외로 사업을 확장하고 있다.
(B) 여러 상을 받았다.
(C) 등록비를 필요로 한다.
(D) 직원을 추가로 고용하는 중이다.

정답 (D)

해설 지문 후반부에 이미 약 30명의 기사들로 구성된 팀을 고용하고 있고 20명을 더 추가하는 과정에 있다고(We already employed a team of around 30 drivers, and are in the process of adding another 20) 알리고 있습니다. 이는 직원을 추가로 고용하는 중임을 의미하는 말이므로 (D)가 정답입니다.

어휘 expand (사업 등을) 확장하다, 확대하다 overseas 해외로 win an award 상을 받다 several 여럿의, 몇몇의 require ~을 필요로 하다 registration 등록 fee 요금, 수수료

3-5 다음 편지를 참조하시오.

> 고용 담당자님께,
>
> **3** 글로벌 트랜짓 사의 웹사이트에 게시된 영업이사 직책과 관련해 검토해 보실 수 있도록 첨부해 드린 제 이력서를 확인해 보시기 바랍니다. 저는 직접적인 소비자 영업 영역에 폭넓은 경험을 지니고 있으며, 현재 새로운 취업 기회를 찾고 있습니다. 저는 특히 귀사에 관심이 있는데, 제가 최근에 글로벌 트랜짓 사가 아주 많은 사업을 하고 있는 지역으로 이사했기 때문입니다.
>
> 이전의 영업직에서, 저는 기존의 시장을 확장하고 새로운 시장에서 사람들과 접촉함으로써 영업 수익을 늘렸습니다. **4** 저는 4년 연속으로 최고의 영업사원 상을 받았으며, 매우 성공적인 영업 설명서를 만든 것에 대해 혁신가 상도 받았습니다.
>
> **5** 첨부해 드린 것에서 연락처가 포함된 여러 추천서와 함께 제 상세 근무 경력을 확인해 보실 수 있습니다. 광고된 직책에 대해 저를 고려해 주시기를 바랍니다.
>
> 안녕히 계십시오.
>
> 마이클 윌슨

어휘 résumé 이력서 attach ~을 첨부하다 review 검토, 평가 in regard to ~와 관련해 sales 영업, 매출, 판매 executive 이사, 임원 position 직책, 일자리 post ~을 게시하다 extensive 폭넓은, 광범위한 direct 직접적인 영업 currently 현재 look for ~을 찾다 career opportunity 취업 기회 particularly 특히 be interested in ~에 관심이 있다 recently 최근에 conduct ~을 수행하다, 실시하다 a great deal of 아주 많은 previous

이전의, 과거의 role 역할, 직책 increase ~을 늘리다, 증가시키다 revenue 수익 by (방법) ~해서, ~함으로써 expand ~을 확장하다, 확대하다 existing 기존의 make a contact 접촉하다 receive ~을 받다 for four consecutive years 4년 연속으로 create ~을 만들다 highly 매우, 아주 successful 성공적인 manual 설명서 detailed 상세한 several 여럿의, 몇몇의 a letter of reference 추천서 consider ~을 고려하다 advertised 광고된

3. 편지의 목적은 무엇인가?
(A) 공석을 알리기 위해
(B) 더 많은 정보를 요청하기 위해
(C) 한 일자리에 대한 관심을 나타내기 위해
(D) 한 직원을 기리기 위해

정답 (C)

해설 첫 단락 시작 부분에 글로벌 트랜짓 사의 영업이사 직책과 관련해 검토할 수 있도록 첨부한 이력서를 확인해 달라고 요청하는(Please find my résumé attached for your review in regard to the sales executive position) 말이 있습니다. 이는 그 자리에 대한 관심을 보임으로써 자신을 채용 대상자로 고려하도록 요청하는 것이므로 (C)가 정답입니다.

어휘 announce ~을 알리다, 발표하다 job opening 공석 request ~을 요청하다 express (의견, 감정 등) ~을 나타내다, 표현하다 interest in ~에 대한 관심 honor v. ~을 기리다, ~에게 영예를 주다

4. 윌슨 씨에 관해 사실인 것은 무엇인가?
(A) 글로벌 트랜짓 사에서 일한다.
(B) 수상자이다.
(C) 광고 분야에서의 경험이 있다.
(D) 새로운 회사를 차렸다.

정답 (B)

해설 두 번째 단락에 4년 연속 최고의 영업사원 상과 매우 성공적인 영업 설명서를 만든 것에 대해 혁신가 상도 받았다는(I received the Top Salesperson Award for four consecutive years, and also the Innovator Award for creating a highly successful sales manual) 말이 있으므로 (B)가 정답입니다.

어휘 advertising 광고 (활동) experience n. 경험

5. 편지에 동봉된 것은 무엇인가?
(A) 추천서
(B) 대학 성적 증명서
(C) 고객 명단
(D) 명함

정답 (A)

해설 질문에 포함된 enclosed와 동의어인 Attached로 시작되는 마지막 단락에 여러 추천서가 함께 동봉되었음을(Attached you will find my detailed job history with several letters of reference) 알리고 있으므로 (A)가 정답입니다.

어휘 enclosed 동봉된 recommendation letter 추천서 transcript 성적 증명서

Paraphrase Attached ⇒ enclosed

6-8 다음 회람을 참조하시오.

> 수신: 전 지역 영업 사원
> 발신: 카밀 포스터, 운영부장
> 제목: 주간 영업 회의 관련
> 날짜: 4월 3일
>
> **6** **8(A)** 4층 대회의실에 대한 개조 공사 작업으로 인해, 이번 주의 영업 회의는 2층에 있는 윌로우 교육실에서 열릴 것입니다. 회의 시간은 목요일 오전 10시 30분으로 변경되지 않은 상태로 유지되며, **8(B)** 원격 접속도 여전히 오피스넷을 통해 이용 가능할 것입니다. **7** **8(C)** 특히 발표하시는 분인 경우에, 준비에 필요한 시간을 감안하실 수 있도록 10분 일찍 도착하시기 바랍니다.

어휘 regional 지역의, 지방의 sales 영업, 판매(량), 매출 associate 사원, 동료, 동업자 regarding ~와 관련해 due to ~로 인해, ~때문에 renovation 개조, 보수 hold (행사 등) ~을 열다, ~을 개최하다 remain + 형용사: ~한 상태로 유지되다, 계속 ~한 상태이다 unchanged 변경되지 않은 remote 원격의, 멀리 떨어진 access 접속, 접근, 이용 available (사물) 이용 가능한, 구입 가능한, (사람) 시간이 있는 via ~을 통해 arrive 도착하다 allow ~을 감안하다, ~을 허용하다 setup 준비, 설치, 설정 present 발표하다

6. 회람의 주 목적이 무엇인가?
(A) 다가오는 영업 회의를 위해 추가 발표자를 찾는 것
(B) 직원들에게 회의 장소의 변경에 관해 통지하는 것
(C) 정기 회의 시작 시간의 지연을 알리는 것
(D) 직원들에게 대회의실 이용에 관한 새 정책을 알리는 것

정답 (B)

해설 지문 초반부에 4층 대회의실에 대한 개조 공사 작업으로 인해 이번 주의 영업 회의가 2층에 있는 윌로우 교육실에서 열린다고 알리는 것이(Due to renovation work on the 4th floor conference room, this week's sales meeting will be held in the Willow Training Room on the 2nd floor) 주 목적에 해당하므로 (B)가 정답입니다.

어휘 seek ~을 찾다, ~을 구하다 additional 추가적인 presenter 발표자 upcoming 다가오는, 곧 있을 notify

~에게 알리다(= inform) delay 지연, 지체 regular 정기적인, 규칙적인 policy 정책, 방침

Paraphrase 4th floor conference room / will be held in the Willow Training Room ⇒ a change in meeting location

7. 직원들이 왜 일찍 도착하도록 요청 받는가?
(A) 회의가 평소보다 더 일찍 시작할 것이다.
(B) 참석자들이 입구에서 인쇄된 유인물을 받을 것이다.
(C) 장비가 미리 설치되어야 한다.
(D) 보안 점검이 회의 전에 실시될 것이다.

정답 (C)
해설 지문 후반부에 특히 발표하는 사람인 경우에 준비 시간을 감안해 10분 일찍 도착하도록(Please arrive ten minutes early to allow time for setup, especially if you are presenting) 당부하고 있습니다. 따라서 발표 준비 과정의 하나에 해당하는 장비 설치를 언급한 (C)가 정답입니다.

어휘 than usual 평소보다 attendee 참석자 handout 유인물 equipment 장비 set up ~을 설치하다, ~을 설정하다, ~을 마련하다 in advance 미리, 사전에 conduct ~을 실시하다, ~을 수행하다

8. 다음 중 회람에 언급되지 않은 것은 무엇인가?
(A) 회의가 개조 공사로 인해 옮겨졌다.
(B) 참가자들은 오피스넷을 통해 원격으로 참석할 수 있다.
(C) 참석자들은 발표를 한다면 일찍 도착해야 한다.
(D) 모든 사람이 인쇄물을 회의에 가지고 와야 한다.

정답 (D)
해설 지문에서 회의에 가지고 와야 하는 것에 대한 언급은 없으므로 (D)가 정답입니다. 나머지 (A)~(C)의 내용은 모두 언급되어 있습니다.

어휘 join 참석하다 remotely 원격으로 printed 인쇄된 handout 유인물

9-11 다음 후기를 참조하시오.

고객 후기: 메사 오디오 M60 블루투스 스피커
☆☆☆☆☆

후기 작성자: 에드워드 버그
날짜: 8월 7일

9 제가 2주 전에 M60 스피커를 구입했는데, 그 음향 품질에 완전히 사로잡혔습니다. 그 크기에 비해 놀라운 정도로 강력하거든요. 저는 그 미니멀리즘 디자인과 배터리 수명도 마음에 드는데, 완전 충전 시 약 10시간 동안 지속되기 때문입니다. **10** 유일한 단점이라면 제 전화기와 페어링하는데 약간의 시간이 걸린다는 점인데, 특히 처음에 그랬습니다. 그래도, 전반적으로, 가격 대비 좋은 성능이고 평상시 듣기용으로는 완벽합니다. **11** 저는 M60의 휴대성과 강력함의 조화에 대해 제 친구들에게 주저하지 않고 알릴 것입니다.

어휘 review 후기, 평가, 검토 blow away ~을 완전히 사로잡다, ~을 매료시키다 surprisingly 놀라울 정도로 minimalist design 미니멀리즘 디자인(단순함에서 우러나오는 미를 추구) last v. 지속되다 charge 충전 downside 단점, 결점 take a while 약간 시간이 걸리다 still 그럼에도 불구하고, 그래도 overall 전반적으로 value for the price 가성비, 가격 대비 성능 casual 평상시의, 간편한

9. 해당 스피커의 음향 품질에 대한 버그 씨의 의견은 어떠한가?
(A) 실망스럽다.
(B) 예상보다 더 좋다.
(C) 너무 소리가 크다.
(D) 가격에 비해 보통이다.

정답 (B)
해설 지문 초반부에 그 음향 품질에 완전히 사로잡혔다는 사실과 크기에 비해 놀라울 정도로 강력하다는 점을(~ have been blown away by the sound quality—it's surprisingly powerful for its size) 언급하고 있으므로 (B)가 정답입니다.

어휘 disappointing (사람을) 실망시키는 than expected 예상보다, 기대보다 average 보통인, 평균인

Paraphrase have been blown away ⇒ better than expected

10. 버그 씨의 기기의 어떤 특징에 대해 문제가 있었는가?
(A) 배터리 수명
(B) 볼륨 조절
(C) 무선 연결성
(D) 제품 무게

정답 (C)
해설 지문 중반부에 유일한 단점이 전화기와 페어링하는데 약간의 시간이 걸렸다는 점이라고(The only downside is that it takes a while to pair with my phone ~) 언급하고 있으므로 (C)가 정답입니다.

어휘 device 기기, 장치 connectivity 연결

Paraphrase to pair with my phone ⇒ Wireless connectivity

11. 버그 씨와 관련해 알려진 것은 무엇인가?
(A) 대부분 전문적인 목적으로 그 스피커를 이용한다.
(B) 스피커를 곧 반품할 계획이다.
(C) 스피커를 다른 사람들에게 추천할 것이다.
(D) 여러 메사 오디오 제품을 소유해 왔다.

정답 (C)

해설 지문 후반부에 친구들에게 주저하지 않고 M60의 휴대성과 강력함의 조화에 대해 알릴 것이라고(I wouldn't hesitate to let my friends know about the M60's blend of portability and power) 언급하는 내용을 보고 다른 사람들에게 M60을 추천할 것이라는 것을 알 수 있습니다. 따라서 정답은 (C)입니다.

어휘 mostly 대부분, 대체로 plan to do ~할 계획이다 return ~을 반품하다, ~을 반납하다 own ~을 소유하다 several 여럿의, 몇몇의

DAY 14 문맥파악

PRACTICE

1. (A)   2. (D)   3. (B)

서울 테크 엑스포에 참여하세요! 이번 엑스포에서는 AI, 로봇공학, VR 분야의 혁신을 선보이는 50개 이상의 기술 스타트업이 참여할 것입니다. 참가자들은 직접 해볼 수 있는 데모, 기조 연설, 네트워킹 행사에 참여할 수 있습니다. 푸드트럭과 라이브 음악으로 축제 분위기를 완성할 것입니다. www.seoultechexpo.com 에서 방문을 계획해보세요.

1. 첫 번째 단락, 첫 번째 줄의 단어 "feature"와 의미가 가장 가까운 것은 무엇인가?
   (A) 보여주다, 선보이다
   (B) …의 탓으로 하다
   (C) 기능하다
   (D) 대표하다, 나타내다

정답 (A)

해설 첫 문장에서 서울 테크 엑스포에 참여하라는 말이 나오고, 이어서 AI, 로봇공학, VR 분야의 혁신을 선보이는 50개 이상의 기술 스타트업들을 특징으로 보여줄 것이라고 언급합니다. 여기서 사용된 feature는 '보여주다', '선보이다'와 같은 의미로 해석될 수 있으므로, 동의어로 사용할 수 있는 (A) present가 정답입니다.

어휘 feature 특징으로 선보이다 attendee 출석자 atmosphere 분위기

[오후 12:48] 다니엘 헌트: 안녕하세요, 자베스 어패럴로 연락 주셔서 감사합니다. 저는 고객 지원팀의 다니엘 헌트입니다. 무엇을 도와드릴까요?
[오후 12:49] 레이첼 로한: 안녕하세요, 지난주에 환불을 요청했는데 아직 처리되지 않았어요.
[오후 12:50] 다니엘 헌트: 상태를 확인해드릴게요. 주문 번호를 알려주시겠어요?
[오후 12:51] 레이첼 로한: 네, 주문 번호는 #92317이에요. 제가 반품한 백팩이에요.
[오후 12:52] 다니엘 헌트: 아, 그럼 이해되네요. 반품 상품이 아직 저희 창고에 도착하지 않아서 환불이 처리되지 않았어요.
[오후 12:53] 레이첼 로한: 아, 알겠습니다. 저는 그럼 며칠 더 기다릴게요.

2. 오후 12:52에 다니엘 헌트 씨가 "아, 그럼 이해되네요"라고 말한 의도는 무엇인가?
   (A) 그는 더 이상 주문 번호가 필요 없다.
   (B) 그는 고객을 더 이상 도와줄 수 없다.
   (C) 그는 고객이 불만을 제기하기를 원한다.
   (D) 그는 지연된 이유를 파악했다.

정답 (D)

해설 12시 52분에 "Ah, that explains it"이라고 말한 다음에 반품 상품이 아직 창고에 도착하지 않아서 환불이 처리되지 않았다고 레이첼 씨에게 알려줍니다. 이를 통해 다니엘 헌트 씨가 "Ah, that explains it"이라고 말한 것은 레이첼 씨의 환불 요청이 왜 처리되지 않았는지 알게 된 것을 의미하므로 정답은 (D)입니다.

어휘 contact 연락하다 request 요청하다 refund 환불 process 처리하다 status 상태 share 공유하다 backpack 배낭, 백팩 issue 발급하다, 발부하다 warehouse 창고 no longer 더 이상 ~않다 any further 더 이상 file a complaint 불만을 제기하다 figure out 알아내다, 파악하다 delay 지연

시립 도서관은 7월 1일부터 스터디룸 예약에 대한 새로운 정책을 도입합니다. — [1] —. 학생과 교직원은 최대 2주 전까지 스터디룸을 예약할 수 있습니다. — [2] —. 예약을 취소하려면 시작 시간 최소 24시간 전에 해야 하며, 그렇지 않으면 벌금이 부과됩니다. — [3] —. 늦은 취소 시에는 소액의 수수료가 부과됩니다. — [4] —.

3. [1], [2], [3], 그리고 [4]로 표기된 위치들 중에서 다음 문장이 가장 잘 어울리는 위치는 어느 것인가?
   "하지만, 도서관 비회원은 예약을 하기 전에 게스트 패스를 등록해야 합니다."
   (A) [1]
   (B) [2]
   (C) [3]
   (D) [4]

정답 (B)

해설 제시된 문장은 도서관 비회원에 대한 스터디룸 예약 방법을 언급하고 있습니다. 대조적인 내용을 언급할 때 사용하는 접속부사 however가 포함되어 있으므로 해당 문장 앞에는 대조적인 내용이 언급되어야 합니다. 도서관 비회원과 대조적인 학생과 교직원이 언급된 문장 뒤인 [2]의 위치가 가장 적절합니다. 따라서 정답은 (B)입니다.

어휘 policy 방침, 정책 faculty (대학의) 교수진 book 예약하다 in advance 사전에 penalty 벌금 nominal 소액의

실전 TEST

1. (B)	2. (D)	3. (B)	4. (C)	5. (A)
6. (B)	7. (D)	8. (A)	9. (B)	10. (A)
11. (C)	12. (C)			

1-3 다음 온라인 채팅 대화를 참조하시오.

그랜트 [오전 10:35]
안녕하세요, 올리비아 씨… **1** 우리 본사의 꼭대기 층이 개조 공사 작업이 진행되는 다음 주 내내 폐쇄될 겁니다. 이 말은 우리가 마케팅 부서 직원들에게 새 업무 장소를 찾아주어야 한다는 뜻입니다.

올리비아 [오전 10:37]
네, 알고 있어요. **2** 마케팅 팀의 최소 절반이 다음 주에 능력 개발 워크숍 때문에 런던에 가 있을 것이기 때문에, 그 나머지 직원들을 위한 새로운 임시 공간을 찾기만 하면 됩니다.

그랜트 [오전 10:39]
아, 맞아요. 그럼, 다음 주에 약 10명의 부서 직원들만 있게 되는 건가요?

올리비아 [오전 10:40]
맞습니다. 그래서, 저는 우리가 3층에 있는 그래픽 디자인팀과 함께 그 직원들이 들어갈 공간을 만들 수 있을 것이라고 생각하고 있었어요. **3** 제가 지난번에 확인했을 때, 그곳에 빈 책상들이 여럿 있었거든요.

그랜트 [오전 10:42]
상황이 변했습니다. **3** 그들은 최근에 많은 신입사원들을 뽑았어요.

올리비아 [오전 10:45]
음… 그렇다면, 우리가 3번 회의실에 임시 업무 자리를 몇 개 마련할 수 있을지 확인해 보겠습니다. 그곳은 요즘 그렇게 많이 이용되고 있지 않아요.

어휘 headquarters 본사 while ~하는 동안 remodeling 개조, 보수 underway 진행 중인 mean (that) ~임을 의미하다 workspace 업무 공간 at least 최소한, 적어도 skill 능력, 기술 development 개발 temporary 임시의, 일시적인 remaining 나머지의, 남아 있는 about 약, 대략 fit A in: A가 들어갈 공간을 만들다 several 여럿의, 몇몇의 recently 최근에 recruit ~을 뽑다, 모집하다 in that case 그렇다면, 그런 경우라면 see if ~인지 확인하다 set up ~을 마련하다, 설치하다 workstation 업무 자리 that much 그렇게 많이

1. 회사에 관해 언급된 것은 무엇인가?
(A) 새 본사로 이전했다.
(B) 일부 개조 공사 일정이 정해졌다.
(C) 최근에 마케팅 직원들을 추가로 고용했다.
(D) 일주일 동안 문을 닫을 것이다

정답 (B)

해설 그랜트 씨의 첫 메시지에 본사 꼭대기 층이 개조 공사가 진행되는 다음 주에 폐쇄된다고(will be closed all of next week while the remodeling work is underway) 나타나 있으므로 개조 공사 일정이 잡혀있다는 것을 알 수 있습니다. 따라서 이를 언급한 (B)가 정답입니다.

어휘 schedule v. ~의 일정을 잡다 renovation 개조, 보수 recently 최근에 hire ~을 고용하다

Paraphrase remodeling work ⇒ renovations

2. 일부 마케팅 부서 직원들에 관해 올리비아 씨가 언급한 것은 무엇인가?
(A) 자주 그래픽 디자이너들과 협업한다.
(B) 새 업무용 장비를 요청했다.
(C) 런던 지사를 기반으로 한다.
(D) 교육 행사에 참석할 것이다.

정답 (D)

해설 올리비아 씨가 10시 37분에 작성한 메시지를 보면, 마케팅 팀의 최소 절반이 다음 주에 능력 개발 워크숍 때문에 런던에 가 있을 것이라고(At least half of the marketing team will be in London next week for a skills development workshop) 알리는 말이 있습니다. 이는 교육 행사에 참석한다는 말과 같으므로 (D)가 정답입니다.

어휘 collaborate with ~와 협업하다 request ~을 요청하다 equipment 장비 be based at ~에 기반을 두고 있다 branch 지사, 지점 attend ~에 참석하다

Paraphrase skills development workshop ⇒ training event

3. 오전 10시 42분에, 그랜트 씨가 "상황이 변했습니다"라고 쓴 의도는 무엇인가?
(A) 일부 업무가 연기되도록 권하고 있다.
(B) 충분한 업무 공간이 이용 가능할지 의구심을 갖고 있다.
(C) 마케팅 팀이 꼭대기 층에 남아 있어야 한다고 생각한다.
(D) 새 책상들이 몇 개 주문되었다고 생각하고 있다.

정답 (B)

해설 10시 40분 메시지에서 올리비아 씨가 3층의 공간에 빈 책상들이 많이 있었다고(there were several empty desks there) 알리자 그랜트 씨가 '상황이 변했다'고 알리면서 신입 사원들을 많이 뽑은 사실을(They have recently recruited a lot of new workers) 밝히는 흐름입니다. 즉 3층에 공간이 충분하지 않다는 뜻을 나타내는 말에 해당되므로 이와 유사한 의미로 쓰인 (B)가 정답입니다.

어휘 recommend that ~하도록 권하다, 추천하다 postpone ~을 연기하다, 미루다 doubt (that) ~인지 의구심을 갖다, 의심하다 available 이용 가능한 remain 남아 있다 order ~을 주문하다

4-6 다음 편지를 참조하시오.

> 해니건 씨께,
>
> **4** 로얄은행을 대표해, 귀하의 대출 신청이 받아들여져 처리되었음을 알려 드리게 되어 기쁩니다. 따라서, 저희는 동봉해 드린 계약서 내에 제시되어 있는 약관에 따라 총액 만 달러를 드릴 것입니다. ㅡ [1] ㅡ.
>
> **6** 저희는 지난 6개월분의 귀하의 급여 명세서 사본과 우리 주에서 발급된 사진이 들어 있는 2개의 신분증, 그리고 주민등록번호를 이미 받았습니다. ㅡ [2] ㅡ. 자금이 귀하의 법인 계좌로 입금되는 대로, 문자 메시지로 통보받을 것이며, 참고용으로 보관하실 수 있는 서면 확인서를 우편으로 받으시게 될 겁니다. ㅡ [3] ㅡ.
>
> 계약서에 상세히 설명된 바와 같이, 총액과 이자는 반드시 10년 내에 상환되어야 합니다. 저희는 9퍼센트의 이자율을 제공해 드릴 수 있으며, 이는 오리건 주의 은행들 사이에서 상당히 경쟁력 있는 이자율입니다. **5** 저희는 매월 1일에 126달러의 상환금을 예상하고 있으며, 이 조건을 준수하지 못하실 경우에는 추가 행정 처리 부담금 또는 수수료가 초래될 수 있습니다. ㅡ [4] ㅡ.
>
> 어떤 질문이나 우려 사항이든 있으시면 555-1103번으로 언제든지 저에게 직접 연락 주시기 바랍니다.
>
> 안녕히 계십시오.
> 라제시 술만, 기업 대출 관리 책임
> 로얄 은행

어휘 on behalf of ~을 대표해, 대신해 inform A that: A에게 ~라고 알리다 loan 대출 application 신청(서) accept ~을 받아 들이다 process ~을 처리하다 therefore 따라서, 그러므로 grant A B: A에게 B를 주다, 승인하다 sum 총액, 액수 in accordance with ~에 따라 terms and conditions (계약서 등의) 약관 lay out ~을 제시하다 enclosed 동봉된 agreement 계약(서) receive ~을 받다 pay slip 급여 명세서 cover ~을 포함하다 state-issued 주에서 발급한 social security number 주민등록번호 once ~하는 대로, ~하자 마자 fund 자금 deposit ~을 입금하다 account 계좌, 계정 notify ~에게 통보하다 confirmation 확인(서) reference 참고 detail v. ~을 상세히 설명하다 interest 이자 pay back ~을 상환하다, 갚다 offer A B: A에게 B를 제공하다 rate 비율, 요금, 속도, 등급 fairly 상당히, 꽤 competitive 경쟁력 있는 expect ~을 예상하다 repayment 상환(금) failure to do ~하지 못함 adhere to ~을 준수하다, 고수하다 result in ~을 초래하다, ~ 라는 결과를 낳다 additional 추가의 administration 행정 (처리) charge (부과) 요금 fee 수수료, 요금 Please feel free to do 언제든지 ~하세요 contact ~에게 연락하다 concern 우려, 걱정

4. 편지가 왜 해니건 씨에게 보내졌는가?
(A) 계좌의 개설을 확인해 주기 위해
(B) 사업 시작에 관해 조언해 주기 위해
(C) 자금 제공 요청을 승인하기 위해
(D) 추가 정보를 요청하기 위해

정답 (C)

해설 지문 시작 부분에 상대방의 대출 신청이 받아들여져 처리되었음을 알리게 되어 기쁘다는 말이(your bank loan application has been accepted and processed) 쓰여 있습니다. 이는 대출을 통한 자금 제공 요청이 승인되었다는 뜻이므로 (C)가 정답입니다.

어휘 confirm ~을 확인해 주다 provide ~을 제공하다 approve ~을 승인하다 request 요청 financing 자금 제공

Paraphrase your bank loan application has been accepted and processed ⇒ approve a request for financing

5. 해니건 씨는 한달 단위로 무엇을 하도록 요청받는가?
(A) 비용 납입하기
(B) 은행 방문하기
(C) 문서 제출하기
(D) 술만 씨에게 전화하기

정답 (A)

해설 세 번째 단락을 보면 매달 1일에 126달러의 상환금을 예상하고 있다고(We expect a repayment of $126 on the 1st of each month) 알리는 말이 쓰여 있습니다. 이는 해니건 씨에게 매달 비용을 납입하도록 요청하는 말에 해당되므로 (A)가 정답입니다.

어휘 be asked to do ~하도록 요청 받다 on a monthly basis 한 달 단위로 submit ~을 제출하다

Paraphrase
• expect a repayment of $126 ⇒ Make a payment
• on the 1st of each month ⇒ on a monthly basis

6. [1], [2], [3], 그리고 [4]로 표기된 위치들 중에서 다음 문장이 가장 잘 어울리는 위치는 어느 것인가?
"따라서, 저희는 필요한 모든 정보를 갖고 있으며, 다른 어떤 것에 대해서도 귀하를 곤란하게 해 드릴 필요가 없습니다."
(A) [1]
(B) [2]
(C) [3]
(D) [4]

정답 (B)
해설 제시된 문장은 결과를 나타내는 As such로 시작해 필요한 모든 정보를 갖고 있기 때문에 더 이상 문제될 것이 없다는 의미를 나타내고 있습니다. 따라서 특정 정보를 보유하고 있음을 알리는 문장 뒤에 쓰여야 자연스럽다는 것을 알 수 있으므로 급여 명세서 사본과 신분증 등의 개인 정보 자료를 언급한 문장 뒤에 위치한 [2]에 들어가 그 자료들을 받은 것에 따른 결과에 해당되는 말을 전하는 흐름이 되어야 알맞으므로 (B)가 정답입니다.

어휘 as such 따라서, 그러한 이유로 necessary 필요한, 필수의 trouble v. ~을 곤란하게 하다, 애먹이다

7-9 다음 공지를 참조하시오.

7 배송 정책 – 어텀 & 레이크 홈 데코

7 저희는 모든 주문품을 구입 후 영업일로 2일 이내에 8 발송하는 것을 목표로 하고 있습니다. – [1] –. 미국 대륙 내에서 배송되는 주문품은 일반적으로 영업일 5~7일 내에 도착합니다. 9 성수기인 연휴 중에는 처리 시간이 더 길어질 수 있다는 점을 유념하시기 바랍니다. – [2] –. 해외 배송 서비스도 이용 가능하지만, 배송 시간이 지역별로 상이하며, 세관 절차에 의해 영향을 받을 수 있습니다. – [3] –. 특급 배송 선택 사항은 더 빠른 서비스가 필요한 고객들을 위해 결제 시에 제공됩니다. – [4] –.

어휘 shipping 배송, 선적 policy 정책, 방침 aim to do ~하는 것을 목표로 하다 dispatch ~을 발송하다, ~을 파견하다 order 주문(품) purchase 구입(품) continental 대륙의 typically 일반적으로 arrive 도착하다 Please note that ~라는 점을 유념하십시오[주목하십시오] processing 처리 peak 성수기의, 절정의 available (사물) 이용 가능한, 구입 가능한, (사람) 시간이 있는 vary 상이하다, 서로 다르다 region 지역, 지방 affect ~에 영향을 미치다 customs 세관 procedure 절차 express 특급의, 특송의 offer ~을 제공하다 checkout 결제, 계산(대)

7. 공지의 주 목적은 무엇인가?
(A) 할인된 배송 요금을 홍보하는 것
(B) 연휴 기간 중의 매장 영업 시간에 대한 정보를 알리는 것
(C) 결함이 있는 제품에 대한 반품 과정을 설명해 주는 것
(D) 고객들에게 주문 처리 진행 일정을 알리는 것

정답 (D)
해설 상단에 제목이 배송 정책(Shipping Policy)으로 쓰여 있고, 초반부에 모든 주문품을 구입 후 영업일로 2일 이내에 발송하는 것을 목표로 하고 있다는(We aim to dispatch all orders within two business days of purchase) 말과 함께 배송 관련 정보를 제공하고 있으므로 (D)가 정답입니다.

어휘 promote ~을 홍보하다, ~을 촉진하다, ~을 승진시키다 rate 요금, 등급, 비율, 속도 inform A of B: A에게 B를 알리다 fulfillment 주문 처리, 이행, 완수 timeline 진행 일정 confirm ~을 확인해 주다 process 과정 update ~에 대한 정보를 알리다

8. 지문에서, 첫 번째 단락, 첫 번째 줄의 단어 "dispatch"와 의미가 가장 가까운 것은 무엇인가?
(A) 배송하다
(B) 교체하다, 대체하다
(C) 제거하다
(D) 추적하다

정답 (A)
해설 상단에 제목이 배송 정책(Shipping Policy)이며, 해당 문장에서 dispatch 뒤에 '모든 주문품'을 뜻하는 명사구 all orders가 목적어로 쓰여 있는 것으로 볼 때, 주문품을 고객에게 배송하는 것을 의미하는 동사임을 알 수 있으므로 (A) ship이 정답입니다.

9. [1], [2], [3], 그리고 [4]로 표기된 위치들 중에서 다음 문장이 가장 잘 어울리는 위치는 어느 것인가?
"특히 크리스마스에 앞서 몇 주 동안 아마 지연 문제가 있을 것입니다."
(A) [1]
(B) [2]
(C) [3]
(D) [4]

정답 (B)
해설 제시된 문장은 특히 크리스마스에 앞서 몇 주 동안 지연 문제

가 있을 가능성에 대해 언급하고 있습니다. 따라서 처리 시간이 성수기 연휴 중에 더 길어질 수 있다는 점을 알리는 문장 뒤에 위치한 [2]에 들어가 배송 지연 가능성이 특히 더 큰 기간을 구체적으로 밝히는 흐름이 되어야 자연스러우므로 (B)가 정답입니다.

어휘 delay 지연, 지체 particularly 특히 likely 아마 prior to ~에 앞서, ~ 전에

10-12 다음 온라인 채팅 대화를 참조하시오.

[오전 10:12] 아룬 데이비스: 팀 여러분, 에코세이브 캠페인 초안 레이아웃 관련 업데이트가 있나요? 저희는 내일 전에 검토하기를 바라고 있었어요.

[오전 10:14] 리나 젠슨: **10** 고객 측에서 보내줄 제품 치수를 아직 기다리고 있어요. 어제 확인할 것이라고 했는데 아직 아무 소식도 못 들었어요.

[오전 10:16] 제이슨 킴: 제가 오늘 아침에 다시 이메일로 그들에게 후속 연락을 시도했어요. 만약 정오까지 답이 없으면, 제가 임시 레이아웃을 만들게요.

[오전 10:18] 리나 젠슨: 좋은 생각이에요. 또한, 슬로건도 마무리되어야 해요. 마케팅에서 보내온 최신 버전으로 가야 할까요?

[오전 10:20] 아룬 데이비스: **11** 조금 미뤄봅시다. 마케팅팀이 어젯밤 늦게 수정된 버전을 보내주긴 했는데 아직 승인되지 않았어요.

[오전 10:23] 제이슨 킴: 알겠습니다. 이메일에 반응이 없으니 **12** 고객 연락처로 전화해볼게요.

[오전 10:25] 아룬 데이비스: 고마워요, 제이슨. 연락 오면 꼭 알려주세요.

어휘 draft 초안 layout 레이아웃, 배치 hope to do ~하기를 바라다 review 검토하다 dimensions 치수 confirm 확인하다, 확정하다 follow up with ~에 후속 조치를 하다 mock up 모형을 만들다 temporary 임시의 tagline 슬로건, 구호 finalize 마무리하다, 완결 짓다 hold off 미루다, 연기하다 revised 수정된 approve 승인하다 contact number 연락처 respond to ~에 응답하다, ~에 반응하다

10. 대화자들은 주로 어떤 문제에 대해 논의하고 있는가?
(A) 고객과의 연락 지연
(B) 제품 디자인의 결함
(C) 디자인 소프트웨어의 오류
(D) 실패한 마케팅 캠페인

정답 (A)

해설 10시 14분에 리나 젠슨 씨가 고객이 보낼 제품 치수를 기다리고 있는 중이며, 어제 확인했다고 했으나 아직 아무 소식도 못 들었다고(They said they'd confirm yesterday, but we've heard nothing yet) 답하는 것을 보고 고객이 제품 정보를 전달하지 않음으로 인해 레이아웃 작업이 지연되고 있는 상황임을 알 수 있습니다. 따라서 정답은 (A)입니다.

어휘 defect 결함 delay 지연, 연기 fault 고장, 오류 unsuccessful 성공하지 못한, 실패한

11. 오전 10시 20분에, 데이비스 씨가 "조금 미뤄봅시다"라고 말한 의미는 무엇인가?
(A) 작업 마감일을 뒤로 미루고 싶어한다.
(B) 회의는 불필요하다고 생각한다.
(C) 승인을 기다리길 원한다.
(D) 고객을 직접 만나길 원한다.

정답 (C)

해설 10시 16분에 리나 젠슨 씨가 마케팅에서 보낸 최신 버전으로 마무리해야할 지를 묻자, 10시 20분에 아룬 데이비스 씨가 "조금 미뤄보자"고 말한 뒤 아직 승인이 되지 않았다고(it hasn't been approved) 말한 것을 보고, 조금 미루자는 말은 승인을 받을 때까지 기다리자는 의미임을 알 수 있습니다. 따라서 정답은 (C)입니다.

어휘 would like to do ~하기를 원하다, ~하고 싶어하다 unnecessary 불필요한 would prefer to do ~하길 원하다, ~하고 싶다 approval 승인 in person 직접

12. 킴 씨는 다음에 무엇을 할 것 같은가?
(A) 슬로건을 수정한다
(B) 이메일을 보낸다
(C) 전화를 한다
(D) 데이비스 씨와 만난다

정답 (C)

해설 10시 23분에 제이슨 킴 씨는 고객의 연락처에 연락을 해보겠다고(I'll try the client's contact number) 언급하였습니다. 이를 보고 킴 씨는 전화를 할 것이라는 것을 알 수 있으므로 정답은 (C)입니다.

어휘 revise 수정하다 make a phone call 전화하다

DAY 15 다중지문

PRACTICE

1. (B)

솔 컴포트 슈 스토어

고객 만족을 보장하기 위해 솔 컴포트 슈 스토어는 다음과 같은 환불 정책을 제공합니다. **구매 후 7일 이내에 원본의 신발과 영수증을 지참한 반품은 100% 환불을 받을 수 있습니다. 구매 후 8일에서 30일 사이에 원본의 신발과 영수증을 지참한 반품은 50% 환불을 받을 수 있습니다.** 구매 후 30일 이상 경과한 반품은 환불되지 않습니다. 신발은 미착용 상태여야 하며 영수증 원본을 지참해야 합니다.

날짜: 8월 20일

관계자 분께,

저는 8월 10일에 120달러에 "메트로 워크" 로퍼 한 켤레를 구입했습니다. 안타깝게도 제 예상대로 신발이 맞지 않았습니다. 신발은 미착용이며 원본 영수증은 아직 가지고 있습니다. 환불 금액과 다음 단계를 알려주세요. 감사합니다.

리타 해리슨

1. 해리슨 씨는 환불로 얼마를 받을 것인가?
 (A) 0 달러
 (B) 60 달러
 (C) 120 달러
 (D) 90 달러

해설 (B)
해설 두 번째 지문에 따르면 구매자는 8월 10일에 신발을 구입했고, 8월 20일에 환불을 요청했습니다. 첫 번째 지문의 환불 정책에 따르면, 구매 후 8일에서 30일 사이에 반품할 경우 50% 환불이 가능하다고 언급하였습니다. 구매자는 신발을 착용하지 않았고 영수증도 가지고 있으므로 환불 조건을 충족하지만 구매 후 10일이 지났기 때문에 총 구매 금액인 120 달러의 50%인 60달러를 환불 받을 것임을 알 수 있습니다. 따라서 정답은 (B)입니다.

어휘 ensure ~을 보장하다, 확실하게 하다 return 반품 purchase 구매 unworn 착용하지 않은, 미착용의 accompany 동반하다 refund 환불하다

실전 TEST

1. (B) **2.** (A) **3.** (C) **4.** (B) **5.** (A)
6. (D) **7.** (D) **8.** (B) **9.** (C) **10.** (D)

1-5 다음 이메일들을 참조하시오.

제목: 마리포사 비스트로
2 날짜: 11월 4일

관계자께,

2 제가 이틀 전에 몇몇 친구들과 함께 귀하의 레스토랑에서 식사했는데, 저희는 테라스가 있는 바깥에 예약한 테이블에서 방대한 해산물 메뉴와 함께 정말 즐거운 시간을 보냈습니다. 그럼에도 불구하고, **1** 제가 이메일을 쓰는 이유는 귀하의 직원들 중 한 분과 관련된 사건에 주목해 주시기를 바라고 있기 때문입니다. 이름표에 스티븐이라고 확인한 그 직원은 디저트 코스를 내오던 중에 아이스크림 그릇을 부주의하게 떨어뜨렸습니다. 안타깝게도, 이것이 탁자에 놓여 있던 제 휴대 전화기 위로 떨어지면서 화면을 깨트리고 가죽 폰 케이스를 손상시켰습니다.

저는 여전히 이 상황에 대해 매우 불쾌한데, 그분이 당시에 너무 많은 접시를 나르고 있어서 사고가 발생할 가능성이 컸기 때문입니다. 결과적으로, 저는 어제 전화기 매장을 방문해 화면 수리에 120달러를 지불할 수밖에 없었습니다. 폰 케이스는 추가 50달러의 가치가 있는 것이지만, 다행히도, 제가 어떻게든 깨끗하게 할 수 있었고, 거의 원래의 모습으로 복구되었습니다. 따라서, **3** 저는 170달러 전액에 대해 보상받을 것으로 기대하고 있지는 않지만, 최소한 수리 비용이라도 받을 수 있다면 좋겠습니다.

이 문제와 관련해 곧 답변을 들을 수 있기를 바랍니다.

안녕히 계십시오.
리사 멀베이니

어휘 dine 식사하다 extensive 폭넓은, 방대한 reserve ~을 예약하다 patio 테라스 nevertheless 그럼에도 불구하고 incident 사건 bring A to one's attention: A에 ~가 주목하게 하다 regarding ~와 관련된 identify (신원 등) ~을 밝혀내다, 확인하다 carelessly 부주의하게 while ~하는 동안 bring out ~을 내오다 unfortunately 안타깝게도, 아쉽게도 land v. 떨어지다 crack ~을 깨트리다, 갈라지게 하다 damage ~을 손상시키다 leather 가죽 carry ~을 나르다 accident 사고 be bound to do ~할 가능성이 크다 as a result 결과적으로 have no choice but to do ~하는 수

정답 및 해설 **187**

밖에 없다 repair 수리 worth + 비용: ~의 가치가 있는 additional 추가의 manage to do 간신히 ~해내다 appearance 모습, 외관 expect to do ~할 것으로 기대하다, 예상하다 compensate A for B: B에 대해 A에게 보상하다 at least 최소한, 적어도 have A p.p.: A가 ~되게 하다 cover (비용 등) ~을 부담하다, 충당하다

날짜: 11월 5일
제목: 마리포사 비스트로

멀베이니 씨께,

제 레스토랑에서 그것만 아니라면 즐거우실 수도 있었던 경험을 망치게 한 사건에 관한 말씀을 듣게 되어 대단히 유감스럽습니다. 귀하께서 언급하신 직원과 이야기를 나눴으며, 이번 주에 전 직원이 재교육을 받도록 조치해 두었습니다. 호의의 표시로, ③ 수리 비용 및 여전히 완벽하지 않은 상태라고 말씀하신 케이스에 대한 비용 모두를 꼭 부담하겠습니다. ④ 괜찮으시다면 제가 직접 금액을 이체해 드리겠습니다. 가급적 빨리 귀하의 계좌 정보를 알려 주시기 바라며, 즉시 이 문제를 처리해 드리겠습니다. 다시 한번, 사과를 받아 주시기 바라며, 마리포사 비스트로에서 다시 뵐 수 있기를 고대합니다.

안녕히 계십시오.

⑤ 앨런 크랜덜
소유주, 마리포사 비스트로

어휘 terribly 대단히, 몹시 spoil ~을 망치다 otherwise 그렇지 않다면 arrange for A to do: A가 ~하도록 조치하다, 준비하다 undergo ~을 거치다, 겪다 retraining 재교육 as a token of ~의 표시로, 뜻으로 goodwill 호의 insist on -ing 꼭 ~하다 in perfect condition 완벽한 상태인 bank transfer 계좌 이체(금) if that suits you 괜찮으시다면 let A know B: A에게 B를 알려 주다 at your earliest possible convenience 가급적 빨리 take care of ~을 처리하다 immediately 즉시 please accept my apologies 사과를 받아주십시오 look forward to -ing ~하기를 고대하다

1. 첫 번째 이메일의 주 목적은 무엇인가?
(A) 테이블을 예약하기 위해
(B) 불만을 제기하기 위해
(C) 메뉴에 관해 문의하기 위해
(D) 한 직원을 칭찬하기 위해

정답 (B)
해설 첫 번째 이메일의 첫 단락에 직원들 중 한 명과 관련된 일에 주목해 주기를 바란다는(I am writing to you because I wish to bring an incident regarding a member of your staff to your attention) 말과 함께 그 직원이 발생시킨 문제점을 설명하고 있습니다. 이는 불만을 제기하는 것에 해당되므로 (B)가 정답입니다.

어휘 reserve ~을 예약하다 make a complaint 불만을 제기하다, 불평하다 inquire about ~에 관해 문의하다 praise ~을 칭찬하다

2. 멀베이니 씨는 언제 마리포사 비스트로를 방문했는가?
(A) 11월 2일에
(B) 11월 3일에
(C) 11월 4일에
(D) 11월 5일에

정답 (A)
해설 첫 번째 이메일의 시작 부분에 친구들과 이틀 전에 식사한(I dined at your restaurant with some friends two days ago) 사실을 알리고 있는데, 첫 번째의 이메일 작성 날짜가 11월 4일이므로(Date: November 4) 11월 2일에 방문했음을 알 수 있습니다. 따라서 (A)가 정답입니다.

3. 크랜덜 씨는 얼마나 많은 돈을 멀베이니 씨에게 보낼 것인가?
(A) 50달러
(B) 120달러
(C) 170달러
(D) 220달러

정답 (C)
해설 연계 문제입니다. 크랜덜 씨가 쓴 이메일인 두 번째 이메일 중반부에 수리 비용과 케이스에 대한 비용 모두를 부담하겠다고(I insist on covering the cost of both the repairs and the case) 밝히고 있습니다. 그리고 첫 지문 두 번째 단락 후반부에 두 가지 사항에 대한 비용이 각각 120달러와 50달러라고 알리면서 170달러 전액을 보상 받을 것으로 기대하지 않는다는(I do not expect to be compensated for the full $170) 말이 있습니다. 따라서 크랜덜 씨는 170달러를 모두 보상하겠다는 뜻을 나타낸 것이므로 (C)가 정답입니다.

4. 두 번째 이메일에서, 첫 번째 단락, 다섯 번째 줄의 단어 "suits"와 의미가 가장 가까운 것은 무엇인가?
(A) 적응시키다
(B) 만족시키다
(C) 확인해 주다
(D) 갖추어 주다

정답 (B)
해설 suits가 포함된 if절에서 주어로 쓰인 that은 앞서 언급된 일, 즉 금액을 이체하는 일(send you a direct bank transfer)을 가리키며, suits의 목적어로는 상대방을 가리키는 you가 쓰여 있습니다. 따라서 그러한 방법이 상대방에게 괜찮은지

묻는 if절인 것으로 판단할 수 있으며, 이는 상대방에게 만족스러운지 확인하는 것과 같으므로 '만족시키다'를 뜻하는 (B) satisfies가 정답입니다.

어휘 adapt 적응하다, 맞추다 confirm (사실로) 확인해 주다 outfit v. ~을 갖추어 주다 n. 옷, 복장

5. 크랜덜 씨는 누구인가?
(A) 사업주
(B) 청소부
(C) 요리사
(D) 종업원

정답 (A)

해설 크랜덜 씨(Mr. Crandall)는 두 번째 이메일의 마지막 부분에 발신자의 이름에서 확인할 수 있습니다. 그 밑에 그가 마리포사 비스트로의 소유주(proprietor)임이 밝혀져 있으므로 정답은 (A)입니다.

어휘 business owner 사업주 cleaner 청소부 chef 요리사 server 종업원

6-10 다음 웹페이지와 보도자료, 그리고 메시지를 참조하시오.

---

http://www.moscowballetgroup.com/about

| 소개 | 무용수 | 공연 | 연락처 |

모스크바 발레단

모스크바 발레단은 2002년에 드미트리 포포프 씨에 의해 설립되었으며, 처음 설립된 이후로 해마다 전 세계적으로 폭넓게 투어를 해 왔습니다. 러시아 최고의 여러 발레 무용수들이 현재 단원으로 활동 중이며, 여기에는 **6 세계 일류의 현대 발레 무용수로 자주 언급되고 있는** 니콜라이 누레예프 씨도 포함되어 있습니다. 곧 시작될 저희 북미 투어가 3월 20일에 로스앤젤레스에서 시작되어 4월 23일에 뉴욕 시에서 종료됩니다. **10 이 공연들은 저희 훌륭한 안무가이신 올가 바가노바 씨에 의해 고안된 완전히 독창적인 춤 동작들을 포함하며**, 유명 미술가 이반 소모바 씨에 의해 제작된 손으로 페인트칠한 굉장히 멋진 배경을 특징으로 합니다. 저희는 지금까지 중에서 가장 놀라운 공연을 만들기 위해 이 모든 훌륭한 요소들이 조화를 이루도록 해 주신 공연 연출자 나탈리아 겔처 씨께 감사드리고자 합니다.

발레 팬들께서는 저희 모스크바 발레단이 내년에 있을 전 세계적인 투어에 스스로 대비하기 위한 연습과 훈련에 집중하기 위해 **7 올해 남은 기간에 공연을 쉴 예정이라는 점을 알아두시기 바라며**, 그에 따라 이번이 한동안 저희 공연들 중 하나를 관람하실 수 있는 마지막 기회가 될 것입니다. 입장권은 상단의 '공연' 탭을 클릭하셔서 구입하실 수 있습니다.

어휘 performance 공연 found ~을 설립하다(= establish)
extensively 폭넓게, 광범위하게 on an annual basis 해마다, 매년 since ~한 이후로 several 여러 명, 여러 개 currently 현재 active 활동 중인 including ~을 포함해 frequently 자주, 빈번히 be cited as ~로 인용되다 leading 일류의, 선도적인 contemporary 현대의 upcoming 다가오는, 곧 있을 kick off 시작되다 include ~을 포함하다 completely 완전히, 전적으로 original 독창적인 dance routines 춤 동작들 devise ~을 고안하다 choreographer 안무가 feature ~을 특징으로 하다 stunning 굉장히 멋진 backdrop 배경 bring A together: A를 조화시키다, 한데 모으다 element 요소 create ~을 만들다 amazing 놀라운 yet (최상급과 함께) 지금까지 중에서 note that ~임을 알아두다 take A off: A만큼 쉬다 focus on ~에 집중하다 practice 연습 training 훈련, 교육 prepare A for B: B를 위해 A를 대비시키다 for a while 한동안 purchase ~을 구입하다

공식 보도 자료
모스크바 발레단
연락처: inquiries@mbg.com

(4월 5일) – 저희는 현재 진행 중인 저희 북미 투어에 캐나다 공연 날짜들을 충분히 포함하지 않았다는 점에 최근 주목하게 되었습니다. 캐나다 팬들은 저희에게 매우 중요하므로, 저희는 온타리오 주와 퀘벡 주에서 몇몇 별도의 공연을 추가해 투어를 연장하기로 결정했습니다. 추가 공연 상세 정보는 다음과 같습니다.

팰리세이드 뮤직 센터 (퀘벡 시) – 4월 27일
프레데릭 빌딩 (몬트리올) – 4월 29일
9 GQ 컨벤션 센터 (오타와) – 5월 1일
러빗 콘서트 홀 (토론토) – 5월 3일

상기 날짜에 대한 입장권이 현재 판매 중이며, 공연 장소에서 직접 구입하시거나 저희 웹사이트 www.moscowballetgroup.com/performances를 방문해 구입하실 수 있습니다.

어휘 press release 보도 자료 recently 최근에 It has come to one's attention that ~라는 점에 주목하게 되다 include ~을 포함하다 current 현재의 decide to do ~하기로 결정하다 extend ~을 연장하다, 확대하다 by (방법) ~함으로써 add ~을 추가하다 additional 별도의, 추가적인 province (행정 구역) 주 details 상세 정보, 세부 사항 as follows 다음과 같습니다 on sale 판매 중인 directly 직접, 곧장 venue 행사 장소

앤젤라 로우덴 [오후 3:25]

안녕하세요, 셀마 씨. **9** 메리 씨와 저는 GQ 컨벤션 센터에 가서 모스크바 발레단을 꼭 보고 싶은데, 저희는 당신이 저희와 함께 가는 데 관심이 있으실 거라고 **8** 생각했습니다. 아마 이미 아시겠지만, **9** 그 공연 장소가 제 집에서 차로 얼마 걸리지 않는 거리에 있기 때문에, 가서 그 공연을 보기 전에 먼저 당신과 메리 씨를 저녁 식사에 꼭 초대하고 싶습니다. **10** 제가 채널 4에서 모든 무용수들의 동작을 연출한 분의 인터뷰를 봤는데, 정말 놀라웠습니다. 관심 있으시면 저에게 알려 주세요!

어휘 figure (that) ~라고 생각하다, 판단하다 be interested in ~에 관심이 있다 have A over for B: B를 위해 A를 초대하다 choreograph (안무 등) ~을 연출하다 move 동작, 움직임 be amazed at ~에 대해 놀라워하다

6. 니콜라이 누레예프 씨에 관해 언급된 것은 무엇인가?
   (A) 모스크바 발레단을 설립했다.
   (B) 자신의 춤으로 여러 상을 받았다.
   (C) 다가오는 투어에 합류할 수 없다.
   (D) 자신의 전문 능력에 대해 종종 찬사를 받는다.

정답 (D)

해설 누레예프 씨의 이름이 언급된 첫 지문 첫 단락을 보면, 세계 최고의 현대 발레 무용수로 자주 언급된다는 말이(Nikolai Nureyev, who is frequently cited as the world's leading contemporary ballet dancer) 쓰여 있습니다. 이는 그 사람이 지닌 전문 능력에 대해 매우 좋은 평가를 받는다는 뜻이므로 (D)가 정답입니다.

어휘 win an award 상을 받다 be unable to do ~할 수 없다 praise A for B: B에 대해 A를 칭찬하다 expertise 전문 능력, 전문 지식

Paraphrase is frequently cited as the world's leading contemporary ballet dancer ⇒ is often praised for his expertise

7. 웹페이지에 따르면, 모스크바 발레단의 북미 투어에 관해 무엇이 사실인가?
   (A) 3개월 동안 진행된다.
   (B) 뉴욕 시에서 시작된다.
   (C) 독창적인 음악 작품을 포함한다.
   (D) 올해 발레단의 마지막 투어이다.

정답 (D)

해설 웹페이지인 첫 지문 두 번째 단락을 보면, 이번 투어가 끝나면 올해 남은 기간에 공연을 쉴 예정이라는(~ will be taking the rest of the year off) 말이 쓰여 있습니다. 이는 이번 투어가 올해 마지막 투어임을 나타내는 것이므로 (D)가 정답입니다.

어휘 run 진행되다 score (음악) 작품

Paraphrase will be taking the rest of the year off ⇒ is the group's final tour this year

8. 메시지에서, 첫 번째 단락, 두 번째 줄의 단어 "figured"와 의미가 가장 가까운 것은 무엇인가?
   (A) 계산했다
   (B) 생각했다
   (C) 해결했다
   (D) 간략히 말했다

정답 (B)

해설 해당 문장에서 동사 figured 뒤로 상대방이 함께 하는 데 관심이 있을 것이라는 말이 쓰여 있습니다. 이는 앞선 문장에서 공연을 꼭 보러 가고 싶다고 말한 것과 관련해 상대도 관심 있을 것이라고 생각한 부분을 밝히는 내용으로 판단할 수 있습니다. 따라서 '생각하다'를 뜻하는 또 다른 동사인 (B) guessed 가 정답입니다.

어휘 count ~을 계산하다, 세다 guess ~을 생각하다 solve ~을 해결하다, 풀다 outline ~을 간략히 말하다

9. 로우덴 씨는 어느 도시에 거주하고 있을 것 같은가?
   (A) 퀘벡 시
   (B) 몬트리올
   (C) 오타와
   (D) 토론토

정답 (C)

해설 연계 유형입니다. 로우덴 씨가 쓴 메시지의 세 번째 지문 첫 단락에 공연 장소로 GQ 컨벤션 센터가 언급되어 있고(Mary and I would really like to go and see the Moscow Ballet Group at the GQ Convention Center), 그곳이 자신의 집에서 가깝다는(the venue is just a short drive from my house) 말도 함께 쓰여 있습니다. 그리고 공연장 및 개최 도시 정보가 담긴 두 번째 지문에 GQ 컨벤션 센터가 오타와에 있는 것으로(GQ Convention Center (Ottawa)) 나타나 있으므로 (C)가 정답입니다.

10. 로우덴 씨는 누가 텔레비전에서 인터뷰하는 것을 보았는가?
   (A) 이반 소모바
   (B) 나탈리아 겔처
   (C) 드리트리 포포프
   (D) 올가 바가노바

정답 (D)

해설 연계 유형입니다. 로우덴 씨가 쓴 이메일인 세 번째 지문 두 번째 단락에 무용수들의 동작을 연출한 사람의 인터뷰를 텔레비전에서 봤다는(I watched an interview on Channel 4 with the person who choreographs all the dancers' moves) 말이 쓰여 있습니다. 안무가와 관련된 정보가 담긴

첫 지문 첫 단락에 안무가 이름이 올가 바가노바(our brilliant choreographer, Olga Vaganova)라고 언급되어 있으므로 (D)가 정답입니다.

VOCA

DAY 1 명사1

1. (B)	2. (A)	3. (B)	4. (A)	5. (A)
6. (C)	7. (D)	8. (C)	9. (C)	10. (D)
11. (B)	12. (A)			

1.
정답 (B)
해석 온라인 구매는 일정 금액 이상 주문 시 무료 배송이 제공됩니다.
해설 형용사 online과 어울리는 명사로서 무료로 제공받을 수 있는 명사가 필요하므로 '구매'를 뜻하는 (B) purchases가 정답입니다.
어휘 come with ~이 딸려 있다 ship 배송 occasion (특수한) 경우, 때 rate 요금

2.
정답 (A)
해석 그 회사는 직원 성과를 평가하기 위해 연례 검토를 계획했다.
해설 형용사 annual 뒤에는 매년 이루어지는 직원 성과 평가와 관련된 명사가 와야 문맥상 자연스러우므로 '검토, 평가'를 의미하는 (A) review가 정답입니다.
어휘 schedule 일정을 잡다 annual 해마다의, 1년의 assess 평가하다 renovation 개조 공사

3.
정답 (B)
해석 재택근무의 주요 장점 중 하나는 직원들에게 제공되는 유연성이다.
해설 빈칸 앞 형용사 major와 어울려 직원들에게 유연성을 제공한다는 명사가 필요하므로 '장점'을 뜻하는 (B) benefit이 정답입니다.
어휘 major 주요한 remote work 원격근무 flexibility 유연성 response 응답, 대답

4.
정답 (A)
해석 해외 여행은 그녀에게 다양한 문화를 경험할 수 있는 독특한 기회를 주었다.
해설 빈칸 앞 형용사 unique와 어울려 다양한 문화를 경험할 수 있는 의미의 명사가 필요하므로 '기회'를 뜻하는 (A) opportunity가 정답입니다.
어휘 abroad 해외로 exception 제외 preference 선호 progress 전진

5.
정답 (A)
해석 그 공장은 고급 섬유를 생산하며 50년 넘게 운영되어 왔다.
해설 빈칸 앞에는 전치사 in이 있으므로 명사 형태가 와야 합니다. in operation은 '운영 중인', '가동 중인'이라는 뜻으로 사용되며, 문맥상 공장이 섬유를 생산하며 50년 넘게 운영되고 있다는 표현이 자연스러우므로 정답은 (A) operation입니다.
어휘 high-quality 고품질 textile 직물의, 방직의 operation 운영, 작용 function 기능 decision 결정 response 응답

6.
정답 (C)
해석 그 장학금은 뛰어난 학업 성취를 보여주는 개인에게 수여된다.
해설 「to + ＿＿＿＿ + who + 동사」 구조에서 관계대명사 who는 사람명사를 수식하므로 '개인'을 뜻하는 (C) individuals가 정답입니다.
어휘 scholarship 장학금 demonstrate 증명하다 exceptional 예외적인 achievement 달성, 성취 suggestion 제안, 암시

7.
정답 (D)
해석 소프트웨어 업데이트의 핵심 기능 중 하나는 향상된 보안성과 더 빠른 성능이다.
해설 빈칸 앞 형용사 key와 어울려 소프트웨어 업데이트의 성능과 어울리는 명사가 필요하므로 '기능'을 뜻하는 (D) feature이 정답입니다.
어휘 key 핵심적인 improve 향상시키다 prospect 가능성, 전망 term 용어 request v. 요청하다 n. 요청

8.
정답 (C)
해석 고객 만족을 보장하는 것이 올해 회사의 최우선 과제이다.
해설 회사가 고객 만족을 보장한다는 내용과 어울리는 명사로, '우선 과제'라는 의미를 가진 (C) priority가 정답입니다. top priority는 '최우선 과제'라는 의미로 쓰입니다.

어휘 ensure 확실히 하다, 보장하다 satisfaction 만족 excellence 우수성 priority 우선순위 advance 진보

9.
정답 (C)
해석 주민들이 제기한 안전 문제에 대응하여, 시의회는 철거 계획을 중단했다.
해설 주민들이 안전 문제를 제기했기 때문에, 시의회가 철거를 중단했다는 흐름이 자연스러우므로 정답은 '반응' 또는 '대응'을 뜻하는 (C) response가 정답입니다.
어휘 safety 안전 concern 문제 raise (문제 등을) 제기하다 council 의회 halt 중단하다, 멈추다 demolition 철거, 해체 contrast 대조적인 exception 예외 alteration 변경, 수정

10.
정답 (D)
해석 그 채용 공고에는 요구되는 자격 조건과 업무 책임에 대한 자세한 설명이 포함되어 있었다.
해설 빈칸은 detailed의 수식을 받는 명사 자리이며, 자격 조건과 업무 책임에 대한 자세한 설명이 포함되어 있음을 의미하는 명사가 필요하므로 '설명'을 뜻하는 (D) description이 정답입니다.
어휘 required 요구되는 qualification 자격 approval 승인 attention 주의, 관심 prediction 예측

11.
정답 (B)
해석 그 회사는 충성도 높은 고객들에게 독점 할인 혜택을 제공함으로써 감사의 표시를 했다.
해설 show appreciation for은 '~에 대해 감사를 표하다'라는 의미로, 고객에게 혜택을 주는 문맥에서 쓰입니다. 따라서, 감사라는 뜻인 (B) appreciation이 정답입니다.
어휘 loyal customer 충성 고객, 단골 고객 value 가치, 중요성 employment 고용, 직업 complaint 불평

12.
정답 (A)
해석 자선단체는 다가오는 모금 행사에 관한 제안들을 수집하기 위해 온라인 양식을 게시했다.
해설 모금 행사와 관련하여 수집하는 대상에 해당하는 명사가 필요합니다. 따라서 선택지 중에 '제안'을 의미하는 (A) suggestions가 정답입니다.
어휘 charity 자선단체 gather 모으다, 수집하다 regarding ~에 관하여 fundraising 모금 활동 composition 구성 success 성공 evaluation 평가

DAY 2 명사 2

1. (B)	2. (B)	3. (A)	4. (A)	5. (D)
6. (D)	7. (B)	8. (C)	9. (D)	10. (A)
11. (C)	12. (C)			

1.
정답 (B)
해석 전문가 인터뷰는 그 다큐멘터리를 위한 귀중한 정보의 원천 역할을 했다.
해설 빈칸 앞에 형용사 valuable이 있고 문맥상 다큐멘터리를 위한 귀중한 정보의 출처 역할을 했다는 의미가 자연스러우므로 '원천'을 의미하는 (B) source가 정답입니다.
어휘 served as ~로서 역할을 하다 valuable 귀중한 practice 연습, 실행 ability 능력

2.
정답 (B)
해석 인사팀은 신규 채용과 관련된 비용을 줄이기 위해 채용 과정을 개선했다.
해설 신규 채용과 관련된 비용을 줄이기 위해 채용 과정을 개선했다라는 의미가 자연스러우므로 '과정'을 의미하는 (B) process가 정답입니다. recruitment process는 인재를 채용하는 전체 절차를 의미하며, 회사에서 인건비와 운영 효율성을 고려할 때 자주 사용되는 표현입니다.
어휘 recruitment 채용 associated with ~와 관련된 demand 수요, 요구 instance 사례 occasion (특수한) 때, 기회

3.
정답 (A)
해석 컴퓨터 공학 학사 학위는 소프트웨어 엔지니어 역할에 필요한 요건이다.
해설 공학 학위는 소프트웨어 엔지니어 역할에 필요한 요건이라는 의미를 나타내야 자연스러우므로 '요건'을 뜻하는 (A) requirement가 정답입니다.
어휘 bachelor's degree 학사학위 registration 등록 reservation 예약 replacement 교체, 대체

4.
정답 (A)
해석 갑작스러운 수요 증가로 인해, 우리 회사는 새로 출시된 스마트폰의 제조 능력을 즉시 확대할 필요가 있다.
해설 빈칸 앞에는 전치사 in이 있으므로 명사 형태가 와야 합니다. 갑작스럽게 증가될 수 있는 것은 '수요'가 문맥상 자연스러우

므로 (A) demand가 정답입니다.

어휘 sudden 갑작스러운 rise 증가 released 출시된 manufacturing 제조 capacity 능력 immediately 즉시, 곧바로 appearance 외모, 출현 population 인구

5.
정답 (D)
해석 소규모 영화 제작사들은 대형 프랜차이즈 영화와 경쟁할 때 특히 광고 예산이 제한되어 시장에서 어려움을 겪는다.
해설 빈칸에 들어갈 명사는 advertising과 함께 쓰이며, 문장에서 constrained(제한된)의 수식을 받습니다. 문맥상 대형 프랜차이즈 영화와 경쟁할 때 소규모 영화 제작사가 제약 받는 것은 광고(advertising)와 관련된 '예산'으로 보는 것이 자연스러우므로 선택지 중 '예산'을 뜻하는 (D) budgets가 정답입니다.
어휘 frequently 자주, 빈번하게 struggle 애쓰다 due to ~때문에 constrained 제한된, 제약을 받는 advertising 광고 compete 경쟁하다 scene 장면

6.
정답 (D)
해석 좌석이 제한되어 있기 때문에, 식당은 손님들이 저녁 식사 전에 예약을 하도록 권장한다.
해설 동사 make의 목적어로서 저녁 식사 전에 하는 것으로 권장되는 명사가 필요하므로 '예약'을 뜻하는 (D) reservations가 정답입니다.
어휘 limited 제한된 seating 좌석 suggestion 제안 observation 관찰

7.
정답 (B)
해석 축제의 다양한 행사는 모든 연령대와 문화권 사람들의 관심을 충족시킵니다.
해설 다양한 행사가 사람들의 취향이나 관심사를 만족시킨다는 의미가 자연스러우므로 '관심'을 뜻하는 (B) interests가 정답입니다.
어휘 wide 광범위하게 a range of 다양한 cater to 제공하다 selection 선택 action 행동 role 역할

8.
정답 (C)
해석 그 경기장에는 향후 스포츠 행사들을 위해 좌석 수용을 늘리기 위한 개조 공사가 진행될 것이다.
해설 빈칸이 속한 to 부정사구가 뜻하는 '향후 스포츠 행사들을 위해'라는 의미와 어울리도록 seation(좌석)과 함께 쓰일 수 있는 명사가 필요합니다. 따라서 '수용'을 뜻하는 (C) capacity가 정답입니다.

어휘 stadium 경기장 undergo 진행하다 renovation 수리, 개조 duration 기간 intensity 강도, 세기

9.
정답 (D)
해석 연구팀은 현재 소비재를 위한 지속 가능한 포장재의 개발에 매진하고 있다.
해설 문맥상 소비재를 위한 지속 가능한 포장재의 개발을 한다는 의미를 구성해야 자연스러우므로 '개발'을 뜻하는 명사 (D) development가 정답입니다.
어휘 currently 현재 sustainable 지속 가능한 instrument 도구, 악기 shipment 배송, 운송 decising 결정

10.
정답 (A)
해석 업그레이드된 소프트웨어는 그 플랫폼의 기존 기능에 유용한 추가 요소를 특징으로 한다.
해설 빈칸 앞에 위치한 형용사 useful과 함께 업그레이드된 소프트웨어의 특징을 나타낼 수 있는 명사가 위치해야합니다. 업그레이드는 기존 기능에 '추가'되는 것이 일반적이므로 문맥상 '추가', '추가된 것'을 의미하는 명사 (A) addition이 정답입니다.
어휘 feature 특징, 기능 useful 유용한 addition 추가(된 것) treatment 치료 outcome 결과, 성과

11.
정답 (C)
해석 건축 허가를 받기 위해, 도급업체들은 시청에 작성 완료된 신청서를 제출해야 한다.
해설 문맥상 '시청에 작성 완료된 신청서를 제출해야 한다'는 의미를 구성해야 자연스러우므로 '신청서'를 뜻하는 명사 (C) application이 정답입니다.
어휘 permit 허가 contractor 계약자, 도급업체 appointment 예약

12.
정답 (C)
해석 귀하의 결제가 접수되는 즉시, 주문하신 상품의 배송 처리를 시작하겠습니다.
해설 빈칸 앞에 위치한 전치사 Upon은 명사와 함께 쓰여서 '~하자마자'라는 의미를 나타냅니다. 문맥상 지불금(payment)과 관련하여 주문품 배송 처리를 시작할 것이라는 내용이므로, 빈칸은 payment와 함께 '지불금을 수령했다'는 내용이 되는 것이 자연스럽습니다. 따라서 선택지 중에 '수령', '받음'을 나타내는 명사 (C) receipt가 정답입니다.
어휘 upon + 명사: ~하자마자, ~하는 즉시 payment 지불금, 결제(금) process 처리하다 shipment 배송 order 주문(품) entry 입력, 입장, 출품(작) request 요청 receipt 수령, 받음 appeal 매력, 호소

DAY 3 명사 3

1. (A)	2. (A)	3. (A)	4. (B)	5. (C)
6. (D)	7. (B)	8. (B)	9. (A)	10. (D)
11. (B)	12. (C)			

1.
정답 (A)

해석 새로운 교육 정책에 대해 문의 사항이 있으시면 인사부에 연락해 주세요.

해설 동사 have의 목적어로서 인사부에 연락할 용건이 언급되어야 합니다. '새로운 교육 정책에 대해 문의 사항'이 문맥상 자연스러우므로 '문의, 질문'를 뜻하는 명사 (A) inquiries이 정답입니다.

어휘 Human Resource 인사부 instruction 지시사항, 설명서 position 직책, 위치 task 업무, 과업

2.
정답 (A)

해석 프로젝트 관리의 중요한 측면 중 하나는, 품질과 업무량의 균형을 맞추면서 현실적인 마감일을 설정하는 것이다.

해설 빈칸 뒤에 형용사 important가 있고 프로젝트 관리의 중요한 하나를 설명하고 있으므로 '측면'을 뜻하는 명사 (A) aspect가 정답입니다.

어휘 realistic 현실적인 deadline 마감일 workload 업무량 overview 개요 ingredient 재료, 성분

3.
정답 (A)

해석 이 박사의 소비자 지출 습관에 대한 관찰은 기존의 경제적 가정에 의문을 제기했습니다.

해설 소비 지출 습관에 대한 행동을 관찰함으로써 경제적 가정에 의문을 제기했다라는 점이 문맥상 자연스러우므로 '관찰'를 뜻하는 명사 (A) observations가 정답입니다.

어휘 challenge 도전하다, 의문을 제기하다 existing 기존의 economic 경제적인 assumption 가정, 추정 standard 기준 instinct 본능

4.
정답 (B)

해석 실내 개조 공사로 인해 추후 통보가 있을 때까지 사무실은 계속 폐쇄됩니다.

해설 실내 개조공사로 인해 사무실이 폐쇄된다는 내용이며, 빈칸은 전치사 until과 형용사 further과 함께 쓰이는 명사여야 합니다. 문맥상 '추후 통보가 있을 때까지'라는 의미가 적절하므로, '통보'를 의미하는 명사 (B) notice가 정답입니다.

어휘 remain 유지하다 until further notice 추후 통보가 있을 때까지 care 애정, 보살핌 redard 관심, 고려, 존경 concern 걱정, 우려

5.
정답 (C)

해석 고객 여러분의 지속적인 지원에 감사드리며, 선정된 기기에 대해 연장된 보증을 제공할 것입니다.

해설 문맥상 고객이 회사에 지속적으로 긍정적인 기여를 했다는 명사가 필요하므로 '지원'을 뜻하는 (C) support가 정답입니다.

어휘 appreciation 감사 extended 연장된 warranty 보증 select a. 엄선된 v. 고르다, 선택하다 transaction 거래 foundation 기반 support 지지, 지원 resouece 원천, 근원

6.
정답 (D)

해석 고객 구매 행동에 대한 철저한 조사는 팀이 전략을 더욱 효과적으로 맞추는 데 도움이 되었다.

해설 빈칸 앞에 형용사 thorough가 있고 고객 구매행동에 대한 철저한 분석이나 조사를 의미하는 명사가 필요하므로 '조사'를 뜻하는 (D) examination가 정답입니다.

어휘 thorough 철저한 behavior 행동 tailor 맞추다, 조정하다 strategy 전략 effectively 효과적으로 abbreviation 약어 agreement 동의, 합의, 계약 permission 허락

7.
정답 (B)

해석 갑작스러운 정전으로 인해 생산 라인이 잠시 중단되었고, 그로 인해 수 시간의 배송 지연이 발생했다.

해설 빈칸 앞에 형용사 brief가 있고 갑작스러운 정전으로 인해 생산 라인이 중단되었다는 내용이 문맥상 적절하므로 '중단'을 의미하는 명사 (B) interruption가 정답입니다.

어휘 sudden 갑작스러운 outage 정전 cause ~을 야기하다 brief 짧은 delay 지연, 연기 interruption 중단, 방해 attendance 참석 outline 개요, 윤곽 statement 진술, 성명

8.
정답 (B)

해석 최근 모바일 뱅킹 앱에 이루어진 기능 개선 사항 덕분에 고객들이 자신의 계좌를 훨씬 더 쉽게 관리할 수 있게 되었다.

해설 모바일 뱅킹 앱에 최근에 이루어진 것이 고객들의 계좌 관리를 더 쉽게 만들었다는 내용이므로, 고객을 위한 긍정적인 변화에 관련된 의미의 명사가 필요합니다. 따라서 선택지 중에서 '향상', '개선'을 뜻하는 (B) enhancements가 정답입니다.

어휘 significantly 상당히 manage 관리하다, 운영하다 account 계좌 continuation 계속, 연속 enhancement 개선, 향상 evaluation 평가 success 성공

9.
정답 (A)
해석 모든 안전 장비는 매월 점검되어야 하며, 손상된 품목은 즉시 관리자에게 보고돼야 한다.
해설 빈칸 앞에 위치한 명사 safety와 함께 쓰이고, 매월 점검되어야 하는 것이 빈칸에 필요합니다. 따라서 선택지 중에 '장비'라는 의미의 (A) equipment가 정답입니다.
어휘 inspect 점검하다 monthle 매월의 damaged 손상된 immediately 즉시 construction 건설, 구조 treatment 치료 security 안전

10.
정답 (D)
해석 불안정한 시장 상황에도 불구하고, 영업부는 서비스 품질에 대한 고객의 기대를 충족하고 그 이상을 달성했다.
해설 빈칸 뒤에는 전치사 on이 있으므로 명사 형태가 와야 한다. 또한, 문맥상 영업부가 서비스 품질에 대한 고객의 기대를 충족한다는 표현이 문맥상 자연스럽기 때문에, '기대'를 뜻하는 명사 (D) expectations가 정답입니다.
어휘 despite ~에도 불구하고 volatile 불안한, 변덕스러운 condition 상태, 조건 meet 충족시키다 exceed 초과하다, 능가하다 quality 품질 computation 계산 endorsement 지지, 보증 adjustment 적응, 조정 expectation 기대, 예상

11.
정답 (B)
해석 인사부는 직원들에게 출장 경비는 출장 후 5일 이내에 제출해야만 환급된다고 상기시켰다.
해설 회사의 출장 관련 경비 처리 규정을 설명하고 있으며 빈칸 앞 명사 travel과 어울리는 명사는 '지출'을 의미하는 (B) expenses입니다. travel expense는 복합명사로 쓰입니다.
어휘 remind 상기시키다 reimburse 환급하다 price 가격 expence 지출, 비용 material 재료

12.
정답 (C)
해석 회사의 개발팀은 지난 1년간 수집된 사용자 피드백에서 영감을 얻었다.
해설 동사 found의 목적어에 어울리는 명사가 위치해야 합니다. 문맥상 지난 1년간 수집된 사용자 피드백에서 얻은 것이라는 의미가 적절하므로 명사 '영감'을 뜻하는 (C) inspiration이 정답입니다.

어휘 past year 지난 1년 suspicion 의심 apprehension 이해 inspiration 영감 construction 건설

DAY 4 명사 4

1. (A)	2. (C)	3. (A)	4. (C)	5. (B)
6. (A)	7. (B)	8. (B)	9. (C)	10. (D)
11. (B)	12. (A)			

1.
정답 (A)
해석 새로운 의료 시설에는 환자 진료실, 진단 장비, 그리고 약국이 포함되어 있다.
해설 환자 진료실과 진단 장비, 그리고 약국을 포함하는 것은 '의료 시설'인 것이 문맥상 자연스러우므로 '시설(물)'을 뜻하는 명사 (A) facility가 정답입니다.
어휘 medical 의료의 patient care room 환자 진료실 diagnostic 진단 pharmacy 약국 device 장치, 기기 facility 시설 product 제품 management 관리, 경영

2.
정답 (C)
해석 모든 금융 기관은 고객 정보를 보호하기 위해 엄격한 보안 조치를 따라야 한다.
해설 빈칸 앞에 명사 security가 있고 고객 정보를 보호하기 위해 엄격한 보안 조치를 따라야 한다는 문맥이 자연스러우므로 '조치'를 뜻하는 명사 (C) measures가 정답입니다.
어휘 financial 재정의, 재무의 institution 협회 be required to do ~하기를 요구받다, ~해야 하다 issue 문제, 사안 measure 조치 ~해야 하다 deposit 보증금

3.
정답 (A)
해석 기술 지원 직원들은 사이버 보안 프로토콜에 중점을 둔 전문 교육 세션에 참여했다.
해설 빈칸 앞에 명사 training과 함께 쓰는 명사이어야 하고 사이버 보안 프로토콜에 중점을 둔 전문 교육 세션이라는 문맥이 자연스러우므로 '(특정 활동을 위한) 시간'을 뜻하는 명사 (A) sessions이 정답입니다.
어휘 technical 기술적인 specialized 전문화된 focus on ~에 집중된, ~에 초점을 맞춘 protocol 규약, 절차 session (특정 활동을 위한) 시간 material 재료, 자료 position 위치, 직무 feedback 피드백, 의견

4.
정답 (C)

해석 각 승객은 체크인 전에 자신의 수하물이 제대로 라벨링되었는지 확인할 책임이 있다.

해설 빈칸 앞에 소유격 passenger's이 있고 빈칸이 속한 to부정사구가 뜻하는 '수하물이 제대로 라벨링되었는지 확인한다'는 문맥과 어울리는 명사가 필요합니다. 따라서 선택지 중에 '책임'을 뜻하는 명사 (C) responsibility가 정답입니다.

어휘 passenger 승객 ensure 확실히 ~하다, 보장하다 baggage 수하물 properly 적절히, 제대로 label 라벨을 붙이다, 표시하다 status 상태, 지위 reservation 예약 responsibility 책임, 임무 delivery 배달

5.
정답 (B)

해석 조립 라인 작업자들은 LED 모듈과 배터리 셀 같은 깨지기 쉬운 부품들을 다루도록 훈련받는다.

해설 빈칸 앞에 형용사 fragile의 수식을 받고 빈칸 뒤에는 LED 모듈과 배터리 셀 같은 것이 있다고 예를 들어 설명하므로 이를 해당하는 명사가 필요합니다. 따라서, '부품들'을 뜻하는 (B) components가 정답입니다.

어휘 assembly line 조립 라인 handle 다루다, 취급하다 fragile 깨지기 쉬운 instrument 기구 component 부품, 요소 formulation 제형 discovery 발견

6.
정답 (A)

해석 필수 직장 안전 교육에 대한 온라인 등록이 월요일 아침에 시작됩니다.

해설 빈칸 앞에 명사 Online이 있고 빈칸 뒤에 있는 전치사 for가 등록 대상이 무엇인지 설명해주는 구조입니다. 또한 열릴 수 있는 대상인 명사가 필요하므로 '등록'을 뜻하는 (A) registration이 정답입니다.

어휘 mandatory 필수적인 redistration 등록 detection 탐지 installation 설치

7.
정답 (B)

해석 모든 공급업체는 서비스, 요금, 조건을 명시한 서면 제안서를 협상이 시작되기 전에 제출해야 한다.

해설 빈칸 앞에 형용사 written(서면의)이 있고, 빈칸 뒤에 있는 분사구 '서비스, 요금, 조건을 명시한 서면'이라는 의미이므로, '제안서'를 뜻하는 (B) proposal이 정답입니다.

어휘 vendor 공급업체 written 서면의 specify 명시하다 rate 요금 negotiation 협상 invoice 송장 confirmation 확인 reference 참고자료

8.
정답 (B)

해석 새로운 클라우드 서비스 할인 혜택을 활용하기 위해, 고객들은 이번 달 말까지 구독을 업그레이드해야 한다.

해설 동사 take의 목적어에 어울리는 명사가 위치해야 합니다. 새로운 클라우드 서비스 할인 혜택을 활용한다는 문맥이 자연스러우므로 '혜택'을 뜻하는 (B) advantage가 정답입니다. take advantage of '~을 이용하다, ~을 활용하다'라는 숙어 표현입니다.

어휘 subscription 구독 merit 장점 improvement 개선

9.
정답 (C)

해석 재무 부서는 모든 지역 지점의 수익을 상세히 비교한 것을 제공했다.

해설 빈칸 앞에 형용사 detailed이 있고, 빈칸 뒤에는 전치사구가 이어지며 '모든 지역 지점의 수익에 대한'이라는 설명이 나옵니다. 모든 지역 지점의 수익에 대해 비교했다는 문맥이 자연스러우므로 '비교, 대조'를 뜻하는 명사 (C) comparison이 정답입니다.

어휘 finance 금융 revenue 수익, 매출 across 전체에 걸쳐 regional 지역의 deduction 공제, 차감 projection 예상, 투사

10.
정답 (D)

해석 설문 결과에 따르면 직원들은 재택근무 정책에 대해 분명한 선호를 가지고 있는 것으로 나타났다.

해설 빈칸 앞에 형용사 clear이 있고, 빈칸 뒤에는 전치사구가 이어지며 '재택근무 정책에 대해'라는 설명이 나옵니다. 또한, 직원들이 분명한 선호를 가지고 있다는 문맥이 자연스러우므로 명사 '선호'를 뜻하는 (D) preference가 정답입니다.

어휘 indicate 나타내다 employee 직원 remote work 재택근무 amount 양 convenience 편의

11.
정답 (B)

해석 모든 서비스 요금은 설치 및 설정 수수료를 포함하여 최종 청구서에 반영된다.

해설 빈칸 앞에 명사 service가 있고, 빈칸 뒤에는 동사 will be reflected on이 이어지며 '설치 및 설정 수수료를 포함하여 최종 청구서에 반영 될 것이다는'라는 설명이 나오므로, '요금'을 뜻하는 명사 (B) charges가 정답입니다.

어휘 reflect on ~에 대해 깊이 생각하다 final 최종의 invoice 청구서 including ~을 포함하여 installation 설치 setup 설치, 설정 fee 수수료, 요금 requirement 필요, 필요조건 charge 요금 guideline 지침, 안내 delivery 배달

12.
정답 (A)

해석 인사부서 직원들의 해외 프로젝트를 위한 여행 및 숙소를 준비하는 일을 담당한다.

해설 빈칸이 전치사 구에 있고 직원들의 해외 프로젝트를 위해 준비하는 대상에 해당하는 명사가 필요합니다. 따라서 선택지 중에 '숙소'를 뜻하는 명사 (A) accommodations가 정답입니다.

어휘 be responsible for ~에 대해 책임이 있다 organize 준비한다, 조직하다 overseas 해외의 surrounding 주변 환경 certification 자격증 vicinity 근처 지역

DAY 5 명사 5

1. (C)	2. (C)	3. (B)	4. (A)	5. (D)
6. (B)	7. (D)	8. (C)	9. (B)	10. (A)
11. (A)	12. (D)			

1.
정답 (C)

해석 제한된 자원에도 불구하고, 인턴들은 시장 분석 프로젝트를 완수하는 데 있어 놀라운 끈기를 보여주었다.

해설 빈칸 앞에 형용사 remarkable이 있고, 빈칸 뒤에는 전치사구가 이어지며 시장 분석 프로젝트를 완수하는 데 놀라운 것을 보여주었다는 문맥이므로 선택지 중에서 '끈기'를 뜻하는 (C) persistence가 정답입니다.

어휘 despite ~에도 불구하고 resource 자원 remarkable 주목할 만한 analysis 분석, 해석 abundance 풍부함 persistence 끈기 attendance 출석, 참석자 수 frequency 빈도

2.
정답 (C)

해석 조수는 수정된 출발 시간과 호텔 변경 사항을 반영한 업데이트된 일정을 준비했다.

해설 빈칸 앞에 형용사 updated가 있고 동사 prepare의 목적어에 어울리는 명사가 와야 합니다. 출발 시간과 호텔 변경 사항을 반영하는 대상으로 여행 일정이 적절하므로 '여행 일정표'를 뜻하는 (C) itinerary가 정답입니다.

어휘 assistant 조수, 비서 reflect 반영하다 revised 수정된, 변경된 supply 공급품 itinerary 여행 일정(표) memo 회람, 공지 account 계좌, 설명

3.
정답 (B)

해석 그 공장은 올해 말까지 수작업 조립에서 자동화 생산으로의 중요한 전환을 겪게 될 것이다.

해설 문맥상 수작업 조립에서 자동화 생산 방식으로의 전환을 의미하는 하는 것이 자연스러우므로 '전환'을 뜻하는 (B) transition이 정답입니다.

어휘 undergo 겪다, 경험하다 manual 인력을 요하는, 수공의 assembly 집회 cooperation 협력 suspension 중단 solution 해결(책)

4.
정답 (A)

해석 제품 조립에 필요한 모든 부품이 상자에 포함되어 있으며, 그림으로 된 단계별 설명서도 함께 들어 있습니다.

해설 빈칸 앞에는 명사 product가 있고, 빈칸 뒤에는 동사구가 이어지며 주어인 '모든 부품'에 대한 설명이 나옵니다. 문맥상 박스에 설명서와 함께 포함되는 것은 '제품 조립에 필요한 모든 부품'이라는 의미가 자연스러우므로, '조립'을 뜻하는 명사 (A) assembly가 정답입니다.

어휘 require 요구하다 along with 함께, ~을 따라서 illustrate 설명하다 step-by-step 단계별 instruction 설명 promotion 홍보 recommendation 추천, 권고 initiation 시작

5.
정답 (D)

해석 기계 근처에서 일하는 직원들을 보호하기 위해 시설에서는 항상 안전 고글을 착용해야 합니다.

해설 항상 안전 고글을 착용해야 한다는 문장과, 빈칸 앞에 '기계 근처에서 작업하는 직원들의'라는 표현이 있는 점을 고려할 때, 직원들의 '보호'를 의미하는 명사가 문맥상 자연스러우므로 '보호'를 뜻하는 (D) protection이 정답입니다.

어휘 at all times 항상, 언제나 machinery 기계류 identity 정체성 creativity 창의성 growth 성장

6.
정답 (B)

해석 악천후 때문에, 신규 본사의 공사는 다음 주까지 연기되었습니다.

해설 'weather'라는 단어가 빈칸 앞에 위치하고, 본사 건설이 연기되었다는 문맥을 봤을 때, 날씨의 상태를 나타내는 명사 conditions가 적절하므로 명사 (B) conditions가 정답입니다.

어휘 due to ~ 때문에 poor 좋지 않은 headquarter 본사 postpone 연기하다 background 배경 evaluation 평가

7.

정답 (D)

해석 마케팅 부서는 다가오는 브랜딩 워크숍을 위한 등록 요청을 많이 받았다.

해설 '마케팅 부서가 다가오는 브랜딩 워크숍을 위해 많이 받았다'는 내용에서 워크샵에 대해 요청할 수 있는 것으로 적절한 것을 골라야 합니다. 따라서 선택지 중에 '등록'을 뜻하는 (D) enrollment가 정답입니다.

어휘 a volume of 많은 양의 request 요청 upcoming 다가오는 research 연구

8.

정답 (C)

해석 폐회 연설에서, 기조 연설자는 변화하는 비즈니스 환경에서의 적응력을 강조했다.

해설 빈칸 뒤의 문장에서 기조 연설자가 발표한 내용이 언급되었습니다. 이를 통해 회의 장소임을 알 수 있어 이와 어울리는 '진술, 발언'을 뜻하는 (C) statement가 정답입니다. 'closing statement'는 회의나 발표의 마지막을 장식하는 주요 발언을 의미합니다.

어휘 emphasize 강조하다 adaptability 적응력 advancement 발전 donation 기부 illustration 설명

9.

정답 (B)

해석 그 부서는 협업과 전반적인 생산성 향상을 위해 새로운 업무 프로세스 시스템을 도입했다.

해설 to부정사로 쓰인 동사 boost의 목적어로서 collaboration과 함께 향상될 수 있는 대상이 될 수 있는 명사가 쓰여야 하므로 '생산성'을 뜻하는 (B) productivity가 정답입니다.

어휘 launch v. 출시하다 n. 출시 workflow 업무 프로세스 boost 향상시키다 overall 전반적인 adjustment 조정 possibility 가능성

10.

정답 (A)

해석 그의 뛰어난 성과와 리더십 덕분에 그는 짧은 시간 내에 예상치 못한 발전을 하게 되었다.

해설 동사 earned의 목적어로서 짧은 시간 내에 예상치 못한 성과를 나타낼 명사가 쓰여야 자연스러우므로 '발전'을 뜻하는 (A) advancement가 정답입니다.

어휘 outstanding 뛰어난, 현저한 performance 성과, 실적 leadership 지도력, 통솔력 earn 획득하다, 얻다 unexpected 예치치 않은 period 시기 certification 증명, 검정

11.

정답 (A)

해석 채용 담당자는 성공적인 지원자는 회사의 핵심 가치에 익숙해야 한다고 강조했다.

해설 주어가 '채용 담당자'이고, '회사 핵심 가치에 익숙해야'하는 주체가 빈 칸에 들어가야 문맥상 회사에 지원하는 '지원자'를 뜻하는 명사 (A) applicants가 정답입니다.

어휘 recruiter 채용 담당자 emphasize 강조하다 be familiar with ~에 익숙하다 value 가치 core 핵심적인, 가장 중요한 applicant 지원자, 신청자 job 일, 일자리 offer 제안, 제공 account 계정, 계좌, 설명

12.

정답 (D)

해석 연말 연회에서, 이사는 고객 만족에 대한 팀의 헌신을 칭찬했다.

해설 빈칸은 'to customer satisfaction'의 수식을 받으며, 문맥상 고객 만족이라는 긍정적인 가치에 대한 팀의 태도나 자세를 나타냅니다. 이사는 팀의 긍정적인 자질을 칭찬한 것이므로, '헌신'을 뜻하는 명사 (D) commitment가 정답입니다.

어휘 banquet 연말 연회 praise 칭찬하다 collaboration 협업 assignment 과제 assurance 확신 commitment 헌신, 전념

DAY 6 동사1

1. (A)	2. (D)	3. (A)	4. (D)	5. (B)
6. (C)	7. (B)	8. (B)	9. (A)	10. (C)
11. (C)	12. (D)			

1.

정답 (A)

해석 금융 시스템 업그레이드가 예상보다 오래 걸리면 급여 처리가 지연될 수 있다.

해설 업그레이드가 예상보다 오래 걸릴 경우, 급여 처리 작업이 지연됨을 나타내는 동사의 과거분사가 쓰여야 의미가 자연스러우므로 '지연되는'을 뜻하는 (A) delayed가 정답입니다.

어휘 payroll 급료 지불 명부 financial 재정의 processing 처리 longer 더 오래 than expected 예상보다 delayed 지연되는 expected 예상되는 reserved 예약된 enrolled 등록된

정답 및 해설 199

2.
정답 (D)

해석 새로운 교육 매뉴얼을 만들기 위해, 여러 명의 고위 직원들이 자신의 경험에서 나온 예시들을 제공할 예정이다.

해설 교육용 자료를 만드는 과정에서 직원들이 자신의 노하우나 경험을 바탕으로 실제 사례를 제공한다는 의미의 동사가 쓰여야 합니다. 따라서 선택지 중에 '공헌하다'를 뜻하는 (D) contribute가 정답입니다.

어휘 several 몇몇의 senior 상급자인 divide 나누다, 쪼개다 argue 논의하다, 논쟁하다 resist ~에 저항하다

3.
정답 (A)

해석 우리 고객지원팀은 여러 지역의 사용자에게 영향을 준 로그인 오류를 신속히 해결했다.

해설 여러 지역의 사용자에게 영향을 준 로그인 오류를 해결했다는 동사가 쓰여야 의미가 자연스러우므로 '~을 해결하다'를 뜻하는 (A) resolved가 정답입니다.

어휘 promptly 신속하게 affect ~에 영향을 미치다 multiple 여러 개의, 다수의 across 전체에 걸쳐 define 정의를 내리다 announce 알리다

4.
정답 (D)

해석 분기별 검토 회의에서 CEO는 부서 간 내부 커뮤니케이션 개선의 필요성을 강조했다.

해설 CEO는 부서 간 내부 커뮤니케이션 개선의 필요성을 목적어로 두고 CEO가 하는 행동을 나타내는 동사가 쓰여야 의미가 자연스러우므로 '~을 강조하다'를 뜻하는 (D) emphasized가 정답입니다.

어휘 quarterly 분기의 internal 내부의 hesitate 주저하다 emphasize 강조하다 launch 출시하다, 개시하다 dominate 지배하다

5.
정답 (B)

해석 오늘 열린 기자회견에서 마케팅 팀은 새로 디자인된 로고와 업데이트된 브랜딩 가이드를 공개했다.

해설 새 로고와 브랜딩 가이드와 같은 시각적 자료를 공개한다는 문맥으로 동사 '~을 발표하다'를 뜻하는 (B) unveiled가 정답입니다.

어휘 press conference 기자 회견 decline 거절하다 unveil 발표하다, 공개하다 omit 생략하다 retrieve 되찾다, 회수하다

6.
정답 (C)

해석 온보딩 가이드는 직원 복지 혜택을 이용하고 근무 시간표를 제출하는 절차를 자세히 설명한다.

해설 온보딩 가이드에 직원 복지 혜택과 근무 시간표 제출 절차가 나열되어 있다는 점에서, 이러한 내용을 '~을 상세히 설명하다'는 의미가 문맥상 적절합니다. 따라서 동사 (C) details가 정답입니다.

어휘 access ~을 이용하다 expect 기대하다 correspond 일치하다

7.
정답 (B)

해석 정부 관계자들은 안전 규정 준수를 확인하기 위해 다음 주에 그 공장을 점검할 예정이다.

해설 시설을 직접 방문하여 규정 준수를 확인하는 과정을 설명하고 있으므로 '점검하다'를 뜻하는 동사 (B) inspect가 정답입니다.

어휘 government official 정부 관계자 compliance with ~을 지켜서, ~을 준수해서 confirm v. 확인하다 n. 확인 perform 수행하다 reject 거절하다

8.
정답 (B)

해석 귀하가 신생 기업을 시작하든 사업을 확장하든, 저희 팀은 맞춤형 해결책으로 여러분을 도울 준비가 되어있습니다.

해설 빈칸이 속한 to 부정사구가 '맞춤형 솔루션으로 여러분을 지원할 준비가 되어있다'라는 의미를 구성해야 자연스러우므로 '돕다'를 뜻하는 (B) assist가 정답입니다.

어휘 whether ~이든지 아니든지 operation 운영 be ready to 준비가 되다 custom Solution 맞춤형 해결책, 고객의 주문에 따라 맞춤 제작한 것 lend 빌려주다 mention 언급하다

9.
정답 (A)

해석 위원회는 실행 가능성과 잠재적 영향력을 바탕으로 각 제안을 평가할 것이다.

해설 빈칸 뒤에 위치한 목적어가 '각각의 제안서'이고, 위원회가 실행 가능성과 영향력이라는 기준에 따라 제안을 검토한다는 문맥이 자연스러우므로 '평가하다'를 뜻하는 동사 (A) evaluate가 정답입니다.

어휘 committee 위원회 based on ~의 기초로 하다 feasibility (실행) 가능성 potential 잠재적인 impact 영향 object 반대하다 persuade 설득하다 complain 불평하다

10.
정답 (C)

해석 내부 기준을 충족하기 위해, 새로 개발된 모든 제품은 엄격한 안전 테스트 절차를 거쳐야 한다.

해설 '엄격한 안전 테스트 절차'를 목적어로 가지는 동사가 필요하므로 '~을 겪다'를 뜻하는 (C) undergo가 정답입니다. 참고로 examine은 사람이 주체가 되어 대상을 검사할 때 쓰입니다.

어휘 meet 충족시키다 internal 내부의 standard 기준 newly 새로 product 제품 rigorous 엄격한 procedure 절차, 순서 submit 제출하다 transfer 옮기다 examine 조사하다

11.
정답 (C)

해석 귀하가 현재 조건에 만족하지 않으시다면, 저희 양측 모두에게 도움이 되는 수정된 계약을 협상할 의향이 있습니다.

해설 빈칸에 들어갈 동사는 '양 측 모두에게 도움이 되는 수정된 계약'이라는 목적어를 가질 수 있는 의미를 나타내야 합니다. 그리고 빈칸 앞 fi절은 '현재의 조건에 만족하지 않는다면'이라는 의미를 나타내므로, 빈칸은 현재의 조건이 아닌 다른 조건의 계약을 '협상'할 수 있다는 의미가 적절합니다. 따라서 선택지 중에 '협상하다'라는 의미를 나타내는 (C) negotiate가 정답입니다.

어휘 be satisfied with ~에 만족하다 current 현재의 be open to do ~할 여지가 있다, ~할 의향이 있다 agreement 계약 enclose 동봉하다 assign 배정하다

12.
정답 (D)

해석 소셜 미디어 리뷰는 종종 전통적인 광고보다 고객의 구매 행동에 더 강한 영향을 미친다.

해설 제품 리뷰나 사용자 후기가 고객의 구매 결정에 영향을 주는 역할을 하므로 '영향을 미치다'를 뜻하는 동사 (D) influence가 정답입니다.

어휘 often 종종 behavior 행동 effectively 효과적인 traditional 전통의 measure 측정하다 predict 예측하다

DAY 7 동사 2

1. (B)	2. (D)	3. (C)	4. (D)	5. (A)
6. (D)	7. (A)	8. (A)	9. (C)	10. (B)
11. (B)	12. (C)			

1.
정답 (B)

해석 에어럭스 항공은 12월부터 운항하는 서울과 밴쿠버를 연결하는 새로운 항공편 노선을 발표했다.

해설 항공사가 새로운 노선을 대상으로 하는 행위에 대한 동사로, 공식적으로 '~을 발표하다, 알리다'는 뜻이 문맥상 자연스럽습니다. 따라서 (B) announced가 정답입니다.

어휘 route 경로 demonstrate 증명하다 apply 적용되다 load ~에 짐을 싣다

2.
정답 (D)

해석 해안 도시의 호텔 예약은 여행 성수기가 끝난 초가을에 하락하는 경향이 있다.

해설 성수기가 끝나면 관광객 수가 줄어들고, 그에 따라 호텔 예약도 감소하므로 동사 '하락하다'를 뜻하는 (D) decline이 정답입니다.

어휘 booking 예약 coastal 해안의 tend to ~하는 경향이 있다 peak travel season 여행 성수기

3.
정답 (C)

해석 실적 평가를 바탕으로, 이사회는 서 씨를 지역 이사로의 승진을 추천했다.

해설 이사회가 평가 결과를 보고 승진 대상자로 추천했다는 뜻이 자연스러우므로 '(사람을) 추천하다'라는 동사의 과거형 (C) recommended가 정답입니다.

어휘 performance review 실적 평가 board 이사회 promotion 승진 regional 지역의 director 이사, 관리직

4.
정답 (D)

해석 작년에 정부는 소기업 성장을 촉진하기 위해 새로운 세금 정책을 시행했다.

해설 새로운 정책을 대상으로 정부가 할 수 있는 행위를 나타낼 동사가 쓰여야 하므로 '~을 시행하다'를 뜻하는 (D) implemented가 정답입니다.

어휘 tax 세금 promote 촉진하다 growth 성장 estimate 추정하다 investigate 조사하다 repeat 반복하다 implement 시행하다

5.
정답 (A)
해석 합병 후, 법무팀은 계약 전환과 관련된 모든 질문을 처리할 것이다.
해설 법무팀이 계약 전환과 관련된 모든 질문에 대해 할 수 있는 행위를 나타내는 동사가 쓰여야 자연스러우므로 '처리하다'를 뜻하는 (A) handle이 정답입니다.
어휘 legal team 법무팀 related to 관련된 transition 변환 dismiss 무시하다 object 반대하다

6.
정답 (D)
해석 우리는 회의가 시작되기 전에 의자들을 원형으로 준비했다.
해설 회의가 시작되기 전에 의자들을 원형으로 배치한다는 동사가 쓰여야 자연스러우므로 이러한 문맥에 맞는 '~을 준비하다'를 뜻하는 (D) arranged가 정답입니다.
어휘 in a circle 원형으로, 둥글게 divide 나누다 automate 자동화하다 lift 들어올리다

7.
정답 (A)
해석 브라이트 퍼블리싱은 전통적인 인쇄 회사에서 현대적인 디지털 제작 회사로 발전했다.
해설 타동사의 과거분사가 has와 현재완료시제 동사를 구성해야 합니다. 회사가 형태나 기능 면에서 변화하고 성장했다는 의미가 적절하므로 '발전하다'를 뜻하는 evolve의 과거분사 (A) evolved가 정답입니다.
어휘 permit 허락하다 focus 집중하다 determine 결심하다 evolve A into B: A에서 B로 발전하다[진화하다]

8.
정답 (A)
해석 보안 데이터에 접근하기 위해서는 IT 부서에 공식 요청서를 제출하시기 바랍니다.
해설 보안 데이터에 접근하기 위해 필요한 절차를 설명하고 있으므로 to부정사는 '접근 권한을 얻기 위해'라는 의미가 되는 것이 적절합니다. '~을 얻다'를 뜻하는 동사 (A) obtain이 정답입니다.
어휘 access 접근(권) formal 형식적인 request v. 요청하다 n. 요청 observe 관찰하다 eliminate 제거하다

9.
정답 (C)
해석 김 박사는 재생 에너지 연구의 선구자로 널리 인정받고 있다.
해설 빈칸에 들어갈 단어는 부사 widely의 수식을 받으며, be동사 is와 함께 쓰이는 수동태를 구성하기 위해 과거분사가 되어야 합니다. 문맥상 김 박사가 재생 가능 에너지 연구의 선구자라는 내용이므로, '인정 받는'이라는 의미의 과거분사가 적절합니다. 따라서 정답은 (C) recognized입니다.
어휘 widely 널리 pioneer 개척자, 선구자 renewable 재생 가능한 organize 조직하다 confuse 혼란스러워하다 obey 복종하다

10.
정답 (B)
해석 타운홀 미팅 동안, 주민들은 새로운 정책에 대한 우려를 표현했다.
해설 회의에서 주민들이 자신의 새로운 정책에 대한 걱정에 대해 할 수 있는 행위를 나타내는 동사가 적절하므로 '(감정 등) ~을 표현하다'를 뜻하는 (B) expressed가 정답입니다.
어휘 during ~동안 resident 거주자 concern 걱정 explore 탐구하다 exchange 교환하다 eliminate 제거하다

11.
정답 (B)
해석 그 호텔은 다음 달까지 오래된 객실 키를 비접촉식 스마트 카드로 교체할 계획이다.
해설 빈칸에 들어갈 동사 뒤에 목적어 its old room keys와 전치사구 with contactless smart cards가 위치해 있으므로 「A with B」 구조가 쓰였음을 알 수 있습니다. 문맥상 '오래된 객실 키를 비접촉식 스마트 카드로 바꾼다'는 내용이므로 'A를 B로 교체하다'라는 의미로 쓰이는 「replace A with B」 표현이 적절합니다. 따라서 정답은 (B) replace입니다.
어휘 plan to do ~할 계획이다 contactless 비접촉식 repair 수리하다 maintain 유지하다

12.
정답 (C)
해석 도시 교통 당국은 내년에 도심 지역에서 전기 버스 차량을 운영할 계획이다.
해설 빈칸이 속한 to 부정사는 a fleet of buses(여러 대의 버스) 실제 교통수단을 운영하는 행위를 나타내는 동사가 필요합니다. 따라서 '~을 운영하다'를 뜻하는 (C) operate가 정답입니다.
어휘 transportation authority 교통 당국 a fleet of 여러 대의 downtown 도심지의 promise 약속하다

DAY 8 동사 3

1. (C)	2. (A)	3. (B)	4. (D)	5. (C)
6. (B)	7. (A)	8. (A)	9. (D)	10. (B)
11. (C)	12. (D)			

1.

정답 (C)

해석 기자회견 시장은 시민들에게 긴급 구조 서비스가 다가오는 폭풍에 완전히 대비되어 있다고 확신시켰다.

해설 주어가 '시장'(the mayor)이고, 목적어가 '시민'(citizens)이며, 그 뒤에 that절은 문맥상 시장이 말한 내용에 해당합니다. 응급 구조 서비스가 다가오는 태풍에 완전히 대비되어 있다고 말한 내용에 맞는 동사가 필요하므로 선택지 중에 '확신시키다, 장담하다'라는 동사 assure의 과거형 (C) assured가 정답입니다. assure는 「assure + 사람명사 + that절」 구조로 '~에게 ~라는 것을 확신시키다'라는 의미로 쓰입니다.

어휘 mayor 시장 emergency 긴급, 응급 fully 완전히 be prepared for ~을 준비하다, 대비하다 arrange 배열하다, 마련하다 commit 범하다, 저지르다

2.

정답 (A)

해석 저희는 라이브 공연 중 사진 촬영을 삼가주실 참가자 여러분께 정중히 요청드립니다.

해설 관객들이 라이브 공연 중 사진 촬영을 자제해달라는 공손하고 정중한 요청을 설명하고 있으므로 전치사 from과 함께 쓰여 '~하는 것을 삼가다'를 뜻하는 (A) refrain이 정답입니다.

어휘 kindly ad. 친절하게 a. 상냥한, 다정한 participant 참가자 refrain from -ing: ~하는 것을 삼가다, 자제하다 forbid 금하다 resist ~에 저항하다 hesitate 주저하다, 머뭇거리다, 망설이다

3.

정답 (B)

해석 프런트 데스크에서는 직원들이 방문객을 위해 가장 가까운 ATM이나 약국을 찾아줄 수 있다.

해설 목적어가 '장소명사'이며, 문맥상 방문객에게 가장 가까운 ATM이나 약국의 위치를 안내하는 내용이므로 '찾아내다'를 뜻하는 (B) locate가 정답입니다.

어휘 staff member 직원 pharmacy 약국 assist 돕다, 원조하다 conduct 실시하다

4.

정답 (D)

해석 팀원들은 금일 중에 설문조사를 완료하라는 재고지를 받았습니다.

해설 주어인 팀원들이 빈칸 뒤에 언급된 금일 중에 설문 조사를 완료해야 한다는 내용입니다. 보기 중에서 이러한 문맥에 사용될 수 있는 동사는 '상기시키다', '재고지하다'라는 의미를 나타내는 동사 remind의 과거분사 (D) reminded입니다. be reminded to do는 '~하는 것을 재고지받다', '~하는 것이 다시 상기되다'라는 의미로 쓰이는 표현입니다.

어휘 survey n. 설문지 v. 조사하다 before 전에, 이전에 pleased 기쁜 affect ~에 영향을 미치다 allow 허용하다

5.

정답 (C)

해석 데이터코프는 데이터 보호 서비스를 강화하기 위해 최근 한 사이버보안 회사를 인수했다.

해설 '데이터 보호 서비스를 강화하기' 위한 목적으로 기업 간 거래나 확장을 나타낼 수 있는 동사 '인수하다', '획득하다'를 뜻하는 (C) acquired가 정답입니다.

어휘 recently 최근의 firm n. 회사 a. 굳은, 단단한 strengthen 강하게 하다, 튼튼하게 하다 protection 보호 audit (회계를) 감사하다 publish 발표하다, 출판하다

6.

정답 (B)

해석 연례 직원 평가는 회계연도가 시작할때 시행된다.

해설 직원 평가가 매 회계연도 초에 시행된다는 점을 설명하고 있으므로 '실시하다'를 뜻하는 (B) conducted가 정답입니다.

어휘 evaluation 평가 fiscal 회계의, 국고의 retain 계속 유지하다 establish 설립하다 postpone 연기하다

7.

정답 (A)

해석 새로운 정책은 민감한 고객 정보의 기밀성이 유지하는 것을 보장합니다.

해설 고객 정보의 유출 없이 안전하게 보존한다는 문맥이 자연스러우므로 목적어 confidentiality를 대상으로 할 수 있는 행위의 동사가 필요합니다. 따라서 '~을 유지하다'를 뜻하는 (A) maintain가 정답입니다.

어휘 confidentiality 기밀성 sensitive 민감한 restore 회복하다, 복구하다 reduce 줄이다, 감소시키다 run 달리다, 운행하다

정답 및 해설 203

8.
정답 (A)
해석 일정 충돌로 인해, 매니저는 당신의 면접을 다음 주 수요일로 다시 재조정할 것이다.
해설 일정 충돌이 발생하여 면접을 다음주 수요일로 변경할 것이라는 문맥으로 '~의 일정을 재조정하다'를 뜻하는 (A) reschedule가 정답입니다.
어휘 conflict v. (~와) 충돌하다, 다투다 n. 투쟁 recall 상기하다, 생각해내다 resume n. 이력서 v. 다시 시작하다 reconstruct 재건하다

9.
정답 (D)
해석 마케팅 부서는 새로운 제품 브로셔를 각 지역 사무소에 제공해야 한다.
해설 문맥상 새로운 제품 브로셔를 각 지역 사무소에 전달한다는 내용이 적절하므로 '~을 제공하다'를 뜻하는 (D) provide가 정답입니다.
어휘 department 부서 regional 지역의 restrict 제한하다 conceal 숨기다, 감추다

10.
정답 (B)
해석 이사회는 다음 분기를 위해 최대 10만 달러의 자본 지출을 허가했다.
해설 이사회가 특정 금액의 자본 지출을 공식적으로 허락한다는 의미가 자연스러우므로 '허가하다, 권한을 부여하다'를 뜻하는 (B) authorized가 정답입니다.
어휘 capital 자본의, 원래의 expenditure 지출, 비용 upcoming 다가오는 quarter 분기 endorse 보증하다

11.
정답 (C)
해석 인사 정책은 기업들이 인사 기록을 최소 7년간 보관하도록 요구한다.
해설 인사 기록을 일정 기간동안 가지고 있다는 문맥이 자연스러우므로 '보관하다'를 뜻하는 (C) retain이 정답입니다.
어휘 require 필요로 하다, ~을 요구하다 record 기록 (문서) at least 적어도 agree 동의하다 hire 고용하다

12.
정답 (D)
해석 경쟁력을 유지하기 위해 전문 역량 개발 과정 등록을 고려할 만한 가치가 있다.
해설 빈칸에는 동명사 enrolling을 목적어로 취할 수 있는 동사가 와야합니다. 전문성 개발 과정을 등록하는 것을 고려할 가치가 있다는 문맥이 자연스러우므로, '고려하다'를 뜻하는 (D) consider가 정답입니다.
어휘 It's worthwhile to~ ~할 가치가 있다 competitive 경쟁의 aim 목표로 삼다 observe 관찰하다, 주시하다 persuade 설득하다

DAY 9 형용사1

1. (D)	2. (D)	3. (C)	4. (C)	5. (B)
6. (B)	7. (C)	8. (D)	9. (B)	10. (A)
11. (A)	12. (A)			

1.
정답 (D)
해석 개요를 작성할 때, 저자는 자신의 연구에 대한 간결한 요약을 제공해야 한다.
해설 빈칸 뒤에 위치한 명사 'summary'를 수식해 연구에 대한 요약을 나타낼 형용사가 필요하므로 '짧은'을 뜻하는 (D) brief가 정답입니다.
어휘 abstract 개요, 초록 author 저자, 작가 research n. 연구 v. 연구하다, 조사하다 normal 표준의, 보통의 lengthy (시간이) 긴, 오랜 repetitive 되풀이하는

2.
정답 (D)
해석 건물 뒤편에 추가 비용 없이 주차 공간을 이용할 수 있다.
해설 주차 공간이 건물 뒤쪽에 있으며 추가 요금 없이 이용할 수 있다는 문맥이 자연스러우므로 '이용 가능한'을 뜻하는 (D) available이 정답입니다.
어휘 parking space 주차장 around 주위에 charge v. (요금을) 청구하다 n. 청구 금액 capable 유능한, 능력 있는

3.
정답 (C)
해석 그 잡지는 해외 사업 운영의 전직 이사와의 단독 인터뷰를 특종으로 실었다.
해설 빈칸 뒤에 위치한 명사 director를 수식해 직함 앞에 나타낼 수 있는 형용사가 필요하므로 '이전의, 전직의'를 뜻하는 (C) former가 정답입니다.
어휘 feature v. 특징으로 삼다 n. 특색, 특징 exclusive 독점적인, 특종의, 한정된 overseas 해외의 final 마지막의

4.
정답 (C)
해석 해외로 여행하기 전에 여권이 최소 6개월 동안 유효한 상태인지 확인해 주세요.
해설 여행 전 여권을 확인해야 한다는 문맥이므로 여권의 효력 상태를 나타내는 형용사가 필요합니다. 따라서 '유효한'을 뜻하는 형용사 (C) valid가 정답입니다.
어휘 ensure 반드시 ~하게 하다, 확인하다 remain ~한 상태이다. expired 만료된 optional 선택사항인 permanent 영구적인

5.
정답 (B)
해석 많은 소비자들이 포괄적이면서도 비용 부담이 적은 건강 보험 상품을 찾고 있다.
해설 건강보험 상품을 찾는 소비자의 요구사항으로 포괄적인 것과 함께 문맥상 어울리는 형용사가 필요합니다. 가격측면에서 부담이 적은 조건을 나타낸다는 문맥이 자연스러우므로 '(가격이) 저렴한'을 뜻하는 형용사 (B) affordable가 정답입니다.
어휘 seek 찾다, 조사하다 health insurance 건강보험 comprehensive 포괄적인 formal 형식적인 extensive 넓은, 광대한

6.
정답 (B)
해석 장치를 조립할 때, 설명서에 명시된 특정한 순서대로 나사를 조이세요.
해설 빈칸 뒤에 명사 'order'을 수식해 설명서에 명시된 순서대로 나사를 조이라고 하는 것이 자연스러우므로 '특정한'을 뜻하는 형용사 (B) particular가 정답입니다.
어휘 assemble (기계 등을) 조립하다, 모으다 device 장치, 기기 tighten 죄다, 단단하게하다 screw n. 나사 v. 나사로 죄다 order n. 순서 v. 주문하다 manual 수공의, 수동의 approximate a. 대략의, 거의 정확한 v. 가까워지다, 가깝다 random 임의의

7.
정답 (C)
해석 엔지니어들은 업그레이드를 준비했지만, 예상치 못한 장비 고장으로 인해 지연되었다.
해설 빈칸에 들어갈 형용사는 빈칸 뒤 명사 'equipment malfunctions'을 수식하며, 준비는 했지만 예상치 못한 문제로 인해 지연되었다는 문맥에 어울려야 하므로 '예상치 못한'을 뜻하는 형용사 (C) unexpected가 정답입니다.
어휘 delayed 지연된 malfunction 고장 routine 일상적인, 정기적인 qualified 자격 있는

8.
정답 (D)
해석 출간 전에, 편집자들은 기사의 정확성을 보장하기 위해 모든 사실을 검증해야 한다.
해설 문맥상 편집자들이 모든 사실을 검증하는 목적으로 적절한 것은 기사가 정확하도록 하기 위한 것임을 알 수 있습니다. 따라서 '정확한'을 뜻하는 (D) accurate가 정답입니다.
어휘 publish 발표하다 verify 증명하다, 입증하다 fact 사실 ensure 확실하게 하다, 보증하다 article 기사, 논문 biased 편향된 public 공공의, 일반 대중의

9.
정답 (B)
해석 예정된 점검 기간 동안, 사용자들은 제한된 콘텐츠에만 접근할 수 있다.
해설 빈칸은 명사 content 앞에 위치하여, 시스템 정비 중에 사용자가 접근할 수 있는 컨텐츠에 대해 수식하는 형용사의 자리입니다. 문맥상 시스템 정비 중에는 정상적인 컨텐츠 이용이 불가할 것이라는 것을 알 수 있으므로, 선택지 중에 '제한된'이라는 의미를 나타내는 형용사가 빈칸에 적절합니다. 따라서 정답은 (B) limited입니다.
어휘 scheduled 예정된 maintenance 보수 관리, 정비 access to ~에 대한 이용, 접근 preventable 예방 가능한 similar 유사한 leading 선도적인

10.
정답 (A)
해석 판매 데이터는 작년과 비교해 분기 수익이 상당히 감소했음을 보여주었다.
해설 빈칸 뒤에 명사 'decline'을 수식해 감소가 단순한 변화가 아니라 눈에 띄고 중요한 수준을 뜻하는 형용사가 필요하므로 '상당한'을 뜻하는 (A) significant가 정답입니다.
어휘 indicate 나타내다, 가리키다 significant 상당한, 중요한 decline n. 감소 v. 거절하다, 기울다 revenue 수익 compared to ~와 비교하여 additional 추가적인 minimal 최소한의 routine 일상적인

11.
정답 (A)
해석 JS 테크는 고품질 부품을 꾸준히 배송할 수 있는 신뢰할 수 있는 공급업체를 찾고 있습니다.
해설 빈칸 뒤에 위치한 명사 supplier(공급업체)를 수식하는 알맞은 의미의 형용사를 찾는 문제입니다. 공급업체에 대한 부연 설명으로 고품질의 부품을 꾸준히 배송할 수 있다고 언급되어 있으므로 이러한 특징의 공급업체를 '신뢰할 만한', '믿을 수 있는'이라는 의미로 수식하는 것이 적절합니다. 따라서 '신뢰할 만한'이라는 의미의 형용사 (A) reliable이 정답입니다.

어휘 seek 찾다, 구하다 supplier 공급업체 consistently 꾸준히, 끈기 있게 deliver 배송하다 high-quality 고품질의 component 부품 reliable 믿을 수 있는, 신뢰할 만한 vacant 비어 있는 convenient 편리한 representative 대표하는

12.
정답 (A)
해석 전기차의 배터리 관리 시스템이 더 효율적으로 되어 주행 거리가 늘어났다.
해설 주행 거리가 늘어났다는 것은 배터리 관리가 더 효율적으로 작동하고 있다는 것을 의미하므로 '효율적인'을 뜻하는 형용사 (A) efficient가 정답입니다.
어휘 electric 전기의 management 관리 driving range 주행 거리 appropriate 적절한 extensive 광범위한 external 외부의

DAY 10 형용사 2

1. (D)	2. (B)	3. (C)	4. (D)	5. (A)
6. (B)	7. (B)	8. (A)	9. (D)	10. (C)
11. (A)	12. (C)			

1.
정답 (D)
해석 그녀의 바이올린 연주는 너무 뛰어나서, 평론가들조차 말문이 막혔다.
해설 그녀의 바이올린 연주가 평론가들조차 말문이 막히게 했다는 것은, 연주가 매우 뛰어났다는 것을 의미하므로 '뛰어난'을 뜻하는 형용사 (D) exceptional이 정답입니다.
어휘 performance 연주, 성과 so 형용사 that: 너무 ~해서 ~하다 critics 비평가, 평론가 speechless 말문이 막힌 mediocre 평범한 sufficient 충분한

2.
정답 (B)
해석 팀은 다음 달에 있을 다가오는 제품 출시 행사의 세부 사항을 마무리하고 있다.
해설 빈칸 뒤에 명사 'product'를 수식하며 문장에서 '다음 달'이라는 미래 시점이 명시되어 있으므로 '다가올'이라는 의미로 미래의 행사를 의미하는 형용사 (B) upcoming이 정답입니다.
어휘 finalize 마무리하다, 완결하다 launch n. 출시 v. 출시하다 previous 이전의 former 이전의 continuous 지속적인

3.
정답 (C)
해석 저희는 본사로부터 즉각적인 조치가 요구되는 긴급 메시지를 받았습니다.
해설 빈칸 뒤에 명사 'message'를 수식하며 즉각적인 조치를 요구하는 의미를 나타내야 자연스러우므로 '긴급한'을 뜻하는 형용사 (C) urgent가 정답입니다.
어휘 headquarter 본사 immediate 즉각의, 당장의 overdue 기한이 지난 existing 기존의

4.
정답 (D)
해석 기념일을 축하하기 위해, 모든 고객에게 무료 디저트를 제공합니다.
해설 빈칸 뒤에 명사 dessert를 수식하며 기념일을 축하하기 위해 제공된다는 의미와 문맥상 부합해야 하므로 '무료의'를 뜻하는 형용사 (D) complimentary가 정답입니다.
어휘 celebrate 축하하다 anniversary 기념일 refundable 환불 가능한 scheduled 예정된

5.
정답 (A)
해석 고객 서비스를 개선하기 위한 진행 중인 노력이 긍정적인 결과를 보이기 시작했다.
해설 빈칸 뒤에 명사 efforts를 수식하며 그 노력이 긍정적인 결과를 보인다는 의미와 문맥상 어울리는 형용사가 필요하므로 '진행 중인'을 뜻하는 (A) ongoing이 정답입니다.
어휘 effort 노력 outcome 결과 dissolved 해산된, 끝난 restrained 제한된, 억제된 vulnerable 취약한

6.
정답 (B)
해석 세입자들의 지속적인 요청으로, 시의회는 주거 지역의 소음 수준에 대한 새로운 규정을 도입했다.
해설 빈칸 뒤에 명사 'areas'를 수식하며 소음 문제가 발생되는 장소와 관련되는 형용사가 필요합니다. 따라서, '주거의'를 뜻하는 (B) residential이 정답입니다.
어휘 consistent 지속적인 request n. 요청 v. 요청하다 tenant 세입자 council 의회 regulation 규정 noise 소음 spacious 넓은 competitive 경쟁적인 rural 시골의

7.
정답 (B)
해석 그 대학은 공학 학위를 전공하는 학생들을 지원하는 데에 전념하는 장학기금을 설립했습니다.

해설 빈칸에 들어갈 과거분사는 앞에 위치한 명사 a scholarship fund(장학기금)를 수식합니다. 그리고 빈칸 뒤에 전치사 to와 동명사가 위치하고 있으므로 「to 동명사」 구조와 함께 쓰이는 과거분사임을 알 수 있습니다. 문맥상 공학 학위를 전공하는 학생들을 지원하기 위한 장학기금을 설립했다는 내용이므로, 선택지 중에서 이에 어울리는 '전념하는', '헌신하는'이라는 의미를 나타내는 (B) dedicated가 정답입니다.

어휘 establish 설립하다, 기반을 마련하다 scholarship fund 장학기금 support 지원하다, 후원하다 pursue a degree 학위를 전공하다, 학위를 추구하다 engineering 공학 prepare 준비하다 dedicated to -ing: ~하는 데 전념하는[헌신하는] allow 허용하다 compare 비교하다

8.

정답 (A)

해설 집주인은 새 사무실 공간에 대해 합리적인 월세를 제안했다.

해설 빈칸 뒤에 명사 monthly rent를 수식하며 집주인이 월세를 제안했다는 내용과 어울려야 하므로 '합리적인'를 뜻하는 형용사 (A) reasonable이 정답입니다.

어휘 landlord 집주인, 주인 propose 제안하다 monthly 매달의 outstanding 뛰어난 notable 주목할 만한 invaluable 매우 귀중한

9.

정답 (D)

해설 서식지가 줄어드는 멸종 위기 종들은 점점 더 멸종에 취약해진다.

해설 줄어드는 서식지의 멸종 위기 종들이 점점 멸종에 대한 어떠한 상태가 된다는 내용이 되어야 합니다. 따라서 선택지 중에 이러한 문맥에 맞는 '~에 취약한'이라는 의미의 형용사 (D) vulnerable이 정답입니다.

어휘 endangered 멸종 위기인 species (분류상의) 종 shrinking 줄어드는 habitat (동식물의) 서식지 increasingly 증가하는 extinction 멸종 immune 면역이 있는 resistant 저항력이 있는 designed 설계된

10.

정답 (C)

해설 모든 이해관계자가 참석 가능 여부를 확인할 때까지 회의 일정은 잠정적이다.

해설 이해관계자가 참석 가능 여부가 아직 확인되지 않았다는 내용이므로, 이에 회의 일정도 확정되지 않았음을 알 수 있습니다. 따라서 '잠정적인'을 뜻하는 형용사 (C) tentative가 정답입니다.

어휘 stakeholder 이해관계자, 책임자 confirm 확인하다 availability 유효성, 유용성 agreeable 동의할 수 있는 sudden 갑작스러운 considerate 사려 깊은

11.

정답 (A)

해설 그 기관은 지난 5년 동안 연례 회의에 대한 관심이 증가하는 것을 목격해왔다.

해설 빈칸 뒤에 명사 interest를 수식하고 '지난 5년 동안 관심이 목격되어 왔다'는 문맥에서 관심에 대한 점진적인 변화를 나타내는 형용사가 필요합니다. 따라서 '(크기, 수, 정도가) 증가하는'을 뜻하는 형용사 (A) growing이 정답입니다.

어휘 organization 기관, 조직 interest 관심, 흥미 annual 1년의, 해마다 over ~하는 동안 closed 닫힌 unknown 알려지지 않은 costly 비용이 많이 드는

12.

정답 (C)

해설 이번 소프트웨어 업데이트는 사용자 경험과 보안을 개선하기 위한 일련의 포괄적인 특징들을 도입한다.

해설 사용자 경험과 보안이라는 두 가지 주요 영역을 개선한다고 했으므로, 여러 특징을 도입했음을 알 수 있습니다. 이러한 문맥에 어울리는 형용사로 '포괄적인' 의미를 지니는 (C) comprehensive가 정답입니다.

어휘 feature 특성, 특징 minimal 최소한의 initial 초기의 existing 기존의

DAY 11 부사 1

1. (B)	2. (B)	3. (C)	4. (D)	5. (D)
6. (A)	7. (C)	8. (D)	9. (B)	10. (A)
11. (C)	12. (A)			

1.

정답 (B)

해설 재무 실적이 기대에 못 미친 후, CEO는 언론에서 심하게 비판을 받았다.

해설 수동태 동사를 구성하는 be동사 was와 과거분사 criticized 사이에서 과거분사를 수식할 수 있는 부사가 필요하며, 재무 실적이 기대에 못 미쳤다는 부정적인 상황을 설명하고 있으므로 '심하게'를 뜻하는 (B) heavily가 정답입니다.

어휘 criticize 비평하다 press 언론, 출판 short of 부족하다 expectation 기대, 예상 mildly 가볍게 briefly 한결같이, 끊임없이 roughly 거칠게, 대충

2.
정답 (B)
해석 저희 웹사이트는 서버 정비로 인해 현재 기술적인 문제를 겪고 있습니다.
해설 현재진행시제동사 is experiencing 사이에 빈칸이 위치해 있으므로 현재진행시제와 잘 어울리는 부사가 필요합니다. 따라서, '현재'를 뜻하는 (B) currently가 정답입니다.
어휘 technical 기술적인 difficulties 문제 due to ~ 때문에 always 항상 soon 곧 immediately 즉시

3.
정답 (C)
해석 태양광 패널의 운영 비용은 전통적인 에너지원보다 상대적으로 낮다.
해설 태양광 패널의 운영 비용과 전통적인 에너지원을 비교하고 있는 비교급 표현인 lower than을 수식하는 부사가 필요합니다. 따라서 '상대적으로'를 뜻하는 (C) relatively가 정답입니다.
어휘 cost 가격 solar panel 태양광 패널 occasionally 때때로 aggressively 공격적으로 mistakenly 실수로

4.
정답 (D)
해석 공급업체는 부품이 곧 배송될 것이라고 확인했다.
해설 배송 시점에 대한 정보를 언급하고 있으며 will be delivered 라는 미래 시제동사와 함께 쓰이는 부사가 필요하므로 '곧'을 뜻하는 (D) shortly가 정답입니다.
어휘 supplier 공급업체 confirm 확인하다 remarkably 눈에 띄게, 매우 barely 거의 ~않다 indefinitely 무기한으로

5.
정답 (D)
해석 보안팀은 24시간 내내 지속적으로 수상한 활동에 대해 네트워크를 감시한다.
해설 빈칸 뒤에 동사 monitors가 쓰여 있으며 '24시간 내내'라는 표현과 어울리는 부사가 필요하므로 '지속적으로'를 뜻하는 (D) continually가 정답입니다.
어휘 suspicious 수상한, 의심이 가는 activity 활동 around the clock 24시간 내내 alternatively 번갈아, 대안적으로 extremely 극도로 finely 정교하게

6.
정답 (A)
해석 지난 분기 동안 매출 수치는 꾸준한 성장을 끊임없이 보여왔다.
해설 '꾸준한 성장'이라는 긍정적이고 지속적인 흐름을 설명하고 있으므로, 그에 맞는 일관성과 지속성을 나타내는 부사가 필요합니다. 따라서, '끊임없이'를 뜻하는 (A) consistently가 정답입니다.
어휘 sales figure 매출 수치 steady 꾸준한 growth 성장 occasionally 때때로 randomly 무작위로 irregularly 불규칙하게

7.
정답 (C)
해석 커뮤니티 센터는 지역 프로젝트를 지원하기 위해 해마다 기금 모금 활동을 조직한다.
해설 문장의 동사가 현재시제(organizes)이므로 반복적인 일임을 알 수 있습니다. 따라서 빈칸 앞 기금 모금 활동의 시간적 빈도를 강조하는 부사가 필요하므로 '해마다'를 뜻하는 (C) annually가 정답입니다.
어휘 organize 조직하다 fundraising 모금 partially 부분적으로 rapidly 빠르게 immediately 즉시

8.
정답 (D)
해석 전체 재고 점검을 하는 데 매주 대략 2시간이 걸린다.
해설 시간을 나타내는 표현 2 hours를 수식하여 대략적인 시간을 추정을 강조하는 부사가 필요합니다. 따라서 '약, 대략'을 뜻하는 (D) approximately가 정답입니다.
어휘 conduct 실시하다 inventory check 재고조사 take (시간이) 걸리다 quickly 빠르게 little 거의 없는

9.
정답 (B)
해석 새로운 안전 규정은 이번 분기에 직장 내 사고 발생건수를 눈에 띄게 줄였다.
해설 사고 발생건수가 줄었다는 긍정적인 결과를 설명하고 있으며, 그 감소의 정도를 강조하는 부사가 필요하므로 '눈에 띄게, 급격하게'를 뜻하는 (B) dramatically가 정답입니다.
어휘 protocol 규정 the number of ~의 수 quarter 분기 slightly 약간 routinely 일상적으로 scarcely 거의 ~않다

10.
정답 (A)
해석 스페셜 에디션 스마트폰은 공식 온라인 스토어를 통해서만 판매된다.
해설 "official online store"라는 특정한 장소에서만 판매된다는 의미를 강조하는 부사가 필요하므로 '독점적으로'를 뜻하는 (A) exclusively가 정답입니다.
어휘 through ~을 통해 occasionally 때때로 commonly 일반적으로

11.
정답 (C)

해석 팀장들은 주간 회의 동안 각 팀원으로부터 직접 프로젝트 업데이트를 받는다.

해설 빈칸에 들어갈 부사는 '각 팀원들로부터'라는 의미의 전치사구 from each member와 함께 팀장이 프로젝트 업데이트를 받는 방식을 나타내는 의미의 부사여야 합니다. 따라서 이러한 문맥에 어울리는 부사는 선택지 중에서 '직접', '곧바로'라는 의미의 부사 (C) directly입니다.

어휘 automatically 자동으로 roughly 대략적으로 incidentally 우연히, 부수적으로

12.
정답 (A)

해설 시스템이 중요한 보안 업데이트를 받는 동안 연구 데이터베이스에 대한 접근은 일시적으로 제한된다.

해설 수동태 동사를 구성하는 be동사 is와 과거분사 restricted 사이에서 과거분사를 수식해 보안 업데이트를 받는 동안의 일시적인 상황을 나타내는 부사가 필요합니다. 따라서, '일시적으로'를 뜻하는 (A) temporarily가 정답입니다.

어휘 restricted 제한된 critical 중요한, 비평의 competitively 경쟁적으로 recently 최근에 collectively 집단적으로

DAY 12 부사 2

1. (D)	2. (C)	3. (B)	4. (D)	5. (D)
6. (B)	7. (C)	8. (C)	9. (B)	10. (A)
11. (C)	12. (A)			

1.
정답 (D)

해석 공장의 생산은 중요한 부품이 경고 없이 고장 나면서 예기치 않게 중단되었다.

해설 부품 고장이 예고 없이 발생하여 생산이 중단되었음을 나타내는 문맥과 어울리는 부사가 필요하므로 '예기치 않게, 뜻밖에'를 뜻하는 (D) unexpectedly가 정답입니다.

어휘 plant 공장, 식물 halt 멈추다, 정지시키다 fail 고장나다 warning 경고 currently 최근에 indefinitely 무기한으로 commonly 흔히, 일반적으로

2.
정답 (C)

해석 지원자들은 자격과 경력을 확인하기 위해 철저하게 평가된다.

해설 수동태 동사를 구성하는 be동사 are와 과거분사 evaluated 사이에서 과거분사를 수식하여 자격과 경력을 완전하고 정확하게 검토한다는 부사가 필요합니다. 따라서, '철저히'를 뜻하는 (C) thoroughly가 정답입니다.

어휘 candidate 지원자 verify 확인하다 qualification 자격 superficially 피상적으로 partially 부분적으로 hastily 성급하게

3.
정답 (B)

해석 신임 CEO는 9월 15일에 공식적으로 그 직책을 맡을 것이다.

해설 빈칸 뒤에 동사 step into가 쓰여 있으며 CEO 취임은 공식적인 절차를 수반한다는 의미를 나타내는 부사가 필요하므로 '공식적으로'를 뜻하는 (B) officially가 정답입니다.

어휘 step into 직책을 맡다, 취임하다 typically 일반적으로, 보통 quietly 조용히

4.
정답 (D)

해석 그들의 온라인 튜터링 패키지는 다양한 배경을 가진 학생들을 지원하기 위해 합리적인 가격으로 책정되어 있다.

해설 수동태 동사를 구성하는 be동사 are와 과거분사 priced 사이에서 과거분사를 수식하는 부사가 필요합니다. '가격이 정해진'이라는 의미의 priced와 함께 쓰여 '합리적으로'를 뜻하는 (D) reasonably가 정답입니다.

어휘 diverse 다양한 background (사람, 사건의) 배경 virtually 사실상, 거의 gratefully 감사하게 thoroughly 철저하게

5.
정답 (D)

해석 도심의 창고 지구는 이전에 산업 지대였던 곳에서 재개발되었다.

해설 빈칸에 들어갈 부사는 다른 부사들과 달리 명사구 an industrial zone을 수식합니다. 빈칸이 포함된 명사절은 what was an industrial zone으로 과거시제이며, '산업 지대였던 것'이라는 의미를 나타냅니다. 문맥상 도심의 창고지구는 예전에 산업 지대였는데, 지금은 재개발되었다는 내용이므로, 빈칸에 들어갈 부사는 과거시제와 함께 쓰이는 부사여야 합니다. 따라서 정답은 '이전에', '과거에 ~였던'라는 의미를 나타내는 부사 (D) formerly입니다.

어휘 downtown 도심지의 warehouse 창고 district 지구 redevelop 재개발하다 industrial 산업의 harshly 거칠게, 혹독하게 literally 문자 그대로

6.
정답 (B)
해석 고객들은 혁신적인 기능과 사용자 친화적인 디자인을 칭찬하며 호의적으로 새 제품에 반응했다.
해설 고객들은 신제품에 긍정적인 반응을 나타내며, 칭찬을 의미할 수 있는 부사가 필요하므로 '호의적으로'를 뜻하는 (B) favorably가 정답입니다.
어휘 praise 칭찬하다 user-friendly 사용자 친화적인 skeptically 회의적으로 indifferently 무관심하게 reluctantly 마지못해

7.
정답 (C)
해석 유연근무제를 도입한 것은 직원들의 사기와 생산성을 뚜렷하게 신장시켰습니다.
해설 빈칸은 현재완료시제 동사 has boosted의 사이에 위치하고 있으므로 '신장시켰다'라는 의미의 동사를 강조하기 위한 부사 자리임을 알 수 있습니다. 문맥상 유연근무제의 도입이 직원들의 사기와 생산성을 증가시켰다는 긍정적인 내용이므로 이와 어울리는 '뚜렷하게', '현저히'라는 의미의 부사 (C) markedly가 정답입니다.
어휘 introduce 도입하다 flexible 유연한 work hours 근무시간 boost 신장시키다, 증가시키다 morale 사기 productivity 생산성 casually 태평하게, 무심하게 openly 터놓고, 솔직하게 loudly 시끄럽게, 큰 소리로 markedly 뚜렷하게, 현저히

8.
정답 (C)
해석 리브스 씨 합병 및 인수 분야에서 수년간의 경험을 가진 매우 숙련된 협상가이다.
해설 'with years of experience' 전치사구는 리브스 씨가 오랜 기간의 경험을 가지고 있음을 알 수 있어 그녀의 능력과 경험을 강조할 수 있는 부사가 문맥상 필요합니다. 따라서 '매우, 대단히'를 뜻하는 부사 (C) highly가 정답입니다.
어휘 negotiator 협상가 merger 합병 acquisition (기업) 인수, 획득 moderately 적당히 somewhat 다소, 약간 rarely 드물게

9.
정답 (B)
해석 회사의 최근 성공은 업계 리더들과의 주로 전략적 제휴 덕분이다.
해설 전략적 제휴가 주된 성공 요인임을 강조하는 의미를 지니는 부사가 쓰여야 자연스러우므로 '주로'를 뜻하는 (B) largely가 정답입니다.
어휘 strategic 전략적인 beneficently 유익하게 quite 꽤, 상당히 rarely 드물게

10.
정답 (A)
해석 사무실 카페는 주요 회의실 옆에 편리하게 위치해 있어 회의 중에 간편하게 다과를 즐길 수 있다.
해설 beside the main conference hall이라는 장소가 회의 중 쉬는 시간에 쉽게 이용 가능하다는 점에 위치나 시간 등이 사용하거나 접근하기 좋다는 의미를 나타내는 부사가 쓰여야 자연스러우므로 '편리하게'를 뜻하는 (A) conveniently가 정답입니다.
어휘 beside ~의 곁에 refreshment 다과 commonly 일반적으로 consistently 지속적으로 cautiously 조심스럽게

11.
정답 (C)
해석 호라이즌 제약회사는 최근에 유럽과 아시아 전역에 유통망을 확장했다.
해설 문장에 과거동사 expanded가 사용되었기 때문에, 과거 어느 시점에 발생한 일의 의미를 지니는 부사가 쓰여야 자연스러우므로 '최근에'를 뜻하는 (C) recently가 정답입니다.
어휘 distribution 분배 across 전체에 걸쳐 precisely 정확하게 strictly 엄밀히 indefinitely 무기한으로

12.
정답 (A)
해석 저희 물류 제휴사는 제품 신선도 기준을 충족하기 위해 제시간에 해외로 배송합니다.
해설 신선도 기준을 충족시키기 위한 시간에 맞추어 빠른 배송 방식 의미를 강조하는 부사가 쓰여야 자연스러우므로 '지체없이, 제 시간에'를 뜻하는 (A) promptly가 정답입니다.
어휘 logistics 물류 관리 overseas 해외의 shipment 배송 freshness 신선도 occasionally 가끔씩 slowly 느리게 promptly 지체없이, 제 시간에 accidentally 우연히, 실수로

DAY 13 숙어 1

1. (C)	2. (B)	3. (A)	4. (D)	5. (A)
6. (C)	7. (C)	8. (D)	9. (C)	10. (D)
11. (A)	12. (B)			

1.
정답 (C)
해석 그 소프트웨어 플랫폼은 강력한 보안성과 사용자 친화적인 인터페이스로 잘 알려져 있다.
해설 빈칸 앞뒤에 각각 위치한 be동사 is 및 전치사 for과 어울리는 형용사가 필요하므로 이 둘과 함께 '~로 잘 알려져 있다' 의미를 나타내는 「be notable for」를 구성하는 형용사 (C) notable이 정답입니다.
어휘 robust 강력한 user-friendly 사용자 친화적인 outdated 구식의 flawed 결함이 있는

2.
정답 (B)
해석 제품 출시 행사는 도심 컨벤션 센터에서 열릴 예정이다.
해설 빈칸 앞뒤에 각각 위치한 be동사 is 및 전치사 to와 어울리는 형용사가 필요하므로 이 둘과 함께 '~할 예정이다' 의미를 나타내는 「be scheduled to do」를 구성하는 형용사 (B) scheduled가 정답입니다.
어휘 launch n. 출시 v. 출시하다 take place (일·사건 등이) 일어나다 registered 등록된 permitted 허용된 required 요구된, 필수의

3.
정답 (A)
해석 저희 회사는 첫 이용 고객에게 설치 서비스를 무료로 제공합니다.
해설 빈칸 뒤 no cost와 어울리는 전치사는 '무료로'라는 의미의 「at no cost」를 구성하는 (A) at이 정답입니다.
어휘 installation 설치

4.
정답 (D)
해석 참석 희망자는 금요일까지 리더십 워크숍에 등록하도록 권장됩니다.
해설 빈칸 뒤에 위치한 전치사 for와 어울리는 동사가 필요하므로 '등록하다' 의미를 나타내는 「register for」를 구성하는 (D) register이 정답입니다.
어휘 prospective 예상된, 가망있는 be encouraged to do ~하는 것이 권장되다 approve 승인하다 express 표현하다 record 기록하다

5.
정답 (A)
해석 참석자는 교육 시간이 끝날 때 설문지를 작성해야 합니다.
해설 빈칸 뒤에 위치한 명사구 survey form과 어울려 설문지나 신청서와 같은 문서를 '작성하다'를 뜻하는 (A) complete이 정답입니다.
어휘 participant 참가자 survey form 설문지 proceed 진행하다 retrieve 회수하다, 가져오다 enlist 등록하다, 모집하다

6.
정답 (C)
해석 IT 부서는 최근에 발생한 데이터 유출에 대응하여 추가 보안 조치를 시행했다.
해설 빈칸 앞뒤에 각각 위치한 전치사 in 및 to 부정사와 어울리는 명사가 필요하므로 이 둘과 함께 '~에 대응하여' 의미의 「in response to do」를 구성하는 명사 (C) response가 정답입니다.
어휘 apology 사과 effect 효과 confirmation 확인

7.
정답 (C)
해석 연례 회의에는 주요 연설과 워크숍으로 이루어진 연속된 행사가 포함되어 있다.
해설 빈칸 앞뒤에 각각 위치한 정관사 a 및 전치사 of와 어울리는 명사가 필요하므로 이 둘과 함께 '연속된', '일련의'라는 의미의 「a series of」를 구성하는 명사 (C) series가 정답입니다.
어휘 measure 조치, 단위 segment 부분

8.
정답 (D)
해석 몇몇 이사회의 임원들은 새로운 플랫폼 개발에 관여되었고, 모든 특징이 고객의 요구에 맞춰 반드시 조정되도록 하였습니다.
해설 빈칸 앞뒤에 각각 위치한 be 동사 were 및 전치사 in과 어울리는 과거분사가 필요하므로 이 둘과 함께 '~에 관여되다'라는 의미를 나타내는 「be involved in」를 구성하는 (D) involved가 정답입니다.
어휘 board member 이사회 임원 development 개발 ensure 반드시 ~하게 하다 feature 특징, 특성 align with ~에 맞춰 조정하다 requirement 요구 (사항) appoint 임명하다 assign 배정하다 facilitate 용이하게 하다 involve 관여하다, 수반하다

9.

정답 (C)

해석 저희 고객 서비스는 채팅 및 전화 등 다양한 지원 채널을 제공합니다.

해설 빈칸 앞뒤에 각각 위치한 관사 a 및 전치사 of와 어울리는 명사가 필요하므로 이 둘과 함께 '다양한' 의미를 나타내는 「a variety of」를 구성하는 명사 (C) variety가 정답입니다.

어휘 concept 개념 division 부서, 분할

10.

정답 (D)

해석 마케팅 이사는 연간 판촉 전략 개발을 책임지고 있다.

해설 빈칸 앞뒤에 각각 위치한 be동사 is 및 전치사 for과 어울리는 명사가 필요하므로 이 둘과 함께 '~에 대해 책임이 있다' 의미를 나타내는「be responsible for」를 구성하는 명사 (D) responsible이 정답입니다. 어떤 업무나 역할을 맡고 있는 사람을 표현할 때 자주 쓰이며 'developing the promotional strategy'라는 명확한 업무와 직책인 마케팅 이사와 직접적으로 연결됩니다.

어휘 strategy 전략 optional 선택적인 analytical 분석적인 dynamic 활기찬, 역동적인

11.

정답 (A)

해석 궁금한 점이 있으시면 가장 편하실 때 언제든지 전화 주세요.

해설 고객이나 상대방의 일정에 맞춰 연락을 권유할 때 '가급적 빨리' 의미를 나타내는「at your earliest convenience」를 구성하는 명사 (A) convenience가 정답입니다.

어휘 importance 중요성 introduction 소개 probability 가능성

12.

정답 (B)

해석 박물관의 대규모 재개관을 기념하여 주말 내내 입장료가 무료입니다.

해설 빈칸 앞뒤에 각각 위치한 전치사 in 및 전치사 of와 어울리는 명사가 필요하므로 이 둘과 함께 '기념하여' 의미를 나타내는 「In celebration of」를 구성하는 명사 (B) celebration이 정답입니다.

어휘 admission 입장료 throughout (시간) ~동안 demonstration 시위, 증명 charge 요금 exploration 탐험, 탐사

DAY 14 숙어 2

1. (D)	2. (D)	3. (C)	4. (D)	5. (B)
6. (C)	7. (A)	8. (A)	9. (B)	10. (A)
11. (C)	12. (B)			

1.

정답 (D)

해석 구독이 활성화되면 사용자는 프리미엄 기사 및 동영상에 접근할 수 있게 된다.

해설 빈칸 앞뒤에 각각 위치한 동사 have 및 전치사 to와 어울리는 명사가 필요하므로 이 둘과 함께 '~을 이용할 수 있다'라는 의미의「have access to」를 구성하는 명사 (D) access가 정답입니다.

어휘 activated 활성화된 premium 아주 높은, 고급의 article 기사 communication 소통 permission 허가, 허락 opportunity 기회

2.

정답 (D)

해석 연례 성과 평가가 8월 첫째 주로 일정이 잡힐 예정이다.

해설 빈칸 앞뒤에 각각 위치한 be 동사 be 및 전치사 for와 어울리는 과거분사가 필요합니다. for 뒤에 the first week of August라는 시점을 나타내는 명사구가 있으므로 「be scheduled for + 시점」를 구성하는 명사 (D) scheduled가 정답입니다.

어휘 annual 연례의, 해마다의 performance 성과, 실적 review 평가, 검토 be scheduled for 시점: ~로 예정되어 있다 maintained 유지된 heard 들린 organized 준비된

3.

정답 (C)

해석 방문자는 회사 구내에 있을 때 신분증 배지를 착용해야 한다.

해설 빈칸 앞뒤에 각각 위치한 be 동사 are 및 to부정사와 어울리는 과거분사가 필요하며, 어떤 규칙이나 방침에 따라 반드시 수행되어야 하는 행동을 나타내는 것이 자연스러우므로 '~해야 하다' 의미의「be required to do」를 구성하는 (C) required가 정답입니다.

어휘 while ~하는 동안 premise (토지 따위를 포함한) 건물 considered 고려된 regarded 여겨진, 간주된 allowed 허용된

4.

정답 (D)

해석 토론 중에 많은 대표자들이 더 엄격한 안전 법률을 지지하여

발언했다.

해설 빈칸 앞뒤에 각각 위치한 전치사 in 및 전치사 of와 어울리는 명사가 필요하므로 이 둘과 함께 '~에 찬성하여' 의미를 나타내는 「in favor of」가 쓰였음을 알 수 있습니다. 따라서 (D) favor가 정답입니다. (A) regard는 '~에 관하여'를 뜻하는 「in regard to」로, (C) view는 '~을 고려하여'를 뜻하는 「in view of」의 구조로 쓰입니다.

어휘 delegate 대표자 stricter 더 엄격한 regard n. 관련 v. ~으로 여기다 aspect 양상, 외관 view n. 개관, 개설 v. 바라보다, 보다

5.
정답 (B)

해설 그래픽 디자이너는 회사 로고를 합리적인 가격에 제작해 주겠다고 제안했다.

해설 빈칸 뒤에 위치한 명사 price와 어울려 '합리적인' 의미를 나타내는 (B) reasonable이 정답입니다.

어휘 offer 제안하다 premium 아주 높은, 고급의 high 높은 temporary 일시적인

6.
정답 (C)

해설 미니멀하고 다용도적인 디자인 덕분에 이 제품들은 캐주얼한 환경과 전문적인 환경 모두에 적합하다.

해설 빈칸 앞뒤에 각각 위치한 be 동사 are 및 전치사 for와 어울리는 형용사가 필요하므로 이 둘과 함께 '~에 적합하다' 의미를 나타내는 「be suitable for」가 쓰였음을 알 수 있습니다. 따라서 (C) suitable이 정답입니다.

어휘 minimalistic 미니멀리즘의 versatile 다용도적인, 다방면의 highly 매우, 대단히 casual 격식을 차리지 않는, 평상의 professional 전문적인 setting 환경, 배경 exaggerated 과장된 fragile 깨지기 쉬운 apt 적절한, ~하기 쉬운

7.
정답 (A)

해설 회사의 구조조정 계획은 정밀한 재무 분석을 바탕으로 수립되었다.

해설 빈칸 앞뒤에 각각 위치한 be 동사 is 및 전치사 on과 어울리는 과거분사가 필요하므로 이 둘과 함께 '~을 바탕으로 하다' 의미로 「be based on」을 구성하는 (A) based가 정답입니다.

어휘 restructuring 구조조정 detailed 상세한, 정밀한 financial analysis 재무분석 constructed 건설된, 구성된 taken 취해진

8.
정답 (A)

해설 필요한 모든 서류를 제때 제출하는 지원자는 장학금 심사를 받을 자격이 있다.

해설 빈칸 앞뒤에 각각 위치한 be 동사 are 및 전치사 for와 어울리는 형용사가 필요하므로 이 둘과 함께 '~에 대한 자격이 있다' 의미로 「be eligible for」을 구성하는 (A) eligible이 정답입니다.

어휘 required 요구되는, 필수의 on time 제시간에, 제때에 scholarship 장학금 plausible 그럴듯한 flexible 유연한, 융통성 있는 compatible 호환되는, 양립할 수 있는

9.
정답 (B)

해설 최근 예산 삭감의 결과로, 부서는 몇 개의 프로젝트를 취소해야 했다.

해설 문맥상 빈칸 뒤에 위치한 명사구 recent budget cuts에 프로젝트 취소의 원인으로 언급되었음을 알 수 있으므로 '~에 따른 결과로' 의미를 나타내는 (B) As a result of가 정답입니다.

어휘 budget cut 예산 삭감 department 부서 despite 그럼에도 불구하고 so as to ~하기 위해서 in order to ~하기 위해서

10.
정답 (A)

해설 사무실 개조 공사 경영진이 정한 마감일을 맞춰 계획대로 완료되었다.

해설 사전에 준비된 일정이나 전략에 따라 일이 진행되었음을 나타내는 것이 자연스러우므로 '계획대로'라는 의미를 나타내는 (A) planned가 정답입니다.

어휘 renovation 기초 공사 set (기한이나 기준 등을) 정하다 management 경영진, 경영 considered 고려된 noted 언급된, 주목된 examined 검토된 as planned 계획대로

11.
정답 (C)

해설 그 매장은 인기 있는 태블릿이 품절되었음을 알리는 공지를 게시해야 했다.

해설 빈칸 앞 명사구 out of와 어울려 어떤 상품이 모두 팔려서 더 이상 재고가 없는 상태를 나타내는 것이 자연스러우므로 '재고가 없는'라는 의미를 나타내는 「out of stock」이 쓰였음을 알 수 있습니다. 따라서 (C) stock가 정답입니다.

어휘 display v. 게시하다, 전시하다 n. 전시 notice 공지, 통보 supply 공급 inventory 재고 목록, 재고자산 merchandise 상품

12.
정답 (B)
해석 첨부된 제안서를 검토해 주시고 월요일 아침까지 의견과 함께 회신해 주시면 감사하겠습니다.
해설 상대방에게 어떤 일을 정중하고 공손하게 부탁하는 문맥이므로 '~해 주신다면 감사하겠습니다'라는 의미를 나타내는 「I'd appreciate it if」 (B) appreciate가 정답입니다.
어휘 attached 첨부된 review 검토하다 return 돌려주다 welcome 환영하다 require 요구하다

DAY 15 숙어 3

1. (C)	2. (A)	3. (C)	4. (B)	5. (B)
6. (D)	7. (A)	8. (D)	9. (A)	10. (D)
11. (C)	12. (D)			

1.
정답 (C)
해석 공항에 도착하면 컨베이어에서 수하물을 찾는 것을 잊지 마세요.
해설 공항에서 짐을 찾는 행위에 자주 사용되는 표현으로 가장 적절한 것은 '~을 얻다, ~을 들어올리다'라는 의미를 나타내는 (C) pick up이 정답입니다.
어휘 forget to do ~할 일을 잊다 baggage 수하물 carousel 컨베이어 drop off 내려놓다, 맡기다 look after 돌보다 put away 치우다, 정리하다

2.
정답 (A)
해석 앨리스는 사무실에 없을 때마다, 원격으로 이메일을 확인한다.
해설 빈칸 앞 out과 어울려 회사나 사무실에서 자리를 비운 상황을 설명할 때 '사무실에서 부재중인'이라는 의미로 「out of the office」를 구성하는 (A) of가 정답입니다.
어휘 whenever ~할 때는 언제나 remotely 원격으로, 멀리서

3.
정답 (C)
해석 에너지 소비를 줄이기 위한 노력의 일환으로, 회사는 태양광 패널을 설치했다.
해설 빈칸 앞뒤에 각각 위치한 전치사 in 및 to와 어울리는 명사가 필요하므로 이 둘과 함께 '~하기 위한 노력으로'라는 의미를 나타내는 「in an effort to」가 쓰였음을 알 수 있습니다. 따라서 (C) effort가 정답입니다.
어휘 consumption 소비 install 설치하다 solar panel 태양광 패널 output 생산량, 출력 instance 사례, 경우 effort 노력, 수고 account 계좌, 계정, 설명

4.
정답 (B)
해석 운전자는 공공 도로에서 안전을 보장하기 위해 차량을 운행할 때 교통 법규를 준수해야 한다.
해설 빈칸 뒤에 위치한 전치사 with와 어울리는 동사가 필요하며, 법적 의무 이행을 의미하는 것이 자연스러우므로 「comply with」로 '~을 준수하다'라는 의미를 나타내는 (B) comply가 정답입니다.
어휘 vehicle 차량 ensure 보장하다, 확실하게 하다 confront 직면하다, 맞서다 assign 할당하다, 배당하다

5.
정답 (B)
해석 그 연구 기관은 언어 습득과 인지 연구를 전문으로 하고 있다.
해설 빈칸 뒤에 위치한 전치사 in과 어울리는 동사가 필요하며, 특정 분야에 대해 집중적으로 연구한다는 의미가 자연스러우므로 「specialize in」으로 '전문으로 하다'라는 의미를 나타내는 (B) specializes가 정답입니다.
어휘 research institute 연구 기관 acquisition 습득 cognitive 인지의 operate 운영하다 apply 적용하다

6.
정답 (D)
해석 창고에서의 장비 점검은 모든 기계가 안전하게 작동하고 있는지 보장하기 위해 정기적으로 시행된다.
해설 빈칸 앞에 위치한 형용사 regular와 어울리는 명사가 필요하며, 시간적인 빈도나 반복성을 나타내는 의미가 자연스러우므로 「on a regular basis」로 '주기적으로'라는 의미를 나타내는 (D) basis가 정답입니다.
어휘 inspection 점검 warehouse 창고 occur 발생하다 machinery 기계 ensure 보장하다 function 기능하다, 작동하다

7.
정답 (A)
해석 캠페인을 시작하기 전에 마케팅팀은 전략을 조율하기 위해 여러 회의를 마련했다.
해설 빈칸 뒤 명사구 several meetings와 어울리는 동사가 필요하므로, '~을 마련하다, ~을 구성하다' 의미를 나타내는 (A) set up이 정답입니다.
어휘 align 조율하다, 조정하다, 제휴하다 shut down 종료하다 clean up 청소하다 turn away 쫓아내다, 돌려보내다

8.

정답 (D)

해석 우리 휴가 패키지는 항공편, 호텔 숙박, 그리고 가이드 투어로 구성되어 있다.

해설 빈칸 뒤 전치사 of와 어울리는 동사가 필요하며, of 뒤에는 휴가 패키지의 구성 요소가 나열되는 문맥이므로 '~로 구성되다'라는 의미를 나타내는 「consists of」가 쓰였음을 알 수 있습니다. 따라서 (D) consists가 정답입니다. (A) composes는 '구성하다'를 뜻하지만 일반적으로 「be composed of」 형태로 쓰이고, (B) contains는 '포함하다'는 뜻으로 의미상 문맥에 쓰일 수 있지만 전치사 of와 함께 쓰이지 않으므로 오답입니다.

어휘 flight 항공편 hotel stay 호텔 숙박 compose 구성하다, 작곡하다 contain 포함하다 introduce 소개하다, 도입하다

9.

정답 (A)

해석 그 컨퍼런스 센터는 여러 레스토랑까지 도보 거리 내에 위치해 있다.

해설 빈칸 뒤 명사구 walking distance와 어울리는 전치사가 필요하며, 범위나 한계를 나타내는 전치사 within이 문맥상 자연스럽습니다. 「within walking distance of」는 '걸어서 갈 수 있는 거리 이내에'라는 의미를 나타내므로 (A) within이 정답입니다.

어휘 apart 떨어져 throughout ~ 전역에 beyond ~ 너머에

10.

정답 (D)

해석 재무 부서는 비용 환급 청구를 시기적절하게 처리하도록 지시받았다.

해설 빈칸 앞뒤 전치사 in 및 명사 manner와 같이 어울리는 형용사가 필요하며, 업무 지시나 요청을 신속하게 처리한다는 의미가 자연스러우므로 「in a timely manner」이라는 표현으로 '시기 적절하게'라는 의미를 나타내는 (D) timely가 정답입니다.

어휘 instruct 지시하다, 알리다 reimbursement 환급 claim n.청구, 주장 v. 요구하다, 주장하다 variable 변동성 있는 indifferent 무관심한

11.

정답 (C)

해석 스트레스를 받는 상황에서는 집중력을 잃지 않고 압박에 대처하는 것이 중요하다.

해설 빈칸 뒤에 있는 전치사 with와 함께 명사 pressure를 목적어로 가질 수 있는 동사가 필요합니다. 문맥상 스트레스가 많은 상황에서 압박감을 대처하는 것을 언급하는 내용이므로, '~에 대처하다', '~을 다루다'라는 의미의 「deal with」가 쓰였음을 알 수 있습니다. 따라서 정답은 (C) deal입니다.

어휘 it's crucial to do ~하는 것이 중요하다 pressure maintain 유지하다, 관리하다 fix 고치다, 고정시키다 solve 해결하다

12.

정답 (D)

해석 세미나에서는 청중을 진정으로 참여시키고 설득하는 프레젠테이션을 진행하는 방법에 대해 다룰 것이다.

해설 빈칸 뒤 명사 a presentation와 어울리는 동사가 필요하며, 발표를 진행한다는 의미가 자연스러우므로 '발표하다'라는 의미의 「make a presentation」을 구성하는 동사 (D) make가 정답입니다.

어휘 cover (주제를) 다루다 truly 진정으로 engage 착수하다 persuade 설득하다 implement 시행하다 serve 제공하다 catch 잡다, 끌다

PART 1~7 FINAL TEST

PART 1 FINAL TEST

1. (B)   2. (C)   3. (B)   4. (D)   5. (B)
6. (A)   7. (B)   8. (B)   9. (C)   10. (B)
11. (D) 12. (C)

1. (A) Some furniture is being restocked.
   (B) They are examining a kitchen appliance.
   (C) The woman is washing some dishes.
   (D) The man is talking to a server.
   (A) 일부 가구가 다시 채워지고 있다.
   (B) 사람들이 주방 기기를 살펴 보고 있다.
   (C) 여자가 몇몇 접시를 씻고 있다.
   (D) 남자가 종업원에게 이야기하고 있다.

정답 (B)
해설 다인 사진이므로 등장 인물들의 공통된 동작이나 개별 자세, 주변 사물에 함께 초점을 맞춰 들어야 합니다.
   (A) 사람들이 가구를 채워 넣는 동작을 하고 있지 않으므로 오답.
   (B) 사람들이 주방 기기를 살펴 보는 자세를 취하고 있으므로 정답.
   (C) 여자가 접시를 씻는 동작을 하고 있지 않으므로 오답.
   (D) 종업원을 찾아볼 수 없으므로 오답.

어휘 restock (물건 등으로) ~을 다시 채우다 examine ~을 살펴 보다, ~을 점검하다 kitchen appliance 주방 기기 server 종업원

2. (A) She's crossing a busy intersection.
   (B) She's pushing a cart in front of her.
   (C) She's walking away from a parking lot.
   (D) She's talking on the phone.
   (A) 여자가 분주한 교차로를 건너고 있다.
   (B) 여자가 자신의 앞에 있는 카트를 밀고 있다.
   (C) 여자가 주차장에서 벗어나 걸어가고 있다.
   (D) 여자가 전화 통화를 하고 있다.

정답 (C)
해설 1인 사진이므로 등장 인물의 동작이나 자세, 관련 사물에 초점을 맞춰 들어야 합니다.
   (A) 교차로를 찾아볼 수 없으므로 오답.
   (B) 여자가 자신의 앞에 있는 카트를 미는 동작을 하고 있지 않으므로 오답.
   (C) 여자가 주차장에서 벗어나 걸어가고 있는 동작을 하고 있으므로 정답.
   (D) 여자가 전화 통화하는 자세를 취하고 있지 않으므로 오답.

어휘 cross ~을 건너다, ~을 가로지르다 intersection 교차로 cart 카트, 손수레 in front of ~ 앞에 parking lot 주차장

3. (A) They're looking at a camera.
   (B) They're having a picnic at the park.
   (C) A dining area has been prepared for customers.
   (D) Some passengers are sitting in a waiting area.
   (A) 사람들이 카메라를 보고 있다.
   (B) 사람들이 공원에서 소풍을 즐기고 있다.
   (C) 식사 구역이 고객들을 위해 준비되어 있다.
   (D) 몇몇 승객들이 대기 구역에 앉아 있다.

정답 (B)
해설 다인 사진이므로 등장 인물들의 공통된 동작이나 개별 자세, 주변 사물에 함께 초점을 맞춰 들어야 합니다.
   (A) 사람들이 카메라를 보는 자세를 취하고 있지 않으므로 오답.
   (B) 사람들이 공원에서 소풍을 즐기고 있는 자세를 취하고 있으므로 정답.
   (C) 식사 구역을 찾아 볼 수 없으므로 오답.
   (D) 사진 속 배경이 승객 대기 구역이 아니므로 오답.

어휘 have a picnic 소풍하다 dining area 식사 구역 prepared 준비된 passenger 승객

4. (A) One of the people is putting on a vest.
   (B) Some workers are trimming bushes.
   (C) A lamppost is being installed next to a road.
   (D) A pathway is blocked by a vehicle.
   (A) 사람들 중 한 명이 조끼를 착용하는 중이다.
   (B) 몇몇 작업자들이 관목을 다듬고 있다.
   (C) 가로등이 도로 옆에 설치되고 있다.
   (D) 보행로가 차량에 의해 가로막혀 있다.

정답 (D)
해설 다인 사진이므로 등장 인물들의 공통된 동작이나 개별 자세, 주변 사물에 함께 초점을 맞춰 들어야 합니다.

(A) 조끼를 착용하는 동작을 하는 사람이 없으므로 오답.
(B) 작업자들이 관목을 다듬는 동작을 하고 있지 않으므로 오답.
(C) 사람들이 가로등을 설치하는 동작을 하고 있지 않으므로 오답.
(D) 보행로가 차량에 의해 가로막혀 있는 상태이므로 정답.

어휘 put on (동작) ~을 착용하다 vest 조끼 trim ~을 다듬다, ~을 손질하다 bush 관목, 덤불 lamppost 가로등 install ~을 설치하다 next to ~옆에 pathway 보행로, 통로 block ~을 가로막다 vehicle 차량

5. (A) A man is setting up a canopy.
   (B) People are shopping at an outdoor market.
   (C) There are decorations hanging above a window.
   (D) Some potted plants are being watered.
   (A) 한 남자가 천막을 설치하고 있다.
   (B) 사람들이 야외 시장에서 쇼핑하고 있다.
   (C) 장식물들이 창문 위쪽에 걸려 있다.
   (D) 몇몇 화분에 심은 식물에 물이 뿌려지고 있다.

정답 (B)
해설 다인 사진이므로 등장 인물들의 공통된 동작이나 개별 자세, 주변 사물에 함께 초점을 맞춰 들어야 합니다.
   (A) 천막을 설치하는 동작을 하고 있는 남자가 없으므로 오답.
   (B) 사람들이 야외 시장에서 쇼핑하는 자세를 취하고 있으므로 정답.
   (C) 창문을 찾아볼 수 없으므로 오답.
   (D) 식물에 물을 뿌리는 동작을 하는 사람이 없으므로 오답.

어휘 set up ~을 설치하다 canopy (지붕 부분만 있는) 천막, 차양, 덮개 decoration 장식(물) hang 걸려 있다, 매달려 있다 potted plant 화분에 심은 식물 water v. ~에 물을 주다

6. **(A) Some people are waiting to use a ticket machine.**
   (B) One of the people is wearing headphones.
   (C) There are some vending machines at a train station.
   (D) A customer is giving money to a cashier.
   (A) 몇몇 사람들이 매표기를 이용하기 위해 대기하고 있다.
   (B) 사람들 중 한 명이 헤드폰을 착용한 상태이다.
   (C) 기차역에 몇몇 자판기가 있다.
   (D) 한 고객이 계산원에게 돈을 주고 있다.

정답 (A)
해설 다인 사진이므로 등장 인물들의 공통된 동작이나 개별 자세, 주변 사물에 함께 초점을 맞춰 들어야 합니다.
   (A) 몇몇 사람들이 매표기를 이용하기 위해 대기하고 있는 자세를 취하고 있으므로 정답.
   (B) 헤드폰을 착용한 사람을 찾아볼 수 없으므로 오답.
   (C) 사진 속 배경이 기차역이 아니므로 오답.
   (D) 계산원을 찾아볼 수 없으므로 오답.

어휘 wear (상태) ~을 착용하다 vending machine 자판기 cashier 계산원, 계산대

7. (A) Chairs have been lined up side by side.
   (B) Some flower bushes surround a garden set.
   (C) Some merchandise is on a display table.
   (D) A seating area is being cleaned.
   (A) 의자들이 나란히 줄지어 있다.
   (B) 몇몇 화초 덤불이 정원 배경을 둘러싸고 있다.
   (C) 몇몇 상품이 진열 테이블에 놓여 있다.
   (D) 좌석 공간이 청소되고 있다.

정답 (B)
해설 풍경 사진이므로 풍경 속 사물의 명칭과 상태, 위치 관계에 초점을 맞춰 들어야 합니다.
   (A) 의자들이 나란히 줄지어 있는 상태가 아니므로 오답.
   (B) 화초 덤불이 정원 배경을 둘러싸고 있는 상태이므로 정답.
   (C) 상품을 찾아볼 수 없으므로 오답.
   (D) 청소하는 동작을 하는 사람이 없으므로 오답.

어휘 be lined up 줄지어 있다 side by side 나란히 bush 덤불, 관목 surround ~을 둘러싸다 merchandise 상품 display v. 진열(품), 전시(품) v. ~을 진열하다, ~을 전시하다 seating area 좌석 공간

8. (A) Some buildings overlook a beach.
   (B) A walkway runs alongside the water.
   (C) Some passengers are getting into a car.
   (D) One of the people is riding a bicycle.
   (A) 몇몇 건물들이 해변을 내려다보고 있다.
   (B) 보행로가 물과 나란히 이어지고 있다.
   (C) 몇몇 승객들이 자동차에 탑승하고 있다.
   (D) 사람들 중 한 명이 자전거를 타고 있다.

정답 (B)
해설 풍경 사진이므로 풍경 속 사물의 명칭과 상태, 위치 관계에 초점을 맞춰 들어야 합니다.
   (A) 사진 속 배경이 해변이 아니므로 오답.
   (B) 보행로가 물과 나란히 이어지고 있는 상태이므로 정답.
   (C) 자동차에 탑승하는 승객들을 찾아볼 수 없으므로 오답.
   (D) 자전거를 타는 사람을 찾아볼 수 없으므로 오답.

어휘 overlook (건물 등이) ~을 내려다보다 run (길 등이) 이어지다, 뻗어 있다 alongside ~와 나란히 passenger 승객 board ~에 탑승하다 sailboat 돛단배 ride ~을 타다

9. (A) The woman is putting an item into her bag.
(B) A light fixture is being repaired.
(C) Some baskets have been filled with fruit.
(D) A shopper is leaning against a display case.

(A) 여자가 제품 하나를 가방에 넣고 있다.
(B) 조명 기구가 수리되고 있다.
(C) 몇몇 바구니들이 과일로 가득 채워져 있다.
(D) 쇼핑객 한 명이 진열 케이스에 기대고 있다.

정답 (C)
해설 1인 사진이므로 등장 인물의 동작이나 자세, 관련 사물에 초점을 맞춰 들어야 합니다.
 (A) 여자가 제품 하나를 가방에 넣는 동작을 하고 있지 않으므로 오답.
 (B) 조명 기구를 수리하는 동작을 하는 사람을 찾아 볼 수 없으므로 오답.
 (C) 몇몇 바구니들이 과일로 가득 채워져 있는 상태이므로 정답.
 (D) 진열 케이스에 기대고 있는 사람을 찾아 볼 수 없으므로 오답.

어휘 put A into B: A를 B에 넣다 light fixture 조명 기구 repair ~을 수리하다 be filled with ~로 가득 채워져 있다 lean against ~에 기대다 display v. 진열(품), 전시(품) v. ~을 진열하다, ~을 전시하다

10. (A) The people are shaking hands.
(B) Boxes have been placed on shelving units.
(C) There are some curtains covering the windows.
(D) One of the workers is climbing up a ladder.

(A) 사람들이 악수하고 있다.
(B) 상자들이 선반마다 놓여 있다.
(C) 몇몇 커튼들이 창문을 가리고 있다.
(D) 작업자들 중 한 명이 사다리를 오르고 있다.

정답 (B)
해설 다인 사진이므로 등장 인물들의 공통된 동작이나 개별 자세, 주변 사물에 함께 초점을 맞춰 들어야 합니다.
 (A) 사람들이 악수하는 동작을 하고 있지 않으므로 오답.
 (B) 상자들이 선반마다 놓여 있는 상태이므로 정답.
 (C) 창문을 가리고 있는 커튼을 찾아 볼 수 없으므로 오답.
 (D) 사다리를 오르는 동작을 하는 사람을 찾아 볼 수 없으므로 오답.

어휘 shake hands 악수하다 place v. ~을 놓다, ~을 두다 shelving unit 선반 climb up ~을 오르다 ladder 사다리

11. (A) There are some bowls on a counter.
(B) He's using a kitchen sink.
(C) Some food is being removed from an oven.
(D) Some vegetables are being cut on a table.

(A) 조리대에 몇몇 움푹한 그릇들이 있다.
(B) 남자가 주방 싱크대를 이용하고 있다.
(C) 몇몇 음식이 오븐에서 꺼내지고 있다.
(D) 몇몇 채소가 테이블에서 잘리고 있다.

정답 (D)
해설 1인 사진이므로 등장 인물의 동작이나 자세, 관련 사물에 초점을 맞춰 들어야 합니다.
 (A) 움푹한 그릇을 찾아 볼 수 없으므로 오답.
 (B) 주방 싱크대를 찾아 볼 수 없으므로 오답.
 (C) 남자가 오븐에서 음식을 꺼내는 동작을 하고 있지 않으므로 오답.
 (D) 몇몇 채소가 남자에 의해 테이블에서 잘리고 있으므로 정답.

어휘 bowl 움푹한 그릇 counter 조리대, 계산대 sink 싱크대 remove ~을 꺼내다, ~을 제거하다, ~을 없애다

12. (A) There's a traffic light in front of a building.
(B) A vehicle is parked next to a fence.
(C) There's a balcony on a street corner.
(D) Some trees are shading a row of trash cans.

(A) 건물 앞에 교통 신호등이 있다.
(B) 차량 한 대가 울타리 옆에 주차되어 있다.
(C) 거리 모퉁이 쪽에 발코니가 있다.
(D) 몇몇 나무들이 일렬로 늘어선 쓰레기통에 그늘을 드리우고 있다.

정답 (C)
해설 풍경 사진이므로 풍경 속 사물의 명칭과 상태, 위치 관계에 초점을 맞춰 들어야 합니다.
 (A) 교통 신호등을 찾아 볼 수 없으므로 오답.
 (B) 울타리를 찾아 볼 수 없으므로 오답.
 (C) 거리 모퉁이 쪽에 발코니가 있는 상태이므로 정답.
 (D) 일렬로 늘어선 쓰레기통을 찾아 볼 수 없으므로 오답.

어휘 traffic 교통(량), 차량들 in front of ~ 앞에 vehicle 차량 park ~을 주차하다 next to ~ 옆에 shade v. ~에 그늘을 드리우다 a row of 일렬로 늘어선

PART 2 FINAL TEST

1. (C)	2. (C)	3. (B)	4. (B)	5. (A)
6. (A)	7. (B)	8. (B)	9. (C)	10. (B)
11. (B)	12. (A)	13. (B)	14. (C)	15. (B)
16. (C)	17. (A)	18. (B)	19. (B)	20. (B)
21. (C)	22. (A)	23. (B)	24. (B)	25. (C)

1. When is your interview scheduled for?
 (A) It started later than expected.
 (B) I really liked his attitude.
 (C) The last week of April.

당신의 면접은 언제로 예정되어 있나요?
 (A) 그게 예상보다 더 늦게 시작했어요.
 (B) 저는 정말로 그의 태도가 마음에 들었어요.
 (C) 4월 마지막 주요.

정답 (C)
해설 면접이 언제로 예정되어 있는지 묻는 When 의문문입니다.
 (A) 과거 시점의 일에 관해 답변하고 있으므로 미래의 일정을 묻는 질문의 의도에 맞지 않는 오답.
 (B) 대상을 알 수 없는 his의 태도에 대한 의견을 말하고 있으므로 오답.
 (C) When과 어울리는 특정 시점으로 답변하고 있으므로 정답.
어휘 be scheduled for 시점: ~로 예정되어 있다

2. Why is the office so quiet?
 (A) Did you shut it off?
 (B) It's in Room 720.
 (C) Almost everyone is at a workshop.

사무실이 왜 이렇게 조용한 거죠?
 (A) 그걸 차단하셨나요?
 (B) 720호실입니다.
 (C) 거의 모든 사람이 워크숍에 가 있어요

정답 (C)
해설 사무실이 왜 조용한지 묻는 Why 의문문입니다.
 (A) 무언가의 차단 여부를 확인하기 위해 묻는 말이므로 질문의 의도에 맞지 않는 오답.
 (B) Where 의문문에 어울리는 장소로 답변하고 있으므로 오답.
 (C) 거의 모든 사람이 워크숍에 가 있다는 말로 사무실이 조용한 이유를 언급하고 있으므로 정답.
어휘 shut A off: A를 차단하다, A를 끄다

3. Where did you store the contract from Rosemary Enterprises?
 (A) Sure, I'll do it.
 (B) In the filing cabinet.
 (C) They have some space for lease.

로즈메리 엔터프라이즈 사에서 보낸 계약서를 어디에 보관하셨나요?
 (A) 물론이죠, 제가 그걸 할게요.
 (B) 파일 캐비닛에요.
 (C) 그들에게 임대용 공간이 좀 있어요.

정답 (B)
해설 로즈메리 엔터프라이즈 사에서 보낸 계약서를 보관한 곳을 묻는 Where 의문문입니다.
 (A) 의문사 의문문에 어울리지 않는 Sure로 답변하고 있으므로 오답. Yes와 같은 의미로 쓰이는 Sure나 OK, Of course 등은 의문사 의문문에 어울리지 않는 반응이므로 바로 오답 소거해야 합니다.
 (B) Where와 어울리는 특정 위치로 답변하고 있으므로 정답.
 (C) contract에서 연상 가능한 lease를 이용해 혼동을 유발하는 답변이며, 임대용 공간과 관련해 언급하고 있으므로 오답.
어휘 store v. ~을 보관하다, ~을 저장하다 contract 계약(서) lease 임대 계약(서)

4. Did Mr. Devi show you his latest design?
 (A) He majored in fashion and apparel.
 (B) I've been in client meetings all day.
 (C) It's part of our new marketing campaign.

데비 씨가 최신 디자인을 당신에게 보여 줬나요?
 (A) 그는 의류 패션을 전공했어요.
 (B) 저는 하루 종일 고객 회의 중이었습니다.
 (C) 그건 저희 새 마케팅 캠페인의 일환입니다.

정답 (B)
해설 데비 씨가 최신 디자인을 상대방에게 보여 줬는지 확인하기 위해 묻는 일반 의문문입니다.
 (A) 전공 분야를 언급하는 답변이므로 질문의 의도에 맞지 않는 오답.
 (B) 하루 종일 고객 회의 중이었다는 말로 해당 디자인을 볼 기회가 없었음을 의미하는 답변이므로 정답.
 (C) 마케팅 캠페인의 일환임을 언급하는 답변이므로 질문의 의도에 맞지 않는 오답.
어휘 major in ~을 전공하다 apparel 의류, 옷 part of ~의 일환인, ~의 일부인

5. Who should I talk to regarding my late fees?
 (A) The man at the front desk.
 (B) I'm on a free trial.

(C) Only about ten attendees.

제 연체료와 관련해서 누구와 이야기해야 하나요?
(A) 프런트 데스크에 계신 남자분이요.
(B) 저는 무료 체험 서비스 이용 중입니다.
(C) 오직 약 10명의 참석자들만요.

정답 (A)
해설 연체료와 관련해서 누구와 이야기해야 하는지 묻는 Who 의문문입니다.
(A) Who와 어울리는 담당자로 답변하고 있으므로 정답.
(B) 이용 중인 서비스의 종류를 말하는 답변이므로 질문의 의도에 맞지 않는 오답.
(C) How many 의문문에 어울리는 인원수를 알리는 답변이므로 질문의 의도에 맞지 않는 오답.

어휘 regarding ~와 관련해 late fee 연체료 free trial 무료 체험 서비스 about 약, 대략

6. The library will be expanding its non-fiction section next year.
(A) It'd be great to have more resources for research.
(B) The second-floor café has decent sandwiches.
(C) A digital membership card.

그 도서관은 내년에 비소설 구역을 확장할 예정입니다.
(A) 연구에 필요한 자료가 더 많이 있으면 아주 좋을 겁니다.
(B) 2층에 위치한 카페에 준수한 샌드위치가 있어요.
(C) 디지털 회원 카드요.

정답 (A)
해설 특정 도서관이 내년에 비소설 구역을 확장할 예정이라는 정보를 알리는 평서문입니다.
(A) 연구에 필요한 자료가 더 많이 있으면 아주 좋을 것이라는 말로 시설 확장에 따른 장점을 언급하고 있으므로 정답.
(B) 카페에서 판매하는 음식 제품에 관해 언급하고 있으므로 도서관 시설 확장 사실을 알리는 평서문과 어울리지 않는 오답.
(C) 디지털 회원 카드를 의미하는 답변이므로 도서관 시설 확장 사실을 알리는 평서문과 어울리지 않는 오답.

어휘 expand ~을 확장하다, ~을 확대하다 non-fiction 비소설의 resource 자료, 자원, 자산 decent 준수한, 꽤 괜찮은

7. What's the total area of the main parking lot?
(A) This neighborhood is mainly residential.
(B) Around 10,000 square feet.
(C) Yes, some spots are available.

중앙 주차장의 총 면적이 어떻게 되나요?
(A) 이 지역은 주로 주거용입니다.
(B) 대략 10,000 평방 피트요.

(C) 네, 몇몇 자리가 이용 가능합니다.

정답 (B)
해설 중앙 주차장의 총 면적을 묻는 What 의문문입니다.
(A) area에서 연상 가능한 neighborhood을 이용해 혼동을 유발하는 답변이며, 지역적 특성과 관련해 언급하고 있으므로 질문의 의도에 맞지 않는 오답.
(B) What's the total area와 어울리는 면적을 언급하고 있으므로 정답.
(C) 의문사 의문문에 어울리지 않는 Yes로 답변하는 오답. 의문사 의문문에 대해 Yes나 No로 시작되는 답변은 바로 오답 소거해야 합니다.

어휘 area 면적 parking lot 주차장 neighborhood 지역, 인근, 이웃 residential 주거의 around 대략, 약, ~쯤 square feet 평방 피트 spot 자리, 장소, 곳 available (사물) 이용 가능한, 구입 가능한, (사람) 시간이 있는

8. Isn't our company's business plan for next year due this Wednesday?
(A) No, we need more people.
(B) Some items are still being discussed.
(C) A bidding proposal.

우리 회사의 내년 사업 계획서의 제출 기한이 이번 주 수요일이지 않나요?
(A) 아뇨, 우리는 더 많은 사람들이 필요해요.
(B) 몇몇 항목들이 여전히 논의되고 있습니다.
(C) 입찰 제안서요.

정답 (B)
해설 내년 사업 계획서가 이번 주 수요일이 제출 기한이지 않은지 확인하기 위해 묻는 부정 의문문입니다.
(A) 부정을 뜻하는 No 뒤에 제출 기한과 관련 없는 인원 규모에 관한 말이 이어지고 있으므로 오답.
(B) 몇몇 항목들이 여전히 논의되고 있다는 말로 제출 전까지 시간이 더 걸린다는 의미를 나타내고 있으므로 정답.
(C) 입찰 제안서를 언급하는 답변이므로 질문의 의도에 맞지 않는 오답.

어휘 due ~가 기한인 item 항목, 품목, 제품, 물품 discuss ~을 논의하다 bidding 입찰, 응찰, 가격 제시 proposal 제안(서)

9. Could you notify Mr. Baek about the compliance inspection?
(A) It includes a photo compilation.
(B) This machine is brand new.
(C) I left him a message already.

백 씨께 준수 여부 점검에 관해 알려 주시겠어요?
(A) 그건 사진 모음집을 포함하고 있어요.
(B) 이 기계는 완전히 새 것입니다.

(C) 제가 이미 그분께 메시지를 남겼습니다.

정답 (C)

해설 백 씨에게 준수 여부 점검에 관해 알려 주라고 묻는 요청 의문문입니다.
- (A) compliance와 일부 발음이 유사한 compilation을 이용해 혼동을 유발하는 답변이며, 사진 모음집을 포함하고 있다는 사실을 알리는 내용이므로 질문의 의도에 맞지 않는 오답.
- (B) 기계의 특징을 알리는 답변이므로 질문의 의도에 맞지 않는 오답.
- (C) 이미 메시지를 남겼다는 말로 백 씨에게 통보한 상태임을 나타내는 답변이므로 정답.

어휘 notify ~에게 알리다, ~에게 통보하다 compliance (법, 명령 등의) 준수, 따름 inspection 점검, 검사 include ~을 포함하다 compilation 모음집, 편집본 brand new 완전히 새로운 leave ~을 남기다, ~을 놓아 두다, ~을 두고 오다

10. Which car model is the most fuel efficient?
    (A) No, I own an electric vehicle.
    (B) A sales representative can help you by the counter.
    (C) Yes, that's my favorite one.

어느 자동차 모델이 가장 연비가 효율적인가요?
(A) 아뇨, 저는 전기 자동차를 소유하고 있어요.
(B) 영업 직원이 카운터 옆에서 도와 드릴 수 있습니다.
(C) 네, 그게 제가 가장 좋아하는 거예요.

정답 (B)

해설 어느 자동차 모델이 가장 연비가 효율적인지 묻는 Which 의문문입니다.
- (A) 의문사 의문문에 어울리지 않는 No로 답변하는 오답. 의문사 의문문에 대해 Yes나 No로 시작되는 답변은 바로 오답 소거해야 합니다.
- (B) 영업 직원이 도와 줄 수 있다는 말로 관련 정보를 얻을 수 있는 방법을 알려 주고 있으므로 정답.
- (C) 의문사 의문문에 어울리지 않는 Yes로 답변하는 오답. 의문사 의문문에 대해 Yes나 No로 시작되는 답변은 바로 오답 소거해야 합니다.

어휘 fuel efficient 연비가 효율적인 vehicle 차량 representative n. 직원, 대표자 favorite a. 가장 좋아하는 n. 가장 좋아하는 것

11. Ms. Park will be here to welcome the guests, won't she?
    (A) Sure, be my guest.
    (B) She's away on a business trip.
    (C) The feedback forms are on my desk.

박 씨가 손님들을 맞이하기 위해 이곳으로 오시는 거죠, 그렇지 않나요?
(A) 물론이죠, 그렇게 하세요.
(B) 그분은 출장으로 자리를 비우셨어요.
(C) 의견 양식이 제 책상에 있습니다.

정답 (B)

해설 박 씨가 손님들을 맞이하기 위해 오는지 확인하기 위해 묻는 부가 의문문입니다.
- (A) guest를 반복해 혼동을 유발하는 답변이며, 허락 등의 의미로 사용하는 표현이므로 질문의 의도에 맞지 않는 오답.
- (B) Ms. Park을 She로 지칭해 출장으로 자리를 비운 상태라는 말로 손님들을 맞이하러 올 수 없다는 뜻을 나타내고 있으므로 정답.
- (C) 의견 양식이 있는 곳을 알려 주는 말이므로 질문의 의도에 맞지 않는 오답.

어휘 be my guest (허락 등을 나타내어) 그렇게 하세요, 좋으실 대로 하세요 away 자리를 비운, 없는, 멀리 가 있는 feedback 의견, 피드백 form 양식, 서식

12. Which of these tasks would you like me to complete today?
    (A) The first four, at least.
    (B) A spacious workstation.
    (C) She is very hardworking.

이 업무들 중에서 어느 것을 제가 오늘 완료하기를 원하세요?
(A) 첫 네 개요, 적어도요.
(B) 널찍한 업무 공간이요.
(C) 그녀는 아주 근면합니다.

정답 (A)

해설 특정 업무들 중에서 어느 것을 오늘 완료하기를 원하는지 묻는 Which 의문문입니다.
- (A) Which of these tasks와 어울리는 최소한의 업무들을 지칭하는 답변이므로 정답.
- (B) tasks에서 연상 가능한 workstation을 이용해 혼동을 유발하는 답변이며, 업무 공간의 특징을 언급하고 있으므로 질문의 의도에 맞지 않는 오답.
- (C) 대상을 알 수 없는 She의 특성을 말하는 답변이므로 질문의 의도에 맞지 않는 오답.

어휘 task 업무, 일 would like A to do: A에게 ~하기를 원하다 complete ~을 완료하다 at least 적어도, 최소한 spacious 널찍한 workstation 업무 공간 hardworking 근면한

13. How close is the nearest subway station?
    (A) I know he usually rides the bus.
    (B) About five minutes walking.
    (C) Kensington Crossing.

가장 가까운 지하철 역이 얼마나 가까운가요?
(A) 그가 평소에 버스를 타고 다니는 것으로 알고 있어요.
(B) 걸어서 약 15분이요.
(C) 켄싱턴 교차로요.

정답 (B)
해설 가장 가까운 지하철 역이 얼마나 가까운지 묻는 How 의문문입니다.
(A) 대상을 알 수 없는 he가 평소에 이용하는 교통 수단을 말하는 답변이므로 질문의 의도에 맞지 않는 오답.
(B) How close와 어울리는 이동 시간으로 답변하고 있으므로 정답.
(C) 특정 위치의 명칭을 말하는 답변이므로 질문의 의도에 맞지 않는 오답.

어휘 close 가까운(= near) usually 평소에, 일반적으로 ride ~을 타다, ~을 타고 다니다 about 약, 대략

14. Why are you stacking up the conference room chairs?
(A) No, thanks. I can do it myself.
(B) Just in the corner, please.
(C) Because this space is needed for later.

왜 대회의실 의자들을 쌓아 올리고 계시는 건가요?
(A) 아뇨, 괜찮습니다. 제가 직접 할 수 있어요.
(B) 그냥 구석에 놓아 주세요.
(C) 이 공간이 나중에 필요하기 때문입니다.

정답 (C)
해설 왜 대회의실 의자들을 쌓아 올리고 있는지 묻는 Why 의문문입니다.
(A) 의문사 의문문에 어울리지 않는 No로 답변하는 오답. 의문사 의문문에 대해 Yes나 No로 시작되는 답변은 바로 오답 소거해야 합니다.
(B) Where 의문문에 어울리는 위치로 답변하고 있으므로 오답.
(C) Why와 짝을 이루는 Because와 함께 나중에 필요한 공간을 확보하기 위해서라는 의미를 나타내는 말로 이유를 언급하고 있으므로 정답.

어휘 stack up ~을 쌓아 올리다 oneself (부사처럼 쓰여) 직접

15. Will we hold the strategy session next week?
(A) Well, I disagree.
(B) It should be this Friday.
(C) Yes, I reviewed the entire letter.

우리가 다음 주에 전략 회의 시간을 열 예정인가요?
(A) 음, 저는 동의하지 않습니다.
(B) 이번 주 금요일일 겁니다.
(C) 네, 제가 그 편지 전체를 살펴 봤습니다.

정답 (B)
해설 다음 주에 전략 회의 시간을 열 예정인지 확인하기 위해 묻는 일반 의문문입니다.
(A) 동의하지 않는다는 의견을 밝히는 답변이므로 질문의 의도에 맞지 않는 오답.
(B) 이번 주 금요일일 것이라는 말로 상대방이 잘못 알고 있는 시점을 바로잡아 주는 말이므로 정답.
(C) 긍정을 뜻하는 Yes 뒤에 다음 주에 전략 회의 시간을 여는지와 관련 없는 편지 이야기를 하고 있으므로 질문의 의도에 맞지 않는 오답.

어휘 hold (행사 등) ~을 열다, ~을 개최하다 strategy 전략 session (특정 활동을 위한) 시간 review v. ~을 살펴 보다, ~을 검토하다 n. 검토, 후기, 평가

16. The dental clinic still accepts walk-ins, doesn't it?
(A) Thanks, but I should be fine.
(B) There are brochures by the entrance.
(C) Yes, I didn't need an appointment last week.

그 치과는 여전히 사전 예약하지 않은 환자도 받고 있죠, 그렇지 않나요?
(A) 감사합니다만, 저는 괜찮을 겁니다.
(B) 입구 옆에 안내 책자가 있습니다.
(C) 네, 저는 지난주에 예약이 필요하지 않았어요.

정답 (C)
해설 특정 치과가 여전히 사전 예약하지 않은 환자도 받고 있는지 확인하기 위해 묻는 부가 의문문입니다.
(A) 감사 인사와 함께 괜찮아질 거라고 알리는 답변이므로 질문의 의도에 맞지 않는 오답.
(B) 안내 책자를 찾을 수 있는 위치를 알려 주는 말이므로 질문의 의도에 맞지 않는 오답.
(C) 긍정을 뜻하는 Yes와 함께 지난주에 예약이 필요하지 않았다는 말로 질문 내용에 대해 확인해 주고 있으므로 정답.

어휘 dental 치과의, 치아의 accept ~을 받아들이다, ~을 수락하다 walk-in 사전 예약 없는 방문 brochure 안내 책자 by ~ 옆에 appointment 예약, 약속

17. The team gathering can wait until next month.
(A) I'll cancel the reservation.
(B) Did you invite all our clients?
(C) No, she didn't say.

팀 모임 행사는 다음 달까지 미뤄도 됩니다.
(A) 제가 예약을 취소할게요.
(B) 모든 우리 고객들을 초대하셨나요?
(C) 아뇨, 그녀는 말하지 않았어요.

정답 (A)
해설 팀 모임 행사를 다음 달까지 미뤄도 된다는 정보를 제공하는 평서문입니다.
(A) 예약을 취소하겠다는 말로 모임 행사를 미루는 것에 따른

조치를 언급하고 있으므로 정답.
(B) 모든 고객들을 초대했는지 확인하기 위해 되묻는 말이므로 팀 모임 행사 변경과 관련 없는 오답.
(C) 대상을 알 수 있는 she가 과거 시점에 말하지 않은 사실을 알리는 답변이므로 팀 모임 행사 변경과 관련 없는 오답.

어휘 gathering 모임 wait (사물 주어) 미루다 cancel ~을 취소하다 reservation 예약 invite ~을 초대하다

18. How many staplers do we have in the supply cabinet?
(A) I installed wooden ones in my kitchen.
(B) I'm not sure.
(C) OK, don't forget to attach the invoice.

우리가 물품 캐비닛에 얼마나 많은 스테이플러를 갖고 있죠?
(A) 저는 제 주방에 목재로 된 것들을 설치했어요.
(B) 잘 모르겠습니다.
(C) 좋아요, 거래 내역서를 첨부하시는 것을 잊지 마세요.

정답 (B)

해설 물품 캐비닛에 얼마나 많은 스테이플러를 갖고 있는지 묻는 How 의문문입니다.
(A) 답변자 자신이 주방에 설치한 것의 특징을 언급하고 있으므로 질문의 의도에 맞지 않는 오답.
(B) 잘 모르겠다는 말로 자신은 알지 못한다는 뜻을 나타내고 있으므로 정답.
(C) 의문사 의문문에 어울리지 않는 OK로 답변하고 있으므로 오답. Yes와 같은 의미로 쓰이는 OK나 Sure, Of course 등은 의문사 의문문에 어울리지 않는 반응이므로 바로 오답 소거해야 합니다.

어휘 stapler 스테이플러, 호치키스 supply n. 물품, 공급(품) v. ~을 공급하다 install ~을 설치하다 forget to do ~하는 것을 잊다 attach ~을 첨부하다, ~을 부착하다 invoice 거래 내역서

19. Why don't we arrange for a taxi to pick us all up?
(A) He sent us the address in an e-mail.
(B) Jennifer said she'll leave after she finishes an assignment.
(C) That's right down the street.

우리 모두를 태우고 갈 택시를 마련하면 어떨까요?
(A) 그가 이메일로 그 주소를 우리에게 보냈어요.
(B) 제니퍼 씨는 배정된 일을 끝마친 후에 출발하실 거라고 하셨어요.
(C) 그곳은 길 바로 저쪽에 있습니다.

정답 (B)

해설 모두를 태우고 갈 택시를 마련하면 어떨지 묻는 제안 의문문입니다.
(A) 이메일로 주소를 보낸 사실을 언급하고 있으므로 택시를 마련하는 방법과 관련 없는 오답.
(B) 제니퍼 씨가 배정된 일을 끝마친 후에 출발할 거라고 말한 사실을 알리는 것으로 택시로 함께 가는 방법에 대해 반대하는 의미를 나타내고 있으므로 정답.
(C) Where 의문문에 어울리는 위치로 답변하고 있으므로 오답.

어휘 Why don't we ~? ~하는 게 어때요? arrange for ~을 마련하다, ~에 대해 조치하다 pick A up: A를 차로 데려 가다[오다] leave 출발하다, 떠나다 assignment 배정(된 일) down (길 등) ~ 저쪽에, ~을 따라

20. Would you like a summary of the survey responses I collected?
(A) No, I'd prefer not to.
(B) Yes, that should be useful.
(C) A five-page document.

제가 수집한 설문 조사 응답의 요약본을 드릴까요?
(A) 아뇨, 저는 그렇게 하고 싶지 않아요.
(B) 네, 그건 유용할 겁니다.
(C) 5페이지 분량의 문서입니다.

정답 (B)

해설 자신이 수집한 설문 조사 응답의 요약본을 원하는지 묻는 제안 의문문입니다.
(A) 질문에 쓰인 것과 동일한 동사로 된 to부정사일 때 해당 동사를 생략하고 to만 사용할 수 있는데, 이에 해당되는 동사가 질문에 제시되지 않아 to부정사의 to로 대답할 수 없으므로 오답.
(B) 수락을 뜻하는 Yes와 함께 요약본을 that으로 지칭해 그 것의 유용함을 말하고 있으므로 정답.
(C) summary에서 연상 가능한 document를 이용해 혼동을 유발하는 답변이며, 문서의 분량을 말하고 있으므로 질문의 의도에 맞지 않는 오답.

어휘 would like ~을 원하다, ~으로 하고 싶다 summary 요약(본) survey 설문 조사(지) response 응답, 반응 collect ~을 수집하다, ~을 모으다 would prefer (not) to do ~하고 싶다(하고 싶지 않다) useful 유용한

21. How much does this lawn chair cost?
(A) A table on the patio.
(B) We weren't there for long.
(C) Twelve dollars for today only.

이 야외용 접이식 의자는 얼마인가요?
(A) 테라스에 있는 탁자요.
(B) 저희는 그곳에 오래 있지 않았어요.
(C) 오늘만 25달러입니다.

정답 (C)

해설 야외용 접이식 의자가 얼마인지 묻는 How 의문문입니다.

(A) chair에서 연상 가능한 table을 이용해 혼동을 유발하는 답변이며, 특정 장소에 있는 탁자를 언급하므로 질문의 의도에 맞지 않는 오답.
(B) How long 의문문에 어울리는 기간과 관련된 답변이므로 오답.
(C) How much와 어울리는 가격으로 답변하고 있으므로 정답.

어휘 cost ~의 비용이 들다 patio 테라스 for long 오랫동안

22. I'd like to request a fitness consultation.
(A) **Are you a member with us?**
(B) Yes, we have plenty of lockers.
(C) Here is your treatment plan.

피트니스 관련 상담을 요청하고 싶습니다.
(A) 저희 회원이신가요?
(B) 네, 저희는 많은 사물함을 보유하고 있습니다.
(C) 여기 고객님의 치료 계획서입니다.

정답 (A)
해설 피트니스 관련 상담을 요청하고 싶다는 말로 원하는 바를 밝히는 평서문입니다.
(A) 회원인지 되묻는 것으로 피트니스 관련 상담과 관련된 정보를 파악하는 말이므로 정답.
(B) fitness에서 연상 가능한 lockers를 언급해 혼동을 유발하는 답변이며, 사물함 수량을 밝히는 말이므로 피트니스 관련 상담을 요청하는 평서문과 어울리지 않는 오답.
(C) 치료 계획서를 전달할 때 하는 말이므로 피트니스 관련 상담을 요청하는 평서문과 어울리지 않는 오답.

어휘 would like to do ~하고 싶다 request ~을 요청하다 consultation 상담, 상의 plenty of 많은, 충분한 treatment 치료, 처치, (약품 등의) 처리

23. How do you feel about the relocation announcement?
(A) A block away from the train station.
(B) **There's a lot to consider.**
(C) I feel like we have a great team.

위치 이전 공지에 대해 어떻게 생각하세요?
(A) 기차역에서 한 블록 떨어져 있어요.
(B) 고려해야 할 게 많이 있습니다.
(C) 저는 우리가 훌륭한 팀을 보유하고 있는 것 같아요.

정답 (B)
해설 위치 이전 공지에 대해 어떻게 생각하는지 묻는 How 의문문입니다.
(A) How far 또는 How long 의문문에 어울리는 거리와 관련된 답변이므로 오답.
(B) 고려해야 할 게 많이 있다는 말로 위치 이전이 쉬운 문제가 아님을 뜻하는 의견을 제시하고 있으므로 정답.

(C) 팀에 대한 의견을 제시하는 답변이므로 질문의 의도에 맞지 않는 오답.

어휘 How do you feel about ~? ~에 대해 어떻게 생각하세요? relocation 위치 이전, 재배치 announcement 공지, 발표 consider ~을 고려하다 feel like ~인 것 같다

24. Who left these papers on my desk?
(A) The printer is working just fine.
(B) **One of the interns.**
(C) Yes, it's right over there.

누가 이 문서들을 제 책상에 놓아 두었나요?
(A) 프린터가 아주 잘 작동하고 있어요.
(B) 인턴 직원들 중 한 명이요.
(C) 네, 바로 저기 저쪽에 있어요.

정답 (B)
해설 누가 특정 문서들을 책상에 놓아 두었는지 묻는 Who 의문문입니다.
(A) 프린터의 작동 상태를 알리는 답변이므로 질문의 의도에 맞지 않는 오답.
(B) Who와 어울리는 특정 직책을 지닌 사람을 언급하여 답변하고 있으므로 정답.
(C) 의문사 의문문에 어울리지 않는 Yes로 답변하는 오답. 의문사 의문문에 대해 Yes나 No로 시작되는 답변은 바로 오답 소거해야 합니다.

어휘 leave ~을 놓아 두다, ~을 남겨 놓다 work (기계 등이) 작동하다 over there 저기 저쪽에

25. How long will I have to wait to see a doctor?
(A) Just down that hallway.
(B) Yes, we already did.
(C) **Are you a returning patient?**

의사 선생님의 진찰을 받는 데 얼마나 오래 기다려야 할까요?
(A) 저 복도만 따라가시면 됩니다.
(B) 네, 저희는 이미 그랬습니다.
(C) 재방문 환자이신가요?

정답 (C)
해설 의사 선생님의 진찰을 받는 데 얼마나 오래 기다려야 하는지 묻는 How 의문문입니다.
(A) 이동 방향 또는 위치를 묻는 How 의문문이나 Where 의문문에 어울리는 답변이므로 오답.
(B) 의문사 의문문에 어울리지 않는 Yes로 답변하는 오답. 의문사 의문문에 대해 Yes나 No로 시작되는 답변은 바로 오답 소거해야 합니다.
(C) 재방문 환자인지 되묻는 것으로 별도의 절차 없이 더 빨리 진찰을 받을 수 있다는 의미를 담고 있는 답변이므로 정답.

어휘 will have to do ~해야 할 것이다 down (길 등) ~을 따라, ~ 저쪽에 returning (고객 등이) 재방문하는, 다시 찾아 오는

PART 3 FINAL TEST

1. (B)	2. (C)	3. (A)	4. (D)	5. (D)
6. (B)	7. (C)	8. (B)	9. (A)	10. (C)
11. (A)	12. (C)	13. (B)	14. (D)	15. (C)
16. (D)	17. (B)	18. (C)	19. (C)	20. (C)
21. (B)	22. (A)	23. (D)	24. (D)	

Questions 1-3 refer to the following conversation.

W: Hi, Thomas. Can you help me with something?
M: Sure. What do you need?
W: I'm preparing to send the contracts to our new freelance writers, and **1** I need plastic sleeves for the paper documents.
M: **1** Did we already run out?
W: Yes, and **2** the shipment of supplies we recently ordered has been delayed.
M: Really? **2** This happened last time, too!
W: Yeah, I know. It's frustrating.
M: Well, **3** I just finished my client meeting at Brandon's Coffee Shop. I'll drop by the Office Plus on Saratoga Avenue to pick up more sleeves on my way back.

여: 안녕하세요, 토머스 씨. 저 좀 도와 주시겠어요?
남: 물론이죠. 뭐가 필요하신가요?
여: 제가 우리 새 프리랜서 작가들께 계약서를 보내 드릴 준비를 하고 있는데, 종이 문서를 담을 플라스틱 서류 폴더가 필요합니다.
남: 벌써 다 떨어졌나요?
여: 네, 그리고 우리가 최근에 주문한 용품 배송이 지연되었어요.
남: 정말요? 이런 일이 지난 번에도 발생했잖아요!
여: 네, 제 말이요. 불만스러워요.
남: 저, 저는 방금 브랜든스 커피숍에서 고객 회의를 끝마쳤어요. 제가 돌아가는 길에 새러토가 애비뉴에 있는 오피스 플러스에 들러서 서류 폴더를 더 구입할게요.

어휘 **help A with B:** B에 대해 A를 돕다 **prepare to do** ~할 준비를 하다 **contract** 계약서 **agreement** 계약서 **plastic sleeve** 플라스틱 서류 폴더 **run out** 다 떨어지다, 다 쓰다 **shipment** 배송(품) **supplies** 용품, 물품 **recently** 최근에 **order** v. ~을 주문하다 n. 주문(품) **delay** v. ~을 지연시키다 n. 지연 **frustrating** 불만스러운, 좌절시키는 **drop by** ~에 들르다 **pick up** ~을 구입하다 **on one's way back** 돌아가는 길에

1. 여자가 남자에게 자신을 위해 무엇을 하도록 요청하는가?
   (A) 일정표를 확인하는 일
   (B) 제품을 구입하는 일
   (C) 일부 의류를 찾는 일
   (D) 몇몇 사본을 만드는 일

   정답 (B)

   해설 대화 초반부에 여자가 종이 문서를 담을 플라스틱 서류 폴더가 필요하다고(I need plastic sleeves for the paper documents) 알리자, 남자가 벌써 다 떨어졌는지(Did we already run out?) 묻고 있습니다. 따라서, 여자가 해당 제품을 구입하도록 요청하는 상황임을 알 수 있으므로 (B)가 정답입니다.

   어휘 **ask A to do:** A에게 ~하도록 요청하다 **calendar** 일정표, 달력 **purchase** ~을 구입하다 **clothing** 의류 **make a copy** 사본을 만들다, 복사하다

2. 남자는 배송품과 관련해 무슨 말을 하는가?
   (A) 배송 추적 번호를 포함하고 있다.
   (B) 지난주에 주문되었다.
   (C) 전에 지연된 적이 있었다.
   (D) 물품들이 빠져 있다.

   정답 (C)

   해설 여자가 대화 중반부에 최근에 주문한 용품 배송이 지연되었다는(the shipment of supplies we recently ordered has been delayed) 사실을 말하자, 남자가 같은 일이 지난 번에도 발생했다고(This happened last time, too!) 언급하고 있으므로 (C)가 정답입니다.

   어휘 **include** ~을 포함하다 **tracking** 추적, 파악 **miss** ~을 빠트리다, ~을 놓치다, ~을 지나치다

   Paraphrase delayed / happened last time
   ⇒ has been delayed before

3. 남자는 어디에 있는가?
   (A) 카페에
   (B) 인쇄소에
   (C) 시장에
   (D) 우체국에

   정답 (A)

   해설 대화 마지막 부분에 남자가 방금 브랜든스 커피숍에서 고객 회의를 끝마쳤다고(I just finished my client meeting at Brandon's Coffee Shop) 밝히고 있어 커피숍에 있다는 것을 알 수 있으므로 (A)가 정답입니다.

   Paraphrase Brandon's Coffee Shop ⇒ a café

Questions 4-6 refer to the following conversation.

W: Hi, Mr. Johnson. It's Jane Lee from Infinite Timepieces. ④ **I'm so glad you've signed a contract with us. We're really proud to have you as our brand ambassador.**

M: Oh, ④ **it's my honor to represent such a well-known brand.**

W: Well, we hope you can show off our high-quality craftmanship with the state-of-the-art watch samples we've sent you. As written in our agreement, you'll wear one of our pieces whenever there's a large press event.

M: Yes! I'll do that ⑤ **at next week's premiere for my new film.**

W: Wonderful. And ⑥ **don't forget to post a few images with our products on social media after the event, too!**

여: 안녕하세요, 존슨 씨. 저는 인피니트 타임피스의 제인 리입니다. 귀하께서 저희와 계약을 맺으셔서 너무 기쁩니다. 저희 브랜드 홍보 대사로 모시게 되어 정말 자랑스럽습니다.

남: 아, 그렇게 잘 알려진 브랜드를 대표하게 되어 영광입니다.

여: 저, 저희가 보내 드린 최신 시계 샘플에 담긴 높은 수준의 저희 장인 정신을 돋보이게 해 주실 수 있기를 바랍니다. 계약서에 쓰여 있는 바와 같이, 언제든 대규모 언론 행사가 있을 때마다 저희 제품들 중 하나를 착용하시게 될 것입니다.

남: 네! 다음 주에 있을 제 신작 영화의 시사회에서 그렇게 하겠습니다.

여: 아주 좋습니다. 그리고 그 행사 후에 소셜 미디어에 저희 제품을 착용하신 몇몇 이미지를 게시하시는 것도 잊지 마시기 바랍니다.

어휘 sign a contract 계약을 맺다 be proud to do ~해서 자랑스럽다 brand ambassador 브랜드 홍보 대사 it's my honor to do ~해서 영광입니다 represent ~을 대표하다, ~을 대신하다 well-known 잘 알려진 show off ~을 돋보이게 하다, ~을 과시하다 high-quality 높은 수준의, 고품질의 craftmanship 장인 정신 state-of-the-art 최신의, 최첨단의 agreement 계약(서), 합의(서) whenever 언제든 ~할 때마다 press event 언론 행사 premiere 시사회 forget to do ~하는 것을 잊다 post ~을 게시하다

4. 남자가 무엇을 하도록 계약을 맺었는가?
 (A) 광고에서 연기하는 일
 (B) 모델을 디자인하는 일
 (C) 행사를 사진 촬영하는 일
 (D) 제품을 광고하는 일

정답 (D)

해설 대화 초반부에 여자가 남자에게 계약을 맺은 사실과 함께 브랜드 홍보 대사로 모시게 된 것이 자랑스럽다고(I'm so glad you've signed a contract with us. We're really proud to have you as our brand ambassador) 말하자, 남자가 여자 회사의 브랜드를 대표하는 것이 영광이라고(it's my honor to represent such a well-known brand) 대답하고 있습니다. 따라서, 제품 홍보 대사로 계약했음을 알 수 있으므로 (D)가 정답입니다.

어휘 be contracted to do ~하도록 계약을 맺다 commercial n. 광고 (방송) advertise ~을 광고하다

Paraphrase brand ambassador / represent such a well-known brand ⇒ Advertise a product

5. 다음 주에 무슨 일이 있을 것인가?
 (A) 업계 컨퍼런스
 (B) 시상식
 (C) 영화제
 (D) 영화 시사회

정답 (D)

해설 다음 주라는 시점이 언급되는 후반부에 남자가 다음 주에 있을 자신의 신작 영화 시사회를(at next week's premiere for my new film) 언급하고 있으므로 (D)가 정답입니다.

어휘 industry 업계, 산업

6. 여자가 남자에게 무엇을 하도록 상기시키는가?
 (A) 몇몇 음식을 시식하는 일
 (B) 여러 사진을 업로드하는 일
 (C) 후기를 작성하는 일
 (D) 카탈로그를 훑어 보는 일

정답 (B)

해설 대화 맨 마지막 부분에 여자가 남자에게 행사 후에 소셜 미디어에 제품을 착용한 몇몇 이미지를 게시하는 것도 잊지 말아 달라고(don't forget to post a few images with our products on social media after the event, too!) 상기시키고 있으므로 (B)가 정답입니다.

어휘 remind A to do: A에게 ~하도록 상기시키다 sample v. ~을 시식하다, ~을 시음하다 review n. 후기, 평가, 검토 v. ~의 후기를 작성하다, ~을 평가하다, ~을 검토하다 look through ~을 훑어 보다

Paraphrase

don't forget ⇒ remind
post a few images ⇒ Upload several pictures

Questions 7-9 refer to the following conversation.

M: Good morning. My name is Victor. I was told to come here for a meeting with Ms. Paige.
W: Hello. Nice to meet you, Victor. **7 How has work been as a trainee in our program?**
M: Very fulfilling. **8 Working in a plant laboratory has always been my goal.**
W: I'm glad to hear that. Today, we'll practice measuring different types of nutrient concentrations in our soil samples. I guess **9 we can begin by weighing the multiple trays I've set up already here.**

남: 안녕하세요. 제 이름은 빅터입니다. 페이지 씨와의 회의를 위해 이곳으로 오라는 얘기를 들었습니다.
여: 안녕하세요. 만나 뵙게 되어서 반갑습니다, 빅터 씨. 지난 주 우리 프로그램의 수습 직원으로서 일이 어떠셨나요?
남: 아주 성취감이 큽니다. 식물 실험실에서 근무하는 것이 항상 제 목표였거든요.
여: 그 말씀을 들으니 기쁘네요. 오늘, 우리 토양 샘플 속에 담긴 여러 다른 유형의 영양분 농도를 측정하는 작업을 실시할 겁니다. 제가 이미 이곳에 준비해 놓은 여러 받침대에 담긴 것의 무게를 재는 작업으로 시작하면 될 것 같습니다.

어휘 be told to do ~하라는 얘기를 듣다 trainee 수습 직원, 교육생, 훈련생 fulfilling 성취감을 주는 laboratory 실험실 practice -ing ~하는 것을 행하다 measure ~을 측정하다 nutrient 영양분 concentration 농도 soil 토양, 흙 by (방법) ~하는 것으로, ~해서 weigh v. ~의 무게를 재다 multiple 여럿의, 다수의, 다양한 tray 받침대, 쟁반 set up ~을 준비하다, ~을 설치하다, ~을 설정하다

7. 무엇이 지난 주에 시작되었을 것 같은가?
(A) 업체 영업
(B) 채용 모집 기간
(C) 교육 프로그램
(D) 연구 프로젝트

정답 (C)
해설 여자가 담화 초반부에 남자에게 프로그램의 수습 직원으로서 일이 어땠는지(How has work been as a trainee in our program?) 묻고 있어 남자가 지난 주에 교육 프로그램을 시작했음을 알 수 있으므로 (C)가 정답입니다.

어휘 operation 영업, 운영, 가동, 작동 recruitment (인원) 모집, 채용 training 교육, 훈련 research 연구, 조사

8. 화자들이 어디에 근무하고 있는가?
(A) 박물관에
(B) 실험실에
(C) 공장에
(D) 농장에

정답 (B)
해설 대화 중반부에 남자가 일이 성취감을 준다고 언급하면서 식물 실험실에서 근무하는 것이 항상 목표였다고(Working in a plant laboratory has always been my goal) 밝히고 있으므로 (B)가 정답입니다.

9. 화자들이 곧이어 무엇을 할 것인가?
(A) 몇몇 물품의 무게를 재는 일
(B) 샘플을 수집하는 일
(C) 탁자를 설치하는 일
(D) 몇몇 결과를 분석하는 일

정답 (A)
해설 대화 맨 마지막 부분에 여자가 자신이 준비해 놓은 여러 받침대에 담긴 것의 무게를 재는 작업으로 시작하면 된다고(we can begin by weighing the multiple trays I've set up already here) 알리고 있으므로 (A)가 정답입니다.

어휘 collect ~을 수집하다 analyze ~을 분석하다 result 결과(물)

Paraphrase weighing the multiple trays
⇒ Weigh some items

Questions 10-12 refer to the following conversation.

M: Jen, **10 I just heard some surprising news. The Public Utilities director will be transferring to our department starting next week.**
W: Wow, I didn't expect that. Well, **11 we do need new ideas to improve the variety of flowers and trees in our parks**, so I hope she's familiar with them.
M: Right, for our city's landscaping renewal initiative.
W: Yeah, and since **12 our team is holding a brainstorming meeting for that tomorrow morning**, we can discuss preliminary details with everyone first.

남: 젠 씨, 방금 놀라운 소식을 좀 들었어요. 공익 사업 관리국장님께서 다음 주에 우리 부서로 전근하실 예정입니다.
여: 와우, 그건 예상하지 못했어요. 음, 우리 공원들마다 꽃과 나무들의 다양성을 향상시킬 새로운 아이디어들이 필요하기 때문에, 그분께서 그것들을 잘 알고 계시기를 바랍니다.
남: 맞아요, 우리 시의 조경 재개발 계획을 위해서요.
여: 네, 그리고 우리 팀이 내일 오전에 그 부분에 대한 아이디어 회의를 열기 때문에, 모든 사람과 먼저 예비 세부 사항을 논의할 수 있습니다.

어휘 surprising (사람을) 놀라게 하는 transfer 전근하다, 전학하다, 환승하다 department 부서, ~부 expect ~을 예상하다, ~을 기대하다 improve ~을 향상시키다, ~을 개선하다 variety 다양성, 종류, 품종 be familiar with ~을 잘 알다, ~에 익숙하다 landscaping 조경 (작업) renewal 재개발, 갱신, 재개 initiative n. 계획, 솔선 수범, 진취(성) hold (행사 등) ~을 열다, ~을 개최하다 brainstorming meeting 아이디어 회의 preliminary 예비의, 사전 준비의 details 세부 사항, 상세 정보

10. 남자는 어떤 소식을 공유하는가?
(A) 시장이 방문할 예정이다.
(B) 공공 도서관이 이전될 것이다.
(C) 한 국장이 부서를 변경했다.
(D) 새 공익 기업 한 곳이 문을 열었다.

정답 (C)
해설 남자가 대화를 시작하면서 놀라운 소식을 들었다고 언급하면서 공익 사업 관리국장이 다음 주에 자신들의 부서로 전근할 예정이라고(I just heard some surprising news. The Public Utilities director will be transferring to our department starting next week) 알리고 있으므로 (C)가 정답입니다.

어휘 mayor (도시의) 시장 relocate ~을 이전하다, ~을 재배치하다 utility company 공익 기업

Paraphrase The Public Utilities director will be transferring to our department
⇒ A director changed departments

11. 화자들은 어떤 개선 사항을 보기를 바라는가?
(A) 다양한 조경 식물
(B) 에너지 효율이 좋은 기계
(C) 확장된 공원 부지
(D) 추가 급수 시설

정답 (A)
해설 대화 중반부에 여자가 공원에 있는 꽃과 나무들의 다양성을 향상시킬 새로운 아이디어들이 필요하다는(we need new ideas to improve the variety of flowers and trees in our parks) 말로 개선이 필요한 부분을 언급하고 있으므로 (A)가 정답입니다.

Paraphrase the variety of flowers and trees in our parks ⇒ Diverse landscaping plants

12. 무엇이 내일 오전으로 예정되어 있는가?
(A) 이사회 회의
(B) 환영식
(C) 아이디어 회의 시간
(D) 팀 단합 워크숍

정답 (C)
해설 내일 오전이라는 시점이 언급되는 대화 후반부에 여자가 팀에서 내일 오전에 아이디어 회의를 연다고(our team is holding a brainstorming meeting for that tomorrow morning) 알리고 있으므로 (C)가 정답입니다.

어휘 board 이사회 session (특정 활동을 위한) 시간

Paraphrase a brainstorming meeting
⇒ A brainstorming session

Questions 13-15 refer to the following conversation with three speakers.

W1: **13 We've been getting more customer complaints** about the quality of our tablecloths. It's great to see the rise in sales, but it also means more people have been claiming that some of the threading becomes loose after one wash.
M: **14 I think we should use a different sewing technique** for the edges of the cloths. The factory machines would need to be reprogrammed, but that shouldn't be too hard. **15 Any thoughts, Grace?**
W2: I like that idea. **15 I'll also ask our textile supplier** if we can receive a more durable type of fiber for the stitches. **15 I'll phone them later today to get a quote.**

여1: 우리 식탁보의 품질과 관련해 계속 고객 불만 사항을 더 많이 받고 있습니다. 판매량 증가를 겪는 게 아주 좋기는 하지만, 더 많은 사람들이 일부 박음질 부분이 한 차례 세탁 후에 헐거워지고 있다고 계속 주장해 오고 있다는 뜻이기도 합니다.
남: 식탁보의 가장자리에 대해 다른 바느질 기법을 이용해야 할 것 같아요. 공장 기계들이 다시 프로그램되어야 하겠지만, 그게 그렇게 어렵지 않을 겁니다. 좋은 생각이라도 있으세요, 그레이스 씨?
여2: 저는 그 아이디어가 마음에 들어요. 우리가 그 박음질을 위해 내구성이 더 좋은 유형의 섬유를 받을 수 있는지도 직물 공급업체에 물어 볼게요. 제가 오늘 이따가 전화해서 견적서를 받아 보겠습니다.

어휘 complaint 불만, 불평 quality 품질, 질, 수준 tablecloth 식탁보 rise in ~의 증가 sales 판매(량), 영업, 매출 claim that ~라고 주장하다 threading 박음질, 바느질 loose 헐거운, 느슨한 wash n. 세탁, 세척 sewing 바느질 edge 가장자리 reprogram (기계 등) ~을 다시 프로그램하다 thought n. 생각 textile 직물, 천 supplier 공급업체, 공급업자 receive ~을 받다 durable 내구성이 좋은 fiber 섬유 stitch 바느질, 바늘땀 phone v. ~에게 전화하다 quote n. 견적(서)

13. 최근 해당 업체에서 무슨 일이 있었는가?
　　(A) 신입 영업 사원을 모집했다.
　　(B) 계속 더 많은 불만 사항을 받고 있다.
　　(C) 특정 제품이 품절되었다.
　　(D) 다른 회사 한 곳과 합병했다.

정답 (B)

해설 여자 한 명이 대화를 시작하면서 자사의 식탁보 품질과 관련해 계속 고객 불만 사항을 더 많이 받고(We've been getting more customer complaints) 있다고 밝히고 있으므로 (B)가 정답입니다.

어휘 recruit ~을 모집하다, ~을 채용하다 representative n. 직원, 대표 sell out of ~이 품절되다, ~이 매진되다 certain 특정한, 일정한 merge with ~와 합병하다, ~와 통합하다

Paraphrase getting more customer complaints
　　⇒ receiving more complaints

14. 남자의 말에 따르면, 무엇이 업체에 도움이 될 것인가?
　　(A) 직원들에게 보상하는 것
　　(B) 장비를 대여하는 것
　　(C) 안전 정책을 시행하는 것
　　(D) 제조 기술을 변경하는 것

정답 (D)

해설 대화 중반부에 남자가 다른 바느질 기법을 이용해야 할 것 같다고(I think we should use a different sewing technique) 언급하고 있습니다. 이는 식탁보를 제조하는 기술을 변경하는 방법을 의미하므로 (D)가 정답입니다.

어휘 reward v. ~에게 보상하다 n. 보상 rent ~을 대여하다 equipment 장비 implement ~을 시행하다 policy 정책, 방침 manufacturing 제조(업)

Paraphrase use a different sewing technique
　　⇒ Changing a manufacturing technique

15. 그레이스 씨는 오늘 누구에게 전화하겠다고 말하는가?
　　(A) 기계 부품 공급업체
　　(B) 패션 액세서리 공급업체
　　(C) 섬유 공급업체
　　(D) 종이 공급업체

정답 (C)

해설 대화 중반부에 남자가 그레이스 씨에게 좋은 생각이라도 있는지(Any thoughts, Grace?) 묻자, 한 여자가 내구성이 더 좋은 유형의 섬유를 받을 수 있는지도 직물 공급업체에 물어 보겠다고 밝히면서 오늘 이따가 전화해서 견적서를 받겠다고(I'll also ask our textile supplier ~ I'll phone them later today to get a quote) 알리고 있습니다. 따라서, 그레이스 씨는 직물 공급업체에 전화할 것임을 알 수 있으므로 (C)가 정답입니다.

어휘 mechanical 기계와 관련된 part 부품

Paraphrase our textile supplier ⇒ A fabric supplier

Questions 16-18 refer to the following conversation with three speakers.

M: **16 Oasis Fitness, this is Kenta at the front desk. How may I help you?**

W1: Hi, my name is Gina Lee. I was at your gym yesterday at around 10 P.M., but **17 I think I left my water bottle there. Has anyone come across it?**

M: I'll ask one of our members who worked the night shift yesterday. One second, please.

W2: Hello, Ms. Lee. My colleague told me about your situation. So, what color is your water bottle?

W1: It's green with a black handle on top.

W2: Oh, we have that here. You can pick it up whenever you come in next. **18 Let me just take down your phone number so that I can hold it safely in our storage room for you.**

남: 오아시스 피트니스입니다, 저는 프런트 데스크의 켄타입니다. 무엇을 도와 드릴까요?

여1: 안녕하세요, 제 이름은 지나 리입니다. 제가 어제 오후 10시쯤 그곳 체육관에 있었는데, 그곳에 제 물병을 두고 온 것 같아요. 누구든 우연히 발견하신 분이 계신가요?

남: 어제 야간 교대 근무를 한 저희 직원들 중 한 명에게 물어 보겠습니다. 잠시만 기다려 주세요.

여2: 안녕하세요. 리 씨. 제 동료 직원이 고객님 상황과 관련해 제게 이야기해 주었습니다. 그래서, 물병이 어떤 색상인가요?

여1: 상단에 검은색 손잡이가 있는 녹색 병이에요.

여2: 아, 저희가 여기 갖고 있습니다. 언제든 다음 번에 오실 때 가져가시면 됩니다. 고객님을 위해 저희 보관실에 안전하게 넣어 둘 수 있도록 제가 전화번호만 받아 적겠습니다.

어휘 around ~쯤, 약, 대략 leave ~을 두고 오다 come across ~을 우연히 발견하다 shift 교대 근무(조) colleague 동료 (직원) situation 상황 pick A up: A를 가져가다[오다] whenever 언제든 ~할 때 take down ~을 받아 적다 so that (목적) ~하도록, (결과) 그래서, 그러므로 hold ~을 갖고 있다, ~을 유지하다 storage 보관, 저장

16. 남자는 누구일 것 같은가?
　　(A) 여행사 직원
　　(B) 신체 운동 트레이너
　　(C) 호텔 직원
　　(D) 체육관 직원

정답 (D)

해설 남자가 대화 시작 부분에 오아시스 피트니스임을 밝히면서 자신이 프런트 데스크에 근무하는 켄타라고(Oasis Fitness, this is Kenta at the front desk. How may I help you?) 알리고 있으므로 (D)가 정답입니다.

어휘 agent 직원, 대리인, 중개인   physical 신체의, 육체의

Paraphrase   Oasis Fitness / Kenta at the front desk
⇒ A gym employee

17. 리 씨는 왜 전화하는가?
(A) 더 빠른 배송이 필요하다.
(B) 소지품 중 하나를 분실했다.
(C) 무료 제품을 받지 못했다.
(D) 요금이 부정확하게 청구되었다.

정답 (B)

해설 대화 초반부에 지나 리라고 이름을 밝히는 여자가 자신의 물병을 두고 온 것 같다고 알리면서 우연히 발견한 사람이 있는지(I think I left my water bottle there. Has anyone come across it?) 묻고 있으므로 (B)가 정답입니다.

어휘 expedite ~을 더 빨리 처리하다   misplace ~을 분실하다, ~을 둔 곳을 잊다   belongings 소지품   receive ~을 받다   complimentary 무료의   incorrectly 부정확하게   charge A B: A에게 B를 청구하다

Paraphrase   left my water bottle there
⇒ misplaced one of her belongings

18. 리 씨는 곧이어 무엇을 할 것 같은가?
(A) 보관실로 가는 일
(B) 통화를 끊지 않고 기다리게 하는 일
(C) 전화번호를 제공하는 일
(D) 가져갈 시간을 정하는 일

정답 (C)

해설 대화 맨 마지막 부분에 여자 한 명이 리 씨에게 물병을 안전하게 보관하기 위해 리 씨의 전화번호를 받아 적겠다고(Let me just take down your phone number so that I can hold it safely in our storage room for you) 알리고 있으므로 (C)가 정답입니다.

어휘 put A on hold: 통화를 끊지 않고 A를 기다리게 하다   provide ~을 제공하다   schedule ~의 일정을 정하다

Questions 19-21 refer to the following conversation.

W: Hi, Johnson. **19** I just received the large poster design from the agency we contracted. Take a look. This ad is going to be great for promoting our air-fryers at retail stores.
M: Wow, it looks awesome! They're getting printed tomorrow, right?
W: Yep. **20** It's unfortunate that they couldn't make several versions though.
M: Well, it does cost more time and effort to make new designs.
W: That's true. But even just swapping some colors would do.
M: Hmm… you have a good point. I'll ask **21** David from the digital marketing team to see if he can help us.

여: 안녕하세요, 존슨 씨. 우리가 계약한 대행사로부터 방금 대형 포스터 디자인을 받았습니다. 한번 보세요. 이 광고가 소매점에서 우리 에어 프라이어를 홍보하는 데 아주 좋을 겁니다.
남: 와우, 아주 멋져 보이네요! 내일 인쇄되는 게 맞죠?
여: 네. 하지만, 우리가 여러 가지 버전을 만들 수 없어서 아쉬워요.
남: 음, 새로운 디자인을 만드는 데 분명 더 많은 시간과 노력이 듭니다.
여: 맞아요. 하지만 심지어 몇몇 색상을 바꾸기만 해도 될 거예요.
남: 흠… 일리 있는 말씀이에요! 제가 디지털 마케팅팀의 데이빗 씨에게 우리를 도우실 수 있는지 알아볼 수 있도록 여쭤 볼게요.

어휘 receive ~을 받다   agency 대행사, 대리점   contract ~와 계약하다   take a look 한번 보다   ad 광고   promote ~을 홍보하다, ~을 촉진하다, ~을 승진시키다   retail 소매(업)   look + 형용사: ~하게 보이다, ~한 것 같다   awesome 아주 멋진, 굉장한, 훌륭한   get p.p.: ~되다, ~된 상태가 되다   It's unfortunate that ~해서 아쉽다, ~해서 유감이다   though (문장 끝이나 중간에서) 하지만   cost (시간, 비용 등) ~이 들다   effort 노력   swap ~을 맞바꾸다   do 되다, 충분하다   you have a good point 일리 있는 말씀입니다   see if ~인지 알아보다

19. 화자들은 무엇을 논의하기 위해 만나고 있는가?
(A) 재무 현황
(B) 생산 과정
(C) 소매 광고
(D) 제품 평가

정답 (C)

해설 여자가 대화를 시작하면서 대행사로부터 방금 대형 포스터 디

자인을 받은 사실과 함께 그것을 소매점에 쓸 광고라고 지칭하고 있습니다(I just received the large poster design ~ This ad is going to be great for promoting our air-fryers at retail stores). 따라서, 소매 광고물과 관련해 논의하는 상황임을 알 수 있으므로 (C)가 정답입니다.

어휘 financial 재무의, 재정의, 금융의 status 현황, 상태, 상황 process 과정 advertisement 광고 evaluation 평가(서)

Paraphrase the large poster / This ad / at retail stores
⇒ A retail advertisement

20. 남자가 "새로운 디자인을 만드는 데 분명 더 많은 시간과 노력이 듭니다" 라고 말할 때 무엇을 의미하는가?
(A) 변화를 주기 위해 자원하고 있다.
(B) 몇몇 결과에 대해 실망했다.
(C) 추론을 제공하려 하고 있다.
(D) 제품 개발을 총괄하게 되어 들떠 있다.

정답 (C)

해설 대화 중반부에 여자가 여러 가지 버전을 만들 수 없어서 아쉽다고(It's unfortunate that they couldn't make several versions though) 말하자, 남자가 '새로운 디자인을 만드는 데 분명 더 많은 시간과 노력이 듭니다'라고 대답하는 흐름입니다. 이는 여러 현실적인 조건을 고려해야 하는 상황에 대한 추론으로 볼 수 있으므로 (C)가 정답입니다.

어휘 volunteer v. 자원하다 n. 자원 봉사자 make a change 변화를 주다, 변경하다 be disappointed with ~에 실망하다 result 결과(물) attempt to do ~하려 하다, ~하기 위해 시도하다 reasoning 추론, 추리 oversee ~을 총괄하다, ~을 감독하다 development 개발, 발전

21. 데이빗 씨는 누구일 것 같은가?
(A) 판화 제작자
(B) 마케팅 담당자
(C) 소매업자
(D) 그래픽 디자이너

정답 (B)

해설 대화 맨 마지막 부분에 남자가 마케팅팀의 데이빗 씨를(David from the digital marketing team) 언급하고 있으므로 (B)가 정답입니다.

Questions 22-24 refer to the following conversation.

W: Howard, I'm trying to purchase train tickets online for our out-of-state conference, but 22 **the payment system keeps on rejecting our company credit card.**
M: 23 **Have you checked the billing address you inputted? It needs to be for our headquarters, not our branch here.**
W: I think I have the correct one. But 24 **this error message isn't specifying what exactly the issue is. You used the company card recently, right?**
M: Yes, but I made a purchase in-store.

여: 하워드 씨, 다른 주에서 열리는 우리 컨퍼런스를 위해 온라인으로 기차표를 구입하려 하고 있는데, 결제 시스템이 계속 우리 회사 법인 카드를 거부하고 있어요.
남: 입력하신 청구서 발송 주소를 확인해 보셨나요? 그게 우리 본사에 대한 것이어야 합니다, 이곳 우리 지사가 아니고요.
여: 정확한 것으로 한 것 같아요. 하지만 이 오류 메시지는 정확히 무엇이 문제인지 명시하지 않고 있어요. 최근에 법인 카드를 이용하신 게 맞죠?
남: 네 하지만 저는 매장 내에서 구입했어요.

어휘 try to do ~하려 하다, ~하려 노력하다 purchase v. ~을 구입하다 n. 구입(품) out-of-state 다른 주의 keep on -ing 계속 ~하다 reject ~을 거부하다, ~을 거절하다 billing 청구서 발송 input ~을 입력하다 headquarters 본사 branch 지사, 지점 correct 정확한, 제대로 된 specify ~을 명시하다 exactly 정확히 issue 문제, 사안 recently 최근에 in-store 매장 내에서

22. 여자는 어떤 문제를 언급하는가?
(A) 거래가 처리될 수 없다.
(B) 기차가 지연되었다.
(C) 행사가 연기되었다.
(D) 몇몇 교통 요금이 상당히 인상되었다.

정답 (A)

해설 여자가 대화 초반부에 결제 시스템이 계속 자신의 회사 법인 카드를 거부하고 있다는(the payment system keeps on rejecting our company credit card) 문제를 언급하고 있습니다. 이는 결제가 되지 않아 거래가 처리되지 않는다는 뜻이므로 (A)가 정답입니다.

어휘 transaction 거래 process v. ~을 처리하다 n. 처리 delay v. ~을 지연시키다 n. 지연 postpone ~을 연기하다, ~을 미루다 fare 교통 요금 increase 인상되다, 증가되다 significantly 상당히, 많이

정답 및 해설 **231**

Paraphrase   the payment system keeps on rejecting our company credit card
⇒ A transaction cannot be processed

23. 남자는 무엇을 제안하는가?
(A) 서비스 공급업체에 연락해 볼 것
(B) 사용 설명서를 읽어 볼 것
(C) 본사에 전화해 볼 것
(D) 주소를 확인해 볼 것

정답 (D)

해설 대화 중반부에 남자가 여자의 문제와 관련해 청구서 발송 주소를 확인해 봤는지 물으면서 그것이 자신들이 있는 지사가 아니라 본사에 대한 것이어야 한다고(Have you checked the billing address you inputted? It needs to be for our headquarters, not our branch here) 알리고 있으므로 (D)가 정답입니다.

어휘 contact ~에 연락하다   manual 사용 설명서   verify ~을 확인하다, ~을 인증하다

Paraphrase   checked the billing address
⇒ Verifying an address

24. 남자가 "저는 매장 내에서 구입했어요"라고 말할 때 무엇을 암시하는가?
(A) 구매 증명서를 요구하고 있다.
(B) 자신이 왜 사무실에 있지 않은지 설명하고 있다.
(C) 대체 해결책을 제안하고 있다.
(D) 여자를 도울 방법이 확실치 않다.

정답 (D)

해설 대화 후반부에 여자가 온라인상의 오류 메시지가 정확히 무엇이 문제인지 명시하지 않고 있다고 밝히면서 남자에게 최근에 법인 카드를 이용한 게 맞는지(this error message isn't specifying what exactly the issue is. You used the company card recently, right?) 묻자, 남자가 '저는 매장 내에서 구입했어요'라고 대답하는 흐름입니다. 이는 남자가 회사 법인 카드로 매장에서 구입한 경험만 있기 때문에 온라인상의 결제와 관련된 문제를 해결할 방법을 알지 못한다는 뜻이므로 (D)가 정답입니다.

어휘 request ~을 요구하다, ~을 요청하다   proof 증명(서)   explain ~을 설명하다   alternative a. 대체의, 대안의 n. 대안   solution 해결책   how to do ~하는 방법

PART 4 FINAL TEST

1. (A)	2. (A)	3. (B)	4. (D)	5. (A)
6. (B)	7. (D)	8. (C)	9. (B)	10. (A)
11. (C)	12. (C)	13. (D)	14. (A)	15. (C)
16. (D)	17. (B)	18. (C)	19. (D)	20. (C)
21. (A)	22. (B)	23. (B)	24. (D)	

Questions 1-3 refer to the following excerpt from a meeting.

■ **Thank you for joining today's factory-wide meeting.** Before diving into our latest product development projects, I want to take a moment to recognize the hard work of our Operations Team. ■ **Their efforts in signing a contract with a logistics provider have made it easier for us to deliver our products across wider regions.** To ensure everyone is familiar with our new business partner, we'll be sending an informational e-mail later today. Now, ■ **let's review these designs we're considering for our new microwave.** We need to assess them together.

공장 전 직원을 대상으로 하는 오늘 회의 시간에 함께 주셔서 감사합니다. 우리의 최근 제품 개발 프로젝트들에 대한 이야기로 더 깊이 들어가기 전에, 잠시 시간을 갖고 우리 운영팀의 노고를 인정해 드리고 싶습니다. 물류 서비스 제공업체와 계약을 맺는 과정에서 이분들의 노력으로 인해 우리가 더 넓은 지역들에 걸쳐 우리 제품을 배송하는 일이 더 수월해졌습니다. 반드시 모든 분이 우리의 새 사업 제휴 업체에 익숙해지시도록 하기 위해, 오늘 이따가 정보 제공용 이메일을 보내 드릴 예정입니다. 이제, 우리의 새 전자레인지를 위해 우리가 고려하고 있는 이 디자인들을 살펴 보겠습니다. 우리가 함께 이것들을 평가해야 합니다.

어휘 join ~에 함께 하다, ~에 합류하다   factory-wide 공장 전체의   dive into ~에 대한 이야기로 더 깊이 들어가다   latest 최신의   development 개발, 발전   take a moment to do 잠시 시간을 갖고 ~하다   recognize ~을 인정하다, ~을 표창하다   operation 운영, 영업, 가동, 작동   effort 노력   sing a contract 계약을 맺다   logistics 물류(서비스), 실행 계획   A make it 형용사 for B to do: A로 인해 B가 ~하는 것이 … 되다   region 지역   ensure (that)

반드시 ~하도록 하다, ~임을 보장하다 **be familiar with** ~에 익숙하다, ~을 잘 알다 **informational** 정보를 제공하는 **review** v. ~을 살펴 보다, ~을 검토하다 n. 검토, 후기, 평가 **consider** ~을 고려하다 **microwave** 전자레인지 **assess** ~을 평가하다

1. 화자는 어디에 있을 것 같은가?
   (A) 제조 공장에
   (B) 공사 현장에
   (C) 화물선에
   (D) 배송 센터에

정답 (A)

해설 화자가 담화를 시작하면서 공장 전 직원을 대상으로 하는 회의 시간에 함께 하는 것에 대해 감사하다고(Thank you for joining today's factory-wide meeting) 인사하고 있으므로 (A)가 정답입니다.

2. 화자는 왜 팀의 공로를 인정해 주는가?
   (A) 그 팀이 유익한 제휴 관계를 확립했다.
   (B) 그 팀이 운영 지출 비용을 감소시켰다.
   (C) 시에서 허가증을 승인했다.
   (D) 그 책임자가 승진되었다.

정답 (A)

해설 담화 중반부에 화자가 운영팀을 언급하면서 물류 서비스 제공 업체와 계약을 맺는 과정에서 그 팀원들의 노력으로 인해 제품을 배송하는 일이 더 수월해진(Their efforts in signing a contract with a logistics provider have made it easier for us to deliver our products across wider regions) 사실을 언급하고 있습니다. 이는 회사 입장에서 더 유익한 계약 관계, 즉 사업 제휴 관계를 맺은 것에 해당하므로 (A)가 정답입니다.

어휘 **establish** ~을 확립하다 **beneficial** 유익한 **partnership** 제휴 관계 **reduce** ~을 감소시키다, ~을 줄이다 **expenditure** 지출 (비용), 경비 **grant** ~을 승인하다, ~을 주다 **permit** n. 허가증 v. ~을 허가하다 **promote** ~을 승진시키다, ~을 홍보하다, ~을 촉진하다

Paraphrase made it easier for us to deliver our products across wider regions ⇒ beneficial

3. 청자들은 무엇을 해야 하는가?
   (A) 이메일을 읽는 일
   (B) 몇몇 디자인을 살펴 보는 일
   (C) 한 명의 이름에 대해 투표하는 일
   (D) 웹사이트에 로그인하는 일

정답 (B)

해설 화자가 담화 후반부에 새 전자레인지를 위해 고려하고 있는 디자인들을 살펴 보겠다고(let's review these designs we're considering for our new microwave) 알리고 있으므로 (B)가 정답입니다.

어휘 **be required to do** ~해야 하다, ~할 필요가 있다 **look over** ~을 살펴 보다, ~을 검토하다 **vote** 투표하다 **sign-in** 로그인하다

Paraphrase review these designs
⇒ Look over some designs

Questions 4-6 refer to the following recorded message.

Hi, you've reached the production team for *Artist Insider*, the radio show that goes in depth on any and all musicians every week. **4** **If you'd like an artist to be featured on our show, we're always taking artist requests!** To submit one, press 3 to leave a message. **5** **Please include the artist's official stage name, country of origin, and why you like them. We will not consider entries without this information.** **6** **Your voice recording may be used during our broadcast, so make sure to speak clearly!**

안녕하세요, 귀하께서는 매주 누구든 모든 음악가에 관해 깊이 있게 살펴 보는 라디오 프로그램 <아티스트 인사이더>의 제작팀에 연락 주셨습니다. 한 아티스트가 저희 프로그램에서 특별 소개되기를 원하시는 경우, 저희는 항상 아티스트 관련 요청을 받고 있습니다! 요청 내용을 제출하시려면, 3번을 눌러 메시지를 남겨 주십시오. 해당 아티스트의 공식 무대명과 출생 국가, 그리고 왜 마음이 드시는지를 포함하시기 바랍니다. 저희가 이 정보 없이는 제출 사항을 고려할 수 없습니다. 귀하의 음성 녹음이 저희 방송 중에 이용될 수 있으므로, 반드시 명확히 말씀해 주시기 바랍니다!

어휘 **reach** ~에 연락하다 **production** 제작, 생산 **go in depth** 깊이 있게 살펴 보다 **would like A to do:** A가 ~하기를 원하다 **feature** v. ~을 특집으로 소개하다, ~을 특징으로 하다 n. 특징 **request** n. 요청, v. ~을 요청하다 **submit** ~을 제출하다 **leave** ~을 남기다 **include** ~을 포함하다 **official** 공식적인, 정식의 **consider** ~을 고려하다 **entry** 제출된 것, 출품작 **broadcast** n. 방송 v. ~을 방송하다 **make sure to do** 반드시 ~하도록 하다

4. 청자는 무엇을 하도록 요청 받는가?
   (A) 아티스트와 만나는 일
   (B) 스튜디오를 방문하는 일
   (C) 질문하는 일
   (D) 제출하는 일

정답 (D)

해설 화자가 담화 중반부에 한 아티스트가 화자의 프로그램에서 특별 소개되기를 원하는 경우에 항상 아티스트 관련 요청을 받고 있다고(If you'd like an artist to be featured on our show, we're always taking artist requests!) 알리고 있으므로 이에 해당하는 (D)가 정답입니다.

어휘 be invited to do ~하도록 요청 받다 submission 제출(물)

5. 화자가 어떤 가이드라인을 강조하는가?
(A) 구체적인 상세 정보를 제공하는 것
(B) 천천히 말하는 것
(C) 전화번호를 포함하는 것
(D) 온라인에서 등록하는 것

정답 (A)

해설 담화 중반부에 화자가 해당 아티스트의 공식 무대명과 출생국가, 그리고 왜 마음에 드는지를 포함하도록 요청하면서 그 정보 없이는 제출 사항을 고려할 수 없다고(Please include the artist's official stage name, country of origin, and why you like them. We will not consider entries without this information) 강조하고 있습니다. 이는 구체적인 정보를 제공하도록 강조하는 것이므로 (A)가 정답입니다.

어휘 specific 구체적인, 특정한 details 상세 정보, 세부 사항 register 등록하다

Paraphrase include the artist's official stage name, country of origin, and why you like them ⇒ Provide specific details

6. 화자의 말에 따르면, 방송 중에 무슨 일이 일어날 수 있는가?
(A) 후원 받은 제품이 광고될 것이다.
(B) 음성 녹음이 이용될 것이다.
(C) 특별 초대 손님을 인터뷰할 것이다.
(D) 신곡을 틀어 줄 것이다.

정답 (B)

해설 화자가 담화 맨 마지막 부분에 청자의 음성 녹음이 방송 중에 이용될 수 있기 때문에 반드시 명확히 말해 달라고(Your voice recording may be used during our broadcast, so make sure to speak clearly!) 당부하고 있으므로 (B)가 정답입니다.

어휘 sponsor ~을 후원하다 advertise ~을 광고하다

Paraphrase Your voice recording may be used ⇒ An audio recording will be used

---

Questions 7-9 refer to the following speech.

7 Welcome to Book Trove's first community reading festival! For decades, our bookstore has been known for offering consumers a wide selection of novels at affordable prices. While we've previously led reading campaigns and giveaways on social media, we've finally decided to create an in-person event and bring the simple joy of reading to life. **8 This free experience is our way of giving back to local residents.** Feel free to choose a book, find a comfortable seat or space, and relax! **9 If you can't find something you like, our knowledgeable associates are here to help and give recommendations.**

북 트로브의 첫 지역 사회 독서 축제에 오신 것을 환영합니다! 수십 년 동안, 저희 서점은 소비자들께 알맞은 가격으로 아주 다양한 소설을 제공하는 것으로 알려져 왔습니다. 저희가 전에는 소셜미디어에서 독서 캠페인과 증정 행사를 진행해 왔지만, 마침내 직접 참여하는 행사를 만들어 독서의 단순한 즐거움에 활기를 불어넣기로 결정했습니다. 이 무료 경험은 저희가 지역 주민들께 보답해 드리는 방식입니다. 부담 갖지 마시고 책을 한 권 선택해, 편안한 자리나 공간을 찾으신 다음, 느긋한 시간을 보내 보십시오! 마음에 드시는 것을 찾으실 수 없는 경우, 풍부한 지식을 갖춘 저희 직원들이 도와 드리고 추천해 드리기 위해 자리하고 있습니다.

어휘 community 지역 사회, 지역 공동체 decade 10년 be known for ~로 알려져 있다 offer A B: A에게 B를 제공하다 consumer 소비자 a wide selection of 아주 다양한 affordable (가격이) 알맞은, 저렴한 previously 이전에, 과거에 lead ~을 진행하다, ~을 이끌다 giveaway 증정 (행사), 증정품 decide to do ~하기로 결정하다 in-person 직접 가서 하는 bring A to life: A에 활기를 불어넣다 free 무료의 give back to ~에게 보답하다 local 지역의, 현지의 resident 주민 Feel free to do 부담 갖지 말고 ~하세요, 마음껏 ~하세요 choose ~을 선택하다 comfortable 편안한, 편한 relax 느긋한 시간을 보내다 knowledgeable 지식이 풍부한, 박식한 associate n. 직원, 동료, 동업자

7. 어떤 종류의 행사가 개최되는가?
(A) 미술 공예 박람회
(B) 지역 사회 경연대회
(C) 음악 공연
(D) 지역 축제

정답 (D)

해설 화자가 담화를 시작하면서 북 트로브의 첫 지역 사회 독서 축제에 온 것을 환영한다고(Welcome to Book Trove's first community reading festival!) 인사하는 부분을 통해 지역 축제 행사장임을 알 수 있으므로 (D)가 정답입니다.

어휘 take place 개최되다, 진행되다, 발생하다 arts-and-crafts 미술 공예의 fair 박람회, 축제 마당 performance 공연, 연주(회), 성과, 수행 (능력)

Paraphrase community reading festival
⇒ A local festival

8. 왜 회사가 변화를 주었는가?
(A) 몇몇 시 규정을 충족하기 위해
(B) 자사의 서비스를 홍보하기 위해
(C) 지역 사회 구성원들을 지원하기 위해
(D) 자사의 브랜드 이미지를 업그레이드하기 위해

정답 (C)
해설 담화 중반부에 화자가 축제를 개최하는 목적과 관련해 그 경험이 지역 주민들에게 보답하는 방식이라고 (This free experience is our way of giving back to local residents) 설명하고 있습니다. 이는 지역 주민들에게 일종의 서비스를 지원하는 방식에 해당하므로 (C)가 정답입니다.

어휘 make a change 변화를 주다, 변경하다 meet (조건 등) ~을 충족하다 regulation 규정, 규제 promote ~을 홍보하다, ~을 촉진하다, ~을 승진시키다 support ~을 지원하다, ~을 지지하다, ~을 후원하다

Paraphrase giving back to local residents
⇒ support community members

9. 청자들은 왜 직원과 이야기해야 하는가?
(A) 양식에 서명하기 위해
(B) 제안을 받기 위해
(C) 좌석을 찾기 위해
(D) 물품을 빌리기 위해

정답 (B)
해설 담화 맨 마지막 부분에 화자가 마음에 드는 것을 찾지 못하는 경우에 풍부한 지식을 갖춘 직원들이 도움도 주고 추천도 해 준다고(If you can't find something you like, our knowledgeable associates are here to help and give recommendations) 알리고 있습니다. 이는 직원들이 마음에 들만한 것을 제안해 주는 방식을 의미하므로 (B)가 정답입니다.

어휘 sign ~에 서명하다 form 양식, 서식 receive ~을 받다 suggestion 제안, 의견 borrow ~을 빌리다

Paraphrase give recommendations
⇒ receive a suggestion

Questions 10-12 refer to the following podcast.

Let me begin today's podcast with a story of my own. As you may know, 10 **I help plan big events for a living**. Over the years, I've worked with a lot of different people. I remember one celebrity dinner I managed, where I was so proud to get a very popular band to perform. But when they arrived, they didn't bring any microphones! So, we had to improvise. 11 **That experience taught me how crucial it is to effectively communicate with external partners in every business agreement.** 12 **That's the topic of Elena Hartman's latest book, which I'm going to give my thoughts on next.**

제 자신의 이야기로 오늘 팟캐스트를 시작해 보겠습니다. 아실지 모르겠지만, 저는 대규모 행사를 계획하는 것을 돕는 일을 업으로 삼고 있습니다. 수년 동안에 걸쳐, 저는 많은 다른 사람들과 일해 왔습니다. 제가 총괄했던 한 유명 인사의 저녁 만찬 행사가 기억이 나는데, 이곳에서 아주 인기 있는 한 밴드를 공연하게 한 것이 아주 자랑스러웠습니다. 하지만 이분들이 도착했을 때, 어떤 마이크도 가져오지 않았습니다! 그래서, 저희는 즉흥적으로 해야 했습니다. 그 경험은 저에게 모든 비즈니스 관련 계약에 있어 외부의 제휴 업체들과 효과적으로 의사 소통하는 것이 얼마나 중대한지 가르쳐 주었습니다. 이것이 바로 엘리나 하트먼 씨의 최신 도서에 담긴 주제이며, 이 도서에 관한 제 생각은 다음 순서로 전해 드리겠습니다.

어휘 help do ~하는 것을 돕다 for a living 업으로 삼아, 생계를 위해 celebrity 유명 인사 be proud to do ~해서 자랑스럽다 get A to do: A에게 ~하게 하다 perform 공연하다, 연주하다 arrive 도착하다 improvise 즉흥적으로 하다, 즉석에서 만들다 crucial 중대한, 아주 중요한 effectively 효과적으로 communicate with ~와 의사 소통하다 external 외부의 agreement 계약(서), 합의(서) thought n. 생각

10. 화자는 무엇을 생계로 일한다고 말하는가?
(A) 행사를 편성한다.
(B) 업체를 총괄한다.
(C) 라이브 음악을 공연한다.
(D) 구직 지원자들을 면접 본다.

정답 (A)
해설 화자가 담화 초반부에 대규모 행사를 계획하는 것을 돕는 일을 업으로 삼고 있다고(I help plan big events for a living) 밝히고 있으므로 (A)가 정답입니다.

어휘 coordinate ~을 편성하다, ~을 조정하다 oversee ~을 총괄하다, ~을 감독하다 candidate 지원자, 후보자

Paraphrase plan big events ⇒ coordinates events

235

11. 화자가 "저희는 즉흥적으로 해야 했습니다"라고 말할 때 무엇을 암시하는가?
(A) 관객들이 크게 실망했다.
(B) 그는 도움을 받기 위해 전문가에게 전화하려고 했다.
(C) 의사 소통상의 오류가 있었다.
(D) 그가 회사 정책을 반복하는 것을 잊었다.

정답 (C)

해설 화자가 담화 중반부에 한 밴드가 마이크를 가져오지 않은 사실과 함께 '저희는 즉흥적으로 해야 했습니다'라고 말한 뒤로 그 경험이 모든 비즈니스 관련 계약에 있어 외부의 제휴 업체들과 효과적으로 의사 소통하는 것이 얼마나 중대한지 가르쳐 주었다고(That experience taught me how crucial it is to effectively communicate with external partners in every business agreement) 강조하고 있습니다. 이는 의사 소통상의 문제로 인해 마이크를 가져오지 않은 문제가 발생했음을 뜻하는 것이므로 (C)가 정답입니다.

어휘 try to do ~하려고 하다 for (목적) ~을 위해 reiterate 반복하다

12. 청자들은 곧이어 무엇을 들을 것 같은가?
(A) 전문적인 분석
(B) 뉴스 보도
(C) 후기
(D) 광고

정답 (C)

해설 담화 맨 마지막 부분에 화자가 엘리나 하트먼 씨의 최신 도서에 담긴 주제임을 언급하면서 그 도서에 관한 자신의 생각을 다음 순서로 전해 주겠다고(That's the topic of Elena Hartman's latest book, which I'm going to give my thoughts on next) 알리고 있습니다. 따라서, 그 도서를 읽은 후의 후기를 이야기할 것으로 볼 수 있으므로 (C)가 정답입니다.

어휘 expert 전문적인 analysis 분석

Paraphrase the topic of Elena Hartman's latest book / my thoughts ⇒ A review

Questions 13-15 refer to the following announcement.

Good afternoon, folks. Sorry for the slight delay in beginning the hiking tour – **13 there's been an issue with the guide's earlier group running slightly over time**. While waiting for them to wrap up, please help yourselves to some free juice and snacks at the visitor center entrance. **14 Be sure to have your water bottles all filled up** before we head out, too. **15 The first highlight of the hike will be the old stone tower, and the guide will tell you all about the fascinating legends surrounding it.**

안녕하세요, 여러분. 하이킹 투어를 시작하는 데 있어 약간의 지연 문제에 대해 사과 드리며, 가이드의 앞선 그룹이 약간 시간을 초과해 진행되는 문제가 있었습니다. 그분들이 마무리되기를 기다리시는 동안, 방문객 센터 입구에서 무료 주스와 간식을 마음껏 드시기 바랍니다. 출발하기에 앞서 꼭 여러분의 물병도 모두 가득 채워 놓으시기 바랍니다. 이번 하이킹의 첫 번째 하이라이트는 오래된 석탑이며, 가이드가 그곳을 둘러싼 매혹적인 전설에 관해 모두 이야기해 드릴 것입니다.

어휘 folks 사람들 slight 약간의, 조금의 delay n. 지연, 지체 v. ~을 지연시키다 issue 문제, 사안 run 진행되다, 운영되다 wrap up 마무리되다 help yourselves to ~을 마음껏 드세요 be sure to do 꼭 ~하다 have A p.p.: A를 ~되게 하다 fill up ~을 가득 채우다 head out 출발하다, 밖으로 향하다 fascinating 매혹적인, 아주 흥미로운 legend 전설 surround ~을 둘러싸다

13. 투어가 왜 지연되었는가?
(A) 등산로가 치워지고 있다.
(B) 일정 관리상의 오류가 있었다.
(C) 일부 방문객들이 장비를 잊었다.
(D) 앞선 투어가 늦게 끝나고 있다.

정답 (D)

해설 화자가 담화를 시작하면서 지연 문제에 대한 사과의 말과 함께 가이드의 앞선 그룹이 약간 시간을 초과해 진행되는 문제가 생긴(there's been an issue with the guide's earlier group running slightly over time) 사실을 알리고 있으므로 (D)가 정답입니다.

어휘 trail 등산로, 산길 clear ~을 치우다, ~을 깨끗하게 하다 scheduling 일정 관리 forget ~을 잊다 equipment 장비 previous 앞선, 이전의, 과거의

Paraphrase the guide's earlier group running slightly over time ⇒ A previous tour is ending late

14. 청자들은 무엇을 하도록 상기되는가?
(A) 물병을 가득 채우는 일
(B) 자외선 차단제를 바르는 일
(C) 약간의 음식을 구입하는 일
(D) 방문객 센터를 둘러 보는 일

정답 (A)

해설 담화 중반부에 화자가 출발하기 전에 물병을 모두 가득 채워 놓으라고(Be sure to have your water bottles all filled up) 상기시키고 있으므로 (A)가 정답입니다.

어휘 be reminded to do ~하도록 상기되다 sun protection 자외선 차단제 explore ~을 둘러 보다, ~을 탐방하다

Paraphrase have your water bottles all filled up
⇒ Fill their water bottles

15. 가이드는 무엇에 관해 먼저 이야기할 것인가?
(A) 하이킹 지속 시간
(B) 토종 식물
(C) 탑에 관한 이야기
(D) 인기 있고 경치 좋은 지점

정답 (C)

해설 담화 마지막 부분에 화자가 하이킹의 첫 번째 하이라이트가 오래된 석탑이며 가이드가 그곳을 둘러싼 매혹적인 전설에 관해 모두 이야기해 줄 것이라고(The first highlight of the hike will be the old stone tower, and the guide will tell you all about the fascinating legends surrounding it) 알리고 있으므로 (C)가 정답입니다.

어휘 duration 지속 시간[기간] native 토종의 scenic 경치 좋은 viewpoint 보는 지점, 관점

Paraphrase the old stone tower / the fascinating legends surrounding it
⇒ Stories about a tower

Questions 16-18 refer to the following telephone message.

Hi, this is Alan. **16** I'm reaching out about the latest curtain designs your team submitted. The ones with lace finishes are absolutely stunning, and I'm confident those will get approval for production in a range of colors. The flower-themed patterns are also very beautiful. **17** Your team did an amazing job with the details on those designs. However, **18** for the polka-dot patterns you sent – the issue is – many customers don't tend to prefer them. Please call me back so we can discuss this further.

안녕하세요, 저는 앨런입니다. 귀하의 팀에서 제출해 주신 최근의 커튼 디자인과 관련해 연락 드립니다. 레이스 마감 처리가 된 것들이 전적으로 굉장히 아름다워서, 이것들이 다양한 색상으로 생산되도록 승인될 것으로 확신합니다. 꽃을 주제로 한 패턴들도 아주 아름답습니다. 귀하의 팀이 그 디자인상의 세부 사항에 대해 놀라운 작업을 해주셨습니다. 하지만, 보내 주신 폴카 도트 패턴에 대해서는, 그 문제가, 많은 고객께서 그것을 선호하시지 않는 경향이 있습니다. 이 부분을 추가로 논의할 수 있도록 제게 다시 전화 주십시오.

어휘 reach out 연락하다 submit ~을 제출하다 finish n. 마감(처리) absolutely 전적으로, 완전히 stunning 굉장히 아름다운, 정말 멋진 be confident (that) ~임을 확신하다 approval 승인 production 생산, 제작 a range of 다양한 A-themed: A를 주제로 한 details 세부 사항, 상세 정보 however 하지만, 그러나 issue 문제, 사안 tend to do ~하는 경향이 있다 prefer ~을 선호하다 call A back: A에게 다시 전화하다 discuss ~을 논의하다, ~을 이야기하다 further ad. 추가로, 한층 더 a. 추가적인, 한층 더 한

16. 화자의 회사는 무엇을 판매하는가?
(A) 담요
(B) 꽃
(C) 카펫
(D) 커튼

정답 (D)

해설 화자가 담화 초반부에 청자가 속한 팀에서 제출한 커튼 디자인과 관련해 연락한다고(I'm reaching out about the latest curtain designs your team submitted) 언급한 뒤로, 그것을 칭찬하면서 생산 가능성에 대해 이야기하고 있으므로 (D)가 정답입니다.

17. 화자는 청자의 팀과 관련해 무엇을 칭찬하는가?
(A) 실현 가능성에 대한 강조
(B) 세부 요소에 대한 주의력
(C) 독특한 접근법
(D) 책임감

정답 (B)

해설 화자가 담화 중반부에 청자의 팀을 칭찬하면서 디자인상의 세부 사항에 대해 놀라운 작업을 했다고(Your team did an amazing job with the details on those designs) 알리고 있습니다. 이는 세부 요소에 대해 신경 써서 작업한 것을 칭찬하는 말이므로 (B)가 정답입니다.

어휘 praise ~을 칭찬하다 emphasis 강조 practicality 실현 가능성, 실질적인 측면 attention 주의(력), 관심, 주목 unique 독특한, 특별한 approach n. 접근(법) v. 접근하다

sense ~감, 감각, 의식 responsibility 책임, 책무

Paraphrase did an amazing job with the details
⇒ attention to detail

18. 화자가 왜 "많은 고객들께서 그것을 선호하시지 않는 경향이 있습니다"라고 말하는가?
(A) 한 제품의 품질이 부족하다.
(B) 소비자 경향이 계속 바뀌어 오고 있다.
(C) 한 가지 디자인이 아마 이용되지 않을 것이다.
(D) 설문 조사에서 놀라운 결과가 드러났다.

정답 (C)

해설 화자가 담화 후반부에 청자가 보낸 폴카 도트 패턴에 문제가 있음을(for the polka-dot patterns you sent - the issue is -) 언급하면서 '많은 고객들께서 그것을 선호하시지 않는 경향이 있습니다'라고 말하는 흐름입니다. 따라서, 고객들이 선호하지 않는 폴카 도트 패턴이 이용되지 않을 것임을 알 수 있으므로 (C)가 정답입니다.

어휘 quality 품질, 질 lacking 부족한 trend 경향, 추세, 유행 likely 아마 survey 설문 조사(지) reveal ~을 드러내다, ~을 밝히다 surprising (사람을) 놀라게 하는 result 결과(물)

Questions 19-21 refer to the following podcast.

Welcome back to the *Future Makers* podcast! For those who've been listening to us for a while, today's guest may sound familiar — she joined us for an episode last summer. **19** **Product designer Vanessa Kim has returned to discuss 20 how 3D printing machines are being adopted by small businesses** to create customized, practical products. These machines have become simplified for home usage, making them very accessible nowadays. Before we begin, a quick heads-up: **21** **we will now be uploading full videos of our episodes so that listeners can engage with us visually.**

<퓨처 메이커스> 팟캐스트를 다시 찾아 주신 것을 환영합니다! 한동안 저희 방송을 계속 청취해 오고 계시는 분들께는, 오늘 초대 손님이 익숙하게 들리실 수 있는데, 이분께서 지난 여름에 한 방송분을 위해 저희와 함께 해 주셨습니다. 제품 디자이너이신 바네사 킴 씨께서 3D 프린팅 기계들이 어떻게 맞춤 제작되는 실용적인 제품들을 만들기 위해 소기업들에 의해 채택되고 있는지 이야기해 주시기 위해 다시 찾아 주셨습니다. 이 기계들이 가정용으로 간소화되어 오면서, 요즘 아주 이용하기 쉬워졌습니다. 시작하기에 앞서, 간단한 공지 사항을 말씀 드리자면, 청취자들께서 시각적으로 저희와 교류하실 수 있도록 이제 저희 방송분의 전체 동영상을 업로드할 예정입니다.

어휘 those who ~하는 사람들 for a while 한동안 sound + 형용사: ~하게 들리다, ~한 것 같다 familiar 익숙한, 잘 아는 join ~와 함께 하다, ~에 합류하다 episode 1회 방송분 adopt ~을 채택하다 create ~을 만들어 내다 customized 맞춤 제작되는 practical 실용적인, 현실적인 simplified 간소화된 make A 형용사: A를 ~하게 만들다 accessible 이용 가능한, 접근 가능한 heads-up 공지, 알림 so that (목적) ~하도록, (결과) 그래서, 그러므로 engage with ~와 교류하다, ~와 소통하다 visually 시각적으로

19. 바네사 킴 씨는 누구인가?
(A) 정비사
(B) 미술가
(C) 기자
(D) 디자이너

정답 (D)

해설 화자가 담화 중반부에 바네사 킴 씨를 소개하면서 제품 디자이너라고(Product designer Vanessa Kim) 언급하고 있으므로 (D)가 정답입니다.

20. 오늘 팟캐스트 방송분의 중점은 무엇인가?
(A) 도서 출판
(B) 주택 개조
(C) 프린팅 기계
(D) 가상 비서

정답 (C)

해설 화자가 담화 중반부에 오늘 초대 손님인 바네사 킴 씨가 3D 프린팅 기계들이 어떻게 소기업들에 의해 채택되고 있는지에 관해(how 3D printing machines are being adopted by small businesses) 이야기할 것이라고 알리고 있으므로 (C)가 정답입니다.

어휘 improvement 개조, 개선, 향상 virtual 가상의 assistant 비서, 보조, 조수

21. 화자는 청자들에게 무엇을 알리는가?
(A) 새로운 시각적 콘텐츠
(B) 전용 상품
(C) 구독 프로그램
(D) 구직 기회

정답 (A)

해설 화자가 담화 맨 마지막 부분에 청취자들이 시각적으로 자신들과 교류할 수 있도록 방송분의 전체 동영상을 업로드할 예정이라고(we will now be uploading full videos of our episodes so that listeners can engage with us visually) 밝히고 있으므로 (A)가 정답입니다.

어휘 alert A to B: A에게 B를 알리다 exclusive 전용의, 독점적인 merchandise 상품 subscription (서비스

등의) 구독, 가입 opportunity 기회

Paraphrase full videos / engage with us visually
⇒ visual content

Questions 22-24 refer to the following excerpt from a meeting and floor plan.

Soon, we'll be introducing a new line of cultural heritage artwork to feature in the gallery. This will be our first time showcasing art from various cultures, so **22** **I'm confident these pieces will help increase our visitor numbers.** The creators will send us everything we need within the next few days. **23** **I'd like to arrange the new exhibit near the front entrance, which means we'll need to move the current display to make room.** If anyone can help out for a few hours after closing on Sunday, **24** **I'll buy dinner that night.**

곧, 우리 미술관에서 특별히 선보일 새로운 라인의 문화 유산 예술품을 소개할 예정입니다. 이는 우리가 처음으로 다양한 문화권의 예술을 선보이는 것이기 때문에, 저는 이 작품들이 우리 방문객 숫자를 늘리는 데 도움이 될 것으로 확신합니다. 창작자들께서 앞으로 며칠 내에 우리가 필요로 하는 모든 것을 보내 주실 것입니다. 저는 정면 입구 근처에 새로운 전시회 자리를 마련하고자 하며, 이는 우리가 공간을 확보하기 위해 현재의 전시품을 옮겨야 할 것임을 의미합니다. 누구든 일요일에 문을 닫은 후에 몇 시간 동안 도와 주실 수 있는 경우, 제가 그날 밤에 저녁을 사 드리겠습니다.

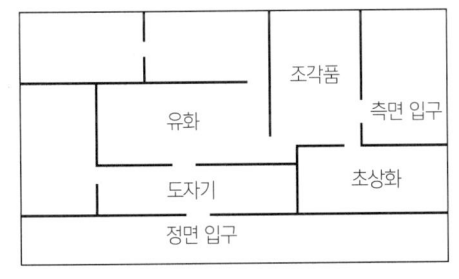

어휘 introduce ~을 소개하다, ~을 도입하다 line 제품 라인, 제품군 cultural heritage 문화 유산 artwork 예술품 feature v. ~을 특별히 선보이다, ~을 특징으로 하다 n. 특징 showcase ~을 선보이다 be confident (that) ~임을 확신하다 piece (글, 그림, 음악 등의) 작품 help do ~하는 데 도움이 되다 increase ~을 늘리다, ~을 증가시키다 creator 창작자 would like to do ~하고자 하다, ~하고 싶다 arrange ~을 마련하다, ~을 조치하다 exhibit 전시회, 전시품 will need to do ~해야 할 것이다 current 현재의 display n. 전시(품), 진열(품) v. ~을 전시하다, ~을 진열하다 make room 공간을 확보하다 help out 도와

주다 oil painting 유화 sculpture 조각품 ceramic 도자기 portrait 초상화

22. 회의는 왜 개최되고 있는가?
(A) 행사 개최 장소를 논의하기 위해
(B) 방문객 숫자를 개선하기 위해
(C) 몇몇 예술가를 기리기 위해
(D) 교대 근무 일정을 업데이트하기 위해

정답 (B)

해설 담화 초반부에 화자가 새로운 예술품을 선보이는 전시회를 언급하면서 방문객 숫자를 늘리는 데 도움이 될 것으로 확신한다고(I'm confident these pieces will help increase our visitor numbers) 언급하고 있으므로 (B)가 정답입니다.

어휘 take place 개최되다, 진행되다, 발생하다 venue 개최 장소, 행사장 improve ~을 개선하다 honor v. ~을 기리다, ~에게 영예를 주다 n. 영예, 영광 shift 교대 근무(조)

23. 시각자료를 보시오. 어느 미술품이 일요일에 옮겨질 것인가?
(A) 유화
(B) 도자기
(C) 조각품
(D) 초상화

정답 (B)

해설 화자가 담화 중반부에 정면 입구 근처에 새로운 전시회 자리를 마련하고 싶다고 알리면서 공간을 확보하기 위해 현재의 전시품을 옮기는 일을 일요일에 할 생각임을(I'd like to arrange the new exhibit near the front entrance, which means we'll need to move the current display to make room. If anyone can help out for a few hours after closing on Sunday) 밝히고 있습니다. 시각자료에서 정면 입구와 가까운 곳에 Ceramics로 표기되어 있으므로 (B)가 정답입니다.

24. 화자는 무엇을 할 것이라고 말하는가?
(A) 레스토랑에 연락하는 일
(B) 추가 보상을 제공하는 일
(C) 초대장을 발송하는 일
(D) 식사 비용을 충당해 주는 일

정답 (D)

해설 화자가 담화 맨 마지막 부분에 일요일에 도와 주는 사람에게 저녁 식사를 사겠다고(I'll buy dinner that night) 알리고 있으므로 (D)가 정답입니다.

어휘 contact ~에 연락하다 extra 추가의, 별도의 compensation 보상(금) invitation 초대(장) cover (비용 등) ~을 충당하다, ~을 포함하다 expense (지출) 비용, 경비

Paraphrase buy dinner ⇒ Cover meal expenses

PART 5 FINAL TEST 1

1. (A)	2. (B)	3. (A)	4. (A)	5. (D)
6. (B)	7. (C)	8. (A)	9. (C)	10. (A)
11. (B)	12. (D)	13. (B)	14. (C)	15. (D)
16. (B)	17. (D)	18. (D)	19. (C)	20. (C)

1.
정답 (A)
해석 그 박물관의 최근 전시회는 전국 각지에서 수만 명의 미술 애호가들을 끌어들였다.
해설 문장의 동사 has attracted 앞에 소유격 The museum's 와 형용사 recent만 쓰여 있으므로 빈칸은 이 둘의 수식을 받으면서 주어 역할을 할 명사 자리입니다. 또한, 단수동사 has attracted와 수 일치되는 단수명사가 주어로 쓰여야 하므로 (A) exhibit이 정답입니다.
오답 (B) exhibiting: 동명사 또는 현재분사의 형태이며, 동명사가 주어 역할은 할 수 있지만 소유격의 수식을 받을 수 없으므로 오답입니다.
(C) exhibited: 동사의 과거형 또는 과거분사형이므로 명사 자리인 빈칸에 쓰일 수 없는 오답입니다.
(D) exhibits: 복수명사의 형태이므로 주어 자리에 쓰이면 단수동사와 수 일치되지 않으므로 오답입니다.
어휘 recent 최근의 attract ~을 끌어들이다 tens of thousands of 수만 명의, 수만 개의 exhibit n. 전시회, 전시품 v. ~을 전시하다

2.
정답 (B)
해석 분기 판매량 수치가 매달 말일에 이메일로 이사회 임원들에게 보내집니다
해설 빈칸 앞에 위치한 The quarterly sales figures가 복수명사 구이므로 수 일치되는 복수동사의 형태인 (B) are가 정답입니다.
오답 (A) is: 복수명사구 주어와 수 일치되지 않는 단수동사이므로 오답입니다.
(C) was: 복수명사구 주어와 수 일치되지 않는 단수동사이므로 오답입니다.
(D) has: 복수명사구 주어와 수 일치되지 않는 단수동사이므로 오답입니다.
어휘 quarterly 분기의 sales 판매(량), 영업, 매출 figure 수치, 숫자 board 이사회, 이사진

3.
정답 (A)
해석 처리 지연 문제를 피하기 위해 마감 기한 전에 사무용품 주문 양식을 제출하는 것이 필수적입니다.
해설 '~하는 것이 하는 것이 필수적이다'를 의미하는 가주어/진주어 구문 「It is essential + to do」를 구성해야 알맞으므로 진주어 역할을 하는 to부정사 (A) to submit이 정답입니다.
오답 (B) submit: 가주어/진주어 구문에서 진주어 역할을 할 수 없는 동사원형이므로 오답입니다.
(C) submitted: 가주어/진주어 구문에서 진주어 역할을 할 수 없는 과거형 또는 과거분사형이므로 오답입니다.
(D) submitting: 가주어/진주어 구문에서 진주어 역할을 할 수 없는 동명사 또는 현재분사의 형태이므로 오답입니다.
어휘 essential 필수적인 supply 용품, 공급(품) order 주문(품) form 양식, 서식 deadline 마감 기한 avoid ~을 피하다 processing 처리 delay 지연, 지체

4.
정답 (A)
해석 스무 명의 사람들로 구성된 팀이 그 모바일 앱을 고안했지만, 그들 중 오직 두 사람만 잠재 투자자들을 대상으로 발표를 실시할 것이다.
해설 전치사 of의 목적어 역할을 할 수 있으면서 앞서 언급된 twenty people을 가리킬 목적격대명사가 필요하므로 (A) them이 정답입니다.
오답 (B) they: 전치사의 목적어 역할을 할 수 없는 주격대명사이므로 오답입니다.
(C) their: 전치사의 목적어 역할을 할 수 없는 소유격대명사이므로 오답입니다.
(D) theirs: 전치사의 목적어 역할은 할 수 있지만, '그들의 것'을 뜻하는 소유대명사로서 twenty people 자체를 가리키지 않으므로 오답입니다.
어휘 conduct ~을 실시하다, ~을 수행하다 presentation 발표(회) potential 잠재적인 investor 투자자

5.
정답 (D)
해석 건축가가 고객의 의견을 받은 뒤로 몇 가지 중요한 변경이 건물 설계도 초안에 이뤄졌다.
해설 문장의 동사 were made 앞에 두 개의 형용사 Several과 significant만 쓰여 있으므로 빈칸은 이 둘의 수식을 받으면서 주어 역할을 할 명사 자리입니다. 따라서 선택지에서 유일하게 명사인 (D) alterations가 정답입니다.
오답 (A) alter: 동사이므로 명사 자리인 빈칸에 쓰일 수 없는 오답입니다.
(B) altered: 동사의 과거형 또는 과거분사형이므로 명사 자리인 빈칸에 쓰일 수 없는 오답입니다.

(C) altering: 동명사 또는 현재분사의 형태이며, 동명사가 주어 역할은 할 수 있지만 형용사의 수식을 받을 수 없으므로 오답입니다.

어휘 **several** 몇몇의, 여럿의 **significant** 중요한, 상당한, 많은 **first draft** 초안 **blueprint** 설계도, 청사진 **architect** 건축가 **receive** ~을 받다 **feedback** 의견 **alter** ~을 변경하다, ~을 개조하다, ~을 수선하다 **alteration** 변경, 개조, 수선

6.

정답 (B)

해석 고객 서비스부에 곧장 연락하시는 것이 결함 제품을 교환하시는 데 필요한 시간을 크게 줄일 수 있습니다.

해설 문장에 이미 조동사 can과 동사 reduce가 있으므로 빈칸은 동사 자리가 아닙니다. 또한, 빈칸 뒤에 위치한 명사구 the customer service department를 목적어로 취함과 동시에 부사 directly의 수식을 받을 수 있는 동명사가 빈칸에 쓰여 문장의 주어 역할을 하는 동명사구를 구성해야 알맞으므로 (B) Contacting이 정답입니다.

오답 (A) Contact: 동사 자리가 아닌 빈칸에 쓰일 수 없는 동사원형이므로 오답입니다.
(C) Contracts: 복수명사 형태의 경우, 뒤에 명사 목적어를 가질 수 없으므로 오답입니다.
(D) Contacted: 주어 역할을 할 수 없는 동사의 과거형 또는 과거분사형이므로 오답입니다.

어휘 **department** ~부, 부서 **directly** 곧장, 바로 **greatly** 크게, 대단히, 매우 **reduce** ~을 줄이다, ~을 감소시키다 **require** ~을 필요로 하다 **exchange** ~을 교환하다 **defective** 결함이 있는 **contact** ~에 연락하다

7.

정답 (C)

해석 모든 결함 제품은 품질 보증 관리팀에 의해 즉시 조립 라인에서 제외됩니다.

해설 결함이 있는 제품이 사람에 의해 제외되는 것이므로 이러한 수동의 의미를 나타낼 수 있도록 타동사 remove가 수동태로 쓰여야 알맞습니다. 따라서 선택지에서 유일하게 수동태인 (C) are removed가 정답입니다.

오답 (A) remove: 능동태 동사이므로 오답입니다.
(B) removed: 능동태 동사이므로 오답입니다.
(D) removes: 능동태 동사이므로 오답입니다.

어휘 **faulty** 결함이 있는 **assembly** 조립 **immediately** 즉시 **quality assurance** 품질 보증 **remove** ~을 없애다, ~을 제거하다

8.

정답 (A)

해석 공장 직원들에게 조립 라인 기계들 중 어떤 것이든 작동하기 전에 안전 장비를 착용하도록 상기시켜 주시기 바랍니다.

해설 빈칸 앞에 위치한 명사 factory는 무언가를 하도록 상기시키는 remind의 대상으로 맞지 않습니다. 따라서 factory와 복합명사를 구성해 동사 remind의 목적어로서 상기시키는 대상이 될 수 있는 사람을 나타낼 명사가 쓰여야 알맞으므로 (A) employees가 정답입니다.

오답 (B) employ: 동사이므로 명사 factory와 복합명사를 구성해 동사 remind의 목적어 역할을 할 수 없는 오답입니다.
(C) employment: 명사이기는 하지만, 상기시키는 대상이 되는 사람을 나타내는 명사가 아니므로 오답입니다.
(D) employing: 동명사이며, 명사 factory와 복합명사를 구성하지 않으므로 오답입니다.

어휘 **remind A to do:** A에게 ~하도록 상기시키다 **put on** (동작) ~을 착용하다 **gear** 장비 **operate** ~을 작동하다, ~을 가동하다, ~을 운영하다 **assembly** 조립 **employment** 고용, 채용, 취업 **employ** ~을 고용하다

9.

정답 (C)

해석 재무이사는 다음 분기의 수익 예상에 관한 전체 보고서를 준비하실 생각이다.

해설 빈칸 앞에 위치한 동사 intend는 to부정사를 목적어로 취해 '~할 생각이다, ~할 작정이다'라는 의미를 나타내므로 (C) to prepare가 정답입니다.

오답 (A) prepares: 동사 intend의 목적어 역할을 할 수 없는 동사의 형태이므로 오답입니다.
(B) preparing: 동사 intend의 목적어 역할을 할 수 없는 동명사 또는 현재분사의 형태이므로 오답입니다.
(D) prepared: 동사 intend의 목적어 역할을 할 수 없는 과거형 또는 과거분사형이므로 오답입니다.

어휘 **finance** 재무, 재정, 금융 **intend to do** ~할 생각이다, ~할 작정이다 **full** 전체의, 모든, 완전한, 최대의 **quarter** 분기 **revenue** 수익 **projection** 예상 **prepare** ~을 준비하다

10.

정답 (A)

해석 리베라 씨에게 그분의 항공편 일정표가 오늘 오전에 그분께 보내졌다고 알려 주시기 바랍니다.

해설 전치사 to의 목적어로서 앞서 언급된 Ms. Rivera를 가리킬 목적격대명사가 쓰여야 알맞으므로 (A) her가 정답입니다.

오답 (B) she: 전치사의 목적어 역할을 할 수 없는 주격대명사이므로 오답입니다.
(C) hers: 전치사의 목적어 역할은 할 수 있지만, '그녀의 것'을 뜻하는 소유대명사로서 Ms. Rivera 자체를 가리키지

않으므로 오답입니다.

(D) herself: 전치사의 목적어 역할은 할 수 있지만, 행위 주체와 대상이 동일인일 때 사용하는 재귀대명사이므로 문장의 의미에 맞지 않는 오답입니다

어휘 inform A that: A에게 ~라고 알리다 itinerary 일정(표)

11.
정답 (B)

해석 그 도시 개발 계획의 완료는 세 부서 사이의 조화를 필요로 할 것입니다.

해설 정관사 The와 전치사 of 사이에 위치한 빈칸은 The의 수식을 받을 명사 자리이므로 (B) completion이 정답입니다.

오답 (A) complete: 명사 자리에 쓰일 수 없는 동사이므로 오답입니다.
(C) completely: 명사 자리에 쓰일 수 없는 부사이므로 오답입니다.
(D) completing: 동명사 또는 현재분사이며, 동명사는 관사의 수식을 받을 수 없으므로 오답입니다.

어휘 urban 도시의 development 개발, 발전 require ~을 필요로 하다 coordination 조화, 조정, 편성 among ~ 사이에서, ~ 중에서 department 부서, ~부 complete ~을 완료하다 completion 완료, 완성 completely 완전히, 전적으로

12.
정답 (D)

해석 인사부의 여러 직원들이 부재 중인 것으로 인해 라일 씨는 직접 오리엔테이션 시간을 진행하겠다고 제안했다.

해설 빈칸 앞에 주어와 동사(has offered), 그리고 to부정사구로 이어지는 완전한 절이 쓰여 있고, 빈칸 뒤에는 전치사구만 있으므로 이미 문장이 완전한 상태입니다. 따라서 '직접'이라는 의미로 부가적인 요소인 부사처럼 쓰일 수 있는 재귀대명사 (D) himself가 정답입니다.

오답 (A) him: 부사와 같은 부가적인 역할을 할 수 없는 목적격대명사이므로 오답입니다.
(B) his: 부사와 같은 부가적인 역할을 할 수 없는 소유격 또는 소유대명사이므로 오답입니다.
(C) he: 부사와 같은 부가적인 역할을 할 수 없는 주격대명사이므로 오답입니다.

어휘 offer to do ~하겠다고 제안하다 lead ~을 진행하다, ~을 이끌다 session (특정 활동을 위한) 시간 due to ~로 인해, ~ 때문에 several 여럿의, 몇몇의 HR 인사(부), 인적자원 absent 부재 중인, 결근한, 결석한 oneself (부사처럼 쓰여) 직접, 스스로

13.
정답 (B)

해석 저희 고객들 중 많은 분들께서 호텔을 둘러싸고 있는 삼림 지역 및 자연 등산로를 둘러보시는 것을 즐거워하고 계십니다.

해설 빈칸 앞에 위치한 동사 enjoy는 동명사를 목적어로 취해 '~하는 것을 즐기다'라는 의미를 나타내므로 (B) exploring이 정답입니다.

오답 (A) explore: 동사 enjoy의 목적어 역할을 할 수 없는 동사의 형태이므로 오답입니다.
(C) to explore: 동사 enjoy의 목적어 역할을 할 수 없는 to부정사이므로 오답입니다.
(D) explored: 동사 enjoy의 목적어 역할을 할 수 없는 과거형 또는 과거분사형의 형태이므로 오답입니다.

어휘 woodland 삼림 (지대) trail 등산로, 산길, 오솔길 surround ~을 둘러싸다 explore ~을 둘러보다, ~을 탐험하다

14.
정답 (C)

해석 고객 만족도의 하락으로 인해, 그 레스토랑은 여러 소셜 미디어 플랫폼에 홍보 캠페인을 시작했다.

해설 빈칸 앞에 위치한 명사 customer는 하락이나 감소의 대상으로 맞지 않습니다. 따라서 customer와 복합명사를 구성해 전치사 in의 목적어로서 하락 대상이 될 수 있는 것을 나타낼 또 다른 명사가 쓰여야 알맞으므로 (C) satisfaction이 정답입니다.

오답 (A) satisfy: 동사이므로 명사 customer와 복합명사를 구성해 전치사 in의 목적어 역할을 할 수 없는 오답입니다.
(B) satisfied: 과거분사 또는 형용사이므로 명사 customer와 복합명사를 구성해 전치사 in의 목적어 역할을 할 수 없는 오답입니다.
(D) satisfying: 현재분사 또는 형용사이므로 명사 customer와 복합명사를 구성해 전치사 in의 목적어 역할을 할 수 없는 오답입니다.

어휘 due to ~로 인해, ~ 때문에 decline in ~의 하락, ~의 감소 launch ~을 시작하다, ~을 출시하다 promotional 홍보의, 판촉의 satisfy ~을 만족시키다 satisfied (사람이) 만족한 satisfaction 만족(도) satisfying (사람을) 만족시키는

15.
정답 (D)

해석 글로벌핀 솔루션스는 신규 고객들이 업그레이드된 대시보드를 통해 재무 기록에 접근할 수 있도록 할 것입니다.

해설 빈칸 앞에 들어갈 알맞은 동사를 고르는 문제입니다. 빈칸 뒤에 목적어 new clients가 있고, 그 뒤에 to부정사(to access)가 위치해 있는데, 문맥상 '신규 고객들이 ~ 접근하게 하다'라는 의미를 나타내야 하므로 to부정사가 목적보어로 사용되었

음을 알 수 있습니다. 따라서 보기 중에 5형식 동사 (D) allow 가 정답입니다.

오답 (A) offer: 4형식 동사로, 「목적어 + 목적보어」 구조와 함께 쓰일 수 없으므로 오답입니다.
(B) send: 4형식 동사로, 「목적어 + 목적보어」 구조와 함께 쓰일 수 없으므로 오답입니다.
(C) find: 5형식 동사이지만, 목적보어 자리에 형용사가 위치해야 하므로 오답입니다.

어휘 access 접근하다, 이용하다 financial 재무의, 재정의 record 기록 though ~을 통해

16.
정답 (B)
해석 고객 설문 조사에 따르면, 응답자들 중 대부분이 샤이닝 테크의 최신 웨어러블 기기를 다른 사람에게 추천하겠다고 말했다.
해설 빈칸 뒤에 「of 복수명사」가 위치해 있으므로 이 구조와 함께 쓰일 수 있는 대명사를 고르는 문제입니다. 보기 중에 '~ 중에 대부분'이라는 의미를 나타낼 수 있는 (B) most가 정답입니다.

오답 (A) that: 「명사1 of 명사2」의 구조가 앞서 언급될 경우 '명사1' 대신에 쓰일 수 있는 대명사이며, 빈칸 앞에는 해당 구조가 없으므로 오답입니다.
(C) every: 항상 형용사로 쓰이며, 「of 복수명사」 앞에 쓰일 수 없으므로 오답입니다.
(D) both: 두 개의 항목이 앞서 언급될 경우 그 둘 모두를 가리킬 때 사용되는 대명사이며, 빈칸 앞에 두 개의 항목에 해당하는 것이 없으므로 오답입니다.

어휘 according to ~에 따르면 survey 설문조사 respondent 응답자 recommend 추천하다 newest 최신의 wearable 착용 가능한, 웨어러블의 device 기기

17.
정답 (D)
해석 시설팀은 생산량이 많은 시간대에 공기 중 입자를 줄이기 위해 건물 곳곳에 공기청정기를 설치했습니다.
해설 빈칸에 들어갈 알맞은 동사의 형태를 고르는 문제입니다. 빈칸 앞에는 주어 The facilities team, 동사 installed, 목적어 air purifiers가 갖춰진 완전한 절이 위치해 있습니다. 따라서 빈칸에 들어갈 동사 reduce는 부사의 역할을 해야 하므로 '~하기 위해'라는 의미를 나타내는 부사적 용법으로 쓰일 수 있는 to부정사 형태 (D) to reduce가 정답입니다.

오답 (A) reduce: 동사원형이며, 빈칸 앞에 동사 installed가 있으므로 또다른 동사를 쓸 수 없습니다.
(B) reduction: 명사이며, 빈칸 뒤에 위치한 airborne particles를 목적어로 취할 수 없으므로 오답입니다.
(C) reduced: 동사의 과거형 또는 과거분사형이며, installed가 문장의 동사이므로 과거형 동사를 쓸 수 없고, 과거분사는 빈칸 뒤에 있는 목적어를 가질 수 없으므로 오답입니다.

어휘 facility 시설 install 설치하다 air purifier 공기 청정기 throughout 곳곳에, 도처에 airborne 공중에 떠있는, 공기로 운반되는 particle 입자 peak 최고조의, 최상의 production 생산

18.
정답 (D)
해석 카터 씨의 제안은 오늘 아침 회의 시간 동안 이사회에 의해 논의되었습니다.
해설 빈칸에 들어갈 동사의 알맞은 형태를 고르는 문제입니다. 빈칸 뒤에는 「by + 행위자」로 '~에 의해'라는 의미를 나타내는 전치사구가 위치해 있으므로 타동사인 discuss가 능동태로 쓰일 수 없으므로 수동태인 (D) was discussed가 정답입니다.

오답 (A) discusses: 능동태이므로 오답입니다.
(B) discussing: 빈칸은 동사 자리이므로 현재분사 형태가 들어갈 수 없습니다.
(C) discussed: 능동태 과거시제일 경우 목적어가 없으므로 오답이며, 과거분사이더라도 동사 자리에 위치할 수 없으므로 오답입니다.

어휘 proposal 제안(서) board member 이사회 (임원) discuss 논의하다

19.
정답 (C)
해석 베리타스 메디컬 솔루션즈의 장비에 대한 신규 주문은 무역 박람회 이후 증가할 것으로 기대된다.
해설 빈칸에 들어갈 동사의 알맞은 형태를 고르는 문제입니다. 빈칸 뒤에 to부정사가 위치해 있으므로 「be expected to 부정사」 구조로 '~할 것으로 기대되다'라는 의미를 나타내는 문장임을 알 수 있습니다. 따라서 정답은 수동태인 (C) are expected 입니다.

오답 (A) was expected: 수동태이지만 주어가 복수명사(New orders)이므로 단수동사 was와 수일치가 되지 않으므로 오답입니다.
(B) is expecting: 능동태 현재진행시제로, '신규 주문이 기대하고 있다'라는 의미가 되므로 어색하며, 단수동사 is와도 수일치가 되지 않으므로 오답입니다.
(D) to expect: 동사 자리이므로 to부정사는 위치할 수 없습니다.

어휘 order 주문 equipment 장비 be expected to do ~할 것으로 기대되다, 예상되다 following ~후에 trade show 무역 박람회

20.

정답 (C)

해석 웨비나를 주최하는 것과 더불어, DLS 컨설팅은 10월에 일련의 대면 워크숍을 시작할 것이다.

해설 빈칸에 들어갈 동사의 알맞은 형태를 고르는 문제입니다. 빈칸 앞에는 전치사 In addition to가 위치해 있으므로 빈칸에는 동명사가 위치해야 합니다. 따라서 정답은 (C) hosting입니다.

오답 (A) host: 동사원형이며, 전치사 뒤에 동사는 쓸 수 없으므로 오답입니다. 빈칸 앞에 있는 to는 to부정사에 쓰이는 to가 아닙니다.
(B) hosts: 동사에 -s가 붙은 형태이며, 전치사 뒤에 동사는 쓸 수 없으므로 오답입니다.
(D) hosted: 동사의 과거형 또는 과거분사이며, 전치사 뒤에는 명사, 대명사, 동명사가 위치할 수 있으므로 오답입니다.

어휘 in addition to ~와 더불어, ~외에도, ~뿐만 아니라 webinar 웨비나(온라인 세미나) launch 시작하다, 출시하다 a series of 일련의 in-person 대면의, 직접 만나는

PART 5 FINAL TEST 2

1. (C)	2. (A)	3. (B)	4. (D)	5. (B)
6. (A)	7. (D)	8. (C)	9. (B)	10. (D)
11. (D)	12. (A)	13. (C)	14. (B)	15. (A)
16. (A)	17. (D)	18. (B)	19. (C)	20. (D)

1.

정답 (C)

해석 인쇄된 문서가 제품 시연회에 참석한 모든 사람에게 배부되었습니다.

해설 정관사 The와 명사 documents 사이에 위치한 빈칸은 명사를 수식할 형용사 또는 분사가 필요한 자리입니다. 선택지에 형용사가 없어 현재분사 (B) printing과 과거분사 (C) printed 사이에서 하나를 골라야 하는데, 문서(documents)는 사람에 의해 인쇄되는 것이므로 이러한 수동의 의미를 나타낼 수 있는 과거분사 (C) printed가 정답입니다.

오답 (A) print: 동사 또는 명사이며, 명사로 쓰일 때 documents와 복합명사를 구성하지 않으므로 오답입니다.
(B) printing: 수동의 의미를 나타낼 수 없는 현재분사이므로 오답입니다.
(D) prints: 동사 또는 명사이며, 명사로 쓰일 때 documents와 복합명사를 구성하지 않으므로 오답입니다.

어휘 distribute ~을 배부하다, ~을 나눠 주다 attend ~에 참석하다 demonstration 시연(회), 시범

2.

정답 (A)

해석 그 기조 연설자는 유전 공학에 관한 강연을 시작하기에 앞서 모든 손님들을 따뜻하게 맞이해 주었다.

해설 명사구 목적어 all guests와 전치사 before 사이에 위치한 빈칸은 동사를 뒤에서 수식할 부사가 쓰여야 알맞은 자리이므로 (A) warmly가 정답입니다.

오답 (B) warm: 명사구 목적어와 전치사 사이에서 동사를 수식하는 역할을 할 수 없는 형용사이므로 오답입니다.
(C) warmest: 명사구 목적어와 전치사 사이에서 동사를 수식하는 역할을 할 수 없는 최상급 형용사이므로 오답입니다.
(D) warmth: 명사구 목적어와 전치사 사이에서 동사를 수식하는 역할을 할 수 없는 명사이므로 오답입니다.

어휘 keynote speaker 기조 연설자 greet 맞이하다, 인사하다 genetic 유전의, 유전학의 warmly 따뜻하게 warm 따뜻한 warmth 따뜻함, 온기

3.
정답 (B)
해석 모든 구직 지원서들을 쿠퍼 씨 책상에 있는 받침대에 놓아 주십시오.
해설 선택지가 모두 전치사이므로 의미가 알맞은 것을 찾아야 합니다. 빈칸 뒤에 위치한 the tray가 지원서들을 놓아 둘 수 있는 '받침대, 쟁반'을 의미합니다. 따라서 동사 place와 어울려 'A를 B에 놓다[두다]'를 뜻하는 「place A in B」를 구성해야 알맞으므로 (B) in이 정답입니다.
오답 (A) at: 동사 place와 함께 쓰여 물건을 놓아 두는 곳을 의미하는 전치사로 어울리지 않으므로 오답입니다.
(C) to: '~으로'라는 의미로 동사 place와 함께 쓰여 물건을 놓아 두는 곳을 의미하는 전치사로 어울리지 않으므로 오답입니다.
(D) over: '~위로', '~넘어'라는 의미로 동사 place와 함께 쓰여 물건을 놓아 두는 곳을 의미하는 전치사로 어울리지 않으므로 오답입니다.
어휘 place v. ~을 놓다, ~을 두다 application 지원(서), 신청(서) form 양식, 서식 tray 받침대, 쟁반

4.
정답 (D)
해석 아르고 스포츠웨어 사의 주 유통 창고는 9번 고속도로에서 바로 벗어난 곳에 있는 산업 단지 내에 위치해 있다.
해설 선택지가 모두 전치사이므로 의미가 알맞은 것을 찾아야 합니다. 유통 창고의 위치와 관련해 '산업 단지 내에'를 의미해야 자연스러우므로 '(거리, 기간, 범위 등) ~ 이내에'를 뜻하는 전치사 (D) within이 정답입니다.
오답 (A) among: 산업 단지라는 공간 범위에 포함된 위치를 나타낼 수 없는 전치사이므로 오답입니다. 참고로, among은 그 의미 특성상 복수명사(구)를 목적어로 취합니다.
(B) across: 산업 단지라는 공간 범위에 포함된 위치를 나타낼 수 없는 전치사이므로 오답입니다.
(C) through: 산업 단지라는 공간 범위에 포함된 위치를 나타낼 수 없는 전치사이므로 오답입니다.
어휘 main 주된, 주요한 distribution 유통, 분배, 분포 warehouse 창고 be located 위치해 있다 industrial park 산업 단지 just off ~에서 바로 벗어난 곳에 (있는) among ~ 사이에서, ~ 중에서 across ~을 가로질러, ~ 건너편에, ~ 전역에 걸쳐 through (이동) ~을 통과해, ~을 거쳐, (수단) ~을 통해, (기간) ~ 동안 내내, ~까지, (장소) ~을 전역에 걸쳐

5.
정답 (B)
해석 저희의 여름 할인 판촉 행사에 포함되는 상품은 노란색 스티커로 표시되어야 합니다.
해설 빈칸 뒤에 주어 없이 동사 is included로 시작하는 절이 있고, 그 뒤에 조동사 should가 이어지는 구조입니다. 따라서 is included로 시작하는 절이 주어를 뒤에서 수식하는 관계대명사절이 되어야 하므로 사물명사를 수식할 수 있는 주격관계대명사 (B) that이 정답입니다.
오답 (A) what: 선행사를 수식하는 역할을 하지 않으므로 오답입니다.
(C) it: 선행사를 수식하는 관계대명사가 아니므로 오답입니다.
(D) this: 선행사를 수식하는 관계대명사가 아니므로 오답입니다.
어휘 merchandise 상품 include ~을 포함하다 promotion 판촉 (행사), 홍보, 승진, 촉진 label (라벨로) ~을 표시하다

6.
정답 (A)
해석 모든 부서는 회사 조직 개편이 시작되기 전에 명확한 계획을 세워 둬야 합니다.
해설 부정관사 a와 명사 plan 사이에 위치한 빈칸은 명사를 수식할 형용사가 필요한 자리이므로 (A) clear가 정답입니다.
오답 (B) clearly: 명사를 수식할 수 없는 부사이므로 오답입니다.
(C) clarity: 명사이며, 복합명사를 구성하는 경우를 생각해 볼 수는 있지만, plan과 복합명사를 구성하지는 않으므로 오답입니다.
(D) clearing: 동명사, 현재분사, 또는 명사이며, 현재분사로서 명사 plan을 수식하거나 명사로서 plan과 복합명사를 구성하지 않으므로 오답입니다.
어휘 department 부서, ~부 develop a plan 계획을 세우다 reorganization 조직 개편, 구조 조정 clear a. 명확한, 분명한, 깨끗한 v. ~을 치우다 clearly 명확히, 분명히 clarity 명확성, 명료성, 투명도

7.
정답 (D)
해석 안전 조사관은 개선될 수 있는 몇 가지 사항들을 확인했지만, 그 레스토랑에 높은 점수를 주었다.
해설 선택지가 모두 접속사이므로 의미가 알맞은 것을 찾아야 합니다. 빈칸 뒤에 위치한 절이 '개선될 수 있는 몇 가지 사항들을 확인했지만'이라는 의미로 레스토랑에 높은 점수를 준 것과 대조적인 사실을 나타내야 자연스러우므로 ~함에도 불구하고, (비록) ~지만'을 뜻하는 (D) although가 정답입니다.
오답 (A) unless: '~하지 않는다면, ~가 아니라면'을 뜻하는 접속사이므로 의미가 맞지 않는 오답입니다.
(B) because: '~하기 때문에'를 뜻하는 접속사이므로 의미가 맞지 않는 오답입니다.
(C) so that: '(목적) ~하도록, (결과) 그래서, 그러므로'를 뜻하는 접속사이므로 의미가 맞지 않는 오답입니다.

어휘 **inspector** 조사관, 점검관 **identify** ~을 확인하다, ~을 식별하다 **several** 몇몇의, 여럿의 **improve** ~을 개선하다, ~을 향상시키다

8.
정답 (C)
해석 할인 쿠폰은 오직 썬라이즈 버블 티의 참여 지점에서만 제품으로 교환될 수 있습니다.
해설 전치사 at과 명사 목적어 branches 사이에 위치한 빈칸은 명사를 수식할 형용사 또는 분사가 필요한 자리입니다. 선택지에 형용사가 없어 현재분사 (B) participating과 과거분사 (D) participated 사이에서 하나를 골라야 하는데, participate 같은 자동사는 현재분사의 형태로만 명사를 수식할 수 있으므로 (C) participating이 정답입니다.
오답 (A) participant: 사람명사이며, branches와 복합명사를 구성하지 않으므로 오답입니다.
(B) participate: 전치사 at과 명사 목적어 사이에 쓰일 수 없는 동사원형이므로 오답입니다.
(D) participated: 과거형 또는 과거분사형이며, 자동사의 과거분사는 명사를 수식할 수 없으므로 오답입니다.
어휘 **voucher** 쿠폰, 상품권 **redeem** (쿠폰 등) ~을 상품으로 교환하다 **branch** 지점, 지사 **participant** 참가자 **participate (in):** (~에) 참여하다, 참가하다

9.
정답 (B)
해석 새로운 기술 지원 웹 채팅 기능이 대단히 효과적이어서, 대응 시간을 30퍼센트 감소시키고 있다.
해설 be동사 is와 형용사 보어 effective 사이에 위치한 빈칸은 형용사를 수식할 부사가 필요한 자리이므로 (B) highly가 정답입니다.
오답 (A) high: 형용사 또는 부사이며, 부사로 쓰일 때 형용사를 수식하는 역할을 하지 않으므로 오답입니다.
(C) higher: 형용사를 수식하는 역할을 할 수 없는 비교급 형용사/부사이므로 오답입니다.
(D) highest: 형용사를 수식하는 역할을 할 수 없는 최상급 형용사/부사이므로 오답입니다.
어휘 **technical** 기술적인 **support** 지원 **feature** 특징, 특성 **effective** 효과적인 **reduce** 줄이다 **response** 대응, 응답 **high** 높은, 높이 **highly** 대단히, 매우

10.
정답 (D)
해석 회계 시스템이 기술적인 문제들을 겪었기 때문에 그 고객에 대한 비용 지급이 지연되었습니다.
해설 선택지가 모두 접속사이므로 의미가 알맞은 것을 찾아야 합니다. 빈칸 뒤에 위치한 절이 '회계 시스템이 기술적인 문제들을 겪었기 때문에'라는 의미로 고객에 대한 비용 지급이 지연된 이유를 나타내야 자연스러우므로 '~하기 때문에'를 뜻하는 (D) because가 정답입니다.
오답 (A) however: 접속사일 때 '아무리 ~해도'를 뜻하므로 의미가 맞지 않는 오답입니다.
(B) but: '하지만, 그러나'를 뜻하는 접속사이므로 의미가 맞지 않는 오답입니다.
(C) so: '(목적) ~하도록, (결과) 그래서, 그러므로'를 뜻하는 접속사이므로 의미가 맞지 않는 오답입니다.
어휘 **payment** 지급, 지불, 결제 **delay** ~을 지연시키다 **accounting** 회계 **experience** ~을 겪다, ~을 경험하다 **issue** 문제, 사안 **however** conj. 아무리 ~해도 ad. 하지만

11.
정답 (D)
해석 새로운 에어컨 기기들이 우리 업무 흐름에 대한 지장을 최소화하기 위해 주말 중에 설치될 것입니다.
해설 선택지에 전치사와 접속사가 섞여 있으므로 빈칸 뒤의 구조 및 문장의 의미에 어울리는 것을 찾아야 합니다. 빈칸 뒤에 명사구와 to부정사구가 있어 명사구 the weekend를 목적어로 취할 전치사가 필요하며, 설치 시점과 관련해 '주말 중에'라는 의미를 나타내야 자연스러우므로 '~ 중에, ~ 동안'을 뜻하는 전치사 (D) during이 정답입니다.
오답 (A) despite: 전치사이기는 하지만, 의미가 맞지 않으므로 오답입니다.
(B) until: 접속사 또는 전치사이며, 전치사일 때 '~까지'를 뜻하므로 의미가 맞지 않는 오답입니다.
(C) while: 주어와 동사를 포함한 절을 이끄는 접속사이므로 오답입니다.
어휘 **air conditioning** 에어컨 **unit** 기기, 장치, (상품의) 하나, 구성 단위 **install** ~을 설치하다 **minimize** ~을 최소화하다 **disruption** 지장, 방해 **workflow** 업무 흐름 **until** conj. (지속) ~할 때까지 prep. ~까지 **while** ~하는 동안, ~하는 반면 **despite** ~에도 불구하고

12.
정답 (A)
해석 우리가 지난 달에 고용한 컨설턴트는 재생 가능 에너지 프로젝트를 전문으로 합니다.
해설 주어 The consultant와 동사 specializes 사이에 주어와 동사를 포함한 절 we hired last month가 위치해 있는 구조입니다. 따라서 이 절이 주어를 뒤에서 수식하는 관계대명사절이 되어야 하는데, 주어 The consultant가 사람명사이므로 선행사가 사람명사일 때 사용하는 관계대명사 (A) who가 정답입니다.
오답 (B) which: 사람명사를 수식하는 관계대명사가 아니므로 오답입니다.
(C) them: 선행사를 수식하는 관계대명사가 아니므로 오답

입니다.
(D) where: 사람명사를 수식하는 관계대명사가 아니므로 오답입니다.

어휘 consultant 컨설턴트, 상담 전문가, 자문 hire ~을 고용하다 specialize in ~을 전문으로 하다 renewable 재생 가능한

13.
정답 (C)
해석 라자루스 엔지니어링 사가 경쟁력 있는 입찰액을 제출했는데, 그것이 그 회사를 모노레일 개발 프로젝트에 있어 강력한 경쟁사로 만들었습니다.
해설 부정관사 a와 명사 bid 사이에 위치한 빈칸은 명사를 수식할 형용사가 필요한 자리이므로 (C) competitive가 정답입니다.
오답 (A) compete: 명사를 수식할 수 없는 동사이므로 오답입니다.
(B) competitor: 명사이며, 복합명사를 구성하는 경우를 생각해 볼 수는 있지만, bid와 복합명사를 구성하지는 않으므로 오답입니다.
(D) competitively: 명사를 수식할 수 없는 부사이므로 오답입니다.

어휘 submit ~을 제출하다 bid 입찰(액) make A B: A를 B로 만들다 firm 회사, 업체 contender 경쟁자, 도전자 development 개발, 발전 competitive 경쟁력 있는, 경쟁하는 competitor 경쟁자, 경쟁사 compete 경쟁하다 competitively 경쟁적으로

14.
정답 (B)
해석 사용자 설명서에 따르면, 깜빡이는 붉은색 점멸등은 기계가 과열되고 있음을 나타냅니다.
해설 형용사 red와 명사 light 사이에 위치한 빈칸은 명사를 수식할 형용사 또는 분사가 필요한 자리입니다. 선택지에 형용사가 없어 현재분사 (B) blinking과 과거분사 (D) blinked 사이에서 하나를 골라야 하는데, (D) blink 같은 자동사는 현재분사의 형태로만 명사를 수식할 수 있으므로 (B) blinking이 정답입니다.
오답 (A) blink: 동사 또는 명사이며, 명사로 쓰일 때 light과 복합명사를 구성하지 않으므로 오답입니다.
(C) blinks: 동사 또는 명사이며, 명사로 쓰일 때 light과 복합명사를 구성하지 않으므로 오답입니다.
(D) blinked: 과거형 또는 과거분사형이며, 자동사의 과거분사는 명사를 수식할 수 없으므로 오답입니다.

어휘 according to ~에 따르면, ~에 따라 manual 설명서, 안내서 indicate that ~임을 나타내다, ~임을 가리키다 overheat 과열되다 blink 점멸하다, 깜빡이다

15.
정답 (A)
해석 그 테니스 토너먼트의 주최측은 예기치 못한 지연 문제로 인해 일정을 조정해야 할 것입니다.
해설 선택지가 모두 전치사이므로 의미가 알맞은 것을 찾아야 합니다. 빈칸 뒤에 위치한 명사구 unforeseen delays가 '예기치 못한 지연'을 뜻하므로 '예기치 못한 지연 문제에 대해 일정을 조정해야 할 것이다'와 같은 의미를 구성해야 자연스럽습니다. 따라서 '~로 인해, ~에 대해, ~을 위해' 등의 의미로 이유나 대상, 목적 등을 나타낼 때 사용하는 전치사 (A) for가 정답입니다.
오답 (B) of: 일정 조정의 이유나 원인을 나타낼 수 있는 전치사가 아니므로 오답입니다.
(C) about: 일정 조정의 이유나 원인을 나타낼 수 있는 전치사가 아니므로 오답입니다.
(D) between: 일정 조정의 이유나 원인을 나타낼 수 있는 전치사가 아니므로 오답입니다.

어휘 organizer 주최자, 조직자 will need to do ~해야 할 것이다 adjust ~을 조정하다, ~을 조절하다 unforeseen 예기치 못한, 뜻밖의 delay 지연, 지체 between (A and B): (A와 B) 사이에

16.
정답 (A)
해석 우리가 그 회계 법인과 맺은 계약이 이번 회계 연도 종료 시점까지 계속 유효한 상태입니다.
해설 선택지가 모두 전치사이므로 의미가 알맞은 것을 찾아야 합니다. 빈칸 뒤에 위치한 명사구 the end of the fiscal year가 계약이 유효한 상태가 끝나는 시점인 것으로 볼 수 있으므로 '~까지'라는 의미로 지속 상태가 종료되는 시점을 나타낼 때 사용하는 (A) until이 정답입니다.
오답 (B) since: 지속 상태가 종료되는 시점을 나타낼 수 없는 전치사이므로 오답입니다.
(C) toward: 지속 상태가 종료되는 시점을 나타낼 수 없는 전치사이므로 오답입니다.
(D) across: 지속 상태가 종료되는 시점을 나타낼 수 없는 전치사이므로 오답입니다.

어휘 contract 계약(서) accounting firm 회계 법인 remain + 형용사: 계속 ~한 상태이다, ~한 상태로 유지되다 valid 유효한 fiscal year 회계 연도 until prep. (지속) ~까지 conj. ~할 때까지 since prep. ~ 이후로 conj. ~한 이후로, ~하기 때문에 ad. 그 이후로 toward (이동, 방향 등) ~쪽으로, ~을 향해, (목적) ~을 위해, (시간의 접근) ~ 무렵 across ~을 가로질러, ~ 건너편에, ~ 전역에 걸쳐

17.
정답 (D)

해석 회사들이 연말 연회를 개최할 대연회장이 시설 관리 직원들에 의해 철저히 청소되어 있습니다.

해설 선택지가 모두 관계대명사이므로 선행사 및 빈칸 뒤에 위치한 절의 구조를 파악해 알맞은 것을 골라야 합니다. 선행사 The function rooms가 장소사물명사이며, 이를 수식하는 절 companies will hold their year-end banquets가 빠진 요소 없이 구성이 완전한 상태이므로 장소사물명사를 수식하면서 완전한 절을 이끄는 관계부사 (D) where가 정답입니다.

오답 (A) what: 선행사를 수식하는 역할을 하지 않으므로 오답입니다.
(B) when: 시간명사(구)를 수식하는 관계부사이므로 오답입니다.
(C) which: 장소사물명사를 수식할 수는 있지만, 주어나 목적어 등이 빠진 불완전한 절을 이끄는 관계대명사이므로 오답입니다.

어휘 function room 대연회장, 대회의장 hold ~을 개최하다 year-end 연말의 banquet 연회 thoroughly 철저히, 꼼꼼히 clean ~을 청소하다 housekeeping staff 시설 관리 직원들

18.
정답 (B)

해석 높은 수요로 인해, 엘름우드 컨퍼런스의 거의 모든 좌석이 2시간 내에 예약되었다.

해설 빈칸 뒤에 위치한 all seats를 수식할 부사가 들어가야 합니다. 문맥상 '거의 모든 좌석'이라는 의미가 적절하므로 '거의'라는 의미의 부사 (B) nearly가 정답입니다.

오답 (A) next to: '~옆에'라는 의미의 전치사이며, 문장의 주어인 all seats와 함께 쓰일 수 없으므로 오답입니다.
(C) somewhat: '어느 정도', '약간'이라는 의미의 부사이며, 의미상 명사 all seats를 수식할 수 없으므로 오답입니다.
(D) approximately: '대략'이라는 의미의 부사이며, 주로 숫자 또는 수치를 수식하는 부사이므로 오답입니다.

어휘 due to ~로 인해 demand 수요 seat 좌석 reserve 예약하다, 따로 두다 within ~내에 next to ~옆에 nearly 거의 somewhat 어느 정도, 약간 approximately 대략

19.
정답 (C)

해석 라미레즈 씨가 여러 차질에도 상관없이 일정을 앞당겨 프로젝트를 완료했기 때문에 그는 성과급을 받았다.

해설 빈칸 뒤에 명사구가 위치해 있으므로 빈칸은 전치사 자리입니다. 문맥상 '여러 차질에 상관없이 일정을 앞당겨 프로젝트를 완료하였다'는 내용이므로, 보기 중에서 '~에 상관없이'라는 의미의 전치사 (C) regardless of가 정답입니다.

오답 (A) against: '~에 대항하여'라는 의미의 전치사로, 반대의 의미를 나타내므로 오답입니다.
(B) except for: '~을 제외하고'라는 의미의 전치사로, '여러 차질들'이 제외의 대상이 아니므로 오답입니다.
(D) nevertheless: '그럼에도 불구하고'라는 의미의 접속부사로, 의미는 적절하지만, 빈칸은 전치사 자리이므로 접속부사는 오답입니다.

어휘 complete 완료하다 ahead of schedule 일정을 앞당겨, 일정보다 빨리 multiple 여러 개의 setback 차질, 문제 performance bonus 성과급 against ~에 대항하여, ~에 반대하여 except for ~을 제외하고 regardless of ~에 상관없이 nevertheless 그럼에도 불구하고

20.
정답 (D)

해석 '스타트업 피치 대회'의 결승전은 너무 흥미진진해서 여러 관객들이 기립 박수를 보냈다.

해설 빈칸에 들어갈 동사의 알맞은 형태를 고르는 문제입니다. 빈칸 앞에 be동사 was와 부사 so가 있으므로 주격보어이자 so의 수식을 받는 형용사가 위치해야 합니다. thrill은 '열광시키다, 흥미진진하게 하다'라는 타동사이므로, 문맥상 주어인 스타트업 피치 대회의 결승전이 흥미진진하게 만드는 것이기 때문에 현재분사형태인 (D) thrilling이 정답입니다.

오답 (A) thrill: 동사원형으로, 문장의 동사 was가 있으므로 또 다른 동사를 쓸 수 없습니다.
(B) thrills: 동사에 -s를 붙인 형태로, 문장의 동사 was가 있으므로 또 다른 동사를 쓸 수 없습니다.
(C) thrilled: 과거분사로, '흥미진진한'이라는 의미로 감정을 느끼는 사람을 수식하거나 보어로 사용할 수 있으므로 오답입니다.

어휘 final round 결승전 contest 대회 so + 형용사 + that …: 너무 ~해서 …하다 audience 관객 standing ovation 기립 박수

PART 6 FINAL TEST

1. (A)　2. (C)　3. (D)　4. (D)　5. (A)
6. (D)　7. (C)　8. (C)　9. (D)　10. (A)
11. (B)　12. (B)　13. (C)　14. (A)　15. (D)
16. (B)

1-4 다음 회람을 참조하시오.

날짜: 3월 3일
제목: 분기 보고서 제출

직원 여러분,

이 회람은 모든 분기 재무 보고서가 반드시 3월 10일, 금요일까지 제출되어야 한다는 점을 상기시키는 메시지입니다. 보고서는 **1** 정확성을 위해 제출 전에 철저히 점검되어야 합니다. 어떤 오류든 반드시 바로잡고 부서장의 승인을 받아야 합니다. 소속 부서에서 추가 시간이 **2** 필요할 경우, 늦어도 화요일까지 제게 알려 주시기 바랍니다. 지체된 모든 보고서는 우리의 내부 회계 감사 절차 준수에 **3** 영향을 미칠 것입니다. 이 사안에 대해 여러분의 협조에 감사 드립니다. **4** 문서는 이메일로 제게 직접 보내 져야 합니다.

안녕히 계십시오.

매리솔 그랜트
재무 이사

어휘 quarterly 분기의 submission 제출(물) reminder (메시지 등의) 상기시키는 것 submit ~을 제출하다 by (기한) ~까지 thoroughly 철저히, 꼼꼼히 correct ~을 바로잡다, ~을 정정하다 approve ~을 승인하다 require ~을 필요로 하다 additional 추가적인 notify ~에게 알리다 no later than 늦어도 ~까지 compliance with ~에 대한 준수 internal 내부의 audit 회계 감사 procedure 절차 appreciate ~에 대해 감사하다 cooperation 협조, 협력 matter 사안, 문제 financial 재무의, 재정의, 금융의

1.

정답 (A)
해설 선택지가 모두 명사이므로 의미가 알맞은 것을 찾아야 합니다. 해당 문장에서 빈칸이 속한 for 전치사구는 제출하기 전에 보고서를 철저히 점검하는 목적을 나타내야 하므로 '정확성'을 뜻하는 (A) accuracy가 정답입니다.

오답 (B) efficiency: '효율(성)'을 뜻하므로 문장의 의미에 어울리지 않는 오답입니다.
(C) diligence: '근면, 성실'을 뜻하므로 문장의 의미에 어울리지 않는 오답입니다.
(D) potential: '잠재력'을 뜻하므로 문장의 의미에 어울리지 않는 오답입니다.

어휘 efficiency 효율(성) diligence 근면, 성실 potential n. 잠재력 a. 잠재적인

2.

정답 (C)
해설 빈칸 뒤에 이어지는 두 개의 절을 읽어 보면, '소속 부서에서 추가 시간이 필요할 경우, 늦어도 화요일까지 제게 알려 주십시오'와 같은 의미를 나타내야 자연스럽습니다. 따라서 조건을 나타내는 If절 If your department should require additional time에서 If가 생략되고 주어와 조동사 should가 도치된 구조를 이루는 (C) Should가 정답입니다.

오답 (A) If: If가 쓰이려면 단수주어인 명사구 your department와 수 일치되는 단수동사의 형태인 requires로 써야 하므로 오답입니다.
(B) Because: '~하기 때문에'라는 의미로 이유를 나타내는 접속사이므로 오답입니다.
(D) Provided: If와 같은 의미로 지니는 접속사로서, 빈칸에 쓰이려면 단수주어인 명사구 your department와 수 일치되는 단수동사의 형태인 requires로 써야 하므로 오답입니다.

어휘 provided 만약 ~한다면

3.

정답 (D)
해설 선택지가 모두 동사의 형태이고 시제와 태가 다르므로 시점 및 능/수동 관련 단서를 찾아야 합니다. 우선, 빈칸 뒤에 명사구 목적어 our compliance가 있으므로 타동사 affect가 능동태로 쓰여야 합니다. 또한, 첫 문장에 제출 시점으로 언급된 by Friday, March 10이 상단의 이메일 작성 날짜보다 미래 시점인데, 늦은 제출에 따른 영향은 그보다 더 나중의 미래에 있을 일이므로 능동태 미래시제인 (D) will affect가 정답입니다.

오답 (A) have affected: 미래의 일을 나타낼 수 없는 현재완료시제이므로 오답입니다.
(B) were affecting: 미래의 일을 나타낼 수 없는 과거진행시제이므로 오답입니다.
(C) is affected: 목적어를 취할 수 없는 수동태 동사이므로 오답입니다.

어휘 affect ~에 영향을 미치다

249

4.

정답 (D)

해석 (A) 여러 핵심 상세 정보가 당신의 보고서에 빠져 있습니다.
(B) 새로운 절차가 회사 웹사이트에 개괄적으로 설명되어 있습니다.
(C) 이 문제에 대한 즉각적인 해결책을 찾는 것이 중요합니다.
(D) 문서는 이메일로 제게 직접 보내셔야 합니다.

해설 지문 전체적으로 분기 재무 보고서 제출 일정 및 그 제출 과정에서 알아 두어야 하는 주의 사항을 설명하고 있습니다. 따라서 해당 보고서 제출과 관련된 정보로서 문서 전달 방법을 언급하는 (D)가 정답입니다.

오답 (A) 빈칸 앞 문장들의 내용이 특정 인물의 보고서가 지닌 특징과 관련된 것이 아니므로 흐름상 맞지 않는 오답입니다.
(B) 빈칸 앞 문장들의 내용이 새로운 절차와 관련된 것이 아니므로 흐름상 맞지 않는 오답입니다.
(C) 빈칸 앞 문장들의 내용이 특정 문제에 대한 조치와 관련된 것이 아니므로 흐름상 맞지 않는 오답입니다.

어휘 several 여럿의, 몇몇의 details 상세 정보, 세부 사항 missing 빠진, 없는, 사라진 procedure 절차 outline ~을 개괄적으로 설명하다 seek ~을 찾다, ~을 구하다 prompt 즉각적인 resolution 해결책

5-8 다음 공지를 참조하시오.

스프링필드 박물관: 연장된 운영 시간

저희 스프링필드 박물관은 4월 1일부터, 새로운 운영 시간이 화요일부터 일요일, 오전 9시부터 오후 8시까지가 될 것이라는 사실을 알려 드리게 되어 기쁩니다. **5** 매주 월요일에는 시설 관리로 인해 계속 문을 닫은 상태로 유지될 것입니다. 이러한 변화로 인해 더 많은 손님들께서, 특히 직장이 있는 전문직 종사자 가들께서 저희 전시물을 **6** 즐기시는 것이 더욱 쉬워질 것입니다. 늘 그렇듯이, 입장료는 매달 첫째 일요일에는 무료입니다. 다른 날에는, 저희 일반 입장권 가격이 8.50달러 **7** 이기는 하지만, 저희가 현재 '원하는 대로 결제하기' 입장 정책을 제공해 드리고 있습니다. 금전적 어려움으로 인해 이 가격을 **8** 감당하실 수 없는 분은 누구든 얼마든지 더 적은 액수를 결제하시거나 무료로 박물관을 방문하셔도 좋습니다. 단체 투어는 저희 웹사이트를 통해 미리 예약될 수 있습니다.

어휘 extend ~을 연장하다, ~을 확장하다 be pleased to do ~해서 기쁘다 A through B: (기간) A부터 B까지 exhibit 전시물, 전시회 professional n. 전문직 종사자, 전문가 as always 늘 그렇듯이 admission 입장(료) free 무료인 currently 현재 offer ~을 제공하다, ~을 제안하다 pay-what-you-please 원하는 대로 결제하는[지불하는] policy 정책, 방침 due to ~로 인해, ~ 때문에 financial 금전적인, 재정적인 be welcome to do 얼마든지 ~해도 좋다 for free 무료로 book ~을 예약하다 in advance 미리, 사전에

5.

정답 (A)

해석 (A) 매주 월요일에는 시설 관리로 인해 계속 문을 닫은 상태로 유지될 것입니다.
(B) 저희는 성대한 개장식 행사에서 여러분을 뵐 수 있기를 바랍니다.
(C) 저희는 이 일시적인 불편함에 대해 사과 드립니다.
(D) 저희는 해당 작업이 4월 말까지 마무리될 것으로 예상하고 있습니다.

해설 상단의 제목이 '연장된 운영 시간'이고, 빈칸 앞 문장에 구체적인 운영 시간이 제시되어 있어 박물관 운영 시간과 관련된 정보를 담은 문장이 쓰여야 흐름이 자연스러우므로 운영하지 않는 요일 및 그 이유를 밝히는 (A)가 정답입니다.

오답 (B) 빈칸 앞뒤 문장이 개장식과 관련된 내용이 아니므로 흐름상 맞지 않는 오답입니다.
(C) 빈칸 앞뒤 문장이 일시적인 불편함과 관련된 내용이 아니므로 흐름상 맞지 않는 오답입니다.
(D) 빈칸 앞뒤 문장이 특정 작업의 진행과 관련된 내용이 아니므로 흐름상 맞지 않는 오답입니다.

어휘 remain + 형용사: 계속 ~한 상태로 유지되다 maintenance 시설 관리, 유지 관리 apologize for ~에 대해 사과하다 temporary 일시적인, 임시의 inconvenience 불편함 expect A to do: A가 ~할 것으로 예상하다 by (기한) ~까지

6.

정답 (D)

해설 빈칸 앞에 위치한 동사 make는 「make it 형용사 for A to do」의 가목적어/진목적어 구조로 쓰여 'A가 ~하는 것을 …하게 만들다'라는 의미를 나타내므로 진목적어인 to부정사 (D) to enjoy가 정답입니다.

오답 (A) are enjoying: 동사 make와 함께 가목적어/진목적어 구조에 쓰이는 형태가 아니므로 오답입니다.
(B) enjoy: 동사 make와 함께 가목적어/진목적어 구조에 쓰이는 형태가 아니므로 오답입니다.
(C) have enjoyed: 동사 make와 함께 가목적어/진목적어 구조에 쓰이는 형태가 아니므로 오답입니다.

7.

정답 (C)

해설 선택지가 모두 접속사이므로 의미가 알맞은 것을 찾아야 합니다. 빈칸 뒤에 위치한 절이 '저희 일반 입장권 가격이 8.50달러이기는 하지만'이라는 의미로 주절에서 말하는 '원하는 대로 결제하기' 정책과 대조적인 사실을 나타내야 알맞으므로 '(비록) ~하기는 하지만, ~함에도 불구하고'를 뜻하는 (C) although가 정답입니다.

오답 (A) unless: '~하지 않는다면, ~가 아니라면'을 뜻하는 접속사이므로 의미가 맞지 않는 오답입니다.
(B) before: '~하기 전에'를 뜻하는 접속사이므로 의미가 맞지 않는 오답입니다.
(D) since: '~한 이후로, ~하기 때문에'를 뜻하는 접속사이므로 의미가 맞지 않는 오답입니다.

어휘 unless ~하지 않는다면, ~가 아니라면 since conj. ~한 이후로, ~하기 때문에 prep. ~ 이후로 ad. 그 이후로

8.

정답 (C)

해설 선택지가 모두 동사이므로 의미가 알맞은 것을 찾아야 합니다. 빈칸이 속한 who절 뒤에 얼마든지 더 적은 액수를 결제하거나 무료로 박물관을 방문해도 좋다는 말이 쓰여 있습니다. 따라서 Anyone을 수식하는 who의 동사는 cannot과 함께 '금전적 문제로 인해 유료 입장을 감당할 수 없는'이라는 의미를 나타내야 자연스러우므로 '~을 감당하다, ~에 대한 여유가 있다'를 뜻하는 동사 (C) afford가 정답입니다.

오답 (A) attend: '~에 참석하다'를 뜻하는 동사이므로 의미가 맞지 않는 오답입니다.
(B) invest: '(~을) 투자하다'를 뜻하는 동사이므로 의미가 맞지 않는 오답입니다.
(D) exchange: '~을 교환하다'를 뜻하는 동사이므로 의미가 맞지 않는 오답입니다.

어휘 attend ~에 참석하다 invest (~을) 투자하다 exchange ~을 교환하다

9-12 다음 회람을 참조하시오.

제목: 시제품 제출 절차상의 변동 사항
날짜: 2월 14일

연구개발부 직원 여러분,

다음주 월요일부터, 모든 시제품 제출은 반드시 변경된 디지털 추적 시스템을 통해 처리되어야 한다는 점을 알아 두시기 바랍니다. 이는 모든 손전등 모델이 지속적으로 **9** 문서로 기록되고 때에 맞춰 평가되도록 보장하는 데 도움을 줄 것입니다. 모든 팀원들은 이번 주 말까지 개인 로그인 정보 및 사용자 가이드를 받을 것입니다. **10** 따라서, 이것들을 금요일 퇴근 전에 이메일로 반드시 확인하시기 바랍니다. 시스템은 신제품 버전들을 공식 승인 받을 때 발생한 최근의 지연 문제에 대한 **11** 대응으로 시작되는 것이며, 이는 수기 문서 기록 작업상의 공백에서 비롯되었습니다. **12** 우리는 이러한 변화가 투명성과 업무 흐름 효율성 둘 모두를 개선해 줄 것으로 생각합니다.

켄드라 마수라
제품 개발 책임

어휘 prototype 시제품, 원형 submission 제출(물) procedure 절차 Please be aware that ~라는 점에 유의하시기 바랍니다 go through ~을 거치다 revised 변경된, 수정된 process 처리하다 tracking 추적, 파악 help do ~하는 데 도움을 주다 ensure that ~임을 보장하다, 반드시 ~하도록 하다 consistently 지속적으로, 한결같이 review ~을 평가하다, ~을 검토하다 in a timely manner 때에 맞춰, 적시에 receive ~을 받다 login credentials 개인 로그인 정보 by (기한) ~까지 launch ~을 시작하다, ~을 출시하다 in response to ~에 대한 대응으로, ~에 대한 답변으로 recent 최근의 delay 지연, 지체 approval 승인 be traced back to A: A에서 비롯되다[시작되다] gap 공백, 격차, 틈 manual 수작업의 improve ~을 개선하다, ~을 향상시키다

9.

정답 (D)

해설 빈칸은 that 명사절의 동사 자리이며, 빈칸 뒤에는 목적어가 없이 부사만 있기 때문에 타동사인 document가 수동태가 되어야 한다는 것을 알 수 있습니다. 따라서 정답은 (D) is documented입니다.

오답 (A) documented: 능동태의 과거시제 동사이며, 타동사인 document 뒤에는 목적어가 필요하므로 오답입니다.
(B) to document: 빈칸은 동사 자리이므로 to부정사는 위치할 수 없습니다.
(C) documenting: 빈칸은 동사 자리이므로 현재분사는 위치할 수 없습니다.

어휘 document v. ~을 문서로 기록하다

10.

정답 (A)

해설 빈칸에 들어갈 알맞은 접속부사를 고르는 문제입니다. 앞문장에서는 팀원들이 이번 주말까지 로그인 정보와 가이드를 받을 것이라고 언급하였고, 그 뒤의 문장에서 금요일 전에 이메일을 확인하라는 내용이 이어지므로, 두 문장은 인과 관계로 이어져야 한다는 것을 알 수 있습니다. 따라서 보기 중에 '따라서', '그러므로'라는 인과 관계를 나타내는 접속부사 (A) Therefore가 정답입니다.

오답 (B) However: '하지만'이라는 의미로 대조 관계를 나타내는 접속부사이므로 오답입니다.
(C) Meanwhile: '그 동안에'라는 의미로 동시 발생 관계를 나타내는 접속부사이므로 오답입니다.
(D) On the other hand: '다른 한편으로는'이라는 의미로 앞서 언급된 것과 대조적 관계에 있는 것을 설명하기 위한 접속부사이므로 오답입니다.

어휘 therefore 따라서, 그러므로 however 그러나, 하지만 meanwhile 그 동안에 on the other hand 다른 한편으로는

11.
정답 (B)

해설 빈칸에 들어갈 알맞은 단어를 고르는 문제입니다. 빈칸 뒤에는 recent delays라는 명사구가 위치해 있으므로 전치사 자리임을 알 수 있습니다. 문맥상 변경된 시스템이 출시되는 이유에 대해 '최근의 지연'을 설명하는 내용이므로, 보기 중에서 '~에 대한 대응으로'라는 의미의 (B) in response to가 정답입니다.

오답 (A) regardless of: '~에 상관없이'라는 의미의 전치사로, 해당 문맥과 거리가 먼 양보의 의미를 나타내므로 오답입니다.

(C) concerning: '~에 관하여'라는 의미의 전치사로, 해당 문맥과 거리가 먼 관련성을 나타내므로 오답입니다.

(D) while: '~동안에', '반면에'를 나타내는 접속사이므로 전치사로 쓰일 수 없습니다.

어휘 regardless of ~에 상관없이 in response to ~에 대한 대응으로 concerning ~에 관하여 while ~동안, 반면에

12.
정답 (B)

해석 (A) 새로운 손전등 제품 디자인은 직접 제출해주시기 바랍니다.

(B) 우리는 이러한 변화가 투명성과 업무 흐름 효율성 둘 모두를 개선해 줄 것으로 생각합니다.

(C) 모든 제품 개발은 수기 문서 과정을 사용하여 진행될 것입니다.

(D) 이 새로운 시스템은 제작 비용을 줄이기 위해 주로 시행되었습니다.

해설 빈칸 앞 문장에서 새로운 제품 버전을 공식 인증 받을 때 여러 번 지연된 일에 대한 대응으로 변경된 시스템이 시작되고 있다고 설명하고, 그게 수기 문서 작성의 공백으로부터 비롯되었다고 설명하고 있습니다. 이는 디지털 추적 시스템이 시작되기 전에 발생했던 문제점을 언급한 것이므로, 빈칸에 들어갈 문장은 새로운 시스템이 가지는 개선점을 설명하는 것이 적절합니다. 따라서 투명성과 업무 흐름의 효율이 개선될 것이라고 설명하는 (B)가 정답입니다.

오답 (A) 제품 디자인을 직접 제출하는 것은 디지털 추적 시스템의 성격과 상반되는 내용이므로 오답입니다.

(C) 수기 문서 과정은 디지털 추적 시스템과 상반되는 성격을 가지므로 오답입니다.

(D) 새로운 시스템은 다음주 월요일에 시행될 것이므로 과거시제(was implemented)로 설명하는 것은 시점 오류가 됩니다. 또한 제작 비용(production costs)은 앞문장에서 언급된 문제점이 아니므로, 새로운 시스템의 개선점으로 보기 어렵기 때문에 오답입니다.

어휘 in person 직접 transparency 투명성 workflow 업무 흐름 efficiency 효율(성) carry out 실행하다 documentation 서류, 기록, 문서화 process 과정, 처리 implement 시행하다 primarily 주로 reduce 줄이다, 감소시키다 production cost 제작 비용, 생산비

13-16 다음 웹페이지를 참조하시오.

---

palmeradigitalcamera.com/question

질문 7월 24일 13시 14분

제가 막 디지털 카메라 C300을 구입했는데, 이미지가 실내에서 지나치게 어두워 보입니다. 이 문제를 바로잡기 위해 무엇을 하면 되나요?

→ 전문가 답변 (크리스 스타인): 이 문제는 아마 초기 광민감도(ISO) 설정이 실내 환경에 대해 너무 낮기 때문일 겁니다. 저희는 빛이 약한 상태에서 **13** 촬영하실 때 ISO를 800까지 또는 더 높게 올리시기를 권해 드립니다. **14** 이는 플래시를 사용하지 않고 카메라가 더 많은 빛을 담아 내는 데 도움을 줍니다. 반드시 셔터 속도도 **15** 조정하셔야 하는데, 그것이 노출 시간에 영향을 미치기 때문입니다. 그리고, 삼각대를 이용하시면 빛이 어두운 공간에서 사진의 질을 향상시키실 수 있습니다. 계속 문제를 **16** 겪으시는 경우, 안내를 통한 문제 해결을 위해 저희 지원팀에 연락주시기 바랍니다.

어휘 look + 형용사: ~하게 보이다, ~한 것 같다 overly 지나치게 fix ~을 바로잡다, ~을 고치다 expert 전문가 likely 아마 due to ~ 때문에, ~로 인한 default 초기 설정(출시될 때의 표준 상태) sensitivity 민감도 setting (기기 등의) 설정 indoor 실내의 increase ~을 높이다, ~을 증가시키다 when -ing ~할 때 shoot 촬영하다 condition 상태, 조건, 환경 make sure to do 반드시 ~하다 as well ~도, 또한 affect ~에 영향을 미치다 exposure 노출 tripod 삼각대 improve ~을 향상시키다, ~을 개선하다 poorly lit 빛이 어두운(lit은 light의 과거분사) continue -ing 계속 ~하다 contact ~에 연락하다 guided 안내 받는 troubleshooting 문제 해결

13.
정답 (C)

해설 빈칸 뒤에 동사의 -ing형태가 위치해 있으므로 전치사 또는 접속사가 위치해야 합니다. 보기 중에 '~할 때'라는 의미를 나타내는 시간 부사절 접속사 (C) when이 정답입니다. 시간 부사절 접속사 뒤에 주어를 생략하고 동사를 현재분사로 써서 「when + ing」 형태로 '~할 때'라는 의미를 나타내는 분사구문입니다.

오답 (A) then: '그 때', '그러고 나서'라는 의미를 나타내는 부사이며, 빈칸은 부사 자리가 아니므로 오답입니다.

(B) so: 접속사 '그래서', 부사 '그렇게'라는 의미를 나타내며, 빈칸은 접속사나 부사 자리가 아니므로 오답입니다.

(D) though: '그래도', '~이긴 하지만'이라는 의미의 부사절

접속사이며, 문맥상 어울리지 않으므로 오답입니다.

14.
정답 (A)

해석 (A) 이는 플래시를 사용하지 않고 카메라가 더 많은 빛을 담아 내는 데 도움을 줍니다.
(B) 게다가, 촬영 세션을 야외에서 진행해 주시기를 정중히 요청드립니다.
(C) 현재 귀하의 지역에서는 팰머라 C300 모델을 구입하실 수 없습니다.
(D) 고객님의 제품은 영업일 기준 7일 이내에 수리 및 발송될 예정이오니 참고 바랍니다.

해설 빈칸 앞 문장에서 빛이 약한 상태에서 촬영할 때 ISO를 800까지 또는 더 높게 올리는 것을 권장한다는 내용이 언급되었는데, 이렇게 권장한 이유나 효과에 대해 설명하는 내용이 뒤에 이어지는 것이 적절합니다. 따라서 보기 중에서 지시어 this를 사용하여 권장한 내용을 지칭하고, 플래시를 사용하지 않고 카메라가 더 많은 빛을 담는 데 도움이 되기 때문이라고 설명한 (A)가 정답입니다.

오답 (B) 앞 문장에서 실내 환경에서 촬영할 때 도움이 되는 방법을 권장하였으므로 실외 촬영을 요청하는 내용은 어울리지 않습니다.
(C) 카메라 제품을 현재 구입할 수 없다는 내용과 문맥상 어울리지 않으므로 오답입니다.
(D) 수리 및 배송에 관한 내용이 앞문장에 언급되어 있지 않으므로 오답입니다.

어휘 help A do: A가 ~하는 데 도움을 주다 capture ~을 담아내다, ~을 포착하다 without -ing ~하지 않고, ~하지 않은 채 additionally 게다가 kindly 정중히 conduct 실시하다 outdoors 야외에서 available 구입할 수 있는, 이용할 수 있는 region 지역 at the moment 현재 note that ~라는 것을 알아 두세요, ~라는 점을 참고하세요 within ~내에 business day 영업일

15.
정답 (D)

해설 앞선 문장에서 ISO를 높이도록 권장하는 내용이 언급되고, 빈칸 뒤의 목적어가 셔터 속도를 뜻하는 the shutter speed인 것으로 볼 때, 해당 문장이 셔터 속도도 변경하도록 당부하는 의미임을 알 수 있습니다. 따라서 '조정하다, 변경하다'를 뜻하는 (D) adjust가 정답입니다.

오답 (A) run: 타동사로 쓰일 경우 '운영하다'라는 의미를 나타내므로 문맥과 어울리지 않습니다.
(B) purchase: '구입하다', '사다'라는 의미를 나타내므로 문맥과 어울리지 않습니다.
(C) compare: '비교하다'라는 의미를 나타내므로 문맥과 어울리지 않습니다.

어휘 run 운영하다 purchase 사다, 구입하다 compare 비교하다 adjust ~을 조정하다, ~을 조절하다

16.
정답 (B)

해설 빈칸에 들어갈 동사의 알맞은 형태를 고르는 문제입니다. 빈칸 앞에는 타동사 continue가 위치해 있는데, continue는 동명사를 목적어로 가질 수 있으며 '계속해서 ~하다'라는 의미를 나타냅니다. 따라서 동명사 형태인 (B) experiencing이 정답입니다.

오답 (A) experience: 동사원형이며, 빈칸 앞에 동사 continue가 있으므로 동사원형을 쓸 수 없습니다.
(C) experienced: '능숙한', '경험이 많은'이라는 의미의 과거분사이며 과거분사는 continue의 목적어가 될 수 없고, 정관사 the가 포함된 명사구를 수식할 수 없으므로 오답입니다.
(D) were experienced: 수동태이며, 빈칸 뒤에 명사 목적어인 the same problem이 위치해 있으므로 수동태는 빈칸에 위치할 수 없습니다.

PART 7 FINAL TEST

1. (B) 2. (B) 3. (C) 4. (D) 5. (C)
6. (A) 7. (B) 8. (D) 9. (C) 10. (A)
11. (D) 12. (B) 13. (C) 14. (A)

1-4 다음 이메일을 참조하시오.

발신: 라비 나이르 <rnair@helixlogistics.com>
수신: 모든 창고 관리자들
제목: 지게차 안전 수료증 시간
날짜: 10월 5일

팀원 여러분,

우리 시설 전체에 걸쳐 최고의 안전 수준을 유지하기 위해 지속되는 노력으로, 우리가 10월 13일 금요일, 오전 10시부터 오후 12시까지, 4번 하역장 근처의 중앙 선적 구역에서 **1** 의무적인 지게차 운전 안전 과정을 주최할 예정입니다. 이 시간은 **2(D)** 안전한 조작 절차에 대한 상세한 안내, **2(C)** 간단한 동영상 시연회, 그리고 **2(A)** 공인 안전 조사관과 함께 하는 현장 질의 응답 시간을 포함할 것입니다.

모든 지게차 운전자들께서 반드시 통보 받아 전체 교육 시간에 참석하시도록 해 주시기 바랍니다. **3** 이 과정을 수료하시는 운전자들께서는 공식 수료증을 받으시게 될 것이며, 이후 18개월 동안 유효합니다. 인증을 위해 도착하자 마자 각자의 사원증을 지참하고 오시도록 참석자들에게 정중히 상기시켜 주시기 바랍니다. **4** 어느 팀원이든 일정상의 충돌 문제가 있거나 어떤 이유로 참석할 수 없는 경우, 늦어도 10월 9일, 월요일까지 이메일을 통해 제게 알려 주시기 바랍니다, 그래야 다른 조치들이 이뤄질 수 있습니다.

이 사안에 대한 여러분의 관심에 대해, 그리고 작업 공간 안전에 대한 여러분의 지속적인 헌신에 대해 미리 감사 드립니다.

안녕히 계십시오.

라비 나이르
물류 안전 조정관

어휘 warehouse 창고 supervisor 관리자, 상사, 감독 forklift 지게차 certification 수료증, 자격증, 증명(서) session (특정 활동을 위한) 시간 ongoing 지속되는, 계속되는 effort 노력 uphold ~을 유지하다 facility 시설(물) host ~을 주최하다 compulsory 의무적인 operation 운전, 작동, 가동, 영업, 운영 loading bay 선적 구역 adjacent to ~ 근처의, ~에 인접한 include ~을 포함하다 detailed 상세한 walk-through (자세한) 설명 handling 조작, 처리 procedure 절차 demonstration 시연(회), 시범 certified 공인된, 자격증이 있는 inspector 조사관, 점검관 ensure that 반드시 ~하도록 하다, ~임을 보장하다 notify ~에게 알리다 attend ~에 참석하다 entire 전체의 duration 지속 시간 training 교육, 훈련 complete ~을 수료하다, ~을 완료하다 valid 유효한 remind ~에게 상기시키다 attendee 참석자 verification 인증, 확인 upon arrival 도착하자마자 scheduling conflict 일정상의 충돌 be unable to do ~할 수 없다 via ~을 통해 no later than 늦어도 ~까지 so that (결과) 그래야, 그러므로, (목적) ~하도록 arrangement 조치, 처리, 마련 in advance 미리, 사전에 attention 관심, 주의(력), 주목 matter 사안, 문제 continued 지속적인 commitment 헌신

1. 이메일의 목적이 무엇인가?
   (A) 직원 회의 일정을 잡는 것
   (B) 교육 과정을 알리는 것
   (C) 취업 기회를 설명하는 것
   (D) 관리자들에게 의견을 요청하는 것

   정답 (B)
   해설 첫 번째 단락에서 의무적인 지게차 운전 안전 과정을 주최할 예정임을(we will be hosting a compulsory forklift operation safety course ~) 밝힌 다음, 그 행사의 진행 및 참석과 관련된 정보를 제공하고 있으므로 (B)가 정답입니다.
   어휘 describe ~을 설명하다, ~을 묘사하다 opportunity 기회 request ~을 요청하다 feedback 의견

   Paraphrase a compulsory forklift operation safety course → a training course

2. 10월 13일에 일어나지 않을 일은 무엇인가?
   (A) 한 전문가가 질문에 답변할 것이다.
   (B) 한 작업 구역이 일시적으로 폐쇄될 것이다.
   (C) 직원들이 동영상을 시청할 것이다.
   (D) 몇몇 절차가 설명될 것이다.

   정답 (B)
   해설 첫 번째 단락에 언급된 안전한 조작 절차에 대한 상세한 안내(a detailed walk-through of safe handling procedures)에서 (D)를, 간단한 동영상 시연회(a short video demonstration)에서 (C)를, 그리고 공인 안전 조사관과 함께 하는 현장 질의 응답 시간(a live Q&A with a certified safety inspector)에서 (A)를 각각 확인할 수 있습니다. 하지만, 폐쇄되는 구역과 관련된 정보는 제시되어 있지 않으므로 (B)가

정답입니다.

어휘 expert 전문가 temporarily 일시적으로, 임시로 explain ~을 설명하다

Paraphrase
- a live Q&A with a certified safety inspector → (A) An expert will answer questions
- a detailed walkthrough of safe handling procedures → (D) Some procedures will be explained

3. 나이르 씨가 수료증과 관련해 언급하는 것은 무엇인가?
(A) 오직 정규직 창고 직원들에게만 발급될 것이다.
(B) 직원 사원증에 포함될 것이다.
(C) 일년 반 동안 계속 유효한 상태로 유지될 것이다.
(D) 한 온라인 과정의 수료를 필요로 한다.

정답 (C)

해설 두 번째 단락에 해당 과정을 수료하는 운전자들이 공식 수료증을 받는다는 사실과 함께, 이후 18개월 동안 유효하다고(Operators who complete the course will receive official certification, valid for the next 18 months) 알리고 있으므로 (C)가 정답입니다.

어휘 issue ~을 발급하다, ~을 지급하다

Paraphrase valid for the next 18 months → remain valid for one and a half years

4. 한 직원이 10월 13일 세션에 참석할 수 없는 경우에 관리자들이 무엇을 해야 하는가?
(A) 안전 조사관에게 연락한다
(B) 추가 교육일을 마련한다
(C) 온라인으로 교육 과정을 실시한다
(D) 나이르 씨에게 그들의 결석을 알린다

정답 (D)

해설 두 번째 단락에 어느 팀원이든 일정상의 충돌 문제가 있거나 어떤 이유로 참석할 수 없는 경우 이메일을 통해 자신에게 알려 달라고(If any team member has a scheduling conflict or is unable to attend for any reason, please notify me via e-mail by no later than Monday, ~) 요청하고 있으므로 (D)가 정답입니다.

어휘 contact ~에게 연락하다 organize ~을 마련하다, ~을 조직하다 additional 추가적인 inform A of B: A에게 B를 알리다 absence 부재, 결근, 결석 conduct ~을 실시하다, ~을 수행하다

Paraphrase unable to attend / notify → Inform / absence

5-9 다음 기사와 메시지를 참조하시오.

9 『헬시 오피스 다이제스트』
3월호

바쁜 전문직 종사자들을 위한 작은 건강 습관

하루 종일 근무하는 동안 건강한 상태를 유지하는 것은 어려울 수 있으며, 특히 장시간 근무하는 직원이나 책상을 기반으로 하는 업무를 맡은 직원에게 그렇습니다. 하지만, 몇 가지 간단한 건강 습관을 기르는 것이 시간이 흐를수록 의미 있는 차이를 만들어 낼 수 있습니다.

- 몸을 움직일 시간을 만들어 보십시오. 사무실 주변을 한 바퀴 도는 것뿐이라 할지라도, **5(A)** 1시간마다 한 번씩 몇 분 동안 서 있거나 걸어 보도록 하십시오. 시간이 흐를수록, 이것이 뻣뻣함을 감소시키고 에너지 수준을 향상시키는 데 도움이 될 수 있습니다.
- **5(B)** 근처에 영양가 있는 간식을 두십시오. 감자칩이나 사탕을 향해 팔을 뻗는 대신, 미리 얇게 썬 과일이나 혼합된 견과류를 준비해 개인 용기에 보관해 놓으십시오.
- **5(D)**, **6** 물을 더 많이 마십시오. 많은 사람들이 갈증을 배고픔으로 혼동하는데, 이는 불필요한 군것질로 이어집니다. 수분이 충전된 상태를 유지하는 것은 집중력도 향상시켜 줍니다.

7 여러분만의 직장 건강 팁이 있으신가요? 저희에게 글을 써서 보내 주시면, 다가오는 호에 특별히 실어 드릴 수도 있습니다!

어휘 wellness 건강(함) habit 습관 professional n. 전문직 종사자, 전문가 stay + 형용사: ~한 상태를 유지하다 while -ing ~하는 동안 A-based: A를 기반으로 하는 make a difference 차이를 만들어 내다 meaningful 의미 있는 over time 시간이 흐를수록 lap 한 바퀴 (돌기) help do ~하는 데 도움이 되다 reduce ~을 감소시키다 stiffness 뻣뻣함 improve ~을 향상시키다, ~을 개선하다 nutritious 영양가 있는 instead of ~ 대신 reach for ~을 향해 팔을 뻗다 slice ~을 얇게 썰다 in advance 미리, 사전에 store v. ~을 보관하다 individual 개인의, 개별적인 container 보관 용기, 그릇 confuse ~을 혼동하다 thirst 갈증 lead to ~로 이어지다 unnecessary 불필요한 snacking 군것질 hydrated 수분이 충전된 concentration 집중(력) feature ~을 특별히 포함하다, ~을 특징으로 하다 upcoming 다가오는, 곧 있을 issue (출판물의) 호

독자 제출 의견

9 귀사의 최근 기사에 실린 훌륭한 제안에 감사 드립니다. 제가 전에 모이라 통신회사에 근무했는데, 항상 제 동료 직원들에게 하루 일과 내내 건강에 좋은 습관을 유지하도록 권하곤 했습니다. 제게 효과가 있었던 한 가지 전략은 오전에 커피를 과일 스무디로 바꾸는 것이었습니다. 그것이 카페인 부족에 따른 무력감 없이 정신이 맑은 상태를 유지하는 데 도움을 주었습니다.

또한, 제가 통근 중에 계속 음료를 흘렸기 때문에, 스무디에 완벽하면서 재사용 가능한 병을 고안했습니다. **8** 완전히 새로운 저희 회사, 리버믹스에서 프레시고 플라스크를 막 출시했습니다. 이 제품은 보냉 보온 처리가 되어 있고, 새지 않으며, 자동차 컵 홀더와 업무용 가방에 쉽게 들어갑니다. 저희는 바쁜 전문직 종사자들께서 더 건강한 방식을 하루를 시작하시는 데 도움을 드리기 위해 이 제품을 고안했습니다.

— 키이라 놀란

어휘 submission 제출(물) suggestion 제안, 의견 recent 최근의 used to do 전에 ~했다 encourage A to do: A에게 ~하도록 권하다 strategy 전략 work for ~에게 효과가 있다 switch from A to B: A를 B로 바꾸다 caffeine crash 카페인 부족에 따른 무력감 keep -ing 계속 ~하다 spill ~을 흘리다, ~을 엎지르다 commute 통근, 통학 reusable 재사용 가능한 brand new 완전히 새로운 release ~을 출시하다, ~을 발매하다 insulated 보냉 보온 처리가 된, 단열 처리된 leakproof 새지 않는 fit into (크기 등이) ~에 잘 맞다, ~에 맞아 들어가다 in a ~ way ~한 방식으로

5. 기사에서 추천되지 않은 것은 무엇인가?
(A) 하루 중에 간단히 걷는 것
(B) 건강에 좋은 간식을 먹는 것
(C) 근무 시간 중에 추가로 자는 것
(D) 물을 더 많이 마시는 것

정답 (C)

해설 첫 지문 두 번째 단락에 1시간마다 한 번씩 몇 분 동안 서 있거나 걷는 것(Try to stand or walk for a few minutes every hour), 근처에 영양가 있는 간식을 두고 먹는 것(Keep nutritious snacks nearby), 그리고 물을 더 많이 마시는 것이(Drink more water) 언급되어 있습니다. 하지만, 추가로 잠은 더 자는 것과 관련된 정보는 제시되어 있지 않으므로 (C)가 정답입니다.

어휘 brief 간단한, 짧은 extra 추가의, 별도의 consume 마시다, 먹다, 소비하다 fluid 물, 액체

Paraphrase
· walk for a few minutes ⇒ (A) Taking brief
· walks nutritious snacks ⇒ (B) healthy snacks
· Drink more water ⇒ (D) Consuming more fluids

6. 기사에서 적절히 수분을 섭취한 상태를 유지하는 것과 관련해 무엇을 언급하는가?
(A) 식욕을 줄이는 데 도움을 줄 수 있다.
(B) 질병 발생 가능성을 낮춰 줄 수 있다.
(C) 더 잦은 휴식으로 이어질 수 있다.
(D) 운동 능력을 향상시켜 준다

정답 (A)

해설 첫 지문 두 번째 단락에 물을 많이 마시라는 조언과 함께 많은 사람들이 갈증을 배고픔으로 혼동해 불필요한 군것질로 이어진다고(Drink more water. Many people confuse thirst for hunger, which leads to unnecessary snacking) 알리고 있습니다. 따라서 수분을 섭취한 상태를 유지하는 것이 식욕 억제 효과가 있는 것으로 볼 수 있으므로 (A)가 정답입니다.

어휘 properly 적절히, 제대로 decrease ~을 낮추다, ~을 감소시키다(= reduce) likelihood 가능성 illness 질병 desire 욕구, 욕망 lead to ~로 이어지다 frequent 잦은, 빈번한 break 휴식 athletic 운동의, 체육의 performance 수행 (능력), 성과, 실적, 공연, 연주

7. 『헬시 오피스 다이제스트』와 관련해 언급된 것은 무엇인가?
(A) 모이라 통신회사에 의해 매일 출판된다.
(B) 독자들로부터 건강 관련 아이디어를 받는다.
(C) 제품 후기에 초점이 맞춰져 있다.
(D) 오직 의료 전문가들만을 대상으로 한다.

정답 (B)

해설 첫 지문 마지막 단락에 자신만의 직장 건강 팁이 있는지 물으면서 글을 써서 보내면 다가오는 호에 실을 수 있다고(Have your own workplace wellness tips? Write to us and we might feature them in an upcoming issue!) 알리고 있으므로 (B)가 정답입니다.

어휘 accept ~을 받아들이다, ~을 수용하다 A-related: A와 관련된 be focused on ~에 초점이 맞춰져 있다 review 후기, 평가, 검토 be intended for ~을 대상으로 하다

Paraphrase your own workplace wellness tips / Write to us ⇒ accepts health-related ideas from readers

8. 프레시고 플라스크와 관련해 사실인 것은 무엇인가?
  (A) 한 건강 잡지에 후기가 실렸다.
  (B) 한 디자인 경연대회에서 영감을 받았다.
  (C) 많은 다른 색상으로 이용 가능하다.
  (D) 최근 시장에 출시되었다.

정답 (D)
해설 두 번째 지문 두 번째 단락에 글쓴이의 회사 리버믹스에서 프레시고 플라스크를 막 출시했다는(My brand new company, Rivermix, just released the FreshGo Flask) 사실을 밝히고 있으므로 (D)가 정답입니다.

어휘 review ~의 후기를 작성하다, ~을 평가하다, ~을 검토하다 inspire ~에 영감을 주다 available (사물) 이용 가능한, 구입 가능한, (사람) 시간이 있는 launch ~을 출시하다, ~을 시작하다 recently 최근

Paraphrase just released ⇒
  was launched onto the market recently

9. 놀란 씨와 관련해 유추할 수 있는 것은 무엇인가?
  (A) 모이라 통신회사의 설립자이다.
  (B) 여러 출판물을 위해 기사를 쓴다.
  (C) 『헬시 오피스 다이제스트』의 3월호를 읽었다.
  (D) 더 이상 과일 스무디를 마시지 않는다.

정답 (C)
해설 두 번째 지문 첫 단락에 상대방 출판사의 최근 기사에 실린 훌륭한 제안에 감사하다는(Thanks for the great suggestions in your recent article) 인사를 전하는 말이 쓰여 있고, 그 기사에 해당하는 첫 지문 상단에 헬시 오피스 다이제스트 3월호(Healthy Office Digest, March Edition)로 표기되어 있으므로 (C)가 정답입니다.

어휘 founder 설립자, 창립자 several 여럿의, 몇몇의 publication 출판(물) no longer 더 이상 ~ 않다

10-14 다음 두 이메일과 거래 내역서를 참조하시오.

수신: info@blossomandbelleweddings.com
발신: clara.finchley@hawthornmedia.co.uk
제목: 결혼식 피로연 계획
날짜: 4월 4일

안녕하세요,

다가오는 5월 18일에 있을 제 결혼식 피로연과 관련해 이메일을 쓰며, 이 행사를 진행하도록 귀사에서 도움을 주시고 계십니다. 아시다시피, **10 제가 이미 귀사를 통해 출장 요리 서비스와 꽃 장식물을 마련해 두었으며**, 귀사는 계획 과정 전반에 걸쳐 의사 소통도 아주 잘 되고 큰 도움이 되었습니다. 하지만, **11 최근의 예측 불가능한 날씨로 인해, 저는 지금 정원 구역에 대한 예방 조치로서 대형 천막을 설치하는 것을 고려하고 있습니다.**

12 약 60명의 초대 손님들을 수용할 수 있는 야외 천막에 대해 이용 가능한 선택 사항과 가격 정보를 제게 보내 주시겠습니까? 제 예산이 이미 빠듯해진 상태이기 때문에, **12** 가격을 1,400달러 미만으로 유지해야 할 겁니다.

감사합니다.
클라라 핀칠리

어휘 wedding reception 결혼식 피로연 upcoming 다가오는, 곧 있을 coordinate ~을 진행하다, ~을 편성하다 arrange ~을 마련하다, ~을 조치하다 catering 출장 요리(업) decoration 장식(물) firm 회사, 업체 communicative 의사 소통도 잘 되는 process 과정 due to ~로 인해, ~ 때문에 unpredictable 예측 불가능한 consider -ing ~하는 것을 고려하다 set up ~을 설치하다, ~을 준비하다 large-scale 대형의, 대규모의 precaution 예방 조치 available (사물) 이용 가능한, 구입 가능한, (사람) 시간이 있는 pricing 가격 (책정) accommodate ~을 수용하다 approximately 약, 대략 budget 예산 be stretched thin 빠듯해지다, 다 떨어지다 would have to do ~해야 할 것이다

수신: clara.finchley@hawthornmedia.co.uk
발신: info@blossomandbelleweddings.com
제목: 회신: 결혼식 피로연 계획
날짜: 4월 5일

핀칠리 씨께,

귀하의 메시지에 감사 드립니다. 저희는 기꺼이 귀하의 행사를 위해 천막을 마련해 드릴 것입니다. 첨부된 가격 목록을 참고하시기 바라며, 이는 크기와 스타일, 그리고 포함된 비품에 따른 여러 천막 선택 사항들을 개괄적으로 설명해 드립니다. 귀하께서 비용을 낮게 유지하시기를 바라고 계신다는 점을 이해하지만, **13 완전히 새로운 스타일을 고려해 보시기를 권해 드리며, 이는 목판 바닥재와 세련된 조명을 포함합니다.**

귀하의 추정 초대 손님 숫자에 대해서는, 가든 뷰와 헤리티지 스타일이 적합할 것입니다. 저희가 귀하의 예약을 확보하고 설치 여부를 확인할 시간이 있도록 4월 12일까지 선호하시는 바를 저희에게 알려 주시기 바랍니다. 이를 전화로 추가적인 논의를 하시고자 하는 경우, 555-4921번으로 언제든지 제게 직접 연락 주시기 바랍니다.

안녕히 계십시오.

아만다 영
행사 진행 관리 책임
블러썸 & 벨 웨딩스

어휘 refer to ~을 참고하다 attach ~을 첨부하다, ~을 부착하다 outline ~을 개괄적으로 설명하다 depending on ~에 따라 (다른), ~에 달려 있는 include ~을 포함하다 furnishings 비품, 집기 keep A 형용사: A를 ~하게 유지하다 encourage A to do: A에게 ~하도록 권하다 brand new 완전히 새로운 flooring 바닥재 sophisticated 세련된, 정교한 estimated 추정된 suitable 적합한, 알맞은 let A know: A에게 알리다 preference 선호(하는 것) so that (목적) ~하도록, (결과) 그래서, 그러므로 secure v. ~을 확보하다 booking 예약 confirm ~을 확인하다 setup 설치, 설정, 준비 further 더 깊이 있게, 한층 더 feel free to do 언제든지 ~하세요 reach ~에게 연락하다

야외 천막 대여 선택 사항 – 봄 결혼 시즌

천막 종류	수용 인원	특징	가격 (고정 요금)
베이직 파빌리온	최대 40명	측면 개방형, 비품 미포함	800달러
12 가든 뷰	50-80명	줄 조명과 측면 벽판 포함	1,200달러
헤리티지 스타일	40-90명	13 샹들리에와 목판 바닥재	1,550달러
그랜드 파빌리온	최대 150명	전체 조명, 무대, 카펫 포함	2,100달러

메모:
14 예약은 반드시 행사 날짜보다 최소 10일 전에 확인되어야 합니다.
모든 천막은 설치 및 해체 작업을 포함합니다.
바람이 강할 경우에 대비해, 측면 벽판이 안전을 위해 제거될 수 있습니다.

어휘 rental 대여, 임대 capacity 수용 인원, 수용 규모 feature 특징, 기능 flat rate 고정 요금 open-sided 측면이 개방되어 있는 at least 최소한, 적어도 dismantling 해체 in the event of ~의 경우에 (대비해) remove ~을 제거하다, ~을 없애다

10. 핀칠리 씨가 이미 무엇을 했다고 말하는가?
(A) 음식과 꽃을 예약한 것
(B) 초대 손님 숫자를 늘린 것
(C) 행사 날짜를 변경한 것
(D) 자신의 행사에 대해 전액 지불한 것

정답 (A)

해설 핀칠리 씨의 이메일인 첫 지문 초반부에 이미 상대방 회사를 통해 출장 요리 서비스와 꽃 장식물을 마련해 둔(I've already arranged catering and floral decorations through your firm) 상태임을 언급하고 있으므로 (A)가 정답입니다.

어휘 in full 전액, 전부, 모두 increase ~을 늘리다, ~을 증가시키다

Paraphrase arranged catering and floral decorations
⇒ Booked food and flowers

11. 원래의 피로연 계획과 관련해 암시된 것은 무엇인가?
(A) 야외에서 열릴 의도였다.
(B) 예비 장소를 포함하고 있었다.
(C) 베이직 파빌리온을 필요로 했다.
(D) 대형 천막을 수반하지 않았다.

정답 (D)

해설 핀칠리 씨의 이메일인 첫 지문 중반부에 최근의 예측 불가능한 날씨로 인해 정원 구역에 대한 예방 조치로서 대형 천막을 설치하는 것을 고려하고 있다는(due to the unpredictable weather lately, I'm now considering setting up a large-scale tent as a precaution for the garden area) 말이 쓰여 있습니다. 이는 애초에 필요하지 않을 것으로 생각되었던 대형 천막이 필요해진 상황임을 의미하므로 (D)가 정답입니다.

어휘 original 애초의, 원래의 be intended to do ~할 의도이다, ~하기 위한 것이다 backup 예비의 location 장소, 위치, 지점 involve ~을 수반하다, ~와 관련되다 require ~을 필요로 하다

12. 핀칠리 씨가 필요로 하는 것에 대해 어느 선택 사항이 가장 적합할 것인가?
(A) 베이직 파빌리온
(B) 가든 뷰
(C) 헤리티지 스타일
(D) 그랜드 파빌리온

정답 (B)

해설 핀칠리 씨의 이메일인 첫 지문 후반부에 대형 천막 이용과 관련된 조건을 약 60명의 초대 손님들을 수용할 수 있는 천막이면서(approximately 60 guests) 가격을 1,400달러 미만으로 유지하는 것이(keep the price below $1,400) 언급되어 있습니다. 따라서 세 번째 지문에서 수용 인원은 50-80으로, 가격은 $1,200으로 표기되어 있는 Garden View가 적합하므로 (B)가 정답입니다.

어휘 appropriate 적합한, 적절한

13. 해당 회사의 최신 대형 천막 종류에 대한 대여 가격은 얼마인가?

(A) 800달러
(B) 1,200달러
(C) 1,550달러
(D) 2,100달러

정답 (C)

해설 두 번째 지문 첫 단락에 완전히 새로운 스타일의 대형 천막이 목판 바닥재와 세련된 조명을 포함한다고 언급되어 있습니다. 세 번째 지문에 특징으로 chandeliers와 wooden flooring이 쓰여 있는 Heritage Style의 가격이 $1,550로 표기되어 있으므로 (C)가 정답입니다.

14. 모든 대형 천막 선택 사항과 관련해 언급된 것은 무엇인가?

(A) 반드시 미리 예약되어야 한다.
(B) 가구와 조명을 포함한다.
(C) 반드시 고객에 의해 설치되어야 한다.
(D) 일년 내내 동일한 가격이다.

정답 (A)

해설 세 번째 지문 마지막 단락에 예약이 반드시 행사 날짜보다 최소 10일 전에 확인되어야 한다고(Bookings must be confirmed at least 10 days before event date) 쓰여 있어 모든 대형 천막이 미리 예약되어야 한다는 점을 알 수 있으므로 (A)가 정답입니다.

어휘 in advance 미리, 사전에 set up 설치하다 all year-round 일년 내내

Paraphrase Bookings must be confirmed at least 10 days before event date ⇒ must be booked in advance

기본토익 700+

700+ 필수
최빈출 정답 어휘

DAY 01-05	최빈출 정답 어휘_명사	2
DAY 06-08	최빈출 정답 어휘_동사	32
DAY 09-10	최빈출 정답 어휘_형용사	50
DAY 11-12	최빈출 정답 어휘_부사	62
DAY 13-15	최빈출 정답 어휘_숙어	74

DAY 01 | 최빈출 정답 어휘: 명사 ①

핵심 단어들을 확인한 후, 오른쪽의 기출 예시를 통해 각 단어의 쓰임새를 익혀보세요.

01 **purchase**	명 구입(품) 동 ~을 구입하다	the receipt for your recent purchase 귀하의 최근 구입품에 대한 영수증
02 **request**	명 요청 동 ~을 요청하다	process one's request ~의 요청을 처리하다
03 **increase**	명 증가, 인상 동 증가하다, ~을 증가시키다	an increase in our sales 우리 매출의 증가
04 **review**	명 검토, 평가, 후기 동 ~을 검토하다, 살펴보다	a positive review of the proposal 제안서에 대한 긍정적인 평가
05 **result**	명 결과 동 결과로서 생기다, 결과를 낳다	the results from the latest analysis 최근의 분석을 통해 얻은 결과
06 **experience**	명 경험, 경력 동 ~을 경험하다	three years of accounting experience 3년의 회계 경력 experienced 형 숙련된, 경험 많은

07 **location**	명 지점, 위치	open a new location in New York 뉴욕에 새로운 지점을 열다 locate 동 ~을 두다, ~의 위치를 찾다
08 **response**	명 반응, 대응, 답장	response to your presentation 당신의 발표에 대한 반응 respond 동 응답하다, 대응하다
09 **benefit**	명 혜택, 이득, (급여 외의) 특전	offer attractive benefits 매력적인 혜택을 제공하다 beneficial 형 유익한, 이로운
10 **approval**	명 승인, 허가	need the approval of the manager 책임자의 승인을 필요로 하다 approve 동 ~을 승인하다
11 **feature**	명 특징, 기능 동 ~을 특집으로 다루다, ~을 포함하다	have more useful features than any other brands 다른 어떤 브랜드들보다 유용한 특징들을 더 많이 갖고 있다
12 **view**	명 견해, 관점, 경관 동 ~을 보다, ~을 (…라고) 생각하다	rooms with a view of the ocean 바다 경관을 지닌 객실들
13 **opportunity**	명 기회	an opportunity to join the team 팀에 합류할 기회
14 **defect**	명 결함, 하자, 흠	discover serious product defects 심각한 제품 결함을 발견하다 defective 형 결함이 있는

15 **renovation**	명 개조, 보수	close the store due to the renovation 개조 공사로 인해 매장을 닫다 renovate 동 ~을 개조하다, 보수하다
16 **employment**	명 고용, 취업, 일자리	be looking for employment 일자리를 찾는 중이다 employ 동 ~을 고용하다, ~을 활용하다
17 **release**	명 출시, 공개, 발표 동 ~을 출시하다, 공개하다	the release of a new book 신간 도서의 출시
18 **priority**	명 우선 순위, 우선 과제	a top priority for our division 우리 부서의 최우선 과제
19 **advance**	명 발전, 진보 형 사전의	recent advances in technology 기술에 있어서 최근의 발전 advanced 형 발전된
20 **rate**	명 요금, 등급, 비율, 속도 동 ~을 평가하다	at reasonable rates 합리적인 요금으로
21 **operation**	명 운영, 작동, 조작, 운행	has been in operation for 10 years 10년 동안 운영되어 왔다 operational 형 운영 중인, 가동되는 operate 동 ~을 운영하다, 가동하다
22 **value**	명 가치, 값어치 동 ~을 소중하게 여기다	could be of great value to the company 회사에 대단한 가치가 있을 수 있다

23 **purpose**	명 목적	for business purpose 사업상의 목적으로 purposely 부 고의로
24 **term**	명 조건, 기간, 용어	according to the terms in the contract 계약서 내의 조건에 따라
25 **individual**	명 개인, 사람 형 개별적인, 개인의	seek talented individuals 재능 있는 사람들을 찾다
26 **cause**	명 이유, 원인 동 ~을 야기하다	determine the cause of the error 오류의 원인을 알아내다
27 **suggestion**	명 제안, 의견, 암시	be open to customer suggestions 고객 제안에 대해 열린 마음을 갖다
28 **complaint**	명 불만, 불평	take care of customer complaints 고객 불만을 처리하다 complain 동 불만을 제기하다, 불평하다
29 **description**	명 설명, 묘사	a detailed description of the position 그 직책에 대한 상세한 설명 describe 동 ~을 설명하다
30 **appreciation**	명 감사(의 뜻)	express[show] one's appreciation for ~에 대해 감사를 표하다 appreciate 동 ~에 대해 감사하다

실전 TEST

1 Online ------- come with free shipping on orders over a certain amount.

(A) occasions
(B) purchases
(C) meetings
(D) rates

2 The company scheduled an annual ------- to assess employee performance.

(A) review
(B) result
(C) budget
(D) renovation

3 One major ------- of remote work is the flexibility it offers employees.

(A) interest
(B) benefit
(C) control
(D) response

4 Traveling abroad gave her a unique ------- to experience different cultures.

(A) opportunity
(B) exception
(C) preference
(D) progress

5 The factory has been in ------- for over 50 years, producing high-quality textiles.

(A) operation
(B) function
(C) decision
(D) response

6 The scholarship is awarded to ------- who demonstrate exceptional academic achievement.

(A) locations
(B) materials
(C) individuals
(D) suggestions

7 A key ------- of the software update is improved security and faster performance.

(A) prospect
(B) term
(C) request
(D) feature

8 Ensuring customer satisfaction is the company's top ------- this year.

(A) experience
(B) excellence
(C) priority
(D) advance

9 In ------- to safety concerns raised by residents, the city council halted the demolition project.

(A) contrast
(B) exception
(C) response
(D) alteration

10 The job posting included a detailed ------- of the required qualifications and responsibilities.

(A) approval
(B) attention
(C) prediction
(D) description

11 The company showed ------- for its loyal customers by offering exclusive discounts.

(A) value
(B) appreciation
(C) employment
(D) complaint

12 The charity posted an online form to gather ------- regarding upcoming fundraising events.

(A) suggestions
(B) compositions
(C) successes
(D) evaluations

DAY 02 | 최빈출 정답 어휘: 명사 ②

핵심 단어들을 확인한 후, 오른쪽의 기출 예시를 통해 각 단어의 쓰임새를 익혀보세요.

01 **source**	몡 근원, 출처	a useful source of information 유용한 정보 출처
02 **figure**	몡 수치, 인물	a decrease in our sales figures 우리 매출 수치의 감소
03 **process**	몡 과정, 처리 동 ~을 처리하다, 가공하다	questions about the recycling process 재활용 과정에 관한 질문
04 **appearance**	몡 외관, 외형, 외모, 등장, 출연	redesign the product's appearance 제품의 외관을 다시 디자인하다
05 **order**	몡 주문(품), 순서, 지시, 명령 동 ~을 주문하다	The order should be placed by midnight. 주문은 자정까지 이뤄져야 한다.
06 **confirmation**	몡 확인(서)	received an e-mail confirmation 이메일 확인서를 받았다 confirm 동 ~을 확인해주다
07 **relocation**	몡 위치 이전, 재배치	the scheduled relocation to the new building 새 건물로의 예정된 위치 이전 relocate 동 ~을 이전하다

08 **position**	명 직책, 일자리, 위치, 입장 동 ~을 위치시키다	will apply for the position 그 직책에 지원할 것이다
09 **addition**	명 추가(물), 추가 인원	the addition of a new dish to the special menu 특별 메뉴에 대한 새로운 요리의 추가
10 **application**	명 신청(서), 지원(서), 적용	a completed application 작성 완료된 지원서
11 **appointment**	명 예약, 약속, 임명	make an appointment for ~에 대한 예약을 하다
12 **cancellation**	명 취소	apologize for the cancellation 취소에 대해 사과하다 cancel 동 ~을 취소하다
13 **capacity**	명 수용 규모, 용량	have greater storage capacity than ~ ~보다 더 큰 저장 용량을 지니다
14 **receipt**	명 영수증, 수령, 받음	submit a receipt for reimbursement 비용 환급을 위해 영수증을 제출하다 receive 동 ~을 받다
15 **agreement**	명 동의(서), 계약(서)	sign a rental agreement 임대 계약서에 서명하다 agree 동 동의하다, 합의하다

16	**expansion**	명 확대, 확장	our company's expansion into the Asian market 우리 회사의 아시아 시장으로의 확장 expand 동 확대(확장)되다, ~을 확대(확장)하다
17	**accomplishment**	명 성취, 성과	noteworthy accomplishments 주목할 만한 성과 accomplish 동 ~을 성취하다, 달성하다
18	**removal**	명 제거, 없앰	removal of unnecessary devices 불필요한 기기의 제거 remove 동 ~을 제거하다
19	**budget**	명 예산 형 저가의	work on the advertising budget 광고 예산 작업을 하다
20	**reservation**	명 예약	confirm a reservation by e-mail 이메일로 예약을 확인해주다 reserve 동 ~을 예약하다
21	**demand**	명 수요, 요구 동 ~을 요구하다	anticipate the higher demand for ~에 대한 더 높은 수요를 예측하다
22	**improvement**	명 개선, 향상	the improvement of our working conditions 우리 업무 환경의 개선 improve 동 ~을 개선하다, 향상시키다
23	**aim**	명 목적, 목표 동 ~을 목표로 하다	The aim of this seminar is to share ~. 본 세미나의 목적은 ~을 공유하는 것입니다.

24 **repair**	명 수리 (작업) 동 ~을 수리하다	call a technician for a repair 수리를 위해 기사를 부르다
25 **profit**	명 수익, 이익 동 수익을 얻다, ~에게 이익을 주다	an increase in net profits 순이익의 증가 profitable 형 수익성이 있는
26 **interest**	명 관심(사), 흥미, 이자 동 ~의 관심을 끌다	have an interest in working as a volunteer 자원봉사자로 일하는 데 관심을 갖고 있다 interested 형 (사람이) 관심을 가진 interesting 형 흥미로운
27 **decision**	명 결정	before you make a final decision 최종 결정을 내리기 전에 decide 동 ~을 결정하다
28 **requirement**	명 요구 (사항), 요건	if you think you meet the job requirements 직무 자격 요건을 충족한다고 생각하신다면 require 동 ~을 필요로 하다, ~에게 요구하다
29 **development**	명 개발, 발전	the development of our new products 우리의 신제품 개발 develop 동 ~을 개발하다, 발전시키다
30 **departure**	명 출발, 떠남	prior to departure 출발 전에 depart 동 출발하다, 떠나다

실전 TEST

1 Expert interviews served as a valuable ------- of information for the documentary.

(A) group
(B) source
(C) practice
(D) ability

2 The HR team improved the recruitment ------- to reduce costs associated with new hires.

(A) instance
(B) process
(C) occasion
(D) demand

3 A bachelor's degree in computer science is a ------- for the software engineer role.

(A) requirement
(B) registration
(C) reservation
(D) replacement

4 Due to a sudden rise in ------- for our newly released smartphone, we need to boost manufacturing capacity immediately.

(A) demand
(B) percentage
(C) population
(D) appearance

5 Smaller studios frequently struggle in the market due to their constrained advertising -------, especially when competing with major film franchises.

(A) fees
(B) viewers
(C) scenes
(D) budgets

6 Because of limited seating, the restaurant recommends that customers make ------- before arriving for dinner.

(A) suggestions
(B) exceptions
(C) observations
(D) reservations

7 The festival's wide range of events caters to the ------- of people of all ages and cultures.

(A) selections
(B) interests
(C) actions
(D) roles

8 The stadium will undergo renovations to increase the seating ------- for future sports events.

(A) duration
(B) preparation
(C) capacity
(D) intensity

9 The research team is currently working on the ------- of sustainable packaging for consumer products.

(A) instrument
(B) decision
(C) shipment
(D) development

10 The upgraded software feature is a useful ------- to the platform's existing capabilities.

(A) addition
(B) response
(C) treatment
(D) outcome

11 To obtain a building permit, the contractor must submit a completed ------- to the city office.

(A) process
(B) appointment
(C) application
(D) experience

12 Upon ------- of your payment, we will begin processing the shipment of your order.

(A) entry
(B) request
(C) receipt
(D) appeal

DAY 03 | 최빈출 정답 어휘: 명사 ③

핵심 단어들을 확인한 후, 오른쪽의 기출 예시를 통해 각 단어의 쓰임새를 익혀보세요.

01 **launch**	명 출시, 공개, 시작 동 ~을 출시하다, 시작하다	the successful launch of computer models 컴퓨터 모델의 성공적인 출시
02 **part**	명 부분, 부품	order engine parts 엔진 부품을 주문하다
03 **notice**	명 통보, 알림 동 ~을 인지하다, 알아채다	advance notice 사전 통보
04 **support**	명 지원, 지지, 도움, 후원 동 ~을 지원하다, 지지하다	call for technical support 기술 지원을 요청하다
05 **equipment**	명 장비, 설비	inspect all the safety equipment 모든 안전 장비를 점검하다
06 **celebration**	명 기념 행사, 축하 행사	our company's 25th anniversary celebration 우리 회사의 25주년 기념 행사 celebrate 동 ~을 기념하다, 축하하다
07 **investigation**	명 조사	a thorough investigation 철저한 조사
08 **examination**	명 조사, 검사	further examination of ~에 대한 추가적인 조사 examine 동 조사하다, 검사하다

09 **enhancement**	명 향상, 강화, 증강	for the purpose of career enhancement 경력 향상의 목적으로 enhance 동 ~을 향상시키다, 강화하다
10 **observation**	명 관찰, 주시	make a comprehensive observation 포괄적인 관찰을 하다 observe 동 ~을 관찰하다, 준수하다
11 **appraisal**	명 (가치 등에 대한) 평가, 감정	performance appraisals 업무 성과 평가 appraise 동 ~을 평가하다
12 **expectation**	명 기대(치), 예상	didn't meet our customers' expectations 우리 고객들의 기대를 충족시키지 못했다 expect 동 ~을 기대하다, 예상하다
13 **inconvenience**	명 불편함	apologize for any inconvenience 어떠한 불편함에 대해서도 사과하다 inconvenient 형 불편한
14 **success**	명 성공(작)	a great success in the field of tourism 관광업 분야에서의 엄청난 성공 successful 형 성공적인
15 **interruption**	명 중단, 방해	a brief interruption in ~의 일시적인 중단
16 **attendance**	명 참석, 참석자 수	high attendance at the quarterly workshop 분기별 워크숍에 대한 높은 참석자 수 attend 동 ~에 참석하다 attendee 명 참석자

DAY 3

17 **evaluation**	몡 평가	a careful evaluation of the survey data indicates that ~ 설문 조사 결과의 신중한 평가가 ~라는 것을 나타내다 evaluate 동 ~을 평가하다
18 **transaction**	몡 거래, 매매	unauthorized transactions 허가되지 않은 거래
19 **distribution**	몡 배부, 유통	distribution of handouts 유인물 배부 distribute 동 ~을 배부하다, 나눠주다
20 **feedback**	몡 의견	valuable feedback from our customers 우리 고객들에게서 받은 소중한 의견
21 **expense**	몡 지출 (비용), 경비	remove unnecessary expenses from the budget 예산에서 불필요한 지출을 없애다
22 **construction**	몡 건설	the construction of a new parking lot 새 주차장의 건설 construct 동 ~을 건설하다, 구성하다
23 **advertisement**	몡 광고(물)	plan to place an online advertisement 온라인 광고를 낼 계획을 세우다 advertise 동 ~을 광고하다 advertising 몡 광고 (활동)
24 **consent**	몡 동의, 승낙 동 동의하다, 승낙하다	without the client's written consent 고객의 서면 동의 없이

25 **disruption**	몡 중단, 장애, 지장	a temporary disruption in our order processing system 우리 주문 처리 시스템에 발생한 일시적인 장애 disrupt 동 ~에 지장을 주다
26 **inspiration**	몡 영감(을 주는 것)	with inspiration from natural surroundings 자연 환경에서 받은 영감으로 inspire 동 ~에게 영감을 주다, 자극하다
27 **preparation**	몡 준비, 대비	in preparation for the annual inspection 연례 점검을 위한 준비로 prepare 동 ~을 준비하다
28 **inquiry**	몡 문의, 질문	deal with customer inquiries 고객 문의 사항들을 처리하다 inquire 동 문의하다
29 **resident**	몡 주민	interesting activities for local residents 지역 주민들을 위한 흥미로운 활동들 residential 형 주거의 residence 몡 주택, 거주지
30 **aspect**	몡 측면, 양상	be involved in all aspects of marketing 마케팅의 모든 측면에 관여되어 있다

실전 TEST

1 If you have any ------- about the new training policy, please contact Human Resources.

(A) inquiries
(B) instructions
(C) tasks
(D) positions

2 One important ------- of project management is setting realistic deadlines while balancing quality and workload.

(A) aspect
(B) overview
(C) ingredient
(D) category

3 Dr. Lee's ------- on consumer spending habits challenged existing economic assumptions.

(A) observations
(B) reasons
(C) standards
(D) instincts

4 The office remains closed until further ------- due to interior renovations.

(A) care
(B) notice
(C) regard
(D) concern

5 In appreciation of our customers' continued -------, we are providing an extended warranty on select devices.

(A) transaction
(B) foundation
(C) support
(D) resource

6 A thorough ------- of customer purchasing behavior helped the team tailor their strategies more effectively.

(A) abbreviation
(B) agreement
(C) permission
(D) examination

7 A sudden power outage caused a brief ------- in the production line, resulting in shipment delays of several hours.

(A) attendance
(B) interruption
(C) outline
(D) statement

8 Recent ------- to the mobile banking app have made it significantly easier for customers to manage their accounts.

(A) continuations
(B) enhancements
(C) evaluations
(D) success

9 All safety ------ must be inspected monthly, and any damaged items should be reported immediately to the manager.

(A) equipment
(B) construction
(C) treatment
(D) security

10 Despite volatile market conditions, the sales department met and exceeded client ------- on service quality.

(A) computations
(B) endorsements
(C) adjustments
(D) expectations

11 The HR department reminded staff that travel ------- will only be reimbursed if submitted within five days of returning from a business trip.

(A) experiences
(B) expenses
(C) materials
(D) prices

12 The company's development team found its ------- in user feedback collected over the past year.

(A) suspicion
(B) apprehension
(C) inspiration
(D) construction

DAY 04 | 최빈출 정답 어휘: 명사 ④

핵심 단어들을 확인한 후, 오른쪽의 기출 예시를 통해 각 단어의 쓰임새를 익혀보세요.

01 **performance**	명 성과, 실적, 수행 능력, 공연	outstanding performance 뛰어난 성과 perform 동 ~을 수행하다, 연주하다
02 **facility**	명 시설(물)	visit overseas manufacturing facilities 해외에 있는 제조 시설을 방문하다 facilitate 동 ~을 용이하게 하다, ~을 촉진하다
03 **advantage**	명 장점, 유리한 점	have a significant competitive advantage 상당한 경쟁 우위를 가지다 advantageous 형 이로운, 유리한
04 **comparison**	명 비교, 대조	in comparison with other businesses 다른 업체들과 비교할 때 compare 동 ~을 비교하다
05 **item**	명 제품, 품목, 항목	will release many new items in the coming year 내년에 다양한 신상품들을 출시할 것이다

06 **presence**	명 존재(감), 출석, 참석	request your presence at a meeting 귀하의 회의 참석을 요청하다 present 동 ~을 제시하다, ~을 제공하다 형 현재의, 참석한, 존재하는
07 **promotion**	명 승진, 홍보, 판촉	This promotion ends on May 31. 이 판촉 행사는 5월 31일에 끝납니다.
08 **firm**	명 회사 형 굳건한, 확고한, 튼튼한	an architectural firm 건축 회사
09 **approach**	명 접근법, 접근 동 접근하다	an innovative approach to product development 제품 개발에 대한 혁신적인 접근법
10 **inventory**	명 재고	reduce the inventory 재고를 줄이다
11 **measure**	명 조치, 측정 동 ~을 재다, 측정하다	take strict measures 엄격한 조치를 취하다
12 **permission**	명 허락, 허가, 승인	without the permission from the author 저자의 허락 없이 permit 동 ~을 허가하다 명 허가증
13 **session**	명 (특정 활동을 위한) 시간	be required to participate in the training session 교육 시간에 참가해야 한다
14 **merchandise**	명 상품	sell various merchandise on the Web site 웹사이트에서 다양한 상품을 판매하다

15 **proposal**	명 제안(서)	rejected his proposal for the new project 새로운 프로젝트에 대한 그의 제안을 거절했다 propose 동 ~을 제안하다
16 **charge**	명 (청구) 요금, 책임 동 ~을 청구하다	a delivery charge 배송 요금 in charge of the project 프로젝트 담당인
17 **delivery**	명 배송(품)	await delivery of ~의 배송을 기다리다 deliver 동 ~을 배송하다
18 **cost**	명 비용, 경비 동 ~의 비용이 들다	try to reduce our operating costs 우리의 운영 비용을 줄이려 노력하다
19 **replacement**	명 교체(품), 후임(자)	receive a replacement part 교체 부품을 받다 replace 동 ~을 교체하다
20 **accommodation**	명 숙소, 숙박 시설	make a reservation for accommodations 숙박 시설을 예약하다 accommodate 동 ~을 수용하다
21 **responsibility**	명 책임, 담당 업무, 직무	It is your responsibility to do ~. ~하는 것은 당신의 직무입니다. responsible 형 책임 있는
22 **sales**	명 매출(액), 판매(량), 영업	experience an increase in our quarterly sales 우리 분기별 매출의 증가를 경험하다

23 **participant**	명 참가자	participants in the local event 지역 행사 참가자들 participate 동 참가하다
24 **supervision**	명 감독, 관리	under the supervision of the manager 매니저의 감독 하에 supervise 동 ~을 감독하다
25 **deal**	명 거래, 협상 동 거래하다, 처리하다	negotiate a deal 거래를 성사시키다
26 **registration**	명 등록	registration procedures 등록 절차 register 동 등록하다
27 **alternative**	명 대안 형 대체하는	be used as an alternative to ~ 대신 사용되다 alternatively 부 그 대신
28 **compliance**	명 준수	in compliance with safety standards 안전 기준을 준수하여 comply 동 준수하다
29 **component**	명 구성 요소, 부품, 부속	damage to product components 제품 부품의 손상
30 **preference**	명 선호, 취향, 선호하는 것	an increasing preference for online shopping 온라인 쇼핑에 대한 증가하는 선호 prefer 동 선호하다

DAY 4

실전 TEST

1 The new medical ------- includes patient care rooms, diagnostic equipment, and a pharmacy.

(A) facility
(B) product
(C) management
(D) device

2 All financial institutions are required to follow strict security ------- to protect customer information.

(A) issues
(B) interests
(C) measures
(D) deposits

3 Technical support staff participated in specialized training ------- focused on cyber-security protocols.

(A) sessions
(B) materials
(C) positions
(D) feedback

4 It is each passenger's ------- to ensure their baggage is properly labeled before check-in.

(A) status
(B) reservation
(C) responsibility
(D) delivery

5 Assembly line workers are trained to handle fragile ------- such as LED modules and battery cells.

(A) instruments
(B) components
(C) formulations
(D) discoveries

6 Online ------- for the mandatory workplace safety training opens on Monday morning.

(A) registration
(B) information
(C) detection
(D) installation

7 All vendors must send a written ------- specifying services, rates, and terms before negotiations begin.

(A) invoice
(B) proposal
(C) confirmation
(D) reference

8 To take ------- of the new cloud-service discounts, customers must upgrade their subscription before the end of the month.

(A) merit
(B) advantage
(C) service
(D) improvement

9 The finance department provided a detailed ------- of revenue across all regional branches.

(A) expression
(B) deduction
(C) comparison
(D) projection

10 The survey results indicate that employees have a clear ------- for a remote work policy.

(A) revision
(B) amount
(C) convenience
(D) preference

11 All service ------- will be reflected on the final invoice, including installation and setup fees.

(A) requirements
(B) charges
(C) guidelines
(D) deliveries

12 The HR department is responsible for organizing travel and ------- for employees' overseas projects.

(A) accommodations
(B) surroundings
(C) certifications
(D) vicinities

DAY 05 | 최빈출 정답 어휘_명사 ⑤

핵심 단어들을 확인한 후, 오른쪽의 기출 예시를 통해 각 단어의 쓰임새를 익혀보세요.

01 **manufacturer**	명 제조업체	a leading manufacturer of kitchen appliances 주방기기 제조업체의 선두주자
02 **persistence**	명 인내, 끈기, 지속	require persistence in the face of difficulties 난관에 직면하여 인내를 요구하다 persistent 형 끈질긴, 지속적인 persistently 부 끈질기게, 지속적으로
03 **itinerary**	명 여행 일정표	the itinerary for your trip 귀하의 여행 일정
04 **standard**	명 표준, 기준 형 일반의, 표준의	maintain high safety standards 높은 안전 기준을 유지하다
05 **transition**	명 전환, 이전	concerns about the system transition 시스템 전환에 대한 우려
06 **presentation**	명 발표, 제시, (선물, 상) 증정	give [make] a presentation 발표하다
07 **reputation**	명 평판, 명성	gain a reputation as ~로서의 명성을 얻다

| 08 **advancement** | 몡 승진, 발전 | be considered for advancement to management positions
관리직으로 승진이 고려되다
advanced 혱 상급의, 진보한, 첨단의 |
| --- | --- | --- |
| 09 **investment** | 몡 투자 | the initial investment in real estate
부동산에 들인 초기 투자금
invest 동 투자하다
investor 몡 투자자 |
| 10 **transportation** | 몡 교통, 운송 | an efficient public transportation system
효율적인 대중 교통 시스템
transport 동 수송하다
몡 수송, 수송 수단 |
| 11 **vendor** | 몡 판매업체, 상인, 판매자 | order the item from a different vendor
다른 판매상으로부터 물건을 주문하다 |
| 12 **commitment** | 몡 헌신, 전념, 약속 | show remarkable commitment to improving work environments
근로환경을 개선하는 데 대단한 헌신을 보이다
committed 혱 헌신적인, 전념하는 |
| 13 **destination** | 몡 (여행) 목적지, 도착지 | a popular tourist destination
인기 있는 관광 목적지
destined 혱 예정된, 운명의 |
| 14 **assembly** | 몡 조립 | assembly instructions
조립 설명서
assemble 동 조립하다, 모이다, 모으다 |

DAY 5

15 **client**	명 고객	a potential [prospective] client 잠재 고객
16 **publication**	명 출판, 발행, 출판물, (신문 등을 통한) 발표	submit the draft to a proofreader to prepare it for upcoming publication 다가오는 출판을 준비하기 위해 초안을 교정자에게 제출하다
17 **productivity**	명 생산성	increase employee productivity 직원들의 생산성을 높이다 produce 동 생산하다 명 농산품 productive 형 생산적인
18 **competition**	명 경쟁, 대회	amid rising [increasing] competition 늘어나는 경쟁 속에서 compete 동 경쟁하다
19 **protection**	명 보호	an organization engaged in wilderness protection 원시림 보호 활동을 하는 단체 protect 동 보호하다
20 **reception**	명 환영식, 접수처, 수신 (상태)	attend a reception to welcome the new CEO 신임 최고경영자를 맞이하는 환영식에 참가하다 receive 동 받다
21 **condition**	명 상태, 조건, 환경	arrive in damaged condition 손상된 상태로 도착하다

22 **patronage**	명 단골거래, 후원	in appreciation of your frequent patronage 자주 거래하는 것에 대한 감사의 표시로 patron 명 (단골) 고객 patronize 동 단골로 다니다, 후원하다
23 **applicant**	명 지원자, 신청자	qualified applicants 자질이 있는 지원자들 apply 동 지원하다, 신청하다
24 **enrollment**	명 등록(자 수), 입회	complete an online enrollment form 온라인 등록 양식을 작성하다
25 **statement**	명 진술, 성명, 내역	one's billing statement 대금 청구서 state 동 말하다, 진술하다, 명시하다 명 상태
26 **admission**	명 입장, 입회, 허가, 시인	receive free admission to ~에 무료 입장 허가를 받다 admit 동 인정하다, 허가하다 admissible 형 인정되는, 허용되는
27 **subscriber**	명 구독자	subscribers to *Market Weekly* magazine 『마켓 위클리』지의 구독자들
28 **proximity**	명 인접(성), 근접	because of its proximity to the convention center 컨벤션 센터와의 인접성 때문에
29 **surplus**	명 과잉, 흑자 형 초과하는, 잉여의	have a surplus of fund 여분의 자금이 있다
30 **transit**	명 운송, 교통 동 운송하다	items lost in transit 운송 중에 분실된 물건

DAY 5

실전 TEST

1 Despite limited resources, the interns showed remarkable ------- in completing the market analysis project.

(A) abundance
(B) attendance
(C) persistence
(D) frequency

2 The assistant prepared an updated ------- that reflects the revised departure time and hotel change.

(A) supply
(B) memo
(C) itinerary
(D) account

3 The factory will undergo a major ------- from manual assembly to automated production by the end of the year.

(A) cooperation
(B) transition
(C) suspension
(D) solution

4 All parts required for product ------- are included in the box, along with illustrated step-by-step instructions.

(A) assembly
(B) promotion
(C) recommendation
(D) initiation

5 Safety goggles must be worn at all times in the facility for the ------- of employees working near machinery.

(A) identity
(B) growth
(C) creativity
(D) protection

6 Due to poor weather -------, construction on the new headquarters has been postponed until next week.

(A) choices
(B) conditions
(C) backgrounds
(D) evaluations

7 The marketing department received a high volume of ------- requests for the upcoming branding workshop.

(A) research
(B) subscriber
(C) evaluation
(D) enrollment

8 In his closing -------, the keynote speaker emphasized adaptability in a changing business environment.

(A) advancement
(B) donation
(C) statement
(D) illustration

9 The department launched a new workflow system to boost collaboration and overall -------.

(A) adjustment
(B) productivity
(C) harvest
(D) possibility

10 His outstanding performance and leadership earned him an unexpected ------- in a short period.

(A) advancement
(B) certification
(C) standard
(D) presentation

11 The recruiter emphasized that successful ------- must be familiar with the company's core values.

(A) applicants
(B) jobs
(C) offers
(D) accounts

12 During the year-end banquet, the director praised the team's ------- to customer satisfaction.

(A) collaboration
(B) assignment
(C) assurance
(D) commitment

DAY 06 | 최빈출 정답 어휘: 동사 ①

MP3 바로 듣기

핵심 단어들을 확인한 후, 오른쪽의 기출 예시를 통해 각 단어의 쓰임새를 익혀보세요.

01 **delay**	동 ~을 연기하다, 지연시키다 명 연기, 지연	delay the process 처리를 연기하다
02 **assist**	동 돕다, ~을 돕다	assist with the negotiation 협상을 돕다 assistance 명 지원, 보조
03 **contribute**	동 공헌하다, ~을 기부하다	contribute money toward ~에 돈을 기부하다 contribution 명 기부(금), 공헌, 기여
04 **address**	동 (문제 등) ~을 다루다, 처리하다, ~에게 연설하다 명 주소, 연설	address customer complaints politely 고객 불만을 정중하게 처리하다
05 **thrive**	동 번창하다, 잘 자라다	thrive in a competitive market 경쟁이 심한 시장에서 번창하다
06 **continue**	동 계속되다, 계속 ~하다	if your computer continues to malfunction 컴퓨터가 계속 제대로 작동하지 않으면
07 **evaluate**	동 ~을 평가하다	evaluate one's performance ~의 실적을 평가하다 evaluation 명 평가

08 **enhance**	동 ~을 강화하다, ~을 향상시키다	enhance one's security ~의 보안을 강화하다
09 **describe**	동 ~을 묘사하다, 설명하다	describe the missing item clearly 분실물을 명확하게 설명하다 description 명 묘사, 설명
10 **resolve**	동 ~을 해결하다	be trained to resolve mechanical problems on the spot 기계적 문제를 현장에서 해결하도록 교육 받다 resolution 명 해결책
11 **offer**	동 ~을 제공하다, ~을 제안하다 명 제공(되는 것), 제안	offer a 10 percent discount 10% 할인을 제공하다 take advantage of the store's special offer 그 매장의 특가 제공 서비스를 이용하다
12 **display**	동 ~을 진열하다, 전시하다, 보여주다 명 진열(품), 전시(품)	must display the parking permit at all times 반드시 항상 주차증을 보이게 해야 하다 new items on display 진열 중인 신상품
13 **utilize**	동 ~을 이용하다, 활용하다	utilize robot technology in various sectors 다양한 분야에서 로봇 기술을 활용하다
14 **undergo**	동 ~을 거치다, ~을 겪다	will undergo a renovation next week 다음 주에 개조 공사를 거칠 것이다

15 **negotiate**	동 ~을 협상하다, 성사시키다, 타결하다	skillfully negotiate a contract 능숙하게 계약을 협상하다
16 **introduce**	동 ~을 소개하다, ~을 도입하다	introduce a new system for our employees 우리 직원들을 위해 새로운 시스템을 도입하다
17 **hold**	동 ~을 개최하다, ~을 보유하다	will hold the annual event soon 곧 그 연례 행사를 개최할 것이다
18 **estimate**	동 추산하다, 추정하다 명 견적(서)	estimate the time of delivery 배송 시간을 추정하다
19 **unveil**	동 ~을 발표하다, 공개하다	unveil one's plan to do ~할 계획을 공개하다
20 **analyze**	동 ~을 분석하다	analyze the survey responses 설문 조사 응답을 분석하다
21 **emphasize**	동 ~을 강조하다	emphasize its fuel efficiency and affordability 그것의 연료 효율성과 가격 적절성을 강조하다
22 **prove**	동 ~을 증명하다, 입증하다, ~한 것으로 드러나다	will prove to be valuable for your research 귀하의 연구에 있어 가치가 있는 것으로 증명될 것이다
23 **install**	동 ~을 설치하다	install a new security system 새 보안 시스템을 설치하다 installation 명 설치 (작업) installment 명 (시리즈물 등의) 한 회분, 분할(납부)

#	단어	뜻	예문
24	**influence**	동 ~에 영향을 미치다 명 영향, 작용	positively influence market trends 시장 경향에 긍정적으로 영향을 미치다
25	**detail**	동 ~을 상세히 설명하다	a report that details our monthly expenses 우리의 월간 지출을 상세히 설명하는 보고서 details 명 상세 정보, 세부 사항 detailed 형 상세한
26	**reveal**	동 ~을 공개하다, 드러내다, 보여주다	reveal a strong preference for SUVs over sedans 세단보다 SUV에 대한 강한 선호도를 보여주다
27	**inspect**	동 ~을 점검하다	inspect the system regularly 정기적으로 시스템을 점검하다 inspection 명 점검, 검사
28	**recover**	동 회복되다, ~을 회복시키다	recover from a health problem 건강 문제에서 회복되다 recovery 명 복구, 회복
29	**cover**	동 (범위에) ~을 포함하다, (비용 등) ~을 부담하다, (주제 등) ~을 다루다 명 덮개	cover many topics 많은 주제를 다루다 cover travel expenses 출장 비용을 부담해주다
30	**refer**	동 참조하다, 나타내다(to), 조회하다	Please refer to the guidelines issued by ~ ~에서 발행한 지침을 참조하시기 바랍니다. referral 명 참조, 소개, 위탁, 추천된 사람

실전 TEST

1 Payroll processing may be ------- if the financial system upgrade takes longer than expected.

(A) delayed
(B) expected
(C) reserved
(D) enrolled

2 To create the new training manual, several senior employees will ------- examples from their experience.

(A) divide
(B) argue
(C) resist
(D) contribute

3 Our support team promptly ------- the login error affecting multiple users across regions.

(A) resolved
(B) requested
(C) defined
(D) announced

4 During the quarterly review, the CEO ------- the need to improve internal communication across departments.

(A) hesitated
(B) dominated
(C) launched
(D) emphasized

5 During today's press conference, the marketing team ------- a redesigned logo and updated branding guide.

(A) declined
(B) unveiled
(C) omitted
(D) retrieved

6 The onboarding guide ------- procedures for accessing employee benefits and submitting timesheets.

(A) prepares
(B) expects
(C) details
(D) corresponds

7 Government officials will ------- the factory next week to ensure compliance with safety regulations.

(A) confirm
(B) inspect
(C) perform
(D) reject

8 Whether you're launching a startup or expanding your operations, our team is ready to ------- you with custom solutions.

(A) lend
(B) assist
(C) explain
(D) mention

9 The committee will ------- each proposal based on feasibility and potential impact.

(A) evaluate
(B) object
(C) persuade
(D) complain

10 To meet internal standards, all newly developed products must ------- rigorous safety testing procedures.

(A) submit
(B) transfer
(C) undergo
(D) examine

11 If you're not satisfied with the current terms, we're open to ------- a revised agreement that benefits both sides.

(A) enclose
(B) express
(C) negotiate
(D) assign

12 Social media reviews often ------- customer purchasing behavior more effectively than traditional advertising.

(A) measure
(B) predict
(C) monitor
(D) influence

DAY 07 | 최빈출 정답 어휘: 동사 ②

핵심 단어들을 확인한 후, 오른쪽의 기출 예시를 통해 각 단어의 쓰임새를 익혀보세요.

01 **subscribe**	동 구독하다, 가입하다	If you are interested in subscribing to our services 저희 서비스에 가입하는 데 관심 있으시면 subscription 명 구독, 서비스 가입
02 **exchange**	동 (같은 종류로) ~을 교환하다 명 교환	exchange the printer for a more portable one 프린터를 좀 더 휴대성이 좋은 것으로 교환하다
03 **announce**	동 ~을 발표하다, 알리다	announce the sales figures for December 12월 매출 수치를 발표하다 announcement 명 공지, 안내
04 **investigate**	동 ~을 조사하다	investigate the recent problems with ~에 대한 최근 문제들을 조사하다
05 **decline**	동 하락하다, 줄어들다, ~을 거절하다 명 하락	typically decline during the winter season 보통 겨울철에 감소하다
06 **apply**	동 지원하다, 신청하다, 적용하다, 바르다	apply for a position 일자리에 지원하다 application 명 지원(서), 신청(서), 적용

07 **promote**	동 ~을 홍보하다, ~을 승진시키다, ~을 촉진시키다	promote a new line of products 신제품 라인을 홍보하다 promotion 명 홍보, 승진, 촉진
08 **select**	동 ~을 선택하다, 선정하다	select candidates for interviews 면접을 위한 후보자를 선정하다
09 **recommend**	동 (사람을) 추천하다, (~하도록) 권고하다	highly recommend taking a tour to Bali 발리로 여행 가는 것을 적극 추천하다 recommendation 명 추천, 권고
10 **reduce**	동 ~을 줄이다, 낮추다, 감소하다	reduce energy costs 에너지 비용을 줄이다 reduction 명 감소, 할인
11 **operate**	동 ~을 운영하다, 작동하다, 운행하다	operate a new bus route 새 버스 노선을 운행하다 operation 명 운영, 작동, 운행
12 **implement**	동 ~을 시행하다	implement a new plan[policy] 새로운 계획[정책]을 시행하다
13 **handle**	동 ~을 다루다, 처리하다	handle a variety of issues 다양한 문제들을 다루다
14 **arrange**	동 ~을 준비하다, 조치하다	arrange to meet Mr. Cole 콜 씨를 만날 준비를 하다 arrangement 명 준비, 조치
15 **qualify**	동 자격이 있다, ~에게 자격을 주다	qualify for a discounted ticket 할인 티켓을 받을 자격이 있다 qualification 명 자격 (요건)

16 **issue**	동 ~을 발급하다, 지급하다, 발표하다 명 문제, 사안, (잡지 등의) 호	issue a full refund to ~ ~에게 전액 환불금을 지급하다 issue a statement 성명을 발표하다
17 **anticipate**	동 ~을 예상하다, 기대하다	anticipate significant revenue increases 상당한 수입 증가를 예상하다 anticipation 명 예상, 기대
18 **determine**	동 ~을 결정하다, ~을 알아내다	determine what caused the damage 무엇이 손상을 초래했는지 알아내다
19 **replace**	동 ~을 교체하다, 대체하다, ~의 후임이 되다	replace the device with a new model 그 기기를 새로운 모델로 교체하다 replacement 명 교체(품), 후임(자)
20 **leave**	동 떠나다, ~에서 나가다, ~을 놓다, ~을 …한 상태로 두다 명 휴가	when you leave the building 건물에서 나가실 때 leave the package in the room 그 방 안에 소포를 놓다
21 **accept**	동 ~을 받아들이다, 수락하다	accept an invitation 초대를 수락하다 acceptance 명 수락, 승인
22 **respond**	동 응답하다, 반응하다	respond promptly to ~에 신속하게 응답하다

23 **obtain**	동 ~을 얻다, 획득하다	obtain approval from the head office 본사로부터 승인을 얻다
24 **evolve**	동 진화하다, 발전하다	evolve into a robust business district 아주 탄탄한 상업 지구로 발전하다 evolution 명 진화, 발전
25 **boost**	동 ~을 증대하다, ~을 촉진시키다, ~을 향상시키다 명 증대, 촉진	boost the economy 경제를 향상시키다
26 **express**	동 (감정 등) ~을 표현하다, 표출하다 형 급행의, 신속한	express concerns about the new regulations 새 규정에 대해 우려를 표하다
27 **encourage**	동 ~을 권장하다, ~에게 권고하다	encourage employees to submit suggestions 직원들에게 의견을 제출하도록 권고하다
28 **accompany**	동 ~을 동반하다, (~와) 동행하다	children accompanied by their parents 자신들의 부모를 동반한 어린이들
29 **ensure**	동 ~을 보장하다, ~임을 확실히 하다	ensure that employees turn off their devices 직원들이 각자의 기기들을 끄도록 확실히 해두다
30 **recognize**	동 ~을 알아보다, ~을 인정하다, ~을 표창하다	be recognized for outstanding performances 뛰어난 성과로 인정 받다 recognition 명 인식, 인정, 표창

실전 TEST

1 AirLux Airways ------- a new flight route connecting Seoul and Vancouver starting in December.

(A) demonstrated
(B) announced
(C) applied
(D) loaded

2 Hotel bookings in coastal towns tend to ------- in early autumn after peak travel season.

(A) expand
(B) develop
(C) impact
(D) decline

3 Based on her performance reviews, the board ------- Ms. seo for promotion to regional director.

(A) challenged
(B) obeyed
(C) recommended
(D) interrupted

4 Last year, the government ------- new tax policies to promote small business growth.

(A) estimated
(B) investigated
(C) repeated
(D) implemented

5 After the merger, the legal team will ------- all questions related to contract transitions.

(A) handle
(B) dismiss
(C) report
(D) object

6 We carefully ------- the chairs in a circle before the meeting started.

(A) lifted
(B) divided
(C) automated
(D) arranged

7 Brightline Publishing has ------- from a traditional printing company into a modern digital production company.

(A) evolved
(B) permitted
(C) focused
(D) determined

8 To ------- access to the secure data, please submit a formal request to the IT department.

(A) obtain
(B) observe
(C) control
(D) eliminate

9 Dr. Kim is widely ------- as a pioneer in renewable energy research.

(A) confused
(B) organized
(C) recognized
(D) obeyed

10 During the town hall meeting, residents ------- their concerns about the new policies.

(A) explored
(B) expressed
(C) exchanged
(D) eliminated

11 The hotel plans to ------- its old room keys with contactless smart cards by next month.

(A) repair
(B) replace
(C) maintain
(D) upgrade

12 The city transportation authority plans to ------- a fleet of electric buses in the downtown area next year.

(A) grow
(B) maintain
(C) operate
(D) promise

DAY 08 최빈출 정답 어휘: 동사 ③

핵심 단어들을 확인한 후, 오른쪽의 기출 예시를 통해 각 단어의 쓰임새를 익혀보세요.

01 **maintain**	동 ~을 유지하다	maintain a broad customer base 넓은 고객층을 유지하다 maintenance 명 유지 관리
02 **run**	동 ~을 운영하다, ~을 진행하다, ~을 운행하다	run more than 50 branches throughout the country 전국에 걸쳐 50개가 넘는 지점을 운영하다
03 **organize**	동 ~을 조직하다, 준비하다	organize a new hiring committee 새 고용 위원회를 조직하다 organization 명 조직(체)
04 **provide**	동 ~을 제공하다	provide free delivery services 무료 배송 서비스를 제공하다 provide employees with regular training 직원들에게 정기 교육을 제공하다
05 **consult**	동 (자료 등) ~을 참고하다, (사람) ~와 상의하다	consult the online user manual 온라인 설명서를 참고하다 consultation 명 상담 consultant 명 상담 전문가
06 **specify**	동 ~을 명시하다, ~을 구체화하다	specify the number of attendees 참석자 수를 명시하다 specification 명 세부 사항, 명세, 규격

44 시원스쿨 기본토익 700+

07 **postpone**	동 ~을 연기하다, 미루다	postpone the workshop until next month 워크숍을 다음 달까지 연기하다
08 **consider**	동 ~을 고려하다, ~을 …로 여기다	consider employee satisfaction (to be) a top priority 직원 만족을 최우선으로 여기다
09 **reschedule**	동 ~의 일정을 재조정하다	reschedule the meeting due to bad weather 악천후로 인해 그 회의 일정을 재조정하다
10 **hesitate**	동 망설이다, 주저하다	Do not hesitate to contact our customer service department. 주저하지 말고 고객서비스부서에 연락하세요. hesitant 형 망설이는, 주저하는 hesitation 명 망설임, 주저함
11 **experiment**	동 실험하다 명 실험	experiment with new materials to improve battery efficiency 배터리 효율을 향상시키기 위해 새로운 소재로 실험하다
12 **establish**	동 설립하다, 수립하다, 확립하다	establish a close relationship with ~와 긴밀한 관계를 확립하다 established 형 자리를 잡은 establishment 명 설립, 시설
13 **conduct**	동 수행하다, 실시하다 명 행동, 처신	conduct an inspection 검사를 수행하다
14 **enclose**	동 동봉하다	enclose an invoice with the product 상품과 함께 운송장을 동봉하다

15 **acquire**	동 (기업을) 인수하다, 취득하다, 습득하다	acquire a company 회사를 인수하다
16 **transfer**	동 (교통을) 갈아타다, (직장을) 전근하다 명 환승, 전근, 이동	transfer to the Beijing office 베이징 사무소로 전근하다
17 **remind**	동 상기시키다	remind tourists to meet in the lobby 관광객들에게 로비에서 만날 것을 상기시켜주다
18 **assign**	동 배정하다, 할당하다	assign one person to handle the issue 그 문제를 해결하도록 한 명을 배정하다
19 **retain**	동 유지하다, 보관하다	retain the receipt for one's records 기록용으로 영수증을 보관하다
20 **conclude**	동 종료하다, 결론 내리다	conclude with a short speech 짧은 연설로 마무리되다 conclusion 명 종료, 결론
21 **risk**	동 ~할 위험을 무릅쓰다, ~을 위태롭게 하다 명 위험, 위험 요소	risk exposing sensitive user data 민감한 사용자 데이터를 노출시킬 위험이 있다 risky 형 위험한
22 **affect**	동 영향을 주다	affect the launch of our new product 우리의 신제품 출시에 영향을 미치다
23 **locate**	동 찾아내다, (장소)에 두다	locate a nearby restaurant 근처의 레스토랑을 찾아내다

24 **revise**	통 수정하다, 개정하다	revise the policy 정책을 개편하다
25 **renew**	통 계약을 갱신하다, 기한을 연장하다	renew one's subscription 정기 구독을 갱신하다
26 **authorize**	통 허가하다, 권한을 부여하다	authorize the payment for ~에 대한 지출을 승인하다
27 **refrain**	통 삼가다, 자제하다	refrain from using mobile phones while driving 운전 중에 휴대폰 사용을 삼가다
28 **instruct**	통 지시하다, 가르치다, 알려주다	instruct all new employees on proper use of ~ ~의 적절한 사용에 관해 모든 신입 직원들을 가르치다 Attendees will be instructed to register at the front desk upon arrival. 참석자들은 도착 시 프런트 데스크에 등록하라는 안내를 받을 것입니다 instruction 명 지시, 설명 instructive 형 유익한
29 **assure**	통 확신시키다, 확신하다	assure one's staff that절 직원들에게 ~라고 확신시키다 assuredly 부 틀림없이, 기필코 assurance 명 확신, 자신
30 **sign**	통 서명하다, 승인하다, 신호하다 명 조짐, 신호	sign an agreement 계약에 서명하다

DAY 8

실전 TEST

1 During the press conference, the mayor ------- citizens that emergency services are fully prepared for the approaching storm.

(A) described
(B) arranged
(C) assured
(D) committed

2 We kindly ask participants to ------- from taking photographs during the live performance.

(A) refrain
(B) forbid
(C) resist
(D) hesitate

3 At the front desk, staff members can ------- the nearest ATM or pharmacy for visitors.

(A) assist
(B) locate
(C) remind
(D) conduct

4 Team members were ------- to complete the survey before the end of the day.

(A) allowed
(B) pleased
(C) affected
(D) reminded

5 DataCorp recently ------- a cybersecurity firm to strengthen its data protection services.

(A) audited
(B) delayed
(C) acquired
(D) published

6 Annual employee evaluations are ------- at the beginning of each fiscal year.

(A) retained
(B) conducted
(C) established
(D) postponed

7 The updated policy ensures we ------ confidentiality of sensitive client information.

(A) maintain
(B) restore
(C) reduce
(D) run

8 Due to a scheduling conflict, the manager will ------- your job interview to next Wednesday.

(A) reschedule
(B) recall
(C) resume
(D) reconstruct

9 The marketing department must ------- the new product brochure to every regional office.

(A) restrict
(B) review
(C) conceal
(D) provide

10 The board has ------- capital expenditures up to $100,000 for the upcoming quarter.

(A) reviewed
(B) authorized
(C) postponed
(D) endorsed

11 The HR policy requires companies to ------- employee records for at least seven years.

(A) agree
(B) hire
(C) retain
(D) continue

12 It's worthwhile to ------- enrolling in professional development courses to stay competitive.

(A) aim
(B) observe
(C) persuade
(D) consider

DAY 09 | 최빈출 정답 어휘: 형용사 ①

핵심 단어들을 확인한 후, 오른쪽의 기출 예시를 통해 각 단어의 쓰임새를 익혀보세요.

01 **additional**	형 추가적인, 여분의	If you need additional information 추가 정보가 필요하다면
02 **particular**	형 특정한	based on one's expertise in a particular area 특정 분야에 대한 전문성을 기반으로
03 **vacant**	형 비어 있는, (자리가) 점유되지 않은	have many vacant positions to fill 충원해야 할 빈 직책들이 많이 있다 vacancy 명 공석, (채용 중인) 빈 자리
04 **limited**	형 제한된, 한정된	remain open for a limited time only 제한된 시간 동안만 문을 연 상태로 있다 limit 명 제한, 한도
05 **effective**	형 효과적인, 효력이 발생되는, 시행되는	highly effective measures to reduce costs 비용을 줄이기 위한 매우 효과적인 조치들
06 **representative**	형 대표하는, 전형적인 명 대표자, 직원	be representative of ~을 대표하다[나타내다] represent 동 ~을 대표하다, ~을 나타내다

07 **responsible**	형 책임 있는	be responsible for marketing planning 마케팅 기획에 대한 책임이 있다
08 **convenient**	형 편리한	whenever it's convenient for you 귀하가 편하신 시간이면 언제든 convenience 명 편의, 편리
09 **affordable**	형 (가격이) 저렴한, 알맞은	can be purchased at an affordable price 저렴한 가격에 구입될 수 있다
10 **reliable**	형 신뢰할 수 있는	provide reliable information 신뢰할 만한 정보를 제공하다 rely 동 의존하다, 신뢰하다
11 **significant**	형 상당한, 중요한	significant savings on the costs 비용에 있어서의 상당한 절약
12 **complete**	형 완료된, 완전한, 철저한 동 ~을 완료하다, ~을 작성하다	after the process is complete 그 과정이 완료된 후에
13 **extensive**	형 광범위한, 폭넓은	have extensive experience in creating advertisements 광고를 만드는 데 있어 폭넓은 경험이 있다
14 **valid**	형 유효한	a valid receipt for a full refund 전액 환불을 위한 유효한 영수증

15 **public**	형 공공의, 일반 대중의	in all public areas of the building 건물의 모든 공공 장소에서
16 **accessible**	형 접근 가능한, 이용 가능한	easily accessible by bus 버스로 쉽게 접근 가능한
17 **unexpected**	형 예상치 못한, 뜻밖의	due to one's unexpected business trip ~의 예상치 못한 출장으로 인해
18 **accurate**	형 정확한	provide accurate information on the problem 그 문제에 관한 정확한 정보를 제공하다
19 **qualified**	형 자격을 갖춘, 적격인	look for qualified applicants 자격을 갖춘 지원자들을 찾다 qualify 동 자격이 있다, ~에게 자격을 주다
20 **appropriate**	형 적합한, 적절한	recommend an appropriate place 적절한 장소를 추천하다 appropriately 부 적합하게, 적절하게
21 **brief**	형 간단한, 짧은, 잠깐의	a brief power failure 잠깐의 정전 briefly 부 간단히, 짧게
22 **former**	형 전직 ~인, 이전의	one's former employer ~의 이전 고용주

23	**efficient**	형 효율적인	in a consistently efficient manner 꾸준히 효율적인 방식으로 efficiency 명 효율(성)
24	**available**	형 (사물) 이용 가능한, 구입 가능한, (사람) 시간이 나는	if the manager is available 책임자가 시간이 나면 currently available at some branches 몇몇 지점에서 현재 구입 가능한
25	**normal**	형 보통의, 정상의, 일반적인	during normal operating hours 정상 영업 시간 동안
26	**equipped**	형 (장비 등이) 갖춰진	be equipped with state-of-the-art appliances 최첨단 기기들이 갖춰져 있다
27	**beneficial**	형 유익한, 이로운	beneficial to the environment 환경에 이로운
28	**overseas**	형 해외의 부 해외에서, 해외로	be supposed to visit some overseas branches 몇몇 해외 지사들을 방문하기로 되어 있다
29	**renowned**	형 유명한	be renowned for vegetarian dishes 채식주의 요리들로 유명하다
30	**committed**	형 전념하는, 헌신적인	be committed to providing quality products 질 좋은 제품을 제공하는 데 전념하다

실전 TEST

1 When writing an abstract, authors must provide a ------- summary of their research.

(A) normal
(B) lengthy
(C) repetitive
(D) brief

2 Parking spaces are ------- around the back of the building at no extra charge.

(A) called
(B) printed
(C) capable
(D) available

3 The magazine features an exclusive interview with a ------- director of overseas operations.

(A) final
(B) best
(C) former
(D) clear

4 Please ensure your passport remains ------- for at least six months before traveling abroad.

(A) expired
(B) optional
(C) valid
(D) permanent

5 Many consumers are seeking health insurance plans that are both comprehensive and -------.

(A) formal
(B) affordable
(C) exclusive
(D) extensive

6 When assembling the device, tighten the screws in the ------- order specified in the manual.

(A) approximate
(B) particular
(C) random
(D) final

7 Engineers prepared for the upgrade, but it was delayed by ------- equipment malfunctions.

(A) routine
(B) qualified
(C) unexpected
(D) standard

8 Before publishing, editors must verify all facts to ensure the article is --------.

(A) biased
(B) convenient
(C) public
(D) accurate

9 During the scheduled maintenance, users will have access only to ------- content.

(A) preventable
(B) limited
(C) similar
(D) leading

10 Sales data indicated a ------- decline in quarterly revenue compared to last year.

(A) significant
(B) additional
(C) minimal
(D) routine

11 JS Tech is seeking a ------- supplier who can consistently deliver high-quality components.

(A) reliable
(B) vacant
(C) convenient
(D) representative

12 The electric car's battery management system has become more -------, extending its driving range.

(A) efficient
(B) appropriate
(C) extensive
(D) external

DAY 10 | 최빈출 정답 어휘: 형용사 ②

핵심 단어들을 확인한 후, 오른쪽의 기출 예시를 통해 각 단어의 쓰임새를 익혀보세요.

01 **impressive**	형 인상적인	an applicant whose résumé is impressive 이력서가 인상적인 한 지원자 impress 동 ~에게 깊은 인상을 남기다
02 **exceptional**	형 보기 드문, 뛰어난	the exceptional service at ~ ~에서의 뛰어난 서비스 exception 명 예외, 특별 사례
03 **complimentary**	형 무료의	attach complimentary dinner coupons 무료 저녁 식사 쿠폰을 첨부하다
04 **comprehensive**	형 종합적인, 포괄적인	conduct a comprehensive inspection 종합적인 점검을 실시하다
05 **invaluable**	형 소중한, 귀중한	invaluable feedback from the customers 고객들로부터 받은 소중한 의견
06 **existing**	형 기존의	much better than existing cell phone models 기존의 휴대전화 모델들보다 훨씬 더 나은
07 **incorrect**	형 정확하지 않은, 오류가 있는	revise incorrect sales figures 부정확한 매출 수치를 수정하다

08 **upcoming**	형 다가오는, 곧 있을	talk about the upcoming corporate event 다가오는 기업 행사에 관해 이야기하다
09 **based**	형 바탕으로 하는, 근거지[본사]를 둔	based on the survey results 설문 조사 결과를 바탕으로 be based in New York 뉴욕에 근거지[본사]를 두고 있다
10 **designed**	형 고안된, 만들어진	be designed for those who are inexperienced 경험이 부족한 사람들을 위해 고안되다
11 **growing**	형 (크기, 수, 정도가) 증가하는, 성장하는	growing seasonal demand 증가하는 계절적 수요
12 **concerned**	형 우려하는, 걱정하는	increasingly concerned about the issue 그 문제에 대해 점점 더 우려하는
13 **extra**	형 추가의, 별도의	receive extra vacation days 추가 휴가일을 받다
14 **familiar**	형 익숙한, 잘 아는	become familiar with the new policies 새 정책에 익숙하게 되다
15 **urgent**	형 긴급한	discuss an urgent matter 긴급한 문제를 논의하다
16 **relevant**	형 관련된	should have experience in a relevant field 관련된 분야에서 경력이 있어야 한다

17 **vulnerable**	형 취약한	be more vulnerable to damage while in normal usage 일반적 사용 환경에서 훼손에 더 취약하다 vulnerability 명 취약성
18 **substantial**	형 상당한	make substantial donations to ~에게 상당한 액수의 기부를 하다 substantially 부 상당히
19 **tentative**	형 임시의, 잠정적인	discuss a tentative agreement with the city council 시의회와 잠정적인 협의를 논의하다 tentatively 부 임시로, 잠정적으로
20 **specific**	형 구체적인, 특정한 명 세부 정보 (복수)	provide specific guidelines on ~에 대한 구체적인 지침을 제공하다 specifically 부 특히
21 **residential**	형 주거의, 가정의	provide both residential and commercial services 가정용 및 기업용 서비스를 모두 제공하다 residence 명 집, 주택 resident 명 주민 reside 동 거주하다
22 **spacious**	형 넓은	a spacious two-bedroom apartment 넓은 침실 2개짜리 아파트

23 **remarkable**	형 눈에 띄는, 주목할 만한	experience a remarkable increase in sales 매출에 있어 눈에 띄는 상승세를 경험하다 remarkably 부 현저하게
24 **ongoing**	형 진행 중인	ongoing research project 현재 진행 중인 연구 프로젝트
25 **numerous**	형 많은, 다수의	offer numerous options 다양한 옵션을 제공하다
26 **outstanding**	형 탁월한, 돋보이는, 미지불 상태의	outstanding balance 미지불 잔고, 지불해야 할 금액
27 **competitive**	형 경쟁력 있는, 경쟁의, 경쟁적인	offer its employees competitive compensation 직원들에게 경쟁력 있는 보수를 제공하다 competitiveness 명 경쟁력
28 **dedicated**	형 헌신하는, 전념하는	a dedicated team of staff 헌신적인 팀 dedicate 동 헌신하다, 전념하다 dedication 명 헌신, 전념
29 **reasonable**	형 합리적인, 합당한, (가격이) 적당한	provide services at reasonable prices 적절한 가격으로 서비스를 제공하다
30 **notable**	형 주목할 만한, 유명한, 훌륭한	produce notable results 주목할 만한 결과를 내다 note 동 주목하다 명 주의, 주목 notably 부 명백히, 현저히

실전 TEST

1 Her performance on the violin was so ------- that even the critics were speechless.

(A) mediocre
(B) sufficient
(C) routine
(D) exceptional

2 The team is finalizing the details for the ------- product launch event next month.

(A) previous
(B) upcoming
(C) former
(D) continuous

3 We received an ------- message from headquarters that required immediate action.

(A) overdue
(B) existing
(C) urgent
(D) upcoming

4 To celebrate our anniversary, we're providing every customer with a ------- dessert.

(A) delayed
(B) scheduled
(C) refundable
(D) complimentary

5 Our ------- efforts to improve customer service have started to show positive outcomes.

(A) ongoing
(B) dissolved
(C) restrained
(D) vulnerable

6 Due to consistent requests from tenants, the city council introduced new regulations for noise levels in ------- areas.

(A) spacious
(B) residential
(C) competitive
(D) rural

7 The university established a scholarship fund ------- to supporting students pursuing engineering degrees.

(A) prepared
(B) dedicated
(C) allowed
(D) compared

8 The landlord proposed a ------- monthly rent for the new office space.

(A) reasonable
(B) outstanding
(C) notable
(D) invaluable

9 Endangered species with shrinking habitats become increasingly ------- to extinction.

(A) immune
(B) resistant
(C) designed
(D) vulnerable

10 The meeting schedule is ------- until all stakeholders confirm their availability.

(A) agreeable
(B) sudden
(C) tentative
(D) considerate

11 The organization has seen a ------- interest in its annual conference over the past five years.

(A) growing
(B) closed
(C) unknown
(D) costly

12 The software update introduces a ------- set of features to improve user experience and security.

(A) minimal
(B) initial
(C) comprehensive
(D) existing

DAY 11 | 최빈출 정답 어휘: 부사 ①

핵심 단어들을 확인한 후, 오른쪽의 기출 예시를 통해 각 단어의 쓰임새를 익혀보세요.

01 **directly**	부 직접적으로, 곧장	be shipped directly from our warehouse 우리 창고에서 직접 발송되다
02 **heavily**	부 (정도 등) 크게, 심하게, 대단히	heavily dependent on tourism 관광 산업에 크게 의존하고 있는
03 **rather**	부 다소, 꽤, 차라리	grow rather slowly 다소 더디게 성장하다
04 **completely**	부 완전히, 전적으로	be completely satisfied with the service 그 서비스에 완전히 만족하다 complete 형 완료한, 완전한 동 완료하다
05 **immediately**	부 즉시, 당장	immediately after signing the contract 계약서에 서명한 후에 즉시 immediate 형 즉각적인
06 **relatively**	부 비교적, 상대적으로	relatively low interest rates 비교적 낮은 이자율

07 **frequently**	🖎 자주, 흔히, 빈번하게	frequently asked questions 빈번하게 묻는 질문들
08 **currently**	🖎 현재, 지금	currently unavailable 현재 이용할 수 없는
09 **generally**	🖎 일반적으로, 보통	generally take 2~3 days to deliver the item 그 제품을 배송하는 데 보통 2~3일 걸리다
10 **definitely**	🖎 명확히, 틀림없이	The dinner at your cabin was definitely the best part of my tour. 귀하의 오두막집에서 했던 저녁 식사는 분명 제 여행에서 최고의 순간이었습니다. definite 🅐 명확한, 한정된
11 **thoroughly**	🖎 완전히, 철저히	should be inspected thoroughly 철저히 점검되어야 하다
12 **shortly**	🖎 곧, 금방	will be finished shortly 곧 끝날 것이다
13 **dramatically**	🖎 급격히, 극적으로	increase dramatically 급격히 증가되다
14 **properly**	🖎 적절히, 제대로	must be properly installed 반드시 적절히 설치되어야 하다

15 **consistently**	부 한결같이, 끊임없이	be consistently late for work 한결같이 직장에 지각하다
16 **briefly**	부 잠시, 간략히	briefly explain the agenda 회의 안건을 간략하게 설명하다
17 **alternatively**	부 그렇지 않으면, 대안으로, 그 대신	Alternatively, you can take a taxi. 그 대신, 택시를 이용하셔도 됩니다.
18 **previously**	부 이전에	as previously discussed 이전에 논의된 것처럼
19 **closely**	부 면밀하게, 꼼꼼하게, 밀접하게, 긴밀하게	closely monitored 면밀하게 관찰되는
20 **continually**	부 계속, 꾸준히	continually update one's equipment ~의 장비를 꾸준히 최신화하다
21 **initially**	부 처음에, 초기에	as initially proposed 처음에 제안된 것처럼 initial 형 처음의, 초기의
22 **remarkably**	부 두드러지게, 현저하게, 놀랍게도	in remarkably good condition 놀라울 정도로 좋은 상태로 remarkable 형 놀랄만한, 주목할 만한
23 **temporarily**	부 일시적으로, 임시로	temporarily out of stock 일시적으로 재고가 없는 temporary 형 일시적인, 임시의

#	단어	뜻	예문
24	**approximately**	🔹 약, 대략	last approximately three hours 약 세 시간 지속되다
25	**exactly**	🔹 정확하게	exactly fifty attendees 정확하게 50명의 참석자들 exact 형 정확한
26	**rapidly**	🔹 빠르게, 신속히	the rapidly changing work environment 빠르게 변화하는 근무 환경
27	**particularly**	🔹 특히, 특별히	particularly popular in Asia 아시아에서 특히 인기 있는 particular 형 특별한, 특정한
28	**exclusively**	🔹 오직, 오로지, 독점적으로	run exclusively on renewable energy 오직 재생 에너지로만 운영되다 exclusive 형 배타적인, 독점적인
29	**extremely**	🔹 대단히, 매우, 극도로	receive extremely positive feedback from customers 고객들로부터 대단히 긍정적인 의견을 받다
30	**annually**	🔹 연례적으로, 해마다	be held annually 해마다 개최되다 annual 형 연례적인, 해마다의

실전 TEST

1 The CEO was ------- criticized in the press after the financial results fell short of expectations.

(A) mildly
(B) heavily
(C) briefly
(D) roughly

2 Our website is ------- experiencing technical difficulties due to server maintenance.

(A) always
(B) currently
(C) soon
(D) immediately

3 The operating costs of solar panels are ------- lower than those of traditional energy sources.

(A) occasionally
(B) aggressively
(C) relatively
(D) mistakenly

4 The supplier has confirmed that the parts will be delivered -------.

(A) remarkably
(B) barely
(C) indefinitely
(D) shortly

5 The security team ------- monitors the network for suspicious activity around the clock.

(A) finely
(B) alternatively
(C) extremely
(D) continually

6 Sales figures have ------- shown steady growth over the last quarter.

(A) consistently
(B) occasionally
(C) randomly
(D) irregularly

7 The community center organizes fundraising activities ------- to support local projects.

(A) partially
(B) rapidly
(C) annually
(D) immediately

8 Conducting a full inventory check takes ------- 2 hours each week.

(A) little
(B) barely
(C) quickly
(D) approximately

9 New safety protocols ------- reduced the number of workplace accidents this quarter.

(A) slightly
(B) dramatically
(C) routinely
(D) scarcely

10 The special edition smartphone is sold ------- through our official online store.

(A) exclusively
(B) occasionally
(C) commonly
(D) randomly

11 Team leaders receive project updates ------- from each member during weekly meetings.

(A) automatically
(B) roughly
(C) directly
(D) incidentally

12 Access to the research database is ------- restricted while the system receives critical security updates.

(A) temporarily
(B) competitively
(C) recently
(D) collectively

DAY 12 | 최빈출 정답 어휘: 부사 ②

핵심 단어들을 확인한 후, 오른쪽의 기출 예시를 통해 각 단어의 쓰임새를 익혀보세요.

01 **unfortunately**	튀 안타깝게도, 아쉽게도	Unfortunately, we cannot accept your proposal. 안타깝게도, 저희는 귀하의 제안을 받아들일 수 없습니다.
02 **unexpectedly**	튀 예기치 않게, 뜻밖에	quit unexpectedly 예기치 않게 그만두다 unexpected 형 예기치 않은, 뜻밖의
03 **typically**	튀 일반적으로, 보통, 전형적으로	typically receive more than 10 e-mails a day 보통 하루에 10개가 넘는 이메일을 받다 typical 형 전형적인, 일반적인
04 **reasonably**	튀 합리적으로	reasonably priced services 합리적으로 가격이 책정된 서비스들 reasonable 형 합리적인, 비싸지 않은
05 **absolutely**	튀 전적으로, 완전히	It is absolutely essential that ~하는 것이 전적으로 필수이다 absolute 형 절대적인, 완전한
06 **markedly**	튀 현저하게, 두드러지게, 뚜렷하게	become markedly better 현저하게 더 나아지다
07 **increasingly**	튀 점점 더	in the increasingly competitive market 점점 더 경쟁적인 시장에서

08 **strictly**	분 엄격히	be strictly implemented 엄격히 시행되다 strict 형 엄격한
09 **primarily**	분 주로	work primarily on 주로 ~에 대한 일을 하다
10 **fully**	분 완전히, 전적으로	remain fully stocked 완전히 재고를 갖춘 상태로 유지하다 full 형 완전한, 가득 찬
11 **recently**	분 최근에	the recently appointed marketing director 최근에 선임된 마케팅 이사 recent 형 최근의
12 **quite**	분 상당히, 꽤	have a quite interesting design 상당히 흥미로운 디자인을 갖고 있다
13 **officially**	분 정식으로, 공식적으로	officially assume the position of ~ ~의 직책을 정식으로 맡다
14 **usually**	분 보통, 일반적으로	usually leave work at 7 P.M. 보통 오후 7시에 퇴근하다
15 **carefully**	분 신중히, 조심스럽게	handle the items very carefully 그 제품들을 매우 조심스럽게 다루다
16 **severely**	분 심하게, 심각하게	severely damaged during the delivery 배송 중에 심각하게 손상된 severe 형 심한, 심각한
17 **accordingly**	분 그에 따라, 따라서, 그러므로	be adjusted accordingly 그에 따라 조정되다 according to 전 ~에 따르면, ~에 따라

DAY 12

18 **formerly**	🖥 전에는, ~의 출신으로	be formerly a famous chef 유명한 요리사 출신이다 former 형 이전의, 전직 ~인
19 **hardly**	🖥 거의 ~아니다[않다]	Mr. Sim could hardly hear the announcement because of the background noise 심 씨는 주변 소음 때문에 거의 안내방송을 듣지 못했다. hard 형 어려운, 단단한 🖥 열심히, 세게, 심하게
20 **occasionally**	🖥 가끔	be occasionally required to work overtime during peak season 성수기에 가끔 초과근무를 요구 받는다 occasional 형 가끔의 occasion 명 (특정한) 때, 기회, 행사
21 **highly**	🖥 대단히, 매우	a highly successful charity event 매우 성공적인 자선 행사 high 형 높은 🖥 높이, 높게
22 **largely**	🖥 주로, 대체로	due largely to the price increases 주로 가격 인상으로 인해
23 **promptly**	🖥 즉시, 제 시간에, 지체 없이	begin promptly at 3 P.M. 오후 3시 정각에 시작하다 prompt 형 신속한, 시간을 엄수하는 동 유발하다, 촉발하다

24 **slightly**	🔵 약간, 근소하게	slightly different from ~ ~와 약간 다른 slight 형 약간의
25 **efficiently**	🔵 효율적으로	handle customer requests efficiently 고객 요청사항을 효율적으로 다루다
26 **conveniently**	🔵 편리하게	conveniently located in the center of the city 시내 중심에 접근이 편리한 곳에 위치한 convenient 형 편리한 convenience 명 편리, 편의 inconvenience 명 불편
27 **gradually**	🔵 점점, 서서히, 점차	gradually increase [decrease] 점차 상승하다[하락하다] gradual 형 점진적인, 완만한
28 **favorably**	🔵 유리하게, 호의적으로	be favorably received by customers 고객들에게 좋게 평가받다 favor 명 호의 동 호의를 베풀다 favorable 형 호의적인, 유리한
29 **financially**	🔵 재정적으로	financially sound 재정적으로 건전한 finance 동 자금을 조달하다 명 재정, 금융 financial 형 재정의, 금융의
30 **significantly**	🔵 상당히, 중요하게	The company's operating costs have been significantly reduced. 회사의 운영비가 상당히 감소했다. significant 형 상당한, 의미가 있는, 중요한

실전 TEST

1. Production at the plant ------- halted when a critical component failed without warning.
   (A) currently
   (B) indefinitely
   (C) commonly
   (D) unexpectedly

2. Job candidates are ------- evaluated to verify their qualifications and experience.
   (A) superficially
   (B) partially
   (C) thoroughly
   (D) hastily

3. The new CEO will ------- step into the position on September 15.
   (A) consistently
   (B) officially
   (C) typically
   (D) quietly

4. Their online tutoring packages are ------- priced to support students from diverse backgrounds.
   (A) virtually
   (B) gratefully
   (C) thoroughly
   (D) reasonably

5. The downtown warehouse district has been redeveloped from what was ------- an industrial zone.
   (A) usually
   (B) harshly
   (C) literally
   (D) formerly

6. Clients responded ------- to the new product, praising its innovative features and user-friendly design.
   (A) skeptically
   (B) favorably
   (C) indifferently
   (D) reluctantly

7 Introducing flexible work hours has ------- boosted employee morale and productivity.

(A) casually
(B) openly
(C) markedly
(D) loudly

8 Ms. Reeves is a ------- skilled negotiator with years of experience in mergers and acquisitions.

(A) moderately
(B) somewhat
(C) highly
(D) rarely

9 The company's recent success is ------- due to its strategic partnerships with industry leaders.

(A) beneficially
(B) largely
(C) quite
(D) rarely

10 The office café is ------- located beside the main conference hall, allowing easy refreshments during meetings.

(A) conveniently
(B) commonly
(C) consistently
(D) cautiously

11 Horizon Pharmaceuticals ------- expanded its distribution network across Europe and Asia.

(A) precisely
(B) strictly
(C) recently
(D) indefinitely

12 Our logistics partner delivers overseas shipments ------- to meet product freshness standards.

(A) promptly
(B) slowly
(C) occasionally
(D) accidentally

DAY 13 | 최빈출 정답 어휘: 숙어 ①

핵심 단어들을 확인한 후, 오른쪽의 기출 예시를 통해 각 단어의 쓰임새를 익혀보세요.

01 **a variety of**
(= a selection of, a range of)
다양한

There will be a variety of interesting events.
다양한 흥미로운 행사들이 있을 것이다.

02 **be involved in**
~에 관여되다, ~에 포함되다

She is involved in all aspects of advertising.
그녀는 광고의 모든 측면에 관여되어 있다.

03 **in response to**
~에 대응하여, ~에 대한 반응으로

In response to the complaints, we will update our menu.
그 불만 사항들에 대응하여, 저희는 메뉴를 업데이트할 것입니다.

04 **a series of**
일련의

A series of workshops will be held at the end of the month.
일련의 워크숍들이 이달 말에 개최될 것이다.

05 **be responsible for**
~에 대해 책임이 있다, ~을 담당하다

He is not responsible for the error.
그는 그 오류에 대해 책임이 있지 않습니다.

06 **look forward to -ing**
~하기를 고대하다

We look forward to hearing from you soon.
귀하로부터 곧 소식을 들을 수 있기를 고대합니다.

07 **fill out** (= fill in, complete)
~을 작성하다

You can fill out the form online.
온라인에서 그 양식을 작성하실 수 있습니다.

08	**at your earliest convenience** 가급적 빨리	Please e-mail us at your earliest convenience. 가급적 빨리 저희에게 이메일을 보내주십시오.
09	**sign up for** ~에 등록하다, ~을 신청하다	You can sign up for the program now. 지금 그 프로그램에 등록하실 수 있습니다.
10	**get in touch with** ~에게 연락하다	I'd like to get in touch with the manager. 저는 그 책임자에게 연락하고자 합니다.
11	**be supposed to do** (= be scheduled to do) ~할 예정이다, ~하기로 되어 있다	Mr. Peterson is supposed to lead the meeting. 피터슨 씨가 그 회의를 이끌기로 되어 있다.
12	**in celebration of** ~을 기념하여, ~을 축하하여	A big music festival will be held in celebration of its tenth anniversary. 10주년을 기념하여 대규모 음악 축제가 열릴 것이다.
13	**be well-known for,** **be famous for,** **be notable for,** **be renowned for** ~로 잘 알려져 있다[유명하다]	He is well-known for his original works. 그는 그의 독창적인 작품으로 잘 알려져 있다.
14	**free of charge** (= for free, at no cost) 무료로	We can make a delivery free of charge. 저희는 무료로 배송해 드릴 수 있습니다.
15	**register for** (= enroll in) ~에 등록하다	All the managers registered for the seminar. 모든 부서장들이 그 세미나에 등록했다.

실전 TEST

1 The software platform is ------- for its robust security and user-friendly interface.

(A) outdated
(B) simple
(C) notable
(D) flawed

2 The product launch event is ------- to take place at the downtown convention center.

(A) registered
(B) scheduled
(C) permitted
(D) required

3 Our company offers installation services ------- no cost for first-time clients.

(A) at
(B) by
(C) over
(D) from

4 Prospective attendees are encouraged to ------- for the leadership workshop by Friday.

(A) approve
(B) express
(C) record
(D) register

5 Participants should ------- the survey form at the end of the training session.

(A) complete
(B) proceed
(C) retrieve
(D) enlist

6 The IT department implemented extra security measures in ------- to recent data breaches.

(A) apology
(B) effect
(C) response
(D) confirmation

7 The annual conference includes a ------- of keynote speeches and workshops.

(A) package
(B) sequence
(C) series
(D) segment

8 Several board members were ------- in the development of the new platform, ensuring every feature aligned with client requirements.

(A) appointed
(B) assigned
(C) facilitated
(D) involved

9 Our customer service offers a ------- of support channels, including chat and phone.

(A) package
(B) concept
(C) variety
(D) division

10 The marketing director is ------- for developing the annual promotional strategy.

(A) optional
(B) analytical
(C) dynamic
(D) responsible

11 Please feel free to call us at your earliest ------- if you have any questions.

(A) convenience
(B) importance
(C) introduction
(D) probability

12 In ------- of the museum's grand reopening, admission will be free throughout the weekend.

(A) demonstration
(B) celebration
(C) charge
(D) exploration

DAY 14 | 최빈출 정답 어휘: 숙어 ②

핵심 단어들을 확인한 후, 오른쪽의 기출 예시를 통해 각 단어의 쓰임새를 익혀보세요.

01 have access to
~을 이용할 수 있다, ~에 접근할 수 있다

Only some of the employees have access to the files.
오직 몇몇 직원들만 그 파일들을 이용할 수 있다.

02 remind A of B
A에게 B를 상기시키다

He reminded us of the scheduled meeting.
그가 우리에게 그 예정된 회의를 상기시켜주었다.

03 at a reasonable price
알맞은 가격에

It can be purchased at a reasonable price.
그것은 알맞은 가격에 구입될 수 있다.

04 out of stock
재고가 없는

The cell phone is currently out of stock.
그 휴대 전화기는 현재 재고가 없습니다.

05 be suitable for
~에 적합하다

The applicant is suitable for the position.
그 지원자가 그 직책에 적합하다.

06 be required to do
~해야 하다, ~할 필요가 있다

New employees are required to attend the orientation.
신입 직원들은 오리엔테이션에 참석해야 한다.

07 be scheduled for + 시점
~로 예정되어 있다

The renovation is scheduled for next week.
개조 공사가 다음 주로 예정되어 있다.

08	**be based on** ~을 바탕으로 하다, ~에 기반을 두다	The report is based on the survey results. 그 보고서는 설문 조사 결과를 바탕으로 한다.
09	**in favor of** ~에 찬성하여	The city council voted in favor of the proposal to build another park. 시의회는 공원을 하나 더 짓고자 하는 제안에 찬성 투표를 했다.
10	**be eligible for** ~에 대한 자격이 있다	You are eligible for the service. 당신은 그 서비스에 대한 자격이 있습니다.
11	**I'd appreciate it if ~** ~하다면 감사하겠습니다	I'd appreciate it if you could send me the file. 그 파일을 저에게 보내주신다면 감사하겠습니다.
12	**be (conveniently) located in/on/at** ~에 (편리하게) 위치해 있다	The center is located in the downtown area. 그 센터는 시내 구역에 위치해 있다.
13	**would like to do** (= would love to do, would prefer to do) ~하고자 하다, ~하고 싶다	I'd like to talk to the manager. 책임자와 이야기하고 싶습니다.
14	**as a result of** ~에 따른 결과로	Our profits have increased as a result of the advertising campaign. 그 광고 캠페인에 따른 결과로 우리 수익이 증가해왔다.
15	**as expected, as planned, as scheduled** 예상대로[계획대로, 예정대로]	The team won the award as expected. 예상대로 그 팀이 그 상을 받았다.

실전 TEST

1 Once the subscription is activated, users will have ------- to premium articles and videos.

(A) communication
(B) permission
(C) opportunity
(D) access

2 The annual performance reviews will be ------- for the first week of August.

(A) maintained
(B) heard
(C) organized
(D) scheduled

3 Visitors are ------- to wear identification badges while on company premises.

(A) considered
(B) regarded
(C) required
(D) allowed

4 During the discussion, many delegates spoke in ------- of stricter safety laws.

(A) regard
(B) aspect
(C) view
(D) favor

5 The graphic designer offered to create the company logo at a ------- price.

(A) premium
(B) reasonable
(C) high
(D) temporary

6 Because of their minimalistic and versatile designs, these products are highly ------- for both casual and professional settings.

(A) exaggerated
(B) fragile
(C) suitable
(D) apt

7 The company's restructuring plan is ------- on detailed financial analysis.

(A) based
(B) constructed
(C) taken
(D) outdated

8 Applicants who submit all required documents on time are ------- for scholarship review.

(A) eligible
(B) plausible
(C) flexible
(D) compatible

9 ------- recent budget cuts, the department had to cancel several projects.

(A) Despite
(B) As a result of
(C) So as to
(D) In order to

10 The renovation of the office was completed as -------, meeting the deadline set by management.

(A) planned
(B) considered
(C) noted
(D) examined

11 The store had to display a notice that the popular tablet was out of -------.

(A) supply
(B) inventory
(C) stock
(D) merchandise

12 I'd ------- it if you could review the attached proposal and return it with comments by Monday morning.

(A) thank
(B) appreciate
(C) welcome
(D) require

DAY 15 최빈출 정답 어휘: 숙어 ③

핵심 단어들을 확인한 후, 오른쪽의 기출 예시를 통해 각 단어의 쓰임새를 익혀보세요.

01 make a presentation
(= give a presentation)
발표하다

He is going to make a presentation at the seminar.
그가 세미나에서 발표할 예정입니다.

02 consist of
~로 구성되다

The committee consists of more than 25 local businesses and organizations.
위원회는 25개 이상의 지역 기업 및 단체로 구성되어 있다.

03 set up
~을 구성하다, ~을 마련하다

The team needs to set up guidelines for onboarding new employees.
그 팀은 신입 직원 온보딩을 위한 가이드라인을 마련할 필요가 있다.

04 deal with (= handle)
~을 처리하다, ~을 다루다

We have to deal with the complaint immediately.
우리는 즉시 그 불만 사항을 처리해야 합니다.

05 on a regular basis
주기적으로, 정기적으로

The device has to be inspected on a regular basis.
그 기기는 주기적으로 점검되어야 한다.

06 in a timely manner
적시에, 시기 적절하게

Ms. Parker always performs her tasks in a timely manner.
파커 씨는 늘 자신의 업무를 적시에 완수한다.

07 **pick up**
~을 얻다, ~을 들어올리다

Kline Pharmacy sends its customers a text message when their prescriptions are ready to be picked up.
클라인 약국은 고객들의 처방약이 가져갈 수 있도록 준비되면 고객들에게 문자 메시지를 발송한다.

08 **out of the office**
사무실에 부재중인

Mr. Kim will be out of the office through next Tuesday.
김 씨는 다음 주 화요일까지 사무실에 부재중이다.

09 **specialize in ~**
~을 전문으로 하다

We specialize in serving freelance writers in the Chicago area.
저희는 시카고 지역 프리랜서 작가들을 위한 서비스 제공을 전문으로 합니다.

10 **in an effort to**
~하기 위한 노력으로

We implemented new software in an effort to increase productivity.
우리는 생산성을 높이기 위한 노력으로 새로운 소프트웨어를 도입했다.

11 **within walking distance of**
걸어서 갈 수 있는 거리 이내에

The hotel is within walking distance of the train station.
호텔은 기차역에서 도보로 갈 수 있는 거리에 있습니다.

12 **comply with**
~을 준수하다

All airlines must comply with international air safety requirements.
모든 항공사는 국제 항공 안전 규정을 준수해야 한다.

실전 TEST

1 When you arrive at the airport, don't forget to ------- your baggage from the carousel.

(A) drop off
(B) look after
(C) pick up
(D) put away

2 Whenever Alice is out ------- the office, she checks her e-mail remotely.

(A) of
(B) into
(C) upon
(D) down

3 In an ------- to reduce energy consumption, the company installed solar panels.

(A) output
(B) instance
(C) effort
(D) account

4 Drivers must ------- with traffic laws when operating a vehicle to ensure safety on public roads.

(A) confront
(B) comply
(C) assign
(D) update

5 The research institute ------- in language acquisition and cognitive studies.

(A) operates
(B) specializes
(C) displays
(D) applies

6 Equipment inspections at the warehouse occur on a regular ------- to ensure all machinery is functioning safely.

(A) increase
(B) meeting
(C) event
(D) basis

7 Before launching the campaign, the marketing team ------- several meetings to align strategies.

(A) set up
(B) shut down
(C) cleaned up
(D) turned away

8 Our holiday package ------- of flights, hotel stays, and guided tours.

(A) composes
(B) contains
(C) introduces
(D) consists

9 The conference center is ------- walking distance of several restaurants.

(A) within
(B) apart
(C) throughout
(D) beyond

10 The finance department is instructed to process reimbursement claims in a ------- manner.

(A) variable
(B) delayed
(C) indifferent
(D) timely

11 In stressful situations, it's crucial to ------- with pressure without losing focus.

(A) maintain
(B) fix
(C) deal
(D) solve

12 The seminar will cover how to ------- a presentation that truly engages and persuades your audience.

(A) bring
(B) serve
(C) catch
(D) make

시원스쿨 LAB